T0213385

Lecture Notes in Artificial Intelligence 9811

Subseries of Lecture Notes in Computer Science

More information about this series at http://www.springer.com/series/1244

Andrey Ronzhin · Rodmonga Potapova
Géza Németh (Eds.)

Speech and Computer

18th International Conference, SPECOM 2016
Budapest, Hungary, August 23–27, 2016
Proceedings

 Springer

Editors
Andrey Ronzhin
SPIIRAS
Saint-Petersburg
Russia

Rodmonga Potapova
Moscow State Linguistic University
Moscow
Russia

Géza Németh
Budapest University of Technology
  and Economics
Budapest
Hungary

ISSN 0302-9743   ISSN 1611-3349   (electronic)
Lecture Notes in Artificial Intelligence
ISBN 978-3-319-43957-0   ISBN 978-3-319-43958-7   (eBook)
DOI 10.1007/978-3-319-43958-7

Library of Congress Control Number: 2016946618

LNCS Sublibrary: SL7 – Artificial Intelligence

Printed on acid-free paper

This Springer imprint is published by Springer Nature
The registered company is Springer International Publishing AG Switzerland

Preface

The Speech and Computer International Conference (SPECOM) has become a regular event since the first SPECOM that was held in St. Petersburg, Russian Federation, in 1996. Twenty years ago, SPECOM was established by St. Petersburg Institute for Informatics and Automation of the Russian Academy of Sciences and State Pedagogical University of Russia thanks to the efforts of Prof. Yuri Kosarev and Prof. Rajmund Piotrowski.

SPECOM is a conference with a long tradition that attracts researchers in the area of computer speech processing (recognition, synthesis, understanding etc.) and related domains (including signal processing, language and text processing, multi-modal speech processing, or human–computer interaction). The SPECOM international conference is an ideal platform for know-how exchange — especially for experts working on Slavic and other highly inflectional languages — including both less-resourced and standard, well-resourced languages.

In its long history, SPECOM conference was organized alternately by the St. Petersburg Institute for Informatics and Automation of the Russian Academy of Sciences (SPIIRAS) and by the Moscow State Linguistic University (MSLU) in their home cities. Furthermore, in 1997 it was organized by the Cluj-Napoca Subsidiary of the Research Institute for Computer Technique (Romania), in 2005 and 2015 by the University of Patras (Greece), in 2011 by the Kazan Federal University (Russian Federation, Republic of Tatarstan), in 2013 by the University of West Bohemia (Pilsen, Czech Republic), and in 2014 by the University of Novi Sad (Serbia).

SPECOM 2016 was the 18th event in the series and this time it was organized by the Budapest University of Technology and Economics (BME) and the Scientific Association for Infocommunications (HTE), in cooperation with Moscow State Linguistic University (MSLU), St. Petersburg Institute for Informatics and Automation of the Russian Academy of Sciences (SPIIRAS) and St. Petersburg National Research University of Information Technologies, Mechanics and Optics (ITMO University). The conference was held during August 23–27, 2016, in the Aquincum Hotel Budapest located in a prime area alongside the river Danube, on the Buda side of this magnificent city and across the river from the serene Margaret Island, with its famous thermal waters.

During the conference the invited talks were given by Prof. Nick Campbell (Speech Processing Lab, Trinity College Dublin, Ireland), Prof. Ralf Schlüter (Faculty of Mathematics, Computer Science and Natural Sciences, Human Language Technology and Pattern Recognition, RWTH Aachen University, Germany), and Attila Vékony (NNG Software Developing and Commercial Llc., Hungary) on the latest achievements in speech technologies and the relatively broad and still unexplored area of human–machine interaction. The invited papers are published as a first part of the SPECOM 2016 proceedings.

This volume contains a collection of submitted papers presented at the conference, which were thoroughly reviewed by members of the Program Committee consisting of around 40 top specialists in the conference topic areas. A total of 85 accepted papers out of 154 submitted for SPECOM and ICR were selected by the Program Committee for presentation at the conference and for inclusion in this book. Theoretical and more general contributions were presented in common (plenary) sessions. Problem-oriented sessions as well as panel discussions brought together specialists in limited problem areas with the aim of exchanging knowledge and skills resulting from research projects of all kinds. This year, the conference had a satellite event – the First International Conference on Interactive Collaborative Robotics — where problems and modern solutions of human–robot interaction were discussed.

We would like to express our gratitude to the authors for providing their papers on time, to the members of the conference reviewing team and Program Committee for their careful reviews and paper selection, and to the editors for their hard work in preparing this volume. Special thanks are due to the members of the local Organizing Committee for their tireless effort and enthusiasm during the conference organization.

August 2016

Andrey Ronzhin
Rodmonga Potapova
Géza Németh

Organization

The conference SPECOM 2016 was organized by the Budapest University of Technology and Economics (BME) and the Scientific Association for Infocommunications (HTE), in cooperation with International Speech Communication Association, the Moscow State Linguistic University (MSLU, Moscow, Russia), St. Petersburg Institute for Informatics and Automation of the Russian Academy of Science (SPIIRAS, St. Petersburg, Russia), St. Petersburg National Research University of Information Technologies, Mechanics and Optics (ITMO University, St. Petersburg, Russia). SPECOM 2016 was sponsored by ASM Solutions Ltd. (Moscow, Russia). The conference website is: http://www.specom2016.hte.hu/.

Program Committee

Elias Azarov, Belarus
Andrey Barabanov, Russian Federation
Vlado Delić, Serbia
Olivier Deroo, Belgium
Vera Evdokimova, Russian Federation
Nikos Fakotakis, Greece
Mais Farkhadov, Russian Federation
Peter French, UK
Todor Ganchev, Bulgaria
Rüdiger Hoffmann, Germany
Oliver Jokisch, Germany
Slobodan Jovicic, Serbia
Alexey Karpov, Russian Federation
Heysem Kaya, Turkey
Irina Kipyatkova, Russian Federation
Daniil Kocharov, Russian Federation
Benjamin Lecouteux, France
Boris Lobanov, Belarus
Elena Lyakso, Russian Federation
Konstantin Markov, Japan
Yuri Matveev, Russian Federation
Péter Mihajlik, Hungary

Wolfgang Minker, Germany
Roman Meshcheryakov,
  Russian Federation
Konstantinos Moustakas, Greece
Iosif Mporas, UK
Géza Németh, Hungary
Alexander Petrovsky, Belarus
Alexey Petrovsky, Russian Federation
Dimitar Popov, Italy
Rodmonga Potapova, Russian Federation
Vsevolod Potapov, Russian Federation
Andrey Ronzhin, Russian Federation
Jesus Savage, Mexico
Milan Secujski, Serbia
Pavel Skrelin, Russian Federation
Mikhail Stolbov, Russian Federation
György Szaszák, Hungary
László Tóth, Hungary
Klára Vicsi, Hungary
Andreas Wendemuth, Germany
Csaba Zainkó, Hungary
Miloš Železný, Czech Republic

Organizing Committee

Géza Németh (*Chair*)
Mátyás Bartalis
Polina Emeleva

Alexey Karpov
Liliya Komalova
Yuri Matveev

Ekaterina Miroshnikova   Andrey Ronzhin
Péter Nagy   Anton Saveliev
Rodmonga Potapova   Mária Tézsla
Alexander Ronzhin   László Tóth

Acknowledgments

Special thanks to the reviewers, who devoted their valuable time to review the papers and thus helped maintain the high quality of the conference review process.

Contents

Invited Talks

Automatic Speech Recognition Based on Neural Networks

Ralf Schlüter$^{(\boxtimes)}$, Patrick Doetsch, Pavel Golik, Markus Kitza, Tobias Menne, Kazuki Irie, Zoltán Tüske, and Albert Zeyer

Lehrstuhl Informatik 6, RWTH Aachen University, 52074 Aachen, Germany
schlueter@cs.rwth-aachen.de
http://www.hltpr.rwth-aachen.de

Abstract. In automatic speech recognition, as in many areas of machine learning, stochastic modeling relies on neural networks more and more. Both in acoustic and language modeling, neural networks today mark the state of the art for large vocabulary continuous speech recognition, providing huge improvements over former approaches that were solely based on Gaussian mixture hidden markov models and count-based language models. We give an overview of current activities in neural network based modeling for automatic speech recognition. This includes discussions of network topologies and cell types, training and optimization, choice of input features, adaptation and normalization, multitask training, as well as neural network based language modeling. Despite the clear progress obtained with neural network modeling in speech recognition, a lot is to be done, yet to obtain a consistent and self-contained neural network based modeling approach that ties in with the former state of the art. We will conclude by a discussion of open problems as well as potential future directions w.r.t. to neural network integration into automatic speech recognition systems.

1 Introduction

Even though artificial neural networks (ANN) have been known for long, their application to automatic speech recognition remained a limited area of research for quite a time. An efficient learning algorithm for the free parameters of neural networks by error backpropagation was introduced in [64]. A few years later, neural networks with a single (non-linear) hidden layer have been shown to have the universal approximator property, meaning that, similar to *Gaussian* mixture models, they are capable of approximating any continuous function to any level of accuracy [44]. In [53], an overview of early approaches to automatic speech recognition using neural network based modeling is given. Notable trends at that time include the time-delay neural network approach [92], the softmax operation for probability normalization on the output layer of neural networks [10], and the introduction of the hybrid concept to hidden *Markov* models (HMM) by interpreting neural network outputs as class posteriors (in the context of

© Springer International Publishing Switzerland 2016
A. Ronzhin et al. (Eds.): SPECOM 2016, LNAI 9811, pp. 3–17, 2016.
DOI: 10.1007/978-3-319-43958-7_1

the squared error criterion), and using them to model HMM emission probabilities [7]. Finally, first results which were competitive to standard *Gaussian* mixture HMMs on the Wall Street Journal task were presented using a recurrent neural network [63]. Nevertheless, only with the new millennium, approaches including neural network modeling started to outperform the former state-of-the-art. Nowadays, ANN-based ASR systems show considerable improvements of 30 % and more relative in word error rate (WER) over *Gaussian* mixture based HMMs, e.g. [73]. In this work, we provide an overview of recent developments and results obtained using ANNs of various flavors in both acoustic and language modeling. In Sect. 2, general approaches to ANN-based acoustic modeling are compared. Section 3 presents network topologies and cell types, followed by a discussion of corresponding training criteria in Sect. 4, regularization methods in Sect. 5, and corresponding optimization methods in Sect. 6. In Sect. 7, input features for ANN-based ASR are discussed. Section 8 shows how multitask learning introduces generalization across multiple languages. Section 9, discusses current approaches to adaptation and normalization for ANN-based ASR. Section 10 gives an overview of ANN-based language modeling. Finally, Sect. 11 discusses recent developments especially in decoding using neural network based modeling, followed by general conclusions in Sect. 12.

2   Acoustic Model Integration

The introduction of neural networks to acoustic modeling can be divided into the *hybrid*, and the *tandem* approach. In the *hybrid* approach [7,8], HMM emission probabilities are modelled explicitly using (appropriately renormalized) neural networks representing phoneme class posteriors, thus dropping the need for *Gaussian* mixture models (GMM). In [63], an early success was obtained on the Wall Street Journal task using recurrent neural networks within the hybrid approach. Nevertheless, GMMs still remained the prevalent acoustic modeling scheme for large vocabulary continuous speech recognition for at least a decade. Meanwhile, the *tandem* approach was proposed [39], where the framewise phoneme classifier neural network output is post-processed and used as additional input feature to a conventional GMM-based recognition system. A powerful extension to the tandem approach was suggested in [33], where the output of one of the hidden layers rather than the output layer is used. Since the size of hidden layers is not constrained, this leaves more freedom to choose its size, position among the layers, and activation function for feature extraction. Due to the usually reduced layer size, this discriminatively learned representation of input data is termed *bottleneck features*.

Universally considered a breakthrough for hybrid modeling, the authors in [73] presented very good results on the widely used conversational telephone speech recognition task *Switchboard*, beating a strong speaker adapted and discriminatively trained GMM baseline. The key to their success was twofold: first, a large number of context-dependent phoneme state targets, instead of monophone targets was modelled. Second, *deep neural networks* (DNN) with a number of large hidden layers were employed. The authors were also among the first groups to transfer training of large models to a *graphics processing unit* (GPU), that offers a great speed-up over CPUs on matrix operations. Both tandem and hybrid approaches have been shown to outperform standard GMM baselines trained on cepstral features [89]. In principle, both methods can be considered a deep stack of non-linear models trained to optimize different objective functions following different schemes for parameter updates [90]. From an even more general point of view, both models consist of a classifier and some representation learning mechanism, although there is no explicit distinction of the two. In [85], both approaches are compared on the Switchboard part of the Hub5'00 test corpus. A hybrid DNN model achieved a word error rate (WER) of 13.7 %, while a comparable tandem system trained w.r.t. the maximum likelihood criterion yielded 14.2 % WER. Same concepts such as speaker adaptation and sequence discriminative training can be applied to both models, making the gap even smaller.

3 Neural Network Topologies

The network topology has a major influence on performance. This includes optimization of the number of hidden layers, their size, the choice of activation functions, the cell types, the connectivity between the layers. Recently, a variety of novel activation functions have been suggested in the literature, including Maxout [26], Exponential Linear Unit [17], and many modifications. Of these, the piece-wise linear function *rectified linear unit* (ReLU) [57] turned out to be very effective. Although unbounded, the ReLU does not violate the universal approximator property of the networks [74]. ReLU networks allow to train very deep models even for hard optimization problems, as shown e.g. in [24,84]. *Bottleneck layers* are not only useful for the tandem approach, but also in a hybrid scenario, allowing to reduce the number of trainable parameters, increasing the processing speed and the generalization ability of the acoustic models [95]. Hierarchical stacking of multiple neural networks [91] provides another choice in network design that has been shown to provide further gains in performance [88]. *Convolutional neural networks* (CNNs) provide another design choice, where a layer with local connectivity shares the weights of its *receptive field* across the positions in the input, to support learning of more robust position-independent features [51]. This concept was applied to speech recognition by defining the convolution layer over a spectrogram, approximated by critical band energies [1]. In [24], convolution in time was used even to jointly learn feature extraction and acoustic model on raw waveform input. Highway networks [76] provide a way to improve information flow across layers and enables training of even deeper networks. Highway networks also were combined with recurrent neural networks in [100]. *Recurrent neural networks* (RNNs) provide another powerful extension of the topology by introducing recurrent connections. Here, hidden layers perform a time-dependent operation taking its own output at the previous time step as input in addition to the output from the previous hidden layer. Optimization of RNNs requires *backpropagation through time* (BPTT), which is known to have the exploding/vanishing gradient effect [42]. Various approaches were suggested to overcome this problem, like gradient clipping [59], or second-order optimization methods [94,95]. However, the most prominent variant is to modify the recurrent model itself, which led to the long short-term memory (LSTM) [43] model which allows for better gradient flow via gating units. Further analyses and variants of LSTMs are presented in [9,16,31,47]. Recently, LSTMs were shown to clearly outperform feed-forward acoustic models [22,66], and can also be stacked to form deep LSTM networks [27]. Also, bidirectional LSTMs were shown to outperform unidirectional LSTMs [30]. Bidirectional LSTMs can also be used in online recognition setups [99]. In recent work [98], based on a fast LSTM implementation [20], we observed an improvement from 15.3 % WER for an highly optimized DNN to 13.1 % WER using LSTM modeling on a 50 h subset of the English Quaero task.

4   Training Criteria

Early approaches to neural network acoustic model training applied the *squared error* criterion [7]. Nevertheless, the common approach is to minimize frame-level *cross entropy* over a training set. The cross entropy criterion was shown to be more robust to poor initialization, than the squared error criterion [23]. The training criterion in *connectionist temporal classification* (CTC) overcomes the necessity for allophone alignment by integrating over all alignments [29], similar to *Baum-Welch* training. Frame-level cross entropy does not take the word level into account, treating all frames independently and with equal weight. Also, both the cross entropy and the frame classification error on a held-out data set are only loosely correlated with the target evaluation measure for speech recognition, word error rate. In the tandem approach, GMM/HMM training can be done with discriminative training [35,36], but usually does not include further optimization of the underlying neural network, even though joint training would be possible [85,90]. Sequence training [49] is the corresponding approach realizing discriminative training criteria for hybrid modeling. The criteria are the same in both cases, comprising *maximum mutual information* (MMI), *minimum phone error* (MPE) (cf. e.g. [35]), and *state-level minimum Bayes risk* (sMBR) criterion [50]. A direct comparison of MMI and MPE can be found e.g. in [93]. For *encoder-decoder* models (cf. Sect. 11), a promising approach using upper estimates on the training error are presented in [5]. In [85], MPE training results are presented on the Switchboard. MPE training reduces the WER of a cross entropy trained hybrid model from 13.7 % to 12.6 %. Further, sequence discriminative training has been found to play a crucial role for performing keyword search [25].

5   Regularization

Neural networks usually have a huge amount of trainable parameters and are thus prone to overfitting, i.e. they fit very good to the training data but perform badly on unseen data. Regularization aims at better generalization by avoiding overfitting in various ways. One approach would be to balance the amount of trainable parameters with the amount of training data available. Nevertheless, it has been shown that depth boosts neural network performance, both theoretically [56] and experimentally [98]. A straight-forward approach to reduce the amount of parameters is to use a reduced matrix representation such as linear bottlenecks [95], cf. Sec. 3. Also, constraints can be introduced on the parameters or to penalize them in various ways, where minimizing the L_1 or L_2 norm is the simplest solution. This is usually added as an additional term to the optimization criterion. Another class of methods stochastically modifies the network architecture so that the overall model can be seen as an ensemble model of all the stochastic variants. The most prominent method of this kind is dropout [75], where hidden nodes are randomly dropped. Another recent promising method is stochastic depth [45], where hidden layers are randomly dropped. In [98] we studied the effect of different regularization methods for LSTM based acoustic models and we found a combination of L_2 and dropout to perform best.

6 Optimization

Neural network weights usually are trained by using error backpropagation and stochastic gradient descent (SGD) on the corresponding training criterion [64]. Improving the initial starting point of the optimization was addressed by so called *pretraining* techniques [41]. Here, the weights are initialized layer-by-layer using unsupervised restricted Boltzmann machines or supervised methods like *discriminative pretraining* [72]. As an alternative to SGD, also batch methods are possible, usually applying second-order information, e.g. LBFGS, Rprop, or the Hessian-Free approach [95]. Second-order optimization can also be transferred to SGD by normalizing mean and variance within a batch [34,95]. The step size for the adjustment is usually treated as hyperparameter and various methods have been proposed to improve the estimate of the optimal step size, like AdaGrad [21], Adadelta [97], or Adam [48], which was reported to give very stable optimization. Also, gradient clipping and noise addition are commonly used methods to improve convergence.

Table 1 shows the performance of these methods on an ASR task. In order to benefit from modern computing architectures like GPUs, algorithms have to be designed to perform simple operations on large amounts of data in parallel. The workload of each single operation can be distributed on several machines. More commonly, training times are reduced and a direct extension to gradient descent is obtained by *data parallelism*, where samples are partitioned into batches and considered as single step in the optimization procedure, c.f. e.g. [19,20].

Table 1. Word error rate on 50 hours of English spoken sentences from the Quaero corpus using different optimization methods. The results are taken from [98].

Systems	WER [%]
Gradient Descent	15.0
AdaGrad	15.6
Adadelta	15.1
Adam	14.8
+ gradient noise	14.6

7   Input Features

Despite similarities in standard feature extraction pipelines like MFCC, PLP, or Gammatone [18,38,70], they can be expected to complement each other when combined. Using these features as concatenated input to neural networks, about 5–10% relative WER reduction was observed on a broadcast news and conversation task in [60,84]. Further investigation also revealed that the optimal cepstral/critical band energy features for MLP requires higher resolution (up to 50–60 dimensional) than for GMM (15–20 dimensional) [85]. Recent studies demonstrated that feature extraction can even be learned completely from data [65,84]. However, this usually requires a large amount of transcribed speech. In low-resource scenarios, well-established static standard feature extraction procedures still show a significant performance margin over data-driven feature extraction. Using 50 hours of broadcast news and conversations data showed about 10 % relative performance loss [24,85] for data driven feature extraction, even if the modeling was informed by standard feature extraction steps. In acoustically challenging recognition tasks, with only a few hours of speech available, well-established preprocessing steps like RASTA filtering [37] of critical band energies and feature combination can still be beneficial [83].

8   Multilingual Modeling

Cepstral features typically capture formant related information and are a good starting point to develop acoustic models for any language. As neural networks have become a major component of recent HMM based ASR techniques, it was observed that neural network based posterior features possess language independent properties to a certain degree. This can be exploited in the tandem approach [61,77,82]. Taking advantage of multiple language acoustic data poses the question of how to handle differing phoneme sets. Language independent mappings can be done using international phonetic alphabets like IPA or SAMPA [71], or by various data driven approaches [12,81]. Nevertheless, this often introduces ambiguities. In another approach, a joint phoneme set was generated by having language dependent phonemes [32], although this might introduce unnecessary discrimination between similar phonemes. The inherent layer-wise structure of an MLP also allows to train the model on multiple languages by sharing only hidden layers across languages [68], which forces the network to learn a *language independent* representation on a deeper level. This multiple output training is closely related to multi-task training proposed by [13] and to subspace methods [11]. One of the biggest advantages of multilingual modeling is that the training can be done without knowing the target language. Thus, system development on a new, unseen language becomes more efficient and even leads to significant performance gains. In [87], multilingual features gave relative gains of 9–11% in WER, and 30–40% in key word search on low resource tasks for a number of quite different languages within the Babel project [2]. Also, performance benefits from using more languages, with their relation to the target language becoming less important. Even for tasks with large training sets, significant improvements were observed. Between 3–7% relative WER reduction was observed on broadcast news and conversation LVCSR tasks for four languages using between 110 h and 320h for training per language, and 700 h overall for training the multilingual net [88]. In summary, multilingual features and corresponding initialization schemes provide an efficient acoustic modeling framework for unseen qalanguages, and could reduce system development time and costs significantly.

9   Adaptation and Normalization

Adaptation and normalization w.r.t. to speaker, environment, or recording channel usually provides significant improvements in ASR. Using GMMs, vocal tract length normalization (VTLN), maximum likelihood linear regression (MLLR), as well as feature space/constrained MLLR (CMLLR), together with speaker adaptive training work well, and have already been transferred to neural network based ASR successfully [33,69,72]. Although many approaches still necessitate GMMs as target models in the background, optimization within the neural network structure also is possible [72]. E.g., for the real test set on the noisy, multi-channel CHiME3 task we observed an improvement from 8.6 % to 6.9 % WER using CMLLR over an LSTM-based hybrid system and using beamforming kindly provided by the authors of [40]. I-vectors are a well known low-dimensional speaker representation used in the domain of speaker recognition/verification, which can be used to inform neural network acoustic models with speaker information. Using i-vectors, in [67] a 5–6% relative improvement in WER over a DNN baseline trained on already speaker adapted features was obtained on the Switchboard task. Neural networks can also be used to generate a variety of adaptation codes, by using speakers or environmental conditions as classification targets for a network [54,62]. Besides CMLLR, different affine transformations can be used throughout the network for speaker adaptation [52,96].

10   Neural Network Based Language Modeling

The earliest ANN-based approach to language modeling known to us was proposed in [58] and termed *NETgram*. However, the first application of ANN-based language models in ASR only appeared in [6]. While competitive results against the conventional count-based models were already reported with feed-forward ANN-based n-gram models, neural networks have become truly popular for language modeling only after introducing recurrent neural networks into language modeling [55]. As opposed to the count model and feed-forward ANN, the recurrent neural network effectively can handle unlimited context by compressing it into a fixed size context vector. This property is an elegant solution to the context length problem which is fundamental in language modeling. Finally, the long short-term memory recurrent network was first applied for language modeling in [79], which is considered the state-of-the-art architecture for language modeling today. In practice, the combination of count-based and neural network-based

Table 2. Standalone perplexities on the Quaero English 2012. Training data of 50M running words. The results are taken from [46,86].

Model type	PPL
4-gram Count	163.0
MLP (20-gram, 4 layers)	109.2
LSTM (2 layers)	98.3

Table 3. Interpolated perplexities and word error rate on Quaero English 2013 [46, 86]. 250h acoustic training data, 3B/50M running words for training count/neural models. CN decoding.

Model type	PPL	WER[%]
4-gram Count	131.1	10.5
+ MLP (20-gram, 4 layers)	97.2	9.5
+ LSTM (2 layers)	90.5	9.0

approaches gives best results in ASR. Linear interpolation is the most popular and effective combination method (a small improvement by an alternative back-off level combination has been reported in [15]). Due to the high computational complexity of neural language models and the context-induced search complexity, ANN-based language models mostly are applied in a rescoring step using N-best lists, or lattices [80] generated using count models. Overall, the relative improvements from a 4-gram count model in perplexity of about 30 % and in word error rate of 16 % were reported in [78] by using a neural network with two LSTM layers. Further recent results can be found in Tables 2 and 3.

11   Recent Developments - Integrated Modeling

While neural networks proved a powerful tool in local and sequential classification tasks, segmentation and length modeling is still entirely done within an HMM framework. Although CTC [29] provides a simpler topology, it could still be seen as realizing a specific HMM topology, where search can be done using standard HMM-based implementations. Recently, a new approach was introduced to integrate segmentation and length modeling into a recurrent topology [3]. These so called *end-to-end* systems separate the input and output handling into two different models: an *encoder*, which reads the input and is trained to compute discriminative features from the observations, and a *decoder*, which produces the desired output target sequence label-by-label by utilizing the encoded features. The decoder includes modeling of label (word) context, thus even integrating language modeling to the extent of utilizing labeled acoustic training data, while the encoder is designed to generate significant representations that are neither constrained by input nor output length. The topology of these models is furthermore closely related to generative RNNs [28] and has been applied to ASR tasks, already [4,14]. In the decoder, length modeling is done by including and hypothesizing an *end-of-sequence* symbol. In its simplest form, the encoder only produces a single final activation that is subsequently used to initialize the decoder. However, the performance of these models quickly degrades even for moderately long sequences (around 10 symbols, depending on the recurrent cell used) [3]. It is furthermore commonly seen as unfavorable that an output sequence of arbitrary size is encoded into a fixed size representation and the effective capacity of those representations is not entirely understood. To account for arbitrary input length, several so-called *attention-mechanisms* were developed [3,14]. Here, at each decoder step, an expected input is computed as a normalized and statistically localized linear combination of all features provided by the encoder. End-to-end approaches usually employ beam search with static beams of limited sizes; their recognition results do not yet outperform hybrid HMM approaches [14]. Nevertheless, improvements can be expected from more dynamic pruning and improved external language model integration.

12   Conclusions

In this work, an overview of recent developments in automatic speech recognition using neural network based modeling approaches was presented. Approaches for both acoustic and language modeling already show considerable improvements, especially using recurrent topologies, and combined with discriminative sequence training criteria. Already, relative improvements of 30 % and more in WER are observed compared to standard GMM/HMM models with count-based language modeling, only. Nevertheless, additional improvements are to be expected. More independence from e.g. GMM-based model initialization, or separate modeling aspects like CART would be desirable to obtain more consistent neural network based modeling. Also, further exploitation of the high potential of neural network based modeling, especially w.r.t. the integration of recurrent models into the decision rule, as well as consistent modeling, training, and decoding w.r.t. the target evaluation measure word error rate seem worthwhile.

References

1. Abdel-Hamid, O., Mohamed, A., Jiang, H., Penn, G.: Applying convolutional neural networks concepts to hybrid NN-HMM model for speech recognition. In: IEEE International Conference on Acoustics, Speech, and Signal Processing (ICASSP), Kyoto, Japan, pp. 4277–4280, March 2012
2. Babel: US IARPA Project (2012–2016). http://www.iarpa.gov/Programs/ia/Babel/babel.html
3. Bahdanau, D., Cho, K., Bengio, Y.: Neural machine translation by jointly learning to align and translate. In: International Conference on Learning Representations (ICLR), San Diego, CA, USA, May 2015
4. Bahdanau, D., Chorowski, J., Serdyuk, D., Brakel, P., Bengio, Y.: End-to-End attention-based large vocabulary speech recognition. In: IEEE International Conference on Acoustics, Speech, and Signal Processing (ICASSP), Shanghai, China, pp. 4945–4949, March 2016
5. Bahdanau, D., Serdyuk, D., Brakel, P., Ke, N.R., Chorowski, J., Courville, A.C., Bengio, Y.: Task loss estimation for sequence prediction. CoRR abs/1511.06456 (2015). http://arxiv.org/abs/1511.06456
6. Bengio, Y., Ducharme, R., Vincent, P.: A neural probabilistic language model. In: Advances in Neural Information Processing Systems (NIPS), Denver, CO, USA, vol. 13, pp. 932–938, November 2000

7. Bourlard, H., Wellekens, C.J.: Links between markov models and multilayer perceptrons. In: Touretzky, D. (ed.) Advances in neural information processing systems i, pp. 502–510. Morgan Kaufmann, San Mateo, CA (1989)
8. Bourlard, H.A., Morgan, N.: Connectionist Speech Recognition: A Hybrid Approach. Kluwer Academic Publishers, Norwell (1993)
9. Breuel, T.M.: Benchmarking of LSTM Networks. arXiv preprint (2015). arxiv:1508.02774
10. Bridle, J.S.: Probabilistic interpretation of feedforward classification network outputs with relationships to statistical pattern recognition. In: Soulié, F.F., Hérault, J. (eds.) Neurocomputing: Algorithms, Architectures and Applications. Nato ASI Series F: Computer and Systems Sciences, vol. 68, pp. 227–236. Springer, Heidelberg (1989)
11. Burget, L., Schwarz, P., Agarwal, M., Akayazi, P., Feng, K., Ghoshal, A., Glembek, O., Goel, N., Karafiát, M., Povey, D., Rastrow, A., Rose, R.C., Thomas, S.: Multilingual acoustic modeling for speech recognition based on subspace gaussian mixture models. In: IEEE International Conference on Acoustics, Speech, and Signal Processing (ICASSP), pp. 4334–4337 (2010)
12. Byrne, W., Beyerlein, P., Huerta, J.M., Khudanpur, S., Marthi, B., Morgan, J., Peterek, N., Picone, J., Vergyri, D., Wang, W.: Towards language independent acoustic modeling. In: IEEE International Conference on Acoustics, Speech, and Signal Processing (ICASSP), vol. 2, pp. 1029–1032 (2000)
13. Caruana, R.: Multitask learning: A knowledge-based source of inductive bias. In: International Conference on Machine Learning (ICML), pp. 41–48 (1993)
14. Chan, W., Jaitly, N., Le, Q.V., Vinyals, O.: Listen, Attend and Spell. CoRR abs/1508.01211 (2015)
15. Chen, X., Liu, X., Gales, M., Woodland, P.: Investigation of back-off based interpolation between recurrent neural network and N-gram language models. In: IEEE Automatic Speech Recognition and Understanding Workshop (ASRU), Scottsdale, AZ, USA, pp. 181–186, December 2015
16. Chung, J., Gülçehre, Ç., Cho, K., Bengio, Y.: Empirical Evaluation of Gated Recurrent Neural Networks on Sequence Modeling. CoRR abs/1412.3555 (2014)
17. Clevert, D., Unterthiner, T., Hochreiter, S.: Fast and accurate deep network learning by exponential linear units (ELUs). In: International Conference on Learning Representations (ICLR), San Juan, Puerto Rico, May 2016
18. Davis, S., Mermelstein, P.: Comparison of parametric representations for monosyllabic word recognition in continuously spoken sentences. IEEE Trans. Acoust. Speech Signal Process. **28**(4), 357–366 (1980)
19. Dean, J., Corrado, G., Monga, R., Chen, K., Devin, M., Mao, M., Ranzato, M.A., Senior, A., Tucker, P., Yang, K., Le, Q.V., Ng, A.Y.: Large scale distributed deep networks. In: Pereira, F., Burges, C.J.C., Bottou, L., Weinberger, K.Q. (eds.) Advances in Neural Information Processing Systems (NIPS), pp. 1223–1231. Nips Foundation (2012). http://books.nips.cc
20. Doetsch, P., Zeyer, A., Voigtlaender, P., Kulikov, I., Schlüter, R., Ney, H.: RETURNN: the RWTH extensible training framework for universal recurrent neural networks. In: Interspeech, San Francisco, CA, USA, September 2016, submitted
21. Duchi, J., Hazan, E., Singer, Y.: Adaptive Subgradient Methods for Online Learning and Stochastic Optimization. Technical Report UCB/EECS-2010-24, EECS Department, University of California, Berkeley, March 2010

22. Geiger, J.T., Zhang, Z., Weninger, F., Schuller, B., Rigoll, G.: Robust speech recognition using long short-term memory recurrent neural networks for hybrid acoustic modelling. In: Interspeech, pp. 631–635 (2014)
23. Golik, P., Doetsch, P., Ney, H.: Cross-entropy vs. squared error training: a theoretical and experimental comparison. In: Interspeech, Lyon, France, pp. 1756–1760, August 2013
24. Golik, P., Tüske, Z., Schlüter, R., Ney, H.: Convolutional neural networks for acoustic modeling of raw time signal in LVCSR. In: Interspeech, pp. 26–30. Dresden, Germany, September 2015
25. Golik, P., Tüske, Z., Schlüter, R., Ney, H.: Multilingual features based keyword search for very low-resource languages. In: Interspeech, Dresden, Germany, pp. 1260–1264, September 2015
26. Goodfellow, I.J., Warde-Farley, D., Mirza, M., Courville, A., Bengio, Y.: Maxout networks. In: International Conference on Machine Learning (ICML), Atlanta, GA, USA, June 2013
27. Graves, A., Mohamed, A.R., Hinton, G.: Speech recognition withdeep recurrent neural networks. In: IEEE International Conference on Acoustics, Speech, and SignalProcessing (ICASSP), pp. 6645–6649. IEEE (2013)
28. Graves, A.: Generating Sequences with Recurrent Neural Networks. CoRR abs/1308.0850 (2013). http://arxiv.org/abs/1308.0850
29. Graves, A., Fernández, S., Gomez, F., Schmidhuber, J.: Connectionist temporal classification: labelling unsegmented sequence data with recurrent neural networks. In: International Conference on Machine Learning (ICML), NY, USA, pp. 369–376 (2006). http://doi.acm.org/10.1145/1143844.1143891
30. Graves, A., Schmidhuber, J.: Framewise phoneme classification with bidirectional LSTM and other neural network architectures. Neural Netw. **18**(5), 602–610 (2005)
31. Greff, K., Srivastava, R.K., Koutník, J., Steunebrink, B.R., Schmidhuber, J.: LSTM: A Search Space Odyssey. arXiv preprint (2015). arxiv:1503.04069
32. Grézl, F., Karafiát, M., Janda, M.: Study of probabilistic and bottle-neck features in multilingual environment. In: IEEE Automatic Speech Recognition and Understanding Workshop (ASRU), pp. 359–364 (2011)
33. Grézl, F., Karafiát, M., Kontár, S., Černocký, J.: Probabilistic and bottle-neck features for LVCSR of meetings. In: IEEE International Conference on Acoustics, Speech, and Signal Processing (ICASSP), Honolulu, HI, USA, pp. 757–760, April 2007
34. Gülçehre, Ç., Bengio, Y.: ADASECANT: Robust Adaptive Secant Method for Stochastic Gradient. CoRR abs/1412.7419 (2014). http://arxiv.org/abs/1412.7419
35. He, X., Deng, L., Chou, W.: Discriminative learning in sequential pattern recognition - a unifying review for optimization-oriented speech recognition. IEEE Signal Process. Mag. **25**(5), 14–36 (2008)
36. Heigold, G., Schlüter, R., Ney, H., Wiesler, S.: Discriminative training for automatic speech recognition: Modeling, criteria, optimization, implementation, and performance. IEEE Signal Process. Mag. **29**(6), 58–69 (2012)
37. Hermansky, H., Morgan, N.: RASTA processing of speech. IEEE Trans. Speech Audio Process. **2**(4), 578–589 (1994)
38. Hermansky, H.: Perceptual linear predictive (PLP) analysis of speech. J. Acoust. Soc. Am. **87**(4), 1738–1752 (1990)

39. Hermansky, H., Ellis, D., Sharma, S.: Tandem connectionist feature extraction for conventional HMM systems. In: IEEE International Conference on Acoustics, Speech, and Signal Processing (ICASSP), Istanbul, Turkey, vol. 3, pp. 1635–1638, June 2000

40. Heymann, J., Drude, L., Chinaev, A., Häb-Umbach, R.: BLSTM supported GEV beamformer front-end for the 3rd CHiME challenge. In: Automatic Speech Recognition and Understanding Workshop (ASRU), December 2015

41. Hinton, G.E., Osindero, S., Teh, Y.W.: A fast learning algorithm for deep belief nets. Neural Comput. **18**(7), 1527–1554 (2006)

42. Hochreiter, S., Bengio, Y., Frasconi, P., Schmidhuber, J.: Gradient flow in recurrent nets: The difficulty of learning long-term dependencies. In: Kolen, J., Kremer, S. (eds.) A Field Guide to Dynamical Recurrent Networks. IEEE Press, New York (2001)

43. Hochreiter, S., Schmidhuber, J.: Long short-term memory. Neural Comput. **9**(8), 1735–1780 (1997)

44. Hornik, K., Stinchcombe, M.B., White, H.: Multilayer feedforward networks are universal approximators. Neural Netw. **2**(5), 359–366 (1989)

45. Huang, G., Sun, Y., Liu, Z., Sedra, D., Weinberger, K.: Deep Networks with Stochastic Depth. arXiv preprint (2016). arxiv:1603.09382

46. Irie, K., Tüske, Z., Alkhouli, T., Schlüter, R., Ney, H.: LSTM, GRU, highway and a bit of attention: an empirical overview for language modeling in speech recognition. In: Interspeech, San Francisco, CA, USA, September 2016, submitted

47. Jozefowicz, R., Zaremba, W., Sutskever, I.: An empirical exploration of recurrent network architectures. In: International Conference on Machine Learning (ICML), pp. 2342–2350 (2015)

48. Kingma, D.P., Ba, J.: Adam: A Method for Stochastic Optimization. CoRR abs/1412.6980 (2014). http://arxiv.org/abs/1412.6980

49. Kingsbury, B.: Lattice-based optimization of sequence classification criteria for neural-network acoustic modeling. In: IEEE International Conference on Acoustics, Speech, and Signal Processing (ICASSP), Taipei, Taiwan, pp. 3761–3764, April 2009

50. Kingsbury, B., Sainath, T.N., Soltau, H.: Scalable minimum bayes risk training of deep neural network acoustic models using distributed hessian-free optimization. In: Interspeech, Portland, OR, USA, September 2012

51. LeCun, Y., Boser, B., Denker, J.S., Henderson, D., Howard, R.E., Hubbard, W., Jackel, L.D.: Handwritten digit recognition with a back-propagation network. In: Advances in Neural Information Processing Systems (NIPS), Denver, CO, USA, vol. 2, November 1990

52. Li, B., Sim, K.C.: comparison of discriminative input and output transformations for speaker adaptation in the hybrid NN/HMM systems. In: Interspeech, Makuhari, Japan, pp. 526–529, September 2010

53. Lippmann, R.P.: Review of neural networks for speech recognition. Neural Comput. **1**(1), 1–38 (1989)

54. Miao, Y., Metze, F.: Distance-aware DNNs for robust speech recognition. In: Interspeech, Dresden, Germany, pp. 761–765, September 2015

55. Mikolov, T., Karafiát, M., Burget, L., Cernockỳ, J., Khudanpur, S.: Recurrent neural network based language model. In: Interspeech, Makuhari, Japan, pp. 1045–1048, September 2010

56. Montufar, G.F., Pascanu, R., Cho, K., Bengio, Y.: On the number of linear regions of deep neural networks. In: Advances in Neural Information Processing Systems (NIPS), pp. 2924–2932 (2014)

57. Nair, V., Hinton, G.E.: Rectified linear units improve restricted boltzmann machines. In: International Conference on Machine Learning (ICML), Haifa, Israel, pp. 807–814, June 2010
58. Nakamura, M., Shikano, K.: A study of english word category prediction based on neural networks. In: IEEE International Conference on Acoustics, Speech, and Signal Processing (ICASSP), Glasglow, UK, pp. 731–734, May 1989
59. Pascanu, R., Mikolov, T., Bengio, Y.: On the difficulty of training recurrent neural networks. arXiv preprint (2012). arxiv:1211.5063
60. Plahl, C., Kozielski, M., Schlüter, R., Ney, H.: Feature combination and stacking of recurrent and non-recurrent neural networks for LVCSR. In: IEEE International Conference on Acoustics, Speech, and Signal Processing (ICASSP), Vancouver, Canada, pp. 6714–6718, May 2013
61. Plahl, C., Schlüter, R., Ney, H.: Cross-lingual portability of Chinese and English neural network features for French and German LVCSR. In: IEEE Automatic Speech Recognition and Understanding Workshop (ASRU), pp. 371–376 (2011)
62. Qian, Y., Tan, T., Yu, D., Zhang, Y.: Integrated adaptation with multi-factor joint-learning for far-field speech recognition. In: IEEE International Conference on Acoustics, Speech, and Signal Processing (ICASSP), Shanghai, China, pp. 1–5 (2016)
63. Robinson, T., Hochberg, M., Renals, S.: IPA: Improved phone modelling with recurrent neural networks. In: IEEE International Conference on Acoustics, Speech, and Signal Processing (ICASSP), vol. I, pp. 37–40, April 1994
64. Rumelhart, D.E., Hinton, G.E., Williams, R.J.: Learning representations by back-propagating errors. Nature **323**, 533–536 (1986)
65. Sainath, T.N., Weiss, R.J., Senior, A., Wilson, K.W., Vinyals, O.: Learning the speech front-end with raw waveform CLDNNs. In: Interspeech, pp. 1–5 (2015)
66. Sak, H., Senior, A., Beaufays, F.: Long short-term memory recurrent neural network architectures for large scale acoustic modeling. In: Interspeech, Singapore, pp. 338–342, September 2014
67. Saon, G., Soltau, H., Nahamoo, D., Picheny, M.: Speaker adaptation of neural network acoustic models using i-Vectors. In: IEEE Automatic Speech Recognition and Understanding Workshop (ASRU), Olomouc, Czech Republic, pp. 55–59, December 2013
68. Scanzio, S., Laface, P., Fissore, L., Gemello, R., Mana, F.: On the use of a multilingual neural network front-end. In: Interspeech, pp. 2711–2714 (2008)
69. Schaaf, T., Metze, F.: Analysis of gender normalization using MLP and VTLN features. In: Interspeech, pp. 306–309 (2010)
70. Schlüter, R., Bezrukov, I., Wagner, H., Ney, H.: Gammatone features and feature combination for large vocabulary speech recognition. In: IEEE International Conference on Acoustics, Speech, and Signal Processing (ICASSP), pp. 649–652 (2007)
71. Schultz, T., Waibel, A.: Fast bootstrapping Of LVCSR systems with multilingual phoneme sets. In: European Conference on Speech Communication and Technology (Eurospeech) (1997)
72. Seide, F., Li, G., Chen, X., Yu, D.: Feature engineering in context-dependent deep neural networks for conversational speech transcription. In: IEEE Automatic Speech Recognition and Understanding Workshop (ASRU), Waikoloa, HI, USA, pp. 24–29, December 2011
73. Seide, F., Li, G., Yu, D.: Conversational speech transcription using context-dependent deep neural networks. In: Interspeech, Florence, Italy, pp. 437–440, August 2011

74. Sonoda, S., Murata, N.: Neural network with unbounded activation functions is universal approximator. Appl. Comput. Harmonic Anal. (2016, in Press), Corrected Proof, Available online 17 December 2015

75. Srivastava, N., Hinton, G., Krizhevsky, A., Sutskever, I., Salakhutdinov, R.: Dropout: a simple way to prevent neural networks from overfitting. J. Mach. Learn. Res. **15**(1), 1929–1958 (2014)

76. Srivastava, R.K., Greff, K., Schmidhuber, J.: Training very deep networks. In: Advances in Neural Information Processing Systems (NIPS), pp. 2368–2376 (2015)

77. Stolcke, A., Grézl, F., Hwang, M.Y., Lei, X., Morgan, N., Vergyri, D.: Cross-domain and cross-language portability of acoustic features estimated by multilayer perceptrons. In: IEEE International Conference on Acoustics, Speech, and Signal Processing (ICASSP), pp. 321–324 (2006)

78. Sundermeyer, M., Ney, H., Schlüter, R.: From feedforward to recurrent LSTM neural networks for language modeling. IEEE/ACM Trans. Audio Speech Lang. Process. **23**(3), 517–529 (2015)

79. Sundermeyer, M., Schlüter, R., Ney, H.: LSTM neural networks for language modeling. In: Interspeech, Portland, OR, USA, pp. 194–197, September 2012

80. Sundermeyer, M., Tüske, Z., Schlüter, R., Ney, H.: Lattice decoding and rescoring with long-span neural network language models. In: Interspeech, Singapore, pp. 661–665, September 2014

81. Thomas, S., Ganapathy, S., Hermansky, H.: Cross-lingual and multistream posterior features for low resource LVCSR systems. In: Interspeech, pp. 877–880 (2010)

82. Tóth, L., Frankel, J., Gosztolya, G., King, S.: Cross-lingual portability of MLP-based tandem features-a case study for English and Hungarian. In: Interspeech, pp. 2695–2698 (2008)

83. Tüske, Z., Golik, P., Nolden, D., Schlüter, R., Ney, H.: Data augmentation, feature combination, and multilingual neural networks to improve ASR and KWS performance for low-resource languages. In: Interspeech, Singapore, pp. 1420–1424, September 2014

84. Tüske, Z., Golik, P., Schlüter, R., Ney, H.: Acoustic modeling with deep neural networks using raw time signal for LVCSR. In: Interspeech, Singapore, pp. 890–894, September 2014

85. Tüske, Z., Golik, P., Schlüter, R., Ney, H.: Speaker adaptive joint training of gaussian mixture models and bottleneck features. In: IEEE Automatic Speech Recognition and Understanding Workshop (ASRU), Scottsdale, AZ, USA, pp. 596–603, December 2015

86. Tüske, Z., Irie, K., Schlüter, R., Ney, H.: Investigation on log-linear interpolation of multi-domain neural network language model. In: IEEE International Conference on Acoustics, Speech, and Signal Processing (ICASSP), pp. 6005–6009, Shanghai, China, March 2016

87. Tüske, Z., Nolden, D., Schlüter, R., Ney, H.: Multilingual MRASTA features for low-resource keyword search and speech recognition systems. In: IEEE International Conference on Acoustics, Speech, and Signal Processing (ICASSP) (2014)

88. Tüske, Z., Schlüter, R., Ney, H.: Multilingual hierarchical MRASTA features for ASR. In: Interspeech, pp. 2222–2226, Lyon, France, August 2013

89. Tüske, Z., Sundermeyer, M., Schlüter, R., Ney, H.: Context-dependent MLPs for LVCSR: TANDEM, hybrid or both? In: Interspeech, Portland, OR, USA, pp. 18–21, September 2012

90. Tüske, Z., Tahir, M.A., Schlüter, R., Ney, H.: Integrating gaussian mixtures into deep neural networks: Softmax layer with hidden variables. In: IEEE International Conference on Acoustics, Speech, and Signal Processing (ICASSP), Brisbane, Australia, pp. 4285–4289, April 2015

91. Valente, F., Vepa, J., Plahl, C., Gollan, C., Hermansky, H., Schlüter, R.: Hierarchical neural networks feature extraction for LVCSR system. In: Interspeech, Antwerp, Belgium, pp. 42–45, August 2007

92. Waibel, A., Hanazawa, T., Hinton, G., Shikano, K., Lang, K.: Phoneme recognition: neural networks vs. hidden markov models. In: IEEE International Conference on Acoustics, Speech, and Signal Processing (ICASSP), vol. 1, pp. 107–110, April 1989

93. Wiesler, S., Golik, P., Schlüter, R., Ney, H.: Investigations on sequence training of neural networks. In: IEEE International Conference on Acoustics, Speech, and Signal Processing (ICASSP), Brisbane, Australia, pp. 4565–4569, April 2015

94. Wiesler, S., Li, J., Xue, J.: Investigations on hessian-free optimization for cross-entropy training of deep neural networks. In: Interspeech, Lyon, France, pp. 3317–3321, August 2013

95. Wiesler, S., Richard, A., Schlüter, R., Ney, H.: Mean-normalized stochastic gradient for large-scale deep learning. In: IEEE International Conference on Acoustics, Speech, and Signal Processing (ICASSP), Florence, Italy, pp. 180–184, May 2014

96. Xue, J., Li, J., Yu, D., Seltzer, M., Gong, Y.: Singular value decomposition based low-footprint speaker adaptation and personalization for deep neural network. In: IEEE International Conference on Acoustics, Speech, and Signal Processing (ICASSP), Florence, Italy, pp. 6359–6363, May 2014

97. Zeiler, M.D.: ADADELTA: An Adaptive Learning Rate Method. CoRR abs/1212.5701 (2012)

98. Zeyer, A., Doetsch, P., Voigtlaender, P., Schlüter, R., Ney, H.: A comprehensive study of deep bidirectional LSTM RNNs for acoustic modeling in speech recognition. In: Interspeech, San Francisco. CA, USA, September 2016, submitted

99. Zeyer, A., Schlüter, R., Ney, H.: Towards online-recognition with deep bidirectional LSTM acoustic models. In: Interspeech, San Francisco, CA, USA, September 2016, submitted

100. Zhang, Y., Chen, G., Yu, D., Yao, K., Khudanpur, S., Glass, J.: Highway Long Short-Term Memory RNNs for Distant Speech Recognition. arXiv preprint (2015). arxiv:1510.08983

Machine Processing of Dialogue States; Speculations on Conversational Entropy

Nick Campbell[✉]

Speech Communication Lab, ADAPT Centre, Trinity College Dublin,
Dublin, Ireland
nick@tcd.ie

Abstract. This keynote talk presents some ideas about 'conversational' speaking machines, illustrated with examples from the Herme dialogues. Herme was a small device that initiated conversations with passers-by in the Science Gallery at Trinity College in Dublin and managed to engage the majority in short conversations lasting approximately three minutes. No speech recognition was employed. Experience from that data collection and analyses of human-human conversational interactions has led us to consider a theory of Conversational Entropy wherein tight couplings become looser through time as topics decay and are refreshed by speaker changes and conversational restarts. Laughter is a particular cue to this decay mechanism and might prove to be sufficient information for machines to intrude into human conversations without causing offence.

Keywords: Interactive speech synthesis · Human-machine-interaction · Conversational engagement · Laughter · Interactional entropy · Intrusive machines

1 Introduction

People talk with machines a lot. Sometimes intentionally, sometimes unknowingly, and sometimes just for the sheer fun of it. We sit in from of our computers and many of us do actually say things in the direction of that machine, though not always with the intention of being understood. Sometimes those words are unrepeatable. Speech-based interfaces are now ubiquitous. Siri, Cortana, Hi-Google, and the rest, have become tools in our pockets that provide a short-cut to the internet; saving our thumbs for better uses than typing.

In the Speech Communication Lab (SCL) in Dublin, part of the School of Computer Science and Statistics (SCSS) at Trinity College (TCD, the University of Dublin), we are designing machines that know how to talk back. Speech synthesis is an old technology now, and can be found in many places - often unrecognised for what it is - but it is a rare synthesiser that knows it is being listened to. Yet how many people can talk to someone without checking that what they say is being heard, comprehended, understood, taken in?

Our SCL research task is the delivery of information derived from electronic content in various forms, and our need is to be sure that the person we are talking to ('we' is a machine in this case) has got the message.

© Springer International Publishing Switzerland 2016
A. Ronzhin et al. (Eds.): SPECOM 2016, LNAI 9811, pp. 18–25, 2016.
DOI: 10.1007/978-3-319-43958-7_2

So we use cameras, movement detection, and tone-of-voice changes; any data that we can sense from the outside world to inform our computers that . . .
. . . well, in the first place, that there is a person present, and that the person has functioning ears, and is listening . . . and that he or she can follow what is being said (i.e., that we speak the same language), and that they are following mentally . . . and even (one day) that they have understood.

Then we adapt what we have to say to the way that they are taking it in - perhaps by speaking faster or slower, or by using simpler words, or more intricate ones - adjusting our style of speech and manner in a way that makes it easier for the person to follow. That is the goal. This is still work in progress.

As a first step to learning more about how we should be doing this, we implemented a conversational robot, called Herme, and left it out in a public space to talk with people for three months. That was some years ago.

2   The Herme Dialogues

Herme didn't listen; like many people, she spoke a lot and she watched the person she was talking to, so as to sense their reactions, and then she just carried on speaking - drawing the interlocutor into her dialogue but not paying much attention to their replies. She could keep people 'chatting' with her for about three to five minutes before her conversation came to an end. She asked simple questions like "What's your name?" and "Why are you here today?" and waited while they replied, sometimes interjecting a "Really!" or an "Oh?" to keep them talking. Her main task was to get them, eventually, to sign a consent form so that we could use the material we were filming of their interaction. By showing them that she had found their face in her environment[1], she managed to persuade people that she was listening to them. She was certainly watching them . . . she needed to see when their face stopped moving so that she could start her next utterance. A very simple technique, but one that we found most effective.

We collected dialogues from about 1500 people of whom about two-thirds voluntarily signed our consent-form. All were recorded. Laughter was common. People were charmed by her voice (like that of a small child) and she was cute, and told them a joke, and even managed to get them to tell her a joke themselves; well, a 'knock-knock' joke anyway. Anyone can tell a knock-knock joke. And everyone laughs when they're chatting. Herme has a cute laugh.

Laughter seems to be a special form of lubricant that keeps the conversations going, but not all laughter has to do with jokes. People laugh when they're embarrassed, when they don't know what to say (if they are relaxed) and when they get the point of what you are trying to say to them. Laughs work as a sign that the conversation is going well. They're a great signal to process.

---

[1] There was a large screen behind Herme's stand showing passers-by what she could see, with a coloured circle drawn around each face in the scene.

3   Conversational Speech Synthesis

Herme used a very old speech synthesiser, Apple's *'Princess'* voice, warped by compressing the formants and raising the pitch to make it sound as if it came from a smaller body. We used a hardware filter for this[2] but it is trivial to do in software nowadays.

For laughs, she could only say "tee hee hee" and "ho-ho-ho" but it was enough. People responded to her laugh with great warmth and it relaxed them enough to keep them listening through the next stage of her spiel.

Herme was a testbed for one type of conversational interaction, but the need for more flexible conversational speech synthesis is probably great and growing. Machines must learn how to speak. They can talk already; talking machines have been around for a long time, but speaking is different: speaking needs a partner. A partner is not the same as a listener. Students listen when the professor speaks, but that is a complicated form of partnership. Most people speak in informal environments, and they intersperse their speech with chat.

We have shown that a machine can chat with a person - Herme was proof of that - but it was an unbalanced conversation. The robot took the lead and the conversation didn't get beyond the early getting-to-know-you stages. She couldn't have held a sustained conversation or spoken easily with the same people on different days without being caught out.

The machines that we use to deliver our spoken digital content will need to have a memory of what has been said (or spoken about) and will need a sense of timing or knowing when to speak. There are strong social rules for that.

3.1   A Talking Fridge

Let's imagine the smart home of the near future. Each room is wired up with sensors that stream information into the home-server (a computer that links the home with the outside world of information). It will probably be part of the fridge. The refrigerator is the one device that doesn't get switched off when people go out so there'll be a constant supply of power. The fridge is also in the place where people gather most. They might relax in front of a large screen but they probably eat round a table in the kitchen. It's the family place.

Like Herme, the fridge (or the home-server, an interactional device) can monitor what is going on in the room around it. It doesn't have to listen to what is being said or talked about; just know enough about who is doing what to be able to interrupt with a message if it has one. If the people around the table are deep in conversation (i.e., their heads are moving in a certain pattern and sounds are being made), then it might be wiser to wait for a lull in the talk before butting in with what it has to say. If they are watching the news, then it might be better to wait until the adverts come on.

It would good for our machine if it had a notion of conversational states and of the types of engagement of each conversational participant in the real world around it. The fridge needs awareness.

---

[2] A Roland Sound Canvas.

3.2   Entropy (An Interlude)

Erwin Schrodinger [5] was at TCD when he gave his lectures on "What is life? The Physical Aspect of the Living Cell"[3]. He said:

> Every process, event, happening - call it what you will; in a word, every-thing that is going on in Nature means an increase of the entropy of the part of the world where it is going on. Thus a living organism continually increases its entropy - or, as you may say, produces positive entropy - and thus tends to approach the dangerous state of maximum entropy, which is of death. It can only keep aloof from it, i.e. alive, by continually drawing from its environment negative entropy -which is something very positive as we shall immediately see. What an organism feeds upon is negative entropy. Or, to put it less paradoxically, the essential thing in metabolism is that the organism succeeds in freeing itself from all the entropy it cannot help producing while alive.

Conversation is a living organism. Entropy kills conversation. Laughter reduces entropy by resetting the topic, and so keeps conversation alive.

He also said (in the same lectures):

> The disintegration of a single radioactive atom is observable (it emits a projectile which causes a visible scintillation on a fluorescent screen). But if you are given a single radioactive atom, its probable lifetime is much less certain than that of a healthy sparrow. Indeed, nothing more can be said about it than this: as long as it lives (and that may be for thousands of years) the chance of its blowing up within the next second, whether large or small, remains the same.

but this is a matter for discussion elsewhere.

Google's definition of entropy :

entropy

/ˈɛntrəpi/ ◀)

noun

1.   PHYSICS
     a thermodynamic quantity representing the unavailability of a system's thermal energy for conversion into mechanical work, often interpreted as the degree of disorder or randomness in the system.
     "the second law of thermodynamics says that entropy always increases with time"

2.   lack of order or predictability; gradual decline into disorder.
     "a marketplace where entropy reigns supreme"

---

[3] Lectures delivered under the auspices of the Dublin Institute for Advanced Studies at Trinity College, Dublin, in February 1943.

4   A Notion of Conversational Entropy

After Herme, we became more interested in laughter and especially how it punctuates a discourse. Francesca Bonin's PhD [2] examined the structure of conversational interaction and explored the relation between social signals and discourse phenomena such as topic changes, investigating whether social signals have a discourse function in addition to their social function. Different analyses that investigated the temporal dynamics of laughter, backchannels, silences and overlaps, were explored, finding a relation between topic changes and a decrease of social signals. Specifically, it was found that immediately after a topic change there is a significant drop in social activity, defined by her as interactional entropy: *"The interactional entropy of a segment x is defined as the number of occurrences of social signals in x"* (ibid p.71).

Through comparing topic changes in two corpora of spontaneous spoken interaction, she concluded that a constant trend emerges in both TableTalk and AMI: topic terminations (wt) show a significantly higher presence of signals if compared to topic beginnings (wb). In AMI [4], among all the distributions of frequencies of laughter, overlaps, silences, lexical and non-lexical backchannels in wt and wb the non-parametric Wilcoxon test rejects the null hypothesis of wb = wt and validates the alternative hypothesis of $wb < wt, p < 0.0005$. In TableTalk [1] the same applies to laughter, overlaps, and lexical backchannels. In other words, topic terminations reveal higher interactional entropy than topic beginnings.

> In fact a drop in social signals appears to occur immediately after a topic change when the interactional entropy [...] is reduced. Participants show the tendency to limit the interaction immediately after a topic change, probably to leave the floor to the speaker who has introduced the new topic (ibid p.128).

She clearly showed that after a topic change a decrease of interactional entropy occurs, and concludes that this information might be used to better understand the discourse structure via non-linguistic information such as laughter, overlaps, backchannels, and silence, and thereby shed new light upon the discourse functionality of social signals.

It seems that introducing a new topic reduces the entropy of a conversation ('feeding it', as Schrodinger would say). Conversely, by observing the amount of non-verbal behaviour in speech (particularly laughter) we can estimate the likelihood of a forthcoming topic change, and thereby enable our device to interrupt at a timely point without having to listen in on the actual content of any conversations.[4]

The system can be aware of its environment through sensing movement and the dynamics of vocal activity around it. It doesn't need to listen. Perhaps that is what many people do too? Conversation is a uniquely human form of behaviour.

---

[4] The idea that household devices might be capable of eavesdropping on nearby conversations is rightly anathema to many kitchen owners and occupants.

5   Social Interactions and Signal Processing

For our system though, a conversation is a data source; a signal that is available to be processed. With Herme, we avoided the use of ASR (automatic speech recognition) for several reasons; it often fails in a noisy environment, it needs specialised domain dictionaries and language models, and it is intrusive. It is the last point that is of most concern to us now. Herme was in a public space and engaged in trivial social chat with a large number of unknown people. Nothing sensitive or really personal was discussed. In the home though, the situation is different. The potential for misuse of available information has been much in the news recently and people in general are now becoming quite wary of devices that leak or pass on information. The law may be clear (voluntary sign-in usually absolves the supplier of legal responsibility), and the ethical issues are certainly of concern to most scientists, but the technology must be made watertight against leaks if our work is to be trusted in society-at-large.

5.1   Natural Human-Machine Conversational Interaction

The 'listening & watching' fridge that may host our technology in the future should be able to observe the goings-on in its environment much as a pet dog may watch and be aware of the happenings of the home. It will of course have to 'listen' carefully when commands or instructions are given, but when in 'sleep mode', it should not be hearing everything.

The work presented above may offer a solution to this conundrum. If the device keeps a measure of the entropy of conversations in the home, without listening to what is being said, through processing of non-verbal and behavioural information, then it can perhaps be considered safe.

At the same time, the amount of processing that is required from a 'conversational agent' can also perhaps be significantly reduced; if the machine only has to devote energy to processing linguistic/semantic propositional information at certain isolated points in the signal then its energy can be greatly preserved, and more time may be devoted to the arduous symbolic processing needed to 'understand' speech.

By maintaining an awareness of the social energy in its environment, perhaps our speaking device will appear well-mannered, only interrupting when necessary and maybe often with a delicate or appropriate sense of timing? It might be far-fetched to imagine the machine joining in with a joke as Herme did, but if it has the sense to 'understand' what processes are happening in the human sphere, then like a pet cat or dog at home, it might be a welcome guest.

6   Conclusions

This paper describes some ideas to be presented in a Keynote at Specom 2016. The invitation tentatively specified "Overview of speech technology results, challenges, trends, promising directions in Social Interactions and Signal Processing" as a title. We chose instead to present some current work from our lab in Dublin as the basis for speculation about higher matters. The facts of current research are perhaps well represented by other papers in these proceedings.

The concept of entropy was introduced at the beginning of the previous century and has been well-understood by physicists, chemists, and information engineers, among others, but has failed to take hold in the humanities. This is sad. Our entire world is subject to entropy, and its concepts may throw light on more than mere mechanics or thermodynamics. The actions of people in society, and particularly the structured actions of participants in conversation are subject to the same laws, and the same probabilistic processes.

Addendum Gibbs' definition of free energy : (something good to think about)

> the greatest amount of mechanical work which can be obtained from a given
> quantity of a certain substance in a given initial state, without increasing its
> total volume or allowing heat to pass to or from external bodies, except such
> as at the close of the processes are left in their initial condition [3].

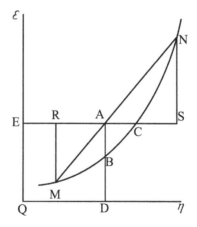

Fig. 1. Graphical representation of the free energy of a body. The figure shows a plane of constant volume, passing through the point A that represents the body's initial state. The curve MN is the section of the "surface of dissipated energy". AD and AE are, respectively, the energy (ϵ) and entropy (η) of the initial state. AB is the "available energy" (now called the Helmholtz free energy) and AC the "capacity for entropy" (i.e., the amount by which the entropy can be increased without changing the energy or volume). From Gibbs, J.W. (1873). "A method of geometrical representation of the thermodynamic properties of substances by means of surfaces". Transactions of the Connecticut Academy of Arts and Sciences 2: 382–404., Public Domain, https://commons.wikimedia.org/w/index.php?curid=3279793

Acknowledgments. This research is supported by Science Foundation Ireland under Grant No. 13/RC/2016, through the ADAPT Centre for Digital Content Technology (www.adaptcentre.ie) at Trinity College, Dublin. We are grateful to the School of Computer Science and Statistics at Trinity College Dublin for their support of the Speech Communication Lab.

References

1. Tabletalk is a multimodal multimedia corpus of free flowing natural conversations, recorded at the advanced telecommunication research labs in Japan (2005). http://sspnet.eu/2010/02/freetalk/
2. Bonin, F.: Unpublished Ph.D. thesis: "Content and Context in Conversations: The Role of Social and Situational Signals in Conversation Structure". Trinity College Dublin, Ireland (2015)
3. Gibbs, J.W.: A method of geometrical representation of the thermodynamic properties of substances by means of surfaces. Connecticut Academy of Arts and Sciences (1873)
4. McCowan, I., Carletta, J., Kraaij, W., Ashby, S., Bourban, S., Flynn, M., Guillemot, M., Hain, T., Kadlec, J., Karaiskos, V., et al.: The AMI meeting corpus. In: Proceedings of the 5th International Conference on Methods and Techniques in Behavioral Research, vol. 88 (2005)
5. Schrödinger, E.: What Is Life? the physical aspect of the living cell and mind. Dublin (1943)

Speech Recognition Challenges in the Car Navigation Industry

Attila Vékony[✉]

Component Architect, NNG LLC, Budapest, Hungary
attila.vekony@nng.com

Abstract. Until a few decades ago, machines talking and understanding human speech were only the subject of science fiction. Nowadays, Text to Speech (TTS) and Automatic Speech Recognition (ASR) became reality, but they are still being considered to be fancy. Automotive infotainment is a selling point for car manufacturers, it is a symbol of being hi-tech, and car commercials often feature the display of the head unit for a few seconds. As avoiding Driver Distraction has grown a major design aspect, ASR is becoming trendy and almost compulsory. But let us see how far we have gotten. In the first part, this talk will summarize the most popular Speech features in today's car navigation systems, and will look into the underlying technology, solutions and limitations widely applied in the industry. We will mention typical context designs, dialogue systems and address search, and we will show how the common technology leads to typical HMI solutions. We will point out the possibilities and limitations of on-board and server-based recognition, and consider why we need to resort to exclusively offline solutions for a while in this industry. At this point we will have an overview of the ingredients, so the talk will focus on problematic and sub-optimal ASR features requested by automotive manufacturers, explaining why they negatively affect recognition accuracy. A workaround often leads to troublesome and seemingly unnecessary questions for the user, so it is not easy to compromise. In the last part, we will examine a certain address search scenario which is trivial for users, and is feasible with a server-based ASR, however being an open question when done offline.

Keywords: Car navigation · On-board speech technology · Connected car

1 Infotainment in a Car

Entertainment with information technology has entered vehicles: airplanes, trains, buses and cars. You have a couple of loud speakers, a radio and a digital audio player at minimum. But contemporary cars tend to have multiple displays. A main display in the dashboard, the smaller *cluster display* behind the steering wheel, and on higher grade cars there may be displays in the back of the front seats, for the passengers. Also, contemporary cars tend to have multiple microphones. What to do with so many displays, microphones and loud speakers? Automotive manufacturers want to offer more and more. They want to provide a cutting edge driver experience: it should be natural, fun and off course it should be safe. They want to entertain you, but also, they want to

© Springer International Publishing Switzerland 2016
A. Ronzhin et al. (Eds.): SPECOM 2016, LNAI 9811, pp. 26–40, 2016.
DOI: 10.1007/978-3-319-43958-7_3

protect you. Today, the vision is an intelligent car integrated to your everyday life via cloud-based technology, caring about your well-being and safety. The industry regards speech recognition as having the *fun* and *safe* property, and according to the gossips about upcoming regulations, lawmakers do.

Another motivation in the car industry, which is affecting in the opposite way, is that manufacturers want a 5 to 10 years of life cycle for their products. The investment per unit is considerable, so it is in the OEM's interest to have the same model on the market for a couple of years. It is not like the mobile phone industry, where several models are released within each year. Car makers typically negotiate a ten years support with a navigation provider, though mainly content update is expected. The car industry has a certain inertia, changes come more slowly.

2 Most Popular Speech Features in a Car

The first line-fit speech-based features were telephony and turn-by-turn navigation. With the development of the hardware and navigation data, the list has grown longer in the recent decade, but although ASR appeared, telephone and turn-by-turn navigation are still considered to play a key role in avoiding user distraction.

Voice prompts
- *Turn-by-turn navigation (pre-recorded audio files)*
- *Turn-by-turn navigation (with a real Text-to-Speech engine)*
- *Warnings (speed limit and other restrictions)*
- *Traffic information*
- *Speech recognition prompts and reading out pick lists*

Telephony
- *Accept call*
- *Ignore call*
- *Ignore call with predefined messages*
- *Digit dialing*
- *Contact dialing*

Places of Interest (POI)
- *Petrol station*
- *Parking*
- *Food*
- *Accommodation*
- *POI categories and subcategories*
- *POI brands*

Address entry
- *One-shot address entry*
- *Step-by-step address entry*
- *Taxi mode*
- *Country selection*
- *Home address*
- *Work address*
- *Favourites*
- *Previous desinations*

3 Talking Cars: A Few TTS Questions in Car Navigation

3.1 Who has the Right to Speak?

In an automotive head unit, a few applications and their modules are competing for the access of the TTS engine. The speech engine is a shared resource, and components have to request for an exclusive access, tagging the request to let the system know the intention. It is up to the HMI designer to prioritize components or intentions. Here are some generic rules that are considered, often contradicting each other. Unfortunately, it is not possible to have everything at the topmost level. Each customer has some reasoning why the priorities should be like that, for example that surveys had proven so. The software has to have the flexibility to support whatever the customer wants.

- Prompts should not be interrupted. (Let us queue requests instead, manage priority and timeout. Sources should be able to create sentences with various verbosity levels.)
- An incoming phone call is very important, because it requires immediate high priority actions.
- Phone calls should not be disturbed with voice prompts. (Short sound effects may be all right, letting the user about what is happening meanwhile.)
- Warnings must have high priority, due to safety reasons. (The whole announcement flow may have to be rearranged.)
- Speech recognition sessions may be interrupted, so that the user does not miss important events.
- Speech recognition sessions should not be interrupted, as the driver is just about expressing their wish.

3.2   Pre-recorded Voice or TTS?

Although technically different only by granulation, pre-recorded voices and a TTS voice have different pros and cons. A pre-recorded voice, although more flexible regarding the sentence collection, is limited to a scale of available languages of a particular TTS engine. A pre-recorded voice requires a real speaker, a "talent", whose voice is recorded in audio files per word or expression. Thus, it is possible to implement any languages or dialects with fine-tuned, high quality material, at the cost of storage space and flexibility. An important feature is missing: being able to read out place names. (With the notable exception of Japan, where a map supplier recorded a raw audio data filling seven DVD's. This data is rarely used due to its high price.) In general, a TTS voice being able to announce street names is considered to be more desirable, but celebrity or themed voices certainly add some fun factor. What is for sure is that having excellent prompts is expensive.

3.3   Timing and Verbosity

In turn-by-turn navigation, automotive customers often define the distances from the maneuver, at which the voice guidance has to speak. Then, it is a typical task for the navigation to generate a similar sentence about the maneuver at different verbosity levels, e.g. depending on how far the maneuver is:

- *"In* 100 m *turn right on Wellington St West, then take next left."*
- *"In* 70 m*, turn right on Wellington St West."*
- *"In* 50 m*, turn right."*
- *"Take the next right."*

The aim is to inform the driver in time so that they have the chance to react. The algorithm needs to measure how much time a given sentence takes a TTS engine has to support that. If it is not supported, the navigation algorithm has to estimate the time, based on the sentence itself. Observe the difference between these two possibilities:

- *"Turn right in* **50** m. *"*
- *"In* **50** m, *turn right. "*

It is the matter of localization, and customers may prefer one of them, but there is an important difference regarding timing. The sentence has to be aligned so that the display shows exactly 50 m by the time it is announced. The first sentence tells the user what to do, and only then does it mention the distance. However, the user may miss the direction, because they are not prepared to receive the information after a long silence from the voice guidance. With the second sentence, the direction is mentioned in the end, leaving more time for the user to prepare. A popular trick is to play a short sound effect, have a little pause and only then comes the announcement. But still, the exact time is to be calculated, at which the whole process starts. The heuristics rely on the data delivered by the hardware, but current speed and direction may change unexpectedly, leading to misaligned announcements (and bug reports).

3.4   Is Phonetical Data Always Beneficial for the Driver?

Phonetical data is meant to polish the pronunciation of the TTS. (Additionally, it is an essential ingredient for the ASR content.) Although map suppliers provide an increasing phonetical coverage of place names, it is not evident that users benefit of this feature. As a native speaker, they definitely do, but driving abroad may be a challenge, when you have to match what you hear with what you see. The original pronunciation in a voice guidance announcement may not help you to identify foreign street names - maybe it would be better to let the engine make a guess without phonetics - just as the user would. The best practice is to have it as an option in Settings, with Enabled as a default.

3.5   Grammatically Correct Monolingual Sentences

Another aspect of the dilemma is that many languages require the alteration of names, when fit in a sentence. It is so easy to say in English: *"Traffic jam ahead on S Franklin St"* or *"I heard S Franklin St. Is that correct?"* where *S Franklin St, Chicago* and *IL* are to be substituted with their corresponding phonetical transcription. But what about Russian or German? *"Traffic jam ahead on Presnenskiy Pereulok"* is problematic, because *"Пресненский переулок"* becomes *"на Пресненском переулке"* in the Russian sentence, which does not have its phonetical form in the data. So the only thing to do here is to play the string as is, and let the TTS engine guess the pronunciation. This use case is somewhat easier in German, where *"die Bahnhofstrasse"* has to be fit with the correct definite article: *"Stau vor an der Bahnhofstrasse"*. But in general, having a grammatically correct sentence with perfect pronunciation requires deeper linguistic processing, which does not usually happen in this industry. It is up to the creativity of translators, to find a sentence where the original form can be used. Then the phonetics is positively useful.

3.6 Multilingual Sentences

Lately, TTS engines feature the ability of being able to use more languages within an announcement. This is not trivial, even from the perspective of the integration in the navigation. Here are some challenging use cases.

- English name in a Chinese sentence - different scripts are be involved.
- Polish driver in Germany - no Polish phonetics available in Germany.
- French driver in Spain - there is phonetical coverage in Spanish, but it is a language-dependent phonetical alphabet.

Each TTS speaker has a list of supported languages, and the navigation software has to select orthography or phonetics accordingly. The engine is capable of using the phonetical alphabet of a few selected languages. The pronunciation is quite good, but nowhere perfect. It sounds like when a German person is speaking Russian name. The integration of such feature is easier if the TTS engine supports a language-independent phonetical alphabet.

3.7 Sound Quality

Human ear is very tolerant human speech is well intelligible in the worst conditions - it may be a result of our evolution. Still, car manufacturers want to provide the best possible quality. A voice guidance announcement at the quality of 22 kHz, 16 bit mono is acceptable on a small speaker, but it may sound cheesy on the loud speaker system of an expensive car.

As of 2016, the TTS speakers in a typical car are neutral, calm and polite. Embedded TTS engines are offered in scalable packages regarding footprint, audio format and expressiveness, it is the matter of disk space, processing capacity and price. But TTS engine suppliers are developing cloud-based solutions with more interesting qualities, trying to make the dreams of automotive manufacturers come true. Upcoming connected digital assistants feature semantic analysis, advanced machine learning based on neural networks and artificial intelligence techniques. The purpose is to help the driver keeping their eye on the road, and reduce the cognitive load of the interaction with the machine. The more natural the interaction, the safer the vehicle - this is what the main motivation is. As nothing is more natural to a human then speech, ASR is regarded as one of the safest means of communication in a vehicle.

4   When the Driver is Speaking: ASR Solutions in Navigation

An ASR context is the representation of the search space, that describes the recognizable elements. The aim is to identify the driver's intention uttered in a certain language or dialect, so that the system can perform an action accordingly. Before looking at challenging scenarios, let us quickly run through the techniques used in automotive speech recognition, as of 2016. Unfortunately, we are living in the dawn of speech recognition, the available solutions in the industry is rather limited.

4.1 Contexts for On-board Recognizers

In case of an on-board recognition, the whole search space is phonetized and optimized off-line. Then, the generated contexts are deployed to the head unit, in order to provide the least possible processing at run time. As part of this optimization, it is typical to assign unique numbers to phonetic buffers, which represent intentions or names, so that the context can get rid of the orthographic form. After the recognition has returned a hypothesis list as a vector of ID's, a pre-generated ASR dictionary is used to map identifiers to intention tokens or real names.

4.1.1 Voice Commands

In case of simple voice commands, even if the context contains alternative phonetics, they are typically mapped to the same ID to represent one certain intention, like ASR_KEY_PARKING. Then this token is localized in the HMI to be displayed or to be read back for the driver.

> *<ASR_KEY_PARKING>: ([rechercher]|[trouver]) [un] (parking | parc de stationnement);*
> *<ASR_KEY_PARKING_ALONG_ROUTE>: ([rechercher]|[trouver]) [un] parking sur l'itinéraire |*
> *([rechercher]|[trouver]) [un] parc de stationnement sur l'itinéraire;*
> *<ASR_KEY_PARKING_AT_DESTINATION>: ([rechercher]|[trouver]) [un] parking ([près de*
> *la]|[à]) destination | ([rechercher]|[trouver]) [un] parc de stationnement ([près de la]|[à])*
> *destination;*
> *<ASR_KEY_PARKING_NEARBY>: ([rechercher]|[trouver]) [un] parking près d'ici |*
> *([rechercher]|[trouver]) [un] parc de stationnement près d'ici | ([rechercher]|[trouver]) [un]*
> *parking proche d'ici | ([rechercher]|[trouver]) [un] parc de stationnement proche d'ici;*

The essential rules about voice commands are:

- The language of voice commands must match that of the GUI.
- Whatever is displayed in the GUI as a caption, it has to be represented in the context. (If the driver reads "Fuel Station", then it is not enough to recognize only "petrol station" and "gas station".)
- Localize the voice commands so that they are distant enough phonetically. (It is unfortunate to have "Answer" and "Cancel" to accept or ignore an incoming phone call, because they are easy to be misrecognized.)

In most Speech UI designs, the hypothesis list or voice command is never displayed for the driver, the item with the best confidence level is accepted instead, if the confidence is above a certain threshold.

4.1.2 Destination Entry

A wildly used approach is to organize the context in a way, that the address structure is defined for the country in terms of fields (like state-city-street), and then all the valid addresses are listed. Then the phonetical data is used to generate ASR data for this region, then a hypothesis is a well-structured address, consisting of fields. It is also possible to select a block from this context, like street recognition York, AL.

Alabama|Abbeville|Abbeville Parrish Bridge Rd
Alabama|Abbeville|Alberta Dr

...

Alabama|York|Wrenn St
Alabama|York|Wright Rd
Alabama|York|York Ave

...

Wyoming|Yoder|W 3rd Ave
Wyoming|Yoder|W 4th Ave
Wyoming|Yoder|Williams St

In scenarios like this, where larger lists are involved, localized place names are not included in the context. Names are represented by numerical identifiers, and the mapping is described in ASR dictionaries, localized in a certain language. (E.g. there are alternative names in Switzerland in multiple languages, and unless the recognizer has multilingual capabilities, you cannot have *Genève* in a German context.) The best practice is to assign the same ID to homonyms, e.g. all of the cities called *Saint-Julien* get the same ID, and all of the places called *Saint-Junien* have another common ID. The first question for the driver after resolving the ID's is whether they want *Saint-Julien* or *Saint-Junien*, and the selected name is used as a keyword in an address search on navigation side. Then the navigation lists the matching addresses, disambiguating the name.

4.1.3 Address Points

Note that, house numbers and address points are not represented in the previous design, as adding a house number field would make the context explode. Instead, address points are recognized with an unconstrained grammar, meaning that it implements a relatively free dictation along predefined rules, and it is optimized for recognition accuracy. The result may be an invalid address point, which has to be handled later on. E.g. a Russian address point grammar would look like this.

```
<enter_house_number>: <template_1> | <template_2> | <template_3> | <template_4> |
<template_5> | <template_6> | <template_7>;

<template_1>: <number> [<letter>];
<template_2>: <number> (<per> | <korp>) <number>;
<template_3>: <number> <korp> <number> <stro> <number> [<letter>];
<template_4>: <number> [<letter>] <stro> <number> [<letter>];
<template_5>: <number> <per> <number> <korp> <number> [(<stro> <number>)];
<template_6>: <number> <per> <number> <stro> <number> [<letter>];
<template_7>: <number> <letter_ze> <stro> <number> [<letter>];

<street_center>: центр улицы | середина улицы;
<per>: дробь;
<korp>: корпус;
<stro>: строение | дом;
<letter>: А | Бэ | Вэ | Гэ| Дэ | Е | Жэ | Зэ;
   <number>: ...
```

4.2   Contexts for Server-Based Recognizers

Server based generic recognizers typically return simple text in the hypothesis list, paired with some confidence scores. The client cannot define a certain domain, only a language is to be set. In this scenario there have to be two contexts. A rather large and complex context on server side, and a smaller context on client side. The server is powerful with great processing capacity, so the search space may be huge, not necessarily described in the form of lists, as flexible grammars and statistical models may be involved. The capacity on client side is more modest, so the task is restricted to string parsing, finding things in the output that are meaningful in the realm of navigation. Although the user can say anything eventually, it is important to point out that it is always clear on client side what the driver is expected to say. The reason is that the system is not listening continuously, we either have a Push to Talk (PTT) button or a wake up word. The navigation is not prepared to get lyrics or food ingredients, but it is prepared to get some navigation related voice commands, place names, an address or some combination of these. With a clever string parsing, it is possible to implement some NLU-like behavior. (Natural Language Understanding).

4.2.1   Voice Commands on Client Side

In order to extract the driver's intention from the text result on a basic level, it is enough to define certain keywords, and have some heuristics to measure the confidence. Confidence levels coming from the server are not enough. Even if the server is quite sure the user said *"Heat olive oil in a large Dutch oven"*, it's not meaningful, it is out of context. But if the result text is *"Is there a car park around here?"* or *"Find parking around my destination."* we can have an algorithm to make the user happy. In these cases, the basic POI categories are regarded as simple voice commands.

4.2.2   Destination Entry on Client Side

It is possible to implement more sophisticated destination entry with a server-based recognizer, because the server has such a large search space. Recognition-wise, an utterance may contain a command, a POI brand name and a city/suburb name, like *"Drive me to a Shell station in Berkely, MI."* Although it is not trivial to parse this string on client side, the processing complexity cannot be compared that of phonetizing and typing the utterance.

5   Dialogue Systems in a Car

The dialogue between user and the system involves a series of voice prompts and answers from the user, refining the data in order to define a certain action. There is a trend of replacing the usual speech menu with an all-commands-at-top-level solution.

It is very common in the industry to create a UI flow dedicated to speech recognition, separating them from the corresponding haptic interface. In an ordinary GUI, it is acceptable to feature lots of visual information in a single screen, but the Speech UI is typically streamlined to be easy to comprehend. Although distraction is a concern, manufacturers often expect multi-modality: you can control the system by either speech or touch, and it is expected to implement a fluent transition between the two worlds. (People may want to use voice destination entry before even starting the engine, simply because it is faster than typing all of those historical names. Still, the UI flow has to be the same no matter if the car is moving or not.)

5.1 Professional Approach

The leader speech engine provider in the automotive market does not only offer the basic TTS and ASR engines, they also offer the service of providing a customized dialogue system. This is quite attracting to automotive Tier1's because they get a professional service, which has proven in many products for many cultures. Another advantage is that the whole head unit becomes ASR-capable, as the Professional Service covers a couple of domains.

This approach is rather expensive, though, and the reason is not only the cost of this service. A unique property of this approach is that the speech flow is controlled by the Dialogue, and not by a GUI flow consisting of screens. The Dialogue keeps track of the details of the topic, and asks more questions if necessary. So from the perspective of integration, an address search by speech scenario is one of the most complex things on an automotive head unit. There may be multiple parties involved:

- Map supplier
- Speech engine provider, often implementing a speech-only dialogue system
- (Optionally, another professional speech company, adding value to the basic TTS and ASR engines, sometimes also supplying the ASR graphical interface.)
- Automotive Tier1 providing hardware, and the graphical interface
- An IT company providing the OS or communication between applications.

The address search dialogue requires the communication between the dialogue system and the navigation, running through the software layers in between. So when a modification is necessary, there are multiple layers involved, multiple parties with whom the matter has to be discussed. So such ASR projects have a rather long integration phase. Off course, after a larger investment in the first product in a series, other regions may require a shorter development.

5.2 Unique Dialogue System on Navigation Side

Lower cost projects require speech features only on navigation side, generally excluding other applications. In these cases, the TTS and ASR engines are integrated by their provider, they are in the navigation app or in Tier1 software instead. Since the speech UI and GUI is also there, this approach has less integration cost. This approach is more demanding for the integrators, requiring a deeper understanding in speech technology.

5.3 Similar Designs in the Industry

Although automotive manufacturers are eager to differentiate their products by customization, there is a certain standard in the industry. Manufacturers design their own appearance, menu structure and speech error handling, but since the underlying speech engine is the same, they end up at about the same level of quality. It is true that the main speech technology provider improves the engine, continuously increasing accuracy and the language portfolio, but this is available to all automotive OEM's. As a result, no matter who implements the dialogue, navigation related ASR content is generated on navigation side, and similar context designs lead to the same recognition accuracy. And the limitation of offline contexts lead to similar refinement questions for the user, leading to similar HMI flows. On the other hand, the professional dialogue approach has a certain set of recommendations and best practices, which affect in the same direction.

6 Limitations and Sub-optimal ASR Features

6.1 Connected Cars are Coming Soon

If the infotainment system in a car has access to external data, then it may be regarded as connected. However, in the strict meaning a connected car has access to resources on the Internet. The possibilities of a connected car are very exciting, almost all of the usual features can be greatly improved with the processing power and knowledge base of distant servers. Still, as of 2016, the era of connected cars has not come. As there are huge areas without mobile net coverage, and mobile charges are rather pricey, car manufacturers still not willing to provide sufficient hardware. However, it is possible to use the driver's mobile phone for connectivity, either with direct HTTP based inquiries to certain data sources, or via a branded companion application. In urban scenarios this may work, and it may provide improved functionality.

This kind of hybrid solution seems to be the best approach, but major companies are reluctant to provide features that behave in a different way without an Internet connection. The main reason is that drivers are used to a certain flow, and it is disturbing to get something else sometimes. We may argue with it, and the future is inevitably connected, but still, providing offline solutions is compulsory in this industry.

The limited size of the content, limited amount of memory and the limited processing capacity lead to significant restrictions in the embedded on-board speech recognition. We have to find the balance between tolerable response time and recognition accuracy. Following the recommendations from the ASR engine provider, it is possible to get the optimum from this limited system. Still, automotive customers are often not willing to compromise, they ask for sub-optimal use cases, which then lead to bug reports and unnecessary cycles in the development. In some cases, that certain feature is modified even in the first model in the series, and sometimes it happens only in 2.0 or higher. Let us mention a few problematic scenarios in the embedded on-board recognition.

6.2 Separate Address Recognition and Address Disambiguation

Although among engineers there is a general consensus about the best practice, customers sometimes want to get rid of unnecessary questions for the driver. Assigning the same ID to homonyms is a necessary step in optimizing recognition accuracy for large field contexts. This means that the recognizer is unable to differentiate among cities of identical names or streets of identical names. For instance, the driver says *"5 Church Hill London"*. The recognizer does not differentiate instances of Church Hill, they have the same ID throughout the country. In the dialogue, the first question typically refers to phonetically similar ASR hypothesis list:

(1) *London*
(2) *Longdon.*

Once the driver selected London for instance, then the matching addresses are looked up in the map database, and there is a second question if the address is ambiguous:

(1) *5 Church Hill, Winchmore Hill (London) N21 1*
(2) *5 Church Hill, Wimbledon (London) SW19 7.*

Automotive partners would like to have these two questions in a single list:

(1) *5 Church Hill, Winchmore Hill (London) N21 1*
(2) *5 Church Hill, Wimbledon (London) SW19 7*
(3) *Church Hill, Longdon (Rugekey) WS15 4.*

Looking at this example, this sounds reasonable. The problem is that in Europe, there may be dozens or even hundreds of places with identical names. There are 109 places in France called *Saint-Julien* and more than 200 places called *Berg* in Germany. Although only 9 of the 109 Saint-Julien's have that exact name, the rest have *Saint-Julien* as an alternative name, so they should be represented indeed. The separation of the *hypothesis list* from the *address disambiguation list* is necessary, because ASR is dealing with phonetics (or even orthography), so for the sake of accuracy, the only thing the recognizer has to decide whether it is *London* or *Longdon*, *Saint-Julien* or *Saint-Junien*. With one-shot address entry over a field context, there is a geographical-based connection between the fields, but this is merely for the sake of accurate one-shot recognition, to be able to decide what the user wants. And then, let the navigation do the address search job.

6.3 Recognition of All Address Points in One-Shot

In Western Europe and North America, house numbers are simple integers, however they may be spelled in a different fashion, like digit by digit or grouping digits. Although recognizing the house number digits alone would give pretty high confidence, pairing the unconstrained grammar with the large field lists will decrease the confidence of the address. And as one-shot address entry is expected so much in car navigation, this decrease is tolerated. The situation becomes more complicated in cultures where the house number describes an address point which is not necessarily accessible by car, lying in a pedestrian area, in the certain side of a house block. We mentioned the house numbers in Russia, but could also mention Poland, Taiwan, Korea, etc. The more complex an address point system is the less accurate one-shot address entry becomes. The worst scenario we came across is the addressing system of India, where a wide variety of digit-letter combination exists, separated by two special characters, which must also be recognized. ("-" is *"dash"*, "/" is *"by"*.)

1-14	*101AJ28*
1-66/3	*A1546*
1-C/1	*A19A*
1/10-4/10	*A1B26*
1/10062A	*A2/16-23/24-30*
1/10101/5	*RZ283/64A*
1/15/16/17	*RZ46/AA1*
1/UA	*RZB18/B*

The result is a disaster, and all we can do is separate the address point recognition from the rest of the address. Actually, the most accurate method to recognize such strings currently is the building of spelling trees. Unfortunately, with this very popular ASR engine, spelling trees cannot be used in a single recognition with large field contexts.

6.4   Address Search with NLU at Top Level

NLU at top level is a common feature in navigation. It is convenient for the user: simply press the button and say what you want. With the professional approach, it is implemented with statistical language modelling. By training the NLU buffers, and processing a gate command to branch to a relevant domain, it is possible for the driver to say *"Destination 121 Jackson St, Trenton, NJ"* or *"Drive me to 121 Jackson St, Trenton, NJ"*. There are more problems here. The address recognition involves a large list, which is demanding enough. Then the accuracy is decreased with an unconstrained house number recognizer, which may consume some of the syllables by mistake. And finally, there comes the audio of the voice command. The feature vector is extracted from the utterance, and the vector is processed against multiple contexts, but the NLU approach allows uncertainty in the voice command. So the syllables of the command, and the syllables for the unconstrained grammar definitely reduce the recognition accuracy of the large list.

By removing NLU and restricting this voice command to a single expression (*"Destination ..."*) would help, but then the driver would have to remember that certain phrase. For optimal accuracy, two separate utterances are required: a command to enter address entry mode, and another one to recognize the address.

6.5   Places in a City

The typical approach for POI category selection, POI brands and addresses involves large lists, and alone they are all feasible with embedded recognition. But automotive customers would like to have the convenient feature of having the place and the city in a single utterance: *"Shell station in Berkeley, MI."* This is natural for the user, and it is generally available in a cloud-based environment. People are used to it in the world of smart phones. However, in case of embedded recognition, this feature is rather challenging, as there is size limitation on ASR content. What projects do is they pair the POI context and the address context, creating a very large search space, as those two contexts are independent. This leads to really bad recognition results.

The easiest solution is to implement this feature in two questions: "What place?", "In what city?", but customers are unwilling to accept this one. Another solution could be to sacrifice some space, and generate a dedicated large field context, listing all the places with city names per state: $< place > <city > <state >$. Such a context returns valid hypothesis items, because this is guaranteed at compilation time. And it has optimal accuracy. Unfortunately, the size of such content file is comparable to a full one-shot context, so the Place in a City feature is a challenge.

6.6   Step-by-Step Address Entry with the One-Shot Context

The aforementioned content size reasoning leads the speech engine provider to develop the technology to use the same content for one-shot and set-by-step recognition. This is a workaround, having some drawbacks, but the result is quite satisfying, so this solution is featured in millions of cars. The context is optimized for one-shot address entry, homonyms have identical ID's. And when it comes to step-by-step, and the city is selected, the streets of a super *Saint-Julien* is activated: all the streets in the union of *Saint-Julien*'s. Suppose the user has disambiguated the city, and specified one certain *Saint-Julien*. But then, certain streets names in the street hypothesis list may be invalid in that certain city. What happens if the user happens to select that one? The workaround is that the navigation has to filter the hypothesis list, removing non existing addresses. And what happens, if all of the elements in the street hypothesis list belong to another city? The problem is that automotive ASR systems typically show the best 3 or 5 items, and phonetically similar items may push at the top results.

7   Open Questions

The previous scenarios were problematic, but there is always a workaround, and despite their drawbacks they are applied in the car navigation industry. As a last topic, let me mention two problems that the industry is facing, without a satisfying answer in 2016.

7.1   Address Entry in India

Several languages are spoken in India, and although many of them are related, they cannot understand each other. The common language is English and Hindi, so these languages are suitable for address entry by speech. But a speaker of one Indian language does not know how to pronounce a name in another language, so users are guessing when navigating to another part of the country. We can state that address entry by speech is only feasible if the expectation of the user meets the expectation of the recognizer. A viable approach could be if we used phonetics for well-known places, and have the engine guess everything else. Unfortunately, this question is not decided yet, there is no best practice here. The customers should not expect to get a decent voice destination entry in India, not even in English, not even separating the address point from the one-shot recognition.

7.2 Fixing a Wrong Address in the USA

Here comes the problem that gives the biggest headache to engineers. It's not about a multilingual scenario or exotic languages. It's about the long streets of the United States, which often run through more suburbs. Here is the challenge: "Even if the user speaks an out of context combination, the systems has to intelligently offer an existing one." People may be not sure about the suburb, points of the compass or read type. What really counts there, is the house number, and the partial street name. So when the confidence level for the city is lower, we can guess that the driver said something else, and start look for similar places within a certain radius.

Examples:

- The driver speaks *"L"4490 Buckingham Avenue, Birmingham, Michigan"* then the system has to realize that it is actually *4490 Buckingham Road and* belongs to *Royal Oak*, so the system has to offer *"4490 Buckingham Rd, Royal Oak, Michigan"*.
- The driver speaks *"6412 South Telegraph Road, Redford, Michigan"* then the system has to realize that *6412* belongs to *North Telegraph Road* and is actually in *Dearborn Heights, Michigan* as they all belong to *Detroit, Michigan.*

It is feasible with a server, just try it in one of the net search engines. But what can we do if the spoken address is out of context? Then the recognizer will return with something phonetically similar and in-context. To understand this, let us look into a small context, like this: *{A, B, C}* What if the user speaks an out-of-context *D*? We will get a similar item from the context with pretty high confidence: *B*. So it is not a good idea for large contexts to have smart algorithms based on confidence level, because there may be phonetically similar item, in a great geographical distance from the user's intention.

8 Vision

As I mentioned, we are living in the dawn of speech recognition, there is so much yet to come. These years, car infotainment industry is searching for offline solutions, at least as a fallback, due to the pure mobile net coverage and high mobile prices. On the other hand, the industry wants the same features, as with the server-based variant. Currently the server is a required for two reasons:

- To perform operations that are not possible on an embedded system.
- To access community resources and other dynamic data.

I believe the first reason is temporary, and it won't take a huge server park to do NLU and advanced machine learning in the future. Why should command and control messages travel around the world to get processed? Why aren't they handled locally?

The time will come when powerful embedded systems can handle the natural interaction between human and machine. Whoever will make that come true, they will start a new era in automotive infotainment.

Conference Papers

A Comparison of Acoustic Features of Speech of Typically Developing Children and Children with Autism Spectrum Disorders

Elena Lyakso[✉], Olga Frolova, and Aleksey Grigorev

Saint Petersburg State University, Saint Petersburg, Russia
lyakso@gmail.com

Abstract. The goal of this study is to find out the acoustic features specific for ASD children vocalizations and speech. Three types of experiments were conducted: emotional speech, spontaneous speech, and the repetition of words. Participants in the study were children with ASD (F 84.0 according to ICD-10), biologically aged 5–14 years (n = 25 children) and typically developing (TD) children aged 5–14 years (n = 60). We compare acoustic features that are widely used in speech recognition and speech perception: pitch values, max and min values of pitch, pitch range, formants frequency, energy and duration. Formant triangles were plotted for vowels with apexes corresponding to the vowels [a], [u], and [i] in F1, F2 coordinates, and their areas were compared. For all children with ASD voice and speech is characterized by high values of pitch, abnormal spectrum, and well-marked high-frequency. Stressed vowels from the words of children (TD & ASD), spoken in discomfort, have higher values of pitch and the third (emotional) formants than spoken in a comfortable condition. ASD children showed higher values of pitch in spontaneous speech than in repetition speech. The current results are a first step toward developing speech based bio-markers for early diagnosis of ASD.

Keywords: Acoustic features · Pitch · Formants frequency · Energy · Children typically developing · ASD children · Speech

1 Introduction

Autism spectrum disorders (ASD) are pervasive developmental disorders that have been defined as a triad of impairment: atypical development of reciprocal social interaction, atypical communication, and restricted, stereotyped, and repetitive behaviors. Since the first delineation of the autistic syndrome [1], abnormal prosody has been identified as a core feature for individuals who speak [2]. Monotonic or machine-like intonation, varying from flat and monotonous to variable, sing-song, or pedantic [1]. Problems in vocal quality, the control of volume, and use of aberrant stress patterns have also been widely reported [3–5]. Abnormal prosody production is a consistent feature of the ASD communication profile [6–8].

© Springer International Publishing Switzerland 2016
A. Ronzhin et al. (Eds.): SPECOM 2016, LNAI 9811, pp. 43–50, 2016.
DOI: 10.1007/978-3-319-43958-7_4

Studies of the acoustic properties of prosody production in height functional autism (HFA) [e.g. 3], generally showing that participants with ASD produce longer utterance durations even when their prosody is perceived as appropriate by listeners. In another study it was found larger spectral variability in the ASD group, which "blurs" or averages out the harmonic structure [6]. These authors note that the ASD children had a significantly larger pitch range and variability across time. The increased pitch range was found in speakers with HFA during both conversation and structured communication. Although the HFA group demonstrated an increased acoustic pitch range, listeners did not rate speakers with HFA as having increased pitch variation [5]. The same was noted in an earlier study [7]. In the studies of ASD pre-school children living in the Japanese language environment the negative correlation between the pitch variation and the domain of social reciprocal interaction scores of Japanese Autism Screening Questionnaire was revealed. Monotonous speech in school-aged children with ASD was detected [9].

So, given literature data indicate contradictory data regarding the prosodic speech features of children with ASD. The goal of this study is to find out the acoustic features specific for ASD children vocalizations and speech.

2   Method

2.1   Data Collection

Participants in the study were children with ASD (F84.0 according to ICD-10), biologically aged 5–14 years (n = 25 children) and typically developing (TD) children (coevals, n = 60). For this study the ASD sample was divided into two groups according developmental features: presence of development reversals at the age 1.5–3.0 years (first group - ASD-1) and developmental risk diagnosed at the infant birth (second group - ASD-2). For these children, the ASD is a symptom of neurological diseases associated with brain disturbed. Mean Child Autism Rating Scale [10] total scores was calculated for each group. In order to assess whether differences in autism severity varied across groups, a one-way ANOVA was conducted for two groups. The groups don't differ significantly.

Three types of experiments were conducted: emotional speech, spontaneous speech, and the repetition of words. For first experiment recording conditions for a TD the model experiment included playing with toys (a standard set of toys); repetition of words from a toy-parrot in the game store situation; watching the cartoon and the retelling of the story; for ASD children - playing with toys, and the pictures description [11]. Child speech recording of the second experiment was carried out in a situation of child dialogue with the experimenter (neutral theme as possible as), in the third - when the child repeated the words of the experimenter or parent (for ASD children). Places of recording were at home, in the laboratory and kindergarten for TD children and in the laboratory and the swimming pool for ASD children. The recordings were made by the "Marantz PMD222" recorder with a "SENNHEIZER e835S" external microphone.

2.2   Data Analysis

The child's emotional state was revealed based on recording situation and video frag-ment analysis by 5 speech experts. The test sequences were presented to 140 adults (native Russian speakers) for perceptual analysis. Spectrographic analysis of speech was carried out in the Cool Edit (Syntrillium Soft. Corp. USA) sound editor. We analyzed and compared pitch values, max and min values of pitch, pitch range, formants frequency (F1 - first formant, F2 - second formant, F3 - third formant), energy and duration. Along with the absolute values of the F1 and F2 formants, their relative values, /F2 – F1/, were compared. Formant triangles were plotted for repetition vowels with apexes corre-sponding to the vowels /a/, /u/, and /i/ in F1, F2 coordinates, and their areas were compared. Vowel formant triangle areas were calculated as described in [12] modified for Russian [13]. To consider word stress development the vowel duration and its stationary part duration were compared in the stressed versus the unstressed vowels, as well as the pitch and formants values in the stationary parts. The same parameters were compared using the Mann-Whitney criterion in /a/, /i/ and /u/ after the following conso-nants: /k/ and /d/ for /a/, /b/ and /g/ for /u/ and /t'/ for /i/. These consonants cause the minimal articulator and hence acoustic influence on the corresponding vowels in Russian. The values of the amplitudes (energy) of pitch and the first three formants of vowels by the dynamic spectrogram were determined. The normalized values of formants amplitude concerning to the amplitude of the pitch (E0/En, where E0 – amplitude of pitch, En – amplitude of formants, where n = 1 for F1, n = 2 for F2, n = 3 for F3). All statistical tests were conducted using Statistica 10.0.

All procedures were approved by the Health and Human Research Ethics Committee (HHS, IRB 00003875, St. Petersburg State University) and written informed consent was obtained from parents of the child participant.

3   Result

3.1   Acoustic Features of TD and ASD Child Emotional Speech

Different emotional states were used for comparing TD children and RAS children that allowed finding the variable characteristics of the voice. Both discomfort and comfort conditions in the speech of TD children were recognized by adults with the perception rate of 0.75–1.0 better compared to the neutral condition. Positive correlation between TD age and recognition of discomfort state $r = 0.9747$ ($p < 0.05$ Spearman) was revealed. Discomfort state in the vocalizations and speech of ASD children, adults recognized better ($p < 0.01$ Mann-Whitney test) than comfort and neutral state. Spectrographic analysis revealed that speech interpreted by listeners as discomfort, neutral and comfort is characterized by a set of acoustic features. Discomfort TD children's speech sample are characterized by highest maximum pitch values ($p < 0.01$), average pitch values ($p < 0.05$) and pitch variation values (F0max–F0min) ($p < 0.05$) vs. neutral speech sample. Discomfort state significantly don't differ from comfort state on the base of average pitch values of stress vowels from words. Correctly recognized by adults discomfort and comfort speech do not differ in pitch variation values. Changes of comfort and neutral state recognition with a child's age are bonded together: positive correlations between recognition of comfort and neutral test samples were revealed r = 0.9. Discomfort state is mostly characterized by falling pitch contour type, comfort state – by rising and neutral – by flat pitch contour.

Discomfort ASD children's speech sample are characterized by vowels' highest average pitch values, pitch range, and third formant frequency of vocalizations and words ($p < 0.001$) than comfort and neutral speech samples (Fig. 1A, B).

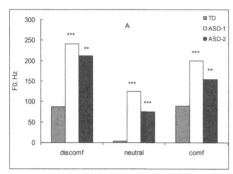 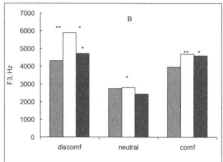

Fig. 1. Vowel's pitch range value (F0max–F0min) (A) and third formant frequency of vowels in discomfort, neutral and comfort (B). * - $p < 0.05$, ** - $p < 0.01$, *** - $p < 0.001$ Mann-Whitney test.

Pitch variation values (F0max–F0min) in ASD-1 child's discomfort, neutral and comfort speech significantly higher ($p < 0.001$) than in ASD-2 child's speech. Pitch contour type does not change depending on the emotional state of ASD children. The F3 values in discomfort speech of ASD-1 children significantly higher than in corresponding voice features in ASD-2 children ($p < 0.01$) and TD peers ($p < 0.01$).

Child membership to an ASD group $F(5.13) = 8.536$ $p < 0.0009$ associated with average pitch values (Beta $= -0.364$, $R^2 = 0.7665$), values of third formant (emotional) (Beta $= -0.743$, $R^2 = -0.7665$), the level of speech (Beta $= -0.484$, $R^2 = 0.7665$ – Multiple Regression analysis). The relation between the heaver child disease, the higher pitch values and third formant values, and the lower speech level was revealed.

3.2 Acoustic Features of TD and ASD Spontaneous Child Speech

The purpose of this experiment is to examine the process of the acoustic features of the vowel from ASD spontaneous speech approaching corresponding values in the TD speech. For all children with ASD voice and speech is characterized by high values of the pitch, abnormal spectrum, and well-marked high-frequency. Pitch values of spontaneous speech of ASD children higher ($p < 0.001$) than pitch values of TD children, pitch values of ASD-1 children higher ($p < 0.01$) than in ASD-2 were shown. Comparison of formant frequency values showed differences for the vowel /a/ by F1 and [F2–F1] values between ASD-1 and ASD -2 ($p < 0.05$), ASD-1 and TD ($p < 0.001$); for the vowel /u/ between ASD-1 and TD ($p < 0.05$); for the vowel /i/ - between [F3–F2] values between ASD-1 and TD ($p < 0.05$). Comparison of vowel formant triangle areas showed that areas were greatest for the vowels of ASD-2 children than ASD-1 ones. Decrease the area of the vowel formant triangle of TD child speech was shown.

In our study, in the ASD-1 were more boys than girls. Therefore additionally only boy's spontaneous speech was analyzed. Belonging to a group $F(6.443) = 57.861$ $p < 0.0000$ was a predictor of the acoustical features of vowels: vowels duration (Beta = 0.1175, $R^2 = 0.4393$), average pitch values (Beta = -0.6811, $R^2 = 0.4393$), values of F1 (Beta = -0.1237, $R^2 = 0.4393$), and values of F2 (Beta = -0.1024, $R^2 = 0.4393$ – Multiple Regression analysis). Boy's age $F(6.443) = 11.455$, $p < 0.0000$ was a predictor of the same acoustical features of vowels as a group. Child's membership to a groups (data for all ASD & TD children) $F(4.59) = 43.902$ $p < 0.0000$ correlated with average pitch values (Beta = -0.4027, $R^2 = 0.7485$), values of third formant (Beta = -0.5647, $R^2 = -0. 4027$– Multiple Regression analysis).

A specific characteristic of the dynamic spectrum of the vowels of the ASD –1 child is the intensity of the third formant (Fig. 2). The intensity of the vowel formants ASD-2 children was not significantly different from the TD corresponding data, except for F3/E0 for vowel /a/.

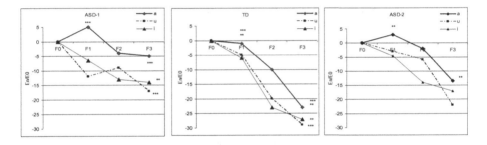

Fig. 2. The distribution of the three first format's amplitudes normalized to the amplitude of pitch for vowels /a/, /u/, /i/ is spontaneous speech. Vertical axis – En/E0 (normalized amplitude), horizontal axis – F0 and formants (F1, F2, F3).

3.3 Acoustic Features of TD and ASD Repetition vs. Spontaneous Child Speech

In speech task - words repetition child membership to an ASD group (first & second) $F(18.163) = 2.7161$ $p < 0.0004$ associated with child sex (Beta = 0.4168, $R^2 = 0.2307$), and stress vowel duration (Beta = 0.1804, $R^2 = 0.2307$).

At 5 years of age in all the TD children the stressed vowel and its stationary part duration, as well as their difference, is higher in the stressed vowels than in unstressed ones. This is unusual for Russian language where the stress is expressed by the duration of vowels. For ASD children stressed vowels don't differ significantly from unstressed vowels on the base of the vowel duration was shown. Stressed vowel extracted on the high pitch values or vowel duration and pitch with a typical allocation of each child was revealed. The context (/a/, /i/ and /u/ after the following consonants) influence on the characteristics of vowels in speech repeated was not significant for ASD and TD children.

Type of speech task (spontaneous and repetition) was revealed as predictor for stress vowels duration $F_{(6.337)} = 3,965$ p < 0.007 (Beta $= 0.1234$, $R^2 = 0.065$), and for average pitch values p < 0.0001 (Beta $= -0.2625$, $R^2 = 0.065$) – Multiple Regression analysis. Child's membership to a group (ASD & TD) was revealed as predictor for speech task realization $F_{(7.336)} = 106.33$ p < 0.0000 (Beta $= -0.6932$ $R^2 = 0.6889$), words duration p < 0.003 (Beta $= -0.0092$, $R^2 = 0.6889$), stress vowels average pitch values p < 0.0000 (Beta $= -0.667$, $R^2 = 0.6889$), and F1 values p $< 0.019\,0000$ (Beta $= 0.0916$, $R^2 = 0.6889$ – Multiple Regression analysis).

Pitch values don't differ significantly in stress vowels from TD children's words in twice task. Pitch values of the ASD-1children was significantly higher (p < 0.001) then in the ASD-2 child's spontaneous speech. Pitch values variation (F0max–F0min) significantly higher in spontaneous speech ASD-1 children than ASD -2 и TD children, and in repetition words ASD-2 children were revealed.

The formant triangles of vowels from the words from the spontaneous speech of ASD children were shifted on the two-formant plane to the higher-frequency region (for vowels /a/ and /u/, and F1 for vowel /i/) as compared with the formant triangles of vowels from repetition words (Fig. 3A). The largest shifts in the values of the first two formants of the vowels /a/, /i/, and /u/, leading to displacement of the formant triangles into the higher-frequency area, were seen for the vowels of ASD -1 children vs. ASD-2 peers (Fig. 3B). The differences in the location on the two coordinate plot of formant triangles from the twice types of speech for TD children was not revealed. Comparison of vowel formant triangle areas showed that areas were greatest for the vowels of TD children's repetition speech (Fig. 3C) and ASD-1 children's repetition speech (Fig. 3D).

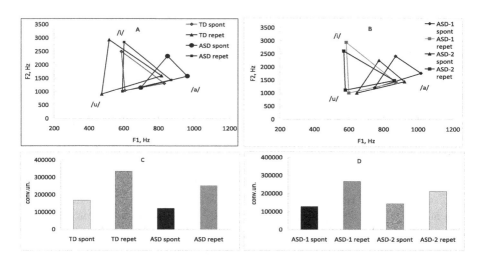

Fig. 3. The vowels formant triangles with apexes /a/, /u/, /i/: A - of ASD and TD children in twice speech tasks (spontaneous and repetition), B - of ASD children (ASD-1 - group 1, ASD-2 - group 2). Horizontal axis values are F1, Hz, vertical axis values are F2, Hz. Areas of vowels formant triangles (in conventional unit): C - data for TD and ASD child's areas of vowels formant triangles in twice speech tasks, D - ASD children (ASD-1 - group 1, ASD-2 - group 2).

These data indicate a clearer articulation of repetition words vs. word articulation in spontaneous speech.

The values of the normalized intensities of formants in repetition speech demonstrate a distribution pattern similar to that in spontaneous speech.

4   Discussion

We present the first data for Russian ASD children of acoustic measures of participant's speech. This study has shown that the ASD children differ from TD children on the base of higher values of pitch, pitch values variability and formant characteristics. These acoustic features and well-marked high-frequency in spectrum more clearly presented in the speech of the first group ASD children than the second group ASD children. ASD children from the first group have diagnosis ASD (F 84.0) as a primary. A common data about the high values of pitch and pitch variability of children with ASD was obtained on the base of three complementary experiments. Our data confirm other studies with similar results [5, 6, 14, 15]. Contrary to the common impression of monotonic speech in autism, the ASD children had a significantly larger pitch range and variability across time. These results indicate that speech abnormalities in ASD are reflected in their spectral content and pitch variability [6]. Paul et al. [15] reported prosodic deficits in only 47 % of the 30 adult speakers with HFA studied. They compared participants with HFA and a typical control group on both the perception and production of a range of specific prosodic elements. Results suggested between-group differences in both the perception and production of prosodic stress, suggesting that both understanding and producing appropriate stress patterns appear to be difficult for participants with HFA [15].

The current results are one of the first steps toward developing speech based biomarkers for early diagnosis of ASD. We believe that the acoustic features of speech of children with different neurological state are perspective for early diagnosis of developmental risk.

5   Conclusions

Differences between children with ASD and TD on the basis of higher values of pitch, pitch variability and formant characteristics of ASD children were revealed. In general, for all children with ASD voice and speech is characterized by high values of pitch and pitch variability. These acoustic features and well-marked high-frequency in spectrum were more clearly presented in the speech of the first group ASD children than the second group ASD children.

Acknowledgements. This study is financially supported by the Russian Foundation for Basic Research (projects № 13-06-00281a, 15-06-07852a, 16-06-00024a).

References

1. Kanner, L.: Autistic disturbances of affective contact. Nerv. Child **2**, 217–250 (1943)
2. Tager-Flusberg, H.: On the nature of linguistic functioning in early infantile autism. J. Autism Dev. Disord. **11**, 45–56 (1981)
3. Diehl, J., Paul, R.: Acoustic and perceptual measurements of prosody production on the profiling elements of prosodic systems by children with autism spectrum disorders. Appl. Psychol. **34**, 135–161 (2013)
4. Grossman, R.B., Bemis, R.H., Plesa, S.D., Tager-Flusberg, H.: Lexical and affective prosody in children with high-functioning autism. J. Speech Lang. Hear. Res. **53**, 778–793 (2010)
5. Nadig, A., Shaw, H.: Acoustic and perceptual measurement of expressive prosody in high-functioning autism: increased pitch range and what it means to listeners. J. Autism Dev. Disord. **42**, 499–511 (2012)
6. Bonneh, Y.S., Levanov, Y., Dean-Padro, O., Lossos, L., Adini, Y.: Abnormal speech spectrum and increased pitch variability in young autistic children. Front. Hum. Neurosci. **4** (2011) doi:10.3389/fnhum.2010.00237
7. Shriberg, L.D., Paul, R., McSweeny, J.L., Klin, A., Cohen, D.J., Volkmar, F.R.: Speech and prosody characteristics of adolescents and adults with high functioning autism and asperger syndrome. J. Speech Lang. Hear. Res. **44**, 1097–1115 (2001)
8. Shriberg, L.S., Paul, Rh., Black, L.M., van Santenc, J.P.: The hypothesis of apraxia of speech in children with autism spectrum disorder. J. Autism Dev. Disord. **41**(4), 405–426 (2011)
9. Nakai, Y., Takashima, R., Takiguchi, T., Takada, S.: Speech intonation in children with autism spectrum disorder. Brain Dev. **36**(6), 516–522 (2014)
10. Schopler, E., Reichler, R.J., DeVellis, R.F., Daly, K.: Toward objective classification of childhood autism: childhood autism rating scale (CARS). J. Autism Dev. Disord. **10**(1), 91–103 (1980)
11. Lyakso, E., Frolova, O., Dmitrieva, E., Grigorev, A., Kaya, H., Salah, A.A., Karpov, A.: EmoChildRu: emotional child russian speech corpus. In: Ronzhin, A., Potapova, R., Fakotakis, N. (eds.) SPECOM 2015. LNCS, vol. 9319, pp. 144–152. Springer, Heidelberg (2015)
12. Vorperian, H., Kent, R.D.: Vowel acoustic space development: a synthesis of acoustic and anatomic data. J. Speech Lang. Hear. Res. **50**(6), 1510–1545 (2007)
13. Lyakso, E.E., Grigor'ev, A.S.: Dynamics of the duration and frequency characteristics of vowels during the first seven years of life in children. Neurosci. Behav. Physiol. **45**(5), 558–567 (2015)
14. Sharda, M., Subhadra, T.P., Sahaya, S., Nagaraja, Ch., Singh, L., Sen, A., Singhal, N., Erickson, D., Singh, N.: Sounds of melody — pitch patterns of speech in autism. Neurosci. Lett. **478**, 42–45 (2010)
15. Paul, R., Augustyn, A., Klin, A., Volkmar, F.: Perception and production of prosody by speakers with autism spectrum disorders. J. Autism Dev. Disord. **35**, 205–220 (2005)

A Deep Neural Networks (DNN) Based Models for a Computer Aided Pronunciation Learning System

Mohamed S. Elaraby[1(✉)], Mustafa Abdallah[1,2],
Sherif Abdou[1,3], and Mohsen Rashwan[1,4]

[1] Research and Development International (RDI®), Giza, Egypt
mohamed.salem@rdi-eg.net, {sabdou,mrashwan}@rdi-eg.com
[2] Department of Engineering Mathematics and Physics, Cairo University, Giza, Egypt
m.a.elhosiny@eng.cu.edu.eg
[3] Department of IT, Faculty of Computers and Information, Cairo University, Giza, Egypt
[4] Department of Electronics and Communication Engineering, Cairo University, Giza, Egypt

Abstract. Gaussian Mixture Models (GMM) has been the most common used models in pronunciation verification systems. The recently introduced Deep Neural Networks (DNN) has proved to provide significantly better discriminative models of the acoustic space. In this paper, we introduce our efforts to upgrade the models of a Computer Aided Language Learner (CAPL) system that is used to teach the Arabic pronunciation for Quran recitation rules. Four major enhancements were introduced, firstly we used SAT to reduce the inter-speakers variability, secondly, we integrated a hybrid DNN-HMM models to enhance the acoustic model and decrease the phone error rate. Third, we integrated Minimum Phone Error (MPE) with the hybrid DNN. Finally, in the testing phase, we used a grammar-based decoding graph to limit the search space to the frequent errors types. A comparison between the performance of the conventional GMM-HMM and the hybrid DNN-HMM was performed with results showing significant performance improvements.

Keywords: Pronunciation learning · Deep neural networks · Speaker adaptive training

1 Introduction

Computer Aided Pronunciation Learning (CAPL) has recently been considerable in the research community. Many efforts have been done for enhancement of such systems specifically in the field of second language teaching [1]. One of the most challenging applications of a (CAPL) system is Holy Qur'an training for correct recitation. Training foreign languages can be tolerant to a wide variety of different pronunciations, however; Qur'an recitation has to be done as in the classical Arabic dialect which makes it a more challenging task. Several research works were done to overcome this problem [2].

As technology advanced, attempts have become more mature and it was possible to build more advanced CAPL systems. For example [3], a commercial system for automatic system of recitation of Holy Qur'an (HAFSS©) was presented. Much more efforts in enhancing usability of the (HAFSS©) system was presented in [4] by using SAT training

© Springer International Publishing Switzerland 2016
A. Ronzhin et al. (Eds.): SPECOM 2016, LNAI 9811, pp. 51–58, 2016.
DOI: 10.1007/978-3-319-43958-7_5

to boost system performance. Another modification was suggested in order to reduce the amount of the enrolment time while keeping the system accuracy at the same level.

The hybrid CD-DNN-HMM architectures have been proposed for phoneme recognition [5, 6] and have reached noticeable competitive performance. An acoustic model, using the context-dependent CD-DNN-HMM presented in [7], was successfully applied to large vocabulary speech recognition data. Word error rate was reduced up to one-third in conversational speech transcription tasks compared to the CD-GMM-HMM systems [8]. An application for using DNN-HMM in verification pronunciation system was suggested in [9]. In this research, a comparison between GMM-HMM and hybrid DNN-HMM was applied for Assessment of childhood Apraxia of speech. Further research work in using DNN-HMM in CAPL systems was presented in [10].

In this paper, we enhance our earlier pronunciation verification method in [4] by utilizing the power of various recent ASR algorithms to boost the performance of our baseline system on the basis of phoneme accuracy. First, Speaker Adaptive Training (SAT) technique [11] was used during the training phase to reduce the inter-speakers variability in training data. Second, Hybrid DNN-HMM was used to enhance the acoustic model and utilize the discriminative nature of the Neural Networks to decrease the phone error rate. Third, we integrated Minimum Phone Error (MPE) with the hybrid DNN. Finally, in the testing phase, we used a grammar-based decoding graph for forcing the output to current arbitrated statement to avoid nonsense pronunciations. A comparison between the performance of the conventional GMM-HMM and the hybrid DNN-HMM was performed. We also compare the performance of different ASR toolkits: Kaldi and HTK. The correlation between the system judgment and linguistic judgments was also improved. The remainder of this paper is structured as follows. Section 2 presents the baseline CAPL system description and the new proposed enhancements. It also explains the proposed Grammar-based decoding graph creation. Section 3 describes the speech corpus used. Section 4 shows the experiments performed and results. Finally, the conclusions are summarized in Sect. 5.

2   Baseline System Description

Our baseline system is a speech-enabled Computer Aided Pronunciation Learning (CAPL) system that helps non-native speakers to learn Arabic pronunciations. First, the input speech is segmented into a sequence of phonemes clusters. Comparing the sequence of reference with the given hypothesized sequence generates substitution, insertion and deletion errors. Second, these units are tested by trained HMM models. Then, it could assess the quality of a user's recitation and produce a feedback messages to help him locate his pronunciation errors and eventually overcome them.

Figure 1 shows the block diagram of the HAFSS© system [12]. Its main blocks are:

1. **Verification HMM Models**: Traditional HMM acoustic models for the system.
2. **Speaker Adaptation**: Maximum Likelihood Linear Regression (MLLR) speaker adaptation algorithm is used to adapt acoustic models to each user acoustic properties.
3. **Pronunciation Hypotheses Generator:** It analyzes current verse and all possible pronunciation variants are generated in order to test them against the spoken utterance.

4. **Confidence Score Analysis:** It receives n-best decoded word sequence from the decoder, then analyzes their scores to determine whether to report that result or not.
5. **Phoneme Duration Analysis:** For phonemes that have variable duration according to its location in the Holy Qur'an, this layer determines whether these phonemes have correct lengths or not.
6. **Feedback Generator:** Recognizer results are then analyzed and appropriate feedback message appeared to the user.

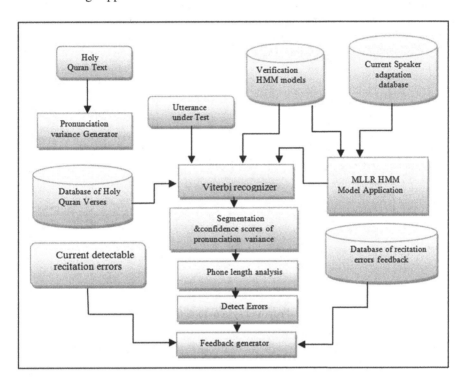

Fig. 1. Baseline system description

2.1 Enhancements in Proposed System

The main enhancements were in two branches; acoustic modeling and language modeling. Block diagram of the new proposed system is shown in Fig. 2.

Acoustic Model Modifications:

- **SAT + FMLLR**: Is used to adapt acoustic models to each user by using speaker adaptive training. It uses FMLLR features which are based on (MLLR) speaker adaptation.
- **Hybrid DNN-HMM:** A deep structure of neural network was trained using back propagation algorithm. Output nodes replaced GMM-HMM states in the decoding process. This stage is considered the main concept of hybrid DNN-HMM approach

since it represents the state better than Gaussians since it comes from a discriminative model – the neural network – while GMM-HMM is a generative model.

- **DNN-MPE:** The final training block was DNN-MPE which is sequence-discriminative training of deep neural networks implemented in the open-source Kaldi toolkit.

Language Model Modifications:

Decoding Graph. The most challenging part in grammar modification was converting classical lattice-based grammar generated from lattice-generator described in [12] into a finite-state transducer to fit the decoding graph creation process. The Grammar is produced depending on the current verse to be arbitrated according to rules of Quran.

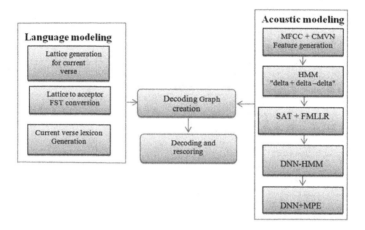

Fig. 2. Proposed system modification

3 Data Description

The training dataset is about 24 h of Quran. The overall utterances used in training are about 17050 utterances. The dataset was manually transcribed by experts. It contains verses from all the thirty parts of the Holy Quran. It was collected from many speakers. It is mainly divided to two countries of native speakers which are Egypt and Kuwait. The variety of speakers and verses gives a significant impact on the acoustic model which will be built using that data. The model includes all the pronunciations with two dialects. It also includes most of recitation rules in the Holy Quran. There are two types of speakers: reference speaker who knows all recitation rules clearly and nearest speaker who are also native, but have some errors in their pronunciations. The test dataset is divided into two main sets. One of which for development and the other is for testing as shown below:

- **Development Testing Corpus**: It consists of 270 utterances from 12 speakers. Each speaker has 23 utterances. The total number of phonemes in this corpus is about 5,000 phones. The disadvantage of that corpus is the small size.

- **Core Testing Corpus**: It consists of 1500 utterances from 45 speakers. It is about six times of the above testing corpus. Utterances consist of a lot of small verses. The total number of phonemes in this corpus is about 32,000 phones. The advantage of that corpus that is its size is moderate so it can give reliable conclusions and results.

Two types of lexicons were used for our proposed system:

- **Lexicon Dedicated for Training**: A phoneme to phoneme lexicon in order to guarantee best model for each phoneme individually.
- **Lexicon Dedicated for Testing**: Which contains the all possible pronounced phonemes of the verse which to be detected at the moment.

4 Experimental Setup

Extracted features – in most of our experiments – from speech utterances were Mel Frequency Cepstral Coefficients (MFCCs) and energy, along with their first and second temporal derivatives. As such, the length of feature vector is of dimension 39. Extracted features are then normalized to make the whole training data as a real Gaussian random variable with zero mean and unit variance. In Kaldi setup, adjusting the number of Gaussians and number of leaves depends on number of hours of speech to avoid over fitting and under fitting. We started from Resource Management example setup since its training hours closer to ours. The initial number of leaves was 1900 and the total number of Gaussians was 9000. After tuning we reached the best performance at 1800 leaves and 8000 Gaussians.

5 Results and Discussion

First, an acoustic model based on HMM with HTK toolkit was built. On the other hand, a similar HMM model with the same configuration was built with Kaldi toolkit. The phone error rates of the baseline systems are presented in Table 1. Second trial was to improve the performance of the first system implemented by HTK toolkit, a proportion of half-hour of speech data extracted from test-speakers was used for doing MLLR adaptation on the acoustic model. This experiment made an absolute improvement on the error rate by about two percent. On the other hand, SAT training with feature likelihood linear regression (fmllr) was performed on the second implementation. Results training are tabulated in Table 2.

Table 1. HMM baseline phone error rates

System	Development-set	Core-test
GMM-HMM (HTK)	10.92 %	9.7 %
GMM-HMM (Kaldi)	9.3 %	8.5 %

Table 2. Effect of adapting acoustic models

System	Development-set	Core-test
GMM + MLLR (HTK)	8.7 %	7.6 %
GMM + SAT (Kaldi)	8.2 %	7.2 %

The next enhancement was by applying the Hybrid DNN-HMM training. In all of the experiments 40-dimensional fmllr were used as the input representation. Finally, input was represented as context frames. For all experiments, we fixed the main parameters for the Viterbi decoder. Specifically, we used a one phone insertion probability and a language model scale factor of 1.0. Since the phonemes of Quran consume more frames, it was a noticeable note to take more care of the context frames. It appeared that increasing the context enhances the performance of the system.

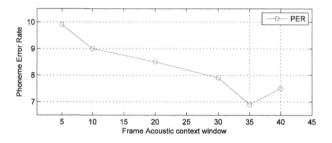

Fig. 3. Changing the context size effect on phoneme accuracy

From results in Table 3, we can see that the system performance has improved significantly with using Hybrid DNN-HMM with absolute 2.4 % improvement in phone error rate with respect to the best results of GMM-HMM.

Table 3. Comparison between hybrid DNN-HMM and classical GMM

System	Development-set	Core-test
GMM	9.3 %	8.5 %
GMM + SAT	8.2 %	7.2 %
Hybrid DNN-HMM	6.9 %	6.5 %

Another important metric in CAPL system evaluation is correlation matrix between CAPL system judgment and Human experts' judgment. First, Human expert listened to each verse under test and made his decision. Second, CAPL system produces its decision based on the acoustic model. Finally, a correlation matrix between the two decisions is calculated.

From results in Table 4. For correct speech segments which constitute about 94.2 % of the data, the system yielded "correct" for about 93.2 % of the total correct words and the system made false rejection for about 1 % of them. For wrong speech segments, which constitute 5.8 % of the data, the system correctly identified the error in 0.3 % of pronunciation errors and it made false acceptance for 5.5 % of the mispronounced phones. This phone recognition accuracy is better than the best performance described in [4] with an absolute improvement of 1.3 %.

Table 4. CAPL system evaluation results for development test data

		Human Judgment		
		Correct	Wrong	Total
System judgment	Correct	93.2 %	5.5 %	98.7%
	Wrong	1 %	0.3 %	1.3%
	Total	94.2 %	5.8 %	100%

The final experiment was sequence discriminative training with Neural Network (DNN + MPE). We performed 5-iterations and achieved a phoneme error rate of 6.9 (Figs. 3 and 4).

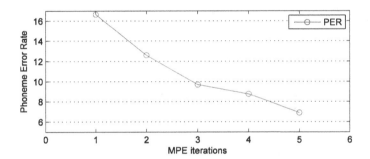

Fig. 4. Minimum phone error iterations VS phone error rate

6   Conclusion

The work in this paper presented a modified verification pronunciation system HAFSS©. Our main aim was minimizing the phoneme error rate by enhancing the acoustic model using DNN-HMM. A comparative study was also performed between the baseline GMM-HMM system and the proposed DNN-HMM system to determine the best configuration for our CAPL system. The DNN-HMM system reached an overall phoneme error rate of 6.9 % thus, it can accurately classify mispronunciation errors. Also, decoding-graph size was moderate which make it applicable to be used in portable devices. However, the classical GMM-HMM achieved a PER of 8.5 %. In classical GMM-HMM, the Kaldi toolkit gave better performance than HTK. For the DNN-HMM increasing context frame window size results in decreasing PER.

References

1. Franco, H., Neumeyer, L., Ramos, M., Bratt, H.: Automatic detection of phone-level mispronunciation for language learning. In: Proceedings of Eurospeech 1999, vol. 2, pp. 851–854. Budapest, Hungary (1999)
2. El-Kasasy, M.S.: An Automatic Speech Verification System. Ph.D. Thesis, Cairo University, Faculty of Engineering, Department of Electronics and Communications, Egypt (1992)
3. Hamid, S.: Computer Aided Pronunciation Learning System using Statistical Based Automatic Speech Recognition. Ph.D. thesis, Cairo University, Cairo, Egypt (2005)
4. Samir, A., Abdou, S.M., Khalil, A.H., Rashwan, M.: Enhancing usability of CAPL system for Qur'an recitation learning. In: 8th Annual Conference of the International Speech Communication Association, at Antwerp, Belgium (2007)
5. Mohamed, A., Dahl, G.E., Hinton, G.E.: Acoustic modeling using deep belief networks. IEEE Trans. Audio Speech Lang. Proc. **20**(1), 14–22 (2012)
6. Mohamed, A., Yu., D., Deng, L.: Investigation of full-sequence training of deep belief networks for speech recognition. In: Proceedings of Interspeech, Makuhari, pp. 1692–1695. Japan (2010)
7. Dahl, G.E., Yu, D., Deng, L., Acero, A.: Context-dependent pre-trained deep neural networks for large-vocabulary speech recognition. IEEE Trans. Audio Speech Lang. Proc. **20**(1), 30–42 (2010)
8. Seide, F., Li, G., Yu, D.: Conversational speech transcription using context dependent deep neural networks. In: Proceedings of Interspeech, pp. 437–440, Florence, Italy (2011)
9. Shahin, M., Ahmed, B., McKechnie, J., Ballard, K., Gutierrez-Osuna, R.: A comparison of GMM-HMM and DNNHMM based pronunciation verification techniques for use in the assessment of childhood apraxia of speech. In: Interspeech 2014, Singapore (2014)
10. Lee, Y.Z., Glass, J.: Mispronunciation detection via dynamic time wrapping on deep belief network-based posterior grams. In: ICASSP (2013)
11. Anastasakos, T., McDonough, J., Schwartz, R., Makhoul, J.: A compact model for speaker-adaptive training. In: Proceedings of the Spoken Language, ICSLP, vol. 2, pp. 1137–1140 (1996)
12. Sherif, M.A., Salah, E.H., Mohsen, R., Abdurrahman, S., Ossama, A.-H., Mostafa, S., Waleed, N.: Computer aided pronunciation learning system using speech recognition techniques. In: INTERSPEECH 2006, ICSLP, Pittsburgh, PA, USA (2006)

A Linguistic Interpretation of the Atom Decomposition of Fundamental Frequency Contour for American English

Tijana Delić[1], Branislav Gerazov[2], Branislav Popović[1], and Milan Sečujski[1(✉)]

[1] Faculty of Technical Sciences, University of Novi Sad, Novi Sad, Serbia
{tijanadelic,bpopovic,secujski}@uns.ac.rs
[2] Faculty of Electrical Engineering and Information Techologies,
Ss. Cyril and Methodius University, Skopje, Macedonia
gerazov@feit.ukim.edu.mk

Abstract. One of the most recently proposed techniques for modeling the prosody of an utterance is the decomposition of its pitch, duration and/or energy contour into physiologically motivated units called atoms, based on matching pursuit. Since this model is based on the physiology of the production of sentence intonation, it is essentially language independent. However, the intonation of an utterance in a particular language is obviously under the influence of factors of a predominantly linguistic nature. In this research, restricted to the case of American English with prosody annotated using standard ToBI conventions, we have shown that, under certain mild constraints, the positive and negative atoms identified in the pitch contour coincide very well with high and low pitch accents and phrase accents of ToBI. By giving a linguistic interpretation of the atom decomposition model, this research enables its practical use in domains such as speech synthesis or cross-lingual prosody transfer.

Keywords: Atom decomposition · Pitch contour · ToBI

1 Introduction

A relatively small number of widely used intonational modeling techniques make direct reference to the physiology of the production of sentence intonation, despite their inherent advantage of being language independent [1–3], with the assumption of language independence coming from the fact that the same physiological apparatus is used to produce the intonation in any language. The reason for this is, most probably, that the language independence of these modeling techniques is exactly what makes them less practical for use in speech processing and speech technology for a particular language. For this reason, it is of particular practical interest to give a linguistic interpretation to a physiologically based model, preferably one that would easily extend to a number of languages.

One of the most recently proposed techniques for the modeling of sentence prosody is based on the decomposition of its pitch, duration and/or energy contour into units called atoms, which originate in the physiology of the production of prosody [4, 5]. Most of the research in this area focuses on the atom decomposition of the pitch contour,

© Springer International Publishing Switzerland 2016
A. Ronzhin et al. (Eds.): SPECOM 2016, LNAI 9811, pp. 59–66, 2016.
DOI: 10.1007/978-3-319-43958-7_6

having in mind its particularly important role in the perception of prosody. However, atoms to which the pitch contour is decomposed do not have any *a priori* linguistic explanation, which is not convenient from the point of view of a practical speech technology system faced with a task of e.g. synthesizing a pitch contour from a given text in a particular language. The problem of describing the intonation of a sentence using sets of linguistically motivated discrete events, on the other hand, has been a matter of extensive research, and a number of practical intonational models have been proposed, including phonological tone sequence models such as Pierrehumbert's theory of intonation [6] or ToBI (tone and break indices) [7], phonetic sequential models involving acoustic stylization [8], phonetic superpositional models [9, 10] and prosodic models [11, 12]. This research focuses on ToBI, as one of the most widely used standards for linguistic annotation of speech prosody, initially developed for American English, but since extended to a number of other variants of English and other languages [13]. As is the case with all other mentioned models, ToBI avoids making direct reference to the physiology of prosody production in the sense of articulatory effort or specific activity of relevant muscles, but it does recognize sequences of high and low tones attached to prominent words or relevant boundaries between intermediate or full intonational phrases. Having in mind the obvious relationship between prominence and articulatory effort, this research attempts to prove a high degree of correlation between the high and low tonal events of ToBI, on one side, and the positive and negative atoms, as identified by the atom decomposition algorithm. Due to the limited availability of ToBI annotated material, the research at present focuses on the case of American English.

The remainder of the paper is organized as follows. Section 2 presents the basics of the atom decomposition intonation modeling, while Sect. 3 gives an overview of the ToBI system for American English. Section 4 presents our experiments on the Boston University Radio Speech Corpus of American English [14], which show a very good match between atoms of positive and negative amplitudes identified by the atom decomposition algorithm, and high and low tonal events of ToBI. Section 5 concludes the paper, giving an outline of the future work as well.

2 Intonation Modeling by Atom Decomposition

The intonation modeling approach analysed in this paper is based on decomposing the pitch, duration, and energy contour into meaningful units called "atoms", focusing on the pitch contour as the primary source of information in prosody perception. The weighted correlation atom decomposition (WCAD) model represents a generalization of the command-response (CR) model [1] and has the advantage of having a simple method for the extraction of parameters. It is based on the matching pursuit algorithm [15] relying on the perceptually relevant weighted correlation as a cost function [16].

The command-response (CR) model defines intonation in terms of the physiological process behind its production. It has been shown [1] that, with respect to the influence of the muscles ruling the vocal folds on their tension, the f_0 contour can be decomposed into several additive components in the log domain. In this model two types of components are related to the translation and rotation of the cricoid in respect to the thyroid, effected by the cricothyroid (CT) muscle. The influence of some other muscles as well as the subglottal pressure has been identified in [2], and in [4] the CR model was generalized in order to take into account more than two types of movements related to the control of the fundamental frequency (f_0). The components of the model were defined as impulse responses to a second-order critically damped system, as they are assumed to be the responses of the muscles involved in the production of intonation. Based on previous research [17], the CR model defines the logarithm of f_0 as the sum of a baseline level, phrase components, and accent components [1], assuming that the global shape of an utterance's log f_0 is generated from the response to phrase command impulses, while the local variations are accounted for by responses to accent commands, which are basically step functions. However, if these step functions are viewed as trains of impulses, all parameters of the CR model can be defined in terms of impulse responses of the following type [4]:

$$G_{pi}(t) = \alpha_i^2 t e^{-\alpha_i t}, \text{ for } t \geq 0, \tag{1}$$

or, if higher order models are used, which has been shown to improve performance [18], the previous expression assumes the general gamma functional form

$$G_{k,\theta}(t) = \frac{1}{\theta^k \Gamma(k)} t^{k-1} e^{-t/\theta}, \text{ for } t \geq 0, \tag{2}$$

Following this line of reasoning, the log f_0 contour is decomposed into a linear combination of "atoms" by the matching pursuit algorithm [15], given a dictionary of kernel functions:

$$x(t) = \sum_{m=1}^{M} \sum_{i=1}^{I_m} \alpha_{m,i} \varphi_m (t - \tau_{m,i}) + \epsilon(t), \tag{3}$$

where $\{\varphi_1, \dots \varphi_M\}$ is the dictionary, $\alpha_{m,i}$ is the gain of the instance i of kernel φ_m and $\tau_{m,i}$ its time delay, and ϵ is the residual error. The decomposition is achieved up to the error ϵ by greedy iterative optimization. At each step, the correlation between the signal and every atom from the dictionary is computed, the atom with the highest correlation is found and its weighted version is subtracted from the signal. These steps are repeated until a predefined accuracy threshold is reached or some other exit criterion is met. Having in mind the global character of the intonation phrase component, log f_0 is decomposed in a two pass process: first an iteration of matching pursuit is applied on the continuous f_0 contour to get the single intonation phrase component, using a dictionary of long atoms that can span more than the length of the utterance, and the second step consists of applying matching pursuit on the residual obtained in the first step.

3   An Overview of ToBI System for Prosodic Labeling

Tone and Break Indices (ToBI) is a set of conventions for prosodic transcription and annotation of speech. Primarily developed for English [7], it has since been extended into a number of other languages [13]. Here only a brief overview of ToBI will be given, with the aim of providing the reader with a good understanding of prosodic events considered in this research.

A ToBI transcription minimally indicates the tonal events in an utterance as well as the intended prosodic grouping of its elements. The term *tonal event* refers to pitch accents and boundary tones. Pitch accents, occurring as combinations of high (H) and low (L) tones, give prosodic prominence to a word, and their use is to some extent ruled by the semantics as well as specific user intention. In each pitch accent either a high or a low tone can be aligned with the stressed syllable, and thus they can be divided into two broad groups of high pitch accents (such as H*) and low pitch accents (such as L*). ToBI also provides means for indexing breaks, i.e. boundary strength between adjacent words. Sentences are composed of intonational phrases (IPs), delimited with breaks of type 4, and each intonational phrase is divided into intermediate phrases (ips), delimited with breaks of type 3. The edges of ips are marked with phrase accents (L-, !H- and L-, where '!' marks a downstep) while the edges of IPs are marked by boundary tones (L% and H%). Having in mind that each IP consists of one or more ips, each edge of an IP is also an edge of an ip, and thus IPs end in one of six possible combinations of phrase accents and boundary tones (L-L%, L-H%, etc.). Initial IP boundary tones (%L and %H), whose use is less regular, could not be taken into account in this research as they were not marked in the corpus used for the research.

4   Experiment Results

In our experiments we investigated the relationship between positive and negative atoms of the atom decomposition paradigm and high and low tonal events of ToBI, along the lines of [19]. The assumption that we tried to prove was that, provided the atoms are relatively wide, which depends on the parameter θ of Eq. (2), positive atoms tend to coincide with high pitch accents (such as H*) or high boundary tones, while negative atoms tend to coincide with the low pitch accents (such as L*) or low boundary tones. If proven true, this would provide a very convenient linguistic interpretation of the atom decomposition approach.

All our experiments were carried out on the Boston University Radio Speech Corpus of American English [14] (more precisely, a portion of this corpus restricted to the female speaker marked as F2, whose 910 utterances were ToBI annotated). It should be noted that the prosodic annotation in the corpus was far from perfect, not only in terms of the accuracy of prosodic tags used, but also in terms of basic consistency. For instance, in the analyzed 904 recordings[1] there were 2,726 intonational phrases, and in 30 % of cases

---

[1] Six recordings from the initial set of 910 recordings were excluded because they contained the ERROR tag where a boundary tone was expected.

the time difference between the phrase break of type 4 and the corresponding boundary tone was more than 50 ms, while in 11 % of cases the difference was more than 100 ms. As boundary tones are intrinsically linked to breaks of type 4, they should obviously be located at the same time instants, corresponding to word endings. Regardless of the fact that such errors would give a negative bias on the experiment results, we decided to conduct the experiment on the corpus "as is", to allow others to replicate it.

Atom decomposition of each utterance was carried out (with $k = 6$ and θ ranging from 0.02 to 0.09), and then the discovered atoms were compared to the ToBI pitch accents and boundary tones as illustrated in Fig. 1 (phrase accents at breaks of type 3 were not taken into account). The discovered atom was considered to coincide with a pitch accent if its peak was located within the stressed vowel or adjacent stressed vowel (if there is one). Boundary tones were also modeled by atoms (with the possible exception of L-L%, see below), and the discovered atom was considered to coincide with a boundary tone if its peak was located within the last word in the IP.

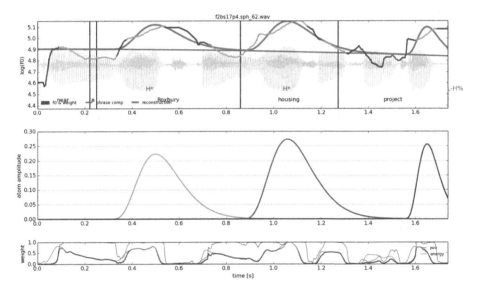

Fig. 1. The atom decomposition of the $\log f_0$ contour of the intonational phrase "near a Roxbury housing project". Two positive atoms correspond to two H* pitch accents, while the remaining positive atom corresponds to the L-H% boundary tone.

In our experiments we introduced the following three variables:

(a) The atom decomposition algorithm can be allowed to discover only the number of atoms defined by ToBI annotations, or it can be allowed to discover as many atoms as it can, using its standard exit criterion. In the following text, these two variants will be denoted as A and $\bar{A}$ respectively.

(b) The experiment can be conducted on L-L% IPs only (1,238 IPs), or on all six types of IPs (2,750 IPs). These two variants will be denoted as B and $\bar{B}$. In the latter case boundary tones other than L-L% were all considered to correspond to positive atoms.

(c) The boundary tone of L-L% IPs can be modeled with a negative atom, or with the absence of an atom. These two variants will be denoted as C and $\bar{C}$.

To illustrate the introduced notation, the experiment referred to e.g. as $\bar{A}\bar{B}C$ allows the atom decomposition algorithm to discover as many atoms as it can, it is carried out on all six types of IPs, and models the L-L% boundary tone with a negative atom.

The evaluation of the success rate of the algorithm is expressed through standard measures used in binary classification, including precision and recall. In this specific case, if a tonal event is expected and a coinciding atom is found, it is considered a true positive if it is of appropriate polarity. A non-coinciding atom or an atom with inappropriate polarity is considered as false positive, while the failure to detect an atom where a tonal event exists is considered as false negative. A true negative represents the case when no atom has been detected on a stressed vowel without tonal events. Success rate measures are calculated according to their standard definitions and are given in Table 1.

Table 1. Experiment results

	ABC	$AB\bar{C}$	$A\bar{B}C$	$A\bar{B}\bar{C}$	$\bar{A}BC$	$\bar{A}B\bar{C}$	$\bar{A}\bar{B}C$	$\bar{A}\bar{B}\bar{C}$
Precision	0.74	**0.88**	0.78	0.86	0.74	**0.88**	0.78	0.86
Recall	0.80	**0.97**	0.86	0.95	0.86	**0.97**	0.89	0.95
Accuracy	0.73	0.93	0.81	0.91	0.75	0.93	0.82	0.91
FNR	0.20	0.03	0.14	0.05	0.14	0.03	0.11	0.05
TNR	0.64	0.90	0.76	0.88	0.62	0.90	0.75	0.87
FDR	0.26	0.12	0.22	0.14	0.26	0.12	0.22	0.14

It can be seen that the best results are achieved in cases where the analysis is limited to the case of L-L% (declarative) IPs, and the boundary tone is modeled with the absence of an atom rather than with a negative atom ($\bar{B}\bar{C}$). This is in line with previous research, which focused on declarative phrases and did not find evidence of atoms occurring at phrase endings particularly frequently [4]. Firstly, a relatively high precision and recall, which reach 0.88 and 0.97 in the most favourable case, show that there is indeed a strong connection between positive and negative atoms and high and low tonal events of ToBI. In other words, atom decomposition modeling as a physiologically based and thus language independent modeling technique, can also be given a linguistic interpretation. When comparing the results of the experiments under different conditions, other interesting conclusions can be drawn. Firstly, the results are quite similar in the case where the algorithm is restricted to finding only the number of atoms equal to the expected number of tonal events and in the case when it is allowed to find as many atoms as it can (A vs. $\bar{A}$). This shows that the algorithm does not tend to find linguistically irrelevant atoms even if it is given the opportunity to do so. Secondly, not modeling the boundary tone instead of modeling it with a negative atom ($\bar{C}$ instead of C) invariably leads to a significant increase of precision and affects other measures as well, particularly if the analysis is restricted only to L-L% phrases (B). It is also interesting to note that the algorithm was much more successful in matching high pitch accents with coinciding atoms (69 % to 87 %, depending on the conditions), than in matching low ones (34 % to 49 %), which is reminiscent of the fact that for a human labeller as well it is more difficult to identify a low pitch accent than a high one. It should also be noted that the frequency of low pitch accents in the corpus is much lower than the frequency of high ones (3.5 % or 4.8 %, depending on the conditions), which explains a relatively low impact of the accuracy of matching low pitch accents on the overall results.

5 Conclusion

By showing that positive and negative atoms to which an intonation contour can be decomposed have a high degree of correspondence with high and low tonal events of the ToBI prosody annotation system (with precision and recall reaching 0.88 and 0.97 in the most favourable case), we have provided a linguistic interpretation to the atom decomposition paradigm, at least for the case of American English. However, since the experiment results clearly indicate the relationship between positive/negative atoms and an effort of the speaker to reach a high/low intonation target, which is arguably a language independent phenomenon, there are grounds to expect similar results for other languages, which remains to be verified. Our future work will also include the construction of a framework that will enable the construction of f_0 contours from ToBI annotations, which would enable the use of the atom decomposition modeling technique in tasks such as expressive text-to-speech synthesis.

Acknowledgments. The presented study was supported in part by the Ministry of Education, Science and Technological Development of the Republic of Serbia (grant TR32035), and was carried out within the SCOPES project "SP2: SCOPES Project for Speech Prosody" (No. CRSII2-147611/1), supported by Swiss National Science Foundation. The authors are grateful to the company Speech Morphing, Inc. from Campbell, CA, USA, for providing the speech corpus used in the experiments.

References

1. Fujisaki, H., Nagashima, S.: A model for the synthesis of pitch contours of connected speech. Technical Report, Engineering Research Institute. University of Tokyo, Japan (1969)
2. Strik, H.: Physiological control and behaviour of the voice source in the production of prosody, Ph.D. thesis, Department of Language and Speech, University of Nijmegen, Netherlands (1994)
3. Kochanski, G.P., Shih, C.: Stem-ML: Language independent prosody description. In: International Conference on Spoken Language Processing (ICSLP), vol. 3, pp. 239–242 (2000)
4. Honnet, P.-E., Gerazov, B., Garner, P.N.: Atom decomposition-based intonation modeling. In: IEEE International Conference on Acoustics, Speech and Signal Processing – ICASSP (2015)
5. Gerazov, B., Honnet, P-E., Gjoreski, A., Garner, P.: Weighted correlation based atom decomposition intonation modeling. In: INTERSPEECH (2015)

6. Pierrehumbert, J.B.: The phonetics and phonology of English intonation (Ph.D. thesis). MIT, Cambridge, MA, USA (1980)
7. Silverman, K., Beckman, M., Pitrelli, J., Ostendorf, M., Wightman, C., Price, P., Pierre-humbert, J., Hirschberg, J.: ToBI: A standard for labeling English prosody. In: Proceedings of the International Conference on Spoken Language Processing (ICSLP), pp. 867–870 (1992)
8. Taylor, P.: Analysis and synthesis of intonation using the Tilt model. J. Acoust. Soc. Am. **107**(3), 1697–1714 (2000)
9. Aubergé, V.: Prosody modeling with a dynamic lexicon of intonative forms: Application for text-to-speech synthesis. In: Proceedings of the ESCA Workshop on Prosody, pp. 62–65 (1993)
10. Holm, B,. Bailly G.: Generating prosody by superposing multi-parametric overlapping contours. In: Proceedings of the International Conference on Spoken Language Processing (ICSLP), pp. 203–206 (2000)
11. Kohler, K.J.: Studies in German intonation, Arbeitsberichte des Instituts für Phonetik und digitale Sprachverarbeitung. Universität Kiel, vol. 25, 295–360 (1991)
12. Kohler, K.J.: Parametric control of prosodic variables by symbolic input in TTS synthesis. In: van Santen, J., Sproat, R., Olive, J., Hirschberg, J. (eds.) Progress in Speech Synthesis, pp. 459–475. Springer, New York (1997)
13. Beckman, M.E., Hirschberg, J., Shattuck-Hufnagel, S.: The original ToBI system and the evolution of the ToBI framework. In: Jun, S.-A. (ed.) Prosodic Typology: The Phonology of Intonation and Phrasing, pp. 9–54. Oxford University Press, UK (2005)
14. Ostendorf, M., Price, P., Shattuck-Hufnagel, S.: The Boston University Radio News Corpus. Linguistic Data Consortium (1995)
15. Mallat, S.G., Zhang, Z.: Matching pursuits with time-frequency dictionaries. IEEE Trans. Signal Process. **41**(12), 3397–3415 (1993)
16. Hermes, D.J.: Measuring the perceptual similarity of pitch contours. J. Speech Lang. Hear. Res. **41**(1), 73–82 (1998)
17. Öhman, S.: Word and sentence intonation: A quantitative model. Speech Transmission Laboratory, Department of Speech Communication, Royal Institute of Technology (1967)
18. Prom-on, S., Xu, Y., Thipakorn, B.: Modeling tone and intonation in Mandarin and English as a process of target approximation. J. Acoust. Soc. Am. **125**, 405–424 (2009)
19. Mixdorff, H.: A novel approach to the fully automatic extraction of Fujisaki model parameters. In: ICASSP 2000, vol. 3, pp. 1281–1284 (2000)

A Phonetic Segmentation Procedure Based on Hidden Markov Models

Edvin Pakoci[1], Branislav Popović[1(✉)], Nikša Jakovljević[1], Darko Pekar[2], and Fathy Yassa[3]

[1] Faculty of Technical Sciences, University of Novi Sad, Novi Sad, Serbia
{edvin.pakoci,bpopovic,jakovnik}@uns.ac.rs
[2] AlfaNum Speech Technologies, Novi Sad, Serbia
darko.pekar@alfanum.co.rs
[3] Speech Morphing Inc., Campbell, CA, USA
fathy@speechmorphing.com

Abstract. In this paper, a novel variant of an automatic phonetic segmentation procedure is presented, especially useful if data is scarce. The procedure uses the Kaldi speech recognition toolkit as its basis, and combines and modifies several existing methods and Kaldi recipes. Both the specifics of model training and test data alignment are explained in detail. Effectiveness of artificial extension of the starting amount of manually labeled material during training is examined as well. Experimental results show the admirable overall correctness of the proposed procedure in the given test environment. Several variants of the procedure are compared, and the usage of speaker-adapted context-dependent triphone models trained without the expanded manually checked data is proven to produce the best results. A few ways to improve the procedure even more, as well as future work, are also discussed.

Keywords: Kaldi · Phonetic segmentation · Hidden Markov models

1 Introduction

In recent years, there is an evident increase in the amount of available multimedia data including speech. This data is interesting for research in social sciences, as well as for speech technologies. These studies usually require audio content and the corresponding phonetic transcription synchronized with it. Manual alignment of audio and text data is very laborious and expensive (30 s of audio data requires about an hour of manual work [1]), thus many automatic and semi-automatic procedures have been developed.

All these procedures can be classified into two broad groups depending on whether or not additional acoustic information about phone identities are used. The first group is comprised of methods which for phonetic segmentation use the information contained in the given audio signal, and order of phones in the corresponding phoneme sequence. These methods are referred to as text-independent or linguistically unconstrained segmentation methods. They exploit

© Springer International Publishing Switzerland 2016
A. Ronzhin et al. (Eds.): SPECOM 2016, LNAI 9811, pp. 67–74, 2016.
DOI: 10.1007/978-3-319-43958-7_7

the fact that sudden changes in speech signal characteristics usually coincide with phone boundaries. Exceptions of this rule are plosives/affricates consisted of occlusion and explosion/friction parts as well as transitions between successive vowels or vowels and semi-vowels [2]. These changes are usually detected in the spectral or cepstral domain [3–5]. Additionally, the level of feature similarity can be exploited in segmentation as in [6]. An advantage of these methods is their independence from language, but the accuracies of obtained phone boundaries are significantly poorer compared to accuracies of text-dependent methods.

Text-dependent or linguistically constrained segmentation methods align audio signal with corresponding phone sequence using phone models similar to those used in the automatic speech recognition (ASR) task. The dominant approach to phone modeling is hidden Markov models (HMMs), and interesting results are obtained in [7–13], among others. Besides HMMs, dynamic time warping [14] and artificial neural networks - ANNs [15,16] are used as well.

The width of analysis frames varies from 10 ms up to 30 ms, and frame shift varies from 1/5 of the frame width up to whole frame width. There are some variations of the extracted features in existing methods, but most of them include 12–14 mel-frequency cepstral coefficients (MFCCs), normalized energy and their first and second order time derivatives. In some studies, the set of features additionally includes a spectral variation function [17], perceptual loudness, measure of periodicity [9] and fundamental frequency (f_0) contour [15]. The basic modeling units can be monophones, triphones or tied-state triphones. The choice between those depends primarily on the size of the training corpus. Sometimes the improvement in alignment accuracy, which is usually obtained with context-dependent modeling units, is not sufficient to justify the increase of duration of the training procedure. Since the objective function for estimation of HMM parameters does not involve accurate position of phone boundaries after alignment, additional boundary refinement is possible. It is usually based on principles exploited in linguistically unconstrained methods [10,17] or using trained GMM or ANN models for boundaries [15,16]. The proposed procedure belongs to the group of linguistically constrained methods based on HMMs in case of scarce data. The procedure is tested on several databases in English whose description is given in Sect. 2. Detailed description of the procedure is presented in Sect. 3, and results of evaluation with discussion in Sect. 4. Section 5 concludes the paper.

2   Speech Corpora

Appen "USE_ASR001" database [18] of natural English (US) speech in studio quality, resampled to 16 kHz, 16 bits per sample, mono PCM, was used in our research. The database contains more than 80000 utterances (almost 7 GB of data, 100 male and 101 female speakers), or approximately 41 h of speech and 20 h of silence segments, and it is transcribed in SAMPA format. Only a small part of the database (in further text referred to as the bootstrapped part), containing around 35 min of speech and 15 min of silence segments, was manually labeled. This part of the database consists of short cropped audio files (around 1900) containing only about 2 to 3 words, which are selected in a way to cover all phone pairs (one after the other) which exist in the source database among all the given speakers. The extraction of audio segments is done automatically using information from initial forced alignment using flat-start models. These phone boundaries are manually checked and corrected by trained annotators. It has been shown that by applying manual alignments on a part of the database throughout the procedure, significant improvement can be obtained in comparison to flat-start training (e.g. [9]). Additionally, in our procedure the bootstrapped part of the database was artificially expanded several times, by modifying pitch and duration (i.e., by applying spectral warping and tempo modifications). It was feared that such a procedure could not provide sufficient data variability, so it was only applied in a limited amount. The original tempo was increased or decreased by 10 % and 20 % and the original pitch was increased (for males) or decreased (for females) by 1, 2 or 3 semitones. Male speakers whose pitch was increased by 1 and 2 semitones, along with the original unmodified male speakers, and female speakers whose pitch was decreased by 3 semitones, were used for the training of specialized male models. The bootstrapped part of the database (along with all the mentioned extensions) was then additionally doubled by marking all the words and phonemes as damaged in the copied instance. This was done in order to provide minimal number of samples needed to train the damaged phoneme models - they were needed primarily since the starting and ending phones in cropped segments had to be marked as damaged, as these are not full sentences by themselves, but segments not necessarily surrounded by silence. Therefore, the bootstrapped part of the database was increased 40 times for male speakers ([male + male pitch $\{+1, +2\}$ + female pitch $\{-3\}$] × tempo $\{-20, -10, 0, +10, +20\}$ × 2 for damaged phonemes). A special characteristic of our training was that the phone boundaries on the whole bootstrapped set (expanded) were kept fixed during the entire procedure, so they could have a greater influence on the accuracy of alignment in the remainder of the database.

Our test database, on which the results presented in this paper were calculated, included an array of phonetically rich utterances, spoken by 3 male speakers - Sean, Doug and Ben - from completely independent single-speaker databases, provided by Speech Morphing Inc. All the utterances for testing were manually labeled, so that automatically aligned phone boundaries could be compared to them. Sean's test database contains 50 utterances (around 1800 phonemes), which added up to 2 min 13 s of speech and 33 s of silence. Ben's test database contains 43 slightly longer utterances, 4 min 17 s of speech and 1 min 5 s of silence in total (around 2700 phonemes). Finally, Doug's test database contains 50 utterances - 2 min 28 s of speech and 23 s of silence (around 1800 phonemes). At the time of tests, no similar female databases were at our disposal. Nevertheless, the obtained results confirm our previous assertions and they were highly comparable among all test databases, as shown by the experiments (see Sect. 4).

3   Segmentation Procedure

The complete training procedure has been done using the Kaldi speech recognition toolkit [19] and modified Kaldi recipes. Inputs were Kaldi data files created using an input lexicon (in SAMPA format), which included all needed words and their pronunciations with multiple alternative pronunciations in some cases, as well as utterance transcriptions with marked speaker identifiers. Model topologies were initialized to 3 states for non-silence phones, and 5 states for silence phones, with a possibility to skip one state at a time (for a minimum of 3 states). For decoding purposes, as in all Kaldi training procedures, a lexicon FST (i.e., finite state transducer) is created based on the input lexicon. In our procedure, this FST is modified by adding alternative arcs for all arcs that have a vowel as their input label, and it concerns vowel stress - if the vowel is stressed, alternative arc with the unstressed version of the same vowel as input label is created, and vice versa. Also, for the arc containing the optional silence between and after each spoken word, an arc with optional glottal stop is created as an alternative. This was done because a lot of places in the database were identified where the gap between words includes rather a glottal stop then something than can be considered as a silence (which would lead to a "dirty" silence model).

The feature vectors include energy and 14 MFCCs, calculated by using a filter bank of 26 overlapping triangular windows, along with their first and second order time derivatives. They were extracted on 30 ms frames, with 7 ms frame shift. Multiplication coefficient of 0.33 was additionally applied to static MFCCs (excluding energy) to bring their value variability closer to that of energy. On the other hand, delta and delta-delta energy values were multiplied by coefficient 20, to effectively change their dynamic range. The mentioned coefficient values were concluded to be appropriate through several previous tests and extracted feature values analysis. No cepstral mean or variance normalization is performed, as the training type (explained below) makes it unnecessary.

The first stage of model training, which is the training of monophones on bootstrapped data set only, comes next. This step included manual alignments as the starting point and a 10 iterations of model and alignment reestimation. After each internal alignment, phone boundaries were reset to manually-given positions, but the within-phone frames per state distributions were saved. Output was the final monophone model set with 1000 Gaussians in total. Afterwards, these models were used to create the initial context-dependency tree for the speaker-adapted training (SAT) step, and to produce initial alignments for the rest of the database. The first pass of SAT started from the aforementioned alignments, i.e., there is no equidistant initial alignment at all. The bootstrapped data set is still used, alongside the whole regular database. The context-dependency tree which is created here has a goal of 1500 leaves (i.e., states). Next, initial fMLLR transforms are calculated using initial alignments, producing a diagonal transform matrix for each of the speakers in the database. Then 10 iterations of model reestimation follow, with periodic internal alignments and fMLLR transform matrices updates, ending with a goal of 4500 Gaussians for final models. Manually set boundaries are also forced throughout the stage (in the bootstrapped part of the database). In the end, the so-called "alignment model" is created - it is computed with speaker-independent (SI) features, but matches Gaussian-for-Gaussian with the speaker-adapted model.

The training procedure ends with the final SAT training pass. The alignment model is first used to align the whole database. Also, a new tree is created, slightly more complex with 2500 leaves, using these new, better alignments. The rest of the stage is very similar to the previous stage, with 12 iterations and a goal of 7000 Gaussians. It outputs the final SAT model set, as well as the final alignment model set. In all internal alignments a large decoding beam is used, to prevent potentially important tokens from being discarded in the early stages of utterance decoding. All the selected numbers - of iterations, states and Gaussians - have shown the best performance on a validation set (a part of the bootstrapped set) during exhaustive testing where these numbers were varied. Now that the models are ready, they can be used to align the given test data. The start is the same as for the training – there are given transcriptions matched to an audio file name each with marked speaker identifiers, and a lexicon containing all the words in transcriptions with possible pronunciations. These are converted to appropriate Kaldi data files. The procedure setup has to be the same as for model training - number of states for certain phones, list of used phones, MFCC and energy extraction specifications. Firstly, lexicon FST is created and modified the same way as in training, which is followed by static feature extraction. Delta and delta-delta features are added later on the fly. Decoding graphs are created from lexicon FST, provided models and corresponding tree. This is followed by first-pass alignment using SI features and the alignment model, the output of which is used to estimate fMLLR transforms, producing a diagonal matrix for each speaker in the test database, used to transform features (on the fly). In the end, the final alignment is performed, using transformed features and provided SAT models. The results are phone alignments within a label file.

4   Results and Discussion

Our test data sets include exclusively male speakers, so the results were obtained using male models. Several experiments were conducted. First, the possibility of using simple monophone models to align test data directly using just SI features is examined [9]. This of course shortens the training procedure a lot, but monophone models may not be precise enough. Then, the described procedure with triphones and SAT is evaluated. Both of these experiments are performed both by using the basic bootstrapped set (without tempo and pitch modifications), and the fully extended bootstrapped set. All the given results were obtained by calculating the difference between the phone start times in the manually labeled set and in the automatically obtained labels, then putting each of those numbers in the appropriate category based on the difference, e.g. up to 10 ms, up to 20 ms, and so on. In the special cases of inserted and deleted optional silences and glottal stops, they are instead compared to the previous phone in the manually marked database (if inserted) or automatic labels (if deleted).

Results for monophones with the extended bootstrapped set are given in Fig. 1 (left). Percentages for phones within 10 ms on all test sets are around 60 %, with more than 80 % within 20 ms, around 90 % within 30 ms and 95 % within 50 ms, and around 5 % of outliers. Outliers mostly include silences or phones after silences, especially if the neighboring phone is a plosive, affricate or a silent fricative. If silences and their adjacent phones are excluded from the results, around 85 % of phone boundaries fall within 20 ms of manual ones. The remaining outliers are mostly boundaries between two plosives, two similar vowels and finally borders between some vowels and lateral 'L' or approximant 'R', which is not that surprising as these borders are hard to put in the correct place even by hand (at most times there is actually no clear border). These kinds of outliers appear in other experiments as well. As for context-dependent triphones trained with the SAT procedure, the results are given in Fig. 1 (right). For the percentage of phones within 20 ms of manual boundaries, a 4–7% improvement was obtained at average, which is a lot when talking about segmentation quality. After excluding silence borders, these improve to over 90 %. The usage of triphones and SAT is justified, even considering the longer training.

The results with the non-extended bootstrapped set are shown in Fig. 2. The results are better then with artificial extension. It can be assumed that the artificial extension of the bootstrapped set results in significant feature dispersion which could not be covered with the monophone models using the same target

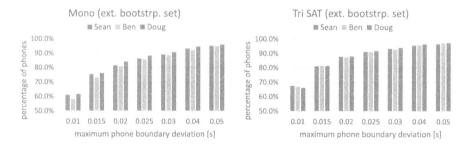

Fig. 1. Results for extended bootstrapped set.

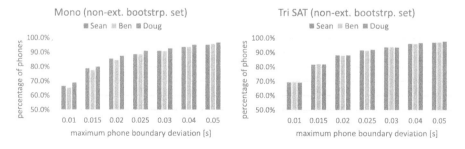

Fig. 2. Results for non-extended bootstrapped set.

number of Gaussians. On the other hand, in case of tied-state triphones it is largely compensated by fMLLR. It will be a subject of further research.

5 Conclusion and Further Directions

In this paper, a novel approach to automatic phone segmentation of an arbitrary speech database in case of scarce data is presented. It is concluded that context-dependent SAT models produce best and most stable overall results, but monophones are not too far behind, if procedure speed is of more concern. Artificial extension of the manually labeled part of the database is examined as well, and it was not proven to improve the results, at least if used in the way described. In the near future, more experiments will be done with versions of the expansion procedure which will conclude what exactly went wrong here. For now, it is assumed that either bad modification parameters are chosen, or the expansion went too far (the part with manual boundaries became too significant compared to the rest of the database). Future work will also include training parameter variations, other speech databases (including other languages as well), and finally improving the alignment analysis tool to get even more data which can help with pointing in the right direction. The greatest value of the described procedure is that the obtained correctly aligned speech databases can be used relatively quickly and successfully for any given application.

Acknowledgments. This research was supported in part by the Ministry of Education, Science and Technological Development of the Republic of Serbia, under Grant No. TR32035. The authors are grateful to the company "Speech Morphing, Inc." from Campbell, CA, USA, for providing the speech corpora for the experiments.

References

1. Brognaux, S., Roekhaut, S., Drugman, T., Beaufort, R.: Train&Align: a new online tool for automatic phonetic alignment. In: Spoken Language Technology Workshop (SLT), pp. 416–421. IEEE Signal Processing Society (2012)
2. Scharenborg, O., Ernestus, M., Wan, V.: Segmentation of speech: child's play? In: 8th Annual Conference of the International Speech Communication Association (INTERSPEECH), Antwerp, pp. 1953–1956 (2007)
3. Esposito, A., Aversano, G.: Text independent methods for speech segmentation. In: Chollet, G., Esposito, A., Faundez-Zanuy, M., Marinaro, M. (eds.) Nonlinear Speech Modeling. LNCS (LNAI), vol. 3445, pp. 261–290. Springer, Heidelberg (2005)
4. Leow, S.J., Chng, E.S., Lee, C.H.: Language-resource independent speech segmentation using cues from a spectrogram image. In: IEEE International Conference on Acoustics, Speech and Signal Processing (ICASSP), South Brisbane, pp. 5813–5817 (2015)
5. Priyadarsini, S., Kumar, A.: Automatic speech segmentation in syllable centric speech recognition system. J. Speech Technol. **19**(1), 9–18 (2016)

6. Almpanidis, G., Kotti, M., Kotropoulos, C.: Robust detection of phone boundaries using model selection criteria with few observations. IEEE Trans. Audio Speech Lang. Process. **17**(2), 287–298 (2009). IEEE Signal Processing Society
7. Bigi, B.: SPPAS: a tool for the phonetic segmentations of speech. In: 8th International Conference on Language Resources and Evaluation (LREC), Istanbul, pp. 1748–1755 (2012)
8. Boeffard, O., Charonnat, L., Le Maguer, S., Lolive, D., Vidal, G.: Towards fully automatic annotation of audio books for TTS. In: 8th International Conference on Language Resources and Evaluation (LREC), Instanbul, pp. 975–980 (2012)
9. Brognaux, S., Drugman, T.: HMM-based speech segmentation: improvements of fully automatic approaches. IEEE/ACM Trans. Audio Speech Lang. Process. **24**(1), 5–15 (2016). IEEE Signal Processing Society
10. Hoffmann, S., Pfister, B.: Fully automatic segmentation for prosodic speech corpora. In: 10th Annual Conference of the International Speech Communication Association (INTERSPEECH), Makuhari, pp. 1389–1392 (2010)
11. Hoffmann, S., Pfister, B.: Text-to-speech alignment of long recordings using universal phone models. In: 14th Annual Conference of the International Speech Communication Association (INTERSPEECH), Lyon, pp. 1520–1524 (2013)
12. Matoušek, J.: Automatic pitch-synchronous phonetic segmentation with context-independent HMMs. In: Matoušek, V., Mautner, P. (eds.) TSD 2009. LNCS, vol. 5729, pp. 178–185. Springer, Heidelberg (2009)
13. Stan, A., Mamiya, Y., Yamagishi, J., Bell, P., Watts, O., Clark, R.A.J., King, S.: ALISA: an automatic lightly supervised speech segmentation and alignment tool. J. Comput. Speech Lang. **35**, 116–133 (2016)
14. Adell, J., Bonafonte, A., Gomez, J., Castro, M.: Comparative study of automatic phone segmentation methods for TTS. In: 30th IEEE International Conference on Acoustics, Speech and Signal Processing (ICASSP), Philadelphia, pp. 309–312 (2005)
15. Toledano, D., Gomez, L., Grande, L.: Automatic phonetic segmentation. IEEE Trans. Speech Audio Process. **11**(6), 617–625 (2003). IEEE Signal Processing Society
16. Wang, L., Zhao, Y., Chu, M., Zhou, J., Cao, Z.: Refining segmental boundaries for TTS database using fine contextual-dependent boundary models. In: IEEE International Conference on Acoustics, Speech and Signal Processing (ICASSP), Montreal, pp. 641–644 (2004)
17. Brugnara, F., Falavigna, D., Omologo, M.: Automatic segmentation and labeling of speech based on hidden Markov models. J. Speech Commun. **12**(4), 357–370 (1993)
18. Appen, Product Catalog. http://catalog.appenbutlerhill.com/
19. Povey, D., Ghoshal, A., Boulianne, G., Burget, L., Glembek, O., Goel, N., Hannemann, M., Motlícek, P., Qian, Y., Schwarz, P., Silovský, J., Stemmer, G., Veselý, K.: The kaldi speech recognition toolkit. In: IEEE Workshop on Automatic Speech Recognition and Understanding (ASRU), pp. 1–4. IEEE Signal Processing Society (2011)

A Preliminary Exploration of Group Social Engagement Level Recognition in Multiparty Casual Conversation

Yuyun Huang[1]([✉]), Emer Gilmartin[1], Benjamin R. Cowan[1,2], and Nick Campbell[1]

[1] Speech Communication Laboratory, School of Computer Science and Statistics, Trinity College Dublin, Dublin, Ireland
{huangyu,gilmare,nick}@tcd.ie
[2] SILS, University College Dublin, Dublin, Ireland
benjamin.cowan@ucd.ie

Abstract. Sensing human social engagement in dyadic or multiparty conversation is key to the design of decision strategies in conversational dialogue agents to decide suitable strategies in various human machine interaction scenarios. In this paper we report on studies we have carried out on the novel research topic about social group engagement in non-task oriented (casual) multiparty conversations. Fusion of hand-crafted acoustic and visual cues was used to predict social group engagement levels and was found to achieve higher results than using audio and visual cues separately.

Keywords: Acoustic and visual signal processing · Human social behaviours · Social engagement recognition

1 Introduction

Although engagement can be expressed through the voice and body gestures of interlocutors and easily perceived by human beings, machines have no ability to sense such human social cognitive behaviours. Levels of engagement are also referential parameters that can be used for conversation assessment and topic detection. In this paper, we describe engagement concepts and highlight relevant works in both group and dyadic conversational engagement. We then outline our proposed engagement recognition methodology and report on several evaluations based on a multiparty casual conversation corpus.

The most widely used definition of social engagement in human - human or human - machine conversation is that formulated by Sidner as: *the process by which two (or more) participants establish, maintain and end their perceived connection. This process includes: initial contact, negotiating a collaboration, checking that other is still taking part in the interaction, evaluating whether to stay involved and deciding when to end the connection* [20]. In measuring engagement it is also vital to take account of auditory and visual non-verbal

© Springer International Publishing Switzerland 2016
A. Ronzhin et al. (Eds.): SPECOM 2016, LNAI 9811, pp. 75–83, 2016.
DOI: 10.1007/978-3-319-43958-7_8

cues, as they have been reported to contain much of the affective information transferred during conversations [9].

2   Related Works

There has been much valuable research into social engagement in various conversation scenarios. Many perceptible non-verbal cues have been analysed in social conversations. Eye gaze has been widely studied in terms of social engagement or interest during dialogues. Argyle and Cook (1976) [3] noted that the failure to attend other's gaze contact was evidence of having no interests and attention. Cassell et al. (1999) [7] examined the relationship between information structure and gaze behavior. They suggested that interlocutors' gaze behaviour served to integrate turntaking cues with the information structure of the propositional content of an utterance. They found that the beginnings of themes were frequently accompanied by a look-away from the hearer, while speakers frequently looked towards the hearer at theme endings. Rich et al. (2010) [19] built a computational model to recognize engagement by using manually annotated data on mutual facial gaze, directed gaze, adjacency pairs, and back-channels. Nakano and Ishii (2010) also used eye-gaze behaviours to estimate user engagement between human users and virtual agents [16].

Gustafson and Neiberg (2010) demonstrated that prosodic cues in Swedish, including change in syllabicity, pitch slope and loudness in non-lexical response tokens, could be used to detect engagement, and investigated prosodic alignment as a cue to engagement between speaker and listener [12]. Gupta et al. (2012) used speech cues to analyse childrens' engagement behavior, with results showing that vocal cues were informative in detecting children's engagement. [11] Hsiao et al. (2012) also investigated engagement level estimation using higher level speech cues like turntaking extracted from low level cues such as MFCCs and intensity [13].

Oertel et al. (2011) [18] used multimodal cues to predict the degree of group involvement during spontaneous conversation, extracting acoustic features including pitch level and intensity and visual features including eye blinking and mutual gaze from manually annotated data. The resulting automatic prediction was based on Support Vector Machines (SVM) with three classes of involvement. Oertel and Salvi (2013) [17] modelled individual engagement and group involvement in an eight-party dialogue corpus. Their results showed that engagement and involvement can be modelled by using gaze pattern. In order to describe engagement, they introduced presence, entropy, symmetry and MaxGaze features to summarize different eye-gaze pattern aspects. Their group involvement classification using Gaussian Mixture Models got accuracies of 71.0 % on training sets and 71.3 % on test sets. Lai et al. (2013) used turn-taking features to detect group involvement and used the involvement cues to predict extractive summary content in meeting segments; they concluded that automatically derived measures of group level involvement, like participation equality and turn-taking freedom, could help in identifying relevant meeting segments for summarization [15].

Bohus et al. (2009) introduced an approach to detect human participants' engagement intentions during dialogue with an avatar agent [4]. Yu et al. (2015) built an engagement awareness dialogue system named TickTock [21], which has a social engagement model to offer information to dialogue manager where conversational strategy was decided.

In this work, we focus more on studying group engagement level recognition, considering the group as a whole rather than individuals. We investigated features which can take all interlocutors into account and contribute to the whole conversation. Visual and acoustic cues like group head movement distance, optical flow, direction of head address (yaw), leaning forward or backward, voice quality and intensity were used for the recognition task.

3 Methodology

We propose a set of features which can represent group talking traits. These comprise visual and auditory visual and auditory cues, which are used in combination for engagement prediction. Figure 1 shows a flowchart overview of our methodology, while the features and steps are described in more detail below.

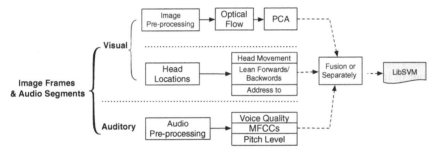

Fig. 1. Methodology overview

3.1 Optical Flow with Principal Component Analysis (PCA)

Optical flow is used to compute the motion of the pixels of an image sequence. It provides a dense (point to point) pixel correspondence over the entire scene, and thus provides an indication of how much movement is occurring overall. We used the algorithm proposed by Gunnar Farnback [10] based on polynomial expansion, which provides all the motion of all the pixels between previous and current frames. PCA was also used for dimensionality reduction.

3.2 Head Pose Related Features

The face detection and the yaw head position library were used from the work of [1], Camshift tracking [6] was also used tracking the detected faces. Yaw angle range from −90 degrees to +90 degrees. Backward or forward body movement (leaning) was computed by comparing the size of participants' faces across sequential frames in 10-frame steps on 30 fps videos.

3.3   Auditory Features

Audio recordings were down-sampled to 16 kHz for feature extraction in this work. The features extracted from the audio signal comprised pitch level, 12 MFCCs, MFCC energy, and glottal parameters.

3.4   Applying Additional Windows

The auditory features were extracted in a small window size, and the video data was recorded at 30 frames per second. However, changes in human cognitive state occur over a longer time frame, up to several minutes. To model these events more reliably, we tested additional window lengths. To make the visual results more reliable, we downsampled the video data from 30 frames per second to 3 frames per second. The method was motivated from previous studies [13]. For the audio, we calculated average feature values across longer window lengths.

4   Experiments and Results

To test the general performance of our engagement model, the LibSVM package [8] with RBF kernel was used for binary classification tasks with grid search method for best parameters selection, cost (set Cost, search from 2^{-5} to 2^{15})and gamma (set gamma, search from 2^{-15} to 2^3) to avoid overfit and underfit. The number of instances of each class used for training was balanced with an baseline accuracy of 50 %.

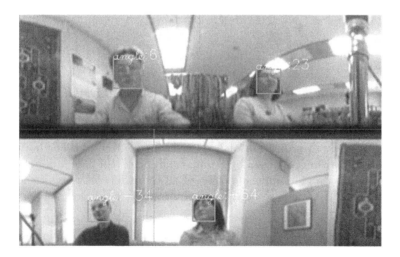

Fig. 2. Screenshot of TableTalk with face detection and head yaw angle

4.1   Data Sets and Annotation

TableTalk [2] is a 210-min corpus of group social conversations collected at the ATR Research Labs in Japan. A 360-degree camera was used to capture the frontal faces of participants chatting around a table. Audio was captured using a centre mounted microphone. Figure 2 shows a screen shot of the video of the corpus with face detection. The TableTalk corpus has been widely studied for social tasks e.g. Scherer [14] studied it for visual interaction management; Bonin F. investigated the engagement annotation study based on TableTalk corpus [5]. We annotated engagement levels on a 0–4 scale in maintain segment as shown in Table 1 and Fig. 3, and the binary classes of engaged (A) and not engaged (C) were analysed in this paper. The maintenance or central phase part engagement was annotated into different degrees, and was the focus of this analysis, rather than the initial phase or approach phase examined in other works [4].

4.2   Feature Analysis

Box plots of several features are shown in Fig. 4. The first two box plots from the left show the distributions of two selected visual cues - head pose (yaw)

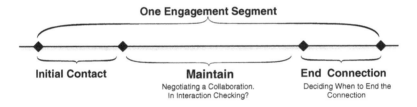

Fig. 3. One engagement segment

Table 1. Annotation rules

5-level Engagement Annotation			
End of the previous segment			
Engagement Initialization			
Maintain	0. Strong Engaged	A. Engaged	Very engaged and strongly want to maintain the conversation
	1. Engaged		Interest but not very high, e.g. willing to talking with no passion
	2. Neutral	B. Neutral	Neither show interest or lack of interest
	3. Disengaged	C. Disengaged	Less interest in the conversation
	4. Strong Disengaged		No interest to continue the conversation at all, want to leave the conversation
End Connection			

and move distance. We observe that for these visual cues, as expected, the non-engaged category has lower values (p<0.005). The two plots on the right show the distributions of MFCC energy and Open Quotient (OQ). Again, non-engaged has lower values. Optical Flow visualization using Munsell Color System is shown in Fig. 5.

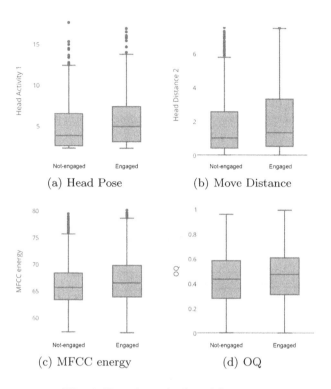

Fig. 4. Box plots of selected features

4.3 Visual Cues Results

Table 2 shows the results for different combinations of visual features. The head backward/forward movement obtained the lowest accuracy rate. A higher result was obtained when head movement distance, optical flow and head yaw angle were considered together.

4.4 Acoustic Cues Results

Table 3 shows the results for the auditory features. Glottal and MFCCs features achieve a higher accuracy of 71 % than other acoustic feature sets.

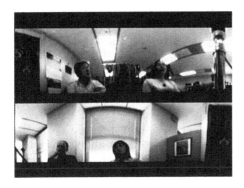

Fig. 5. Optical flow visulization

Table 2. Classification results of group engagement using visual features

Feature set	Accuracy
Head forward/backward	65.0024 %
Head move distance	71.0875 %
Head Pose	71.2081 %
Optical flow with PCA	73.4748 %
Head move distance + Optical flow + Head yaw angle	74.1741 %

Table 3. Classification results of group engagement using auditory features

Feature set	Accuracy
F0	60.9187 %
Glottal	71.9074 %
MFCCs	72.2691 %
Glottal + MFCCs	72.679 %

4.5 Fusion Feature Set Results

A 'fusion' feature set consisting of both audio and video features was obtained by concatenating the visual and auditory vectors which had been time-aligned. The mean values of head move distance and head pose for the four speakers were calculated. The auditory features were extracted from a single recorded audio file containing all participants. Table 4 shows the results of the combination of these audio-visual feature sets with 82.23 % prediction rate. These results indicate that the combined audio-visual feature is better for detecting engagement than using the auditory and visual feature sets separately.

Table 4. Prediction results of combined features

Feature set	Accuracy	Recall	Precision	F-Score
Auditory and visual combined	82.23 %	0.822	0.816	0.815

5 Conclusion

Low level visual and auditory cues of engagement have been analysed in the TableTalk corpus. In general, the visual parameters performed slightly better than the auditory parameters in recognition of engagement in this work. We compared recognition results using feature fusion and using visual/audio features separately, and found that audio-visual fusion gave higher accuracy. As a shallow analysis, we believe that advanced detailed visual and audio features can definitely increase the prediction accuracy, deep learning may also increase the results, which is conducted in the future works. Model-level and decision-level fusion will also be investigated in the future.

Acknowledgement. This research is supported by Science Foundation Ireland through the CNGL Programme (Grant 12/CE/I2267) in the ADAPT Centre and CHISTERA-JOKER project at Trinity College Dublin.

References

1. Libfacedetection. https://github.com/ShiqiYu/libfacedetection
2. Campbell, N.: The freetalk database. http://freetalk-db.sspnet.eu/files/
3. Argyle, M., Cook, M.: Gaze and mutual gaze (1976)
4. Bohus, D., Horvitz, E.: Learning to predict engagement with a spoken dialog system in open-world settings. In: Proceedings of the SIGDIAL 2009 Conference: The 10th Annual Meeting of the Special Interest Group on Discourse and Dialogue, pp. 244–252. Association for Computational Linguistics (2009)
5. Bonin, F., Böck, R., Campbell, N.: How do we react to context? annotation of individual and group engagement in a video corpus. In: Privacy, Security, Risk and Trust (PASSAT), 2012 International Conference on and 2012 International Confernece on Social Computing (SocialCom), pp. 899–903. IEEE (2012)
6. Bradski, G.R.: Computer vision face tracking for use in a perceptual user interface. Intel Technol. J. **Q2**, 214–219 (1998)
7. Cassell, J., Bickmore, T., Billinghurst, M., Campbell, L., Chang, K., Vilhjálmsson, H., Yan, H.: Embodiment in conversational interfaces: Rea. In: Proceedings of the SIGCHI Conference on Human Factors in Computing Systems, pp. 520–527. ACM (1999)
8. Chang, C.C., Lin, C.J.: LIBSVM: a library for support vector machines. ACM Trans. Intell. Syst. Technol. (TIST) **2**(3), 27 (2011)
9. Ekman, P., Friesen, W.V.: The repertoire of nonverbal behavior: categories, origins, usage, and coding. Semiotica **1**(1), 49–98 (1969)
10. Farnebäck, G.: Two-frame motion estimation based on polynomial expansion. In: Bigun, J., Gustavsson, T. (eds.) SCIA 2003. LNCS, vol. 2749, pp. 363–370. Springer, Heidelberg (2003)

11. Gupta, R., Lee, C.C., Bone, D., Rozga, A., Lee, S., Narayanan, S.: Acoustical analysis of engagement behavior in children. In: WOCCI, pp. 25–31 (2012)
12. Gustafson, J., Neiberg, D.: Prosodic cues to engagement in non-lexical response tokens in swedish. In: DiSS-LPSS, pp. 63–66. Citeseer (2010)
13. Hsiao, J.C.y., Jih, W.r., Hsu, J.Y.: Recognizing continuous social engagementlevel in dyadic conversation by using turntaking and speech emotion patterns. In: Activity Context Representation Workshop at AAAI (2012)
14. Jokinen, K., Scherer, S.: Embodied communicative activity in cooperative conversational interactions-studies in visual interaction management. Acta Polytech. Hung. **9**(1), 19–40 (2012)
15. Lai, C., Carletta, J., Renals, S., Evanini, K., Zechner, K.: Detecting summarization hot spots in meetings using group level involvement and turn-taking features. In: INTERSPEECH, pp. 2723–2727 (2013)
16. Nakano, Y.I., Ishii, R.: Estimating user's engagement from eye-gaze behaviors in human-agent conversations. In: Proceedings of the 15th International Conference on Intelligent User Interfaces, pp. 139–148. ACM (2010)
17. Oertel, C., Salvi, G.: A gaze-based method for relating group involvement to individual engagement in multimodal multiparty dialogue. In: Proceedings of the 15th ACM on International Conference on Multimodal Interaction, pp. 99–106. ACM (2013)
18. Oertel, C., Scherer, S., Campbell, N.: On the use of multimodal cues for the prediction of involvement in spontaneous conversation. In: Interspeech 2011, pp. 1541–1544 (2011)
19. Rich, C., Ponsler, B., Holroyd, A., Sidner, C.L.: Recognizing engagement in human-robot interaction. In: 2010 5th ACM/IEEE International Conference on Human-Robot Interaction (HRI), pp. 375–382. IEEE (2010)
20. Sidner, C.L., Lee, C., Kidd, C.D., Lesh, N., Rich, C.: Explorations in engagement for humans and robots. Artif. Intell. **166**(1), 140–164 (2005)
21. Yu, Z., Papangelis, A., Rudnicky, A.: Ticktock: a non-goal-oriented multimodal dialog system with engagement awareness. In: 2015 AAAI Spring Symposium Series (2015)

An Agonist-Antagonist Pitch Production Model

Branislav Gerazov[1(✉)] and Philip N. Garner[2]

[1] Faculty of Electrical Engineering and Information Technologies,
University of Ss. Cyril and Methodius in Skopje, Skopje, Macedonia
gerazov@feit.ukim.edu.mk
[2] Idiap Research Institute, Martigny, Switzerland
phil.garner@idiap.ch

Abstract. Prosody is a phenomenon that is crucial for numerous fields of speech research, accenting the importance of having a robust prosody model. A class of intonation models based on the physiology of pitch production are especially attractive for their inherent multilingual support. These models rely on an accurate model of muscle activation. Traditionally they have used the 2nd order spring-damper-mass (SDM) muscle model. However, recent research has shown that the SDM model is not sufficient for adequate modelling of the muscle dynamics. The 3rd order Hill type model offers a more accurate representation of muscle dynamics, but it has been shown to be underdamped when using physiologically plausible muscle parameters. In this paper we propose an agonist-antagonist pitch production (A2P2) model that both validates and gives insight behind the improved results of using higher-order critically damped system models in intonation modelling.

Keywords: Prosody · Intonation · Muscle models · Resonant frequency · Damping

1 Introduction

Prosody is a multidimensional phenomenon comprising the intonation, energy, and duration contours of the speech signal, which carries both linguistic and paralinguistic information [3,15]. Prosody is crucial in speech technology systems, especially in Text to Speech synthesis (TTS) where it is necessary for generating natural speech output, but also in Automatic Speech Recognition (ASR), Speech Emotion Recognition (SER) [19], emotional speech synthesis [2], and emphatic human-machine dialogue systems. Intonation is arguably the most studied and modelled dimensions of prosody [14]. Most intonation models follow one of two general approaches: (i) modelling the pitch contour directly, and (ii) modelling the underlying mechanisms, i.e. the physiology of pitch production. The physiology-based models are especially attractive because they offer insight into the way prosody is produced, and because of their inherent multilinguality.

One of the most well-known physiological models is the command-response (CR) model of Fujisaki [4], which models the pitch contour as a sum of global,

© Springer International Publishing Switzerland 2016
A. Ronzhin et al. (Eds.): SPECOM 2016, LNAI 9811, pp. 84–91, 2016.
DOI: 10.1007/978-3-319-43958-7_9

phrase components, and local, accent components. Both components are output from a 2nd order critically damped system that models laryngeal muscle activation based on the Spring-Damper-Mass (SDM) muscle model [5]. More recently, research has shown that using higher order system models increases intonation modelling performance. The quantitative target approximation (qTA) model, for example, uses a 3rd order system to generate the surface pitch contours [13]. We have also observed improved performance in our Weighted Correlation Atom Decomposition (WCAD) based intonation model[1], when higher 6th order system responses are used [8,9]. These findings necessitate a closer examination of the muscle model used in intonation modelling.

There are different muscle models suggested in literature, which go from very detailed ones – modelling the internal mechanics of the muscle fibre, to more general ones – modelling only the output to a given input of the muscle as a whole [20]. Recently, we have analysed the two most commonly used muscle models: the 2nd order SDM model and the 3rd order Hill type model [7]. Research suggests that the SDM model is too simple to capture the basic mechanics of muscle activation [10]. On the other hand, the Hill type model while offering improved modelling of muscle-tendon dynamics, exhibits underdamped behaviour when using physiologically plausible muscle parameters [11]. In this paper we propose an agonist-antagonist pitch production (A2P2) model [12] and analyse how it relates to recent results in physiological intonation modelling. The analysis shows that the A2P2 model validates and gives insight behind the improved results of using higher-order critically damped system models in intonation modelling.

2 SDM and Hill Muscle Models

The spring-damper-mass (SDM) model shown to the left in Fig. 1 is the simplest model of muscle activation. It comprises a parallel elasticity (PE) k, a damper c and a force generator F. If we assume steady state initial conditions and an impulse driving force its transfer function is given by (1) [6]. From it, we can extract the damping ratio ζ and the undamped resonant frequency ω_0, which are given by (2). If we plug in physiologically plausible parameters taken from the elbow muscles [11] into the SDM, we obtain the zero-pole diagram and corresponding impulse responses in Fig. 2. The diagram shows that the system reaches critical damping only for $c = 10$, which is at the extreme end of the physiologically plausible range:

$$y(s) = \frac{1}{\frac{m}{k}s^2 + \frac{c}{k}s + 1},\tag{1}$$

$$\zeta^2 \triangleq \frac{c^2}{4mk}, \qquad \omega_0^2 \triangleq \frac{k}{m}.\tag{2}$$

The three-element Hill muscle model [20] is shown in its Poynting-Thomson (PT) form to the right of Fig. 1. It improves on the SDM by adding a series elasticity

---

[1] The WCAD implementation code is available on gitHub at https://github.com/dipteam/wcad.

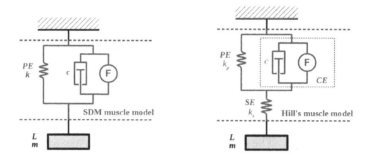

Fig. 1. The 2nd order spring-damper-mass (SDM) muscle model (left), and the Hill three element model (right).

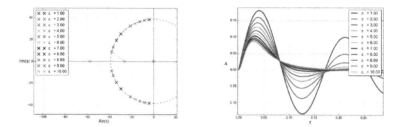

Fig. 2. Zero-pole diagram (left) and impulse response (right) of the SDM model, for a sweep of values of $c \in [1, 10]$, for $k = 178$ and $m = 0.12$.

(SE) k_s that models the tendons connecting the muscle to the bone. It is the simplest model that takes into account the essential interactions arising from the stiffness of the tendon [10]. Its transfer function under steady state initial conditions and an impulse driving force is given in (3). To derive its resonant frequency ω_0 (4) we can use the impedance electro-mechanical analogy [1] to draw the equivalent electrical circuit, find its input impedance $Z_i(j\omega)$, and equate its imaginary part to 0 [7]. Unfortunately, there is no straightforward solution for the damping ratio ζ [11]:

$$y_o(s) = \frac{1}{\frac{cm}{k_s}s^3 + m\frac{k_s+k_p}{k_s}s^2 + cs + k_p}, \tag{3}$$

$$\omega_0^2 = \frac{k_p k_s}{m(k_p + k_s)}. \tag{4}$$

The movement of the poles is shown in Fig. 3 for a sweep of muscle damping c and an increasing SE to PE ratio $k = k_s/k_p$. We can see that the system reaches critical damping only for $k \geq 8$, when the two imaginary poles reach the real axis, and is underdamped over most of the parameter range. In fact, for $k \geq 8$ the Hill model exhibits underdamped oscillatory behaviour independent of its damping c [11].

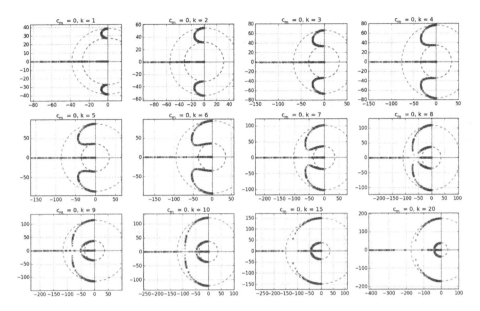

Fig. 3. Movement of the poles for the Hill model for a sweep of $c \in [0.1, 1000]$.

3 Physiology of Pitch Production

It is clear the the SDM, and even the Hill muscle model, with their underdamped behaviour cannot on their own account for the dynamics of the laryngeal muscle system. In order to build a better model we have to take a examine more closely the physiology of pitch production. Such a detailed analysis reveals four physiological sources of pitch change [16]:

(i)   Cricothyroid (CT) muscle that rotates the thyroid cartilage in respect to the cricoid, stretching the vocal folds and raising pitch,

(ii) Vocalis (VOC) muscle, whose contraction decreases vocal cord length, but increases their tensile stress, effecting a rise in pitch [18],

(iii) Sternohyoid (SH) muscle that lowers the larynx decreasing vocal fold tension and pitch, and

(iv) Subglottal pressure (P_{SB}), which linearly correlates to pitch.

Other researchers have suggested that thyrohyoid (TH), rather than the SH muscle effectuates the drop in pitch [5], but these muscle have been found to activate in unison.

4 The Agonist-Antagonist Pitch Production Model

Reflecting the complexity of the laryngeal muscle system we propose an agonist-antagonist pitch production (A2P2) model to capture the opposing muscle physiological environment of pitch production [5,16]. The agonist-antagonist concept was first proposed by Plamondon and colleagues [12], mainly in the context of handwriting analysis. Plamondon's model is built around the velocity of muscles following a lognormal profile. The lognormal in turn arises as a limiting case where complex muscles are driven by signals travelling some distance from the brain, and driving large masses. In considering the Hill model (and derivatives), we rather model the absolute offsets of individual muscle fibres. Of course, complex muscles lead to higher order models which likely tend towards lognormal profiles. It is an open question whether the muscles associated with prosody are small enough to be modelled as individual fibres. At least, the thrust of the present work is to understand what can be gained from assuming so. Conversely, the difference between a lognormal and the gamma-like profiles that arise from such analysis is not large, and probably below the noise level of measurements of prosody.

The A2P2 model is shown in Fig. 4 and consists of an agonist Hill muscle that models the CT and VOC muscles, an antagonist Hill muscle that models the SH-TH muscle complex, and a mass with its damper and elasticity that represents the thyroid cartilage held in place by the elasticity of the vocal folds and whose movements are damped by the friction at its joint with the cricoid. Although P_{SB} is not explicitly modelled, it is indirectly included in the two opposing muscle models, as it is also due to the activation of muscles in the respiratory system. The physiological plausibility of the proposed model is grounded on the assumption that we can group all of the muscles responsible for the production of the pitch into two equivalent opposing muscles, whilst still being small enough to merit the small muscle assumption in the Hill model. This has been common practice when modelling muscle systems [11] and is also justified by the correlation seen in the activation of the CT and the VOC [16].

Transfer Function. To obtain the transfer function of the proposed model we can use the impedance electro-mechanical analogy [1] to obtain the equivalent electrical circuit shown in Fig. 5. When solving in the Laplace domain [17] we find that the proposed system is 4th order with one zero. It is possible to simplify the equivalent circuit by applying Thévenin's theorem between the connection points of the two muscles, here marked A and B and thus calculating a joint equivalent Hill model for the opposing muscles. If we assume that the two opposing muscles have identical parameters, which is physiologically plausible, then the system simplifies to a 3rd order system, whose impulse is given by (5) response for steady state initial conditions, and an impulsive driving force:

$$y_o(s) = \frac{1}{\frac{c_p m}{k_s}s^3 + \frac{c_m c_p + m(k_p+k_s)}{k_s}s^2 + \frac{c_m(k_p+k_s)+c_p(k_m+k_s)}{k_s}s + \frac{k_m k_p}{k_s} + k_m + k_p} \quad (5)$$

Resonant Frequency ω_0. We can now find the input impedance of the system and use it to calculate the resonant frequency ω_0. A simplified analysis, which disregards the elasticity k_m, gives (6), showing that the A2P2 model has two resonant frequencies. It is interesting to note that if we let $c_m = 0$, the simplified A2P2 model reduces to the Hill model, and as solutions of (6) we have (7).

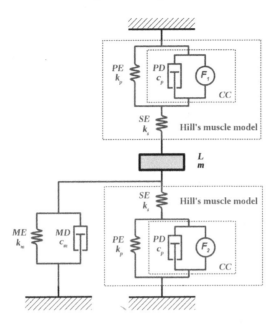

Fig. 4. The agonist-antagonist pitch production (A2P2) model.

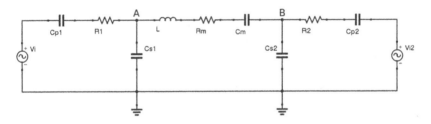

Fig. 5. Equivalent electrical circuit of the A2P2 model.

While the first solution ω_0 is equivalent to (4), ω_1 explains the outer resonant frequency seen in the movement of the poles in Fig. 3:

$$\omega_0^2 = \frac{1}{2}\left(-\frac{c_m^2}{m^2} + \frac{k_s(2k_p + k_s)}{(k_p + k_s)m} \pm \sqrt{\frac{c_m^4}{m^4} - \frac{2c_m^2 k_s(2k_p^2 - 3k_p k_s - k_s^2) - k_s^4 m}{m^3(k_p + k_s)^2}}\right), \quad (6)$$

$$\omega_0 = \sqrt{\frac{k_p k_s}{m(k_p + k_s)}}, \qquad \omega_1 = \sqrt{\frac{k_p k_s + k_s^2}{m(k_p + k_s)}}. \quad (7)$$

Pole Movement. To understand the A2P2 model's behaviour and compare it to the Hill model, we will look at the movement of the poles in the simplified model for various k-s keeping $c_m = 2$, shown in Fig. 6. We can see that (i) for $k = 1$ the two resonant frequencies coincide, (ii) the asymptotic movement of the poles towards ω_0 and ω_1 is from the outside rather than from in between as

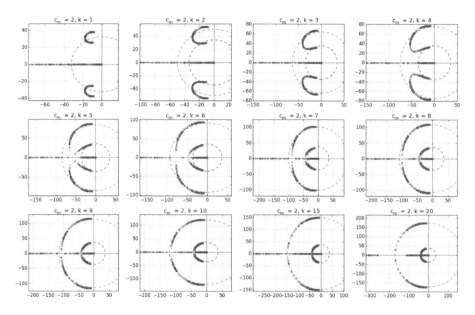

Fig. 6. Movement of the poles for the AA model for $c_m = 2$ and a sweep of $c_p \in [0.1, 1000]$.

for the Hill model, and (iii) we have critical damping already for $k = 5$, instead of $k = 8$ as was the case for the Hill model. Thus, the added damping c_m in the A2P2 compensates for the underdamped behaviour of the individual Hill model, granting critical damping and overdamping for a physiologically plausible set of parameters. This effect is emphasised if we let $c_m > 2$.

5   Conclusions

The proposed agonist-antagonist pitch production model appears to be a reasonable hypothesis for the model that is being implicitly assumed when higher orders are used in prosody models. Combined with the feedback assumption of Prom-on, it justifies use of a model order somewhere between the 2nd order of the CR model and the limiting lognormal case of Plamondon. Moreover, the A2P2 model also grants physiological plausibility to the use of critically damped system models in intonation modelling.

Acknowledgements. The authors would like to thank the support of the Swiss National Science Foundation via the joint research project *"SP2: SCOPES Project on Speech Prosody"* (No. CRSII2-147611/1).

References

1. Beranek, L.: Acoustics Sound Fields and Transducers. Academic Press, Waltham (2012). S.l

2. Burkhardt, F., Campbell, N.: Emotional speech synthesis. In: The Oxford Handbook of Affective Computing, p. 286 (2014)
3. Cutler, A., Dahan, D., Van Donselaar, W.: Prosody in the comprehension of spoken language: a literature review. Lang. Speech **40**(2), 141–201 (1997)
4. Fujisaki, H.: A model for synthesis of pitch contours of connected speech. Annu. Rep. Eng. Res. Inst. Univ. Tokyo **28**, 53–60 (1969)
5. Fujisaki, H.: The roles of physiology, physics and mathematics in modeling prosodic features of speech. In: Proceedings of Speech Prosody (2006)
6. Garner, P.N.: A derivation of a second order damped system. http://www.idiap.ch/~pgarner/appendices/damping.pdf
7. Gerazov, B., Garner, P.N.: An investigation of muscle models for physiologically based intonation modelling. In: Proceedings of the 23rd Telecommunications Forum, Belgrade, Serbia, pp. 468–471, November 2015
8. Gerazov, B., Honnet, P.E., Gjoreski, A., Garner, P.N.: Weighted correlation based atom decomposition intonation modelling. In: Proceedings of Interspeech, Dresden, Germany, September 2015
9. Honnet, P.E., Gerazov, B., Garner, P.N.: Atom decomposition-based intonation modelling. In: Proceedings of the IEEE International Conference on Acoustics, Speech and Signal Processing, Brisbane, Australia. IEEE, April 2015
10. Kistemaker, D.A., Rozendaal, L.A.: *In Vivo* dynamics of themusculoskeletal system cannot be adequately described using astiffness-damping-inertia model. PLoS ONE **6**(5), e19568 (2011). http://dx.doi.org/10.1371%2Fjournal.pone.0019568
11. Piovesan, D., Pierobon, A., Mussa Ivaldi, F.A.: Critical damping conditions for third order muscle models: implications for force control. J. Biomech. Eng. **135**(10), 101010 (2013)
12. Plamondon, R.: A kinematic theory of rapid human movements: part I: movement representation and generation. Biol. Cybern. **72**(4), 295–307 (1995)
13. Prom-on, S., Xu, Y., Thipakorn, B.: Modeling tone and intonation in Mandarin and English as a process of target approximation. J. Acoust. Soc. Am. **125**, 405–424 (2009)
14. van Santen, J., Mishra, T., Klabbers, E.: Prosodic processing. In: Benesty, J., Sondhi, M.M., Huang, Y. (eds.) Springer Handbook of Speech Processing, pp. 471–488. Springer, Heidelberg (2008)
15. Schuller, B., Batliner, A.: Computational Paralinguistics: Emotion, Affect and Personality in Speech and Language Processing. Wiley, Hoboken (2013)
16. Strik, H.: Physiological control and behaviour of the voice source in the production of prosody. Ph.D. thesis, Dept. of Language and Speech, Univ. of Nijmegen, Nijmegen, Netherlands, October 1994
17. Thomas, R.E., Rosa, A.J., Toussaint, G.J.: The Analysis and Design of Linear Circuits, 7th edn. Wiley Publishing, Chichester (2012)
18. Titze, I.R., Martin, D.W.: Principles of voice production. J. Acoust. Soc. Am. **104**(3), 1148 (1998)
19. Vogt, T., André, E., Wagner, J.: Automatic recognition of emotions from speech: a review of the literature and recommendations for practical realisation. In: Peter, C., Beale, R. (eds.) Affect and Emotion in Human-Computer Interaction. LNCS, vol. 4868, pp. 75–91. Springer, Heidelberg (2008)
20. Zatsiorsky, V., Prilutsky, B.: Biomechanics of Skeletal Muscles. Human Kinetics, Champaign (2012)

An Algorithm for Phase Manipulation in a Speech Signal

Darko Pekar[1], Siniša Suzić[2], Robert Mak[2], Meir Friedlander[3], and Milan Sečujski[2(✉)]

[1] AlfaNum – Speech Technologies, Novi Sad, Serbia
darko.pekar@alfanum.co.rs
[2] Faculty of Technical Sciences, University of Novi Sad, Novi Sad, Serbia
{sinisa.suzic,robert.mak,secujski}@uns.ac.rs
[3] Speech Morphing, Inc., Campbell, CA, USA
meir@speechmorphing.com

Abstract. While human auditory system is predominantly sensitive to the amplitude spectrum of an incoming sound, a number of sound perception studies have shown that the phase spectrum is also perceptually relevant. In case of speech, its relevance can be established through experiments with speech vocoding or parametric speech synthesis, where particular ways of manipulating the phase of voiced excitation (i.e. setting it to zero or random values) can be shown to affect voice quality. In such experiments the phase should be manipulated with as little distortion of the amplitude spectrum as possible, lest the degradation in voice quality perceived through listening tests, caused by the distortion of amplitude spectrum, be incorrectly attributed to the influence of phase. The paper presents an algorithm for phase manipulation of a speech signal, based on inverse filtering, which introduces negligible distortion into the amplitude spectrum, and demonstrates its accuracy on a number of examples.

Keywords: Phase perception · Parametric speech synthesis · Zero phase · Random phase · Inverse filtering

1 Introduction

Due to the early studies of sound perception, it has been assumed for a long time that human auditory system recovers all information from the amplitude spectrum of the incoming signal and that it does not rely on phase spectrum at all [1, 2][1]. However, more recent studies have shown that, on the contrary, our sound perception is sensitive to phase information to a certain degree [4–6]. In practice this dependence is still often ignored. For example, most contemporary automatic speech recognition systems still rely on features extracted from amplitude spectra only [7], and in speech enhancement it is common practice to modify the magnitude spectrum and keep the corrupt phase spectrum [8, 9]. Nevertheless, a number of recent studies have shown that pitch information has particular relevance in case of speech signals [10], and that, e.g. the

---

[1] A review of most important early studies in phase perception can be found e.g. in [3].

© Springer International Publishing Switzerland 2016
A. Ronzhin et al. (Eds.): SPECOM 2016, LNAI 9811, pp. 92–99, 2016.
DOI: 10.1007/978-3-319-43958-7_10

accuracy of both human and automatic speech recognition can be improved if phase information is taken into account in some way [7, 11, 12].

Most practical studies related to the influence of phase to speech perception are based on listening tests in which listeners are presented with speech samples containing a number of different versions of the same utterance, which are assumed to have identical amplitude spectra and different phase spectra. A direct consequence of this approach is that any difference in quality that is perceived between sound samples will inevitably be attributed to the influence of the phase information. However, in reality it is not possible to modify the phase spectrum of an utterance in an arbitrary way without affecting the amplitude spectrum as well, which implies that the interpretation of the results of such studies has to take into account the specific algorithm used to modify the phase spectrum. For instance, some representative phase perception studies, including most notably [13], are based on the manipulation of either excitation signal or speech itself by superimposing overlapping frames previously shifted in time, which is known to affect the amplitude spectrum as well. This paper presents an alternative approach, based on the decomposition of the speech signal according to the source-filter model and phase modification by using an all-pass filter whose phase response varies from sample to sample of the input signal.

The remainder of the paper is organized as follows. Section 2 presents the source-filter separation algorithm which enables subsequent manipulation of the phase spectrum. Section 3 presents the proposed algorithm for phase manipulation in detail, Sect. 4 presents the results of a simple experiment carried out on recordings of four speakers of Serbian and English, and Sect. 4 concludes the paper, giving an outline of the future work as well.

2 Source-Filter Separation Algorithm

The source-filter separation algorithm used in this research is based on inverse filtering with filters obtained through the estimation of MFCC coefficients of the spectrum, as outlined in Fig. 1. Since this study is concerned with phase information, the discussion will be restricted to the case of voiced speech segments, with well-defined fundamental frequency (f_0). The speech signal under analysis is firstly separated into individual frames using overlapping Hamming windows, positioned pitch-synchronously, which requires the knowledge of f_0 as well as glottal closure instants. A slightly modified

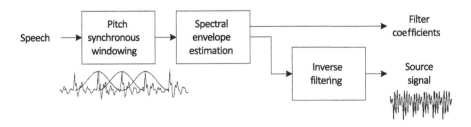

Fig. 1. Outline of the source-filter separation algorithm for voiced speech.

approach can be used even if these are not available, but with inferior results. The spectral envelope for each frame is estimated in the following steps:

(1) FFT of size N is calculated for each frame in a sufficient number of points.
(2) Obtained values are used to calculate the estimated value of the spectrum at integer multiples of f_0, using linear interpolation.
(3) Based on the values of the spectrum at integer multiples of f_0, FFT coefficients are re-interpolated.
(4) Thus obtained FFT coefficients are passed through a filter bank of K overlapping mel-spaced triangular filters, where K is one of the analysis parameters.

The estimates of filter bank outputs at equidistant reference time instants (the distance d between them being another analysis parameter) are obtained by linear interpolation between filter bank outputs previously obtained at glottal closure instants (i.e. pitch-synchronously). Thus obtained values are used to interpolate the full spectrum envelope in L points (where L is also specified as input parameter) for each reference time instant. Linear interpolation is used, since some other techniques, which were also investigated, did not lead to an improvement. In the i-th reference time instant the spectrum envelope is normalized by:

$$norm_i = \sqrt{\frac{1}{WL} \sum_{k=0}^{L-1} X^2(k)}, \tag{1}$$

where $X(k)$ is the interpolated spectrum and W is the length of the analysis window.

Thus obtained spectrum envelope can be converted into the impulse response of the corresponding filter using IFFT. The actual frequency response of the inverse filter at each sample between reference time instants $n - 1$ and n is given by:

$$I(f) = \frac{1}{H(f)} = \frac{1}{c_1 H_{n-1}(f) + c_2 H_n(f)}, \tag{2}$$

where $H_{n-1}(f)$ and $H_n(f)$ are the frequency responses at reference time instants $n - 1$ and n, and c_1 and c_2 represent the relative distance of the sample under consideration from time instants $n - 1$ and n respectively. It is important to note that the inverse filter obtained in this way varies with each sample of the speech signal. The excitation signal $e(n)$ can now be easily obtained by inverse filtering.

It should be noted that the described procedure is computationally too demanding to be performed at real time due to the necessity of calculating the inverse filter coefficients for each sample. However, having in mind its purpose, this is only a minor disadvantage, particularly having in mind that the resynthesis process does not suffer from the same drawback. Namely, for resynthesis purposes it is possible to keep only the filters related to reference time instants and to perform linear interpolation in time domain.

3 Phase Manipulation

In this approach phase manipulation is performed on the excitation signal, which is processed within symmetrical rectangular windows of length equal to the current T_0. The windows are centered around glottal closure instants (GCIs), which are also used for calculating the current T_0 and as reference points during the analysis. Assuming that the aim is to obtain zero phase spectrum, the phase spectrum for each voiced frame is manipulated in the following steps:

(1) Firstly, the T_0 of each fundamental period is calculated by subtracting two adjacent GCIs, and this value is assigned to the centre of that period (i.e. it will be assumed that at that point T_0 has this value). Then, each sample is assigned its current T_0, calculated by interpolating the values of T_0 of the two adjacent fundamental periods between whose centres the sample in question is located.

(2) A DFT of size T_0 (in samples) is calculated for each sample, using a symmetrical rectangular window, without zero padding. The obtained phase spectrum is unwrapped in order to avoid phase discontinuities, using an appropriate function from *Matlab*.

(3) For each sample, the corresponding phase spectrum is calculated from the previously obtained unwrapped phase spectrum by adding the term $2k\pi\delta$, where k is the index of a particular spectral component and δ is the parameter that provides the relative distance of the relevant sample of the signal from the previous GCI $(0 \leq \delta < 1)$. In this way a phase spectrum that varies with each sample of the excitation signal is obtained.

(4) For each sample it is now possible to obtain an all-pass filter with a phase spectrum exactly the inverse of the phase spectrum obtained in the previous step. By filtering the excitation signal $e(n)$ using the time-variant all-pass filter, a modified excitation signal $e'(n)$ with zero-phase spectrum is obtained. It is important to note that all-pass filtering is carried out on a sample-by-sample basis, i.e. although the all-pass filter obtained for sample i of the input signal operates on a number of samples in the neighbourhood of i, it produces only one sample of the output signal. For each new sample of the input signal, a new filter has to be obtained.

The algorithm is summarized by the pseudocode given in Fig. 2.

It should be noted that it would be possible to shape the phase spectrum in any other way by applying an obvious modification to the step 3. However, to obtain a random-phase excitation signal it is not necessary to perform a sample-by-sample modification proposed above, i.e. it is sufficient to manipulate the excitation signal all at once, by using a time-invariant all-pass filter. Figure 3 illustrates a segment of the excitation signal for the vowel /a/ before and after phase manipulation. The modified speech segment belongs to the corpus of studio recordings of a female speaker of Serbian (referred to as D in the following section), used for expressive speech synthesis [14]. It should be noted that the excitation signal modified in this way has the most of its energy concentrated around GCIs, which makes it more robust to windowing. This, in turn, is beneficial for a number of speech processing techniques that include overlap-add modifications of excitation signals. Figure 4 illustrates the difference between the original phase spectrum, the phase spectrum set to zero using the proposed algorithm, and the phase spectrum of the generic HTS (Hidden Markov model based TTS) excitation [15], shown here as a reference.

```
algorithm phase_mod is
  input: Excitation signal e
  output: Modified excitation signal e'
  for each sample i in e do
    if voiced(i) then
        find 3 closest GCIs to i and calculate T₀₁ and T₀₂
        let d₁ and d₂ be distances to centres of periods T₀₁ and T₀₂
        T₀ ← (d₂ * T₀₁ + d₁ * T₀₂)/(d₁ + d₂)
        let f be the array of samples from i - T₀/2 to i + T₀/2
        F ← DFT(f)
        phase(F) ← unwrap(phase(F))
        let i₁ and i₂ be positions of previous and next GCI in e
        delta ← (i - i₁)/(i₂ - i₁)
        for each spectral sample F(k) in F do
            phase(F(k)) ← phase(F(k)) + 2 * k * delta * pi
        let AP be the all-pass filter with phase -phase(F(k))
        e'(i) ← AP(e(i))
    else
        e'(i) ← e(i)
    end if
  return e'
```

Fig. 2. Pseudocode of the phase modification algorithm.

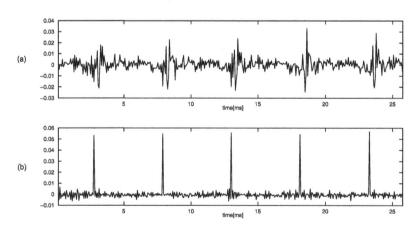

Fig. 3. A segment of voiced speech excitation (vowel /a/) (a) with original phase distribution (b) with phase spectrum set to zero using the proposed method.

4 Experiment Results

Preliminary experiments aimed at the verification of the proposed methods for source-filter separation and phase manipulation were carried out on speech recordings of four speakers – one female and one male speaker of Serbian, as well as one female and one male speaker of English. Five recordings from each speaker were analyzed, selected at random from large speech corpora recorded for the purposes of expressive speech synthesis. All of the corpora were made in a professional studio using high quality equipment. The selected recordings were downsampled to 16 kHz and the original bit depth of 16 bits per sample was kept.

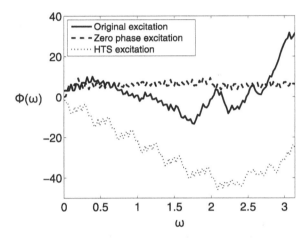

Fig. 4. Phase spectra of the original excitation, the excitation with phase spectrum set to zero, and the generic HTS excitation (pulse train with noise).

Firstly, in order to verify the proposed method for source-filter separation, the selected recordings were separated into their source and filter components and then resynthesized, with no phase manipulation (Experiment 1). The amplitude spectra of the original recordings were then compared frame by frame to the amplitude spectra of their resynthesized versions, and the results are shown in Table 1. The comparison was carried out on the full frequency range by calculating the amplitude of the FFT at 30 ms long successive overlapping frames with a shift of 5 ms, and then averaging the result. A very small distortion of the amplitude spectrum occurs, which was con-firmed by informal listening tests, where no perceptual difference between the original and the resynthesized sample was detected by any of the listeners.

Secondly, in order to verify the proposed phase manipulation algorithm and to examine the extent of the distortion of the amplitude spectrum that it introduces, the source component obtained in Experiment 1 was re-created with zero phase spectrum at voiced segments, while on unvoiced segments it was not modified in any way. It has been confirmed by listening tests that the different treatment of frames due to the difference in their voicing does not lead to audible discontinuities in resulting speech. The phase modification was limited to the frequencies below 5 kHz. The signal was then resynthesized from the source component modified in this way, using the filter component which was not altered (Experiment 2). The difference in the amplitude spectra was then calculated in the same way as in Experiment 1, and the results are shown in Table 2. The distortion that occurs is somewhat greater than in the first case, but can still be considered very small, while the informal listening tests reveal only a slight perceptual difference between the original and the resynthesized signal.

Table 1. Results of Experiment 1: Original vs. resynthesized recordings.

	Serbian		English		Average
	D (female)	J (male)	K (female)	D (male)	
Mean [%]	1.38	0.71	1.42	0.56	1.02
Variance [%]	0.36	0.14	0.23	0.06	0.20

Table 2. Results of Experiment 2: Original vs. zero-phase resynthesized recordings.

	Serbian		English		Average
	D (female)	J (male)	K (female)	D (male)	
Mean [%]	5.21	9.65	5.24	5.86	6.49
Variance [%]	0.63	0.98	0.66	1.07	0.83

5   Conclusion

In this paper we have proposed a novel technique for manipulating the phase spectrum of a speech signal by firstly decomposing the signal into its source and filter components by inverse filtering and then modifying the phase of the excitation on a sample-by-sample basis. The proposed technique thus avoids the need for overlap-add, which is often used for phase manipulation regardless of the fact that it can affect the amplitude spectrum significantly. The results of the preliminary experiments, including the resynthesis of the original speech using the original excitation signal and the excitation signal with phase spectra set to zero, confirm that the distortion of the amplitude spectrum caused by phase manipulation is indeed relatively small. This makes the proposed technique useful in a range of speech processing scenarios which require the modification of excitation phase spectrum, including the construction of excitation signals for parametric speech synthesis or speech vocoding. Our future work will include the re-implementation of most widely used phase modification algorithms from their descriptions in the literature, and their direct comparison with the proposed algorithm, both through objective measurements as well as more extensive listening tests.

Acknowledgments. The presented study was supported in part by the Ministry of Education and Science of the Republic of Serbia (grant TR32035), in part by the project "SP2: SCOPES Project for Speech Prosody" (No. CRSII2-147611/1), financed by the Swiss National Science Foundation, and in part by the company Speech Morphing, Inc. from Campbell, CA, USA, which also provided some of the speech corpora used in the experiments.

References

1. Ohm, G.S.: Über die Definition des Tones, nebst daran geknüpfter Theorie der Sirene und ähnlicher tonbildender Vorrichtungen. Annalen der Physik und Chemie **135**(8), 513–565 (1843)
2. von Helmholtz, H.L.F.: Über die Klangfarbe der Vocale. Annalen der Physik und Chemie **18**, 280–290 (1859)
3. Plomp, R., Steeneken, H.J.M.: Effect of phase on the timbre of complex tones. J. Acoust. Soc. Am. **46**(2B), 409–421 (1969)
4. Schroeder, M.R.: Models of hearing. Proc. of the IEEE **63**, 1332–1350 (1975)
5. Oppenheim, A.V., Lim, J.S.: The importance of phase in signals. Proc. IEEE **69**, 529–541 (1981)
6. Patterson, R.D.: A pulse ribbon model of monaural phase perception. J. Acoust. Soc. Am. **82**(5), 1560–1586 (1987)
7. Paliwal, K.K., Alsteris, L.D.: On the usefulness of STFT phase spectrum in human listening tests. Speech Commun. **45**(2), 153–170 (2005)
8. Lim, J.S., Oppenheim, A.V.: Enhancement and bandwidth compression of noisy speech. Proc. IEEE **67**, 1586–1604 (1979)
9. Wang, D.L., Lim, J.S.: The unimportance of phase in speech enhancement. IEEE Trans. Speech Signal Process. **30**(4), 679–681 (1982)
10. Pobloth, H., Kleijn, W.B: On phase perception in speech. In: Proceedings of IEEE International Conference on Acoustics, Speech and Signal Processing (ICASSP), vol. 1, pp. 29–32 (1999)
11. Shi, G., Shanechi, M.M., Aarabi, P.: On the importance of phase in human speech recognition. IEEE Trans. Audio Speech Lang. Process. **14**(5), 1867–1874 (2006)
12. Schluter, R., Ney, H.: Using phase spectrum information for improved speech recognition performance. In: Proceedings of IEEE International Conference on Acoustics, Speech and Signal Processing (ICASSP), vol. 1, pp. 133–136 (2001)
13. Raitio, T., Juvela, L., Suni, A., Vainio, M., Alku, P.: Phase perception of the glottal excitation and its relevance in statistical parametric speech synthesis. Speech Communication (in press, 2016)
14. Sečujski, M., Ostrogonac, S., Suzić, S., Pekar, D.: Speech database production and tagset design aimed at expressive text-to-speech in Serbian. In: Proceedings of Digital Signal and Image Processing (DOGS), Novi Sad, Serbia, pp. 51–54 (2014)
15. Zen, H., Nose, T., Yamagishi, J., Sako, S., Masuko, T., Black, A.W., Tokuda, K.: The HMM-based speech synthesis system version 2.0. In: Proceedings of ISCA Speech Synthesis Workshop (2007)

An Exploratory Study on Sociolinguistic Variation of Russian Everyday Speech

Natalia Bogdanova-Beglarian, Tatiana Sherstinova$^{(\boxtimes)}$, Olga Blinova, and Gregory Martynenko

Saint Petersburg State University, 7/9 Universitetskaya nab., St. Petersburg 199034, Russia
{n.bogdanova,t.sherstinova,o.blinova,g.martynenko}@spbu.ru

Abstract. The research presented in this paper has been conducted in the framework of the large sociolinguistic project aimed at describing everyday spoken Russian and analyzing the special characteristics of its usage by different social groups of speakers. The research is based on the material of the ORD corpus containing long-term audio recordings of everyday communication. The aim of the given exploratory study is to reveal the linguistic parameters, in terms of which the difference in speech between different social groups is the most evident. An exploratory subcorpus, consisting of audio fragments of spoken communication of 12 respondents (6 men and 6 women, 4 representatives for each age group, and representatives of different professional and status groups) with the total duration of 106 min and of similar communication settings, was created and fully annotated. The quantitative description of a number of linguistic parameters on phonetic, lexical, morphological, and syntax levels in each social group was made. The biggest difference between social groups was observed in speech rate, phonetic reduction, lexical preferences, and syntactic irregularities. The study has shown that the differences between age groups are more significant than between gender groups, and the speech of young people differs most strongly from the others.

Keywords: Russian everyday speech · Sociolinguistics · Multilevel linguistic analysis · Phonetics · Vocabulary · Syntax · Social groups · Speech corpus

1 Introduction

The speech of any person inevitably reflects features of the sociolects that are connected to those social groups or strata to which this person belongs to and in the scope of which he or she mainly communicates with other people. Nowadays, it seems quite impossible to study speech in any language independently of speaker's gender and age parameters. The examples of sociolinguistic studies of spoken Russian may be found in [1–4] and other works.

Therefore, "making a speech portrait" not of an individual but of a particular social group has become a challenging topic that attracts the linguists' attention. The decision of this problem is important for solution of many theoretical and practical tasks (e.g., for creation of speech synthesis and recognition systems, speaker's verification and identification, elaboration of speaker adaptive dialogue systems, forensic phonetics, etc.) [5].

© Springer International Publishing Switzerland 2016
A. Ronzhin et al. (Eds.): SPECOM 2016, LNAI 9811, pp. 100–107, 2016.
DOI: 10.1007/978-3-319-43958-7_11

The research presented in this paper has been conducted in the framework of the large sociolinguistic project aimed at describing everyday spoken Russian and analyzing the special characteristics of its usage by different social groups of speakers.

The study is based on the material of the ORD corpus containing long-term audio recordings of everyday communication [6, 7], which is one of the most representative corpus of spoken Russian and the largest multimedia resource of Russian everyday discourse, containing more than 1200 h of recordings gathered from 127 respondents and hundreds of their interlocutors. The respondents which took part in the ORD recordings represent different gender groups (66 men and 61 women), different age groups (with individual ages of participants ranging from 18 to 77 years), different professional and status groups [8].

The aim of the given exploratory study is to reveal the linguistic parameters, in terms of which the difference in speech between different social groups is the most evident. Taking into account the high labor requirements of spoken data transcription and annotation [9], it was decided firstly to conduct an exploratory study on the limited speech sample in order to detect linguistic parameters that are the most indicative for different social groups (mainly, for the age and gender groups). The results of this research are presented in the given article.

2   The Exploratory Subcorpus and the Methodology of the Pilot Study

For this study, the pilot subcorpus, containing fragments of everyday communication of 12 respondents and their 10 interlocutors, lasting 1 h 46 min in total, was formed and completely annotated. The episodes for this subcorpus have been selected from everyday (non-professional) conversations of respondents with their relatives, friends or colleagues in alike communicative situations [10]. The amount of the explored speech material is comparable to a well-known spoken Russian corpus "Rasskazy o snovideniyax" (Night Dream Stories) [11].

The subcorpus contains episodes of speech communication of the balanced sample of respondents, representing two gender groups (6 men and 6 women), three age groups (four representatives for each – youth, middle-aged and seniors – group) and at least one representative of 4 social class groups: (a) high-level personnel, businessmen and self-employed individuals, (b) salaried employees, (c) students, (d) unoccupied people, including non-working pensioners. Besides, the subcorpus contains speech of representatives of the following professions: (1) a worker, (2) a soldier, (3) an engineer, (4) an IT-specialist, (5) a teacher, (6) a physicist, (7) an art historian, (8) a marketer, (9) a lawyer, and (10) a musician.

All speech data have been segmented into utterances, phrases, words and allophones. Phonemic and phonetic transcriptions have been performed. Linguistic annotation is made on phonetic, lexical, morphological and syntax levels.

In total, the subcorpus contains 16060 tokens of speech transcripts (10259 of which are word tokens), 2039 clauses, and 41850 allophones. Multilevel statistical analysis of annotations has been conducted on all levels for the whole subcorpus and separately for two gender and three age groups.

3   The Phonetic Level

On phonetic level, the statistical data concerning the distribution of individual phonemes and allophones have been obtained, and the duration of sounds, words and phrases has been measured; the speech rate has been analyzed, and the realization of reduced forms has been described in detail.

It proved that in speech of all social groups, the phonemes /a/ (18 %), /i/ (9 %), /t/ (6 %), /o/ (5 %), /u/ (4 %) are the most frequent. At least, there is no difference between the groups up to the 10th rank. In the allophone frequency ranging, the stressed [a0] (7 %) predictably ranked first, the second is [t] (6 %), followed by two unstressed allophones of /a/ – [a1] (5.3 %) and [a4] (4.9 %), the stressed [o0] holds the fifth position (4.9 %). No evident difference between social groups has been observed in this aspect.

The analysis of duration of allophones, words and phrases has been made. The average allophone duration for the whole subcorpus was 66.81 ms (61.54 ms for men vs. 69.51 ms for women). Speech rate, being an integrative factor for time values of units from different linguistic levels, was specially investigated. The average speech tempo in the subcorpus is 5.32 words/s (SD = 8.28). It turned out that in general men speak a little bit faster than women: 5.46 words/s vs. 5.25 words/s (SD = 2 and SD = 10 respectively). The speech of young people is characterized by the highest speech rate – 5.91 words/s (SD = 12). Thus, the previously suggested hypothesis concerning correlation between the age of speakers and their speech ratio was confirmed [12].

Further, all reduced forms have been found in the pilot subcorpus and their acoustical analysis has been performed. The overall number of all reduced word forms is 350 that adds up to 3.4 % of the whole subcorpus vocabulary, and refers to 111 different variants of reduced forms. The examples of variants are the following: *gar'ú*, *gr'ú*, *gu* and *gru* for *govor'ú* ('*I say*') or *tos'* and *tóis'* for *tó est'* ('*I mean*', '*so*'), etc.

On top of the frequency list there are the forms *š':as* (*seichas* '*now*'; 10.6 %) and *ch'o* (*chto* '*what*'; 10.3 %). They are followed by *búit* (*búd'et* '*will be*'; 4.3 %), *ch'ó-to* (*chtó-to* '*something*'; 4.0 %), *nich'ó* (*nichego* '*nothing*'; 3.1 %), *gar'ú* (*govor'ú* '*I say*'; 3.1 %) and *t'a* (*teb'á* '*you*'– Gen. or Acc.; 3.1 %), *tóka* (*tól'ko* '*only*', '*just*'; 2.6 %), *kadá* (*kogdá* '*when*'; 2.3 %) and *tos'* (*to est'* '*that is*'; 2.3 %).

The upper zones of the frequency lists analyzed separately for men's and women's speech show certain differences. Men's "priorities" have appeared to be *ch'o* (14.5 %), *š':as* (7.2 %), *búit* (6.5 %), *nich'ó* (4.3 %) and *t'a* (3.6 %). Women prefer *š':as* (12.9 %), *ch'o* (7.1 %), *ch'o-to* (5.7 %), *gar'ú* (4.3 %), *tos'* (3.3 %), *búit* (2.9 %), *gyt* (*govorit* '*s/he says*'; 2.9 %). It may be seen that the most popular reduced form *š':as* is used by women almost twice more often than by men (12.9 vs. 7.2 %). Men in their turn use forms *ch'o*, *búit* and *nich'ó* more often: *ch'o* (14.5 vs. 7.1 %), *búit* (6.5 vs. 2.9 %) and *nich'ó* (4.3 vs. 2.4 %). It's only in the men's speech, that the forms *disítna* (*deistvítel'no* '*really*'), *kadá* (*kogdá* '*when*') and *sho* (*chto* '*what*') are frequent. In women's speech, the reduced form *gyt* (*govorít 's/he says'*; 2.9 %) is on top of the frequency list, while it is not observed in men's conversations.

Further, it turned out that the most popular reduced form *š':as* is on top of the frequency lists only for the middle and senior age groups (17.9 and 7.4 % respectively). In the youth group, however, the reduced form *ch'o* (14.5 %) turned out to be the most "popular", with *š':as* taking only the second position (9.8 %). The data show that only the younger generation actively uses the form *vaš'é*, whereas the forms of politeness *pozhálsta* (*pozhaluista 'please'*) and *pasíb(a)* (*spasíbo 'thank you'*) are found mainly in the speech of the middle-aged respondents.

The study of the phonetic realization of discourse markers and hesitation phenomena has not revealed any regularities. The intonation contours of phrases were not analyzed on this stage of the research.

4   The Lexical Level

The lexical study in the given research involves the analysis of usage of stylistically marked words, professional words, neologisms, slang words, etc. in everyday speech data, the comparison of words' functional activity in speech of different social groups and their lexical richness, as well as describing the usage of pragmatic items and constructions in everyday spoken Russian.

The frequency word lists have been compiled for the whole subcorpus and for individual social groups. For subcorpus in total, the rank distribution of the upper zone of the frequency word list is the following: *ya* (*I*) (3.1 %), *nu* (*well/er*) (2.9 %), *ne* (*no*) (2.6 %), *da* (*yes/but*) (2.4 %), *i* (*and/here*) (2.2 %), *vot* (*here is/well/now*) (2.1 %), *eto* (*this*) (1.95 %), *v* (*in/at*) (1.9 %), *chto* (*what*) (1.83 %), *a* (*and/but/ah*) (1.58 %). This ranking is repeated in all gender and age groups' frequency lists with slight variations. For studying of less-frequent word distribution, it is necessary to conduct the research on more representative speech sample.

The index of lexical diversity which is defined as the ratio of words occurring only once to the whole number of words is 0.164 for the total sample. For men's speech it is slightly higher (0.169) and for women's speech it is considerably lower (0.128).

The distribution of neologisms is strongly correlated with the speakers' age. Thus, the share of neologisms is maximum in speech of the youth (0.42 %), it is less in speech of the middle-aged (0.32 %) and is exceptionally low in speech of seniors (0.02 %). The youth's speech is also characterized by the high rank of the words such as *ayfon* (*iPhone*) and *KASKO* (*a car insurance package*), thereby indicating some dominants of their interests and priorities.

The analysis of the youth slang did not bring any surprises. Thus, youth speakers give preference to low-style words at least twice as often as other age groups. Swear words are especially frequent here.

One of the brightest features of everyday speech is the verbal elements that cannot be indisputably identified neither as lexical nor lexicogrammatical items. For example: *(tak) skazhem, (ne) eto samoye, (ya) ne znayu, kak (yego, yeyo, ikh, eto), (i) vsyo takoye (procheye), vse dela, tuda-syuda* etc. These items unambiguously mark the oral spontaneous speech and are very frequent in everyday communication. In recent works, such items are usually called "pragmatic markers", "pragmatic constructions", or "pragmatemes" [13, 14].

17 pragmatic constructions have been found in the research material. On top of the list, there are metacommunicative markers (or, "contact verbs") *znayesh/znayete* (*you know*), *ponimayesh* (*you understand*), *vidish* (*you see*), *slushay* (*listen*), etc., that form 19.4 % of all pragmatemes in the sample. The other popular pragmatic markers are used less frequently: *koroche* (*in short*) (15.5 %) and *v obschem* (*generally*) (10.7 %). The usage of approximating constructions *i tak dalee* and *to-syo* is sporadic, as well as the use of uncertainty markers *tipa* (6.3 %) and *vrode* (3.4 %).

Sociolinguistic variation of these markers is difficult to be analyzed on these data because their number in the subcorpus is rather small. However, women used them twice as often as men (67.5 and 32.5 % correspondently), giving preference to metacommunicative markers, which are used to attract and keep interlocutor's attention (80 % of their realizations took place in female speech). The "favourite" male pragmateme is *koroche*; 56.3 % of its use was observed in speech of men, predominantly of the youth age group. One-third of all pragmatic markers was found in speech of seniors, mainly female, who give preference to the pragmateme *v obschem*.

5   The Morphological Level

On the morphological level, the distributions of parts of speech, grammatical forms, agrammatical and occasional forms, as well as some "rare" or "complicated" forms, have been analyzed in speech of various social groups.

There was not observed much difference in parts of speech usage among men and women. Cf. two lists: (1) POS distribution in men's speech: PART (11.0 %), V (10.0 %), SPRO (9.9 %), APRO (2.7 %), S (9.0 %), PR (5.0 %), ADV (6.0 %), CONJ (4.64 %), INTJ (2.58 %), A (2.4 %); and (2) POS distribution in women's speech: V (11.0 %), SPRO (11.0 %), PART (10.0 %), S (8.9 %), ADV (6.0 %), PR (4.8 %), CONJ (4.5 %), ADVPRO (2.9 %), APRO (2.5 %), A (2.2 %). As for the differences among the age groups, the younger respondents use significantly more emotional speech markers, discourse markers and particles (11.36 %). The speech of seniors is characterized by the dominance of substantive pronouns (especially *ya* (*I/me*)) (11.52 %).

No agrammatical forms have been detected in the exploratory subcorpus. The occurrence of "rare" grammatical forms (e.g., the second genitive case and the second prepositional case) is lower than expected. As for grammatically complicated forms, only 26 participles (0.25 %) were found in the whole sample; no adverbial participles were observed. Nouns in vocative case have 20 occurrences, being used mainly by women addressing to women.

6   The Syntax Level

The syntactic analysis involved the following aspects: (1) the study of verbal and noun syntactic branches, (2) the identification of the most frequent syntactic structures of spoken Russian, (3) the description of their complexity, and (4) measuring the frequency of some syntactic phenomena which are typical to spontaneous speech (parcellation, ellipsis, incomplete utterances, self-correction, etc.).

Altogether, 2039 clauses have been found in the given subcorpus and annotated in terms of syntactic structures. The highest frequency for the speech of all social groups has been shown by the most simple structures, consisting of one or two elements, namely *SV* (a simple clause consisting of *noun (subject) + verb (predicate)*; 2.75 %), *V* (verb predicate without dependent words, 1.8 %), *S* (a single subject noun, 1.6 %), and *Q?* (a single interrogative word, 0.8 %).

As for the noun groups, the most frequent structures are *S* (subject), *xS* (prepositional group), AS (attributive construction with preposition attribute), *xAS* (prepositional group with preposition attribute). No significant difference in preferences between different social groups under study has been discovered.

Sixteen non-projective dependency trees have been found in speech data of the pilot subcorpus. It is impossible to draw any research conclusions based on such low number of occurrences. However, it's worth noticing that non-projective syntactic structures are more frequently used by young people with poor educational background.

Further, the analysis of syntactic structures has shown that left-branching verbal groups prevail over the right-branching ones in everyday oral Russian speech in contrast to Russian written language where symmetrical structures dominate [15]. This feature of oral speech is characteristic to all social groups.

The biggest difference between social groups is observed in the following syntactic irregularities of speech: the number of interrupted or incompleted utterances (CUT), ellipsis (EL), parcellation (PARS), and self-correction (COR). From all analyzed clauses (2039 units), interrupted utterances prevail covering 6.9 %, further goes (in descending order) EL (4.2 %), PARC (1.8 %) and COR (1.2 %). All these features occur mainly in women's speech, in which 63.6 % of incomplete utterances, 78.5 % of ellipses, 65.7 % of parcellation, and 65.2 % of self-corrections have been found.

The similar tendency has been discovered in speech of youth: 54.4 % CUT, 68.1 % EL, 85.7 % PARC, and 66.7 % COR. The lowest index in this respect is typical for seniors' speech: 11.4 % CUT, 7.2 % EL, 3.6 % PARC, and 6.7 % COR respectively. In other words, it can be cautiously supposed that the peculiarities of Russian everyday speech are concentrated mainly in women's language as against to men's and in the speech of youth as against to the speech of middle-agers and seniors.

The analysis of syntactic features in respect with informants' social status has been also performed. It turned out that incomplete syntactic structures prevail noticeably in speech of employees and businessmen (29.4 and 32.1 % respectively) and are very scarcely represented in speech of retired pensioners' (8.3 %). Elliptic structures most often appear in the speech of students (35.9 %), often enough in managers' speech (26.6 %), having the minimum in speech of retired pensioners (1.6 %). Parcellations that clearly prevail in students' speech (66.7 %) did not appear at all in speech of retired pensioners' and turned out to be evenly distributed among the rest social groups: 11.1 % for employees, 7.4 % for managers and 14.8 % for businessmen. The cases of self-correction have shown the following distribution: businessmen – 30.0 %, employees and managers – 25.0 % each, students – 15.0 %, retired pensioners – 5.0 %.

It can be also observed that syntactical correctness of speech is most common for the group of retired pensioners.

7   Conclusion

This study has shown that the differences in usage of everyday language between age groups are more significant than between gender groups, and the speech of young people differs most strongly from the others. The biggest difference between social groups is observed in speech rate, phonetic reduction, lexical preferences, POS distribution, pragmatic markers, and in some syntactic irregularities of speech (namely incomplete utterances, ellipsis, parcellation, and self-correction). No principle differences in speech between different gender and age groups were detected in terms of the other linguistic parameters that have been analyzed in this study.

The results of this study are of exploratory nature. This sociolinguistic research is planned to be further continued on the expanded sample of the ORD corpus with a focus on those linguistic parameters which have turned out to be the most indicative for different social groups. Statistical hypothesis testing should be obligatory for obtaining reliable results. Taking into consideration high variability of such parameters as prosodic patters (in particular, intonation contours), lexical preferences and syntactic structure distribution, their further study should be also undertaken on a more representative speech sample.

Acknowledgement.   The research is supported by the Russian Science Foundation, project # 14-18-02070 "Everyday Russian Language in Different Social Groups".

References

1. Larin, B.A.: On the linguistic characteristics of a City (a few assumptions). In: The History of the Russian Language and General Linguistics, pp. 189–199. Prosveshhenie, Moscow (1977) (In Russian)
2. Krysin, L.P.: Sociolinguistic Aspects of Studying Contemporary Russian Language. Nauka, Moscow (1989) (In Russian)
3. Erofeeva, E.V.: Social Component of Lexical Connotation. Perm Univ. Herald Russ. Foreign Philol. **5**, 16–23 (2009) (In Russian)
4. Sirotinina, O.B.: Urban speech: problems, aspects and difficulties of studying. In: Proceedings of International Conference 8th Shmelevsky Readings, Language of the Modern City, Moscow, pp. 146–148 (2008) (In Russian)
5. Potapova, R.K., Potapov, V.V.: Language, speech, personality. In: Languages of Slavic Cultures, Moscow, 496 p. (2006) (In Russian)
6. Asinovsky, A., Bogdanova, N., Rusakova, M., Ryko, A., Stepanova, S., Sherstinova, T.: The ORD speech corpus of Russian everyday communication "One Speaker's Day": creation principles and annotation. In: Matoušek, V., Mautner, P. (eds.) TSD 2009. LNCS, vol. 5729, pp. 250–257. Springer, Heidelberg (2009)

7. Bogdanova-Beglarian, N.V., Asinovsky, A.S., Blinova, O.V., Markasova, E.V., Ryko, A.I., Sherstinova, T.Y.: Speech Corpus of Russian Language: New Methodology of Speech Analysis. Lang. Method **2**, 357–372 (2015)
8. Bogdanova-Beglarian, N., Martynenko, G., Sherstinova, T.: The "One Day of Speech" corpus: phonetic and syntactic studies of everyday spoken Russian. In: Ronzhin, A., Potapova, R., Fakotakis, N. (eds.) SPECOM 2015. LNCS, vol. 9319, pp. 429–437. Springer, Heidelberg (2015)
9. Romaine, S.: Corpus linguistics and sociolinguistics. In: Lüdeling, A., Kytö, M. (eds.) Corpus Linguistics: An International Handbook, vol. 1, pp. 96–111. Mouton de Gruyter, Berlin-New York (2008)
10. Sherstinova, T.: Macro episodes of Russian everyday oral communication: towards pragmatic annotation of the ORD speech corpus. In: Ronzhin, A., Potapova, R., Fakotakis, N. (eds.) SPECOM 2015. LNCS, vol. 9319, pp. 268–276. Springer, Heidelberg (2015)
11. Kibrik, A., Podlesskaya, V. (eds.): Night Dream Stories: A Corpus Study of Spoken Russian Discourse. Languages of Slavic Cultures, Moscow (2009) (In Russian)
12. Stepanova, S.: Speech rate as reflection of speaker's social characteristics. Approaches Slavic Interact. Dialogue Stud. (DS) **20**, 117–129 (2013)
13. Bogdanova-Beglarian, N.V.: Pragmatemes in spoken everyday speech: definition and general typology. Perm Univ. Herald. Russ. Foreign Philol. **3**(27), 7–20 (2014) (In Russian)
14. Bogdanova-Beglarian, N.V. (ed.): Speech Corpus as a Base for Analysis. Collective Monograph. Part 2. Theory and Practice of Speech Analysis, vol. 2. Speech Corpus as a Base for New Lexicographical Projects, Sankt Petersburg (2015) (In Russian)
15. Martynenko, G.Y.: Syntax of live spontaneous speech: the symmetry of linear orders. In: Zakharov, V.P., Mitrofanova, O.A., Khokhlova, M.V. (eds.). Proceedings of the International Conference "Corpus Linguistics-2015", pp. 371–378 (2015)

Adaptation of DNN Acoustic Models Using KL-divergence Regularization and Multi-task Training

László Tóth[1(✉)] and Gábor Gosztolya[1,2]

[1] MTA-SZTE Research Group on Artificial Intelligence, Szeged, Hungary
{tothl,ggabor}@inf.u-szeged.hu
[2] Institute of Informatics, University of Szeged, Szeged, Hungary

Abstract. The adaptation of context-dependent deep neural network acoustic models is particularly challenging, because most of the context-dependent targets will have no occurrences in a small adaptation data set. Recently, a multi-task training technique has been proposed that trains the network with context-dependent and context-independent targets in parallel. This network structure offers a straightforward way for network adaptation by training only the context-independent part during the adaptation process. Here, we combine this simple adaptation technique with the KL-divergence regularization method also proposed recently. Employing multi-task training we attain a relative word error rate reduction of about 3 % on a broadcast news recognition task. Then, by using the combined adaptation technique we report a further error rate reduction of 2 % to 5 %, depending on the duration of the adaptation data, which ranged from 20 to 100 s.

Keywords: Deep neural net · Speaker adaptation · Multi-task learning

1 Introduction

In the recent years, deep neural network (DNN) based acoustic models have become the state-of-the-art in speech recognition, replacing the Gaussian mixture (GMM) component of hidden Markov models (HMM). However, there are several refinements of HMM/GMM systems that cannot be trivially transferred to HMM/DNNs. One such issue is the construction and training of context-dependent (CD) units. Currently, the CD states of HMM/DNN systems are usually created by training and aligning a conventional HMM/GMM [2,7,12]. Although alternative solutions that try to get rid of GMMs have been proposed, these are not yet widely accepted [4,14,19]. As regards training, it was found recently that the learning of CD units by DNNs can be improved by multi-task training. Namely, Bell et al. found that the training of CD targets can be regularized by also showing context-independent (CI) targets to the net in a multi-task fashion [1]. Here, we follow the multi-task training recipe of Bell for training CD units, and we report a gain of 3 % in the word error rate.

© Springer International Publishing Switzerland 2016
A. Ronzhin et al. (Eds.): SPECOM 2016, LNAI 9811, pp. 108–115, 2016.
DOI: 10.1007/978-3-319-43958-7_12

Another task where regularization can help a lot is the adaptation of DNN-based acoustic models. The DNNs we use usually have a lot of parameters (many wide layers), hence they can easily overfit the adaptation data, especially when the adaptation set is small. Perhaps the most common solution is to extend the network with a linear layer, and adapt only this layer that allows only linear transformations [3,16]. One might also control overfitting by reducing the number of layers or weights that are adapted [9,10]. A further possibility is to adapt only the biases [17] or the amplitudes of hidden unit activations [15]. Yet another group of solutions applies some sort of regularization during training on the adaptation data. Li et al. proposed a form of L2 regularization to penalize the difference between the adapted and the unadapted weights [8]. Gemello introduced "conservative training", which uses the outputs of the unadapted network as adaptation targets for the classes not seen in the adaptation set [3]. Yu et al. proposed getting the training targets by interpolating between the output of the unadapted model and the (estimated) transcripts of the adaptation data. Mathematically, this corresponds to a Kullback-Leibler divergence-based regularization of the network outputs [18].

The use of CD models makes the adaptation task even more challenging, as it decreases the number of adaptation samples per class. Hence, Price et al. came up with the idea of using a hierarchy of two output layers, the lower corresponding to the CD classes, and the upper to the CI classes [11]. This construct allows the use of CD units during training and evaluation, while one can use the CI output layer during adaptation, when only a much smaller amount of data is available.

Here, we propose an adaptation method that is similar to the approach of Price et al., but the network structure applied is different. While they positioned the layers corresponding to the CD and CI targets on top of each other, we place them side by side, following the arrangement used for multi-task training. This structure yields a straightforward way for adaptation using only the CI data: while we present both CD and CI samples to the network during full (multi-task) training, during adaptation just the CI output layer receives input. This way, we can exploit the regularization benefit of CI samples during both training and adaptation. While Huang et al. have recently published a similar approach [6], our solution is different in that we combine the multi-task training strategy with the KL-regularization method of Yu et al. [18]. We found that this regularization step is vital for reducing the chance of overfitting, and thus for obtaining good results for our data set, especially when the adaptation data set was very small. With the combined method, in an unsupervised adaptation task with 20–100 s of adaptation data we report relative word error rate reductions of 2 % to 5 %, depending on the duration of the adaptation utterances.

2 Multi-task Training

Multi-task learning was proposed as a method for improving the generalization ability of a classifier by learning more tasks at the same time. To our knowledge, it was first applied to DNN acoustic models by Seltzer and Droppo [13]. They

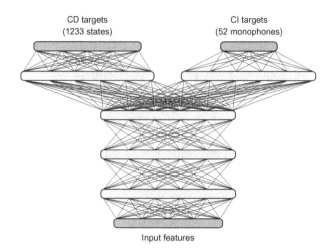

Fig. 1. The structure of the multi-task network.

found that besides training the network to recognize the actual frame, the phone recognition accuracy can be improved by also training on the phone context as a secondary task. More recently, Bell et al. applied CI labels as the secondary task during the training of CD states, and they obtained a 3 %–10 % relative improvement in the word error rate compared to conventional training [1].

Figure 1 shows the structure of the network we applied here. As can be seen, there are two output layers, one dedicated to the CD states, and the other to the CI targets. We also split the uppermost hidden layer, which is different from the work of Bell et al., where all the hidden layers were shared between the CD and the CI training paths [1]. We obtained slightly better results with this structure, although the improvements were not significant.

Following Bell et al. [1], we did not model the monophone states separately, so the CI targets corresponded to the monophone labels. During training, the network training routine received both the CD and CI labels as input, and each mini-batch was randomly assigned to the CD or the CI output layer. Based on this assignment, we either presented the given batch of CD targets to the CD output layer or the corresponding CI targets to the CI output layer. Naturally, while the shared hidden layers were updated for each batch, the weights were not updated for that target-specific output layer and uppermost hidden layer pair which was inactive for the given batch. We give an analysis of how this weight update technique affects convergence in the next section.

3   Experiments with Multi-task Training

The data used in the experiments was the "Szeged" Hungarian broadcast news corpus [5]. It contains 28 h of broadcast news recordings taken from eight TV channels. The train-dev-test division was the same as that used in our earlier

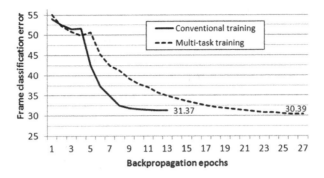

Fig. 2. The convergence of CD frame error rates on the development set for conventional and multi-task training.

work [5], and the language model was also the same. To create the CD state targets we applied the KL-divergence based state tying method described in [4], which resulted in 1233 triphone states. The number of monophone labels used during multi-task training was 52.

The deep neural network which served as the baseline contained 4 hidden layers with 2000 rectified linear units (ReLU) in each hidden layer [5]. For multi-task training, the network structure was modified according to Fig. 1. This network contained two output layers, one for the CD targets and one for the CI targets, and the uppermost hidden layer also had a separate copy of 2000-2000 units for the cases of CD and CI training. During multi-task training, the network receives a batch of training data for either the CD or the CI output layer in a random fashion. The error is computed and propagated down only on the active side, while the weights of the other, inactive output and uppermost hidden layer remain unchanged. The training was performed using the backpropagation algorithm with the conventional frame-level cross-entropy error function.

During experimentation, we tried to tune the probability of the network receiving CD or CI data batches. Compared to the 0.5-0.5 ratio preferred by Bell et al., a weighting of 0.75-0.25 (in favor of CD input) gave slightly better CD frame error rates, but this did not influence the word error rate significantly.

Learning two things at the same time slows down the convergence of the backpropagation training process. We applied the usual "newbob" learning rate schedule, which basically corresponds to an exponential decay of the learning rate. We found that multi-task training required a slower decay rate, hence we applied a multiplying factor of 0.8 instead of 0.5. Using the same stopping criterion, multi-task training required about twice as many training epochs as with conventional training. Figure 2 shows how the CD error rate dropped during training for conventional versus multi-task training.

Table 1 shows the error rates obtained with conventional and with multi-task training. Multi-task training yielded a relative word error rate reduction of about 3%, which is similar to the findings of Bell et al. [1]. However, while they reported that the frame error rate of CD units actually *increased* in spite of the

Table 1. Frame and word error rates for conventional and multi-task training.

Training method	FER %		WER %	
	Train set	Dev. set	Dev. set	Test set
Conventional	25.9 %	31.4 %	17.7 %	17.0 %
Multi-task	23.5 %	30.4 %	17.4 %	16.5 %

drop in word error rate, in our case the CD frame error rate also decreased. This difference might be due to our uneven balancing of the distribution of the CD and CI data blocks, which put more emphasis on the CD frame error rate.

4   Acoustic Adaptation with the Multi-task Model

The number of CD states used in a recognition system is chosen in accord with the amount of training data available. That is, we work with as many CD states as can be safely trained on the *full* training set without risking overfitting. However, during adaptation the amount of adaptation data available is much smaller than the size of the full train set. Hence, training the network with CD output units on the adaptation set will almost inevitably result in overfitting. However, the multi-task framework yields a straightforward solution for alleviating overfitting: during adaptation we do not train the CD part of the network, as for most of the CD units there would be no training examples in the adaptation data. Instead, we adapt the network only through the CI output layer, which is much less affected by the data scarcity problem.

Deep neural networks have a huge amount of parameters (i.e., weights), which increases their flexibility when training on a large data set, but it also increases the chance of overfitting on a small set of adaptation data. Several authors suggested that one should update only a small set of parameters – for example, only one hidden layer – during adaptation [10]. Besides alleviating overfitting, it also reduces the amount of time required by the adaptation process. We decided to restrict the adaptation to only the uppermost hidden layer that is shared by the CD and CI paths of the multi-task network (Fig. 1). Even doing it this way, we had difficulties finding the optimal learn rate for unsupervised adaptation. We observed that while smaller learn rates gave stable but moderate improvements for all files, larger learn rates resulted in a much larger error rate reduction for some files, while significantly increasing the error for others. Supposing that this unstable behavior was caused by the incorrect adaptation labels, we decided to apply some sort of regularization. We chose the KL-divergence based regularization technique recently proposed by Yu et al. [18]. Mathematically, this approach can be formulated as penalizing the output of the adapted model straying too far from the output of the unadapted model. As the DNN outputs form a discrete probability distribution, a natural choice for measuring this deviation is the Kullback-Leibler divergence. After some reorganization (cf. [18]), the formulas boil down to smoothing the target labels estimated for the adaptation data by

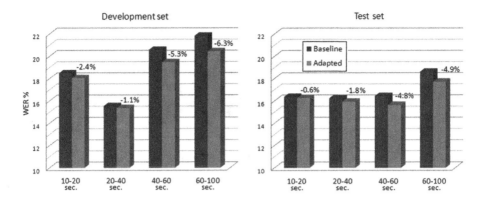

Fig. 3. The reduction of word error rate as a function of the duration of adaptation data.

the probability output produced by the unadapted model. That is, the training targets are got by applying the linear interpolation:

$$(1 - \alpha)p(y|x) + \alpha p_{un}(y|x),$$

where $p(y|x)$ are the "hard" targets obtained during the recognition pass (or alignment pass in the supervised case), $p_{un}(y|x)$ are the probability values yielded by the unadapted model, and α is the parameter that controls the strength of smoothing.

5   Experiments with Unsupervised Adaptation

The development set of our broadcast news corpus contained 448 files (about 2 h in length), while the test set consisted of 724 files (about 4 h in length). The duration of the files ranged from just one sentence (a couple of seconds) to about 100 s. For the adaptation experiments, we threw away the files with a duration less than 10 s, as we judged these to be too short for adaptation. It was known that the identity of the speaker and the acoustic conditions do not change within a file, but besides this, no further speaker information was available. The silence ratio of the corpus was very low, as the manual verification of the transcripts included the removal of long silent segments. In all our adaptation experiments we sought unsupervised adaptation, which means that we recognized the given file with the unadapted model, and then used the transcript obtained this way as target labels for the adaptation. This was followed by a second pass of recognition using the adapted model.

The adaptation process involved several parameters that we had to tune on the development set. These included the learn rate, the number of training iterations and the α parameter of KL-divergence regularization. In the initial experiments we found that the optimal learning rate varied from file to file,

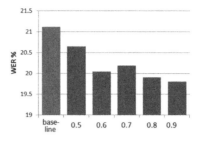

Fig. 4. The influence of the α parameter of KL-divergence regularization on the word error rate.

making it difficult to chose one global value. However, after the introduction of KL-divergence the scores become much less sensitive to the actual choice of the learn rate and the number of iterations. Eventually, we got the best results by going five training epochs with a relatively large learning rate.

Figure 3 shows the word error rates attained before and after adaptation as a function of the duration of adaptation data, for both the development set and the test set. For this evaluation the files were arranged into four groups, according to their duration. As can be seen, the error rate improvement on the test set was minimal for the files with duration between 10 and 20 s, and it was still slightly below 2 % for the duration range of 20 to 40 s. However, for the recordings longer than 40 s the relative error rate reduction went up to 5–6% on the development set and to 5 % on the test set. Unfortunately, our database did not contain longer recordings, so we could not test the algorithm for adaptation durations longer than 100 s.

Figure 4 shows how the α parameter of KL-divergence regularization influences the word error rate of the adapted model. The scores are plotted for those files of the development set that were longer than 40 s. The figure clearly shows that the use of KL-divergence regularization significantly contributed to our good results. Actually, we had to use a large α value around 0.8–0.9 to attain the best results, even for the file group with the longest duration (60–100 s).

6   Conclusions

The adaptation of DNN acoustic models has become a very active topic recently. The use of context-dependent DNNs presents a special challenge because it increases the scarcity of the adaptation data labels. As the recently introduced multi-task training method makes direct use of the monophone training labels, it was straightforward to extend it to model adaptation by just using only the monophone labels of the adaptation set. Even by doing this, we had to apply the recently proposed KL-divergence regularization method of Yu et al. [18] to get good results. On a broadcast news recognition task we obtained a relative word error rate reduction of about 3 % using multi-task training, and a further 2 % to 5 % error rate reduction by applying the proposed adaptation technique.

References

1. Bell, P., Renals, S.: Regularization of deep neural networks with context-independent multi-task training. In: Proceedings of ICASSP, pp. 4290–4294 (2015)
2. Dahl, G.E., Yu, D., Deng, L., Acero, A.: Context-dependent pre-trained deep neural networks for large vocabulary speech recognition. IEEE Trans. ASLP **20**(1), 30–42 (2012)
3. Gemello, R., Mana, F., Scanzio, S., Laface, P., de Mori, R.: Linear hidden transformations for adaptation of hybrid ANN/HMM models. Speech Commun. **49**(10–11), 827–835 (2007)
4. Gosztolya, G., Grósz, T., Tóth, L., D., I.: Building context-dependent DNN acoustic models using Kullback-Leibler divergence-based state tying. In: Proceedings of ICASSP, pp. 4570–4574 (2015)
5. Grósz, T., Tóth, L.: A comparison of deep neural network training methods for large vocabulary speech recognition. In: Proceedings of TSD, pp. 36–43 (2013)
6. Huang, Z., Li, J., Siniscalchi, S., Chen, I.F., Wu, J., Lee, C.H.: Rapid adaptation for deep neural networks through multi-task learning. In: Proceedings of Interspeech, pp. 3625–3629 (2015)
7. Jaitly, N., Nguyen, P., Senior, A., Vanhoucke, V.: Application of pretrained deep neural networks to large vocabulary speech recognition. In: Proceedings of Interspeech (2012)
8. Li, X., Bilmes, J.: Regularized adaptation of discriminative classifiers. In: Proceedings of ICASSP, Toulouse, France (2006)
9. Liao, H.: Speaker adaptation of context dependent deep neural networks. In: Proceedings of ICASSP, pp. 7947–7951, Vancouver, Canada (2013)
10. Ochiai, T., Matsuda, S., Lu, X., Hori, C., Katagiri, S.: Speaker adaptive training using deep neural networks. In: Proceedings of ICASSP, pp. 6399–6403 (2014)
11. Price, R., Iso, K., Shinoda, K.: Speaker adaptation of deep neural networks using a hierarchy of output layers. In: Proceedings of SLT, pp. 153–158 (2014)
12. Seide, F., Li, G., Chen, L., Yu, D.: Feature engineering in context-dependent deep neural networks for conversational speech transcription. In: Proceedings of ASRU, pp. 24–29 (2011)
13. Seltzer, M., Droppo, J.: Multi-task learning in deep neural networks for improved phoneme recognition. In: Proceedings of ICASSP, pp. 6965–6969 (2013)
14. Senior, A., Heigold, G., Bacchiani, M., Liao, H.: GMM-free DNN training. In: Proceedings of ICASSP, pp. 307–312 (2014)
15. Swietojanski, P., Renals, S.: Learning hidden unit contributions for unsupervised speaker adaptation of neural network acoustic models. In: Proceedings of SLT, pp. 171–176 (2014)
16. Trmal, J., Zelinka, J., Müller, L.: Adaptation of a feedforward artificial neural network using a linear transform. In: Sojka, P., Horák, A., Kopeček, I., Pala, K. (eds.) TSD 2010. LNCS, vol. 6231, pp. 423–430. Springer, Heidelberg (2010)
17. Yao, K., Yu, D., Seide, F., Su, H., Deng, L., Gong, Y.: Adaptation of context-dependent deep neural networks for automatic speech recognition. In: Proceedings of SLT, pp. 366–369, Miami, Florida, USA (2012)
18. Yu, D., Yao, K., Su, H., Li, G., Seide, F.: KL-divergence regularized deep neural network adaptation for improved large vocabulary speech recognition. In: Proceedings of ICASSP, pp. 7893–7897 (2013)
19. Zhang, C., Woodland, P.: Standalone training of context-dependent deep neural network acoustic models. In: Proceedings of ICASSP, pp. 5597–5601 (2014)

Advances in STC Russian Spontaneous Speech Recognition System

Ivan Medennikov[1,2(✉)] and Alexey Prudnikov[2,3]

[1] STC-innovations Ltd, St. Petersburg, Russia
[2] ITMO University, St. Petersburg, Russia
{medennikov,prudnikov}@speechpro.com
[3] Speech Technology Center Ltd, St. Petersburg, Russia

Abstract. In this paper we present the latest improvements to the Russian spontaneous speech recognition system developed in Speech Technology Center (STC). Significant word error rate (WER) reduction was obtained by applying hypothesis rescoring with sophisticated language models. These were the Recurrent Neural Network Language Model and regularized Long-Short Term Memory Language Model. For acoustic modeling we used the deep neural network (DNN) trained with speaker-dependent bottleneck features, similar to our previous system. This DNN was combined with the deep Bidirectional Long Short-Term Memory acoustic model by the use of score fusion. The resulting system achieves WER of 16.4 %, with an absolute reduction of 8.7 % and relative reduction of 34.7 % compared to our previous system result on this test set.

Keywords: Spontaneous speech recognition · Bottleneck features · Deep neural networks · Recurrent neural networks

1 Introduction

Spontaneous conversational speech recognition is one of the most difficult tasks in the field of automatic speech recognition (ASR). The difficulties are due to the following characteristics of spontaneous conversational speech: high channel and speaker variability, presence of additive and non-linear distortions, accents and emotional speech, diversity of speaking styles, speech rate variability, reductions and weakened articulation.

There is a large number of studies on recognizing English spontaneous speech, such as [1–5]. Systems proposed in these papers demonstrate high effectiveness, which makes it possible to use them in commercial applications. As far as we know, the state-of-the-art English spontaneous speech recognition system [4] achieves word error rate (WER) of 8.0 % on the Switchboard part and 14.1 % on the CallHome part of the HUB5 2000 evaluation set. This impressive results were obtained by combining various effective techniques of acoustic and language modeling.

© Springer International Publishing Switzerland 2016
A. Ronzhin et al. (Eds.): SPECOM 2016, LNAI 9811, pp. 116–123, 2016.
DOI: 10.1007/978-3-319-43958-7_13

Our goal is to build a speaker-independent system for high-quality Russian spontaneous speech recognition. At present none of the Russian spontaneous speech recognition systems provide recognition accuracy comparable with the above-mentioned English systems. We would like to highlight two reasons of this. First, there are not available training and evaluation datasets for the Russian language, such as the Switchboard and Fisher English speech corpora and the HUB5 2000 evaluation set. Second, Russian is an inflective language with a several times larger number of unique words than English. Moreover, the Russian language is characterized by a relatively free word order in a sentence. This considerably complicates the recognition task [6]. Our previous system achieved WER of 25.1 % [7]. In this work we present the set of recent improvements of the system.

The rest of this paper is organized as follows. Section 2 contains the experimental setup description. Section 3 presents the acoustic modeling approach based on speaker-dependent bottleneck features. Section 4 describes deep BLSTM acoustic models and score fusion of DNN and BLSTM acoustic models (AMs). Section 5 presents the experiments on hypothesis rescoring with language models (LMs) based on Recurrent Neural Networks (RNNs). Finally, Sect. 6 concludes the paper and discusses future work.

2 Experimental Setup

For experiments we used the Kaldi speech recognition toolkit [8]. AM training was performed using a 390 h Russian spontaneous speech dataset (telephone channel, several hundreds of speakers). A test set consisted of about 1 h of Russian telephone conversations. Both training and test sets are the same as used in our previous work [7].

Language models training data consisted of 2 datasets. The first one contained the transcriptions of the AM training dataset. The second one was a large amount (about 200 M words) of texts from Internet forum discussions, books and subtitles from the OpenSubtitles site. The baseline 3-g language model with a vocabulary of 214 K words was built in the SRILM Toolkit [9]. It was obtained by interpolation of 3-g LMs trained on the first and second datasets using Modified Kneser-Ney smoothing. The size of this model was reduced to 4.16 M bigrams and 2.49 M trigrams by the use of pruning.

3 Speaker-Dependent Bottleneck Features

Here we describe the acoustic modeling approach based on speaker-dependent bottleneck (SDBN) features. This approach was proposed in our previous works [7,10]. Its underlying idea is to extract high-level features from the DNN model, which is adapted to the speaker and acoustic environment by the use of i-vectors. The extracted features are applied to training another acoustic model (Fig. 1).

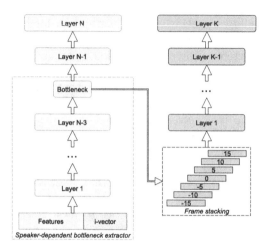

Fig. 1. Speaker-dependent bottleneck approach scheme

Our approach consists of the following main steps:

1. Training the DNN model on the source features using the Cross-Entropy (CE) criterion.
2. Expanding an input layer of the DNN trained at the first step and retraining using an input feature vector appended with i-vector. The regularizing term

$$R = \lambda \sum_{l=1}^{L} \sum_{i=1}^{N_l} \sum_{j=1}^{N_{l-1}} (\mathbf{W}_{ij}^l - \bar{\mathbf{W}}_{ij}^l)^2 \qquad (1)$$

is added to the CE criterion for penalizing parameters deviation from the source model. Here $\mathbf{W}^l$ and $\bar{\mathbf{W}}^l$ are weight matrices of l-th layer ($1 \leq l \leq L$) of the current and the source DNNs, N_l is the size of l-th layer, and N_0 is the dimension of the input feature vector.
3. Transforming the last hidden layer into two layers. The first one is a bottleneck layer with the weight matrix $\mathbf{W}_{bn}$, a zero bias vector and linear activation function. The second one is a non-linear layer with the dimension of the source layer, with weight matrix $\mathbf{W}_{out}$ and the original bias vector $\mathbf{b}$, activation function f and the dimension of the source layer:

$$\mathbf{y} = f(\mathbf{W}\mathbf{x} + \mathbf{b}) \approx f(\mathbf{W}_{out}(\mathbf{W}_{bn}\mathbf{x} + \mathbf{0}) + \mathbf{b}). \qquad (2)$$

These layers are formed by applying Singular Value Decomposition (SVD) to the weight matrix $\mathbf{W}$ of the source layer:

$$\mathbf{W} = \mathbf{U}\mathbf{S}\mathbf{V}^T \approx \tilde{\mathbf{U}}_{bn}\tilde{\mathbf{V}}_{bn}^T = \mathbf{W}_{out}\mathbf{W}_{bn}, \qquad (3)$$

where $_{bn}$ designates reduced dimension.

4. Retraining the network formed at the previous step using the CE criterion with the penalty (1) for parameters deviation from original values.
5. Discarding all layers after the bottleneck and extracting high-level SDBN features using the resulting DNN.
6. Training the GMM-HMM acoustic model using the constructed SDBN features and generating the senone alignment of the training data.
7. Training the final DNN-HMM acoustic model using SDBN features and the generated alignment.

The extractor of 120-dimensional SDBN features was trained using the presented approach. Training was carried out using 23-dimensional log mel filterbank energy (FBANK) features with Cepstral Mean Normalization (CMN), appended with the first and second order derivatives. These features were taken with the temporal context of 11 frames ($\pm$ 5) and appended with an i-vector. We applied 50-dimensional i-vectors extracted by the use of the Universal Background Model with 512 Gaussian, which was trained with our toolset [11] on the full 390 hour training set. We applied the following configuration of the basic network: 6 hidden layers with 1536 sigmoidal neurons in each, the output softmax layer with about 13000 neurons corresponding to senones of the GMM-HMM acoustic model. DNN parameters were updated using the Nesterov Accelerated Gradient algorithm with the momentum value equal to 0.7. Extractor training was initialized using the algorithm presented in the paper [12].

DNN training with the constructed SDBN features (SDBN-DNN) was performed using the temporal context of 31 frames taking every 5th frame. We applied the following DNN configuration: 4 sigmoidal hidden layers with 2048 neurons in each, the output softmax layer with about 13000 neurons corresponding to senones of the GMM-HMM model, which was trained using the same SDBN features. The training was carried out with the CE criterion and the state-level Minimum Bayes Risk (sMBR) sequence-discriminative criterion.

Table 1. SDBN results

Acoustic model	Training criterion	WER, %
DNN-ivec	CE	23.8
SDBN-DNN	CE	22.0 (-1.8)
DNN-ivec	sMBR	21.7
SDBN-DNN	sMBR	19.5 (-2.2)

Table 1 gives the comparison of SDBN-DNN and DNN trained in a speaker adaptive manner using i-vectors (DNN-ivec). It can be seen that the SDBN approach provides a significant gain. Note that SDBN-DNN WER of 19.5 % is much lower than the result of our previous system (25.1 % WER). This is due to the larger SDBN features extractor, more careful tuning of the AM training procedure and the larger language model.

4   Deep Bidirectional Long Short-Term Memory Recurrent Neural Networks

Acoustic models based on deep Bidirectional Long Short-Term Memory (BLSTM) recurrent neural networks demonstrate high effectiveness in various ASR tasks [5,13]. In this section we describe our experiments with these models carried out with the *nnet3* setup of the Kaldi speech recognition toolkit.

We used BLSTM architecture with projection layers described in the paper [13]. The following configuration of the network was applied: 3 forward and 3 backward layers, 1024 cell and hidden dimensions, 128 recurrent and non-recurrent projection dimensions. Training examples consisted of chunks of 20 frames with additional left context of 40 frames and right context of 40 frames. We performed 8 epochs of cross-entropy training with an initial learning rate of 0.0003 and final learning rate of 0.00003. Model parameters were updated using BPTT algorithm with the momentum value equal to 0.5. The models obtained at the iterations of the last epoch were combined into the final BLSTM model. For BLSTM training we used 23-dimensional log mel filterbank energy (FBANK) features with CMN with the first and second order derivatives, appended with the 50-dimensional i-vector described before. Training data alignments prepared using the SDBN-DNN acoustic model were used for the training.

4.1   Score Fusion of SDBN-DNN and BLSTM Acoustic Models

The underlying idea of the score fusion technique is in combining the benefits of both different model architectures and different input features. In this subsection we analyze effectiveness of this technique applied to SDBN-DNN and BLSTM acoustic models. We used log-likelihoods (LLH) determined by the formula

$$\text{LLH} = \alpha \log \left(\frac{P_1(\mathbf{s}|\mathbf{x})}{P_1(\mathbf{s})} \right) + (1 - \alpha) \log \left(\frac{P_2(\mathbf{s}|\mathbf{x})}{P_2(\mathbf{s})} \right) \qquad (4)$$

for the decoding with fusion of these acoustic models. Here $P_1(\mathbf{s}|\mathbf{x})$ and $P_2(\mathbf{s}|\mathbf{x})$ are posterior probabilities of state $\mathbf{s}$ given an input vector $\mathbf{x}$ on the current frame, $P_1(\mathbf{s})$ and $P_2(\mathbf{s})$ are prior probabilities of state $\mathbf{s}$ for SDBN-DNN and BLSTM models respectively. We estimated prior probability of state $\mathbf{s}$ as average posterior probability calculated with the corresponding model on the training data. α value was chosen equal to 0.5. The results of deep BLSTM acoustic model and score fusion are given in Table 2.

Table 2. Deep BSLTM acoustic models and score fusion results

Acoustic model	WER, %
SDBN-DNN	19.5
BLSTM	19.8
score fusion	17.8 (−1.7)

5 RNN-based Language Models

In this section we describe the experiments with sophisticated language models based on recurrent neural networks. Word lattices obtained on the decoding pass with the 3-g LM and the best DNN+BLSTM models fusion in subsection 4.1 were taken as a starting point for these experiments.

We trained two RNN-based language models on shuffled utterances from transcriptions of the AM training dataset. To speed-up the training we used the vocabulary of 45 K most frequent words. All other words were replaced with the <UNK> token. Utterances were divided into two parts: a valid set (15 K utterances) and a train set (all other, 243 K utterances).

Table 3. Rescoring results

Language model	WER, %
3-g	17.8
RNNLM	17.4 (−0.4)
LSTM-LM (medium)	16.7 (−1.1)
LSTM-LM (large)	16.4 (−1.4)

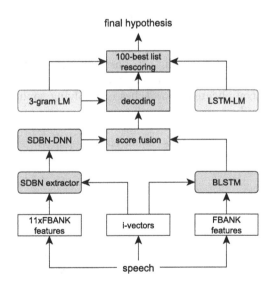

Fig. 2. System architecture

The first RNN-based LM was the Recurrent Neural Network Language Model (RNNLM) [14] which significantly outperforms n-gram LMs in various speech recognition tasks. We applied the following RNNLM configuration: 256 neurons in the hidden layer and 200 classes in the output layer.

The second RNN-based LM was the LSTM recurrent neural network LM (LSTM-LM) trained with dropout regularization [15]. We trained two LSTM-LMs using the Tensorflow toolkit [16]: "medium" (2 layers with 650 units each, 50 % dropout on the non-recurrent connections) and "large" (2 layers with 1500 units each, 65 % dropout on the non-recurrent connections) configurations from the paper [15].

The trained RNNLM and both LSTM-LMs were applied for hypothesis rescoring. We generated 100-best lists from the word lattices using Kaldi scripts. For the rescoring we took the weighted sum of n-gram LM and RNN-based LM scores. If the sentence contained a word missing in the 45K RNN vocabulary, we added an unigram score of this word from the 3-g model to the RNN score. The results of the rescoring are given in Table 3. It can be seen that RNNLM provided substantial improvement over the n-gram LM, as well as LSTM-LM over RNNLM.

6   Conclusion

The architecture of our system is depicted in Fig. 2. The system achieves WER of 16.4 %, with an absolute reduction of 8.7 % and relative reduction of 34.7 % over our previous system.

We consider several ways of further improvement of our system. First, BLSTM acoustic models improving techniques, such as sequence-discriminative training and dropout regularization, can lead to substantial WER reduction. Second, significant acoustic models improvement can be obtained by the use of the data augmentation approach [17]. Last but not least, we plan to carry out experiments with other promising language model architectures as well as to investigate more complicated approaches of applying sophisticated language models than simple n-best rescoring.

Acknowledgement. This work was financially supported by the Ministry of Education and Science of the Russian Federation, Contract 14.579.21.0057 (ID RFMEFI57914X0057).

References

1. Vesely, K., Ghoshal, A., Burget, L., Povey, D.: Sequence-discriminative training of deep neural networks. In: 14th Annual Conference of the International Speech Communication Association (Interspeech), pp. 2345–2349. Lyon (2013)
2. Saon, G., Soltau, H., Nahamoo, D., Picheny, M.: Speaker adaptation of neural network acoustic models using i-vectors. In: IEEE workshop on Automatic Speech Recognition and Understanding (ASRU), pp. 55–59. Olomouc (2013)
3. Soltau, H., Saon, G., Sainath, T.N.: Joint training of convolutional and non-convolutional neural networks. In: 39th International Conference on Acoustics, Speech and Signal Processing (ICASSP), pp. 5572–5576. Florence (2014)

4. Saon, G., Kuo, H.-K., Rennie, S., Picheny, M.: The IBM 2015 english conversational telephone speech recognition system. In: 16th Annual Conference of the International Speech Communication Association (Interspeech). Dresden (2015)
5. Mohamed, A., Seide, F., Yu, D., Droppo, J., Stolcke, A., Zweig, G., Penn, G.: Deep bi-directional recurrent networks over spectral windows. In: IEEE workshop on Automatic Speech Recognition and Understanding (ASRU), pp. 55–59. Scottsdale (2015)
6. Tampel, I.B.: Automatic speech recognition -the main stages over last 50 years. Sci. Tech. J. Inf. Technol. Mech. Opt. **15**(6), 957–968 (2015). doi:10.17586/2226-1494-2015-15-6-957-968
7. Prudnikov, A., Medennikov, I., Mendelev, V., Korenevsky, M., Khokhlov, Y.: Improving acoustic models for russian spontaneous speech recognition. In: Ronzhin, A., Potapova, R., Fakotakis, N. (eds.) SPECOM 2015. LNCS, vol. 9319, pp. 234–242. Springer, Heidelberg (2015)
8. Povey, D., et al.: The kaldi speech recognition toolkit. In: IEEE Workshop on Automatic Speech Recognition and Understanding (ASRU), pp. 1–4. Big Island (2011)
9. Stolcke, A.: SRILM – an extensible language modeling toolkit. In: Seventh International Conference on Spoken Language Processing, vol. 3, pp. 901–904 (2002)
10. Medennikov, I.P.: Speaker-dependent features for spontaneous speech recognition. Sci. Tech. J. Inf. Technol. Mech. Opt. **16**(1), 195–197 (2016). doi:10.17586/2226-1494-2016-16-1-195-197
11. Kozlov, A., Kudashev, O., Matveev, Y., Pekhovsky, T., Simonchik, K., Shulipa, A.: SVID speaker recognition system for NIST SRE 2012. In: Železný, M., Habernal, I., Ronzhin, A. (eds.) SPECOM 2013. LNCS, vol. 8113, pp. 278–285. Springer, Heidelberg (2013)
12. Medennikov, I.P.: Two-step algorithm of training initialization for acoustic models based on deep neural networks. Sci. Tech. J. Inf. Technol. Mech. Opt. **16**(2), 379–381 (2016). doi:10.17586/2226-1494-2016-16-2-379-381
13. Sak, H., Senior, A., Beaufays, F.: Long short-term memory recurrent neural network architectures for large scale acoustic modeling. In: 15th Annual Conference of the International Speech Communication Association (Interspeech). Singapore (2014)
14. Mikolov, T., Karafiat, M., Burget, L., Cernocky, J., Khudanpur, S.: Recurrent neural network based language model. In: 11th Annual Conference of the International Speech Communication Association (Interspeech), pp. 1045–1048. Makuhari (2010)
15. Zaremba, W., Sutskever, I., Vinyals, O.: Recurrent neural network regularization. arXiv preprint (2014). arXiv:1409.2329
16. Abadi, M., et al.: TensorFlow: Large-Scale Machine Learning on Heterogeneous Systems (2015). http://tensorflow.org/
17. Ko, T., Peddinti, V., Povey, D., Khudanpur, S.: Audio augmentation for speech recognition. In: 16th Annual Conference of the International Speech Communication Association (Interspeech). Dresden (2015)

Approaches for Out-of-Domain Adaptation to Improve Speaker Recognition Performance

Andrey Shulipa[1]([⊠]), Sergey Novoselov[1,2], and Aleksandr Melnikov[2]

[1] ITMO University, Saint Petersburg, Russia
{shulipa,novoselov}@speechpro.com
[2] Speech Technology Center, Saint Petersburg, Russia
a-melnikov@speechpro.com
http://en.ifmo.ru/
http://speechpro.com/

Abstract. In last years satisfactory performance of speaker recognition (SR) systems have been achieved in evaluations provided by NIST. It was possible due to using large datasets to train system parameters and accurate speaker variability modeling. In such a cases test and train conditions are similar and it ensures good performance for the evaluations. However in practical applications when training and testing conditions are different the problem of mismatching of the optimal SR system parameters occurs. It is the main problem in the deployment of the real application systems. It leads to reducing SR systems effectiveness. This paper investigates discriminative and generative approaches for the adaptation of the parameters of the speaker recognition systems and proposes effective solutions to improve their performance.

Keywords: Speaker recognition · Domain adaptation · Mismatch conditions

1 Introduction

Recent progress in speaker recognition has been built on using large speaker labeled speech databases to train model parameters [5,10,11]. Such datasets with thousands of multisession speakers allow to estimate within class variability characterizing distortions and interclass variability to derive speaker information with high accuracy. It ensures the speaker recognition performance with low error rates. Such results are obtained due to using in-domain data for the evaluation. However in spite of the large amount speech data available the lack of generalization of the speaker recognition systems application is the main problem in their deployment. It occurs when speech data of development set to train the model parameters and evaluation set are mismatched. Differences in background noise, microphone settings, specific channel distortions reduce speaker recognition performance. So the adaptation of the model parameters for the mismatch compensation is needed. It allows to find the optimal settings of the speaker recognition system when evaluation environment is out of target domain.

A. Ronzhin et al. (Eds.): SPECOM 2016, LNAI 9811, pp. 124–130, 2016.
DOI: 10.1007/978-3-319-43958-7_14

In practice there are no large amount labeled speech datasets for retraining the speaker recognition system to use at new (out-of-domain) conditions. But as a rule very small amounts speech data to make adaptation are available. The data may be speaker labeled so it can be used for supervised out-of-domain adaptation [7]. Also very common case when data is not speaker labeled so the preliminary clusterisation have to be used [8].

This work explores the approaches to the supervised out-of-domain adaptation on the limited speech dataset. The state-of-the-art PLDA speaker recognition system to be trained on development set with large amount speaker labeled data was considered in our investigation. The PLDA model parameters were adapted on the small amount out-of-domain dataset using generative and discriminative ways detailed in [7,13] respectively.

We considered the generative approach of the adaptation based on the estimation of within and inter speaker variability matrix by using maximum a posterior criterion (MAP). There were two covariance matrices to be estimated within indomain dataset as prior parameters in the approach. Then the covariance matrix were corrected on the small out-of-domain dataset to maximize posterior probability.

Also the discriminative adaptation approach was investigated in our work. In contrast mentioned above probabilistic generative approach the estimation of the covariance matrix of the PLDA model was obtained by optimization of the cost function [13]. We made recognition trials on small part of out-of-domain dataset and used all trial scores to estimate the gradient of the objective function. As initial settings for solution of the optimization problem we used the PLDA model parameters that were estimated on the in-domain set.

There is a description of the speaker recognition system and experimental speech bases in Sects. 2 and 3 respectively in the paper. Different approaches for the out-of-domain adaptation and their performance measures are detailed in Sects. 4 and 5. Conclusion of the paper is presented in Sect. 6.

2   Speaker Recognition System

In our experiments we used the text independent speaker recognition system based on total variability space. In this case i-vectors in low dimension space [4] are applied for speaker modeling. We used probabilistic linear discriminant analysis (PLDA) [9] to model i-vectors distribution. The variability factors were assumed to have multivariate Gaussian Distribution and we considered only speaker variability factors. Channel variability factors had been excluded from the PLDA model. I-vector length normalization and covariance normalization [6] were applied preliminarily at the testing stage for optimal recognition performance.

We trained our PLDA model using out-of-domain speaker labeled data detailed in the next section. As mentioned above in PLDA model we took into account only speaker factors and their number was 400. We report performance in terms of equal error rate (EER) and normalized minimum detection cost function (DCF)] [3] with probability of target trials set to 10^{-3}.

3   Databases

We followed the DAC setup detailed as follows. The i-vector extractor uses 40-dimensional MFCCs (20 base + deltas) with short-term mean and variance normalization. It uses a 2048-component gender-independent UBM with a 600 dimensional gender-independent i-vector extractor. As for our previous experiments [12], the SRE10 telephone data (condition 5 extended task, males) was used for evaluation. This evaluation set consists of 3,465 target and 175,873 non-target trials. For parameter training two datasets are defined. The out-of-domain SRE set includes telephone calls from 1,115 male speakers and 13,628 speech cuts taken from SRE 04, 05, 06, and 08 collections. The in-domain SWB set includes calls from 1,461 male speakers and 15,164 speech cuts taken from Switchboard [2]. More details of this setup can be found at [1]. In our experiments, the small amount of out-of-domain SRE dataset was used only for the supervised adaptation of *in-domain PLDA trained parameters* to out-of-domain conditions.

4   Adaptation Approaches

In the section we present two different approaches to the out-of-domain adaptation using speaker labeled data. The first is a generative approach that based on definition of inter and intra speaker covariances from MAP estimation [7]. Assuming μ the center of the PLDA model is an observed variable so the matrices can be obtained separately from equation:

$$\Sigma_{map} = (1 - \alpha)\Sigma_{in} + \alpha\Sigma_{out}, \tag{1}$$

where Σ_{in} and Σ_{out} are covariances computed on the large in-domain and small part out-of-domain datasets respectively. Parameter α defines the strength of the prior and can be chosen experimentally. It depends on the extent of confidence to the out-of-domain adaptation data. The smaller the value of the α the weaker the adaptation. The larger the interpolation parameter $\alpha \in [0, 1]$ the stronger the contribution of the out-of-domain data.

The second adaptation technique we considered is the discriminative approach. We used discriminative training of the PLDA model developed in [13]. The main distinctive features of the discriminative approach are using target and not target trials and minimizing detection cost function computed on trial scores to determine the parameters of the PLDA model. The approach allows to take into account the requirements on balance between the recognition errors (FR/FA) in objective function [3]. If we denote PLDA model parameters as θ then objective function to be optimized for the supervised out-of-domain adaptation can be written as:

$$E(\theta) = \sum_{i=1}^{N} \sum_{j=1}^{N} \beta_{ij} l(t_{ij}, s_{ij}(\theta)) + \lambda \|\theta - \bar{\theta}\|. \tag{2}$$

where $\theta = \mathrm{vec}([B, W])$ is a vectorized B between and W within speaker covariance matrices, $\bar{\theta}$ denotes initial PLDA model parameters that are obtained on out-of-domain development set, t_{ij} is a trial indicator that equals to 1 if i-vector voice models with indices i and j are from the same speakers and -1 if otherwise, N is a total number of trials and $l(\cdot)$ is a trial loss function [13]. Finally s_{ij} and β_{ij} are denoted as trial scorers and weights. Weights determine the contributions of errors FR/FA in the objective function and have to be specified accordingly to the application dependent requirements. It should be noted that trial scores in (2) are obtained on the out-of-domain small dataset but not the evaluation dataset. Parameter λ allows to control the deviation of the adapted PLDA model from the initial state.

Also we propose effective supplementation to the discriminative approach based on using self-target trials (STT). The trials are obtained when compared voice models are identical. They give max possible scores and can be effectively used to regularize optimization problem. This regularization can be done by using the restriction of search region for the PLDA model parameters. In this way we can label the self-target scores as non-target. Thus target scores occur to be bounded by non-target scores on the left and self-target scores on the right sides, as it is shown in Fig. 1a. This regularization trick allows us to get more stabilized scores.

We studied the approaches in respect to the adaptation of the covariance matrices of the PLDA model with the exception of the mean. In both the generative and discriminative cases the mean of the model is computed separately on the same data that is used for the adaptation of the covariance matrix.

5   Experiment Results

In the section we present the analysis of adaptation approaches and experimental results. We used three types of dataset for our investigation that are defined as out-of-domain, in-domain and small speaker labeled dataset that is similar to

Table 1. Evaluation results for the adaptation

Num speakers/files from in-domain set N_s/N_f	Adaptation approaches		
	Generative EER(%)/DCF$_{min}$	Discriminative	
		Conv EER(%)/DCF$_{min}$	STT EER(%)/DCF$_{min}$
10(100)	3.97/0.56	3.91/0.59	**3.33/0.54**
50(563)	3.28/0.45	3.83/0.53	**2.94/0.42**
100(1126)	2.97/0.43	3.47/0.50	**2.60/0.42**
200(2252)	2.79/0.40	3.13/0.43	**2.55/0.37**

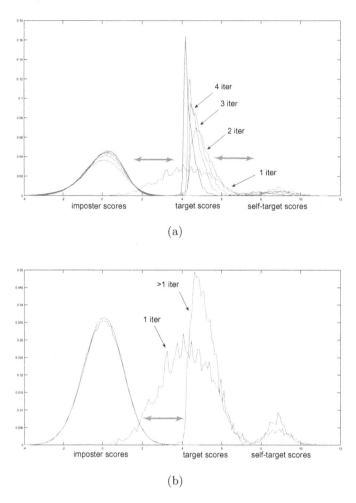

Fig. 1. Distributions of the trial scores obtained on the adaptation dataset during discriminative training of the PLDA model parameters: (a) with self-target trial (STT) scores (b) conventional approach. (Color figure online)

in-domain dataset. The datasets applied for training, testing and the supervised adaptation of the PLDA model respectively.

It is important to note that the adaptation is needed when properties of voice models are different. The difference between test and train conditions we considered in our investigation occur due to mismatch on telephone channels between SWB and SRE datasets. The distributions of the i-vectors from these dataset do not have general center in the multidimensional space and are localized in different areas. Proposed adaptation approaches allow to compensate the mismatch on the PLDA model level. The results of using the discriminative and the generative approaches are presented in the Table 1. We reported the performance of the speaker recognition system in terms equal error rate (EER) and minimum of the detection cost function. The amount of speakers and files in dataset used for the adaptation is presented in the first column of the table. We investigated the speaker recognition system performance depending on amount of speakers/files. We considered the generative and discriminative approaches to tune the parameters of the PLDA model. The conventional discriminative approach and supplemented with self-target trials were investigated.

Our results have shown the generative approach more effective in compare with the conventional discriminative approach for all amounts of speakers/files in the adaptation dataset. The supplementation of the discriminative approach with the self-target trials allows to increase the effectiveness of the adaptation and to improve the performance of speaker recognition system. It is reached due to the restriction of searching area on the parameters of the PLDA model so it permits to get suitable conditions for resolution of the optimization problem. The distributions of target and non target scores in the cases of using the self-target trial scores and without ones are shown in Fig. 1. The distributions that are presented in the figure are obtained on the adaptation dataset during the iterations of the optimization problem solving. It can be seen that improvement of the adaptation using of the self-target trials gives possibility to avoid local extremum and to update the model parameters on each iteration. In the second case the update of the parameters ceases after a few iterations. Green double arrows show directions change of target distribution accordingly to class labels during the discriminative training. It is shown that using additional regularization restriction with the help of self-target trials let us to improve significantly the results of the adaptation of the discriminative method (see Table 1).

6   Conclusion

In this paper a comparative investigation of the supervised domain adaptation approaches has been presented. The problem occurs when development and evaluation dataset are mismatched. The reason of mismatch is a difference of channel, environment conditions that impact on speech signal. So the adaptation system recognition to new conditions is needed for improving effectiveness in real applications. We considered two approaches to the supervised adaptation based on the generative and discriminative techniques. Also we proposed supplementation of the discriminative approach with using self-target trials to increase the performance of the adaptation. All results were obtained using a state-of-the-art PLDA speaker recognition system with Gaussian priors for speaker factors and length normalized i- vectors.

The investigation results presented in the paper demonstrate that generative adaptation approach is superior than discriminative one in terms of $minDCF$ performance measure. But using additional regularization restriction with the help of self-target trials let us to improve significantly the results of the adaptation of the discriminative method. Improving composes on average about 15 % relative in the $minDCF$ point.

Acknowledgments. This work was partially financially supported by the Government of the Russian Federation, Grant 074-U01.

References

1. Jhu 2013 speaker recognition workshop. http://www.clsp.jhu.edu/workshops/13-workshop/speaker-and-language-recognition/
2. The lingusitic data consortium (ldc) catalog. http://catalog.ldc.upenn.edu
3. Brümmer, N., de Villiers, E.: The bosaris toolkit: theory, algorithms and code for surviving the new dcf. arXiv preprint (2013). arXiv:1304.2865
4. Dehak, N., Kenny, P.J., Dehak, R., Dumouchel, P., Ouellet, P.: Front-end factor analysis for speaker verification. IEEE Trans. Audio, Speech Lang. Process. **19**(4), 788–798 (2011)
5. Doddington, G.R., Przybocki, M.A., Martin, A.F., Reynolds, D.A.: The NIST speaker recognition evaluation-overview, methodology, systems, results, perspective. Speech Commun. **31**(2), 225–254 (2000)
6. Garcia-Romero, D., Espy-Wilson, C.Y.: Analysis of i-vector length normalization in speaker recognition systems. In: Interspeech, pp. 249–252 (2011)
7. Garcia-Romero, D., McCree, A.: Supervised domain adaptation for i-vector based speaker recognition. In: 2014 IEEE International Conference on Acoustics, Speech and Signal Processing (ICASSP), pp. 4047–4051. IEEE (2014)
8. Garcia-Romero, D., McCree, A., Shum, S., Brummer, N., Vaquero, C.: Unsupervised domain adaptation for i-vector speaker recognition. In: Proceedings of Odyssey: The Speaker and Language Recognition Workshop (2014)
9. Kenny, P.: Bayesian speaker verification with heavy-tailed priors. In: Odyssey, p. 14 (2010)
10. Novoselov, S., Pekhovsky, T., Simonchik, K.: STC speaker recognition system for the NIST i-vector challenge. In: Odyssey: The Speaker and Language Recognition Workshop, pp. 231–240 (2014)
11. Novoselov, S., Pekhovsky, T., Simonchik, K., Shulipa, A.: RBM-PLDA subsystem for the NIST i-vector challenge. System **8**, 9 (2014)
12. Pekhovsky, T., Novoselov, S., Sholohov, A., Kudashev, O.: On autoencoders in the i-vector space for speaker recognition
13. Rohdin, J., Biswas, S., Shinoda, K.: Discriminative PLDA training with application-specific loss functions for speaker verification. In: Odyssey, The Speaker and Language Recognition Workshop (2014)

Assessment of the Relation Between Low-Frequency Features and Velum Opening by Using Real Articulatory Data

Alexander Sepulveda-Sepulveda[1]([✉]) and German Castellanos-Dominguez[2]

[1] Escuela de Ingenierías Eléctrica, Electrónica y de Telecomunicaciones, Universidad Industrial de Santander, Bucaramanga, Colombia
`fasepul@uis.edu.co`
[2] Universidad Nacional de Colombia, Signal Processing and Recognition Group, Campus La Nubia, km 7 via al Magdalena, Manizales, Colombia

Abstract. This work aims to assess the relation between low-frequency speech features and velum opening by using data coming from an electromagnetic articulograph system (EMA). In previous works, features related to frequency content below first formant has been proposed in order to detect nasalized sounds and hypernasality; however, those low-frequency features have not yet been assessed on real articulatory data regarding the dynamical behavior of velum opening. In order to evaluate the relationship between low-frequency features and velum opening, statistical association between acoustic information and velum movement is measured. In addition, the parameters are evaluated in an acoustic-to-articulatory system based on radial basis neural networks. Results suggest the existence of low-frequency features related to velum position. Therefore, this kind of parameters could be useful in acoustic-to-articulatory mapping systems.

Keywords: Velum opening · Electromagnetic articulograph (EMA) · Low-frequency features · Acoustic-to-articulatory mapping · Articulatory phonetics

1 Introduction

The analysis of soft palate movements using voice signals is of interest in several areas as articulatory inversion, and, classification and detection of hypernasality and nasal sounds. In particular, hypernasality is characterized by an excessive sound coming from the nasal cavity during the utterance of speech sounds since the soft palate is not closed properly [8]. Still, these episodes should be not always assumed as irregular, in fact, those sounds that are close to the nasal phonemes have nasality to a some degree. Furthermore, previous studies have documented some properties of the speech spectral representation allowing detection of hypernasality and nasalized sounds. Among the properties related to nasalized sounds the following are worth of mentioning: (*i*) widening of the bandwidth of formants

© Springer International Publishing Switzerland 2016
A. Ronzhin et al. (Eds.): SPECOM 2016, LNAI 9811, pp. 131–139, 2016.
DOI: 10.1007/978-3-319-43958-7_15

F_1 and F_2 [17]; (*ii*) introduction of additional resonances that cause flattening of nasalized spectra [13]; and (*iii*) introduction of a resonance below F_1 due to acoustic coupling to a sinus [10]. Nonetheless, in this work we pay particular importance to the spectral changes arising below the first formant.

For detection of hypernasal and nasalized sounds, several works have been formulated recently, for instance, the ratio of energies between $[0, 320]$ and $[320, 5360]$ Hz as the energy proportion to detect nasal sounds in [12]. Since cleft palate patients tend to concentrate the emitted acoustic energy on these low-frequency bands, authors in [6] introduce a parameter accounting for the energy shift towards the low frequencies that is by the ratio $R = E_{fc}/E_{fs/2}$, where E_{fc} is the energy within the bandwidth from 0 to fc Hz, and $E_{fs/2}$ is the total energy of the signal. The parameter (termed *voice low tone to high tone ratio*) is also computed in [9], but as the ratio between low-frequency and high-frequency powers split by specific cutoff frequency at 600 Hz. Besides, other aspects of the spectral distribution are considered like in [18] where the appearance of an additional resonance frequency below the first formant in nasalized sounds is reported. Thus, estimations of group delay function around the first peak frequency (resonance nasalised) and the second peak (first formant) are involved as well. Although these approaches have been tested in the detection of hypernasality and nasalized sounds, works that directly assess the relationship of this kind of parameters with the movement of the velum are scarce or even carried out using only vocal tract simulations [10,13,17].

We evaluate the relationship between the acoustic parameters related to information located below the first formant with the degree of velum opening. Consequently, we concurrently make use of the signals measuring (speech recordings) acoustic emission as well the movement of the soft palate (electromagnetic articulography). Firstly, the non-linear statistical correlation between low-frequency related acoustic and measured articulatory information is estimated. Then, these acoustic parameters are evaluated on an acoustic-to-articulatory mapping system based on radial basis neural network. The following parameters are tested: (*i*) energy ratio [13]; (*ii*) ratio of group delay [18]; (*iii*) frame energy (*iv*) energy filter related to the higher value of statistical association below the first formant. As a result, we detect a peak confidently by the used statistical association measure; this peak is related to the frequency band just below the first formant. Finally, we show that the low-frequency parameters allow improving performance of the acoustic-to-articulatory mapping of the soft palate.

2   Methods

2.1   Database

The present study uses the MOCHA-TIMIT database consisting of a collection of sentences that are designed to provide a set of phonetically diverse utterances [19]. The MOCHA-TIMIT database includes four data streams recorded concurrently: the acoustic waveform (16 kHz sample rate, with 16 bit precision), laryngograph, electropalatograph, and EMA data where the EMA system corresponds

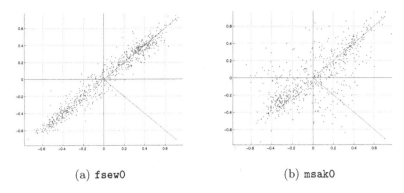

(a) fsew0   (b) msak0

Fig. 1. PCA basis vectors resulted for each considered speakers, in blue. Original data in red. (Color figure online)

a to 2D electromagnetic articulography (AG100) device. Movements of receiver coils attached to the articulators are sampled by the EMA system at 500 Hz. Coils are affixed to the lower incisors (li), upper lip (ul), lower lip (ll), tongue tip (tt), tongue body (tb), tongue dorsum (td), and velum (vl). The two coils at the bridge of the nose and upper incisors provide reference points to correct errors produced by head movements. The EMA trajectories are resampled from 500 to 100 Hz after a filtering process with an 8th order Chebyshev Type II low–pass filter of 20 Hz cut-off frequency. Then, the normalization process described in [14] is carried out. In the present study, we use the horizontal and vertical information provided by the coil attached to the velum $[v_x \, v_y]$.

2.2   Feature Extraction

Representation of the Velum Position. EMA data provide information about the movement of the velum along the directions (x, y) using a sensor placed at approximately 1–2 cm beyond the hard palate. Yet, we only make use of the direction having the maximum variability of EMA data. To this end, we apply the principal component analysis (PCA) fixing as the variance explained the values of 98.7 % and 86 % for fsew0 and msak0 speakers, respectively. In both cases, the angle of major component is approximately 45°. The velum position representation is given by $\nu = [v_x \, v_y]a_p$; where, a_p is the 2×1 vector, inside PCA transformation matrix, related to the highest eigenvalue of the covariance matrix of the EMA vector $[v_x \, v_y]$. Figure 1 shows scatter plot of EMA data and the PCA vectors.

In the velopharyngeal mechanism, the levator veli palatini (LVP) is the muscle mainly engaged in the movement of the soft palate, and it has an orientation angle close to 122.4° (i.e. 57.6° in its complementary version) [15]. This difference in the values of orientation angle (57.6° and 45°, respectively) can be explained by the disagreement of the references between the EMA and the plane used in [2].

Acoustic Feature Extraction. Computation of the considered acoustic parameters is as follows:

- *Filter-banks*, ξ_1. Grounded on the fact that the filter banks simulating the human hearing process supply less uncertainty in articulatory inference tasks [3], we implement a 20-order Mel filter bank for representing the spectrum of speech, where the center frequency of the first filter is located at 110 Hz while the center frequency of the last triangular filter – at 7026 Hz. As a result, we get 20 values representing the energy of frequency domain, denoted as $z = [z_1 \ldots z_k \ldots z_{20}]$ where the selected configuration of the spectral banks has equivalent filtering areas. However, we only use the energy value of greater statistical association located immediately below the first formant (denoted as ξ_1).
- *Energy ratio (ER)*, ξ_2. Since the energy of the very low-frequency bands increases in nasalized and nasal sounds, ER measures the relation between the energies within the bandwidth $[0, 320]$ to the range $[320, 5360]$ Hz [12].
- *Center of mass of modified group delay function (CM-MGDF)*, ξ_3. The group delay spectrum (MGDS), denoted as δ_g, allows improving the resolution of the low-frequency speech spectrum for the detection of hypernasal speech [18]. To avoid the influence of the outliers, however, we compute the center of mass of the approximated version of MGDS, $\tilde{\delta}_g$, as follows:

$$\xi_3 = \frac{\sum_{f \in F} f \tilde{\delta}_g(f)}{\sum_{f \in F} \tilde{\delta}_g(f)} \tag{1}$$

where $F = [0, 800]$ Hz, and the approximated group delay $\tilde{\delta}_g(f)$ of the signal $x(n)$ (corresponding to speech segment at current time frame) is obtained as:

$$\tilde{\delta}_g(f) = \text{sgn}(\delta_g(f)) \left(\frac{X_R(f)Y_R(f) + X_I(f)Y_I(f)}{\tilde{X}(f)^{2\gamma}} \right)^\alpha$$

where $X(f)$ and $Y(f)$ are the N-point discrete Fourier transform (DFT) of the sequences $x(n)$ and $nx(n)$, respectively. α and γ are the tuning parameters, resulting in $\alpha = \gamma = 0.8$ [1]. The subscripts R and I denote the real and imaginary parts, respectively. In turn, $\tilde{X}(f)$ is the cepstrally smoothed version of $X(f)$; and notation $\text{sgn}(\cdot)$ stands for the sign function computed for the expression: $\delta_g(f) = (X_R(f)Y_R(f) + X_I(f)Y_I(f))/X(f)^2$.
- *Frame energy*, ξ_4. This parameter infers the way the energy is varying along the time, and is calculated in the sliding window mode where each frame lasts 20 ms with overlaps of 10 ms.

2.3   Measure of Statistical Association

Correlation measures are typically developed only for an assumed linear piecewise relationship between random variables. Nonetheless, the correlated variables (acoustic and articular ones) mostly should be related through a nonlinear relationship. To this end, we can capture nonlinear statistical relationships between the articulatory and the acoustic variables through the widely used the Kendall's coefficient or χ^2 information measures [16]. Several reasons account for the choice of the former measure: It is implemented by robust and simple algorithms [4]. Besides, the estimation of the information measure χ^2 may be not confident as the number of samples drops.

Given a bivariate distribution model of $z_k(t)$ and $\nu(t)$ random variables, the Kendall coefficient (noted $\tau \in [-1, 1]$) is a measure of random association defined in terms of probability P as follows:

$$\tau_k = \tau(z_k(t), \nu(t)) \tag{2}$$

$$= P((z_k^i(t) - \nu^i)(z_k^j(t) - \nu^j) > 0)$$

$$- P((z_k^i(t) - \nu^i(t))(z_k^j(t) - \nu^j(t)) < 0) \tag{3}$$

Both terms of τ in Eq. (3) are estimated from the given set of independent observations pairs $(z_k^i(t), \nu^i(t))$, $(z_k^j(t), \nu^j(t))$, selected from the N samples. So, the measure $\tau(\cdot, \cdot)$ becomes 1 if there is a perfect concordance, i.e., if the direct relationship holds, $z_k^i(t) \lessgtr z_k^j(t)$ whenever $\nu^i(t) \lessgtr \nu^j(t)$. On the contrary, the measure of perfect discordance yields -1 meaning that the inverse relationship holds: $z_k^i(t) \lessgtr z_k^j(t)$ whenever $\nu^i(t) \gtrless \nu^j(t)$. If neither the concordant criterion nor discordant criterion is true, the measure between pairs will lie within the interval $(-1, 1)$.

Given the specific set of pairs $(z_k^i(t), \nu^i(t))$, $(z_k^j(t), \nu^j(t))$, the respective elemental pair indicator of association measure $a^{ij} \in [-1, 1]$ is defined as:

$$a_k^{ij} = \mathrm{sgn}(z_k^i(t) - \nu^i(t))\,(\,z_k^j(t) - \nu^j(t))$$

Therefore, the value of $\tau_k = \mathbb{E}\left\{a_k^{ij}\right\}$ (notation $\mathbb{E}\{\cdot\}$ stands for the expectation operator), denoting the Kendall coefficient is provided by the following expected value:

$$\tau_k = \sum\sum_{1 \leq i < j \leq N} \frac{a_k^{ij}}{\binom{N}{2}}.$$

2.4   Acoustic-Articulatory Mapping

For evaluation of the proposed acoustic-to-articulatory mapping system, we perform testing of all the above extracted acoustic parameters that are compared further to the baseline system based on MFCC parameters. The mapping function is accomplished using radial basis neural network (RBNN). Although there are more sophisticated approaches of regression that may provide better performance, we make use of the RBNN because of its ease implementation.

The following three feature sets are tested. $S_1 = [\xi_1\,\xi_2\,\xi_3\,\xi_4]$, the proposed feature set; S_2 containing 13 MFCC (Mel-frequency cepstral coefficients) parameters; and, S_3 corresponding to the union of S_1 and S_2 sets.

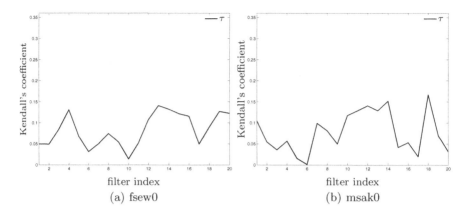

Fig. 2. Kendall's coefficient values between filter-bank's energy values and velum opening measure.

3   Results and Discussion

Relevant Frequencies. As seen in Fig. 2 showing the piecewise Kendall's coefficient, several peaks arise including the one for the fourth triangular filter and located near the first formant frequency. The appearance of these peaks in the first formant proximity has been already reported. In fact, the presence of an additional peak before the first formant is reported in [5], especially in nasal sounds, within the bandwidth ranging from 250 to 450 Hz for utterance of French and Japanese vowels. Besides, authors in [10], based on simulations of the nasal tract, state that the sinuses cause low-frequency peaks neighboring the first formant. This finding is proved too in [13] using volumetric MRI images for creating simulations of the vocal tract.

Low-Frequency Parameters. Estimation of the statistical association of the ER (ξ_2) and CM-MGDF (ξ_3) parameters, both related to the movement of the soft palate, provides higher values than those computed by the filter bank. Namely, $\tau(\xi_2(t), \nu(t)) = -0.29$ and $\tau(\xi_3(t), \nu(t)) = -0.15$ for msak0 speaker, and $\tau(\xi_2(t), \nu(t)) = -0.25$ and $\tau(\xi_3(t), \nu(t)) = -0.16$ for the fsew0 speaker. On the other hand, in [7] it was used the results of previous works ([18]) showing the appearance of nasal resonance below first formant to formulate a parameter they named as Energy Amplified Frequency Bands (EAFB); however, as reported, the feature EAFB did not achieve good results. In present work, based on first observations, it was not seen any relational pattern between the velum movement and the distance from first to second peak on group delay function; but, in contrast, the centre of mass over group delay function (ξ_3) showed better results.

Test of the Proposed Parameters with the RBNN-Based Acoustic-to-Articulatory System. As seen in Fig. 3 showing the resulting components of the

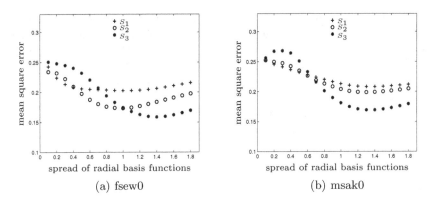

(a) fsew0   (b) msak0

Fig. 3. Mean square error results when testing sets S_1, S_2 and S_3 on RBN acoustic-to-articulatory mapping system.

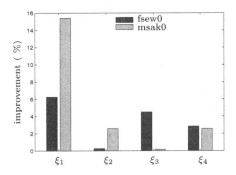

Fig. 4. Percentage of improvement in acoustic-to-articulatory mapping task when forming the feature sets MFCC $\oplus \xi_i$; $i = 1, \ldots, 4$.

acoustic-to-articulatory mapping system, the use of just S3 (MFCC $\oplus$ low-frequency parameters) leads to improve the performance. Consequently, rates of gain are 14.8 % and 8.5 % for msak0 and fsew0 speakers respectively. Although the low-frequency based set S2 outperforms the proposed MFCC-based S1 (5 % and 14.4 % for msak0 and fsew0, respectively), we only employ one-third of the amount of the parameters for S2. It is worth noting that the former set aims at representing only part of spectral information while the latter set extracts information from the whole spectrum. Finally, when adding the features ξ_i to the MFCC set (S_2) such that new sets are obtained $S_2 \oplus \xi_i$; $i = 1, \ldots, 4$, the accuracy increased. Figure 4 shows these results.

4 Conclusions

This work provides enough evidence for the presence of peak values of statistical association between velum position and fourth filter energy. We support this finding in the light of previously obtained results stating the effects of nasalization within the first formant region. Also, we suggest the use of low-frequency energy parameters for estimating the velum position. Although the performance of these low frequency based parameters are a bit less than using MFCCs, it is important to note that the proposed feature set aims to represent only part of spectral information while MFCC parameters provide information about whole spectrum. Finally, as a future work, we propose to test a greater set of acoustic features in a larger database, for instance, by using the recently developed USC-TIMIT database [11].

References

1. Belalcazar, E., Serna, F., Garcés, F., Orozco, R., Vargas, F.: Detección de hipernasalidad en el español usando funciones de retardo de grupo. In: XVI Symposium of Image, Signal Processing, and Artificial Vision, septiembre 2011
2. Ettema, S.L., Kuehn, D.P., Perlman, A.L., Alperin, N.: Magnetic resonance imaging of the levator veli palatini muscle during speech. Cleft Palate Craniofac. J. **39**(2), 130–144 (2012)
3. Ghosh, P.K., Goldstein, L.M., Narayanan, S.S.: Processing speech signal using auditory-like filterbank provides least uncertainty about articulatory gestures. J. Acoust. Soc. Am. **129**(6), 4014–4022 (2011)
4. Gibbons, J.D., Chakraborti, S.: Nonparametric Statistical Inference. Marcel Dekker, Inc., New York (2003)
5. Hattori, S., Yamamoto, K., Fujimura, O.: Nasalization of vowels in relation to nasals. J. Acoust. Soc. Am. **30**(4), 267–274 (1958)
6. He, L., Zhang, J., Liu, Q., Yin, H., Lech, M.: Automatic evaluation of hypernasality and consonant misarticulation in cleft palate speech. IEEE Signal Process. Lett. **21**(10), 1298–1301 (2014)
7. He, L., Zhang, J., Liu, Q., Yin, H., Lech, M., Huang, Y.: Automatic evaluation of hypernasality based on a cleft palate speech database. J. Med. Syst. **39**(5), 61 (2015)
8. Kummer, A.: Speech evaluation for patients with cleft palate. Clin. Plast. Surg. **41**(2), 241–251 (2014)
9. Lee, G.S., Wang, C.P., Yang, C., Kuo, T.: Voice low tone to high tone ratio: a potential quantitative index for vowel [a:] and its nasalization. IEEE Trans. Biomed. Eng. **53**(7), 1437–1439 (2006)
10. Maeda, S.: The role of the sinus cavities in the production of nasal vowels. In: Acoustics, Speech, and Signal Processing, IEEE International Conference on ICASSP 1982, May 1982, pp. 911–914 (1982)
11. Narayanan, S., et al.: Real-time magnetic resonance imaging and electromagnetic articulography database for speech production research (TC). J. Acoust. Soc. Am. **136**(3), 1307 (2014)
12. Pruthi, T., Espy-Wilson, C.Y.: Acoustic parameters for automatic detection of nasal manner. Speech Commun. **43**, 225–239 (2004)
13. Pruthi, T., Espy-Wilson, C.Y., Story, B.H.: Simulation and analysis of nasalized vowels based on magnetic resonance imaging data. J. Acoust. Soc. Am. **121**(6), 3858–3873 (2007)

14. Richmond, K.: Estimating articulatory parameters from the acoustic speech signal. Ph.D. thesis, The Centre for Speech Technology Research, Edinburgh University (2001)
15. Scott, A.D., Wylezinska, M., Birch, M.J., Miquel, M.E.: Speech MRI: morphology and function. Physica Medica **30**(6), 604–618 (2014)
16. Sepulveda-Sepulveda, A., Capobianco-Guido, R., Castellanos-Domínguez, G.: Estimation of relevant time frequency features using Kendall coefficient for articulator position inference. Speech Commun. **55**(1), 99–110 (2013)
17. Stevens, K.S.: Acoustic phonetics (2000)
18. Vijayalakshmi, P., Reddy, M., O'Shaughnessy, D.: Acoustic analysis and detection of hypernasality using a group delay function. IEEE Trans. Biomed. Eng. **54**(4), 621–629 (2007)
19. Wrench, A.: The MOCHA-TIMIT articulatory database. Technical report, Queen Margaret University College (1999). www.cstr.ed.ac.uk/research/projects/artic/mocha.html

Automatic Summarization of Highly Spontaneous Speech

András Beke[1] and György Szaszák[2(✉)]

[1] Research Institute for Linguistics,
Hungarian Academy of Sciences, Budapest, Hungary
beke.andras@mta.nytud.hu
[2] Department of Telecommunications and Media Informatics,
Budapest University of Technology and Economics, Budapest, Hungary
szaszak@tmit.bme.hu

Abstract. This paper addresses speech summarization of highly spontaneous speech. Speech is converted into text using an ASR, then segmented into tokens. Human made and automatic, prosody based tokenization are compared. The obtained sentence-like units are analysed by a syntactic parser to help automatic sentence selection for the summary. The preprocessed sentences are ranked based on thematic terms and sentence position. The thematic term is expressed in two ways: TF-IDF and Latent Semantic Indexing. The sentence score is calculated as linear combination of the thematic term score and a sentence position score. To generate the summary, the top 10 candidates for the most informative/best summarizing sentences are selected. The system performance showed comparable results (recall: 0.62, precision: 0.79 and F-measure 0.68) with the prosody based tokenization approach. A subjective test is also carried out on a Likert scale.

Keywords: Speech summarization · Latent semantic indexing · Spontaneous speech

1 Introduction

Automatic summarization is used to extract the most relevant information from various sources: text or speech. Although speech is most often transcribed and summarization is carried out on text, the automatically transcribed text contains several linguistically incorrect words or structures resulting from the spontaneity of speech and also from speech-to-text errors. Spontaneous speech is "ill-formed" and very different from written text: it is characterized by disfluencies, filled pauses, repetitions, repairs and fragmented words, but behind this variable acoustic property, syntax can also deviate from standard.

Another challenge originates in the speech-to-text conversion. Errors can propagate into the text-based analysis phase. The recognition of spontaneous speech is probably the hardest recognition task, due to the extreme variable

© Springer International Publishing Switzerland 2016
A. Ronzhin et al. (Eds.): SPECOM 2016, LNAI 9811, pp. 140–147, 2016.
DOI: 10.1007/978-3-319-43958-7_16

acoustics, environmental noise (especially other's speech), and language coverage (or language model perplexity) [10].

A possible approach of summarizing written text is to extract important sentences from a document based on keywords or cue phrases. Automatic sentence segmentation (tokenization) is crucial before such a sentence based extractive summarization [5]. The difficulty comes not only from recognition errors, but also from missing punctuation marks, which would be fundamental in syntactic parsing and POS tagging (disambiguation). In current work we propose a prosody based automatic tokenizer which recovers intonational phrases (IP) and use IPs as sentence like units in further analysis. Summarization will also be compared to a baseline version using tokens available from human annotation The baseline tokenization relies on acoustic (silence) and syntactic-semantic (sintactically or semantically closely together belonging) axes.

Other research showed that using speech-related features beside textual-based features can improve the performance of summarization [6]. Prosodic features such as speaking rate; minimuma, maximuma, mean, and slope of fundamental frequency and those of energy and utterance duration can also be exploited.

In this work we present an initial effort to develop a Hungarian speech summarization system. In Hungarian, both speech recognition [10] and text-based syntactical analysis [1] are difficult compared to English due to the very rich morphology of the language. Mainstream works on extractive summarization use two major steps: the first step is ranking the sentences based on their scores which are computed by combining features such as term frequency (TF), positional information and cue phrases; the second step consists in selecting a few top ranked sentences to prepare the summary.

2 Material and Speech-to-Text

2.1 Speech Material

For the summarization experiments, we use 4 interviews from the BEA Hungarian Spontaneous Speech database [8]. Participants talk about their jobs, family, and hobbies. Three of the speakers are male and one of them is female. All speakers are native Hungarian, living in Budapest (aged between 30 and 60). The total material is 28 min long (average duration was 7 min per participant).

2.2 The Speech-to-Text System

We use 160 interviews from BEA, accounting for 120 h of speech (the interviewer discarded) to train Speech-to-text (S2T) acoustic models. Speakers involved in the 4 interviews used for summarization are held out.

Using the Kaldi toolkit we train 3 hidden layer DNN acoustic models with 2048 neurons per layer and tanh non-linearity on 160 interviews from BEA (Hungarian). Input data is 9x spliced MFCC13 + CMVN +LDA/MLLT. A trigram language model is trained on transcripts of the 160 interviews after text normalization, with Kneser-Ney smoothing. Dictionaries are obtained using a rule-based phonetizer (spoken Hungarian is very close to the written form).

Word Error Rate (WER) was found around 44 % for this task. This relative high WER is justified by the high spontaneity of speech. Stem error rate was found to be somewhat smaller, 39 %.

2.3   The IP Tokenizer

A segmentation tool capable of recovering phonological phrases (PP) was presented in [11]. This system uses phonological phrase models and aligns them to the input speech based on prosodic features F0 and mean energy. The PP alignment is conceived in such a manner that it encodes upper level intonational phrase (IP) constraints (as IP starter and ending PPs, as well as silence are modelled separately), and hence is de facto capable of yielding an IP segmentation, capturing silence, but also silence markers (often not physically realized as real silence). The algorithm is described in detail in [11], in this work we use it to obtain sentence-like tokens from speech-to-text output. We use the IP tokenizer in an operating point with high precision (96 % on read speech) and lower recall (80 % on read speech) as we consider less problematic missing a token boundary (merge 2 sentences) than inserting false ones (splitting the sentence into 2 parts).

3   The Summarization Approach

Once speech-to-text conversion and tokenization for sentence-like units took place, text summarization is split into three main modules. The first module does the preprocessing of the output of the ASR (Automatic Speech Recognizer, S2T), the second module is responsible for sentence ranking, and the final module generates the summary. This approach is based on [9], but we modify the thematic term calculation method. The overall scheme of the system is depicted in Fig. 1.

3.1   Pre-processing

Stop words are removed from the tokens and stemming is performed. Stop-words are collected into a list, which contains (i) all words tagged as fillers by the S2T component (speaker noise) and (ii) a predefined set of non-content words such as articles, conjunctions etc.

Hungarian is an agglutinating language, with a very rich morphology, and consequently, grammatical relations are expressed less by the word order but rather by case endings (suffixes). The *magyarlánc* toolkit [13] was used for the stemming and POS-tagging of the Hungarian text. In case of Hungarian, stemming is very important and often ambiguous due to the rich morphology. Thereafter, the POS-tagger module was applied to determine a word as corresponding to a part-of-speech. The words are filtered to keep only nouns.

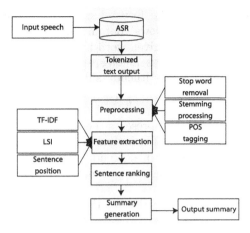

Fig. 1. Block scheme of the speech summarization system.

3.2 Textual Feature Extraction

In order to rank sentences based on their importance, some textual features need to be extracted:

TF-IDF. (Term Frequency - Inverse Document Frequency) reflects the importance of a sentence and is generally measured by the number of keywords present in it. The importance value of a sentence is computed as the sum of TF-IDF values of its constituent words (in this work: nouns) divided by the sum of all TF-IDF values found in the text. TF shows how frequently a term occurs in a document divided by the length of the document, whereas IDF shows how important a term is. In raw word frequency each word is equally important, but, of course, not all equally frequent words are equally meaningful. For this reason it can be calculated using the following equation:

$$IDF(t) = ln\frac{Total \quad number \quad of \quad documents}{Number \quad of \quad documents \quad containing \quad term \quad t}. \quad (1)$$

TF-IDF weighting is the combination of the definitions of term frequency and inverse document frequency, to produce a composite weight for each term in each document, calculated as a dot product:

$$TF * IDF. \quad (2)$$

Latent Semantic Analysis. (LSA) exploits context to try to find words with similar meaning. LSA is able to reflect both word and sentence importance. Singular Value Decomposition (SVD) is used to assess semantic similarity.

LSA based summarization needs the calculation of the following items [3]:

– Represent the input data in the form of a matrix (input matrix), where columns contain sentences and rows contain words. In each cell, a measure reflecting the importance of the given word in the given sentence is stored.
– use SVD to capture relationships among words and sentences. The input matrix is decomposed into 3 constituents (sub-matrices):

$$A = U\Sigma VT, \tag{3}$$

where A is the input matrix U represents the description of the original rows of the input matrix as a vector of extracted concepts, Σ is a diagonal matrix containing scaling values sorted in descending order, and V represents the description of the original columns of input matrix as a vector of the extracted concepts [3].
– The final step is the sentence selection for the summary.

Positional Value. Generally, a reasonable a priori assumption is that the more meaningful sentences can be found at the beginning of the document. This is even more true in case of spontaneous narratives, as the interviewer asks the participant to tell something about her/his life, job, hobbies. The following equitation was used [9]:

$$P_k = 1/\sqrt{k}, \tag{4}$$

where the P_k is the positional score of kth sentence.

Sentence Length. Sentences are of different length (they contain more or less words) in documents. Usually a short sentence is less informative than a longer one and hence, readers or listeners are more prone to select a longer sentence than a short one when asked to find good summarizing sentences in documents [9]. However, a too long sentence may contain redundant information. The idea is then to eliminate or de-weight sentences which are too short or too long (compared to an average). If a sentence is too short or too long, it is assigned a ranking score of 0.

Sentence Ranking. The ranking score RS_K is calculated as the linear combination of the so-called thematic term based score S_k and positional score P_k. The final score of a sentence k is:

$$RS_k = \begin{cases} \alpha S_k + \beta P_k, & if L_k \geq L_L \quad \& \quad L_k \leq L_U; \\ 0 & otherwise, \end{cases} \tag{5}$$

where α is the lower, β is the upper cut-off for the sentence position ($0 \leq \alpha, \beta \leq 1$) and L_L is the lower and L_U is the upper cut-off on the sentence length L_k [9].

3.3 Summary Generation

The last step is to generate the summary. In this process the N-top ranked sentences are selected from the text [9]. We set N to 10, so the final text summary contains the top 10 sentences.

4 Results

4.1 Metrics

The most commonly used information retrieval evaluation metrics are precision and recall, which are appropriate to measure summarization performance as well [7]. Beside recall and precision, we use the F_1-measure:

$$F_1 = \frac{2 * precision * recall}{precision + recall}. \tag{6}$$

The challenge of evaluation consists rather in choosing or obtaining a reference summary. For this research we decided to obtain a set of human made summaries, whereby 10 participants were asked to select up to 10 sentences that they find to be the most informative for a given document (presented also in spoken and in written form). Participants used 6.8 sentences on average for their summaries. For each narrative, a set of reference sentences was created: sentences chosen by at least 1/3 of the participants were added to the reference summary. Overlap among human preferred sentences was ranging from 10 % to 100 %, with an average overlap of 28 %. Sentences are appended to the summaries in the order of their appearance in the original text. When used for comparison, we filter stop words, fillers (ASR output) and require at least a 2/3 overlap ratio for the content words. We will refer to this evaluation approach as *soft comparison*.

An automatic evaluation tool is also considered to obtain more objective measures. The most commonly used automatic evaluation method is ROUGE [4]. However, ROUGE performs strict string comparison and hence recall and precision are commonly lower with this approach [7]. We will refer to this evaluation approach as *hard comparison*.

4.2 Experiments

Text summarization was then run with 3 setups regarding pre-processing (how the text was obtained and tokenized):

- OT-H: Use the original transcribed text as segmented by the human annotators into sentence-like units.
- S2T-H: Use speech-to-text conversion to obtain text, but use the human annotated tokens.
- S2T-IP: Use speech-to-text conversion to obtain text and tokenize it based on IP boundary detection from speech.

Summary generation is tested for all the 3 setups with both TF-IDF and LSA approaches to calculate the thematic term S_k in Eq. (5). Results are shown in Table 1.

Overall results are in accordance with known peformance for similar tasks [2]. When switching to the speech-to-text output, there is no significant difference in performance regarding the soft comparison, but we notice a decrease

Table 1. Recall, precision and F_1.

Setup	Approach	Soft comparison			Hard comparison (ROUGE)		
		Recall [%]	Precision [%]	F_1	Recall [%]	Precision [%]	F_1
OT-H	TF-IDF	0.51	0.76	0.61	0.36	0.28	0.32
	LSA	0.36	0.71	0.46	0.36	0.30	0.32
S2T-H	TF-IDF	0.51	0.80	0.61	0.34	0.29	0.31
	LSA	0.49	0.77	0.56	0.39	0.27	0.32
S2T-IP	TF-IDF	0.62	0.79	0.68	0.33	0.28	0.30
	LSA	0.59	0.78	0.65	0.33	0.32	0.32

(rel. 8 %) in the hard one (comparing OT-H and S2T-IP approaches). This is due to speech-to-text errors, however, keeping in mind the high WER for spontaneous speech, this decrease is rather modest. Indeed, it seems that content words and stems are less vulnerable to speech-to-text errors: in [12] it is shown that 35 % WER in the S2T output results in 12 % POS-tag error for nouns.

An important outcome of the experiments is that the automatic, IP detection based prosodic tokenization gave almost the same performance as the human annotation based one (in soft comparison it is even better).

4.3   Subjective Assessment of Summaries

In a separate evaluation step, participants were asked to evaluate the system generated summaries on a Likert scale. Thereby they got the system generated summary as is and had to rate it according to the question "How well does the system summarize the narrative content in your opinion?". The Likert scale was ranging from 1 to 5: "Poor, Moderate, Acceptable, Good, Excellent". Results of the evaluation are shown in Fig. 2. Mean Opinion score was 3.2. Regarding redundance ("How redundant is the summary in your opinion?") MOS value was found to be 2.8.

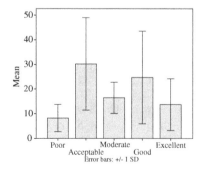

Fig. 2. Likert scale distribution of human judgements.

5   Conclusions

This paper addressed speech summarization for highly spontaneous Hungarian. Given this high degree of spontaneity and also the heavy agglutinating property of Hungarian, we believe the obtained results are promising as they are comparable to results published for other languages [2]. The proposed IP detection based tokenization was as successful as the available human one. The overall best results were 62 % recall and 79 % precision ($F_1 = 0.68$). Subjective rating of the summaries gave 3.2 mean opinion score.

Acknowledgment. The authors would like to thank the support of the Hungarian National Innovation Office (NKFI) under contract IDs *PD-112598* and *PD-108762*.

References

1. Babarczy, A., Gábor, B., Hamp, G., Rung, A., Szakadát, I.: Hunpars: a rule-based sentence parser for hungarian. In: Proceedings of the 6th International Symposium on Computational Intelligence. Citeseer (2005)
2. Campr, M., Ježek, K.: Comparing semantic models for evaluating automatic document summarization. In: Král, P., Matoušek, V. (eds.) TSD 2015. LNCS, vol. 9302, pp. 252–260. Springer, Heidelberg (2015). doi:10.1007/978-3-319-24033-6_29
3. Landauer, T.K., Foltz, P.W., Laham, D.: An introduction to latent semantic analysis. Discourse Processes **25**(2–3), 259–284 (1998)
4. Lin, C.Y.: Rouge: A package for automatic evaluation of summaries. In: Proceedings of the ACL-04 Workshop, Text Summarization Branches Out, vol. 8 (2004)
5. Liu, Y., Xie, S.: Impact of automatic sentence segmentation on meeting summarization. In: 2008 IEEE International Conference on Acoustics, Speech and Signal Processing, ICASSP 2008, pp. 5009–5012. IEEE (2008)
6. Maskey, S., Hirschberg, J.: Comparing lexical, acoustic/prosodic, structural and discourse features for speech summarization. In: INTERSPEECH, pp. 621–624 (2005)
7. Nenkova, A.: Summarization evaluation for text and speech: issues and approaches. In: INTERSPEECH. pp. 1527–1530 (2006)
8. Neuberger, T., Gyarmathy, D., Gráczi, T.E., Horváth, V., Gósy, M., Beke, A.: Development of a large spontaneous speech database of agglutinative hungarian language. In: Sojka, P., Horák, A., Kopeček, I., Pala, K. (eds.) TSD 2014. LNCS, vol. 8655, pp. 424–431. Springer, Heidelberg (2014)
9. Sarkar, K.: Bengali text summarization by sentence extraction. In: Proceedings of International Conference on Business and Information Management ICBIM12, pp. 233–245 (2012)
10. Szarvas, M., Fegyó, T., Mihajlik, P., Tatai, P.: Automatic recognition of Hungarian: Theory and practice. Int. J. Speech Technol. **3**(3), 237–251 (2000)
11. Szaszák, G., Beke, A.: Exploiting prosody for automatic syntactic phrase boundary detection in speech. J. Lang. Model. **0**(1), 143–172 (2012)
12. Tündik, M.A., Szaszák, G.: Szövegalapú nyelvi elemzö kiértékelése gépi beszédfelismerö hibákkal terhelt kimenetén. In: Proceedings of the 12th Hungarian Conference on Computational Linguistics (MSZNY), pp. 111–120 (2016)
13. Zsibrita, J., Vincze, V., Farkas, R.: magyarlanc: A toolkit for morphological and dependency parsing of hungarian. In: Proceedings of RANLP, pp. 763–771 (2013)

Backchanneling via Twitter Data for Conversational Dialogue Systems

Michimasa Inaba[✉] and Kenichi Takahashi

Hiroshima City University, 3-4-1 Ozukahigashi, Asaminami-ku, Hiroshima, Japan
{inaba,takahashi}@hiroshima-cu.ac.jp

Abstract. Backchanneling plays a crucial role in human-to-human communication. In this study, we propose a method for generating a rich variety of backchanneling, which is not just limited to simple "hm" or "sure" responses, to realize smooth communication in conversational dialogue systems. We formulate the problem of what the backchanneling generation function should return for given user inputs as a multi-class classification problem and determine a suitable class using a recurrent neural network with a long short-term memory. Training data for our model comprised pairs of tweets and replies acquired from Twitter. Experimental results demonstrated that our method can appropriately select backchannels to given inputs and significantly outperform baseline methods.

Keywords: Conversational dialogue systems · Recurrent neural network · Backchanneling

1 Introduction

Backchanneling plays a crucial role in human-to-human communication. Clancy defined backchanneling as a short utterance produced by an interlocutor playing the role of a listener during another interlocutor's speakership [4]. In human conversation, the listener's active participation is important because the backchanneling, i.e., the listener's reaction and positive attitude, are essential for most speakers to talk and communicate effectively. Moreover, a previous study has reported that dialogues in which a listener uses backchanneling more frequently tend to be more enthusiastic [16].

Overall, in the field of dialogue systems, the importance of backchanneling has been recognized; moreover, suitable backchanneling generation has been extensively studied [6,10,19]. Okato et al. proposed a method for backchanneling using particular pitch patterns in the human user's utterances [12]. Similarly, Kobayashi et al. estimated the user's degree of interest about the current topic and selected suitable backchannels using the estimated degree [9]. Kitaoka estimated suitable timings of backchannels using a decision tree [8]. The key problem with these and other previous studies is that they employ a limited set of backchannels such as "hm" or "sure" or repeat a part of the user's previous utterance. This is particularly true of conversational dialogue systems (also called

© Springer International Publishing Switzerland 2016
A. Ronzhin et al. (Eds.): SPECOM 2016, LNAI 9811, pp. 148–155, 2016.
DOI: 10.1007/978-3-319-43958-7_17

non-task-oriented or chat-oriented dialogue systems) that use various backchannels for their dialogues.

Given the above issues, in this study, we propose a method for generating a rich variety of backchanneling to realize smooth communication in conversational dialogue systems. We employ Twitter data to train our model to be able to reply with suitable backchannels given a human user's input. Because backchanneling is frequently used by Twitter users, we acquire a large amount of backchanneling data in response to various types of tweets. Therefore, we collect backchanneling replies and the corresponding tweets they respond to by using this data as training data for our model. In our proposed method, we use a recurrent neural network (RNN) to determine suitable backchannels.

2   Proposed Method

We formulate the problem of what the backchanneling function should return for given utterances as a multi-class classification problem. Thus, we consider given utterances as input and suitable responses as one of the many output classes. In short, we determine replies using this multi-class classifier. To train our classifier, we first determine the reply (output) classes in advance. In this study, we used the 44 reply classes shown in Table 1.

In the subsections that follow, we describe the training data acquisition and response selection mechanisms in detail.

2.1   Data Acquisition

We employed tweet—reply pairs as our training data, with data acquired through the Twitter API. To increase the size of the acquired data, we searched Twitter not only for the reply classes shown in Table 1 but also for other expressions. For example, in the "That's incredible (すごいね)" class, we used "凄いね" a kanji expression with the same pronunciation and meaning as "That's incredible" as an additional search query. Moreover, we searched Twitter using reply classes and these other expressions (hereafter called reply expressions) and acquired corresponding tweets. From the search results, we extracted tweets that satisfied the following conditions:

- Tweet is a reply tweet with a corresponding target tweet
- Containing a reply expression at the beginning of a reply tweet

Finally, we acquired the target tweet corresponding to the extracted one. From the above procedures, we acquired the training data for our model. We used the acquired target tweets as inputs and the reply classes of the reply expressions as the correct classes for the target tweets.

Table 1. Reply classes used in our proposed method. Note that these replies were originally in Japanese and then translated by the authors. The original Japanese replies are shown in parentheses.

That's tough (大変だね)	Never mind (ドンマイ)	Congratulations (おめでとう)	I understand (わかるよ)
So cute (かわいいよね)	So cool (かっこいいよね)	Sounds good (いいですね)	That's difficult (難しいね)
Thank you (ありがとう)	I'm sorry (ごめんね)	Looks that way (そうみたい)	That's funny (笑えるね)
I'm impressed (さすが)	Are you OK? (大丈夫ですか)	No kidding (そうだね)	I feel sorry for that (辛いね)
Awesome! (やばいよね)	That's good (よかった)	Good for you (よかったね)	I'll do my best (頑張るよ)
I see (そうなんだ)	That's OK (大丈夫だよ)	That's incredible (すごいね)	It's no go (だめだよ)
No kidding (本当だね)	That looks fun (楽しそう)	I'm looking forward to it (楽しみです)	That's interesting (面白いね)
That's really yammy (美味しいよね)	I'm jealous (羨ましいな)	You are right (確かにね)	I'm counting on you (よろしく)
I'm happy (嬉しいな)	Good luck (頑張ってね)	Let's do our best (頑張ろう)	Sure (もちろん)
Strewth (マジか)	No way (それはないね)	That would be fine (了解です)	Is that true? (本当ですか)
I agree (同感です)	That's horrible (怖いね)	That's too bad (残念です)	You must be tired (お疲れさま)

2.2 Backchanneling Learning

Long Short-Term Memory. For suitable backchanneling learning, we used a RNN with long short-term memory (LSTM) (LSTM-RNN) [7]. We proposed our RNN models to handle sequential data; however, normal RNNs have a problem called vanishing gradients [2] when learning with backpropagation.

The LSTM takes in and holds errors selectively into memory cell c_t to preserve vanishing gradients. The LSTM has input, forget and output getes for managing functions when it takes in, deletes and outputs errors respectively. Mathematical expressions of the LSTM are as follows:

$$i_t = \sigma(W_i x_t + U_i h_{t-1} + b_i);$$

$$f_t = \sigma(W_f x_t + U_f h_{t-1} + b_f);$$

$$o_t = \sigma(W_o x_t + U_o h_{t-1} + V_o c_t + b_f;)$$

$$c_t = i_t \odot \tanh(W_c x_t + U_c h_{t-1} + b_c) + f_t \odot c_{t-1};$$

$$h_t = o_t \odot \tanh(c_t).$$

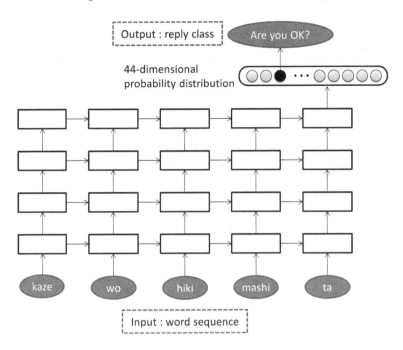

Fig. 1. Illustrative example of our four-layer LSTM backchanneling model in which the input is "Kaze wo hiki mashi ta (I caught a cold)" and the output is "Are you OK?". The LSTM-RNN reads each word sequentially and outputs a 44-dimensional probability distribution. The highest probability in this distribution indicates the suitable reply class identified by our model.

Here $\mathbf{x_t}$ is a input vector at time t, $\mathbf{h_t}$ is output, σ is the sigmoid function, $\mathbf{i_t}, \mathbf{f_t}$ and $\mathbf{o_t}$ are input, forget, and output gates respectively, and $\mathbf{c_t}$ is the memory cell. Note that $\odot$ indicates element-wise multiplication.

Recently, application of statistical machine translation methods using RNNs to dialogue models has been proposed [14,17]. These models receive word sequences (of target sentences or user input) and output word sequences (of translated sentences or system output). Our model receives word sequences but outputs a reply class rather than a translated sentence.

Proposed Model. An illustration of our model is shown in Fig. 1. The LSTM-RNN reply model reads one word at a time and outputs a 44-dimensional probability distribution corresponding to each reply class. When the last word in the input sequence is read, the model checks the output distributions and identifies the reply class with the highest probability. For our experiments (described in the next section), we used a four-layer LSTM with 1000 memory cells. In the learning phase, the cross-entropy function calculates the error between the output distribution and the answer distribution with a probability of correct reply class of 1.0; subsequently, the weights in the model are updated via backpropagation of the errors. Input words are converted into a 1000-dimensionally distributed representation using the method proposed by Mikolov et al. in [11], which was implemented in Word2Vec. We used 120 GB of Twitter data to train Word2Vec.

3   Experiment

To evaluate our proposed method, we conducted experiments and made both automatic and manual evaluations. In the automatic evaluation, performance is evaluated by calculating the co-incidence ratio between our method's outputs and the original replies in the acquired pairs of tweets and replies; however, a given utterance may yield multiple "correct" replies. Therefore, to better mimic real human conversations, we employed human subjects to evaluate the generated replies.

3.1   Data

For our dataset, we collected 460 K Japanese pairs of tweets and replies in advance, from which, we used 455 K pairs for training the model and 5 K pairs for evaluation in our experiments. Note that we constructed this data to obtain 44 equally distributed reply classes.

3.2   Experimental Procedure

We used the following two baseline methods for comparison.

Baseline 1: Random. The first baseline method randomly selects a reply class from among the 44 classes, using it as output to a given input utterance.

Baseline 2: Multi-class Support Vector Machine. The second baseline method learns and classifies replies via a multi-class support vector machine (SVM) with a linear kernel using unigram and trigram features. Here we used LIBSVM [3], an SVM library implemented by Chang et al. Multi-class classification in the LIBSVM adopts the one-versus-one strategy, where the LIBSVM builds classifiers for all possible pairs of classes and determines a class by majority.

We evaluated our proposed and baseline methods via both automatic and manual methods. The automatic method used 5000 pairs of tweets and replies, which were not previously used as training data. We inputted tweets into each method and calculated the co-incidence rates between each method's outputs and the original replies.

For the manual method, we randomly extracted 200 data points from 5 K pairs, and then had two human subjects (not authors of this paper) evaluate outputs from each method for each given tweet. The subjects judged the natural quality of replies to tweets using a five-point Likert scale, in which 1 was the

Table 2. Accuracy, average natural quality, and acceptable rate of our proposed method and the two baseline methods. The accuracy is calculated by comparing each model's output to replies in the original data. The natural quality and acceptable rate values are calculated by averaging the results of the two human judges.

	Random	Multi-class SVM	**Proposed**	Original data
Accuracy	0.02	0.31	**0.34**	1.00
Naturality	1.69	3.08	**3.28**	3.57
Acceptable rate	0.18	0.63	**0.68**	0.73

worst and 5 was the best; the average score from the two subjects was used for our evaluation. Moreover, each backchanneling method was evaluated based on its acceptable rate, which is the number of three or more natural quality outputs versus the number of total outputs. This measure indicates that the system forms a suitable response in conversation using the target method.

3.3 Results

Table 2 shows the results of our evaluations. Original data in the table indicates that original replies in the test data were regarded as outputs; hence, the accuracy of the original data is shown as 1.00. The results show that the performance of our proposed method is better than the two baseline methods for all evaluation indices.

Regarding the accuracy and acceptable rate values, McNemar's test demonstrates that our proposed method and the other methods significantly differ at the 1 % level. Moreover, in terms of natural quality, the t-test shows that our proposed method significantly differs, with our proposed method and multi-class SVM meeting the significance level of 5 % and others meeting 1 %.

When we look further at accuracy, the absolute value of our proposed method (0.34) is not very high; however, in terms of natural quality and acceptable rate values, our proposed method outperformed the multi-class SVM and is closer to the results of the original data. On the other hand, the acceptable rate of the original data is far from perfect (0.73) regardless of using actual human-to-human conversation data. We consider this last point is due to a substantial amount of noise in the Twitter data, i.e., the data is not as clean as news articles or an annotated corpus. At present, our proposed method does not contain countermeasures for the noise; therefore, we note that our proposed method could potentially be improved by decreasing noise from the initial training data.

4 Related Work

Existing well-known conversational dialogue systems, such as ELIZA [20], PARRY [5] and Artificial Linguistic Internet Computer Entity (A.L.I.C.E.) [18], typically use response rules for utterance generation. dialogue systems that employ such rule-based strategies require a large amount of time and cost to construct rules, primarily because these rules are manually created. Therefore, researchers have more recently focused on response methods using Web data. For example, Shibata et al. and Yoshino et al. proposed dialogue systems that employ text acquired from websites (the text obtained via search engines) as system utterances [15, 21].

Similar to our current study, research involving response methods that utilize social media data has been conducted. Banch et al. proposed a method that searches a dialogue database based on user input, selecting an utterance that follows after the most similar input as a response [1]. Ritter et al. applied a statistical machine translation method to response generation [13]. More specifically, they used Twitter data and regarded pairs of tweets and replies as pairs of inputs and translated sentences. For example, using their method, "Today is my birthday" would translate into "Happy birthday". Other studies based on the statistical machine translation method include [14, 17].

5   Conclusions

In this study, we proposed a method for generating a rich variety of backchanneling for conversational dialogue systems to realize smooth human–machine communication. Our proposed method formulates the problem of what backchannel to return for a given utterance as a multi-class classification problem that determines a suitable reply class using a LSTM-RNN. The training data for the LSTM-RNN comprises pairs of tweets and replies acquired from Twitter. Experimental results demonstrated that our method significantly outperformed two baseline methods, i.e., random and multi-class SVM classification.

In a future study, we plan to reduce noise in the training data by implementing a filtering technique. We conjecture that the performance of our model will improve using cleaner training data. Furthermore, we aim to study backchanneling timing control to build a spoken conversational dialogue system.

References

1. Banchs, R.E., Li, H.: Iris: a chat-oriented dialogue system based on the vector space model. In: Proceedings of the ACL 2012 System Demonstrations, pp. 37–42. Association for Computational Linguistics (2012)
2. Bengio, Y., Simard, P., Frasconi, P.: Learning long-term dependencies with gradient descent is difficult. IEEE Trans. Neural Netw. **5**(2), 157–166 (1994)
3. Chang, C.C., Lin, C.J.: Libsvm: a library for support vector machines. ACM Trans. Intell. Syst. Technol. (TIST) **2**(3), 27 (2011)
4. Clancy, P.M., Thompson, S.A., Suzuki, R., Tao, H.: The conversational use of reactive tokens in English, Japanese, and Mandarin. J. Pragmatics **26**(3), 355–387 (1996)
5. Colby, K.: Modeling a paranoid mind. Behav. Brain Sci. **4**(4), 515–560 (1981)
6. Hirasawa, J., Miyazaki, N., Nakano, M., Kawabata, T.: Implementation of coordinative nodding behavior on spoken dialogue systems. In: Fifth International Conference on Spoken Language Processing, pp. 2347–2350 (1998)

7. Hochreiter, S., Schmidhuber, J.: Long short-term memory. Neural Comput. **9**(8), 1735–1780 (1997)
8. Kitaoka, N., Takeuchi, M., Nishimura, R., Nakagawa, S.: Response timing detection using prosodic and linguistic information for human-friendly spoken dialog systems. Trans. Jpn. Soc. Artif. Intell. **20**(3), 220–228 (2005)
9. Kobayashi, Y., Yamamoto, D., Doi, M.: Word co-occurrence analysis with utterance pairs for spoken dialogue system. Trans. Jpn. Soc. Artif. Intell. **28**(2), 141–148 (2013)
10. Koiso, H., Horiuchi, Y., Tutiya, S., Ichikawa, A., Den, Y.: An analysis of turn-taking and backchannels based on prosodic and syntactic features in Japanese map task dialogs. Lang. Speech **41**(3–4), 295–321 (1998)
11. Mikolov, T., Sutskever, I., Chen, K., Corrado, G.S., Dean, J.: Distributed representations of words and phrases and their compositionality. In: Advances in Neural Information Processing Systems, pp. 3111–3119 (2013)
12. Okato, Y., Kato, K., Kamamoto, M., Itahashi, S.: Insertion of interjectory response based on prosodic information. In: Third IEEE Workshop on Interactive Voice Technology for Telecommunications Applications, Proceedings, pp. 85–88. IEEE (1996)
13. Ritter, A., Cherry, C., Dolan, W.B.: Data-driven response generation in social media. In: Proceedings of the Conference on Empirical Methods in Natural Language Processing, pp. 583–593. Association for Computational Linguistics (2011)
14. Shang, L., Lu, Z., Li, H.: Neural responding machine for short-text conversation. arXiv preprint arXiv:1503.02364 (2015)
15. Shibata, M., Tomiura, Y., Nishiguchi, T.: Method for selecting appropriate sentence from documents on the www for the open-ended conversation dialog system. Trans. Jpn. Soc. Artif. Intell. **24**(6), 507–519 (2009)
16. Toyoda, K., Miyakoshi, Y., Yamanishi, R., Kato, S.: Dialogue mood estimation focusing on intervals of utterance state. Trans. Jpn. Soc. Artif. Intell. **27**(2), 16–21 (2012)
17. Vinyals, O., Le, Q.: A neural conversational model. arXiv preprint arXiv:1506.05869 (2015)
18. Wallace, R.: The anatomy of alice. In: Epstein, R., Roberts, G., Beber, G. (eds.) Parsing the Turing Test, pp. 181–210. Springer, The Netherlands (2009)
19. Ward, N., Tsukahara, W.: Prosodic features which cue back-channel responses in English and Japanese. J. Pragmatics **32**(8), 1177–1207 (2000)
20. Weizenbaum, J.: Eliza-a computer program for the study of natural language communication between man and machine. Commun. ACM **9**(1), 36–45 (1966)
21. Yoshino, K., Mori, S., Kawahara, T.: Spoken dialogue system based on information extraction using similarity of predicate argument structures. In: Proceedings of the SIGDIAL 2011 Conference, pp. 59–66. Association for Computational Linguistics (2011)

Bio-Inspired Sparse Representation of Speech and Audio Using Psychoacoustic Adaptive Matching Pursuit

Alexey Petrovsky, Vadzim Herasimovich[(⊠)],
and Alexander Petrovsky

Belarusian State University of Informatics and Radioelectronics, Minsk, Belarus
alexey@petrovsky.eu, {gerasimovich, palex}@bsuir.by

Abstract. Current paper devoted to the sparse audio and speech signal modelling via the matching pursuit (MP) algorithm. Redundant dictionary of the time-frequency functions is constructed through the frame-based psychoacoustic optimized wavelet packet (WP) transform. Anthropomorphic adaptation of the time-frequency plan allows minimizing perceptual redundancy of the signal modelling. Psychoacoustic information at MP stage for the best atom selection from the dictionary is used. It improves algorithm performance in terms of human hearing system and computational complexity. Described signal model can be applied in many audio and speech processing tasks such as source separation, watermarking, classification and so on. Presented research focused on the signal encoding. Universal audio/speech coding algorithm that is suitable for the input signals with different sound content is proposed.

Keywords: Sparse approximation · Matching pursuit · Wavelet packet · Audio/speech coding

1 Introduction

A sparse signal approximation represents the input signal with the minimum amount of nonzero elements. It is very suitable tool for audio/speech processing since such type of the signals has a big informational redundancy. MP is a greedy iterative algorithm, which maps the input signal onto redundant dictionary of the time-frequency functions [1].

A signal modelling based on MP uses in various works. In [2] perceptual MP with Gabor dictionary is introduced. The time-frequency masking model utilized after MP decomposition to select only audible atoms. Modified Discrete Cosine Transform (MDCT) based dictionary is proposed in [3]. This approach shows decomposition with two types of dictionary consist of MDCT bases. Switching between them is based on the decomposition residual energy decay. Some approaches use MP not for the entire input frame but for some part of it [4, 5]. Such models separate the input signal into three fundamental parts: harmonic (sinusoidal), transient and noise (*HTN* or *STN* model), and work with them separately. MP is used for modelling of some part of the signal. *STN* allows rather robust parameterization since every part of the signal is processed with a suitable model in terms of its nature.

© Springer International Publishing Switzerland 2016
A. Ronzhin et al. (Eds.): SPECOM 2016, LNAI 9811, pp. 156–164, 2016.
DOI: 10.1007/978-3-319-43958-7_18

The proposed approach uses an idea of the transients modelling via MP from [5] but with the application to the entire input signal frame. MP with the time-frequency dictionaries that are formed out from the input signal by WP decomposition (*WPD*) parameterize the signal. Perceptually motivated cost functions can minimize atoms amount and the psychoacoustic criterion allows improving MP stage for the best parameter selection.

One of the fast developing field of audio/speech processing for which signal modelling highly necessary is coding. Modern transmission technologies such as *VoIP*, *VoLTE*, *DAB* allow to work with the wideband signal and require high quality of the transmitted signal. Many state-of-the-art algorithms work well with a specific type of the input data. Transform audio coders are suitable for the high quality music processing but they do not work in real time scale and do not provide high compression rate for the speech signals that vocoders do for example. Therefore, a task of the development of the universal audio/speech coder is highly relevant. One of such coders is Opus [6, 7]. It shows high quality of the reconstructed signal but its model is composite that process audio and speech separately.

In this work universal scalable audio/speech coding algorithm based on the developed bio-inspired sparse signal representation is proposed. One of the main goals of the conducted research is effectively work with all known types of sound content.

2   MP Algorithm with Perceptually Optimized WP Dictionary

MP is a procedure that maps a signal onto an over-complete set of functions called atoms which are selected from the dictionary D. The dictionary determined in the following way:

$$D = \{g_m(n), m = 0..M, n = 0..N - 1, \|g_m\| = 1\}, \qquad (1)$$

where M is the dictionary size, N is a function length. MP selects such atoms that has the best matching with the modelled signal, i.e. has the biggest inner product [1, 8]:

$$r_k(n) = a_k g_k + r_{k+1}(n), \qquad (2)$$

where $g_k[n] \in D \, with \, \max | < g_k, r_k > |$, $a_k = \, < g_k, r_k >$, r_k – residue at the current iteration k. Atoms must be related to the signal structure to make such decomposition useful. Based on this fact the redundant dictionary must contain functions that have good time-frequency resolution. These properties can be produced by WP based dictionary.

WP has a tree structure E with the corresponding scale level: $0 \le l < L$ and the node number on the scale level: $0 \le n < 2^l$. Each node $(l, n) \in E$ of WP tree is associated with the frequency band.

MP with the perceptually optimized WP based dictionary consist of two parts. At the first part of the algorithm, *WPD* tree growth is considered. This part is based on the cost functions minimization [5, 9]. One function estimates the information density of WP tree level (wavelet time entropy – *WTE*). The other one computes perceptual entropy (*PE*) for each node. The optimization stops when *WTE* or *PE* (or both of them) start to grow, or when the limiting tree structure is reached. In contrast of [5] in this work, the limiting tree is different from the critical band *WPD* (*CB-WPD*).

Second part of the algorithm performs MP procedure [5]. The input information for this stage is the signal frame; optimized WP tree structure; masking threshold and temporal masker; auditory excitation salogram. The goal of this stage is to select the most perceptual relevant atom g_γ from the WP-based dictionary. Selection is made by the best matching the original and the modelled scalograms. For the signals of N samples each atom is indexed in the following way: $\gamma \in (l, n, k)$, where $0 \leq l < \log_2 N$, $0 \leq n < 2^l$, $0 \leq k < N/2^l$. Figure 1 shows an example of the scalogram for the original frame and modelled with 200 atoms.

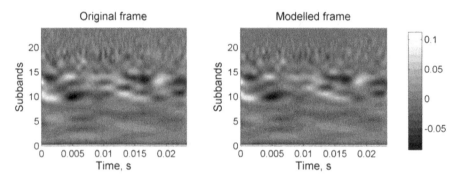

Fig. 1. Auditory excitation scalograms for one frame

MP stops when the desirable atoms number is reached. The energy threshold can also be a stop criterion of MP and this provides a scalability of the scheme.

3   Time-Frequency Plan Adaptation

The structure of WP based dictionary depends on the time-frequency (*TF*) plan of *WPD*. The reconstructed signal quality at the decoder side depends on how good *TF* plan adjusted to the input frame at the encoder side. The most appropriate tuning of *TF* plan for audio and speech processing is adaptation to the human auditory system. *CB-WPD* form [9] is chosen as the maximum tree structure and in most cases a huge amount of the input frames are decomposed based on this one. According to the numerical experiments, it was defined that the decomposition of the low frequency nodes is not suitable for sparse representation. As it is known from the uncertainty principle [10] it's impossible to obtain high frequency and time resolution simultaneously. Therefore, the terminal nodes at level 8 of *CB-WPD* tree have almost frequency resolution and scale factor can be expanded through frame segment length.

The modification of *WPD* tree structure growing procedure is consist in *PE* cost function optimization that responds to the individual nodes splitting. Therefore, the estimation of *PE* was reviewed based on the original expression [5]:

$$PE_{l,n} = \sum_{k=0}^{K_{l,n}-1} \log_2 \left(2 \left(nint \left(\frac{|X_{l,n,k}|}{\sqrt{12 \cdot T_{l,n}/K_{l,n}}}\right)\right)+1\right), \tag{3}$$

where $K_{l,n}$ is a number of WP coefficients $X_{l,n,k}$, k is the coefficient index, $T_{l,n}$ is the masking threshold, $\sqrt{12 \cdot T_{l,n}/K_{l,n}}$ is the maximum quantization step $\Delta_{l,n}$ in a corresponding node $(l, n) \in E$.

The cost function optimization is obtained by *PE* calculation based on selecting the most perceptually relevant coefficients $X_{l,n}^* = \{X_{l,n,0}^*, \ldots, X_{l,n,M-1}^*\}$ that is chosen according to:

$$X_{l,n,m}^* = X_{l,n,k}(\forall X_{l,n,k}/\Delta_{l,n} > 1), \tag{4}$$

where $m = 0, \ldots, M_{l,n} - 1$ is an index and $M_{l,n}$ is a number of the chosen coefficients $X_{l,n,m}^*$ of the node $(l, n) \in E$ and $k = 0, \ldots K_{l,n} - 1$ is an index of the input coefficient $X_{l,n,k}$. Then, applying $X_{l,n,m}^*$, $M_{l,n}$ in (3) instead of $X_{l,n,k}$, $K_{l,n}$ for *PE* computation and involving it in *WPD* tree structure growing procedure, allows to obtain a calibrated *WPD* tree that provides flexible *TF* plan for the low frequency nodes. Resulting WP tree has 24 instead of 25 frequency bands of *CB-WPD* and they are shown in Fig. 2. The objective assessments of the reconstructed signals of encoder/decoder solution using the calibrated *WPD* tree and *CB-WPD* as a maximum one is described in Sect. 5.

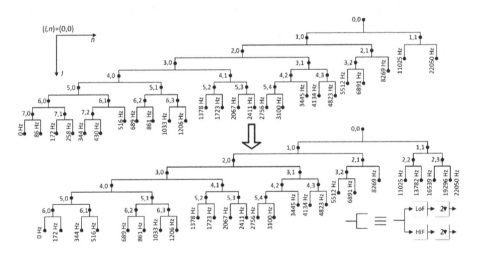

Fig. 2. *CB-WPD* (top) and the calibrated *WPD* (bottom) tree structures

4 Coding Algorithm Structure

The described modelling approach is used in the development of the universal audio coding algorithm that can effectively work with both audio and speech input signal. Its structure is illustrated in Fig. 3. The algorithm consist of the following main parts: adaptive *WPD* with psychoacoustical model, parameters selection based on MP, coding and quantization.

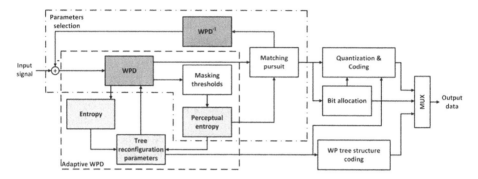

Fig. 3. Encoder structure

The audio encoding flow can be described as follows. The input signal is divided into the frames of 1024 samples length (for 44.1 kHz sampling rate) with the overlap between neighboring frames in 1/8 of the frame size. Adaptive *WPD* part computes the decomposition tree structure for each frame. Reconfiguration is based on the perceptual features of the input data. The decomposed signal and the psychoacoustic information are transferred to MP. At this stage, the algorithm is choose the most relevant in terms of the human hearing atoms from WP dictionary. The parameters are represented by the weights and their position in WP tree structure. The scalar non-uniform quantizer is used for the weights quantization and the tree structure is encodes via estimation of the difference between the frames in the quantization and coding block that produces compact representation of the selected parameters and provides the output data to the decoder side.

Fig. 4. Decoder structure

The input data is reconstructed at the decoder according to Fig. 4 where the parameters are recovered and dequantize and then they are allocated into the full WP reconstruction tree structure due to each atom position is obtained. The inverse *WPD* located in the signal reconstruction block produces the output signal.

5 Experimental Results

For the objective quality assessment of the proposed audio coding scheme *PEMO-Q* model [11] was used. This metric estimates the perceptual similarity measure (*PSM*). This mark can be mapped into the objective deference grade (*ODG*) and has the following scale: 0.0 – imperceptible impairment; −1.0 – perceptible, but not annoying; −2.0 – slightly annoying; −3.0 – annoying; −4.0 – very annoying impairment. As a test sequence, samples with a different content were used (Table 1). They are one-channel signals with 44.1 kHz sampling rate and 16-bit resolution.

Table 1. Test sequence

Test item	Description	Test item	Description
es01	Vocal (Suzan Vega)	si01	Harpsichord
es02	German speech	si02	Castanets
es03	English speech	si03	Pitch pipe
sc01	Trumpet solo and orchestra	sm01	Bagpipes
sc02	Orchestra piece	sm02	Plucked strings
sc03	Contemporary pop music		

The average bit budget for the atom encoding can be estimated in the following way. During the implementation of Huffman coding, bits distribution per each level of WP tree was determined. Sum of this number divided by the maximum number of the frequency bands (24 in the proposed case) shows the mean bit budget per parameter. Adding certain bit budget for the structure and the atom position coding shows that 200 atoms have the average bitrate 36.4 kbps, and each 50 atoms add 8.6 kbps for the bitrate.

Objective quality difference between the encoding based on the calibrated tree and *CB-WPD* expressed in *ODG* improvement is shown in Fig. 5.

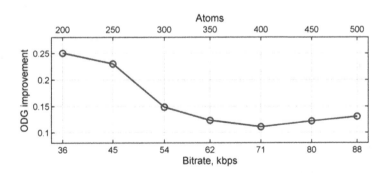

Fig. 5. Improvement of the calibrated tree

The enhancement of the assessment of the calibrated tree can be seen at every atoms set. The biggest improvement is in the low bitrate part. Moreover, for 250 atoms, the difference is 0.23 and thus the overall mark for the new tree structure is moved to the "imperceptible" impairment area.

The objective quality of each test sample is shown in Fig. 6. None of the test samples is located below the "slightly annoying" impairment. At the lowest bitrate, only three sounds are in the "slightly annoying" area. Speech sequences *es*02, *es*03 have the "imperceptible" impairment with the 200 atoms number. Speech-like sample – *es*01 (vocal, Suzan Vega), has mark in the "perceptible, but not annoying" impairment diapason, but closer to the "imperceptible". With the growth of the bitrate, the objective marks distribution moves to the "imperceptible" area. For 350 atoms (or 62 kbps), all of the samples have marks from −1 to 0 (only *sm*01 is at the border of −1 mark).

So as it seen, proposed universal audio/speech coding algorithm provides good quality of the reconstructed signals and effectively works with the different types of input sound content.

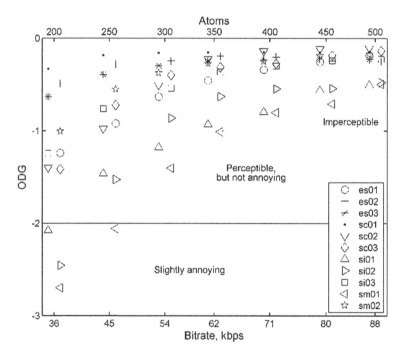

Fig. 6. Quality distribution of the test samples encoded by the proposed algorithm

With the help of the scalability scheme, it can run with the "imperceptible" impairment for all of the test samples by changing the atoms number on the go for each frame.

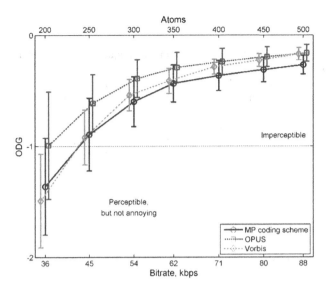

Fig. 7. Overall quality comparison

Comparison of the overall objective quality of the provided coding algorithm with the state-of-the-art coders (Opus and Vorbis) viewed in Fig. 7 (confidence interval is 95 %). It is seen that from 45 kbps and higher all three coders are in the "imperceptible" diapason. Opus mark for 36 kbps is on the border of this area. As for Vorbis and the proposed algorithm, they have "perceptible, but not annoying" impairment both.

6   Conclusions

The method of an audio/speech modeling based on MP with the psychoacoustic optimized WP dictionary is shown. This model allows preserving perceptual features of the processed signal and selecting only relevant for the human hearing components. The cost function optimization approach is proposed and applied into the encoder/decoder solution where it allows limiting WP tree structure for better sparse representation. The objective quality assessment of the reconstructed audio/speech signals of the presented algorithm is compared with Opus and Vorbis and demonstrated similar performance.

Further research will be focused on: MP procedure optimization that improves model even more; the encoding algorithm quantization scheme enhancement for the output signal quality increase.

Acknowledgement.   This work was supported by ITForYou company.

References

1. Mallat, S., Zhang, Z.: Matching pursuits with time-frequency dictionaries. IEEE Trans. Sig. Process. **41**(12), 3397–3415 (1993)
2. Chardon, G., Necciari, T., Balazs, P.: Perceptual matching pursuit with gabor dictionaries and time-frequency masking. In: ICASSP 2014, Florence, Italy, pp. 3126–3130 (2014)
3. Ravelli, E., Richard, G., Daudet, L.: Matching pursuit in adaptive dictionaries for scalable audio coding. In: EUSIPCO 2008, Lausanne, Switzerland, pp. 1–5 (2008)
4. Ruiz Reyes, N., Vera Candeas, P.: Adaptive signal modeling based on sparse approximations for scalable parametric audio coding. IEEE Trans. Audio Speech Lang. Process. **18**(3), 447–460 (2010)
5. Petrovsky, Al., Azarov, E., Petrovsky, A.: Hybrid signal decomposition based on instantaneous harmonic parameters and perceptually motivated wavelet packets for scalable audio coding. Sig. Process. **91**, 1489–1504 (2011). Special Issue "Fourier Related Transforms for Non-Stationary Signals". Elsevier
6. Valin, J.-M., Maxwell, G., Terriberry, T., Vos, K.: High-quality, low-delay music coding in the opus codec. In: AES 135th Convention, paper 8942, New York, USA (2013)
7. Vos, K., Sørensen, K.V., Jensen, S.S., Valin, J.-M.: Voice coding with opus. In: AES 135th Convention, paper 8941, New York, USA (2013)
8. Goodwin, M., Vetterli, M.: Atomic decompositions of audio signals. In: IEEE Audio Signal Processing Workshop (1997)
9. Petrovsky, A., Krahe, D., Petrovsky, A.A.: Real-time wavelet packet-based low bit rate audio coding on a dynamic reconfiguration system. In: AES 114th Convention, paper 5778, Amsterdam, The Netherlands (2003)
10. Strang, G., Nguyen, T.: Wavelets and Filter Banks. Wellesley-Cambridge Press, Wellesley (1997)
11. Huber, R., Kollmeier, B.: PEMO-Q – a new method for objective audio quality assessment using a model of auditory perception. IEEE Trans. Audio Speech Lang. Process. **14**(6), 1902–1911 (2006)

Combining Atom Decomposition of the F0 Track and HMM-based Phonological Phrase Modelling for Robust Stress Detection in Speech

György Szaszák[1]([✉]), Máté Ákos Tündik[1], Branislav Gerazov[2], and Aleksandar Gjoreski[2]

[1] Department of Telecommunications and Media Informatics,
Budapest University of Technology and Economics, Budapest, Hungary
{szaszak,tundik}@tmit.bme.hu
[2] Faculty of Electrical Engineering and Information Technologies,
University of Ss. Cyril and Methodius in Skopje, Skopje, Macedonia
gerazov@feit.ukim.edu.mk, aleksandar@gjoreski.mk

Abstract. Weighted Correlation based Atom Decomposition (WCAD) algorithm is a technique for intonation modelling that uses a matching pursuit framework to decompose the F0 contour into a set of basic components, called atoms. The atoms attempt to model the physiological activation of the laryngeal muscles responsible for changes in F0. Recently, WCAD has been upgraded to use the orthogonal matching pursuit (OMP) algorithm, which gives qualitative improvements in the modelling of intonation. A possible exploitation of the OMP based WCAD is the automatic detection of stress in speech, which we undertake for the Hungarian language. Correlation is demonstrated between stress and atomic peaks, as well as between stress and atomic valleys on the previous syllable. The stress detection technique based on WCAD is compared to a baseline system using HMM/GMM stress/phrase models. 7 % improvement is noticed in the F-measure compared to baseline when evaluating on hand-made reference. Finally, we propose a hybrid approach which outperforms both individual systems (by 11 % compared to the baseline).

Keywords: Prosody · Atom decomposition · Orthogonal matching pursuit · Intonation modelling · Phrasing · Stress

1 Introduction

The contribution of speech prosody in human speech perception and speech understanding is a well-known issue. Prosody provides cues revealing the information structure (by layering of the content in terms of its relevance) and adds information linked to emotions and attitudes. Automatic stress detection and phrasing are important, open problems in spoken language understanding.

Stress detection implies relying on some intonation models. The plethora of models can be split roughly into two groups: (i) surface models, which model

© Springer International Publishing Switzerland 2016
A. Ronzhin et al. (Eds.): SPECOM 2016, LNAI 9811, pp. 165–173, 2016.
DOI: 10.1007/978-3-319-43958-7_19

the pitch contour directly, such as ToBI, INSINT, Tilt, and SFC, and (ii) physiological models, that model the underlying mechanisms of pitch production, such as StemML, qTA and the Fujisaki model [1]. Recently, the physiologically based Weighted Correlation Atom Decomposition (WCAD) model has been proposed that models intonation by decomposing it into elementary atoms [3]. As these atoms pertain to model the activation of laryngeal muscles that change pitch, they can be used to infer higher linguistic meaning, such as the detection of emphasized words in an utterance [4]. In this paper, we assess the WCAD approach to automatic stress and phrase boundary detection in Hungarian.

The paper is organized as follows: Sect. 2 introduces the weighted correlation based atom decomposition algorithm for the F0 track. Section 3 presents the material used for experiments and the proposed approach for the alignment of the extracted atoms to syllables, as stress is related to the syllables. Thereafter, Sects. 4 and 5 presents the results of the WCAD based approach, using the hand-made reference phrase annotations as ground truth, and Sect. 5 compares them to the results obtained with the Gaussian Mixture Model (GMM)/Hidden Markov Model (HMM) stress detection system relying on statistical modelling. Finally, conclusions are drawn.

2   The Atom Decomposition Algorithm

The Weighted Correlation based Atom Decomposition (WCAD) algorithm[1] decomposes the pitch contour into a set of superposed elementary gamma distribution based atoms (1). The whole decomposition of the pitch contour takes place in the log frequency domain:

$$G_{k,\theta}(t) = \frac{1}{\theta^k \Gamma(k)} t^{k-1} e^{-t/\theta} \quad \text{for} \quad t \geq 0. \tag{1}$$

WCAD is built on the basis of a matching pursuit framework that uses the weighted correlation (WCORR) as a cost function, due to its perceptual significance [5]. The WCAD algorithm decomposes the pitch contour into two types of elementary atoms: (1) a global phrase atom, and (2) local accent atoms. While the accent atoms are calculated using (1), the phrase atom is calculated using a concatenation of a two gamma functions, in order to capture its dynamics [3].

The steps taken by the WCAD algorithm are outlined in Algorithm 1. First, the energy contour e, as well as the pitch f_0 and probability of voicing (POV) p contours are extracted. Then, the weighting function w used for the WCORR is calculated, and the algorithm uses the provided annotations, or alternatively the energy, to estimate the moments when phonation starts t_s and ends t_e. The phrase atom a_{phrase} is then extracted by determining the θ that gives the maximum WCORR for the whole intonation contour minus an offset t_{off} meant to compensate for phrase-final tones. The phrase atom is then subtracted from f_0 to obtain f_{diff} and forms the initial pitch contour reconstruction f_{recon}.

---

[1] The WCAD implementation code is available on gitHub at https://github.com/dipteam/wcad.

Algorithm 1. Weighted Correlation Atom Decomposition algorithm.

```
1: procedure WCORR ATOM DECOMPOSITION
2:     Extract f_0, e and p from waveform.
3:     w = e · p
4:     Extract t_s and t_e from annotation.
5:     Extract a_phrase at position t_s with maximum WCORR.
6:     Calculate a_phrase amplitude using CORR.
7:     f_diff = f_0 − a_phrase.
8:     f_recon = a_phrase.
9:     repeat
10:        Extract a_loc with maximum WCORR.
11:        Calculate a_loc amplitude using CORR.
12:        f_diff = f_diff − a_loc.
13:        f_recon = f_recon + a_loc.
14:    until WCORR(f_recon) > WCORR_thresh or a_loc < a_thresh
```

Next, local atoms a_{loc} are iteratively extracted from f_{diff} using the WCORR as a measure, by selecting the atom that maximises it at each iteration. Each new atom is subtracted from f_{diff}, and added to f_{recon}. Local atom extraction ends when either a) the reconstruction f_{recon} reaches a selected WCORR threshold, or b) when the amplitude of the atoms goes below a set threshold.

The selection of the local atoms is based on an orthogonal matching pursuit (OMP) approach [6] in which the amplitudes of all of the previously selected atoms are recalculated before calculating the new reconstruction and thus the residual for the next iteration. In this way, OMP takes into account the inter-atom interference due to atom overlap and uses it in the modelling process. Improved efficiency has been demonstrated by OMP over MP in terms of a faster diminishing residual energy. In our WCAD algorithm, OMP was implemented again using the WCORR as a cost function. The use of the OMP gives qualitative improvements in the WCAD algorithm with equal quantitative performance [2].

Two example atom decompositions are shown in Fig. 1 demonstrating the difference between the OMP and MP based WCAD implementations. Here, the top plot shows the waveform, the 2nd the F0 contour, phrase atom and the F0 reconstruction, the OMP extracted local atoms are shown in the 3rd plot, the MP atoms in the 4th, and finally the bottom plot shows the weighting function. We can see that although the two approaches give similar results, there are subtle differences in that the OMP atoms work together rather than against each other. This is for example evident in the atom complex around 0.3 s in which the MP algorithm extracts two small negative atoms that counteract the big positive atom at its edges. The OMP in contrast, produces three positive atoms with reduced amplitudes, eliminating the need for compensation.

3   Materials and Methods

We use passages composed of 5–6 sentences from the Hungarian BABEL speech database [7] (404 utterances in total). Word, syllable and phone annotations are available in parallel to a hand-made labelling of phonological phrases, which is used as a reference.

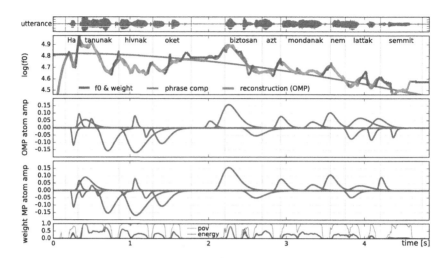

Fig. 1. Example WCAD output using MP and OMP for the Hungarian sentence "Ha tanúnak hívnák őket, biztosan azt mondanák, nem láttak semmit. [If they were warranted to appear they would say having seen nothing, undoubtedly.]"

Phonological phrases (PP) constitute a prosodic unit, characterized by its own stress and some preceding/following intonation contour. A PP by definition contains one and exactly one stressed position on its first syllable. Given Hungarian stress is fixed on the first syllable, phrasing (for PP) and stress detection are almost equivalent tasks (stress follows PP onset).

3.1   Stress Detection Based on WCAD

The F0 track of all utterances is decomposed by the WCAD algorithm (Sect. 2). The number of iterations of the atom decomposition, which directly influences atom density, is determined based on the duration of the utterance. We control atom density with an incrementation factor in the range 0.025–1.

The extracted atoms are then divided into positive (peaks) and negative atoms (valleys) and are associated to underlying syllables (atom position is also known). In Fig. 1, syllables peaks are labelled 'H' (high accent), and those with valleys 'L' (low accent).

If atom density is higher, one syllable can have several matching atomic peaks or valleys. Ambiguity becomes a problem if a syllable has both associated peaks and valleys. In such occasions, we apply a majority decision. If there is an equal amount of peaks and valleys, the atom which appears first is considered to be the dominant.

Given the fixed stress on the first syllable in Hungarian we hypothesize that (i) peaks coincide with initial (or singleton) syllables when revealing stress, and may appear on word-terminal syllables when associated to a continuation rise; (ii) valleys coincide with terminal (or singleton) syllables. Indeed, this valley is thought to be equivalent to a peak on the next syllable.

Following this logic, it is easy to construct a PP segmentation from atoms linked to syllables. We keep silence regions longer than 200 ms from the phone segmentation (and hence we know the intonational phrase segmentation), then proceed as follows: (i) a peak (H) signals a PP onset if it is associated with the first syllable of any word; (ii) a peak (H) signals a PP is ending with a continuation rise if it is associated with the last syllable of any word; (iii) a valley (L) signals a PP ending. If it is followed by silence, also the intonational phrase (IP) ends.

3.2 The Baseline GMM/HMM Approach

This system is documented in detail in [9]. The baseline relies on machine learning of a small set of PP types, based on their stress and intonation contour, using F0 and energy as acoustic-prosodic features. A labelled dataset is necessary for the training of the PP models. The Viterbi alignment is used to match PPs to the input speech, which yields a phrasing. The density of phrase boundaries can be controlled by an insertion likelihood-like parameter. This phrasing can be compared to that derived from WCAD.

4   Assessing Correlation Between Atoms and Stress

To test out hypotheses, we use the following relative frequency-like measures: the ratio of word-initial (WI) or singleton (WS) syllables associated with an atomic peak (H) vs. all syllables (syl):

$$R1_{H,I} = \frac{c(H|syl \in WI \cup WS)}{c(H)}, \tag{2}$$

where $c()$ is a count operator and $\cup$ refers to set union and $|$ to auxiliary conditions.

The ratio of word-terminal (WT) or singleton (WS) syllables associated with a valley (L) vs. all syllables:

$$R2_{L,T} = \frac{c(L|syl \in WT \cup WS)}{c(L)}. \tag{3}$$

As peaks can be also associated with WT syllables, we calculate another score, reflecting the ratio of peaks which are potentially IP boundary markers:

$$R3 = \frac{c(H|syl \in WI \cup WS \cup WT)}{c(H)}. \tag{4}$$

Results are shown in Fig. 2. Around 60 % of WI (or WS) syllables get marked by an atom peak (R1), and around 50 % of WT (or WS) them by atom valleys (R2). Around 85 % of peaks can be potentially relevant in signalling an IP boundary (see R3). For all measures, results are significantly better than chance, which confirms our hypotheses.

Two more additional measures intend to reflect the ratio of peak (or valley) syllables with respect to all potential WI (or WT) syllables, respectively. These measures are intended to give a recall related feedback, i.e. the ratio of words potentially stressed. For this, singleton words are distributed and added to the WI and WT mass according to their ratio seen in atom labelling (H or L).

The ratio of syllables with peak (H) out of all potential word-initial (WI') syllables:

$$R4_{I',H} = \frac{c(WI'|atom = H)}{c(WI')}, \text{where} \tag{5}$$

$c(WI') = c(WI) + c(WS|atom = H) + c(WS|atom \notin (H \cup L))\frac{(WS|atom=H)}{(WS|atom\in(H\cup L))}.$
The ratio of syllables with valley (L) out of all potential word-terminal (WT') syllables:

$$R5_{T',L} = \frac{c(WT'|atom = L)}{c(WT')}, \text{where} \tag{6}$$

$c(WT') = c(WT) + c(WS|atom = L) + c(WS|atom \notin (H \cup L))\frac{(WS|atom=L)}{(WS|atom\in(H\cup L))}.$

Results are shown in Fig. 3. As not all words are stressed, the theoretical maximum is well below 100 %: approximately 33–50 % of the words are stressed on average in Hungarian read speech [8]. Taking this into account, these recall rates are rather satisfactory.

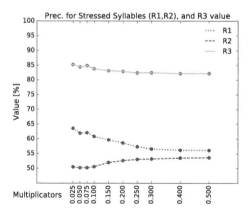

Fig. 2. Precision-like measures of PP recovery R1, R2 and R3.

An exact evaluation of stress detection can be performed if phonological phrasing is addressed. With this approach, both peaks and valleys can be simultaneously taken into account, and the evaluation is closer to possible applications as well. This is presented in the next section.

5   Robust Stress Detection

Once all utterances have the automatic PP segmentation ready, recall, precision and F-measures F_1 and F_2 are calculated to evaluate performance. Evaluation

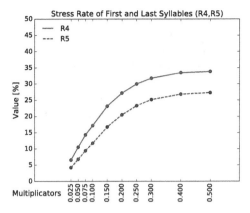

Fig. 3. Recall-like measures of stress recovery R4 and R5.

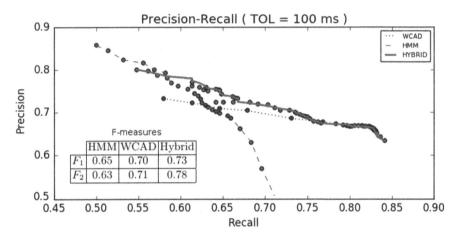

Fig. 4. Recall and precision of the HMM/GMM (baseline), the WCAD system and the hybrid system in phonological phrasing.

of PP segmentation is done with a leaving-one-out cross-validation in case of the HMM system, hence it is based on machine learning and most of the samples are needed for training.

The automatically generated (WCAD and HMM/GMM) PP alignment is compared to the hand-made reference. Detection is regarded to be correct if the boundary is detected within 100 ms compared of the reference one. In the respective sections we have seen that both the baseline and the WCAD methods allow for the control of PP insertion "willingness" of the systems. We use these parameters (insertion log-likelihood in HMM/GMM and multiplier factor in WCAD) to obtain plots of operation curves in the precision and recall space.

Precision-recall plots and F-measures can be seen in Fig. 4. In some operating points, the WCAD algorithm perform betters than the baseline. Regarding the F-measure, the WCAD system outperforms the baseline by 7 %.

Observing that the two systems yield different PP boundaries several times, a hybrid approach is tested. The combination of the systems occurs in the terminal phase, the two PP alignment predictions are merged so that only boundaries further apart than 250 ms are kept (to avoid overlapping intervals from the two alignments). The precision, recall and F-measures for the hybrid system are also shown in Fig. 4. The hybrid approach outperforms both individual systems (11 % improvement in F-measure compared to baseline). The average deviation between detected and reference PP boundaries was found 21 ms for the baseline; 23 ms for WCAD and 22.5 ms for the hybrid approach, because HMM system marked less phrases but more accurately than WCAD and hybrid system.

6   Conclusions

In PP detection for Hungarian, results confirmed the high correlation between atom peaks and stress and between atom valleys and upcoming stress on the next word. The evaluation of the two methods shows comparable performance: higher precision for the HMM/GMM baseline system and higher recall and F-measure for the WCAD system. A hybrid architecture was proposed which outperformed both systems in F-measure. The results have also confirmed the plausibility of using the WCAD algorithm as a means for inferring higher linguistic meaning from the intonation contour.

Acknowledgments. This work was supported by the Hungarian National Innovation Office (*OTKA-PD-112598*, *"Automatic Phonological Phrase and Prosodic Event Detection for the Extraction of Syntactic and Semantic/Pragmatic Information from Speech"* and by the Swiss National Science Foundation (No. CRSII2-147611/1, *"SP2: SCOPES Project on Speech Prosody"*).

References

1. Fujisaki, H.: The roles of physiology, physics and mathematics in modeling prosodic features of speech. In: Speech Prosody, Dresden, Germany, May 2006
2. Gerazov, B., Gjoreski, A., Ivanovski, Z.: Implementation of optimized matching pursuit techniques in weighted correlation based atom decomposition intonation modelling. In: 3rd International Acoustics and Audio Engineering Conference TAK-TONS, Novi Sad, Serbia, pp. 68–69, November 2015
3. Gerazov, B., Honnet, P.E., Gjoreski, A., Garner, P.N.: Weighted correlation based atom decomposition intonation modelling. In: Proceedings of Interspeech, Dresden, Germany, pp. 1601–1605, September 2015
4. Gjoreski, A., Gerazov, B., Ivanovski, Z.: Atom-decomposition based analysis for the purpose of emphatic word detection. In: XII International Conference ETAI, Ohrid, Macedonia, September 2015

5. Hermes, D.J.: Measuring the perceptual similarity of pitch contours. J. Speech Lang. Hear. Res. **41**(1), 73–82 (1998)
6. Pati, Y.C., Rezaiifar, R., Krishnaprasad, P.: Orthogonal matching pursuit: recursive function approximation with applications to wavelet decomposition. In: 1993 Conference Record of the Twenty-Seventh Asilomar Conference on Signals, Systems and Computers, pp. 40–44. IEEE (1993)
7. Roach, P.S., et al.: Babel: an eastern european multi-language database. In: International Conference on Speech and Language, pp. 1033–1036 (1996)
8. Szaszák, G., Beke, A., Olaszy, G., Tóth, B.P.: Gépi beszéd természetességének növelése automatikus, beszédjel alapú hangsúlycímkézö algoritmussal. In: Proceedings of 12th Hungarian Conference on Computational Linguistics (MSZNY), pp. 144–153 (2016)
9. Szaszák, G., Tulics, M.G., Tündik, M.A.: Analyzing f0 discontinuity for speech prosody enhancement. Acta Univ. Sapientiae Elect. Mech. Eng. **6**(1), 59–67 (2014)

Comparative Analysis of Classifiers for Automatic Language Recognition in Spontaneous Speech

Konstantin Simonchik[1,2], Sergey Novoselov[1,2], and Galina Lavrentyeva[1,2(✉)]

[1] ITMO University, Saint-Petersburg, Russia
{simonchik,novoselov,lavrentyeva}@speechpro.com
[2] Speech Technology Center, Krasutskogo street 4, 196084 Saint-Petersburg, Russia

Abstract. In this paper we consider a language identification system based on the state-of-the-art i-vector method. Paper presents a comparative analysis of different methods for the classification in the i-vector space to determine the most efficient for this task. Experimental results show the reliability of the method based on linear discriminant analysis and naive Bayes classifier which is sufficient for usage in practical applications.

Keywords: Language recognition · i-vectors · SVM · LDA · Naive bayes

1 Introduction

Speech technologies for various applications are widely developing in today's world. These are synthesis, identification, speech recognition. The last two technologies allow to extract different types of information from the speech signal: "who" is talking on the soundtrack and "what" it is said. However, it is also possible to obtain other type of information from the voice recording: speaker gender, emotional state, etc. This article deals with the problem of speaker language determination on the spontaneous speech recording [1].

Information about the speaker's language is important for a variety of applications. For example, application of the appropriate acoustic models for speech recognition can depend on the speaker language. This is particularly true for countries where there are two or more official languages. Language detection in automated processing of voice calls in a call centers and the Internet make it possible to improve its efficiency.

The most popular approaches in acoustic space modelling for language detection problem currently are based on Gaussian Mixture Models (GMM) [2] and their representation in the form of so-called i-vectors [3]. Also recently, much research has been proposed using Deep Neural Networks (DNN) and Restricted Boltzmann Machines (RBM) for speech, speaker and language modeling [4–6]. It should be mentioned that the problem of language identification is a multiclass, and the key issue here is the selection of efficient classifier for this purpose. In this paper, we investigate different approaches for the solution of the language identification problem: support vector machines, linear discriminant analysis, and Naive Bayes classifier.

© Springer International Publishing Switzerland 2016
A. Ronzhin et al. (Eds.): SPECOM 2016, LNAI 9811, pp. 174–181, 2016.
DOI: 10.1007/978-3-319-43958-7_20

2   The Structure of Language Identification System

The structure of language identification system by spontaneous speech recordings is a sequential processing of the input signal by the following modules: voice activity detector, speech features extractor, i-vector voice modelling, i-vector classification to determine the target language. The system scheme is performed in Fig. 1.

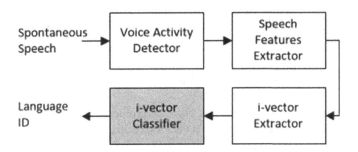

Fig. 1. Language identification scheme.

In this paper we use state-of-the-art methods for feature and i-vector extraction and concentrate on the problem of i-vector classifier investigation for language identification of the proceeding utterance.

3   Front-End Features Extraction

Speech detecting module consists of several preprocessing algorithms, including energy, clipping, tonal noise, overload and clicks detectors, briefly described in [7].

Acoustic features extraction module includes signal windowing by the segments of 22 ms length and 50 % overlap. Feature vector, used in language identification system, is a contaminated vector of the original MFCC features with its smoothed first order derivatives along some continuous time interval (Shifted Delta Cepstrum, SDC) [8]. These features are characterized by four parameters: M-d-p-k. M parameters means the amount of MFCC coefficients, using for SDC-features building, d – is degree of the smoothed derivatives, p – is a shift, that is used for SDC features extracting and k – is amount of MFCC derivatives vectors, taken for building the result vector. In this paper we used well-proven feature set of SDC features 7-1-3-7 with 56 features length.

For the acoustic space modelling we used Total Variability super-vectors (so called i-vectors) to achieve state-of-the-art performance. According to this approach, the distribution of the i-vectors can be expressed as following:

$$\mu = m + T\omega + \varepsilon.$$

where μ is the super-vector of the Gaussian Mixture Models (GMM) parameters of the speaker model,

m is the super-vector of the Universal Background Model (UBM) parameters,

T is the matrix defining the basis in the reduced feature space,

ω is the i-vector in the reduced feature space, $\omega \in N(0, 1)$,

ε is the error vector.

In our system the dimension of i-vector space was 600 and UBM was gender-independent with 512 components. UBM was obtained by standard ML-training. UBM and i-vector extractor were trained on the telephone part of the NIST's SRE 1998-2012 [9] and NIST LRE 2003-2011 [10] datasets (all languages, both genders).

In our study we used 10844 files with spontaneous speech in total. We also used a diagonal, not a full-covariance GMM UBM.

4 Multiclass Classification Problem

The language identification problem is a classical problem of multiclass identification, where the input data are multidimensional vectors. In this case, we are talking about the "open" task, as it is possible for input vector to be from the other language set. In this case input vector won't match any of the detecting classes and the detector should make an appropriate decision that language on the input recording was not included in the training set and it is impossible to detect this language or mark it as the "unknown" language.

The dimension of the input i-vector was set to be 600. The number of target languages was 10: Arabic, Chinese, English, French, Japanese, Korean, Russian, Spanish, Tamil, Vietnamese.

For training we used speech database with 15 languages with several dialects or accents for each language (28 accents in total). For testing we used NIST LRE 2007 database [9] that was not included in training, with 18 languages, 10 of which were target languages and 8 were used to simulate the situation of non-target languages.

In this research we investigated different classifiers in i-vector space. These were support vector machine (SVM), linear discriminant analysis (LDA), and Naive Bayes classifier. The brief description of these classifiers is presented further.

4.1 SVM Based Classifier

SVM classifier was firstly proposed by Vapnik in [12]. The main idea of SVM is to find the optimal separating hyperplane between two classes. The distance from a test i-vector x to the SVM hyperplane can be defined by the formula:

$$f(x) = \sum_{i=1}^{N} w_i K(x, x_i) + w_0,$$

where N - number of supporting vectors,

x_i - i-th supporting vector,

$K(.,.)$ - SVM kernel.

Since SVM classifier is designed to separate a set of input data into 2 classes, and language detection problem includes more than 2 languages, then individual SVMs were trained for each language, which should separate this language from all the others. At the decision making stage all SVMs output scores were compared to each other and the maximum score denoted the result language.

During the SVM training all accents and dialects of each language were combined into a single class. Thus, only 27 SVM classifiers were trained. We used linear kernel for our SVM classifiers. The choice of this kernel function was based on the fact that the amount of data for the majority of languages was comparable to the dimension of data equal to 600. Using complex non-linear kernels in these cases can lead to strong overfitting of classifiers on the training dataset.

4.2 LDA Based Classifier

Linear discriminant analysis (LDA) is a generalization of Fisher's linear discriminant, a method used in statistics, pattern recognition and machine learning to find a linear combination of features that characterizes or separates two or more classes of objects or events. The resulting combination may be used as a linear classifier, or, more commonly, for dimensionality reduction before later classification.

In the case where there are more than two classes, the analysis used in the derivation of the Fisher discriminant can be extended to find a subspace which appears to contain all of the class variability. This Due to generalization in [13], we suppose that each of N classes has a mean ω_i and the same covariance Σ. Then the scatter between class variability may be defined by the sample covariance of the class means:

$$\Sigma_b = \frac{1}{N} \sum_{i=1}^{N} (\omega_i - \omega)(\omega_i - \omega)^T,$$

where ω - is the mean of the class means. The class separation in a direction $\vec{\phi}$ in this case be given by:

$$S = \frac{\vec{\phi}^T \Sigma_b \vec{\phi}}{\vec{\phi}^T \Sigma \vec{\phi}}.$$

This means that when $\vec{\phi}$ is an eigenvector of $\Sigma^{-1}\Sigma_b$ the separation will be equal to the corresponding eigenvalue.

During the LDA training, similarly to SVM, all accents and dialects of each language were combined into a single class. Thus, only 27 LDA classifiers were trained. On the decision step testing vector was compared to the center of each cluster with the use of cos-metrics. Belonging to the concrete class was determined by the maximum value of cos-metrics.

4.3   Naive Bayes Based Classifier

Naive Bayes classifier is a simple probabilistic classifier based on applying Bayes' theorem with strong (naive) independence assumptions between the features. Abstractly, naive Bayes is a conditional probability model: given a problem instance to be classified, represented by a vector ω representing some features (independent variables), it assigns to this instance probabilities:

$$p(C_n|\omega) = \frac{P(C_n)p(\omega|C_n)}{p(\omega)}$$

for each of N possible outcomes or classes [14].

In this work we used Gaussian Bayes classifier, thus the value of $p(\omega|C_n)$ was modelling by Gaussian Mixture Model. However, it should be noticed, that this classifier used the information about all accents and dialects of each language. This means that the model of each language was represented as the mixture of multivariate normal distributions, which amount was equal to amount of all accents and dialects corresponding to this language:

$$p(\omega|C_n) = \sum_{k=1}^{K_n} \alpha_{n,k} N(\omega|\mu_{n,k}, \Sigma),$$

where K_n is number of dialects and accents of n-th language;

$\alpha_{n,k} = \dfrac{1}{K_n}$ is weight coefficient of k-th accent of n-th language;

$\mu_{n,k}$ is a mean of k-th accent of the n-th language.

Thus, one dialect or accent was modeled by one Gaussian distribution. It should be noted that, given amount of the training data for some accents were not enough. In order to ensure the classifier robustness we used one "shared" Σ for all Gaussian mixtures, and we used LDA before the Bayes classifier to reduce the dimensionality of data from 600 to 26 (the number of classes minus 1).

5   Experiments

We used NIST LRE 2007 speech data base [11] for our experiments. As quality evaluation metrics for classifiers we used the following:

1. The probability of correct language identification P. We accept the correct language classification if the classifier was applied to the input recording corresponding to the one of the 10 target languages, and the output language index matched the correct answer. At the same time the output of the classification $Score$ for that language had to be more than a certain threshold value T.

2. The probability of false acceptance *FA* (false acceptance). This is a situation when the input recording corresponds to non-target language, and the output classification *Score* is above the threshold T at least for one target languages.

3. Equal error identification rate P_{opt}. That is the point on the ROC curve, where the probability P is equal to $1-FA$.

We produced a comparison of the methods described in Sects. 4.1 (SVM), 4.2 (LDA-cos) and 4.3 (LDA-Bayes) on the evaluation data base (Table 1).

Table 1. Comparison of the classifiers on the base of NIST LRE 2007.

Classifier	P_{opt}
SVM	88.9 %
LDA-cos	87.0 %
LDA-Bayes	**89.5 %**

After that we produced a comparative analysis of the language detector robustness against the changing duration of the speech signal, which the i-vector was extracted from (Table 2).

Table 2. Dependency of identification reliability on the duration of the speech signal.

Classifier	P_{opt}			
	13 s	8 s	5 s	3 s
SVM	**84.4 %**	76.1 %	66.7 %	55.0 %
LDA-cos	82.6 %	75.3 %	67.0 %	55.5 %
LDA-Bayes	84.0 %	**77.3 %**	**69.2 %**	**57.1 %**

Figure 2 demonstrates the ROC curve of the identification reliability dependency P on the false acceptance for language detector based on the LDA-Bayes method.

After that we simulated the situation when the number of non-target languages increases. We propose that the classifier should be resistant to the change of the non-target languages amount. This was done by using an additional database with speech recordings in languages that were included neither in training set, nor in the first test data set. The experimental results are summarized in Table 3.

Table 3. Investigation of the classifiers resistance against the amount of non-target languages.

Classifier	P_{opt}							
	8 (original)	9	10	11	12	13	14	15
SVM	88.9 %	87.4 %	86.4 %	**85.9 %**	**86.0 %**	**86.1 %**	**86.0 %**	**86.2 %**
LDA-cos	87.0 %	85.4 %	84.2 %	82.6 %	82.8 %	83.0 %	83.3 %	83.3 %
LDA-Bayes	**89.5 %**	**88.0 %**	**86.6 %**	84.7 %	84.6 %	84.7 %	84.6 %	84.9 %

Interesting result in Table 3 is that SVM classifier is more resistant against increasing amount of non-target languages. Thus, for language amount increasing from 8 to 15 the

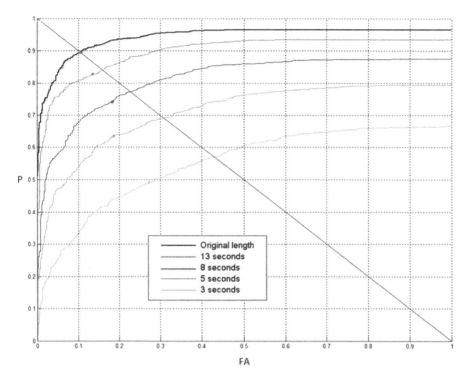

Fig. 2. ROC for different speech length (LDA-Bayes classifier).

reliability LDA-Bayes classifier dropped down by 4.6 %, while the reliability of SVM classifier by only 2.7 %.

6   Conclusions

This paper presents the investigation of the state-of-the-art language identification system by the spontaneous speech recordings. The aim of this research was to produce the comparative analysis of different approaches for classification in i-vector space for the most efficient problem solution. Experiments results for long and short speech recordings demonstrated slight advantage of the LDA based and naive Bayes classifiers. However, investigation of the system resistance against the amount of non-target languages show high performance of the SVM based classifier.

Acknowledgement. This work was financially supported by the Ministry of Education and Science of the Russian Federation, Contract 14.578.21.0126 (ID RFMEFI57815X0126).

References

1. Singer, E., Torres-Carrasquillo, P.A., Gleason, T.P., Campbell, W.M., Reynolds, D.A.: Acoustic, phonetic and discriminative approaches to automatic language identification. In: Proceedings of Eurospeech, pp. 1345–1348, September 2003
2. Torres-Carrasquillo, P.A., Singer, E., Kohler, M.A., Greene, R.J., Reynolds, D.A., Deller Jr., J.R.: Approaches to language identification using Gaussian mixture models and shifted delta cepstral features. In: Proceedings of the Annual Conference of the International Speech Communication Association (INTERSPEECH), September 2002
3. Dehak, N., Torres-Carrasquillo, P.A., Reynolds, D.A., Dehak, R.: Language recognition via i-vectors and dimensionality reduction. In: Proceedings of the Annual Conference of the International Speech Communication Association (INTERSPEECH), pp. 857–860, August 2011
4. Lei, Y., Scheffer, N., Ferrer, L., McLaren, M.: A novel scheme for speaker recognition using a phonetically-aware deep neural network. In: Acoustics, Speech and Signal Processing (ICASSP), pp. 1695–1699, May 2014
5. Lopez-Moreno, I., Gonzalez-Dominguez, J., Plchot, O., Martinez, D., Gonzalez-Rodriguez, J., Moreno, P.: Automatic language identification using deep neural networks. In: Acoustics, Speech and Signal Processing (ICASSP), pp. 5337–5341, May 2014
6. Novoselov, S.A., Pekhovsky, T.S., Simonchik, K.K., Shulipa, A.K.: RBM-PLDA subsystem for the NIST i-vector challenge. In: Proceedings of the Annual Conference of the International Speech Communication Association (INTERSPEECH), pp. 378–382 (2014)
7. Simonchik, K., Aleinik, S., Ivanko, D., Lavrentyeva, G.: Automatic preprocessing technique for detection of corrupted speech signal fragments for the purpose of speaker recognition. In: Ronzhin, A., Potapova, R., Fakotakis, N. (eds.) SPECOM 2015. LNCS, vol. 9319, pp. 121–128. Springer, Heidelberg (2015)
8. Kohler, M.A., Kennedy, M.: Language identification using shifted delta cepstra. In: Circuits and Systems, vol. 3, pp. 69–72, August 2002
9. NIST Speaker Recognition Evaluation. http://www.nist.gov/itl/iad/mig/sre.cfm
10. NIST Language Recognition Evaluation. http://www.nist.gov/itl/iad/mig/lre.cfm
11. The 2007 NIST Language Recognition Evaluation Plan. http://www.itl.nist.gov/iad/mig/tests/lre/2007/LRE07EvalPlan-v8b.pdf
12. Vapnik, V.N.: Statistical Learning Theory. Wiley, New York (1998)
13. Rao, R.C.: The utilization of multiple measurements in problems of biological classification. J. Roy. Stat. Soc. B 10(2), 159–203 (1948)
14. Narasimha Murty, M., Susheela Devi, V.: Pattern Recognition: An Algorithmic Approach. Springer, London (2011)

Comparison of Retrieval Approaches and Blind Relevance Feedback Methods Within the Czech Speech Information Retrieval

Lucie Skorkovská[(⊠)]

Faculty of Applied Sciences, Department of Cybernetics
and New Technologies for the Information Society, University of West Bohemia,
Univerzitní 8, 306 14 Plzeň, Czech Republic
lskorkov@ntis.zcu.cz

Abstract. This article has several objectives. First, it is to compare the most used information retrieval methods on a single speech retrieval collection. The collection, used in the CLEF 2007 Czech task, contains automatically transcribed spontaneous interviews of holocaust survivors and is to our knowledge the only Czech collection of spontaneous speech intended for speech information retrieval. Apart from the first experiments presented in the CLEF competition, no comprehensive experiments have been published on this collection to compare the different information retrieval methods. The second objective of this paper is to compare the results of using the blind relevance feedback methods with the individual retrieval methods and introduce the possibility of using the score normalization methods for the selection of documents for the blind relevance feedback. The third objective of this article is to compare different normalization methods among themselves. Exhaustive experiments were performed for each method and its settings. For all information retrieval methods used, the experiments results showed that the use of score normalization methods significantly improves the achieved retrieval score.

Keywords: Query expansion · Blind relevance feedback · Spoken document retrieval · Score normalization · Czech malach collection

1 Introduction

The focus of the information retrieval (IR) field shifted in the past years from the text IR to the speech IR. It is only natural that researchers from many fields like history, arts or culture request comfortable and easy access to the large audio-visual documents available nowadays. Listening to every audio document is impossible. With the improving quality of the automatic speech recognition (ASR) systems, the most frequent approach to handling this problem is the use of ASR to transcribe the speech into the text and then use the IR methods to search in them. To deal with the query words not present in the searched

© Springer International Publishing Switzerland 2016
A. Ronzhin et al. (Eds.): SPECOM 2016, LNAI 9811, pp. 182–190, 2016.
DOI: 10.1007/978-3-319-43958-7_21

documents the query expansion techniques are often used. One of these methods often used in the IR field is the relevance feedback method. The idea behind this method is that the relevant documents retrieved in the first run of the search are used to enrich the query for the second run of the search. In most cases, the retrieval system does not have the feedback from the user and thus it does not know which documents are relevant. The blind relevance feedback (BRF) method can be used, where the system "blindly" selects some documents, which it considers to be relevant and uses them for the enrichment of the query.

The paper presents the comparison of the two most used methods in IR and also the use of the BRF method. Experiments aimed at the better automatic selection of the relevant documents for the BRF method are presented. Our idea is to apply the score normalization techniques originally used in the open-set text-independent speaker identification problem.

2   Information Retrieval Collection

All the experiments were performed on the spoken document retrieval collection used in the Czech task of the Cross-Language Speech Retrieval track organized in the CLEF 2007 evaluation campaign [1]. The collection contains automatically transcribed spontaneous interviews of the holocaust survivors (segmented by a fixed-size window into 22 581 "documents") and two sets of TREC-like topics - 29 training and 42 evaluation topics. Each topic consists of 3 fields - <title> (T), <desc> (D) and <narr> (N). The training topic set was used for our experiments and the queries were created from all terms from the fields T, D and N, stop words were omitted. All terms were also lemmatized [2].

The mean Generalized Average Precision (mGAP) measure that was used in the CLEF 2007 Czech task was used as an evaluation measure. The measure (described in detail in [3]) is designed for the evaluation of the retrieval performance on the conversational speech data, where the topic shifts in the conversation are not separated as documents. The mGAP measure is based on the evaluation of the precision of finding the correct beginning of the relevant part of the data.

3   Information Retrieval System

In this paper, we wanted to compare the two still most used IR methods in the speech retrieval task. For our experiments, we have selected the vector space retrieval model and language modeling approach with several smoothing variants. In our previous work, we have experimented separately with the use of the score normalization methods for the blind relevance feedback in the vector space model [4] and in the language modeling environment - basic query likelihood model [5,6]. This paper presents experiments with more complex smoothing methods for the language modeling - the Dirichlet prior smoothing method [7] and the Two-stage smoothing method presented by Zhai and Lafferty in [8].

3.1 Language Modeling

For the previous experiments [5,6], the language modeling (LM) approach [9] was used as the information retrieval method, specifically the query likelihood model with a linear interpolation of the unigram language model of the document M_d with an unigram language model of the whole collection M_c (Jelinek-Mercer smoothing). The idea of this method is to create a language model from each document d and then for each query q to find the model which most likely generated that query, that means to rank the documents according to the probability $P(d|q)$. The final ranking of the documents according to the query is:

$$P(d|q) \propto \prod_{t \in q} (\lambda P(t|M_d) + (1 - \lambda)P(t|M_c)), \tag{1}$$

where t is a term in a query and λ is the interpolation parameter.

Dirichlet Prior Method. With the Dirichlet prior smoothing method the Eq. (1) changes to the form:

$$P(d|q) \propto \prod_{t \in q} \frac{tf_{t,d_j} + \alpha P(t|M_c)}{L_{d_j} + \alpha}, \tag{2}$$

where α is the smoothing parameter, tf_{t,d_j} is the term frequency and L_{d_j} is the length of the document d.

Two-Stage Smoothing Method. The Two-stage smoothing method is a combination of the Dirichlet prior smoothing and the Jelinek-Mercer smoothing methods. It is defined:

$$P(d|q) \propto \prod_{t \in q} \lambda \frac{tf_{t,d_j} + \alpha P(t|M_c)}{L_{d_j} + \alpha} + (1 - \lambda)P(t|M_U), \tag{3}$$

where $P(t|M_U)$ is a language model of the query user environment.

3.2 Vector Space Model

In the vector space model VSM [10] the document d_j and query q are represented as vectors containing the importance weights $w_{i,j}$ of each of its terms:

$$d_j = (w_{1,j}, w_{2,j}, ..., w_{n,j}), \qquad q = (w_{1,q}, w_{2,q}, ..., w_{n,q})$$

For the $w_{i,j}$ we have used the TF-IDF weighting scheme:

$$w_{i,j} = tf_{t_i,d_j} \cdot idf_{t_i}, \qquad idf_{t_i} = \log \frac{N}{n_i}, \tag{4}$$

where N is the total number of documents and n_i is the number of documents containing the term t_i. The similarity of a document d_j and a query q is then computed using the cosine similarity of vectors:

$$sim_{d_j,q} = \frac{d_j \cdot q}{\|d_j\| \|q\|} = \frac{\sum_{i=1}^{t} w_{i,j} w_{i,q}}{\sqrt{\sum_{i=1}^{t} w_{i,j}^2} \sqrt{\sum_{i=1}^{t} w_{i,j}^2}}. \tag{5}$$

The most similar documents are then considered to be the most relevant.

3.3   Blind Relevance Feedback

Query expansion techniques based on the blind relevance feedback (BRF) method has been shown to improve the results of the information retrieval [2]. The idea behind the blind relevance feedback is that amongst the top retrieved documents most of them are relevant to the query and the information contained in them can be used to enhance the query for acquiring better retrieval results. First, the initial retrieval run is performed, documents are ranked according to some similarity or likelihood function. Then the top N documents are selected as relevant and the top k terms (according to some term importance weight L_t, for example *TF-IDF*) from them is extracted and used to enhance the query. The second retrieval run is then performed with the expanded query.

In the standard approach to the BRF, the number of documents and terms is defined experimentally in advance the same for all queries. In our experiments, we would like to find the best setting of the standard BRF method and then compare it with the use of the score normalization methods.

BRF in Vector Space Model. First, for each document its similarity $sim_{d_j,q}$ is computed and the documents are sorted accordingly. For the selection of terms we have used the TF-IDF weight defined in (4).

BRF in Language Modeling. In the language modeling approach, the importance weight L_t defined in [9] was selected for weighting the terms for the BRF method, R is the set of relevant documents:

$$L_t = \sum_{d \in R} \log \frac{P(t|M_d)}{P(t|M_c)}. \tag{6}$$

4   Score Normalization Methods

In the previous work, the score normalization methods were derived for the language modeling IR system [6] and for the vector space system [4]. In the following, the derivation process will be summarized for the language modeling environment since its principle is the most similar to the open-set text-independent speaker identification (OSTI-SI) and then it will be shown how the normalization methods are used in the VSM system.

After the initial run, we have the ranked list of the document likelihoods $p(d|q)$. Similarly as in the OSTI-SI [11], we can define the decision formula:

$$p(d_R|q) > p(d_I|q) \rightarrow q \in d_R \quad \text{else} \quad q \in d_I, \tag{7}$$

where $p(d_R|q)$ is the score given by the relevant document model d_R and $p(d_I|q)$ is the score given by the irrelevant document model d_I. By the application of the Bayes' theorem, formula (7) can be rewritten as:

$$\frac{p(q|d_R)}{p(q|d_I)} > \frac{P(d_I)}{P(d_R)} \rightarrow q \in d_R \quad \text{else} \quad q \in d_I, \tag{8}$$

where $l(q) = \frac{p(q|d_R)}{p(q|d_I)}$ is the normalized likelihood score and $\theta = \frac{P(d_I)}{P(d_R)}$ is a threshold that has to be determined. Setting θ a priori is a difficult task, since we do not know the prior probabilities $P(d_I)$ and $P(d_R)$. Similarly as in the OSTI-SI task the document set can be open - a query belonging to a document not contained in our set can easily occur. A frequently used form to represent the normalization process [11] can therefore be modified for the IR task:

$$L(q) = \log p(q|d_R) - \log p(q|d_I), \tag{9}$$

where $p(q|d_R)$ is the score given by the relevant document and $p(q|d_I)$ by the irrelevant document. Since the normalization score $\log p(q|d_I)$ of an irrelevant document is not known, there are several possibilities how to approximate it:

World Model Normalization (WMN). The unknown model d_I can be approximated by the collection model M_c created as a language model from all documents in the retrieval collection. This technique was inspired by the World Model normalization [12]. The normalization score of a model d_I is defined as:

$$\log p(q|d_I) = \log p(q|M_c). \tag{10}$$

Unconstrained Cohort Normalization (UCN). For each document model, a set (cohort) of N similar models $C = \{d_1, ..., d_N\}$ is chosen [13]. These models are the most competitive models with the document model, i.e. models which yield the next N highest likelihood scores. The normalization score is given by:

$$\log p(q|d_I) = \log p(q|d_{UCN}) = \frac{1}{N} \sum_{n=1}^{N} \log p(q|d_n). \tag{11}$$

Standardizing a Score Distribution. Another solution called Test normalization (T-norm) stated in [13] is to transform a score distribution into a standard form. The formula (9) now has the form:

$$L(q) = (\log p(q|d_R) - \mu(q))/\sigma(q), \tag{12}$$

where $\mu(q)$ and $\sigma(q)$ are the mean and standard deviation of the distribution.

4.1 Score Normalization in VSM

The likelihood $p(d|q)$ in the normalization formula (9) can be replaced with the similarity $sim_{d_j,q}$, but since the likelihoods are in logarithms of probabilities the formula has to be changed to the form:

$$l(q) = sim_{d_R,q}/sim_{d_I,q}. \tag{13}$$

Then the actual score normalization methods can also be rewritten. We have done our experiments with the UCN and the T-norm methods since they are easily transformed for the use in VSM system. The WMN on the other hand, requires replacing the "world" model defined with the collection model M_c with some equivalent in the vector space. The UCN method can be rewritten as:

$$sim_{d_I,q} = \frac{1}{N}\sum_{n=1}^{N} sim_{d_n,q}, \tag{14}$$

and the T-norm method will now have the form:

$$l(q) = (sim_{d_R,q} - \mu(q))/\sigma(q). \tag{15}$$

Threshold Selection. Even when we have the scores normalized, we still have to set the threshold for verifying the relevance of each document in the list. Selecting a threshold defining the boundary between the relevant and the irrelevant documents in a list of normalized scores is more robust because the normalization removes the influence of the various query characteristics. Since in the former experiments the threshold was successfully defined as a percentage of the normalized score of the best scoring document, the threshold θ will be similarly defined as the ratio k of the best normalized score.

5 Experiments

First, we have done experiments with the setting (smoothing parameters) of each presented method to find the best one. Then thorough experiments with the standard blind relevance feedback method (the selection of the number of documents and the number of terms) were done for each presented method. We have found the best parameters settings and selected it for our baseline. Finally, detailed experiments with the score normalization methods were performed.

5.1 IR Methods

According to the experiments, the parameter λ in Jelinek-Mercer smoothing was set to the best value - $\lambda = 0.1$. The Dirichlet prior smoothing parameter α was set to the best value $\alpha = 10000$ and for the Two-stage smoothing method the parameters achieving the best results were found to be $\lambda = 0.99$ and $\alpha = 5000$.

Number of Documents for Standard BRF. We have experimented with the number of documents to select equal to 5, 10, 20, 30, 40, 50, 100. For all methods except Jelinek-Mercer (JM) smoothing it seems that the best results are achieved with higher number of documents. But we have found out that the number of documents and the number of terms to select are dependent on each other, so with 40 terms and 100 documents the result of JM is almost the same as presented in the results table.

Number of Terms. We have done experiments with the number of terms to select with all the described methods in this paper. The number of terms was selected from 5 to 45 terms, with 5 term interval (5, 10, 15...). For all methods, the experiments show that best results are achieved with a moderate number of terms selected - around 30 terms.

Score Normalization. In score normalization methods, the number of documents to select for the BRF is dependent on the threshold θ defined as the ratio k of the best normalized score. The final number of documents selected this way is different for each query. The experiments with the different ratio setting (from 0.1 to 0.95 with 0.05 distance) were done for all the methods presented. In the **UCN method** apart from the ratio k also the size C has to be set. Experiments with C from 5 to 800 with distance 10 were performed. The ratio k and the cohort size C depends on each other directly, because the normalization score in (11) is bigger (an average from the higher likelihoods) for a smaller cohort.

The final comparison of the vector space model (VSM) and language modeling methods with Jelinek-Mercer (JM), Dirichlet prior (DP) and Two-stage (TS) smoothing methods can be seen in Table 1. As can be seen from the table, in all cases the BRF methods achieved a better score than without BRF. All the score normalization methods achieved a better mGAP score than the standard BRF, except the WMN method in TS smoothing. The best score for all IR methods achieved the UCN score normalization method.

Table 1. IR results for all methods (mGAP score) for no blind relevance feedback, with standard BRF and BRF with score normalization.

Method	No BRF	Standard BRF	WMN	UCN	T-norm
params VSM	-	# doc.= 100	-	**k=0.95, C=295**	**k=0.35**
VSM(25 terms)	0.0456	0.0560	-	*0.0602*	*0.0597*
params JM	-	# doc.= 20	**k=0.5**	**k=0.25, C=85**	**k=0.55**
JM (30 terms)	0.0392	0.0513	*0.0568*	*0.0570*	0.0564
params DP	-	# doc.= 100	**k=0.5**	**k=0.35, C=710**	**k=0.4**
DP (35 terms)	0.0413	0.0523	*0.0572*	*0.0576*	0.0569
params TS	-	# doc.= 100	**k=0.9**	**k=0.3, C=245**	**k=0.55**
TS (30 terms)	0.0445	0.0574	0.0557	*0.0614*	*0.0614*

6   Conclusions

We have compared the most used methods in the information retrieval task in the environment of the speech retrieval. We have also compared these methods with the use of the standard blind relevance feedback method. For the standard BRF method, the extensive experiments have been done to find the best possible setting to be able to further compare it with the use of the score normalization methods. In all cases, the results were better with the use of the BRF method than without it and also were better with the use of the score normalization methods for the selection of documents for the BRF than with the standard blind relevance feedback. It also seems that the Two-stage smoothing method is the best method for incorporating the blind relevance feedback, the results show the biggest improvement when comparing without and with the use of BRF.

Acknowledgments. The work was supported by the Ministry of Education, Youth and Sports of the Czech Republic project No. LM2015071 and by the grant of the University of West Bohemia, project No. SGS-2016-039.

References

1. Ircing, P., Pecina, P., Oard, D.W., Wang, J., White, R.W., Hoidekr, J.: Information retrieval test collection for searching spontaneous Czech speech. In: Matoušek, V., Mautner, P. (eds.) TSD 2007. LNCS (LNAI), vol. 4629, pp. 439–446. Springer, Heidelberg (2007)
2. Ircing, P., Psutka, J.V., Vavruška, J.: What can and cannot be found in Czech spontaneous speech using document-oriented IR methods — UWB at CLEF 2007 CL-SR Track. In: Peters, C., Jijkoun, V., Mandl, T., Müller, H., Oard, D.W., Peñas, A., Petras, V., Santos, D. (eds.) CLEF 2007. LNCS, vol. 5152, pp. 712–718. Springer, Heidelberg (2008)
3. Liu, B., Oard, D.W.: One-sided measures for evaluating ranked retrieval effectiveness with spontaneous conversational speech. In: Proceedings of ACM SIGIR 2006, SIGIR 2006, pp. 673–674. ACM, New York (2006)
4. Skorkovská, L.: Relevant documents selection for blind relevance feedback in speech information retrieval. In: Text, Speech, and Dialogue, TSD 2016. LNCS. Springer International Publishing, Cham (2016)
5. Skorkovská, L.: First experiments with relevant documents selection for blind relevance feedback in spoken document retrieval. In: Ronzhin, A., Potapova, R., Delic, V. (eds.) SPECOM 2014. LNCS, vol. 8773, pp. 235–242. Springer, Heidelberg (2014)
6. Skorkovská, L.: Score normalization methods for relevant documents selection for blind relevance feedback in speech information retrieval. In: Král, P., Matoušek, V. (eds.) TSD 2015. LNCS, vol. 9302, pp. 316–324. Springer, Heidelberg (2015). doi:10.1007/978-3-319-24033-6_36
7. MacKay, D.J., Peto, L.C.B.: A hierarchical dirichlet language model. Nat. Lang. Eng. **1**, 1–19 (1994)
8. Zhai, C., Lafferty, J.: A study of smoothing methods for language models applied to information retrieval. ACM Trans. Inf. Syst. **22**(2), 179–214 (2004)

9. Ponte, J.M., Croft, W.B.: A language modeling approach to information retrieval. In: Proceedings of SIGIR 1998, pp. 275–281. ACM, New York (1998)

10. Salton, G., Wong, A., Yang, C.S.: A vector space model for automatic indexing. Commun. ACM **18**(11), 613–620 (1975)

11. Sivakumaran, P., Fortuna, J., Ariyaeeinia, A.M.: Score normalisation applied to open-set, text-independent speaker identification. In: Proceedings of Eurospeech, Geneva, pp. 2669–2672 (2003)

12. Reynolds, D.A., Quatieri, T.F., Dunn, R.B.: Speaker verification using adapted gaussian mixture models. In: Digital Signal Processing (2000)

13. Auckenthaler, R., Carey, M., Lloyd-Thomas, H.: Score normalization for text-independent speaker verification systems. Digital Sig. Process. **10**(1–3), 42–54 (2000)

Convolutional Neural Network in the Task of Speaker Change Detection

Marek Hrúz[1(✉)] and Marie Kunešová[1,2]

[1] Faculty of Applied Sciences, NTIS - New Technologies for the Information Society,
University of West Bohemia in Pilsen, Univerzitní 8, 306 14 Pilsen, Czech Republic
{mhruz,mkunes}@ntis.zcu.cz
[2] Faculty of Applied Sciences, Department of Cybernetics,
University of West Bohemia in Pilsen, Univerzitní 8, 306 14 Pilsen, Czech Republic

Abstract. This paper presents an approach to detect speaker changes in telephone conversations. The speaker change problem is presented as a classification problem. We use a Convolutional Neural Network to analyze short audio segments. The Network plays a role of a regressor. It outputs higher values for segments that are more likely to contain a speaker change. Upon thresholding the regressed value the decision about the segment is made. The experiment shows that the Convolutional Neural Network outperforms a baseline system based on the Bayesian Information Criterion. It behaves very well on previously unseen data produced by previously unheard speakers.

Keywords: Convolutional neural network · Speaker change detection · Spectrogram

1 Introduction

Speaker change detection is the task of identifying the instances in an audio stream when a change of speakers occurs. This procedure yields segments in which the audio sources are constant. From this point of view the segments can be generated by one speaker, by more (but the same) overlapping speakers, by noises, or by silence. These segments can then be used in different tasks, e.g. speaker identification, speech recognition, speaker adaptation and so on. The standard approaches are based on computing dissimilarities of two neighboring regions. They are usually based on the Bayesian Information Criterion [1] or other forms of distances such as the Generalized Likelihood Ratio or the Kullback-Leibler divergence. Energy-based approaches can also be found in literature [2]. Other approaches are based on classification [3]. In such setup each segment of speech is analyzed whether a speaker change is present or not. In this paper we present an approach with a Convolutional Neural Network (CNN) in a role of regressor. When a threshold is applied to the regressed value the decision about the segment is made.

© Springer International Publishing Switzerland 2016
A. Ronzhin et al. (Eds.): SPECOM 2016, LNAI 9811, pp. 191–198, 2016.
DOI: 10.1007/978-3-319-43958-7_22

2   Convolutional Neural Network

CNNs are deep neural networks with a special kind of layer - the convolution layer. In this layer the weights of the neurons are bound together into kernels. The layer performs a convolution of its input with the kernels. First experiments were conducted on images of handwritten postal codes [4]. Later the CNNs were redesigned to be able to classify a huge amount of images [5]. CNNs proved to be useful for regression. In this scenario they have been successfully used for estimating hand pose [6]. In speech, the CNNs have been used for speaker recognition [7,8], speaker diarization [9], speech recognition [10], or speaker adaptation [11].

2.1   Architecture of the CNN

The architecture of our CNN consists of three convolution layers with ReLU activation functions. Each convolution layer is followed by a max pooling layer and a batch normalization layer [12]. The last two layers are fully connected with sigmoid activation function.

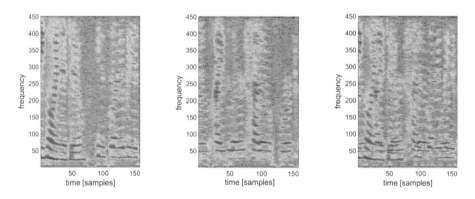

Fig. 1. Examples of typical spektrograms. The first depicts a segment where a speaker change occurs. In the second one there is no speaker change. The third is an example of overlapping speech.

There are 50 kernels in the first convolution layer with the shape of 16-by-8 samples. The 16 samples are in the time domain and the 8 samples are in the frequency domain. This reflects the usually rectangular shapes of high energy wrinkles in the spectrograms of speech (see Fig. 1) which correspond to formants and higher harmonics. The first layer serves as a "visual" features detector. The kernels should learn typical shapes of the energy wrinkles. The kernels are shifted by 2-by-2 samples. There are 200 kernels in the second layer with the shape of 4-by-4 samples, and 300 kernels in the last convolution layer with the shape of 3-by-3 samples. In these layers the shift is 1-by-1 sample. The role of the latter layers is the accumulation of responses of the shape filters from the first layer.

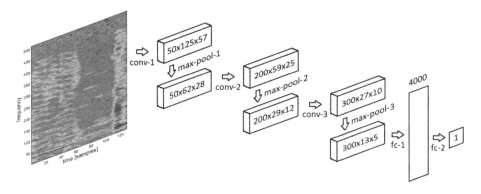

Fig. 2. Architecture of the CNN with the dimensionality of intermediate outputs.

Max pooling layers use windows of size 2-by-2 samples and are shifted by 2-by-2 samples. The first fully connected layer consists of 4000 neurons. The last fully connected layer has only one neuron. The scalar output of the last layer represents the likelihood that a speaker change is present in the analyzed spektrogram. To avoid any confusion it needs to be noted that this likelihood does not behave as a probability of the speaker change in the sense of absolute values (e.g. likelihood grater than 0.5 does not mean that a change is present). The CNN can be used for inferences about speaker change given a spektrogram. The architecture can be seen in Fig. 2 and is summarized in Table 1.

Table 1. Summary of the architecture of the CNN.

Layer	Kernels	Size	Shift
Convolution	50	16×8	2×2
Max pooling		2×2	2×2
Batch norm			
Convolution	200	4×4	1×1
Max pooling		2×2	2×2
Batch norm			
Convolution	300	3×3	1×1
Max pooling		2×2	2×2
Batch norm			
Fully connected	4000		
Fully connected	1		

2.2 Training of the CNN

The training of the CNN is a process of finding the optimal parameters according to a criterion given some data. We use the binary cross-entropy criterion

$$L(\omega) = -\frac{1}{N} \sum_{n=1}^{N} \left[y_n \log \hat{y}_n + (1 - y_n) \log(1 - \hat{y}_n) \right], \tag{1}$$

where y_n is the desired output, $\hat{y}_n$ is the output of the CNN, and ω are the parameters of the net - weights and biases. The desired output is either equal to one when there is a speaker change present in the spektrogram and zero otherwise. The criterion needs to be minimized and the optimal parameters are

$$\omega^* = \arg \min_{\omega} L(\omega). \tag{2}$$

For the minimization we used Stochastic Gradient Descent (SGD) on mini-batches of data. The batch size was set to 64. We used the Nesterov momentum [13] in the gradient updates, which has been shown to yield good results [14]. Similar to [5] we use momentum of 0.9, weight decay of 0.0005, and learning rate of 0.01. The update of the parameters is then

$$\omega^{t+1} = \omega^t + \Delta\omega^t - \gamma \nabla L(\omega^t + \Delta\omega^t), \tag{3}$$

where γ is the learning rate and

$$\Delta\omega^t = 0.9\Delta\omega^{t-1} - 0.0005.\gamma.\omega^t - \gamma \nabla L(\omega^t) \tag{4}$$

is the momentum variable.

3 Data

For the training purposes we used a fraction of telephone conversation data from CallHome [15] corpus. The data are sampled at 8 kHz and are in English. We consider only the conversations where two speakers are present. This gives us a total of 112 conversations. The input for the CNN is a spectrogram computed on a 1.4 s window of the waveform. The window is shifted by 0.2 s where another spektrogram is computed and so on. We compute 1024 frequencies with a window shift of 800 samples. Due to the symmetry of the spectrum we can omit half of the frequencies. Preliminary experiments have shown that the lower frequencies are sufficient to discriminate between audio sources. Thus the final shape of the CNN input is 256×128 samples (frequency $\times$ time).

3.1 Labeling of Data

The data are annotated according to the speech segments. The beginning and the end of a speech segment is labeled as well as the identity of the speaker in the segment and the transcribed speech. These are so called "turns".

From these annotations we create labeling of the data. These labels are then used in the training phase of the CNN. We define a tolerance threshold $\tau = 0.1$ s. We look at the boundary of each turn. The boundary represents the time of the speaker change. In our window the local time of the change is 0.7 s i.e. the middle of the window. We shift the window by $\pm\tau$ seconds. This gives us three spectrograms that represent the speaker change and we label them as "1". The negative samples are generated from segments of speech that last longer than the window size (=1.4 s). These are given a label of "0" and two consecutive windows must be at least 0.2 s away from each other.

4   Experiment

To test the efficiency of our proposed system we compare it to a baseline system of speaker change detection.

4.1   Baseline System

The baseline system uses a simple distance-based approach with a pair of fixed-length sliding windows. We use the Bayesian Information Criterion (BIC) [1] as the distance using Gaussians with full covariance matrices. In order to allow us to more easily compare the two systems, we adjusted the BIC decision process by replacing the selection of a penalty factor with the use of a distance threshold.

The Gaussians were computed on features based on Linear Frequency Cepstral Coefficients (LFCCs) of the signal using Maximum Likelihood Estimation. We used a Hamming window of length 25 ms with a 10 ms shift. There were 25 triangular filter banks which were spread linearly across the frequency spectrum and 20 LFCCs were extracted. Delta coefficients were added to the vector leading to a 40-dimensional feature vector. The parameters were chosen according to the work of Machlica et al. [16].

4.2   Evaluation

The probability of the speaker change is proportional to the ΔBIC value. The same holds for the output of our CNN. The comparison of the systems is based on the shapes of the Detection Error Tradeoff (DET) curves [17] and Equal Error Rate (EER). A point laying on the DET curve represents the relative false alarm and relative miss rate for a given threshold imposed on the output values of the analyzed system. The false alarm represents how many detections were produced in instances where there is no change present relative to the length of the audio data stream. The miss rate represents the number of speaker changes that were not detected relative to the number of all changes in the audio stream. A better system produces a DET curve that is closer to the origin (zero) point. EER is such a point on the DET curve for which the false alarm rate is equal to the miss rate. A better system has lower EER.

The baseline system does not require any training phase. Our CNN system was trained on 35 conversations. The duration of the training data is 5 h and 48 min. The remaining 77 conversations with unheard speakers were used for testing of both systems. The testing data have duration of 11 h and 20 min. The speech signal was analyzed window by window with shifts of 0.2 s. For the CNN we used window of length 1.4 s. For the BIC system we used a pair of windows of length 0.7, 2.0 or 5.0 s. The resulting DET curves and EERs can be seen in Fig. 3 and Table 2 respectively. We used tolerance of 0.4 s which is due to imperfect annotations and the 0.2 s shift of input window.

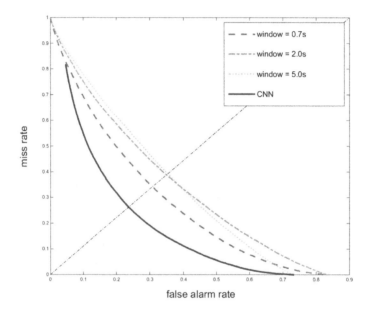

Fig. 3. DET curves for different systems.

The CNN performed notably better. It has to be noted that the telephone conversations are "wild". They are recorded as they were. No filtering was done. The turns are very frequent. One speech segment is usually shorter than one second. The BIC system is comparing the speech characteristics from neighboring windows. We experiment with windows of different lengths. When the length of the window is shorter the performance is better. But in such short times the extracted features seem to be not fully descriptive and a speaker change can occur based on the phonemes uttered rather than an actual change of speakers. When longer windows are used the system is failing because the utterances are shorter than the window and the speech characteristics of a single speaker cannot be modeled. The CNN handles short utterances well. It seems that the model is learning the shapes of the wrinkles in the spectrograms and finds out when a sudden change happens. The localization of the speaker change is not perfect.

Table 2. EER values for different systems.

System	BIC 0.7	BIC 2.0	BIC 5.0	CNN
EER	0.3229	0.3679	0.3704	**0.2482**

This is given by the length of the window used in training and by the shift of this window. The phenomena need to be looked into in the future.

5 Conclusion

In this paper we presented an approach for speaker change detection in telephone conversations. The conversations were unscripted and natural with relatively fast speaker turns. We used a Convolutional Neural Network trained on mini-segments of the speech (1.4 s) as a regressor. The CNN maps the input spectrogram to a value between zero and one where higher values mean a higher probability of a speaker change in the given segment. The CNN performs very well on unseen test data. Since the unseen data are produced by speakers not available in the training process it can be concluded that the CNN was able to detect the speaker changes via the visual changes in the spectrogram rather than by learning the acoustic parameters of the speakers. The presented CNN can be used as a filter of speech segments that can be helpful for recognition, identification, or adaptation of speaker/speech. In the future we plan to experiment with the architecture of the network more thoroughly. We want to test the capabilities of the network by presenting test data from different sources (e.g. TV broadcast) and different languages.

Aknowledgments. This research was supported by the Grand Agency of the Czech Republic, project no. P103/12/G084. We would also like to thank the grant of the University of West Bohemia, project No. SGS-2016-039. Access to computing and storage facilities owned by parties and projects contributing to the National Grid Infrastructure MetaCentrum, provided under the programme "Projects of Large Research, Development, and Innovations Infrastructures" (CESNET LM2015042), is greatly appreciated.

References

1. Chen, S., Gopalakrishnan, P.: Speaker, environment and channel change detection and clustering via the bayesian information criterion. In: Proceedings DARPA Broadcast News Transcription and Understanding Workshop, vol. 8, pp. 127–132 (1998)
2. Kemp, T., Schmidt, M., Westphal, M., Waibel, A.: Strategies for automatic segmentation of audio data. In: Proceedings of IEEE International Conference on Acoustics, Speech, and Signal Processing (ICASSP 2000), vol. 3, pp. 1423–1426 (2000)

3. Kartik, V., Satish, D.S., Sekhar, C.C.: Speaker change detection using support vector machines. In: ISCA Tutorial and Research Workshop (ITRW) on Non-Linear Speech Processing (2005)

4. LeCun, Y., Boser, B., Denker, J.S., Henderson, D., Howard, R.E., Hubbard, W., Jackel, L.D.: Backpropagation applied to handwritten ZIP code recognition. Neural Comput. **1**(4), 541–551 (1989)

5. Krizhevsky, A., Sutskever, I., Hinton, G.: Imagenet classification with deep convolutional neural networks. In: Advances in Neural Information Processing Systems, pp. 1097–1105 (2012)

6. Tompson, J., Stein, M., Lecun, Y., Perlin, K.: Real-time continuous pose recovery of human hands using convolutional networks. ACM Trans. Graph. (TOG) **33**(5), 169 (2014)

7. Lei, Y., Ferrer, L., McLaren, M.: A novel scheme for speaker recognition using a phonetically-aware deep neural network. In: Proceedings of IEEE International Conference on Acoustics, Speech and Signal Processing (ICASSP), pp. 1695–1699 (2014)

8. Kenny, P., Gupta, V., Stafylakis, T., Ouellet, P., Alam, J.: Deep neural networks for extracting baum-welch statistics for speaker recognition. In: Proceedings of Odyssey, pp. 293–298 (2014)

9. Sell, G., Garcia-Romero, D., McCree, A.: Speaker diarization with I-Vectors from DNN senone posteriors. In: Proceedings of Interspeech (2015)

10. Abdel-Hamid, O., Mohamed, A.R., Jiang, H., Penn, G.: Applying convolutional neural networks concepts to hybrid NN-HMM model for speech recognition. In: Proceedings of IEEE International Conference on Acoustics, Speech and Signal Processing (ICASSP), pp. 4277–4280 (2012)

11. Zajíc, Z., Zelinka, J., Vaněk, J., Müller, L.: Convolutional neural network for refinement of speaker adaptation transformation. In: Ronzhin, A., Potapova, R., Delic, V. (eds.) SPECOM 2014. LNCS, vol. 8773, pp. 161–168. Springer, Heidelberg (2014)

12. Ioffe, S., Szegedy, C.: Batch normalization: accelerating deep network training by reducing internal covariate shift. arXiv preprint (2015). arXiv:1502.03167

13. Nesterov, Y.: A method of solving a convex programming problem with convergence rate O (1/k2). Sov. Math. Dokl. **27**(2), 372–376 (1983)

14. Sutskever, I., Martens, J., Dahl, G., Hinton, G.: On the importance of initialization and momentum in deep learning. In: Proceedings of the 30th International Conference on Machine Learning (ICML 2013), pp. 1139–1147 (2013)

15. Canavan, A., Graff, D., Zipperlen, G.: CALLHOME American English Speech LDC97S42. DVD. Philadelphia: Linguistic Data Consortium (1997)

16. Machlica, L., Zajíc, Z.: Analysis of the influence of speech corpora in the PLDA verification in the task of speaker recognition. In: Sojka, P., Horák, A., Kopeček, I., Pala, K. (eds.) TSD 2012. LNCS, vol. 7499, pp. 464–471. Springer, Heidelberg (2012)

17. Martin, A., Doddington, G., Kamm, T., Ordowski, M., Przybocki, M.: The DET Curve in Assessment of Detection Task Performance. National Inst of Standards and Technology Gaithersburg MD (1997)

Design of a Speech Corpus for Research on Cross-Lingual Prosody Transfer

Milan Sečujski[1(✉)], Branislav Gerazov[2], Tamás Gábor Csapó[3], Vlado Delić[1],
Philip N. Garner[4], Aleksandar Gjoreski[2], David Guennec[5], Zoran Ivanovski[2],
Aleksandar Melov[2], Géza Németh[3], Ana Stojković[2], and György Szaszák[3]

[1] Faculty of Technical Sciences, University of Novi Sad, Novi Sad, Serbia
secujski@uns.ac.rs
[2] Faculty of Electrical Engineering and Information Technologies,
University of Ss. Cyril and Methodius, Skopje, Macedonia
gerazov@feit.ukim.edu.mk
[3] Department of Telecommunications and Media Informatics,
Budapest University of Technology and Economics, Budapest, Hungary
[4] Idiap Research Institute, Martigny, Switzerland
[5] IRISA Research Institute, Rennes, France

Abstract. Since the prosody of a spoken utterance carries information about its discourse function, salience, and speaker attitude, prosody models and prosody generation modules have played a crucial part in text-to-speech (TTS) synthesis systems from the beginning, especially those set not only on sounding natural, but also on showing emotion or particular speaker intention. Prosody transfer within speech-to-speech translation is a recent research area with increasing importance, with one of its most important research topics being the detection and treatment of salient events, i.e. instances of prominence or focus which do not result from syntactic constraints, but are rather products of semantic or pragmatic level effects. This paper presents the design and the guidelines for the creation of a multilingual speech corpus containing prosodically rich sentences, ultimately aimed at training statistical prosody models for multilingual prosody transfer in the context of expressive speech synthesis.

Keywords: Prosody · Speech corpus · Speech synthesis · Speech-to-speech translation

1 Introduction

The ambition of current state-of the art systems is not only to produce intelligible and natural sounding speech, but also to approach humans in their ability to convey emotion or a particular speaker intention [6,16,24,25]. For that reason, prosody modeling and prediction are arguably the most important research challenges in the domain of text-to-speech (TTS) synthesis [1,6,26]. The relevance of prosody for automatic speech recognition (ASR) has also begun to gain

© Springer International Publishing Switzerland 2016
A. Ronzhin et al. (Eds.): SPECOM 2016, LNAI 9811, pp. 199–206, 2016.
DOI: 10.1007/978-3-319-43958-7_23

appreciation, particularly with the advent of speech-to-speech (STS) translation systems [2]. Just as humans disambiguate spoken utterances and give them
a proper linguistic interpretation relying on prosody, automatic systems now
attempt do the same, which can be of particular importance in the context of
STS [22]. Furthermore, by taking sentence intonation and other prosodic features
into account, salient prosodic events, which represent intentional speaker deviations from the canonical prosody, can be detected and, if properly modelled, can
be carried over to the target language and introduced into synthesized speech,
with the ultimate goal of preserving the original speaker intention. However, the
treatment of salient prosodic events is a complex task, since their realization constitutes an interplay between the basic prosody features (intonation, timing and
dynamics), just as is the case with canonical prosody, which is generally determined by the morphology and syntax of the utterance (e.g. by stress patterns
and ordering of sentence constituents).

Since prosody transfer within speech-to-speech translation is a recent research
area, there have so far been relatively few approaches to analyse source speech
prosody in terms of salient events and carry them over to the target language.
The assumption that there exists some isomorphism between the source and the
target language greatly simplifies the problem. For instance, the research in [2],
using a bilingual speech corpus as training material, was based on performing
unsupervised clustering of intonation patterns in the source speech in order to
directly map them to corresponding intonation clusters in the target speech.
However, a general case where such an assumption cannot be made requires a
more high-level approach. In [19] the generation of pitch accent information was
integrated into statistical translation models using factored translation models
[14], in order to avoid possibly erroneous reconstruction of prosody of the target
utterance based on the translated text only. However, besides focusing on the
intonation contour and excluding other prosodic features from consideration,
both approaches are based on the detection of each and every pitch accent and
translating them to the output speech, rather than explicitly considering salient
prosodic events which occur relatively unfrequently.

The modeling and treatment of salient prosodic events is closely related to
prosodic labeling, i.e. annotating speech corpora for prosodic events (stress,
accent, boundary between prosodic constituents, emphasis etc.). Prosodically
annotated corpora are an indispensable tool for training statistical prosody models for a range of applications including speech synthesis or syntactic analysis of
spoken utterances [22]. However, the construction of such corpora is an extremely
time-consuming task, requiring a lot of manual effort, which makes such corpora relatively scarce and prompts the need for the development of automatic
prosodic labeling techniques [17]. To this date, a number of various classifiers for
automatic prosodic labeling of speech have been proposed (cf. e.g. [13,20,27]),
based on annotation systems such as Tone and Break Indices (ToBI) [3] or other
conventions for marking tones and breaks (cf. e.g. [9]), but their accuracy is
still below the one that can be achieved by expert humans. This paper presents
the design and the guidelines for the creation of a multilingual speech corpus

containing prosodically rich sentences, representing an invaluable resource for the research in the domain of cross-lingual prosody transfer in the context of expressive speech synthesis. The corpus has been created within the research project "SP2: SCOPES Project on Speech Prosody" supported by the Swiss National Science Foundation [23], covers 5 languages at the moment, and to the best knowledge of the authors, represents the only existing multilingual corpus specifically aimed at supporting the research into salient prosodic events and their cross-lingual transfer.

The remainder of the paper is organized as follows. Section 2 will present the content of the speech corpus in more detail and discuss the motives behind several choices that have been made. Section 3 will present the annotation guidelines and present several characteristic examples. Section 4 will briefly illustrate the utility of the corpus with an example research based on it, and Sect. 5 will conclude the paper with an outline of the future work.

2   Contents of the SP2 Speech Corpus

At the moment, the SP2 Speech Corpus contains sections covering English, French, Hungarian, Serbian and Macedonian, and each section contains recordings from one or two speakers so far, amounting to 7 speakers in total.[1] Following the existing guidelines for new contributions, the corpus can be easily extended to new speakers and new languages.

The set of sentences for a single speaker contains 50 prosodically rich sentences, with the same text translated into different languages. Each utterance has one or more words marked in bold to indicate emphasis. When translating the text into a new language, care was taken to preserve the original meaning of the sentence, but just as importantly, to preserve the emphasis in the translation without signaling it by other means such as a particular choice of words. For instance, for the Serbian sentence:

Đorđe$_{[n.\ George]}$ im$_{[pron.\ to\ them]}$ je$_{[aux.v.]}$ to$_{[pron.\ about\ it]}$ saopštio$_{[v.\ told]}$.

the translation into English "**George** told them about it" would be preferable to a translation that introduces a cleft sentence, such as "It was **George** who told them about it." The sentences are divided into the following 5 groups of 10 sentences:

- Emphasis on a single word. ("It turned out that it was a **fake** gun".)
- Emphasis early in the sentence. ("**Money** is what I like the most".) This specific case is treated separately in order to give a better insight into post-focus compression [5,8], i.e. the perceptible reduction of pitch range and intensity after prosodic focus.
- Emphasis marking an explicit contrast. ("Since he cannot **buy** it, he's going to **rent** it".) This section is expected to provide an insight into the differences in prosodic realization of the opposed syntactic constituents in various languages.

---

[1] The SP2 Speech Corpus can be downloaded from https://github.com/SP2-Consortium/SP2-Speech-Corpus, and contributions are welcome.

- Emphasis marking an explicit contrast in a question. ("Are you **emotional** or **rational**?")
- Emphasis as a result of semantic focus on a relatively large constituent. ("**It was because she felt so lonely** that she decided to move".) This section is expected to provide an insight into the speaker dependence of focus projection, i.e. the degree of variability with which different speakers map the semantic focus on a certain constituent into emphasis or pitch accent on particular words [18].

Each speaker was required to deliver:

- the described 50 sentences *with* particular emphasis on the words or parts of sentences marked in bold,
- the same 50 sentences *without* particular emphasis on the marked word or parts of sentences, to the degree to which it is reasonably possible, having in mind that in some sections, especially ones dealing with explicit contrast, it can be difficult to pronounce a particular sentence without emphasis, as emphasis "comes naturally".

The set of recordings for each speaker thus contains 100 utterances. The number of the sentences per speaker is arguably too small for the corpus to be directly used for training statistical prosody models, but it offers a possibility to study inter-speaker variability in using prosodic cues to signal emphasis in a particular language, as well as the relations between their use in different languages in a number of typical situations.

3   Annotation Guidelines

The existing speaker sets have been annotated with *Praat* [4], using the following interval tiers:

- **Emphasis**. The only mandatory tier, in which the emphasized word(s) are marked with '+', while other words are not marked. If the word is pronounced with an unusually strong emphasis, '++' is used instead. Clearly, not all words marked in bold in the text get a '+' or '++', but only ones actually emphasized. For each word marked with '+' or '++' in the emphasized utterance, there is a corresponding '(+)' or '(++)' in the neutral utterance (the non-emphasized counterpart), indicating the position of the corresponding word.
- **Contrast**. This is a semantic tier, which marks the opposing sentence constituents in sentences with explicit contrast (e.g. "Instead of getting a **rest**, I got **tired**"). Here, words in contrast ("rest" and "tired") are marked with '1' and '2' respectively. In some cases, where more than one element is emphasized on either of the opposing sides, multiple '1' or '2' tags are assigned. If a word is marked with a '1' or '2' in the emphasized utterance, it carries the same tag in the neutral utterance, regardless of the fact that it is may not be actually emphasized there.

- **Words**. This tier indicates boundaries between words, which are given in their orthographic forms in order to be matched with the text more easily.
- **Syllables**. This tier indicates boundaries between syllables, which are also given in their orthographic forms.
- **Lexical stress**. This tier marks lexically stressed syllables with a '+'. If the speaker stressed a different syllable than the one required by the standard pronunciation, a syllable actually stressed is marked with a '+' (in general, at least for some languages and particular words, there can be more than one acceptable location of the lexical stress).
- **Lexical tone**. This tier is applicable only to tonal languages or languages with pitch accent, and indicates the tone or pitch accent of a particular syllable (according to the conventions adopted for the langauge in question).
- **Phones**. This tier indicates phone boundaries and gives a phonetic transcription in SAMPA format. The purpose of this tier is to enable a more detailed analysis of pitch contours, since stress is usually related primarily to the vowel in the syllable.

The following point tier can also be used:

- **Breaks**. This tier indicates the positions of phrase breaks which significantly affect pitch in either of the two versions of the utterance. The purpose of this tier is to indicate possible sources of major pitch variations which are not due to emphasis. Unless otherwise specified for a particular language, such breaks are indicated by 'B' in both versions of the utterance even if their impact is significant in only one of them.

The following example (Fig. 1) shows the full annotation of the following Macedonian sentence (version with emphasis): "Сите мислеа дека тој **знаел** за заговорот." ("Everybody thought that he **knew** about the plot."). The contrastive stress is not marked, as there is none in this example. Similarly, lexical tones are not applicable to Macedonian, so this tier is empty, as well as the phrase breaks tier.

4   Example Research

In the course of the SP2 project several sections of the SP2 Speech Corpus have been used in research focused on salient prosodic event analysis and detection. Specifically we have looked at how emphasis is communicated in the three dimensions of prosody, through the comparison between emphasized and non-emphasized renditions of the same utterance. In the English language, both syllable duration [15] and energy [21] were seen as indicative of emphasis. Based on their analysis, emphasis detection algorithms were designed and evaluated using the SP2 Speech Corpus. Moreover, an adapted version of our Weighted Correlation Atom Decomposition (WCAD) based intonation modelling algorithm [10,12] was used to decompose the energy contour, achieving results in emphasis detection [11] comparable to the state-of-the-art [7]. The database is currently being used for the design of more sophisticated emphasis detection algorithms, as well as cross-lingual transfer of emphasis.

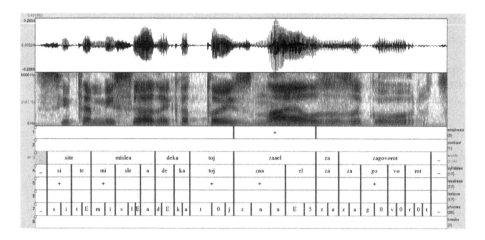

Fig. 1. Annotation of an emphasized sentence in Macedonian. In the corresponding non-emphasized sentence, the absence of emphasis would be indicated by a '(+)' marker on the emphasis tier, positioned at the corresponding word ('знаел').

5   Conclusions and Future Work

The prosodically rich SP2 Speech Corpus has been specifically designed for the research in salient prosodic event detection and their cross-lingual transfer. This is an area of research gaining particular importance with the introduction of STS translation systems which aim at conveying not only the information contained in *what* was said but also in *how* it was said. The corpus in its current form covers 5 languages and includes voices of 7 speakers, each having delivered 50 pairs of unemphasised-emphasised utterances, divided into 5 categories based on the type and/or location of emphasis. Our team has, thus far, used the corpus to successfully design and evaluate emphasis detection algorithms. It is our intention that the corpus should be of use for research conducted by the whole scientific community. Moreover, owing to well-defined guidelines for preparing contributions to the corpus, it is our hope that the community will help the corpus to expand to other languages soon.

Acknowledgments. The authors would like to acknowledge the support of the Swiss National Science Foundation via the research project "SP2: SCOPES Project on Speech Prosody".

References

1. Adámek, J.: Neural networks controlling prosody of Czech language. Magister thesis, Univerzita Karlova v Praze, Matematicko-fyzikaln fakulta (2002)
2. Agüero, P.D., Adell, J., Bonafonte, A.: Prosody generation for speech-to-speech translation. In: Proceedings of the IEEE International Conference on Acoustics, Speech and Signal Processing, pp. 557–560 (2006)

3. Beckman, M.E., Hirschberg, J.B., Shattuck-Hufnagel, S.: The original ToBI system and the evolution of the ToBI framework. In: Prosodic Models and Transcription: Towards Prosodic Typology, pp. 9–54 (2004)
4. Boersma, P., et al.: Praat, a system for doing phonetics by computer. Glot Int. 5(9/10), 341–345 (2002)
5. Botinis, A., Fourakis, M., Gawronska, B.: Focus identification in English, Greek and Swedish. In: Proceedings of The 14th International Congress of Phonetic Sciences, San Francisco, pp. 1557–1560 (1999)
6. Bulut, M., Narayanan, S.S., Syrdal, A.K.: Expressive speech synthesis using a concatenative synthesizer. In: Proceedings of Interspeech (2002)
7. Cernak, M., Honnet, P.E.: An empirical model of emphatic word detection. In: Proceedings of Interspeech, Dresden, Germany, September 2015
8. Chen, S., Wang, B., Xu, Y.: Closely related languages, differentways ofrealizing focus. In: Proceedings of Interspeech, pp. 1007–1010 (2009)
9. Gallwitz, F., Niemann, H., Nöth, E., Warnke, V.: Integrated recognition of words and prosodic phrase boundaries. Speech Commun. 36(1), 81–95 (2002)
10. Gerazov, B., Honnet, P.E., Gjoreski, A., Garner, P.N.: Weighted correlation based atom decomposition intonation modelling. In: Proceedings of Interspeech, pp. 1601–1605, Dresden, Germany, September 2015
11. Gjoreski, A., Gerazov, B., Ivanovski, Z.: Atom-decomposition based analysis for the purpose of emphatic word detection. In: XII International Conference ETAI, Ohrid, Macedonia, September 2015
12. Honnet, P.E., Gerazov, B., Garner, P.N.: Atom decomposition-based intonation modelling. In: Proceedings of the IEEE International Conference on Acoustics, Speech and Signal Processing, pp. 4744–4748. IEEE, Brisbane, Australia, April 2015
13. Jeon, J.H., Liu, Y.: Syllable-level prominence detection with acoustic evidence. In: Eleventh Annual Conference of the International Speech Communication Association (2010)
14. Koehn, P., Hoang, H.: Factored translation models. In: EMNLP-CoNLL, pp. 868–876 (2007)
15. Melov, A., Gerazov, B., Ivanovski, Z.: Emphatic word detection based on syllable durations. In: XII International Conference ETAI, Ohrid, Macedonia, September 2015
16. Pitrelli, J.F., Bakis, R., Eide, E.M., Fernandez, R., Hamza, W., Picheny, M.A.: The IBM expressive text-to-speech synthesis system for American English. IEEE Trans. Audio Speech Lang. Process. 14(4), 1099–1108 (2006)
17. Rosenberg, A.: Automatic detection and classification of prosodic events. Ph.D. thesis, Columbia University, NY, USA (2009)
18. Selkirk, E.: Sentence prosody: intonation, stress, and phrasing. In: Goldsmith, J.A. (ed.) The Handbook of Phonological Theory, Blackwell Handbooks in Linguistics, vol. 1, chap. 16, pp. 550–569. Blackwell Publishers, Oxford, UK (1995)
19. Sridhar, V.K.R., Bangalore, S., Narayanan, S.S.: Factored translation models for enriching spoken language translation with prosody. In: Proceedings of Interspeech, pp. 2723–2726 (2008)
20. Sridhar, V.K.R., Nenkova, A., Narayanan, S., Jurafsky, D.: Detecting prominence in conversational speech: pitch accent, givenness and focus. In: Proceedings of Speech Prosody, vol. 453, p. 456 (2008)
21. Stojkovic, A., Gerazov, B., Ivanovski, Z.: Emphatic word detection based on relative phoneme energies within syllables. In: XII International Conference ETAI, Ohrid, Macedonia, September 2015

22. Szaszák, G., Beke, A.: Exploiting prosody for automatic syntactic phrase boundary detection in speech. J. Lang. Model. **1**, 143–172 (2012)
23. Szaszák, G., Gábor Csapó, T., Garner, P.N., Gerazov, B., Ivanovski, Z., Németh, G., Tóth, B., Sečujski, M., Delić, V.: The SP2 SCOPES project on speech prosody. In: Proceedings of the DOGS - Digital Speech and Image Processing Conference, pp. 2–10, Novi Sad, Serbia, October 2014
24. Szekely, E., Csapó, T.G., Toth, B., Mihajlik, P., Carson-Berndsen, J.: Synthesizing expressive speech from amateur audiobook recordings. In: Spoken Language Technology Workshop, SLT 2012, pp. 297–302. IEEE (2012)
25. Tatham, M., Morton, K.: Developments in Speech Synthesis. Wiley, New York (2005)
26. Taylor, P.: Text-to-Speech Synthesis. Cambridge University Press, Cambridge (2009)
27. Vicsi, K., Szaszák, G.: Using prosody to improve automatic speech recognition. Speech Commun. **52**(5), 413–426 (2010)

Designing High-Coverage Multi-level Text Corpus for Non-professional-voice Conservation

Markéta Jůzová[1,2]([✉]), Daniel Tihelka[2], and Jindřich Matoušek[1,2]

[1] Faculty of Applied Sciences, Department of Cybernetics,
University of West Bohemia, Pilsen, Czech Republic
[2] NTIS-New Technologies for the Information Society, Faculty of Applied Sciences,
University of West Bohemia, Pilsen, Czech Republic
{juzova,dtihelka,jmatouse}@ntis.zcu.cz

Abstract. The paper focuses on building a text corpus suitable for the conservation of the voices of non-professional speakers, who are loosing their voices due to serious healthy problems. Since we do not know in advance, how many sentences a speaker will be able to record, we propose a multi-level greedy algorithm which can ensure the coverage of selected texts by various phonetic and prosodic units. The comparison of such coverage is presented for various corpus sizes, and compared to the generic TTS corpus recorded by a healthy professional speaker.

Keywords: Voice conservation · Voice banking · Speech synthesis · Text corpus · Phone · Diphone · Greedy algorithm

1 Introduction

In the last decade, speech technology became extremely useful helping handicapped people to improve their quality of life. Let us name, above all, the support programmes for the blind or vision impaired (so-called screen readers which utilize text-to-speech (TTS) technology to read out the contents of the screen) and for the dumb or speech impaired (so-called speaking aids which use TTS to enable the speech impaired to communicate with voice).

Recent advances in speech synthesis have also shown that TTS technology is mature enough to offer synthetic speech of a reasonable quality, also in a very specific application so-called *personalised speech synthesis*. Such an application can primarily be used by persons loosing their ability to speak due to a severe illnesses or degradations of their vocal tract, and it enables them to communicate somehow with their original voice. However, prior to the creation of the personalised synthesizer, a person must record a number of samples, ideally in high quality, which will serve as the source for the personalization. Such process is usually called as *voice conservation*, or *voice banking*. The main problem is

The research has received funding from the Norwegian Financial Mechanism 2009–2014 and the Ministry of Education, Youth and Sports under Project Contract no. MSMT-28477/2014, Project no. 7F14236 (HCENAT).

A. Ronzhin et al. (Eds.): SPECOM 2016, LNAI 9811, pp. 207–215, 2016.
DOI: 10.1007/978-3-319-43958-7_24

that we do not know in advance, how many samples will those people be able to record. For example, patients diagnosed with severe laryngeal cancer have in average approximately 2 weeks between the diagnosis and the total laryngectomy, but sometimes there are only few days from a diagnosis to the surgery — and besides other consequences, the patient permanently loses the ability to communicate with voice [5,13]. As a result, a significantly lower amount of speech recordings are obtained from such patients when compared to healthy professional speakers used to record "generic" TTS. In addition, the quality of the recordings is often considerably deteriorated, as the patients usually has no experience with speech recording and/or with using a computer, they are most likely rather distressed with a progressing disease, and the quality of their voice is often very affected by the disease. All the aforementioned facts make the design of a personalised speech synthesizer which would "speak" in the patient's own voice very challenging.

The limited amount of recorded samples is often coped with using a statistical parametric speech synthesis framework (HMM based), in which an average statistical model trained from many voices is adapted by a small number of the particular target conserved recordings [15]. A different approach was chosen by [11] who used voice conversion to convert alaryngeal speech produced by the laryngectomised patient to a more human-like speech. However, both the quality of synthetic/converted speech and the resemblance of synthetic/converted voice to the original one still suffer from the principle of speech vocoding/conversion given the limited amount of the target speech data.

Our primary goal is, in the contrary, to prepare source material allowing to efficiently record as much speech data from a non-proffesional speakers as possible, given their limited time and speaking abilities. In this way, the voice of the patient can be conserved forever, and later used to create a high-quality personalised synthesizer for a pocket device like a smartphone, or, in a distant future, for a device implanted into the body of the speaker.

We also try to design the material for recording in such a way, that it can be used to create a synthetic voice directly, avoiding any voice conversion or adaptation technique. Depending on the amount of recorded data, HMM synthesis mentioned above (for smaller number of recordings) and unit selection (yielding very good quality when more recordings are available) could be used as the actual speech synthesis methods. To achieve this, we propose an algorithm for text corpus design which, in multiple levels, optimises its both phonetic and prosodic coverage. The resulting text prompts are then recorded in a level-by-level fashion.

2   Text Corpus Building

As mentioned in Sect. 1, the aim is to prepare a (smaller) text corpus for the voice conservation recording. Our primary requirement is to maximize the coverage of appropriate speech units, no matter the number of sentences will finally be recorded. Since the unit selection synthesis is considered to be more natural compared to HMM synthesis [10], we focus primary to that, while HMM represents a backup solution when too few recordings are available.

2.1   Source Text Data Analysis

For the purpose of our TTS system research and development, we have at disposal a large collection of Czech texts – 524,481 sentences from various domains (news, culture, economy, sport, etc.). In the phonetic form, converted into by our TTS frontend using letter-to-phone rules ([9], we intentionally work on finer level than on phonemes), these texts contain all 44 Czech phones, with the rarest phone being e_u, one of three Czech diphthongs occurring in loanwords, with 1,412 occurrences (0.0034 % of the whole phone set). Theoretically, the total number of diphones[1] should be $44^2 = 1,936$. Nevertheless, as follows from our text materials and linguistic rules, some phone combinations are inapplicable in Czech (even at word boundaries). Thus, the text collection contains only 1,397 of diphones, with 41 of them occurring only once.

The average sentence length is 13.8 words in the whole collection. Nevertheless, since we are building a text corpus for voice banking, the speakers are usually not professionals, not used to talk publicly, often with only basic computer control skills. Long sentences, in general, are thus quite difficult to concentrate on and to read them fluently without any stammering, spoonerisms and mispronunciations. Also, the final synthetic voice is expected to be used mainly for common communication in which rather shorter sentences are used. On the other hand, however, very short sentences (containing 3 words and less) have different prosodic structure comparing to "average" sentences. Therefore, we decided to leave only sentences with the length from 5 to 8 words in our source data. In addition, also those containing some very long, usually foreign-like words difficult for reading, were excluded. Note that we can do that because all theoretically synthesized foreign-like words are ordinarily transcribed with Czech phones. The proposed length preselection should be a good compromise between the number of words non-professionals are able to read fluently, and the need to keep the natural sentence structure. The number of available sentences thus decreases to 97,033, approximately one fifth being questions.

Our further attention was focused on the missing diphones. We stated above that the collection does not contain all theoretically possible diphones and the removal of long and short sentences has also caused a further loss. To encourage the presence of rare, yet meaningful, diphones, the additional set of almost 1,500 sentences was prepared manually to cover the rare or missing diphones. Since we are aware that these sentences are a bit more difficult for reading (they contain shorter, but not very common words), we added them into higher levels of the source data (see Sect. 2.3, step 4).

---

[1] We consider here a *diphone* as TTS system unit, i.e. signal from a middle of one phone to the middle of the next phone. Nevertheless, the numbers presented will be the same when considering a diphone as the join of any two neighbouring phones.

To ensure not only phonetically, but also prosodically covered corpus, the phonetic form was tied with prosodeme–based symbolic prosody description [12]. It means that words in the collection sentences were first joined into prosodic words, each of them was then assigned with the following base prosodeme types: 0 - "null" prosodeme, 1 - declarative prosodeme, 2 - interrogative prosodeme and 3 - non-terminating prosodeme (for details see [12]). Such a description allows us to capture the base, but the most prominent prosodic patterns of each sentence as expected[2] to be pronounced. Having the prosodeme labels, each phonetic unit can be tied with the prosodeme type according to the prosodic word it belongs to (see prosodic grammar description in [14] for the example) – we will call these couple units phone-in-prosodeme and diphone-in-prosodeme, respectively.

2.2 Greedy Algorithm for Sentences Selection

When recording a phonetically and prosodically rich corpus for a generic high-quality TTS system, we can presume that a professional or semi-professional speaker will record the whole corpus, and thus we can use a single criterion for the text corpus building – e.g. 10,000 sentences with uniformly balanced diphones-in-prosodeme with at least 5 occurrences of each [7,8]. However, not knowing the number of sentences finally recorded, we cannot use such a global requirement – when maximizing one criterion, there is no guarantee that other requirements (e.g. at least 50 phone occurrences) will be satisfied as well.

To deal with this, we have split the corpus building process into several steps, where in each step a different *level* of units is used to maximize their coverage. In each step (i.e. units level), we have used the greedy algorithm, described in [8], which ensures that with each selected sentence it maximizes the given criteria. Thus, no matter the number of sentences a speaker is able to record, we can guarantee the highest coverage reached by the last recorded sentence at the level the sentence belongs to, as well as the fulfilment of all lower-level criteria.

2.3 Multi-level Text Corpus Building

Let us describe the details of the whole process of the multi-level text corpus building. We will use R to describe the set of sentences from which we select (i.e. $|R| = 97,033$ as explained in Sect. 2.1), and $\bar{R}$ the set of sentences selected. It is clear, that with each selected sentence s it is true that $s \in \bar{R}$ and $s \notin R$. Also, once a sentence is stored to $\bar{R}$, it will remain there forever.

Step 1: At the beginning, we consider a unit being raw phone and we require at least 15 occurrences of every phone in the selected sentences. The algorithm ends with $|\bar{R}| = 96$ sentences fulfilling this criterion.

Step 2: At this level, the unit is the phone-in-prosodeme, since we need to ensure enough units in the various basic prosodic positions. We also demand at least

---

[2] Let us emphasize that we work with text now, so we can only *expect* how the sentence will, or should be pronounced.

15 occurrences for each unit. The algorithm selected 380 additional sentences, $|\bar{R}| = 476$ in total. 14 units did not reach the required minimum number of occurrences (the worst case is 1 occurrence for 2 out of 162 different units), but as all the occurrences available in the source text collection were selected (see Table 1), no other sentence in the source text collection could improve the criterion.

Step 3: Since our unit-selection synthesizer [9] works with diphones, this level focuses on diphones' coverage; the requirement of at least 2 occurrences of each diphone in $\bar{R}$ was set. The number of selected sentences stopped at $|\bar{R}| = 1,040$, where no further sentence was available to improve the required coverage.

Step 4: Having selected more than 1,000 sentences so far, we have changed the paradigm of the corpus preparation. Until this point, the input texts were chosen with respect to the speakers, however when they are able and willing to record this number of sentences, we can start to optimize the corpus with respect to the speech synthesis method we use. Here, the manually created sentences covering rare Czech diphones (see Sect. 2.1) were added to the source text collection. Therefore, still the same algorithm but with extended R was used to select sentences with at least 5 occurrences of each diphone in $\bar{R}$, after that $|\bar{R}| = 2,317$. There are 77 diphones not fulfilling the requirement, but again, no further sentence could improve it.

Step 5: In the last step we demanded at least 3 occurrences of diphones-in-prosodeme units. However, it would enlarge the set to almost 7,000 sentences, which is impossible to record by our target speakers. Therefore, the selection process was stopped when the number 2,500 was achieved.

Step 6: Finally, the algorithm tried to uniformly balance the distribution of diphones-in-prosodemes – see [8] for details – until $|\bar{R}| = 3,500$ sentences were selected, when the process was stopped.

Only one patient has managed to record the whole prepared corpus yet; nevertheless, the number 3,500 was chosen to be sure that the text corpus is well prepared and large enough even for very capable speakers with more time. This amount of sentences also guarantees enough data for high-quality unit selection synthesis being considered the most natural method of speech synthesis.

3   Final Text Corpus Statistics

The sequential selection process described above guarantees the widest possible coverage of speech units (phones, diphones in different prosodemes) in the group of sentences selected in the particular step. Some more detailed statistics of the corpus are shown in Table 1, as well as the comparison with the full sentence collection, the reduced set used in greedy algorithm and a general corpus used for standard TTS. Since it is expected that people undergoing voice conservation are usually not able to record the whole corpus, we also counted the statistics for corpus subsets, meaning the sets of first N sentences from the prepared corpus.

Table 1. Text corpus statistics presented for *full* text corpus (0.5 M sentences), *reduced* corpus with sentences 5–8 words long plus the manually created sentences (98 k in total), *corpus* being the final selection from *reduced*, and *corpus subsets* representing the first N selected sentences from the *corpus*. Also, *general* corpus represents the set selected from *full* and recorded by a professional female voice talent [4] for our generic–purpose TTS. P_x means a prosodeme X.

Statistics		Full	Reduced	Corpus	Corpus subsets			General
No. sentences		524, 481	98, 498	3, 500	2, 000	1, 000	300	12, 151
Average sent. length		13.8	6.7	6.9	7.2	7.0	7.0	9.8
No. different phones		44	44	44	44	44	44	44
No. different diphones		1, 397	1, 449	1, 449	1, 449	1, 284	934	1430
Units	I							
Phones	15x	44	44	44	44	44	44	44
Phones in P_0	15x	44	44	44	44	44	41	44
Reduced texts coverage		100.00 %	100.00 %	100.00 %	100.00 %	100.00 %	99.96 %	100.00 %
Phones in P_1	15x	42	42	42	42	42	37	42
Reduced texts coverage		94.38 %	94.38 %	94.38 %	94.38 %	94.38 %	94.27 %	94.38 %
Phones in P_2	15x	39	37	37	37	37	32	39
Reduced texts coverage		94.34 %	94.27 %	94.27 %	94.27 %	94.27 %	91.48 %	94.34 %
Phones in P_3	15x	42	39	39	39	39	37	41
Reduced texts coverage		94.38 %	94.34 %	94.34 %	94.34 %	94.34 %	94.27 %	94.36 %
Diphones	5x	1, 397	1, 280	1, 280	1, 203	801	527	1, 249
Reduced texts coverage		99.99 %	99.99 %	99.99 %	99.90 %	98.55 %	92.32 %	99.97 %

As follows from the table, not all required minimum occurrences were met in the process of sentence selection, e.g. the requirement of at least 15 occurrences of all phones-in-prosodemes in the step 2. The source sentence collection used to select from, however, does not contain enough units in prosodemes 2 and 3, so having the number of sentences selected in a particular step, selection of no additional sentence would increase the given criterion (i.e. none of the missing units is added). We have considered further extension of the set with those missing units, but it has been finally refused, since there are too many units missing, and it would mean extremely large amount of manual work. Moreover, even if the required number of occurrences was not fulfilled, the algorithm guarantees that at least one instance of every unit (except the step 5) is selected. Also, considering the rare nature of the units, unnatural artefacts possibly caused by their inappropriate placement in synthetic speech will not be very frequent.

The second part of the table contains more detailed information about the units as used in the individual selection steps. The numbers in cells correspond to the numbers of units with the required occurrence appearing in the individual corpora. The percentage, then, illustrates the coverage of the reduced set by occurrences of those units which appeared at least the given number of times in the particular set of selected sentences. For example, there are 1, 280 different diphones, each with at least 5 occurrences in the reduced set. All the occurrences of those diphones then cover 99.99 % of all the diphone occurrences in this set.

Table 2. The base statistics of speech corpora recorded by 12 laryngectomees (marked as Px) whose voice was conserved before the surgery. The duration of speech in the corpus is excluding pauses.

	# Sent.	Speech dur.		# Sent.	Speech dur.		# Sent.	Speech dur.
P1	3,500	227.6 min	P5	856	79.5 min	P9	555	34.7 min
P2	2,014	116.6 min	P6	769	41.3 min	P10	469	46.2 min
P3	1,431	99.0 min	P7	700	73.3 min	P11	403	26.2 min
P4	1,038	62.8 min	P8	683	52.6 min	P12	300	17.2 min

When, for example, the first 300 selected sentences (full step 1 and part of step 2) are recorded, we will get (theoretically) 527 various diphones with the given minimum occurrence amount. While this is lower amount of diphones, they still cover 92.32 % of all the diphone occurrences in the reduced set. It is clear that the percentage is sometimes higher for the full collection, as there is the higher number of different units with the required minimum occurrences.

From the TTS engine point of view, it is interesting to look at the diphones coverage for the selected corpus and its subsets. The percentage value can be interpreted as the chance that unit selection synthesis will require a diphone not having at least 5 occurrences, so this is the worst–scenario estimate of the frequency of unnatural artefact appearance due to a missing unit[3]. For example, having 300 recorded sentences, there is 7.68 % such a chance, but when a speaker is capable to record at lest 1, 000 sentence, this chance is only 1.45 %.

4   Conclusion

Although the paper describes mainly the procedure of text corpus building, using the set of 3500 sentences, we have already conserved voices of several patients undergoing total laryngectomy surgery. Due to their various social status, technical capabilities and speak difficulties, most of them were able to record only a subset of the whole sentence set, ranging from 300 to 2, 000 sentences; the details are listed in Table 2. For all of them, the personalised TTS system was built from their recordings (see [6]) and it was given to them to simplify they everyday communication. The samples can be listened in table online (please see [3]) and it can be heard that even the unit selection version has a reasonable quality, leaving aside some audible artefacts caused by insufficient coverage of some diphones. Let us also note that the recordings of the patients are the most valuable source of their original voice which will never be returned them.

In our future work, we would like to keep recording patients' voices. As for speech synthesis, we plan to research into incremental speech synthesis framework [1]. We would also like to propose a fully automatic process of voice building

---

[3] Let us note that the real unnatural artefacts appearance will be much lower and it will be influenced by other factors like recording style, speech units segmentation, unit selection criteria etc. Those will not be influenced by the speech corpus per se.

without any need of human intervention. We are testing the possibility to collect recordings at patients' homes, but unfortunately, it brings some problems relating to speech quality, proper loudness etc. Similarly to [2], a more patient-friendly recording application is being implemented within this process.

References

1. Baumann, T., Schlangen, D.: Evaluating prosodic processing for incremental speech synthesis. In: INTERSPEECH, pp. 438–441, Portland, OR, USA (2012)
2. Erro, D., Hernaez, I., Alonso, A., García-Lorenzo, D., Navas, E., Ye, J., Arzelus, H., Jauk, I., Hy, N.Q., Magariños, C., Pérez-Ramón, R., Sulír, M., Tian, X., Wang, X., Vitoria, B.: Personalized synthetic voices for speaking impaired: website and app. In: INTERSPEECH, pp. 1251–1254, Dresden, Germany (2015)
3. Examples: Personalised speech synthesis samples. https://docs.google.com/presentation/d/1iWeeWFW-jYIO1fMV9CxImC261QoPUUiZKOsT9w8UxXc/present#slide=id.gc411cf050_0_0
4. Hanzlíček, Z., Matoušek, J., Tihelka, D.: Experiments on reducing footprint of unit selection TTS system. In: Habernal, I. (ed.) TSD 2013. LNCS, vol. 8082, pp. 249–256. Springer, Heidelberg (2013)
5. Hanzlíček, Z., Romportl, J., Matoušek, J.: Voice conservation: towards creating a speech-aid system for total Laryngectomees. In: Kelemen, J., Romportl, J., Zackova, E. (eds.) Beyond Artificial Intelligence. TIEI, vol. 4, pp. 205–214. Springer, Heidelberg (2013)
6. Jůzová, M., Romportl, J., Tihelka, D.: Speech corpus preparation for voice banking of Laryngectomised patients. In: Král, P., Matoušek, V. (eds.) TSD 2015. LNCS, vol. 9302, pp. 282–290. Springer, Heidelberg (2015)
7. Matoušek, J., Psutka, J., Krůta, J.: Design of speech corpus for text-to-speech synthesis. In: Eurospeech 2001 - Interspeech, Proceedings of the 7th European Conference on Speech Communication and Technology, pp. 2047–2050, Aalborg, Denmark (2001)
8. Matoušek, J., Romportl, J.: On Building phonetically and Prosodically rich speech corpus for text-to-speech synthesis. In: Proceedings of the 2nd IASTED International Conference on Computational Intelligence, pp. 442–447. ACTA Press, San Francisco (2006)
9. Matoušek, J., Tihelka, D., Romportl, J.: Current state of Czech text-to-speech system ARTIC. In: Sojka, P., Kopeček, I., Pala, K. (eds.) TSD 2006. LNCS (LNAI), vol. 4188, pp. 439–446. Springer, Heidelberg (2006)
10. Merritt, T., Clark, R.A.J., Wu, Z., Yamagishi, J., King, S.: Deep neural network-guided unit selection synthesis. In: Proceedings of ICASSP (2016)
11. Nakamura, K., Toda, T., Saruwatari, H., Shikano, K.: The use of air-pressure sensor in electrolaryngeal speech enhancement based on statistical voice conversion. In: INTERSPEECH, pp. 1628–1631, Makuhari, Japan (2010)
12. Romportl, J., Matoušek, J.: Formal prosodic structures and their application in NLP. In: Matoušek, V., Mautner, P., Pavelka, T. (eds.) TSD 2005. LNCS (LNAI), vol. 3658, pp. 371–378. Springer, Heidelberg (2005)
13. Romportl, J., Řepová, B., Betka, J.: Vocal rehabilitation of Laryngectomised patients by personalised computer speech synthesis. In: Phoniatrics. European Manual of Medicine. Springer, Heidelberg (2015) (in press)

14. Tihelka, D., Matoušek, J.: Unit selection and its relation to symbolic prosody: a new approach. In: INTERSPEECH 2006 – ICSLP, Proceedings of 9th ICSLP, vol. 1, pp. 2042–2045. ISCA, Bonn (2006)
15. Yamagishi, J., Veaux, C., King, S., Renals, S.: Speech synthesis technologies for individuals with vocal disabilities: voice banking and reconstruction. Acoust. Sci. Technol. **33**, 1–5 (2012)

Designing Syllable Models for an HMM Based Speech Recognition System

Kseniya Proença[1(✉)], Kris Demuynck[2], and Dirk Van Compernolle[1]

[1] ESAT - PSI, KULeuven, Kasteelpark Arenberg 10, 2441, 3001 Leuven, Belgium
{kseniya.proenca,dirk.vancompernolle}@esat.kuleuven.be
[2] ELIS, UGent, Sint-Pietersnieuwstraat 41, 9000 Ghent, Belgium
Kris.Demuynck@elis.ugent.be

Abstract. In this paper we present novel ways of incorporating syllable information into an HMM based speech recognition system. Syllable
based acoustic modelling is appealing as syllables have certain acoustic-
phonetic dependencies that can not be modeled in a pure phone based
system. On the other hand, syllable based systems suffer from sparsity
issues. In this paper we investigate the potential of different acoustic
units such as phone, phone clusters, phones-in-syllables, demi-syllables
and syllables in combination with a variety of back-off schemes. Experimental results are presented on the Wall Street Journal database. When
working with traditional frame based features only, results only show
minor improvements. However, we expect that the developed system will
show its full potential when incorporating additional segmental features
at the syllable level.

Keywords: Hidden Markov Models · Syllables · Continuous speech
recognition · Back-off schemes

1 Introduction

Hidden Markov Models (HMM) are a very powerful statistical method of characterizing the observed data samples of discrete-time series [7]. HMM are a
standard approach used in speech recognition for acoustic modeling. In recent
years, great progress has been made in the modeling of the frame observation
probabilities by the introduction of deep neural nets (DNNs). While improving
on accuracy, thanks to the powerful discriminative training of the DNNs, the
HMM-DNN framework still suffers from some of the intrinsic simplifications and
limitations in the HMM architecture. In particular, the traditional approach to
use beads-on-a-string to model states in (context-dependent)-phones is known
to be overly simple for many reasons: there is the HMM frame-by-frame independence assumption; it does not allow to incorporate segmental information;
and mismatches between canonical phonetic transcriptions and the observed
acoustics are common. In this paper we focus on the latter two problems.

© Springer International Publishing Switzerland 2016
A. Ronzhin et al. (Eds.): SPECOM 2016, LNAI 9811, pp. 216–223, 2016.
DOI: 10.1007/978-3-319-43958-7_25

A syllable is an attractive unit for usage in speech technology applications for several reasons: it is much more salient than the shorter phone-unit, co-articulation tends to be stronger within than across syllables, and it is the shortest unit that contains all acoustic attributes relating to phonetics, rhythm and prosody. All syllabifications used in this paper are derived from our syllabification algorithm proposed in [11]. While using syllables as basic units is not novel, we believe that there is still room for improvement on how such syllabic information can be used best in an HMM based system.

The rest of the paper is organized as follows. We first talk about similar research. Then we describe the problem of the unit selection. Next, phone syllable-based labeling system is explained. In the end we give conclusions, discussions and further work.

2   Related Work

Decision trees, HMM, neural networks and trajectory models have all been used for speech recognition where syllable information is incorporated in the system.

Liao et al. [9] examine the use of the word or syllable context as a feature in the decision tree. This way, they introduce word- and syllable-specific models into the recognition system. Since they employ finite state transducer based ASR the syllable information is incorporated as features on the arcs in the transducer.

Jones and others [8] analyzed a phonetically annotated telephony database at the syllable level and built a set of syllable-based HMMs. Recognition performance was improved with syllable-level bigram probabilities and both word- and syllable-level insertion penalties. They built prototype HMMs for each syllable with the number of states set proportional to the number of phonemes in the syllable.

Zhang and Edmondson showed how a model of syllable articulation can be used with Pseudo-Articulatory Representations (PARs) to provide a general articulatory transcription of speech without phonetic labeling [14]. First, they establish the mapping between PARs and acoustic parameters. After that they perform recognition in three steps. The first step is the transition from the acoustic representation of the incoming signal to the PAR with feature trajectories available as a function of time. The second step makes a move from the PARs to the syllable structures and produces a sequence of the recovered syllables. The third stage focuses on the transition from the syllable patterns to the phonetic level and produces a sequence of phone labels.

Hu and colleagues proposed a recognition strategy which uses syllable-like units as the basic unit for recognition [6]. They define the criterion of grouping phonemes into syllable-like units as follows: phoneme sequences for which the boundary is difficult to detect are grouped together forming a new set of base recognition units. After syllable-like units are defined according to the set of predefined rules, word pronunciation models are generated using these units. Statistical trajectory models [4] are computed for each defined unit. Artificial neural networks or Gaussian mixture models are then trained to estimate probabilities of the units. The search is implemented using the Viterbi algorithm in a time-asynchronous manner.

Hauenstein [5] applied a hybrid Hidden Markov Model - Artificial Neural Network (HMM-ANN) recognition system to small and medium vocabulary recognition tasks using syllables as basic modelling units. Features are kept the same as in the phoneme-based baseline.

Syllable-level acoustic units were also used in [3] for large vocabulary continuous speech recognition (LVCSR) on telephone-bandwidth speech. The major innovation of their syllable system is the smooth integration of a large inventory of syllable models and a mixture of acoustic models ranging from monosyllabic words to CD phones.

3   Unit Selection

The main modeling unit in our system is a syllable. To make an accurate statistical model, it is essential to have enough data. The original phone-based recognition system had 43 context independent phones for which the problem of sparsity does not exist. The situation with syllables is different: there exist quite a lot of rare syllables. Therefore a back-off mechanism to smaller units is required.

The first back-off option we investigate are demi-syllables: a syllable-initial consonant cluster plus the first half of the vowel or a second half of the vowel and syllable-final consonant cluster [12]. If there is still not enough data to model a demi-syllable, we back-off to the phone sequence. For example, the word "`string`" is transcribed as "`strIN`". Demi-syllable back-off looks like "$\langle$`strI=`$\rangle\langle$`=IN`$\rangle$".

There are two main problems with this approach. The first one is sparsity. The second is how to divide the vowel in the middle and how to model it. To overcome this issue we propose another back-off mechanism. Instead of using demi-syllables, we model the syllable by three parts namely onset, vowel and coda in which onset and coda are optional consonant clusters. We call this the "cvc-scheme". The same example for "`string`" in cvc-version is "$\langle$`str.`$\rangle\langle$`.I.`$\rangle\langle$`.N`$\rangle$".

The other question is how to decide, how many examples are needed to train a unit, and when to back-off. In this research we set this threshold to a 100 examples. The statistics were counted on the WSJ database training data [10]. We will report statistics for cvc-scheme in two ways: measured on the syllable lexicon independently of the number of occurrences and measured on running text. The database contains 5648 unique syllables. 78 % of the syllables do not occur more than 100 times and hence need to use the back-off scheme (going to cvc). On the other hand, if we take into consideration the syllable frequency, the back-off from syllable to cvc needs to be done only in 7.5 % of the cases. The same happens with the back-off from cvc to phones. On running text this happens in less than 0.5 % of times. Based on these results only the CVC backoff scheme will be considered in the remainder of this paper.

4   HMM with Syllables

For all our experiments we use the WSJ database [10], the CMU dictionary [13] and the SPRAAK toolkit [2]. SPRAAK (Speech Processing, Recognition and Automatic Annotation Kit) is an open source speech recognition package. It is an efficient and flexible tool that combines many of the recent advancements in automatic speech recognition with a very efficient decoder in a proven HMM architecture. Our speech recognition system consists of a preprocessing unit, the acoustic models and the language model, a lexicon and a search-engine. Preprocessing for all systems is the same consisting of filterbank features with vocal track length normalization and mida transformation [1]. Acoustic models are made for phones, onsets, codas, vowels and syllables separately. The lexicon includes phone, cvc and syllable descriptions of words. A semi-continuous HMM-GMM with a common pool of gaussians for all states is used. Decoding is done using Viterbi alignments.

4.1   CI Syllable Units

To create the initial context-independent (ci) syllable HMM model, we start from an existing cd-phone HMM system. Based on the phone segmentation we create ci-syllables. After the first iteration of training we regenerate segmentation of the training corpus and retrain the system. The number of states per unit depends on its length: 3 states for phones and between 3 and 19 states for the various syllables. We create three sub-models: syllables, consonant clusters+vowels, phones. These sub-models are independent, except for the shared Gaussian set.

4.2   CD Syllable Units

Modeling context-dependent (cd) syllables can be done in several ways. In our research we started from the ci-syllable system and use a phone-based context i.e. context-dependency is determined by the first or last phone of the neighbouring right/left syllable. We split all syllables, cvc and phones into two groups of long and short units. Units of 3 states are considered short units (su). Units having more than three states are called long units (lu). All states of the short units are context-dependent. In long units, only the first and last states are context-dependent. In the other words, a long unit is split as follows:

[lu]	→ [lu]:L [lu]:C [lu]:R
[lu]:L, [lu]:R	left/right context-dependent states
[lu]:C	the remaining 2 to 17 context-independent states in the syllable model.

4.3   Results

For our work we used the WSJ-based speaker independent acoustic training data [10]. We report word error rates (ERR, %) for the nov92 bigram 5 K closed-vocabulary test set (b05) and for the trigram 20 K open-vocabulary test set (t20). The results of our initial experiments are presented in Table 1. While creating the ci-syllable system, we trained it twice (as described above). The first line, first column shows the results after the first iteration. The second iteration was based on the retrained syllable system and improved the recognition result as shown in the second line, first column of the table.

We made extra analysis to find the problems of the recognition. Firstly, we evaluated the sub-models (syllable/cvc/phone) in two different ways: separately and in parallel and also investigated which unit was used (syllable/consonant cluster/phone) more often. Separate evaluation of the sub-models of the system means that the we limit the used units by the sub-model (last three columns). That means that if cvc sub-model is evaluated, we don't present any full-syllable information. The back-off to phones in the canonical transcription is used only with the limited amount of training data. Parallel evaluations means that all the units are presented in the canonical transcription and the system can choose which unit to use (first and second columns).

Secondly, we improved the Gaussians initialization. It is possible to initialize Gaussians from the phone model only and to share Gaussians only within the same model. This improved the result on 0.5 %. The results are shown in the third row of the table. cd-results are presented in the last line of the table.

Table 1. Results for the HMM system, WSJ, nov92, b05, phone ci-result: 6.86

	syl/cvc/ph	cvc/ph	syl	cvc	ph
Syllable system, 1st iteration	6.09	7.1	6.67	7.08	8.16
Syllable system, 2nd iteration	**5.66**	6.46	7.01	5.58	6.87
Gaussians initialization from phone model	6.63	7.6	9.42	7.58	6.95
cd-syllable system	4.15				

There are still a number of uncertainties and difficulties to solve. The main one is the sparsity issue: for long units (such as syllables and some conso-nant cluster) we don't have enough training data. To solve this, we need to have another back-off mechanism. Though, developing such a mechanism is not a trivial task. Another uncertainty concerns the system initialization and Gaussians distribution among units of different size. Pronunciation ambiguity also causes some problems. Depending on the phonetic writing, there might be several syllabification versions.

5   Phones with Syllabic Labels

In this approach we use phones as units, but all phones get a label indicating it's position in a syllable or/and word. This helps to solve the sparsity issues that we faced in the previous approach. Label is always added after the phone: <phone>:<label>. After that we train the system as it was done with regular phones. We worked out several labeling schemes. The first one (called **SylPosit**) is a simple indication the position of a phone in a syllable.

We use 4 labels :I, :C, :F, :S to indicate initial, central, final or single position of the phone in a syllable. For 2-phone syllables, the central label is not used.

The rest of the labeling schemes have the same idea and are explained in Table 2.

Table 2. Different schemes of syllabic labels

WordPosit	
Position in a word; Initial Central Final	I:I f:C I!:C S:C @:C n:C s:C i:F
PWPosit	
Both word and syllable positions; ":CF": a center phone in a word and final in a syllable. We use 8 labels (3 for words and 4 for syllables)	I:IS f:CI I!:CF S:CI @:CC n:CF s:CI i:FF
SylPositBound	
Mark only a syllable boundary; :I(initial), :C(central), :F(final) for position in a syllable. First phone can be marked as :F is it is an only phone in a syllable	I:F f:I I!:F S:I @:C n:F s:I i:C
SylPositCC	
Vowels :I(initial), :M(middle), :F(final), :S(single); and consonants :O(onset), :C(coda) in a syllable	I:S f:O I!:F S:O @:M n:C s:O i:F
SylPositVC	
Position-independent vowel (:V); position dependent consonant (initial, center, final)	INCIDENTS I!n-s@-d@nts
	I!:V n:f s:i @:V d:i @:V n:C t:C s:f

6   Modelling Syllable Boundary (SylBound)

In this approach we again use phones as basic units, but now we add syllable boundary ([:S:]) in the phonetic transcriptions. No observations or state are associated with it. For example:

PREDICTION [pri[:S:]dI!k[:S:]S@n]

By adding an extra syllable boundary marker and by using tri-phones only (looking one phone or syllable boundary marker to the left/right), the obtained phones models are fully context-dependent within a syllable only. Phones in a syllable initial or syllable final position are conditioned only on the presence of a syllable boundary and no longer on the specific left/right phone.

7   Experiments and Results

Experiments were carried on the same data as in previous research (WSJ). CI results are not presented as they are the same in all the labeling schemes. The starting point is the cd-phone HMM system. The results are presented in the Table 3.

Table 3. Results for WSJ experiments with phone labels.

	phon	WordPosit	SylPosit	PWPosit	SylPositCC	SylPositVC	SylPositBound	SylBound
b05	3.92	3.36	3.66	3.53	3.59	3.75	3.42	5.06
t20	7.6	7.27	7.66	7.57	7.50	7.64	7.74	8.24

The results indicate that loosing (or reducing) context-dependency information at syllable boundaries is not a good idea. That means that it is important to retain the phone-boundary dependency at syllable boundaries. The best results was shown with "word position" labeling system though all of the systems gave very similar results between each other and original phone system.

8   Discussion and Conclusions

In this research we tried two approaches for speech recognition using syllables. The first one is modelling syllables and making the back-off to onset-vowel-coda structure. The second one is done with labeling phones depending on their position in a syllable/word. We also tried the approach with inserting a syllable boundary that gave very poor results. We showed that the HMM with syllable position dependent phones gives better accuracy result than modelling complete syllable. The observed difference in results may be connected with the lack of training data or unefficient gaussians initialization and estimation.

Our work is similar to the research in [9] from Google though there are a few relevant some differences. While Liao and others take extra information about the syllable boundary, we model the syllable in more detail. For example, in the labeling system we model separately phones depending on the syllable position.

This system is being used as starting point for an exemplar-based system with syllable information. It is a done because we get consistent results with a well-established approach. This research is still carried on.

References

1. Demuynck, K., Duchateau, J., Compernolle, D.V.: Optimal feature sub-space selection based on discriminant analysis. In: Sixth European Conference on Speech Communication and Technology, EUROSPEECH 1999, Budapest, Hungary, 5–9 September 1999
2. Demuynck, K., Roelens, J., Compernolle, D.V., Wambacq, P.: Spraak: an open source "speech recognition and automatic annotation kit". In: INTERSPEECH, p. 495 (2008)
3. Ganapathiraju, A., Hamaker, J., Picone, J., Ordowski, M., Doddington, G.R.: Syllable-based large vocabulary continuous speech recognition. IEEE Trans. Speech Audio Process. **9**(4), 358–366 (2001)
4. Goldenthal, W.D.: Statistical trajectory models for phonetic recognition. Ph.D. thesis, Massachusetts Institute of Technology, Department of Aeronautics and Astronautics (1994)
5. Hauenstein, A.: Using syllables in a hybrid HMM-ANN recognition system. In: EUROSPEECH (1997)
6. Hu, Z., Schalkwyk, J., Barnard, E., Cole, R.A.: Speech recognition using syllable-like units. In: ICSLP (1996)
7. Huang, X., Acero, A., Hon, H.W.: Spoken Language Processing: A Guide to Theory, Algorithm and System Development. Prentice Hall PTR, Prentice-Hall, Inc., Upper Saddle River (2001)
8. Jones, R.J., Downey, S., Mason, J.S.: Continuous speech recognition using syllables. In: EUROSPEECH (1997)
9. Liao, H., Alberti, C., Bacchiani, M., Siohan, O.: Decision tree state clustering with word and syllable features. In: INTERSPEECH, pp. 2958–2961 (2010)
10. Paul, D.B., Baker, J.M.: The design for the wall street journal-based CSR corpus. In: ICSLP (1992)
11. Rogova, K., Demuynck, K., Van Compernolle, D.: Automatic syllabification using segmental conditional random fields. Comput. Linguist. Neth. J. **3**, 34–48 (2013)
12. Syrdal, A., Bennett, R., Greenspan, S.: Applied Speech Technology. Taylor & Francis, Oxford (1994). http://books.google.be/books?id=kyJBjxw3ducC
13. Carnegie Mellon Universit: CMU pronouncing dictionary (2008). http://svn.code.sf.net/p/cmusphinx/code/trunk/cmudict
14. Zhang, L., Edmondson, W.H.: Speech recognition using syllable patterns. In: INTERSPEECH (2002)

Detecting Filled Pauses and Lengthenings in Russian Spontaneous Speech Using SVM

Vasilisa Verkhodanova$^{(\boxtimes)}$ and Vladimir Shapranov

SPIIRAS, St. Petersburg, Russia
verkhodanova@iias.spb.su, equidamoid@gmail.com

Abstract. Spontaneous speech differs from any other type of speech in many ways. And the presence of speech disfluencies is its prominent characteristic. These phenomena are important feature in human-human communication and at the same time a challenging obstacle for the speech processing tasks. This paper reports the experiment results on automatic detection of filled pauses and sound lengthenings basing on the automatically extracted acoustic features. We have performed machine learning experiments using support vector machine (SVM) classifier on the mixed and quality diverse corpus of Russian spontaneous speech. We applied Gaussian filtering and morphological opening to post-process the probability estimates from an SVM classifier. As the result we achieved F1–score of 0.54, with precision and recall being 0.55 and 0.53 respectively.

Keywords: Speech disfluencies · Filled pauses · Lengthenings · Speech processing · Support vector machines

1 Introduction

Speech disfluencies are common in spontaneous speech. They consist of hesitations, self-repairs, repetitions, substitutions, etc. They do not add the semantic information to the speech signal, but may play a valuable role such as helping a speaker to hold a conversational turn or expressing the speakers thinking process of formulating the upcoming utterance fragment [4,17].

However human language technologies are often developed for other than spontaneous type of speech, and the occurrence of disfluencies is one of the factors that makes the spontaneous speech processing challenging [19]. The need of detecting them automatically emerged mainly from the problems of automatic speech recognition (ASR): disfluencies are known to have an impact on ASR results, they can occur at any point of spontaneous speech, thus they can lead to misrecognition or incorrect classification of adjacent words.

Speech disfluencies occur quite often: for example, in conversational speech in American English about 6 per 100 words are disfluent [21]. Though evidence on filled pauses and lengthenings (jointly reffered as FPs later on) differs across languages, genres, and speakers, on average there are several disfluencies per 100 syllables, FPs being the most frequent disfluency type [16]. According to [25] in

© Springer International Publishing Switzerland 2016
A. Ronzhin et al. (Eds.): SPECOM 2016, LNAI 9811, pp. 224–231, 2016.
DOI: 10.1007/978-3-319-43958-7_26

the conversational Switchboard database [7], about 39.7 % of the all disfluencies contain a filled pause. In the corpus of Portuguese lectures LECTRA filled pauses correspond to 1.8 % of all the words and to 22.9 % of all disfluency types being the most frequent type in the corpus [14]. In Russian speech FPs occur at a rate of about 4 times per 100 words, they also occur at approximately the same rate inside clauses and at the discourse boundaries [13].

FPs exhibit universal as well as linguistic and genre specific features. FPs are represented mainly by vocalizations with rare cases of prolonged consonants (which was shown to be a peculiarity of Armenian hesitational phenomena [12]). These vocalizations in FPs are usually phonetically different from the lexical items, since they are pronounced with minimal movements of the articulatory organs due to the articulatory economy [24]. However, it was also shown that phonological system of the language may influence the quality of FPs vocalizations [6]. Even universal characteristics of FPs, such as lengthenings being accompanied by creaky voice, may operate differently in different languages: e.g. in Finnish it was proposed that creaky voice may indicate turn-transitional locations [17], which is not the case for English [22].

Although the speech technologies, and particularly ASR systems, have to account for all types of disfluencies (filled pauses, prolongations, repetitions, deletions, substitutions, fragments, editing expressions, insertions, etc.), in the present study we focus on the detection of the most frequent disfluent categories: filled pauses and sound lengthenings. In this paper we present the results of experiments on detection of FPs on the mixed and quality diverse corpus of Russian spontaneous speech. We used an SVM classifier and two methods applied at the stage of post-processing: Gaussian filtering and morphological opening.

2   Related Work

During last years speech disfluencies and particularly FPs have received more attention in the field of speech processing due to speech recognition tasks: ASR systems are usually trained on the structured data without any types of speech disfluencies.

It has been shown that along with duration the prominent characteristic of FPs is a gradual fall of fundamental frequency (F0) [18]: FPs tend to be low in F0 as well as displaying a gradual, roughly linear F0 fall. In [23] it was shown that for fair detection of FPs these two characteristics and distance to a pause are enough. In [28] authors used duration and statistical characteristics of F0, first three formants and energy for the experiments based on gradient decent optimizing parameters for maximization of F1–score; achieved result was F1–score = 0.46.

In [8], filled pauses are detected on a basis of two features (small fundamental frequency transition and small spectral envelope deformation) using as material 100 utterances extracted from a Japanese spoken language corpus where 91.5 % precision and 84.9 % recall were achieved. In [26] authors developed a detection system in order to improve the speech recognizer performance, achieving precision of 85 % at a recall rate of 70 %.

In [15] authors focused on detection of filled pauses basing on acoustic and prosodic features as well as on some lexical features. Experiments were carried on a speech corpus of university lectures in European Portuguese Lectra. Several machine learning methods have been applied, and the best results were achieved using Classification and Regression Trees. The performance achieved for detecting words inside of disfluent sequences was about 91 % precision and 37 % recall, when filled pauses and fragments were used as a feature, without it, the performance decayed to 66 % precision and 20 % recall. Further experiments on filled pauses detection in European Portuguese were carried out using prosodic and obtained from ASR lexical features; the best results were achieved using J48, corresponding to about 61 % F-measure [14].

The INTERSPEECH 2013 Paralinguistic Challenge [11] raised interest in automatic detection of fillers providing a standardised corpus and a reference system. The winners of the Social Signals Sub-Challenge introduced a system, built upon a DNN classifier complemented with time series smoothing and masking [9].

In [20] authors presented a method for filled pauses detection using an SVM classifier, applying a Gaussian filter to infer temporal context information and performing a morphological opening to filter false alarms. For the feature set authors used the same as was proposed for [11], extracted with the openSMILE toolkit [5]. Experiments were carried out on the LAST MINUTE corpus of naturalistic multimodal recordings of 133 German speaking subjects in a so called Wizard-of-Oz (WoZ) experiment. The obtained results were recall of 70 %, precision of 55 %, and AUC of 0.94.

3   Material

The material we have used in this study consists of several parts. The first part is the corpus of task-based dialogs collected at SPIIRAS in St. Petersburg in the end of 2012 - beginning of 2013 [27]. It consists of 18 dialogs from 1.5 to 5 min, where people in pairs fulfilled map and appointment tasks. Recording was performed in the sound isolated room. Participants were students: 6 women and 6 men from 17 to 23 years old with technical and humanitarian specialization. Recordings were annotated manually into different types of disfluencies, the FPs being the majority - 492 phenomena (222 filled pauses and 270 lengthenings).

For the second part of our material we used part of Multi-Language Audio Database [29]. This database consists of approximately 30 h of sometimes low quality, varied and noisy speech in each of three languages, English, Mandarin Chinese, and Russian. For each language there are 900 recordings taken from open source public web sites, such as http://youtube.com. All recordings have been orthographically transcribed at the sentence/phrase level by human listeners. The Russian part of this database consists of 300 recordings of 158 speakers (approximately 35 hours). The casual conversations part consists of 91 recordings (10.3 h) of 53 speakers [29]. From this Russian part we have taken the random 6 recordings of casual conversations (3 female speakers and 3 male speakers) that were manually annotated into FPs. The number of annotated phenomena is 284 (188 filled pauses and 96 sound lengthenings).

The third part is the corpus of scientific reports from seminar devoted to analysis of conversational speech held at SPIIRAS in 2011. Recordings of reports of 6 people (3 female and 3 male speakers) were manually annotated into speech disfluencies. Since speakers didn't base their reports on a written text, these recordings ontain considerable amount of speech disfluencies. 951 FPs were manually annotated: 741 filled pauses and 210 lengthenings.

Another part we added for making our corpus more quality and situation diverse is the the records from the appendix No5 to the phonetic journal "Bulletin of the Phonetic Fund" belonging to the Department of Phonetics of Saint-Petersburg University [1]. The 12 recorded reports concerned different scientific topics (linguistics, logic, psychology, etc.). They were all recorded in 70s-80s in Moscow except one that was recorded in Prague. All speakers (6 men and 6 women) were native Russian speakers, and were recorded while presenting on conferences and seminars. The number of manually annotated FPs is 285 (225 filled pauses and 60 lengthenings).

In total, the data set we used is about 3 h and comprises 2012 filled pauses. Distribution of FP duration over the corpus is shown on Fig. 1. The duration of a single FP lies between 6 ms and 2.3 s, the average duration is 388 ms.

The data has been separated into two classes: "FPs" and "Other". First one consists of FPs only, while the other comprises the rest of the frames. Each 10th file was selected for train set, then again each 10th - for development set, and the rest was used as the test set. This operation was performed 10 times producing 10 different triplets of train, development and test sets.

Since the classes were not balanced (there were about 12 times more Other instances than FPs ones) we downsampled the train set to avoid the bias towards the class Other [20]. Thus we created subset containing randomly chosen 8 % of the instances of the class Other and all the FPs data. To train the classifier we use these downsampled training set.

4   Filled Pauses and Lengthenings Detection

In our study we have followed [20], basing our experiments on support vector machine (SVM) classifier. The extreme learning machines (ELM) in our unreported study shows that SVM provides better detection accuracy with better harmonized mean of precision and recall (with ELM we got F1–score $= 0.4$). We used a scikit-learn Python library [2] implementation of SVM with polynomial kernel, that enables the probability estimates by means of C-Support Vector Classification, the implementation is build upon libsvm [3].

The feature set is based in the set that was used for the INTERSPEECH 2013 Social Signals Sub-Challenge [11]. Features were extracted with the openS-MILE toolkit [5] on the frame-level basis (25 ms window, 10 ms shift). This set is derived from 54 low-level descriptors (LLDs): 14 mel-frequency cepstral coefficients (MFCCs), logarithmic energy as well as their first and second order delta

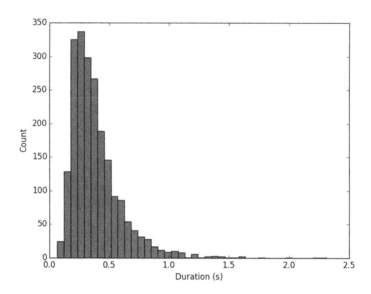

Fig. 1. The distribution of FPs duration

and acceleration coefficients; there are also voicing probability, F0 and zero-crossing rate, together with their deltas. For each frame-wise LLD the arithmetic mean and standard deviation across the frame itself and eight of its neighbouring frames (four before and four after) are used as the actual features. As the result we have in 162 values per frame.

After training our SVM classifier, as the post-processing step we applied Gaussian filter and morphological opening [10,20] that proved to be reasonably efficient for improving both precision and recall rates due to the usage of contextual information. Both these techniques are applied in the signal and image processing tasks for noise removal. Gaussian filter was used to smooth the spikes and remove the outliers on the probability estimates. Morphological opening is proved to be useful for making the detection of FPs more balanced by filtering false alarms and improving F1–score [20]. The parameters for Gaussian and morphological opening, as well as the decision threshold were determined using grid search on the development set.

The Gaussian filter allows us ahieve 12 % improvement for F1–score (precision rate improving by 17 % and recall rate by 5 %). Morphological opening gave us only 2 % improvement for F1–score, precision and recall, reducing false alarm rate. The example of dependence of results from varying decision threshold on SVM output is shown on Fig. 2.

As the result we achieved F1–score = F1–score = 0.54 ± 0.027, with precision and recall being 0.55 ± 0.05 and 0.53 ± 0.04 respectively. Measures on the test set are reported in terms of mean and standard deviation over the ten evaluations using classifiers trained on ten training subsets.

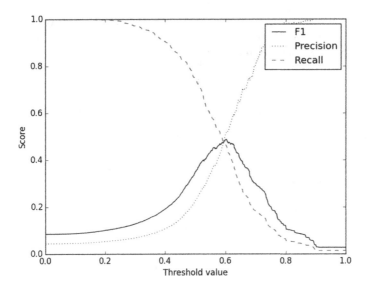

Fig. 2. The dependence of results from decision threshold

5   Conclusion

In this paper we present the experimental results on the detection of filled pauses and lengthenings in Russian spontaneous speech. For the purposes of this study we have united several corpora, that differ in quality, recording sites and situations, into one corpus that was used for the experiments. We used an SVM classifier and applied Gaussian filtering and morphological opening to post-process the probability estimates from an SVM, since these two techniques make use of contextual information. As the result we achieved F1–score = 0.54 ± 0.027, with precision and recall being 0.55 ± 0.05 and 0.53 ± 0.04 respectively. The future work will be aimed at addressing the remaining problem of false positives and false negatives by tuning SVM and introducing more contextual information.

Acknowledgments. This research is supported by the grant of Russian Foundation for Basic Research (project No 15-06-04465) and by the Council for Grants of the President of the Russian Federation (project No. MK-5209.2015.8).

References

1. Department of Phonetics of Saint Petersburg University. http://phonetics.spbu.ru/
2. Scikit-Learn: Machine Learning in Python. http://scikit-learn.org
3. Chang, C.C., Lin, C.J.: LIBSVM: A library for support vector machines. ACM Trans. Intell. Syst. Technol. (TIST) **2**, 1–27 (2011). http://www.csie.ntu.edu.tw/cjlin/libsvm
4. Clark, H.: Using Language. Cambridge University Press, Cambridge (1996)

5. Eyben, F., Wöllmer, M., Schuller, B.: OpenSMILE: the Munich versatile and fast open-source audio feature extractor. In: Proceedings of the 18th ACM International conference on Multimedia, pp. 1459–1462. ACM (2010)

6. Giannini, A.: Hesitation phenomena in spontaneous italian. In: Proceedings of the 15th International Congress of Phonetic Sciences, Barcelona, Spain, pp. 2653–2656 (2003)

7. Godfrey, J.J., Holliman, E.C., McDaniel, J.: SWITCHBOARD: Telephone speech corpus for research and development. In: Proceedings of the International Conference on Acoustics, Speech, and Signal Processing (ICASSP 1992), vol. 1, pp. 517–520. IEEE (1992)

8. Goto, M., Itou, K., Hayamizu, S.: A real-time filled pause detection system for spontaneous speech recognition. In: Proceedings of the Eurospeech, Budapest, Hungary, pp. 227–230. ISCA (1999)

9. Gupta, R., Audhkhasi, K., Lee, S., Narayanan, S.: Paralinguistic event detection from speech using probabilistic time-series smoothing and masking. In: Proceedings of the INTERSPEECH 2013, Lyon, France, pp. 173–177. ISCA (2013)

10. Heijmans, H.J.: Mathematical morphology: a modern approach in image processing based on algebra and geometry. SIAM Rev. **37**(1), 1–36 (1995)

11. INTERSPEECH: Computational Paralinguistic Challenge (2013). http://emotion-research.net/sigs/speech-sig/is13-compare

12. Khurshudian, V.: Hesitation in typologically different languages: An experimental study. In: Proceedings of the International Conference on Computational Linguistics Dialogue, pp. 497–501 (2005)

13. Kibrik, A., Podlesskaya, V. (eds.): Rasskazy o Snovideniyah: Korpusnoye Issledovaniye Ustnogo Russkogo Diskursa [Night dream stories: Corpus study of Russian discourse]. Litres (2014)

14. Medeiros, H., Batista, F., Moniz, H., Trancoso, I., Meinedo, H.: Experiments on automatic detection of filled pauses using prosodic features. In: Actas de Inforum 2013, pp. 335–345 (2013)

15. Medeiros, H., Moniz, H., Batista, F., Trancoso, I., Nunes, L., et al.: Disfluency detection based on prosodic features for university lectures. In: Proceedings of the INTERSPEECH 2013, Lyon, France, pp. 2629–2633 (2013)

16. O'Connell, D., Kowal, S.: The history of research on the filled pause as evidence of the written language bias in linguistics. J. Psycholinguist. Res. **33**(6), 459–474 (2004)

17. Ogden, R.: Turn-holding, turn-yielding and laryngeal activity in finnish talk-in-interaction. J. Int. Phonetics Assoc. **31**(1), 139–152 (2001)

18. O'Shaughnessy, D.: Recognition of hesitations in spontaneous speech. In: Proceedings of the International Conference on Acoustics, Speech, and Signal Processing, (ICASSP 1992), vol. 1, pp. 521–524. IEEE (1992)

19. Ostendorf, M., Shriberg, E., Stolcke, A.: Human Language Technology: Opportunities and Challenges. Technical report, DTIC Document (2005)

20. Prylipko, D., Egorow, O., Siegert, I., Wendemuth, A.: Application of image processing methods to filled pauses detection from spontaneous speech. In: Proceedings of the INTERSPEECH 2014, Singapore, pp. 1816–1820. ISCA (2014)

21. Shriberg, E.: Spontaneous speech: how people really talk and why engineers should care. In: Proceedings of the INTERSPEECH 2005, Lisbon, Portugal, pp. 1781–1784. ISCA (2005)

22. Shriberg, E.: To 'Errrr' is human: Ecology and acoustics of speech disfluencies. J. Int. Phonetic Assoc. **31**(1), 153–169 (2001)

23. Shriberg, E., Bates, R.A., Stolcke, A.: A prosody only decision-tree model for disfluency detection. In: Proceedings of the 5th European Conference on Speech Communication and Technology Eurospeech 1997, Rhodes, Greece, pp. 2383–2386 (1997)
24. Stepanova, S.: Some features of filled hesitation pauses in spontaneous Russian. In: Proceedings of the 16th International Congress of Phonetic Sciences, Saarbrucken, Germany, vol. 16, pp. 1325–1328 (2007)
25. Stolcke, A., Shriberg, E., Bates, R.A., Ostendorf, M., Hakkani, D., Plauche, M., Tür, G., Lu, Y.: Automatic detection of sentence boundaries and disfluencies based on recognized words. In: ICSLP (1998)
26. Stouten, F., Martens, J.P.: A feature-based filled pause detection system for Dutch. In: Workshop on Automatic Speech Recognition and Understanding, ASRU 2003, pp. 309–314. IEEE (2003)
27. Verkhodanova, V., Shapranov, V.: Automatic detection of filled pauses and lengthenings in the spontaneous russian speech. In: Proceedings of the 7th International Conference Speech Prosody, Dublin, Ireland, pp. 1110–1114 (2014)
28. Verkhodanova, V., Shapranov, V.: Multi-factor method for detection of filled pauses and lengthenings in russian spontaneous speech. In: Ronzhin, A., Potapova, R., Fakotakis, N. (eds.) SPECOM 2015. LNCS, vol. 9319, pp. 285–292. Springer, Heidelberg (2015)
29. Zahorian, S.A., Wu, J., Karnjanadecha, M., Vootkur, C.S., Wong, B., Hwang, A., Tokhtamyshev, E.: Open-source multi-language audio database for spoken language processing applications. In: Proceedings of the INTERSPEECH 2011, Florence, Italy, pp. 1493–1496 (2011)

Detecting Laughter and Filler Events by Time Series Smoothing with Genetic Algorithms

Gábor Gosztolya[1,2(✉)]

[1] Institute of Informatics, University of Szeged,
Dugonics tér 13, Szeged 6720, Hungary
ggabor@inf.u-szeged.hu
[2] MTA-SZTE Research Group on Artificial Intelligence,
Tisza Lajos krt. 103, Szeged 6720, Hungary

Abstract. Social signal detection, where the aim is to identify vocalizations like laughter and filler events (sounds like "eh", "er", etc.) is a popular task in the area of computational paralinguistics, a subfield of speech technology. Recent studies have shown that besides applying state-of-the-art machine learning methods, it is worth making use of the contextual information and adjusting the frame-level scores based on the local neighbourhood. In this study we apply a weighted average time series smoothing filter for laughter and filler event identification, and set the weights using genetic algorithms. Our results indicate that this is a viable way of improving the Area Under the Curve (AUC) scores: our resulting scores are much better than the accuracy of the raw likelihoods produced by both AdaBoost.MH and DNN, and we also significantly outperform standard time series filters as well.

Keywords: Social signals · Laughter and filler event detection · Time series filter · Genetic algorithms

1 Introduction

In speech technology an emerging area is paralinguistic phenomenon detection, which seeks to detect non-linguistic events (laughter, conflict, etc.) in speech. One task belonging to this area is the detection of social signals, from which, perhaps laughter and filler events (vocalizations like "eh", "er", etc.) are the most important. Many experiments have been performed with the goal of detecting laughter (e.g. [11,12]), and this task might prove useful in emotion recognition and in general man-machine interactions. Apart from laughter, the detection of filler events has also become popular (e.g. [14,18]). Besides serving to regulate the flow of interaction in discussions, it was also shown that filler events are an important sign of hesitation; hence their detection could prove useful during the automatic detection of various kinds of dementia such as Alzheimer's Disease [10] and Mild Cognitive Impairment [18].

In the tasks of detecting laughter and filler events, it is well known (see e.g. [3,6,9]) that although classification and evaluation are performed at the frame

© Springer International Publishing Switzerland 2016
A. Ronzhin et al. (Eds.): SPECOM 2016, LNAI 9811, pp. 232–239, 2016.
DOI: 10.1007/978-3-319-43958-7_27

level, it is worth making use of the contextual information and adjusting the frame-level scores based on the local neighborhood. Gupta et al. [9] applied probabilistic time series smoothing; Brueckner et al. [3] trained a second neural network on the output of the first, frame-level one to smooth the resulting scores; while Gosztolya [6] used the Simple Exponential Smoothing method on the frame-level posterior likelihood estimates.

What is common in these studies is that first they trained a frame-level classifier such as Deep Neural Networks (DNN) to detect the given phenomena, and then, as a second step, they aggregated the neighbouring posterior estimates to get the final scores. It is not clear, however, what type of smoothing may prove to be optimal. In this study we compute the weighted mean of the neighbouring scores as a time series smoothing filter; but even with this type of aggregation, the optimal weight values have to be determined. We treated this task as an optimization one in the space of frame-level weights, where we seek to maximize the Area Under the Curve (AUC) score for the phenomena we are looking for (now laughter and filler events). To find the optimal weight values, we applied genetic algorithms. Using the optimal filters found on the development set, we significantly outperformed both the unsmoothed ("raw") values and some standard time series filters of the same size on the test set of a public English dataset containing laughter and filler events.

2   Genetic Algorithms

Genetic Algorithms (GAs) are adaptive methods which may be used to solve search and optimization problems [1]. The concept and mechanisms applied are based on the genetic processes of biological organisms. Mimicking the evolution of biological populations by selection and recombination, genetic algorithms are able to "evolve" solutions to real world problems.

Genetic Algorithms use a direct analogy of natural behaviour. They work with a *population* of *individuals*, each representing a valid solution to the given problem. Each individual consists of a number of parameters (*genes*). To each individual, a *fitness score* is assigned, which is based on how good a solution it is to the given task. Individuals with higher fitness scores are given opportunities to "reproduce" by "cross breeding" (*crossover*) with other individuals in the population. In this way new individuals are generated that share some features taken from each parent. Then, to each child, *mutation* is applied, which usually means that with a small probability (e.g. 0.001), a gene is changed to some random value. The traditional view is that, from the two recombination steps, crossover is the more important one for rapidly exploring the search space, but mutation provides a small amount of random search [1]. The individuals constructed in this way will form the population of the next *generation*. Traditional GAs start from a randomly generated population and repeat the above steps for several generations. Lastly, the best solution will be the individual in the last population with the highest fitness score.

3   Experimental Setup

3.1   The SSPNet Vocalization Corpus

The SSPNet Vocalization Corpus [14] consists of 2763 short audio clips extracted from telephone conversations of 120 speakers, containing 2988 laughter and 1158 filler events. We used the feature set provided for the Interspeech 2013 Computational Paralinguistics Challenge (ComParE, [16]). It consisted of the frame-wise 39-long $MFCC + \Delta + \Delta\Delta$ feature vector along with voicing probability, HNR, F0 and zero-crossing rate, and their derivatives. To these 47 features their mean and standard derivative in a 9-frame long neighbourhood were added, resulting in a total of 141 features [16]. Each frame was labeled as one of three classes, namely "laughter", "filler" or "garbage" (meaning both silence and non-filler non-laughter speech).

We followed the standard routine of dividing the dataset into training, development and test sets published in [16]. As evaluation metrics, we used the method of evaluation which is the de facto standard for laughter detection: we calculated the Area Under Curve (AUC) score for the output likelihood scores of the class of interest. As we now seek to detect two kinds of phenomena (laughter and filler events), we calculated AUC for both social signals; then these AUC values were averaged, giving the Unweighted Average Area Under Curve (UAAUC) score [16].

3.2   Frame-Level Classification

Before applying a time series filter, first we have to somehow get a likelihood estimate for each class and frame of the utterances. For this, we utilized two state-of-the-art machine learning methods, which we will briefly describe below.

AdaBoost.MH. AdaBoost.MH [15] is an efficient meta-learner algorithm, which seeks to build a strong *final classifier* from a linear combination of simple, scalar *base classifiers*. For more complex problems, the state-of-the-art performance of AdaBoost.MH is usually achieved using *decision trees* as base learners, parametrized by their number of leaves.

We utilized an open source implementation (the *multiboost* tool [2]), and followed a multi-armed bandit (MAB) setup, which can speed up training significantly. In it, for each boosting iteration step, the optimal base learner is found using only a small subset of features, and the usefulness of these subsets are learned from the accuracy of these basic classifiers [4]. We sampled the over-represented "garbage" class, and included the feature vectors of 8 neighbouring frames on each side. We then used 8-leaved decision trees as base learners, and trained our model for $100,000$ iterations. For the details, see [7].

Deep Rectifier Neural Networks. Deep neural networks differ from conventional ones in that they consist of several hidden layers. This deep structure can provide significant improvements in results compared to earlier techniques used, but the conventional backpropagation algorithm has problems when training such networks. For this, one possible solution is deep rectifier neural networks [5].

In deep rectifier neural networks, rectified linear units are employed as hidden neurons, which apply the rectifier activation function $\max(0, x)$ instead of the usual sigmoid one [5]. The main advantage of deep rectifier nets is that they can be trained with the standard backpropagation algorithm, without any tedious pre-training (e.g. [8]). We used our custom implementation, originally developed for phoneme classification. On the TIMIT database, frequently used as a reference dataset for phoneme recognition, we achieved the best accuracy known to us [17].

For the actual task, we trained our model on 31 consecutive neighbouring frame vectors. (Due to shorter execution times, we were able to carry out more experiments with neural networks than with AdaBoost.MH.) After preliminary tests, we used five rectified hidden layers, each consisting of 256 neurons, and we had neurons that used the softmax function in the output layer.

3.3 Frame-Level Likelihood Aggregation

After obtaining the frame-level likelihood estimates of our classifiers (the "raw" scores), in the next part we will aggregate the values in the local neighbourhood in order to improve the AUC scores. We chose the weighted form of the moving average time series filter; that is, for a filter with a width of $2N + 1$ we define the weight values as $w_{-N}, w_{-N+1}, \ldots, w_N \geq 0$ and $\sum_{i=-N}^{N} w_i = 1$. Afterwards, for the jth frame with the raw likelihood estimate a_j we calculate

$$a'_j = \sum_{i=-N}^{N} w_i a_{j+i}. \tag{1}$$

(Here we used the simplification that, for an utterance consisting of k frames, $a_j = a_1$ for $\forall j \leq 0$, and $a_j = a_k$ for $\forall j > k$.) We then optimized the w_i weight values using genetic algorithms. To test whether the (possible) improvements in the AUC scores come from the actual weight vector and not from the fact that we use some kind of aggregation, we also tested two simple approaches. In the first one, we took the unweighted average of the raw likelihood estimates; that is, we had $w_i = \frac{1}{2N+1}$ (*constant* filter). In the second approach we randomly generated the w_i values (*random* filter).

3.4 Applying Genetic Algorithms

We represented each time series filter by a vector of the w_i weights (i.e. each gene corresponded to a w_i weight). We used filters of size of 129 (64 frames at both sides), based on the results of preliminary tests. We supposed that the optimal weights of the neighbouring frames are not completely independent of each other, so we only stored one weight for every eight frames, while we linearly interpolated

Table 1. The AUC scores for the laughter and filler events got by using the different classification and aggregation methods.

ML method	Filter type	Dev. set			Test set		
		Lau.	Fil.	Both	Lau.	Fil.	Both
AdaBoost.MH	—	94.0	94.9	94.5	91.9	87.9	89.9
	Random	97.7	94.2	95.9	94.6	87.5	91.0
	Constant	97.8	94.1	95.9	94.7	87.6	91.2
	Genetic alg.	**98.0**	**96.4**	**97.2**	**95.0**	**89.5**	**92.2**
DNN	—	92.9	95.5	94.2	91.3	87.9	89.6
	Random	96.7	94.4	95.5	94.2	86.9	90.5
	Constant	**96.9**	94.3	95.6	**94.4**	86.9	90.7
	Genetic alg.	96.7	**96.5**	**96.6**	94.3	**88.8**	**91.6**
DNN + Prob. time series smoothing [9]		95.1	94.7	94.9	93.3	89.7	91.5
DNN + DNN [3]		98.1	96.5	97.3	94.9	89.9	92.4
ComParE 2013 baseline [16]		86.2	89.0	87.6	82.9	83.6	83.3

the weight values for the intermediate frames. This approach resulted in a more compact weight vector (only 17 values overall instead of 129), which should be easier to optimize.

We utilized the JGAP Java Genetic Algorithm Package [13]. The population size was 250, while we evolved for 100 generations. We used averaging crossover, while for mutation we randomly changed the value of one weight in the weight vector (with the default probability value of 0.001). To keep the frame weight values on the same scale, for each step we normalized each weight vector so that the weights summed up to one. We optimized the filter of the laughter and the filler phenomena independently; the fitness function was the AUC score of the given phenomenon on the development set.

4   Results

Table 1 lists the output AUC and UAAUC scores we got for the two classifier methods and the time series filter approaches. The first thing to notice is that the raw scores (indicated by the "—" filter type) are quite competitive, compared to the ComParE baseline, which were not smoothed over time either. As for the two classifier methods, AdaBoost.MH performed somewhat better; the reason for this is probably that we sampled the database during classifier model training, therefore the distribution of the three classes (that of garbage, laughter and filler events) was more balanced, resulting in more precise likelihood estimations for the laughter and filler classes.

Upon examining the two basic smoothing approaches used for reference (filters "random" and "constant"), we can see that applying these approaches alone brings a significant improvement over the raw likelihood scores. This indicates

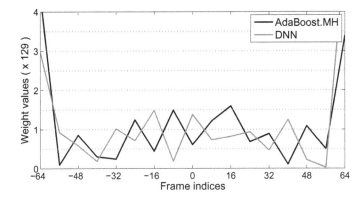

Fig. 1. The optimal filters found using the genetic algorithm for laughter events

that just by utilizing a smoothing filter of this width (which is over a second long) we can noticeably improve the AUC values of the likelihood estimates. Over these scores, however, the weight vectors optimized by the genetic algorithm gives an additional 1 % gain in AUC on the test set, which, in our opinion, justifies our approach of utilizing a weighted average time series filter over the raw likelihood estimates, and optimizing the weights using genetic algorithm. Of course, the width of the filter has to be set carefully, which requires further investigation, just as the number of weights in the weight vector (recall that now for each eight frame we optimized only one weight, while the remaining ones were linearly interpolated). Furthermore, the application of other crossover operators besides the averaging one (for example single point crossover, or a crossover operator which takes the mean of neighbouring filter weight values, therefore smoothing the whole time series filter) could be tested as well, but this falls outside the scope of this study.

4.1 The Time Series Filters Found

Figures 1 and 2 show the time series smoothing filters got by using a genetic algorithm for the laughter and filler events, respectively. The weight values were scaled up to 129 times for better readability (i.e. a weight value of 1 means average importance for the given frame). The large straight sections are due to the linear interpolation of the intermediate frames. It can be seen that the filters are not really smooth themselves, which is probably due to the optimization technique used. Despite this, the two filters belonging to the two different machine learning methods are quite similar to each other for both phenomena.

The filters found for the laughter events have slightly higher weight values around the central frame than those further away (although this tendency is disturbed by the noise present in the weight vectors, which is probably due to the random population initialization of GA). However, what is quite interesting is that the first and last weight values for both machine learning methods are quite

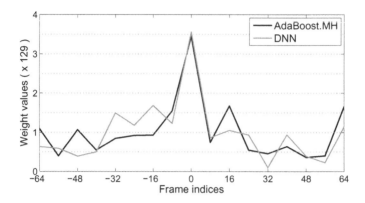

Fig. 2. The optimal filters found using the genetic algorithm for filler events

high, being 3–4 times the average weight. For an explanation of this phenomenon recall that our classifier models were trained using the feature vectors of the 8-8 and 15-15 neighbouring frames on both sides for AdaBoost.MH and DNNs, respectively. This means that the posterior estimate provided by a DNN for the first frame in the smoothing filter already includes some information about the 15 preceding frame, and using the likelihood estimate of the last frame we can "peek" into the 15 consecutive frames. This makes the first and last frames in the averaged filter more important than the inner ones, while the values of the inner frames are redundant to some extent.

This effect is present on the time series smoothing filters found for the filler events, although surprisingly only at the end of the filter. Here, however, the middle frames seem to be very important, having a relative importance of about 3.5 times that of an average frame. This holds for the filters found for both machine learning methods.

5   Conclusions

In this study, we investigated the task of laughter and filler detection. As was shown earlier, after some frame-level posterior estimation step performed via some machine learning method, it is worth smoothing the output likelihood scores of the consecutive frames; so we applied a weighted averaging time series smoothing filter. To set the weights in the filter, we applied genetic algorithms, using the development set of a public English dataset. Our AUC scores got on the test set significantly outperformed both the unsmoothed likelihood values and standard time series filters of the same size.

Acknowledgments. The Titan X graphics card used for this research was donated by the NVIDIA Corporation.

References

1. Beasley, D., Bull, D.R., Martin, R.R.: An overview of genetic algorithms: part 1, fundamentals. Univ. Comput. **15**(2), 58–69 (1993)
2. Benbouzid, D., Busa-Fekete, R., Casagrande, N., Collin, F.D., Kégl, B.: Multi-Boost: a multi-purpose boosting package. J. Mach. Learn. Res. **13**, 549–553 (2012)
3. Brueckner, R., Schuller, B.: Hierarchical neural networks and enhanced class posteriors for social signal classification. In: Proceedings of ASRU, pp. 362–367 (2013)
4. Busa-Fekete, R., Kégl, B.: Fast boosting using adversarial bandits. In: Proceedings of ICML, vol. 27, pp. 143–150 (2010)
5. Glorot, X., Bordes, A., Bengio, Y.: Deep sparse rectifier networks. In: Proceedings of AISTATS, pp. 315–323 (2011)
6. Gosztolya, G.: On evaluation metrics for social signal detection. In: Proceedings of Interspeech, Dresden, Germany, pp. 2504–2508, September 2015
7. Gosztolya, G., Busa-Fekete, R., Tóth, L.: Detecting autism, emotions and social signals using AdaBoost. In: Proceedings of Interspeech, Lyon, France, pp. 220–224, August 2013
8. Tóth, L., Grósz, T.: A comparison of deep neural network training methods for large vocabulary speech recognition. In: Habernal, I. (ed.) TSD 2013. LNCS, vol. 8082, pp. 36–43. Springer, Heidelberg (2013)
9. Gupta, R., Audhkhasi, K., Lee, S., Narayanan, S.S.: Speech paralinguistic event detection using probabilistic time-series smoothing and masking. In: Proceedings of InterSpeech, pp. 173–177 (2013)
10. Hoffmann, I., Németh, D., Dye, C., Pákáski, M., Irinyi, T., Kálmán, J.: Temporal parameters of spontaneous speech in Alzheimer's disease. Int. J. Speech-Language Pathol. **12**(1), 29–34 (2010)
11. Knox, M.T., Mirghafori, N.: Automatic laughter detection using neural networks. In: Proceedings of Interspeech, pp. 2973–2976 (2007)
12. Neuberger, T., Beke, A., Gósy, M.: Acoustic analysis and automatic detection of laughter in Hungarian spontaneous speech. In: Proceedings of ISSP, pp. 281–284 (2014)
13. Rotstan, N.: JGAP: Java Genetic Algorithms Package (2005). http://jgap.sourceforge.net/
14. Salamin, H., Polychroniou, A., Vinciarelli, A.: Automatic detection of laughter and fillers in spontaneous mobile phone conversations. In: Proceedings of SMC, pp. 4282–4287 (2013)
15. Schapire, R., Singer, Y.: Improved boosting algorithms using confidence-rated predictions. Mach. Learn. **37**(3), 297–336 (1999)
16. Schuller, B., Steidl, S., Batliner, A., Vinciarelli, A., Scherer, K., Ringeval, F., Chetouani, M., Weninger, F., Eyben, F., Marchi, E., Salamin, H., Polychroniou, A., Valente, F., Kim, S.: The interspeech 2013 computational paralinguistics challenge: social signals, conflict, emotion, autism. In: Proceedings of Interspeech (2013)
17. Tóth, L.: Phone recognition with hierarchical convolutional deep maxout networks. EURASIP J. Audio, Speech, Music Process. **2015**(25), 1–13 (2015)
18. Tóth, L., Gosztolya, G., Vincze, V., Hoffmann, I., Szatlóczki, G., Biró, E., Zsura, F., Pákáski, M., Kálmán, J.: Automatic detection of mild cognitive impairment from spontaneous speech using ASR. In: Proceedings of Interspeech, Dresden, Germany, pp. 2694–2698, September 2015

Detecting State of Aggression in Sentences Using CNN

Denis Gordeev[✉]

Moscow State Linguistic University, Ostozhenka. 38, 119034 Moscow, Russia
gordeev-d-i@yandex.com

Abstract. In this article we study verbal expression of aggression and its detection using machine learning and neural networks methods. We test our results using our corpora of messages from anonymous imageboards. We also compare Random forest classifier with convolutional neural network for "Movie reviews with one sentence per review" corpus.

Keywords: Word2vec · CNN · Random forest · Verbal aggression · Sentiment analysis · Imageboards

1 Introduction

With the development of the Internet, verbal aggression and cyberbullying have become a problem on the Net. For example, the US government has proposed an incentive to stop cyberbullying [2] and Russian criminal code [20] persecutes verbal aggression both in oral and written speech, but there is no clear definition of what is aggression and what is not. For this reason many researchers study expression of aggression both on all levels nowadays. A lot of studies have been devoted to the analysis of the semantic field of aggression [14] and its aspects in multicultural communities both for written [15,17] and oral speech [13,18].

In recent years the number of works using neural network and machine learning techniques has seen a dramatic increase. While neural networks per se or combined with machine learning methods such as Random forest [4] or SVM [5] make it possible to discard vocabulary-based methods and to switch from these and other similar methods requiring manual editing. That is why the field of sentiment analysis, being already studied [7], has become even more prominent with the advent of machine learning and neural networks as it can be efficiently solved using these methods. Word2vec [10], glove [11] and other word vector models have shown better results than usual bigram and trigram models and helped to overcome the computational difficulties of larger n-gram spaces. They provided an efficient and computationally affordable method of finding similarity between different words and building semantic vector space. They require no manual annotation, only large corpora of texts, thus any set of texts can be used as a corpus. Skip-gram models combined with deep learning methods are widely

© Springer International Publishing Switzerland 2016
A. Ronzhin et al. (Eds.): SPECOM 2016, LNAI 9811, pp. 240–245, 2016.
DOI: 10.1007/978-3-319-43958-7_28

used now for sentiment analysis [21], for object labeling [9] and for other NLP tasks.

CNN neural networks first used for image object classification and detection and other computer vision tasks, have been shown to be efficient for NLP tasks. Kim [8] has proposed to combine CNN's and Word2vec for sentiment analysis tasks. His model outperformed other deep learning models for the majority of tasks on different corpora. His model included word2vec [10] word embeddings for every word of the text and a set of convolutional filters. Chunting Zhou et al. [22] have showed close results to Kim's CNN using a LSTM-model. It was also [19] proposed to decrease the size and number of filters for such a tiny corpus as "Movie reviews with one sentence per review" [12].

In this article we compare the results of a CNN-model with usual machine learning techniques (Random forest) for the task of analysis of aggression.

We used a corpus of movie reviews by Pang and Lee and our tiny corpus of aggressive imageboard messages for this task and compared the results with our Random Forest classifier.

2   Methods and Materials

We selected imageboards (4chan.org, 2ch.hk) as the material for our tiny corpus because these communities are considered to be extremely aggressive and messages containing expression of verbal aggression are abundant there [16]. Bernstein who has conducted research on imageboard culture supports this statement [3]. By verbal aggression we understand a personality trait that predisposes persons to attack the selfconcepts of other people instead of, or in addition to, their positions on topics of communication [6].

Movie reviews corpus is a subset of Stanford Sentiment Treebank containing only one-sentence reviews. Data is labeled there as positive or negative (Table 1).

Imageboard aggression corpus of English messages consists of about 2000 annotated messages for Russian and English languages. Both parts consist of about 1000 messages. They are labeled as positive or negative, neutral reviews are removed. There is no test data, so 90 % of data was used training and 10 % for evaluation (see Table 1). From the table we can see that the vocabulary is much more diverse for movie reviews, while imageboards suffer from primitive lexics.

We used a CNN model with backpropagation of embeddings (CNN-nonstatic) similar to Kim's with some adjustments suggested by Rakhlin. Thus, we decreased the number of filter sized from 3 to 2 and However, instead of using Google-news corpus or training word2vec vectors we used model based on 4chan.org threads with about 600-dimensional vector trained on about 1,089,000 messages and containing about 30 million words for the American corpus. For 2ch.hk and the Russian language we used our corpus of 974654 messages containing 13640000 sentences, For the task of aggression classification we treated messages as single sentences. There is also no test data, and 90 % of data was used training and 10 % for evaluation.

Table 1. Comparison of movie reviews and aggressive messages corpora

Corpora	Classes (N)	Avg. sentence length	Dataset (sent.)	Voc. size	Voc. in model
Movie reviews	2	20	10662	18765	17121
SVAggr. (eng.)	2	19	19732	3765	3690
SVAggr. (rus.)	2	13	5101	1030	989

Movie reviews is a corpus of on sentence per movie review, SVAggr.(eng.) is the corpus of American anonymous messages, SVAggr.(rus) is the corpus of Russian anonymous messages

Other CNN models were trained to compare the results. We also tried to use some language features to improve CNN-predictions. As linguistic information we used preprocessed part-of-speech (POS) tags. Tags were gained using nltk library. Its efficiency rate is between 88 % and 94 % [1]. These tags were combined in another convolutional network (CNN POS). We tried to implement these tags into a neural model, so we added another neural model in parallel and then merged its results with the neural network that uses embeddings (CNN-non-static). CNN-neural network that used word embeddings into a final neural network. We tried several models for the POS neural network.

For the Random forest classifier, first, we chose a set of words and phrases using our background knowledge of typical expressions for aggressive messages. Then after clearing and tokenizing raw data we computed features F used for Random forest training and evaluation:

$$F_{1,i} = \{f_1 \, f_2, ..., f_i\}, \tag{1}$$

where $\{f_1, f_2, ..., f_i\}$ is a set features for sentences $\{s_1, s_2, ..., s_i\}$ and

$$\dot{f}n = \{\textstyle\sum_{i=1}^{z}(w2v(\{w_1, w_2, ..., w_z\})), mean(w2v(s_n)), \\ max(w2v(s_n)) - min(w2v(s_n)), len(s_n))\}, \tag{2}$$

where s_n is a sentence with words $\{w_1, w_2, ..., w_z\}$ and $w2v$ is a function that computes distance between a given word and a chosen set of aggressive words and phrases for sentence s_n, len is a length of the sentence s_n.

3   Results and Discussions

Results of CNN-based and Random forest models are listed in Table 2. Random Forest classifier outperforms CNN-based methods for aggression detection task for the English language. It can be a result of overfitting, although train and test sets are not mixed and properly divided. Also it is possible to consider that word2vec distance performs well enough for the task of aggression detection and that features were selected successfully or that concatenating sentences is not effective. Moreover, with the increase of the set, the results are prone to worsen

Table 2. Results of CNN and random forest classificators

Classifier	MR (%)	Verb. Aggr. (eng.) (%)	Verb. Aggr. (rus.)
Random forest	58.39	88.4	59.13
CNN-non-static	81.1	81.39	66.68
CNN (POS)	80.9	81.17	62.37
CNN-non-static, CNN (POS) combined	81	81.22	64.53

MR - Movie reviews corpus, Verb. aggr. (eng.)- is a corpus of American image-board messages annotated with consideration of containing or not state of aggression, Verb. Aggr. (rus.) is the corpus of Russian anonymous messages

because more types of aggression will be included and it will be expressed in other wording. We can see that it performed poorly for movie reviews classification task, also we failed to select a good set of feature words. Moreover, as said by Chunting Zhou [8] a simple SVM algorithm with hand-crafted features outperformed more robust and complicated models, however, it requires manual featuring.

We also supported the results of the article by [19]. It is asserted there that the result of the work by Kim is caused not by the amount and complexity of convolutional layers. So Kim's model may be greatly simplified without affecting the performance. We should also admit that Kim says himself that the philosophy of his work is that pretrained deep learning features work well for other tasks as well and asserts it in conclusion as well.

Also using not a Google news word2vec model, but a model from another domain having substantial vocabulary did not affect the results.

Adding POS-tags did not help to improve the results. At first we tried usual recurrent network, it gained decent 76 % after the 5th epoch for the aggression

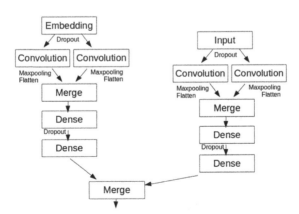

Fig. 1. The structure of neural networks. *On the right is a branch using POS-tags, on the left is CNN with word-embedding vectors*

detection corpus, however, it overfitted soon after it. Then we tried the same model as used for the word2vec embeddings. The only difference was that we changed word2vec embeddings with random coefficients, it helped to get decent 81.1 % for the same task, almost the same as with using word2vec embeddings. After that, we tried to combine two models, unfortunately, we increased the results above the threshold of CNN-rand model that used nothing besides part-of-speech tags only a little (see Fig. 1).

4   Conclusion

In this article we have considered ways of automatic determining of state of aggression. We used two classifiers for this task and later compared them. We used Random forest classifier and a convolutional neural network for this task. They were tested on two different corpora: "Movie reviews with one sentence per review" containing positive and negative movie reviews and a 2-language Anonymous imageboards corpus annotated whether a message is aggressive or not. Random forest classifier surpassed CNN for the task of detecting aggression for the English language, however, the gap between two classifiers is very significant for the task of sentiment analysis of movie reviews and Random forest performed poorly for the Russian language. That is why convolutional neural network (and deep learning, in general) classifiers are considered more perspective and promising. We also tried implementing linguistic features, such as part of speech tagging, but it did not lead to better results. However, the results are promising and in future works we will continue their implementation.

Acknowledgments. The survey is being carried out with the support of the Russian Science Foundation (RSF) in the framework of the project 14-18-01059 at the Institute of Applied and Mathematical Linguistics of the Moscow State Linguistic University and with the support of the Russian Foundation for Basic Research (RFBR) in the framework of the project 16-29-12986.

References

1. A Good Part-of-Speech Tagger in about 200 Lines of Python. https://spacy.io/blog/part-of-speech-pos-tagger-in-python. Accessed 24 Oct 2015
2. ASPA, What is Cyberbullying (2012). http://www.stopbullying.gov/cyberbullying/what-is-it/. Accessed 24 Oct 2015
3. Bernstein, M., Monroy-Hernndez, A., Harry, D., Andr, P., Panovich, K., Vargas, G.: 4chan and /b/: an analysis of anonymity and ephemerality in a large online community. In: Proceedings of Fifth International AAAI Conference on Weblogs Social Media, pp. 50–57 (2011)
4. Breiman, L.: Random forests. Mach. Learn. **45**, 5–32 (2001)
5. Hearst, M.A., Dumais, S.T., Osman, E., Platt, J., Scholkopf, B.: Support vector machines. IEEE Intell. Syst. **13**, 18–28 (1998)
6. Infante, D.A., Wigley, C.J.: Verbal aggressiveness: an interpersonal model and measure. Commun. Monogr. **53**, 61–69 (1986)

7. Kharlamov, A.A., Yermolenko, T.V., Zhonin, A.A.: Modeling of process dynamics by sequence of homogenous semantic networks on the base of text corpus sequence analysis. In: Ronzhin, A., Potapova, R., Delic, V. (eds.) SPECOM 2014. LNCS, vol. 8773, pp. 300–307. Springer, Heidelberg (2014)
8. Kim, Y., Jernite, Y., Sontag, D., Rush, A.: Character-Aware Neural Language Models. arXiv Prepr. arXiv:1508.06615 (2015)
9. Lazaridou, A., Pham, N., Baroni, M.: Combining language and vision with a multimodal skip-gram model. arXiv Prepr. arXiv:1501.02598 (2015)
10. Mikolov, T., Chen, K., Corrado, G., Dean, J.: Distributed representations of words and phrases and their compositionality. In: Nips, pp. 1–9 (2013)
11. Pennington, J., Socher, R., Manning, C.D.: GloVe: global vectors for word representation. In: Proceedings of the 2014 Conference on Empirical Methods in Natural Language Processing, pp. 1532–1543 (2014)
12. Pang, B., Lee, L.: Seeing stars: exploiting class relationships for sentiment categorization with respect to rating scales. In: Proceedings of the 43rd Annual Meeting (2005)
13. Potapova, R., Komalova, L., Bobrov, N.: Acoustic markers of emotional state "aggression". In: Ronzhin, A., Potapova, R., Fakotakis, N. (eds.) SPECOM 2015. LNCS, vol. 9319, pp. 55–64. Springer, Heidelberg (2015)
14. Potapova, R., Komalova, L.: On principles of annotated databases of the semantic field "aggression". In: Ronzhin, A., Potapova, R., Delic, V. (eds.) SPECOM 2014. LNCS, vol. 8773, pp. 322–328. Springer, Heidelberg (2014)
15. Potapova, R., Komalova, L.: Lingua-cognitive survey of the semantic field "aggression" in multicultural communication: typed text. In: Železný, M., Habernal, I., Ronzhin, A. (eds.) SPECOM 2013. LNCS, vol. 8113, pp. 227–232. Springer, Heidelberg (2013)
16. Potapova, R., Gordeev D.: Determination of the internet anonymity influence on the level of aggression and usage of obscene lexis. In: Proceedings of the 17th International Conference Speech and Computer (SPECOM 2015), Athens, Greece, 20–24 September 2015, vol. 2, pp. 29–36. University of Patras Press, Patras (2015)
17. Potapova, R., Komalova, L.: Auditory-perceptual recognition of the emotional state of aggression. In: Ronzhin, A., Potapova, R., Fakotakis, N. (eds.) SPECOM 2015. LNCS (LNAI), vol. 9319, pp. 89–95. Springer, Heidelberg (2015)
18. Potapova, R., Potapov, V.: Cognitive mechanism of semantic content decoding of spoken discourse in noise. In: Ronzhin, A., Potapova, R., Fakotakis, N. (eds.) SPECOM 2015. LNCS, vol. 9319, pp. 153–160. Springer, Heidelberg (2015)
19. Rakhlin, A.: Convolutional Neural Networks for Sentence Classification. https:// github.com/alexander-rakhlin/CNN-for-Sentence-Classification-in-Keras
20. Russian Criminal Code, art. 282
21. dos Santos, C., Gatti, M.: Deep convolutional neural networks for sentiment analysis of short texts. In: COLING (2014)
22. Zhou, C., Sun, C., Liu, Z., Lau, F.C.M.: A C-LSTM Neural Network for Text Classification (2015)

DNN-Based Acoustic Modeling for Russian Speech Recognition Using Kaldi

Irina Kipyatkova[1,2(✉)] and Alexey Karpov[1,3]

[1] St. Petersburg Institute for Informatics and Automation of the Russian Academy
of Sciences (SPIIRAS), St. Petersburg, Russia
{kipyatkova,karpov}@iias.spb.su
[2] St. Petersburg State University of Aerospace Instrumentation (SUAI), St. Petersburg, Russia
[3] ITMO University, St. Petersburg, Russia

Abstract. In the paper, we describe a research of DNN-based acoustic modeling for Russian speech recognition. Training and testing of the system was performed using the open-source Kaldi toolkit. We created tanh and p-norm DNNs with a different number of hidden layers and a different number of hidden units of tanh DNNs. Testing of the models was carried out on very large vocabulary continuous Russian speech recognition task. We obtained a relative WER reduction of 20 % comparing to the baseline GMM-HMM system.

Keywords: Deep neural networks · Acoustic models · Automatic speech recognition · Russian speech

1 Introduction

Investigations of combining artificial neural networks (ANNs) and hidden Markov models (HMMs) for acoustic modeling were started between the end of the 1980s and the beginning of the 1990s [1]. At present the usage of ANNs in automatic speech recognition (ASR) becomes very popular because of increasing performance of computers.

For acoustic modeling, ANNs are often combined with HMMs using hybrid and tandem methods [1]. In the hybrid method, ANNs are used for estimating the posterior probabilities of an HMM state. In the tandem method, outputs of ANNs are used as an additional stream of input features for HMM-GMM (Gaussian Mixture Models) system.

In this paper, we present a study on deep neural network (DNN) based acoustic models (AMs) for Russian speech recognition. For training and testing the speech recognition system we have used the open-source Kaldi toolkit [2]. The Kaldi software is written in C++ and based on the OpenFST library, and uses BLAS and LAPACK libraries for linear algebra. There are two implementations of DNNs in Kaldi. The first one is Kerel's implementation [3]. It supports Restricted Boltzmann Machines (RBM) pre-training, stochastic gradient training using graphics processing units (GPU), and discriminative training. The second implementation is Dan's implementation [4]. It does not support Restricted Boltzmann Machine pre-training; instead a method similar to the greedy layer-wise supervised training [5] or the "layer-wise backpropagation" [6] is

© Springer International Publishing Switzerland 2016
A. Ronzhin et al. (Eds.): SPECOM 2016, LNAI 9811, pp. 246–253, 2016.
DOI: 10.1007/978-3-319-43958-7_29

used. For the given research, we have chosen the latter DNN implementation because it supports parallel training on multiple CPUs.

The paper is organized as follows. In Sect. 2 we give a survey of various DNNs acoustic modeling, in Sect. 3 we give a description of DNN-based AMs in our Russian speech recognition system, in Sect. 4 we present our own training and test speech corpora, finally experiments on speech recognition using DNN-based AMs are presented in Sect. 5.

2 Related Works

In many recent papers, it was shown that DNN-HMM models outperform traditional GMM-HMM models. In [7], context-depended model based on a deep belief network for large-vocabulary speech recognition is presented. Deep belief networks have undirected connections between the 2 top layers and directed connections to all other layers from the layer above. In that research, a hybrid DNN-HMM architecture was used; it was shown that DNN-HMM model can outperform GMM-HMMs and the authors have achieved a relative sentence error reduction of 5.8 %.

In [8], context-depended DNNs-HMMs (CD-DNN-HMMs) are described. CD-DNN-HMMs combine ANN-based HMMs with tied-state triphones and deep-belief-network pre-training. Efficiency of the models was evaluated on the phone call transcription task. The application of CD-DNN-HMMs has reduced the word error rate (WER) from 27.4 % to 18.5 %.

An application of the tandem approach to acoustic modeling is presented in [9]. The input of the network was a window of successive feature vectors. Training of the network was performed according to the standard procedure that is used for a hybrid DNN-HMM system. Then extracted features were fed to the GMM-HMM system. The training was performed according to the standard expectation-maximization procedure. The authors have obtained a relative WER reduction of 31 % over baseline MFCC and PLP acoustic features with the context-independent models.

In [10], the possibility of obtaining the features directly from DNN without a conversion of output probabilities to features suitable for GMM-HMM system was researched. Experiments with the use of a 5-layer perceptron in a bottle-neck layer were conducted. After training the DNN, the outputs of the bottle-neck layer were used as features for GMM-HMM system for speech recognition system. There was obtained the reduction of WER comparing to the system with probabilistic features, as well as the reduction of model size because only a part of the network was used.

A research of DNN for acoustic modeling for large vocabulary continuous speech recognition (LVCSR) was also presented in [11]. In this paper, the authors have conducted an empirical investigation on what aspects of the DNN-based AM design are most important for performance of a speech recognition system. It was shown that increasing model size and depth is effective only up to a certain point. In addition, a comparison of standard DNNs, convolution NNs and deep locally untied NNs was made. It was found out that deep locally untied NNs perform slightly better.

In [12], the Kaldi toolkit was used for DNN-based children speech recognition for Italian. Karel's and Dan's DNN training was explored. Speech recognition results obtained using the Karel's implementation were slightly better than the Dan's DNN, but both implementations significantly outperformed non-DNN configuration.

The Kaldi toolkit was used for Serbian speech recognition in [13]. The DNN models were trained using the Karel's implementation on a single CUDA GPU. Depending on the test set a relative WER reduction of 15–22 % comparing to the GMM-HMM system was obtained.

In [14], Kaldi was used in conjunction with PDNN (Python deep learning toolkit) developed under Theano environment (http://deeplearning.net/software/theano/). The authors used Kaldi for training GMMs. DNN was trained with the help of PDNN, and then obtained DNN models were loaded into Kaldi for speech recognition. Four receipts were described in [14]: DNN Hybrid, Deep Bottleneck Feature (BNF) Tandem, BNF+DNN Hybrid, convolution NN Hybrid.

A continuous Russian speech recognition system with DNNs was described in [15]. The DNNs were used to calculate probabilities of states for a current observation vector. The speech recognition was performed with the help of finite state transducers (WFST). Feature vectors were represented as a sequence of characters, which were used as an input to the finite state transducer. In that paper, it was shown that the proposed method allows increasing speech recognition accuracy comparing to HMMs.

Another research of DNN for Russian speech recognition system is presented in [16], where a speaker adaptation method for CD-DNN-HMM AM was proposed. GMM-derived features were used as an input to DNN. There was obtained a relative WER reduction of 5 %–36 % on different adaptation sets comparing to the speaker-independent CD-DNN-HMM systems.

DNN-based acoustic modeling using Kaldi for Russian speech is presented in [17]. The authors applied the main steps of the Kaldi Switchboard recipe to one Russian speech database. The obtained results of speech recognition were compared with those for English speech. The absolute difference between WERs for Russian and English speech was over 15 %. So, the authors have proposed two methods for spontaneous Russian speech recognition, namely i-vector based DNN adaptation and speaker-dependent bottle-neck features, which provided 8.6 % and 11.9 % relative WER reductions respectively.

3   DNN-Based Acoustic Modeling for Russian ASR

A general architecture of the DNN-HMM hybrid system is presented in Fig. 1. The DNN is trained to predict posterior probabilities of each context-depended state with given acoustic observations. During decoding the output probabilities are divided by the prior probability of each state forming "pseudo-likelihood" that is used in place of the state emission probabilities in the HMM [18].

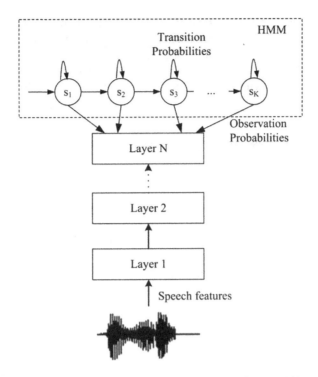

Fig. 1. Architecture of the DNN-HMM hybrid system [1]

The first step in training DNN-HMM model is to train GMM-HMM model using training data. The standard Kaldi receipt for DNN-based acoustic modeling consists of the following steps:

- feature extraction (13 MFCCs can be used as the features);
- training a monophone model;
- training a triphone model with delta features;
- training a triphone model with delta and delta-delta features;
- training a triphone model with Linear Discriminative Analysis (LDA) and Maximum Likelihood Linear Transform (MLLT);
- Speaker adapted training (SAT), i.e. training on feature space maximum likelihood linear regression (fMLLR) adapted features;
- training the final DNN-HMM model.

The DNN-HMM model is trained using fMLLR-adapted features; the decision tree and alignments are obtained from the SAT-fMLLR GMM system. We have tried DNNs with two types of nonlinearities (activation functions): tanh and p-norm. The p-norm generalization was proposed in [18], it is calculated as follows:

$$y = \|x\|_p = \left(\sum_i |x_i|^p \right)^{1/p},$$

where vector *x* represents a small group of inputs. The value of p is configurable. In [18], it was shown that p = 2 provides better results. The output layer is softmax layer with output dimension equal to the number of context-depended states (1609 in our case). The DNN was trained on top of FMLLR features. The system was trained for 15 epochs with the learning rate varying from 0.02 to 0.004 and then for 5 epochs with a constant final learning rate (0.004).

4   Training and Test Speech Datasets

For training and testing the Russian ASR system we used our own Russian speech corpora recorded in SPIIRAS. The training speech corpus consists of two parts; the first part is the speech database developed within the framework of the EuroNounce project [19]. The database consists of 16,350 utterances pronounced by 50 native Russian speakers (25 men and 25 women). Each speaker pronounced a set of 327 phonetically rich and meaningful phrases and texts. The second part of the corpus consists of recordings of other 55 native Russian speakers. Each speaker pronounced 105 phrases: 50 phrases were taken from the Appendix G to the State Standard P 50840-95 [20] (these phrases were different for each speaker), and 55 common phrases were taken from a phonetically representative text, presented in [21]. The total duration of the entire speech corpus is more than 25 h.

To test the system we used a speech dataset of 500 phrases pronounced by 5 speakers [19]. The phrases were taken from the materials of one Russian on-line newspaper that was not used in the training data.

The recording of speech data was carried out with the help of two professional condenser microphones Oktava MK-012. The speech data were collected in clean acoustic conditions, with 44.1 kHz sampling rate, 16-bit per sample. The signal-to-noise ratio (SNR) is about 35 dB. For the recognition experiments, all the audio data were down-sampled to 16 kHz. Each phrase was stored in a separate wav file. Also a text file containing orthographical representation (transcription) of utterances was provided.

5   Experiments with DNN-Based AMs

ASR was performed with the *n*-gram language model trained on Russian text corpus of on-line newspapers [22] using Kneser-Ney smoothing method [23]. The language model was created using the SRI Language Modeling Toolkit (SRILM) [24]. For Russian speech recognition 150 K vocabulary was used. Phonetic transcriptions for the words from vocabulary were made automatically by applying a set of G2P rules [25, 26].

At first, we made experiments using the GMM-HMM AMs. The obtained results are presented in Table 1.

Then, we made experiments on Russian speech recognition using the DNN-based AMs. We have created some DNNs with a different number of hidden units. Our DNNs with the tanh function have 3–5 hidden layers with 1024–2048 units in each hidden layer. The speech recognition results obtained with these tanh DNN-based AMs are presented in Table 2. The obtained results show that the number of layers has only slightly influence

Table 1. Speech recognition results with the baseline GMM-HMM models

AM	WER %
Triphone model with deltas	30.30
Triphone model with deltas and delta-deltas	30.04
LDA_MLLT	28.88
SAT_fMLLR	25.32

on speech recognition results. The best result was obtained when DNN with 6 hidden layers and 1024 units in each hidden layer was used. Increasing the number of hidden units led to increasing the WER, it can be caused by small amount of training data.

Table 2. WER with tanh-based DNN-HMM models (%)

Number of hidden layers	Number of units in each hidden layer	
	1024	2048
3	22.58	24.10
4	21.87	24.25
5	21.91	23.11
6	21.80	22.70

For the p-norm DNNs, there is no parameter of hidden layer dimension. Instead, there are two other parameters: (1) p-norm output dimension and (2) p-norm input dimension. The input dimension needs to be an exact integer multiple of the output dimension; normally a ratio of 5 or 10 is used [18]. We have tried p-norm DNNs with input/output dimensions of 2000/200 and 4000/400 respectively. The obtained results are presented in Table 3.

Table 3. WER with p-norm DNN-HMM models (%)

Number of hidden layers	Input/output dimension	
	2000/200	4000/400
3	20.99	22.66
4	21.61	23.41
5	21.48	23.33
6	20.30	23.69

The lowest WER was achieved with the p-norm DNN, it was equal to 20.30 %. It was obtained using the DNN with 6 hidden layers and input/output dimension of 2000/200.

6 Conclusion and Future Work

We have studied some DNN-based AMs for continuous Russian speech recognition with very large vocabulary using the Kaldi toolkit. We have experimented with DNNs with two types of nonlinearity (tanh and p-norm), different numbers of hidden layers and hidden units in tanh-based DNNs. The speech recognition experiments showed that the best results were obtained with the p-norm DNN-based AM. The relative WER reduction was 20 % comparing to the baseline system with fMLLR features (the absolute WER reduction was 5 %). In further research, we will investigate some other DNN's configurations as well as make experiments with tandem models.

Acknowledgments. This research is partially supported by the Council for Grants of the President of the Russian Federation (projects No. MK-5209.2015.8 and MD-3035.2015.8), by the Russian Foundation for Basic Research (projects No. 15-07-04415 and 15-07-04322), and by the Government of the Russian Federation (grant No. 074-U01).

References

1. Yu, D., Deng, L.: Automatic Speech Recognition - A Deep Learning Approach. Springer, London (2015)
2. Povey, D. et al.: The Kaldi speech recognition toolkit. In: IEEE Workshop on Automatic Speech Recognition and Understanding ASRU (2011)
3. Veselý, K. et al.: Sequence-discriminative training of deep neural networks. In: INTERSPEECH 2013, pp. 2345–2349 (2013)
4. Povey, D., Zhang, X., Khudanpur, S.: Parallel training of DNNs with natural gradient and parameter averaging. preprint arXiv:1410.7455 http://arxiv.org/pdf/1410.7455v8.pdf (2014)
5. Bengio, Y., Lamblin, P., Popovici, D., Larochelle, H.: Greedy layer-wise training of deep networks. Adv. Neural Inf. Process. Syst. (NIPS) **19**, 153–160 (2007)
6. Seide, F., Li, G., Yu, D.: Conversational speech transcription using context-dependent deep neural networks. In: INTERSPEECH-2011, pp. 437–440 (2011)
7. Dahl, G., Yu, D., Deng, L., Acero, A.: Context-dependent pre-trained deep neural networks for large vocabulary speech recognition. IEEE Trans. Audio Speech Lang. Process. **20**(1), 30–42 (2012)
8. Seide, F., Li, G., Yu, D.: Conversational speech transcription using context-dependent deep neural networks. In: INTERSPEECH-2011, pp. 437–440 (2011)
9. Ellis, D.P.W., Singh, R., Sivadas, S.: Tandem acoustic modeling in large-vocabulary recognition. In: International Conference on Acoustics, Speech and Signal Processing ICASSP 2001, pp. 517–520 (2001)
10. Grezl, F., Karafiat, M., Kontar, S., Cernocky, J.: Probabilistic and bottle-neck features for LVCSR of meetings. In: ICASSP 2007, pp. 757–760 (2007)
11. Maas, A.L. et al.: Building DNN Acoustic Models for Large Vocabulary Speech Recognition. preprint arXiv:1406.7806, http://arxiv.org/pdf/1406.7806.pdf (2015)
12. Cosi, P.: A KALDI-DNN-based ASR system for Italian. In: IEEE International Joint Conference on Neural Networks IJCNN 2015, pp. 1–5 (2015)
13. Popović, B., Ostrogonac, S., Pakoci, E., Jakovljević, N., Delić, V.: Deep neural network based continuous speech recognition for Serbian using the Kaldi toolkit. In: Ronzhin, A., Potapova, R., Fakotakis, N. (eds.) SPECOM 2015. LNCS, vol. 9319, pp. 186–192. Springer, Heidelberg (2015)
14. Miao, Y.: Kaldi+PDNN: building DNN-based ASR systems with Kaldi and PDNN. arXiv preprint arXiv:1401.6984, https://arxiv.org/abs/1401.6984 (2014)
15. Zulkarneev, M.Yu., Penalov, S.A.: System of speech recognition for Russian language, using deep neural networks and finite state transducers. Neurocomput. Dev. Appl. **10**, 40–46 (2013). (in Russia)

16. Tomashenko, N., Khokhlov, Y.: Speaker adaptation of context dependent deep neural networks based on MAP-adaptation and GMM-derived feature processing. In: INTERSPEECH 2014, Singapore, pp. 2997–3001 (2014)
17. Prudnikov, A., Medennikov, I., Mendelev, V., Korenevsky, M., Khokhlov, Y.: Improving acoustic models for Russian spontaneous speech recognition. In: Ronzhin, A., Potapova, R., Fakotakis, N. (eds.) SPECOM 2015. LNCS, vol. 9319, pp. 234–242. Springer, Heidelberg (2015)
18. Zhang, X. et al.: Improving deep neural network acoustic models using generalized maxout networks. In: ICASSP 2014, pp. 215–219 (2014)
19. Karpov, A., Markov, K., Kipyatkova, I., Vazhenina, D., Ronzhin, A.: Large vocabulary Russian speech recognition using syntactico-statistical language modeling. Speech Commun. **56**, 213–228 (2014)
20. State Standard P 50840-95. Speech transmission by communication paths. Evaluation methods of quality, intelligibility and recognizability, Moscow. Standartov Publ. (1996) (in Russia)
21. Stepanova, S.B.: Phonetic features of Russian speech: realization and transcription. Ph.D. Thesis (1988) (in Russia)
22. Kipyatkova, I., Karpov, A.: Lexicon size and language model order optimization for Russian LVCSR. In: Železný, M., Habernal, I., Ronzhin, A. (eds.) SPECOM 2013. LNCS, vol. 8113, pp. 219–226. Springer, Heidelberg (2013)
23. Kneser, R., Ney, H.: Improved backing-off for m-gram language modeling. In: ICASSP 1995, pp. 181–184 (1995)
24. Stolcke, A., Zheng, J., Wang, W., Abrash, V.: SRILM at sixteen: update and outlook. In: ASRU 2011, Waikoloa, Hawaii, USA (2011)
25. Kipyatkova, I., Karpov, A., Verkhodanova, V., Zelezny, M.: Analysis of long-distance word dependencies and pronunciation variability at conversational Russian speech recognition. In: Federated Conference on Computer Science and Information Systems, FedCSIS 2012, pp. 719–725 (2012)
26. Karpov, A., Kipyatkova, I., Ronzhin, A.: Very large vocabulary ASR for spoken Russian with syntactic and morphemic analysis. In: INTERSPEECH 2011, Florence, Italy, pp. 3161–3164 (2011)

DNN-Based Duration Modeling
for Synthesizing Short Sentences

Péter Nagy[(⊠)] and Géza Németh

Department of Telecommunications and Media Informatics (TMIT),
Budapest University of Technology and Economics (BME),
Magyar tudósok krt. 2, 1117 Budapest, Hungary
{nagyp,nemeth}@tmit.bme.hu

Abstract. Statistical parametric speech synthesis conventionally utilizes decision tree clustered context-dependent hidden Markov models (HMMs) to model speech parameters. But decision trees are unable to capture complex context dependencies and fail to model the interaction between linguistic features. Recently deep neural networks (DNNs) have been applied in speech synthesis and they can address some of these limitations. This paper focuses on the prediction of phone durations in Text-to-Speech (TTS) systems using feedforward DNNs in case of short sentences (sentences containing one, two or three syllables only). To achieve better prediction accuracy hyperparameter optimization was carried out with manual grid search. Recordings from a male and a female speaker were used to train the systems, and the output of various configurations were compared against conventional HMM-based solutions and natural speech. Experimental results of objective evaluations show that DNNs can outperform previous state-of-the-art solutions in duration modeling.

Keywords: Speech synthesis · Deep neural network · Hidden markov model · Duration modeling

1 Introduction

With state-of-the-art text-to-speech (TTS) systems high quality, intelligible artificial speech can be generated. However the naturalness of synthesized speech is still below the levels of human speech [1]. One of the key aspects that makes machine speech sound unnatural or inadequate is the generated synthetic prosody. Studies on the dimensions of perceptual speech quality found that naturalness of voice and prosodic quality are correlated [2, 3]. Sound duration is an important prosodic feature that contributes not only to naturalness but to the meaning of speech also. The influence duration has on naturalness and intelligibility of speech has been extensively studied [4]. Explicit modeling of speech-sound durations in statistical parametric speech synthesis improves the naturalness of synthetic speech [5].

In the last decade among statistical parametric speech synthesis methods the hidden Markov model (HMM) based approach [6] has become the most promising and it went through significant improvements. The open source HMM-based speech synthesis system (HTS) [7] uses context dependent decision tree clustered hidden semi Markov

© Springer International Publishing Switzerland 2016
A. Ronzhin et al. (Eds.): SPECOM 2016, LNAI 9811, pp. 254–261, 2016.
DOI: 10.1007/978-3-319-43958-7_30

models (HSMMs) with Gaussian duration distributions. The quality of HMM-based systems is limited by state-level averaging across differing linguistic contexts that can degrade the naturalness of synthesized speech [8]. Decision trees are inefficient at modeling complex and specific dependencies between linguistic features, and model parameters are learned only on a subset of the training material [9, 10]. In order to improve duration modeling, multi-level duration models were introduced where pho-neme- and syllable-duration distributions were also taken into account [11]. Although this approach improves duration prediction there is much space for improvements. Deep neural networks (DNNs) can overcome the limitation of the modeling ability of HMMs and they can achieve significantly better performance than decision tree clus-tered HMMs [9, 12]. Besides feed-forward DNN-based acoustic modeling [9] there have been investigations with promising results utilizing deep belief networks [13], unidirectional [14] and bidirectional [15] long short-term memory recurrent neural networks (LSTM-RNNs).

In this paper we investigate the use of feed-forward neural networks for duration prediction for short sentences in Hungarian speech synthesis. In the study utterances with only one, two or three syllables are considered as short sentences. Phoneme durations are context dependent [16] and the sound durations are highly dependent on the length of the given word and utterance [17]. Intelligibility is highly degraded in the Hungarian HMM-based framework due to the state-level inherent averaging addressed earlier. In this study we investigate if DNNs are capable to model these kind of utterances better.

The rest of the paper is organized as follows. Section 2 describes the architecture and methods used to train the DNN, together with the assessment of a HMM-based system used as a baseline in the study. The parameter optimization and the performed evaluation is presented in Sect. 3 including the results of objective assessments. Sec-tion 4 summarizes the work and describes future directions.

2 Methods

2.1 Database

The Hungarian PPSD (Parallel Precision Speech Database) corpus [18] contains recordings from 14 (7 male and 7 female) speakers. This corpus contains 1992 sen-tences that were selected from different novels. The aim of the corpus was to cover all possible different sound transitions, thus the database is considered phonetically bal-anced. The original corpus was expanded with 522 additional sentences in earlier studies. The extension contains one, two and three syllable sentences in equal pro-portion. The PPSD corpus with the extension contains 2514 utterances per speaker (3 h of speech on average). The recordings were annotated and segmented using HMM forced alignment. The resulting segmented database thereafter was corrected and refined manually based on auditory and visual inspection of the waveforms. The combined automatic and manual methods allow us to use it as a reference in com-prehensive studies. To compare the HMM and DNN-based duration prediction for short sentences 2 speakers (1 male, 1 female) were selected from this corpus. For DNN duration modeling [19] introduced robust statistical methods to overcome the issues caused by the errors and excess variation in common databases. These statistical methods were not applied in this study, since this database was manually corrected to be suitable for speech synthesis.

2.2 HMM Training

In this study we wanted to compare the modeling capability of HMM and DNN statistical methods for duration prediction. Three different voices were trained for both speakers. Two speaker adapted voices: in the first case the adaptation corpus contains 500 utterances with normal length denoted in the study by HMM-NO. The second adaptation corpus contains 400 short sentences and 100 normal length sentences (HMM-SH). Besides these, a speaker dependent voice was trained with 2300 sentences for both speakers (HMM-SI). The feature vectors consist of 39 mel-cepstral coefficients (including the 0th coefficient), log(F0), and aperiodicity measures with their dynamic features. Decision tree-based context clustering was used with context dependent labeling applied in the Hungarian derivative of HTS 2.3beta [20]. Independent decision trees are built for the spectral and excitation parameters, and for duration also, using a maximum likelihood criterion.

2.3 DNN Training

In this study we focused on using feed-forward deep neural networks. The input features to train the network are introduced in Table 1 together with the output features. The training samples were randomly shuffled and both input and output features were transformed. The input features were standardized to zero mean and unit variance, while the output feature was normalized between 0.01 and 0.99. Due to its robustness as an optimization function we employed Adadelta [21]. This optimization function gives the opportunity to adaptively control the learning rate, and instead of accumulating all past gradients, the window size for accumulation is fixed. It is able to handle noisy gradients well, converges fast and can handle a number of data representations. The loss function used during training was the mean squared error function. In hidden layers we used parametric rectified linear units (PReLUs) [22] as an activation function. PReLUs can adaptively learn the shape of activation function and this additional parameter means negligible computational overhead compared to non-parametric rectifiers. In the output layer linear activation was applied. Between hidden layers orthogonal weight initialization was used and in case of input-hidden and hidden-output layers Glorot weight initialization [23] was performed. In order to avoid feature co-adaptation, after each layer (except the output layer) dropout with 50 % probability was applied during training. To avoid overfitting early stopping regularization was used with patience set to 50 epochs.

Table 1. Input and output features of the deep neural network of this study

Feature type	Feature	#	Type
Input	Quinphone	5*68	One-hot
	Forward/backward position of actual phoneme/syllable/word/phrase in syllable/word/phrase/sentence	4*2	Numerical
	Number of phonemes/syllables/words/phrases in the previous/current/next syllable/word/phrase/sentence	4*3	Numerical
	Number of phonemes/syllables/words in the current sentence	3	Numerical
	The previous/current/next phoneme is a vowel of a short sentence	3	Binary
Total number of input features: 366			
Output	Duration	1	Continuous
Total number of output features: 1			

3 Evaluation

During the evaluation durations predicted by decision tree clustered HSMMs were compared to DNN predicted ones. In case of DNNs the training, validation and test data were 80, 14 and 6 percentage of the corpus, respectively. In order to find the optimal hyperparameter set, we performed optimization with manual grid search. In the optimization step only the number of hidden layers, number of neurons and minibatch size parameters were taken into account, other hyperparameters were set according to the previous section. In this phase the number of hidden layers, the number of neurons and minibatch size were set between 1..7, 64..2048, 16..256, respectively. Altogether 89 training cycles were performed with the female and 74 with the male corpus. The 4 best combinations of hyperparameters in case of both the female and the male voice together with the validation mean squared error are shown in Table 2.

Table 2. The 4 best performing hyperparameter sets as a result of manual grid search

Voice	# of Layers	# of Neurons	Minibatch	Epochs	MSE
Female	7	900	128	292	0.0029671
	5	1024	128	230	0.0030813
	5	1800	64	317	0.0030924
	7	2048	128	142	0.0031296
Male	7	750	64	126	0.0030007
	5	2048	128	147	0.0030062
	3	1024	64	65	0.0030277
	5	1024	128	230	0.0030813

3.1   RMSE and Correlation

After hyperparameter optimization we measured the RMSE and correlation between the sound durations of the natural utterances and those predicted by the HMM and DNN-based methods. The measurements were done on the 5 percent test data selected during the DNN training. Neither the DNN, nor the HMM training corpus included the utterances that were present in the test set. The test set contained 120 short sentences and 30 utterances with normal length.

The RMSE values for normal length and short sentences are shown in Fig. 1. In case of normal length sentences it can be seen, that DNN-based duration prediction in case of the female speaker resulted slightly better and in case of the male speaker slightly worse results, but the difference between the measured error values are not statistically significant. If we consider only predicted durations for segments in prominent words the DNN based solution outperforms all the HMM-based ones, but the difference is still not statistically significant. Nevertheless in case of short sentences, DNN-based prediction resulted significantly ($p < 0.05$) lower errors than any HMM-based voice. It is also worth mentioning that while the differently trained HMM-based voices resulted in relatively similar results for both male and female voices, the measured error values are lower for the female voice with DNN-based duration prediction. This may occur as a consequence of the selected voice talents unique characteristics. While the female speaker is a trained professional announcer, the male speaker has no such qualifications.

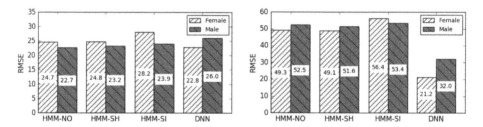

Fig. 1. RMSE between natural and predicted durations in case of normal length (left) and short (right) sentences for both speakers

The correlation values are shown in Fig. 2. The results here are also presented separately for normal length and for short utterances. In general DNN-based duration prediction resulted in both cases and for both speakers significantly ($p < 0.05$) higher correlation values than any HMM-based solutions. An important result is clearly visible in case of short sentences: while HMM-based systems could not perform equally for both of the speakers, DNN-based prediction resulted in consistently high values. Based on the results of this objective evaluation we concluded that the selected contextual features are appropriate to train DNNs for duration prediction, but there is still room for improvements.

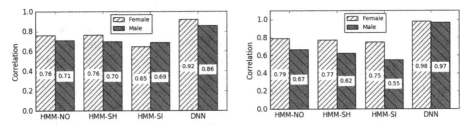

Fig. 2. Correlation between natural and predicted durations in case of normal length (left) and short (right) sentences for both speakers

3.2 Mean Durations

In a comprehensive study Olaszy [17] found that speech sound durations are related to the syllable count of the utterance. An inverse proportion can be observed between the two quantities in natural speech. The fewer syllables a sentence contains, the longer the mean phoneme duration becomes. In order to evaluate if the investigated approaches follow this behavior, we measured the mean durations for vowels and consonants separately for each system. The results are summarized in Table 3.

Table 3. Mean duration values in [ms] for the systems under study, separated by speaker and utterance length (No.-Normal, Sh.-Short), compared to natural speech

			Natural speech	HMM-NO	HMM-SH	HMM-SI	DNN
Female	No.	V	101.9	103.3	104.5	101.1	109.6
		C	70.6	70	71.1	69.8	74.7
	Sh.	V	176.7	138.3	148.5	137.7	174.9
		C	114.9	95.5	97.5	85.1	113.9
Male	No.	V	85.1	82.6	83.7	82.2	96.1
		C	65.5	65.3	65.8	67.9	74.6
	Sh.	V	153	105.2	111.3	122.8	162.4
		C	101.6	83.5	86.4	93.8	109.9

Generally we can see that both HMM and DNN-based methods were able to capture the syllable count dependency of durations, but at different rates. All three HMM-based voices for both speakers resulted in significantly shorter sound durations in case of short sentences than expected. This may produce degraded intelligibility for these utterance in synthetic speech. It is also worth mentioning that for male voice HMM-SI preformed the best approximation, while for female voice the speaker adapted HMM-SH system. It can also be seen that HMM-based prediction of sound durations in short sentences performed significantly better for the female voice, regardless of the used training method. In contrast, DNN-based prediction tends to predict longer durations for both vowels and consonants in normal length sentences than expected. In this preliminary study no subjective evaluation was performed, but in order to determine hów such a behavior affects the perceived naturalness, further studies are necessary. If we only consider short sentences it can be seen, that DNN prediction is much closer to natural speech than any of the HMM-based ones. Similarly to the RMSE evaluation, we can see that DNN prediction performs better for the female voice, the mean sound durations are closer to natural ones. Based on this comparison we concluded that DNNs are able to capture the duration changes in short sentences and they outperform traditional HMM-based prediction for both speakers.

4   Conclusions and Future Work

The aim of our preliminary study was to evaluate the DNN-based duration prediction to synthetize short sentences. The results show that the selected contextual features are suitable for DNN-based duration prediction. For normal length sentences the trained DNNs could reach the modeling performance of previous state-of-the-art HMM-based solutions. However if the results are discussed with taking into account only prominent parts DNNs can outperform HMMs in these type of sentences. However further evaluation is necessary to address the phenomenon. Nevertheless DNNs outperformed HMM-based solutions regarding duration prediction for short sentences. Duration is predicted with lower error rates and higher correlation in this case. Although results of the objective evaluation show improvements, subjective preference tests are necessary for assessing the possible naturalness improvement.

One limitation of the feed-forward DNN-based acoustic modeling used in this study is that the sequential nature of speech is ignored. In order to overcome this issue, and to further improve duration modeling we plan to apply different architectures such as long short-term memory recurrent neural networks. In addition involve further contextual features that could further improve duration prediction for short sentences.

Acknowledgments. This research is partially supported by the Swiss National Science Foundation via the joint research project (SCOPES scheme) SP2: SCOPES project on speech prosody (SNSF n° IZ73Z0_152495-1).

References

1. Prahallad, K., Vadapalli, A., Kesiraju, S., Murthy, H.A., Lata, S., Nagarajan, T., Presanna, M., Patil, H., Sao, A.K., King, S., Black, A.W., Tokuda, K.: The blizzard challenge 2014. In: Proceedings of the Blizzard Challenge Workshop (2014)
2. Hinterleitner, F., Möller, S., Norrenbrock, C., Heute, U.: Perceptual quality dimensions of text-to-speech systems. In: Proceedings of the Interspeech 2011, pp. 2177–2180 (2011)
3. Hinterleitner, F., Norrenbrock, C., Möller, S.: Is intelligibility still the main problem? A review of perceptual quality dimensions of synthetic speech. In: Proceedings of the 8th ISCA Speech Synthesis Workshop, pp. 147–151 (2013)

4. Mayo, C., Clark, R.A., and King, S.: Multidimensional scaling of listener responses to synthetic speech. In: Proceedings of the Interspeech 2005, pp. 1725–1728 (2005)
5. Zen, H., Tokuda, K., Masuko, T., Kobayashi, T., Kitamura, T.: Hidden semi-markov model based speech synthesis system. Proc. IEICE – Trans. Inf. Syst. **E90-D**(5), 825–834 (2007)
6. Zen, H., Tokuda, K., Black, A.W.: Statistical parametric speech synthesis. Speech Commun. **51**(11), 1039–1064 (2009)
7. Zen, H., Nose, T., Yamagishi, J., Sako, S., Masuko, T., Black, A.W., Tokuda, K.: The HMM-based speech synthesis system (HTS) version 2.0. In: Proceedings of the SSW6, pp. 294–299 (2007)
8. Watts, O., Henter, G.E., Merritt, T., Wu, T., King, S.: From HMMs to DNNs: where do the improvements come from? In: Proceedings of the ICASSP, p. 5 (2016)
9. Zen, H., Senior, A., Schuster, M: Statistical parametric speech synthesis using deep neural networks. In: Proceedings of the ICASSP, pp. 7962–7966 (2013)
10. Zen, H.: Acoustic modeling in statistical parametric speech synthesis – from HMM to LSTM-RNN. In: Proceedings of the MLSLP, Invited paper (2015)
11. Gao, B.-H., Qian, Y., Wi, Z.-Z., Soong, F.-K.: Duration refinement by jointly optimizing state and longer unit likelihood. In: Proceedings of the Interspeech, pp. 2266–2269 (2008)
12. Qian, Y., Fan, Y., Hu, W., Soong, F.K.: On the training aspects of deep neural network (DNN) for parametric TTS synthesis. In: Proceedings of the ICASSP, pp. 3857–3861 (2014)
13. Kang, S., Qian, X., Meng, H.: Multi-distribution deep belief network for speech synthesis. In: Proceedings of the ICASSP, pp. 8012–8016 (2013)
14. Zen, H., Sak, H.: Unidirectional long short-term memory recurrent neural networks with recurrent output layer for low-latency speech synthesis. In: Proceedings of the ICASSP, pp. 4470–4474 (2015)
15. Fan, Y., Qian, Y., Xie, F.-L., Soong, F.K.: TTS synthesis with bidirectional LSTM based recurrent neural networks. In: Proceedings of the Interspeech 2014, pp. 1964–1968 (2014)
16. Van Santen, J.P.: Contextual effects on vowel duration. Speech Commun. **11**(6), 513–546 (1992)
17. Olaszy, G.: Hangidőtartamok és időszerkezeti elemek a magyar beszédben [Sound durations and time structure elements in Hungarian speech] (in Hungarian). In: Nyelvtudományi Értekezések, Akadémiai Kiadó, p. 141 (2006)
18. Olaszy, G.: Precíziós, párhuzamos magyar beszédadatbázis fejlesztése és szolgáltatásai [Development and services of a Hungarian precisely labeled and segmented, parallel speech database] (in Hungarian). Beszédkutatás 2013 [Speech Research 2013], pp. 261–270 (2013)
19. Henter, G.E., Ronanki, S., Watts, O., Wester, M., Wu, Z., King, S.: Robust TTS duration modelling using DNNs. In: Proceedings of the ICASSP, p. 5 (2016)
20. Tóth, B., Németh, G.: Improvements of Hungarian hidden Markov model-based text-to-speech synthesis. Acta Cybern **19**(4), 715–731 (2010)
21. Zeiler, M.D.: ADADELTA: An adaptive learning rate method. In arXiv preprint, arXiv: 1212.5701 (2012)
22. He, K., Zhang, X., Ren, S., Sun, J.: Delving deep into rectifiers: surpassing human-level performance on ImageNet classification. In arXiv preprint, arXiv:1502.01852 (2015)
23. Glorot, X., Bengio, Y.: Understanding the difficulty of training deep feedforward neural networks. In: Proceedings of the International Conference on Artificial Intelligence and Statistics (AISTATS), pp. 249–256 (2010)

Emotional Speech of 3-Years Old Children: Norm-Risk-Deprivation

Olga Frolova[✉] and Elena Lyakso

Saint-Petersburg State University, Saint-Petersburg, Russia
olchel@yandex.ru

Abstract. The goal of the study is to compare emotional speech and vocalizations of 3-years old healthy children (control) and children with neurological disorders (risk), brought up in families and children from the orphanage (deprivation). Audio and video recording of the child's speech and behavior were made in model situations, designed to evoke the emotional expressions of children during interaction with their mothers and the experimenter. Perceptual analysis was conducted to estimate the possibility of child's emotional state recognition when listening the child's speech and vocalizations by groups of native speakers: parents, experts, adults who do not have their own children. Native speakers have been attributed child's utterances to the state of comfort, discomfort, neutral and to clarify the emotional state as anger, fear, sadness, happiness, surprise, calm. The acoustic characteristics of the child's speech and vocalizations: pitch values, the range of pitch values, duration of utterances, duration of vocalizations and stressed vowels, formant frequencies were measured. Dialogues of children with mothers and experimenter were described for evaluation of the level of the child's speech mastering. Phonetic analysis of child's emotional utterances was made. Differences in recognition of emotional state between groups of children were revealed: native speakers identified emotional state in the voice of healthy children grown up at families better than in orphans' voice, whereas experts recognized emotional state better compared to parents and adults without experience of interaction with their own children. The communication between children of risk and deprivation groups and adults is obstructed due to the features of the acoustic characteristics of their emotional speech.

Keywords: Emotional state · Orphanage · Acoustic features · Perceptive analysis · Neurological disorders

1 Introduction

The child begins to manifest an emotional state from the moment of birth in facial expression and vocalizations. Adults able to detect gradations of emotions listening two months old child's vocalizations [1]. Age and emotion-related changes are studied during first year of child's life by acoustic analysis [2]. Infant's cries features are studied on the base of their perception by adults and acoustic analysis [3]. The study of acoustic characteristics of early vocalizations and speech of children up to the age of three years is difficult, because high values and variability of the pitch

© Springer International Publishing Switzerland 2016
A. Ronzhin et al. (Eds.): SPECOM 2016, LNAI 9811, pp. 262–270, 2016.
DOI: 10.1007/978-3-319-43958-7_31

make automatic measurements inaccurate [4]. However, at the present time research on speech based automatic recognition of child's emotional state is carried out, but most of them is devoted to the speech of children older than 5 years [5, 6]. Such studies of younger children, especially on the material of the Russian language are single [7].

The determination of the acoustic features of child's emotional speech and vocalizations could be useful for early diagnostics of emotional disorders in children [8]. At the present time much attention is paid to study of acoustics of emotional manifestations in the speech of children with different disorders: autistic children [9], children with cochlear implants [10]. As a course of these researches, our study is aimed at comparing of emotional speech and vocalizations features of 3-years old healthy children and children with neurological disorders, brought up in families and children from the orphanage.

2   Method

Participants in the study were Russian healthy children (n = 15) brought up in families – control group; children with light neurological disorders diagnosed after birth (P.91.8 - ICD 10, n = 10) from families – risk group; children (F83 - ICD 10, n = 10) brought up in an orphanage (Child Home) – deprivation group. The age of children was 36 months. Audio registration of mother-child (control and risk group) and experimenter-child (deprivation group) dialogues at play with toys and book reading model situations, designed to evoke the emotional expressions of children, was made by the digital recorder "Marantz PMD660" with external microphone "SENNHEIZER e835S". Two experts with professional experience of work with children selected typical for the child's age and group utterances, which were pronounced by children at the discomfort, neutral and comfort state (by viewing video and using recording protocol). There were 90 utterances – speech samples of children: 30 for each investigated group (10 in each state). Then native speakers listened speech samples organized in the test sequences. Native speakers had to determine: 1. child's state as discomfort, comfort, neutral; 2. emotional state of child as anger, fear, sadness, gladness, surprise, and calm. Native speakers were selected in three groups: experts (n = 5) with professional experience of work with child's speech, parents (n = 5, age 37 ± 6) and auditors - adults without their own children (n = 95, age 18.4 ± 2). Spectrographic analysis of speech was carried out in the Cool Edit (Syntrillium Soft. Corp. USA) sound editor. We evaluated the duration of utterances, maximum (F0 max) and minimum (F0 min) pitch values and variability of pitch (the difference between maximum and minimum values: F0 max - F0 min) in utterance; stressed vowels' and their stationary fragments' duration, pitch (F0) and formant frequencies (F1, F2).

Ethical approval was obtained from the Ethics Committees (Health and Human Services, HHS, IRB 00003875, St. Petersburg State University).

3   Results

3.1   Speech Level of Children from Control, Risk and Deprivation Groups

Speech level of 3-years old children from a control, risk and deprivation groups significantly differ. Analysis of dialogues of children with their mothers and with experimenter (for deprivation group) revealed that replicas of children could be represented by sound combinations (vocalizations and syllables), separate words, simple phrases, and constructions of several phrases. Simple phrases occurred more often in speech of the control group children. Separate words were most frequent in speech of risk group children. Sounds combinations prevailed in the speech of deprivation group children. On the base of phonetic analysis the number of different consonants in children's utterances that could characterize the complexity of child's articulation was calculated. Amount of different consonants in the utterances of deprivation group children was lower than in the utterances of risk and control groups children. Deprivation group children used 9 different consonants in discomfort, 11 in neutral and 10 in comfort state. Risk group children used 14 different consonants in all states. Control group children used 14 different consonants in discomfort, 19 in neutral and 18 in comfort state. Children of control and deprivation group used in discomfort state less different consonants than in neutral and comfort state.

So the assessment of the level of speech development in children allowed to choose the utterances that are typical for children of investigated groups in different states for future perceptive and acoustic analysis.

3.2   Recognition of Discomfort, Comfort and Neutral State of Children by Native Speakers: Experts, Parents and Auditors

Experts recognized child's state on the base of listening of the child's speech samples better than other native speakers. The average recognition accuracy in a group of experts was 84% at children of the control group, 75% at risk group and 68% at deprivation group. So errors in experts answers were mainly connected with recognition of state in deprivation group children: speech samples uttered by children in comfort state were recognized as neutral (Table 1).

Table 1.   Confusion matrices for state recognition of children from control, risk and deprivation groups by experts, amount of responses (%).

State	Groups								
	Control			Risk			Deprivation		
	disc	neutral	comf	disc	neutral	comf	disc	neutral	comf
disc	**92**	6	2	**64**	14	22	**84**	14	2
neutr	12	**78**	10	4	**84**	12	16	**74**	10
comf	8	10	**82**	4	20	**76**	10	48	**42**

Experts correctly recognized with perception rate 0.75–1.0 state in 80 % speech samples at control group children, 67 % at risk group children, and 53 % at deprivation group children. Though experts in some utterances defined incorrectly with high perception rate (0.75–1.0) state of risk group children (single discomfort speech samples were described by experts as comfort) and deprivation group children (single comfort speech samples were determined as neutral).

The average recognition accuracy of children's state by parents was 67 % at control group, 67 % at risk group and 54 % at deprivation group. Most mistakes in state classification were associated with attribution of comfort state to neutral state. Neutral state more often was recognized by parents as a comfort than discomfort state in control and risk groups. In deprivation group neutral state was attributed as discomfort and comfort state with equal probability (Table 2). Parents correctly recognized with perception rate 0.75–1.0 state in 57 % speech samples at control group children, 53 % at risk group children and 30 % at deprivation group children. Parents incorrectly recognized with perception rate 0.75–1.0 single comfort speech samples as neutral and neutral speech sample as comfort in the control group, single discomfort and comfort speech samples as neutral in the risk group. Parents made more kinds of errors with speech samples of deprivation group children: single discomfort samples were recognized with perception rate 0.75–1.0 as comfort, comfort samples as neutral, and neutral samples as comfort and discomfort.

Table 2. Confusion matrices for state recognition of children from control, risk and deprivation groups by parents, amount of responses (%).

State	Groups								
	Control			Risk			Deprivation		
	disc	neutral	comf	disc	neutral	comf	disc	neutral	comf
disc	**70**	20	10	**60**	16	24	**56**	26	18
neutr	14	**64**	22	4	**72**	24	22	**54**	24
comf	0	34	**66**	4	30	**68**	4	48	**48**

The average recognition accuracy in group of auditors (young people without their own children) was 63 % at control group, 58 % at risk group and 55 % at deprivation group. Errors in classification were connected mainly with the determination of neutral speech samples as comfort (Table 3).

Table 3. Confusion matrices for state recognition of children from control, risk and deprivation groups by auditors, amount of responses (%).

State	Group								
	Control			Risk			Deprivation		
	disc	neutral	comf	disc	neutral	comf	disc	neutral	comf
disc	**72**	11	17.5	**57**	15	28	**70**	15	15
neutr	12	**44.5**	43.5	11	**53**	36	22	**39**	39
comf	11.5	15	**73.5**	9	21	**70**	12	33	**55**

Auditors recognized with perception rate 0.75–1.0 state in 40 % speech samples at control group children, 30 % at risk group children, and 23 % at deprivation group children.

As a whole discomfort and comfort state are recognized rather than a neutral state in the control group. Neutral and comfort state are recognized well in the risk group. All native speakers recognized rather discomfort state than comfort state in deprivation group. Experts and parents recognized with perception rate 0.75–1.0 discomfort, comfort and neutral speech sounds of children. Auditors could not recognize unambiguously (with perception rate 0.75–1.0) speech sounds uttered by children in a neutral state.

3.3   Recognition of Base Emotional States of Children by Native Speakers

Experts and parents mainly described discomfort speech samples as sadness and anger. Neutral samples were mainly described as calm; rarely as sadness or gladness. Comfort speech samples were attributed as gladness in control and risk groups, but as calm in deprivation group. Experts and parents did not answer "I don't know" about the child's emotional state. Auditors (without their own children) attributed discomfort speech samples as sadness and anger, but a large number of responses were fear. Neutral samples were mainly determined as calm, but also as sadness in control and risk groups and surprise in deprivation group. Comfort speech samples were determined as gladness and calm in control and risk groups, and as calm, gladness and surprise in deprivation group (Table 4). Answer surprise was given by auditors more frequently in deprivation group children than in other groups.

Table 4. Amount of auditors' responses (%) in emotional state recognition task.

state	state group	anger	fear	sadness	gladness	surprise	calm	don't know
disc	control	**32.5**	21	**25**	4	12,5	5	0
	risk	**26**	11	**33**	13	10	4	3
	deprivation	**28**	21	**24**	7	13	5	2
neutr	control	3	3	**21**	10	16	**47**	0
	risk	1,5	3	**15**	13,5	13,5	**51.5**	2
	deprivation	12	8	10	13	**23**	**32**	2
comf	control	3	4	6	**55**	8	**23**	1
	risk	6	2	6	**58**	11,5	**16.5**	0
	deprivation	5	4	10	**25**	24	**31**	1

In this task with perception rate 0.75–1.0 experts recognized emotional state in 70 % speech samples at control group children, 63 % at risk group children, and 47 % at deprivation group children; parents recognized emotional state in 43 % speech samples at control group children, 50 % at risk group children, and 17 % at deprivation group children; auditors recognized emotional state in 23 % speech samples at control group children, 20 % at risk group children, and 13 % at deprivation group children.

3.4 Acoustic Features of Speech and Sounds Uttered by Children in Discomfort, Neutral and Comfort State

Speech samples correctly recognized by at least one group of native speakers as discomfort, comfort or neutral state were analyzed spectrographically for the estimation of their acoustic features underlying successful recognition.

The speech samples correctly recognized as discomfort is characterized by higher pitch values (pitch of stressed vowels, maximum and minimum pitch values in an utterance) and duration of stressed vowels than comfort and neutral speech samples. Lowest values of these characteristics were in neutral speech samples. Comfort speech samples are characterized by high values of second formant and common duration of utterances (Table 5). The tendency to decrease of stressed vowels' stationary fragments was revealed in comfort samples versus discomfort samples. Pitch contour of vowels from discomfort samples was mainly falling. The rising pitch contour of stressed vowels was more common in comfort speech samples. Flat and falling pitch contours were more typical for neutral state speech samples.

Table 5. Differences in the acoustic features of speech samples correctly recognized by native speakers as comfort, neutral and discomfort.

Number	Features	Differences
1	T utterance	C>N>D
2	T vowel	D>C>N (D>N**, D>C*)
3	T stationary fragment	D>N>C
4	F0 max	D>C>N (D>N***, D>C*)
5	F0 min	D>C=N (D>N**, D>C**)
6	F 0 stressed vowel	D>C=N (D>N**, D>C**)
7	F1	D>C>N (D>N*)
8	F2	C>D>N (C>N*)

Note: D-discomfort, C – comfort, N-neutral state. Comparing of the corresponding features of states D, C, N. Measured values: > - higher, < - lower, = - equal. * - $p < 0.05$, ** - $p < 0.01$, *** - $p < 0.001$ – Mann-Whitney test.

Comparing of the acoustic features of speech samples unambiguously attributed by at least one group of native speakers (perception rate 0.75–1.0) as sadness and anger revealed differences between these emotional states. Speech samples attributed as anger have higher values of minimum pitch in utterance, duration, pitch and formant frequency values of stressed vowels than sadness. Speech sample recognized with high perception rate as a surprise is characterized by the high value of pitch range of stressed vowel and high maximum pitch.

It is important to note that instrumental analysis of all test material revealed differences between groups of children. The acoustic features, which underlie the allocation of speech samples to discomfort, neutral and comfort state categories, more realized in the speech samples of the control group children. Thus neutral and comfort speech samples were not differed in pitch values of stressed vowels and in maximum pitch values of utterances in risk group children. The duration of stressed vowels and maximum pitch values in the comfort and neutral speech samples of deprivation group children were not differed. The formant triangle of vowels of the control group children constructed for stressed vowels from discomfort, neutral and comfort speech samples occupy different positions on two-formant plot. The formant triangle of vowels for discomfort speech samples of the control group children is shifted to high frequency region of two-formant plot than the formant triangle of vowels for neutral speech samples (Fig. 1). The formant triangle of vowels for the discomfort and comfort speech samples of risk group children are located on the joint area of two-formant plot. All three formant triangles of vowels of deprivation group children are located on the common area of two-formant plot.

The connection between the perception rate and acoustic features for every state was revealed (Spearman Correlation, Multiple Regression analysis).

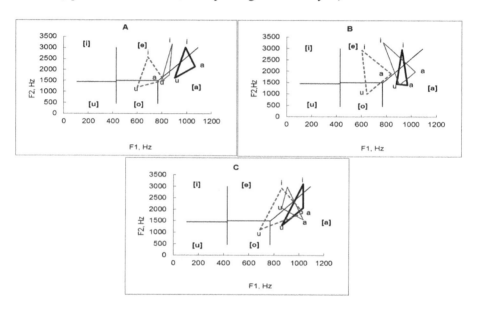

Fig. 1. The formant triangles of vowels (medians) of children. Perceptive bounds for adult Russian vowels. A – data for control group; B – risk group; C – deprivation group. Bold black lines – discomfort, dropped lines – neutral, thin line – comfort.

4   Discussion and Conclusion

Significant differences were revealed between experts and auditors - adults without their own children: experts recognized state of children better. Parents detected emotion state of children better than the auditors, but worse than the experts. In other studies [11] no differences were found between the results for parents and nonparents in cry perception. We can assume that professional and parental experience plays a role in the recognition of emotions in the speech of 3-years old children. The results showed differences in recognition of emotional state between groups of children: native speakers identified emotional state in the voice of healthy children grown up at families better than in orphans' voice. These results are consistent with the facts about emotional development problems in children from the orphanage. Orphanage staff did not respond to vocalizations and other attempts to attract their attention by children that leads to a mismatch of interaction between nurses and children. In our work, discomfort state was recognized better both for children from deprivation group and for children from control groups. That is in line with previous studies about better recognition of discomfort emotional state reflection in the voice of adults, children, chimpanzees [8]. Neutral and comfort state is recognized well in risk group children that could be interpreted as specificity of children's behavior reactions. So it was shown that very preterm infants with neurological problems demonstrate at the age of 12 month the level of facial and vocal joy the same as heathy full-term children, but the very preterm born infants exhibited higher levels of positive motor activity [12]. The communication between children of risk and deprivation groups and adults is obstructed due to the features of the acoustic characteristics of their emotional speech. These data could be used in the future as an additional criterion for diagnostic of emotional development disorders, also in systems of automatic recognition of the child's emotional state and developmental risks by child's voice.

Acknowledgements. This study is financially supported by the Russian Foundation for Basic Research (projects N 15-06-07852a, 16-06-00024a).

References

1. Shimura, L., Imaizumi, S.: Emotional information in young infant's vocalizations. In: ICP 1995, vol. 3, p. 412 (1995)
2. Scheiner, E., Hammerschmidt, K., Jürgens, U., Zwirner, P.: Acoustic analyses of developmental changes and emotional expression in the preverbal vocalizations of infants. J. Voice **16**(4), 509–529 (2002)
3. Protopapas, A., Eimas, P.D.: Perceptual differences in infant cries revealed by modifications of acoustic features. J. Acoust. Soc. Am. **102**(6), 3723–3734 (1997)
4. McGowan, R.W., McGowan, R.S., Denny, M., Nittrouer, S.: A longitudinal study of very young children's vowel production. J. Speech, Lang. Hear. Res. **57**(1), 1–15 (2014)
5. Gerosa, M., Giuliani, D., Brugnara, F.: Acoustic variability and automatic recognition of children's speech. Speech Commun. **49**(10), 847–860 (2007)
6. Potamianos, A., Narayanan, S., Lee, S.: Automatic speech recognition for children. Eurospeech **5**, 2371–2374 (1997)
7. Lyakso, E., Frolova, O., Dmitrieva, E., Grigorev, A., Kaya, H., Salah, A.A., Karpov, A.: EmoChildRu: emotional child Russian speech corpus. In: Ronzhin, A., Potapova, R., Fakotakis, N. (eds.) SPECOM 2015. LNCS, vol. 9319, pp. 144–152. Springer, Heidelberg (2015)
8. Lyakso, E., Frolova, O.: Emotion state manifestation in voice features: chimpanzees, human infants, children, adults. In: Ronzhin, A., Potapova, R., Fakotakis, N. (eds.) SPECOM 2015. LNCS, vol. 9319, pp. 201–208. Springer, Heidelberg (2015)
9. Hubbard, J., Trauner, D.A.: Intonation and emotion in autistic spectrum disorders. Psycholinguist. Res. **36**(2), 159–173 (2007)

10. Mildner, V., Koska, T.: Recognition and production of emotions in children with cochlear implants. Clin. Linguist. Phon. **28**(7–8), 543–554 (2014)
11. Gustafson, G.E., Green, J.A.: On the importance of fundamental frequency and other acoustic features in cry perception and infant development. Child Dev. **60**(4), 772–780 (1989)
12. Langerock, N., van Hanswijck de Jongeb, L., Bickle Graz, M., et. al.: Emotional reactivity at 12 months in very preterm infants born at <29 weeks of gestation. Infant. Behav. Devel. **36**, 289– 297 (2013)

Ensemble Deep Neural Network Based Waveform-Driven Stress Model for Speech Synthesis

Bálint Pál Tóth[✉], Kornél István Kis, György Szaszák, and Géza Németh

Department of Telecommunications and Media Informatics,
Budapest University of Technology and Economics, Budapest, Hungary
{toth.b,szaszak,nemeth}@tmit.bme.hu, kis.kornel@outlook.com

Abstract. Stress annotations in the training corpus of speech synthesis systems are usually obtained by applying language rules to the transcripts. However, the actual stress patterns seen in the waveform are not guaranteed to be canonical, they can deviate from locations defined by language rules. This is driven mostly by speaker dependent factors. Therefore, stress models based on these corpora can be far from perfect. This paper proposes a waveform based stress annotation technique. According to the stress classes, four feedforward deep neural networks (DNNs) were trained to model fundamental frequency (F0) of speech. During synthesis, stress labels are generated from the textual input and an ensemble of the four DNNs predict the F0 trajectories. Objective and subjective evaluation was carried out. The results show that the proposed method surpasses the quality of vanilla DNN-based F0 models.

Keywords: Text-to-speech · TTS · Deep learning · Deep neural networks · F0 · Ensemble learning · Stress annotation

1 Introduction

For training statistical parametric speech synthesis systems a speech corpus is required that contains utterances from a natural speaker, the phonetic transcriptions of the utterances and additional metadata is defined automatically or annotated manually. Prosodic stress is one of these features. While the importance of prosodic stress in human conversations is unquestionable, in speech corpora usually this feature is calculated automatically based on the phonetic transcriptions.

Generally, language rules unambiguously define the positions where prosodic stress should occur, however, even in case of planned speech, the location of stress greatly depends on the speaker. Thus it is likely to observe a high number of mismatches between the prosodic and syntactic stress labels. Therefore the statistical models neglect stress labels and attempt to model the emphasized parts based on other features, like the position of the current phoneme/syllable/word within the actual syllable/word/sentence. The result is synthetic prosody with monotonous, slight stress patterns. To improve the pitch variance (and thus the emphases) the first and second derivatives of the fundamental frequency can also be modeled and used during speech parameter generation [1],

© Springer International Publishing Switzerland 2016
A. Ronzhin et al. (Eds.): SPECOM 2016, LNAI 9811, pp. 271–278, 2016.
DOI: 10.1007/978-3-319-43958-7_32

as well as global variance [2]. However the prosodic stress in synthetic speech probably will still have low correlation with the actual stress model of the original speaker.

Another approach is to annotate prosodic stress in speech corpora manually. The disadvantage of this solution is the relatively high cost of manual stress annotation and it is also very time consuming. Furthermore, human work introduces subjectivity. For example, inter-annotator agreement scores using ToBI annotation are usually found between 70–80 % for pitch-accents in English [3]. Our experience shows that the interpretation of syntax greatly influences manual annotators, even if they are high-qualified experts.

Given these difficulties of stress annotation, and the fact that even manual labelling is ambiguous (consensus labeling results in about only 80 % overlap) a method that predicts prosodic stress extracted from audio could be effective for speech synthesis systems.

In this paper, an automatic stress labelling approach is used [4], which relies on acoustic-prosodic parameters. Regarding prosodic stress, the smallest unit which by definition contains one and a single stress is called phonological phrase. The idea of stress detection is to perform a Viterbi-alignment for phonological phrases, and then locate the stressed syllable within each phrase. In case of Hungarian, which is stressed on the first syllable, the stress occurs at the left edge of the phonological phrase. The Viterbi alignment requires a pre-trained set of phrase models, which are HMM/GMMs having fundamental frequency and energy as input features. Labelling the text-to-speech corpus with this approach is shown to augment naturalness of synthesized speech [4], and the accuracy of stress detection is fairly comparable to inter-annotator agreement rates (75–90 % depending on the exact setup) [5].

This paper is organized as follows: in the next section the waveform inspired stress model is introduced, and the general deep neural network based F0 modeling technique is described. Next a novel deep ensemble based F0 model is proposed and eventually, the stress annotation from transcripts for F0 trajectory generation is shown. In Sect. 3 objective and subjective evaluation, including a CMOS (Comparison Mean Opinion Score) listening test, take place. Finally, in Sect. 4, the conclusions are drawn.

2   Proposed Method

Our proposed method for modeling the fundamental frequency (F0) of human speech uses an ensemble of Deep Neural Network (DNN) models. Properly assembled ensemble models have been shown to outperform single-model deep learning solutions in several cases [6]. During this research, a single Multi-Layer-Perceptron model was trained and compared against an ensemble model which consists of four smaller Multi-Layer-Perceptron networks.

The main idea was that each network in the ensemble specializes on modeling the F0 frequency at a distinct stress level. Unlike in the case of the single, larger model, where the stress level appears just as a single input to the neural network, the training database of the networks were split into four parts before training, based on the stress level obtained directly from the waveform. Each of the four networks represents a different stress level, and was trained on its appropriate part of the database. In realistic text-to-speech use case scenarios, waveform based stress levels are not available, therefore all the testing was performed with stress levels produced by applying the language rules. During the testing of the ensemble model, the ensemble member network from which the given frame is obtained is chosen based on the stress level.

2.1 Waveform Inspired Stress Model

The waveform inspired automatic stress labelling approach relies on an automatic phonological phrasing of speech. Exploiting the fact that phonological phrases carry one and a single stressed syllable each, this latter should be identified within the phrase once the phrase boundaries are known. In fixed stress Hungarian, the stressed syllable follows the onset phrase boundary, as stress is realized always on the first syllable (if present, as usually not all words are stressed in an utterance).

Phonological phrasing is obtained by Viterbi alignment using a phonological phrase model set (Hidden Markov Models with Gaussian Mixture Models). The model set consists of 7 different models, including silence. The remaining 6 models model phonological phrases with different properties regarding the strength of the stress and the following intonation contour. The overall approach is documented in [7] in detail. For the current application, the intonation contour is irrelevant (at this stage) only the strength of the stress is extracted to derive a 3 level stress labelling schema: unstressed, stressed and strongly stressed syllables are differentiated. These levels correspond to the levels used by stress labelling based on text (transcripts). Indeed, we know syllable boundaries from a phone level segmentation, and compute phonological phrase boundaries by the Viterbi alignment. The first syllable in a phrase gets a stressed or a strongly stressed marking (depending on the detected phrase type), the remaining syllables get an unstressed label.

2.2 Single Deep Neural Network Based F0 Modeling

Recently deep neural network based solutions became widespread in the field of artificial speech synthesis. Various test architectures were presented [8, 9] using either Recurrent Neural Networks (RNN) or feedforward neural networks. When working with feedforward models, deep MLP networks are often used for modeling the fundamental frequency (F0) of human speech. Input and output data for the networks are usually collected from the transcription of recorded waveforms. Our training database consisted of the transcripted form of 1984 short declarative sentences. Obtaining reference F0 values from the waveforms is possible with pitch extractors. In this research, the SWIPE software [10] was used with the resolution of 5 ms per frame. The extracted sequence is non-continuous, since F0 is not defined for unvoiced phonemes, therefore a linear interpolation of the unvoiced frames of the sentences was implemented before training.

Training a deep MLP requires supervised learning techniques and a labeled database of input-output pairs. In this research, each model was trained using mini-batch gradient descent with Nesterov accelerated gradient [11]. Early stopping and a 30 % dropout was used in each training case. The input array contained information about phonemes with context using the quinphone model and 25 numerical features. The single model used an extra input feature, the stress level itself. The output of the networks were the natural logarithm of the F0 value, and a binary voiced/unvoiced flag. For training, the input features were transformed to have a mean of zero, and unit variance, the output features were minmax scaled between 0.01–0.99.

Several network architectures were trained and compared against each other. For the single feedforward model, a network with 3 hidden layers where each layer contains 3000 neurons gave the best results. The hidden layers used ReLU as an activation function, the output layer was equipped with a sigmoid activation.

2.3 Ensemble Deep Neural Network Based F0 Modeling

The main goal of an ensemble model is to improve output performance by creating smaller, more specialized networks whose aggregated knowledge may result in a better performance. This approach is especially useful when dealing with sparse signal modeling. In the case of F0 modeling, training data with higher prosodic stress level is significantly less frequent in the database, therefore a large, single model is likely to ignore the effect of these data elements, resulting in a reduced performance of the whole model. To address this problem, an ensemble of four smaller feedforward networks was trained on different parts of the training database. The distinction was performed according to the prosodic stress levels. During testing, each ensemble member calculated its associated frames, again based on the prosodic stress levels. The end result was compiled from these frames. Each ensemble member model had the same 3 hidden layer architecture, but it contained only 1000 neurons in each hidden layer. The learning strategy, and the input-output values were also the same.

2.4 Stress Annotation from Text

After the F0 models are trained, in the evaluation phase, the stress annotations are determined from the input text. First morphological and syntactic analysis and preprocessing is performed. Then a dependency grammar is used for further analysis [12]. Stress annotation is performed based on the results of this analysis. Generally, four levels of stress are distinguished:

1. Very strong stress. It is assigned based on an exception list, typically covering contrastive negation.
2. Strong stress, also assigned based on an exception list (different than in case of very strong stress).
3. Medium stress assigned by linguistic rules. The basic principles are the following:
   a. Sentence initial words are medium stressed with predefined exceptions.
   b. All words following an article or conjunction word 'és' ('and') are medium stressed.
   c. All words following a comma have medium stress–exceptions may apply based on a list.
   d. The last word of a sentence is never medium stressed.

   Neutral stress (unstressed) form.

The details of these stress categories can be found in [13]. In current paper the first and second stress categories are merged, consequently 3 levels of stress are distinguished: strongly stressed, stressed and neutral. This way the stress levels predicted from the text for evaluation is in accordance with the waveform inspired stress levels, which were introduced in Sect. 2.1.

3   Evaluation

In the evaluation part single and ensemble DNNs were trained as described in Sects. 2.2 and 2.3. For training a female speaker was selected from the Precisely Labelled Hungarian Database (PLHD) containing 1984 sentences [14]. Precise labelling refers to manually corrected phonetic transcription and phone boundaries. In this research declarative sentences were investigated only. The training, validation and test data were the 70, 20 and 10 percentage of the corpus, respectively. In the evaluation part phone durations from natural utterances were used for the temporal information of the input vector. The spectral parameters were also obtained from the natural utterances. The F0 trajectories were generated by the different DNN models. The stress annotation of the input sentence was calculated according to Sect. 2.4. The deep neural networks introduced in Sect. 2 was implemented in Keras deep learning framework [15], and the calculations were done on high performance NVidia GPUs.

Both in subjective and objective evaluation three systems were involved: (1) vocoded natural utterances; (2) vocoded natural utterances with F0 trajectories generated by single deep neural networks; (3) vocoded natural utterances with F0 trajectories generated by ensemble deep neural networks. The three systems will be referred to as NAT, SINGLE and ENSEMBLE throughout the evaluation.

3.1   Objective Evaluation

To get an objective picture of how the two approaches (single model versus the ensemble model) perform during evaluation, Pearson correlation (Eq. 1) was calculated on the sentences of the testing database twice:

$$r(x, y) = \frac{\sum_{i=1}^{n} (x_i - \bar{x})(y_i - \bar{y})}{\sqrt{\sum_{i=1}^{n} (x_i - \bar{x})^2} \sqrt{\sum_{i=1}^{n} (y_i - \bar{y})^2}}. \tag{1}$$

First, the correlation between the NAT and the SINGLE trajectories, then the correlation between the NAT and the ENSEMBLE was calculated. A higher value shows a better fit to the natural trajectory of the sentence. The results show that in approximately 61 % of the sentences, the ensemble model had a slightly worse Pearson value than the large model. The remaining 39 % of the sentences gave a larger Pearson value for the ensemble model. The differences between the two models were very small, 75 % of the sentences had a difference of the Pearson correlation smaller than 0.05.

To better understand the differences between the two systems, the F0 trajectories of test sentences were plotted. These sentences were not part of the training corpus. An example sentence can be seen in Fig. 1. The blue line shows the NAT system (reference), the green shows the SINGLE configuration, and the red is the ENSEMBLE model. Frames between 500 and 800 are of particular interest, since these show the benefits of using the ensemble model. This part of the trajectory has a large prosodic stress, and the ensemble model is able to provide much better result than the single configuration.

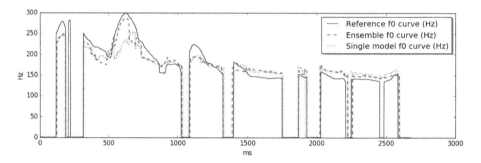

Fig. 1. An example F0 trajectory (Color figure online)

3.2   Subjective Evaluation

In order to measure the perceived improvement in intonation modeling with deep ensemble models compared to single deep neural networks a CMOS (Comparison Mean Opinion Score) type listening test was carried out [16]. In this listening test the subjects had to compare pairs of utterances in a three level scale if the first or second utterance has more emphases. Altogether, 72 utterances were included in the test (1 speaker × 3 types × 24 sentences). Before the test, listeners were asked to listen to an example from the male speaker to adjust the volume. The utterances were presented in a randomized order (different for each participant). Altogether 16 listeners participated in the test (5 females, 11 males). All subjects were native Hungarian speakers, between 22–70 years (mean: 36 years). On average the test took 8 min to complete. The CMOS scores of the listening test are presented in Fig. 2.

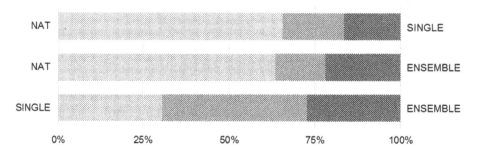

Fig. 2. The results of the CMOS listening test

The results of the listening test show that deep ensemble outperformed the single model when the intonation of natural utterances was compared to deep ensemble and to single feedforward deep neural network separately (NAT-SINGLE versus NAT-ENSEMBLE). However, when the ensemble was directly compared to the single model significant preference was not traceable (SINGLE-ENSEMBLE).

4   Conclusions and Discussion

The results of objective and subjective evaluation show that the deep ensemble models trained with waveform-driven stress annotations can produce more precise F0 trajectories and emphases than the vanilla DNN intonation model. The enhancement generally occurs – according to the test samples – in the first emphasis of the declarative sentences – that is the sentence stress in Hungarian. Thus we can conclude, that the deep ensemble model helps to approach the natural sentence stress.

Naturally there is space for improvements. Continuous F0 with Maximum Voices Frequency excitation model has been proven to produce more natural F0 trajectories than the vanilla vocoder [17]. Introducing uni- and bidirectional Long Short-Term Memory (LSTM) networks to intonation modeling is expected to further increase the quality of the stress model. Furthermore the effect of dynamic components besides the static F0 values to the proposed stress model is planned to be investigated as well.

Acknowledgments. We would like to thank to Mátyás Bartalis for his help in creating the subjective listening test and to the listeners for participating in it. Bálint Pál Tóth gratefully acknowledges the support of NVIDIA Corporation with the donation of an NVidia Titan X GPU used for his research. This research is partially supported by the Swiss National Science Foundation via the joint research project (SCOPES scheme) SP2: SCOPES project on speech prosody (SNSF n° IZ73Z0_152495-1).

References

1. Yoshimura, T., Tokuda, K., Masuko, T., Kobayashi, T., Kitamura, T.: Simultaneous modeling of spectrum, pitch and duration in HMM-based speech synthesis. In: Eurospeech, pp. 2347–2350 (1999)
2. Tomoki, T., Tokuda, K.: A speech parameter generation algorithm considering global variance for HMM-based speech synthesis. IEICE Trans. Inf. Syst. **90**(5), 816–824 (2007)
3. Pitrelli, J.F., Beckman, M.E., Hirschberg, J.: Evaluation of prosodic transcription labeling reliability in the ToBI framework. In: International Conference on Spoken Language Processing, vol. 1, pp. 123–126 (1994)
4. Szaszák, G., Beke, A., Olaszy, G., Tóth, B.P.: Using automatic stress extraction from audio for improved prosody modeling in speech synthesis. In: 16th Annual Conference of the International Speech Communication Association, pp. 2227–2231 (2015)
5. Pitrelli, J.F., Beckman, M.E., Hirschberg, J.: Evaluation of prosodic transcription labeling reliability in the ToBI framework. In: International Conference on Spoken Language Processing, vol. 1, pp. 123–126 (1994)

6. Hannun, A., et al.: Deep speech: scaling up end-to-end speech recognition. arXiv preprint arXiv:1412.5567 (2014)
7. Szaszák, G., Beke, A.: Exploiting prosody for syntactic analysis in automatic speech understanding. J. Lang. Model. **1**, 143–172 (2012)
8. Zen, H., Senior, A., Schuster, M.: Statistical parametric speech synthesis using deep neural networks. In: IEEE International Conference on Acoustics, Speech and Signal Processing (ICASSP), pp. 7962–7966 (2013)
9. Fan, Y., Qian, Y., Xie, F.L., Soong, F.K.: TTS synthesis with bidirectional LSTM based recurrent neural networks. In: Interspeech, pp. 1964–1968 (2014)
10. Camacho, A., Harris, J.G.: A sawtooth waveform inspired pitch estimator for speech and music. J. Acoust. Soc. Am. **124**(3), 1638–1652 (2008)
11. Nesterov, Y.: Gradient methods for minimizing composite objective function, UCL (2007)
12. Koutny, I.: Parsing Hungarian sentences in order to determine their prosodic structure in a multilingual TTS system. In: Eurospeech, pp. 2091–2094 (1999)
13. Olaszy, G., Németh, G., Olaszi, P., Kiss, G., Zainkó, C., Gordos, G.: Profivox – a Hungarian TTS system for telecommunications applications. Int. J. Speech Technol. **3**(3-4), 201–215 (2000)
14. Olaszy, G.: Precíziós, párhuzamos magyar beszédadatbázis fejlesztése és szolgáltatásai [Development and services of a Hungarian precisely labeled and segmented, parallel speech database] (in Hungarian)," Beszédkutatás 2013 [Speech Res. 2013], pp. 261–270 (2013)
15. Chollet, F.: Keras: Theano-based deep learning library (2015). https://github.com/fchollet, Documentation: http://keras.io/
16. ITU-T recommendation p. 800: Methods for subjective determination of transmission quality (1996)
17. Tóth, B., Csapó, G.: Continuous fundamental frequency prediction with deep neural networks. In: European Signal Processing Conference (2016, in review)

Evaluation of Response Times on a Touch Screen Using Stereo Panned Speech Command Auditory Feedback

Hunor Nagy and György Wersényi[✉]

Széchenyi István University, Győr, Hungary
{nagy.hunor,wersenyi}@sze.hu

Abstract. User interfaces to access mobile and handheld devices usually incorporate touch screens. Fast user responses are in general not critical, however, some applications require fast and accurate reactions from users. Errors and response times depend on many factors such as the user's abilities, feedback types and latencies from the device, sizes of the buttons to press, etc. We conducted an experiment with 17 subjects to test response time and accuracy to different kinds of speech-based auditory stimuli over headphones. Speech signals were spatialized based on stereo amplitude panning. Results show significantly better response times for 3 directions than for 5, as well as for native language compared to English, and more accurate judgements based on the meaning of the speech sounds rather than their direction.

Keywords: Speech stimuli · Spatial sound · Response time · Mobile device

1 Introduction

Reaction times to different auditory stimuli are important in many cases, especially when dangerous situations arise and users have to act and respond as quickly and reliably as possible [1–3]. Such situations include both real safety issues and simulated scenarios. Good examples are flight and combat simulators, driving assistance systems, auditory games, and alarm systems [4–9]. The relative importance of fast reactions and precision varies depending on the application: sometimes errors are less important than the reaction itself, while in other cases, errors are required to be small, and longer response times are tolerated.

Reaction time depends on the measurement setup, first of all on the auditory stimuli (signal type) and the device itself. Furthermore, additional information such as vibration, or spatialization of sound can influence the results. In general, visual information cannot be relied upon when testing auditory performance. However, in practice contradictory information via concurrent sound sources or spatial information can also influence the outcome.

Selection of sound types to respond to is one of the key elements during the design of any audio feedback-based system. Loudness, length and type play a significant role [10–17]. If it is required to recognize the sound itself, recognition (processing) time adds to the time needed for physical perception. In the case of speech commands, subjects have to wait and "understand" what to do, but the same is also true in the case of iconic

© Springer International Publishing Switzerland 2016
A. Ronzhin et al. (Eds.): SPECOM 2016, LNAI 9811, pp. 279–286, 2016.
DOI: 10.1007/978-3-319-43958-7_33

sounds, such as auditory icons, alarms etc. which produce a minimum limit of temporal and spectral cues for perception.

Focusing on speech, short iconic commands can be used in some scenarios. If reaction time is a key issue, long sentences are insufficient. One-syllable words indicating directions, interference etc. are well-suited and even applicable for non-native speakers. Thus, one of the main drawbacks of speech (language dependence) can be eliminated or reduced. Speech is a special signal even if it is of iconic length [18–22]. Sounds with meaning–independent of whether they are intuitive (auditory icons) or have to be learned (earcons)–are meant to also be processed based on the meaning and not just based on the sound's physical parameters. Meaningless sounds, such as noise signals, sinusoidal samples are the same over time and fully active from the beginning of playback. On the other hand, speech samples can differ according to the first vocals. Meaningless sounds can be sonified based on their physical parameters, e.g. sinusoidal signals with different frequency or loudness can initialize different actions [20].

Regarding the equipment, the device collecting the responses also influences response time. The required reaction can be any kind of movement (e.g. turning a wheel or pressing a button) or speech input. Most generally, users are required to press a button, such as a key on a keyboard, a mouse button, or some other button on dedicated equipment or on a virtual touch-screen. The actual recorded response time is always a summed value of the reaction of the subject and the latencies of the device. This latency may or may not be important. For example, when it is approximately the same for all subjects, it can be deducted from the results.

As mobile and handheld devices often incorporate touch-screens, reaction times can be evaluated separate from other hardware devices. Our former experiment compared reaction times using smartphones and a dedicated hardware architecture to test various acoustic stimuli [23, 24]. This focused mainly on sinusoidal and noise signals, and as expected, reaction times were higher in the case of a touch-screen. However, the same tendencies and preferences were observed among the signal types. This paper presents more recent results using speech excitations from two languages (Hungarian and English), prompting users through short commands to press different buttons in different directions on the touch-screen. Sound is also spatialized in the horizontal plane using stereo panning, and this spatialization can be in alignment or in contradiction with the meaning of the speech commands. The experiment was aimed at testing whether subjects use the spatial information or the meaning of the speech in their judgements. Furthermore, error rates in case of 3 and 5 directions should be evaluated.

2 Measurement Setup

For testing, an Android-based application was developed and installed on a Samsung mobile device (Samsung Galaxy S2 smartphone) [24]. During operation, users listen to speech commands indicating various directions and buttons on the touchscreen that have to be accessed based on the direction of the sound source. Each subject performed the following tests in the same order:

3-direction Hungarian
5-direction Hungarian
3-direction English
5-direction English
3-direction Hungarian (mixed–source directions differed from commands)
3-direction English (mixed–source directions differed from commands)

Each test consisted of a minimum of three runs of 10 trials (in randomized order). In the case of three directions, possible answers were left, right and front (see Fig. 1). In the case of five directions, left middle and right middle directions were added. In the first four tests, speech commands were in alignment with the simulated direction of sound source. All samples were pre-recorded TTS samples in Hungarian and English suing the same engine [25]. Stereo amplitude panning was applied as follows:

- "left" is 90 degrees to the left, so that only the left speaker of the headphone is active,
- "right" is 90 degrees to the right, so that only the right speaker of the headphone is active,
- "front" is in the middle, so that each speaker contributes 50–50 % to the mono-aural signal
- "left front" and "right front" are simulated 45 degrees to the left and right respectively, with appropriate percentages contributed from each of the speakers.

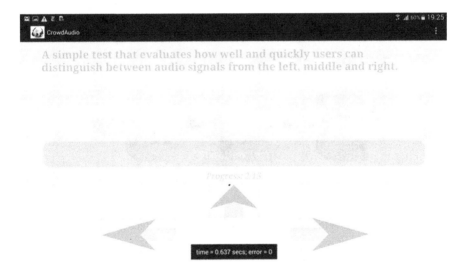

Fig. 1. Feedback on correctness and measured time delay following a test question.

In tests 5 and 6, the simulated direction was different from that indicated by the speech sample (e.g. the sample "left" was played back from the right or from the middle). In all cases, users had to indicate the direction of the sound source. The number of errors and response times were collected. Furthermore, gender, age and a unique ID were recorded for each test subject.

In the application, different environmental parameters can be set. For this test, an idle time of 2 s between each sample (pause time) was set. The maximum (random) delay before playing back a sound was also 2 s. Thus, after responding to one sound, a random delay between 2–4 s was inserted before the next sound. If the response time was greater than 5 s the test was aborted. If all 10 questions were answered, the results (number of errors, response times for each direction and user data) were saved in CSV format.

17 test subjects (8 males and 9 females) participated in the test, all of whom were native Hungarian speakers. One full testing procedure including all 6 tests took about 20-25 min for one subject. The Sennheiser HD 595 headphone was used. Playback level was set to equal loudness for all subjects.

3   Results

In the tests 17 participants (min. age 20, max. age 40, mean age 25.7) participated. In total, 3350 answers were collected. Out of this number, 184 were incorrect (5,5 %). The largest error statistics were obtained on test 5 (67) followed by test 6 (24)–i.e. the mixed tests in Hungarian and English. Figure 2 shows the number of errors for these two tests.

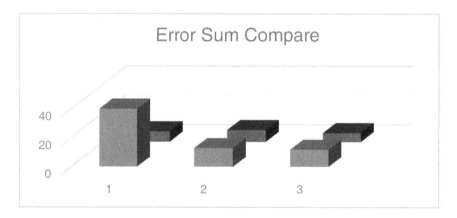

Fig. 2. Number of errors for the first three answers in tests 5 and 6 (blue Hungarian, red English). (Color figure online)

Mean and SD values for response times are shown in Table 1. Results larger than 2,5 s in case of 5 directions and larger than 1,75 s for 3 directions were deleted as outliers. For statistical analysis a Kolmogorov-Smirnov test was performed for normality, followed by ANOVA. ANOVA could be performed on the four 3-direction tests and results were controlled by paired Welch T-tests as well. Table 2 and Fig. 3 show corresponding ANOVA results.

Table 1. Mean and SD values for response times.

	Eng mixed	Hun mixed	Eng 5	Eng 3	Hun 5	Hun 3
Mean	0.89	0.99	1.35	0.85	1.0	0.82
SD	0.21	0.31	0.41	0.23	0.24	0.24

Table 2. ANOVA table for the four 3-direction tests.

	SS	df	MS	F	Prob > F
Groups	10.99	3	3.66	69.83	4.38e-43
Error	1.12e + 02	2143	0.0525		
Total	1.23e + 02	2146			

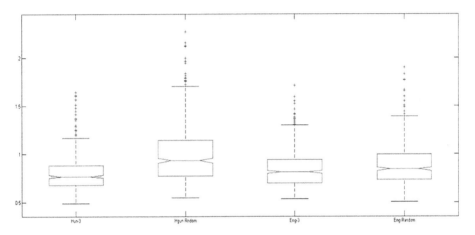

Fig. 3. Boxplot for the ANOVA based on Table 2.

4 Discussion

As results indicate, 5,5 % of total error was measured. This was strongly biased by the mixed version tests, so if we extract these, the total error is reduced to 2,8 %. Based on the normality tests, after filtering the outliers, all results could be analyzed with ANOVA.

Comparing English and Hungarian 5-direction tests through the Welch T-test, the response times for English were significantly worse (slower) than for Hungarian (p = 7,3e-05). The same comparison for 3-direction tests showed a similar result: the Hungarian test was significantly better (p = 6,7e-04).

Based on Fig. 2, most of the errors were due to the shift in the test from regular to mixed. As the first mixed test was in Hungarian, subjects tended to answer the first question based on the meaning rather than the direction. It took 2-3 questions to accommodate and after this, both Hungarian and English test errors were around the mean value. This conclusion is also supported by the response times, i.e. the English version was significantly faster (p = 1,4e-10), but we assume that this effect is mainlydue to the fact that the Hungarian test was performed first, followed by the English version. On the other hand, it also seems somewhat likely that even when test subjects answered correctly, the meaning of the speech commands still had an influence on their reactions. First, error rates were generally higher in the mixed as opposed to the normal tests. Second, in the case of 45-degree directions, subjects waited for a relatively longer time, so as to hear the second part of the speech sample (as in "straight right"). Table 1 shows the mean and SD values of the response times in the tests.

We can also compare the 3-direction regular test with the mixed ones. As expected, for both languages, the regular test results are significantly faster and better than the mixed tests' results (p = 2,1e-04 for English; p = 1,5e-24 for Hungarian). Comparing all results, the best was achieved in the 3-direction regular Hungarian (test 1). Mean response times of about 0,8–0,9 s were measured for three directions, and 1–1,3 s for five directions. Native Hungarian samples were detected faster, meaning that subjects still made their judgements based on the meaning and not on the direction, even if they were clearly instructed to rely only on the latter. This is also supported by the mixed tests, where response times were higher and errors more frequent.

Our conclusion is that stereo panning can be used for directional simulation, but by increasing the possible directions, both error rates and reaction times increase. Given more options, subjects need more processing time and have to "think" about making the correct judgements based on the directions of the stimuli only.

Future work will include statistical analysis and comparison of speech samples and former results with noise and sinusoidal signals [24]. Furthermore, multiple (concurrent) sound sources and different reaction methods (such as tilting the handheld device) are planned to be included into the test scenarios. As the application is able to use vibration as feedback, this could also enhance reaction times.

5 Conclusion

Auditory response times and error rates to speech commands indicating 3 or 5 directions in Hungarian and English were recorded with 17 subjects. Users responded on a touch-screen according to the direction of the sound source. Directions were emulated using stereo panning at left, right, middle and 45 degree directions. Mean response times of about 0.8–0.9 s (for three directions) and 1–1.3 s (for five directions) were measured. These results are similar to other experiments' results. Native speakers responded significantly better for the native language. The tests with mixed directions-commands, where the semantic meaning (e.g. "left") of the speech sample was different from the spatially panned direction revealed that subjects made their judgements based on the meaning and not on the direction. It takes 2–3 questions for users to handle this confusion and give correct answers–nevertheless, error rates were higher and response times increased.

Acknowledgement. This project received funding from the European Union's Horizon 2020 research and innovation programme under grant agreement No 643636 "Sound of Vision".

References

1. Hyman, R.: Stimulus information as a determinant of reaction time. J. Exp. Psychol. **45**(3), 188–196 (1953)
2. Kosinski, R.J.: A literature review on reaction time. http://biae.clemson.edu/bpc/bp/lab/110/reaction.htm, Accessed 03 March 2016
3. Pain, M.T.G., Hibbs, A.: Sprint starts and the minimum auditory reaction time. J. Sports Sci. **25**(1), 79–86 (2007)
4. El-Shimy, D., Grond, F., Olmos, A., Cooperstock, J.: Eyes-free environmental awareness for navigation. J. Multimodal User Interfaces **5**, 131–141 (2012)
5. Hourlier, S., Meehan, J., Léger, A., Roumes, C.: Relative effectiveness of audio tools for fighter pilots in simulated operational flights: a human factors approach. In: New Directions for Improving Audio Effectiveness, Meeting Proceedings RTO-MP-HFM-123, Neuilly-sur-Seine, France, pp. 23-1–23-8 (2005)
6. Ho, C., Spence, C.: Assessing the effectiveness of various auditory cues in capturing a driver's visual attention. J. Appl. Exp. Psychol. **11**(3), 157–174 (2005)
7. Simpson, B., Brungart, D., Gilkey, R., McKinley, R.: Spatial audio displays for improving safety and enhancing situation awareness in general aviation environments. In: New Directions for Improving Audio Effectiveness, Meeting Proceedings RTO-MP-HFM-123, Neuilly-sur-Seine, France, pp. 26-1–26-16 (2005)
8. Gillard, J., Schutz, M.: Improving the efficacy of auditory alarms in medical devices by exploring the effect of amplitude envelope on learning and retention. In: Proceeding of the International Conference on Auditory Display (ICAD 2012), Atlanta, 240–241 (2012)
9. Suzuki, K., Jansson, H.: An analysis of driver's steering behavior during auditory or haptic warnings for the designing of lane departure warning system. JSAE Rev. **24**(1), 65–70 (2003)
10. Mynatt, E.D.: Transforming graphical interfaces into auditory interfaces for blind users. Hum. Comput. Interact. **12**, 7–45 (1997)
11. Gaver, W.W.: Auditory icons: using sound in computer interfaces. Hum. Comput. Interact. **2**(2), 167–177 (1986)
12. Blattner, M.M., Sumikawa, D.A., Greenberg, R.M.: Earcons and Icons: their structure and common design principles. Hum. Comput. Interact. **4**, 11–44 (1989)
13. Gygi, B., Shafiro, V.: From signal to substance and back: insights from environmental sound research to auditory display design. In: Proceeding of the 15th International Conference on Auditory Display (ICAD 09), Copenhagen, pp. 240–251 (2009)
14. Gygi, B., Kidd, G.R., Watson, C.S.: Spectral-temporal factors in the identification of environmental sounds. J. Acoust. Soc. Am. **115**(3), 1252–1265 (2004)
15. Ballas, J.A.: Common factors in the identification of an assortment of brief everyday sounds. J. Exp. Psychol. Hum. **19**(2), 250–267 (1993)
16. Wersényi, G.: Auditory representations of a graphical user interface for a better human-computer interaction. In: Ystad, S., Aramaki, M., Kronland-Martinet, R., Jensen, K. (eds.) CMMR/ICAD 2009. LNCS, vol. 5954, pp. 80–102. Springer, Heidelberg (2010)
17. Csapó, Á., Wersényi, G.: Overview of auditory representations in human-machine interfaces. J. ACM Comput. Surv. (CSUR) **46**(2), 19 (2013). Article No. 19
18. Vargas, M.L.M., Anderson, S.: Combining speech and earcons to assist menu navigation. In: Proceeding of the International Conference on Auditory Display (ICAD 2003), Boston, pp. 38–41 (2003)
19. Walker, B.N., Nance, A., Lindsay, J.: Spearcons: speech-based earcons improve navigation performance in auditory menus. In: Proceeding of the International Conference on Auditory Display (ICAD 2006), London, pp. 63–68 (2006)

20. Hermann, T., Hunt, A., Neuhoff, J.G. (eds.): The Sonification Handbook. Logos Publishing House, Berlin (2011). http://sonification.de/handbook/chapters
21. Csapó, Á., Wersényi, G., Nagy, H., Stockman, T.: Survey of assistive technologies and applications for blind users on mobile platforms - a review and foundation for research. J. Multimodal User Interfaces 9(3), 11 (2015)
22. Jeon, M., Walker, B.N.: Spindex (speech index) improves auditory menu acceptance and navigation performance. J. ACM Trans. Access. Comput. (TACCESS) 3(3), 10 (2011). Article No. 10
23. Nagel, F., Stöter, F-R., Degara, N., Balke, S., Worrall, D.: Fast and accurate guidance–response times to navigational sounds. In: Proceeding of the 20th International Conference on Auditory Display (ICAD 2014), New York, p. 5 (2014)
24. Wersényi, G., Nagy, H., Csapó, Á.: Evaluation of reaction times to sound stimuli on mobile devices. In: Proceeding of the International Conference on Auditory Display (ICAD 2015), Graz, pp. 268–272 (2015)
25. http://www.oddcast.com/home/demos/tts/tts_example.php

Evaluation of the Speech Quality During Rehabilitation After Surgical Treatment of the Cancer of Oral Cavity and Oropharynx Based on a Comparison of the Fourier Spectra

Evgeny Kostyuchenko[1]([⊠]), Mescheryakov Roman[1], Dariya Ignatieva[1], Alexander Pyatkov[1], Evgeny Choynzonov[2], and Lidiya Balatskaya[2]

[1] Tomsk State University of Control Systems and Radioelectronics, Lenina str. 40, 634050 Tomsk, Russia
key@keva.tusur.ru, mrv@tusur.ru
[2] Tomsk Cancer Research Institute, Kooperativniy av. 5, 634050 Tomsk, Russia
nii@oncology.tomsk.ru
http://www.tusur.ru, http://www.oncology.tomsk.ru/

Abstract. In this paper, we propose the selection of parameters for quality evaluation criterion of pronunciation of certain phonemes. Is presented a comparison of the different options and criteria for the selection of the parameter metric serving their basis - the Minkowskian metric. This approach is used for the comparative assessment of the quality of their utterances in the process of voice rehabilitation of patients after surgical treatment of cancer of the oral cavity and oropharynx. The pronunciation before surgery, taken as a etalon, and after the operation in the course of employment with a speech therapist are compared. The proposed criterion is calculated based on a comparison of the Fourier spectra of these signals and detect differences on the basis of Minkowskian distance. Pre-signals are subjected to the procedure of normalization for the comparability of the spectra. At the end of the experiment the value of the Minkowskian distance parameter to ensure the greatest legibility signals in comparing the quality of pronunciation was suggested. Various approaches to the formation of the quality evaluation criteria pronouncing phonemes are presented. The applicability of the proposed approach for an objective comparative evaluation of the quality of pronouncing phonemes [k] and [t] in patients before and after surgery is confirmed.

Keywords: Speech quality · Speech rehabilitation · Cancer of the oral cavity and oropharynx · Speech quality criteria

1 Introduction

The problem of speech rehabilitation of patients after surgical treatment of cancer of the oral cavity and oropharynx is relevant. The higher incidence of these diseases says in favor of the relevance of this problem. In 2014 in Russia the

© Springer International Publishing Switzerland 2016
A. Ronzhin et al. (Eds.): SPECOM 2016, LNAI 9811, pp. 287–295, 2016.
DOI: 10.1007/978-3-319-43958-7_34

incidence of cancer of the oral cavity and pharynx was 5.6 per 100 thousand. The prevalence −36.5 per 100 thousand. Thus, each year in the country revealed near 13,000 new cancers oropharyngeal localization, and the total number of patients suffering from this disease calculated over 53,000 people [1,2]. One of the main problems in the treatment is the need of learning the speech of patients after partial or complete surgical removal of some organs of speech production path, for example, tongue. During rehabilitation it is necessary to estimate the quality of the patient's speech. Until recently, this problem was solved only by subjective evaluation of speech quality. In previous studies we have proposed a method based on the use of GOST R-50840-95 Speech transmission over varies communication channels. Techniques for measurements of speech quality, intelligibility and voice identification [3]. This technique allows to obtain a quantitative assessment of the quality of speech, for example, syllable intelligibility. However, to obtain objective assessments in the framework of this method requires an estimate of not less than 5 auditors. In terms of the actual process of voice rehabilitation, this requirement is at least exigent. There is a task of automation of the patient's quality of speech estimation while minimizing the participation of a speech therapist. Such assessment may be obtained by comparing the reference speech (speech of patient before the surgery), and the speech in the rehabilitation process. This approach solves the problem of taking into account the characteristics of different speakers - comparisons are made only in one speaker, that simplifies the solution of the problem. This paper presents one of the steps to solve this problem - the formation of the quality criteria of pronouncing certain phonemes.

2   The Current State of Research

In previous stages of research was carried out the analysis of groups of the phonemes at the greatest change at a surgical treatment of cancer of the oral cavity and oropharynx. Using developed software for automation the evaluation of speech quality on the basis of GOST R 50840-95 [4,5] it have been received the list of the phonemes at the greatest change, namely [r], [t], [s], [f], [k], and also their softened options. In many cases, there was a modification of the softening feature. Comparison of the received list with classical sources, that contains information about the phonemes at the greatest change by this disease, was carried out [6] (referencing to earlier work of the authors team I. Bolov, M. Solovyev, L. Dushak, D. Podgornykh, A. Shenderov, 1974.), high extent of coincidence confirms reliability of the obtained data. Besides, it has been made a preliminary research of Fourier spectrums of phonemes which are most prone to change that has allowed to make the assumption of the greatest susceptibility to change of the top part of a spectrum (areas with a frequency of 2 kHz and above). The example of these spectrum is presented in the Fig. 1. On the basis of the analysis of the received results the task on the current stage of implementation of the project has been formulated.

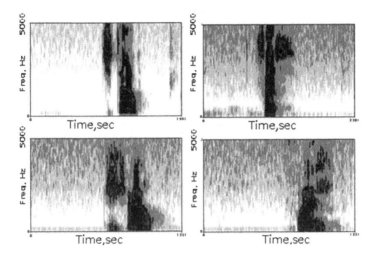

Fig. 1. Fourier spectrogram for russian syllable [ʦtał] (left half). Top part of figures contain spectrogram for syllables records before surgery, down part spectrogram for syllables records after surgery. Fourier spectrogram for russian syllable [səs'] (right half). Top part of figures contain spectrogram for syllables records before surgery, down part spectrogram for syllables records after surgery. The X axis - the time in seconds, Y - frequency in hertz, the upper limit of 5000 Hz

3   Setting Objectives for Research

In this stage it was proposed to form a simple measure to estimate the differences between the normal pronunciation of sounds (as a reference are used the sounds obtained from patient records syllables recorded in the preliminary examination before surgery) and sounds in process of rehabilitation. The first step is to make assumptions based on the analysis of the spectra of healthy speakers, who in the first instance pronounced syllables in normal mode, and in the second - with the minimization of the use of language in speech production. It was set the task of definition of localization of the used range to form a measure of distinction: does it better to use the whole syllable or changed phoneme only, as well as the whole spectrum or only the upper part. The task of the choice of a concrete measure of distinction at determination of distance between the received ranges is also set. As part of this task is carried out research of the application of the Minkowskian distance (1) at different values of parameters. At the same time are considered special cases of this distance - the Euclidian distance (2) and the Manhattan distance (3) (p = 2, p = 1) [7]:

$$\rho(x,y) = \left(\sum_{i=1}^{n} |x_i - y_i|^p \right)^{1/p}, \tag{1}$$

$$d(x,y) = \sqrt{\sum_{i=1}^{n}(x_i - y_i)^2}, \tag{2}$$

$$m(x,y) = \sum_{i=1}^{n}|x_i - y_i|, \tag{3}$$

where x is a first signal, y is a second signal, i is a position in the signal, ρ is the Minkowskian distance, d is the Euclidian distance, m is the Manhattan distance, p is a parameter of Minkowskian distance.

Minkowskian distance is used to solve the problem for different values of its parameters. The following values of parameter p are selected: $p = [-10 - 9.9 - 9.8 \ldots 9.9\,10]$. This involves a consideration of the practical application of these values, in spite of the fact that for $p < 1$ considered distance is not a metric. After receiving the values of distances between different implementations of phonemes in the normal and modified pronunciation it was carried out consideration of some preliminary approaches to formation the criterion of phonemes pronouncing quality on the basis of the distance. The details of these criteria and their characteristics are given in the appropriate section. It is carried out the assessment of the received results at various parameters of determination of Minkowskian distance on the basis of the offered criteria and also it is made the preliminary choice of parameter for practical use. After the choice of a measure for a distance assessment between realization of syllables or phonemes, and also the analysis of criteria for evaluation of quality of pronouncing it is carried out an inspection of the received assumptions with use of records of real patients and it is made the decision on applicability of the offered approach.

4 The Basic Signal Processing Steps in Determining the Quality of the Pronunciation of Syllables or Phonemes

Speech signal processing can be represented as a sequence of performing the following steps:

1. normalization of all studied speech signals on duration;
2. normalization of all studied speech signals on signal power;
3. definition of the Fourier spectrum [8] of all signals. The calculation is carried out with an analysis window of 256 samples and the offset between the windows in a 1 count;
4. determination of paired distances between all signals on the basis of Minkowskian distance;
5. calculation of an assessment of quality of pronouncing of a syllable or phoneme on the basis of the analysis of paired distances between various realizations of a syllable (phoneme).

As a result of this procedure it turns out the criterion or a set of the criteria allowing to estimate quality of pronouncing a syllable (phoneme).

5   Preliminary Normalization of a Speech Signal

5.1   Normalization of All Studied Speech Signals on Duration

It is carried out a reduction of each phoneme to duration equal 0.050 s with application of interpolation. Using of this value is based on the fact that there is no loss of information because it is certainly more than the duration of a single phoneme.

5.2   Normalization of all Studied Speech Signals on Middle Power of Signal

It is carried out a reduction of signals to identical power if they contain identical number of phonemes. Coefficient of normalization can be defined by square root of Middle power of a signal. Middle power of a signal is determined by a formula [9]:

$$MP = \sum_{i=1}^{n} \frac{A_i^2}{n},\tag{4}$$

where A is the amplitude of signal on descrete number i, MP is the middle power value, n is the length of signal.

This normalization is non-obvious and disputable at application in the syllables consisting of several phonemes differing in the compared syllables. The reason is different contribution of phonemes to the overall energy value, but when used in a single phoneme this deficiency is absent.

6   Determination of Paired Distances on the Basis of Minkowskian Distance

Taking into account the processed spectrum of signal and the normalization of the spectrum length the measure takes the form below:

$$l(x, y) = \left(\frac{\sum_{j=1}^{n_f} \sum_{i=1}^{n_t} |x_{ij} - y_{ij}|^p}{n_f \cdot n_t} \right)^{1/p},\tag{5}$$

where x is the first specrum, y is the second spectrum, i is the number of time discrete, j is the number of frequency discrete, n_i is the count of time discrete, n_j is the count of frequency discrete.

Results of calculation are brought in the diagonal matrix presented in Fig. 2. In this case area S_1 corresponds to comparison of the initial and modified signals, area S_2 to comparison only of initial signals and area S_3 to comparison only of the modified signals. n_1 is a quantity of initial signals, n_2 is a quantity of modified signals. l_{ij} is a distance between spectrums of signals number i and j.

Average distance by each area are determined on the basis of this matrix using formulas:

$$\overline{l_1} = \frac{\sum_{i,j \in S_1} l_{ij}}{n_1 \cdot n_2},\tag{6}$$

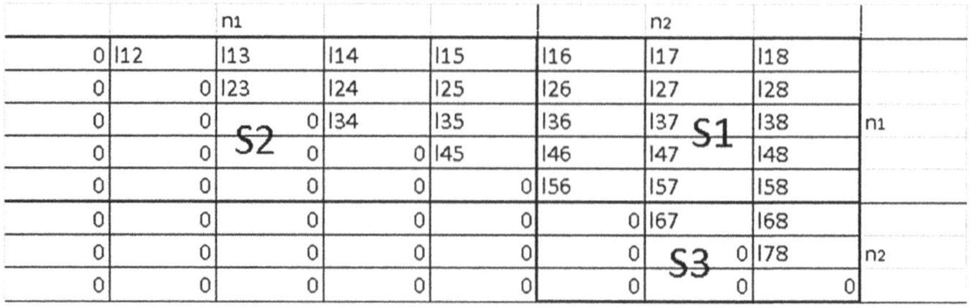

	n1					n2			
0 l12	l13	l14	l15	l16	l17	l18			
0	0 l23	l24	l25	l26	l27	l28			
0	0	0 l34	l35	l36	l37 S1	l38	n1		
0	0 S2	0	0 l45	l46	l47	l48			
0	0	0	0	0 l56	l57	l58			
0	0	0	0	0	0 l67	l68			
0	0	0	0	0	0 S3	0 l78	n2		
0	0	0	0	0	0	0	0		

Fig. 2. View of matrix of distances between spectrum.

$$\overline{l_2} = \frac{2\sum_{i,j\in S_2} l_{ij}}{n_1 \cdot (n_1 - 1)}, \tag{7}$$

$$\overline{l_3} = \frac{2(\sum_{i,j\in S_2, S_3} l_{ij})}{n_1 \cdot (n_1 - 1) + n_2 \cdot (n_2 - 1)} \tag{8}$$

and also the minimum distance on area S_1 and the maximum distance on area S_2.

$$l_{1min} = min_{i,j\in S_1} l_{ij}, \tag{9}$$

$$l_{2max} = max_{i,j\in S_2} l_{ij}. \tag{10}$$

These values are used to form criterion of phoneme pronouncing quality. As criteria for evaluation of phoneme pronouncing quality is offered:

1. The ratio between average distance between the initial and modified signals to average distance between initial signals.

$$Cr_1 = \overline{l_1}/\overline{l_2}. \tag{11}$$

The closer this value to 1, the closer modified signal to initial and vice versa. Among the shortcomings can be noted the possibility of almost complete determination of the final value by stands out in big side values;

2. The ratio between average distance between the initial and modified signals to average distance between signals of one type.

$$Cr_2 = \overline{l_1}/\overline{l_3}. \tag{12}$$

The closer this value to 1, the closer modified signal to initial and vice versa. Among the shortcomings can be noted the possibility of almost complete determination of the final value by stands out in big side values. Use of distinctions between the modified signals is doubtful because Fof their smaller stability and, as a result, great values of distances. However the possibility of application of this criterion demands additional practical check.

3. The ratio between the minimum distinction between the initial and modified signals to the maximum distinction between initial signals.

$$Cr_3 = l_{1min}/l_{2max}. \tag{13}$$

If this value more than 1, then obviously metrics for classes aren't crossed and the farther they from each other, the better created criterion. However in reality the similar assessment is defined by extreme values dropping out of the general set and in practice will almost always be less than 1. Then, on the one hand, the closer this value to 1, the less an area of crossing of sets of value of distances for the initial and modified signals. With another, it isn't considered the quantity or a share of the signals getting to this area.

4. A share of couples of initial signals between which distance exceeds the minimum distance between couples of initial and modified signals, and also a share of couples of initial and modified signals between which distance is less maximum between couples of initial signals.

$$Cr_{41} = 2 \cdot count_{i,j \in S_2}(l_{ij} > l_{1min})/n_1(n_1 - 1), \tag{14}$$

$$Cr_{42} = count_{i,j \in S_1}(l_{ij} < l_{2max})/n_1 n_2. \tag{15}$$

Ideally shares have to be equal 0, is really the less value, the better because the crossings of distances of couple of signals getting to the area are leveled by application of the averaging criterion 1 (on condition of a small amount of such couples).

7   Analysis of the Signal of Healthy Speaker with Using the Proposed Approach

On this stage research conducted on records of one male and one female speakers. 10 records were made by every speaker, herein 5 first and 5 last syllables differed, but they contain the same phoneme in same part inside the syllable.

Further comparison was made for every individual speaker. Comparison of different speakers between each other obviously less important, because accounting of several factors in the same time (specific speaker and condition of speech formation tract), that lead to a change in pronunciation is problematic.

Below in Fig. 3 is shown the values of obtained criteria of quality for all area of studied values with step in 1 (on left half). Values of criteria are also presented for the most characteristic part on the results of the previous stage of the experiment (on right half).

At the result is possible to say, that most appropriate Minkovskian distance when the parameter p is between 1.6 and 3.1. Moreover, Fig. 4 shows a similar addiction, obtained by upper half of the spectrum (3–6 kHz).

Results showed that on this stage of considered range of values is sufficient to preselect the Minkovskian distance parameter and it not requires further expansion. The usefulness of localization in upper range of frequency, potentially more informative according to the results of preliminary experiments, it is not confirmed and requires further research.

Preliminary experiment on recordings of real patients was conducted to confirm the results. It is possible to talk about the correctness of the findings, but in this article is not enough space for its detailed description and it will be

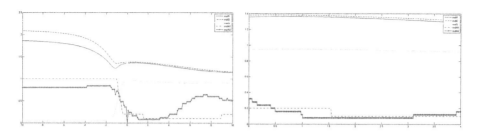

Fig. 3. Values of criteria for $p = -10 \ldots 10$ (left) and $-0.5 \ldots 0.5$ (right)

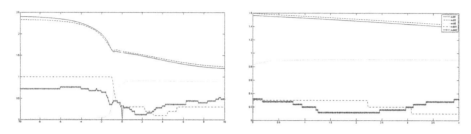

Fig. 4. Values of criteria for $p = -10 \ldots 10$ (left) and $-0.5 \ldots 0.5$ (right)

made in subsequent publications. In addition, the next step will be the using of mel-cepstral coefficients [10], linear prediction coefficients [11] and autocorrelation [12] for evaluation of speech quality. Automation of the segmentation of syllables into phonemes also is a problem for next stage of research [13].

8   Conclusion

As part of this work presents the results of phase for the formation of the quality evaluation criteria pronouncing phonemes by patient in the process of speech rehabilitation after surgery for cancer of the oral cavity and oropharynx. The criteria on the basis of Minkowskian distance between normalized spectra defective phonemes was formed. Preliminary parameter of the distance for the most informative criterion was selected. The approbation of the proposed method of assessing the quality of pronouncing phonemes [t] and [k] on a real patient records was implemented. The tasks for the next phase of the study were set. This work is one part of the big task of assessing the quality of speech in the speech rehabilitation.

Acknowledgments. The study was performed by a grant from the Russian Science Foundation (project 16-15-00038).

References

1. Kaprin, A.D., Starinskiy, V.V., Petrova, G.V.: Status of cancer care the population of Russia in 2014. Moscow, MNIOI name of P.A. Herzen, Moscow (2015)
2. Kaprin, A.D., Starinskiy, V.V., Petrova, G.V.: Malignancies in Russia in 2014 (Morbidity and mortality). MNIOI name of P.A. Herzen, Moscow (2015)
3. Standard GOST R 50840–95 Voice over paths of communication. Methods for assessing the quality, legibility and recognition. Publishing Standards, Moscow (1995)
4. Balatskaya, L.N., Choinzonov, E.L., Chizevskaya, S.Y., Kostyuchenko, E.U., Meshcheryakov, R.V.: Software for assessing voice quality in rehabilitation of patients after surgical treatment of cancer of oral cavity, oropharynx and upper jaw. In: Železný, M., Habernal, I., Ronzhin, A. (eds.) SPECOM 2013. LNCS, vol. 8113, pp. 294–301. Springer, Heidelberg (2013)
5. Kostyuchenko, E.Y., Mescheryakov, R.V., Balatskaya, L.N., Choynzonov, E.L.: Structure and database of software for speech quality and intelligibility assessment in the process of rehabilitation after surgery in the treatment of cancers of the oral cavity and oropharynx, maxillofacial area. SPIIRAS Proc. **32**, 116–124 (2014)
6. MedFind. Oncology. Plastic surgery in the surgical treatment of tumors of the face, jaws. http://medfind.ru/modules/sections/index.php?op=viewarticle&artid=324
7. Kim, D.O., Myuller, C.U., Klekka, U.R.: Factorial, Discriminant and Cluster Analysis. Finance and Statistics, Moscow (1989)
8. Sergienko, A.B.: Digital Signal Processing. Peter, St. Petersburg (2006)
9. Max, J.: Methods and signal processing equipment for physical measurements. In: 2 vols, Translation from French. Mir, Moscow (1983)
10. Rabiner, L.R., Schafer, R.W.: Introduction to Digital Speech Processing. Foundations and Trends in Signal Processing (2007)
11. Benesty, J., Sondhi, M.M., Huang, Y. (eds.): Springer Handbook of Speech Processing. Springer, Heidelberg (2008)
12. Shuyin, Z., Ying, G., Buhong, W.: Auto-correlation property of speech and its application in voice activity detection. In: First International Workshop on Education Technology and Computer Science. ETCS 2009, pp. 265–268 (2009)
13. Gold, K., Scassellati, B.: Audio speech segmentation without language-specific knowledge. In: Cognitive Science, pp. 1370–1375 (2006)

Experiments with One–Class Classifier as a Predictor of Spectral Discontinuities in Unit Concatenation

Daniel Tihelka[1]([✉]), Martin Grůber[1], and Markéta Jůzová[2]

[1] NTIS – New Technologies for the Information Society, Faculty of Applied Sciences,
University of West Bohemia, Pilsen, Czech Republic
{dtihelka,gruber}@ntis.zcu.cz
[2] Department of Cybernetics, Faculty of Applied Sciences, University of West
Bohemia, Pilsen, Czech Republic
juzova@kky.zcu.cz

Abstract. We present a sequence of experiments with one–class classification, aimed at examining the ability of such a classifier to detect spectral smoothness of units, as an alternative to heuristics–based measures used within unit selection speech synthesizers. A set of spectral feature distances was computed between neighbouring frames in natural speech recordings, i.e. those representing natural joins, from which the per–vowel classifier was trained. In total, three types of classifiers were examined for distances computed from several different signal parametrizations. For the evaluation, the trained classifiers were tested against smooth or discontinuous joins as they were perceived by human listeners in the ad–hoc listening test designed for this purpose.

Keywords: Speech synthesis · Unit selection · One–class classification · Concatenation cost · Speech parametrization · Spectral distance

1 Introduction

Although unit selection speech synthesis systems are still often preferred in the commercial sphere, according to [5] and our own experience, it is clear that heuristics–based approaches of unit selection features tuning basically fail. For example, papers such as [1,6,7,15,17,19,20,23–25] examined various concatenation cost features, but the results are rather inconsistent and sometimes even in contradiction. Therefore, instead of manual features tuning, we have started to examine machine–learning techniques for a data–driven automatic per–voice unit selection tuning.

One of the interesting ideas was introduced in [4], where the one–class classification (OCC) technique was used as a replacement for a classic spectral–related smoothness measure in concatenation cost computation. In [22], we tried to validate the results of the original research on our own speech database. In this paper, we present extended results, primarily focusing on parametrizations computed

© Springer International Publishing Switzerland 2016
A. Ronzhin et al. (Eds.): SPECOM 2016, LNAI 9811, pp. 296–303, 2016.
DOI: 10.1007/978-3-319-43958-7_35

from various speech signal framings and their impact on the ability of OCC to detect the joins of speech units where unnatural artefacts are perceived by humans.

2   One–Class Classification in Unit Selection

One–class classification [10,21], also known as *anomaly* or *novelty detection*, is used to address the problem of finding such occurrences in data that do not conform to expected behaviour. This is very advantageous and not yet widely used for unit selection speech synthesis, where usually large speech databases with natural recordings are available. However, it is common in this synthesis technique that unnatural disturbing artefacts may occur when incompatible units are concatenated. The reason is that the target and concatenation costs are generally designed to prefer units minimizing the trade-off of features evaluating *similarity to the requirements*, instead of reflecting whether the units will sound natural in the sequence they are used in. These artefacts, obviously not occurring in the source speech corpus, can thus be viewed as "anomalies" or "outliers". However, the occurrence of the artefacts can be considered as a random process (if they could be predicted, they can be avoided), which makes their collection and the reliable analysis of their causes rather difficult. Therefore, the existence of natural sequences and the unavailability of unnatural anomalies lead to the idea of exploring the abilities of OCC to detect, and thus to avoid, those anomalies.

2.1   Distances to Train the Classifiers on

For the initial experiment [22], we focus only on spectral continuity classification (following [4]) but using our Czech male speech corpus [3] containing approximately 15 h of speech, designed as described in [11,14].

To capture natural spectral transitions, for every two consecutive speech frames, with signal pre–emphasized by value 0.95 and Hamming–windowed, we computed *Euclidean* and *Mahalanobis* distances between MFCC vectors, *Itakura–Saito* distance between LPC coefficients and *symmetrical Kullback–Leibler* distance between spectral envelopes obtained from the LPC and between power FFT spectrum (referred to as "targets" or "references"); each distance vector thus consists of 5 values. Contrary to [4,22], however, we examined several different framings of the signals:

async 20/20 is the original scheme from the initial experiment, where the signal frames are 20 ms long without overlap (20 ms shift). Since we compute feature distances on rather stable vowel parts (see Fig. 1), it is supposed that the spectrum does not change very much within a particular phone. Thus, the natural transition of neighbouring frames should lead to rather small features distance, contrary to a spectral change perceived as an artefact.

async 04/25 is a scheme with frames 25 ms long, shifted by 4 ms. This scheme was chosen as it provides the most accurate automatic phone segmentation for this voice. The significant signal overlap, and thus accented spectral similarity of the consecutive frames, was assumed to emphasize the effect of natural and smooth signal transition pattern which the OCC is required to train.

async 12/25 scheme, having 25 ms long frames with 12 ms shift, was chosen as
a compromise between large overlap (4 ms shift) and no overlap at all, while
there is still slight preference towards frame overlapping.

psync pm/25 is a pitch–synchronous framing, where 25 ms long frames are
centred around pitch–marks [8,9]. In this way, the MFCC, energy and F_0
are computed for the "classic" concatenation cost computation in our TTS
system. Contrary to the previous schemes, the shift is always one pitch period
long and the overlap varies dynamically as pitch changes. In unvoiced regions,
the distances were not computed.

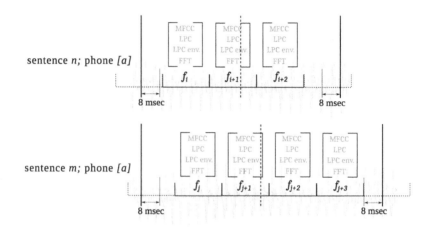

Fig. 1. The example of non-overlapped framing for two illustrative variants of phone
[a] with phone boundaries and centre marked by bold and dashed, respectively, vertical
lines. Feature vectors are outlined for each frame.

As already mentioned, we limit the experiment to vowels only, as unnatural
artefacts are perceived more strongly due to their larger amplitude. Nevertheless,
the extension to other voiced phones is planned as soon as reliable results are
obtained.

For all the various signal framings, the target (natural) distance vectors used
to train OCC were collected per–vowel from:

- all the consecutive frames covering the signal of the vowel, except frames spanning 8 ms at the vowel's beginning and end, i.e. for $(f_i, f_{i+1}), (f_{i+1}, f_{i+2})$ and
  $(f_j, f_{j+1}), (f_{j+1}, f_{j+2}), (f_{j+2}, f_{j+3})$ pairs from Fig. 1. By using of diphones in
  our TTS system, with boundaries approximately in the middle of the under-
  lying phone, this exclusion allows us to avoid distances near phone (vowel)
  transitions in the training/testing set.
- the two consecutive frames nearest to the middle of each vowel, i.e. for
  (f_{i+1}, f_{i+2}) and (f_{j+1}, f_{j+2}) pairs from Fig. 1 — we will mark it as *mid.only*
  in Table 1. This might seem to be a natural choice reflecting the fact that

only signal around phone centre is examined for smoothness during diphones concatenation.

2.2 Evaluation of Real Concatenations

When using only (smooth) distances computed on the corpus data, we do not know much about how well a trained classifier is able to detect real non–continuous spectral transitions. Therefore, we created artificial join in the middle vowel of several words by concatenating two halves of the words from different parts of the corpus. Around the join, the distance was computed in the way that when $[a]$ from sentence m is to be concatenated with $[a]$ from sentence n (see Fig. 1), (f_{i+1}, f_{j+2}) vectors are used — f_{i+1} is nearest to the middle of the initial vowel half and f_{j+2} is the one after the vector nearest to the middle of the final vowel half. Each such distance was coupled with the listeners evaluation whenever a concatenation discontinuity is perceived in the word (further referred to as outlier distances) or not. Since details can be found in [22], we just summarize here that only examples where at least two of three listeners agreed were taken for further processing.

2.3 Classifiers Examined

Having obtained positive experience with OCC [12,13], we examined 3 classifier types, all implemented in *Scikit-learn toolkit* [16]. The first one is *Multivariate Gaussian distribution* (MGD), with all the distances modelled together in one go, tied through covariance matrix. The second one is *One-class SVM* (OCSVM), mapping distances into a high dimensional feature space via a kernel function, and iteratively finding the maximal margin hyperplane which best separates the training data from the outliers [18]. And the last one is *Grubbs' test* [2] modified as described in [12] to detect multidimensional distance vector as outlier when any of the individual features is detected outlying (GRT).

Prior the training, the whole per–vowel set of target distances was reduced to $4,000$ randomly selected vectors, mostly due to speeding up the training process, but also to prevent potential OCC overfitting (see [22] for the total number of distances in *async 20/20*, which is the lowest of all used here). This reduced set was then further randomly split into 80 % for training distances targets and 20 % distances being held out for the final evaluation (see Sect. 3). From the training targets, 20 % were randomly chosen for 10–fold cross–validation. All the classifiers were trained to minimize F1 score, the details about parameters setup can be found in [22].

To further increase the robustness of the training, we added 50 % of the outlier distances (with discontinuity perceived, see Sect. 2.2) to the cross–validation process, if these were available for the corresponding vowel.

3 Results

Once the classifiers are trained, the 20 % of target corpus distance vectors and all the distance vectors for smooth joins evaluated by listeners (i.e. those without an

Table 1. The classification performance when the given number of target distances (for all the words without artefacts perceived) and the remaining 50 % of outlier distances (those not used for cross–validation), obtained by evaluations described in Sect. 2.2 and computed for the given framing, were passed to the classifier trained on the corresponding data. All the values are in %.

phones		a	e	i	o	a:	a	e	i	o	a:
		No. of examples to classify									
targets		60	45	30	50	17					
outliers		9	18	10	21	52					
		async 20/20					async 20/20, mid.only				
OCSVM	TPR	48.3	82.2	93.3	72.0	100.0	56.7	77.8	80.0	86.0	94.1
	TNR	55.6	33.3	50.0	23.8	0.0	44.4	33.3	80.0	0.0	96.2
	F1	62.4	78.7	88.9	70.6	73.9	68.7	76.1	85.7	75.4	91.4
MGD	TPR	100.0	95.6	96.7	98.0	100.0	100.0	75.6	96.7	100.0	88.2
	TNR	0.0	0.0	0.0	4.8	78.8	0.0	22.2	10.0	0.0	94.2
	F1	93.0	81.1	84.1	82.4	75.6	93.0	73.1	85.3	82.6	85.7
GRT	TPR	55.0	86.7	83.3	96.0	100.0	63.3	82.2	86.7	94.0	100.0
	TNR	44.4	33.3	40.0	4.8	53.8	33.3	27.8	70.0	0.0	82.7
	F1	67.3	81.2	82.0	81.4	58.6	73.1	77.9	88.1	79.7	79.1
		async 04/25					async 04/25, mid.only				
OCSVM	TPR	8.3	0.0	0.0	8.0	5.9	6.7	0.0	0.0	2.0	5.9
	TNR	100.0	100.0	100.0	100.0	100.0	100.0	100.0	100.0	100.0	100.0
	F1	15.4	n/a	n/a	14.8	11.1	12.5	n/a	n/a	3.9	11.1
MGD	TPR	41.7	44.4	26.7	36.0	58.8	38.3	42.2	30.0	34.0	29.4
	TNR	100.0	88.9	90.0	95.2	100.0	100.0	88.9	90.0	95.2	100.0
	F1	58.8	59.7	41.0	52.2	74.1	55.4	57.6	45.0	50.0	45.5
GRT	TPR	53.3	24.4	63.3	44.0	29.4	46.7	17.8	23.3	38.0	17.6
	TNR	88.9	100.0	100.0	100.0	100.0	88.9	100.0	100.0	100.0	100.0
	F1	68.8	39.3	77.6	61.1	45.5	62.9	30.2	37.8	55.1	30.0
		async 12/25					async 12/25, mid.only				
OCSVM	TPR	56.7	44.4	63.3	58.0	100.0	45.0	37.8	50.0	50.0	64.7
	TNR	100.0	72.2	90.0	85.7	100.0	100.0	94.4	100.0	0.5	100.0
	F1	72.3	57.1	76.0	70.7	100.0	62.1	54.0	66.7	64.9	78.6
MGD	TPR	46.7	51.1	70.0	54.0	100.0	55.0	44.4	66.7	44.0	58.8
	TNR	100.0	72.2	50.0	66.7	84.6	55.6	88.9	80.0	90.5	92.3
	F1	63.6	63.0	75.0	64.3	81.0	68.0	59.7	76.9	59.5	64.5
GRT	TPR	65.0	51.1	73.3	66.0	100.0	68.3	46.7	56.7	72.0	88.2
	TNR	88.9	61.1	70.0	66.7	90.4	44.4	77.8	100.0	57.1	100.0
	F1	78.0	61.3	80.0	73.3	87.2	77.4	60.0	72.3	75.8	93.8
		psync pm/25					psync pm/25, mid.only				
OCSVM	TPR	38.3	37.8	43.3	46.0	58.8	30.0	22.2	40.0	30.0	11.8
	TNR	100.0	88.9	100.0	90.5	100.0	100.0	88.9	90.0	100.0	100.0
	F1	55.4	53.1	60.5	61.3	74.1	46.2	35.1	55.8	46.2	21.1
MGD	TPR	65.0	26.7	26.7	50.0	76.5	45.0	33.3	46.7	48.0	47.1
	TNR	55.6	88.9	80.0	95.2	92.3	100.0	88.9	60.0	90.5	96.2
	F1	75.7	40.7	40.0	65.8	76.5	62.1	48.4	58.3	63.2	59.3
GRT	TPR	53.3	48.9	70.0	52.0	100.0	63.3	35.6	63.3	56.0	100.0
	TNR	100.0	83.3	90.0	81.0	100.0	100.0	88.9	90	85.7	100.0
	F1	69.6	62.9	80.8	65.0	100.0	77.6	50.8	76.0	69.1	100.0

artefact perceived) were used to evaluate the ability of classifiers to recognize target distances never seen. Also, the remaining 50 % of outlier distances not used in cross–validation were used to enumerate the reliability of probable artefacts detection.

In Table 1 we present results for all the framings mentioned in Sect. 2.1 and all the classifiers described in Sect. 2.3. In the table, the abbreviation TP describes *true positives* (targets detected as targets) and TPR is then percentage of TP from all the targets to be classified (also called *recall*). Similarly, TN stands for *true negatives* (correct outliers classification) and TNR is its percentage (*specificity*). Due to space limitation, we exclude here vowels with a smaller number of examples to evaluate (both due to less joined words evaluated and lower mutual agreement of listeners on artefact absence/presence, see Sect. 2.2). Also, we do not present here the classification of the 20 % target distances being held out.

It can clearly be seen that the results are rather shuffled, with no significant preference for a framing and/or classifier type. In general, the *mid.only* variant behaves worse than when distances taken through the whole vowels are taken into account. Another surprising fact is that the larger overlap leads to worse results – although the distances to train are computed from very similar signals, the classifiers are not able to recognise outlier distances. It can be said that distances between non–overlapping frames are better in recognising targets, while distances between frames with large overlap recognise outliers instead. The best compromise seems to be *async 12/25*, for which *OCSVM* can reliably classify phone [a:] and rather successfully detect outliers for other phones as well.

Looking at raw F1 scores, most of the best results are for *async 20/20* framing, spread through various classifiers. However, taking for example phone [a] with F1 = 93 % (*MGD*), none of the 9 outliers was detected successfully. Similar situation is for [i] (F1 = 88.9 %, *OCSVM*), where only 5 out of 10 outliers were detected. From the point of view of unit selection, where the classifiers should finally be used, we would prefer reliable detection of outliers at the expense of higher FN (continuous joins classified as outliers). This would ensure that no audible artefact (or minimum of them) will appear in the synthesized speech. On the other hand, however, discarding wrongly classified smooth joins can easily lead to the inability of following the required target specifications (those with better match were discarded), which is not a desirable situation either.

4   Conclusion

Hopefully, we have shown that this alternative approach to feature hand–tuning may have its potential despite the fact that there is no ultimate answer to the question of what features/classifiers to use to avoid unnatural artefacts sometimes occurring in unit selection generated speech (neither did in [4]).

To address further research directions, it is important to start with an error analysis, i.e. to examine the causes of the classification failures. Our hypothesis for them is that the cause of the artefacts perceived is either due to a mismatch of non–spectral related features, or due to a spectral mismatch not covered well by the features and distance scheme computations chosen. Therefore, we need to search for another set of features, not necessarily entirely spectral–related, which has a better capability of capturing the causes of artefacts perception — this may affect both concatenation and target cost features. And since the vowel joins evaluated by listeners (described in Sect. 2.2 and in details in [22]) were intentionally not limited with respect to spectral features anyway, they can be gradually extended and reused when searching for and experimenting with some other mismatch–describing features.

To make our results verifiable as well as to provide a solid springboard for prospective followers, we put all the data required to repeat the experiment on github under **ARTIC-TTS-experiments/2016_SPECOM/** repository. Also, more detailed results can be found there. Do not hesitate to contact us in case of any questions.

Acknowledgments. This work was supported by the Grant Agency of the Czech Republic, project No. GA16-04420S and by the grant of the University of West Bohemia, project No. SGS-2016-039. Computational resources were provided by the CESNET LM2015042 under the program "Projects of Large Research, Development, and Innovations Infrastructures".

References

1. Bellegarda, J.R.: A novel discontinuity metric for unit selection text-to-speech synthesis. In: Proceedings of the 5th Speech Synthesis Workshop (SSW5), pp. 133–138. Pittsburgh, PA, USA (2004)
2. Grubbs, F.E.: Procedures for detecting outlying observations in samples. Technometrics **11**, 1–21 (1969)
3. Hanzlíček, Z., Matoušek, J., Tihelka, D.: Experiments on reducing footprint of unit selection TTS system. In: Habernal, I. (ed.) TSD 2013. LNCS, vol. 8082, pp. 249–256. Springer, Heidelberg (2013)
4. Karabetsos, S., Tsiakoulis, P., Chalamandaris, A., Raptis, S.: One-class classification for spectral join cost calculation in unit selection speech synthesis. IEEE Signal Process. Lett. **17**(8), 746–749 (2010)
5. King, S.: Measuring a decade of progress in text-to-speech. Loquens **1**(1), e006 (2014)
6. Klabbers, E., Veldhuis, R.N.J.: Reducing audible spectral discontinuities. IEEE Trans. Speech Audio Process. **9**(1), 39–51 (2001)
7. Legát, M., Matoušek, J.: Analysis of data collected in listening tests for the purpose of evaluation of concatenation cost functions. In: Habernal, I., Matoušek, V. (eds.) TSD 2011. LNCS, vol. 6836, pp. 33–40. Springer, Heidelberg (2011)
8. Legát, M., Matoušek, J., Tihelka, D.: On the detection of pitch marks using a robust multi-phase algorithm. Speech Commun. **53**(4), 552–566 (2011)
9. Legát, M., Tihelka, D., Matoušek, J.: Pitch marks at peaks or valleys? In: Matoušek, V., Mautner, P. (eds.) TSD 2007. LNCS (LNAI), vol. 4629, pp. 502–507. Springer, Heidelberg (2007)
10. Markou, M., Singh, S.: Novelty detection: a review-part 1: statistical approaches. Signal Process. **83**(12), 2481–2497 (2003)

11. Matoušek, J., Romportl, J.: On building phonetically and prosodically rich speech corpus for text-to-speech synthesis. In: Proceeding of the 2nd IASTED International Conference on Computational Intelligence, pp. 442–447. ACTA Press, San Francisco (2006)
12. Matoušek, J., Tihelka, D.: Voting detector: A combination of anomaly detectors to reveal annotation errors in TTS corpora. Submitted to the Interspeech (2016)
13. Matoušek, J., Tihelka, D.: Anomaly-based annotation errors detection in TTS corpora. In: Proceedings of the 16th Annual Conference of the International Speech Communication Association (Interspeech 2015), pp. 314–318. Dresden, Germany (2015)
14. Matoušek, J., Tihelka, D., Romportl, J.: Building of a speech corpus optimised for unit selection TTS synthesis. In: Proceedings of 6th International Conference on Language Resources and Evaluation, LREC 2008. ELRA (2008)
15. Pantazis, Y., Stylianou, Y.: On the detection of discontinuities in concatenative speech synthesis. In: Stylianou, Y., Faundez-Zanuy, M., Esposito, A. (eds.) COST 277. LNCS, vol. 4391, pp. 89–100. Springer, Heidelberg (2007)
16. Pedregosa, F., Varoquaux, G., Gramfort, A., Michel, V., Thirion, B., Grisel, O., Blondel, M., Prettenhofer, P., Weiss, R., Dubourg, V., Vanderplas, J., Passos, A., Cournapeau, D., Brucher, M., Perrot, M., Duchesnay, E.: Scikit-learn: machine learning in Python. J. Mach. Learn. Res. **12**, 2825–2830 (2011)
17. Přibil, J., Přibilová, A.: Evaluation of influence of spectral and prosodic features on GMM classification of Czech and Slovak emotional speech. EURASIP J. Audio Speech Music Process. **33**(3), 1–22 (2013)
18. Schölkopf, B., Platt, J.C., Shawe-Taylor, J.C., Smola, A.J., Williamson, R.C.: Estimating the support of a high-dimensional distribution. Neural Comput. **13**(7), 1443–1471 (2001)
19. Stylianou, Y., Syrdal, A.K.: Perceptual and objective detection of discontinuities in concatenative speech synthesis. In: Proceedings of the IEEE Acoustics, Speech, and Signal Processing (ICASSP), pp. 837–840 (2001)
20. Syrdal, A.K., Conkie, A.D.: Data-driven perceptually based join costs. In: Proceedings of the 5th Speech Synthesis Workshop (SSW5), pp. 49–54. Pittsburgh, PA, USA (2004)
21. Tax, D.M.J.: One-class classification: concept learning in the absence of counter-examples. Ph.D. thesis, Technische Universiteit Delft (2001)
22. Tihelka, D., Grůber, M., Matoušek, J., Jůzová, M.: Examining the ability of one-class classifier to ensure the spectral smoothness of concatenated units. Submitted to the 13th IEEE International Conference on Signal Processing (ICSP) 2016. If not accepted, the paper will be placed to github, under ARTIC-TTS-experiments/2016_SPECOM/ repository where the experiment data are
23. Vepa, J.: Join cost for unit selection speech synthesis. Ph.D. thesis, The University of Edinburgh, College of Science and Engineering, School of Informatics (2004)
24. Vepa, J., King, S.: Kalman-filter based join cost for unit-selection speech synthesis. In: Proceedings of the EUROSPEECH 2003 - INTERSPEECH 2003. Proceedings of 8th European Conference on Speech Communication and Technology, pp. 293–296. ISCA (2003)
25. Vít, J., Matoušek, J.: Concatenation artifact detection trained from listeners evaluations. In: Habernal, I. (ed.) TSD 2013. LNCS, vol. 8082, pp. 169–176. Springer, Heidelberg (2013)

Exploring GMM-derived Features
for Unsupervised Adaptation of Deep Neural
Network Acoustic Models

Natalia Tomashenko[1,2,3(✉)], Yuri Khokhlov[1],
Anthony Larcher[3], and Yannick Estève[3]

[1] STC-Innovations Ltd., Saint-petersburg, Russia
{tomashenko-n,khokhlov}@speechpro.com
[2] ITMO University, Saint-petersburg, Russia
[3] University of Le Mans, Le Mans, France
{anthony.larcher,yannick.esteve}@univ-lemans.fr

Abstract. In this paper we investigate GMM-derived features recently introduced for adaptation of context-dependent deep neural network HMM (CD-DNN-HMM) acoustic models. We present an initial attempt of improving the previously proposed adaptation algorithm by applying lattice scores and by using confidence measures in the traditional maximum a posteriori (MAP) adaptation algorithm. Modified MAP adaptation is performed for the auxiliary GMM model used in a speaker adaptation procedure for a DNN. In addition we introduce two approaches - data augmentation and data selection, for improving the regularization in MAP adaptation for DNN. Experimental results on the Wall Street Journal (WSJ0) corpus show that the proposed adaptation technique can provide, on average, up to 9.9 % relative word error rate (WER) reduction under an unsupervised adaptation setup, compared to speaker independent DNN-HMM systems built on conventional features.

Keywords: Speaker adaptation · Deep neural networks (DNN) · MAP · CD-DNN-HMM · GMM-derived (GMMD) features · Speaker adaptive training (SAT) · Confidence scores

1 Introduction

Nowadays, deep neural networks (DNNs) have replaced conventional GMM-HMMs in most state-of-the-art automatic speech recognition (ASR) systems, because it has been shown that DNN-HMM models outperform GMM-HMMs in different ASR tasks. However, various adaptation algorithms that have been developed for GMM-HMM systems cannot be easily applied to DNNs because of the different nature of these models. Many new adaptation methods have recently been developed for DNNs, and a few of them [4,7,10,13–15] take advantage of robust adaptability of GMMs. However, there is no universal method for efficient transfer of all adaptation algorithms from the GMM framework to DNN

© Springer International Publishing Switzerland 2016
A. Ronzhin et al. (Eds.): SPECOM 2016, LNAI 9811, pp. 304–311, 2016.
DOI: 10.1007/978-3-319-43958-7_36

models. The purpose of the present work is to make a step in this direction using GMM-derived features for training DNN models.

Most of the existing methods for adapting DNN models can be classified into several types: (1) linear transformation, (2) regularization techniques, (3) auxiliary features, (4) multi-task learning, (5) combining GMM and DNN models. **Linear transformation** can be applied at different levels of the DNN system: to the input features, as in linear input network transformation (LIN) [2] or feature-space discriminative linear regression (fDLR); to the activations of hidden layers, as in linear hidden network transformation (LHN) [2]; or to the softmax layer, as in LON or in output-feature discriminative linear regression. The second type of adaptation consists in re-training the entire network or only a part of it using special **regularization techniques** for improving generalization, such as L2-prior regularization [6], Kullback-Leibler divergence regularization [16] and conservative training. The concept of **multi-task learning** (MTL) has recently been applied to the task of speaker adaptation and has been shown to improve the performance of different model-based DNN adaptation techniques, such as LHN and learning speaker-specific hidden unit contributions [12]. **Using auxiliary features** is another approach in which the acoustic feature vectors are augmented with additional speaker-specific or channel-specific features computed for each speaker or utterance at both training and test stages. An example of effective auxiliary features is i-vectors [11]. Alternative methods are adaptation with speaker codes [1] and factorized adaptation [5]. The most common way of **combining GMM and DNN models** for adaptation is using GMM-adapted features, for example fMLLR, as input for DNN training [10]. In [4] likelihood scores from DNN and GMM models, both adapted in the feature space using the same fMLLR transform, are combined at the state level during decoding. The authors of [7] propose combining the GMM and DNN models using the temporally varying weight regression framework.

In this work we investigate a novel approach for SAT of DNNs based on using GMM-derived features as the input to DNNs [13,14]. We present an initial attempt of improving the previously proposed scheme for DNN adaptation by using recognition lattices in MAP adaptation and by the data augmentation and data selection approaches.

2   SAT for DNN-HMM Based on GMM-derived Features

Construction of GMM-derived features for adapting DNNs was proposed in [13,14], where it was demonstrated, using MAP and fMLLR adaptation as an example, that this type of features makes it possible to effectively use GMM-HMM adaptation algorithms in the DNN framework.

Our features are obtained as follows (Fig. 1). First, 39-dimensional Mel-frequency cepstral coefficients (MFCC) with delta and acceleration coefficients are extracted with per-speaker cepstral mean normalization (CMN). Then an auxiliary GMM monophone model is used to transform cepstral feature vectors into log-likelihoods vectors. At this step, speaker adaptation of the auxiliary

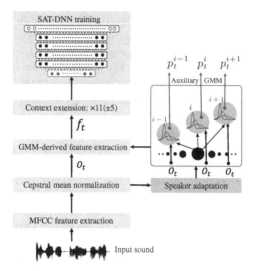

Fig. 1. Using speaker adapted GMMD features for SAT DNN training.

speaker-independent (SI) GMM model is performed for each speaker in the training corpus and the new speaker-adapted (SA) GMM model is obtained in order to extract SA GMM-derived features.

In the auxiliary model, each phoneme is modeled using a three state left-right context-independent GMM-HMM. For a given acoustic MFCC-feature vector, a new GMM-derived feature vector is obtained by calculating log-likelihoods across all the states of the auxiliary GMM monophone model on the given vector. Suppose o_t is the acoustic feature at time t, then the new GMM-derived feature vector f_t is calculated as follows:

$$f_t = [p_t^1, \ldots, p_t^n], \tag{1}$$

where n is the number of states in the auxiliary GMM model,

$$p_t^i = \log\left(P(o_t \mid s_t = i)\right) \tag{2}$$

is the log-likelihood estimated using the GMM. Here s_t denotes the state index at time t. In our case n is equal to 132 ($39 \times 3 + 3 \times 5$), coming from: 39 three-state phones, one five-state silence model, and two five-state (speech and non-speech) noise models. Hence this procedure leads to a 132-dimension feature vector per speech frame. After that, the features are spliced in time taking a context size of 11 frames (i.e., ± 5). We will refer to these resulting features as GMMD features. The dimension of the resulting features is equal to 1452 (11×132). These features are used as the input for training the DNN. The proposed approach can be considered a feature space transformation technique with respect to DNN-HMMs trained on GMMD features.

3   MAP Adaptation Using Lattices Scores

The use of lattice-based information and confidence scores [3] is a well-known method for improving the performance of unsupervised adaptation. In this work we use the MAP adaptation algorithm for adapting the SI GMM model. Speaker adaptation of a DNN-HMM model built on GMMD features is performed through the MAP adaptation of the auxiliary GMM monophone model, which is used for calculating GMMD features. We modify the traditional MAP adaptation algorithm by using lattices instead of alignment from the first decoding pass as follows. Let m denote an index of a Gaussian in SI acoustic model (AM), and μ_m the mean of this Gaussian. Then the MAP estimation of the mean vector is

$$\widehat{\mu}_m = \frac{\tau\mu_m + \sum_t \gamma_m(t)p_s(t)o_t}{\tau + \sum_t \gamma_m(t)p_s(t)}, \tag{3}$$

where τ is the parameter that controls the balance between the maximum likelihood estimate of the mean and its prior value; $\gamma_m(t)$ is the posterior probability of Gaussian component m at time t; and $p_s(t)$ is the confidence score of state s at time t in the lattice obtained from the first decoding pass by calculating arc posteriors probabilities. The forward-backward algorithm is used to calculate these arc posterior probabilities from the lattice as follows:

$$P(l|O) = \frac{\sum_{q \in Q_l} p_{acc}(O|q)^{\frac{1}{\alpha}} P_{lm}(w)}{P(O)}, \tag{4}$$

where α is the language model scale factor; q is a path through the lattice corresponding to the word sequence w; Q_l is the set of paths passing through arc l; $p_{acc}(O|q)$ is the acoustic likelihood; $P_{lm}(w)$ is the language model probability; and $p(O)$ is the overall likelihood of all paths through the lattice. In a particular case, when $p_s(t) = 1$ for all states and t, formula (3) represents the traditional MAP adaptation. In addition to this frame-level weighting scheme, we apply confidence base selection scheme, when we use in (3) only those observations, which confidence scores exceed the given threshold.

4   Data Augmentation and Data Selection for SAT

In this work we explore two approaches to improve the performance of SAT DNN models with MAP adaptation. The first approach is based on using different values of τ (in formula (3)) when extracting adapted GMMD features for DNN training. In this approach we extract features for all training corpus several times for a set of τ values. And then the DNN models are trained on the union of the obtained features. The intuition behind this approach is similar to that used in data augmentation.

The second approach, which we call data selection strategy, consists in splitting training data for each speaker in the training corpus into several parts and then performing MAP adaptation independently on each of the part. In this paper we use a simple implementation of this strategy - we randomly separate training data for each speaker into several subsets so that the total amount of data in each subset is approximately equal to the average amount of data per speaker in the test set. This strategy serves as a regularization and is supposed to make adaptation more robust to the size of the adaptation set.

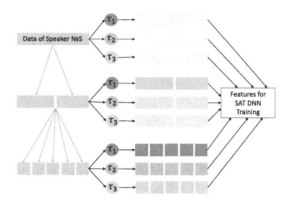

Fig. 2. Data augmentation and data selection scheme for SAT

Hence, the original data from the training corpus are used in AM training several times with different values of τ and inside different subsets of data chosen for adaptation. The motivation for these two approaches lies in obtaining more robust SAT DNN models for MAP adaptation, especially when the training corpus is relatively small.

The GMMD feature dynamic in the training corpus for different values of τ and for different data selection strategies is shown in Fig. 2. In both pictures "full" means that during the SAT training for a given speaker all data of that speaker from the training corpus are used for MAP adaptation, whereas "selection" means that data selection strategy is applied and training data for this speaker is randomly split into two subsets so that MAP adaptation is performed for each subset independently. Let denote T_1 and T_2 two types of features, (or more precisely, to GMMD features extracted with different parameters). Every curve in Fig. 3a and b, marked as "T_1–T_2", corresponds to the average differences between T_1 and T_2 features and is calculated as follows. First, we subtract coordinatewise features T_2 from T_1 on the training corpus. Then we found mean (Fig. 3a) and standard deviation values (Fig. 3b) for each feature vector coordinate. Finally, we sort the obtained values for each feature vector dimension by descending order. We can see that GMMD features calculated for various τ and with (or without) data selection strategy have different amplitude and dynamic characteristics, therefore they can contain complementary information. Hence data augmentation might improve AM by making them more robust to τ and to the size of the adaptation set.

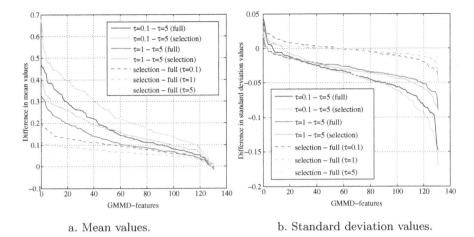

a. Mean values.   b. Standard deviation values.

Fig. 3. Differences in GMMD-features.

5   Experimental Results

The experiments are conducted on the WSJ0 corpus [8]. For AM training we use 7138 utterances of 83 speakers from the standard SI-84 training set, which correspond to approximately 15 hours of data, recorded with the Sennheiser microphone, 16 kHz. AMs are trained using the Kaldi speech recognition toolkit [9], following mostly Kaldi WSJ recipe (except for GMMD-features and adaptation). We use conventional 11×39MFCC features (39-dimensional MFCC (with CMN) spliced across 11 frames (± 5)) as baseline features and compare them to the proposed GMMD features. We train four DNN models: SI model on 11×39MFCC; SI and two SAT models on GMMD features. These four DNNs have identical topology (except for the dimension of the input layer) and are trained on the same training dataset. An auxiliary GMM is also trained on the same data.

The first SAT DNN on GMMD features is trained as described in Sect. 2 with parameter τ for adaptation equal to 5. The second SAT DNN on GMMD features is trained using data augmentation (with τ equal to 0.1, 1 and 5) and data selection strategy, as described in Sect. 4. For training SI-DNN on GMMD features, we apply the scheme shown in Fig. 1, but eliminate the speaker adaptation step. All four CD-DNN-HMM systems had six 2048-neuron hidden layers and 2355-neuron output layer. The neurons in the output layer correspond to context-dependent states determined by tree-based clustering in CD-GMM-HMM. The DNN is initialized with the stacked restricted Boltzmann machines by using layer by layer generative pre-training. It is trained with an initial learning rate of 0.008 using the cross-entropy objective function. After that five iterations of sequence-discriminative training with per-utterance updates, optimizing state Minimum Bayes Risk (sMBR) criteria, are performed.

In all experiments further we consider SI DNN trained on 11×39MFCC features as the baseline model and compare the performance results of the other models with it. Evaluation is carried out on the standard WSJ0 evaluation test **si_et_20**, which consists of 333 read utterances (5645 words) from 8 speakers. A WSJ trigram open NVP LM with a 20k word vocabulary is used during recognition. The OOV rate is about 1.5 %. The LM is pruned as in the Kaldi [9] WSJ recipe with the threshold 10^{-7}. The adaptation experiments are conducted in an unsupervised mode on the test data using transcripts or lattices obtained from the first decoding pass. For adapting an auxiliary GMM model we use MAP adaptation algorithm. We perform two adaptation experiments: (1) with traditional MAP and (2) with lattice-based MAP using confidence scores, as described in Sect. 3. For lattice-based MAP the value of confidence threshold is 0.6. The performance results in terms of word error rate (WER) for SI and adapted DNN-HMM models are presented in Table 1. We can see that using confidence scores can give an additional slight improvement in MAP adaptation for DNN models over adaptation, which uses an alignment. The best result is obtained using data augmentation and data selection strategies. For comparison purposes we also train six DNN models with τ values 0.1, 1 and 5 with and without data selection strategies, but in all cases the results are worse than the one obtained combining both strategies, so we do not report other results here.

Table 1. Summary of WER (%) results on WSJ0 evaluation set si_et_20. Δ WER - relative WER reduction.

Type of Features	Adaptation	WER, %	Δ WER, %
11×39MFCC	SI	7.51	baseline
GMMD	SI	7.83	–
	MAP (alignment)	7.09	5.6
	MAP (lattice-based)	6.93	8.4
	MAP (data augmentation & selection)	6.77	9.9

6   Conclusion

In this work we have investigated GMM-derived features recently introduced for adaptation of DNN AMs. MAP adaptation algorithm is performed for the auxiliary GMM model used in a SAT procedure for a DNN. We present an attempt of improving the previously proposed adaptation algorithm by using confidences scores in adaptation. In addition we introduced two approaches, so called data augmentation and data selection strategies, for improving the regularization in MAP adaptation for DNN. The proposed approaches are especially suitable when the training corpus is small, or when the amount of adaptation data is not known in advance and can vary. Experimental results on the WSJ0 corpus demonstrate that, in an unsupervised adaptation mode, the proposed adaptation technique can provide, approximately, up to 9.9 % relative WER reduction compared to the SI DNN system built on conventional 11×39MFCC features.

Acknowledgements. This work was partially financially supported by the Ministry of Education and Science of the Russian Federation, Contract 14.579.21.0057, ID RFMEFI57914X0057.

References

1. Abdel-Hamid, O., Jiang, H.: Fast speaker adaptation of hybrid NN/HMM model for speech recognition based on discriminative learning of speaker code. In: Proceedings of the ICASSP, pp. 7942–7946. IEEE (2013)
2. Gemello, R., Mana, F., Scanzio, S., Laface, P., De Mori, R.: Adaptation of hybrid ANN/HMM models using linear hidden transformations and conservative training. In: Proceedings of the ICASSP, vol. 1. IEEE (2006)
3. Gollan, C., Bacchiani, M.: Confidence scores for acoustic model adaptation. In: Proceedings of the ICASSP, pp. 4289–4292. IEEE (2008)
4. Lei, X., Lin, H., Heigold, G.: Deep neural networks with auxiliary gaussian mixture models for real-time speech recognition. In: Proceedings of the ICASSP, pp. 7634–7638. IEEE (2013)
5. Li, J., Huang, J.T., Gong, Y.: Factorized adaptation for deep neural network. In: Proceedings of the ICASSP, pp. 5537–5541. IEEE (2014)
6. Liao, H.: Speaker adaptation of context dependent deep neural networks. In: Proceedings of the ICASSP, pp. 7947–7951. IEEE (2013)
7. Liu, S., Sim, K.C.: On combining DNN and GMM with unsupervised speaker adaptation for robust automatic speech recognition. In: Proceedings of the ICASSP, pp. 195–199. IEEE (2014)
8. Paul, D.B., Baker, J.M.: The design for the wall street journal-based CSR corpus. In: Proceedings of the Workshop on Speech and Natural Language, pp. 357–362. Association for Computational Linguistics (1992)
9. Povey, D., Ghoshal, A., et al.: The Kaldi speech recognition toolkit. In: IEEE 2011 Workshop on Automatic Speech Recognition and Understanding (2011)
10. Rath, S.P., Povey, D., Veselỳ, K., Cernocky, J.: Improved feature processing for deep neural networks. In: Interspeech, pp. 109–113 (2013)
11. Senior, A., Lopez-Moreno, I.: Improving DNN speaker independence with i-vector inputs. In: Proceedings of the ICASSP, pp. 225–229 (2014)
12. Swietojanski, P., Bell, P., Renals, S.: Structured output layer with auxiliary targets for context-dependent acoustic modelling. In: Interspeech (2015)
13. Tomashenko, N., Khokhlov, Y.: Speaker adaptation of context dependent deep neural networks based on MAP-adaptation and GMM-derived feature processing. In: Proceedings of the Interspeech, pp. 2997–3001 (2014)
14. Tomashenko, N., Khokhlov, Y.: GMM-derived features for effective unsupervised adaptation of deep neural network acoustic models. In: Proceedings of the Interspeech, pp. 2882–2886 (2015)
15. Tomashenko, N., Khokhlov, Y., Larcher, A., Estève, Y.: Exploration de paramètres acoustiques dérivés de GMM pour l'adaptation non supervisée de modèles acoustiques à base de réseaux de neurones profonds. In: Proceedings of the 31éme Journées d'Études sur la Parole (JEP) (2016)
16. Yu, D., Yao, K., Su, H., Li, G., Seide, F.: KL-divergence regularized deep neural network adaptation for improved large vocabulary speech recognition. In: Proceedings of the ICASSP, pp. 7893–7897. IEEE (2013)

Feature Space VTS with Phase Term Modeling

Maxim Korenevsky[1,2(✉)] and Aleksei Romanenko[1]

[1] ITMO University, Saint Petersburg, Russia
[2] STC-Innovations Ltd., Saint Petersburg, Russia
{korenevsky,romanenko}@speechpro.com

Abstract. A new variant of Vector Taylor Series based features compensation algorithm is proposed. The phase-sensitive speech distortion model is used and the phase term is modeled as a multivariate gaussian with unknown mean vector and covariance matrix. These parameters are estimated based on Maximum Likelihood principle and EM-algorithm is used for this. EM formulas of parameter update are derived as well MMSE estimate of the clean speech features. The experiments on Aurora2 database show that taking phase term into account and data-driven estimation of its parameters result in relative WER reduction of about 20 % compared to phase-insensitive VTS version. The proposed method is also compared to the VTS with constant phase vector and this approximation is shown to be very efficient.

Keywords: Robust speech recognition · Feature compensation · Vector taylor series · Distortion model · Phase-sensitive · Aurora2

1 Introduction

Vector Taylor Series (VTS) is an effective and popular approach widely used in robust speech recognition. Its simplest form was proposed in the middle 90's [18,19] and since then many improvements and generalizations have been made. The scope of VTS comprises the compensation of the acoustic features distortion [10,14,21], the acoustic models adaptation to the environment [2,10–13] and various forms of noise adaptive training [8,9,14]. Besides, VTS is often used in combination with other approaches, for instance Join Uncertainty Decoding (JUD) [15–17] and Support Vector Machines (SVM) [5].

The important assumption used in almost all VTS papers is a possibility to approximate the distribution of the clean speech features with Gaussian Mixture Model (GMM). Due to the linearity of the VTS distortion model it can be shown that the distribution of noisy speech features can be also described by GMM. This property makes it possible to effectively use VTS for GMM-HMM acoustic model adaptation to the environment. However, in the last decade the GMM-HMM acoustic models have been superseded by models based on various neural networks such as DNN, CNN, LSTM etc. [1,3,6]. That's why the use of VTS in the feature space to compensate feature distortions due to channel and additive noise becomes more demanded.

© Springer International Publishing Switzerland 2016
A. Ronzhin et al. (Eds.): SPECOM 2016, LNAI 9811, pp. 312–320, 2016.
DOI: 10.1007/978-3-319-43958-7_37

The "phase-sensitive" feature distortion model was first introduced in [4]. In comparison to previously considered models, it includes extra summand which depends on the phase difference between complex noise and channel-passed speech spectra. It was proposed to model phase-dependent vector as a multivariate gaussian random vector with zero mean and diagonal covariance estimated from the training data. It was shown that using this model improves the results of the VTS acoustic model adaptation. The same distortion model was used in [13] again in the acoustic model space but there the phase vector was assumed to be deterministic and all its elements were equal. The experiments demonstrated that such an approach provides the recognition improvement and the optimal value of phase vector elements was found to be 2.5. This result is at odds with the theoretical estimates which state that these elements magnitude must not be greater that 1. The authors of [13] proposed several explanations for this and one of them is that the phase vector is stochastic by its nature but it was forced to be deterministic.

This paper considers the usage of phase-sensitive distortion model for the feature compensation. It assumes the phase vector to be a multivariate gaussian vector as in [4] but with the unknown mean vector and covariance matrix which are estimated from the noisy features by means of EM-algorithm in spirit of [10]. The experiments on Aurora2 database confirm the significant WER reduction of the proposed approach in comparison to not using phase-dependent term.

2 Phase-Sensitive Speech Feature Distortion Model

Most of the VTS papers rely on the following clean speech distortion model:

$$y(t) = x(t) * h(t) + n(t), \tag{1}$$

where $x(t)$, $h(t)$, $n(t)$ and $y(t)$ represent the clean speech, channel impulse response, noise and noisy speech signal respectively and $*$ stands for the convolution operation. As shown in [4], such model generates the corresponding distortion models for various acoustic features, which have the same algebraic form

$$\mathbf{y} = \mathbf{x} + g(\mathbf{x}, \mathbf{h}, \mathbf{n}, \boldsymbol{\alpha}), \tag{2}$$

for both linear and mel-frequency log-power spectra as well as for MFCCs. These models differ only in form of nonlinearity g. Here $\mathbf{h}$ is a corresponding feature vector of an impulse response $h(t)$ and $\boldsymbol{\alpha}$ is a vector which depends on phase difference between complex spectra of $n(t)$ and $x(t) * h(t)$. As shown in [4], all the components of $\boldsymbol{\alpha}$ meet the condition $|\alpha^{(l)}| \leqslant 1$.

The form of function g for the MFCC is[1]

$$g(\mathbf{x}, \mathbf{h}, \mathbf{n}, \boldsymbol{\alpha}) = \mathbf{h} + C \log \left(1 + e^{D(\mathbf{n} - \mathbf{x} - \mathbf{h})} + 2\boldsymbol{\alpha} \bullet e^{D(\mathbf{n} - \mathbf{x} - \mathbf{h})/2} \right), \tag{3}$$

---

[1] In what follows we deal with only mel-cepstral domain since log-spectral domain is similar but more simple to explore.

where exponent and logarithm are applied element-wise, $\bullet$ means element-wise multiplication and C and D stand for DCT matrix and its right pseudo-inverse matrix respectively.

By expanding $g(\mathbf{x}, \mathbf{h}, \mathbf{n}, \boldsymbol{\alpha})$ into the Taylor series around the point $(\mathbf{x}_0, \mathbf{h}_0, \mathbf{n}_0, \boldsymbol{\alpha}_0)$ up to the first order terms it is possible to obtain a linearized version of the expression (2):

$$
\begin{aligned}
\mathbf{y} &= \mathbf{x} + g(\mathbf{x}_0, \mathbf{h}_0, \mathbf{n}_0, \boldsymbol{\alpha}_0) \\
&\quad + \nabla_{\mathbf{x}} g^T(\mathbf{x} - \mathbf{x}_0) + \nabla_{\mathbf{h}} g^T(\mathbf{h} - \mathbf{h}_0) + \nabla_{\mathbf{n}} g^T(\mathbf{n} - \mathbf{n}_0) + \nabla_{\boldsymbol{\alpha}} g^T(\boldsymbol{\alpha} - \boldsymbol{\alpha}_0) \\
&= (I + \nabla_{\mathbf{x}} g^T)\mathbf{x} + \nabla_{\mathbf{h}} g^T \mathbf{h} + \nabla_{\mathbf{n}} g^T \mathbf{n} + \nabla_{\boldsymbol{\alpha}} g^T \boldsymbol{\alpha} + f(\mathbf{x}_0, \mathbf{h}_0, \mathbf{n}_0, \boldsymbol{\alpha}_0), \quad (4)
\end{aligned}
$$

where for the brevity $\nabla_{\mathbf{var}} g$ stands for the gradient of g with respect to variable $\mathbf{var}$ taken in the point $(\mathbf{x}_0, \mathbf{h}_0, \mathbf{n}_0, \boldsymbol{\alpha}_0)$ and

$$
f(\mathbf{x}_0, \mathbf{h}_0, \mathbf{n}_0, \boldsymbol{\alpha}_0) = g(\mathbf{x}_0, \mathbf{h}_0, \mathbf{n}_0, \boldsymbol{\alpha}_0) - \nabla_{\mathbf{x}} g^T)\mathbf{x}_0 - \nabla_{\mathbf{h}} g^T \mathbf{h}_0 - \nabla_{\mathbf{n}} g^T \mathbf{n}_0 - \nabla_{\boldsymbol{\alpha}} g^T \boldsymbol{\alpha}_0.
$$

The model (4) takes into account the dependence of distorted features on phase vector $\boldsymbol{\alpha}$ which is assumed to be gaussian with unknown mean vector $\mu_{\boldsymbol{\alpha}}$ and covariance matrix $\Sigma_{\boldsymbol{\alpha}}$:

$$
\boldsymbol{\alpha} \sim \mathcal{N}(\boldsymbol{\alpha}; \mu_{\boldsymbol{\alpha}}, \Sigma_{\boldsymbol{\alpha}}). \quad (5)
$$

The similar assumption is made for the noise features vector, $\mathbf{n} \sim \mathcal{N}(\mathbf{n}; \mu_{\mathbf{n}}, \Sigma_{\mathbf{n}})$, and the channel feature vector $\mathbf{h}$ is considered to be unknown but deterministic and constant during the whole recording. Notice that the dimension of the vector $\boldsymbol{\alpha}$ is equal to the number of mel-frequency bands while vectors $\mathbf{x}, \mathbf{h}, \mathbf{n}$ dimensions are equal to the number of cepstral coefficients, so they a generally different.

The gradients of the non-linearity g is easy to compute. The gradients with respect to $\mathbf{h}$ and $\boldsymbol{\alpha}$ look like

$$
\nabla_{\mathbf{h}} g(\mathbf{x}, \mathbf{h}, \mathbf{n}, \boldsymbol{\alpha}) = D^T \mathrm{diag} \left\{ \frac{1 + \boldsymbol{\alpha} \bullet e^{D(\mathbf{n} - \mathbf{x} - \mathbf{h})/2}}{1 + e^{D(\mathbf{n} - \mathbf{x} - \mathbf{h})} + 2\boldsymbol{\alpha} \bullet e^{D(\mathbf{n} - \mathbf{x} - \mathbf{h})/2}} \right\} C^T, \quad (6)
$$

$$
\nabla_{\boldsymbol{\alpha}} g(\mathbf{x}, \mathbf{h}, \mathbf{n}, \boldsymbol{\alpha}) = \mathrm{diag} \left\{ \frac{2e^{D(\mathbf{n} - \mathbf{x} - \mathbf{h})/2}}{1 + e^{D(\mathbf{n} - \mathbf{x} - \mathbf{h})} + 2\boldsymbol{\alpha} \bullet e^{D(\mathbf{n} - \mathbf{x} - \mathbf{h})/2}} \right\} C^T, \quad (7)
$$

and the gradients with respect to $\mathbf{x}$ and $\mathbf{n}$ are equal to

$$
\nabla_{\mathbf{x}} g(\mathbf{x}, \mathbf{h}, \mathbf{n}, \boldsymbol{\alpha}) = -\nabla_{\mathbf{n}} g(\mathbf{x}, \mathbf{h}, \mathbf{n}, \boldsymbol{\alpha}) = I + \nabla_{\mathbf{h}} g(\mathbf{x}, \mathbf{h}, \mathbf{n}, \boldsymbol{\alpha}). \quad (8)
$$

It should be also noted that the gradient with respect to $\boldsymbol{\alpha}$ is in general a rectangular but not a square matrix of dimensions equal to those of matrices D and C^T.

Let's assume as usual in VTS that the distribution of the clean speech features is described by GMM:

$$
p(\mathbf{x}) = \sum_{k=1}^{K} P(k) p(\mathbf{x} \mid k) = \sum_{k=1}^{K} P(k) \mathcal{N}(\mathbf{x}; \mu_{\mathbf{x},k}, \Sigma_{\mathbf{x},k}). \quad (9)
$$

Then the linearized distortion model (4) application entails that the distribution of the noisy speech features is also described by GMM:

$$p(\mathbf{y}) = \sum_{k=1}^{K} P(k)p(\mathbf{y} \mid k) = \sum_{k=1}^{K} P(k)\mathcal{N}(\mathbf{y}; \mu_{\mathbf{y},k}, \Sigma_{\mathbf{y},k}) \tag{10}$$

which has the same weights and whose other parameters are defined by the following expressions[2]

$$\mu_{\mathbf{y},k} = (I + \nabla_{\mathbf{x}}g^T)\mu_{\mathbf{x},k} + \nabla_{\mathbf{h}}g^T\mathbf{h} + \nabla_{\mathbf{n}}g^T\mu_{\mathbf{n}} + \nabla_{\alpha}g^T\mu_{\alpha} \tag{11}$$
$$+ f(\mathbf{x}_0, \mathbf{h}_0, \mathbf{n}_0, \alpha_0), \tag{12}$$
$$\Sigma_{\mathbf{y},k} = (I + \nabla_{\mathbf{x}}g^T)\Sigma_{\mathbf{x},k}(I + \nabla_{\mathbf{x}}g) + \nabla_{\mathbf{n}}g^T\Sigma_{\mathbf{n}}\nabla_{\mathbf{n}}g + \nabla_{\alpha}g^T\Sigma_{\alpha}\nabla_{\alpha}g. \tag{13}$$

It is important to notice that for different GMM components the Taylor expansion points may generally differ from each other, so they should have the corresponding index k which is omitted for brevity. Usually, the point $(\mu_{\mathbf{x},k}, \overline{\mathbf{h}}, \overline{\mu}_{\mathbf{n}}, \overline{\mu}_{\alpha})$ is taken as an expansion point for the k-th GMM component, where $\overline{\mathbf{h}}, \overline{\mu}_{\mathbf{n}}, \overline{\mu}_{\alpha}$ are the current estimates of the distortion model parameters.

3   Estimation of the Distortion Model Parameters

To estimate the set of distortion model parameters $\lambda = (\mathbf{h}, \mu_{\mathbf{n}}, \Sigma_{\mathbf{n}}, \mu_{\alpha}, \Sigma_{\alpha})$ the maximum likelihood method is used conventionally. Unfortunately, the direct likelihood optimization is infeasible so we have to use EM-algorithm for the iterative parameters reestimation. We use the approach from [10] where vectors $\mathbf{h}$ and $\mathbf{n}_t$ (as well as α_t in this paper) are considered as hidden variables and the EM auxiliary function has the following form:

$$Q(\lambda, \overline{\lambda}) = \sum_{t=1}^{T}\sum_{k=1}^{K}\int_{\mathbf{n}_t}\int_{\alpha_t} p(\mathbf{n}_t, \alpha_t, k \mid \mathbf{y}_t, \overline{\lambda}) \log p(\mathbf{y}_t, \mathbf{n}_t, \alpha_t, k \mid \lambda) d\alpha_t d\mathbf{n}_t, \tag{14}$$

where $\overline{\lambda}$ is current parameters vector, and its new value is determined as a solution of an optimization problem

$$\widetilde{\lambda} = \arg\max_{\lambda} Q(\lambda, \overline{\lambda}). \tag{15}$$

The optimization task (15) is more complicated then in [10], because even if $\mathbf{n}$ and α are considered to be independent, they are no longer independent given $\mathbf{y}_t$. Nonetheless it is possible to derive their conditional distributions given $\mathbf{y}_t$ and they turned out to be gaussian. By differentiating $Q(\lambda, \overline{\lambda})$ with respect

---

[2] The equation (13) holds when noise and phase vectors are considered as independent. Otherwise the additional cross-correlation term appears.

to each component of λ and equating gradients to zero the following update equations can be derived:

$$\tilde{\mathbf{h}} = \overline{\mathbf{h}} + S^{-1} \sum_{k=1}^{K} \nabla_{\mathbf{h}} g \overline{\Sigma}_{\mathbf{y},k}^{-1} \sum_{t=1}^{T} \gamma_k(t)(\mathbf{y}_t - \overline{\mu}_{\mathbf{y},k}), \tag{16}$$

$$\tilde{\mu}_{\mathbf{n}} = \overline{\mu}_{\mathbf{n}} + \frac{1}{T}\overline{\Sigma}_{\mathbf{n}} \sum_{k=1}^{K} \nabla_{\mathbf{n}} g \overline{\Sigma}_{\mathbf{y},k}^{-1} \sum_{t=1}^{T} \gamma_k(t)(\mathbf{y}_t - \overline{\mu}_{\mathbf{y},k}), \tag{17}$$

$$\tilde{\Sigma}_{\mathbf{n}} = \frac{1}{T} \sum_{k=1}^{K}\sum_{t=1}^{T} \gamma_k(t)\left(\breve{\Sigma}_{\mathbf{n},k} + \breve{\mu}_{\mathbf{n},k}(\mathbf{y}_t)\breve{\mu}_{\mathbf{n},k}(\mathbf{y}_t)^T\right) - \tilde{\mu}_{\mathbf{n}}\tilde{\mu}_{\mathbf{n}}^T, \tag{18}$$

$$\tilde{\mu}_{\boldsymbol{\alpha}} = \overline{\mu}_{\boldsymbol{\alpha}} + \frac{1}{T}\overline{\Sigma}_{\boldsymbol{\alpha}} \sum_{k=1}^{K} \nabla_{\boldsymbol{\alpha}} g \overline{\Sigma}_{\mathbf{y},k}^{-1} \sum_{t=1}^{T} \gamma_k(t)(\mathbf{y}_t - \overline{\mu}_{\mathbf{y},k}), \tag{19}$$

$$\tilde{\Sigma}_{\boldsymbol{\alpha}} = \frac{1}{T} \sum_{k=1}^{K}\sum_{t=1}^{T} \gamma_k(t)\left(\breve{\Sigma}_{\boldsymbol{\alpha},k} + \breve{\mu}_{\boldsymbol{\alpha},k}(\mathbf{y}_t)\breve{\mu}_{\boldsymbol{\alpha},k}(\mathbf{y}_t)^T\right) - \tilde{\mu}_{\boldsymbol{\alpha}}\tilde{\mu}_{\boldsymbol{\alpha}}^T, \tag{20}$$

where

$$\breve{\mu}_{\boldsymbol{\alpha},k}(\mathbf{y}_t) = \overline{\mu}_{\boldsymbol{\alpha}} + \overline{\Sigma}_{\boldsymbol{\alpha}}\nabla_{\boldsymbol{\alpha}} g \overline{\Sigma}_{\mathbf{y},k}^{-1}(\mathbf{y}_t - \overline{\mu}_{\mathbf{y},k}), \tag{21}$$

$$\breve{\Sigma}_{\boldsymbol{\alpha},k} = \overline{\Sigma}_{\boldsymbol{\alpha}} - \overline{\Sigma}_{\boldsymbol{\alpha}}\nabla_{\boldsymbol{\alpha}} g \overline{\Sigma}_{\mathbf{y},k}^{-1}\nabla_{\boldsymbol{\alpha}} g^T \overline{\Sigma}_{\boldsymbol{\alpha}}, \tag{22}$$

$$\breve{\mu}_{\mathbf{n},k}(\mathbf{y}_t) = \overline{\mu}_{\mathbf{n}} + \overline{\Sigma}_{\mathbf{n}}\nabla_{\mathbf{n}} g \overline{\Sigma}_{\mathbf{y},k}^{-1}(\mathbf{y}_t - \overline{\mu}_{\mathbf{y},k}), \tag{23}$$

$$\breve{\Sigma}_{\mathbf{n},k} = \overline{\Sigma}_{\mathbf{n}} - \overline{\Sigma}_{\mathbf{n}}\nabla_{\mathbf{n}} g \overline{\Sigma}_{\mathbf{y},k}^{-1}\nabla_{\mathbf{n}} g^T \overline{\Sigma}_{\mathbf{n}}, \tag{24}$$

$$S = \sum_{k=1}^{K} \nabla_{\mathbf{h}} g (I + \nabla_{\mathbf{x}} g)^{-1} \Sigma_{\mathbf{x},k}^{-1}(I + \nabla_{\mathbf{x}} g^T)^{-1}\nabla_{\mathbf{h}} g^T \sum_{t=1}^{T} \gamma_k(t) \tag{25}$$

and the notation $\gamma_k(t) = P(k|\mathbf{y}_t, \overline{\lambda})$ is introduced. Notice that expressions for channel and noise parameters re-estimation are formally identical to those previously obtained in [10] without phase-sensitive term.

However it should be realized that non-linearity gradients and noisy features distribution parameters involved into these expressions do actually depend on phase vector.

4 Estimation of the Clean Speech Features

After the EM-algorithm converged and the final estimates of the distortion model parameters were found the estimate of the clean speech features $\mathbf{x}_t$ should be obtained.

If the minimum mean square error (MMSE) approach is used for this, then the clean features estimate is defined as $\mathbf{x}_t^{MMSE} = E_{\mathbf{x}_t|\mathbf{y}_t}\{\mathbf{x}_t\}$ and it can be shown that

$$\mathbf{x}_t^{MMSE} = \sum_{k=1}^{K} p(k \mid \mathbf{y}_t)\left(\mu_{\mathbf{x},k} + \Sigma_{\mathbf{x},k}(I + \nabla_{\mathbf{x}} g)\Sigma_{\mathbf{y},k}^{-1}(\mathbf{y}_t - \mu_{\mathbf{y},k})\right). \tag{26}$$

Once again one can notice that (26) looks identical to the estimates from [14, 21] obtained without phase-sensitive term, however there is an implicit difference in gradient expressions and noisy speech features distribution parameters.

5 Experiments and Results

In order to evaluate the effectiveness of the proposed approach we produced several experiments on Aurora2 database [7]. This database consists of digits string utterances distorted with several kinds of additive noise at different SNRs as well as lowpass filtering which emulates channel distortions. For our experiments we used "simple backend" [7] based on HTK Toolkit [22].

The clean speech features GMM (9) was trained on the clean trainset of Aurora2 by means of GmmBayes toolkit [20]. Only the full-covariance computations were used throughout the experiments. The initial estimates of noise distribution parameters for a given utterance were obtained from its first ten and last ten frames. The initial parameters of the phase vector distribution were set to zero vector and unit matrix respectively.

We compared recognition accuracy on MFCCs processed with conventional [10] and proposed VTS variants as well as without any processing for both clean and multi-condition training. The results are presented in the Table 1.

Table 1. The recognition accuracy, % on Aurora2 tests (averaged over SNRs from 0 to 20 dB)

Processing of data	Clean training				Multi-condition training			
	Test A	Test B	Test C	Avg	Test A	Test B	Test C	Avg
No processing	59.1	55.5	66.5	59.1	87.0	86.4	85.1	86.4
VTS phase-insensitive	83.8	84.1	82.8	83.7	86.6	85.8	86.4	86.3
VTS phase-sensitive	86.1	86.4	86.2	86.2	88.9	88.3	89.1	88.7

The results from the Table 1 show that the proposed modeling of the phase term improves the recognition accuracy significantly compared to the conventional phase-insensitive VTS. Indeed, the average WER is reduced by 20 % for the clean training scenario and by 18 % for the multi-condition training. Besides, in the clean training scenario the proposed variant of VTS almost fills the large gap which is between clean and multi-condition training results without using any processing. It can be noticed that the largest accuracy gain due to phase modeling is achieved on the Test C, where channel distortion is applied to data.

The simplified version of the phase-sensitive VTS was also tested. It uses the idea from [13] where phase vector is treated as deterministic with equal elements. The dependence of recognition accuracy on elements value α is depicted in the Fig. 1.

The figure shows that constant equal-element vector is indeed a good approximation to the stochastic gaussian model of phase. For the clean training scenario

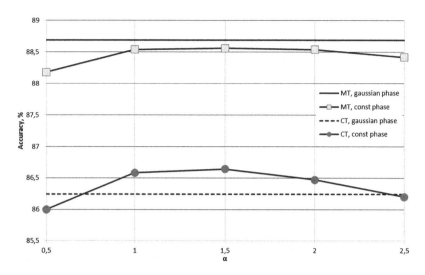

Fig. 1. Comparison of speech recognition accuracy of the proposed phase modeling and deterministic constant phase approximation. CT and MT stand for clean and multi-condition training respectively

this approximation is even slightly better than proposed one while for the multi-condition training the results are slightly worse but the difference is subtle. However, the optimal value of vector elements (1.5) differs from that one obtained in [13] in application to acoustic model adaptation (2.5). So this optimal value is algorithm-dependent and we guess that it may be task and data dependent as well.

6 Conclusions

The feature compensation algorithm based on Vector Taylor Series approximation of phase-sensitive distortion model is proposed. The formulas for parameters update and clean speech features estimate are derived. The comparison of the proposed method to its phase-insensitive analogue made on Aurora2 database shows that it provides WER reduction of about 20 % relative. The simplified variant of phase-sensitive VTS is also tested and shown to be reasonable approximation which provides comparable results at reduced complexity.

Acknowledgments. This work was financially supported by the Ministry of Education and Science of the Russian Federation, Contract 14.575.21.0033 (ID RFMEFI57514X0033).

References

1. Abdel-Hamid, O., Mohamed, A., Jiang, H., Penn, G.: Applying convolutional neural network concepts to hybrid nn-hmm model for speech recognition. In:

Proceedings of IEEE International Conference on Acoustics, Speech, and Signal Processing (ICASSP), pp. 4277–4280 (2012)

2. Acero, A., Deng, L., Kristjansson, T., Zhang, J.: Hmm adaptation using vector taylor series for noisy speech recognition. In: Proceedings of International Conference on Spoken Language Processing (ICSLP), pp. 869–872 (2000)

3. Dahl, G., Yu, D., Deng, L., Acero, A.: Context-dependent pre-trained deep neural networks for large vocabulary speech recognition. IEEE Trans. Audio Speech Lang. Process. **20**(1), 30–42 (2012)

4. Deng, L., Droppo, J., Acero, A.: Enhancement of log mel power spectra of speech using a phase-sensitive model of the acoustic environment and sequential estimation of the corrupting noise. IEEE Trans. Speech Audio Process. **12**(2), 133–143 (2004)

5. Gales, M., Flego, F.: Discriminative classifiers with adaptive kernels for noise robust speech recognition. Comput. Speech Lang. **24**, 648–662 (2014)

6. Graves, A., Jaitly, N., Mohamed, A.: Hybrid speech recognition with deep bidirectional lstm. In: Proceedings of IEEE Workshop on Automatic Speech Recognition and Understanding (ASRU), pp. 273–278 (2013)

7. Hirsch, H., Pearce, D.: The aurora experimental framework for the performance evaluations of speech recognition systems under noisy conditions. In: Proceedings of ISCA ITRWASR2000 on Automatic Speech Recognition: Challenges for the Next Millennium (2000)

8. Hu, Y., Huo, Q.: Irrelevant variability normalization based hmm training using vts approximation of an explicit model of environmental distortions. In: Proceedings of Annual Conference of the International Speech Communication Association (Interspeech), pp. 1042–1045 (2007)

9. Kalinli, O., Seltzer, M., Droppo, J., Acero, A.: Noise adaptive training for robust automatic speech recognition. IEEE Trans. Audio Speech Lang. Process. **18**(8), 1889–1901 (2010)

10. Kim, D., Un, C., Kim, N.: Speech recognition in noisy environments using first-order vector taylor series. Speech Commun. **24**, 39–49 (1998)

11. Li, J., Deng, L., Yu, D., Gong, Y., Acero, A.: High-performance hmm adaptation with joint compensation of additive and convolutive distortions via vector taylor series. In: Proceedings of IEEE Workshop on Automatic Speech Recognition and Understanding (ASRU), pp. 65–70 (2007)

12. Li, J., Deng, L., Yu, D., Gong, Y., Acero, A.: Efficient vts adaptation using jacobian approximation. In: Proceedings of Annual Conference of the International Speech Communication Association (Interspeech), pp. 1906–1909 (2012)

13. Li, J., Seltzer, M., Gong, Y.: A unified framework of hmm adaptation with joint compensation of additive and convolutive distortions. Computer Speech Lang. **23**, 389–405 (2009)

14. Li, J., Seltzer, M., Gong, Y.: Improvements to vts feature enhancement. In: Proceedings of IEEE International Conference on Acoustics, Speech, and Signal Processing (ICASSP), pp. 4677–4680 (2012)

15. Liao, H.: Uncertainty Decoding for Noise Robust Speech Recognition. Ph.D. thesis, Sidney Sussex College University of Cambridge (2007)

16. Liao, H., Gales, M.: Joint uncertainty decoding for noise robust speech recognition. In: Proceedings of Annual Conference of the International Speech Communication Association (Interspeech), pp. 1042–1045 (2005)

17. Liao, H., Gales, M.: Joint uncertainty decoding for robust large vocabulary speechrecognition. Technical report, Cambridge University Engeneering Department (2006)

18. Moreno, P.: Speech Recognition in Noisy Environments. Ph.D. thesis, Department of Electrical and Computer Engineering, Carnegie Mellon University (1996)
19. Moreno, P., Raj, B., Stern, R.: A vector taylor series approach for environment-independent speech recognition. In: Proceedings of IEEE International Conference on Acoustics, Speech, and Signal Processing (ICASSP). vol. 2, pp. 733–736 (1996)
20. Paalanen, P., Kämäräinen, J., Kälviäinen, H.: Gmmbayes toolkit. http://www.it.lut.fi/project/gmmbayes
21. Stouten, V. Van hamme, H., Demuynck, K., Wambacq, P.: Robust speech recognition using model-based feature enhancement. In: Proceedings of 4th Annual Conference of the International Speech Communication Association (Interspeech), pp. 17–20 (2003)
22. Young, S.J., Kershaw, D., Odell, J., Ollason, D., Valtchev, V., Woodland, P.: The HTK Book Version 3.4. Cambridge University Press, Cambridge (2006)

Finding Speaker Position Under Difficult Acoustic Conditions

Evgeniy Shuranov[1], Aleksandr Lavrentyev[1(✉)], Alexey Kozlyaev[1],
Galina Lavrentyeva[1], and Valeriya Volkovaya[1,2]

[1] Speech Technology Center, Krasutskogo-4, St. Petersburg 196084, Russia
{shuranov, lavrentyev, kozlyaev, lavrentyeva,
volkovaya}@speechpro.com
[2] ITMO University, 49 Kronverkskiy Pr., St. Petersburg 197101, Russia

Abstract. In this paper are presented different approaches for speaker position identification that use a microphone array and known voice models. Comparison of speaker positioning is performed by using acoustic maps based on FBF and PHAT. The goal of the experiments is to find best algorithm parameters and their approbation for different types of noises. The proposed approaches allows for better results in automatic positioning under noisy conditions. It enables to identify the target speaker whose speech duration is longer than 10 s.

Keywords: Microphone array · Acoustic map · Speech enhancement

1 Introduction

Microphone arrays are widely used for speech enhancement in noisy environments and different acoustic situations. Using fixed beamforming (FBF), minimum variance distortionless response (MVDR) [1] and other algorithms, speech capturing must be executed in a certain direction. So, to use microphone array as efficiently as possible, direction to the target speaker must be known. Also, it would be useful to have more detailed information about directions of noise sources, to be able to suppress them. For finding target directions usually used sound intensity maps or visual pinpointing. These methods have several disadvantages.

Sound intensity maps (acoustic maps) allow finding the loudest sound source. For the computation of acoustic maps are used algorithms such as FBF and phase transform (PHAT) [14]. One of its main weaknesses is that speaker voice cannot be differentiated from a noisy background, like loud music or conversation of other speakers. Because of the fact that sound is reflects from surfaces, a lot of unwanted sources may appear.

Method of visual pinpointing allows transmitting information about target speaker direction to a microphone array. The process of tracking necessary objects is widely used today. However, this method has restrictions caused by cameras that are used for tracking. As a rule, camera view angle is smaller than possible pointing angle of a microphone array. Camera can have difficulties on providing an accurate image due to poor lightening. There are situations when two speakers turn their back on a

© Springer International Publishing Switzerland 2016
A. Ronzhin et al. (Eds.): SPECOM 2016, LNAI 9811, pp. 321–327, 2016.
DOI: 10.1007/978-3-319-43958-7_38

microphone array and this method cannot find position of a target speaker. Also it is difficult to find position of a target speaker in case of fog or other interference.

In practice, automatic speaker positioning meets many difficulties in many acoustic situations, especially in situations with two or more speakers.

Problem of separation of the target speaker can be resolved with use of identification algorithms. There are solutions that use beamforming to estimate speakers' positions and then identify them [12]. There are solutions that estimate speakers' positions using audio information captured by microphone array and video captured by several camcorders [13]. In this paper we propose to focus on the problem of determining the position of the speakers through audio data only, in difficult listening situations using identification algorithm based on PLDA and NMF.

2 Description of the Used Speaker Identification System [2]

2.1 Total Variability Approach

GMM based approach for i-vector extraction consists of mean values estimation of speaker voice features attributed to each component of Universal Background Model (UBM). The distribution of concatenated mean vectors (mean supervector) is assumed as:

$$s = m_0 + T\omega, \tag{1}$$

where m_0 is mean supervector of UBM, T is the matrix defining the basis in the reduced feature space, ω is the i-vector in the reduced feature space, with prior $p(\omega) = \mathcal{N}(0, I)$.

T and m_0 are global parameters which can be estimated using Factor Analysis and Expectation-Maximization algorithm. The reader can refer to [3] for more details.

UBM is obtained by unsupervised training using huge amount of representative unlabeled speech data. Thus, UBM is used for posteriors calculation on each speech frame followed by Baum-Welch statistics accumulation [4].

2.2 PLDA Based Back-End [5]

Among state-of-the-art speaker verification systems, leading positions are occupied by PLDA-based systems [4, 6–9] working in the i-vector space.

$$i_{s,r} = \mu + V_y y_s + \in_{s,h}, \tag{2}$$

where $i_{s,h}$ is an f-dimensional i-vector from set $\{i_1, \ldots, i_H\}$, obtained from H utterances belonging to speaker s, and $y, \in_{s,h}$ is hidden speaker factors and Gaussian noise, respectively. V_y- is an eigenvoices matrix.

In order to carry out a large number of experiments we did not use costly EM-algorithm [5] to estimate the model parameters. Instead of that, similar to our study [8], we estimated between-speaker and within-speaker covariances, respectively, according to formulas:

$$\Sigma_B = \frac{1}{S} \sum_S (i_s - \mu)(i_S - \mu)^T, \tag{3}$$

$$\Sigma_W = \frac{1}{S} \sum_h \left(i_{s,h} - i_s\right)\left(i_{s,h} - i_s\right)^T. \tag{4}$$

The vector $i_{s,h}$ is an i-vector extracted from the h-th session of the s-th speaker, the vector i_s is the average over all sessions of this speaker. i_s can be viewed as the maximum likelihood estimate in the Gaussian model of within-speaker variability. μ is the dataset mean and S is the number of speakers in the training set. Given a pair of i-vectors i_1 and i_2, assuming zero mean and skipping the scalar term, the commonly used PLDA verification score can be written as:

$$Score = i_1^T Q i_1 + i_2^T Q i_2 + 2i_1^T P i_2, \tag{5}$$

where square matrices P and Q can be expressed in terms of (3) and (4).

3   Sparse Non-negative Matrix Factorization

Alternative approach that was used for solving speaker targeting problem is SNMF [10]. Let Y be a spectrogram of speech mixture. Y is a non-negative $n \times m$ matrix that can be factorized into an $n \times r$ matrix D and an $r \times m$ matrix H:

$$Y = DH, \tag{6}$$

where D is a dictionary and H is a code matrix. D and H also consist of only non-negative elements and H is sparse. The SNMF minimizes the following cost function:

$$E = \|Y - DH\|^2 + \mu \sum_{ij} H_{ijs} \quad s.t. D, H \geq 0, \tag{7}$$

where μ controls degree of sparsity. D and H are update by following rules:

$$H_{ij} \leftarrow H_{ij} \frac{(D^T Y)_{ij}}{(D^T D H)_{ij} + \mu}, \quad D_{ij} \leftarrow D_{ij} \frac{(Y H^T)_{ij}}{(D H H^T)_{ij}}. \tag{8}$$

We first apply SNMF to learn matrix D of individual speakers. To separate speech mixtures we keep the matrix D fixed and update only the matrix H.

After separation we estimate speech of target speaker and residual noise. Score is calculated like an energy of estimated signal.

4 Comparing Results of Identification with BSS

We recorded data using FBF method [11] from directions in range from -90 to 90 degrees with interval 1. We compared results from each direction with a model, using identification algorithm or SNMF. For each direction, we calculated a score, which are presented in Fig. 1. For this data we also calculated a score that shows situation on acoustic maps based on sound intensity evaluation from a target direction.

Since we know the direction of a target speaker, we introduced metric for characterization of the obtained plots, whether speaker direction is identified well or not:

$$M = \frac{F_d - F_r}{\sigma},\tag{9}$$

where F_d – score corresponding to a speaker direction;
F_r – average score for all directions;
σ – standard deviation.

5 Data

In our experiments we used a microphone array with 66 microphones: 11 microphones in 6 rows with 3.5 cm horizontal distance and 5 cm vertical distance between microphones. Audio data was recorded in rooms with reverberation time of 0.3 s. Audio data was recorded in the following acoustic conditions:

- Speech of one speaker in a calm environment.
- Simultaneous speech of two speakers.
- Speaker with a white noise on a background, SNR $\sim$ 8 dB.

6 Results

For comparing algorithms, we used audio recording with simultaneous speech of two speakers. Results are presented in Table 1.

Table 1. Algorithm comparison

Algorithm	Metric
Identification	1,24
SNMF	2,40
FBF	0,63

Next we are going to analyze more detailed results of optimizing parameters, using identification method.

A microphone array focuses on low frequencies worse than high frequencies; that is why we made a decision to analyze the influence of filter that cuts off low frequencies. The results are shown in Table 2.

Table 2. Dependence between equalizer settings and the metric

Lower frequency limit	Identification	SNMF
50 Hz	1,66	1,34
500 Hz	1,87	1,06
1000 Hz	1,27	2,40
2000 Hz	1,13	2,68

We were highly interested in analyzing this method on short time intervals. Table 3 shows the dependence of supplied metric on duration of an analyzed recording interval.

Table 3. Dependence between duration and the metric

Duration of analyzed interval	Identification	SNMF
7 s	1,59	2,56
15 s	1,77	2,43
30 s	0,92	2,47
60 s	−0,04	2,38

Table 4 shows dependence of metric values on acoustic environment. Fields marked "N/A" means that it's impossible to find target position in this case.

Table 4. Comparison of algorithms by acoustic environment

	FBF	SNMF	Identification
One speaker	1,41	2,40	0
2 speaker	N/A	2,40	1,24
Speaker and white noise SNR 8 dB	N/A	N/A	2,40[a]

[a] In this case two peaks were obtained. We propose to compare SNR in both directions to find real position of target speaker.

Let us consider an example of a simultaneous speech of two speakers. The figure shows an acoustic map that displays the score of finding a target speaker and presents an opportunity of identifying a target speaker position automatically. On this map, the acoustic map (Energy), NMF and identification maps are displayed. In energy map, it is impossible to distinguish direction of target speaker from a direction of another speaker. On NMF and identification maps we achieve result presented in Fig. 1.

On the acoustic map, you can see that the first (target) speaker is significantly quieter than the second speaker, and it is impossible to identify his/her position by a volume level. On the score map, his/her position can be easily seen and automatically identified.

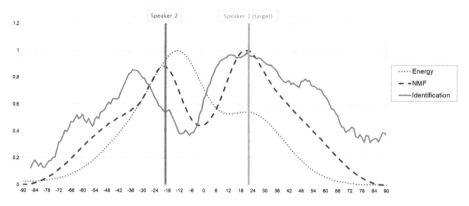

Fig. 1. Score for direction angles

7 Conclusion

In this paper we proposed methods for finding speaker position under difficult acoustic conditions. We achieve that goal using identification or SNMF algorithms and calculating score for each direction. Using those methods, we can achieve positive results for recordings of 7-15 s. SNMF showed better accuracy in direction estimation, but identification was able to work in very noisy environment. The disadvantage of the proposed methods is that their current realizations are too resource and time consuming for an online use. The proposed methods now presents for post-processing mode.

Acknowledgements. This work was partially financially supported by the Govern-ment of the Russian Federation, Grant 074-U01.

References

1. Ba, D.E., Florencio, D., Zhang, C.: Enhanced MVDR beamforming for arrays of directional microphones. In: IEEE International Conference on Multimedia and Expo, pp. 1307–131 (2007)
2. Kudashev, O., Novoselov, S., Pekhovsky, T., Simonchik, K., Lavrentyeva, G.: Usage of DNN in speaker recognition: advantages and problems. In: To be Appear in Proceedings of the 13th International Symposium on Neural Networks (2016)
3. Kenny, P., et al.: A study of interspeaker variability in speaker verification. IEEE Trans. Audio Speech Lang. Process. **16**(5), 980–988 (2008)
4. Kenny, P., Gupta, V., Stafylakis, T., Ouellet, P., Alam, J.: Deep neural networks for extracting baum-welch statistics for speaker recognition. In: Odyssey: The Speaker and Language Recognition Workshop (2014). http://cs.uef.fi/odyssey2014/program/pdfs/28.pdf
5. Pekhovsky, T., Novoselov, S., Sholohov, A., Kudashev, O.: On autoencoders in the i-vector space for speaker recognition. In: Odyssey (2016)

6. Lei, Y., Scheffer, N., Ferrer, L., McLaren, M.: A novel scheme for speaker recognition using a phonetically aware deep neural network. In: IEEE International Conference on Acoustics, Speech, Signal Processing, pp. 1695–1699 (2014)
7. Stafylakis, T., Kenny, P., Senoussaoui, M., Dumouchel, P.: PLDA using gaussian restricted boltzmann machines with application to speaker recognition. In: 13th Annual International Conference Speech Communications Association, pp. 1692–1696 (2012)
8. Novoselov, S., Pekhovsky, T., Kudashev, O., Mendelev, V., Prudnikov, A.: Non-linear PLDA for i-vector speaker verification. In: Interspeech-2015, pp. 214–218 (2015)
9. Prince, S.J.D., Elder, J.H.: Probabilistic linear discriminant analysis for inferences about identity. In: IEEE 11th International Conference on Computer Vision, pp. 1–8 (2007)
10. Schmidt, M. N., Olsson, R. K.: Single-channel speech separation using sparse non-negative matrix factorization. In: International Conference on Spoken Language Processing (2006)
11. Fischer, S., Kammeyer, K., Simmer, K.: Adaptive microphone arrays for speech en-hancement in coherent and incoherent noise fields. In: 3rd meeting of the Acoustical Society of America and the Acoustical Society of Japan, pp. 1–30 (1996)
12. Busso, C., Hernanz, S., Chu, C.-W., Kwon, S.-I., Lee, S., Georgiou, P., Cohen, I., Narayanan, S.: Smart room: participant and speaker localization and identification. In: IEEE International Conference on Acoustics, Speech, Signal Process, pp. 1117–1120 (2015)
13. Khalidov, V., Forbes, F., Hansard, M., Arnaud, E., Horaud, R.: Audio-visual clustering for multiple speaker localization. In: 5th International Workshop on Machine Learning for Multimodal Interaction (2008)
14. Knapp, C.H., Carter, G.C.: The generalized correlation method for estimation of time delay. IEEE Trans. Acoust. Speech Signal Process. **24**(4), 320–327 (1976)

Fusing Various Audio Feature Sets for Detection of Parkinson's Disease from Sustained Voice and Speech Recordings

Evaldas Vaiciukynas[1,2(✉)], Antanas Verikas[1,3], Adas Gelzinis[1],
Marija Bacauskiene[1], Kestutis Vaskevicius[1], Virgilijus Uloza[4],
Evaldas Padervinskis[4], and Jolita Ciceliene[5]

[1] Department of Electrical Power Systems,
Kaunas University of Technology, Kaunas, Lithuania
evaldas.vaiciukynas@ktu.lt
[2] Department of Information Systems, Kaunas University of Technology,
Kaunas, Lithuania
[3] Intelligent Systems Laboratory, Centre for Applied Intelligent Systems Research,
Halmstad University, Halmstad, Sweden
[4] Department of Otolaryngology, Lithuanian University of Health Sciences,
Kaunas, Lithuania
[5] Department of Neurology, Lithuanian University of Health Sciences,
Kaunas, Lithuania

Abstract. The aim of this study is the analysis of voice and speech recordings for the task of Parkinson's disease detection. Voice modality corresponds to sustained phonation /a/ and speech modality to a short sentence in Lithuanian language. Diverse information from recordings is extracted by 22 well-known audio feature sets. Random forest is used as a learner, both for individual feature sets and for decision-level fusion. Essentia descriptors were found as the best individual feature set, achieving equal error rate of 16.3 % for voice and 13.3 % for speech. Fusion of feature sets and modalities improved detection and achieved equal error rate of 10.8 %. Variable importance in fusion revealed speech modality as more important than voice.

Keywords: Parkinson's disease · Audio signal processing · OpenSMILE · Essentia · MPEG-7 · jAudio · YAAFE · Random forest · Information fusion

1 Introduction

Parkison's disease (PD) is the second most common neurodegenerative disease after Alzheimer's [5] and it is expected that the prevalence of PD is going to increase due to population ageing. Medicine and surgical intervention may slow down the progression of PD if it is detected early, resulting in increased life span and life quality for PD patients. Acoustic analysis is considered as an

© Springer International Publishing Switzerland 2016
A. Ronzhin et al. (Eds.): SPECOM 2016, LNAI 9811, pp. 328–337, 2016.
DOI: 10.1007/978-3-319-43958-7_39

important non-invasive tool in screening for PD. Some studies use large feature sets aiming to obtain comprehensive characterization of the voice/speech signal, while others rely on "clinically useful" measures or perform feature selection to obtain a compact set of audio descriptors. There are almost no studies comparing performance of many different feature sets and exploring fusion of feature sets and modalities by a committee of PD detectors.

Size of previously used databases (less than 100 subjects) is a major problem leading to unreliable estimates of reported performance. Another common problem is the lack of conformity to leave-one-subject-out [14] or leave-one-individual-out [15] validation scheme. The need for such scheme arises when subject has several recordings, where all recordings of a subject should be included either in a training or in a testing fold, but not in both. Detailed review of the related work can be found in [14].

2   Voice and Speech Data

Two vocal exercises were recorded as separate voice and speech modalities. Voice modality corresponds to sustained phonation of vowel /a/ vocalized at comfortable pitch and loudness level for at least 5 s and repeated 3 times. Speech modality corresponds to single pronunciation of phonetically balanced sentence in a native Lithuanian language, – "turėjo senelė žilą oželį ", – which translates into "granny had a little greyish goat". Audio samples were recorded in a soundproof booth using an acoustic cardioid microphone AKG Perception 220 (AKG Acoustics). The microphone was placed at ~ 10 cm distance from the mouth at about 90° microphone-to-mouth angle. The audio format was wav (mono PCM, 16 bit samples at 44 kHz rate). A mixed gender database containing 383 subjects was collected. Several subjects had speech modality missing, therefore, fusion of modalities was possible only for 375 subjects. For full details see Table 1.

Table 1. Summary of database: numbers denote amount of subjects (recordings), PD stands for Parkinson's disease patients and HC for healthy control subjects.

Modality:	Voice	Speech	Fusion
PD male	36 (107)	35	35 (103)
PD female	39 (116)	39	39 (116)
PD	75 (223)	74	74 (219)
HC male	105 (312)	101	101 (302)
HC female	203 (599)	200	200 (594)
HC	308 (911)	301	301 (896)
Total	383 (1134)	375	375 (1115)

3 Feature Extraction

Information, contained in audio recordings of voice or speech signal, can be extracted using various signal analysis methods. Resulting measures are commonly known as features. Various feature collections with total number of features are listed in Table 3. All feature sets were published before and have publicly available extractors. Depending on the amount of signal used for extracting features they can be categorized into:

- global features: long-term or recording-based or high-level descriptors;
- local features: short-term or frame-based or low-level descriptors (LLDs).

Short-term parametrization is performed by dividing a recording into short and usually overlapping segments (frames or windows) and applying an algorithm that computes respective local feature for each segment. Short-term features later are compressed into long-term features by computing various statistical functionals. Feature sets # 1 – 12 had their own predefined choice from 42 statistical functionals. Statistical functionals in feature sets # 13 – 17 encompass the following 13 characteristics: minimum, maximum, mean, median, lower quartile (Q_{lo}), upper quartile (Q_{up}), trimean ($\frac{2 \cdot median + Q_{lo} + Q_{up}}{4}$), standard deviation, inter-quartile range, lower range ($median - Q_{lo}$), upper range ($Q_{up} - median$), skewness, and kurtosis. Feature sets # 18 – 22 use mostly mean and standard deviation.

OpenSMILE Features. Feature sets # 1 – 12 are computed using predefined configurations available in **openSMILE** [7] toolkit (version 2.2 RC 1). Name of each feature set is identical to the name of the respective configuration file with `.conf` ending. Most of these configurations are rather similar, therefore, for illustration, only `emobase.conf` is described further. The feature set `emobase`, introduced for emotion recognition, contains 26 LLDs and also the 1st derivative (delta or velocity) of each LLD. To summarize various aspects of frame-based data distribution for each LLD and its delta, a collection of statistical functionals is applied. Details are in Table 2, and the overall size of the feature set is 988 features = (26 LLDs + 26 deltas) × 19 functionals.

Table 2. Overview of the `emobase.conf` file settings.

Low-level descriptors	Statistical functionals
pitch, pitch envelope, intensity, loudness, 12 MFCCs, probability of voicing, 8 frequencies of line spectral pairs, zero-crossing rate	min (or max) value and its respective relative position within a signal, range, arithmetic mean, 2 linear regression coefficients and linear and quadratic error, standard deviation, skewness, kurtosis, 3 quartiles, and 3 inter-quartile ranges

Configuration file `emobase.conf` contains these processing-related settings:

- pitch and pitch envelope are estimated using pre-emphasis (of 0.97) and over-lapping (by a step of 10 ms) Hamming windows (of 40 ms duration);
- other LLDs are obtained without pre-emphasis and the signal is windowed into overlapping (by a step of 10 ms) Hamming windows (of 25 ms duration).

All extracted LLDs are smoothed using a simple moving average filter (with window size 3) before proceeding to compress them by statistical functionals.

Essentia Descriptors. Feature set # 13 was computed using Essentia [1] (version 2.1 beta 2) – an open-source C++ library for audio analysis – out-of-the-box extractor `streaming_extractor_freesound.exe` (version 0.3). Descriptors of `lowlevel` and `sfx` type were selected and descriptors of `tonal` and `rythm` type were discarded. A detailed list of 1915 (17 global + 146 × 13 local) descriptors:

- 1 global descriptor of `lowlevel` type – average loudness;
- 16 global descriptors of `sfx` type – 5 temporal (centroid, decrease, kurtosis, skewness, spread), 4 morphological (the ratio between the index of the maximum value of the envelope of a signal and the total length of the envelope, the ratio of the temporal centroid to the total length of a signal envelope, the weighted average of the derivative after the maximum amplitude, the maximum derivative before the maximum amplitude), pitch centroid, strong decay, flatness, log attack time of a signal envelope, the ratio between the index of the maximum value of the pitch envelope of a signal and the total length of the pitch envelope, the ratio between the index of the minimum value of the pitch envelope of a signal and the total length of the pitch envelope, the ratio between the pitch energy after the pitch maximum to the pitch energy before the pitch maximum;
- 141 local descriptors of `lowlevel` type – spectral energy in 77 bands (28 frequency bands, 4 bands of low/mid-low/mid-high/high frequencies, 18 ERB bands, 27 Bark bands), 3 statistics of spectral energy in Bark bands (kurtosis, skewness, spread), 13 GFCC, 13 MFCC, 15 spectral (energy, entropy, complexity, centroid, strong peak, crest, the high frequency content measure of Masri & Bateman, RMS, roll-off, decrease, flatness in dB, flux, kurtosis, skewness, spread), 6 spectral contrasts, 6 spectral contrast valleys, 3 pitch-related (pitch, instantaneous confidence of pitch, salience of pitch), 3 silence rates (20 dB, 30 dB, 60 dB), dissonance, zero-crossing rate;
- 5 local descriptors of `sfx` type – 3 tristimulus values, inharmonicity, odd-to-even harmonic energy ratio.

MPEG7 Descriptors. Feature set # 14 was combined from some descriptors of the MPEG-7 standard, extracted using Java library `MPEG7AudioEnc` [4] (version 0.4 RC 3). The MPEG-7 audio standard specifies normative for audio content description as a comprehensive form of meta-data to enhance searchability among multimedia content. A detailed list of 527 (7 global + 40 × 13 local) descriptors:

- 7 global descriptors – 4 harmonic spectral (centroid, deviation, variation, spread), 2 centroid (spectral, temporal), log attack time;
- 40 local descriptors – 36 audio spectrum (24 flatness, 10 envelope, centroid, spread), 2 audio harmonicity, audio fundamental frequency, audio power.

KTU Features. Feature set # 15 was introduced for voice pathology screening by [8] at Kaunas University of Technology and later expanded to include additional features. Latest variant of this feature set was devised here by combining feature subsets # 1 – 13 from [19] with MFCC and PLPCC features from [6]. For MFCC and PLPCC features the signal is pre-emphasized by 0.97, frames are computed using the sliding 10 ms (440 samples) Hamming window with 5 ms overlap. Frame-based 19 MFCCs and 19 PLPCCs were characterized by 13 statistical functionals, providing a subset of 494 features. Combining 773 [19] and 494 [6] features resulted in the feature set with a size of 1267 features.

jAudio Features. Feature set # 16 was generated by Java application jAudio [12] (version 0.4.5.1), which was developed as a standardized audio feature extraction system for automatic music classification. All features selected were frame-based with window size of 1024 (corresponding to ∼ 23.3 ms frame length) and window overlap of 50 %. A detailed list of 1794 (138 × 13 local) features: 100 area method of moments, 13 MFCC, 10 LPC, 4 spectral (centroid, flux, rolloff point, variability), 3 strongest frequency (via zero crossings, via spectral centroid, via FFT maximum), 2 partial-based spectral (centroid, flux), peak-based spectral smoothness, compactness, root mean square, fraction of low energy windows, relative difference function, zero crossings.

YAAFE Features. Feature set # 17 was computed by yet another audio features extraction toolbox – YAAFE [11] (version 0.65). Default settings were used for the following list of 1885 (145×13 local) features: 24 loudness, 23 spectral crest factor per band, 23 spectral flatness per band, 13 MFCC, 12 shape statistics (4 envelope, 4 spectral, 4 temporal), 10 LSF, 10 OBSI, 9 OBSIR, 8 amplitude modulation, 6 spectral (decrease, flatness, flux, rolloff, slope, variation), 2 LPC, 2 perceptual (sharpness, spread), complex domain onset detection, energy, ZCR.

Tsanas Features. Feature set # 18 was developed specifically for PD screening. Code to compute these features is publicly available as Voice Analysis Toolbox (version 1.0) for Matlab and the full list of 339 features is described in PhD thesis [17]. Feature sets # 19 – 22 (compact subsets of the feature set # 18) were refined for PD detection task using 4 different wrapper-based feature selection techniques with SVM in [18].

4   Methodology

We have used random forest (RF) [2] as a supervised algorithm to detect Parkinson's disease and also to fuse information in the form of soft decisions, obtained using various audio feature sets from non-invasive modalities – voice and speech.

4.1   Random Forest

Matlab port of original RF algorithm was obtained from [10]. RF is a committee of decision trees, where the final decision is derived by majority voting. The core idea of RF is to combine many (B in total) decision trees, built using different bootstrap samples of the original data set, and a random subset (of predetermined size q) of features $x^1, \ldots, x^p$. RF is known to be robust against over-fitting and as the number of trees increases, the generalization error converges to a limit [2]. For our experiments B was set to 5000, several specific values of q ($\sqrt{p}, 2 \cdot \sqrt{p}, \frac{1}{2} \cdot p$) were tested and the best performing q setting retained.

The generalization performance of RF was evaluated using internal out-of-bag (OOB) validation, where each observation is classified only by the trees which did not have this observation in bootstrap sample during construction. It is well known that OOB validation provides an unbiased estimate of a test set error, similar to leave-one-out scheme. Because of the "repeated measures" aspect in voice data, where each subject is represented by several recordings of sustained vowel, sampling part of the RF had to be modified to ensure that all recordings of each subject are either included in a bootstrap sample or left aside as OOB. Such modification corresponds to leave-one-subject-out scheme, which helps to avoid speaker detection intermingling with pathology detection. Also RF setting, allowing to perform stratified sampling, was configured to preserve class ratio and gender balance of the full dataset in each drawn bootstrap sample.

4.2   Decision-Level Fusion

Individual RFs were built independently on bootstrap sets and decisions of these individual experts were combined in a meta-learner fashion. RF was used both as a base learner and as a meta learner. This implies that outputs from RF models from the first stage are treated as inputs (meta-features) for another RF in the second stage. For the detection task, an input to the meta-learner is the difference between class posteriori probabilities obtained from the base-learner. Given a trained RF, this difference or variant of soft decision is estimated as:

$$d(\{t_1, ..., t_L\}, \mathbf{x}) = \frac{\sum_{i=1}^{L} f(t_i, \mathbf{x}, q = 2)}{L} - \frac{\sum_{i=1}^{L} f(t_i, \mathbf{x}, q = 1)}{L}, \tag{1}$$

where $\mathbf{x}$ is the object being classified, L is the number of trees $t_1, ..., t_L$ in the RF for which observation $\mathbf{x}$ is OOB, q is a class label (1 corresponds to HC and 2 to PD), and $f(t_i, \mathbf{x}, q)$ stands for the qth class frequency in the leaf node, into which $\mathbf{x}$ falls in the ith tree t_i of the forest:

$$f(t_i, \mathbf{x}, q) = \frac{n(t_i, \mathbf{x}, q)}{\sum_{j=1}^{Q} n(t_i, \mathbf{x}, q_j)}, \tag{2}$$

where Q is the number of classes and $n(t_i, \mathbf{x}, q)$ is the number of training data from class q and falling into the same leaf node of t_i as $\mathbf{x}$.

Meta-features were also investigated by performing permutation-based variable importance analysis using mean decrease in accuracy as the variable importance measure. Values of each meta-feature are permuted several times and the mean difference in meta-RF performance on OOB data is estimated.

4.3 Assessing Detection

To evaluate the goodness of detection, detector's scores for OOB data were used. Votes of RF were converted to a proper score vector by normalizing votes for a specific class through division by the total number of times the case was OOB, as in formula (1). Using a score (soft decision) instead of predicted class (hard decision) enables us with a more precise evaluation of the detection, which can be visually summarized by the detection error trade-off (DET) curve, as recommended in [16]. A quick way to compare detectors with different DET curves is the equilibrium point where curve intersects diagonal – the equal error rate (EER). The cost of log-likelihood-ratio C_{llr} is the most comprehensive detection metric, used here as the main criterion for model selection. The log-likelihood-ratio is the logarithm of the ratio between the likelihood that the target (PD) produced the signal and the likelihood that a non-target (HC) produced the signal. The DET curve, EER and C_{llr} measures were estimated using the ROC convex hull method, available in the BOSARIS toolkit [3]. A well-calibrated and useful detector should have $C_{llr} < 1$ and EER $< 50\%$.

5 Experimental Results

Detection performance of individual feature sets and their fusion is summarized in Table 3 and DET curves for the best results are on the left-hand side

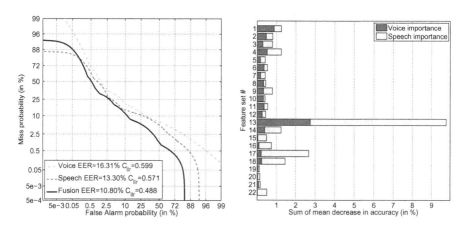

Fig. 1. Evaluation of detection performance by DET curves (**left**). Meta-RF permutation-based variable importance as decrease in fusion accuracy (**right**).

Table 3. Performance of feature sets and their fusion according to C_{llr} and EER.

#	Feature set name	Size	C_{llr}		EER, %	
			Voice	Speech	Voice	Speech
1	avec2011	1941	0.785	0.758	25.95	23.93
2	avec2013	2268	0.783	0.768	26.26	22.95
3	emo_large	6552	0.768	0.731	24.72	21.54
4	emobase	988	0.780	0.700	27.81	18.80
5	emobase2010	1582	0.805	0.758	27.70	19.60
6	IS09_emotion	384	0.836	0.797	30.00	23.72
7	IS10_paraling	1582	0.806	0.760	27.28	20.27
8	IS10_paraling_compat	1582	0.804	0.775	27.83	22.93
9	IS11_speaker_state	4368	0.797	0.783	26.23	24.42
10	IS12_speaker_trait	5757	0.795	0.804	25.38	22.94
11	IS12_speaker_trait_compat	6125	0.787	0.800	26.54	24.47
12	IS13_ComParE	6373	0.782	0.792	25.74	25.03
13	Essentia_descriptors	1915	0.599	0.571	16.31	13.30
14	MPEG7_descriptors	527	0.756	0.697	22.72	20.80
15	KTU_features	1267	0.835	0.766	29.05	22.78
16	jAudio_features	1794	0.806	0.769	26.90	21.26
17	YAAFE_features	1885	0.778	0.674	26.27	18.12
18	Tsanas_features	339	0.788	0.758	26.53	22.81
19	Tsanas_LASSO	14	0.912	0.916	34.26	32.35
20	Tsanas_LLBFS	14	0.913	0.890	33.45	31.23
21	Tsanas_mRMR	15	0.942	0.928	37.60	35.05
22	Tsanas_RELIEF	18	0.939	0.813	36.55	26.01
Decision fusion of sets & modalities		44	0.488		10.80	

of Fig. 1. Top 5 feature sets for the voice modality: (1) Essentia; (2) MPEG-7; (3) emo_large; (4) YAAFE; (5) emobase. Top 5 feature sets for the speech modality: (1) Essentia; (2) YAAFE; (3) MPEG-7; (4) emobase; (5) emo_large. Essentia descriptors provided the best detection performance irrespective of the modality. For all 22 feature sets investigated speech modality outperformed voice.

The fusion of models created using different feature sets and modalities improved detection performance achieving EER of 10.8 %. Variable importance analysis from the meta-RF (see the right-hand side of Fig. 1) indicate that for the most feature sets (except for # 1, 2, 6, 8, 10 – 12) the speech modality appears as more important than voice in decision-level fusion. Top 5 feature sets for the fusion of modalities: (1) Essentia; (2) YAAFE; (3) Tsanas; (4) emobase; (5) avec2011.

Reason behind the worst performing feature sets (# 19 – 22) could be their small size and the fact that they were formed by feature selection in [18], potentially compromising stability and generalization properties of SVM, as elimination of meaningless features is not so critical for obtaining a good performance [9,13]. This also conforms to the findings of [20] indicating that stable algorithm, such as SVM or RF, cannot help in identifying redundant features.

6   Conclusions

Essentia descriptors proved to be the best collection of features for PD detection, achieving 16.3 % EER for voice and 13.3 % EER for speech data. Fusion of 22 feature sets from both modalities improved detection performance down to 10.8 % EER and revealed that decisions from speech appear somewhat more important than decisions from voice. Fusion of diverse information could be recommended over feature selection for robust PD screening from voice and speech recordings.

Acknowledgments. This research was funded by a grant (No. MIP-075/2015) from the Research Council of Lithuania.

References

1. Bogdanov, D., Wack, N., Gómez, E., Gulati, S., Herrera, P., Mayor, O., Roma, G., Salamon, J., Zapata, J., Serra, X.: Essentia: an audio analysis library for music information retrieval. In: International Society for Music Information Retrieval Conference (ISMIR), pp. 493–498. Curitiba, Brazil, 4–8 November 2013. http://essentia.upf.edu
2. Breiman, L.: Random forests. Mach. Learn. **45**, 5–32 (2001)
3. Brümmer, N., de Villiers, E.: The BOSARIS toolkit: Theory, algorithms and code for surviving the new DCF. arXiv 1304(2865v1), 1–23, Presented at the NIST SRE 2011 Analysis Workshop, Atlanta, December 2011.
http://sites.google.com/site/bosaristoolkit/
4. Crysandt, H., Tummarello, G., Piazza, F.: MPEG-7 encoding and processing: MPEG7AUDIOENC + MPEG7AUDIODB. In: 3rd MUSICNETWORK Open Workshop: MPEG AHG on Music Notation Requirements. Munich, Germany, 13–14 March 2004. http://mpeg7audioenc.sf.net
5. de Rijk, M.C., Launer, L.J., Berger, K., Breteler, M.M.B., Dartigues, J.F., Baldereschi, M., Fratiglioni, L., Lobo, A., Martínez-Lage, J.M., Trenkwalder, C., Hofman, A.: Prevalence of Parkinson's disease in Europe: a collaborative study of population-based cohorts. Neurology **54**(11 Supply 5), S21–S23 (2000). Neurologic Diseases in the Elderly Research Group
6. Ellis, D.P.W.: PLP and RASTA (and MFCC, and inversion) in Matlab (2005). Matlab implementation of popular speech recognition feature extraction including MFCC and PLP (as defined by Hermansky and Morgan), http://www.ee.columbia.edu/~dpwe/resources/matlab/rastamat/, http://www.ee.columbia.edu/%7Edpwe/resources/matlab/rastamat/

7. Eyben, F., Weninger, F., Gross, F., Schuller, B.: Recent developments in openSMILE, the Munich open-source multimedia feature extractor. In: Proceedings of the 21st ACM International Conference on Multimedia (MM), pp. 835–838. ACM Press, Barcelona, Spain, 21–25 October 2013. http://audeering.com/research/opensmile/

8. Gelzinis, A., Verikas, A., Bacauskiene, M.: Automated speech analysis applied to laryngeal disease categorization. Comput. Methods Programs Biomed. **91**(1), 36–47 (2008)

9. Guyon, I.: Practical Feature Selection: from Correlation to Causality, NATO Science for Peace and Security Series D: Information and Communication Security, vol. 19, Chap. 3, pp. 27–43. IOS Press (2008)

10. Jaiantilal, A.: Random forest (regression, classification and clustering) implementation for Matlab (and standalone) (2012). http://code.google.com/archive/p/randomforest-matlab/

11. Mathieu, B., Essid, S., Fillon, T., Prado, J., Richard, G.: YAAFE, an easy to use and efficient audio feature extraction software. In: Proceedings of the 11th International Society for Music Information Retrieval Conference (ISMIR), pp. 441–446. Utrecht, Netherlands, 9–13 August 2010. http://yaafe.sf.net

12. McEnnis, D., McKay, C., Fujinaga, I.: jAudio: Additions and improvements. In: Proceedings of the 7th International Conference on Music Information Retrieval (ISMIR), pp. 385–386. University of Victoria, Victoria, British Columbia, Canada, 8–12 October 2006. http://github.com/dmcennis/jAudioGIT

13. Nilsson, R., Peña, J.M., Björkegren, J., Tegnér, J.: Evaluating feature selection for svms in high dimensions. In: Fürnkranz, J., Scheffer, T., Spiliopoulou, M. (eds.) ECML 2006. LNCS (LNAI), vol. 4212, pp. 719–726. Springer, Heidelberg (2006)

14. Orozco-Arroyave, J.R., Hönig, F., Arias-Londoño, J.D., Vargas-Bonilla, J.F., Daqrouq, K., Skodda, S., Rusz, J., Nöth, E.: Automatic detection of Parkinson's disease in running speech spoken in three different languages. J. Acoust. Soc. Am. **139**(1), 481–500 (2016)

15. Sakar, C.O., Kursun, O.: Telediagnosis of Parkinson's disease using measurements of dysphonia. J. Med. Syst. **34**(4), 591–599 (2010)

16. Sáenz-Lechón, N., Godino-Llorente, J.I., Osma-Ruiz, V., Gómez-Vilda, P.: Methodological issues in the development of automatic systems for voice pathology detection. Biomed. Signal Process. Control **1**(2), 120–128 (2006). Voice Models and Analysis for Biomedical Applications

17. Tsanas, A.: Accurate telemonitoring of Parkinson's disease symptom severity using nonlinear speech signal processing and statistical machine learning. Ph.D. thesis, Oxford Centre for Industrial and Applied Mathematics, University of Oxford, Oxford, United Kingdom, http://people.maths.ox.ac.uk/tsanas/software.html

18. Tsanas, A., Little, M.A., McSharry, P.E., Spielman, J.L., Ramig, L.O.: Novel speech signal processing algorithms for high-accuracy classification of Parkinson's disease. IEEE Trans. Biomed. Eng. **59**(5), 1264–1271 (2012)

19. Verikas, A., Gelzinis, A., Vaiciukynas, E., Bacauskiene, M., Minelga, J., Hallander, M., Uloza, V., Padervinskis, E.: Data dependent random forest applied to screening for laryngeal disorders through analysis of sustained phonation: acoustic versus contact microphone. Med.Eng. Phys. **37**(2), 210–218 (2015)

20. Xu, H., Caramanis, C., Mannor, S.: Sparse algorithms are not stable: a no-free-lunch theorem. IEEE Trans. Pattern Anal. Mach. Intell. **34**(1), 187–193 (2012)

HAVRUS Corpus: High-Speed Recordings of Audio-Visual Russian Speech

Vasilisa Verkhodanova[1(✉)], Alexander Ronzhin[1], Irina Kipyatkova[1],
Denis Ivanko[1], Alexey Karpov[1], and Miloš Železný[2]

[1] SPIIRAS, St. Petersburg, Russia
{verkhodanova,ronzhinal,kipyatkova,karpov}@iias.spb.su,
denis.ivanko11@gmail.com
[2] University of West Bohemia, Pilsen, Czech Republic
zelezny@kky.zcu.cz

Abstract. In this paper we present a software-hardware complex for collection of audio-visual speech databases with a high-speed camera and a dynamic microphone. We describe the architecture of the developed software as well as some details of the collected database of Russian audio-visual speech HAVRUS. The developed software provides synchronization and fusion of both audio and video channels and makes allowance for and processes the natural factor of human speech - the asynchrony of audio and visual speech modalities. The collected corpus comprises recordings of 20 native speakers of Russian and is meant for further research and experiments on audio-visual Russian speech recognition.

Keywords: Multimodal database · Audiovisual speech · Speech technology · Automatic speech recognition

1 Introduction

A lot of work has been done already in the field of automatic speech recognition (ASR), but it is still far from human level of performance. The need of making ASR robust to various changes in the environment and channel leads to a search of new approaches and sources to yield ASR improvements. Among these is audio-visual speech recognition (AVSR). The additional modality of visual speech is very helpful for making improvements in the environments with a high level of noises. Visual speech is a source of a great amount of complimentary information to the acoustic signal, being at the same time independent from acoustic noises and environment. At present there are many studies in the field of AVSR done for a number of European languages as well as for Chinese and Japanese, but there are quite few works on Russian AVSR [5,11,12,22]. In 2012 it was proposed to use high-speed cameras along with microphones for the task of audio-visual speech recognition [9], since the high frequency of video frames may improve the performance of AVSR systems allowing more precise analysis of articulation organs.

© Springer International Publishing Switzerland 2016
A. Ronzhin et al. (Eds.): SPECOM 2016, LNAI 9811, pp. 338–345, 2016.
DOI: 10.1007/978-3-319-43958-7_40

This paper presents a description of software architecture meant for recording of AV speech databases by means of a high-speed camera, as well as the corpus of AV Russian speech HAVRUS collected using this software.

2   State-of-the-Art Audio-Visual Databases

Nowadays there are various audio-visual databases, that are collected for different purposes and with different means. For example, there is a European project CHIL (Computers in the Human Interaction Loop) that aims to introduce computers into a loop of humans interacting with humans, realizing computer services that can be delivered to humans in an implicit, indirect and unobtrusive way [2]. For the aims of this project from 2004 till 2007 the audio-visual corpus of English speech was collected in the smart rooms located in five different sites, that were specially equipped for the project: in UKA-ISL (Germany), in AIT (Greece), in ITC (Italy), in UPC (Spain), and in IBM (USA). The use of different places for recording sessions brought variability into the corpus: rooms differ in size, layout, acoustic and visual environment, as well as sensor properties. Two types of interaction scenarios were recorded for the corpus: lectures and meetings.

There are recordings of 46 lectures and 40 meetings in the CHIL corpus. The database contains rich annotations in multiple channels of both audio and visual modalities. Recorded speech as well as environmental acoustic events were segmented and annotated by human transcribers. Video annotations were manually generated using an ad-hoc tool with manual annotating of the 2D face and 3D head location information. Part of the lecture recordings (19 lecture videos) were also labeled with gross information about the lecturer's head pose. The head orientation label corresponded to one of eight discrete orientation classes, ranging from 0° to 315° angle, with an increment of 45° degrees [15,20]

Another project that is worth mentioning is audio-visual corpus of Australian English – AusTalk. It was collected in the scope of the Big Australian Corpus project where 11 Australian universities have collaborated [6]. The main goal of this project was the collection of a big audio-visual corpus of Australian English that would allow researchers to investigate social, regional, ethnic and cultural varieties of the language. Another goal of the project was to provide the standardized infrastructure for audio-visual recordings all around Australia. More than 1000 speakers from different geographical regions and social groups were recorded. The corpus comprises nearly 3000 h of audio-video recordings. There are four parts of read speech and five parts of spontaneous speech. All audio and video data was captured by five microphones and two stereo cameras recording audio and video. Automatic audio-video alignment was provided by a strobe signal recorded on a separate audio channel. Annotation of the corpus includes word-level for the part of read speech and orthographic transcription for the part of spontaneous speech. Corpus was already used for the tasks of multimodal speech recognition [19].

In the University of West Bohemia, several audiovisual corpora were collected. The very first one is UWB-05-HSCAVC, the database of audiovisual

Czech speech (UWB means University of West Bohemia, 05 year 2005 when records were collected, and HSCAVC means Hundred Speakers Czech Audio-Visual Corpus), that consists of 40 h of audio and video data with high resolution [4]. Corpus comprises records of 100 speakers (39 men and 61 women), the average age was 22 years. Speakers read 200 sentences: 50 of them were phonetically representative texts common for all, the rest were different for every speaker and comprised as maximum various triphones as possible. Recording was done with two cameras and two microphones. Annotation included labels marking the beginning and the end of the phrases allowing segmentation of both audio and video data into sentences. Each video file comes with such information as description of mouth position and size. The similar corpus design was used for collection of Czech speech corpus for audio-visual continuous speech recognition [3,4].

The separate trend in audio-visual databases creation is the collection of corpora recorded for the purpose of audio-visual speech recognition in cars, since there are special and difficult acoustical conditions. An example of such databases is AVICAR project [14]. AVICAR is a big corpus of audio-visual speech recorded in the real-life conditions of moving car. It was collected in the University of Illinois (USA) with the financial support of Motorola company in 2003–2004. The similar corpus for Czech speech was collected in the University of West Bohemia in 2003 [23]. The main difference in the design was that for the Czech corpus the speech of driver speech, not passenger, was recorded.

However, at the moment there are almost no audiovisual databases representing continuous speech. Such databases are vital for the training of visual and acoustical models in the scope of statistical method of speech recognition. This type of modeling requires training corpora as close as possible to the real conditions. For the training of Russian speech recognition systems with one modality there is a number of commercially available speech resources, such as RuSpeech, SPEECHDAT, ISABASE, SPEECON, InfantRU/ChildRU. But no audio-visual Russian speech corpora with video and audio annotations exist. Now the only known project concerning the creation of a multimodal database for Russian speech is Multimodal Russian Corpus (MURCO) [8]. This corpus is intended for investigation of emotional speech and has no phoneme or viseme levels of annotation that are necessary for audiovisual speech recognition. Work on Russian AV speech databases has been done previously at SPIIRAS, paving the way to the results of the present study: creating the software for recording the AV speech databases by means of high-speed camera and collecting HAVRUS corpus [9,10].

There are also some other corpora of audio-visual speech like corpus of affective communication Biwi 3D [1], corpus of French news shows REPERE [7], speaker-independent corpus of both connected and isolated digits CUAVE [17].

3   Software Architecture for Recording Audio-Visual Speech Databases

A typical bimodal speech recognition system fuses both audio and visual modalities. Our goal was to develop and implement an efficient software-hardware complex that would allow us to collect the audio-visual corpus for the purposes of bimodal speech recognition.

In our complex, we use one high-speed camera JAI Pulnix RMC-6740 (200 fps at 640 × 480 pixels resolution) and one dynamic microphone Oktava MK-012 in order to capture both video and audio signals. High frequency of video frames is crucial for analysis of dynamical images for at least two reasons. First one is that visible articulation organs (lips, teeth, tip of tongue) change their configuration quite fast during speech production. Second reason is that duration of some phonemes (e.g. explosive consonants) is within 20–30 ms. Duration of each video frame at 25 fps is 40 ms, so recordings made by a standard camera fps cannot catch fast dynamics of lips movements, this results in a lot of the important information missing in these signals.

Figure 1 shows a setup for audiovisual speech recording. There are four types of equipment installed: (a) A separated microphone (one or two, depends on requirements). When one microphone is used, it is placed in front of a user at half-meter distance, when both are used, they are located at the left and right side of table with 45° to a user; (b) A table lamp with a warm light pointed on a user face. This lamp is used to discard illumination conditions; (c) A screen for displaying graphical user interface (GUI) of audiovisual recording system, and interaction with it; (d) A high-speed camera mounted on a tripod. The distance between a user and the camera may be based on parameters of lenses installed on the camera.

For the camera we can use one of the three different lenses: Navitar NMV-25M23 (focal length = 3.5 mm, diagonal angel = 13.2°, and distortion −0.04 %); KOWA LM3NCM (focal length = 3.5 mm, diagonal angel = 66.9°, and distortion −0.46 %); KOWA LM6NCM (focal length = 6mm, diagonal angel = 46.5°, and distortion −0.2 %). Usage of these different lenses allows to increase the

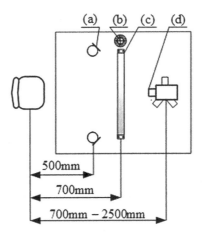

Fig. 1. Setup for audio-visual speech recording

adaptation and robustness of developed system to illumination [21] and other conditions [18], that may degrade facial features [16].

Figure 2 shows the architecture of software for audio-visual speech database recording. The developed software provides synchronization and fusion of both audio and video channels that is suitable for training probabilistic models for the speech recognition system.

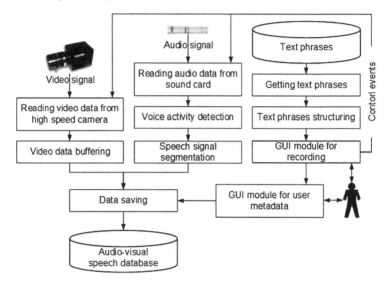

Fig. 2. The architecture of software for audio-visual speech database recording

The software complex consists of four main modules: (1) video data capturing and buffering; (2) audio data capturing, processing and segmentation; (3) text phrases displaying; (4) GUI for interaction with a user (speaker). The developed software has two GUI modules for interaction with the user and receiving his/her metadata. The modules of GUI provide two modes for data recording: (1) a "manual" mode, when the user manages the start and end points for each phrase; (2) an "automatic" mode, when parts of the recording are determined by a voice activity detection (VAD) method. In the "automatic" mode, audio signal capturing and processing is carried out continuously, and video data is buffered in RAM memory for the last 60 frames (300 ms at 200 fps). This buffering option is based on nature of human speech production: asynchrony of both speech modalities. One major problem in automatic audio-visual speech recognition is to implement a correct method for synchronization and unification of different speech modalities. The problem is that the two modalities naturally become desynchronized, i.e., streams of corresponding phonemes and visemes are not perfectly synchronous in real life due to natural constraints in the human speech production process, inertia in human articulation organs, and coarticulation (interdependence and interaction of adjacent elements in spoken speech) which has different effects on acoustic and visual speech components. All these aspects lead to desynchronization [11]. The developed system includes method for calculation of mistiming between audio and video streams based on analysis of semaphores(events) realised on sending and receiving video frames from camera as well as reading audio frames from microphone.

After the recording phrase, audio and video data of a current speaker are saved into the speech database. For synchronizing audio and video signals, the software calculates the frame mistiming.

4   HAVRUS Corpus Description

The developed software was used for recording of the audio-visual corpus of Russian speech - HAVRUS. This corpus consists not only of video files without compression (the optical resolution is 640×460 px with 200 fps) and of audio files also without compression (one channel PCM WAV files with 16 kHz sampling rate), it also includes text files of temporal annotation into phrases, words, phonemes and visemes of the part meant for training. The GUI used for the recording is presented on Fig. 3.

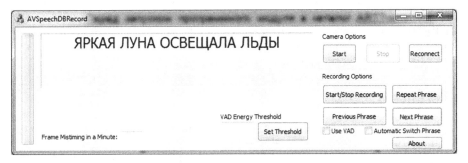

Fig. 3. The dialogue window of the software for the recording of AV speech databases

20 native monolingual Russian speakers (10 male and 10 female speakers) with no language or hearing problems participated in the recordings. Each of them pronounced 200 Russian phrases: (a) 130 phrases for training are 2 phonetically rich texts and are common for all speakers, and (b) 70 phrases for testing are different for every speaker: 20 phrases were commands for the MIDAS information kiosk in SPIIRAS [13] and 50 phrases are telephone numbers. All the recordings were organized into a logically structured database, that comprises a file with information about all the speakers and recording parameters, as well as number of text and audio files for each recorded speaker.

For the audio data Mel-Frequency Cepstral Coefficients (MFCC) are calculated from 26 channel filer bank analysis of 20 ms long frames with 5 ms step, these were stored as acoustical parameters. The video signal processing module produces 10-dimensional articulatory feature vectors with 200 Hz frequency calculated as the result of multi-scale face and mouth detection in video frames using cascaded classifiers with AdaBoost, then applying principal component analysis (PCA) and linear discriminant analysis (LDA) to the normalized graphical mouth region.

5   Conclusion

In this paper we presented the developed software-hardware complex for collection of audiovisual speech databases with a high-speed camera JAI Pulnix RMC-6740 and a dynamic microphone Oktava MK-012, as well as the collected corpus HAVRUS. The developed framework provides synchronization and fusion of both audio and video channels making allowance for the asynchrony of audio and visual speech modalities. Such synchronization is based on calculation of frames mistiming in a video stream per second as well as by joint implementation of voice activity detection and facial features analysis allowing to detect speech start and end time moments. The collected corpus HAVRUS comprises recordings of 20 native monolingual speakers of Russian with no language or hearing problems. Each speaker pronounced 200 Russian sentences. HAVRUS is meant for further research and experiments on audiovisual Russian speech recognition.

Acknowledgments. This research is financially supported by the Ministry of Education and Science of the Russian Federation, agreement No 14.616.21.0056 (reference RFMEFI61615X0056), project "Research and development of audio-visual speech recognition system based on a microphone and a high-speed camera", as well as by the Czech Ministry of Education, Youth and Sports, project No LO1506.

References

1. Biwi 3D Audiovisual Corpus of Affective Communication. http://www.vision.ee.ethz.ch/datasets/b3dac2.en.html
2. CHIL - Computers in the Human Interaction Loop. https://imatge.upc.edu/web/projects/chil-computers-human-interaction-loop
3. Czech Audio-Visual Speech Corpus for Recognition with Impaired Conditions. http://catalog.elra.info/product_info.php?cPath=25&products_id=1082
4. Císař, P., Železný, M., Krňoul, Z., Kanis, J., Zelinka, J., Müller, L.: Design and recording of czech speech corpus for audio-visual continuous speech recognition. In: Proceedings of International Conference on the Auditory-Visual Speech Processing, pp. 1–4 (2005)
5. Císař, P., Zelinka, J., Železný, M., Karpov, A., Ronzhin, A.: Audio-visual speech recognition for slavonic languages (Czech and Russian). In: Proceedings of 11th International Conference SPECOM 2006, St. Petersburg, Russia, pp. 493–498 (2006)
6. Estival, D., Cassidy, S., Cox, F., Burnham, D., et al.: Austalk: an audio-visual corpus of australian english. In: Proceedings of 9th Language Resources and Evaluation Conference LREC 2014, pp. 3105–3109 (2014)
7. Giraudel, A., Carré, M., Mapelli, V., Kahn, J., Galibert, O., Quintard, L.: The REPERE corpus: a multimodal corpus for person recognition. In: Proceedings of 8th Language Resources and Evaluation Conference (LREC 2012), pp. 1102–1107 (2012)
8. Grishina, E.: Multimodal russian corpus (MURCO): first steps. In: Proceedings of 7th Language Resources and Evaluation Conference (LREC 2010), pp. 2953–2960 (2010)

9. Karpov, A., Ronzhin, A., Kipyatkova, I.: Designing a multimodal corpus of audio-visual speech using a high-speed camera. In: Proceedings of 11th International Conference on Signal Processing (ICSP 2012), vol. 1, pp. 519–522. IEEE (2012)

10. Karpov, A., Kipyatkova, I., Železný, M.: A framework for recording audio-visual speech corpora with a microphone and a high-speed camera. In: Ronzhin, A., Potapova, R., Delic, V. (eds.) SPECOM 2014. LNCS, vol. 8773, pp. 50–57. Springer, Heidelberg (2014)

11. Karpov, A., Ronzhin, A., Kipyatkova, I., Železný, M.: Influene of phone-viseme temporal correlations on audiovisual STT and TTS performance. In: Proceedings of 17th International Congress of Phonetic Sciences, pp. 1030–1033 (2011)

12. Karpov, A., Ronzhin, A., Markov, K., Zelezný, M.: Viseme-dependent weight optimization for CHMM-based audio-visual speech recognition. In: Proceedings of INTERSPEECH 2010, Makuhari, Japan, pp. 2678–2681 (2010)

13. Karpov, A.A., Ronzhin, A.L.: Information enquiry kiosk with multimodal user interface. Pattern Recogn. Image Analy. **19**(3), 546–558 (2009)

14. Lee, B., Hasegawa-Johnson, M., Goudeseune, C., Kamdar, S., Borys, S., Liu, M., Huang, T.S.: AVICAR: audio-visual sspeech corpus in a car eenvironment. In: Proceedings of INTERSPEECH 2004, Jeju Island, Korea, pp. 2489–2492 (2004)

15. Mostefa, D., Moreau, N., Choukri, K., Potamianos, G., Chu, S.M., Tyagi, A., Casas, J.R., Turmo, J., Cristoforetti, L., Tobia, F., et al.: The CHIL audiovisual corpus for lecture and meeting analysis inside smart rooms. Lang. Resour. Evalu. **41**(3–4), 389–407 (2007)

16. Nikan, S.: Human face recognition under degraded conditions. University of Windsor (2014)

17. Patterson, E.K., Gurbuz, S., Tufekci, Z., Gowdy, J.N.: CUAVE: a new audio-visual database for multimodal human-computer interface research. In: Proceedings of International Conference on Acoustics, Speech, and Signal Processing (ICASSP), vol. 2, pp. 2017–2020. IEEE (2002)

18. Ronzhin, A.L., Vatamanyuk, I., Ronzhin, A.L., Železný, M.: Mathematical methods to estimate image blur and recognize faces in the system of automatic conference participant registration. Autom. Remote Control **76**(11), 2011–2020 (2015)

19. Togneri, R., B.M., Sui, C.: Multimodal speech recognition with the AusTalk 3D audio-visual corpus. In: Tutorial at ITERSPEECH 2014 (2014)

20. Waibel, A., Stiefelhagen, R., Carlson, R., Casas, J., Kleindienst, J., Lamel, L., Lanz, O., Mostefa, D., Omologo, M., Pianesi, F., et al.: Computers in the human interaction loop. In: Nakashima, H., Aghajan, H., Augusto, J.C. (eds.) Handbook of Ambient Intelligence and Smart Environments, pp. 1071–1116. Springer, Heidelberg (2010)

21. Xie, X.: Illumination preprocessing for face images based on empirical mode decomposition. Signal Process. **103**, 250–257 (2014)

22. Železný, M., Císař, P., Krňoul, Z., Ronzhin, A., Li, I., Karpov, A.: Design of russian audio-visual speech corpus for bimodal speech recognition. In: Proceedings of SPECOM, pp. 397–400 (2005)

23. Zelezný, M., Císar, P.: Czech audio-visual speech corpus of a car driver for in-vehicle audio-visual speech recognition. In: Proceedings of International Conference on Audio-Visual Speech Processing (AVSP 2003), pp. 169–173 (2003)

Human-Smartphone Interaction for Dangerous Situation Detection and Recommendation Generation While Driving

Alexander Smirnov[1,2], Alexey Kashevnik[1,2(✉)], and Igor Lashkov[1,2]

[1] SPIIRAS, St. Petersburg, Russia
[2] ITMO University, St. Petersburg, Russia
{smir,alexey}@iias.spb.su, igor-lashkov@ya.ru

Abstract. The paper presents a human-smartphone interaction system that is aimed at dangerous situation detection in a vehicle while driving. The system implements the driver head position and face tracking to detect if the driver is fine or he/she drowsed or distracted. For the image recognition, the OpenCV computer vision library is used that allows to determine the main head and face parameters that are analyzed to detect dangerous situations. Taking into account detected dangerous situation and current situation in the road (e.g., city or countryside driving; hotels, gas stations, cafes, restaurants around; Internet availability) the system generates recommendations for the driver to prevent accidents caused by dangerous driver behavior.

Keywords: Human-computer interaction · Image recognition · Head tracking · Face tracking · Context-aware recommendations · Dangerous situation detection

1 Introduction

Dangerous situation detection while driving vehicles and accident prevention in the public roads is a popular research direction last years [1–3]. Such kind of systems are offered to increase car and road safety. There are two main research direction in this topic: (1) developed by manufactures complex hardware and software solutions and integration it to the vehicles; (2) developed a smartphone-based application that uses built-in cameras and accessible sensors to understand dangerous situation. Solutions from the first group are very expensive and accessible only in the vehicles from premium segment. In contrast, solutions from the second group are free (or cheap), they suppose to use existing personal smartphone to download an application and use it that makes the second group of application affordable for wide group of drivers. Presented paper aimed at research and development reference model and implementation for human-smartphone interaction using the front camera and detection of one of two dangerous situation: drowsiness and distraction. Based on the detected dangerous situation recommendations for the driver are generated to prevent an accident.

Presented paper extends authors work in the area of dangerous events detection while driving a vehicle. In the paper [4] authors present a comprehensive state-of-the-art analysis of existing systems for dangerous events detection. Paper [5] contains developed approach for two-wheeled self-balancing vehicles driver assisting to enhance their trips.

© Springer International Publishing Switzerland 2016
A. Ronzhin et al. (Eds.): SPECOM 2016, LNAI 9811, pp. 346–353, 2016.
DOI: 10.1007/978-3-319-43958-7_41

In the paper [6] authors present a driver ontology that describes main concepts, possible dangerous states for a driver that have to be taking into account dangerous situations identification and recommendation generation.

The rest of the paper is structured as follows. Section 2 presents the reference model of human-smartphone interaction. Two use cases are presented in Sect. 3. Implementation of proposed reference model is presented in Sect. 4. Main results are summarized in Conclusion.

2 Reference Model of Human-Smartphone Interaction While Driving

For tracking human head and face the reference model has been proposed. Every time when the mobile application gets image from the front camera this image is recognized and situation is estimated (is it dangerous or not). Then the process is repeated until the user closes the application or stops dangerous situation estimation function.

Presented reference model includes three main components: human, smartphone, and cloud (Fig. 1). Smartphone analyses the human head and face and generate recommendations in case of dangerous situation is detected. Information for analyzing the human head and face is collected by the mobile application component from the front camera using the image recognition module. Application is analyzed head movements (head rotation and nods), percentage of closure of eyelid (PERCLOS), eye blink rate and gaze, and yawning using the analysis module that is responsible for extraction of the visual features from the images taken by front camera. User interface is used to show the user determined dangerous state and recommendations. Recommendation module

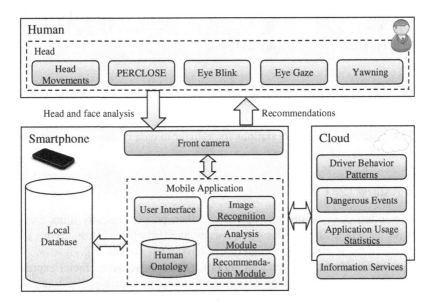

Fig. 1. The reference Model of Human-Smartphone Interaction while Driving

is responsible for generation of context-aware recommendations for the human driver based of the detected dangerous situation and current situation in the road. Local database is responsible for storing a data collected by the smartphone. If the Internet connection is available, the smartphone uses the cloud to exchange useful information with other system users and to store generic information about the driver's behavior.

Such information as smartphone characteristics, application usage statistics, and dangerous events occurred during trip is stored for a deep analysis and using in the future. Smartphone characteristics are GPU, sensors (GPS, Accelerometer, Gyroscope, Magnetometer), front camera, memory & battery capacity, and version of operation system. The cloud also is used for keeping behavior patterns to analyze and create new dangerous situation. Operations that can be carried out in the cloud storage are:

- correctness estimation of dangerous events recognition;
- behavior patterns matching;
- analysis and classification of driver behavior for generating recommendations for safe driving;

The system is focused on the behavioral and physiological signals acquired from the driver to assess his/her mental state in real-time [7]. In the presented approach, the driver is considered as a set of mental states. Each of these states has its own particular control behavior and interstate transition probabilities. The canonical example of this type of model would be a bank of standard linear controllers (e.g., Kalman Filters plus a simple control law). Each controller has different dynamics and measurements, sequenced together with a Markov network of probabilistic transitions. The states of the model can be hierarchically organized to describe the short and long-term behaviors by using the driver ontology that includes visual cues and visual behaviors and determines relationships between them.

The vehicle drivers are faced with a multitude of road hazards and an increasing number of distractions (e.g. music, phone calls, smartphone texting and browsing, advertising information on the road, and etc.).

3   Use Cases

This section contains description of two use cases that have been developed and implemented for generating recommendations for a driver in case of dangerous event recognition: drowsiness and distraction.

3.1   Drowsiness Use Case

Drivers are often unaware of these episodes; rather, people typically think they have been awake the whole time or have lost focus momentarily. As a result, drivers experiencing bouts of micro sleep are at high risk of having an accident [8].

The smartphone's front camera monitors the head movements, facial expressions and the prolonged and frequent eye blinks indicative of micro sleep. Existing research findings have shown that the PERCLOS is an effective indicator for evaluating a driver's drowsiness. A measure of drowsiness, PERCLOS, was generated and associated with degradation in driving performance in a simulated roadway environment. PERCLOS

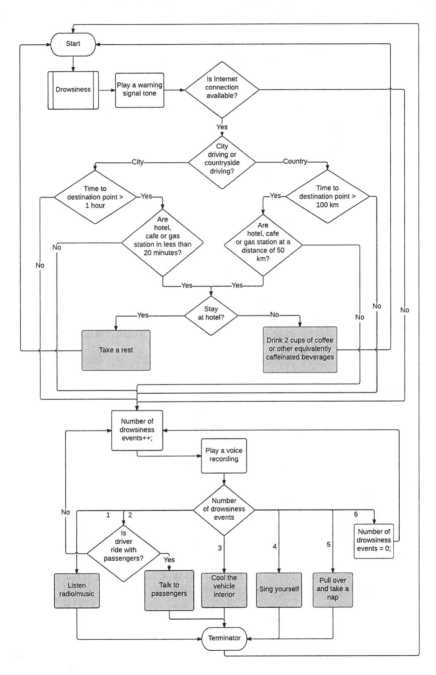

Fig. 2. Flow chart of drowsiness dangerous state

formally represents the proportion of time within one minute that eyes are at least 80 % closed [9]. This driver state information such as PERCLOS and eye-blink speed is provided by smartphone's front-facing camera. We continuously compute PERCLOS and declare the driver "drowsy" if PERCLOS exceeds a threshold (28 %) [10]. Another parameter is the speed of blinking, giving a permissible range of 0.5–0.8 s per blink. One more indicator of drowsiness is a yawning. If the driver makes more than 3 yawns in 30 min, we consider the driver is in the dangerous state. And finally, the fourth indicator of this dangerous event is the head nodding. If the number of head tilts exceeds a threshold (4) in 2 min, the drowsiness is inferred.

If the analysis module detects drowsiness, the application alerts the driver by playing a signal tone. If the Internet connection is available for a smartphone it checks whether the driver in a city or in a countryside. If the driver is on the countryside roads, the recommendation module checks how many kilometers drives has to go to destination point. If it is more than 100 km it tries to find a hotel around the route and makes the driver recommendation to stay in hotel and to take a rest. If the driver declines this proposal, the recommendation module generates recommendation for the driver to drink 2 cups of coffee before continue the trip in the nearest gas station. Otherwise, if driver goes through the city and the observable distance to the destination point is more than 1 h of driving the recommendation module generates the same recommendation. If driver declines the recommendation or destination point is not far or the Internet connection is not available the recommendation module notifies the driver that drowsiness dangerous state is detected and provides one of the following recommendation: listen radio/music, talk to passengers, cool the vehicle interior, sign yourself, pull over and take a nap. The flowchart of the drowsiness state is presented in Fig. 2. Recommendations are highlighted in a grey color in Fig. 2.

3.2 Distraction Use Case

Maintaining eye contact with the road is fundamental to safe driving. The National Highway Transportation Safety Administration (NHTSA) has defined distracted driving as "an activity that could divert a person's attention away from the primary task of driving". Distraction occurs when drivers divert their attention away from the driving task to focus on another activity instead.

Two types of inattentive driving are monitored. In the first type, the output of the face direction classifier based on head movements and head position is tracked. If the driver's face is not facing forward for longer than three seconds while the car is moving forward (i.e., while a positive speed is reported by the accelerometer) and not turning as reported by the turn detector (which is based on the gyroscope readings) then a dangerous driving event is inferred. In the second type, we trace a vehicle movement and determine whether the vehicle made a turn or not.

In this paper four driver's face related categories is recognized. They are: (1) no face is present; or the driver's face is either (2) facing forwards events, towards the road; (3) facing to the left events (i.e., a $\geq 15°$ rotation relative to facing directly forward); and, (4) facing to the right events (another $\geq 15°$ rotation but this time to the right). Each time a turn is detected the historical output of the face direction classifier is checked. If there is no head turn corresponding to a car turning event then the driver did not check that the road is clear before turning – as a result, a dangerous event is inferred. There is a diversity of distraction tasks that can affect driver in different ways. Driver distraction is a contributing factor in many crashes.

If the application detects the driver's distraction, it checks if the driver talks with a passenger if it is talk it provides him/her information that distraction state is detected and recommendation to stop talking with passenger (see Fig. 3). If the driver is not talking with passenger the application checks if he/she is fond of listening to music or radio. If it is true, the application recommends to turn off radio/music. In the both cases the application plays a warning tone and flash the smartphone screen to attract the driver attention that he/she is drowse. The overall scheme of distraction state avoidance is presented in the Fig. 3.

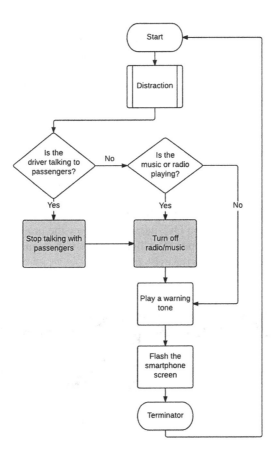

Fig. 3. Flow chart of distraction dangerous state

4   Implementation

Implementation of proposed human-smartphone interaction system for dangerous driving situation detection in the vehicle has been developed for Android-based mobile device. Mobile application has been developed using C and C ++. For the image recognition the open source computer vision (OpenCV) library has been used.

The face recognition process includes following key steps:

- The creation of the face detector.
- Face detection and face tracking.
- Facial landmarks detection like as "left eye", "right eye".
- Facial characteristics classification like as "eyes open", "eyes close".

To provide the functionality for face detection in consecutive video frames the Face API is used and Classification API that is determining whether a certain characteristic is present i.e. a face can be classified with regards to whether its eyes are open or closed. Both of these classifications rely upon landmark detection. A landmark is a point of interest within a face. The left eye, right eye, and nose base are all examples of landmarks. Classification is expressed as a certainty value, indicating the confidence that the facial characteristic is present. In our case, a value of 0.3 or less for the eye state classification indicates that it is likely that person's eyes are in a closed state.

The overall speed and efficiency of the application has been improved by applying several optimization techniques. To improve the frame processing performance, the width and the height of the camera frames to 640 × 480 pixels have been set. Also, the requested frame rate to 30 frames per second has been adjusted.

Figure 4 illustrate the user interface of mobile application. When a face is detected, it is marked by a rectangle around the head in the camera image. The face detector marks landmarks by circles. The Euler Y and Euler Z angles characterize a face's orientation. The "Left eye OP" and "Right eye OP" parameters show the probabilities whether the left or right eye, respectively, is open. The higher value of these measurements is on the image, the higher probability that the eyes are open.

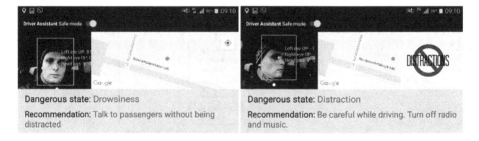

Fig. 4. Prototype example: drowsiness and distraction dangerous state identification

5   Conclusion

The paper present a human-smartphone interaction system for drivers in vehicles that aims at dangerous situation detection while driving and generating recommendations for the driver to prevent an accident in the road. There are two dangerous situation use cases have been considered in the paper: distraction and drowsiness. For every use case a flowchart diagram has been developed for recommendation generation. Implementation of the system has been done for Android OS based mobile device. Evaluation shows that in real situation the calibration is needed that allows to take into account the displacement of smartphone in the vehicle from the driver gaze line.

Acknowledgements. The presented results are part of the research carried out within the project funded by grants# 16-07-00462, 16-29-04349 of the Russian Foundation for Basic Research, programs # I.5, III.3, and # I.31 of the Russian Academy of Sciences. The work has been partially financially supported by Government of Russian Federation, Grant 074-U01.

References

1. Underwooda, G., Ngaia, A., Underwood, J.: Driving experience and situation awareness in hazard detection. Saf. Sci. **56**, 29–35 (2013)
2. Aurichta, M., Stark, R.: How to consider emotional reactions of the driver within the development of advanced driver assistance systems? Procedia CIRP **21**, 70–74 (2014)
3. Biassoni, F., Ruscio, D., Ciceri, R.: Limitations and automation. The role of information about device-specific features in ADAS acceptability. Saf. Sci. **85**, 179–186 (2016)
4. Smirnov, A., Lashkov, I.: State-of-the-art analysis of available advanced driver assistance systems. In: 17th Conference of the Open Innovations Association FRUCT, pp. 345–349 (2015)
5. Smirnov, A., Kashevnik, A., Lashkov, I., Hashimoto, N., Boyali, A.: Smartphone-based two-wheeled self-balancing vehicles rider assistant. In: 17th Conference of the Open Innovations Association FRUCT, pp. 201–209 (2015)
6. Lashkov, I., Smirnov, A., Kashevnik, A., Parfenov, V.: Ontology-based approach and implementation of ADAS system for mobile device use while driving. In: Klinov, P., et al. (eds.) KESW 2015. CCIS, vol. 518, pp. 117–131. Springer, Heidelberg (2015). doi: 10.1007/978-3-319-24543-0_9
7. Rigas, G., Goletsis, Y., Bougia, P., Fotiadis, D.: Towards driver's state recognition on real driving conditions. Int. J. Veh. Technol. **2011**, 1687–5702 (2011)
8. Knipling, R.: PERCLOS, A Valid Psychophysiological Measure of Alertness as Assessed by Psychomotor Vigilance. Technical Report FHWA-MCRT-98-006, Federal Highway Administration, Office of Motor Carrier Research and Standards (1998)
9. Dinges, D.F., Grace, R.: PERCLOS: a valid psychophysiological measure of alertness as assessed by psychomotor vigilance. In: 6th International Driving Symposium on Human Factors in Driver Assessment, Training and Vehicle Design (1998)
10. Wierwille, W.W., Wreggit, S.S., Kirn, C.L., Ellsworth, L.A., Fairbanks, R.J.: Research on Vehicle-Based Driver Status/Performance Monitoring: Development, Validation, and Refinement of Algorithms for Detection of Driver Drowsiness, Technical Report DOT-HS-808-247, National Highway Traffic Safety Administration (1994)

Improving Automatic Speech Recognition Containing Additive Noise Using Deep Denoising Autoencoders of LSTM Networks

Marvin Coto-Jiménez[1,2]($\boxtimes$), John Goddard-Close[1,2],
and Fabiola Martínez-Licona[1,2]

[1] University of Costa Rica, San José, Costa Rica
marvin.coto@ucr.ac.cr
[2] Metropolitan Autonomous University, México D.F., Mexico
{jgc,fmml}@xanum.uam.mx

Abstract. Automatic speech recognition systems (ASR) suffer from performance degradation under noisy conditions. Recent work, using deep neural networks to denoise spectral input features for robust ASR, have proved to be successful. In particular, Long Short-Term Memory (LSTM) autoencoders have outperformed other state of the art denoising systems when applied to the mfcc's of a speech signal. In this paper we also consider denoising LSTM autoencoders (DLSTMA), but instead use three different DLSTMAs and apply each to the mfcc's, fundamental frequency, and energy features, respectively. Results are given using several kinds of additive noise at different intensity levels, and show how this collection of DLSTMA's improves the performance of the ASR in comparison with the LSTM autoencoder.

Keywords: LSTM · Deep learning · Denoising autoencoders

1 Introduction

Real world environments often adversely affect speech signals through the introduction of contaminants such as noise and reverberation. If the speech signal is not too damaged, humans are usually able to understand the original utterance, whilst an Automatic Speech Recognition system (ASR) may experience a degradation in its recognition performance [1,2].

This can be partially explained by the fact that a traditional ASR is HMM-based, and the HMMs are trained using voices from some controlled environment, and then tested differently, on real world environments. In this case, there may be a considerable mismatch between the training and testing data.

As a result of the poorer performance of ASR under noisy conditions, research is currently focused on making ASR systems more robust in such conditions [3–8], trying to achieve recognition accuracy similar to that of quiet, controlled environments. Generally, approaches to noise robustness fall into one of two categories: feature enhancement methods, which attempt to remove the corrupting noise

© Springer International Publishing Switzerland 2016
A. Ronzhin et al. (Eds.): SPECOM 2016, LNAI 9811, pp. 354–361, 2016.
DOI: 10.1007/978-3-319-43958-7_42

from the observations prior to recognition, and model adaptation, which leaves the observations unchanged and instead updates the model parameters of the recognizer to be more representative of the observed speech [9].

Recently, deep neural networks have been shown to be effective for a variety of speech research tasks, for example, robust speech recognition and speech enhancement systems c.f. [10–13]. One technique has been to map spectral features from speech containing noise, into the same spectral features of the corresponding clean speech, using sigmoid neurons in the hidden layers.

Among the recent models of deep learning, a new kind of recurrent neural network, called a Long Short-Term Memory Network (LSTM) has proved to be successful in a variety of machine learning tasks. In particular, LSTM networks have been used in [14] to map noisy and reverberant speech to clean speech, by using spectral features of mfcc and Mel filter banks. Spectral features are the ones primarily used, perhaps because ASR systems are usually based on them. One interesting possibility is to include other acoustic features e.g. fundamental frequency (f0) and energy, in this approach to see if this improves the results obtained.

In this work, we explore an extended LSTM based approach for the feature enhancement of ASR with additive noise, by considering not only the mfcc mapping from noisy to clean speech, but also the mapping of other acoustic features, namely fundamental frequency and energy, by using a collection of deep autoencoders. The collection of autoencoders is trained on part of the CMU ARCTIC databases by mapping utterances with added noise at different levels to the clean utterances. Results are given by testing the utterances using a state-of-the-art commercial ASR system. These results are also compared to the original approach, using only the spectral features, and also to a third approach using multilayer perceptrons instead of LSTMs. The results seem to show the benefits of our proposed system.

The rest of this paper is organized as follows: Sect. 2 briefly presents the LSTM, Sect. 3 describes the proposed system, Sect. 4 presents the experiments, Sect. 5 gives the results together with an analysis, and finally in Sect. 6 we give some conclusions derived from the paper.

2   Long Short-Term Memory Recurrent Neural Networks

Deep learning algorithms which are based on feedforward neural networks have difficulty in modeling sequential information, where present values may depend on previous ones. This type of modeling is desirable when dealing with speech signals. To try to solve this problem, different techniques have been proposed including Recurrent Neural Networks (RNN) [15]. In this case, there will be nonfeedforward feedback from some or all of the neurons in the network, allowing their internal memory to process this sequential information.

An extended type of RNN, which can store information over long or short time intervals, has been presented in [16], giving the lowest recorded error rates on the TIMIT database [17,18]. One advantage of the LSTM is in terms of its training procedure, which doesn't suffer from the vanishing gradient problem common to other RNN architectures.

In a RNN, output vector sequences $\mathbf{y} = (y_1, y_2, \ldots, y_T)$ are computed from input vector sequences $\mathbf{x} = (x_1, x_2, \ldots, x_T)$ and hidden vector sequences $\mathbf{h} = (h_1, h_2, \ldots, h_T)$ iterating Eqs. 1 and 2 from 1 to T [19]:

$$h_t = \mathcal{H}\left(\mathbf{W}_{xh}x_t + \mathbf{W}_{hh}h_{t-1} + b_h\right), \tag{1}$$

$$y_t = \mathbf{W}_{hy}h_t + b_y, \tag{2}$$

where $\mathbf{W}$ is the weight matrix, e.g. $\mathbf{W}_{xh}$ is the weight matrix between input and hidden vectores, b is the bias vector, e.g. b_h is the bias vector for hidden state vectores and $\mathcal{H}$ is the activation function for hidden nodes.

Each cell in the hidden layers of a LSTM, has some extra gates to store values: an input gate, forget gate, output gate and cell activation, so values can be stored in the long or short term. These gates are implemented following the equations:

$$i_t = \sigma\left(\mathbf{W}_{xi}x_t + \mathbf{W}_{hi}h_{t-1} + \mathbf{W}_{ci}c_{t-1} + b_i\right), \tag{3}$$

$$f_t = \sigma\left(\mathbf{W}_{xf}x_t + \mathbf{W}_{hf}h_{t-1} + \mathbf{W}_{cf}c_{t-1} + b_f\right), \tag{4}$$

$$c_t = f_t c_{t-1} + i_t \tanh\left(\mathbf{W}_{xc}x_t + \mathbf{W}_{hc}h_{t-1} + b_c\right), \tag{5}$$

$$o_t = \sigma\left(\mathbf{W}_{xo}x_t + \mathbf{W}_{ho}h_{t-1} + \mathbf{W}_{co}c_t + b_o\right), \tag{6}$$

$$h_t = i_t \tanh\left(c_t\right), \tag{7}$$

where σ is the sigmoid function, i is the input gate activation vector, f the forget gate activation function, o is the output gate activation function, and c the cell memory.

3   Description of the System

In order to improve the accuracy of the ASR system in noisy utterances, we train a collection of networks, each composed of LSTM units, where each network maps a noisy utterance x to a clean utterance y. We call this special kind of network a denoising LSTM autoencoder (DLSTMA). Autoencoders usually consist of the encoder and the decoder; the encoder is a deterministic mapping f that transforms a n-dimensional input vector x into a hidden representation y. The typical form is an affine mapping, followed by a nonlinearity: $f(x) = s(Wx + b)$, with parameter set $\theta = \{W, b\}$, where W is a $n \times n$ weight matrix and b is an offset vector of dimensionality d. The resulting hidden representation y is then mapped back to a reconstructed d-dimensional vector z in input space, with $z = g(y)$. This mapping is called the decoder [20].

Figure 1 outlines the system, where three denoising autoencoders are trained to map noisy features (x) of the waveform to clean features (y). The three autoencoders have the same number of units in each hidden layer.

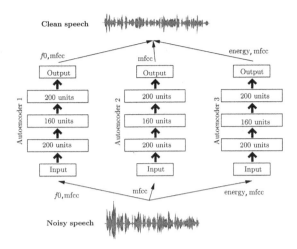

Fig. 1. Proposed system

4 Experiments

The CMU ARCTIC databases were created at the Language Technologies Institute at Carnegie Mellon University, and consist of around 1150 utterances selected from out-of-copyright texts from Project Gutenberg. The databases include US English male and female speakers. A detailed report on the structure and content of the database and the recording conditions is available in the Language Technologies Institute Tech Report CMU-LTI-03-177 [21]. For this paper, the SLT female voice was chosen, and 600 sentences were randomly selected to define training, validation and test sets.

To evaluate the automatic speech transcription performance of the DLSTMA and collection of DLSTMAs, we performed a series of experiments adding several kinds of noise. The white Gaussian noise, brown noise and pink noise were generated synthetically, and 50 randomly selected sentences were tested in a state-of-the art online ASR, Speechmatics [22].

Each sentence was parameterized using the Ahocoder system [23]. Three DLSTMAs were defined after a process of trial and error with three hidden layers of 200, 160 and 200 units, to process separately each group of parameters: $f0$, energy and 39 mfcc. All the acoustic features were extracted from frames of 10ms. The training procedure was accelerated by an NVIDIA GPU system, taking about 7 h to train each DLSTMA.

Four levels of noise of each kind were added to the sentences, thereby affecting the ASR accuracy from negligible to considerable. For comparison purposes, three results were analyzed: transforming only the mfcc spectral features with one DLSTMA (base system), our proposal of transforming three acoustic features with separate DLSTMA, and changing the LSTM units with simple sigmoid functions (Multilayer Perceptron).

5   Results and Analysis

Word Error Rates (WER) were obtained by applying the Speechmatics ASR to the test data. Figure 2 summarizes the WER obtained for the three cases. It is noticeable how the DLSTMAs, in general, show an improvement over the MLP for denoising, when all have the same hidden layer structure. Further, the results obtained by the collection of DLSTMAs are also significantly better than the results of the original DLSTMA (trained only on the mfcc parameters).

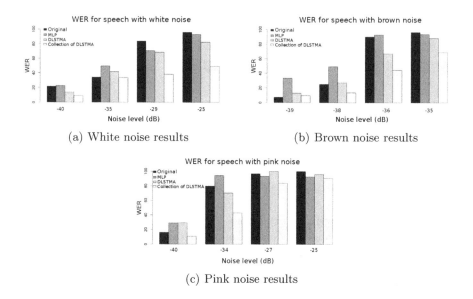

(a) White noise results   (b) Brown noise results

(c) Pink noise results

Fig. 2. Results of WER for the different levels of each noise

The most remarkable results come from the higher noise levels added to the speech signal. Whereas such levels produce a WER close to 100 % on the original waveform, the collection of DLSTMAs reduce it to 49.2 % (white noise), 68.9 % (brown noise) and 90.83 % (pink noise). For the brown and pink noise, the MLP autoencoder seems to degrade its performance, possibly due to the nature of non-homogenous power spectral density of the noise over the frequency range of the voice.

Figure 3 shows four spectrograms of the original signal (a), the higher white noise level added to the signal (b), the denoised spectrogram of the signal using the DLSTMA for the mfcc (c), and the spectrogram of the denoised signal using the collection of DLSTMA for mfcc, fundamental frequency and energy (d). The spectrograms clarify how well the collection of DLSTMA outperforms the denoising of the spectral representation of the waveform, and how it achieves better results for ASR.

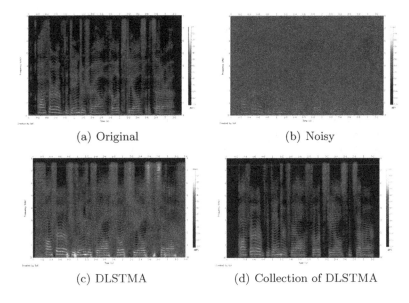

(a) Original   (b) Noisy

(c) DLSTMA   (d) Collection of DLSTMA

Fig. 3. Spectrograms of original, noisy and denoised waveforms

6   Conclusions

In this paper, we have presented an extension of the DLSTMA, which was trained using only the mfcc features of a speech utterance, to a collection of DLSTMAs which also use the fundamental frequency and energy. This has been done in the context of denoising speech utterances in order to improve ASR performance. Our system is based on a collection of denoising autoencoders, each composed of LSTM units.

We evaluated the proposed system on data containing three different noise types, each at four noise levels, using a commercial ASR. The results showed that in all cases the collection of DLSTMAs improved the WER performance in comparison with the DLSTMA trained using only mfccs.

Even for the case where the noise level is high enough to degrade WER to almost 100 %, the collection of DLSTMAs lowers the WER signicantly. These are encouraging initial results.

While this paper presents the preliminary results of our research using DLST-MAs for denoising, there are a number of questions left unanswered:

1. How effective are other combinations of features, such as mfcc features and energy.
2. Do other architectures for the autoencoder change the results we obtain. In particular, how can we reduce the training time.
3. Do other types of noise affect the results we obtain with the proposed approach.

We hope to provide some answers to these questions in future work.

Acknowledgements. This work was supported by the SEP and CONACyT under the Program SEP-CONACyT, CB-2012-01, No. 182432, in Mexico, as well as the University of Costa Rica in Costa Rica.

References

1. Weninger, F., Watanabe, S., Tachioka, Y., Schuller, B.: Deep recurrent de-noising auto-encoder and blind de-reverberation for reverberated speech recognition. In: IEEE International Conference on Acoustics, Speech and Signal Processing (ICASSP), pp. 4623–4627. IEEE (2014)
2. Bagchi, D., Mandel, M.I., Wang, Z., He, Y., Plummer, A., Fosler-Lussier, E.: Combining spectral feature mapping and multi-channel model-based source separation for noise-robust automatic speech recognition. In: Proceedings of IEEE ASRU (2015)
3. Kalinli, O., Seltzer, M.L., Droppo, J., Acero, A.: Noise adaptive training for robust automatic speech recognition. IEEE Trans. Audio Speech Lang. Process. **18**(8), 1889–1901 (2010)
4. Ishii, T., Komiyama, H., Shinozaki, T., Horiuchi, Y., Kuroiwa, S.: Reverberant speech recognition based on denoising autoencoder. In: INTERSPEECH, pp. 3512–3516 (2013)
5. Zhang, Z., Wang, L., Kai, A., Yamada, T., Li, W., Iwahashi, M.: Deep neural network-based bottleneck feature and denoising autoencoder-based dereverberation for distant-talking speaker identification. EURASIP J. Audio Speech Music Process. **2015**(1), 1–13 (2015)
6. Delcroix, M., Yoshioka, T., Ogawa, A., Kubo, Y., Fujimoto, M., Ito, N., Nakamura, A.: Linear prediction-based dereverberation with advanced speech enhancement and recognition technologies for the REVERB challenge. In: Proceedings of REVERB Workshop (2014)
7. Kawase, T., Niwa, K., Hioka, Y., Kobayashi, K.: Selection of optimal array noise reduction parameter set for accurate speech recognition in various noisy environments. In: Western Pacific Acoustics Conference (2015)
8. Zhao, M., Wang, D., Zhang, Z., Zhang, X.: Music removal by denoising autoencoder in speech recognition. In: APSIPA 2015 (2015)
9. Seltzer, M.L., Yu, D., Wang, Y.: An investigation of deep neural networks for noise robust speech recognition. In: IEEE International Conference on Acoustics, Speech and Signal Processing (ICASSP), pp. 7398–7402 (2013)
10. Du, J., Wang, Q., Gao, T., Xu, Y., Dai, L.R., Lee, C.H.: Robust speech recognition with speech enhanced deep neural networks. In: INTERSPEECH, pp. 616–620 (2014)
11. Han, K., He, Y., Bagchi, D., Fosler-Lussier, E., Wang, D.: Deep neural network based spectral feature mapping for robust speech recognition. In: INTERSPEECH, pp. 2484–2488 (2015)
12. Maas, A.L., Le, Q.V., O'Neil, T.M., Vinyals, O., Nguyen, P., Ng, A.Y.: Recurrent neural networks for noise reduction in robust ASR. In: INTERSPEECH, pp. 22–25 (2012)
13. Deng, L., Li, J., Huang, J.T., Yao, K., Yu, D., Seide, F., Seltzer, M., Zweig, G., He, X., Williams, J., Gong, Y.: Recent advances in deep learning for speech research at Microsoft. In: IEEE International Conference on Acoustics, Speech and Signal Processing (ICASSP), pp. 8604–8608 (2013)

14. Geiger, J.T., Weninger, F., Gemmeke, J.F., Wollmer, M., Schuller, B., Rigoll, G.: Memory-enhanced neural networks and NMF for robust ASR. IEEE/ACM Trans. Audio Speech Lang. Process. **22**(6), 1037–1046 (2014)

15. Zen, H., Sak, H.: Unidirectional long short-term memory recurrent neural network with recurrent output layer for lowlatency speech synthesis. In: Submitted to ICASSP (2015)

16. Hochreiter, S., Schmidhuber, J.: Long short-term memory. Neural Comput. **9**(8), 1735–1780 (1997)

17. Graves, A., Navdeep, J., Abdel-Rahman, M.: Hybrid speech recognition with deep bidirectional LSTM. In: IEEE Workshop on Automatic Speech Recognition and Understanding (ASRU) (2013)

18. Graves, A., Fernández, S., Schmidhuber, J.: Bidirectional LSTM networks for improved phoneme classification and recognition. In: Duch, W., Kacprzyk, J., Oja, E., Zadrożny, S. (eds.) ICANN 2005. LNCS, vol. 3697, pp. 799–804. Springer, Heidelberg (2005)

19. Fan, Y., Qian, Y., Xie, F.L., Soong, F.K.: TTS synthesis with bidirectional LSTM based recurrent neural networks. In: Interspeech, pp. 1964–1968 (2014)

20. Feng, X., Zhang, Y., Glass, J.: Speech feature denoising and dereverberation via deep autoencoders for noisy reverberant speech recognition. In: IEEE International Conference on Acoustics, Speech and Signal Processing (ICASSP), pp. 1759–1763 (2014)

21. Kominek, J., Black, A.W.: The CMU Arctic speech databases. In: Fifth ISCA Workshop on Speech Synthesis (2004)

22. Speechmatics. https://www.speechmatics.com

23. Erro, D., Sainz, I., Navas, E., Hernaez, I.: Improved HNM-based vocoder for statistical synthesizers. In: INTERSPEECH, pp. 1809–1812 (2011)

Improving the Quality of Automatic Speech Recognition in Trucks

Maxim Korenevsky[1,3], Ivan Medennikov[1,3], and Vadim Shchemelinin[2,3](✉)

[1] STC-Innovations Limited, St. Petersburg, Russia
[2] Speech Technology Center Limited, St. Petersburg, Russia
[3] ITMO University, St. Petersburg, Russia
{korenevsky,medennikov,shchemelinin}@speechpro.com
www.speechpro.com
www.ifmo.ru

Abstract. In this paper we consider the problem of the DNN-HMM acoustic models training for automatic speech recognition systems on russian language in modern commercial trucks. The speech database for training and testing the ASR system was recorded in various models of trucks, operating under different conditions. The experiments on the test part of the speech database, show that acoustic models trained on the base of specifically modeled training speech database enable to improve the recognition quality in a moving truck from 35 % to 88 % compared to the acoustic models trained on a clean speech. Also a new topology of the neural network was proposed. It allows to reduce the computational costs significantly without loss of the recognition accuracy.

Keywords: ASR · DNN · MFCC · CMVN · Multi-bottleneck · Database · Trucks

1 Introduction

It is hard to imagine modern cars without voice control of media system and onboard computer. But, until recently, trucks were not equipped by voice control functionality of the onboard computer. The implementation of the voice control systems in trucks contains a lot of difficulties for engineers. First of all, the noise level in the truck cabins is much higher than it is in the interiors of the passengers cars. Secondly, the standard trucks operations include movements over the long distances through the territories without a mobile internet connection. This means that it is impossible to use cloud services for the speech recognition.

In recent years, the error rate of automatic speech recognition systems has been substantially reduced. Latest studies [1] show that in conditions with SNR range of -6–9 dB, command recognition reliability can achieve 94.2 %.

At the same time, the current state of up-to-date hardware technologies suggests the possibility of an effective automatic speech recognition implementation under different trucks operation without the use of cloud-based ASR solutions.

© Springer International Publishing Switzerland 2016
A. Ronzhin et al. (Eds.): SPECOM 2016, LNAI 9811, pp. 362–369, 2016.
DOI: 10.1007/978-3-319-43958-7_43

Thus, the aim of our study was to develop the command recognition system that can provide the recognition quality not less than 85 % under different operation conditions for different trucks models. As a prototype of the onboard truck computer the Intel Atom^{TM}(E3827) based PC, 2×1.75 GHz was used with only 2 Gb of RAM. The speed of response of the system on the voice command does not exceed two seconds.

Additional objectives of this study were to choose the efficient microphone model and to determine its optimal location in the cabin of the truck.

2   Speech Database

For solving the task of improving the quality of automatic speech recognition in different models of cargo vehicles, the training and testing speech databases were collected. The speech database was recorded by three different models of microphones, which characteristics are shown in Table 1. Microphones were mounted in two different positions. The first "bottom" position, was located on the dashboard, behind the wheel and before the driver. The second "top" position was also located directly in front of the driver, but on the panel above the windscreen.

Table 1. Characteristics of microphones used for recording the speech database

Specifications	Microphone A	Microphone B	Microphone C
Frequency response	100–10000 Hz	50–20000 Hz	50–18000 Hz
Polar pattern	Omnidirectional	Omnidirectional	Unidirectional
Sensitivity	−53 dB/Pa	−38 dB/Pa	−40 dB/Pa
SPL	74 dB	120 dB	136 dB
Dynamic range	100 dB	102.5 dB	112 dB
SNR	75 dB	75 dB	70 dB

The speech database recording was conducted in six different models of trucks, including long-haul tractor, tractor-trailer, medium-duty trucks and a flatbed truck in manual and automatic transmission versions.

The recorded speech database includes 22 different speakers. For each speaker it contains the prepared list of 334 short phrases in Russian language. Examples of phrases include: "Повторный набор номера." ("Povtornyj nabor nomera." – translated: "Redial the number."); "Сколько километров осталось ехать?" ("Skol'ko kilometrov ostalos' ehat'?" – translated: "How many kilometers do we have to go?"); "Как называется эта песня?" ("Kak nazyvaetsja jeta pesnja?" – translated: "What is the name of this song?"). Table 2 presents the resulting signal characteristics in case of different recording conditions.

In addition to the recorded phrases uttered by the driver, the noise signal was recorded at: the listed conditions, additional possible combinations of conditions, and at the speed of 30 km/h.

Table 2. Speech database recording conditions

Engine	Speed, km/h	Driver's window	Ventilation	SNR, dB	Duration, min
×	0	Closed	Off	20–25	236
∨	0	Closed	Off	5–9	267
∨	0	Closed	Max	4–7	223
∨	0	Open	Max	3–7	52
∨	0	Semi-open	Off	5–8	73
∨	60	Closed	Off	3–6	146
∨	60	Semi-open	Off	3–5	58
∨	90	Closed	Off	2–5	104
∨	90	Semi-open	Off	2–4	82

3   Automatic Speech Recognition System

The architecture of the proposed system of automatic Russian speech recognition in the truck is traditional and it has been successfully applied in a number of Speech Technology Center products (see [2]).

The system consists of a voice activity detector (VAD), acoustic features extraction and normalization module, CD-DNN-HMM acoustic models unit and WFST-decoder. In LVCSR scenario the WFST graph is build on the base of language model, lexicon and set of context-dependent triphones states. In grammar-based recognition, the grammar is also compiled into WFST-graph format.

For successful recognition in case of a strong non-stationary noise we have trained the special acoustic model that takes into account the acoustic conditions in the truck cabin.

3.1   Preparation of the Training Database and the Acoustic Models Training

The amount of speech material recorded in real-life conditions of the truck cabin interior seemed to be insufficient to train high quality acoustic model. Therefore, the collected database was augmented by artificially simulated phonograms. For this purpose we took clean speech microphone recordings from several dictation Russian speech corpora, including the Russian part of the SpeeCon projects [3], RuSpeech corpus [4] etc. Total duration of the selected clean speech collection was about 400 h.

Impulse responses of truck cabins describe the distortion of the drivers speech picked up by a microphone. They were simulated based on the recordings collected in real conditions of the truck cabin interior. It turned out that they can be modeled by a highpass filter with a cutoff frequency at about 150 Hz, which basically simulates signal power attenuation due to the distance to the microphone. Collected clean speech recordings were passed through this filter and then mixed with the additive real noises recorded on different kinds of microphones in the real truck motion conditions. The SNR values for the signal mixing were selected randomly according to the Gaussian distribution with parameters estimated on the base of speech recordings collected in truck cabins.

In our system the DNN-based acoustic model was used. It was trained by Kaldi toolkit [5]. We tested several types of noise robust speech features like PNCC [6], MVA [7] and ESTI AFE [8]. However the best results on test corpus were obtained with the use of conventional MFCC and LMFB (Log-Mel FBanks energies) energies with mean and variance normalization (CMVN) [9]. The Kaldi training recipe was developed on the base of the recipe for Switchboard and includes the following basic steps:

- GMM-HMM models training on the base of MFCC features with delta and acceleration coefficients.
- Computation of LDA transform based on 7 consecutive frames of MFCCs with dimensionality reduction to 40, as well as MLLT transform.
- GMM-HMM models training on the base of LDA-MLLT-transformed features.
- Computation of adapting fMLLR-transforms for each utterance and re-training of the fMLLR-SAT GMM-HMM model to senones (decision tree tied triphone states). The number of senones in our system was about 1900.
- Re-alignment of training data to senones' labels based on obtained models.
- DNN-HMM model training on the base of LMFB features, extracted from 11 consecutive frames, with delta and acceleration coefficients normalized with CMVN that were concatenated into one DNN input vector. The DNN model outputs posteriors of senones for each frame of the utterance.

The first DNN models that we trained contained 6 fully-connected layers with 1024 neurons per layer.

3.2   Retraining Acoustic Models to Improve the Recognition Speed

The results of the first DNN preliminary testing showed that it provides satisfactory recognition accuracy but demonstrates rather low recognition speed and high memory load. In order to speedup recognition process it was proposed to train DNN of alternative topology which was called *multi-bottleneck* (see Fig. 1). In this DNN the number of hidden layers was increased to 10 but layers of size 1000 are interleaved with layers of size 100. This topology reduces the number of model parameters by about 5 times, which leads to significant speedup of DNN computations and the entire recognition process.

Unlike the first DNN which was initialized with a conventional RBM-based greedy layerwise pretraining [10], the multi-bottleneck DNN was initialized with the discriminative pretraining [11]. A step of pretraining consisted of appending two new hidden layers of sizes 1000 and 100 respectively and retraining network to the target senones according to the cross-entropy criterion. The training process is depicted in Fig. 1.

We found out that two epochs of SGD algorithms were sufficient for network retraining after appending each pair of hidden layers. We used a weight decay regularization and Nesterov Accelerated Gradient (NAG) [12] algorithm for training.

After the addition of hidden layers the entire network was fine-tuned with the NAG. We regularized this process by adding the term penalizing the L2-deviation of tuned network weights from the pretrained network ones.

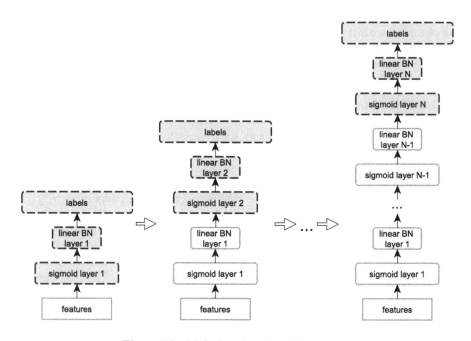

Fig. 1. The Multi-bottleneck DNN training

Despite the fact that multi-bottleneck network has a greatly reduced number of parameters, it provides the recognition accuracy rates comparable to the first DNN results (and even better in some tests). This confirms that using the proposed multi-bottleneck DNN topology leads to impressive speed-up of the recognition process and reduction in memory consumtion without substantial loss of accuracy.

4   Experiments

The quality evaluation of the automatic speech recognition system was carried out in the Direct Phrase Recognition scenario. The first experiments were carried out for the baseline system without the factory fixation of microphones in the truck cabin and with limited options of traffic conditions. Their goal was to determine the type of microphone for further speech database recording and training acoustic models.

The baseline system is based on the acoustic model trained on a large speech corpora of pure Russian language speech dictation, as described in the paper [2].

Preliminary experiments on the baseline system with these types of microphones and their installation options given in Table 3 show that the most efficient microphone location is the top shelf, and the microphone type has no significant impact on the recognition quality. According to these results microphone type A has been selected for further experiments as it is the cheapest one. However, during the experiments with factory fixed microphones, it was found that vibration in the "top" position during the process of truck motion is much higher than in the "bottom" position. Because of that the recognition quality in the "top" position appeared to be 10 % less than in the "bottom" position. According to this, for further experiments we used microphone A fixed on the dashboard, directly in front of the driver.

Table 3. Baseline system results for the different types of microphones and their positions, Acc.

Engine	Speed, km/h	Placement	Microphone A	Microphone B	Microphone C
×	0	Bottom	93.0 %	92.5 %	92.5 %
×	0	Top	97.5 %	96.5 %	96.5 %
∨	0	Bottom	89.5 %	85.5 %	90.9 %
∨	0	Top	95.3 %	96.5 %	89.5 %
∨	60	Bottom	35.0 %	35.0 %	48.0 %
∨	60	Top	36.5 %	40.5 %	40.0 %
∨	90	Bottom	38.5 %	34.5 %	55.5 %
∨	90	Top	43.8 %	46.5 %	41.5 %

The recognition speed of our system was estimated in terms of RT, which is the ratio of the time required for signal processing to the duration of the signal. The experiment results showed that the use of retrained acoustic model with the proposed multi-bottleneck topology leads to the recognition speed increase from 1.25RT to 0.84RT, and reduction of the memory required for the automatic speech recognition from 172 Mb to 119 Mb.

Comparative results of baseline and developed system under various conditions are given in Table 4.

Table 4. Results of baseline and final systems, Acc.

System	Engine off	Engine on, 0 km/h	Engine on, 60 km/h	Engine on, 90 km/h
Baseline	93.0 %	89.5 %	35.0 %	38.5 %
Final	96.0 %	92.1 %	88.9 %	86.9 %

5   Conclusions

This paper describes our investigation of speech recognition task in case of commercial trucks motion conditions. It describes the preparation process of the speech databases and acoustic models training in details. The outcomes of this work are the following conclusions:

1. The recognition system can be used successfully in various truck motion conditions despite the low SNR and other problems (for example, the vibration transmitting to the microphone).
2. Data augmentation by including recordings under emulated truck cabin conditions allows to train efficient recognition model under the noise conditions.
3. Multi-bottleneck topology can significantly speed up the recognition process and reduce memory requirements without loss of quality.

Acknowledgments. This work was financially supported by the Ministry of Education and Science of the Russian Federation, Contract 14.575.21.0033 (ID RFMEFI57514X0033).

References

1. Prudnikov, A., Korenevsky, M., Aleinik, S.: Adaptive beamforming and adaptive training of DNN acoustic models for enhanced multichannel noisy speech recognition. In: IEEE Automatic Speech Recognition and Understanding Workshop, pp. 401–408. IEEE Press, Scottsdale (2015)
2. Levin, K., Ponomareva, I., Bulusheva, A., Chernykh, G., Medennikov, I., Merkin, N., Prudnikov, A., Tomashenko, N.: Automated closed captioning for Russian live broadcasting. In: 16th Annual Conference of the International Speech Communication Association (Interspeech), Singapore, pp. 1438–1442 (2014)
3. Siemund, R., Hoge, H., Kunzmann, S., Marasek, K.: SPEECON speech data for consumer devices. In: Second International Conference on Language Resources and Evaluation, Athens, vol. II, pp. 883–886 (2000)
4. Arlazarov, V.L., Bogdanov, D.S., Krivnova, O.F., Podrabinovitch, A.Y.: Creation of Russian speech databases: design, processing, development tools. In: SPECOM 2004, Saint-Petersburg, Russia, pp. 650–656 (2004)
5. Povey, D., Ghoshal, A., Boulianne, G., Burget, L., Glembek, O., Goel, N., Hannemann, M., Motlicek, P., Qian, Y., Schwarz, P., Silovsky, J., Stemmer, G., Vesely, K.: The kaldi speech recognition toolkit. In: IEEE Workshop on Automatic Speech Recognition and Understanding, ASRU 2011 (2011)
6. Kim, C., Stern, R.: Power-normalized cepstral coefficients (PNCC) for robust speech recognition. In: IEEE International Conference on Acoustics, Speech, and Signal Processing (ICASSP 2012), pp. 4101–4104 (2012)
7. Chen, C.-P., Bilmes, J.: MVA processing of speech features. IEEE Trans. Audio, Speech Lang. Process. **15**(1), 257–270 (2009)
8. European Telecommunications Standards Institute, Speech Processing, Transmission and Quality Aspects (STQ); Distributed Speech Recognition; Advanced Front-end Feature Extraction Algorithm; Compression Algorithms, es 202 050, Rev. 1.1.5 edn. (2007)

9. Viikki, O., Laurila, K.: Cepstral domain segmental feature vector normalization for noise robust speech recognition. Speech Commun. **25**, 133–147 (1998)
10. Mohamed, A., Dahl, G.E., Hinton, G.: Acoustic modeling using deep belief networks. IEEE Trans. Audio, Speech, Lang. Process. **20**(1), 14–22 (2012)
11. Seide, F., Li, G., Chen, X., Yu, D.: Feature engineering in context-dependent deep neural networks for conversational speech transcription. In: 2011 IEEE Workshop on Automatic Speech Recognition and Understanding (ASRU), pp. 24–29. IEEE (2011)
12. Nesterov, Y.: Introductory Lectures on Convex Optimization. A Basic Course. Kluwer Academic Publishers, New York (2004)

Improving Recognition of Dysarthric Speech Using Severity Based Tempo Adaptation

Chitralekha Bhat$^{(\boxtimes)}$, Bhavik Vachhani, and Sunil Kopparapu

TCS Innovation Labs, Mumbai, India
{bhat.chitralekha,bhavik.vachhani,sunilkumar.kopparapu}@tcs.com

Abstract. Dysarthria is a motor speech disorder, characterized by slurred or slow speech resulting in low intelligibility. Automatic recognition of dysarthric speech is beneficial to enable people with dysarthria to use speech as a mode of interaction with electronic devices. In this paper we propose a mechanism to adapt the tempo of sonorant part of dysarthric speech to match that of normal speech, based on the severity of dysarthria. We show a significant improvement in recognition of tempo-adapted dysasrthic speech, using a Gaussian Mixture Model (GMM) - Hidden Markov Model (HMM) recognition system as well as a Deep neural network (DNN) - HMM based system. All evaluations were done on Universal Access Speech Corpus.

Keywords: Dysarthria · Tempo adaptation · Disordered speech · Speech recognition

1 Introduction

Dysarthria is a motor speech disorder resulting from impairment in muscles responsible for speech production. Neurological injury may result in weakness, paralysis, or a lack of co-ordination of the motor-speech system, affecting speech subsystems, giving rise to reduction in intelligibility, audibility, naturalness, and efficiency of vocal communication. For dysarthric speakers, speech is a more efficient/convenient mode of communication with electronic devices as compared to keyboard input [14]. Several techniques have been proposed to improve the performance of automatic recognition of dysarthric speech such as: (1) enhancement of dysarthric speech in the acoustic domain to match that of normal speakers. (2) Automatic speech recognizer (ASR) based speech recognition using speaker adaptation. Research methods to improve intelligibility of dysarthric speech by modifying various aspects of speech such as vowel space [6], energy, fundamental frequency, formants and tempo of dysarthric speech [15] have been proposed. In [12] the impact of manipulation of fundamental frequency on intelligibility has been studied; wherein intelligibility reduced with reduction in variation in $F0$. Several studies have been conducted to understand the ASR performance based on severity levels. Maximum likelihood and maximum *a posteriori* (MAP) adaptation has been used for speaker adaptation in [2,8,17] wherein, the authors

© Springer International Publishing Switzerland 2016
A. Ronzhin et al. (Eds.): SPECOM 2016, LNAI 9811, pp. 370–377, 2016.
DOI: 10.1007/978-3-319-43958-7_44

analyze the performance of different types of ASR systems such as speaker independent (SI), speaker adapted (SA) and speaker dependent (SD) for various severity levels. An interpolation technique along with MAP adaptation on a speaker-wise background model is used in [18] to provide improved ASR performance. In [13], the performances of speaker dependent and speaker adaptive models have been compared, where the speaker adaptive models performed better across various levels of severity of dysarthria.

Automatic recognition of dysarthric speech is poorer as compared to that of normal speech, owing to the inter-speaker and intra-speaker inconsistencies in the acoustic space as well as the sparseness of data. Thus far, three popular dysarthric speech databases, namely Universal Access (UA) speech corpus [7], Nemours [9] and TORGO [16] exist for American English. No known dysarthric speech database is available for Indian languages. The objective of our work is to build an ASR for dysarthric speakers for resource deficient Indian languages, using zero or small amount of dysarthric data for training the acoustic models of an automatic speech recognizer (ASR).

In this paper, we propose a mechanism to improve the recognition of dysarthric speech using tempo adaptation of sonorants (vowels, glides, liquids and nasals) in dysarthric speech, by using acoustic models primarily built from healthy control speakers. We show that severity of dysarthria has a bearing on the duration of sonorants and thereby degree of adaptation can be selected based on severity of dysarthria. Severity classification itself is beyond the scope of this work, and can be done using techniques known in literature [5]. We also compare the performance of speaker independent (SI) and speaker adapted (SA) recognition systems when a small amount of dysarthric data is available and is used for speaker adaptation. The experimental results show that speaker-adapted dysarthric speech recognition further improved with tempo adaptation, indicating that tempo adaptation supplements the speaker-adapted dysarthric speech recognition. This improvement was seen across both Gaussian Mixture Model (GMM) - Hidden Markov Model (HMM) and Deep neural network (DNN) - HMM based recognition system.

The rest of the paper is organized as follows. Section 2 describes the tempo adaptation and its impact on dysarthric speech recognition, Sect. 3 discusses the various experimental setups and a description of the data used, in Sect. 4 we discuss the experimental results and we conclude in Sect. 5.

2 Severity Based Tempo Adaptation

Impairment of the motor nervous system impacts the articulator movements adversely, causing the articulators to move slowly. This manifests as longer durations for sonorants in dysarthric speech as compared to normal speech and tempo adaptation of the sonorants of dysarthric speech leads to improvement in the performance of ASRs [15]. Tempo adaptation involves temporal reduction of the sonorant regions of an utterance using a pre-determined adaptation parameter α.

Tempo adaptation needs to be in a manner such that it does not impact the pitch of the sonorant regions. Hence, a phase vocoder based on short-time Fourier transform (STFT) is used [10]. Magnitude spectrum and phase of the STFT are either interpolated or decimated based on the adaptation parameter, where the magnitude spectrum is directly used from the input magnitude spectrum and phase values are chosen to ensure continuity. This ensures that the pitch of the time-warped sonorant region is intact. For the frequency band at frequency F and frames i and $j > i$ in the modified spectrogram, the phase θ is predicted as

$$\theta'^F_j = \theta^F_j + 2\pi F \cdot (i - j).$$

The modified spectrogram is then converted into a time-domain signal using inverse Fourier transform, wherein the tempo of the sonorant regions are adapted with the pitch unchanged.

2.1   Learning the Adaptation Parameter

We propose a scheme to automatically adapt the tempo of dysarthric speech based on severity of dysarthria. The adaptation parameter α, has been determined empirically using healthy control speech data and dysarthric speech of various severity levels. Both sets of data, healthy control and dysarthric comprise the same words. Initially, tempo adaptation is done for the sonorants at word level, wherein the tempo of the dysarthric speech for the sonorant region in each word was adapted to match the tempo of the sonorant region in the exact same word as spoken by healthy control speakers. Consider a word W whose average sonorant duration for healthy control speakers, is d_{HC} and that for a dysarthric utterance is d_{dys}. The tempo adaptation parameter for the word W is computed as

$$\alpha_{initial} = \frac{d_{HC}}{d_{dys}}.$$

The sonorant region of the dysarthric utterance is adapted using $\alpha_{initial}$ for each dysarthric utterance. It was observed that the severity of the speakers had a clear bearing on the $\alpha_{initial}$ values, as shown in Fig. 1, wherein the letter M and F in speaker code indicate a dysarthric speakers' gender. Speaker-wise relative improvement in recognition of dysarthric speech for both GMM and DNN systems are as shown in Fig. 2. Also, for some speakers with high intelligibility, the word error rate (WER) increased using tempo adaptation. This factor was considered for setting the α parameter. It was also observed that the standard deviation across words was low for a particular severity class, with the highest standard deviation (0.82) being for low intelligibility.

Based on the above empirical evidence, the α parameters selected for different severity levels are as shown in Table 1. Figure 3 shows the proposed system, wherein tempo adaptation for a particular speaker is done based on the severity level. Sonorant region in a speech utterance was identified using a three-class classification technique, wherein an utterance was classified into silence, non-sonorant and sonorant regions using HTK 3.4 toolkit [19]. For this task, acoustic models corresponding to the three classes were trained using TIMIT [4] database.

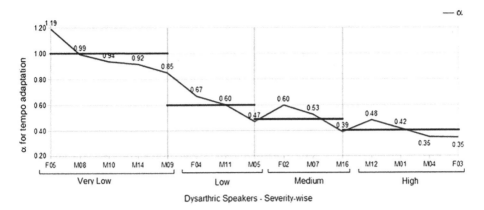

Fig. 1. Variation in initial tempo adaptation parameter $\alpha_{initial}$ across various severity levels of dysarthria

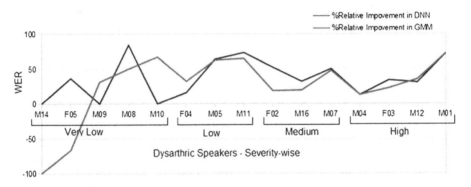

Fig. 2. Relative improvement in WER across various severity levels of dysarthria for GMM and DNN using $\alpha_{initial}$

Table 1. Tempo adaptation parameter α based on severity computed empirically.

Severity	Very low	Low	Mid	High
α	1	0.6	0.5	0.4

3 Experimental Setup

3.1 Data

Data from Universal Access (UA) speech corpus [7] was used for both training and testing of the two ASR systems discussed in this section. UA speech corpus comprises data from 13 healthy control (HC) speakers and 15 dysarthric (DYS) speakers with cerebral palsy. The recording material consisted of 455 distinct words with 10 digits, 26 international radio alphabets, 19 computer commands, 100 common words and 300 uncommon words that were distributed

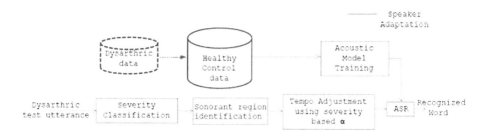

Fig. 3. Proposed system for tempo adapted dysarthric speech recognition

into three blocks. Three blocks of data were collected for each speaker such that in each block speaker recorded the digits, radio alphabets, computer commands, common words and 100 of the uncommon words. Thus each speaker recorded 765 isolated words. Speech intelligibility ratings for each dysarthric speaker, as assessed by five naive listeners is also included in the corpus. Speakers were divided into four different categories based on the intelligibility, namely high, mid, low and very low. We use this information to analyse the performance of our recognition systems at dysarthria severity level.

3.2 Speech Recognition

We use Kaldi toolkit [11] for both GMM-HMM based and DNN-HMM based dysarthric speech recognition. A 3-state HMM with a monophone or a triphone context model is used. GMM-HMM system was trained using a maximum likelihood estimation (MLE) training approach along with 100 senones and 8 Gaussian mixtures. Cepstral mean and variance normalization (CMVN) was applied on each of the above sets of features. Dimensionality reduction was done using Linear Discriminant Analysis (LDA), wherein LDA builds HMM states using feature vectors with a reduced feature space. We use a context of 6 frames (3 left and 3 right) to compute LDA. The feature vector size post LDA is set to 40.

The input layer of DNN has 360 (40×9 $frames$) dimensions using a left and right context of 4 frames. The output layer has a dimension of 96 (number of senones available in the data). 2 hidden layers with 512 nodes in each layer were used. Performance of each of the recognition systems is reported in terms of word error rate (WER).

We use Maximum Likelihood Linear Transform (MLLT) for speaker normalization. MLLT derives a unique transformation for each speaker using the reduced feature space from the LDA. An inter-speaker feature space normalization technique known as feature space maximum likelihood linear regression (fMLLR) [3] is performed for each speaker. Speaker adaptive training (SAT) [1] is applied at the time of training the acoustic models and aims at eliminating the inter-speaker variation. fMLLR based SAT was applied to create speaker adapted (SA) acoustic models; further, fMLLR was applied on the features of

Table 2. Training and testing corpus

System	Training	Testing	Purpose
SI-01	HC-CC	DYS-CC (B1&B3)	$\alpha_{initial}$ and α learning
SI-02	HC-CC	DYS-CC (B2)	α validation
SA-01	HC-CC, DYS-CC (B1&B3)	DYS-CC (B2)	α + Speaker adaptation
SA-02	HC-CC, HC-digits, DYS-CC (B1&B3)	DYS-digits (B2)	α validation for unseen data

the input utterances at the time of decoding. SAT using fMLLR remain common to both GMM-HMM and DNN-HMM based systems.

A specific combination of healthy control (HC) and dysarthric data (DYS) from each of the three blocks (B1, B2 and B3) of computer command (CC) words and digits, were used for various experiments as described in Table 2.

The above experimental setup is used for both GMM-HMM and DNN-HMM recognizers. System SA-02 specifically shows the performance obtained for the recognition of unseen dysarthric data (does not exist in the training set). It is expected that this would be the typical scenario, considering the challenges in collecting dysarthric data. The objective of our work is to be able to recognize dysarthric speech when no or small amount of dysarthric data is available for training. To the best of our knowledge, no other work has reported speech recognition for this specific combination of testing and training data.

4 Evaluation Results and Discussion

The tempo adaptation parameter α was learned for each severity level, as described in Sect. 2. Experiments were conducted to understand the applicability of α under various scenarios such as SI, SA and SA with unseen data (Table 3). The results indicate that the recognition accuracy improved or the WER reduced when the tempo was adapted. Acoustic models were trained using both monophone and triphone contexts. It was observed that across all experimental setups,

Table 3. Relative improvement in WER using tempo-adaptation.

System	GMM-HMM %WER	GMM-HMM-TA %WER	%relative improvement	DNN-HMM %WER	DNN-HMM-TA %WER	%relative improvement
SI-01	77.21	40.84	47.11	75.88	39.12	48.44
SI-02	79.36	48.05	39.45	73.42	44.47	39.43
SA-01	49.59	34.12	31.2	34.67	27.57	20.48
SA-02	72.96	52.22	28.42	52.01	42.83	17.65

Table 4. Impact of tempo adaptation on WER for SA-01 based on severity.

Severity	GMM-HMM %WER	GMM-HMM-TA %WER	%relative improve-ment	DNN-HMM %WER	DNN-HMM-TA %WER	%relative improve-ment
Low	39.68	22.83	42.46	26.32	14.18	46.12
Medium	60.39	45.87	24.04	42.69	31.43	26.38
High	108.86	69.15	36.48	86.52	68.53	20.79

triphone models showed higher relative improvement in recognition performance after tempo adaptation. This indicates that the tempo adaptation improves the triphone acoustic model of a phone as well.

Further, it can be seen from Table 4, that the recognition performance of the best performing system SA-01, improved across all severity levels for both GMM-based and DNN-based system with tempo adaptation (TA). It was observed that the reduction in WER was largely due to the decrease in the number of insertions as compared to substitutions.

5   Conclusion

In this paper, we propose a mechanism to improve the speech recognition of dysarthric speech using tempo adaptation of sonorants in dysarthric speech. We show that severity of dysarthria has a bearing on the duration of sonorants and thereby degree of adaptation can be selected based on severity of dysarthria. This mechanism is especially beneficial when no or less amount of dysarthric data is available in a specific language (e.g. Indian Languages), for training the acoustic models of an ASR. We compare the performance of speaker indepen-dent (SI) and speaker adapted (SA) recognition systems when a small amount of dysarthric data is available and is used for speaker adaptation. The results show that speaker-adapted dysarthric speech recognition further improved with tempo adaptation, indicating that tempo adaptation supplements the speaker-adapted dysarthric speech recognition. This improvement was seen across both Gaussian Mixture Model (GMM) - Hidden Markov Model (HMM) and Deep neural network (DNN) - HMM based recognition system. If we consider the sys-tem wherein only healthy controls are used for training the acoustic models with no tempo-adaptation as baseline, the proposed speaker-independent and speaker-adapted systems provide an improvement of 47.11 % and 55.81 % respectively, for GMM-HMM-TA and 48.44 % and 63.67 % for DNN-HMM-TA respectively. Severity based tempo adaptation using triphone based acostic models showed higher relative improvements than monophone acoustic models across all sys-tems mentioned in Sect. 3. This indicates that the tempo adaptation improves the acoustic phone model in the triphone context as well.

References

1. Anastasakos, T., Mcdonough, J., Schwartz, R., Makhoul, J.: A compact model for speaker-adaptive training. In: Proceedings of ICSLP, pp. 1137–1140 (1996)

2. Christensen, H., Cunningham, S., Fox, C., Green, P., Hain, T.: A comparative study of adaptive, automatic recognition of disordered speech. In: Proceedings of INTERSPEECH 2012, pp. 1776–1779 (2012)
3. Gales, M.: Maximum likelihood linear transformations for HMM-based speech recognition. Comput. Speech Lang. **12**(2), 75–98 (1998)
4. Garofolo, J.S.: Getting started with the darpa TIMIT cd-rom: An acoustic phonetic continuous speech database. NIST (1988)
5. Kadi, K., Selouani, S., Boudraa, B., Boudraa, M.: Discriminative prosodic features to assess the dysarthria severity levels. In: Proceedings of the World Congress on Engineering, vol. 3 (2013)
6. Kain, A.B., Hosom, J.P., Niu, X., van Santen, J.P., Fried-Oken, M., Staehely, J.: Improving the intelligibility of dysarthric speech. Speech Commun. **49**(9), 743–759 (2007)
7. Kim, H., Hasegawa-Johnson, M., Perlman, A., Gunderson, J., Huang, T.S., Watkin, K., Frame, S.: Dysarthric speech database for universal access research. In: Proceedings of INTERSPEECH 2008, pp. 1741–1744 (2008)
8. Kim, M.J., Yoo, J., Kim, H.: Dysarthric speech recognition using dysarthria-severity-dependent and speaker-adaptive models. In: Proceedings of INTER-SPEECH 2013, pp. 3622–3626 (2013)
9. Menendez-Pidal, X., Polikoff, J.B., Peters, S.M., Leonzio, J.E., Bunnell, H.T.: The nemours database of dysarthric speech. In: Proceedings of ICSLP, vol. 3, pp. 1962–1965 (1996)
10. Portnoff, M.: Implementation of the digital phase vocoder using the fast fourier transform. IEEE Trans. Acoust. Speech Signal Process. **24**(3), 243–248 (1976)
11. Povey, D., Ghoshal, A., Boulianne, G., Burget, L., Glembek, O., Goel, N., Hannemann, M., Motlicek, P., Qian, Y., Schwarz, P., et al.: The Kaldi speech recognition toolkit. In: IEEE 2011 Workshop on Automatic Speech Recognition and Understanding, No. EPFL-CONF-192584. IEEE Signal Processing Society (2011)
12. Redd, E.E.: The effect of an artificially flattened fundamental frequency contour on intelligibility in speakers with dysarthria. All Theses and Dissertations. Paper 3229 (2012). http://scholarsarchive.byu.edu/etd/3229
13. Rudzicz, F.: Comparing speaker-dependent and speaker-adaptive acoustic models for recognizing dysarthric speech. In: Proceedings of the 9th International ACM SIGACCESS Conference on Computers and Accessibility, p. 256. ACM (2007)
14. Rudzicz, F.: Learning mixed acoustic/articulatory models for disabled speech. In: Proceedings of NIPS, pp. 70–78 (2010)
15. Rudzicz, F.: Adjusting dysarthric speech signals to be more intelligible. Comput. Speech Lang. **27**(6), 1163–1177 (2013)
16. Rudzicz, F., Namasivayam, A.K., Wolff, T.: The TORGO database of acoustic and articulatory speech from speakers with dysarthria. Lang. Resour. Eval. **46**(4), 523–541 (2011)
17. Sehgal, S., Cunningham, S.: Model adaptation and adaptive training for the recognition of dysarthric speech. In: Proceedings of 6th Workshop on Speech and Language Processing for Assistive Technologies (SLPAT), p. 65 (2015)
18. Sharma, H.V., Hasegawa-Johnson, M.: Acoustic model adaptation using in-domain background models for dysarthric speech recognition. Comput. Speech Lang. **27**(6), 1147–1162 (2013)
19. Young, S.J., Kershaw, D., Odell, J., Ollason, D., Valtchev, V., Woodland, P.: The HTK Book Version 3.4. Cambridge University Press, Cambridge (2006)

Improving Robustness of Speaker Verification by Fusion of Prompted Text-Dependent and Text-Independent Operation Modalities

Iosif Mporas[✉], Saeid Safavi, and Reza Sotudeh

School of Engineering and Technology, University of Hertfordshire, College Lane Campus, Hatfield, Hertfordshire AL10 8PE, UK
{i.mporas,s.safavi,r.sotudeh}@herts.ac.uk

Abstract. In this paper we present a fusion methodology for combining prompted text-dependent and text-independent speaker verification operation modalities. The fusion is performed in score level extracted from GMM-UBM single mode speaker verification engines using several machine learning algorithms for classification. In order to improve the performance we apply clustering of the score-based data before the classification stage. The experimental results indicated that the fusion of the two operation modes improves the speaker verification performance both in terms of sensitivity and specificity by approximately 2 % and 1.5 % respectively.

Keywords: Speaker verification · Fusion · Machine learning

1 Introduction

Biometric technology has widely been used over the last decade to several applications, such as access control to physical places, secure login to computer systems and mobile devices, online banking and ATMs, personalized human-machine interfaces etc. One of the most widely used modalities in this area is voice-based biometrics and particularly speaker verification, due to the convenience that offers to the user as well as due to the fact that the input signal can be captured by a conventional microphone, nowadays available in most electronic devices, and does not need any specialized sensor or other hardware equipment to capture the input biometric signal.

In speaker verification the user provides a speech input, usually after a screened prompted message, and the system decides whether the user is an authorized one or not, i.e. accepts or rejects the claimed by the user identity. Based on the prompted message, speaker verification can roughly be divided into two categories, namely the text-dependent and the text-independent. In text-dependent speaker verification a text message, selected from a predefined and close-set of utterances, is prompted to the user in order for him/her to pronounce it [1–3]. In the case of text-independent speaker verification [4–7] a text generator is used to prompt to the user a text message to be pronounced, which does not belong to an apriori known to the user close-set of utterances. Thus, in the text-independent mode of operation the prompted message is random

© Springer International Publishing Switzerland 2016
A. Ronzhin et al. (Eds.): SPECOM 2016, LNAI 9811, pp. 378–385, 2016.
DOI: 10.1007/978-3-319-43958-7_45

and as a result cannot easily be reproduced by audio replay attacks from impostors. On the other hand, the use of new uttered message to the speaker verification system, which does not appear (as a whole or even partially) in the training data results in the reduction of the verification performance, thus result to a trade-off between performance and robustness against spoofing.

The concurrent technology in speaker verification is based on short-time speech signal analysis followed by machine learning based modeling. In detail, the most commonly used features for speaker recognition are the Mel frequency cepstral coefficients (MFCCs) [8, 9]. Other speech parameterization techniques, as wavelets have also successfully been applied [7]. As considers speaker modeling, the state of the art technology is dominated by the probabilistic Gaussian mixture models (GMMs) [10]. GMM technology has proved to perform well using universal background models (UBMs) trained from a large number of background speakers and maximum a-posteriori (MAP) adaptation or means-only adaptation of the UBM to speaker specific data. Except probabilistic modeling discriminative approaches, such as support vector machines (SVMs) have also successfully been used in the task of speaker verification [11]. SVMs have also been used in combination with GMMs by concatenating the means of the Gaussian components of the GMMs to super-vectors and apply discriminative classification on them [12]. Recently, subspace methods have been proposed for the speaker verification task such as the i-vectors method [13], which are based on joint factor analysis. Although in specific setups subspace methods have proved to outperform probabilistic models, the GMM-UBM approach in general offers more stable results, especially when not enough training and development data are available. For this reason, in the present evaluation we relied in this technology.

In this work, we present a methodology for fusing the speaker verification scores produced by two different modes of operation, namely the text-dependent and the text-independent. The exploitation of the advantages of each of the two modes of operation is achieved using a machine learning based scheme for fusion, in order to get a final speaker verification decision.

The rest of the article is organized as follows. In Sect. 2 the proposed fusion methodology for combining prompted text-dependent and text-independent speaker verification modes is presented. In Sect. 3 the experimental setup that was followed is described and in Sect. 4 the experimental results are presented. Finally, in Sect. 5 the conclusions of this work are given.

2   Fusion of Speaker Verification Operation Modes

In real-life voice based biometrics applications the user is asked to provide voice samples in order the system to verify whether the user is an authorized one or not. Depending on the mode of operation, the speaker verification performance as well as the vulnerability to spoofing attacks are affected. Specifically, when using text-dependent prompts the recognition accuracy is high, while when using text-independent prompts the performance significantly drops. On the other hand, prompted text-dependent operation is easy to be spoofed, for example using audio replay attacks or synthetic speech. In contrast to this, text-independent speaker recognition mode of operation offers robustness against spoofing attacks, since due to the absence of apriori knowledge of the prompted utterance message audio replays cannot be applied, while in synthetic speech based attacks the use of phonetically rich prompted messages (which probably will not appear in the training corpus) can significantly reduce the quality of the output of a text-to-speech engine. Except this, algorithms based on phase detection can be used to identify synthetic speech.

The fusion of the prompted text-dependent (TD) and text-independent (TI) modes of operation is performed on score level. In detail, the user is asked to provide voice response to two prompted messages (usually shown on a screen), which consist of TD and TI utterance messages respectively. Each of these messages is processed by a mode specific speaker verification engine and the TD and TI verification scores are estimated. The two mode-dependent scores are concatenated to constitute a 2-dimentional feature vector which is used as input to a machine learning classification algorithm, in order to decide whether the user is an authorized or an impostor. Since the score values typically present some variation, in order to support the classification stage, we apply in advance clustering in order to separate the 2-dimentional score data to areas with less variation. After clustering the data we apply a cluster-specific classification model and get the verification decision. The block diagram of the proposed methodology is illustrated in Fig. 1.

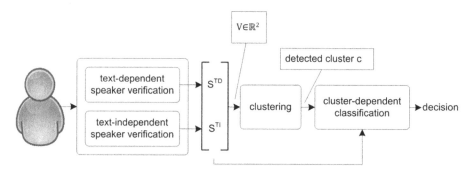

Fig. 1. Block diagram of the proposed methodology for fusion of prompted text-dependent and text-independent modes of speaker verification operation

As can be seen in Fig. 1, the user is providing to the system a prompted text-dependent and a prompted text-independent voice input. These inputs are processed by mode-specific speaker verification engines and one verification score is estimated for each mode, i.e. S^{TD} for text-dependent and S^{TI} for text-independent mode of operation. The two scores are concatenated to a score vector $V \in \mathbb{R}^2$. During the training phase a cluster algorithm separates the score vectors to C clusters. In the test phase each score vector is assigned to a cluster c, with $1 \leq c \leq C$. Based on the detected cluster for each pair of TD and TI inputs a cluster-specific classification model f will be activated and assign an acceptance or rejection decision label to the input score vector V, i.e.:

$$d = f_c(V), \tag{1}$$

where f_c denotes the classification model that is dedicated to classify the inputs V which belong to cluster c.

The number of clusters is manually defined based on evaluation of performance on a bootstrap training data set. The verification in each operation mode-specific speaker verification engine is made on the basis of thresholded scores, while the speaker verification decision of the fusion methodology is made on the basis of classification results.

3 Experimental Setup

The experimental setup for the evaluation of the fusion methodology described in Sect. 2, is presented here. Specifically, we describe the dataset used in the evaluation, the setup of the single-mode speaker verification engines and the setup of the fusion stage.

3.1 Speech Corpus

In this evaluation we relied on the RSR2015 database [3]. RSR2015 consists of recordings from 300 speakers (157 male, 143 female). For each speaker, there are 3 enrolment sessions of 73 utterances each and 6 verification sessions of 73 utterances each. In total there are 657 utterances distributed in 9 sessions per each speaker. The sampling frequency of the speech recordings is 16 kHz and the speech samples are stored with analysis equal to 16 bits.

Except RSR2015, we used TIMIT [14] for training a universal background model. TIMIT consists of recordings of 630 speakers, sampled at 16 kHz with resolution analysis equal to 16 bits per sample.

3.2 Single-Mode Speaker Verification Engines

Each of the two single-mode speaker verification engines, i.e. the text-dependent and the text-independent ones, were based on the well known GMM-UBM technique [10]. Specifically, each voice input was initially pre-processed and parameterized. During pre-processing an energy-based speech activity detector was applied to retain the speech only parts. The speech input was frame blocked using a time shifting Hamming window of 20 ms length with 10 ms overlap between successive frames. For each frame the first 19 Mel frequency cepstral coefficients (MFCCs) were estimated, which were further expanded to their first and second derivatives, thus resulting to a feature vector of length equal 57. In order to reduce the effect of handset mismatch and make the feature more robust RASTA [15] and CMVN processing were applied to the MFCC features.

For both TD and TI speaker models we used the GMM-UBM [10] approach. Specifically the universal background model (UBM) was built by a mixture of 128 Gaussian distributions and was trained using all utterances from 630 speakers from TIMIT. For each of the speakers of the RSR2015 database we applied MAP adaptation (means only adaptation) on the UBM model, using the speaker-specific enrollment data and the speech utterances that corresponded to the text-dependent and the text-independent sessions for the speaker TD and TI models respectively.

3.3   Setup of the Fusion of Speaker Verification Modes

The verification scores produced by the text-dependent and the text-independent speaker verification engines described above were concatenated to 2-dimensional feature vectors as described in Sect. 2. These data were clustered to groups using the k-means algorithm [16]. The number of the clusters produced by the k-means algorithm was manually defined. Based on the clustering results we trained one classification model for each cluster of data.

As considers the classification stage, each pair of TD and TI scores was processed by a cluster-specific classification model, we relied on a number of well known and widely used in the bibliography machine learning algorithms for classification. Specifically, we used the following algorithms: (i) multilayer perceptron neural networks (MLP), (ii) C4.5 decision trees (C4.5), (iii) support vector machines (SVM) using the sequential minimal optimization implementation, (iv) Bayesian networks (BN), (v) classification and regression trees (CART) and (vi) reduced error pruning tree (REP). For the implementation of these machine learning algorithms for classification we relied on the WEKA toolkit [16].

4   Experimental Results

The proposed fusion methodology for speaker verification presented in Sect. 2 was evaluated based on the experimental setup described in Sect. 3. For all evaluations we relied on a 10-fold cross validation protocol. The performance of the proposed methodology was evaluated in terms of sensitivity (i.e. the percentage of the correctly classified instances of the target speakers) and specificity (i.e. the percentage of the correctly classified instances of the impostor speakers).

Table 1. Speaker verification, in terms of percentages of sensitivity and specificity, for different operation mode fusion methods

Method	Sensitivity	Specificity
TD (single mode)	84.65	97.46
TI (single mode)	84.70	91.83
MLP	71.14	99.82
C4.5	72.89	99.79
SVM	71.12	99.82
Bayesian Network	76.33	99.66
CART	72.13	99.81
REP	73.10	99.78

As a first step we evaluated the performance of the fusion scheme without applying clustering. The experimental results for the single-mode TD and TI speaker verification engines as well as their fusion using several classification algorithms is tabulated in Table 1.

As can be seen in Table 1, the single mode speaker verification methods outperform the evaluated fusion methodologies in terms of sensitivity. However, in terms of specificity it seems that fusion of the text-dependent and text-independent modes offers an improvement of more than 2 %. Specifically, the best performing fusion algorithm was the Bayesian network classifier which offered sensitivity equal to 76.33 %, followed by the decision trees (C4.5, CART and REP). In terms of sensitivity, the MLP and SVM discriminative algorithms did not offered high accuracy. All evaluated fusion algorithms proved to offer specificity of more than 99.50 %, while the text-dependent and text-independent single mode methods achieved 97.46 % and 91.83 % respectively.

In a second step we estimated the performance of the fusion methodology using different numbers of clusters. The experimental results are tabulated in Table 2. For direct comparison we replicate the results for the case where no clustering of the data was applied before the classification stage.

Table 2. Speaker verification, in terms of percentages of sensitivity (sens) and specificity (spec), for different operation mode fusion methods and different number of clusters

Method	$c = 1$		$c = 5$		$c = 10$		$c = 20$	
	sens	spec	sens	spec	sens	spec	sens	spec
TD (single mode)	84.65	97.46	–	–	–	–	–	–
TI (single mode)	84.70	91.83	–	–	–	–	–	–
MLP	71.14	99.82	73.30	99.79	73.30	99.78	72.11	99.81
C4.5	72.89	99.79	72.97	99.79	71.92	99.81	71.53	99.82
SVM	71.12	99.82	76.07	99.70	58.89	99.97	68.43	99.88
Bayesian Network	76.33	99.66	78.70	99.57	86.55	98.88	86.47	98.92
CART	72.13	99.81	73.18	99.79	72.37	99.80	72.47	99.81
REP	73.10	99.78	73.33	99.77	72.52	99.78	72.34	99.79

As can be seen in Table 2, the application of fusion of the two modalities on clustered data results to significant improvement of speaker verification both in terms of sensitivity and specificity. In detail, the Bayesian network achieved 86.55 % sensitivity for 10 clusters (i.e. for $c = 10$), which results to an improvement of 2 % comparing to the text-dependent single modality. For the same setup Bayesian network achieved specificity equal to 98.88 %, which corresponds to an absolute improvement of approximately 1.5 % comparing to the TD single mode case. The application of cluster-based fusion of text-dependent and text-independent modes of speaker verification improved the sensitivity accuracy of all evaluated algorithms comparing to the case of fusion without clustering, i.e. for $c = 1$. This is owed to the fact that in the case of cluster-based fusion the classification algorithms are trained on data with less varying characteristics thus can train their free parameters to be dedicated to each specific data subset's characteristics.

5   Conclusions

The score level fusion of prompted text-dependent and text-independent speaker verification modalities is a methodology that can directly be applied to real-world applications related to voice-based biometrics. The experimental evaluation using clustering of the single mode score data followed by application of classification for fusion showed an absolute improvement of more approximately 2 % in terms of sensitivity and an absolute improvement of 1.5 % in terms of specificity. The best performing algorithm for fusing the two modes of speaker verification operation was found to be the Bayesian network classifier. The improvement is owed to the exploitation of the underlying and complementary information between the distributions of the scores of the two modes of operation. We deem the fuse of the two modalities can lead to real-world voice biometrics based applications which will be more accurate and thus more robust to spoofing attacks.

Acknowledgement. This work was partially supported by the H2020 OCTAVE Project entitled "Objective Control for TAlker VErification" funded by the EC with Grand Agreement number 647850. The authors would like to thank Dr Md Sahidullah, Dr Nicholas Evans and Dr Tomi Kinnunen for their support in this work.

References

1. Aronowitz, H., Hoory, R., Pelecanos, J., Nahamoo, D.: New developments in voice biometrics for user authentication. In: Proceedings of the Interspeech (2011)
2. Hébert, M., Sondhi, M., Huang, Y.: Text-Dependent Speaker Recognition. Book Section. In: Springer Handbook of Speech Processing, pp. 743–762 (2008)
3. Larcher, A., Kong, A.L., Bin, M., Haizhou, L.: Text-dependent speaker verification: Classifiers, databases and RSR2015. Speech Commun. **60**, 56–77 (2014)
4. Reynolds, D.A., Quatieri, T.F., Dunn, R.B.: Speaker verification using adapted gaussian mixture models. Digit. Signal Proc. **10**(1–3), 19–41 (2000)
5. Safavi, S., Hanani, A., Russell, M., Jancovic, P., Carey, M.J.: Contrasting the effects of different frequency bands on speaker and accent identification. IEEE Signal Proc. Lett. **19**(12), 829–832 (2012)
6. Safavi, S., Najafian, M., Hanani, A., Russell, M.J., Jancovic, P., Carey, M.J.: Speaker Recognition for Children's Speech. In: Interspeech, pp. 1836–1839 (2012)
7. Ganchev, T., Siafarikas, M., Mporas, I., Stoyanova, T.: Wavelet basis selection for enhanced speech parameterization in speaker verification. Int. J. Speech Technol. **17**(1), 27–36 (2014)
8. Davis, S., Mermelstein, P.: Comparison of parametric representations for monosyllabic word recognition in continuously spoken sentences. IEEE Trans. Acoust. Speech Signal Proc. **28**(4), 357–366 (1980)
9. Furui, S.: Cepstral analysis technique for automatic speaker verification. IEEE Trans. Acoust. Speech Signal Proc. **29**(2), 254–272 (1981)
10. Reynolds, D.A., Rose, R.C.: Robust text-independent speaker identification using Gaussian mixture speaker models. IEEE Trans. Speech Audio Proc. **3**(1), 72–83 (1995)

11. Campbell, W.M., Campbell, J.P., Reynolds, D.A., Jones, D.A., Leek, T.R.: Phonetic speaker recognition with support vector machines. In: Neural Information Processing Systems 16, Neural Information Processing Systems, NIPS 2003, 8–13 December 2003, Vancouver and Whistler, British Columbia, Canada (2003)
12. Campbell, W.M., Sturim, D.E., Reynolds, D.A.: Support vector machines using GMM supervectors for speaker verification. IEEE Signal Proc. Lett. **13**(5), 308–311 (2006)
13. Kenny, P., Boulianne, G., Ouellet, P., Dumouchel, P.: Joint factor analysis versus eigenchannels in speaker recognition. IEEE Trans. Audio Speech Lang. Proc. **15**(4), 1435–1447 (2007)
14. Campbell, J.P., Reynolds, D.A.: Corpora for the evaluation of speaker recognition systems. In: Proceedings of ICASSP 1999, vol. 2, pp. 829–832 (1999)
15. Hermansky, H., Morgan, N.: RASTA processing of speech. IEEE Trans. Speech Audio Proc. **2**(4), 578–589 (1994)
16. Witten, I.H., Frank, E., Hall, M.A.: Data Mining, Practical machine learning tools and techniques, 3rd edn. Morgan Kaufmann, San Francisco (2011)

Improvements to Prosodic Variation in Long Short-Term Memory Based Intonation Models Using Random Forest

Bálint Pál Tóth[✉], Balázs Szórádi, and Géza Németh

Department of Telecommunications and Media Informatics, Budapest University of Technology
and Economics, Budapest, Hungary
{toth.b,nemeth}@tmit.bme.hu, szoradib@gmail.com

Abstract. Statistical parametric speech synthesis has overcome unit selection methods in many aspects, including flexibility and variability. However, the intonation of these systems is quite monotonic, especially in case of longer sentences. Due to statistical methods the variation of fundamental frequency (F0) trajectories decreases. In this research a random forest (RF) based classifier was trained with radio conversations based on the perceived variation by a human annotator. This classifier was used to extend the labels of a phonetically balanced, studio quality speech corpus. With the extended labels a Long Short-Term Memory (LSTM) network was trained to model fundamental frequency (F0). Objective and subjective evaluations were carried out. The results show that the variation of the generated F0 trajectories can be fine-tuned with an additional input of the LSTM network.

Keywords: Text-To-Speech · TTS · Deep learning · Deep neural networks · LSTM · Random forest · Fundamental frequency · Prosodic variability

1 Introduction

In statistical parametric speech synthesis pitch, durations and spectral components are modeled by advanced machine learning methods. The first statistical method that gained in popularity was Hidden Markov Model-based Text-To-Speech synthesis (HMM-TTS) [1]. HMM-TTS has proven to surpass unit selection systems in many aspects, including flexibility and variability (e.g. variable pitch and speaking rate, speaker adaptation, speaker interpolation) and the storage and computational costs can be significantly reduced. Thanks to the scientific results, to the great progress in computation power of GPU (Graphical Processing Unit) based workstations and to the dramatically increased amount of training data the predictive capabilities of neural networks with multiple hidden layers have significantly improved [2]. This new paradigm is called deep learning and the multilayer neural networks, including numerous variants (e.g. convolutional nets, recurrent nets, autoencoders), are often referred to as Deep Neural Networks (DNNs). The recent results of deep learning and statistical parametric speech synthesis were necessary to be able to achieve high quality synthetic speech with DNN-based TTS systems. Generally, in deep learning feedforward multilayer neural networks [3] and Long Short-Term Memory (LSTM) architectures [4] are used to model speech

© Springer International Publishing Switzerland 2016
A. Ronzhin et al. (Eds.): SPECOM 2016, LNAI 9811, pp. 386–394, 2016.
DOI: 10.1007/978-3-319-43958-7_46

parameters. The results show that the DNN-TTS can produce even better synthesized voice quality than the vanilla HMM-TTS. Although state-of-the-art HMM and DNN Text-To-Speech synthesizers have high quality, natural sounding voice, the prosody variation of these systems in case of extended passages becomes monotonous due to the averaging property of statistical models.

Using a large runtime speech corpus, it is possible to inherit and spread the prosody across similar sentences and thus increase the variation [5]. This technique requires large runtime storage capacity and a precisely designed and recorded high quality speech corpus. The prosody variation can be measured automatically, according to [6]. In this research eight repetitions of 200 Mandarin utterances from multiple speakers was compared manually and automatically (including tone, intonation and rhythm). Evaluation shows that the automatic method achieves good correlation with human scoring. Expressive speech synthesis may introduce intense prosodic variation, however the emotional classes have great influence on the semantic meaning [7]. We would like to increase the prosodic variation without modifying the semantics. It has been also shown that modifying default prosodic parameters in a TTS system, such as widening F0 range is generally considered more 'fun' and less 'boring' by Swedish children [8], however the method was not introduced to speech synthesis systems.

Based on the results of these previous studies the current research targets to improve the variability of intonation in LSTM based F0 models and hereby the overall quality of statistical parametric speech synthesis systems.

2   Proposed Method

Our goal was to create a system which can generate fundamental frequency series while allowing the user to determine the desired level of intonation variation for each sentence. The overview of the system is depicted on Fig. 1. First the training corpus of the Text-To-Speech system was extended with labels of pitch variation level by a random forest (RF) classifier. The random forest was trained with a supplementary, manually annotated corpus. Later an LSTM-based neural network was trained with the extended TTS corpus. After training, the neural network can produce fundamental frequency trajectory for arbitrary sentences with three different levels of pitch variation given as an input (corresponding the three classes of the RF classifier).

2.1   Random Forest Based Corpus Classification

We preprocessed the data in such way that a random forest classifier could estimate the perceived pitch variation level of an arbitrary utterance.

To train the classifier, a manually annotated supplementary corpus was set up (Fig. 1, '*Pitch variation corpus*' part). This corpus contained a few hundred utterances. The annotation of such a corpus takes about 5–6 h of manual work. The levels were assigned according to the perceived dynamism of the pitch (later referred as pitch variation level). Rates range on a three-point scale consisting of choices "boring", "average" and "exciting". These levels will be referred to as DYN-LOW, DYN-MEDIUM and DYN-HIGH, respectively.

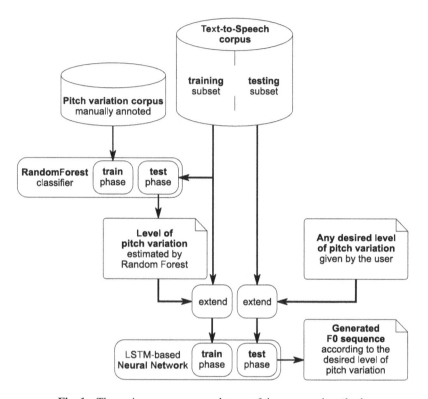

Fig. 1. The main components and steps of the proposed method.

Input feature vectors were calculated from the pitch trajectories of the utterances. SWIPE [9] was used for pitch tracking. Input features included various statistical representations of the pitch trajectories. Some calculations produce one numerical value for each utterance while others can produce more as they can be parameterized further, as shown below. Simple calculations (which produce one numerical output per utterance) include standard deviation of lengths of unvoiced sections; average pitch value; standard deviation of pitch sequence; absolute range of pitch (difference of extremes); relative range of pitch (ratio of extremes); squared sum of the 1st and 2nd derivatives of pitch; maximum of the 1st and 2nd derivatives of pitch and squared sum of the 1st derivatives of lengths of unvoiced sections. Parameterized calculations (that produce more numerical outputs per utterance according to their parameters) include autocorrelation of pitch sequence (*parameters: window length, step length*); standard deviation of partial pitch sequence windows' deviations (*parameter: window length*) and count of relatively extreme jumps in pitch sequence (*parameters: absolute and relative threshold for minimal jump height, minimal and maximal value count per jump*).

These representations were picked on the purpose to support the decision of the classifier as they tend to be linked with the perceived dynamism of pitch [8]. For each utterance of the supplementary corpus we calculated these features. The results formed the input feature vectors that were used to train a random forest (RF) classifier, while the target classes of RF were the manually annotated level of pitch variation. We calculated the same features for the training part (90 %) of the Text-To-Speech corpus and the trained random forest classifier was used to automatically assign a pitch variation level to every utterance of this TTS corpus (see Fig. 1). We used inter alia these labels throughout training the LSTM, as described in Sect. 2.2.

2.2 Long Short-Term Memory Based F0 Modeling

We used unidirectional Long Short-Term Memory-based neural network for learning and generating pitch trajectories [10]. LSTMs are proven to be very effective in modeling the temporal structure of time series and they are free of the adverse effect of exploding/vanishing gradient in vanilla recurrent neural networks [11]. Uni- and bidirectional LSTMs have been successfully applied for speech synthesis [4], however intonation variation is not considered in previous research.

Vanilla vocoders use discontinuous F0 contour controlled by a voiced/unvoiced (V/UV) flag, because F0 is not defined within unvoiced phonemes. However, it has been shown that excitation models with continuous F0 trajectories are advantageous in statistical parametric speech synthesis systems [12]. In such continuous systems, often a separate stream of voicing strength is used for modeling the voicing feature [13]. The V/UV decision can be left to the dynamic voiced frequency feature in a residual-based vocoder [14]. Hence in this research continuous F0 modeling combined with the Maximum Voiced Frequency (MVF) vocoder technique was used [15].

The used TTS corpus contained thousands of studio quality utterances. Various metadata such as pitch trajectories, phonetic transcription with time alignment and numerical linguistic contexts are also stored for each utterance. These data were used for training and testing pitch trajectories as target variable and the others as input features.

The corpus was split into training, validation and testing parts (Fig. 1). For each timestep, input features were quinphone (current phoneme and its environment, one-hot encoded); percentage (position of actual timestep within current phoneme's time-span); duration of current phoneme; numerical linguistic context values (position of current phoneme within current word, position of current word within the utterance etc.) and the level of pitch variation (one-hot encoded–3 binary inputs).

The level of pitch variation was represented using one-hot encoding. At the LSTM training phase, the input vectors contained the corresponding pitch variation level produced by random forest of the utterances as described in the previous section. During the testing phase of the network, the level of pitch variation could be set to any of the three valid values (Fig. 1). This means that the network can produce three different outputs for each utterance based on the chosen pitch variation level. Values were scaled to zero mean and unit variance, except for the one-hot parts. Every input vector included 4 timesteps.

The network architecture contained two layers as shown in Fig. 2. The input layer is made up of 512 LSTM cells while the output layer is a fully connected output layer containing two neurons. The output neurons produce logF0 and logMVF signals. Softplus were used as activation function at both layers. During the learning phase mean squared error was used as loss function and AdaDelta as optimizer. Early stopping was also applied to prevent overfitting.

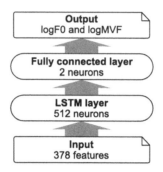

Fig. 2.   Architecture of the used neural network.

3   Evaluation

In the evaluation part an LSTM was trained as described in Sect. 2. For training a male speaker was selected from the Precisely Labelled Hungarian Database (PLHD) containing 1984 sentences [16]. Within this speech corpus the phonetic transcription and phone boundaries are manually corrected. The supplementary corpus for training the random forest classifier contained spontaneous radio conversations with a length of 40 min. In this research declarative, complex sentences with two phrases were under study. For evaluation phone durations from natural utterances were used as the temporal information of the input vector. The spectral parameters were also obtained from the natural utterances. The F0 trajectories were generated by the LSTM. The training, validation and test data were the 76, 14 and 10 percentage of the corpus, respectively. The LSTM was implemented in Keras deep learning framework [17], and the calculations were performed on high performance NVidia GPUs.

Both in subjective and objective evaluation four sentence types were involved: (1) vocoded natural utterances; (2–4) vocoded natural utterances with F0 trajectories generated by the LSTM and setting prosodic variation to low, medium and high. The four types will be referred to as NAT, DYN-LOW, DYN-MEDIUM, DYN-HIGH throughout the evaluation.

3.1   Objective Evaluation

In this paper only the best performing neural network is described, although we built up a number of different networks, using different parameters and methods to improve the results. Quality of the results and the time of learning were mostly affected by the number of layers and neurons, inputs' representation, activation functions as well as batch size and supplementary techniques such as early stopping.

Figure 3 shows an example F0 sequences of the same part of an utterance. NAT is the original F0 curve while DYN-LOW, DYN-MEDIUM and DYN-HIGH are the generated ones made with different levels of pitch variation. Regarding the generated sequences of the whole testing set, diagrams show that usually DYN-HIGH sequences tend to reach higher values and higher deviation than the other two.

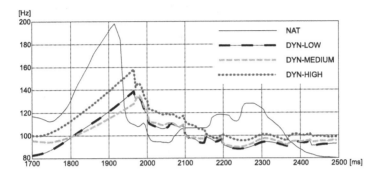

Fig. 3. F0 trajectories of natural utterance and generated by DYN-LOW, DYN-MEDIUM and DYN-HIGH.

For evaluation, we estimated the level of pitch variation of the TTS corpus using the random forest classifier. This formed three disjunctive classes of utterances based on their level of pitch variation. For every utterance in each class the Pearson product-moment correlation coefficient was calculated between the original pitch sequence and their generated pairs. Table 1 shows the average correlation coefficient for each class against their generated pairs of each level. The results show that the generated F0 trajectories with higher level of pitch variation are more correlated to the original F0 curves with lower level of pitch variation in case of DYN-LOW and DYN-MEDIUM. This phenomenon can be explained by that the proposed model lowers the pitch variation in case of these categories. The original and generated F0 curves of DYN-HIGH are correlated most, consequently in this case the variation is preserved the most.

Table 1. Pearson correlation coefficients between utterances with natural and generated F0 trajectories.

		ORIGINAL		
		DYN-LOW	DYN-MEDIUM	DYN-HIGH
GENERA-TED	DYN-LOW	0.665	0.666	0.597
	DYN-MEDIUM	0.672	0.659	0.605
	DYN-HIGH	0.662	0.676	0.642

3.2 Subjective Evaluation

In order to measure the perceived pitch variation in DYN-LOW, DYN-MEDIUM and DYN-HIGH LSTM intonation models a CMOS (Comparison Mean Opinion Score) type listening test was carried out [18]. In this listening test the subjects had to compare pairs of utterances in a three level scale whether the speaker of the first or second utterance is more unexcited. This way the perceived pitch variation is measured indirectly.

Altogether, 96 utterances were included in the test (1 speaker × 4 types × 24 sentences). Before the test, subjects were asked to listen to an example from the male speaker to adjust the volume. The utterances were presented in a randomized order (different for each participant) in order to eliminate 'memory-effect'. Altogether 13 listeners participated in the test (3 females, 10 males). All subjects were native Hungarian speakers, between 23–74 years (mean: 34 years). On average the test took 7 min to complete. The CMOS scores of the listening test are presented in Fig. 4.

The results show that the synthetic voice was considered more unexcited compared to the natural utterances–however with higher levels of pitch variation the generated sentences were perceived less unexcited. Comparing the generated F0 trajectories DYN-LOW and DYN-MEDIUM have almost the same scores, while DYN-HIGH was considered significantly less unexciting than DYN-LOW and DYN-MEDIUM. This result confirms that with the experimental system the perceived pitch variation can be controlled with constraints.

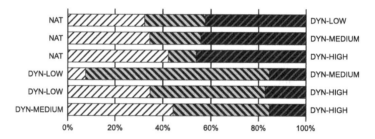

Fig. 4. The results of the CMOS listening test

4   Conclusions and Discussion

From the objective and subjective evaluations we can conclude that prosodic variation in Long Short-Term Memory based intonation models can be improved by extending the inputs with a one-hot encoded value. This input refers to the different classes of the training corpus classified by random forest based on the perceived prosodic variation. The results are promising and the application perspective of the proposed method lies on its simplicity: the prosodic variation of speech synthesis system can be modified by turning single inputs on and off. This type of simple control over the prosodic variation could improve the overall negative judgement related to the monotony of speech synthesis systems.

This research is only the first step towards improving the prosodic variation and thus the overall quality of statistical parametric speech synthesis systems. The annotation of class labels for the random forest should be automated. One approach could be the introduction of the results of Laskowski et al. [19]. They have developed vector-valued representation of pitch variation, inspired by vanishing-point perspective, a technique used in architectural drawing and grounded in projective geometry. The technique is instantaneous, continuous and distributed, it is formalized in four equations and can be successfully applied to statistical parametric modeling techniques, including DNNs. Furthermore, experiments will be carried out with different deep architectures, including deep ensembles.

Acknowledgments. We would like to thank to Mátyás Bartalis for his help in creating the subjective listening test and to the listeners for participating in it. Bálint Pál Tóth gratefully acknowledges the support of NVIDIA Corporation with the donation of an NVidia Titan X GPU used for his research. This research is partially supported by the Swiss National Science Foundation via the joint research project (SCOPES scheme) SP2: SCOPES project on speech prosody (SNSF n° IZ73Z0_152495-1).

References

1. Zen, H., Tokuda, K., Black, A.W.: Statistical parametric speech synthesis. Speech Commun. **51**, 1039–1064 (2009)
2. LeCun, Y., Bengio, Y., Hinton, G.: Deep learning. Nature **521**(7553), 436–444 (2015)
3. Zen, H., Senior, A., Schuster, M.: Statistical parametric speech synthesis using deep neural networks. In: ICASSP, pp. 7962–7966 (2013)
4. Fan, Y., Qian, Y., Xie, F.-L., Soong. F.K.: TTS synthesis with bidirectional LSTM based recurrent neural networks. In:. Interspeech, pp. 1964–1968 (2014)
5. Németh, G., Fék, M., Csapó, T.G.: Increasing prosodic variability of text-to-speech synthesizers. In: INTERSPEECH, pp. 474–477 (2007)
6. Jia, H, Tao, J, Wang, X.: Prosody variation: application to automatic prosody evaluation of Mandarin speech. In: Proceeding Speech Prosody, pp. 547–550 (2008)
7. Gahlawat, M., Malik, A., Bansal, P.: Expressive speech synthesis system using unit selection. In: Prasath, R., Kathirvalavakumar, T. (eds.) MIKE 2013. LNCS, vol. 8284, pp. 391–401. Springer, Heidelberg (2013)
8. Gustafson, K., House, D.: Fun or boring? A web-based evaluation of expressive synthesis for children. In: INTERSPEECH, pp. 565–568 (2001)
9. Camacho, A.: Swipe: a sawtooth waveform inspired pitch estimator for speech and music. Doctoral dissertation at the University of Florida, pp. 47–86 (2007)
10. Hochreiter, S., Schmidhuber, J.: Long short-term memory. Neural Comput. **9**(8), 1735–1780 (1997)
11. Pascanu, R., Mikolov, T., Bengio, Y.: On the difficulty of training recurrent neural networks. arXiv preprint arXiv:1211.5063 (2012)
12. Garner, P.N., Cernak, M., Motlicek, P.: A simple continuous pitch estimation algorithm. IEEE Signal Process. Lett. **20**(1), 102–105 (2013)
13. Zhang, Q., Soong, F. K., Qian, Y., Yan, Z., Pan, J., Yan, Y.: Improved modeling for F0 generation and V/U decision in HMM-based TTS. In: ICASSP, pp. 4606–4609 (2010)

14. Drugman, T., Stylianou, Y.: Maximum voiced frequency estimation: exploiting amplitude and phase spectra. IEEE Signal Process. Lett. **21**(10), 1230–1234 (2014)

15. Csapó, T.G., Németh, G., Cernak, M.: Residual-based excitation with continuous F0 modeling in HMM-based speech synthesis. In: Dediu, A.-H., Martín-Vide, C., Vicsi, K. (eds.) SLSP 2015. LNCS, vol. 9449, pp. 27–38. Springer, Heidelberg (2015). doi: 10.1007/978-3-319-25789-1_4

16. Olaszy, G.: Development and services of a Hungarian precisely labeled and segmented, parallel speech database, (in Hungarian), Speech Res., pp. 261–270 (2013)

17. Chollet, F.: Keras: Theano-based deep learning library, https://github.com/fchollet, Documentation: http://keras.io (2015)

18. ITU-T recommendation p. 800: Methods for subjective determination of transmission quality (1996)

19. Laskowski, K., Heldner, M., Edlund, J.: The fundamental frequency variation spectrum. In: FONETIK-2008, pp. 29–32 (2008)

In-Document Adaptation for a Human Guided Automatic Transcription Service

André Mansikkaniemi[1(✉)], Mikko Kurimo[1], and Krister Lindén[2]

[1] School of Electrical Engineering, Department of Signal Processing and Acoustics, Aalto University, Espoo, Finland
{andre.mansikkaniemi,mikko.kurimo}@aalto.fi
[2] Department of Modern Languages, University of Helsinki, Helsinki, Finland
krister.linden@helsinki.fi

Abstract. In this work, the task is to assist human transcribers to produce, for example, interview or parliament speech transcriptions. The system will perform in-document adaptation based on a small amount of manually corrected automatic speech recognition results. The corrected segments of the spoken document are used to adapt the speech recognizer's acoustic and language model. The updated models are used in second-pass recognition to produce a more accurate automatic transcription for the remaining uncorrected parts of the spoken document. In this work we evaluate two common adaptation methods for speech data in settings that represent typical transcription tasks. For adapting the acoustic model we use the Maximum A Posteriori adaptation method. For adapting the language model we use linear interpolation. We compare results of supervised adaptation to unsupervised adaptation, and evaluate the total benefit of using human corrected segments for in-document adaptation for typical transcription tasks.

Keywords: Automatic speech recognition · Language model adaptation · Acoustic model adaptation · Human guided speech recognition

1 Introduction

Researchers of various fields have an ever increasing access to spoken documents such as audio recordings and videos. Many researchers also produce their own material in the form of interviews or lectures. To make full use of the spoken material, it needs to be transcribed into text one way or the other. Manual transcriptions are time-consuming and many times frustrating to produce. Automatic speech recogniton (ASR) can help but the result depends on how well the ASR models match the data. Automatic recognition results are often disappointing for spoken documents that in terms of topic, style, or recording conditions deviate from the baseline models.

Adaptation of ASR models has previously been studied exstensively. The common approach has been to use a small amount of target data (audio or text)

© Springer International Publishing Switzerland 2016
A. Ronzhin et al. (Eds.): SPECOM 2016, LNAI 9811, pp. 395–402, 2016.
DOI: 10.1007/978-3-319-43958-7_47

from a speaker, recording condition, topic, or style to adapt the general models that are trained on a larger set of data.

In this work we study of how common language and acoustic model adaptation methods can be used for performing in-document adaptation. Our main focus is on how a small amount of manually transcribed speech data can improve the automatic recognition of the rest of the document. We will also compare unsupervised and semi-supervised adaptation where adaptation is either performed based on the first-pass recognition output of the entire document (unsupervised) or on a combination of the manual transcription of a small segment of the document and the automatic transcription of the rest of the document (semi-supervised). The adaptation framework used in this work is illustrated in Fig. 1.

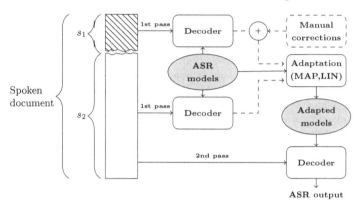

Fig. 1. Framework for in-document adaptation. A short segment s_1 of a spoken document, decoded by the ASR system, is corrected by a human transcriber. Based on the corrected segment the ASR models are adapted. The adapted ASR models are used in second-pass decoding for recognizing the remaining uncorrected segment s_2. Alternatively the uncorrected segments based on first-pass decoding can be used for performing unsupervised adaptation.

The adaptation methods that are used in this work are maximum a posteriori (MAP) for acoustic model adaptation and linear interpolation (LIN) for language model adaptation.

2   Related Works

Exploiting user feedback in speech recognition applications has been studied in several previous works. Cross-document adaptation has often been applied in this context. Fully or partially corrected spoken documents are used to adapt the language or acoustic model. The adapted models are used in recognizing new spoken documents of the same domain.

In [11], partially corrected meeting transcripts were used to adapt the background language model using linear interpolation and unigram rescaling. Significant improvements in recognition accuracy were achieved using the adapted

LM when recognizing new meeting documents. In [9], crowdsourcing was utilized letting anonymous users correct recognition errors for Web podcasts. The corrected transcripts were used for training new component language models. The same crowdsourcing paradigm had also been used earlier for training new acoustic models for podcast transcription [8].

User feedback has also been used for learning new pronunciation variants for words. In [12], in-document pronunciation adaptation was implemented by learning new pronunciation rules for misrecognized words using a phoneme recognizer. The adapted pronunciation dictionary was used in recognizing the remaining part of the spoken document. In our previous work [7], we implemented a system based on user feedback for learning adapted pronunciation variants for foreign names. Pronunciation rules were learned for foreign words by force aligning and re-decoding the misrecognized segment with alternative pronunciation variants generated with a grapheme-to-phoneme (G2P) model. The new pronunciation rules were used in recognizing new spoken documents.

Recently there has also been research on how the quality of the ASR output affects human transcription latency [3]. Results indicate that above a certain error rate threshold, human transcribers are faster at generating the transcript from scratch than correcting erroneous low quality ASR output.

The novelty in this work is the evaluation of in-document acoustic and language model adaptation, based on a short corrected segment at the beginning of a longer spoken document.

3   Adaptation Methods

3.1   Maximum A Posteriori Acoustic Model Adaptation

Maximum A Posteriori is a common acoustic model adaptation method and it has been recently implemented into the Aalto ASR system [6]. A standard GMM-HMM acoustic model is trained based on maximum likelihood (ML) estimates of the training data. MAP adaptation is performed by re-estimating the acoustic model parameters.

Based on the adaptation data x, new ML estimates are calculated. In MAP adaptation, a new estimate is formed by shitfing the original prior parameters to the new ML estimates. The MAP estimate can be defined as follows,

$$\theta_{MAP} = \arg\max_{\theta} f(x|\theta)g(\theta), \tag{1}$$

where $f(x|\theta)$ is the ML estimate of the adaptation data and $g(\theta)$ is the prior distribution.

Compared to maximum likelihood linear regression (MLLR), another acoustic model adaptation method, MAP adaptation requires more adaptation data. In MAP adaptation each parameter of the GMM components are individually estimated. With small amounts of adaptation data only a small margin of all the possible triphones are re-estimated. In previous experiments, MAP adaptation has been found to outperform MLLR when more adaptation data is made available [6]. MAP adaptation has also been found to reduce the acoustic model size which can be useful in otherwise computationally intensive multi-pass recognition environments. In this work we will also observe how MAP adaptation performs in multi-speaker environments.

3.2   Linear Interpolation

In this work linear interpolation is used for in-document LM adaptation. It's a well established adaptation method within the ASR field because of its ease of use. For the intended application in this work, we also value that linear interpolation is a relatively quick and computationally cheap process.

An in-document LM $P_D(w|h)$ is trained on the first-pass ASR output (corrected or uncorrected). Linear interpolation is used to adapt the background LM $P_B(w|h)$ with the in-document LM $P_D(w|h)$. The adapted LM $P_A(w|h)$ is calculated by adding together the weighted probabilities of the two different models:

$$P_A(w|h) = \lambda P_B(w|h) + (1 - \lambda)P_D(w|h). \tag{2}$$

The interpolation weight λ is tuned on the first-pass ASR output of s_2, using an expectation-maximization (EM) estimation procedure. Because the background LM $P_B(w|h)$ is trained on a substantially larger corpus than the in-document LM $P_D(w|h)$, the weight obtained from the EM estimation λ_{EM} is scaled to a minimum value λ_{min} that the background LM weight can have. In this work the λ_{min} value is set to 0.90. The scaled weight λ_{scaled} which is used in the interpolation process is calculated as follows:

$$\lambda_{scaled} = \lambda_{min} + \lambda_{EM}(1 - \lambda_{min}). \tag{3}$$

4   Experiments

4.1   System

Speech recognition experiments were run on the Aalto ASR system [4], which utilizes crossword triphone GMM-HMM acoustic models. The baseline acoustic model was trained on a subset of the Finnish Speecon corpus (20 h speech in 16 kHz, 310 speakers) [5].

The Finnish background language model was trained on three different text sources: the Kielipankki corpus (140 million words) [1], a Web corpus consisting of online news articles (7 million words) and another Web corpus consisting of conversational texts retrieved from discussion forums (76 million words). A model for morpheme segmentation and a 80 k morph lexicon were trained on the LM training corpora using Morfessor [2]. A Kneser-Ney smoothed varigram LM (max n = 6 for n-grams) was trained on the morph-segmented background corpus with the variKN language modeling toolkit [10].

4.2   Evaluation Data

The experiments are run on Finnish speech data. In this work the evaluation data consists of spoken documents which are at least over 50 min long. There are three types of spoken documents we evaluate in this work: audiobooks, conversational speech, and parliament sessions. A detailed description of the different data sets is provided in Table 1.

Table 1. Evaluation data sets used in the experiments.

Data set	Spoken documents	Speakers/ document	Data set size	Average length s_1	Average length s_2
Audiobook	2	1	3 h 56 min	10 min	1 h 47 min
Conversational	5	2	4 h 30 min	10 min	44 min
Parliament	5	5–10	5 h 2 min	10 min	50 min

Audiobooks only have one speaker per document. The type of speech is planned. The language is formal and in terms of content, one audiobook is a novel and the other one is related to European politics.

The conversational data set is made up of 5 different dialogues between two people interviewing each other. The type of speech is unplanned and the language is colloquial.

The parliament data set consists of 5 Finnish parliament sessions recorded during 2015. There are multiple speakers in each session, ranging between 5–10 speakers. The type of speech is a mix between planned and unplanned. There are segments with read speech and there are also segments where speakers are debating and not speaking from a manuscript. The language is mostly formal and related to different political issues.

4.3   Adaptation Experiments

The general adaptation framework was presented in Fig. 1. In this context, there are three different adaptation scenarios that we evaluate: supervised, unsupervised, and semi-supervised adaptation.

Supervised: In the supervised adaptation scenario the adaptation data is only based on the corrected 10 min segment of the spoken document. In this work we denote the supervised adaptation data as $\hat{s}_1$.

Unsupervised: In the unsupervised adaptation scenario the adapation data is based on the uncorrected first-pass ASR output of both the short 10 min segment and the remaining longer segment. We denote this adaptation data as $s_1 + s_2$.

Semi-supervised: In the semi-supervised adaptation scenario the adaptation data is based on the corrected 10 min segment and the uncorrected longer segment. We denote this adaptation data as $\hat{s}_1 + s_2$.

In terms of measuring performance we only use s_2, the longer segment of the spoken document, as evaluation data.

5 Results

Results of the adaptation experiments are presented in Table 2. In this work we measure performance in letter error rate (LER) instead of word error rate (WER). This is motivated by the intended application for this work. It's of more interest for a human transcriber how many letters he/she has to correct instead of how many words are misrecognized.

Table 2. Results of in-document adaptation on the three different data sets.

Adaptation method	Adaptation data	Audiobook LER [%]	Conversational LER [%]	Parliament LER [%]
-		**4.1**	**36.5**	**20.5**
MAP	$\hat{s}_1$	3.3	34.0	19.3
	$s_1 + s_2$	**3.0**	35.3	17.6
	$\hat{s}_1 + s_2$	3.0	35.0	17.6
LIN	$\hat{s}_1$	4.1	36.5	20.5
	$s_1 + s_2$	4.1	36.5	20.6
	$\hat{s}_1 + s_2$	4.1	36.5	20.6
MAP + LIN	$\hat{s}_1$	3.3	**33.8**	19.2
	$s_1 + s_2$	3.0	35.3	17.6
	$\hat{s}_1 + s_2$	3.0	35.0	**17.5**

The baseline results on the first row are a clear indicator of the difference between the data sets. Performance values are best for data that deviate the least from the baseline ASR models. The audiobook data set, which consists of read speech and formal language, has the lowest LER. Worst performance is on the conversational data set, which consists of unplanned speech and colloquial language.

MAP adaptation results are on rows 2–4. Using MAP, the results improve significantly for all data sets in every adaptation scenario. Supervised MAP adaptation (MAP, $\hat{s}_1$) lowers LER for the audibook data set with 20 %. Relative LER reduction for the conversational data set is 7 % and for the parliament data set 6 %. Unsupervised MAP adaptation (MAP, $s_1 + s_2$) further lowers LER for the audiobook and parliament data sets, with 27 % and 14 % respectively (compared to baseline). Unsupervised MAP adaptation performs slightly worse on the conversational data set compared to supervised adaptation. Relative LER reduction is only 3 %. Semi-supervised MAP adaptation (MAP, $\hat{s}_1 + s_2$) does not give any additional improvement compared to unsupervised adaptation, except for the conversational data set where relative LER reduction is 4 %.

Linear interpolation results are on rows 5–7. In general, LM adaptation usually gives less significant improvements compared to acoustic model adaptation. In this case LM adaptation in the form of linear interpolation did not give any performance improvements at all, in any adaptation scenario. It is probable that 10 min of data is simply not enough for improving language modeling substantially.

Results for combining both MAP and linear interpolation are on rows 8–10. Results are quite similar compared to using only MAP adaptation. Letter error rate is only lowered slightly for conversational data using semi-supervised adaptation.

6   Discussion and Conclusions

In this work we implemented and studied a framework for performing in-document adaptation on lengthy spoken documents. In the framework there is an option for a human transcriber to manually correct a short segment at the beginning of the document. Our main focus point was how this short manually transcribed segment could be used in acoustic and language model adaptation, and how much the adapted models could improve the recognition for the remaining part of the document. A comparison was made between supervised adaptation using the short manually corrected segment, and unsupervised adaptation using the first-pass ASR output of the entire document.

Linear interpolation was used for performing LM adaptation and MAP adaptation was used for acoustic model adaptation. Three different types of spoken documents were evaluated in the adaptation experiments: audiobooks, conversational recordings, and parliament sessions.

For acoustic model adaptation, supervised adaptation only outperforms unsupervised adapation on the conversational data set. It seems that human made corrections are only beneficial on data that is very poorly recognized by the baseline ASR models. On the audiobook and parliament data sets unsupervised adaptation gave the best results. It is of course important to remember that the unsupervised adaptation data was larger than the supervised data by a factor of 5–10. It might be worthwhile studying how increasing the supervised adaptation data from 10 min can further improve performance compared to unsupervised adaptation. For lengthy spoken documents supervised adaptation could be called after the corrected segment exceeds a certain threshold.

Language model adaptation did not give any improvements in this work. The size of adaptation data was of course very small and this limits the capability of LM adaptation. Other LM adaptation methods could be explored such as unigram rescaling. The only drawback with many of these methods is that they are computationally expensive and it takes a long time to obtain the adapted model, which is not ideal for the intended application in this work. Another framework could be explored for LM adaptation in this context where the adaptation data is not used as training text but rather as tuning data for finding optimal internal parameters of the baseline LM.

For future work we will explore adjusting the corrected segment to different lengths, and measure the relative improvements compared to unsupervised adaptation. We will also study the use of more advanced LM adaptation setups in the context of in-document adaptation.

References

1. Department of general linguistics, university of helsinki, linguistics and language technology department, university of joensuu, research institute for the languages of finland, and csc "finnish text collection - collection of finnish text documents from years 1990–2000." http://www.csc.fi/kielipankki/
2. Creutz, M., Lagus, K.: Unsupervised morpheme segmentation and morphology induction from text corpora using Morfessor 1.0. Helsinki University of Technology (2005)
3. Gaur, Y.: The effects of automatic speech recognition quality on human transcription latency. In: Proceedings of the 17th International ACM SIGACCESS Conference on Computers and Accessibility, pp. 367–368. ACM (2015)
4. Hirsimaki, T., Pylkkonen, J., Kurimo, M.: Importance of high-order n-gram models in morph-based speech recognition. IEEE Trans. Audio, Speech, Lang. Process. **17**(4), 724–732 (2009)
5. Iskra, D.J., Grosskopf, B., Marasek, K., van den Heuvel, H., Diehl, F., Kiessling, A.: Speecon-speech databases for consumer devices: database specification and validation. In: LREC (2002)
6. Leino, K., et al.: Maximum a posteriori for acoustic model adaptation in automatic speech recognition (2015)
7. Mansikkaniemi, A., Kurimo, M.: Unsupervised and user feedback based lexicon adaptation for foreign names and acronyms. In: Dediu, A.-H., Martín-Vide, C., Vicsi, K. (eds.) SLSP 2015. LNCS, pp. 197–206. Springer, Heidelberg (2015)
8. Ogata, J., Goto, M.: Podcastle: collaborative training of acoustic models on the basis of wisdom of crowds for podcast transcription. In: INTERSPEECH, pp. 1491–1494 (2009)
9. Ogata, J., Goto, M.: Podcastle: collaborative training of language models on the basis of wisdom of crowds. In: INTERSPEECH, pp. 2370–2373 (2012)
10. Siivola, V., Hirsimaki, T., Virpioja, S.: On growing and pruning kneser-ney smoothed-gram models. IEEE Trans. Audio, Speech, Lang. Process. **15**(5), 1617–1624 (2007)
11. Vergyri, D., Stolcke, A., Tur, G.: Exploiting user feedback for language model adaptation in meeting recognition. In: 2009 IEEE International Conference on Acoustics, Speech and Signal Processing, pp. 4737–4740. IEEE (2009)
12. Yu, D., Hwang, M.Y., Mau, P., Acero, A., Deng, L.: Unsupervised learning from users' error correction in speech dictation. In: INTERSPEECH (2004)

Interaction Quality as a Human-Human Task-Oriented Conversation Performance

Anastasiia Spirina[1]([✉]), Olesia Vaskovskaia[2], Maxim Sidorov[1], and Alexander Schmitt[1]

[1] Ulm University, Ulm, Germany
{anastasiia.spirina,maxim.sidorov,
alexander.schmitt}@uni-ulm.de
[2] Siberian State Aerospace University, Krasnoyarsk, Russia
soul.lesuy@mail.ru

Abstract. The spoken dialogue systems (SDSs), which are designed to replace employees in different services, need some indicators, which show what happened in the ongoing dialogue and what the next step in system's behaviour should be. Thus, some indicators for the SDSs come from the field of the call centre's quality evaluation. In turn, some metrics like Interaction Quality (IQ), which was designed for human-computer spoken interaction, can be applied to human-human conversations. Such experience might be used for both call centres and SDSs for service quality improvement. This paper provides the results of IQ modelling for human-human task-oriented conversation with several classification algorithms.

Keywords: Call centres · Classification algorithms · Principal component analysis · Call centre's performances

1 Introduction

Many companies have different services such as: call centres, support/information services, help desk and other. To improve the service quality, to attract and increase the number of customers (which may influence in some cases on company's profit), to detect the problems in company's work and to increase the qualification of employees, different performance metrics are used.

With the development of SDSs and based on the fact, that customer-employee and customer-SDS dialogues are similar, there was a need to introduce some call centre's metrics to evaluate and then to improve the SDSs' work. One of such metrics is user/customer satisfaction (CS). Later, Schmitt et al. have redesigned CS concept in the IQ paradigm [1, 2]. In [1, 3] the authors explained the differences between CS and IQ concepts.

Despite the fact that IQ was developed specifically for SDSs to improve it, this paradigm might be adapted for evaluating dialogues in call centres. The results of such adaptation might be used both for the further improvement of SDSs (implementing the information of the agent's behaviour into SDSs) and call centre's service quality.

© Springer International Publishing Switzerland 2016
A. Ronzhin et al. (Eds.): SPECOM 2016, LNAI 9811, pp. 403–410, 2016.
DOI: 10.1007/978-3-319-43958-7_48

This paper describes the attempts of modelling the adapted version of IQ for human-human conversation (HHC) with several classification algorithms.

The rest of this paper is organised as follows. The description of IQ for human-computer spoken interaction (HCSI) and some call centre's metrics are presented in Sect. 2. Brief information of speech data for our experiments is provided by Sect. 3. In turn, Sect. 4 gives information about experimental setup and results. Discussion of the obtained results can be found in Sect. 5, whereas conclusion and future work are described in Sect. 6.

2 Related Works

In call-centres as well as in SDSs there are many approaches, which are utilized to monitor and to evaluate the quality of spoken interaction between employees/computer systems and customers. Most of such metrics are customer-centric. Some evaluations are based on emotion recognition [4, 5], but the customer's emotion state not necessarily reflects the quality of interaction in dialogues, because this emotion state may be the result of external circumstances or customer can be too/not enough emotional. Other metrics use text mining to identify Customer Orientation Behaviours, described in [6], or the cooperativeness score, presented in [7] as a measure obtained from the argumentative labels.

CS is one of the widely used metrics. There are different scales for CS measurement: in some research works [8, 9] the 5-point scale is used, in other – the 7-point scale [10]. Mostly call centres conduct a manual survey with their customers at the end of calls, but these measurements can be done automatically. In [8] authors described their approach for measuring CS using automatically generated call transcripts. Using the features from the different categories such as: structured features, prosodic features, lexical features, and contextual features, the authors tried to identify CS at the end and in the middle of calls.

Instead of the approach, described in [8], IQ allows to estimate the dialogue performance at any point of an ongoing interaction. The idea of the IQ metric for HHC is based on the research works, presented in [1–3]. The 5-point scale IQ metric from [1–3] was designed to assess the SDS performance. It is based on the features from Automatic Speech Recognition, Natural Language Understanding, and Dialogue Management system modules. All features for IQ modelling are subdivided into the three level: the exchange level, describing the current system-user exchange, the dialogue level, containing information about complete dialogue up to the current exchange, and the window level, comprising information about the n last exchanges. Being beneficial in HCSI scenarios, the IQ metric may be useful for evaluating the quality of HHC, what may be applied then for the service quality improvement.

3 Corpus Description

All computational experiments were conducted using the spoken corpus, described in [11]. This corpus includes 53 dialogues between customers and employees. These 53 dialogues were transformed into 1165 exchanges. Each exchange consists of an agent's and customer's turn and may contain overlapping speech. There are more than 1200 features, which describe an agent's/customer's/overlapping speech and an exchange in general. All features are subdivided into three groups: exchange/window/dialogue levels, which were proposed in [2].

3.1 Interaction Quality

Each exchange from this corpus is associated with two IQ score labels, which are based on the different guidelines. The guideline, described in [1], was used as a basis for the two suggested guidelines. For the first approach of an IQ annotation we used the guideline for HCSI [1] with the small changes in the rules, concerning the difference between HCSI and HHC. This guideline gives an absolute scale for IQ: "1", "2", "3", "4" and "5" [1, 3]. In contrast to the first approach, the second approach consists of two steps. The guideline in this case is similar to the guideline for the first approach, but is considered in terms of a scale of changes. At the first stage, applying the guideline, the scale of changes for IQ may be obtained, which at the next stage is transformed into an absolute scale, using an assumption, that the first exchange in all dialogues has IQ score "5".

The IQ annotation guidelines for both approaches can be found in [11]. For the first approach IQ score was denoted as IQ1, whereas for the second approaches it was designated as IQ2abs. The distributions of the IQ1and IQ2abs scores are shown in Table 1.

Table 1. The IQ score distribution

IQ type	Classes			
	"3"	"4"	"5"	"6"
IQ1	4	38	1123	–
IQ2abs	4	37	1028	96

3.2 Emotions

All speech fragments in the corpus were accompanied with the emotion labels. Based on different research works, we have chosen three emotion sets (denote them as em{1,2,3}), which are described in [11]. For better understanding whether the specific emotions are important for IQ modelling or not, all initial emotion sets were subdivided into neutral and other emotions and into neutral (denote them as em{1,2,3}_2), positive and negative emotions (denote them as em{1,2,3}_3).

4 Experimental Setup and Results

The IQ score identification task can be formulated as a classification problem. For IQ1 it is the three-class classification problem, whereas for IQ2abs it is classification problem with the four classes according to the corpus. For our research we have formulated in total eighteen classification problems, each of them is a combination of an IQ label (IQ1 or IQ2abs) and an emotion set (nine sets: the three main sets and two sets derived from each of them).

For modelling IQ for HHC we used classification algorithms implemented in *Rapidminer* [12] and *WEKA* [13]: Kernel Naïve Bayes classifier (NBK) [14], *k*-Nearest Neighbours algorithm (*k*NN) [15], L2 Regularized Logistic Regression (LR) [16], Support Vector Machines [17, 18] trained by Sequential Minimal Optimisation (SVM) [19].

The settings for these classification algorithms can be found in Table 2. Some parameters of the algorithms were optimized by the Grid optimisation to maximize F1-score [20].

Table 2. The settings for the classification algorithms and parametric optimisation

	Parameter	Parameter's value
NBK	• laplace correction (helps to prevent high influence of zero probabilities)	• true
	• estimation mode	• greedy
	• minimum bandwidth	• [0.01, 0.3], step 0.01
	• number of kernels	• [1, 20], step 1
*k*NN	• *k*	• [1, 20], step 1
	• numerical measure	• KernelEuclideanDistance
	• kernel type	• anova
	• kernel gamma	• [0.5, 5.0], step 0.5
	• kernel degree	• [0.5, 5.0], step 0.5
LR	• *R* (sets set the ridge in the log-likelihood)	• [0.05, 0.95], step 0.05
SVM	• the complexity constant *C*	• 1
	• the tolerance parameter *L*	• 0.001
	• fit logistic models to SVM outputs	• false
	• kernel	• polynomial

As a dimensionality reduction technique Principal Component Analysis (PCA) [21] is applied with the cumulative variance value 0.99. The data were pre-processed: each column (attribute values) was centred and normalised, it means, that the mean of each column is equal to 0 and the variance is equal to 1. Denote the algorithms with using PCA as NBK1, *k*NN1, LR1, SVM1.

For measuring the performance of the classification algorithms, we rely on F1-score, unweighted average recall (UAR) [22] and accuracy, averaged over different train-test splits, generated by 10-fold cross-validation. The obtained results can be found in Tables 3, 4 and 5. The best results are highlighted in bold in these tables.

5   Discussion

According to the one-way analysis of variance (one-way ANOVA) [23] and Tukey's honest significant difference (HSD) test [24], which are implemented in R programming language [25], with the default settings there are statistically significant differences between the means almost for all classification problems and for all classification performance measures for IQ2_abs and for some classification problems for IQ1. These tests determined, that almost in all the cases the results, obtained with NBK/NBK1 statistically significant differ from the other results.

In terms of F1-score and UAR the obtained results outperform the most frequent class baselines, which for F1-score for IQ1 and IQ2_abs equal to 0.327 and 0.234 correspondently. In terms of accuracy the results, obtained with the use of PCA, almost for all algorithms and all classification problems for IQ1 do not outperform the baseline, which is 0.964. For IQ2_abs this value equals to 0.882.

Given the fact that the data is highly unbalanced the results are not reasonable enough, although the obtained results outperform the baselines almost in all the cases. Also the result can be not objective, since emotions and IQ scores were annotated by only one expert rater.

The best results in terms of F1-score and UAR almost in all classification problems were obtained with kNN and kNN1, whereas the best results in terms of accuracy were achieved by LR and SVM.

Finally, based on the statistical tests it can be concluded, that, although the use of the PCA doesn't improve the results of classification without applying of the PCA,

Table 3. F1-score for the classification algorithms

		Emotion sets								
		em1	em12	em13	em2	em22	em23	em3	em32	em33
IQ1	NBK	0.532	**0.518**	0.532	0.502	0.5	0.499	0.521	0.515	0.516
	SVM	0.524	0.5	0.524	0.534	0.522	0.519	**0.548**	0.523	0.544
	kNN	0.509	0.509	0.509	0.48	0.48	0.48	0.509	0.509	0.509
	LR	0.506	0.472	0.506	0.484	0.479	0.492	0.52	0.471	0.504
	NBK1	0.432	0.428	0.432	0.448	0.438	0.437	0.448	0.411	0.452
	SVM1	0.46	0.468	0.46	0.497	0.438	0.493	0.495	0.432	0.499
	kNN1	**0.58**	0.512	**0.58**	**0.581**	**0.527**	**0.57**	**0.548**	**0.535**	**0.55**
	LR1	0.498	0.487	0.498	0.512	0.466	0.512	0.489	0.461	0.5
IQ2abs	NBK	0.452	0.474	0.452	0.455	0.471	0.461	0.441	0.481	0.441
	SVM	0.578	0.579	0.578	0.592	0.589	0.591	0.593	0.585	0.594
	kNN	0.606	**0.606**	0.606	**0.606**	**0.606**	**0.606**	0.604	**0.604**	0.604
	LR	0.563	0.541	0.563	0.548	0.541	0.543	0.541	0.531	0.538
	NBK1	0.398	0.387	0.398	0.39	0.378	0.389	0.382	0.401	0.403
	SVM1	0.498	0.496	0.498	0.504	0.485	0.502	0.487	0.495	0.514
	kNN1	**0.609**	**0.606**	**0.609**	0.6	0.604	0.602	**0.617**	0.603	**0.623**
	LR1	0.538	0.529	0.538	0.532	0.526	0.521	0.521	0.528	0.525

Table 4. UAR for the classification algorithms

		Emotion sets								
		em1	em12	em13	em2	em22	em23	em3	em32	em33
IQ1	NBK	0.501	0.485	0.501	0.477	0.469	0.476	0.493	0.477	0.492
	SVM	0.497	0.469	0.497	0.495	0.478	0.486	0.499	0.478	0.506
	kNN	0.508	0.508	0.508	0.475	0.475	0.475	0.508	0.508	0.508
	LR	0.457	0.44	0.457	0.45	0.441	0.449	0.466	0.44	0.458
	NBK1	0.411	0.426	0.411	0.423	0.436	0.418	0.423	0.42	0.431
	SVM1	0.453	0.462	0.453	0.482	0.435	0.479	0.49	0.435	0.48
	kNN1	**0.592**	**0.523**	**0.592**	**0.606**	**0.532**	**0.581**	**0.558**	**0.541**	**0.558**
	LR1	0.456	0.448	0.456	0.465	0.44	0.465	0.464	0.439	0.465
IQ2abs	NBK	0.435	0.461	0.435	0.452	0.46	0.458	0.434	0.467	0.434
	SVM	0.55	0.547	0.55	0.559	0.553	0.557	0.562	0.551	0.56
	kNN	**0.596**	**0.596**	**0.596**	**0.596**	**0.596**	**0.596**	**0.593**	**0.594**	**0.594**
	LR	0.518	0.497	0.518	0.522	0.5	0.506	0.512	0.486	0.512
	NBK1	0.39	0.406	0.39	0.389	0.393	0.408	0.375	0.406	0.4
	SVM1	0.492	0.497	0.492	0.508	0.483	0.503	0.496	0.495	0.514
	kNN1	0.581	0.566	0.581	0.585	0.579	0.574	0.589	0.573	0.582
	LR1	0.504	0.498	0.504	0.512	0.497	0.498	0.501	0.498	0.506

Table 5. Accuracy for the classification algorithms

		Emotion sets								
		em1	em12	em13	em2	em22	em23	em3	em32	em33
IQ1	NBK	0.971	**0.972**	0.971	0.972	0.971	0.971	0.971	**0.971**	0.97
	SVM	0.969	0.966	0.969	0.973	0.969	0.969	**0.976**	0.969	0.971
	kNN	0.968	0.968	0.968	0.968	0.968	0.968	0.968	0.968	0.968
	LR	**0.973**	0.971	**0.973**	**0.974**	**0.972**	**0.973**	**0.976**	0.971	**0.975**
	NBK1	0.964	0.951	0.964	0.967	0.958	0.953	0.967	0.95	0.967
	SVM1	0.961	0.962	0.961	0.967	0.955	0.967	0.967	0.954	0.968
	kNN1	0.968	0.96	0.968	0.962	0.962	0.961	0.966	0.963	0.966
	LR1	0.97	0.97	0.97	0.973	0.969	**0.973**	0.97	0.967	0.973
IQ2abs	NBK	0.856	0.851	0.856	0.847	0.848	0.849	0.852	0.852	0.852
	SVM	0.934	0.933	0.934	**0.941**	0.936	**0.939**	**0.938**	**0.936**	**0.939**
	kNN	0.927	0.927	0.927	0.927	0.927	0.927	0.926	0.926	0.926
	LR	**0.937**	**0.936**	**0.937**	0.936	**0.937**	0.936	0.934	0.933	0.932
	NBK1	0.694	0.681	0.694	0.688	0.702	0.691	0.685	0.694	0.694
	SVM1	0.897	0.899	0.897	0.906	0.895	0.907	0.894	0.9	0.908
	kNN1	0.925	0.924	0.925	0.924	0.924	0.922	0.925	0.924	0.929
	LR1	0.924	0.923	0.924	0.924	0.921	0.92	0.921	0.922	0.923

there are no any statistically significant differences in general and it makes sense to use the PCA as a dimensionality reduction technique, because it decreases the computational complexity by reducing the number of features approximately in 2.5 times (from $\sim$ 1200 to $\sim$ 470).

Based on the fact, that all emotion and IQ labels have non-normal distributions (it was proved by Shapiro-Wilk test [26]), for determination any dependency between these values the Spearman's rho [27] was applied. According to the obtained results for all combinations of emotion sets and IQ labels (the absolute value of Spearman's rho is less, then 0.25, but not equals to 0) we can conclude, that there are only weak correlations between these values.

6 Conclusion and Future Work

In this paper we presented the results of modelling IQ for HHC as an adaptation of IQ for HCSI. IQ can be considered as a HHC performance metric, which may be used in call centres. Also the results of IQ modelling for HHC can be used for improving SDS in terms of flexibility, user-friendliness and human-likeness.

As a future direction for our research we plan to extend the list of applying classification algorithms and dimensionality reduction techniques. Furthermore, to obtain more objective data the number of expert raters should be increased. In this paper we presented two approaches of the IQ metric adaptation for HHC. One of the suggested metrics, which is based on the scale of changes (IQ2abs), showed some drawbacks of the IQ metric based on the absolute scale (IQ1), but the IQ2abs metric is not an easily interpretable scale. That is why these metrics should be redesigned in order to get an alternative scale, which may be easily interpretable.

Acknowledgements. The work presented in this paper was partly supported by the DAAD (German Academic Exchange Service) within the different programmes.

References

1. Schmitt, A., Schatz, B., Minker, W.: Modeling and predicting quality in spoken human-computer interaction. In: Proceedings of the SIGDIAL 2011 Conference. Association for Computational Linguistics, pp. 173–184 (2011)
2. Schmitt, A., Ultes, S., Minker, W.: A parameterized and annotated corpus of the CMU let's go bus information system. In: International Conference on Language Resources and Evaluation (LREC) (2012)
3. Schmitt, A., Ultes, S.: Interaction Quality: Assessing the quality of ongoing spoken dialog interaction by experts – And how it relates to user satisfaction. Speech Commun. **74**, 12–36 (2015)
4. Devillers, L., Vidrascu, L.: Real-life emotions detection with lexical and paralinguistic cues on human-human call center dialogs. Proc. Interspeech **2006**, 801–804 (2006)
5. Siegert, I., Ohnemus, K.: A new dataset of telephone-based human-human call-center interaction with emotional evaluation. In: Proceedings of the 1st International Symposium on Companion-Technology (ISCT 2015), pp. 143–148 (2015)

6. Rafaeli, A., Ziklik, L., Doucet, L.: The impact of call center employees' customer orientation behaviors on service quality. J. Serv. Res. **10**(3), 239–255 (2008)
7. Pallotta, V., Delmonte, R.: Interaction mining: the new frontier of customer interaction analytics. In: Lai, C., Semeraro, G., Vargiu, E. (eds.) New Challenges in Distributed Inf. Filtering and Retrieval. SCI, vol. 439, pp. 91–111. Springer, Heidelberg (2013)
8. Park, Y., Gates, S.C.: Towards real-time measurement of customer satisfaction using automatically generated call transcripts. In: Proceedings of the 18th ACM Conference on Information and Knowledge Management, pp. 1387–1396 (2009)
9. Walker, M., Kamm, C., Boland, J.: Developing and testing general models of spoken dialogue system performance. In: Proceedings of the 2nd International Conference on Language Resources and Evaluation (LREC), pp. 189–196 (2000)
10. Higashinaka, R., Minami, Y., Dohsaka, K., Meguro, T.: Modeling user satisfaction transitions in dialogues from overall ratings. In: Proceedings of SIGDIAL 2010: the 11th Annual Meetings of the Special Interest Group on Discourse and Dialogue, pp. 18–27 (2010)
11. Spirina, A.V., Sidorov, M.Y., Sergienko, R.B., Semenkin E.S., Minker, W.: Human-human task-oriented conversations corpus for interaction quality modelling. Vestnik SibSAU, **17** (1), 84–90 (2016) (In Russian). http://vestnik.sibsau.ru/images/vestnik/ves%2017%20num%201.pdf
12. RapidMiner. http://rapidminer.com/
13. Hall, M., Frank, E., Holmes, G., Pfahringer, B., Reutemann, P., Witten, I.H.: The WEKA data mining software: an update. SIGKDD Explor. **11**(1), 37–57 (2009)
14. John, G.H., Langley, P.: Estimating continuous distributions in bayesian classifiers. In: Eleventh Conference on Uncertainty in Artificial Intelligence, San Mateo, pp. 338–345 (1995)
15. Witten, I.H., Frank, E., Hall, M.A.: Data mining: practical machine learning tools and techniques, 3rd edn. Morgan Kaufmann, USA (2011)
16. le Cessie, S., van Houwelingen, J.C.: Ridge estimators in logistic regression. Appl. Stat. **41**(1), 191–201 (1992)
17. Cristianini, N., Shawe-Taylor, J.: An introduction to Support Vector Machines and Other Kernel-based Learning Methods. Cambridge University Press, Cambridge (2000)
18. Vapnik, V.N.: The nature of statistical learning theory. Springer-Verlag New York, Inc., New York (1995)
19. Platt, J.: Sequential Minimal Optimisation: A Fast Algorithm for Training Support Vector Machines. TechReport MSR-TR-98-14, Microsoft Research (1998)
20. Goutte, C., Gaussier, E.: A probabilistic interpretation of precision, recall and f-score, with implication for evaluation. Advances in information retrieval. Springer, Heidelberg (2005)
21. Abdi, H., Williams, L.J.: Principal component analysis. Computational Statistics 2, 433–459, John Wiley & Sons, Inc. (2010)
22. Rosenberg, A.: Classifying skewed data: importance to optimize average recall. Proc. Interspeech **2012**, 2242–2245 (2012)
23. Bailey, R.A.: Design of comparative experiments. Cambridge University Press, New York (2008)
24. Kennedy, J.J., Bush, A.J.: An introduction to the design and analysis of experiments in behavioral research. University Press of America, New York (1985)
25. R Core Team: R: A language and environment for statistical computing. R Foundation for Statistical Computing, Vienna, Austria (2015). http://www.r-project.org/
26. Shapiro, S.S., Wilk, M.B.: An analysis of variance test for normality (complete samples). Biometrika **52**(3–4), 591–611 (1965)
27. Spearman, C.: The proof and measurement of association between two things. Am. J. Psychol. **15**(1), 72–101 (1904)

Investigation of Segmentation in i-Vector Based Speaker Diarization of Telephone Speech

Zbyněk Zajíc[1](✉), Marie Kunešová[1,2], and Vlasta Radová[1,2]

[1] Faculty of Applied Sciences, NTIS - New Technologies for the Information Society, University of West Bohemia, Univerzitní 8, 306 14 Plzeň, Czech Republic
zzajic@ntis.zcu.cz
[2] Faculty of Applied Sciences, Department of Cybernetics, University of West Bohemia, Univerzitní 8, 306 14 Plzeň, Czech Republic
{mkunes,radova}@kky.zcu.cz
http://www.zcu.cz

Abstract. The goal of this paper is to evaluate the contribution of speaker change detection (SCD) to the performance of a speaker diarization system in the telephone domain. We compare the overall performance of an i-vector based system using both SCD-based segmentation and a naive constant length segmentation with overlapping segments. The diarization system performs K-means clustering of i-vectors which represent the individual segments, followed by a resegmentation step. Experiments were done on the English part of the CallHome corpus. The final results indicate that the use of speaker change detection is beneficial, but the differences between the two segmentation approaches are diminished by the use of resegmentation.

Keywords: Speaker diarization · Speaker change detection · i-vector · Segmentation

1 Introduction

Speaker diarization is defined as the task of categorizing different speech sources in an unlabeled conversation. Or in other words, determining "Who spoke when", typically without any prior information regarding the number and identities of the speakers.

The majority of diarization systems follow one of two basic approaches. The most common approach consists of the segmentation of the input signal, followed by the merging of the segments into clusters corresponding to the individual speakers [1,2]. The alternative is to combine the segmentation and clustering steps into a single iterative process [3,4].

In systems which have a standalone segmentation step, speaker change detection (SCD) is often applied to this purpose, as it allows to obtain segments which ideally contain only the speech of a single speaker (e.g. [1]). However, due to some of the common obstacles typically present in spontaneous telephone

© Springer International Publishing Switzerland 2016
A. Ronzhin et al. (Eds.): SPECOM 2016, LNAI 9811, pp. 411–418, 2016.
DOI: 10.1007/978-3-319-43958-7_49

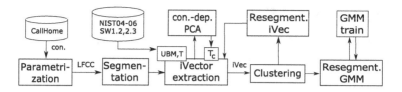

Fig. 1. Diagram of the diarization process.

conversation, namely very short speaker turns and frequent overlapping speech, diarization systems aimed at telephone speech often omit the SCD process and use a simple constant length segmentation of areas of speech found by a speech activity detector (e.g. [2,5]).

In this paper, we compare the two segmentation approaches on telephone data from the CallHome corpus [15]. Our goal is to determine whether the SCD approach offers any improvement under such conditions.For this purpose, we implement an i-vector based speaker diarization system. The use of i-vectors in speaker diarization has become increasingly popular in recent years [2,5], following their success in speaker recognition tasks [6,7].

This paper is organized as follows: The i-vector based speaker diarization system is described in Sect. 2. In Sect. 3, two approaches to segmentation are introduced: segmentation with constant length segments and segmentation based on SCD. The i-vector extraction is explained in Sect. 4, clustering using K-means in Sect. 5 and the resegmentation step is described in Sect. 6. The comparison of the efficiency of the two proposed segmentation approaches is presented in Sect. 7.

2   Speaker Diarization System

Our speaker diarization system is based on the use of i-vectors to represent segments of speech, as introduced in [8]. The diarization process starts with the extraction of acoustic features from the conversation and the identification of the regions of speech by a voice activity detector. Following this, the non-speech regions are discarded and the rest is split into short segments, using SCD-based or constant length segmentation. In the next step, a single i-vector is extracted from each segment and the i-vectors are clustered using cosine distance in order to determine which parts of the signal were produced by the same speaker. Finally, the system iteratively performs resegmentation using a similar i-vector based clustering process, followed by a single iteration using GMMs to refine the final results. A diagram of our diarization system can be seen in Fig. 1 and the main steps are described in detail in the following sections.

3   Segmentation

The purpose of the segmentation step of a speaker diarization system is to divide an audio recording into short segments, so that they can be subsequently merged into clusters corresponding to the individual speakers. The length of the segments should be enough to allow the extraction of speaker-identifying information, in our case represented by an i-vector, while limiting the risk of a speaker change being present within the segment, as may happen in longer segments, depending on the used method. In the following subsections, we describe the two segmentation approaches which were considered.

3.1 Constant Length Segments

The naive approach to segmentation is to simply split the speech regions into short segments of fixed length. The main issue with this simple method is that the segment boundaries do not correspond in any way to the speaker change points and so many of the segments may contain the speech of more than one speaker. For this reason, it is preferable to use very short segments. On the other hand, a certain minimal duration is required for i-vector extraction. Typically, this is selected as 1–2 s of speech. As in [2], segment overlap is used to increase the amount of information contained in a single i-vector while retaining the same precision of the segmentation.

3.2 Speaker Change Detection

The standard approach to speaker change detection consists of applying a pair of sliding windows on the signal and computing the distance between their contents. Speaker changes are then found at the boundary between the two windows, at the points in which the distance achieves a significant local maximum. An example of this approach can be found in [1].

Commonly used distance metrics include the Bayesian Information Criterion (BIC), Generalized Likelihood Ratio (GLR) and Kullback-Leibler divergence.

In our system, we use a GLR-based segmentation. In order to obtain segments of consistent length, comparable to the constant length approach described in Sect. 3.1, we use a two-step algorithm which incorporates a fixed minimum and maximum segment length.

In the first step of the segmentation, we identify a smaller number of the most likely speaker change points by performing standard GLR-based speaker change detection using two neighboring sliding windows of 2 s with a step size of 0.1 s.

The distance between two windows X_i and X_j is calculated as

$$d(X_i, X_j) = -\log GLR(X_i, X_j),\tag{1}$$

where $GLR(X_i, X_j)$ is the generalized likelihood ratio, which is defined as

$$GLR(i, j) = \frac{L(X_i \cup X_j | M)}{L(X_i | M_i) \cdot L(X_j | M_j)}\tag{2}$$

and is used to express whether X_i and X_j are better represented by a single model M or two different ones, M_i and M_j [9]. In our system, M, M_i and M_j are

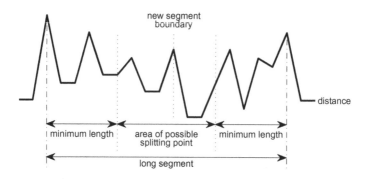

Fig. 2. The process of splitting longer segments.

single Gaussians with full covariance matrices, estimated from the corresponding data.

Likely speaker changes are identified as the locations of significant local maxima of the distances. For this purpose, we calculate the prominence of individual peaks in the distances and select those with values exceeding a threshold.

Peak prominence measures how much a given peak stands out within the signal and is calculated as follows: on each side of the peak, find the minimum of the signal that lies in the area between the peak and either the nearest higher point or the edge of the signal. The prominence of the peak is given as the difference between the value of the peak and the higher of the two minima.

The second step of the segmentation consists of further splitting any segments which are longer than the maximum allowed length. The point where a long segment is split is found in the following manner:

First, the system identifies an area where a split can occur, such that neither of the resulting new segments would be shorter than the minimum allowed length. If there are any peaks within this smaller area, the one with the highest prominence (as calculated during the first step of the segmentation) is selected as the new segment boundary. If no peaks are present, the segment is cut at the edge of the area, at the point where the distance is highest. Figure 2 illustrates this process.

4   Segment Description

For each segment of parametrized conversation the supervector of statistics is accumulated. Subsequently, an i-vector is extracted from the supervector.

4.1   Statistics Extracted on GMM

For each segment of a parametrized conversation the supervector of statistics is accumulated. Supervector of statistics contains the first and zeroth statistical moments of speakers' data related to a Universal Background Model (UBM) based on GMM. This idea has origins in the speaker adaptation process [10], where these statistics are used as a descriptor of a new speaker.

First, a GMM trained on a huge amount of data from different speakers is used as a UBM and consists of a set of parameters $\lambda_{\mathrm{UBM}} = \{\omega_m, \boldsymbol{\mu}_m, \boldsymbol{C}_m\}_{m=1}^{M}$, where M is the number of Gaussians in the UBM, ω_m, $\boldsymbol{\mu}_m$, $\boldsymbol{C}_m$ are the weight, mean and covariance of the mth Gaussian, respectively. In our case, the covariance matrix $\boldsymbol{C}_m$ is diagonal with vector σ_m on diagonal. Let $\boldsymbol{O} = \{\boldsymbol{o}_t\}_{t=1}^{T}$ be the set of T feature vectors $\boldsymbol{o}_t$ of dimension D of one segment of conversation, and

$$\gamma_m(\boldsymbol{o}_t) = \frac{\omega_m \mathcal{N}(\boldsymbol{o}_t; \boldsymbol{\mu}_m, \boldsymbol{C}_m)}{\sum_{m=1}^{M} \omega_m \mathcal{N}(\boldsymbol{o}_t; \boldsymbol{\mu}_m, \boldsymbol{C}_m)} \tag{3}$$

be the posterior probability of mth Gaussian given a feature vector $\boldsymbol{o}_t$. The soft count of the mth Gaussian (zeroth statistical moments of feature vectors) is $n_m = \sum_{t=1}^{T} \gamma_m(\boldsymbol{o}_t)$ and the sum of the first statistical moments of feature vectors with respect to the mth Gaussian is $\boldsymbol{b}_m = \sum_{t=1}^{T} \gamma_m(\boldsymbol{o}_t)\boldsymbol{o}_t$. The speaker's supervector for given data $\boldsymbol{O}$ is a concatenation of the zeroth and first statistical moments of $\boldsymbol{O}$.

4.2   i-Vectors

For i-vectors extraction the Factor Analysis (FA) approach [11] (or extended Joint Factor Analysis (JFA) [12] to handle more sessions of each speaker) is used for dimensionality reduction of the supervector of statistics. The generative i-vector model has the form

$$\psi = \boldsymbol{m}_0 + \boldsymbol{T}\boldsymbol{w} + \epsilon, \quad \boldsymbol{w} \sim \mathcal{N}(\boldsymbol{0}, \boldsymbol{I}), \quad \epsilon \sim \mathcal{N}(\boldsymbol{0}, \boldsymbol{\Sigma}), \tag{4}$$

where $\boldsymbol{T}$ (of size $D \times D_w$) is called the total variability space matrix, $\boldsymbol{w}$ is the segment's i-vector of dimension D_w having standard Gaussian distribution, $\boldsymbol{m}_0$ is the mean vector of ψ, however often the UBM's mean supervector $\boldsymbol{m}_0$ is taken instead as an approximation, and ϵ is some residual noise with a diagonal covariance $\boldsymbol{\Sigma}$ constructed from covariance matrices $\boldsymbol{C}_1, \ldots, \boldsymbol{C}_m$ of the UBM ordered on the diagonal of $\boldsymbol{\Sigma}$. The i-vectors are also length-normalised [7]. Details about training of total variability space matrix $\boldsymbol{T}$ can be seen in [13] or [14].

Because of the differences between each conversation (and the similarity in one conversation), we also compute a conversation dependent PCA transformation, which further reduces the dimensionality of the i-vector $\boldsymbol{w}$. The dimension of the PCA latent space is dependent on the parameter p, the ratio of eigenvalue mass [8] (in our case $p = 0.5$).

5   Clustering

The clustering of all segments is used for determining which segments are produced by the same speaker. Since our data only includes conversations with

2 speakers, we use K-means clustering into 2 clusters, based on cosine distance [8] of two i-vectors:

$$dist(\boldsymbol{w}_1, \boldsymbol{w}_2) = \frac{\boldsymbol{w}_1^T \boldsymbol{w}_2}{\|\boldsymbol{w}_1\| \cdot \|\boldsymbol{w}_2\|}, \tag{5}$$

where $\boldsymbol{w}_1$ and $\boldsymbol{w}_2$ are these i-vectors.

6   Resegmentation

After clustering the segments, the new i-vector of each cluster is computed (only from data of each cluster) and resegmentation is made to get better results. This process is repeated iteratively until the clusters consist of the same segments as in previous iteration (or the maximum number of iterations is reached). After the i-vector resegmentation, data (in the form of acoustic features) belonging to each cluster are used to train the Gaussian Mixture Model (GMM) of this cluster. The whole conversation is then resegmented frame by frame according to the likelihood of each GMM.

7   Experiments

In this paper, we try to answer the question of whether segmentation by SCD can improve the performance of an i-vector based speaker diarization system compared to the use of a naive segmentation with constant length segments. The experiment was carried out on telephone conversations from the English part of CallHome corpus [15], where only two speaker conversations were selected (so the clustering can be limited to two clusters), this is 109 conversation each with about 10 min duration in a single telephone channel sampled at 8 kHz.

The feature extraction was based on Linear Frequency Cepstral Coefficients (LFCCs), Hamming window of length 25 ms with 10 ms shift of the window. There are 25 triangular filter banks which are spread linearly across the frequency spectrum, and 20 LFCCs were extracted. Delta coefficients were added leading to a 40-dimensional feature vector. Instead of the voice activity detector, the reference annotation about missed speech was used.

For naive segmentation, a 2 s window with 1 s of overlap was used. For segmentation by SCD, the length of the segments was set to 4 s maximum and 0.1 s minimum.

The i-vector extraction system was trained using the following corpora: NIST SRE 2004, NIST SRE 2005, NIST SRE 2006, Switchboard 1 Release 2 and Switchboard 2 Phase 3. The number of Gaussians in the UBM was set to 512. The latent dimension (dimension of i-vectors) in the FA total variability space matrix $\boldsymbol{T}$ in the i-vector extraction was set to 400. Finally, the dimension of the final i-vector was reduced by conversation dependent PCA with the ratio of eigenvalue mass $p = 0.5$.

In the resegmentation, the maximum iteration was set to 1000. The GMMs consisted of 1024 components and were trained by adaptation from a UBM.

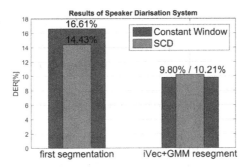

Fig. 3. Comparison of the system using SCD-based segmentation and constant window segmentation, before and after resegmentation. Results are given as given as DER[%].

7.1 Results

For evaluation, the Diarization Error Rate (DER) was used as described and used by NIST in the RT evaluations [16], with 250 ms tolerance around the reference boundaries. DER combines all types of error (missed speech, mislabeled non-speech, incorrect speaker cluster), but with correct information about the silence from the reference annotation, DER represents only the error in speaker cluster. The results are shown in Fig. 3.

The experimental results of two approaches to the segmentation for speaker diarization task indicate, that the segmentation based on SCD brings better information for further clustering. However, the following iterations of resegmentation reduce the impact of inaccurate segmentation, making the final differences between systems with or without SCD negligible.

8 Conclusions

In this work, we compared two approaches to segmentation in an i-vector based speaker diarization system. The SCD segmentation method is based on finding the precise boundaries where the speaker is changing. On the other hand, the segmentation with constant length divides a conversation into short segments and relies on clustering and further resegmentation to refine the boundaries. The experimental results of these two approaches show that the SCD approach offers significantly better performance in the clustering stage, but the differences are diminished by the resegmentation. Therefore the naive segmentation is a sufficient approach for the speaker diarization system based on i-vectors.

Acknowledgments. The work was supported by the Ministry of Education, Youth and Sports of the Czech Republic project No. LO1506 and by the grant of the University of West Bohemia, project No. SGS-2016-039. Access to computing and storage facilities (CESNET LM2015042) is greatly appreciated.

References

1. Rouvier, M., Dupuy, G., Gay, P., Khoury, E., Merlin, T., Meignier, S.: An open-source state-of-the-art toolbox for broadcast news diarization. Technical report, Idiap (2013)
2. Sell, G., Garcia-Romero, D.: Speaker diarization with PLDA i-vector scoring and unsupervised calibration. In: IEEE Spoken Language Technology Workshop, pp. 413–417 (2014)
3. Fredouille, C., Bozonnet, S., Evans, N.: The lia-eurecom RT 09 speaker diarization system. In: RT-09, NIST Rich Transcription Workshop (2009)
4. Shum, S.H., Dehak, N., Dehak, R., Glass, J.R.: Unsupervised methods for speaker diarization: an integrated and iterative approach. IEEE Trans. Audio Speech Lang. Process. 21(10), 2015–2028 (2013)
5. Senoussaoui, M., Kenny, P., Stafylakis, T., Dumouchel, P.: A study of the cosine distance-based mean shift for telephone speech diarization. IEEE Trans. Audio Speech Lang. Process. 22(1), 217–227 (2014)
6. Dehak, N., Kenny, P., Dehak, R., Dumouchel, P., Ouellet, P.: Front-end factor analysis for speaker verification. IEEE Trans. Audio Speech Lang. Process. 19(4), 788–798 (2011)
7. Garcia-Romero, D., Espy-Wilson, C.Y.: Analysis of i-vector length normalization in speaker recognition systems. In: Interspeech 2011, pp. 249–252, Florence (2011)
8. Shum, S., Dehak, N., Chuangsuwanich, E., Reynolds, D., Glass, J.: Exploiting intra-conversation variability for speaker diarization. In: INTERSPEECH, pp. 945–948, August 2011
9. Gish, H., Siu, M.H., Rohlicek, R.: Segregation of speakers for speech recognition and speaker identification. In: ICASSP, pp. 873–876 (1991)
10. Zajíc, Z., Machlica, L., Müller, L.: Initialization of fMLLR with Sufficient statistics from similar speakers. In: Habernal, I., Matoušek, V. (eds.) TSD 2011. LNCS, vol. 6836, pp. 187–194. Springer, Heidelberg (2011)
11. Kenny, P., Dumouchel, P.: Experiments in speaker verification using factor analysis likelihood ratios. In: Odyssey - Speaker and Language Recognition Workshop, pp. 219–226, Toledo (2004)
12. Kenny, P.: Joint factor analysis of speaker and session variability: theory and algorithms. Technical report (2006)
13. Machlica, L., Zajíc, Z.: Factor analysis and nuisance attribute projection revisited. In: Interspeech 2012, pp. 1570–1573, Portland (2012)
14. Kenny, P., Ouellet, P., Dehak, N., Gupta, V., Dumouchel, P.: A study of inters-peaker variability in speaker verification. IEEE Trans. Audio Speech Lang. Process. 16(5), 980–988 (2008)
15. Canavan, A., Graff, D., Zipperlen, G.: CALLHOME American English Speech LDC97S42. LDC Catalog. Philadelphia: Linguistic Data Consortium (1997)
16. Fiscus, J.G., Ajot, J., Michel, M., Garofolo, J.S.: The rich transcription 2006 spring meeting recognition evaluation. In: Renals, S., Bengio, S., Fiscus, J.G. (eds.) MLMI 2006. LNCS, vol. 4299, pp. 309–322. Springer, Heidelberg (2006)

Investigation of Speech Signal Parameters Reflecting the Truth of Transmitted Information

Victor Budkov[1(✉)], Irina Vatamaniuk[1], Vladimir Basov[1], and Daniyar Volf[2]

[1] SPIIRAS, 39, 14th Line, St. Petersburg 199178, Russia
{budkov,vatamaniuk}@iias.spb.su, vovilla@mail.ru
[2] TUSUR, 40, Lenina Avenue, Tomsk 634050, Russia
runsolar@mail.ru

Abstract. A review of the existing methods of transmitted information truth diagnostics is presented. A conclusion concerning the purposefulness of this function realization in polymodal infocommunication systems has been shown. Parameters of speech signal that reflect the truth of transmitted information are considered. The results of testing the developed software are presented. Based on the undertaken study, a conclusion concerning possibility of realization of transmitted information truth in the course of interpersonal communication between subscribers has been drawn and a decisive rule has been formulated.

Keywords: Speech signal · Assessment of the truth of transmitted messages · Lie detector · Polymodal infocommunication system

1 Introduction

The constantly growing loads on the psychological activity of infocommunication systems subscribers make the processes of their communication more and more diverse and emotionally constrained. Despite the constant necessity in solving the problem of the transmitted message falsity (truth) under such conditions, nowadays, the secure methods of the corresponding function realization in the corresponding communication systems do not exist [1–3].

Nowadays for solving the problem of the message falsity determination the method of instrumental diagnostics with the help of a polygraph detector (lie detector) is mostly used. In terms of this method, the conclusion about the falsity of the information transmitted by a person is shown upon his psychophysical reaction changes character. Despite its popularity, a number of conditions significantly limit its application in practice. Particularly, the use of polygraph as a contact method is possible only provided meeting the range of requirements concerning the place of study organization (comfortable temperature, optimal humidity, noise insulation etc.) and of personal character (personal consent to studies, absence of somatic diseases, mental disorder and etc.) [4, 5]. All listed requirements make the use of polygraph in the course of infocommunication systems subscriber's communicative interaction nearly impossible.

A noncontact method of a person's psychophysiological reaction is also known and it resides in the person's psychophysical reaction fixation according to his changing

© Springer International Publishing Switzerland 2016
A. Ronzhin et al. (Eds.): SPECOM 2016, LNAI 9811, pp. 419–426, 2016.
DOI: 10.1007/978-3-319-43958-7_50

electromagnetic field in the process of verbal and nonverbal communication. The disadvantage of this method is in the necessity of instrumental complex implementation and a stimulating verbal exposure, which makes its exploitation in infocommunication systems impossible [6].

The degree of users' replies honesty can be determined with the help of noninvasive video registration of the eye movement parameters registration during verbal communication [7, 8]. The conclusion concerning the emotional psychophysical elevation which may appear as a result of information concealing or garbling, is drawn based on the comparison of numbers of blinking acts, figure's area and pupils diameter with the control value. The suggested approach appears to be contact and requires special equipment (video-oculography) and abiding to a set of rules significant for the research procedure performance, which makes this method complicated for subscribers' communication.

A method of defining the multimodal information falsity transmitted in the course of communication act with the help of these systems has been suggested in [9]. Common tendencies concerning the subscribers' non-verbal behavior parameters dynamics have been formulated. Based on the factor and multiple regressive analyses the factors depending on such dynamics have been distinguished. Based on the research carried out a conclusion concerning the possibility of realization of transmitted information falsity in the course of interpersonal communication between subscribers was drawn and a decisive rule has been formulated.

The truth (falsity) evaluation of the speaker can be carried out on the basis of speaker's emotional-psychological features and states range by a number of experts-observers using the same video fragment of the test with duration not less than 40-60 s [10]. Experts [numbered not less than 10 people] must know the basics of the human expressive body movements on the scale of popular editions [11, 12]. The conclusion concerning the speaker's honesty is drawn with the consideration of visual and audio evaluation correspondence index based on the correspondence degree of the voice intonation and the total of expressive body movements (facial gestures, posture and gestures).

The stated index is defined through the mean estimator for each group of experts as a result of Spearmen's rank-order correlation calculation and accepts it as a psychophysiological measure of the speaker's honesty. The described approach appears to be too subjective as it requires expert group participation and does not allow identifying individual peculiarities of nonverbal behavior of a particular subscriber which significantly reduces the value of the obtained results.

Besides, a great number of medical and special equipment oriented on human functional features assessment including his behavior exists and in this respect the problem was successfully solved a long time ago. However, the problem of lie detection in both technical and methodological respect is far from being simple and requires enhanced solutions and new approaches.

Application of the existing and expected solutions of the signal processing tasks with different modalities during the polymodal infocommunication systems (PICS) synthesis will provide an opportunity of defining the transmitted information falsity [13]. PICS should be understood as an interconnected aggregate of multimodal interfaces, information processing and storing subsets, telecommunication systems, their unifiers functioning under the sole management with the aim of collecting, processing, storing, protection transmission and reallocation, reflection and exploitation of multimodal information to the benefit of the subscribers.

In [14–18] various methods of deceptive speech detection are considered. These methods are based on: (1) application of the fractional Mel cepstral coefficient (FrCC); (2) analysis of speaking rate, response onset time, and frequency and duration of hesitation markers; (3) analysis of nonlinear spectral features derived using a Bark scale and psychoacoustic masking property of human speech; (4) non-linear dynamics (NLD) features and relevance vector machine (RVM) based on sparse Bayesian Learning (SBL) for feature classification.

The main way to improve the accuracy of estimating the truth of transmitted voice messages lies through creation of methods and software for their realization, enabling one to individualize the approach, to implement adjustment, to detect the most informative parameters of communicant speech reflecting the truth of transmitted information in each case [19–22].

2 Software for Investigation of Speech Signal Parameters

The functional flow diagram of the software solution allowing detection of the parameters of speech signal is presented in Fig. 1. Let us consider it in more details.

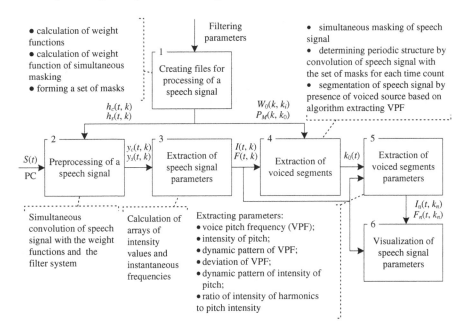

Fig. 1. The functional flow diagram of the developed software for speech processing

The module "Creating files for processing of a speech signal" includes: (1) the module of calculation of weight functions $h_C(t, k)$ and $h_S(t, k)$ of the filter system; (2)

the module of calculation of weight function of simultaneous masking $W_0(k, k_i)$, applied for extraction of frequency domain of strong correlation; (3) the module of forming a set of masks $P_M(k, k_0)$ based on $W_0(k, k_i)$.

The module "Preprocessing of a speech signal" consists of two modules simultaneously committing convolution of speech signal S(t) with the weight functions hC(t, k) and hS(t, k) of the filter system. The module "Extraction of speech signal parameters" includes modules calculating arrays of intensity values I(t, k) and instantaneous frequencies F(t, k) of the filtered speech signal.

The module "Extraction of voiced segments" includes: (1) the module of simultaneous masking of speech signal; (2) the module determining periodic structure by convolution of speech signal with the set of masks for each time count; (3) the module segmenting a speech signal by presence of voiced source based on the algorithm extracting voice pitch frequency.

In this study, the following speech parameters reflecting the truth of transmitted information were considered: the presence of voiced sound, voice pitch frequency (VPF), intensity of pitch, dynamic pattern of VPF, deviation of VPF, dynamic pattern of intensity of pitch, ratio of intensity of harmonics to pitch intensity [23–26]. To extract these parameters the appropriate module was implemented in the software solution (Fig. 1). The module "Visualization of speech signal parameters" allows saving obtained graphs both in automatic and manual mode.

3   Experiment Results

The investigation of a speech signal using developed tests and the software solution yielded results that are partially presented in Table 1 and Figs. 2 and 3. The test included the following sequence of Neutral (N), Control (C) and Important (I) questions, aimed to detect implication of the test person in a laptop theft:

Table 1. Patterns of the speech signal characteristics obtained during the experiments

Case	VPF	Mean value of VPF	Deviation from the mean value
A man answers the neutral questions	120–140 Hz	130 Hz	10 Hz
A man answers the important questions	120–150 Hz	135 Hz	15 Hz
A man answers the control questions	110–140 Hz	125 Hz	15 Hz
A woman answers the neutral questions	200–240 Hz	220 Hz	20 Hz
A woman answers the important questions	160–250 Hz	205 Hz	45 Hz
A woman answers the control questions	180–280 Hz	230 Hz	50 Hz

N1: Were you born in 1985?
C1: Have you ever taken other people's stuff without permission?
I1: Did you steal the laptop?
N2: Is your name Maxim?
C2: Have you ever broken the law?
I2: Have you ever been to his house?
N3: Are you 22 years old?
C3: Have you ever stolen something?
I3: Did you steal the laptop?
N4: Have you had lunch today?
C4: Have you ever lied to somebody to avoid problems?
I4: Are you involved in the theft of the laptop?

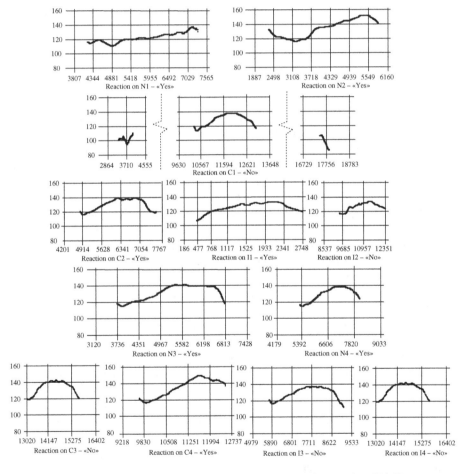

Fig. 2. Reaction patterns of the male test person at the questions N1-I2

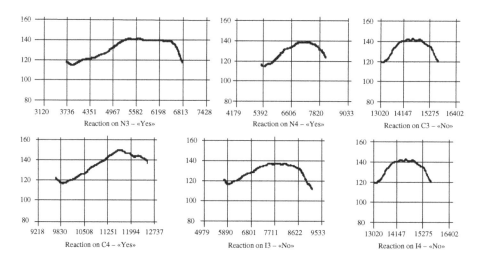

Fig. 3. Reaction patterns of the male test person at the questions N3-I4

The neutral questions belong to the general category; they do not cause anxiety. The special important questions are associated with the crime. The control questions always have generalized nature. They aim is to bring the person being tested into confusion and cause anxiety. The results presented in Table 1 show that when the test person answers the neutral questions, he/she has no strong emotional excitement. This fact allows one to compose a reaction pattern of test person telling a lie and the truth and to compare the reaction to the control and important questions with it. A lie brings a person in a stress state, which is reflected in a change of speech parameters.

For numerical expression of the results the reaction to the important questions and to the subsequent control questions were compared (I1 was compared with C1, I2 was compared with C2, and I3 was compared with C3). The measure of discrepancy of physiological response Pr was considered: (1) if there is no difference in physiological reaction of the test person, the zero rating is assigned, $Pr = 0$; (2) if the difference is noticeable, $Pr = 1$; 3) if the difference is intense or very intense, the $Pr = 2$ or $Pr = 3$ respectively.

If the reaction at the important question is stronger than at the control one, the negative rating is put ($Pr = -1, -2$ or -3) and vice versa, if the reaction at the important question is weaker than at the control one, the positive rating is put ($Pr = +1, +2$ or $+3$). Then the ratings are summed and the total test score is drawn. The final test result is based on this total score. If it falls to -6 or below ($Pr = -7, -8$, etc.), the test person is considered to fail the test and, consequently, he/she have lied. If the final rating reaches $+6$ or above ($Pr = +7, +8$, etc.), the test person is considered to tell the truth. The ratings in the interval ($-5 \leq Pr \leq +5$) point to an uncertain result.

Let us consider an example. It is seen in case of interviewing the test person (Fig. 2) that the reaction at the question C1 is stronger than at the I1; hence, $P_r = +3$. The reaction at the C3 is the same as at the I3, $P_r = 0$. As a result the final score is $P_r = +6$, that allows considering the test passed. Consequently, the person being tested has reported the truth information.

4 Conclusion

The obtained results testify to the possibility of the realization of the suggested method of transmitted multimodal information falsity determination in the real-time mode and in the process of interpersonal communication between PICS subscribers. Its further development and perfection is due to increasing the accuracy of the algorithms for modality identification and estimation of nonverbal parameters of human behavior.

Acknowledgment. This work is supported by the Russian Foundation for Basic Research (project No. 16-37-60085) and by the Council for Grants of the President of Russia (project No. MK-7925.2016.9).

References

1. Basov, O.O.: Reasoning of the transition to polymodal infocommunicational systems. In: Trudy 18 Mezhdunarodnoj Nauchnoj Konferencii "Raspredelennye komp'juternye i telekommunikacionnye seti: upravlenie, vychis-lenie, svjaz' (DCCN-2015)". Moscow, October, 19–22, pp. 418–425 (2015)
2. Budkov, V.Y., Ronzhin, A.L., Saveliev, A.I.: Context-aware mobile applications for communication in intelligent environment. In: Andreev, S., Balandin, S., Koucheryavy, Y. (eds.) NEW2AN/ruSMART 2012. LNCS, vol. 7469, pp. 307–315. Springer, Heidelberg (2012)
3. Budkov, V.Y., Ronzhin, A.L., Glazkov, S.V., Ronzhin, A.: Event-driven content management system for smart meeting room. In: Balandin, S., Koucheryavy, Y., Hu, H. (eds.) NEW2AN 2011 and ruSMART 2011. LNCS, vol. 6869, pp. 550–560. Springer, Heidelberg (2011)
4. Vrij, A.: Detecting lies and deceit: The psychology of lying and implications for professional practice. Wiley, London (2000)
5. Gruzyeva, I.V.: Formal-dynamic and Stylistic Peculiarities of Individuality as Factors of Instrumental Detection of the Concealed Information. Author's Abstract. Cand. Sc. {Psychology} (2006) (In Russian)
6. Gubaidulin, V.I., Zimin, E.V.: Method of Control over Human Psychophysical Reaction and Device for its Fulfilling. Patent RU 2216269, Proprietor: International Federation of Shaping, Application 2000122210/14, 21.08.2000 (2003)
7. Usanov, D.A., Romanova, N.M., Skripal, A.V., Rytik, A.P., Vagarin, A.J., Samokhina, M.A.: Method of estimation of psychophysical condition of person. Patent RU 2337607, Application 2007111403/14, 28.03.2007, Bull. 31 (2008)
8. Romanova, N.M., Rytik, A.P., Samohina, M.A., Skripal, A.V., Usanov, D.A.: Osobennosti glazodvigatel'nyh reakcij cheloveka pri proiznesenii istinnoj i lozhnoj informacii. Izvestija Saratovskogo universiteta. Novaja serija. Serija: Filosofija. Psihologija. Pedagogika, **8**(1), 65–73 (2008) (In Russian)
9. Basov, O., Ronzhin, A., Budkov, V., Saitov, I.: Method of defining multimodal information falsity for smart telecommunication systems. In: Balandin, S., Andreev, S., Koucheryavy, Y. (eds.) NEW2AN/ruSMART 2015. LNCS, vol. 9247, pp. 163–173. Springer, Heidelberg (2015)
10. Morozov, V.P., Morozov, P.V.: Method for estimating sincerity-insincerity of speaking person. Patent RU 2293518, Application 2005124844/14, 04.08.2005, Bull. 5 (2007)

11. Nierenberg, G., Calero, H.H.: How to Read a Person like a Book. Simon and Schuster, New York (1971)
12. Pease, B., Pease, A.: The definitive book of body language. Bantam, New York (2008)
13. Basov, O.O., Saitov, I.A.: Basic channels of interpersonal communication and their projection onto infocommunicational systems. SPIIRAS Proc. **30**, 122–140 (2013)
14. Pan, X., Zhao, H., Zhou, Y.: The application of fractional Mel cepstral coefficient in deceptive speech detection. PeerJ **3**, e1194 (2015)
15. Kirchhübel, C., Stedmon, A.W., Howard, D.M.: Analyzing deceptive speech. Engineering Psychology and Cognitive Ergonomics. Understanding Human Cognition, pp. 134–141. Springer, Berlin Heidelberg (2013)
16. Sanaullah, M., Gopalan, K.: Deception detection in speech using bark band and perceptually significant energy features. In: 2013 IEEE 56th International Midwest Symposium on Circuits and Systems (MWSCAS), pp. 1212–1215. IEEE (2013)
17. Gopalan, K., Chu, T., Miao, X.: An utterance recognition technique for keyword spotting by fusion of bark energy and MFCC features. In: Rudas, I., Demiralp, M., Mastorakis, N. (eds.), WSEAS International Conference. Proceedings. Recent Advances in Computer Engineering (No. 9). WSEAS (2009)
18. Zhou, Y., Zhao, H., Pan, X., Shang, L.: Deception detecting from speech signal using relevance vector machine and non-linear dynamics features. Neurocomputing **151**, 1042–1052 (2015)
19. Basov, O., Ronzhin, A., Budkov, V.: Optimization of pitch tracking and quantization. In: Ronzhin, A., Potapova, R., Fakotakis, N. (eds.) SPECOM 2015. LNCS, vol. 9319, pp. 317–324. Springer, Heidelberg (2015)
20. Basov, O.O., Hahamov, P., Nosov, M.V.: Improving the efficiency of management under the conditions of staff's psychophysiological state changing. SPIIRAS Proc. **34**, 112–135 (2014)
21. Basov, O.O., Nosov, M.V., Shalaginov, V.A.: Pitch-jitter analysis of the speech signal. SPIIRAS Proc. **32**, 27–44 (2014)
22. Meshcheriakov, R.V., Ponizov, A.G.: Quality assessment of hearing based on mobile computing devices. SPIIRAS Proc. **18**, 93–107 (2011)
23. Basov, O., Ronzhin, A., Budkov, V.: Optimization of pitch tracking and quantization. In: Ronzhin, A., Potapova, R., Fakotakis, N. (eds.) SPECOM 2015. LNCS, vol. 9319, pp. 317–324. Springer, Heidelberg (2015)
24. Volf, D.A., Meshcheryakov, R.V.: Software implementation of a singular meter of the pitch frequency of a speech signal. SPIIRAS Proc. **43**, 191–209 (2015)
25. Basov, O., Ronzhin, A., Budkov, V., Saitov, I.: Method of defining multimodal information falsity for smart telecommunication systems. In: Balandin, S., Andreev, S., Koucheryavy, Y. (eds.) NEW2AN/ruSMART 2015. LNCS, vol. 9247, pp. 163–173. Springer, Heidelberg (2015)
26. Volf, D., Meshcheryakov, R., Kharchenko, S.: The singular estimation pitch tracker. In: Ronzhin, A., Potapova, R., Fakotakis, N. (eds.) SPECOM 2015. LNCS, vol. 9319, pp. 454–462. Springer, Heidelberg (2015)

Investigating Signal Correlation as Continuity Metric in a Syllable Based Unit Selection Synthesis System

Sai Sirisha Rallabandi[1(✉)], Sai Krishna Rallabandi[1], Naina Teertha[2],
Kumaraswamy R.[2], and Suryakanth V. Gangashetty[1]

[1] Speech and Vision Laboratory, International Institute of Information Technology,
Hyderabad, India
{sirisha.rallabandi,saikrishna.r}@research.iiit.ac.in, svg@iiit.ac.in
[2] Siddaganga Institute of Technology, Tumkur, Karnataka, India
nainai91i98@gmail.com, hyrkswamy@gmail.com

Abstract. In recent years, text-to-speech (TTS) systems have shown considerable improvement as far as the quality of the synthetic speech is concerned. Data driven synthesis methods using syllable as basic unit for concatenation, have proved to generate high quality speech for Indian Languages because of their advantage of prosodic matching function. However, still there is no acceptable solution to the optimal selection of speech segments in terms of audible discontinuities and human perception. This problem gets aggravated in the cases where there is no enough data for building the voice due to the missing units. In this paper, we continue our efforts in trying to address this by investigating the use of a new continuity measure based on maximum signal correlation for optimal selection of units in concatenative text-to-speech (TTS) synthesis framework. We explore two formulations for calculating the signal correlation: cross correlation (CC) based and average magnitude difference function (AMDF) based. We first perform an initial experiment to understand the significance of the approach and then build 5 experimental systems. Evaluations on 30 sentences for each of these languages by native users of the language show that the proposed continuity measure results in more natural sounding synthesis.

Keywords: Unit selection synthesis · Cross correlation · Forced alignment · Target cost · Average magnitude difference function · Join cost

1 Introduction

Text-to-Speech synthesis systems convert an arbitrary text to a spoken waveform. Current TTS systems employing data-driven synthesis techniques are shown to generate more natural speech than the conventional approaches [5,19]. Data-driven synthesis techniques employ a large speech corpus containing multiple realizations of each unit with differing prosody [12]. During synthesis,

© Springer International Publishing Switzerland 2016
A. Ronzhin et al. (Eds.): SPECOM 2016, LNAI 9811, pp. 427–434, 2016.
DOI: 10.1007/978-3-319-43958-7_51

a particular manifestation of a unit is selected depending on how well it matches with the input specification and on how well it matches with other units in the sequence. Unit selection algorithm tries to select the longest available strings of units that match a sequence of target units [16]. Following a significant research progress, via platforms like Blizzard Challenges [2–4, 10, 13, 14] the unit selection concatenative method and statistical parametric synthesis have become the dominant approaches for building text-to-speech systems. Unit selection systems [6–8, 27] have become popular due to their highly natural-sounding synthetic speech compared to their statistical parametric counterparts. These systems have large speech databases containing many instances of each speech unit, with a varied and natural distribution of prosodic and spectral characteristics. The key idea in unit selection speech synthesis is to use the database as the acoustic inventory and to select at run time, different acoustic units that match better according to a cost function, so as to capture the characteristics of a targeted synthetic speech and at the same time deliver context-specific prosodic behaviour. The cost function is typically a combination of two costs: target cost (how closely a candidate units in the inventory match the required targets) and join cost (how well the neighbouring units are feasible for joining) [12].

1.1 Motivation

In this paper, the motivation for our approach comes from the understanding that the human speech database is fully comprised of naturally evolving adjacent speech frames, forming sequences of audibly perfect joins. The adjacent speech frames are highly correlated with each other. We try to emulate this correlated behavior in our synthesis framework. Specifically, we investigate the use of a continuity metric targeted at maximizing such correlation between the units during synthesis. There are two ways of using the correlation between the units in a unit selection synthesis framework. One way is use the knowledge of signal correlation during the concatenation of the selected units so that they are joined at the point of maximum correlation between the units. We have introduced this approach in [22]. The other way, which we focus on in this paper is to directly use the correlation as a sub cost in the join cost, thereby controlling the selection of the units themselves. We employ two formulations for estimating correlation between the units: Cross correlation based formulation and Average Magnitude Difference Function (AMDF) based formulation. We try to answer the following questions: Is signal correlation an important feature to be considered for obtaining more natural synthesis? Is it sufficient in itself to serve as join cost to ensure good quality synthesis or should it be used in combination with the other sub costs? How many time frames have to be considered from the units to calculate the correlation? Which formulation (CC vs AMDF) has better performance? Does performance improve if we combine both the formulations using appropriate weighting functions? To answer these questions, we build experimental systems and cross validate them. The outline of the paper is as follows: In Sect. 2, we present the current framework which was used in [22]. Section 3 lists the experiments conducted and the systems developed followed by conclusions.

2   Overview of the Current Framework: Baseline System

In this section, we give a brief overview of our synthesis system, as used in [24]. The framework follows a frontend/back-end architecture with Natural Language processing as front end and Digital signal processing module as back end.

2.1   Size of the Unit

The basic units of the writing system in Indian languages are characters which are an orthographic representation of speech sounds. A character in Indian language scripts is close to a syllable and can be typically of the following form: C, V, CV, VC, CCV and CVC, where C is a consonant and V is a vowel. All Indian language scripts have a common phonetic base, and a universal phoneset consists of about 35 consonants and about 18 vowels [15]. Earlier work on Indian languages suggested that a syllable based approach to synthesis could lead to more reliable quality. There are a number of reasons for this, some of them being that (a) the syllable units can capture coarticulation better than phonemes, (b) the number of concatenation points decreases when syllable is used as the basic unit, (c) syllable boundaries are characterized by regions of low energy and therefore audible mismatches at the boundary are hardly perceived, etc. Also in the context of Indian languages, the number of polysyllabic words is huge. Due to these advantages, we have chosen syllable as the basic unit in our concatenative synthesis framework.

2.2   Voice Building

Forced Alignment. For segmenting the audio data we used the procedure described in [21] which is based on an HMM forced alignment algorithm. The alignment has been performed without any change or supervision as it closely developed to the TTS front-end component.

Pre-clustering. It was seen that syllables of the same type can be easily differentiated depending on their position in the word [18]. In addition, syllables occurring at the beginning of the word are of longer duration than the syllables occurring at the middle and end of a word [25,28]. The energy and pitch were also found to vary depending on the position of the syllable in the word [1]. Therefore, we've performed pre-clustering based on position of the syllable in a word, i.e. syllables of the same type were pre-clustered as begin, middle and end by appropriately depending on their position in the word, in the original context. In case a syllable of appropriate position is not available during synthesis, an order of preference is used to pick a syllable of the same type occurring at an alternate position. During synthesis, if the required begin or an end syllable is not present in the database, middle syllable is preferred. If the required middle syllable is not present, a syllable from a word beginning is selected instead.

Target and Join Costs. Typically mel frequency cepstral coefficients (MFCC) are used to calculate distance between two units accompanied by duration and F0 of the unit. Preliminary analysis on the data showed that the energy of units play a major role in syllable unit synthesis. We have therefore included log energy, MFCC, dynamic features of MFCC (deltas and double deltas), F0 and unit durations as the acoustic features. We employed a target cost based on the distance from the mean duration of the syllables in the current version of the framework, following [26]. The mean duration for each of the units is computed using all the occurrences in the database. Thus, the units with minimum distance from this mean value have a higher probability in getting selected when the total cost is obtained. The join cost consists of the sub costs arising from log energy, spectral and pitch based features. We follow the formulation similar to the one proposed in [17,23] and calculate the spectral, f0 and energy based continuity metrics using 1, 4 and 2 boundary frames respectively [24]. The weights of the individual sub costs have been optimized manually over a held out set from the training data.

Table 1. Preference test on Telugu. The percentages are shown for each system.

CC	4F vs 2F	2F vs 1F	4F vs 1F	AMDF	4F vs 2F	2F vs 1F	4F vs 1F
Prefer 4F	23	-	**47**	Prefer 4F	29	-	**46**
Prefer 2F	**51**	**73**	-	Prefer 2F	**46**	**79**	-
Prefer 1F	-	7	21	Prefer 1F	-	9	33
No preference	26	20	32	No preference	25	12	21

Table 2. Preference test on Hindi. The percentages are shown for each system.

CC	4F vs 2F	2F vs 1F	4F vs 1F	AMDF	4F vs 2F	2F vs 1F	4F vs 1F
Prefer 4F	22	-	**42**	Prefer 4F	22	-	**44**
Prefer 2F	**53**	**77**	-	Prefer 2F	**59**	**73**	-
Prefer 1F	-	13	23	Prefer 1F	-	17	30
No preference	25	10	35	No preference	19	10	26

Waveform Similarity Concatenation. In order to obtain smooth joins at the concatenation boundaries we can use overlap addition after finding the suitable temporal point for joining the units so that the concatenation is performed at a point where maximal similarity exists between the units. In other words, we try to ensure that sufficient signal continuity exists at the concatenation point. For this, we use the cross correlation between the units as a measure of similarity between the units. Crossfade technique [11] is used to further remove the phase discontinuities. The number of frames used to calculate the correlation is limited by the duration of the available subword unit. Last two frames of the individual units were used to calculate the cross correlation. We have used reduced vowel epenthesis based backoff [20] strategy to synthesize the missing units and word to native speaker phone mapping [9] for the English words.

3 Experimental Setup

3.1 Data

We have used the database provided as a part of Blizzard Challenge 2015 for the purpose of the current investigation. Although the data was released for 6 languages, we have used Telugu (a Dravidian language) and Hindi (an Indo-Aryan language) databases for our experiments, promarily as they are from different language families. The other reasons for selecting these languages were the availability of native speakers for testing and larger database size (4 h) compared to the other languages (2 h). The training and the test set have been used as is except for leaving out 15 training sentences as a held out set to validate the findings and tune the weighting functions.

3.2 Embedding Correlation

Our goal is to increase the naturalness of the synthesized speech signal, in order to achieve this we have embedded correlation between the units as one of the subcosts in the join cost, which further affects the selection of the units. A simple experiment with a set of 30 words in both the languages were selected included 4 missing syllable units and 3 borrowed words (English words) was carried out to know the perceptual acceptability of the synthesized signals by introducing correlation and Average Magnitude Difference Function based formulation. By varying the number of frames, 3 files were synthesized for each word to calculate the correlation between the units. It is important to note that the correlation score obtained using cross correlation formulation has to be maximized where as the score obtianed via AMDF has to be minimized. Forced preference test was performed by native speakers of both the languages. We have followed the same procedure mentioned in [20] and the results are summarized in Tables 1 and 2. The results indicate that the correlation based approach is indeed preferred by the users, in both the languages and for both the formulations. They also indicate that for both the formulations, using 2 frames to the left and right at the boundary to calculate the correlation has received maximum preference.

3.3 Systems Designed

In this sub-section, we describe the experimental systems designed. Based on the inferences from the preference test, we have used 2 boundary frames to calculate the continuity metric in all of the experimental systems.

Type A Systems. These are the experimental systems built only using cross-correlation and average magnitude difference function as the join cost components. In other words, system CC has only the cross correlation based continuity metric as the join cost and system AMDF has only the average magnitude difference function based continuity metric as the join cost. The intention behind building these systems is to understand if ensuring temporal correlation in the signal alone would suffice as the join cost to produce highly natural speech.

Type B Systems. The systems built were the baseline combined with cross-correlation system and the baseline combined with AMDF system. These wer built to investigate the performance using the continuity measures in combination with the other subcosts. The weighting functions for each of the sub costs were optimized manually using a held out set of 15 utterances from the training set in both the languages.

Hybrid System. Hybrid system has all the three systems in it, the baseline, cross-correlation system and the AMDF system. Here both the formulations were used in addition to the existing sub-costs which has improvised the performance of the system to the greater extent. The weights used for each of these formulations were 0.33 for AMDF and 0.67 for Cross-Correlation.

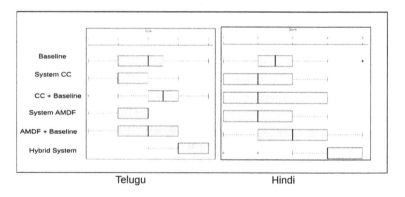

Fig. 1. Results from the Subjective Evaluation. Figure depicts box plots plotted based on the Mean Opinion Scores on a scale of 5.

3.4 Subjective Evaluation

In order to evaluate the systems, we have performed subjective evaluations using procedure similar to Blizzard challenge listening tests [2,13,14,22,24]. A set of 15 participants were made to listen to the synthesized files and rate the naturalness on a scale of 1 to 5, with 5 being the most natural and 1 being the most unnatural.

The results from the listening test are shown in the Fig. 1. Type A systems have performed worser compared to the baseline system in both the languages and both the formulations, showing that the other sub costs have a significant role in the join cost. In line with our hypothesis, type B systems have better MOS scores compared to the baseline system, in both the languages and both the formulations. Further, it is clearly evident that the hybrid system, using both the formulations has significantly outperformed the baseline system.

4   Conclusion

In this paper, we performed an experimental analysis on the usage of signal correlation as join cost in concatenative speech synthesis framework. As answers to the questions posed in Sect. 1, we have observed that the continuity measures do make a perceptual difference and therefore serves as an important feature to be considered for obtaining more natural synthesis. We also found from the preference test that using 2 time frames for calculation of the correlation was preferred for both the formulations. However, when the measures were used in isolation (type-A systems), their performance is not very encouraging. When they are combined with the other costs (type-B systems and hybrid system), they outperform the baseline. Results on systems developed for the Telugu and Hindi languages provide evidence on the effectiveness of the proposed method. The samples and listening test results used in the experiments are available online via this link: https://goo.gl/XJgOUc.

References

1. Bellur, A., Narayan, K.B., Krishnan, K.R., Murthy, H.A.: Prosody modeling for syllable-based concatenative speech synthesis of hindi and tamil. In: 2011 National Conference on Communications (NCC), pp. 1–5, January 2011
2. Bennett, C.L., Black, A.W.: The blizzard challenge 2006. In: Proceedings of the Blizzard Challenge (2006)
3. Black, A., Tokuda, K.: The blizzard challenge 2005: evaluating corpus-based speech synthesis on common databases. In: Proceedings of Interspeech (2005)
4. Black, A.W., King, S., Tokuda, K.: The blizzard challenge 2009 (2009)
5. Black, A.W., Taylor, P.A.: Automatically clustering similar units for unit selection in speech synthesis (1997)
6. Clark, R.A., Richmond, K., King, S.: Festival 2-build your own general purpose unit selection speech synthesiser (2004)
7. Clark, R.A., Richmond, K., King, S.: Multisyn: open-domain unit selection for the festival speech synthesis system. Speech Commun. 49(4), 317–330 (2007)
8. Dutoit, T., Pagel, V., Pierret, N., Bataille, F., Van der Vrecken, O.: The MBROLA project: towards a set of high quality speech synthesizers free of use for non commercial purposes. In: Proceedings of the Fourth International Conference on Spoken Language, 1996. ICSLP 1996, vol. 3, pp. 1393–1396. IEEE (1996)
9. Elluru, N.K., Vadapalli, A., Elluru, R., Murthy, H., Prahallad, K.: Is word-to-phone mapping better than phone-phone mapping for handling english words? In: ACL (2), pp. 196–200 (2013)

10. Fraser, M., King, S.: The blizzard challenge 2007. In: Proceedings of the BLZ3-2007 (in Proceedings SSW6) (2007)
11. Hirai, T., Tenpaku, S.: Using 5 ms segments in concatenative speech synthesis. In: Fifth ISCA Workshop on Speech Synthesis (2004)
12. Hunt, A.J., Black, A.W.: Unit selection in a concatenative speech synthesis system using a large speech database. In: 1996 Proceedings of the IEEE International Conference on Acoustics, Speech, and Signal Processing, 1996. ICASSP-96, vol. 1, pp. 373–376. IEEE (1996)
13. King, S., Clark, R.A., Mayo, C., Karaiskos, V.: The blizzard challenge 2008 (2008)
14. King, S., Karaiskos, V.: The blizzard challenge 2012 (2012)
15. Kishore, S., Black, A.W., Kumar, R., Sangal, R.: Experiments with unit selection speech databases for indian languages. National seminar on Language Technology Tools, Hyderabad, India (2003)
16. Kishore, S., Kumar, R., Sangal, R.: A data driven synthesis approach for indian languages using syllable as basic unit. In: Proceedings of International Conference on NLP (ICON), pp. 311–316 (2002)
17. Lakkavalli, V.R., Arulmozhi, P., Ramakrishnan, A.G.: Continuity metric for unit selection based text-to-speech synthesis. In: 2010 International Conference on Signal Processing and Communications (SPCOM), pp. 1–5, July 2010
18. Murthy, H.A.: Methods for improving the quality of syllable based speech synthesis (2008)
19. Ng, K.: Survey of data-driven approaches to speech synthesis. Spoken Language Systems Group, Massachusetts Institute of Technology, Cambridge, MA (1998)
20. Peddinti, V., Prahallad, K.: Significance of vowel epenthesis in telugu text-to-speech synthesis. In: 2011 IEEE International Conference on Acoustics, Speech and Signal Processing (ICASSP), pp. 5348–5351. IEEE (2011)
21. Prahallad, K., Toth, A.R., Black, A.W.: Automatic building of synthetic voices from large multi-paragraph speech databases. In: INTERSPEECH, pp. 2901–2904 (2007)
22. Prahallad, K., Vadapalli, A., Elluru, N., Mantena, G., Pulugundla, B., Bhaskararao, P., Murthy, H., King, S., Karaiskos, V., Black, A.: The blizzard challenge 2013-indian language task. In: Blizzard Challenge Workshop 2013 (2013)
23. Rajaram, B.S.R., Shiva Kumar, H.R., Ramakrishnan, A.: Mile tts for tamil for blizzard challenge 2014. In: 2010 International Conference on Signal Processing and Communications (SPCOM), pp. 1–5. IEEE (2010)
24. Rallabandi, S.K., Vadapalli, A., Achanta, S., Gangashetty, S.V.: Iiit-h's entry to blizzard challenge 2015. In: Blizzard Challenge Workshop 2015, Interspeech (2015)
25. Rao, K.S., Yegnanarayana, B.: Modeling durations of syllables using neural networks. Comput. Speech Lang. $21(2)$, 282–295 (2007)
26. Shiva Kumar, H.R., Ashwini, J.K., Rajaram, B.S.R., Ramakrishnan, A.G.: Mile tts for tamil and kannada for blizzard challenge 2013. In: Blizzard Challenge 2013 Workshop, Barcelona, Catalonia. CMU (2013)
27. Tsiakoulis, P., Karabetsos, S., Chalamandaris, A., Raptis, S.: An overview of the ILSP unit selection text-to-speech synthesis system. In: Likas, A., Blekas, K., Kalles, D. (eds.) SETN 2014. LNCS, vol. 8445, pp. 370–383. Springer, Heidelberg (2014)
28. Vinodh, M.V., Bellur, A., Narayan, K.B., Thakare, D.M., Susan, A., Suthakar, N.M., Murthy, H.A.: Using polysyllabic units for text to speech synthesis in indian languages. In: 2010 National Conference on Communications (NCC), pp. 1–5, January 2010

Knowledge Transfer for Utterance Classification in Low-Resource Languages

Andrei Smirnov[1,3(✉)] and Valentin Mendelev[2,3]

[1] STC-Innovations, Saint Petersburg, Russia
[2] Speech Technology Center, Saint Petersburg, Russia
[3] ITMO University, Saint Petersburg, Russia
{smirnov-a,mendelev}@speechpro.com

Abstract. The paper deals with a problem of short text classification in Kazakh. Traditional text classification approaches require labeled data to build accurate classifiers. However the amount of available labeled data is usually very limited due to high cost of labeling or data accessibility issues. We describe a method of constructing a classifier without labeled data in the target language. A convolutional neural network (CNN) is trained on Russian labeled texts and a language vector space transform is used to transfer knowledge from Russian into Kazakh. Classification accuracy is evaluated on a dataset of customer support requests. The presented method demonstrates competitive results compared with an approach that employed a sophisticated automatic translation system.

Keywords: Text classification · Language vector space · Word embeddings · CNN · Low-resource

1 Introduction

Text classification tasks are ubiquitous and essential for modern technologies. One may need to categorize documents, detect sentiment, intention or desired action etc. This paper is devoted to users' requests classification for customer support. In modern contact centers all initial appeals are fed to a classifier that determines a request topic and performs an action which may be to forward a message to a responsible staff member or to generate a unique answer automatically. The requests are typically short phrases consisting of only several words and the number of target classes can be fairly large (up to 40). We investigate a problem of building a classifier when training data in a target language are scarce but a sufficient amount of labeled requests in another language is available. Kazakh language was chosen to be the target language while training data were in Russian (the source language).

Distributed vector representations of words are widely used as input features in various natural language processing problems. They can be understood as a mapping from words in a given vocabulary to vectors in a low-dimensional embedded space. We propose to construct a classifier in the low-resource language combining a convolutional neural network (CNN) classifier in the source

© Springer International Publishing Switzerland 2016
A. Ronzhin et al. (Eds.): SPECOM 2016, LNAI 9811, pp. 435–442, 2016.
DOI: 10.1007/978-3-319-43958-7_52

language and a linear mapping between source and target vector spaces. The absence of sufficient amount of training data results in inaccurate mapping which affects the performance of the classifier. We show how classification accuracy improves with the training data increase to eventually outperform the baseline obtained with Google Translate.

The outline of the rest of the paper is as follows. In Sect. 2 a brief overview of the related works is given. Section 3 describes the proposed model. The detailed description of our datasets and training procedure is provided in Sect. 4. Experiments are presented in Sect. 5 and followed by a discussion and conclusions.

2   Related Work

Distributed vector representations (or word embeddings) have become a very useful tool in various Natural Language Processing (NLP) tasks, including language modeling, word-sense disambiguation, word similarity and synonym detection (e.g. [4,7,8,19,21]). Overcoming a data sparsity problem, word embeddings represent words as low-dimensional dense vectors. Methods of their construction (e.g. [17,18], see also [21] for a survey of classical vector space models) require unlabeled text data only.

The two lines of research concerning distributed vector representations are directly connected to our study. The first one is training multilingual word embeddings to transfer linguistic knowledge from one language to another, the other one is learning embeddings for more complex monolingual lexical units like phrases, sentences and documents.

Several methods have been proposed to train and align bi- and multilingual word embeddings. In [1] monolingual models of languages are built separately and then a linear projection between two language vector spaces is learned on a small bilingual dictionary. More sophisticated approaches [3,6,13] optimize monolingual and cross-lingual objectives simultaneously (e.g. by minimizing the sum of monolingual and cross-lingual loss functions). To train such a model one needs a parallel corpus aligned at a sentence level. The quality of vector representations can be evaluated on a cross-lingual document classification task. A common setup was introduced by Klementiev et al. [13]. They used a subset of English and German sections of the Reuters RCV1/RCV2 corpora [16]. There are four topics in the corpus. The classifier is trained on documents belonging to one language and tested on documents in the other language. Coulmance et al. [6] reported a performance of several bilingual word embedding models for the setup.

Word vector representations cannot properly capture the semantic properties of longer phrases, so compositionality has recently received a lot of attention. A number of approaches have been developed for learning mappings from word vectors to sentence vectors. Paragraph Vector introduced in [15] learns a fixed-length feature representations for variable-length texts in an unsupervised manner. Supervised approaches induce task-specific sentence embeddings using labeled text corpora. Among them are recursive neural networks [9,20], convolutional neural networks [11,12] and long short term memory recurrent neural networks [14]. An appealing feature of these models is that in the absence of a large supervised training set to boost the performance one could initialize word vectors with those obtained from an unsupervised neural language model [5,10,19].

We integrate these two lines of research to solve a text classification problem in a low-resource language.

3   Approach

The proposed model includes three main components: word embeddings, CNN trained on top of the embeddings and Transferring Matrix, which is a linear mapping between vector spaces of the target (Kazakh) and source (Russian) languages. The model architecture is shown in Fig. 1.

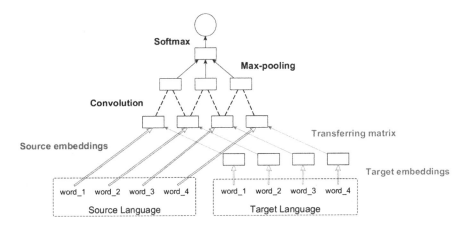

Fig. 1. Model architecture. Data flow for the source language is shown in blue, for the target language in green (Color figure online)

Embeddings. Having the large unannotated text corpora in both the target and source languages we pre-trained vector embeddings. The two well-known algorithms to learn monolingual word embeddings are the skip-gram and continuous bag of words (CBOW). The training objective of CBOW is to predict the word by its context in the sentence while the training objective of the skip-gram model is to predict surrounding words with the word itself. The training of CBOW is known to be faster but skipgram learns better representation when the training corpus is small. According to our experiments, monolingual word embeddings learned by the CBOW model give better results in terms of classification accuracy on both the source and target request datasets. All results reported hereafter were obtained using the CBOW model.

Convolutional Network. A simple CNN with one layer of convolution is trained on top of precomputed word vector representations for the source language as in [12]. During the training phase the word embeddings are fine-tuned. Kim altered the architecture of the CNN to allow for the use of both task-specific and static word vectors. We use only the non-static channel since adding the static channel does not lead to any improvement in classification accuracy for the task.

Transferring Matrix. Following the approach proposed in [9] we trained Transferring Matrix A that maps word vectors from the target into source vector space by minimizing $min_A \sum_{i=0}^{N} ||Av_i^t - v_i^s||^2$, where v_i^t is the word vector in the target language, the v_i^s is the vector of its translation into the source language and N is the size of the dictionary. Some words in the target language do not have one-word equivalents and are translated as short phrases. In such cases v_i^s is calculated by averaging vectors which compose a phrase.

During the prediction phase the word vectors for the target language are translated to the vector space of the source language by Transferring Matrix and then are processed by the CNN.

4   Datasets and Training Details

4.1   Datasets

To evaluate our approach we use the dataset of 6000 users requests in Russian which were manually split into 40 classes according to their topic and also manually translated into Kazakh. The average request length was 7.6 words. Discarding the examples from the least represented classes we generate the datasets with 30, 20, 10, 5 and 2 classes, consisting of 5700, 5200, 4200, 3350, 1980 requests correspondingly. The data for a given number of classes were divided into a train set (80 %), a development set (10 %) and a test set (10 %).

4.2   Training Details

Word2vec. The word2vec tool [2] was used to produce monolingual word embeddings. The architecture of the model was CBOW and it was trained by negative sampling. The training data for the Russian model consisted of transcribed spontaneous conversational speech, fiction and news articles (200M tokens). The Kazakh model was trained on the latest dump of Kazakh Wikipedia and Kazakh news articles (30M tokens). The dimension of vector representation was 100 for the Russian model. We tested vector space dimensions from 100 to 800 for the Kazakh model and found that 500-dimensional word embedding gave the best classification accuracy for 40 classes. We used a 500-dimensional Kazakh vector space for the rest of experiments.

k-NN. As a baseline classifier we considered the k-nearest neighbors (k-NN) algorithm in the space of sentence vectors. The number of neighbors was tuned on the development set and the weight of a neighbor vote was inversely proportional to the cosine distance from this neighbor to the test vector. We averaged single word vectors composing the phrase to get the sentence vector.

CNN. The hyper-parameters of the CNN were tuned on the development set of the full Russian dataset (40 classes) and were held constant for the other datasets. We came up with the following settings: the filter size was 2, the number of feature maps was 192, we used the rectified linear unit activation function, the dropout rate was 0.5, no l_2 regularization was used and the mini-batch consisted of 64 examples.

5 Experiments

5.1 Transfer Techniques

We compare the performance of the k-NN and CNN classifiers on the Kazakh test sets for several transfer techniques:

Transferring Matrix (TM). For each word in a given input phrase corresponding vectors from the target language vector space are calculated and mapped to the source language vector space with Transferring Matrix. The sequence of vector representations in the source space is then classified.

Google Translate (GT). An input request is translated into the source language by Google Translate. The translation is classified.

Manual (Man). The whole source language dataset was translated into the target language by a human expert. We take the source language translation that corresponds to the presented target language test phrase and perform classification.

5.2 Dictionary Variations

The performance of our model strongly depends on the quality of a mapping (Transferring Matrix) between vector spaces of the target and source languages. In turn, the quality of the Transferring Matrix depends on the dictionary used for training it's size, how accurate it is, if the vocabulary of the target domain is included. To examine how the classification accuracy depends on the amount of available manual translations we use the following dictionaries:

GT-dict is a dictionary constructed without manual translation at all. We chose the 5000 most frequent words from the proprietary Russian telecom-related text corpus and translate them into the Kazakh language

Train$X$%. Randomly chosen X% requests from the Russian train set manually translated into Kazakh

Train$\leq N$ includes the manual translation of requests from the Russian train set that did not exceed N words

For each dictionary we discarded the translations that were not present in the vocabulary of the Kazakh word embedding model. Table 1 shows the sizes of the dictionaries in terms of requests and tokens.

Table 1. Statistics of the dictionaries

	Train 10 %	Train 25 %	Train 50 %	Train 100 %	Train≤ 1	Train≤ 2	Train≤ 4	Train≤ 7
# req.	307	793	1559	3137	70	415	1442	2321
# tok.	1623	4447	8763	17478	70	760	4113	8690

5.3   Results

The performance of the proposed approach on the datasets with different numbers of classes is reported in Table 2. We observed that classifiers based on Transferring Matrix constructed with GT-dict (dictionary without manually translated data) perform poorly, significantly worse than classifiers based on Google Translate or manual translation. This may be due to the fact that for the Kazakh-Russian language pair GT-dict contains a noticeable amount of inaccuracies itself. One can also note that CNN outperforms the k-NN classifier for every translation technique and dataset.

Table 2. Classification accuracy for different transfer techniques for test sets with different numbers of classes

# of classes	Manual		GT		TM (GT-dict)	
	k-NN	CNN	k-NN	CNN	k-NN	CNN
40	72.8	84.3	56.8	61.4	32.8	37.6
30	73.5	85.5	57.8	63.4	35	37.9
20	75.7	87.7	61.6	66.5	38.8	45.2
10	78.4	89.1	65.8	71.9	46.7	51.8
5	82.6	92.4	80.2	87.1	57.6	65.6
2	90.5	97.8	93	95	76.4	84.4

Table 3 shows the classification accuracy for several dictionaries on the test set with 10 classes. Adding manually translated examples to the translation dictionary improves the classifier performance significantly. The best accuracy is obtained when the entire training set is used to construct the Transferring Matrix. In that case the CNN-classifier slightly outperforms the one based on

Table 3. Dependence of the classification accuracy on the dictionary used to build the Transferring Matrix

Dictionary	k-NN	CNN	Dictionary	k-NN	CNN
GT-dict	46.7	51.8	GT-dict∪Train≤ 1	47	52.3
GT-dict∪Train10%	52.8	55.6	GT-dict∪Train≤ 2	56.7	60.2
GT-dict∪Train25%	57.4	60.5	GT-dict∪Train≤ 4	60	67.7
GT-dict∪Train50%	60.5	66	GT-dict∪Train≤ 7	62.8	69.3
GT-dict∪Train100%	64.2	69.5	Train100%	66.7	73.3

Google Translate. In the original work [1] only single words constitute the dictionary for the Transferring Matrix. The presented results show that the whole phrases in the dictionary can also be beneficial to the task.

6   Conclusions

In the present work we demonstrate that having some unlabeled data in the target language and labeled data in the source language it is possible to build a classifier accurate enough to solve practical problems in the target language. We exploit a vector space mapping to transfer knowledge from the source to the target language. The performance of the classifier is poor when only the automatically translated word pairs are used to train the transfer mapping. A substantial classification accuracy increase is obtained by adding manually translated phrases to the training data for the mapping. It is also shown that despite of inaccuracies in transfer technique it is beneficial to use a more complex CNN classifier in the source language vector space instead of k-NN one.

Acknowledgments. This work was financially supported by the Ministry of Education and Science of the Russian Federation, Contract 14.579.21.0008, ID RFMEFI57914X0008.

References

1. Mikolov, T., Le, Q.V., Sutskever, I.: Exploiting similarities among languages for machine translation. http://arxiv.org/abs/1309.4168
2. Word2vec. https://code.google.com/archive/p/word2vec/
3. Bengio, Y., Corrado, G.: Bilbowa: Fast bilingual distributed representations without word alignments (2014)
4. Bengio, Y., Ducharme, R., Vincent, P., Jauvin, C.: A neural probabilistic language model. J. Mach. Learn. Res. **3**, 1137–1155 (2003)
5. Collobert, R., Weston, J., Bottou, L., Karlen, M., Kavukcuoglu, K., Kuksa, P.: Natural language processing (almost) from scratch. J. Mach. Learn. Res. **12**, 2493–2537 (2011)
6. Coulmance, J., Marty, J.M., Wenzek, G., Benhalloum, A.: Trans-gram, fast cross-lingual word-embeddings. arXiv preprint arXiv:1601.02502 (2016)
7. Erk, K., Padó, S.: A structured vector space model for word meaning in context. In: Proceedings of the Conference on Empirical Methods in Natural Language Processing, pp. 897–906. Association for Computational Linguistics (2008)
8. Huang, E.H., Socher, R., Manning, C.D., Ng, A.Y.: Improving word representations via global context and multiple word prototypes. In: Proceedings of the 50th Annual Meeting of the Association for Computational Linguistics: Long Papers, vol. 1, pp. 873–882. Association for Computational Linguistics (2012)
9. Irsoy, O., Cardie, C.: Deep recursive neural networks for compositionality in language. In: Advances in Neural Information Processing Systems, pp. 2096–2104 (2014)

10. Iyyer, M., Enns, P., Boyd-Graber, J., Resnik, P.: Political ideology detection using recursive neural networks. In: Proceedings of the Association for Computational Linguistics (2014)
11. Kalchbrenner, N., Grefenstette, E., Blunsom, P.: A convolutional neural network for modelling sentences. arXiv preprint arXiv:1404.2188 (2014)
12. Kim, Y.: Convolutional neural networks for sentence classification. arXiv preprint arXiv:1408.5882 (2014)
13. Klementiev, A., Titov, I., Bhattarai, B.: Inducing crosslingual distributed representations of words (2012)
14. Le, P., Zuidema, W.: Compositional distributional semantics with long short term memory. arXiv preprint arXiv:1503.02510 (2015)
15. Le, Q.V., Mikolov, T.: Distributed representations of sentences and documents. In: ICML, vol. 14, pp. 1188–1196 (2014)
16. Lewis, D.D., Yang, Y., Rose, T.G., Li, F.: Rcv1: a new benchmark collection for text categorization research. J. Mach. Learn. Res. **5**, 361–397 (2004)
17. Mikolov, T., Chen, K., Corrado, G., Dean, J.: Efficient estimation of word representations in vector space. arXiv preprint arXiv:1301.3781 (2013)
18. Pennington, J., Socher, R., Manning, C.D.: Glove: global vectors for word representation. In: EMNLP, vol. 14, pp. 1532–1543 (2014)
19. Socher, R., Pennington, J., Huang, E.H., Ng, A.Y., Manning, C.D.: Semi-supervised recursive autoencoders for predicting sentiment distributions. In: Proceedings of the Conference on Empirical Methods in Natural Language Processing, pp. 151–161. Association for Computational Linguistics (2011)
20. Socher, R., Perelygin, A., Wu, J.Y., Chuang, J., Manning, C.D., Ng, A.Y., Potts, C.: Recursive deep models for semantic compositionality over a sentiment treebank. In: Proceedings of the Conference on Empirical Methods in Natural Language Processing (EMNLP), vol. 1631, p. 1642. Citeseer (2013)
21. Turney, P.D., Pantel, P., et al.: From frequency to meaning: vector space models of semantics. J. Artif. Intell. Res. **37**(1), 141–188 (2010)

Language Identification Using Time Delay Neural Network D-Vector on Short Utterances

Maxim Tkachenko[1(✉)], Alexander Yamshinin[1], Nikolay Lyubimov[3],
Mikhail Kotov[2], and Marina Nastasenko[1]

[1] Vector I LLC, Moscow, Russia
makseq@gmail.com, lex.sapfir@gmail.com, marina.nastasenko@gmail.com
[2] ASM Solutions LLC, Moscow, Russia
kotov.mike@gmail.com
[3] Lomonosov Moscow State University, Moscow, Russia
lubimov.nicolas@gmail.com

Abstract. This paper describes d-vector language identification (LID) system on short utterances using time delay neural network (TDNN) acoustic model for the speech recognition task. The acoustic TDNN model is chosen for ASR system of ICQ messenger and it's applied for the LID task. We compared LID TDNN d-vector results to i-vector baseline. It was found that the TDNN system performance is close at any durations while i-vector shows good results only at long time. Open-set test is conducted. Relative improvement of 5.5 % over the i-vector system is shown.

Keywords: Language identification · I-vector · D-vector · Speech recognition acoustic model · Neural networks

1 Introduction

I-vector is a gold-standard approach for speaker and language identification [1,2]. Whereas neural networks have a rising power. Deep neural networks (DNN) and Long Short-Term Memory (LSTM) were introduced. LSTM has demonstrated a high performance for ASR and LID [3–5] tasks. Auto-encoders and bottleneck features provided by NNs have also improved the performance in all speech processing tasks. D-vectors become popular within DNNs. The goal of our team is to explore the acoustic model of our production ASR based on TDNN for d-vector [6].

We have built Russian ASR in ICQ messenger. More than 15 % of data queries is not in Russian. Under a high load there is a need to truncate unwanted traffic with no Russian speech.

The paper is organized as follows. Section 2 refers to I-Vector Baseline system. Section 3 describes D-vector and TDNN in detail. Section 4 describes dataset and data preparation. Section 5 presents and analyzes the results on 3 s durations. Section 6 presents the conclusions and interesting findings.

© Springer International Publishing Switzerland 2016
A. Ronzhin et al. (Eds.): SPECOM 2016, LNAI 9811, pp. 443–449, 2016.
DOI: 10.1007/978-3-319-43958-7_53

2   I-Vector Baseline System

2.1   About

I-vector is the state of the art technique that effectively represents speech utterance as low dimensional vector. The underlying idea behind i-vectors is based on supervectors over concatenated Gaussian Mixture Models (GMM) means M, factorized as

$$M = m + Tw, \tag{1}$$

where m is concatenated Universal Background Model (UBM) means, T forms the subspace covering the important variability (both language- and session-specific) in the supervector space, and w is a random vector distributed as $N(0, 1)$. For each observation sequence representing an utterance the corresponding i-vector can be estimated using the maximum a posteriori (MAP) method. For more detail on i-vector extraction see [2,8].

2.2   Configuration

First, the UBM GMM is trained. The next step is to calculate Total Variability and Sigma matrices on the special dataset from train. The i-vector extra ctor uses Baum-Welch statistics calculated from voice frames, followed by Support Vector Machine scoring procedure. We have used RBF kernels to model nonlinear relationship in total variability space (Fig. 1).

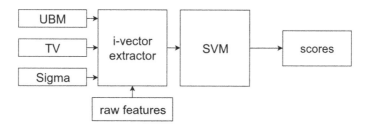

Fig. 1. I-vector system configuration

3   TDNN D-Vector System

3.1   About

In proposed LID system we use d-vectors instead of i-vectors as the input language features for the SVM classifier. D-vectors are obtained using our best for ASR acoustic model. We hypothesize that amount of uncertainty in the neural network output, produced by non-target language, leads to the shift in hidden layer activations behavior relatively target language (Russian in our case). Therefore their averaged representations (d-vectors) must give good discriminative feature for binary identification task, but not for multiclass identification.

3.2   Extracting Improved D-Vector

Assume we have a set of raw features of the whole utterance $X_{utt} = \{x_1, \ldots, x_T\}$ $X_{utt} \in \mathbb{R}^{F x T}$ and the last hidden layer activations corresponding to raw features $H_{utt} = \{h_1, \ldots, h_T\}$ $H_{utt} \in \mathbb{R}^{L x T}$ from TDNN where F is a raw feature dimension, L is a number of neurons in the last hidden layer and T is a number of frames in the utterance. Next we compute mean and standard deviation of H_{utt} and concatenate them into one single vector. Now we have improved version of d-vectors per utterance as compared with [7].

TDNN is chosen as d-vector extractor because it can model long term temporal dependencies with training times comparable to standard feed-forward DNNs and shows better Word Error Rate (WER) in speech recognition tasks [6]. Training TDNN is done using Kaldi toolkit [9].

Scheme below depicts an example of TDNN architecture with sub-sampling $\{-3, 3\}$, $\{-1, +1\}$ and $\{-2, +1\}$ applying to its hidden layers correspondingly (Fig. 2).

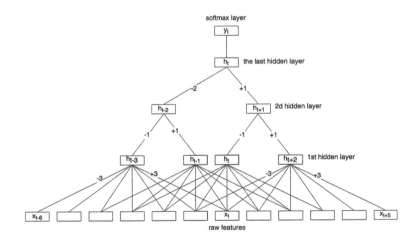

Fig. 2. An example of TDNN architecture with sub-sampling. D-vector is extracted from the last hidden layer activations

3.3   Configuration

To make the comparison clear d-vector is configured as in Subsection 2.2 of I-Vector Baseline System. However, a slight difference is still present — Principal Component Analysis (PCA) was used to whiten d-vectors and reduce the dimensionality (Fig. 3).

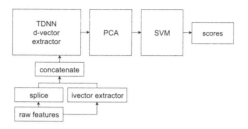

Fig. 3. TDNN d-vector system configuration

4 Experiment Setup

4.1 Dataset

ASR TDNN model, i-vector UBM, TV & Sigma parameters were obtained on the proprietary Russian corpus collected from the microphone and telephone speech.

NIST Language Recognition Evaluation 2007 (LRE07) is a popular corpora and it contains Russian language in train and test sets. We have used the next 11 languages to train the classifier: Russian, Arabic, Bengali, Chinese (Min), Spanish (Mexican), Tamil, Thai, Chinese (Taiwan, Wu, Cantonese), Hindustani (Urdu). It was prepared 26 items for open-set test: Arabic, Bengali, Chinese (Cantonese, Mainland, Taiwan, Min, Wu), English (American, Indian) Farsi, French, German, Hindustani (Hindi, Urdu), Indonesian, Italian, Japanese, Korean, Punjabi, Russian, Spanish (Caribbean, non-Caribbean), Tagalog, Tamil, Thai, Vietnamese.

We run Voice Activity Detector over train set to split long durations of source audio files into small parts (Fig. 4). I-vector and d-vector extractors results were considered at this training corpora.

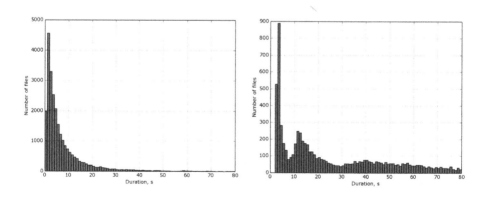

Fig. 4. Train (left) and test (right) durations histogram

4.2 I-Vector

13-dimensional MFCCs with double deltas and no normalization were used as input to the i-vector extractor. UBM has 512 GMMs. Output is 400-dimensional vector. It's about 20 h of audio in UBM training and 50 h for TV & Sigma.

4.3 D-Vector

Perceptual Linear Prediction (PLP) with 13 cepstral coefficients, without cepstral mean and variance normalization, were used as input to the TDNN at the each time step. Also we concatenated a 100-dimensional i-vector with the PLP input.

TDNN consists of 6 nonlinear hidden layers and we use the following subsampling scheme (Table 1) on the first three layers only.

Table 1. Sub-sampling scheme

Layer	Input context
1	$\{-4, 4\}$
2	$\{-2, 2\}$
3	$\{-4, 4\}$

Neural network was trained using stochastic gradient descent after that sequence training based on a state-level variant of the Minimum Phone Error (MPE) criterion was applied to get the final acoustic model.

The output dimension of d-vector after PCA is 400. It's about 450 h of audio for the TDNN train.

5 Results

The research purpose was the investigation of the short utterance LID. Here are presented DET plots of i-vector and d-vector open-set General LR 3 sec test on Russian language (Fig. 5). We used a lot of short audio fragments (after VAD) in train and didn't expect a great work of i-vectors &d-vectors at 10 s and 30 s (Tab. 2). But as you can see d-vectors outperforms at 10 s and 30 s i-vectors too.

Table 2. I-vector and D-vector EER on Russian open-set test, %

System	3 s	10 s	30 s
I-vector	28.08	24.09	22.51
D-vector	22.42	21.23	20.34

We found that d-vectors need less data to reach the best result while i-vectors take more data to train SVM model. It makes SVM very slow because the high number of support vectors increases the computing time.

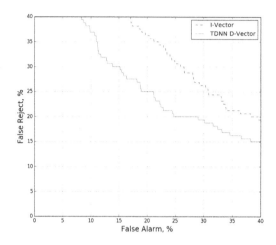

Fig. 5. I-vector (red, dashed) and D-vector (green) DET curves on Russian open-set test (Color figure online)

All the results, scores and other meta information about the experiments are stored in the Testarium — research tool and experiment repository [10]. Using this tool we made a grid search of SVM gamma, C, data limits and other parameters of our setup.

6   Conclusions

In this paper we have successfully applied TDNN framework to model acoustic features within language verification scenario. The feed-forward architecture of TDNN allows training and adapting parameters faster than more sophisticated recurrent nets, whereas gathering sufficiently wide context is important to make the system robust against outliers. The accurate modeling of target language phonemes seems to be crucial step for gaining performance when the small portion of acoustic information is given. Furthermore an interesting observation was concluded: TDNN d-vectors using in training are not so sensitive to audio durations in contrast to i-vectors.

Though only Russian language was the case study, we believe in the same effect for other languages. Also we want to build multiple TDNN acoustic models for other languages and concatenate their d-vectors to reach the best performance. The validation addressed to the future work.

References

1. Dehak, N., Kenny, P., Dehak, R., Dumouchel, P., Ouellet, P.: Front-end factor analysis for speaker verification. IEEE Trans. Audio Speech Lang. Process. **19**, 788–798 (2011). IEEE Press
2. Martinez, D., Plchot, O., Burget, L., Glembek, O., Matejka, P.: Language recognition in ivectors space. In: 12th Annual Conference of the International Speech Communication Association (INTERSPEECH), pp. 861–864. ISCA, Florence (2011)
3. Graves, A., Mohamed, A., Hinton, G.: Speech recognition with deep recurrent neural networks. In: International Conference on Acoustics, Speech and Signal Processing (ICASSP), pp. 6645-6649. IEEE Press, Vancouver (2013)
4. Gonzalez-Dominguez, J., Lopez-Moreno, I., Sak, H., Gonzalez-Rodriguez, J., Moreno, P.: Automatic language identification using long short-term memory recurrent neural networks. In: 16th Annual Conference of the International Speech Communication Association (INTERSPEECH). ISCA, Dresden (2015)
5. Zazo, R., Lozano-Diez, A., Gonzalez-Dominguez, J., Toledano, D., Gonzalez-Rodriguez, J.: Language identification in short utterances using long short-term memory (LSTM) recurrent neural networks. PLoS ONE **11**(1), e0146917 (2016)
6. Peddinti, V., Povey, D., Khudanpur, S.: A time delay neural network architecture for efficient modeling of long temporal contexts. In: 16th Annual Conference of the International Speech Communication Association (INTERSPEECH). ISCA, Dresden (2015)
7. Variani, E., Lei, X., McDermott, E., Moreno, I.L., Gonzalez-Dominguez, J.: Deep neural networks for small footprint text-dependent speaker verification. In: International Conference on Acoustics, Speech and Signal Processing (ICASSP). IEEE Press, Singapore (2014)
8. Kenny, P., Oullet, P., Dehak, N., Gupta, V., Dumouchel, P.: A study of interspeaker variability in speaker verification. IEEE Trans. Audio Speech Lang. Process. **16**, 980–988 (2008). IEEE Press
9. Povey, D., Ghoshal, A., Boulianne, G., Burget, L., Glembek, O., Goel, N., Hannemann, M., Motlicek, P., Qian, Y., Schwarz, P., Silovsky, J., Stemmer, G., Vesely, K.: The kaldi speech recognition toolkit. In: IEEE 2011 Workshop on Automatic Speech Recognition and Understanding, Hawaii (2011)
10. Testarium. Research tool and experiment repository. http://testarium.makseq.com

Lexical Stress in Punjabi and Its Representation in PLS

Swaran Lata[1(✉)], Swati Arora[2], and Simerjeet Kaur[2]

[1] JNU, New Delhi 110067, India
slata@deity.gov.in
[2] WSI, DeitY, Delhi 11003, India
swati.w3cindia@gmail.com, simer.uni@gmail.com

Abstract. Punjabi is a tonal language and belongs to Indo-Aryan family of languages. Punjabi literature reveals that the suprasegmental phonemes such as Tone, Nasalization and stress are realized at the syllable level. There is abundance of geminated words in which stress Co-occurs on the geminated consonant. The disyllabic words have highest frequency of occurrence. There are very few quadrisyllabic/polysyllabic words excluding borrowed words. There is limited work available on Punjabi generative phonology. Initial efforts were made however no conclusive work on linguistic rules for stress is available. Pronunciation lexicon development is a very useful resource for machine learning and is critical for speech technology research. Pronunciation lexicon specification (PLS) of W3C enables development of such data in standard XML format. This PLS data ought to be enriched with stress information encoded in IPA so that the Punjabi Text-to-Speech systems can use it to deliver near natural voice. An attempt has been made in this paper to study Non-tonal disyllabic words for identifying stress patterns. The data was further analyzed to define linguistic contexts in which stress occurs in Punjabi disyllabic words.

Keywords: PLS · Punjabi · IPA · Syllable · Stress · Pitch · Vowel duration · Vowel intensity · Disyllabic · Phonology · Voice browser · TTS · Lexicon · Pronunciation · Acoustic · Articulation · W3C · Phonetics · PRAAT · MATLAB

1 Introduction

1.1 Punjabi Language

Punjabi is a member of Indo-Aryan Language family and it is mainly spoken by inhabitants of north western India and north eastern Pakistan. Punjabi is most commonly written in the Gurmukhi script. Gurmukhi, means proceeding from the mouth of the Guru. Thus it refers to its use in the Granth Sahib, and is written from left to right. The number of letters in the Gurmukhi alphabet accounts for its common name "pẽti akʰəri" 'thirty – five'. According to the ethnologies 2005 estimate, there 88 million native speakers of the Punjabi language, which makes it approximately the 10th most widely spoken language in the world and according to 2001 census of India, there are 29,102,477 Punjabi speakers in India.

© Springer International Publishing Switzerland 2016
A. Ronzhin et al. (Eds.): SPECOM 2016, LNAI 9811, pp. 450–460, 2016.
DOI: 10.1007/978-3-319-43958-7_54

1.2   Punjabi Phonology

Punjabi language uses 42 phonemes (10 vowels and 32 consonants) which are discussed by (Lata 2011) in "Challenges for Design of Pronunciation Lexicon Specification (PLS) for Punjabi Language". According to the generative theory, the syllable has been considered as the hierarchical unit in the phonological representation by Kahn. Subsequently "CV Phonology" (Clements and Keyser 1983), explains CV tier theory of phonology which provides phonological representation to distinguish functional positions within the syllable and proposed a set of constituents smaller than the syllable, taking consonant and vowel segments as members. These constituents may be termed the onset, nucleus and coda. Nucleus plays role in defining the distinction between heavy and light syllables. There is further distinction between a heavy syllable and a light syllable depending on the quality of vowels involved. Punjabi vowels can be classified into (Sharma 1971).

Class I vowels		Class II vowels	
ɪ	ʊ	i	u
	ə	e	o
		ɛ (æ)	ɔ
			a

Initial occurrence of class II vowels is very much restricted in Punjabi (Singh 1991). Thus nucleus of a syllable is a category of prosodic element. Therefore the relative stress of syllables occurring in a word can be studied as per Generative phonology to identify stress patterns in a language.

1.3   PLS

PLS is a standard of World-Wide Web Consortium (W3C) http://www.w3.org/TR/pronunciation-lexicon/ and its current version is PLS 1.0 (2008) produced by Voice Browser Working Group of W3C. The PLS has been designed with a goal to have Inter-operable specifications of pronunciation information which can be used for speech technology development. It provides a mapping between the words or short phrases, their written representations and their pronunciation especially for use by speech engines. PLS specification provides a framework and guideline which can be tailored to the needs of a specific language and consequently the XML tag set can be defined to build the PLS data using IPA & UTF 8 representation. (Lata 2011).

1.4   Stress in Punjabi

Stress is a structural linguistic property of a word that specifies which syllable in the word, in some sense, is stronger than any others. This acoustic characterization of the properties can distinguish the stressed syllable from any other unstressed syllable surrounding it. In Punjabi, the stress falls on the geminated consonant and it also Co-occurs with tone in tonal words. The tone gets realized on a stronger syllable. The stress realization due to presence of tones in Tonemes was examined in (Lata 2012) and Laryngeal tones were studied (Lata 2013). Punjabi has very high frequency of disyllabic words. The current study focuses on stress realization in Non-tonal disyllabic words in Punjabi.

The paper is organized as follows. Section 2 gives the literature survey. In Sect. 3 we have described the syllabic structure of Punjabi language utilizing the generative phonology theory. Section 4 elucidates data collection and methodology of experimental study. In Sect. 5 the data recorded along with the syllabic description. Section 6 presents the methodology for annotation and the annotated data. Section 7 derives the empirical analysis of stress pattern.

2 Literature Survey

2.1 The Problem of Stress

There is a general agreement that stressed syllable is characterized by higher pitch and duration is also a significant Co-variable. (Lehiste 1970) claims that phonetically realized word level stress is the capacity of a syllable in a word to receive sentence level stress. According to (Prakash 2003), stress generally falls on the syllable containing long vowel. Thus the degrees of stress on various syllables in a word should be predictable by rules and therefore be non contrastive. The phonetic correlate of stress is a combination of length and pitch. Unstressed syllables lack length and a high pitch. Emphasized syllables contain a greater amount of energy.

The stress in Punjabi is determined by the phonological form of the word. The phonological processes such as vowel laxing, vowel reduction & schwa deletion can be explained by a single parameter i.e. stress. (Kalra 1982) defined three rules and elaborated their applicability on a limited set of words. He concluded that stress in Punjabi can be predicted by rules.

2.2 Phonetic Stress Placement Rules

In disyllabic words, the initial syllable has a stress if the final syllable is open (Bhatia 1993) e.g. ਮਾਲੀ/'mali/Gardener.

2.3 Stress in Disyllabic Words

Word stress in Punjabi is robustly perceptible and can be independently motivated elsewhere in the phonology of the language. Turning to the details of stress placement in Punjabi, it must be noted that the language has a three way syllable weight distinction as in language like Hindi (Prince and Smolensky 1993). It has monomoraic light syllables (L), bimoraic heavy syllables (H) and trimoraic Super-Heavy syllables (S) which have a long vowel and a coda or a short vowel followed by two coda consonants. Thus the need for scientific study to evolve rules for stress in disyllabic words was identified as discussed by (Vijayakrishnan 2003), through following examples:

ਗਿਲਾਫ	/gɪˈlapʰ/	'pillowcase'
ਜਾਸੂਸ	/d͡ʒaˈsus/	'spy'
ਤਾਰੀਫ	/taˈripʰ/	'praise'

It is observed from these examples that the second syllable is stressed.

No scientific study is available on stress in Non-tonal words in Punjabi language. Therefore 100 Non- tonal disyllabic words of different syllable categories are being examined in this paper for the stress patterns as the frequency of occurrence of disyllabic words in Punjabi is very high.

3 Syllabic Structure of Punjabi

A syllable is a vocalic unit, or a combination of the vocalic unit preceded or followed by a consonantal margin. There are syllables with zero margins also.

3.1 Syllable Peak

Simple peak syllable consists of one of the vowel phonemes of class I or class II. The main difference is in their prominence i.e. class I syllable peaks are phonetically less prominent and have a laxer articulation than class II syllable peaks. Complex peak syllable consists of a simple peak accompanied by a satellite peak consisting of /h (ə), j, w/ or having overlong vowel occurrences.

3.2 Syllable Margin

A syllable margin (onset, coda or onset & coda) consists of one or more of the consonant phonemes or Semi-consonants. Simple margin consists of only one consonant. Complex margin consists of consonant cluster/geminated consonants.

3.3 Syllable Classification

Based on literature survey (Vijayakrishnan 2003), following definition of light syllable, heavy syllable and super heavy syllable has been followed for carrying out this study.

3.3.1 Light Syllable (L)

i. Open syllable containing a class I vowel i.e. V_1 or CV_1.

3.3.2   Heavy Syllable (H)

i. Open syllable containing a class II vowel or a dipthong viz. V_2, CV_2, CV_1V_2.
ii. Any syllable having class I vowel with a coda/onset or both viz. V_1C, CV_1C.

3.3.3   Super Heavy Syllable (S)

i. Long vowel followed by one or more consonants viz. V_2C, $V_2C(C)$ and long vowel having onset as well as coda viz. CV_2C.
ii. Class I vowel followed by one or more consonants viz. V_1CC.

4   Articulatory Features for Syllabic Stress

Co-articulation is a phenomenon in which the articulatory moments required for a syllable are often anticipated (anticipatory Co-articulation) or carried over (carry over Co-articulation) during the production of an adjacent syllable (Sharma 1971). Stress plays an important role and depends on: Quality of syllable peak, Openness or closeness of the syllable, Type of syllable Margin, Position of the syllable in the word under consideration, Presence of Gemination, Presence of Tone.

Syllable peaks and syllable margins show considerable reduction of quantity, quality, intensity and pitch when occurring in weak position of a syllable whereas there is an all around rise in a stronger syllable. Reduction in quality of the initial syllable in disyllabic words is a common feature which needs to be examined.

5   Recording of Data

For the recoding of the Punjabi speech data, standardized procedure for speech corpora development based on the ITU recommendations has been adopted. The recording of data has been done in standard recording environment having SNR $>=$ 45 dB. The recording format is 16 bit, PCM, Mono and sampling rat is 48 kHz and the speech rate is medium with neutral emotion as the words are recorded in isolation however each word has been recorded thrice to avoid contaminating contextual influences.

The number of informants used is 3 male & 2 female native Punjabi speakers from Malwa (Malwai dialect) region between 25–35 age groups. Each informant recorded the entire set of 100 words thrice belonging to four linguistic categories based on the syllable definition as per Sect. 3 i.e. (1) L-H: 36 words, (2) H-H: 44 words, (3) L-S: 16 words, (4) H-S: 04 words. The middle sample of speech data is considered for the analysis to avoid any contaminating contextual influences.

6 Methodology

Pitch and Duration are the main acoustic correlates of stress however intensity being a weak cue also needs to be considered. According to the literature survey various degrees of links between stress and increase in respiratory effort, subglottal pressure, amplitude of sound waves and intensity have been found. This needs to be examined in the context of varying Intra-syllabic linguistic contexts viz Co-occurrence of different categories of syllables.

The spectrographic analysis using PRAAT of all the male & female samples was carried out and phoneme level and syllable level annotation was done. Intensity of both the syllables was recorded for each word by using PRAAT software. MATrix LABoratory (MATLAB) algorithm was developed to get mean pitch and duration for both the syllables.

Graphs are represented below for sample words exhibiting pitch contour, duration and intensity. The pause between the syllables was not accounted while calculating duration, pitch and intensity.

6.1.1: Syllabic Description: L-H: (See Fig. 1).

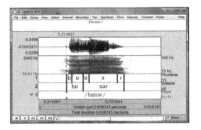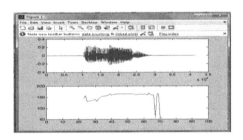

Fig. 1. (a) ਹੁਨਰ /hʊnər /_ Intensity graph. (b) ਹੁਨਰ /hʊnər /_ Pitch & Duration graph

6.1.2: Syllabic Description: H-H: (See Fig. 2).

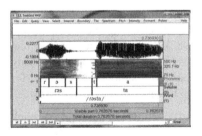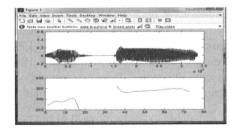

Fig. 2. (a) ਰਸਤਾ /rəsta/_ Intensity graph. (b) ਰਸਤਾ /rəsta/_ Pitch & Duration graph

6.1.3: Syllabic Description: L-S: (See Fig. 3).

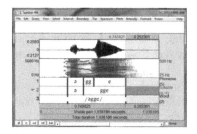 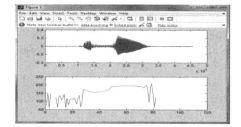

Fig. 3. (a) ਅੱਗੇ /əgge/_ Intensity graph. (b) ਅੱਗੇ /əgge/_ Pitch & Duration graph

6.1.4: Syllabic Description: H-S: (See Fig. 4).

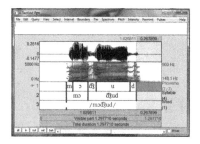 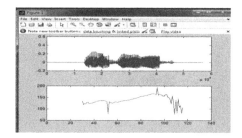

Fig. 4. (a) ਮੌਜੂਦ /mɔdʒud/_ Intensity graph. (b) ਮੌਜੂਦ/mɔdʒud/_ Pitch & Duration graph

7   Data Analysis

7.1   Empirical Formula for Syllabic Stress

The disyllabic words pertaining to different linguistic categories of the collected samples have been analyzed to investigate the Intra-syllabic stress. Duration is most significant parameter in terms of acoustic correlate in determining the stress as discussed in (Sluijter and Van Heuven 1996; Kalra 1982). It has also been found that stressed syllable reflects higher pitch. However, intensity is a weak cue for identifying the linguistic stress. The stress pattern of the recorded samples has been analyzed for identifying weightage of duration, pitch and intensity heuristically as given below:

1. Standard deviations of each of the parameters for 100 words i.e. duration (τ), pitch (P) and intensity (I) were calculated by substituting these respectively as per standard formula given below:

$$\sigma = \sqrt{\frac{1}{N}\sum_{i=1}^{N}(x_i - \bar{x})^2} \tag{1}$$

2. σ_τ, σ_ρ and σ_I were calculated for each of the sample word averaging the ensemble over five speakers.
3. Scatter graphs were plotted for each of the parameters σ_τ, σ_ρ and σ_I for both syllable 1 & syllable 2. The graphs were fitted by the linear curve fitting approach for both the syllables as shown below (Figs. 5, 6 and 7):

Time Duration (σ_τ)

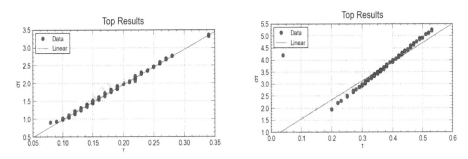

Fig. 5. (a) Syllable 1. (b) Syllable 2

Pitch (σ_ρ)

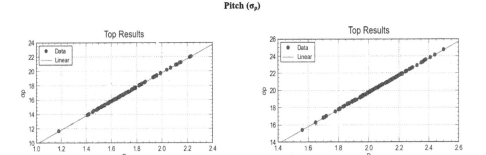

Fig. 6. (a) Syllable 1. (b) Syllable 2

4. It has been observed that σ_τ, σ_ρ, and σ_I follow the equation as given below (Table 1):

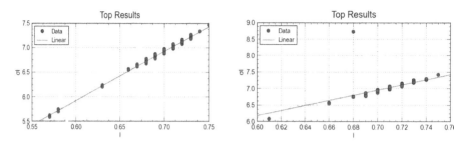

Fig. 7. (a) Syllable 1. (b) Syllable 2

Table 1. Linear equations of standard deviation

Syllable 1	Syllable 2
$\sigma_\tau = 9.84x + 2.73$	$\sigma_\tau = 9.87x + 1.22$
$\sigma_\rho = 9.90x - 2.35$	$\sigma_\rho = 9.9x - 1.84$
$\sigma_I = 1.00x - 7.68$	$\sigma_I = 7.75x + 1.53$

5. Analyzing the above functions and the corresponding weightage factors involving τ, P and I averaging over both the syllables the empirical stress function (ψ) may be expressed as:
$\psi = 0.42\tau + 0.42\,P + 0.16I$ where
τ is the duration (ms)
P is the Pitch measured in terms of frequency (Hz)
I is the Intensity (dB)
This reveals that duration and pitch have higher importance in determining lexical stress as compared to intensity.

7.2   Study of Stress Pattern

Using the above Eq. 1, the stress of syllable 1 and syllable 2 of each word was calculated and percentage increases of stress in syllable 2 with reference to syllable 1 was calculated as per sample data presented below Table 2:

The data reveals that stress is on the second syllable. Percentage increase of second syllable over first syllable has been plotted for each word. The standard deviation of this stress data has been calculated and it is noted from the graph that 14 % of the words carry minor stress on syllable 2.

Table 2. Sample data

Disyllabic word	Category	Syllabic stress		Percentage Increase
		Syb 1	Syb 2	
/səʈək/	L-H	16.14	22.41	38.81
/həzəm/	L-H	18.18	22.17	21.94
/ʃəgən/	L-H	20.14	23.07	14.54
/ʊgər/	L-H	17.89	23.19	29.6
/əgge/	L-H	17.22	22.04	27.98
/rəsta/	L-H	20.09	24.11	20.01
/ʊtsʊk/	H-H	16.59	20.37	22.76
/gərɪpʰt/	H-H	15.41	21.36	38.59
/gadʒər/	H-H	16.14	21.88	35.55
/gɔkul/	H-H	18.58	23.98	29.08
/ɔrət/	H-H	17.58	23.79	35.31
/pakʰə̃d/	H-H	17.09	22.00	28.79
/məjur/	L-S	19.41	25.86	33.26
/ʊdʒɛn/	L- S	15.7	22.4	42.7
/ʋedãt/	H- S	18.55	21.79	17.48
/ɪman/	H- S	18.46	26.33	42.63

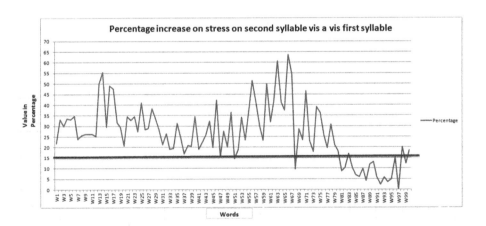

Fig. 8. Threshold graph

8   Conclusion

It is evident from the data analyzed that the Non-tonal disyllabic Punjabi words carry lexical stress on second syllable. Therefore the lexical stress in these words can be represented on the last syllable. The stress parameter is proposed to be incorporated in PLS which will increase the intelligibility of the spoken message via TTS. The PLS data encoded in IPA thus developed incorporating the above study will assist TTS engines in realization of near human voice.

The further analysis reveals that the following categories of words are below the threshold in Fig. 8. (a) nasalized L-H, (b) H-H ending with CV_1C syllable, (c) both syllables of CV_2 category other than few exceptions. The lexical stress may be ignored in these cases.

9   Future Study

This study may be extended by working on more number of speakers and for larger set of data to further validate the research findings. The study also needs to be extrapolated for trisyllabic and polysyllabic words.

References

Alan, P., Smollensky, P.: Optimality Theory, Constraint Interaction in Generative Grammer. Rutgers Cognitive Science Center, Rutgers University (1993)

Bhatia Tej, K.: Punjabi a Congnitive-Descriptive Grammer. Routledge Inc., London and New York (1993)

Clements, Keyser.: CV Phonology A Generative Theory of the Syllable. The MIT press, Cambridge (1983)

Kalra, A.K.: Some Topic in Punjabi Phologogy. University of Delhi, Delhi (1982)

Lata, S.: Challenges for design of Pronunciation Lexicon Specification (PLS) for Punjabi Language. LTC (2011)

Lata, S.: Exploratory analysis of Punjabi tones in relation to orthographic characters: a case study, Istanbul (2012)

Lata, S.: Laryngeal tonal characteristics of Punjabi – an experimental study. ICHCI (2013)

Lehiste: Suprasegmental features are established by a comparison of items (segments) in a sequence (1970)

Prem, P.: Sidhantik Bhasha Vigyan. Madan Publication, Patiala (2003)

Sharma, D.D.: Syllabic Structure of Hindi and Punjabi. Punjab University, Chandigarh (1971)

Singh, H.: Punjabi Deean Bhashai Visheshtava. Punjabi University, Patiala (1991)

Sluijter, A.M.C., Van Heuven, V.J.: Spectral balances an acoustic co-relate of linguistic stress. J. Acoust. Soc. Am. **100**, 2471 (1996)

Panday, P.K.: Syllable dependent process in Mundari, Central Institute of Indian languages, Mysore (1989)

Vijayakrishnan, K.G.: Stress and Tone in Punjabi. CIEFL, Hyderabad (2003)

Low Inter-Annotator Agreement in Sentence Boundary Detection and Annotator Personality

Anton Stepikhov[1(✉)] and Anastassia Loukina[2]

[1] The Russian Language Department, St. Petersburg State University,
7/9 Universitetskaya nab., St. Petersburg 199034, Russia
a.stepikhov@spbu.ru
[2] Educational Testing Service, 660 Rosedale Rd, Princeton, NJ 08541, USA
aloukina@ets.org

Abstract. The paper investigates how the annotators personality affects the result of their segmentation of unscripted speech into sentences. This task is inherently ambiguous and the disagreement between the annotators may result from a variety of factors – from speech disfluencies and linguistic properties of the text to social characteristics and the individuality of a speaker. While some boundaries are marked by the majority of annotators, there is also a substantial number of boundaries marked only by one or several experts.

In this paper we focus on sentence boundaries that are only marked by a small number of annotators. We test the hypothesis that such "uncommon" boundaries are more likely to be identified by experts with particular personality traits. We found significant relationship between uncommon boundaries and two psychological traits of annotators measured by the Big Five personality inventory: emotionality and extraversion.

Keywords: Sentence boundary detection · Segmentation · Personality · Annotation · Spontaneous speech · Unscripted speech · Russian

1 Introduction

In this paper we investigate how the annotators personality affects the result of their segmentation of unscripted speech into sentences.

The main challenge of syntactic analysis of unscripted speech is that speech does not have obvious sentence boundaries. While expert manual annotation is the common way of obtaining sentence boundaries in unscripted speech, a number of studies show that experts rarely reach unambiguous segmentation [1–6]. Previous studies revealed that there is a range of sources of annotators disagreement in segmentation – from speech disfluencies and language-specific features to social characteristics and the individuality of a speaker [2,6–8]. Other reasons for inconsistencies in boundary detection between annotators may be misinterpretation of annotation guidelines [9], different interpretation of the same text or complexity of the task leading to labellers mistakes [10].

© Springer International Publishing Switzerland 2016
A. Ronzhin et al. (Eds.): SPECOM 2016, LNAI 9811, pp. 461–468, 2016.
DOI: 10.1007/978-3-319-43958-7_55

As we earlier showed for Russian, annotated sentence boundaries may have different status depending on the extent of expert agreement [7]. While some boundaries are marked by the majority of annotators, there is also a substantial number of boundaries marked only by one or several experts.

Furthermore, in [8] we explored potential factors contributing to such variability between the annotators. We showed that the differences between the annotators may be related to their personality traits. Thus we found that two traits measured by the Five Factor Personality Questionnaire, "unemotionality vs. emotionality" and "practicality vs. playfulness" accounted for about 20 % of variability in sentence length as marked by the annotators.

In this paper we further investigate the connection between the annotators personality and the sentence boundaries. We focus on boundaries that are only marked by a small number of annotators (we will call them "uncommon boundaries"). We test the hypothesis that such uncommon sentence boundaries are more likely to be identified by experts with particular personality traits – for example, neuroticism, extraversion, etc. The study has practical implications: if our hypothesis is correct, it might be reasonable to select experts according to certain criteria before they start working with speech.

We used the corpus described in [8] which contains boundary annotations and the personality scores for the annotators. The scores were collected using two questionnaires to evaluate personality traits: the Eysenck Personality Inventory (EPI) [11] adopted and validated for Russian by [12] and the Five Factor Personality Questionnaire, or the Big Five (FFPQ) [13] adopted and validated for Russian by [14].

We use linear regression to evaluate whether sentence boundaries with low inter-annotator agreement are related to certain personality traits as measured by the two personality questionnaires.

2   Experimental Design and Data Collection

2.1   Data

The study is based on expert manual annotation of spontaneous monologues. We used three texts taken from the corpus of transcribed spontaneous Russian monologues described in [6,7]. This corpus contains manual transcriptions of different types of monologues recorded by 32 native speakers of Russian.

This paper is based on 3 monologues from this corpus produced by the same male speaker. This speaker had a higher education and was 40 years old at the time of the recording. Since expert manual annotation depends on text genre [7] we included the monologues which covered three different tasks: "Description" (162 words), "Story" (225 words) and "Free comment" (312 words).

2.2   Participants

Fifty native speakers of Russian (9 male and 41 female) took part in the experiment. All participants were students or professors in linguistics and/or

modern languages with a background in linguistics. The age of participants varied between 18 and 68 with a median age of 24.

2.3 Personality Questionnaires

The first task for the participants was the completion of two personality questionnaires. Both questionnaires were administered on paper.

Eysenck Personality Inventory. (EPI) consists of 57 yes/no questions and
the results are interpreted along two scales: introversion vs. extraversion and
stability vs. neuroticism. Each scale ranges from 0 to 24. There is also a separate
lie-scale designed to identify participants who are being insincere and exclude
them from the data.

Five Factor Personality Questionnaire. (FFPQ) includes 75 items with
five-level Likert scale (from -2 to 2 including 0). Each item has two opposite
statements, and a respondent has to choose the closest score on the scale to
one or another statement. The results of FFPQ are interpreted along five scales
corresponding to five super-trait factors to describe personality: (1) introversion
vs. extraversion, (2) separateness vs. attachment, (3) naturality vs. controlling,
(4) unemotionality vs. emotionality, and (5) practicality vs. playfulness.[1] Each
scale ranges from 15 to 75. Both questionnaires were administered on paper.

2.4 Sentence Boundary Annotation

After completing the questionnaires, the participants were given orthographic
transcriptions of the 3 recordings described in Sect. 2.1 and asked to mark the
sentence boundaries using conventional full stops or any other symbol of their
choice (e.g. a slash). The participants did not have access to actual recordings
and were asked to provide annotations based on text only. In addition, the
transcriptions did not contain any punctuation or any other information that
could directly indicate presence of a pause such as graphic symbols of hesitation
(like *eh, uhm*) or other comments (e.g. *[sigh], [laughter]*). Thus, we tried to
focus on semantic and syntactic factors in boundary detection. The experts were
presumed to have a native intuition of what a sentence is and, thus, it was left
undefined. There were no time-constraints.

3   Data Analysis and Results

We computed scores for each scale of the two personality inventories giving us
7 personality scores per each participant.

---

[1] We follow [13] for factor names since this version of FFPQ was used as the basis for
the Russian version.

3.1 Inter-Annotator Agreement

We identified all places where at least one annotator marked a sentence boundary. There were a total of 167 such possible boundaries across the three texts considered in this study. For each location, we assigned 1 to each annotator who marked a boundary at this location, and 0 to those annotators who did not mark the boundary. We then used these labels to compute inter-annotator agreement. We found moderate agreement between the annotators: Fleiss $\kappa = 0.46$ ($p < 0.00001$). We binned the boundaries into the following categories according to the number of annotators who marked each boundary:

- boundaries marked by half (25 subjects) of all experts and more ("common");
- boundaries marked by less than half of all experts ("somewhat rare");
- boundaries marked by less than 10 experts ("rare boundaries");
- boundaries marked by less than 5 experts ("very rare boundaries");
- boundaries marked by a single expert ("unique boundaries").

The distribution of different types of boundaries is shown in Table 1.

Table 1. The frequency of different types of boundaries.

Boundary	Marked by	Number	%
Unique	1	42	25 %
Very rare	2–4	34	20 %
Rare	5–9	21	13 %
Somewhat rare	10–24	21	13 %
Common	25–50	49	30 %

As one can see from Table 1, about one third of all boundaries were marked by the majority of the annotators. At the same time almost half of the boundaries were marked by less than 5 annotators (out of 50) with a quarter of the boundaries marked by just one annotator.

3.2 Unique Boundaries and Annotator Personality

We next performed regression analysis to find whether the number of rare and unique boundaries is associated with personality scores as measured by EPI and FFPQ.

We first used multilevel logistic regression to model the probability of sentence boundary after each word for each annotator. We used position in the text and annotator as random variables and the annotator personality score as the fixed variable.

In agreement with the results for sentence boundary length reported in [8], the personality scores measured by EPI had no significant effect on sentence boundaries ($p = 0.993$ for both scales).

For FFPQ the presence of sentence boundary in the annotation depended on unemotionality vs. emotionality (UE) ($p = 0.02$) and practicality vs. playfulness (PP) ($p = 0.04$) scores of the annotators.

We next focused on the main question of this paper: are annotators with particular personality traits more likely to mark unique boundaries?

For each boundary we computed the average personality score of all annotators who marked that boundary. We then used linear regression to test whether the type of the boundary ("unique", "very rare", "rare", "somewhat rare", "common") had any effect on the average personality score for that boundary.

We found that for unique boundaries the personality score along UE scale was significantly higher than for other types of boundaries ($R^2 = 0.05$, $p = 0.001$). While average UE score for all boundaries was 53.3, the average score for unique boundaries was 57.3, four points above the average. The distribution of scores for different boundary types is shown in Fig. 1.

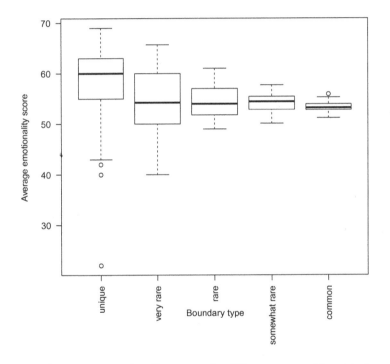

Fig. 1. Annotator emotionality scores for different types of boundaries.

There also was significant relationship between the boundary type and the annotator score on "introversion vs. extraversion" (IE) scale: the average IE score of annotators who marked unique boundaries was 2–3 points higher than for other boundaries ($R^2 = 0.06$, $p = 0.4$). This is shown in Fig. 2.

We saw no significant relationship between the unique boundaries and other scores.

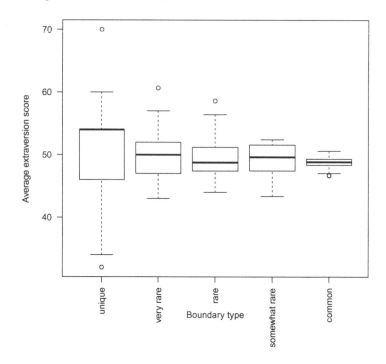

Fig. 2. Annotator extraversion scores for different types of boundaries.

4   Conclusion

In this paper we tested the hypothesis that low inter-annotator agreement in a number of boundaries detected by experts in the process of manual annotation may be related to particular personality traits of annotators. Our attention was focused on unique boundaries (marked by only one person) and very rare boundaries (marked by 2–4 persons, or 4 %–8 % of the annotators who took part in the experiment).

We found that, in general, the presence of sentence boundaries in the annotated texts is related to two personality traits described by Five-Factor Personality Questionnaire as unemotionality vs. emotionality and practicality vs. playfulness.

As for the uncommon boundaries, the analysis revealed the connection between the placement of unique boundaries and two personality traits – emotionality and extraversion. We found that highly emotional and highly extravert people are more likely to mark unique boundaries. Therefore in a situation where the quality of annotation is judged by the inter-annotator agreement, it may be useful to obtain emotionality and extraversion scores of prospective annotators and consider those when creating the gold standard annotation.

We note that it is of course also possible that annotators with particular personality traits are more likely to identify the boundaries missed by other annotators. Testing this hypothesis would require an external validity criterion. It is worth mentioning that, since the five factor model of personality is not universal and cannot encompass all individual traits, there may be other personal characteristics which are related to uncommon segmentation and merely await their identification. Besides, very low inter-annotator agreement in some positions may have another source. We assume, for example, that it might reflect the disfluent character of spontaneous speech which, in its turn, in some cases provokes disfluent annotation.

Acknowledgments. This study was supported by the Russian Foundation for Humanities, project No. 15–04–00165. We thank Keelan Evanini, Su-Youn Yoon and two anonymous reviewers for their comments and suggestions.

References

1. Vannikov, Y., Abdalyan, I.: Eksperimentalnoe issledovanie chleneniya razgovornoj rechi na diskretnye intonacionno-smyslovye edinicy (frazy). In: Sirotinina, O.B., Barannikova, L.I., Serdobintsev, L. Ja. (eds.) Russkaya razgovornaya rech, Saratov, pp. 40–46 (1973). (in Russian)
2. Guaïtella, I.: Rhythm in speech: What rhythmic organizations reveal about cognitive processes in spontaneous speech production versus reading aloud. J. Pragmat. **31**, 509–523 (1999)
3. Strassel, S., Walker, C.: Data and annotation issues in RT-03. In: EARS Rich Transcription Workshop (2003)
4. Liu, Y., Chawla, V.N., Harper, M.P., Shriberg, E., Stolcke, A.: A study in machine learning from imbalanced data for sentence boundary detection in speech. Comput. Speech Lang. **20**(4), 468–494 (2006)
5. Lee, A., Glass, J.: Sentence detection using multiple annotations. In: Proceedings of the Interspeech 2012, pp. 1848–1851 (2012)
6. Stepikhov, A.: Resolving ambiguities in sentence boundary detection in russian spontaneous speech. In: Habernal, I. (ed.) TSD 2013. LNCS, vol. 8082, pp. 426–433. Springer, Heidelberg (2013)
7. Stepikhov, A.: Analysis of expert manual annotation of the russian spontaneous monologue: evidence from sentence boundary detection. In: Železný, M., Habernal, I., Ronzhin, A. (eds.) SPECOM 2013. LNCS, vol. 8113, pp. 33–40. Springer, Heidelberg (2013)
8. Stepikhov, A., Loukina, A.: Annotation and personality: individual differences in sentence boundary detection. In: Ronzhin, A., Potapova, R., Delic, V. (eds.) SPECOM 2014. LNCS, vol. 8773, pp. 105–112. Springer, Heidelberg (2014)
9. Evanini, K., Zechner, K.: Using crowdsourcing to provide prosodic annotations for non-native speech. In: Proceedings of the Interspeech 2011, pp. 3069–3072 (2011)
10. Cuendet, S., Hakkani-Tür, D., Shriberg, E.: Automatic labeling inconsistencies detection and correction for sentence unit segmentation in conversational speech. In: Popescu-Belis, A., Renals, S., Bourlard, H. (eds.) MLMI 2007. LNCS, vol. 4892, pp. 144–155. Springer, Heidelberg (2008)

11. Eysenck, H.J., Eysenck, S.B.G.: Manual of the Eysenck Personality Inventory. University of London Press, London (1964)
12. Shmelev, A.G.: Test-oprosnik Ajzenka. In: Bodalev, A.A., Karpinskaya, et al. (eds.) Praktikum po psikhodiagnostike. Psikhodiagnosticheskie materialy, pp. 11–16. MGU, Moscow (1988). (in Russian)
13. Tsuji, H., Fujishima, Y., Tsuji, H., Natsuno, Y., Mukoyama, Y., Yamada, N., Morita, Y., Hata, K.: Five-factor model of personality: Concept, structure, and measurement of personality traits. Jpn. Psychol. Rev. **40**(2), 239–259 (1997)
14. Khromov, A.B.: Patifactornyj oprosnik lichnosti: Uchebno-metodicheskoe posobie. Izd-vo Kurganskogo gosudarstvennogo universiteta, Kurgan (2000). (in Russian)

LSTM-Based Language Models for Spontaneous Speech Recognition

Ivan Medennikov[1,2]($\boxtimes$) and Anna Bulusheva[1]

[1] STC-innovations Ltd, St. Petersburg, Russia
{medennikov,bulusheva}@speechpro.com
[2] ITMO University, St. Petersburg, Russia

Abstract. The language models (LMs) used in speech recognition to predict the next word (given the context) often rely on too short context, which leads to recognition errors. In theory, using recurrent neural networks (RNN) should solve this problem, but in practice the RNNs do not fully utilize the potential of the long context. The RNN-based language models with long short-term memory (LSTM) units take better advantage of the long context and demonstrate good results in terms of perplexity for many datasets. We used LSTM-LMs trained with regularization to rescore the recognition word lattices and obtained much lower WER as compared to the n-gram and conventional RNN-based LMs for the Russian and English languages.

Keywords: Recurrent neural networks · Long shorm-term memory · Language models · Automatic speech recognition

1 Introduction

Many speech recognition errors are due to the fact that the language model used relies on too short word context to predict the next word. For example, the modern n-gram models [1] usually operate with a context of 2–5 words. The feedforward neural network language models [2,3] always rely on a context of a fixed length, but this is not always sufficient for good prediction. In theory, this could be resolved with the help of the RNN-based language model (RNNLM) [4–6] which takes into account all preceding words. They significantly outperform the n-gram models in various ASR tasks [4,5]. But RNNs are very difficult to train because of the vanishing gradient problem; in practice, RNNs do not fully utilize the potential of the long context [7]. To overcome these difficulties, it has been proposed to apply RNNs with LSTM units [8–13]. But, like the RNNLM, they are prone to overfitting. The regularization techniques commonly used for the feedforward neural networks perform rather poorly on RNN and LSTM networks [14,15]. The RNN regularization technique proposed in [16] successfully solves this problem.

In this research, we apply LSTM language models trained with dropout regularization to rescore the recognition hypotheses. We obtained a significant word

© Springer International Publishing Switzerland 2016
A. Ronzhin et al. (Eds.): SPECOM 2016, LNAI 9811, pp. 469–475, 2016.
DOI: 10.1007/978-3-319-43958-7_56

error rate (WER) reduction as compared to the n-gram and conventional RNN language models for Russian and English languages.

The rest of the paper is organized as follows. In Sect. 2, we describe the LSTM and RNN regularization. In Sect. 3, we give the results of experiments on recognition of Russian and English spontaneous speech, and discuss them in Sect. 4.

2   Description of LSTM Units

In order to overcome the vanishing gradient problem for RNNs, Sepp Hochreiter and Jürgen Schmidhuber proposed RNN architecture elements called long short-term memory units [8]. A rather complex structure of LSTM (see Fig. 1) makes it possible to store long-term information effectively.

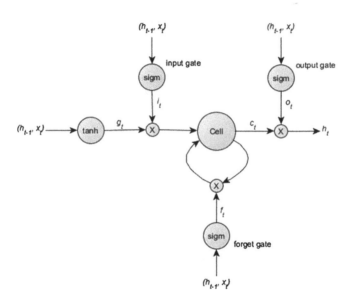

Fig. 1. Structure of LSTM

The long-term memory is implemented with the use of the memory cell vector. LSTM allows to store, change, or delete the information placed in the memory cell. This is controlled by three gates which are presented in every LSTM block. They consist of the sigmoid layer followed by the element-wise multiplication operation. The sigmoid layer outputs take values from zero to one, which indicate what fraction of a component should pass through the gate. For example, zero value means a full forbiddance to pass, while the unit value means the opposite. So, the input gate determines which information from the input is allowed to enter inside the LSTM block, the forget gate determines which information should be removed from the memory cell. Finally, the output is determined by the cell state and the output gate values.

The LSTM is described by the equations

$$\text{LSTM} : h_{t-1}, c_{t-1}, x_t \mapsto h_t, c_t,$$

$$\begin{pmatrix} i_t \\ f_t \\ o_t \\ g_t \end{pmatrix} = \begin{pmatrix} \text{sigm} \\ \text{sigm} \\ \text{sigm} \\ \text{tanh} \end{pmatrix} T_{2n,4n} \begin{pmatrix} x_t \\ h_{t-1} \end{pmatrix}, \tag{1}$$

$$c_t = f_t \odot c_{t-1} + i_t \odot g_t,$$

$$h_t = o_t \odot \tanh(c_t).$$

Here $x_t, h_t, c_t, i_t, f_t, o_t, g_t \in \mathbb{R}^n$ denote the input vector, output vector, memory cell state and the activations of input gate, forget gate, output gate and input modulation gate at time t; $T_{2n,4n} : \mathbb{R}^{2n} \to \mathbb{R}^{4n}$ is a linear transform with a bias; $\odot$ symbol denotes element-wise multiplication; logistic (sigm) and hyperbolic tangent (tanh) activation functions are applied element-wise.

A more detailed description and an algorithm to train the LSTM can be found in [9].

2.1   Regularization with Dropout

The standard regularization techniques that exist for feedforward neural networks [14,15] perform rather poorly on RNN and LSTM networks, which commonly leads to model overfitting. The use of dropout regularization for RNN and LSTM networks is proposed in [16]. The key idea of this technique consists of applying the dropout to non-recurrent connections only. The formulas below describe this method in more detail:

$$\text{LSTM} : h_{t-1}, c_{t-1}, x_t \mapsto h_t, c_t,$$

$$\begin{pmatrix} i_t \\ f_t \\ o_t \\ g_t \end{pmatrix} = \begin{pmatrix} \text{sigm} \\ \text{sigm} \\ \text{sigm} \\ \text{tanh} \end{pmatrix} T_{2n,4n} \begin{pmatrix} \text{D}(x_t) \\ h_{t-1} \end{pmatrix}, \tag{2}$$

$$c_t = f_t \odot c_{t-1} + i_t \odot g_t,$$

$$h_t = o_t \odot \tanh(c_t),$$

where D stands for the dropout operator which sets a random subset of its argument to zero. Its detailed description can be found in [16].

3   Experiments

3.1   Experiments on English Spontaneous Speech

For our experiments, we chose a training set consisted of transcriptions from the *Switchboard-1 Release 2* and *Fisher English* corpora. The 3-gram LM for the first recognition pass was trained with modified Kneser-Ney (MKN) smoothing [1] on the transcriptions of the *Switchboard* corpus with 30 K words vocabulary. The baseline 4-gram model was built following the swbd(s5c) recipe. The vocabulary was around 30 k words and the model was produced by interpolation of two 4-gram models built with MKN smoothing (*Switchboard* and *Fisher*).

In order to train neural language models, we mixed all sentences and partitioned them into two parts: cross-validation(CV) (20 K sentences) and TRAIN (the remaining ones, about 2.5 M sentences). All words which were not found in the vocabulary of the 4-gram model were replaced by the ⟨UNK⟩ token. As the TEST set we chose the transcriptions of the HUB5 2000 evaluation set. We trained RNNLM [4] and LSTM-LM on the TRAIN part, and then evaluated the perplexity on the CV and TEST parts.

For the training of RNNLM we used Tomas Mikolov's utility rnnlm-0.4b from the http://www.rnnlm.org site. The RNNLM topology was the following: 256 neurons in the hidden layer, 200 direct connections, 4 direct order. In order to speed up the training process, we factorized the output layer into 200 classes.

To train LSTM-LM we used the TensorFlow toolkit [17]. We trained two neural networks in the "medium" and "large" configurations given in [16]. LSTMs had two layers and were unrolled for 35 steps. We initialized the hidden states with zeros. Then we used the final hidden states of the current minibatch as the initial hidden state of the subsequent minibatch (successive minibatches sequentially traverse the training set). The size of each minibatch was 100. The "medium" LSTM-LM had 650 units per layer. We applied 50 % dropout to the non-recurrent connections. The "large" LSTM-LM had 1500 units per layer. We applied 65 % dropout to the non-recurrent connections. In addition, for the "large" model forget gate biases were initialized with value of 1.0.

Table 1. Experiment results on English spontaneous speech

Language model	PPL			WER, %	
	Train	CV	Test	SW	Full
4-gram	66.366	62.946	87.039	11.7	17.1
RNNLM	57.982	78.578	76.123	10.8	16.1
LSTM-LM (medium)	51.104	58.964	56.822	10.4	15.4
LSTM-LM (large)	46.033	54.821	52.892	10.1	15.2

The speech recognition experiments performed on the HUB5 2000 evaluation set were carried out with the use of the Kaldi speech recognition toolkit [18]. As the baseline we chose the DNN-HMM acoustic model trained with the state-level Minimum Bayes Risk (sMBR) sequence-discriminative criterion using the nnet1 setup in the Kaldi swbd (s5c) recipe [19]. The recognition was performed with the trigram LM, and then the word lattices were rescored with the use of the 4-gram model. Next, we carried out the rescoring of the 100-best list with the use of neural network language models; in doing so, we calculated the language score by the formula

$$lm_{\text{rescore}} = \lambda lm_{rnn} + (1 - \lambda)lm_{4\text{gr}}, \tag{3}$$

where lm_{rnn} were calculated with the use of RNNLM, LSTM-LM (medium), LSTM-LM (large). Experiment results in terms of perplexity and WER are shown in Table 1. Note that valid PPL of the baseline 4-gram model is low due to the presence of valid texts in the training data for this LM.

3.2   Experiments on Russian Spontaneous Speech

The experiments on Russian spontaneous speech were performed in a similar way. We chose the DNN-HMM acoustic-model trained on 390 h of Russian spontaneous speech (telephone conversations). The model was trained on 120-dimensional speaker-dependent bottleneck features [20,21] extracted from the DNN trained in a speaker adaptive manner using i-vectors. We used 50-dimensional i-vectors constructed with our toolset [22]. The acoustic model training was carried out with the use of the sMBR sequence-discriminative criterion. The experiments were conducted on the same test dataset as in [20] which contained about one hour of Russian telephone conversations.

We chose two datasets to train language models. The first one consisted of the transcriptions of the AM training dataset. The second one contained a large amount (about 200 M words) of texts from Internet forum discussions, books and subtitles from the http://www.opensubtitles.org site. The baseline 3-gram language model with a vocabulary of 214 K words was built in the SRILM toolkit [23]. It was obtained by interpolation of 3-gram LMs trained on the first and second datasets using Modified Kneser-Ney smoothing. The size of this model was reduced to 4.16 M bigrams and 2.49 M trigrams with the use of pruning.

RNNLM and LSTM-LM were trained only on mixed sentences from the training dataset 1 divided into CV (15 K sentences), TEST (4 K sentences) and TRAIN (the remaining ones, 243 K sentences) parts. In order to speed up the training we utilized the vocabulary of 45 K most frequent words; all other words were replaced by the ⟨UNK⟩ token. During RNNLM training we used 256 neurons in the hidden layer and 200 classes in the output layer. LSTM-LMs were trained in the "medium" and "large" configurations described in the paper [16].

The experiments were carried out with the use of the Kaldi toolkit. The word lattices generated during the recognition phase with the 3-gram LM were used to extract the 100-best hypotheses list. The list was then rescored with the neural network language model. Since the 3-gram and the neural network language models contained different vocabularies we had to use unigram weights from the 3-gram LM for words that were absent in the 45 K vocabulary of RNN-based model. The results in terms of perplexity and WER are presented in Table 2. It should be noted that the 3-gram LM was trained using both dataset 1 and dataset 2 with a full vocabulary of 214 K words, while RNN-based models were trained using dataset 1 only with a reduced vocabulary of 45 K words. So, the 3-gram LM perplexity results can not be directly compared with the results of RNN-based models and reported only for reference.

Table 2. Experiment results on Russian spontaneous speech

Language model	PPL			WER, %
	Train	CV	Test	
3-gram	134.26	134.921	228.015	19.5
RNNLM	134.136	164.147	186.757	18.8
LSTM-LM (medium)	110.689	127.358	148.627	17.9
LSTM-LM (large)	105.918	124.618	146.812	17.8

4   Discussion and Conclusion

In this study we used LSTM-LM with regularization to rescore the n-best lists produced by English and Russian spontaneous speech recognition systems. This technique takes into account a longer context to predict the next word as compared with the n-gram and even with the RNN-based models. The LSTM-LMs do not suffer from the vanishing gradient problem while training.

Our experiments demonstrate that LSTM-LM gives much better results than the n-gram model and RNNLM. As compared with the n-gram model, we obtained relative WER reduction by 11.1–13.7 % for the English language and by 8.4 % for the Russian language. As compared with RNNLM, relative WER reduction is 5.6–6.5 % for the English language and 5.3 % for the Russian language.

We plan to apply LSTM-LM to other ASR tasks and study other promising language model architectures, such as character-aware neural language models [13] and end-to-end memory networks [24] in the future.

Acknowledgements. The work was financially supported by the Ministry of Education and Science of the Russian Federation. Contract 14.579.21.0121, ID RFMEFI57915X0121.

References

1. Kneser, R., Ney, H.: Improved backing-off for M-gram language modeling. In: 1995 International Conference on Acoustics, Speech and Signal Processing (ICASSP), vol. 1, pp. 181–184 (1995)
2. Bengio, Y., Ducharme, R., Vincent, P.: A neural probabilistic language model. Adv. Neural Inf. Process. Syst. **13**, 932–938 (2001)
3. Schwenk, H.: Continuous space language models. Comput. Speech Lang. **21**, 492–518 (2007)
4. Mikolov, T., Karafiat, M., Burget, L., Cernocky, J., Khudanpur, S.: Recurrent neural network based language model. In: 11th Annual Conference of the International Speech Communication Association (Interspeech), pp. 1045–1048. Makuhari (2010)
5. Kipyatkova, I., Karpov, A.: A comparison of RNN LM and FLM for Russian speech recognition. In: Ronzhin, A., Potapova, R., Fakotakis, N. (eds.) SPECOM 2015. LNCS, vol. 9319, pp. 42–50. Springer, Heidelberg (2015)

6. Mikolov, T.: Statistical language models based on neural networks. Ph.D. thesis, Brno University Technology (2012)
7. Bengio, Y., Simard, P., Frasconi, P.: Learning long-term dependencies with gradient descent is difficult. IEEE Trans. Neural Netw. **5**(2), 157–166 (1994)
8. Hochreiter, S., Schmidhuber, J.: Long short-term memory. Neural Comput. **9**(8), 1735–1780 (1997)
9. Graves, A., Schmidhuber, J.: Framewise phoneme classification with bidirectional LSTM and other neural network architectures. Neural Netw. **18**(5–6), 602–610 (2005)
10. Józefowicz, R., Vinyals, O., Schuster, M., Shazeer, N., Wu, Y.: Exploring the limits of language modeling (2016). arXiv preprint arXiv:1602.02410
11. Sundermeyer, M., Schlüter, R., Ney, H.: LSTM neural networks for language modeling. In: 13th Annual Conference of the International Speech Communication Association (INTERSPEECH), Portland, pp. 194–197 (2012)
12. Soutner, D., Müller, L.: Application of LSTM neural networks in language modelling. In: Habernal, I. (ed.) TSD 2013. LNCS, vol. 8082, pp. 105–112. Springer, Heidelberg (2013)
13. Kim, Y., Jernite, Y., Sontag, D., Rush, A.: Character-aware neural language models (2015). arXiv preprint arXiv:1508.06615
14. Bayer, J., Osendorfer, C., Chen, N., Urban, S., van der Smagt, P.: On fast dropout and its applicability to recurrent networks (2013). arXiv preprint arXiv:1311.0701
15. Graves, A.: Generating sequences with recurrent neural networks (2013). arXiv preprint arXiv:1308.0850
16. Zaremba, W., Sutskever, I., Vinyals, O.: Recurrent neural network regularization (2014). arXiv preprint arXiv:1409.2329
17. Abadi, M., et al.: TensorFlow: large-scale machine learning on heterogeneous systems (2015). http://tensorflow.org/
18. Povey, D., et al.: The Kaldi speech recognition toolkit. In: IEEE workshop on Automatic Speech Recognition and Understanding (ASRU), Big Island, pp. 1–4 (2011)
19. Vesely, K., Ghoshal, A., Burget, L., Povey, D.: Sequence-discriminative training of deep neural networks. In: 14th Annual Conference of the International Speech Communication Association (Interspeech), Lyon, pp. 2345–2349 (2013)
20. Prudnikov, A., Medennikov, I., Mendelev, V., Korenevsky, M., Khokhlov, Y.: Improving acoustic models for Russian spontaneous speech recognition. In: Ronzhin, A., Potapova, R., Fakotakis, N. (eds.) SPECOM 2015. LNCS, vol. 9319, pp. 234–242. Springer, Heidelberg (2015)
21. Medennikov, I.P.: Speaker-dependent features for spontaneous speech recognition. Sci. Tech. J. Inf. Technol. Mech. Opt. **16**(1), 195–197 (2016). doi:10.17586/2226-1494-2016-16-1-195-197
22. Kozlov, A., Kudashev, O., Matveev, Y., Pekhovsky, T., Simonchik, K., Shulipa, A.: SVID speaker recognition system for NIST SRE 2012. In: Železný, M., Habernal, I., Ronzhin, A. (eds.) SPECOM 2013. LNCS, vol. 8113, pp. 278–285. Springer, Heidelberg (2013)
23. Stolcke, A.: SRILM – an extensible language modeling toolkit. In: Seventh International Conference on Spoken Language Processing, vol. 3, pp. 901–904 (2002)
24. Sukhbaatar, S., Szlam, A., Weston, J., Fergus, R.: End-to-end memory networks (2015). arXiv preprint arXiv:1503.08895

Measuring Prosodic Entrainment in Italian Collaborative Game-Based Dialogues

Michelina Savino[1(✉)], Loredana Lapertosa[1], Alessandro Caffò[1], and Mario Refice[2]

[1] Department of Education, Psychology, Communication, University of Bari, Bari, Italy
{michelina.savino,loredana.lapertosa,alessandro.caffo}@uniba.it
[2] Department of Electrical and Information Engineering,
Polytechnical University of Bari, Bari, Italy
mario.refice@poliba.it

Abstract. In a large number of studies, it has been observed that conversational partners tend to adapt each other's speech over the course of the interaction. This phenomenon, variously named as entrainment, coordination, alignment or adaptation, is widely believed to be crucial to mutual understanding and successful communication in human interaction. Modelling human adaptation in speech behaviour would also be very important for improving naturalness in voiced-based human-machine interaction systems. Recently, a body of research in this field has been devoted to find evidence of prosodic entrainment by measuring a number of acoustic-prosodic parameters in some languages, yet not in Italian. Our study offers a contribution to this research line. We analysed game-based collaborative dialogues between Italian speakers, by measuring their articulation rate, pitch range, pitch level and loudness. Results show some evidence of overall speech coordination (convergence and synchrony) between conversational partners, wherein the combination of specific prosodic parameters involved may vary across dialogues. Our results are in line with those obtained in previous studies on other languages, thus contributing to providing a useful basis for modelling prosodic adaptation in multilingual spoken dialogue systems.

Keywords: Entrainment · Prosody · Collaborative dialogues · Human-machine interaction · Italian

1 Introduction

In a large number of studies, it has been observed that conversational partners show the tendency to adapt their speech over the course of the interaction. This phenomenon, termed in different ways such as convergence (e.g. [1]), entrainment (e.g. [2]), alignment (e.g. [3]), accomodation (e.g. [4]), adaptation (e.g. [5]), or coordination (e.g. [2]), is widely believed to be crucial to mutual understanding and successful communication. The Communication Accomodation Theory [6] motivates this phenomenon in terms of its social function, as it modulates social distance among interactants. The possibility of modelling mutual speech adaptation also in relation to human-machine interaction would be crucial for improving naturalness of communication with spoken dialogue systems, thus allowing users to perceive the system as a more natural and socially

© Springer International Publishing Switzerland 2016
A. Ronzhin et al. (Eds.): SPECOM 2016, LNAI 9811, pp. 476–483, 2016.
DOI: 10.1007/978-3-319-43958-7_57

competent conversational partner (for a comprehensive overview and discussion on this topic see [7]). Currently, instead, entrainment tends to be unidirectional, in that humans are the ones who normally and unconsciously tend to entrain the machine – for example, by adapting their speaking rate to that of the system [5].

Recent research lines on speech entrainment modelling have being focussed on prosodic aspects, attempting to find evidence of prosodic adaptation between conversational partners in spoken interactions both locally (typically, at turn-exchanges) and globally (over the entire dialogue) by measuring a number of prosodic-acoustic features. These studies include a variety of diverse languages, thus highlighting the importance of investigating the cross-linguistic and cross-cultural aspects involved in prosodic adaptation, as much crucial for modelling speech entrainment in multilingual spoken dialogue systems. Languages investigated so far include Swedish [8], varieties of English [2, 9–11], German ([12], in this case articulation rate is the only parameter considered), Japanese [13], Slovak [14] and recently Slovak, English, Spanish, and Chinese in a cross-linguistic direct comparison [15], but not Italian. The present paper represents a preliminary contribution to filling this gap.

We collected and analysed a corpus of cooperative game-based dialogues between pairs of Italian participants and measured a number of prosodic parameters looking for evidence of overall speech coordination at the global level of dialogue session.

2 Materials and Method

2.1 Elicited Dialogues

The interaction paradigm adopted for eliciting our Italian data is the one developed within the PAGE project [16]. It consists of an adapted version of the Tangram Game, a communicative task where participants play with sets of figures from the old Chinese Tangram game, as developed by [17].

In our recording sessions, pairs of participants in a game round were given Tangram figures according to their role in that game round, i.e. Director or Matcher. The Director was provided with a set of four Tangram figures, one of which was marked by an arrow, and the Matcher was given one of the figures belonging to the Director's set. Each of the participants could not see the partner's figure(s), and goal of the game in each round was to establish whether the figure given to the Matcher was the one marked by the arrow in the Director's set or not, by exchanging information about how figures looked like, and so on. The players were explicitly instructed to come to that decision on the basis of a common agreement. In order to encourage a cooperative behaviour, they were told they both gained a score every time they chose well, and they both lost a score when they did not. Even though normally games involve competition between players (thus always implying a winner and a loser), we opted for a cooperative paradigm basing on the assumption that speakers would more likely to entrain each other in a collaborative rather than in a competitive context. The use of a cooperative interaction paradigm makes also possible a more direct comparison with most of previous studies on prosodic adaptation involving other languages, in which a similar paradigm was adopted.

A complete Tangram Game session consists in 22 game rounds. In each round, participants alternate their role as Director or Matcher, i.e., in the whole game dialogue each speaker played 11 times the role of Director, and 11 times that of Matcher in total.

In our experimental setting, participants in a pair sat at desk in front of each other, each of them wearing head-mounted professional microphones (AKG C520) connected to a Marantz PMD 661 digital recorder. A Panasonic HC-V700 camcorder was placed in front of each of the two participants for high quality video-recording (this was done for planned future studies on multimodal aspects of entrainment). The parallel audio-recording via professional microphones and digital recorder was carried out in order to ensure high quality of acquired speech signal and a better dealing with overlapped speech during analysis. A cardboard was inserted between the participants' desks at a suitable height in order to prevent seeing each other's Tangram figures, but preserving eye contact between players. Each recording session lasted approximately 30 min.

2.2 Speakers

Twelve informants participated in the recording sessions. They were selected according to a number of parameters which could influence adaptation, namely age, gender, and familiarity. Accordingly, selected subjects were all young adult females (aged 21–25), and MA student classmates, i.e. they were familiar with each other as they had met before participating in the game session. Also, they all came from the same geolinguistic area (Bari district in Apulia, a southeastern region of Italy). They obtained a course credit as reward for participating, and were all naïve to the research goal of the study.

2.3 Annotation Levels and Prosodic Parameters

All game dialogues were orthographically transcribed, basing on the coding scheme for enriched orthographic transcription developed within the AVIP national corpus of spoken varieties of Italian [18]. Beginning and end of each game round were also reported in the orthographic transcriptions.

Speech signal of the twelve speakers was manually annotated along the following levels:

- Tangram Game rounds
- InterPausal Units (where each IPU corresponds to speaker's speech bounded by silence longer than 100 ms)
- Words
- Syllables (trascribed in SAMPA)

All annotations were carried out manually by using Praat software tool for speech analysis [19]. In a post-processing step, consistency of annotations was checked by means of specifically designed and developed home-made tools, and errors were manually corrected. In measuring prosodic entrainment, the following parameters were taken into account and automatically extracted via Praat scripts implementation (taking IPU as speech unit of analysis): pitch range (F0max-F0 min, Hz), pitch level (F0 median, Hz), loudness (intensity, dB) and articulation rate (number of syll/sec).

2.4   Measuring Overall Speech Coordination: Convergence and Synchrony

Speech entrainment can be basically defined as a phenomenon where speakers increase similarity in their speech features over the course of their interaction. Even though such a definition would imply that speech adaptation is a linear process, recent research has proposed frameworks of analysis describing it as a quite complex phenomenon which can imply a number of strategies (proximity, convergence, synchrony), and can occur both globally (over the entire dialogue) and locally (typically, at turn-exchanges) [2, 15]. Given the preliminary nature of our study, in this paper we will focus on global aspects of speech coordination, i.e. those referring to similarity process undergoing at the level of the whole dialogue. In particular, we basically follow the approach proposed by [8] and substantially drawn on by [10] in defining similarity as underlined by two phenomena: convergence and synchrony. In particular:

Convergence is the process by which conversational partners' speech features become more similar over time (i.e. over the course of the interaction) until they converge;

Synchrony implies that speakers' speech happen to have similar patterns over time (in [8] terms, when they "happen at the same time or work at the same speed").

Note that since convergence and synchrony are two possible modalities of entrainment manifestation, they could but do not have to necessarily co-occur in the same dialogue. Moreover, both convergence and synchrony can be realised on the opposite direction as complementary manifestation of entrainment. According to Communication Adaptation Theory [6], intra-speaker coordination dynamics can also imply divergence, i.e. that speakers can sound more dissimilar over the course of the interaction, in this way marking their social distance (complementary convergence or divergence [20]). For the same reason, also anti-synchrony (or negative synchrony) can be considered as a possible manifestation of overall speech coordination (see also [10]).

Moreover, coordination process at the global level cannot exclude that speakers can converge by some speech features yet diverge by some others in the same interaction (see, for example, in [8]).

As to measurements, we looked for evidence of convergence at the overall game session level by identifying cases in which speakers mean values were more similar (or, in case of divergence, more distant) to each other later in the dialogue. Accordingly, we splitted each game session into two halves, i.e. a window consisting of game rounds 1–11 vs another window including game rounds 12–22. Within each of the two windows, we compared (paired t-tests) mean values of speaker1 vs speaker2. Mean values found as significantly different in the first half but not significantly different in the second half were considered as evidence for convergent entrainment (i.e. speakers becoming more similar to each other later in the dialogue). Mean values found as not significantly different in the first half but significantly different in the second half were considered as evidence of complementary convergence or divergence (i.e. speakers increasing mutual distance later in the dialogue). Cases other from these two (mean values either significantly different or not different in both first and second halves of the sessions) were not taken as evidence for convergence or divergence.

In measuring synchrony, we followed [8] in using Pearson's correlation for capturing the dynamicity involved in the overall coordination process. We correlated speaker1 with speaker2 mean values, at the game round level, over the whole dialogue session. We assumed positive correlation as evidence of synchrony, and negative correlation as evidence of anti-synchrony, in the terms described above in this section.

3   Results

Table 1 shows results of speaker1-speaker2 mean values comparison, for each prosodic parameter, within the first vs second halves of each game-based dialogue session. According to the criterion described above, (two-tailed) t-tests show statistical evidence of convergence/divergence in four out of our six dialogues. In particular, speakers in dialogue CD show to use F0 voice features for manifesting entrainment: they converge in pitch range and diverge in pitch level. Speakers in dialogue PZ become more similar in their voice loudness in the second part of the dialogue (convergence), whereas speakers in dialogue RC show complementary entrainment by significantly diverging in their articulation rate in the second half of the game session. Finally, speakers in dialogue DS converge in their articulation rate, and diverge in the loudness of their voices. As to participant pairs in the two game sessions PP and BV, instead, our measurements do not provide statistical evidence of prosodic convergence (or divergence).

As to synchrony, results in Table 2 show that significant positive correlations between speaker pairs in game sessions were found in five out of our six dialogues, each for a variable number of prosodic parameters. In particular, pitch range appears the most widely used prosodic cue across dialogue partners for manifesting synchrony (dialogues RC, PP, and DS), followed by articulation rate (dialogues PZ and DS) and loudness (only dialogue PP). Among these, we registered one case of anti-synchrony, that for pitch level in dialogue DS.

Participants in the game session BV – one of the two dialogues for which no statistical evidence of convergence has been recorded on the basis of our measurements – do not appear to manifest overall coordination by synchronising their speech either, for any of the prosodic parameters considered.

By combining results on convergence with those on synchrony, it can be noted that speakers in each dialogue use different strategies for cueing prosodic entrainment. For example, in dialogues PZ, RC and DS conversational partners both converge (or diverge) and synchronise their speech through a variable number of prosodic parameters, whereas in dialogue CD conversational partners converge without synchronising, and in dialogue PP they synchronise without converging. As to the prosodic parameters involved, only in dialogue DS speech coordination is consistently realised between speakers via both synchronising and converging by the same prosodic feature – in this case, articulation rate. In all the remaining dialogues where both similarity processes are combined, prosodic parameters involved are diverse.

Finally, conversational partners in game session BV do not appear to display overall speech coordination by any of the two modalities investigated in this study, namely convergence and synchrony. This result does not necessarily imply that speakers in this case did not entrain at all, but that they possibly coordinated their speech at a local level (for example, at turn-exchanges), and/or that they used speech (or other linguistic) parameters different from those measured in this study.

Table 1. Comparison of speaker1 vs speaker2 mean values in the first vs second halves of each dialogue (two-tailed t-test, t values only when significant (*=p<.05, **=p<.01, ***=p<.001). Light gray shaded boxes indicate convergence, dark gray shaded ones indicate divergence. Dialogue sessions are identified by participants' initial names (e.g. CD = game session run by participants C and D)

Dialogue	Convergence/divergence *speaker1-speaker2 mean values comparison, 1 half vs 2 half of dialogue*							
	Art. rate		Pitch range		Pitch level		Loudness	
	1st half	2nd half	1st half	2nd half	1st half	2nd half	1st half	2nd half
CD	n.s.	n.s	2.18*	n.s.	n.s.	4.18***	2.29*	2.58*
PZ	n.s.	n.s.	n.s.	n.s.	-10.46***	-6.71***	-3.52**	n.s.
RC	n.s.	-2.69*	n.s.	n.s.	n.s.	n.s.	4.88***	4.89***
PP	n.s.	n.s.	n.s.	n.s.	-8.27***	-4.94***	4.66***	7.10***
DS	3.21**	n.s.	2.14*	2.16*	n.s.	n.s.	n.s.	2.16*
BV	-3.73**	-3.97***	-2.33*	-2.34*	-6.42***	-9.35***	6.63***	8.75***

Table 2. Pearson's correlation (r values) of speaker1 with speaker2 mean values (at the game round level) in the whole dialogue session (*=p<.10, **=p<.05)

Dialogue	**Synchrony**			
	Art. rate	Pitch range	Pitch level	Loudness
CD	.034	.185	−.120	−.295
PZ	.465**	−.204	.177	−.053
RC	−.098	−.078	.401*	.047
PP	−.097	−.217	.452**	.425**
DS	.523**	.191	−.381*	−.071
BV	.053	−.346	.048	.219

4   Discussion and Conclusions

Results of this explorative study on prosodic entrainment between Italian speakers involved in a collaborative game-based dialogue indicate that, at the global level of the entire dialogue session, conversational partners tend to coordinate their speech through a variable number of prosodic parameters. Modalities and direction of the overall speech coordination process may also vary, i.e. convergence and synchrony can or cannot co-occur (yet in our data they do in most of the cases), and complementary convergence (divergence) and anti-synchrony can also characterise the process (as accounted for by social-oriented theories of adaptation like Communication Accomodation Theory [6]).

Strategies and manifestation of prosodic entrainment vary from dialogue to dialogue in our data, and this result simply confirms widely-acknowledged accounts of adaptation phenomena as being very complex since they include a number of interpersonal and social factors (for a review, see for example [21]), which we have planned to take into account in our future research. Such a complex picture of different strategies and prosodic parameters involved in speech entrainment as derived by our preliminary study is consistent with that offered by the literature on prosodic adaptation as briefly sketched in the introduction.

As to prosodic parameters involved in speech entrainment, our results on Italian data indicate that vocal pitch features, articulation rate and loudness can be all involved in the overall speech coordination process between native speakers of that language. These outcomes are also generally in line with those obtained in the other languages investigated so far (e.g. in [2, 11, 14, 15]). With this respect, this preliminary work contributes to providing a common basis not only for accounting for cross-linguistic and cross-cultural aspects of speech coordination, but also for modelling prosodic entrainment in multilingual spoken dialogue systems.

References

1. Pardo, J.: On phonetic convergence during conversational interaction. JASA **119**(4), 2382–2393 (2006)
2. Levitan, R., Hirschberg, J.: Measuring acoustic-prosodic entrainment with respect to multiple levels and dimensions. In: Proceedings of Interspeech 2011, pp. 28–31. Florence (2011)
3. Pickering, M., Garrod, S.: Alignment as the basis for successful communication. Res. Lang. Comput. **4**, 203–228 (2006)
4. Giles, H., Taylor, D.M., Bourhis, R.Y.: Toward a theory of interpersonal accomodation through speech: Some Canadian data. Lang. Soc. **2**(2-3), 177–192 (1973)
5. Bell, L., Gustafson J., Heldner M.: Prosodic adaptation in human-computer interaction. In: Proceedings of ICPhS 2003, vol. 3, pp. 833–836. Barcelona (2003)
6. Giles, H., Coupland, N., Coupland, J.: Accomodation Theory: communication, context and consequence. In: Giles, H., Coupland, N., Coupland, J. (eds.) Contexts of accomodation: developments in applied sociolinguistics, pp. 1–68. CUP, Cambridge (1991)
7. Benus, S.: Social aspects of entrainment in spoken interaction. Cogn. Comput. **6**, 802–813 (2014)
8. Edlund, J., Heldner, M., Hirschberg, J.: Pause and gap length in face-to-face interaction. In: Proceedings of Interspeech 2009, pp. 2779–2782. Brighton (2009)
9. Kousidis, S., Dorran, D., Wang, Y., Vaughn, B., Cullen, C.: Towards measuring continuous acoustic feature convergence in unconstrained spoken dialogues. In: Proceedings of Interspeech 2008, pp. 1692–1695. Brisbane (2008)
10. De Looze, C., Rauzy, S.: Measuring speakers' similarity in speech by means of prosodic cues: methods and potential. In: Proceedings of Interspeech 2011, pp. 1393–1396. Florence (2011)
11. Truong, K.P., Heylen, D.: Measuring prosodic alignment in cooperative task-based conversations. In: Proceedings of Interspeech 2012, pp. 843–846. Portland (2012)
12. Schweitzer, A., Lewandowski, N.: Convergence of articulation rate in spontaneous speech. In: Proceedings of Interspeech 2013, pp. 525–529. Lyon (2013)

13. De Looze, C., Scherer, S., Vaughan, B., Campbell, N.: Investigating automatic measurements of prosodic accomodation and its dynamics in social interaction. Speech Commun. **58**, 11–34 (2014)
14. Benus, S., Hirschberg, J., Levitan, R., Gravano, A., Darjaa, S.: Entrainment in Slovak collaborative dialogues. In: Proceedings of the 5th IEEE Conference on Cognitive Infocommunications, pp. 309–313. Vietri sul Mare (2014)
15. Levitan, R., Benus, S., Gravano A., Hirschberg, J.: Acoustic-prosodic entrainment in Slovak, Spanish, English and Chinese: A cross-linguistic comparison. In: Proceedings of SIGDIAL Conference, pp. 325–334. Prague (2015)
16. PAGE (Prosodic And Gestural Entrainment in conversational interactions across diverse languages) project funded by VolksWagen Stiftung. http://page.home.amu.edu.pl/
17. Clark, H.H., Wilkes-Gibbs, D.: Referring as a collaborative process. Cognition **22**, 1–39 (1986)
18. Refice, M., Savino, M., Altieri, M., Altieri, R.: SegWin: a tool for segmenting, annotating and controlling the creation of a database of spoken italian varieties. In: Proceedings of LREC 2000 (2nd International Conference on Language Resources and Evaluation), pp. 1531–1536. Athens (2000)
19. Boersma, P.: Praat, a system for doing phonetics by computer. Glot Int. **5**(9/10), 131–151 (2001)
20. Healey, P., Purver, M., Howes, C.: Divergence in dialogue. PloS one **9**(6), 1–6 (2014). e98598
21. Pardo, J.: Reflections on phonetic convergence: speech perception does not mirror speech production. Lang. Linguist. Compass **6**(12), 753–767 (2012)

Microphone Array Directivity Improvement in Low-Frequency Band for Speech Processing

Mikhail Stolbov[1,2] and Sergei Aleinik[2,3(✉)]

[1] Speech Technology Center, Krasutskogo-4, St. Petersburg 196084, Russia
stolbov@speechpro.com
[2] ITMO University, 49 Kronverkskiy pr., St. Petersburg 197101, Russia
sergealeinik@gmail.com
[3] Alango Technologies Ltd., St. Petersburg, Russia

Abstract. This paper presents a new method of improving microphone array directivity in the low-frequency band. The method is based on a sub-band processing technique. We also evaluate the parameters and characteristics of the method and consider some of its practical implementations.

Keywords: Microphone array · Sub-band processing · Directivity pattern · Directivity index

1 Introduction

It is well known that conventional microphone arrays (MA) for speech processing have poor directivity in the low-frequency band (lower than 1000 Hz) [1–4]. At the same time, it is known that this frequency band is important for speech processing systems, since a large part of both speech signal and noise is concentrated in this band. There are two basic ways to solve this problem: (1) applying different superdirectivity algorithms [2–4] and (2) increasing the size of the MA by using the harmonically nested microphone subarrays technique with sub-band processing [3, 5].

However, superdirectivity algorithms perform badly in non-stationary noise environments, are very sensitive to noise (or signal + noise) covariance matrix estimation errors [6], as well as to microphone gain mismatch [7], etc., which limits their use in speech signal processing.

On the other hand, non-adaptive nested microphone subarrays with sub-band processing show good results, as noted in [3, 5]. A typical scheme of microphone layout for a MA with 9 microphones and 3 subarrays is described in detail in [5]. Here we note that in such schemes all subarrays have the same numbers of microphones but different distances between microphones, and improvement of directivity in the low-frequency (LF) band is achieved by increasing the length of the MA while keeping the total number of microphones constant. In the present paper we propose a different approach.

© Springer International Publishing Switzerland 2016
A. Ronzhin et al. (Eds.): SPECOM 2016, LNAI 9811, pp. 484–490, 2016.
DOI: 10.1007/978-3-319-43958-7_58

2 The Proposed Method

2.1 The Basic Idea

Typically, the distance d between microphones in a discrete MA is chosen based on the absence of side lobes with a large amplitude [1]:

$$d < \frac{c}{2f_{max}}, \tag{1}$$

where: c is speed of sound in the air (343.1 m/s for 20 °C) and f_{max} is the maximum frequency of the operating range of the MA in Hz. Let us denote the total number of microphones in the MA as N, and the aperture length of the MA as L: $L = d(N-1)$.

It is known that if (1) is satisfied, further increasing N with a fixed L (i.e. decreasing d) does not lead to directivity improvement. On the other hand, (1) shows that for the low frequency range it is not necessarily to use all MA microphones. We can take, for example, only the edge microphones (the 0-th and $N-1$). It turns out that for the low-frequency range, we obtain improved directivity even in comparison with the case where all MA microphones are used.

Let us consider a standard equidistant linear MA with the number of microphones $N = 9$ and the distance between microphones $d = 0.05$ m. Consequently, the aperture length L of the MA is equal to: $L = d(N-1) = 0.4$ m. The normalized horizontal amplitude directivity pattern $D(f, \varphi_d, \varphi)$ of such an MA (for far-field assumption) can be obtained as [1]:

$$D(f, \varphi_d, \varphi) = \left| \frac{1}{N} \sum_{n=0}^{N-1} \exp\left(j\frac{2\pi f}{c} nd(\sin(\varphi) - \sin(\varphi_d)) \right) \right|, \tag{2}$$

where: f is the signal frequency in Hz; φ is the direction of arrival; φ_d is the desired look direction and '$|\cdot|$' denotes the "magnitude of complex value" operator.

The directivity pattern (DP), calculated using (2), for MA with $N = 9$, $d = 0.05$, $\varphi_d = 0$ and $f = 428.87$ Hz is shown in Fig. 1, solid line.

It is clear that the MA has poor directivity for the given f. At the same time, if we take only the edge microphones (0-th and 8-th, $d_{0,8} = L = 0.4$) and calculate the DP for the same f for this 2-microphone sub-array, we get the dashed curve shown in Fig. 1, i.e. we get better DP.

It seems strange, but when signal frequency is lower than some threshold level, it is better to use the edge microphones rather than all microphones in the MA.

2.2 Detailed Study of the Method

In fact there is nothing strange about the above mentioned result. It is known that for a dual-microphone array with a 0.4 m distance between microphones, the first zeroes in the DP for $\varphi = \pm90$ can be calculated as: $\lambda/2 = 0.4$ (where λ is the wavelength); which implies that $f = c/0.8 = 343.1/0.8 = 428.875$ Hz. At the same time, for an MA with a continuous aperture (and the same length) we will have the condition of first

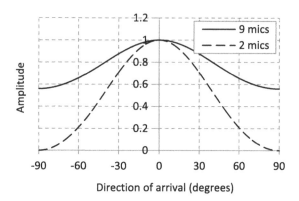

Fig. 1. Directivity patterns, calculated using all 9 (solid line) and 2 edge (dashed line) microphones of the MA for $f = 428.87$ Hz.

zeroes at $\varphi = \pm 90$ as: $\lambda = 0.4$ [1] i.e. the frequency in this case is two times higher. Frequency for a discrete MA with $N = 9$ occupies an intermediate position.

Now consider the directivity index (DI), $G(f, \varphi_d)$ of a linear MA. $G(f, \varphi_d)$ characterizes the directivity of the MA: the greater $G(f, \varphi_d)$, the better the directivity. Without loss of generality we can calculate it in Cartesian coordinates, using a single-dimensional horizontal DP (as in Fig. 1) and $-90 \leq \varphi \leq 90$ in degrees. In this case $G(f, \varphi_d)$ can be obtained as:

$$G(f, \varphi_d) = \frac{180}{\int_{-90}^{90} |D(f, \varphi_d, \varphi)|^2 \cos(\varphi) d\varphi} \tag{3}$$

Figure 2 demonstrates the directivity index $G(f, \varphi_d)$ for $\varphi_d = 0$ and for the initial MA ($N = 9$, $d = 0.05$ m); for the MA created using two microphones on the edges

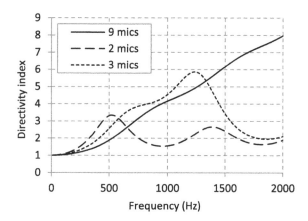

Fig. 2. Directivity index as function of signal frequency for three MA's with the same length and different number of microphones.

($N = 2$, $d = 0.4$ m) and for the MA created using three (the central and the edges) microphones, i.e. $N = 3$, $d = 0.2$ m.

It can be seen that up to 600 Hz the MA with $N = 2$ has the best directivity. The MA with $N = 3$ has the best directivity in the interval 600–1300 Hz. The MA with $N = 9$ works best only when $f > 1300$ Hz. It should also be noted that the difference in $G(f, \phi_d)$ for $N = 3$ and $N = 9$ is not so large, so we will further focus only on the MA with $N = 2$.

Maximizing (3) for $N = 2$, $d = 0.4$ and $\varphi_d = 0$ we find that $G(f, \varphi_d)$ has a maximum when $f = 523$ Hz. The corresponding DP as well as the DP of the initial MA with $N = 9$ are shown in Fig. 3.

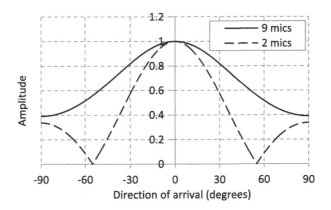

Fig. 3. Directivity patterns, calculated using all 9 (solid line) and 2 edge (dashed line) microphones of the MA for $\phi_d = 0$, $f = 523$ Hz.

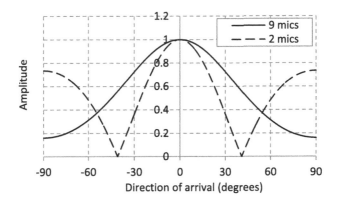

Fig. 4. Directivity patterns, calculated using all 9 (solid line) and 2 edge (dashed line) microphones of the MA for $\phi_d = 0$, $f = 654.54$ Hz.

Figure 3 demonstrates the advantages of using the two microphone scheme instead of the total number of microphones in the LF band. Further increase of signal frequency leads to the point of intersection of $G(f, \varphi_d)$ for $N = 2$ and $N = 9$: $f = 654.54$ Hz. The corresponding DPs are shown in Fig. 4.

In our opinion, Fig. 4. shows performance deterioration for $N = 2$, as the side-lobe level of the DP increases rapidly. Figures 3 and 4 suggest that the boundary frequency between using 2 and 9 microphones should be chosen in the interval [523, 654] Hz.

2.3   Dependence on the Look Direction

The above suggestions were obtained when the look direction was perpendicular to the line of the microphones, i.e. for $\varphi_d = 0$. In real life we often have $\varphi_d \neq 0$ and it is clear that directivity patterns, directivity indexes and, consequently, boundary frequencies depend on the φ_d. These dependences for the MA with $L = 0.4$ m are shown in Fig. 5.

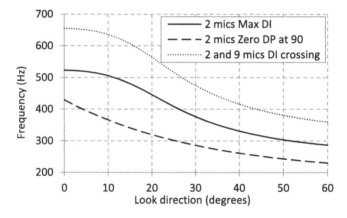

Fig. 5. Three basic frequencies as functions of the look direction ϕ_d.

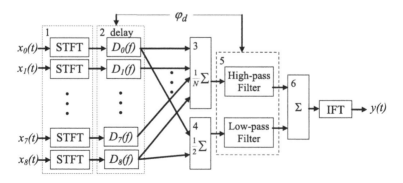

Fig. 6. Flow-chart of the MA with the proposed method.

It can be seen that all frequencies decrease when φ_d increases. So the boundary frequency of the filters should be controlled depending on the φ_d. We suggest choosing Max DI frequency (solid curve on Fig. 5) or the arithmetical mean between Max DI frequency and the frequency at which the 2 and 9 mics DI cross.

The structure of the MA with the proposed method is shown in Fig. 6.

The first two blocks of the chart are well-known: they are the short time Fourier transform (Block 1) that transforms input signals $x_i(t)$, $i = 0, N - 1$ into the frequency domain, and the frequency-domain delay (Block 2) where all signals are delayed by multiplication by the complex steering vector $D_m(f, \varphi_d)$ [9] to move the MA beam to the look direction. After the delay, all signals $X_i(f, \varphi_d)$, $i = 0, N - 1$ are summed and normalized to $1/N$ in Block 3. At the same time the two signals $X_0(f, \varphi_d)$ and $X_{N-1}(f, \varphi_d)$ are summed and normalized to $1/2$ in Block 4. Then both sums are filtered in Block 5 where the cut-off frequency is calculated according to the look direction φ_d (Fig. 5). Finally, both filtered sums are added together, after which inverse Fourier transform is performed for the resulting signal.

As a result, we have the following: high-frequency components of the input signal are passed to the MA output through Block 3 and the high-pass filter (all MA microphones work); at the same time, the LF components of the input signal are passed to the MA input through Block 4 and the low-pass filter, i.e. only $X_0(f, \varphi_d)$ and $X_{N-1}(f, \varphi_d)$ are used, which gives us better MA directivity in the LF band.

3   Conclusion

In this paper we describe a new method for improving MA directivity in the low-frequency band. This method can be useful for speech processing in MAs in different areas, for example in speaker verification [8], in multimodal systems [9], etc.

Note that it is easy to implement a 3-microphones scheme (two microphones on the edges and the central one) in the flowchart in Fig. 6. In order to do this, it is necessary to add the third sum block and the third band-pass filter to Block 5. However, the improvement will not be significant (see Fig. 2).

It is clear that the proposed method can be used for LF direction improvement not only in equidistant MAs but in all MAs that include a set of microphones, even for nested microphone subarrays described in [5].

The method can also be used in planar MAs. For circular planar MAs, for example, the microphone ring with the highest diameter is the analog of two microphones on the edges for linear MAs. The proposed scheme may be improved by using adaptive superdirectivity algorithms, for example, those presented in [10]. This will further strengthen the MA directivity in the LF band, but will cause a shift in boundary frequency. This modification of the method remains to be studied in future work.

Acknowledgement. This work was financially supported by the Government of the Russian Federation, Grant 074-U01.

References

1. McCowan, I.: Microphone arrays: a tutorial (2001). URL: http://www.idiap.ch/~mccowan/arrays/tutorial.pdf
2. Bitzer, J., Simmer, K.U.: Superdirective microphone arrays. In: Brandstein, M., Ward, D. (eds.) Microphone Arrays: Signal Processing Techniques and Applications, pp. 19–38. Springer, Heidelberg (2001)
3. Aleinik, S., Stolbov, M.: A comparative study of speech processing in microphone arrays with multichannel alignment and zelinski post-filtering. In: Ronzhin, A., Potapova, R., Fakotakis, N. (eds.) SPECOM 2015. LNCS, vol. 9319, pp. 34–41. Springer, Heidelberg (2015)
4. Löllmann, H.W., Vary, P.: Post-filter design for superdirective beamformers with closely spaced microphones. In: Proceedings of IEEE Workshop on Applications of Signal Processing to Audio and Acoustics (WASPAA 2007), pp. 291–294 (2007)
5. Fischer, S., Kammeyer, K.D.: Broadband beamforming with adaptive postfiltering for speech acquisition in noisy environment. In: Proceedings of International Conference on Acoustics, Speech, and Signal Processing, pp. 359–362 (1997)
6. Carlson, B.: Covariance matrix estimation errors and diagonal loading in adaptive arrays. IEEE Trans. Aerosp. Electron. Syst. **24**(3), 397–401 (1988)
7. Ba, D.E., Dinei, F., Cha, Z.: Enhanced MVDR beamforming for arrays of directional microphones. In: IEEE Conference on Multimedia and Expo, pp. 1307–131 (2007)
8. Kozlov, A., Kudashev, O., Matveev, Y., Pekhovsky, T., Simonchik, K., Shulipa, A.: SVID speaker recognition system for NIST SRE 2012. In: Železný, M., Habernal, I., Ronzhin, A. (eds.) SPECOM 2013. LNCS, vol. 8113, pp. 278–285. Springer, Heidelberg (2013)
9. Karpov, A., Akarun, L., Yalcin, H., Ronzhin, A., Demiroz, B., Coban, A., Zelezny, M.: Audio-visual signal processing in a multimodal assisted living environment. In: Proceedings of INTERSPEECH 2014, pp. 1023–1027 (2014)
10. Buck, M., Roessler, M.: First order differential microphone arrays for automotive applications. In: Seventh International Workshop on Acoustic Echo and Noise Control (IWAENC 2001), Darmstadt, pp. 19–22 (2001)

Modeling Imperative Utterances in Russian Spoken Dialogue: Verb-Central Quantitative Approach

Olga Blinova[(✉)]

Saint Petersburg State University,
7/9 Universitetskaya nab., St. Petersburg 199034, Russia
o.blinova@spbu.ru

Abstract. The study is aimed at detecting stable wording patterns of the utterances with directive function in Russian, and based on the material of speech corpus containing long-term audio recordings of everyday spoken communication. The lemmatized and morphologically annotated mini-corpus in question includes 2030 utterances with 2nd person Sg and Pl verb forms in imperative mood and consists of 11075 word forms. The research involves the data on frequencies of (co-)occurrences of word forms, lemmas, parts of speech within the mini-corpus.

Keywords: Speech corpus · Russian · Everyday speech · Spoken dialogue · Imperative utterances · Pragmatics · Dialogue acts

1 Introduction

This paper presents some results of the description of imperative utterances in the corpus of Russian everyday communication «One day of speech» (ORD). By now the ORD includes transcripts and multi-level linguistic annotation for audio recordings representing daily speech by 127 informants and their numerous interlocutors. Creation principles of the corpus are described in detail in [1].

The main goal of the ORD corpus creation is to fix Russian spontaneous speech in natural communicative situations, and to get authentic data from everyday speech and spontaneous interaction. Face-to-face dialogues are the main part of the corpus. The linguistic material of such type is especially well suited for the studies in real linguistic behavior, in particular, for the analysis of the ways of "doing things with words" in Austin's sense [2].

2 Illocutionary Force Indicating Devices or Dialogue Act Cues

One of the central challenges of the corpus pragmatics is the dialogue acts annotation. «Dialogue act» (DA) loosely means a «speech act used in dialogue» [3]. The important question is: what kind of search approaches can be used in a corpus for

© Springer International Publishing Switzerland 2016
A. Ronzhin et al. (Eds.): SPECOM 2016, LNAI 9811, pp. 491–498, 2016.
DOI: 10.1007/978-3-319-43958-7_59

identification of given linguistic expressions as utterances with certain pragmatic meaning?

There are the features for marking the illocutionary force of utterances, the so called «illocutionary force indicating devices», IFIDs. According to [4] IFID is «any element of a natural language which can be literally used to indicate that an utterance of a sentence containing that element has a certain illocutionary force or range of illocutionary forces». We can use standard IFIDs as search strings. There are lexical, morphosyntactic and prosodic IFIDs, such as lexemes, word order, intonation [5]. However, there are speech acts, which ostensibly «do not appear in routinized forms or in reliable combination with IFIDs», and directive speech acts in English fall into this category [6].

As reported by D. Jurafsky, there are lexical, syntactic, prosodic, and discourse cues for dialogue act identification, including in particular lexical cues, so called 'cue phrases' [7]. The inventory of cross-linguistically common lexical or syntactic cues for imperatives (commands) includes particles, verbal clitics, special verb morphology, subject omitting etc. [7, 8]. In Russian we can distinguish several types of devices which serve to indicate the type of dialogue act, first of all, it is a grammatical mood.

3   Types of Form/Function Correspondence in Russian Verb Utterances

As A. Aikhenvald explains, «imperative mood is the commonest way of expressing commands in languages of the world» [9]. In terms of theory of speech acts, commands belong to the group of directives [10]. Using directive, the speaker tries to cause the hearer to do or not to do something. Russian has a special morphological imperative forms, and the imperative occurs in its prototypical directive function above all.

Imperative forms also can occur in 'transposed' uses, «which are not directive in the prototypical sense but only express directivity in a very weakened form» [11]. E. Fortuin in [12] speaks about

(1) necessitive use: *Все ушли, а я сиди дома* [13, §1948]
    all gone but I-Nom sit-Imp.2Sg at home
    'Everybody has gone, but I have to stay at home'
(2) narrative use: *Мы возьми и напиши на сайт президенту* [14]
    we-Nom take-Imp.2Sg and write-Imp.2Sg to the website to the president
    'We suddenly wrote to the website to the president'
(3) optative use: *Награди вас господь за вашу добродетель* [12, 162]
    reward-Imp.2Sg you-Acc god-Nom for your goodness
    'May God reward you for your goodness'
(4) conditional use: *Будь я помоложе, и позволила бы комплекция, сам бы полез* [12, 177]
    be-Imp.2Sg I-Nom younger and allowed Irr bodily constitution, self Irr climb
    'Had I been younger, and had my bodily constitution allowed it, I would have climbed myself'
(5) concessive use: *В какую сторону ни гляди, выхода нет* [12, 216]

in which side not look-Imp.2Sg escape not
'No matter in which direction you look, there is no way out'.

There are semantic-syntactic features, which can provide identification of directive versus non-directive uses of imperative. Some relevant features are: aspect, possibility of expressing subject, occurrence of the suffix -*me*, presence of particle -*ка*, presence of particle *бы*, word order [12]. Thus, we can involve the information about co-occurrences of imperative forms for the semantic qualification of the imperative utterances.

In Russian, **commands also can be regularly expressed by the non-imperative verb forms,** by using: (1) present tense forms *В эти игры ты больше не играешь* 'Don't play these games any more', (2) future tense forms *Пойдёшь со мной* 'Go with me', (3) past tense forms *Пошёл отсюда* 'Get off', (4) infinitive *Стоять* 'Stay put', 'Freeze!', (5) irrealis *Сходил бы ты в магазин* 'Maybe you should go to the shop'.[1]

N. Stojnova in the paper devoted to imperative uses of indicative present and future forms in Russian [16] indicates, that there are some formal features, which can mark pragmatic similarity of the non-imperative utterance to prototypical directive use of the imperative. So, there are certain patterns of non-imperative commands formation. The features she mentions are as follows: presence of the subjective pronouns *ты*, *вы* etc., occurrence with particles of the type *ну-ка*, aspect.

Thus, the three possibilities of form/function correspondence for the verb utterances have been identified: directive imperatives, non-directive imperatives, and non-imperative directives. Certain morphological, morpho-syntactic and lexical features can indicate pragmatic meaning of the utterance created on the basis of imperative or non-imperative verb form.

4   Study Design, Material and Method

The actual study is aimed at detecting stable wording patterns of the utterances with directive function, and detection of formal markers, which can indicate pragmatic meaning of a directive.

The subcorpus used for this research encompasses mainly face-to-face dialogues between 42 informants and their interlocutors which include 240000 word forms. The paper concentrates on utterances in the imperative mood with the verb in the second person Sg or Pl. All utterances of this kind were extracted from a subcorpus. The lemmatized and morphologically annotated mini-corpus includes 2030 imperative utterances and consists of 11075 word forms. So, the mini-corpus here under analysis is composed of the imperative utterances only. The mini-corpus in question is small, but highly homogeneous: it consists of the utterances with prototypical imperative forms mainly in prototypical directive function.

As D. Jurafsky indicates, the simplest way to build a probabilistic model for detection of lexical and phrasal cues (resp. lexical and morphosyntactic IFIDs)

---

[1] For details, see [15]. In the listing the so called «whimperatives» and other indirect ways of expressing commands, as well as verbless directives are not taken into account.

«is simply to look at which words and phrases occur more often in one dialogue act than another» [7, 597]. N-gram model is used successfully in practical implementations of dialogue act detection, e.g. yes-no-questions in English often have bigram sequences of the type *do you, are you, was he* (or trigram sequences of the type *<start> do you*) [7, 17].[2]

The actual research is based on the information about occurrences of word forms, lemmas, parts of speech, inflectional forms, and about co-occurrences of word forms, parts of speech, inflectional forms within the exploratory subcorpus of directives. Thus, frequency-ordered lists of the unigrams, lemmas, POSs, some forms of inflection, as well as lists of most common bigrams with an imperative component are considered.

An utterance in the actual research usually is a fragment of the text transcript between two marks of phrasal division '//', '?' et al. However, in the mini-corpus there are many single-word utterances of the type *слушай, послушай* 'listen', *смотри* 'look', *подожди* 'wait'. E.g., the following phrase is divided by two parts – the part consisting of the attention getting device, the imperative *слушай*, and subsequent statement: *Слушай в буфете я не беру сосиски //* 'Listen at the lunchroom I don't take the sausages'.

5   Results and Discussion

Firstly, the data on frequency distribution of POS classes was obtained.[3] The most frequent parts of speech in the mini-corpus are: the verb, the particle, the noun, the pronoun. It is worth noting the high position of the particle in the list (Table 1).

Secondly, the list of most commonly used colligations (including colligations with verbs in the imperative mood in the second person Sg or Pl) was created. The list is based on bigram co-occurrence data of tags of POS classes. Table 2 lists top ten colligations. The data demonstrate in particular a high degree of co-occurrence between imperative forms and particles (which use in front of the verb), another imperative forms, and nouns (which usually use in front of the verb).

Thirdly, the lists of most frequent unigrams and most frequent lemmas were created. The stopword list at present includes prepositions only, and does not include particles, conjunctions, pronouns etc. The stop words are *в, на, у, с, к, по* etc.

The list of top thirty most frequent unigrams includes: PART *ну* 'well' (#332), NEG PART *не* (#278), PART *вот* (#269), imperative which usually functions as an attention-getting device *слушай* 'listen-Imp.2Sg'(#228), SPRO *ты* 'you-Nom.Sg'

---

[2] See [18] for a detailed overview of the approaches to dialogue act recognition, based on intra-utterance features or on inter-utterance context.

[3] Morphological annotation is carried out using the analyzer MyStem, developed for Russian by I. Segalovich and V. Titov at «Yandex». The list of POS-tags includes: S = noun, A = adjective, NUM = numeral, ANUM = numeral adjective, V = verb, ADV = adverb, PRAEDIC = predicative, SPRO = pronoun, APRO = adjectival pronoun, ADVPRO = adverbial pronoun, PR = preposition, CONJ = conjunction, PART = particle, INTJ = interjection, COM = part of compound word; «foreign» means a word of a foreign language. The abbreviations NEG = negative (negation), IRR = irrealis are used in the glosses above.

Table 1. Frequency distribution of POS classes

POS	Count	Percent	POS	Count	Percent
V	3142	28,37	APRO	308	2,78
PART	1752	15,82	A	239	2,16
S	1574	14,21	INTJ	209	1,89
SPRO	1418	12,80	NUM	120	1,08
PR	650	5,87	ANUM	45	0,40
ADV	641	5,79	Foreign	2	0,02
CONJ	603	5,45	COM	2	0,02
ADVPRO	370	3,34	**Total**	**11075**	**100**

Table 2. Commonly used colligations

Colligation	Count	Illustration	Translation
PART + V-Imp-2	589	ну смотри	Well look
V-Imp-2 + V-Imp-2	443	иди иди	Go go
S + V-Imp-2	408	Маш бери	Masha-Voc take
V-Imp-2 + PART	405	слушай ну	Listen well
PART + PART	328	ну вот	Well
V-Imp-2 + SPRO	313	подожди ты	Wait you-Sg
V-Imp-2 + S	311	дай ложку	Give a spoon
PR + S	300	в холодильник	In the fridge
S + PART	268	Коля ну	Kolya well
SPRO + V	266	я говорю	I say

(#200), CONJ *и* 'and' (#195), SPRO *я* 'I-Nom' (#185), CONJ, INTJ or PART *а* (#164), PART or CONJ *да* (#148), SPRO or CONJ *что* (#144), PART, APRO or CONJ *так* (#130), SPRO, PART or APRO *это* (#124), SPRO or APRO *все* (#115), PART or ADVPRO *там* (#114), V *смотри* 'look-Imp.2Sg' (#105), SPRO *мне*, 'I-Dat', 'to me' (#103), V *подожди* 'wait-Imp.2Sg' (#103), PART or V *давай* 'let's', 'give-Imp.2Sg' (#95), INTJ *э* (#94), SPRO *вы* 'you-Nom.Pl' (#94), PART *пожалуйста* 'please' (#87), ADVPRO, PART or CONJ *как* (#70), ADV *сейчас* 'now'(#69), SPRO *меня* 'I-Gen (Acc)' (#57), PART, SPRO or CONJ *то* (#56), V *иди* 'go- Imp.2Sg'(#55), V *смотрите* 'look-Imp.2Pl' (#49), PART *нет* (#47), PART or ADV *еще* (#44), *он* 'he-Nom' (#44).

The data obtained show a predominant use of a range of particles including *ну, вот, так, давай*. The presence of most common polite formula *please* should be noted and the absence of the post verbal particle *-ka* in the list of top 30 unigrams. The subject pronoun *я* 'I' appears in the occurrences of the type *я и говорю, я тебе говорю, я же говорю* 'I'm saying', *я сказала* 'I said' et al., see the following example: *не лезь к девочке/я тебе/десять раз уже сказала //* 'Do not bother the girl/I told you ten times already'.

As it was expected, the frequency list of verb forms shows a predominance of imperative. However, among frequently occurring verb forms there are two indicative forms: the one mentioned above *говорю* 'I'm saying', and *хочешь*, which usually occurs in the form, as in the utterance *хочешь ночуй/хочешь уезжай//* 'You can stay if you want or leave if you want'.

The most frequent lemmas that have inflected forms are represented in Table 3 below.

Table 3. Top-thirty most frequent lemmas

Rank	Lemma	Count	Rank	Lemma	Count
1	*я* 'I'	337	15	*идти* 'go'	64
2	*ты* 'you-Sg'	267	16	*извинить* 'excuse'	62
3	*слушать* 'listen'	252	17	*мы* 'we'	57
4	*смотреть* 'look'	155	17	*давай* 'let's'	57
5	*вы* 'you-Pl'	151	18	*они* 'they'	50
6	*это* 'it'	133	18	*говорить* 'say'	50
7	*быть* 'be'	127	19	*давать* 'give'	49
8	*подождать* 'wait'	118	20	*взять* 'take'	37
9	*он* 'he'	106	21	*делать* 'do'	36
10	*все* 'everyone'	103	22	*такой* 'such'	33
11	*сказать* 'say'	99	23	*знать* 'know'	30
12	*она* 'she'	82	23	*держать* 'hold'	30
13	*посмотреть* 'look'	67	23	*хотеть* 'want'	30
14	*дать* 'give'	65	24	*мочь* 'can'	29
14	*этот* 'this'	65	25	*написать* 'write'	28

The lemma *я* 'I' has the leading position due to the large amount of entries of the type *дай мне* 'give it to me', *позвони мне* 'call me', *скажи мне* 'tell me', *послушай меня* 'listen to me' etc. Lemmas *ты*, *вы* represent subjective pronouns (those that serve as non-omitted subjects) above all.

Fourthly, the list of bigram sequences on word forms was created. Table 4 lists 20 most frequent bigrams with verbs in the second person Sg or Pl in the data. As it can be seen, sequences with particles predominate, while sequences with content words encompass only insignificant part of the list.[4]

Whereas the most frequent bigrams may be considered as collocation candidates, the values of t-score for the most frequent two-word sequences were counted. Some sequences with relatively high t-score are not fully compositional, indeed. Thus, *говорить* with negation (t-score 3,99) is used in the utterances of the type *и не говори* 'don't even say this' that usually express agreement with the other communicant: *ага// вот именно//не говори* 'yes//sure//don't even say this'.

---

[4] The sequences *слушай слушай* 'listen listen'(#148), *подожди подожди* 'wait wait'(#33) and *слушайте слушайте* 'listen-Pl listen-Pl'(#17) are not under consideration, as their presence in the data is caused by the multiplicity of single-word utterances *слушай, слушайте, подожди*.

Table 4. Most frequent bigram sequences on word forms

2-gram	Count	2-gram	Count
не говори 'don't say'	16	*ну слушай* 'well listen-Sg'	6
ну смотри 'well look-Sg'	15	*ну смотрите* 'well look-Pl'	6
вот смотри 'here look-Sg'	15	*дай ей* 'give-Sg it to her'	6
сейчас подожди 'now, wait-Sg (just a minute)'	11	*иди иди* 'go-Sg go-Sg'	6
слушай ну 'listen-Sg well'	11	*извини меня* 'excuse-Sg me'	6
вот смотрите 'here look-Pl'	9	*не лезь* 'don't meddle'	5
иди сюда 'come-Sg here'	9	*ну посмотри* 'well look-Sg'	5
скажите пожалуйста 'tell-Pl please'	9	*ну попробуй* 'well try-Sg'	5
скажите а 'tell-Pl me'	8	*ну расскажи* 'well tell-Sg'	5
ну подожди 'well wait-Sg'	7	*вы посмотрите* 'have-Pl a look at it'	5

6 Conclusion

The results of the study confirm the significant role of «small words» in wording of the utterances with imperatives in directive function. Thus, most frequent parts of speech in the mini-corpus of directives are the verb and the particle; the most frequent unigrams are the particles *ну*, *не*, *вот*; the sequences with particles predominate in the list of most frequent bigram sequences. By now it is clear that the features, which can indicate pragmatic meaning of a directive in Russian, are the colligations of the type *ну* + V-Imp-2, *вот* + V-Imp-2, *пожалуйста* + V-Imp-2.

Imperative forms in 'transposed' uses can hardly demonstrate such sequential patterns. Thus, the incorporation of *пожалуйста* 'please' in all types of 'transposed' uses looks equally unacceptable, cf.: **Все ушли а я дома пожалуйста сиди*, **Мы пожалуйста возьми и напиши <...>* etc.[5] Combinations with most common particles *ну* and *вот* 'well' seem to be acceptable to varying degrees, cf.: **Все ушли, а я ну сиди дома*, but *Все ушли а я вот сиди дома*. However, these findings need to be verified with the use of corpus material. It is also worth noting that we do not know, whether the 'transposed' uses occur in the colloquial speech, or in the fiction texts and academic grammars only. Consequently, the directions of further study are: the improvement of using n-gram model due to addition of the position numbering, and the corpus study of 'transposed' uses of imperative forms.

Acknowledgement. The research is supported by the Russian Science Foundation (RSF), project #14-18-02070 «Everyday Russian Language in Different Social Groups».

---

[5] The asterisk marks unacceptable sentences.

References

1. Asinovsky, A., Bogdanova, N., Rusakova, M., Ryko, A., Stepanova, S., Sherstinova, T.: The ORD speech corpus of russian everyday communication "one speaker's day": creation principles and annotation. In: Matoušek, V., Mautner, P. (eds.) TSD 2009. LNCS, vol. 5729, pp. 250–257. Springer, Heidelberg (2009)
2. Austin, J.L.: How to Do Things with Words, 2nd edn. Oxford University Press, Oxford (1976)
3. Bunt, H.: The dit++ taxonomy for functional dialogue markup. In: Decker, S., Sichman J., Sierra, C., Castelfranchi, C. (eds.) Proceedings of 8th International Conference on Autonomous Agents and Multiagent Systems (AAMAS 2009), pp. 13–20 (2009)
4. Searle, J.R., Vanderveken, D.: Speech acts and illocutionary logic. In: Vanderveken, D. (ed.) Logic, Thought and Action, pp. 109–132. Springer, Heidelberg (2005)
5. Weisser, M.: Landmarks in 'Traditional' Pragmatics. http://martinweisser.org/courses/intro/pragmatics.html
6. Flöck, I., Geluykens, R.: Speech acts in corpus pragmatics a quantitative contrastive study of directives in spontaneous and elicited discourse. In: Romero-Trillo, J. (ed.) Yearbook of Corpus Linguistics and Pragmatics 2015: Current Approaches to Discourse and Translation Studies, pp. 7–37. Springer, Heidelberg (2015)
7. Jurafsky, D.: Pragmatics and computational linguistics. In: Horn, L., Ward, G. (eds.) The Handbook of Pragmatics, pp. 578–604. Blackwell Publishing, Oxford (2006)
8. Sadock, J.M., Zwicky, A.M.: Speech acts distinctions in syntax. In: Shopen, T. (ed.) Language Typology and Syntactic Description, pp. 155–196. Cambridge University Press, Cambridge (1985)
9. Aikhenvald, AYu.: Imperatives and Commands. Oxford University Press, New York (2010)
10. Searle, J.R.: Expression & Meaning: Studies in the Theory of Speech Act. Cambridge University Press, Cambridge (1979)
11. Fortuin, E.L.J., Boogaart, R.J.U.: Imperative as conditional: from constructional to compositional semantics. Cogn. Linguist. **20**(4), 641–673 (2009)
12. Fortuin, E.L.J.: Polysemy or monosemy: Interpretation of the imperative and the dative-infinitive construction in Russian, Ph.D. thesis, Amsterdam, Institute for Logic, Language and Computation (2000). https://www.illc.uva.nl/Research/Publications/Dissertations/
13. Russkaya Grammatika, t.2: Sintaksis [The Russian Grammar, vol. 2: Syntax] (1980). http://rusgram.narod.ru/
14. Russian National Corpus. http://www.ruscorpora.ru/
15. Khrakovskij, V.S., Volodin, A.P.: Semantika i Tipologija Imperativa: Russkij Imperativ [Semantics and Typology of Imperative: Russian Imperative]. Nauka, Leningrad (1986)
16. Stojnova, N.: Pobuditel'nye upotreblenija form nastojashhego i budushhego vremeni [imperative use of forms of present and future tense]. In: Proceedings of the 3rd Conference «Issues of the language: The view of young scientists», pp. 227–243. Kanzler, Moscow (2014)
17. Stolcke, A., Ries, K., Coccaro, N., Shriberg, E., Bates, R., Jurafsky, D., Taylor, P., Martin, R., Van Ess-Dykema, C., Meteer, M.: Dialogue act modeling for automatic tagging and recognition of conversational speech. Comput. Linguist. **26**(3), 339–373 (2000)
18. Kral, P., Cerisara, Ch.: Dialogue act recognition approaches. Comput. Inform. **29**(2), 227–250 (2010)

Multimodal Perception of Aggressive Behavior

Rodmonga Potapova and Liliya Komalova[✉]

Institute of Applied and Mathematical Linguistics,
Moscow State Linguistic University, Moscow, Russia
{RKPotapova,GenuinePR}@yandex.ru

Abstract. The paper proposes the results of the comparative auditory-perceptual and visual-perceptual analyses of Russian, English, Spanish and Tatar experimental samples representing the emotional-modal complex aggression. It describes statistically valid differences between auditory and visual types of perception of aggressive (physical and verbal) behavior, influenced by such factors as emotional-modal state of a recipient and language of communication.

Keywords: One-channel perception · Multimodal (different channel) perception · Communicative act of aggression · Aggressive verbal behavior · Emotional-modal state

1 Introduction

Methodology of the present research bases on the works in pragmaphonetics and forensic linguistics on the material of German and Russian texts/discourses [7,9–13]. The researchers substantiate the necessity of complex analysis of verbal and non-linguistic (extra- and paralinguistic) speech communication parameters, affirming that auditory and visual image processing in perception of speech communication realizes in a complimentary regime [13, p. 607]. Similar methodology we find, e.g. in the investigation of visual and verbal perception (not evaluating emotional state of a recipient) by Kharkwal and Stromswold [4].

At the same time, the same emotional-modal state of a communicant or the emotional background of communication can be perceived differently depending on the situation and the current emotional-modal state of a recipient (see, e.g. [1,2,15]). Possible implementation of the methodology based on evaluation of visual and acoustic types of perception in correlation with the emotion estimation in real-life situations are described in [14].

2 Method and Procedure

The aim of the research is to reveal relations between auditory and visual types of perception in assessment of the emotional-modal state of an exterior communicant. We try to clarify, how the changes in the emotional-modal state of

© Springer International Publishing Switzerland 2016
A. Ronzhin et al. (Eds.): SPECOM 2016, LNAI 9811, pp. 499–506, 2016.
DOI: 10.1007/978-3-319-43958-7_60

a recipient correlate with the changes in the perception of communicants negative emotional-modal states, classified by the recipient as aggressive behavior, in native language (Russian), foreign language the recipient studies (English) and in unknown language (Spanish, Tatar). We also intend to specify the correlation between auditory and visual perception in the system of multimodal perception of emotional-modal states of a speaker.

Hypothesis 1: Current emotional-modal state of a recipient has an influence upon the assessment of the current emotional-modal state of another communicant.

Hypothesis 2: In conditions of one-channel perception, in spite of the language of communication, a recipient tends to rely more on the visual type of perception than on the auditory one.

27 native Russian speakers studying English, but unacquainted with Spanish and Tatar languages (22 female and 5 male; 19–22 years old), participated in the research. They analyzed 48 samples (identical 24 speech utterances and 24 sound-tracks representing the scenes of physical and verbal aggressive behavior) in Russian, English, Spanish and Tatar languages (time duration of the samples being from 25 s to 2 min., performed by male and female informants).

Before the analysis all the subjects went through a psychological test (by A. Uesman and D. Ricks method) [3, p. 39–40] determining their current emotional-modal state (EMS). A total point of three scales (composure - anxiety; exultant mood - depression; self-confidence - feeling of helplessness) constitutes current EMS index. According to the test results, the subjects were divided in three groups:

- with low current EMS (dominant indices: anxiety, tiredness, depression, feeling of helplessness);
- with higher current EMS (calmness, vitality, vigor, exultant mood, self-confidence);
- with neutral current EMS (average points in all scales).

The research was carried out in two stages.[1] At the first stage the subjects analyzed video samples; at the second audio samples. A special questionnaire included the following tasks:

- to determine the quality of the dominant emotional background of communication: (a) neutral background, (b) positive (friendly, joyful, cheerful communication), (c) negative (aggressive, angry, malicious communication);
- to point out the name of the dominant emotional/emotional-modal state of the communicant(s);
- to indicate the intensity of communication emotionality according to the scale from 0 to 10 points, where 0–3 points corresponds with the low emotionality of communication, 4–6 means medium intensity of emotionality, 7–10 means high emotionality;
- to determine, what means the communicants use mostly to create the dominant emotional background of communication:

---

[1] Detailed results of one channel auditory-perceptual recognition of aggressive speech behavior see in [5,8].

- at the first stage of the experiment one should choose one of the following parameters: (a) mimics, (b) gestures, (c) body movement, (d) distance between the communicants (proxemics), (e) all the mentioned parameters together in relatively equal extend;
- at the second stage the subjects should choose one of the following parameters: (a) intonation (speech melodic contours, rhythm, tempo, pauses), (b) verbal means (semantics, vocabulary, grammar, syntax, stylistics), (c) all the mentioned parameters together in relatively equal extend.

Statistical validity of the experimental data was verified by means of such nonparametric methods as T-criterion by Wilcoxon, tendency L-criterion by Page and Spearman's rank correlation coefficient [16].

3   Results

According to the experimental results (Table 1), there're less differences between visual and auditory types of perception in assessment of the dominant emotional background of communication within the subjects with neutral current EMS (n = 9). The tendency extends to all the languages under investigation and three types of the dominant emotional background of the communication: (a) neutral, (b) positive, (c) negative.[2]

The most differences between visual and auditory perception are registered within the evaluations of *the subjects with low current EMS* (n = 9) when the perception of emotionally marked communication bases mostly on the visual channel.

The subjects with higher current EMS (n = 9) mostly rely on the auditory channel of perception, while assessing the dominant emotional background.

In one-channel perception three groups of the subjects equally determine the experimental material as the communication with predominance of the negative emotional and emotional-modal states (for all the languages under investigation) ($\rho \leq 0,001$). Meanwhile, we didn't register any statistically valid differences between visual and auditory types of perception of the samples, while assessing the dominant emotional communication background quality.

The majority of the subjects recognized the dominant EMS of the communicant(s) as related to the emotional-modal complex aggression. In one channel perception Russian samples are evaluated more clearly in comparison with the samples in other languages ($\rho \leq 0,001$). The tendency is that the more unknown the language of communication is the more difficult it becomes to recognize the dominant EMS of a communicant. It's interesting, that only for the Russian samples statistically valid differences between visual and auditory types of perception were registered (Table 2).

---

[2] Symbolic notation: "0" means no statistically valid differences between visual and auditory perception; "+" − there's statistically valid difference. "+ auditory" means that auditory perception parameters statistically exceed visual perception parameters. "+ visual" − visual perception parameters statistically exceed auditory perception parameters.

Table 1. Relevance of the dominant emotional background of communication ($\rho \leq 0,05$).

Groups of the subjects	Quality of the dominant emotional background of communication	Language of communication			
		Russian	English	Spanish	Tatar
		Differences between visual and auditory perception			
with *higher* current EMS	negative	0	0	0	0
	positive	+ auditory	+ auditory	+ auditory	+ auditory
	neutral	0	0	0	0
with *low* current EMS	negative	0	+ visual	+ visual	+ visual
	positive	+ visual	+ visual	0	0
	neutral	0	0	0	0
with *neutral* current EMS	negative	0	0	0	0
	positive	0	0	0	+ auditory
	neutral	0	0	0	0

Table 2. Name relevance of the dominant EMS of the communicant(s) ($\rho \leq 0,05$).

Name of the dominant EMS of the communicant(s)	Language of communication			
	Russian	English	Spanish	Tatar
	Differences between visual and auditory perception			
emotional complex aggression	+ visual	0	0	0
anger	+ visual	0	0	0
rage	+ auditory	0	0	0
malice	+ visual	0	0	0
hatred	+ auditory	0	0	0
insult	+ auditory	0	0	0
irritation	+ visual	0	0	0
outrage	+ visual	0	0	0
tension	+ auditory	0	0	0
sadness	+ auditory	0	0	0
fear	+ visual	0	0	0

Groups of *the subjects with higher/low current EMS* marking the intensity of communication emotionality as high mostly rely on the auditory perception; meanwhile the same groups rely more on visual perception marking the intensity of communication emotionality as low (Table 3).

In evaluations of the dominant emotional-modal state of an exterior communicant we found no statistically valid differences connected with the parameter "language of communication" in one channel perception. At the same time, there are still statistically valid differences related with the parameter "emotional-modal state of a recipient" (mostly $\rho \leq 0,01$, and $\rho \leq 0,05$ for the subjects with low current EMS in visual perception). The tendency is that in one channel perception *the subjects with high EMS* are more likely to overestimate the intensity of the communication emotionality; *the subjects with low and neutral EMS* have a tendency to overage out the intensity of the communication emotionality.

Table 3. Relevance of communication emotional intensity ($\rho \leq 0,05$).

Groups of the subjects	Intensity of communication emotionality	Language of communication			
		Russian	English	Spanish	Tatar
		Differences between visual and auditory perception			
with *higher* current EMS	high	+ auditory	+ auditory	+ auditory	+ auditory
	medium	0	0	0	0
	low	+ visual	+ visual	+ visual	+ visual
with *low* current EMS	high	0	+ visual	+ visual	+ visual
	medium	+ auditory	+ auditory	+ auditory	+ auditory
	low	+ visual	0	+ visual	+ visual
with *neutral* current EMS	high	0	0	0	0
	medium	+ visual	+ auditory	+ visual	0
	low	0	+ visual	+ visual	+ visual

In *one channel visual perception* for the three groups of the subjects the main supporting means to recognize the dominant emotional background of communication are mimics and gestures, no matter what linguaculture an exterior communicant belongs to (Table 4).

In *one channel auditory perception* the subjects of the three groups in most cases rely on the intonation features in the process of recognition of the dominant emotional background of communication (Table 5). The subjects *with higher/low EMS* ($\rho \leq 0,05$) tend to rely more on the intonation features the more unacquainted the language of communication is. The experimental data is statistically relevant ($\rho \leq 0,01$) for the subjects *with neutral EMS*.

Comparing visual and auditory perception categories, we can see that the majority of the correlations are tight or of the middle tightness (Table 6). The predominant type of correlation is positive; which means that with the growth of the visual perception significance the significance of the auditory perception also raises. Statistically relevant correlations are marked by gray color filling; bold type shows the data statistically relevant at $\rho \leq 0,01$ and italic type $\rho \leq 0,05$; the rest correlations are statistically invalid.

Table 4. Supporting means in the recognition of the dominant emotional background of communication, visual channel of perception ($\rho \leq 0,01$).

Groups of the subjects	Features of visual perception	Language of communication/frequency			
		Russian	English	Spanish	Tatar
with *higher* current EMS	mimics	**4,5**	**5,6**	**5**	**5**
	gestures	**5**	2, 2	**5**	1, 8
	body movement	3, 5	2, 9	2	4, 6
	distance between the communicants	1	1, 3	1, 2	2
	all the mentioned parameters together in relatively equal extend	0, 5	1, 5	2	0, 4
with *low* current EMS	mimics	**5**	**6,1**	**4,5**	**5**
	gestures	3	2, 4	4, 2	1, 8
	body movement	1	2, 6	1, 7	3, 6
	distance between the communicants	1	0, 8	0, 8	0, 2
	all the mentioned parameters together in relatively equal extend	1, 5	1, 5	2, 8	1, 4
with *neutral* current EMS	mimics	**8,5**	**6,5**	**5,2**	**6,4**
	gestures	2, 5	2, 5	**5,8**	2, 4
	body movement	2, 5	2, 5	2, 7	3, 2
	distance between the communicants	0, 5	0, 7	0, 3	0, 6
	all the mentioned parameters together in relatively equal extend	0, 5	1, 3	2	0, 8

Table 5. Supporting means in the recognition of the dominant emotional background of communication, auditory channel of perception.

Groups of the subjects	Auditory perception features	Language of communication/frequency			
		Russian	English	Spanish	Tatar
with *higher* current EMS	intonation	2	2, 8	**6,7**	**5,6**
	verbal means	3	2, 3	0,2	1,2
	all the mentioned parameters together in relatively equal extend	**4**	**3,9**	2,2	2,2
with *low* current EMS	intonation	1, 5	**3,5**	**6,3**	**4,6**
	verbal means	**4,5**	3, 3	2,2	3,4
	all the mentioned parameters together in relatively equal extend	3	2, 6	0,2	1,2
with *neutral* current EMS	intonation	2	3	3,5	**3,8**
	verbal means	2	**3,2**	**4,2**	3,4
	all the mentioned parameters together in relatively equal extend	**3,5**	2, 4	0,7	1,6

Table 6. Rank correlations between visual and auditory types of perception.

Category of the evaluation	Language of communication			
	Russian	English	Spanish	Tatar
Quality of the dominant emotional background of communication	+.94	+.93	+.91	+.86
Name of the dominant emotional / emotional-modal state of communicant(s)	+.49	+.87	+.74	+.37
Intensity of the communication emotionality	+.54	+.58	+.92	+.60
Means marking the dominant emotional background of communication	.69	+.15	+.53	+.64

4   Conclusion

The results of the experimental research give the possibility to formulate the following conclusions:

– current emotional-modal state of a recipient has an impact on the estimation of the emotional-modal state of another (exterior) communicant;
– in conditions of one channel perception of negative emotional-modal states of an exterior communicant the significance of visual/auditory perception fluctuates in dependence with the current EMS of a recipient;
– there're more evident differences in the evaluations of the communication emotionality made by the subjects with higher/low current EMS;
– the subjects with higher current EMS tend to rely more on the results of the auditory perception, and the subjects with low current EMS are more likely to rely on the visual type of perception;
– presumably, in the system of multimodal perception of the negative emotional-modal states of an exterior communicant visual and auditory types of perception correlate according to the rule of direct proportionality.

5   Prospects of Investigation

Further investigation can be related with the gender factor influence on the (one-channel/multimodal) perception of EMS of an exterior communicant.

Acknowledgements. The research is being carried out with the support of Russian Science Foundation (RSF) in the framework of the project N14-18-01059. Methodological concepts of the project are described in [6].

References

1. Bandura, A.: Aggression: a social learning analysis. Prentice Hall Inc, Englewood Cliffs, New Jersey (1973)

2. Ekman, P., Friesen, W.V.: Unmasking the Face: A Guideline to Recognizing Emotions from Facial Clues. Malor Books, Cambridge (2003)
3. Karelin, A.: Bol'shaja Enciklopedija Psikhologicheskikh Testov. Eksmo, Moskva (2007). (in Russian)
4. Kharkwal, G., Stromswold, K.: Good-enough language processing: evidence from sentence-video matching. J. Psycholinguist. Res. **43**(1), 27–43 (2014)
5. Komalova, L.R.: Vosprijatie negativnykh emocional'nykh sostojanij po slukhovomu kanalu (na materiale mnogojazychija). Vestnik Minsk. gos. lingvist. un-ta. Serija 1. Filologija **3**(58), 5–17 (2012). (in Russian)
6. Potapova, R.: From deprivation to aggression: verbal and non-verbal social network communication. In: 6th International Scientific Conference on Global Science and Innovation, pp. 129–137. Accent Graphics Communications Publishing Office, Chicago (2015)
7. Potapova, R.K.: Perceptivno-slukhovaja divergencija v ocenke emocional'no-modal'nogo sostojanija inojazychnogo partnera po kommunikacii. In: International Conference Events in Communication and Cognition. Moscow State Linguistic University, Moscow (preprint) (2016). (in Russian)
8. Potapova, R., Komalova, L.: Auditory-perceptual recognition of the emotional state of aggression. In: Ronzhin, A., Potapova, R., Fakotakis, N. (eds.) SPECOM 2015. LNCS, vol. 9319, pp. 89–95. Springer, Heidelberg (2015)
9. Potapova, R., Potapov, V.: Auditory and visual recognition of emotional behaviour of foreign language subjects (by Native and Non-native Speakers). In: Železný, M., Habernal, I., Ronzhin, A. (eds.) SPECOM 2013. LNCS, vol. 8113, pp. 62–69. Springer, Heidelberg (2013)
10. Potapova, R.K., Potapov, V.V.: Jazyk, rech', lichnost'. Jazyki slavjanskoj kul'tury, Moskva (2006). (in Russian)
11. Potapova, R.K., Potapov, V.V.: Kommunikative Sprechtaetigkeit: Russland u. Deutschland im Vergleich. Boehlau Verlag, Koeln, Weimar, Wien (2011). (in German)
12. Potapova, R.K., Potapov, V.V.: O dvukhkanal'nom dekodirovanii emotivnoj informacii v akte inojazychnoj kommunikacii. In: 19th Sessija RAO, pp. 8–11. GEOS, Nizhnij Novgorod (2007). (in Russian)
13. Potapova, R.K., Potapov, V.V.: Vosprijatie emocional'nogo povedenija inojazychnykh i inokul'turnykh kommunikantov. In: Fonetika i Nefonetika. K 70-letiju Sandro V. Kodzasova, pp. 602–616. Jazyki Slavjanskikh kul'tur, Moskva (2008). (in Russian)
14. Rabie, A., Handmann, U.: Fusion of audio- and visual cues for real-life emotional human robot interaction. In: Mester, R., Felsberg, M. (eds.) DAGM 2011. LNCS, vol. 6835, pp. 346–355. Springer, Heidelberg (2011)
15. Rejkovskij, J.: Eksperimental'naja psikhologija emocij. Progress, Moskva (1979). (in Russian)
16. Sidorenko, E.V.: Metody matematicheskoj obrabotki v psikhologii. Social'no-Psikholog, Centr, SPb (1996). (in Russian)

On Individual Polyinformativity of Speech and Voice Regarding Speakers Auditive Attribution (Forensic Phonetic Aspect)

Rodmonga Potapova[1(✉)] and Vsevolod Potapov[2]

[1] Institute of Applied and Mathematical Linguistics,
Moscow State Linguistic University, Ostozhenka 38, Moscow 119034, Russia
rkpotapova@yandex.ru
[2] Faculty of Philology, Lomonosov Moscow State University, GSP-1, Leninskie Gory,
Moscow 119991, Russia

Abstract. This paper considers the role of the auditive recognition of speakers regarding the attribution of speech and voice individual features. Our study investigates how well listeners can attribute a set of individual features of speakers: verbal, paraverbal, extraverbal, physiological, anthropometric, physical, emotional, social, etc. The main task of this investigation was to indicate which attributes of a speaker should be auditive recognized: universal, group or idiosyncratic ones. For auditive analysis special questionnaires were used. Two types of speech and voice were analysed: interindividual, intraindividual ones.

Keywords: Speaker · Listener · Auditive analysis · Interindividual · Intraindividual · Speaker's profile · Speech and voice attribution

1 Introduction

Subjective (auditive) and objective (acoustic) events of speech behavior are of great interest for several professional groups. In the science of forensic phonetics investigations in the field of acoustic and auditory features of voice and spoken language of subjects under the intoxication by drugs are very important. The aim of the present study is to obtain new auditive data in order to expand the knowledge of a variety of personal characteristics of speech of Russian native speakers. The term personal characteristics of speech expresses the well-known fact that speakers can be distinguished and recognized by their voices and speech. Personal characteristics of speech may be described as a complex of those sound qualities which enable us to identify the speaker. Our research is focused on the problem of auditive definition of speech qualities resulting from the psychic or psychosomatic conditions of Russian-speaking individuals. It should be noted that in our investigations we use scientific principles of auditory analysis in the field of forensic phonetics [6,7], [10, pp. 81–138], [14,18]. Perceptual analysis

© Springer International Publishing Switzerland 2016
A. Ronzhin et al. (Eds.): SPECOM 2016, LNAI 9811, pp. 507–514, 2016.
DOI: 10.1007/978-3-319-43958-7_61

aimed at the determination of a set of perceptual cues relevant to the description of the peculiarities of voice, segmental and suprasegmental characteristics of speech of native Russian speaker introduced by the alterations of emotional, psychic, psychosomatic and physiological state [1–5]. Voice-based evidence is an important part of many criminal investigations and has commonly included such things as threats left on an answering machine, a robbery caught on videotape, or a confession recorded during a police interrogation. In the technological age of mobile telephones, voicemail, and voice-recognition software applications, the potential for voice-based evidence continues to increase, on the domain of personality identification and attribution in the communication by means of Skype, You Tube, com. and in the case of telephone terrorism, Internet pranker communication, etc.

2   Method, Experiment, Results

The speech signal therefore contains at least two kinds of information. As a linguistic signal, it conveys the communicative content of the utterance. The speech signal also conveys information about certain features of the speaker, such as his sex, age, regional origin, etc. An important distinction may be drawn here between whether these kinds of information are intentionally introduced or not. Laver [8,9,12] proposes a classification of the different kinds of indexical information present in speech: biological information (size, physique, sex, age and medical state); psychological information (personality); social information (mainly accent information of regional origin, social status, etc.). The main reason for the specifics of the speech signal may be neurophysiological and psychological features of the phonation and articulation process, the implementation of which is controlled by the speakers central and autonomic nervous systems [14,17]. It is important to distinguish between two types of speech signal variability: **interindividual** variability due to individual anatomical and physiological, psychological and social characteristics of speakers which is the basis of individually-significant attributes; **intraindividual** variability caused by a number of non-semantic factors and expressed in spontaneous variation of voice and speech, even within an unchanged speech segment according to various uncontrollable factors related to multi-component vocal apparatus functioning. Speech is both a mechanism of intellectual activity, which allows to perform operations of abstraction and generalization that provides the basis of categorical thinking, and a mechanism of semantic programming enabling the transition from the semantic level to the syntactic level with the help of psycho-physiological mechanism called internal (implicit) speech [12].

Human speech is characterized by an operating component, the first element of which is physical or sound matter, the analysis of which allows to determine the relationship between individual voice production with an invariant and variants of sound and intonation patterns on the basis of a specific language. The next link of the operating component of the speech process is a lexical-semantic organization of verbal material including implementation of the lexical-morphological code of the language that converts images and concepts to their verbal forms. The above determines the conceptual basis of the successful development of attributes and identification of the speaker in forensic phonetics [11,12,15–17,19]. Based on the basic premise that human speech is individually organized on the basis of individual phonational and articulatory gestures in close connection with the social phonological representation of an utterance and its lexical and semantic features, it seems reasonable to build an acoustic-linguistic algorithm of the speaker identification analysis taking into account the following factors: acoustic (hardware and software) processing of the speech signal; anatomical and physiological-based decoding of the speech signal; social- and psychological-based decoding of the speech signal; intellectual and meaningful decoding of the speech signal; tiered global linguistic decoding.

In this regard, all solvable problems can be roughly described as tasks of drawing up an individual portrait of the speaker, which includes phonational (voice), articulatory (segmental) and prosodic (suprasegmental) correlates of his/her speech. The basis of the acoustic-linguistic analysis are iterative speech wave processing procedures. It seems reasonable to divide acoustic and linguistic features of the speech signal into primary and secondary ones. The primary ones include: phonational features (typology of voice mimics, such as forced or gentle phonation/with correlation of the speech signal analyzed to one of the phonation types; articulatory features (articulatory typology of generating speech signal (e.g., tense or relaxed articulation) with correlation of the speech signal to one of the articulation types).

Primary features are directly dependent on the specific anatomical and physiological nature. Secondary (prosodic) features are of conditionally superstructural character with respect to the primary ones and are implemented on their basis. Suprasegment implementation of secondary features of the speech signal leads to formation of a kind of structurally-organized speech figures and their concatenation of strictly individual character. According to recent data, voice features that characterize the speaker as well as the specificity of his/her individual character formation (i.e. idiosyncrasy) contain two types of information: **communicative and individual** one. As a linguistic (verbal) signal, speech includes communicative content of a message, and as an extralinguistic (nonverbal) signal, it correlates with the information about such speakers features as gender, age, region of origin, etc.

In portrait attributes of the speaker by voice and speech there are three types of norms: **universal, group** and **idiosyncratic** ones. A special role belongs to speech and voice information decoded at the level of auditory perception [18]. The purpose of our experiment was to identify key features of the perceptual-auditory perception of speech necessary and sufficient to answer the question: what individual features of the speaker may be used by an expert making up a portrait of the speaker. In addition, it was necessary to answer the question whether the information content of features was identical to establish the speakers profile. Special questionnaires [13,14,18–20] were used for the experiment. Listeners were asked to listen to some phonograms and then record their answers in a special questionnaire. The material (phonograms for each speaker) was played repeatedly. There were no restrictions in time and number of plays.

The listeners were to note those features in their questionnaires, which, in their view, matched the profile of the speaker. The listeners of the experiment were represented by 4 groups of listeners: 2 groups of experts who were people from various business dimensions and had fundamental knowledge in the field of speaker identification by voice and speech (n = 21); and non-experts students of Moscow State Linguistic University (n = 45). The subjects belonged to various age, gender, social and territorial groups. One of the hypotheses put forward to test the empirical data, was the assumption according to which the subjects (in this case, the listeners) possess different levels of language competence and skills of listening, which affects the final results of the perceptual-auditory analysis. Along with listening to the phonograms presented, the listeners were to perform special questionnaires giving their opinion on speakers profile characteristics. Speakers were presented by: males and females (the subjects also had an option transvestite in their questionnaires); people of various social groups (high school students, teachers, politicians, etc.); representatives of various age groups; representatives of regional groups (residents of various regions in Russia).

Speakers speech was recorded under various conditions: physical (various rooms with varying degrees of noise insulation) and communication (radio interviews, spontaneous speech, lectures, reports, phrases from polylogues, dialogues, etc.). According to the experiment procedure, the listeners had no information on speakers in advance. The listeners were to fill in the questionnaire while listening, focusing solely on their auditory impressions. The listeners had a task to analyze the acoustic part of the sounding material (expression plan) rather than specific semantic content of speech fragments (content plan). Data obtained as a result of the perceptual-auditory experiment were analyzed and statistically processed. For each of the 4 groups of speakers personal characteristics, namely speakers phonetic characteristics, language characteristics; physiological and anthropometric characteristics of the speakers appearance, his/her physical and emotional state, tables were drawn containing the results of the perceptual-auditory analysis. Thus, for each group 2 tables were drawn showing the number of listeners reactions to the presence/absence of a characteristic proposed in the questionnaire (as well as the parameter of this characteristic, for example, voice pitch medium) in absolute and relative units (%).

Further evaluation of the results obtained was carried out by two vectors: vertical vector for perceptual-auditory definition of interspeaker features (and parameters) essential for each speaker separately; horizontal vector for classification of parameters singled out for each speaker (intraspeaker section) on the basis of the statistical weight of each parameter. The horizontal vector gives an insight into the intraspeaker mechanism of perception by speech. Classification of parameters within each feature is based on statistical weights (W, %) attributable to each parameter according to the following formula:

$$W = \frac{a * 100}{A},\tag{1}$$

where a is the number of positive responses of the subjects received for a specific parameter for all speakers (i.e. how many times the listeners noted this parameter during the experiment); A is the total number of positive responses regarding specific features for the entire group of speakers. Next, each parameter was assigned a rank value (it takes with respect to the appropriate feature).

The parameters that are well perceived by the subjects by ear (most listeners noted their presence) have, respectively, a greater statistical weight (W) and, as a consequence, a higher rank. The empirical evidence also showed that the features do have various weights and various significance for the completion of the task, that is drawing up the speaker's portrait. In each of the 4 groups under consideration, the characteristics were assigned ranks according to their statistical weights in the group. This ranking of the features can be interpreted as follows: the higher rank is assigned to a particular feature of any group of characteristics (phonetic, linguistic, physiological and anthropometric or physical and emotional characteristics), the more accessible and more important it is for the expert studying speaker's characteristics. This classification can be perceived as a kind of guide for an audio expert indicating which attributes of the speaker should be considered and analyzed in the first place, what indicators are reliable and meaningful to perform such a task as drawing up the speakers portrait. It is seen from the obtained data that the listeners best perceived the following characteristics: generation in the process of speech breathing, strength of voice and specific features of pronunciation; temporal peculiarities, melodic patterns, distinguishing stressed and unstressed syllables, speech rhythm; language (native/foreign), language (standard vs. dialect) and a communicative act specificity (group of verbal features); gender, age and size of the speaker's head (physiological and anthropometric features); physical state of a speaker (group of features that describe the speaker's physical and emotional state). The following features were most difficult for auditive speaker attribution: voice timpre and strength (group of phonetic features); type of speech activity, functional style and language (in opposition to the standard vernacular; group of linguistic features); speaker's height, weight, age and hair color, width of his/her chest (physiological and anthropometric attributes); defects in speech and pronunciation; emotional and emotional-modal state (group of features that describe the speaker's emotional state).

3   Conclusion

Conclusions regarding the speakers attributes, which can be made in an intraspeaker (horizontal) analysis, have the greatest practical value. The resulting information can be used particularly in forensic purposes in solving diagnostic tasks. The purpose of this type of analysis is to identify a common mechanism of formation of listeners' interpretation of the speaker (author of a spoken text) image. The statistical analysis is used to determine which speaker's attributes are perceived by the listeners, what personality characteristics are difficult to determine by ear, and what parameters are perceived by the listeners equally, etc.

With the <u>vertical</u> vector of data obtained in the course of the experiment, inter-speaker identification features are determined. Statistics show that it is possible to single out key features for each speaker who took part in the experiment. For classification of parameters, the ranking method was used again. To this end, each parameter was assigned a numerical index, which reflects the number of positive responses to the presence of this parameter for each speaker (in %). Dominating parameters build the speaker's profile.

Next, to assess the relevant parameters in the speakers personality profile, a sample of the maximum values (the highest values of the parameters) has been split into three intervals: (a) [0 – 50] parameters with values within this range, may be declared as those least perceived by the listeners. A small value of the parameter means that either the listeners are not able to auditive define what value of a speech parameter may be attributed to the speaker, or these characteristics are not strongly marked, which prevents the listeners from determining whether the speaker has this feature; (b) [50 – 75] parameters with values within this range are more perceptually significant. However, features of this interval cannot be considered as basic points in a forensic expertise; (c) [75 – 100] parameters with values within this range are most perceptible. Considering the fact that most of the most listeners answers are identical on this particular subject, the speaker will likely be attributed these values of features. Moreover, high values of the parameter indices of this interval indicate that the respective features may be included in a palette of an expert creating the speaker's portrait. Next, values were considered from the upper range [75–100] including features whose values are both statistically and perceptually marked. It can be assumed that the parameters within of this interval, provide specific information about the speaker's identity, and therefore they should be taken into account when drawing up his/her portrait.

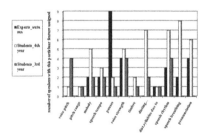
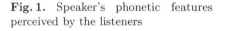
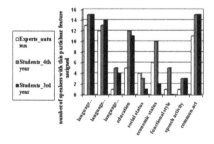

Fig. 1. Speaker's phonetic features perceived by the listeners

Fig. 2. Speaker's language features perceived by the listeners

Bar charts were built for these features (Figs. 1, 2, 3 and 4). Features that are included in the top interval are distributed along the X-axis; and the number of speakers whose portrait has this particular feature is shown on the Y-axis. Thus, according to Figs. 1, 2, 3 and 4 the features attributed to most speakers (n = 15) include *pauses, speech rhythm, speech breathing and distinguishing*

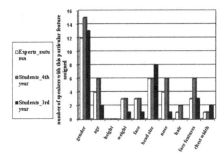 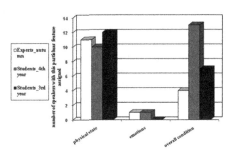

Fig. 3. Speaker's physiological and anthropometric features perceived by the listeners

Fig. 4. Features of the speaker's physical and emotional state perceived by the listeners

stressed/unstressed syllables (phonetic features); *language* (native vs. foreign), *communicative act, language* (standard vs. dialect), *education and economic status* (linguistic features); *speakers gender and size of his/her head* (physiological and anthropometric features), *speakers overall condition* (features of speaker's physical and emotional state). Features that are assigned by the subjects to a minority of speakers (n = 1–6) are either purely individual and make the speaker's voice and speech exclusive (these characteristics distinguish the speaker's voice from all the others), or are difficult to determine by listeners. To answer these questions it is necessary to conduct an additional series of experiments to increase speakers' and listeners' samples.

Acknowledgment. This research is supported by Russian Science Foundation, Project N14-18-01059 (2014–2016).

References

1. Brown, R.: Auditory Speaker Recognition. Helmut Buske Verlag, Hamburg (1987)
2. Buzik, O.Z., Rychkova, O.V., Agibalova, T.V., Gurevich, G.L., Shalaeva, E.V., Potapova, R.K.: Emotional and cognitive disturbances in addictions: interactions and correlations. Zhurnal nevrologii i psikhiatrii imeni S.S. Korsakova, pp. 79–83 (2014) (in Russian)
3. Fazakis, N., Karlos, S., Kotsiantis, S., Sgarbas, K.: Speaker identification using semi-supervised learning. In: Ronzhin, A., Potapova, R., Fakotakis, N. (eds.) SPECOM 2015. LNCS, vol. 9319, pp. 389–396. Springer, Heidelberg (2015)
4. French, P.: An overview of forensic phonetics with particular reference to speaker identification. Forensic Linguist. Int. J. Speech Lang. Law **1**(2), 169–181 (1994)
5. Hollien, H.: Forensic Voice Identification. Academic Press, London (UK), San Diego (California) (2002)
6. Jessen, M.: Phonetische und linguistische Prinzipien des forensischen Stimmenvergleichs. Lincom, Muenchen (2012)
7. Kuenzel, H.J.: Sprechererkennung. Kriminalistik Verlag, Heidelberg (1987)
8. Laver, J.: The Phonetic Description of Voice Quality. Cambridge University Press, Cambridge (1980)

9. Laver, J.: Voice quality and indexical information. Br. J. Disord. Commun. **3**, 43–54 (1968)
10. Polzehl, T.: Personality in Speech: Assessment and Automatic Classification. T-Labs Series in Telecommunication Services. Springer, Heidelberg (2015)
11. Potapova, R.K.: Speech: Communication, Information, Cybernetics, 5th edn. URSS, Moscow (2015) (in Russian)
12. Potapova, R.K.: The subject-oriented perception of foreign speech. Voprosy jazykoznanija **2**, 46–64 (2005) (in Russian)
13. Potapova, R., Potapov, V.: Associative mechanism of Foreign spoken language perception (Forensic Phonetic Aspect). In: Ronzhin, A., Potapova, R., Delic, V. (eds.) SPECOM 2014. LNCS, vol. 8773, pp. 113–122. Springer, Heidelberg (2014)
14. Potapova, R., Potapov, V.: Auditory and visual recognition of emotional behaviour of Foreign language subjects (by Native and Non-native speakers). In: Železný, M., Habernal, I., Ronzhin, A. (eds.) SPECOM 2013. LNCS, vol. 8113, pp. 62–69. Springer, Heidelberg (2013)
15. Potapova, R.K., Potapov, V.V.: Kommunikative Sprechtaetigkeit: Russland und Deutschland im Vergleich. Boehlau Verlag, Koeln; Weimar; Wien (2011)
16. Potapova, R.K., Potapov, V.V.: Language, Speech, Personality. Publishing House Languages of Slavic Cultures, Moscow (2006) (in Russian)
17. Potapova, R.K., Potapov, V.V.: On the correlation between attribute characteristics of a speaker and the speech signal. In: Proceedings of the XVI International Scientific Conference Informatization and Information Security of Low and Order Bodies, Moscow, RF, pp. 330–336 (2007) (in Russian)
18. Potapova, R.K., Potapov, V.V.: Speech Communication: From Sound to Utterance. Publishing House Languages of Slavic Cultures, Moscow (2012) (in Russian)
19. Potapova, R.K., Potapov, V.V.: Spoken language as an object of fundamental and applied linguistic investigation. In: Annual Report of the Russian Acoustical Society Speech Acoustics and Applied Linguistics, Moscow, pp. 6–28 (2002) (in Russian)
20. Potapova, R.K., Potapov, V.V., Lebedeva, N.N., Agibalova, T.V.: Interdisciplinarity in the Investigation of Speech Polyinformativeness. Publishing House Languages of Slavic Cultures, Moscow (2015) (in Russian)

Online Biometric Identification with Face Analysis in Web Applications

Gerasimos Arvanitis$^{(\boxtimes)}$, Konstantinos Moustakas, and Nikos Fakotakis

Electrical and Computer Engineering Department,
University of Patras, Rio, Patras, Greece
{arvanitis,moustakas}@ece.upatras.gr, fakotaki@upatras.gr

Abstract. Internet security is an important issue that concerns everyone who uses it without exception. Over the past few years, there has been a significant improvement in internet security but little attention has been paid to protect careless users. This paper introduces a user-based security application that could replace the classic login frame on websites in order to offer an extra security level that allows a biometric identification of the user that prevents unauthorized login to his personal page.

Keywords: Face recognition · Biometric identification · Online safety · User-based security

1 Introduction

More and more people every day choose internet as a tool to communicate with others, shop products from all over the world, disclose sensitive information like personal photos and videos, make money transactions from their bank account etc. The most common problem that seems to exist is the difficulty in using a variety of strong passwords. For example, older users are less concerned about choosing a secure password because it is harder to remember and they rarely change it or use the same one on every web application they use. On the other hand, even though younger people are more diligent in choosing a secure password, they are more careless with the personal information they upload. Researches have shown that heavy web users have an average of 21 passwords, 81 % of users select a common password and 30 % write their passwords down or store them in a file [1]. Security system engineers aim to make websites safer by using secure protocols (https, sftp), encryptions and other security techniques. A common technique that hackers use, even those who do not have much experience, is the brute force that is easy to apply and most of the time brings the desirable results. They use a set of common passwords and iteratively try to login. No secure system can prevent them and the results depend only on the strength of user's password. Therefore, it is obvious that there is a need for more secure systems to protect individuals when logging in.

© Springer International Publishing Switzerland 2016
A. Ronzhin et al. (Eds.): SPECOM 2016, LNAI 9811, pp. 515–522, 2016.
DOI: 10.1007/978-3-319-43958-7_62

1.1 Related Works

In recent years, there has been a remarkable improvement in face detection and recognition. Most of the techniques are very robust, fast and operate satisfactorily under any circumstances. Principal component analysis (PCA) has demonstrated its success in face recognition, detection, and tracking at [12]. At [7] a study is conducted to optimize the time complexity of PCA (eigenfaces). One extension of PCA, known as multilinear principal components analysis (MPCA) is described at [6]. Linear Discriminant Analysis aims to maximum between class (across users) variance and minimum within class (within user) variance [8]. At [2] is presented ICA which is a generalization of PCA in that it tries to identify high-order statistical relationships between pixels to form a better set of basis vectors. The use of neural networks for face recognition is shown at [3]. At [5] a new method is introduced, SIFT, according to which features are extracted from images for matching between different poses of the same subject. A lot of applications, which use face information for security reasons, have been created and some examples of these are being presented at Table 1.

Table 1. Examples of applications which use face recognition [10]

Area	Examples
Security	access control to buildings, airports/seaports, ATM machines, email authentication on multimedia workstations
Surveillance	a large number of CCTVs can be monitored to look for known criminals, drug offenders, thieves
identity verification	electoral registration, banking, electronic commerce, identifying newborns, national IDs, passports, drivers' licenses, employee IDs
Criminal justice systems	mug-shot/booking systems, post-event analysis, forensics
Image database investigations	searching image databases of licensed drivers benefit recipients, missing children, immigrants and police bookings
Smart Card	SIM Card

1.2 Originality of This Work

In this paper we present an application which uses face recognition at websites for security purposes. Until now no technique or application has ever given emphasis on user-based security. The main originality of this work is that it aims to protect careless users who are inattentive considering the safety of their personal password. Additionally, the identification becomes very fast because it takes into account only the stored images of the user and not all the images of the database which is ideal for real time procedures. We use robust and reliable algorithms for face detection and user's identification with a combination of the latest web technologies. The paper is organized as follows: In Sect. 2 we present the main steps of the proposed login with the extra security level. In Sect. 3 we discuss the techniques we use in order to achieve the user's identification. In Sect. 4 we show a presentation of the application and some basic steps of image processing. In Sect. 5 we mention the limitations of this work and future extensions as well.

2 Proposed Login Procedure

The interaction between user and application starts with a login frame which has no difference with the other login frames that the user is already familiar with. When the user fills the gaps of username and password, two possible scenarios could happen (Fig. 1).

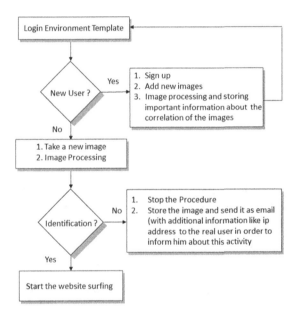

Fig. 1. Schematic algorithm of the login procedure

1. If it is the first time that the user visits the website then he should create an account. In this case, the new user needs to sign up like he would do on any website, but he has to upload additionally some images of his face. At least three images are required but it is recommended to upload as much as possible in order to achieve better processing results.
2. If a user is already subscribed then only one new image is required to be uploaded. Image processing techniques are being applied in order to verify users identification.

Fig. 2. (a) example of a login form (b) interface for taking images (c) face detection using Viola–Jones algorithm

Finally, if the new image is identified as the user's image, he can have access to his account; otherwise the image is being stored and marked as "a potential threat". Next, an email is being sent to the user, with the ip address of the computer that was used to login with the marked image as attachment (Fig. 2).

3   Online Face Recognition and Image Processing

3.1   Viola and Jones

For face detection we use the Viola–Jones algorithm which is a robust and fast technique ideal for real time applications. The algorithm has four stages that are described below [11]:

Haar Feature Selection. Each feature results in a single value which is calculated by subtracting the sum of the white rectangle(s) from the sum of the black rectangle(s) (Fig. 3).

Fig. 3. The different types of features

Creating an Integral Image. The integral image at location x, y contains the sum of the pixels above and to the left of x, y, inclusive:

$$ii(x, y) = \sum_{x' \leq x, y' \leq y} i(x', y'),$$

where $ii(x, y)$ is the integral image and $i(x, y)$ is the original image (Fig. 4).

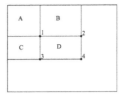

Fig. 4. The sum of the pixels within rectangle D can be computed with four array references.

Adaboost Training. Each feature is considered to be a potential weak classifier. A weak classifier is mathematically described as:

$$h(x, f, p, \theta) = \begin{cases} 1 & if \quad pf(x) < p\theta \\ 0 & otherwise \end{cases},$$

where f feature, θ threshold and p polarity that indicate the direction of the inequality.

Cascading Classifiers. The cascaded classifier is composed of stages each containing a strong classifier. The job of each stage is to determine whether a given sub-window is definitely not a face or maybe a face. When a sub-window is classified to be a non-face by a given stage it is immediately discarded. Conversely a sub-window classified as a maybe-face is passed on to the next stage in the cascade. It follows that the more stages a given sub-window passes, the higher the chance the sub-window actually contains a face. The concept is illustrated with two stages in Fig. 5 [4].

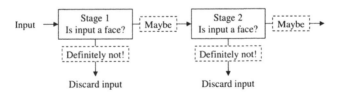

Fig. 5. The cascaded classifier.

3.2   PCA for Recognition

We use PCA [9] for user identification. Firstly we assume that we have N normalized images n x n that are stored at user's file system. These N images make up our training set $\{I_1 \, I_2 \, ... \, I_N\}$. The next step is to reshape them and create image vectors that are represented by Φ:

$$I_i = \begin{bmatrix} p_{1,1} & p_{1,2} & \cdots & p_{1,n} \\ p_{2,1} & p_{2,2} & \cdots & p_{2,n} \\ \vdots & \vdots & \ddots & \vdots \\ p_{n,1} & p_{n,2} & \cdots & p_{n,n} \end{bmatrix}_{n \times n} \Rightarrow \begin{bmatrix} p_{1,1} \\ \cdots \\ p_{1,n} \\ \cdots \\ p_{2,n} \\ \cdots \\ p_{n,n} \end{bmatrix}_{n^2 \times 1} = \Phi_i.$$

All N images of the training set are taken into account to determine the mean image vector:

$$M = \frac{1}{N} \sum_{i=1}^{N} \Phi_i.$$

We remove the common information $L_i = \Phi_i - M$, and we find the covariance matrix $C = XX^T$ *where* $X = [L_1\ L_2\ ...\ L_N]$ Next, we select the best K Eigenvectors. Each face in the training set, Φ_i can be represented as a linear combination of these Eigenvectors u_i:

$$L_i = \sum_{j=1}^{K} w_j u_j.$$

The weights are calculated as follows, $w_j = u_j^T L_i$. Each normalized training image is represented in this basis as a vector $W = \begin{bmatrix} w_1 & w_2 & w_3 & \cdots & w_k \end{bmatrix}^T$. The vector is stored and subsequently is compared with a new vector W' when a new image is received. The same procedure is followed for the calculation of W' as well, with the difference that now N+1 images exist:

$$e_r = min \left\| W - W' \right\|.$$

If $e_r < \Theta$ the image is deemed to belong to the user. If $e_r > \Theta$ the image is deemed that it does not belong to the user.

3.3 Auto-Learning and Image Database Update

In order to create a strongly autocorrelated database, a function that finds the ideal combination of images is executed every time that a new image is verified that actually belongs to the user. Images with low correlation factor are removed. More recent images have higher weights because they represent the current situation. Considering the fact that physical characteristics change with time, the latest images represent better the current features of the user and make more efficient a future recognition process. The new mean image is determined by the following formula taking into account the weighted average:

$$M' = \frac{1}{N'} \sum_{i=1}^{N} a_i \Phi_i \ where \ N' > N \ and \ N' = \sum_{i=1}^{N} a_i.$$

4   Assumptions - Presentation of the Application

In this section we will explain some basic steps of the processing procedure. Firstly, it is important to make sure that the face is located inside the frame, as shown Fig. 6, in order to eliminate the limitation of different poses.

Fig. 6. (a) wrong face placement without frame (b) correct face placement with frame (c) wrong face placement with frame

When the face is detected, the background of the image is removed and is kept only the face as shown at Fig. 2(c). After that, the new image is converted into gray scale and is normalized so that there are only images with the same number of pixels 250×250 (it is likely that the user has logged in from different computers with different web camera resolution). Next, a query is made in the database to find the path of the file system where the user's images are located. The PCA method is applied and vector W' is calculated. This vector is being compared with the value of vector W that is stored in the database. The length of the vectors is 5 equal to the number of eigenvectors that we have decided to keep. If the euclidean distance between two vectors is lower than the threshold: $\Theta = 0.03$ twe assume that the new image is located in the subspace of user's images and it is considered as the correct image, otherwise it is marked as unacceptable as it may belong to someone else.

Tools That We Used: Contemporary internet technologies (html, php, Javascript, css), Database (msql), Python for image processing and machine learning techniques.

5   Limitations and Extensions at Future Work

There are some limitations that are possible to affect the identification result such as (a) the variations in lighting conditions, (b) the differences in pose or head orientation, (c) Image quality, CCTV, Web-cams (d) expressions and partial occlusion (hats, glasses, different haircut, beards etc.). To overcome some of these problems one could take into account other biometric or distinctive features of the users, like the sound of voice (e.g. a specific phrase) or a short duration video with a distinctive motion or gesture of the user. This will be the direction of our future work.

6   Conclusion

In this paper we present a way to create a more secure login environment to websites. This extra safety level protects mainly the more careless users who use weak passwords. The proposed method uses face detection and recognition in order to identify the user. The algorithms that are used are robust and trust-worthy and additionally, real time processing is very fast and ideal for online usage.

References

1. http://passwordresearch.com/stats/study64.html
2. Bartlett, M.S., Movellan, J.R., Sejnowski, T.J.: Face recognition by independent component analysis. IEEE Trans. Neural Netw. **13**(6), 1450–1464 (2002)
3. Fan, X., Verma, B.: A comparative experimental analysis of separate and combined facial features for ga-ann based technique. In: Sixth International Conference on Computational Intelligence and Multimedia Applications (ICCIMA 2005), pp. 279–284. IEEE (2005)
4. Jensen, O.H.: Implementing the Viola-Jones face detection algorithm. Ph.D. thesis, Technical University of Denmark, DTU, DK-2800 Kgs. Lyngby, Denmark (2008)
5. Križaj, J., Štruc, V., Pavešić, N.: Adaptation of SIFT features for robust face recognition. In: Campilho, A., Kamel, M. (eds.) ICIAR 2010. LNCS, vol. 6111, pp. 394–404. Springer, Heidelberg (2010)
6. Lu, H., Plataniotis, K.N., Venetsanopoulos, A.N.: Multilinear principal component analysis of tensor objects for recognition. In: 18th International Conference on Pattern Recognition (ICPR 2006), vol. 2, pp. 776–779. IEEE (2006)
7. Abdullah, M., Wazzan, M., Bo-saeed, S.: Optimizing face recognition using PCA. Int. J. Artif. Intell. Appl. (IJAIA), **3**(2) (2012)
8. Martínez, A.M., Kak, A.C.: PCA versus LDA. IEEE Trans. Pattern Anal. Mach. Intell. **23**(2), 228–233 (2001)
9. Turk, M., Pentland, A.: Eigenfaces for recognition. J. Cogn. Neurosc. **3**(1), 71–86 (1991)
10. Upadhayay, R., Yadav, R.K.: Kernel principle component analysis in face recognition system: a survey. Int. J. Adv. Res. Comput. Sci. Softw. Eng. **3**(6), 348–353 (2013)
11. Viola, P., Jones, M.: Robust real-time object detection. Int. J. Comput. Vis. **4**, 34–47 (2001)
12. Yang, M.H., Ahuja, N., Kriegman, D.: Face recognition using kernel eigenfaces. In: 2000 Proceedings International Conference on Image Processing, vol. 1, pp. 37–40. IEEE (2000)

Optimization of Zelinski
Post-filtering Calculation

Sergei Aleinik[1,2(✉)]

[1] ITMO University, 49 Kronverkskiy pr., St. Petersburg 197101, Russia
sergealeinik@gmail.com
[2] Alango Technologies Ltd., St. Petersburg, Russia

Abstract. This paper describes a new optimized method for calculating Zelinski post-filter transfer function for a microphone array. Optimized algorithm requires less memory and fewer arithmetical multiplications. We demonstrate that for the known algorithm computational complexity increases quadratically as a function of the number of microphones. In contrast, the computational complexity of the proposed algorithm increases linearly. This provides a considerable acceleration in the calculation of the post-filter transfer function.

Keywords: Zelinski · Post-filtering · Microphone array

1 Introduction

Zelinski post-filtering is one of the widely used method for digital speech signal processing in microphone array [1–5]. Zelinski post-filter (ZPF) is good for spatially uncorrelated noise suppression [6–8]. A generalized block diagram of a microphone array (MA) with post-filtering (for an array with 4 microphones and frame-based frequency domain processing) is shown in Fig. 1.

The input signals $x_n(t)$ of each n-th microphone (n, $n = 0, N − 1$) are transformed into spectra $X_n(f, k)$ using short-time Fourier transform (STFT), where N is total number of microphones; f is the frequency bin index and k is the frame index (block 1). Then each signal $X_n(f, k)$ is delayed by multiplication by the complex steering vector $D_n(f, \theta)$ (block 2):

$$Y_n(f, k) = D_n(f, \theta)X_n(f, k),\qquad(1)$$

where θ is the desired source direction. At the third step (block 3) the frequency-domain output signal is calculated:

$$Z(f, k) = \frac{1}{N}\sum_{n=0}^{N-1} Y_n(f, k).\qquad(2)$$

Block 4 estimates the post-filter transfer function $W(f, k)$ using the signals $Y_n(f, k)$ and $Z(f, k)$. Then the post-filter (block 5) calculates the frequency-domain output:

© Springer International Publishing Switzerland 2016
A. Ronzhin et al. (Eds.): SPECOM 2016, LNAI 9811, pp. 523–530, 2016.
DOI: 10.1007/978-3-319-43958-7_63

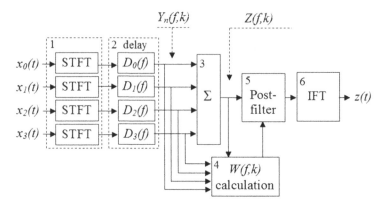

Fig. 1. Block diagram of a microphone array processing with post-filtering

$Z_{out}(f,k) = Z(f,k)W(f,k)$. Finally, the time-domain output signal $z(t)$ is calculated as the inverse Fourier transform (IFT) of $Z_{out}(f,k)$.

The main question in this kind of processing is how to calculate the post-filter transfer function $W(f,k)$.

2   Zelinski Post-filter Transfer Function

In this paper for ZPF calculation we used "classical" equation equivalent to the one given in [7, 8]:

$$W(f,k) = \text{HR}\left\{ \frac{C_N \text{Re}\left[\sum_{n=0}^{N-2}\sum_{m=n+1}^{N-1} \langle \Phi_{Y_n Y_m}(f,k)\rangle\right]}{\frac{1}{N}\sum_{n=0}^{N-1} \langle \Phi_{Y_n Y_n}(f,k)\rangle} \right\}, \tag{3}$$

where the operator $\langle \cdot \rangle$ is the exponential smoothing over frames; $\text{Re}[\cdot]$ marks the real part; $HR\{x\} = \max\{x, 0\}$ is the rectification operator; and $C_N = 2/(N^2 - N)$ is the normalization factor. The difference between formula (3) and the formula presented in [7] is that we used different symbols for smoothing, frequency and frame indices and changed the limits of microphones indices to $n = 0, N - 1$. The smoothed over frames cross-spectra $\langle \Phi_{Y_n Y_m}(f,k)\rangle$ are calculated as follows [7]:

$$\langle \Phi_{Y_n Y_m}(f,k)\rangle = \alpha\langle \Phi_{Y_n Y_m}(f,k-1)\rangle + (1-\alpha)Y_n(f,k)Y_m^*(f,k), \tag{4}$$

where $0 \leq \alpha < 1$ is smoothing factor.

3   Drawbacks of the Classical Implementation

There are two disadvantages in the calculation of (3): required memory (minor) and required number of complex multiplications (major). Let us denote the number of frequency bins in signals $Y_n(f, k)$ as F, so $f = 0, F - 1$. In that case the calculation of a single smoothed cross-spectrum (4) for the frame index k and some specific indices n and m requires:

- Complex array with the size F (to store smoothed cross-spectrum).
- $F + 2$ complex multiplications.

   In the numerator in (3) there are two nested loops where indices n and m vary as follows: $n = 0, N - 2$ and $m = n + 1, N - 1$. It is clear that the total number of calculation steps is equal to $(N^2 - N)/2$ (see normalization factor C_N in (3)). Hence, the calculation of the numerator in (3) takes $(N^2 - N)/2$ complex arrays of size F and $(F + 2)(N^2 - N)/2$ complex multiplications: the computational complexity of (3) is $O(N^2)$. The main problem, of course, is multiplications, as (3) has to be calculated for every input signal frame in real time applications.

4   Accelerated Algorithm Derivation

First we note that it is easy to show that arithmetic summation and exponential smoothing in the nominator of (3) may be reversed. This statement is also true for the exponential smoothing and the $\mathrm{Re}[\cdot]$ operator. Hence (3) may be rewritten as:

$$
W(f, k) = \mathrm{HR} \left\{ \frac{C_N \left\langle \mathrm{Re} \left[\sum_{n=0}^{N-2} \sum_{m=n+1}^{N-1} \Phi_{Y_n Y_m}(f, k) \right] \right\rangle}{\frac{1}{N} \left\langle \sum_{n=0}^{N-1} \Phi_{Y_n Y_n}(f, k) \right\rangle} \right\}.
\tag{5}
$$

It is clear that (5) and (3) are mathematically equivalent, but to store the nominator of (5) we need only a single complex array of size F.

   Second, let us take a closer look at the cross-spectrum matrix $\Phi(f, k)$. This is the matrix of the following form (for our example when $N = 4$):

$$
\begin{bmatrix}
\Phi_{Y_0 Y_0}(f) & \Phi_{Y_1 Y_0}(f) & \Phi_{Y_2 Y_0}(f) & \Phi_{Y_3 Y_0}(f) \\
\Phi_{Y_0 Y_1}(f) & \Phi_{Y_1 Y_1}(f) & \Phi_{Y_2 Y_1}(f) & \Phi_{Y_3 Y_1}(f) \\
\Phi_{Y_0 Y_2}(f) & \Phi_{Y_1 Y_2}(f) & \Phi_{Y_2 Y_2}(f) & \Phi_{Y_3 Y_2}(f) \\
\Phi_{Y_0 Y_3}(f) & \Phi_{Y_1 Y_3}(f) & \Phi_{Y_2 Y_3}(f) & \Phi_{Y_3 Y_3}(f)
\end{bmatrix}.
\tag{6}
$$

Here we omit the frame index k for the sake of simplicity. Then the sum in the numerator of (5) is the sum of the elements of a strictly lower triangular matrix:

$$
\begin{bmatrix}
0 & 0 & 0 & 0 \\
\Phi_{Y_0 Y_1}(f) & 0 & 0 & 0 \\
\Phi_{Y_0 Y_2}(f) & \Phi_{Y_1 Y_2}(f) & 0 & 0 \\
\Phi_{Y_0 Y_3}(f) & \Phi_{Y_1 Y_3}(f) & \Phi_{Y_2 Y_3}(f) & 0
\end{bmatrix}.
\tag{7}
$$

Since (6) is a Hermitian matrix (i.e. $\Phi_{Y_n Y_m}(f) = \Phi^*_{Y_m Y_n}(f)$ and, correspondingly, $\mathrm{Re}[\Phi_{Y_n Y_m}(f)] = \mathrm{Re}[\Phi_{Y_m Y_n}(f)]$) we can write the sum of the real part of all elements of (6) as:

$$
\mathrm{Re}\left[\sum_{n=0}^{N-1}\sum_{m=0}^{N-1}\Phi_{Y_n Y_m}(f,k)\right] = 2\mathrm{Re}\left[\sum_{n=0}^{N-2}\sum_{m=n+1}^{N-1}\Phi_{Y_n Y_m}(f,k)\right] + \sum_{k=0}^{N-1}\Phi_{Y_k Y_k}(f,k),
\tag{8}
$$

from which it follows that the expression under the operator $\langle \cdot \rangle$ in the numerator of (5) is:

$$
\mathrm{Re}\left[\sum_{n=0}^{N-2}\sum_{m=n+1}^{N-1}\Phi_{Y_n Y_m}(f,k)\right] = \frac{1}{2}\left(\mathrm{Re}\left[\sum_{n=0}^{N-1}\sum_{m=0}^{N-1}\Phi_{Y_n Y_m}(f,k)\right] - \sum_{k=0}^{N-1}\Phi_{Y_k Y_k}(f,k)\right).
\tag{9}
$$

Hence (5) can be rewritten as:

$$
W(f,k) = \frac{1}{2}NC_N\mathrm{HR}\left\{\frac{\left\langle \mathrm{Re}\left[\sum_{n=0}^{N-1}\sum_{m=0}^{N-1}\Phi_{Y_n Y_m}(f,k)\right] - \sum_{k=0}^{N-1}\Phi_{Y_k Y_k}(f,k)\right\rangle}{\left\langle \sum_{n=0}^{N-1}\Phi_{Y_n Y_n}(f,k)\right\rangle}\right\}.
\tag{10}
$$

Note that we moved factors $\frac{1}{2}$, C_N and $\frac{1}{N}$ to the beginning of (10).

Note also that we already have the output sum $Z(f,k)$ calculated using (2). Consider the cross-spectra of the signals $Y_n(f, k)$ and $Z(f,k)$:

$$
\Phi_{Y_n Z}(f, k) = Y_n(f, k) \cdot Z(f, k)^* = \frac{1}{N}Y_n(f, k)\left(\sum_{m=0}^{N-1}Y_m(f, k)\right)^*
$$

$$
= \frac{1}{N}\sum_{m=0}^{N-1}Y_n(f, k)(Y_m(f, k))^* = \frac{1}{N}\sum_{m=0}^{N-1}\Phi_{Y_n Y_m}(f, k),
\tag{11}
$$

i.e.:

$$
\sum_{m=0}^{N-1}\Phi_{Y_n Y_m}(f, k) = N\Phi_{Y_n Z}(f, k).
\tag{12}
$$

Putting (12) into (10) we get:

$$W(f,k) = D_N \text{HR} \left\{ \frac{\left\langle N\text{Re}\left[\sum_{n=0}^{N-1} \Phi_{Y_n Z}(f,k)\right] - \sum_{k=0}^{N-1} \Phi_{Y_k Y_k}(f,k) \right\rangle}{\left\langle \sum_{n=0}^{N-1} \Phi_{Y_n Y_n}(f,k) \right\rangle} \right\}, \tag{13}$$

where $D_N = 1/(N-1)$. Hence

$$W(f,k) = D_N \text{HR} \left\{ \frac{\left\langle N\text{Re}\left[\sum_{n=0}^{N-1} \Phi_{Y_n Z}(f,k)\right] \right\rangle}{\left\langle \sum_{n=0}^{N-1} \Phi_{Y_n Y_n}(f,k) \right\rangle} - 1 \right\}. \tag{14}$$

Simplifying the numerator of (14) we finally get the equation for the accelerated Zelinski post-filter transfer function:

$$W(f,k) = D_N \text{HR} \left\{ \frac{\left\langle N^2 \Phi_{ZZ}(f,k) \right\rangle}{\left\langle \sum_{n=0}^{N-1} \Phi_{Y_n Y_n}(f,k) \right\rangle} - 1 \right\}. \tag{15}$$

5 Analysis of the Accelerated Algorithm Equation

First, note that the classical Eqs. (3) and (15) are mathematically equivalent and gives the same results. At the same time, we avoid nested loops in the numerator, so the computational complexity of (15) is $O(N)$ instead of $O(N^2)$ for (3). Thus, we have a significant gain in computational speed, especially for MAs with a large number of microphones.

Second, (15) requires less memory: the numerator requires a single real array of size F and the numerator of (3) requires $(N^2 - N)/2$ complex arrays of size F.

Third, in real-life applications a small "regularization constant" δ is usually used in the denominator of (3) (to avoid a "zero divide" error for zero signal):

$$W(f,k) = \text{HR} \left\{ \frac{C_N \text{Re}\left[\sum_{n=0}^{N-2} \sum_{m=n+1}^{N-1} \left\langle \Phi_{Y_n Y_m}(f,k) \right\rangle\right]}{\frac{1}{N} \sum_{n=0}^{N-1} \left\langle \Phi_{Y_n Y_n}(f,k) \right\rangle + \delta} \right\}. \tag{16}$$

If we simply add δ to the denominator of (15) the new equation gives us a result similar, but not equivalent to (15) (although the differences are small). Simplifying (13) with δ in the denominator, it is easy to show that the right equation is:

$$W(f,k) = V_N\text{HR}\left\{\frac{\langle N\Phi_{ZZ}(f,k)\rangle + \frac{\delta}{N}}{\left\langle\sqrt{\sum_{n=0}^{N-1}\Phi_{Y_nY_n}(f,k)}\right\rangle + \delta} - \frac{1}{N}\right\}, \tag{17}$$

where $V_N = N/(N-1)$. Eqs. (16) and (17) are also mathematically equivalent.

6   Experiments and Results

In our experiments we used an equally spaced MA with the well-known OLA (Overlap and Add) technique and parameters fully described in [9, 10]. Parallel calculation of $W(f,k)$ using (3) and (15) yielded absolutely identical transfer functions. The same was true for (16) and (17). Computational speed testing was conducted using a real processing scheme (Fig. 1) for Eqs. (16) and (17) for different numbers of microphones in the MA. A computer with Intel(R) Core (TM) i5-4670 CPU 3.4 GHz was used. The test signal was a real human speech WAV-file with 16 kHz sampling frequency, 200 s in duration. The number of trials for the estimation of the computational time for every number of microphones in the MA was 64. The result (processing time: mean values and 95 % confidence intervals) is shown in Fig. 2.

We can see that for a small number of microphones $(N < 32)$ processing times for both (16) and (17) equation are almost equal. As the number of microphones increases,

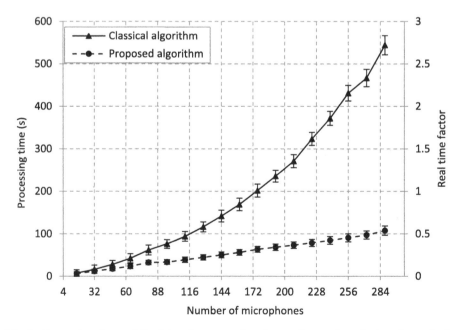

Fig. 2. Processing time and Real time factor as a function on the number of microphones in the MA

the processing time for (16) also increases in quadratic dependence on the number of microphones. On the other hand, the processing time for (17) is smaller and increases linearly. When the number of microphones reaches 176, the processing time for Eq. (16) becomes equal to signal time (correspondingly, the real time factor is 1). Hence, when $N > 176$ it is not possible to provide real-time processing for the MA on the given computer using (16). On the other hand, processing time for (17) when $N = 176$ is 63.2 s (the real time factor is 0.316). Even for $N = 288$ real time processing is possible for Eq. (17).

7 Conclusions

In this paper we presented a novel algorithm for calculating the transfer function of the Zelinski post-filter. The proposed algorithm has the computational complexity $O(N)$ and therefore it is much faster than the classical algorithm (which has the complexity of $O(N^2)$). The proposed algorithm also requires significantly less memory. These properties are particularly useful for MAs with a large number of microphones. The proposed algorithm can be applied in various MA applications, for example in speech recognition [2], in speaker verification [11] and multimodal systems [12], etc.

Acknowledgement. This work was financially supported by the Government of the Russian Federation, Grant 074-U01.

References

1. Zelinski, R.: A microphone array with adaptive post-filtering for noise reduction in reverberant rooms. In: Proceedings of International Conference on Acoustics, Speech, and Signal Processing (ICASSP), New York, pp. 2578–2581 (1988)
2. Aleinik, S., Stolbov, M.: A comparative study of speech processing in microphone arrays with multichannel alignment and Zelinski post-filtering. In: Ronzhin, A., Potapova, R., Fakotakis, N. (eds.) SPECOM 2015. LNCS, vol. 9319, pp. 34–41. Springer, Heidelberg (2015)
3. Junfeng, L., Akagi, M.: Theoretical analysis of microphone arrays with post-filtering for coherent and incoherent noise suppression in noisy environments. In: Proceedings of IWAENC2005-International Workshop on Acoustic Echo and Noise Control, pp. 85–88 (2005)
4. Fischer, S., Kammeyer, K.D., Simmer, K.U.: Adaptive microphone arrays for speech enhancement in coherent and incoherent noise fields. In: Proceedings of 3rd Joint Meeting Acoustical Society of America and Acoustical Society of Japan (1996)
5. McCowan, I.A., Bourlard, H.: Microphone array post-filter based on noise field coherence. IEEE Trans. Speech Audio Process. **11**(6), 709–716 (2003)
6. Cheng, N., Liu, W., Li, P., Xu, B.: An effective microphone array post-filter in arbitrary environments. In: Proceedings of INTERSPEECH-2008, pp. 439–442 (2008)
7. Löllmann, H.W., Vary, P., Post-filter design for superdirective beamformers with closely spaced microphones. In: Proceeding of IEEE Workshop on Applications of Signal Processing to Audio and Acoustics (WASPAA 2007), pp. 291–294 (2007)

8. Wolff, T., Buck. M., A generalized view on microphone array postfilters. In: Proceedings of International Workshop on Acoustic Signal Enhancement (2010)
9. Stolbov, M., Aleinik, S.: Speech enhancement with microphone array using frequency-domain alignment technique. In: Proceedings of 54-th Conference on Audio Forensics Techniques, Technologies and Practice, no. 54, pp. 1–5 (2014)
10. Stolbov, M., Aleinik, S.: Improvement of microphone array characteristics for speech capturing. Modern Appl. Sci. **9**(6), 343–352 (2015)
11. Kozlov, A., Kudashev, O., Matveev, Y., Pekhovsky, T., Simonchik, K., Shulipa, A.: SVID speaker recognition system for NIST SRE 2012. In: Železný, M., Habernal, I., Ronzhin, A. (eds.) SPECOM 2013. LNCS, vol. 8113, pp. 278–285. Springer, Heidelberg (2013)
12. Karpov, A., Akarun, L., Yalcin, H., Ronzhin, A., Demiroz, B., Coban, A., Zelezny, M.: Audio-visual signal processing in a multimodal assisted living environment. In: Proceedings of INTERSPEECH-2014, pp. 1023–1027 (2014)

Phonetic Aspects of High Level of Naturalness in Speech Synthesis

Vera Evdokimova$^{(\boxtimes)}$, Pavel Skrelin, Andrey Barabanov, and Karina Evgrafova

Saint Petersburg State University,
7/9 Universitetskaya Nab., St. Petersburg 199034, Russia
{postmaster,skrelin,evgrafova}@phonetics.pu.ru,
andrey.barabanov@gmail.com

Abstract. The paper is concerned with the phonetic aspects of speech synthesis of Russian vowels with the use of a voice source signal. An original method of recording the glottal wave synchronously with an output speech signal was employed to obtain the experimental material. Several types of perceptual experiments were carried out. The comparison of the recorded signals allowed us to analyze the structure of the speech signal at different stages of its generation. The source-filter interaction is analyzed by speech signal filtering. The transfer functions of the articulation for the Russian vowels were obtained. The transfer functions and voice source signals of different vowels were used to generate new signals. The resulted signals were analyzed. We examined the way the fundamental frequency, voice quality and a type of phoneme influence the source-filter interaction. In the paper the perceptual experiments, acoustic analysis and signal generation results are presented.

Keywords: Phonetics · Voice source · Source-filter interaction · Formants · Formant synthesis

1 Introduction

For the last 50 years four basic approaches to modeling and synthesis of speech have been developed at many research centers. These are articulatory, formant, concatenative and parametric ones [1]. The most flexible models for speech synthesis are the articulatory and the formant. However, the synthesized speech tends to be of bad quality in terms of intelligibility and naturalness. The concatenative synthesis for a long time (since 80s of the 20th century) has provided the best compromise between price and quality of the synthesized speech. However, its main drawback is low naturalness of sound caused by a large number of joints between the basic elements in the compilation process and a need to modify the acoustic parameters (primarily, pitch, duration and spectral components). As a result, HMM-based Unit-Selection synthesis has been focused on. Recently this model has been of great interest for research and speech applications [2–5]. However, those systems require large speech corpora (up to 100 h of

© Springer International Publishing Switzerland 2016
A. Ronzhin et al. (Eds.): SPECOM 2016, LNAI 9811, pp. 531–538, 2016.
DOI: 10.1007/978-3-319-43958-7_64

speech). The annotated large speech corpora make it possible to concatenate any speech phrase using available sound units and sequences with proper acoustic characteristics and correct intonation (Unit-Selection). Besides, it is possible to generate speech signal employing method of parametric synthesis. The advantage of this model is high naturalness of speech signal. The acoustic modification of speech sounds is significantly reduced. However, on the other hand, this model is cost and effort consuming as it requires large speech annotated corpora. Besides, this system cannot be adapted to a new speaker without recording a new corpus. Moreover, the systems of automatic speech synthesis are usually limited in intonation modelling.

Traditionally, the process of speech production is described as having several successive stages which are initialization, phonation, articulation and radiance of speech signal [6–10].The observed interaction between the two parts of the vocal tract does not make the classic linear source-filter theory completely consistent. It is important to obtain the voice source signal and analyze its nature for different fields of speech science and speech technology. There exist different voice source models that are applied to the majority of linguistic research and speech applications. Apart from LF-model [11–13] there are biomechanical models of the voice source and the vocal folds [14–17]. The source-filter interactions that involve changes in vocal fold vibration have been demonstrated by investigators [9, 16, 18–20].

Our research is aimed at analyzing the signal of the voice source and the output speech signal to consider the non-linearity of the vocal tract system. The main task was to produce synthesized vowels of high naturalness which can be obtained without recording a large speech corpus for a new speaker. The coprocessing of these signals allowed us to construct the transfer functions of the articulatory component for vowels, the frequency constituents of different kinds of vowels and their variations. We used the transfer functions of certain vowels and the voice source signals of others to synthesize vowel sounds (Sect. 4). A group of expert phoneticians were involved into the auditory tests of the obtained speech signals.

This paper is organized as follows. In Sect. 2, we introduce the equipment and subjects. Section 3 presents the perceptual analysis. Section 4 describes the acoustic analysis and the procedure of generating new signals. In Sect. 5 we discuss the results. In Sect. 6 we formulate our conclusions.

2   Equipment and Subjects

The recordings were made in the recording studio. Multichannel recording system Motu Traveler and WaveLab program were used. The recordings had a sample rate of 44100 Hz and a bitrate of 16 bits. Two types of microphones were used. The capacitor microphone AKG HSC200 was placed in the output of the speakers mouth (Microphone External - ME). The miniature microphone QueAudio (d = 2.3 mm, waterproof) was located in the proximity of the speaker's vocal folds (Microphone Internal - MI) with the use of special medical equipment. This procedure was performed by a phoniatrician [21–24].

The subjects of the experiment were 3 male and 3 female speakers. Each speaker pronounced each of the 6 Russian vowels: /a/, /e/, /i/, /ɨ/, /o/ and /u/ in different pitch modes: comfort, high, low, rising and falling. Apart from the isolated vowels the speakers were asked to read a set of words.

3   Perceptual Analysis

The aim of the experiment was to find out if a voice source signal could be identified as a speech sound and which Russian vowel it could be associated with. A group of informants (23 individuals) were involved into perceptual tests. The samples were organized on a random basis. The informants were asked to assign each stimulus to one of the six Russian vowel phonemes. The questionnaire had also *no decision* option.

The tests results showed that the vowel [a] stayed most intelligible and were identified correctly in most cases. The vowels [e], [o] and [u] were second intelligible (Table 1). However, there were strong confusions of [i] and [u], [i] and [ɨ] and [u] and [ɨ]. Besides, some informants reported that all vowel types were perceived as labialized.

Table 1. Confusion matrix of vowel identification (in percentage)

	decisions (%)						
	a	*e*	*i*	*ɨ*	*o*	*u*	no decision
a	75	16	0	1	4	1	2
e	18	52	0	2	18	4	6
i	1	2	25	30	2	33	5
ɨ	0	5	6	38	7	40	5
o	2	12	0	7	57	18	5
u	1	1	5	25	9	51	8

Table 1 above shows the identification strategy. Each row contains percentage of answers of recognition for an input vowel indicated in the first column.

4   Acoustic Analysis and New Speech Signals Generation

The analysis of the vowel spectra shows that the signal from MI contains the frequency constituents of the vowel formants (resonance frequencies of the set of pharynx, nasal and oral cavities) However, the frequency constituents are weakened in amplitude. It can be assumed that it is caused by the reflection of the acoustic energy from the articulation system upstream [22, 25]. As well as this the plots show that the signals can be very different for the two microphones. For example, see the plot for the vowel [ɨ] (Fig. 1).

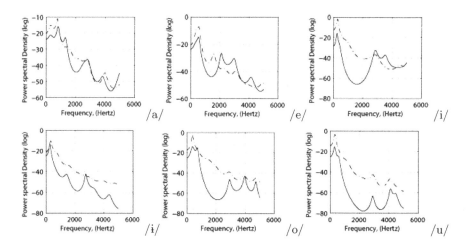

Fig. 1. Spectral densities for Russian vowels [a], [e], [i], [ɨ], [o], [u]. The solid line shows the spectral density of ME signal and the dashed line shows the spectral density of MI signal.

The comparison of the recorded signals and the simulated ones including the source-filter interaction was performed in previous work [26]. Thus, the reflected energy in the nonlinear acoustic system of the vocal tract affects the work of the voice source and the glottal wave characteristics. This energy is reflected again to the articulation system and its frequency constituents are changed. The next step was the discrimination and modelling of the transfer functions of the articulation. The transfer functions and the formant positions were estimated using the algorithm described in the research by Evdokimova [22, 24, 27].

The transfer functions were estimated as the Fourier transform of the pulse response. The pulse response of the length of $2^{16} = 65536$ samples was estimated by the LS approach. The superfast Schur algorithm for Toeplitz matrix inversion was implemented. The resulting transfer function was then smoothed to prevent a jitter between support frequencies where the estimates are reliable. The program uses the synchronized signals from both microphones and calculates the transfer functions of the vowels.

5   Results of Vowel Synthesis

The obtained transfer functions of the vowels were used to generate new signals. The voice source signals of different vowels with different fundamental frequency characteristics were the input for these transfer functions. Our aim was to find out which of the following would influence the resulted signal more: the characteristics of the voice source signal or the transfer function of the articulation system.

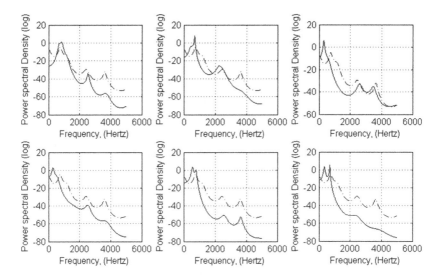

Fig. 2. Spectral densities for ME signal of the input vowel [a] (the dashed line in all six figures) and the resulted output vowels with added transfer function of articulation system for the vowels [a], [e], [i], [ɨ], [o], [u] (solid line). Female speaker.

- The first experiment was the generation of the vowels using their own voice source input signal. The results showed that the produced sound had a good quality.
- The next step was the filtering of the voice source signals of higher or lower fundamental frequency. The results showed that the synthesized vowels and the input signals had similar pitch.
- The third step was to mix the transfer functions of vowel type with voice source signals of the other vowel types for the same speaker. In Figs. 2 and 3 the results for two vowels are presented.
  The MI signal of the [a] realization was used as an input signal for the transfer functions of another [a], [e], [i], [ɨ], [o], [u], realizations. The same procedure was performed with voice source signal of the vowel [ɨ]. The choice of the input signals was influenced by the results of the perceptual analysis which showed that [a] MI signal was identified as [a] in most cases. Also the auditory analysis showed [ɨ] MI signal as the most unintelligible.
- The final step in the filtering procedure was to mix the voice source signals and the transfer functions of the same vowel phonemes for different speakers. The MI signal of the one [a] realization was used as an input signal for the transfer function of the [a] of another speaker. The mixing of the male voices showed that the resulted vowel had the same formants as the transfer function had. However, the perceived voice quality had the characteristics of the speaker whose input voice source signal was used.

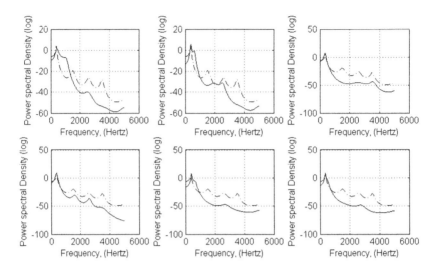

Fig. 3. Spectral densities for ME signal of the input vowel [ɨ] (the dashed line in all six figures) and the resulted output vowels with added transfer function of articulation system for the vowels [a], [e], [i], [ɨ], [o], [u] (solid line). Female speaker.

6   Conclusions

1. The acoustic analysis and perception experiments allowed us to specify and improve the source-filter model. The results confirmed the fact of the interaction between the two parts of the vocal tract.
2. The used approach allowed reliable automatic discrimination of the vowel formant structure by processing the speech signal.
3. In experiments with mixing voice source signals and articulatory component of different vowels and speakers the resulted signal had the voice quality of the input signal.
4. The reflected signal of the feedback section was sometimes stronger and influenced the resulting signal more in the experiments of using voice source signal of one phoneme realisation with the transfer function of other vowel phoneme. Therefore we can conclude that the speech synthesis system should have the voice source signals for different phoneme types.
5. The constructed model of the filter part of the vocal tract completely corresponds to the basic phonetic laws. It adds the accuracy to the existing models of the speech production and can be used for solving specific problems of speech technologies.

Acknowledgement. The authors would like to thank the Saint Petersburg State University. This work has been carried out in the framework of SPbSU projects n. 31.37.353.2015 and n. 6.37.349.2015.

References

1. Lobanov, B.M., Tsirulnik, L.I.: Computer synthesis and speech cloning. Belarussian science (2008)
2. Mizutani, T., Kagoshima, T.: Concatenative speech synthesis based on the plural unit selection and fusion method. IEICE Trans. Inf. Syst. **E88–D**(11), 2565–2572 (2005)
3. Ni, J., Shiga, Y., Hori, Ch., Kidawara, Y.: A targets-based superpositional model of fundamental frequency contours applied to HMM-based speech synthesis. In: INTERSPEECH 2013, pp. 1052–1056 (2013)
4. Raitio, T., Kane, J., Drugman, T., Gobl, Ch.: HMM-based synthesis of creaky voice. In: INTERSPEECH 2013, pp. 2316–2320 (2013)
5. Nurminen, J., Sil'en, H., Gabbouj, M.: Speaker-specific retraining for enhanced compression of unit selection text-to-speech databases. In: INTERSPEECH 2013, pp. 388–391 (2013)
6. Bondarko L.V. Phonetics of Russian modern language. SPbSU (1998). (in Russian)
7. Kodzasov S.V., Krivnova O.F.: General Phonetics. Moscow (2001)
8. Fant, G.: Acoustic Theory of Speech Production. Mouton, Netherlands (1960)
9. Flanagan, J.L.: Source-system interaction in the vocal tract. Ann. N.Y. Acad. Sci. **155**, 9–17 (1968)
10. Flanagan, J.L.: Speech Analysis, Synthesis, and Perception. Springer, New York (1972)
11. Fant, G.: The voice source in connected speech. Speech Commun. **22**(2–3), 125–139 (1997)
12. Fant, G., Liljencrants, J., Lin, Q.: A four-parameter model of glottal flow. Technical Report, STL-QPSR (1985)
13. Alzamendi, G.A., Schlotthauer, G., Torres, M.E.: Formulation of a stochastic glottal source model inpired on deterministic Lilencrants-Fant model. In: International Workshop on Models and Analysis of Vocal Emissions for Biomedical Applications - MAVEBA 2015, Florence, pp. 15–18 (2015)
14. Stevens, K.: Acoustic Phonetics. The MIT Press, Cambridge (1998). 02141
15. Howe, M.S., McGowan, R.S.: On the single-mass model of the vocal folds. Fluid. Dyn. Res. **42**(1), 15001 (2010). doi:10.1088/0169-5983/42/1/015001
16. Titze, I.R.: Non-linear source-filter coupling in phonation Theory. J. Acoust. Soc. Am. **123**, 2733–2749 (2008). doi:10.1121/1.2832337
17. Zanartu, M., Mongeau, L., Wodicka, G.R.: Influence of acoustic loading on an effective single mass model of the vocal folds. J. Acoust. Soc. Am. **121**, 1119–1129 (2007). doi:10.1121/1.2409491
18. Hatzikirou, H., Fitch, W.T.S., Herzel, H.: Voice instabilities due to source-tract interactions. Acta Acust. Acust. **92**, 468–475 (2006)
19. Miller, D.G., Schutte, H.K.: Mixing the registers: Glottal source or vocal tract. Folia Phoniatr. Logop. **57**, 278–291 (2005)
20. Mergell, P., Herzel, H.: Modeling biphonation - The role of the vocal tract. Speech Commun. **22**, 141–154 (1997). doi:10.1016/S0167-6393(97)00016-2
21. Evgrafova, K., Evdokimova, V., Skrelin, P., Chukaeva, T., Shvalev, N.: A new technique to record a voice source signal. In: International Workshop on Models and Analysis of Vocal Emissions for Biomedical Applications - MAVEBA 2013, Florence, pp. 181–182 (2013)

22. Evdokimova, V., Evgrafova, K., Skrelin, P., Chukaeva, T., Shvalev, N.: Detection of the frequency characteristics of the articulation system with the use of voice source signal recording method. In: Železný, M., Habernal, I., Ronzhin, A. (eds.) SPECOM 2013. LNCS, vol. 8113, pp. 108–115. Springer, Heidelberg (2013)
23. Barabanov, A., Evdokimova, V., Skrelin, P.: Estimation of vowel spectra near vocal chords with restoration of a clipped speech signal. In: Ronzhin, A., Potapova, R., Fakotakis, N. (eds.) SPECOM 2015. LNCS, vol. 9319, pp. 209–216. Springer, Heidelberg (2015)
24. Evdokimova, V., Skrelin, P., Evgrafova, K., Chukaeva, T., Shvalev, N.: Investigating voice source signal filtering be articulation component. Teoreticheskaya i prikladnaya lingvistika **1**(3), 37–49 (2015). (in Russian)
25. Evdokimova V., Evgrafova K., Skrelin P.: Investigating source - filter interaction to specify classic speech production theory. In: Proceedings of the 18th International Congress of Phonetic Sciences. The Scottish Consortium for ICPhS 2015. The University of Glasgow, Glasgow, UK. ISBN 978-0-85261-941-4. Paper number 04.621.1-5. http://www.icphs2015.info/pdfs/Papers/ICPHS0462.pdf. Retrieved from (2015)
26. Fraile, R., Evdokimova, V.V., Evgrafova, K.V., Godino-Llorente, J.I., Skrelin, P.A.: Analysis of measured and simulated supraglottal acoustic waves. J. Voice (2015). doi:10.1016/j.jvoice.2015.08.006
27. Evdokimova, V.V.: The use of vocal tract model for constructing the vocal structure of the vowels. In: SPECOM 2006, Saint-Petersburg, pp. 210–214, 25–29 June 2006

Polybasic Attribution of Social Network Discourse

Rodmonga Potapova[1]([✉]) and Vsevolod Potapov[2]

[1] Institute of Applied and Mathematical Linguistics,
Moscow State Linguistic University, Ostozhenka 38, Moscow 119034, Russia
`rkpotapova@yandex.ru`
[2] Faculty of Philology, Lomonosov Moscow State University,
GSP-1, Leninskie Gory, Moscow 119991, Russia

Abstract. Nowadays a number of studies have demonstrated the great interest in discourse differences on the domain of monologue, dialogue and polylogue communication on the Internet. This paper describes the results of our investigation regarding relations between some types of deprivation, on the one hand, and, on the other hand, its verbal, paraverbal and non-verbal determinants from emotional and emotional-modal point of view, on the basis of spoken Russian communication by means of YouTube.com, Skype and ok.ru videohostings. The research is aimed at developing a knowledge database for the decision-making system and the computer-aided analysis of Russian spoken and written discourses in social network communication on Internet.

Keywords: Deprivation · Social network discourse · Verbal · Paraverbal and non-verbal information · Monologues · Dialogues · Polylogues · Emotional and emotional-modal states

1 Introduction

The fundamental model of human emotional and emotional-modal behaviour regarding interpersonal, socioeconomic, interethnic, interconfessional, political, geopolitical and other types of **deprivation** should include such variables as **value expectations** (expectations, hopes, prospects of future etc.) and **value opportunities** of certain individuals and communities [7,9]. The discrepancy between these values can be defined as a measure of relative **deprivation** (RD) [3,7], which is the principal cause of individual and mass frustration that can lead to realization of conflicts, individual and mass destructive behaviour, all types of aggression, and finally, to terror actions. The research is aimed at handling a major scientific problem of detecting the verbal, paraverbal and non-verbal characteristics of the formation and functioning of a new communication type (electronic social network discourse (SND)) in the global electronic media environment [11–13,23]. The final result of this new type of communication is the social network communication (as a material product) which reflects interpersonal, interethnic, interconfessional, political, geopolitical and socioeconomic

© Springer International Publishing Switzerland 2016
A. Ronzhin et al. (Eds.): SPECOM 2016, LNAI 9811, pp. 539–546, 2016.
DOI: 10.1007/978-3-319-43958-7_65

relations. This is expressed in the specifics of verbal, paraverbal and non-verbal correlates of written and spoken utterances. The original assumption of the current research would be that spoken and written language is a product of complex polyfunctional human activity, the system which includes all components of psychophysical, functional-motoric and mental-cognitive-intellectual subsystems regarding the scientific aspects of biology, psychology, physiology, biomechanics, anthropophonics, semiotics, cognitology, cogitology, and sociopsychology [1,8,14–16,21]. At the same time the additional multitude of various components of human speech activity constitutes **a qualitatively new integral product**, whose features do not make the sum of the features of its components, being realized both in spoken and written form. The functioning of the emotional and emotional-modal mechanism is regarded as a special feature of the speech product and has a direct cause-and-effect relationship with all its components, which has been thoroughly studied regarding the functioning of psychological and value-oriented mechanisms of human life activities.

2   Research, Method, Results

The special issue of this research is to establish the relationship between peculiarities of human speech activity and various manifestations of deprivation (Fig. 1). It is known that *the verbal, paraverbal and non-verbal mechanism* of deprivation manifestation concerning the emotional and emotional-modal level with reference to specific features of speech production and speech perception of written and spoken language at the initial stage has been examined [7–16,22,24].

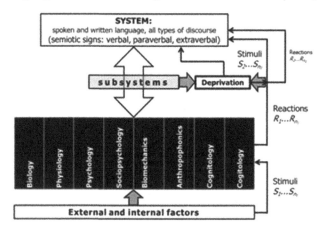

Fig. 1. Mechanism of influence of deprivation factors on the discourse production system

Addressing the abovementioned problem (regarding social networks; video hosting service YouTube.com and Skype VoIP technology) in order to define verbal, paraverbal and non-verbal determinants of emotional and emotional-modal human behaviour under conditions of multifactor deprivation will allow one to establish the system of semantic content determinants used for manipulating the recipients consciousness with destructive intentions. This refers first of all to pronunciation correlates of the means, used to communicate various types of deprivation, and to establishment of the forms of dependence between the auditory-perceptual and acoustic determinants of human emotional and emotional-modal behaviour under conditions of the presence of various types of deprivation on the basis of communication and social media tools. Revealing of verbal, paraverbal and non-verbal specificity of SND formation and functioning in the global electronic media environment is based on the definition of the SND as a special electronic macropolylogue, considering the relevant categories of its form, content and functional weight [17]: SND form types of electronic macropolylogue: distant, indirect, real-time (on-line) and put off-time (off-line), single-vector polyvector, monochronous polychronous; SND content types of electronic macropolylogue: monothematic polythematic, high contextual low contextual, provoking debates, actions, deeds not provoking debates, actions, deeds; SND function types of electronic macropolylogue: informative with the senders point of view, influencing, containing certain verbal, paraverbal and non-verbal means which can produce influence on recipient of the message, provoking with a certain aim to commit specific actions (particularly destructive, realized according to the "stimulus → pragmatic reaction in a form of specific destructive action" scheme), recipients consciousness manipulation, aimed at a limited target group of users aimed at an infinite number of users; types of factors of electronic macropolylogue SND that influence upon the specificity of communication: psycho-physiological (e.g., age-specific, gender-related, pathological, emotional, etc.), ethnic, socio-economic, political and geopolitical, confessional, cultural [4,5], pragmatic, moral and ethical.

Thus, the SND in the global network is characterized by irreversibility, contextuality, dynamism, social relations hierarchy violation (democratic character/pseudodemocratic character), the combination of monochronism and polychronism considering the high speed (tempo) of information dissemination, the combination of statements of low- and high-context culture representatives, the increase in interpersonal space, an infinite number of themes, causal conditionality, recipients conscience manipulation, emotional and emotional-modal richness. It is obvious that all the above mentioned SND characteristics contribute to the formation of a cognitive, cogitive/verbal and emotional and emotional-modal portrait of the electronic personality [7,9]. Problem domain analysis as well as the study of earlier researches of emotionally coloured speech together with speech correlates of various emotional states made it possible to form an approximate list of emotions and emotional-modal states which provided the basis for a single-purpose survey intended for conducting perceptual-auditory experiments in order to assess and describe the emotional content of speech in target phonograms as well as to model the range of identifiable emotions on the basis of clusterization of characteristic values with a view to creating a multimedia based atlas of emotional and emotional-modal states in real conditions. Experimental studies aimed at finding possible sources of target phonograms and videograms determined the following ways of collecting speech material: hidden audio or video recording of people in real-world situations which involve emotionally coloured utterances (primarily in conflicts or emergencies); the analysis of audio and video recordings of one of the abovementioned types on the Internet in the public domain.

Within the framework of the present research a primary analysis of verbal, paraverbal and non-verbal features of informants communicative behavior was performed, enabling to correlate these features with manifestation of various types of deprivations associated with political, geopolitical, socio-economic and confessional issues. The material of the research is based on videos posted on the most visited video hosting YouTube.com, as well as those posted in social network ok.ru/video and Skype. The purpose of the research is identification of the main explicit features of informants verbal behavior, correlation of these features with demonstrated emotional and emotional-modal state and degree of deprivation, as well as an analysis of videos as SND elements. The research objectives at this stage of project are as follows: to create a database of video fragments posted on YouTube.com, ok.ru/video and Skype sites; to classify selected video contents by types of deprivation; to conduct a perceptual-auditory and visual analysis for subsequent identification of verbal, paravererbal and non-verbal markers of emotional and emotional-modal states and to correlate the obtained data with types of deprivation; to formalize the obtained data by constructing tables including SND parameters regarding its form, content, function, types of influence, emotional and emotional-modal coloring (SND forms are: distant, mediated, real-time (on-line) and postponed (off-line), single vector polyvector, monochronous polychronous; SND content types are: monothematic polythematic, informationally rich (highly contextual) informationally poor (low contextual), provoking debates, actions, deeds not provoking debates, actions, deeds; SND functions are: informing, containing the message senders point of view; influencing, containing special linguistic means of influencing the recipient; rousing a specific action or deed (in particular, destructive ones implemented by the scheme stimulus → pragmatic response in the form of a specific destructive action), manipulating the recipients consciousness; aimed at limited group of users aimed at an unlimited number of users; factors influencing the specifics of SND communication: psycho-physiological (e.g., age, gender, pathological, emotional, etc.); ethnic; socio-economic; political and geopolitical; confessional; cultural; pragmatic; moral and ethical) [7,9].

The objects of this research are spoken statements within the SND (monologues, dialogues [2], macropolylogues). At this stage of the study 287 videos were selected for a database that had been posted during the period from 02.04.2011 to 29.10.2015. The main focus was on the videos of 2014–2015 (80 % of the total number of records) as the most relevant and suitable ones in the current situation in the Russian Federation. The material subjects regarding deprivation were as follows: internal Russian politics (government; legal systems, opposition, etc.); geopolitical relations (Ukraine, Ukrainian immigrants/refugees; Syria, etc.); socio-economic relations (crisis, ruble fall/price increases; sanctions;

pensions, wages, living conditions; stores; ecology; migrants/guest workers); interpersonal relationships (family and children, disabled people); confessional issues (Christianity, Islam). The share of video records for each thematic group in the database is shown in the diagram (Fig. 2). Thematically, the analyzed material shows a significant prevalence of Russias internal policy and socio-economic relations as subjects of the SND.

At the preliminary stage 45 video records (105 subjects) were analyzed on political, geo-political and socio-economic issues. For each subject, a perceptual-auditory analysis (according to the instructions developed for perceptual-auditory and visual analysis) were performed [12]. The number of listeners and visual recipients was N = 60. Thus, for each subjects speech a description was drawn up, which included such parameters as: nonverbal behavior: gestures, e.g. hands crossed on his/her chest; hand movements in time with speech; facial motions, etc.; speech style: e.g. strained; prosodic means of conveying the emotional and emotional-modal state: melodic register; melodic range; predominance of melodic finalization forms; tempo; loudness; presence of certain segments of maximum loud singled out within an utterance; pausation; duration of pauses; predominance of unfilled pauses; timbre (mellow, harsh, etc.); rhythm patterns [6]; lexis used in the SND; emotion/emotional-modal state shown: e.g. pretentiousness, dissatisfaction; SND parameters by its form: e.g. not mediated, in real time; polyvector; monochronous (Fig. 3); SND parameters by its content: e.g. monothematic, informationally poor, not provoking debates; SND parameters by its functions: e.g. containing the message senders point of view, aimed at an unlimited number of users; SND parameters by factors influencing the specifics of communication: e.g. geopolitical factors. Thus, for each subject, verbal, paraverbal and non-verbal markers of emotional and emotional-modal state were obtained, and these markers were correlated with some types of deprivation. The following results were obtained (Figs. 3, 4 and 5).

Regarding SND forms, the following results were obtained: for off-line discourses: monochronous polyvector types are predominant; for on-line discourses: single-vector types prevail. SND content types are distributed as follows (Fig. 4). As can be seen, the following SND content types dominate: monothematic, informationally unsaturated, not provoking debates. As for polythematic types, those discourses that are informationally rich and provoking debates form the vast majority. Thus, there are less polythematic discourses than monothematic ones, but they are richer in information and provoke debates. Speech activity types in the SND is represented as follows (Fig. 5). The SND is characterized by the predominance of males in all types of speech activity - monologues, dialogues and polylogues. The monological form is the primary one. The negative emotional-modal states anxiety, depression, sorrow and sadness form the dominant group of analysed states of SND-communicants. And all negative emotional-modal states in the SND were evaluated as strong and weak ones. Our results on the domain of emotional-modal state recognition show that the analyzed SND states were evaluated first of all as strong and weak negative ones. Main determinants of all types of deprivation are depression, anxiety, sorrow, sadness.

Fig. 2. Thematic distribution of material on YouTube.com video hosting, as well as in social network Odnoklassniki (ok.ru) and in Skype for 2014–2015

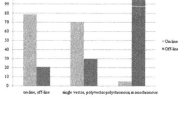

Fig. 3. SND forms compared (in %)

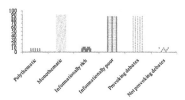

Fig. 4. SND content types (in %)

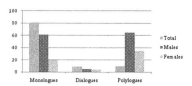

Fig. 5. SND by speech activity types (participation of males/females in various types in %)

3   Conclusion

The SND can be regarded as a special lingua-technological phenomenon with its own form, content and functions. The SND is intended for a wide range of audience like a macropolylogue, which comprises an open set of dialogues, whose communicants can be both in non-antagonistic dialogical and in antagonistic antidialogical relations to each other. Special mention should go to pseudo-dialogues, i.e. absurd conversations, chatter, gossip, demagogy etc. [2]. A huge number of pseudo-dialogues have recently been recorded. They form pseudo-polylogues which include "likes", "reposts", "fakes", thus increasing the index of "self-worth" of social network users, the so called "electronic personality" in the world of information technology. In view of the SND global dimension, its main features, taking into account its categories, forms and functions, can be characterized by the presence of **the combinatorial set of simultaneity and non-simultaneity as well as the one of monochronism and polychronism. The combinatorial set of high contextuality and low contextuality is characteristic of the SND semantic aspect** [4,5,7,9]. The essential features of culture as well as its distinctiveness for ethnic models are supposed to diffuse for the objective reasons of informational globalization. As a consequence, they form a new **multiple-purpose combination, which manifests itself as the**

SND, which, in its turn, is charged with **communicative, informing, influencing and provocative functions**. In consideration of the foregoing the aim of our research in the future is as follows: to determine the role of verbal, paraverbal and non-verbal means in defining peoples vision of extremism as well as hatred, enmity and discord incitement on the basis of deprivation phenomenon; to determine verbal, paraverbal and non-verbal means used to manipulate the recipients conscience; to systematize lexical and prosodic means, used to form conceptual categories, concepts criteria and frame knowledge structures for the semantic field of deprivation; to classify verbal, paraverbal and non-verbal means, used to represent and form conceptual metaphors in the SND; to develop major criteria of the destructively oriented SND expertise considering deprivation forms reconstruction with the aim of forecasting.

As a result, to the fore comes the problem of various interpretations of the range of implicit meanings of discourse fragments based on the verbal, paraverbal and non-verbal communication [17–20], inclusive of presupposition, implication, connotation, metamessage and background knowledge, on the one hand, and the written and spoken language segment/suprasegment information, on the other. This will directly serve as a conceptual tool for solving problems related to SND nature and functions.

Acknowledgments. This research is supported by Russian Science Foundation, Project N14-18-01059 (2014–2016).

References

1. Bertau, M.C.: Voice as heuristic device to integrate biological and social sciences. A comment to Sidtis & Kreimans in the beginning was the familiar voice. Integr. Psychol. Behav. Sci. **46**(2), 160–171 (2012)
2. Bush, G.: Dialogue Studies and Creation. Avots, Riga (1985) (in Russian)
3. Gurr, T.: Why Men Rebel. Princeton University Press, Princeton (1970)
4. Hall, E.T.: Beyond Culture. Anchor Press, New York (1976)
5. Hall, E.T., Hall, M.R.: Understanding Cultural Differences: Germans, French and Americans. Intercultural Press, Yarmouth (1990)
6. Potapov, V.: Speech rhythmic patterns of the Slavic languages. In: Ronzhin, A., Potapova, R., Delic, V. (eds.) SPECOM 2014. LNCS, vol. 8773, pp. 425–434. Springer, Heidelberg (2014)
7. Potapova, R.K.: From deprivation to aggression: verbal and non-verbal social network communication. In: Materials of the VI International Conference Global Science and Innovation, Chicago, USA, vol. 1, pp. 129–137 (2015)
8. Potapova, R.K.: Speech: Communication, Information, Cybernetics, 5th edn. URSS, Moscow (2015) (in Russian)
9. Potapova, R.K.: Social network discourse as an object of interdisciplinary research. In: Proceedings of the 2nd International Scientific Conference Discourse as Social Activity: Priorities and Perspectives, pp. 20–22. Moscow State Linguistic University, Moscow, RF (2014) (in Russian)
10. Potapova, R., Komalova, L.: Auditory-perceptual recognition of the emotional state of aggression. In: Ronzhin, A., Potapova, R., Fakotakis, N. (eds.) SPECOM 2015. LNCS, vol. 9319, pp. 89–95. Springer, Heidelberg (2015)

11. Potapova, R., Potapov, V.: Associative mechanism of Foreign spoken language perception (Forensic Phonetic Aspect). In: Ronzhin, A., Potapova, R., Delic, V. (eds.) SPECOM 2014. LNCS, vol. 8773, pp. 113–122. Springer, Heidelberg (2014)
12. Potapova, R., Potapov, V.: Auditory and visual recognition of emotional behaviour of foreign language subjects (by Native and Non-native speakers). In: Železný, M., Habernal, I., Ronzhin, A. (eds.) SPECOM 2013. LNCS, vol. 8113, pp. 62–69. Springer, Heidelberg (2013)
13. Potapova, R., Potapov, V.: Cognitive mechanism of semantic content decoding of spoken discourse in noise. In: Ronzhin, A., Potapova, R., Fakotakis, N. (eds.) SPECOM 2015. LNCS, vol. 9319, pp. 153–160. Springer, Heidelberg (2015)
14. Potapova, R.K., Potapov, V.V.: Kommunikative Sprechtaetigkeit. Russland und Deutschland im Vergleich. Boehlau Verlag, Koeln, Weimar, Wien (2011)
15. Potapova, R.K., Potapov, V.V.: Language, Speech, Personality. Publishing House Languages of Slavic Cultures, Moscow (2006) (in Russian)
16. Potapova, R.K., Potapov, V.V.: Speech Communication: From Sound to Utterance. Publishing House Languages of Slavic Cultures, Moscow (2012) (in Russian)
17. Potapova, R.K., Potapov, V.V.: XIV International conference Speech and computer (SPECOM2011). Voprosy jazykoznanija 5, 146–154 (2012) (in Russian)
18. Potapova, R.K., Potapov, V.V.: XV International conference Speech and computer (SPECOM2013). Voprosy jazykoznanija 3, 138–140 (2014) (in Russian)
19. Potapova, R.K., Potapov, V.V.: XVI International conference Speech and computer (SPECOM2014). Voprosy jazykoznanija 4, 147–154 (2015) (in Russian)
20. Potapova, R.K., Potapov, V.V.: XVII International conference Speech and computer (SPECOM2015). Voprosy jazykoznanija 3, 151–154 (2016) (in Russian)
21. Potapova, R.K., Potapov, V.V., Lebedeva, N.N., Agibalova, T.V.: Interdisciplinarity in the Investigation of Speech Polyinformativeness. Publishing House Languages of Slavic Cultures, Moscow (2015) (in Russian)
22. Potapova, R., Sobakin, A., Maslov, A.: On the possibility of the skype channel speaker identification (on the Basis of Acoustic Parameters). In: Ronzhin, A., Potapova, R., Delic, V. (eds.) SPECOM 2014. LNCS, vol. 8773, pp. 329–336. Springer, Heidelberg (2014)
23. Ronzhin, A., Budkov, V.: Speaker turn detection based on multimodal situation analysis. In: Železný, M., Habernal, I., Ronzhin, A. (eds.) SPECOM 2013. LNCS, vol. 8113, pp. 302–309. Springer, Heidelberg (2013)
24. Zhenilo, V., Potapov, V.: Invariant components of speech signals: analysis and visualization. In: Ronzhin, A., Potapova, R., Fakotakis, N. (eds.) SPECOM 2015. LNCS, vol. 9319, pp. 251–258. Springer, Heidelberg (2015)

Precise Estimation of Harmonic Parameter Trend and Modification of a Speech Signal

Andrey Barabanov$^{(\boxtimes)}$, Valentin Magerkin, and Evgenij Vikulov

Saint Petersburg State University,
Universitetskaya nab., 7/9, Saint Petersburg, Russia
Andrey.Barabanov@gmail.com, magerkin93@gmail.com, jenyav94@gmail.com

Abstract. The high frequency part of the voiced speech signal beyond 4 kHz is very difficult to study and to decompose into harmonics. In the HNM this spectrum part is assumed to be noise. In this paper it is shown that the main problem is numerical. Faster harmonics have faster trends. It is necessary to implement precise estimation technique to estimate a high frequency complex amplitude on a short time interval. An illustrative example is supplied. In the second part of the paper a new modification technique is proposed for interpolation of the complex amplitudes in the case of intonation modification. Reliable estimates of harmonic complex amplitudes are necessary as inputs. Then a nonlinear rule is formulated that incorporates specific features of formants and their slopes.

Keywords: Harmonic speech model · Parameter estimation · Speech modification

1 Introduction

The parametric model analysis and synthesis is a powerful tool for speech signal description with various applications. The Harmonic-plus-Noise Model (HNM) and its modifications was the base of the parametric approach [1,2]. The high frequency spectrum can be studied in more detail and the noise model is replaced by harmonic trends. Another approach is based on instantaneous harmonic parameters and wavelet packets [3,4].

At the stage of analysis, a speech signal is divided in a sequence of overlapping frames. A signal in a frame is to be approximated by a parametric formula, that is, a full set of parameters is estimated. The obtained model can be used for various purposes including synthesis, modification, recognition. The most popular models are stationary and linear. The stationary harmonic model in the frame is given by the following equation:

$$\widehat{s}_t = \sum_{m=-M}^{M} a_m e^{2\pi i m f t}$$

© Springer International Publishing Switzerland 2016
A. Ronzhin et al. (Eds.): SPECOM 2016, LNAI 9811, pp. 547–554, 2016.
DOI: 10.1007/978-3-319-43958-7_66

where t is the time instant, f is the fundamental, M is the number of harmonics, a_m is the complex amplitude. It holds $a_{-m} = \bar{a}_m$ because the value of $\widehat{s}_t$ is real. The full set of parameters consists of a single value of f and of a set of amplitudes $A = (a_m)_{m=-M}^{M}$.

Each term in the sum can be considered as an independent harmonic that changes from frame to frame. This is clearly seen for the low frequency part of spectrum. A low frequency harmonic has a couple of periods and is nearly stationary in the frame. That is enough to estimate the harmonic parameters.

High frequency harmonic signals can be recognised by the ear on a short time interval because it contains many periods. This time interval can be shorter than the interval of analysis. Therefore, a transient may occur in the high frequency part of spectrum inside the time interval of analysis. This can be a reason to declare the high frequency spectrum of the voiced speech signal as a noise and to apply the harmonic model to the low frequency spectrum only.

The another problem is a contradiction between the time and frequency resolution. Any pair of neighbouring harmonics in the sum of the harmonic model has the frequency difference f. An interference of the harmonics occurs on short time intervals or under nonstationary conditions. It is very difficult to estimate model parameters if there are a couple of interfered pairs of harmonics.

In this paper, a precise implementation of the LS algorithm is presented that finds a minimum of the mean square error:

$$E(A, f) = \sum_{t \in \Delta} |w_t(s_t - \widehat{s}_t)|^2,$$

where $w = (w_t)_{t \in \Delta}$ is an appropriate window.

2   High Frequency Spines Separation

The speech signal in Fig. 1 is examined as an illustrative example. It contains a syllable /zu/.

A spectrogram of the central part containing the allophone /z/ is shown in Fig. 2.

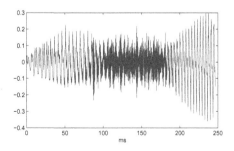

Fig. 1. The speech signal /zu/

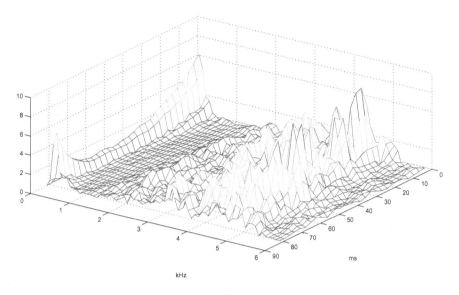

Fig. 2. The spectrogram of the allophone /z/. The energy is concentrated around 5 kHz

Notice that there are several spines in the high frequency part of the spectrogram that are located closely. Nevertheless, the precise technique of harmonic separtion in the LS estimation identifies the spines that are the trends of harmonic signals constituting the high frequency consonant /z/. This precise estimation is necessary for the accurate modification of intonation.

Frequencies of harmonics in the high frequency part of the spectrum are very sensitive to the Pitch value. Estimation error of a harmonic frequency of a voiced signal leads to complete failure in amplitude and phase estimation. Therefore, accuracy of the Pitch estimation is especially important for high frequency consonants.

The central part of the signal contains the allophone /z/. Spectra of two frames of this signal of the length of 50 ms are shown in Figs. 3 and 4.

There are two basic approaches to modelling of this type of the spectrum. In the HNM approach this part is assumed to be not structured and therefore its model is a noise. The later modifications of HNM incorporate some regular structure of the high frequency spectrum. In this paper, we consider the pure harmonic model of the full frequency spectrum and try to estimate all the parameters of the harmonic trends.

The Pitch, amplitude and phase parameters were estimated by algorithms described in [5], and the decoder algorithm was described in [6]. The result of the signal resynthesis is shown in Fig. 4. The high frequency harmonics are successively estimated and reproduced (Fig. 5).

The low frequency harmonics change their amplitudes as a rule together with the full sound energy or in transients between allophones. If the high frequency

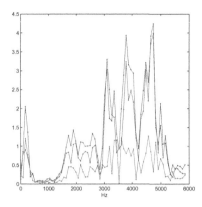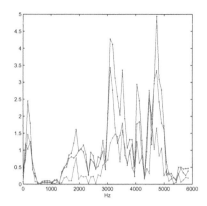

Fig. 3. Spectra of two frames of the allophone /ʑ/, the estimated signal by the harmonic model, and the estimation error

band of the speech signal is relatively wide then it contains much more harmonics than the low frequency band. A distribution of amplitudes and phases of the high frequency harmonics is perceived by the ear. This distribution may change faster than intonation or energy of the full signal. Accuracy of estimation of the model parameters depends on the frame length.

Trends of high frequency harmonics with big amplitudes are shown in Fig. 6.

3   Nonlinear Interpolation of Complex Amplitudes

The main problem of the intonation modification of the speech given by the parametric model consists of phase interpolation. Both the initial model and the modified model are represented by the harmonic models that are decomposed into sums of harmonics with multiple frequencies [6].

The necessary condition for successful implementation of this harmonic-by-harmonic modification is a precise estimation of both frequency and complex amplitude of all the harmonics of the voiced speech signal that was discussed above. In this section, two nonlinear approaches are presented for calculation of complex amplitudes after modification of the Pitch period.

3.1   Direct Complex Smoothing

Let a pair of harmonics with known complex amplitudes have neighbouring frequencies and it is required to estimate a complex amplitude of a harmonic with frequency between them. If the amplitudes of the known harmonics are equal or close then the interpolated harmonic has the same amplitude and its phase is a convex combination of the phases. If one of the known harmonics dominates the other in amplitude then the convex combination can be applied to the complex amplitudes. This idea is implemented in the following rule.

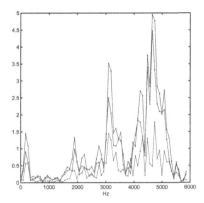

Fig. 4. Spectrum of the another frame of the allophone /ʑ/. The distance between neighbouring peaks of the model is exactly the same (Fundamental) for all harmonics

Consider a harmonic model of a signal. Assume the modified signal is also a sum of harmonics with fixed frequencies. Take one of them with frequency f. The closest left frequency of the harmonics from the initial model and the closest right frequency of the harmonics from the initial model will be denoted by f_l and f_r, respectively. The complex amplitudes are denoted, respectively, by A, A_l and A_r. It is required to estimate A given all other parameters.

It was noticed in experiments that linear interpolation

$$A = A_l \frac{f_r - f}{f_r - f_l} + A_r \frac{f - f_l}{f_r - f_l}$$

is admissible basically at the slope condition, where $|A_l| \gg |A_r|$ or $|A_l| \ll |A_r|$.

The opposite case takes place when both harmonics belong to a formant and they are relatively big. Then the amplitudes $|A_l|$ and $|A_r|$ should be interpolated smoothly and the phases can be interpolated linearly.

The aggregated rule is nonlinear. Denote

$$A_l = a_l e^{i\phi_l}, \qquad A_r = a_r e^{i\phi_r}.$$

Then

$$A = \gamma_r A_l e^{i\delta\gamma_l(\phi_r - \phi_l)} + \gamma_l A_r e^{i\delta\gamma_r(\phi_l - \phi_r)},$$

where

$$\gamma_l = \frac{f - f_l}{f_r - f_l}, \qquad \gamma_r = \frac{f_r - f}{f_r - f_l}$$

and

$$\delta = \frac{2\min\{a_l, a_r\}}{a_l + a_r}.$$

The tests have shown that the smoothing procedure works correctly and does not produce clicks. But it can weaken spectrum peaks in the second formant band. This leads sometimes to a vague sound.

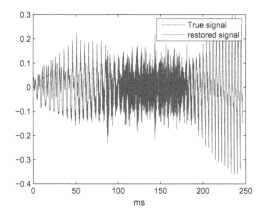

Fig. 5. The input and restored signals. The high frequency consonant was estimated and restored by the harmonic model with a high accuracy

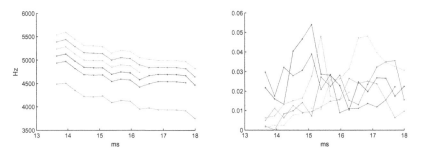

Fig. 6. Frequency trend (left) and amplitude trend (right) of the main harmonics of the allophone from Fig. 1

3.2   Linear Phase Correction

The local formant structure of a sound in a short time analysis is very sensitive to a small deviation of the spectral envelope. The formants do not necessarily correspond to the local maxima of the envelope. Sometimes the second formant is recognised as a small amount of extra energy in the slope of the big first formant. Therefore, smoothing of the spectral envelope by a rough interpolation as in the previous Section is not accurate enough.

The spline interpolation of the real spectral amplitudes has proved to be a stable approach for correct speech signal modification that preserves the formant structure.

Consider the phase interpolation problem. It was studied for a long time [1]. Assume the voiced signal under consideration is locally close to periodic. Then its Fourier transform of the fixed length nearly does not depend on the window position. More precisely, the signal s_t can be expand as:

$$s_t = \sum_{m=0}^{M} a_m \cos\left(\frac{2\pi}{P}mt + \phi_m\right), \qquad t - t_0 = 1, 2, \ldots, T,$$

where T is the length of the interval of the analysis, t_0 is the beginning time instant, P is the Pitch period, M is the number of harmonics, a_m is the (real) amplitude, ϕ_m is the (initial) phase of the m-th harmonic.

The signal s_t contains a constant term and M harmonics with the angle frequencies $f_m = mF$, $F = 2\pi/P$, $1 \le m \le M$. After modification the new period R generates harmonics with the frequencies $g_k = 2\pi k/R$, $1 \le k \le N$. Assume g is a frequency of a new harmonic and $h_m < g < h_{m+1}$. If ϕ_m and ϕ_{m+1} are close then interpolation can be reduced to a simple convex combination. But if the distance between ϕ_m and ϕ_{m+1} is close to π then it is not obvious should we add or subtract this value of π.

The initial phases $(\phi_m)_{m=0}^{M}$ for a periodic signal s_t are defined up to an arbitrary linear function. Indeed, consider a translated time interval with $t_c = t_0 - c$. Then

$$s_t = \sum_{m=0}^{M} a_m \cos\left(\frac{2\pi}{P}mt + \left(\phi_m + \frac{2\pi c}{P}m\right)\right), \qquad t - t_c = 1, 2, \ldots, T.$$

We see that the phases changed by the linear function

$$\phi_m^c = \phi_m + \ell(mF), \qquad \ell(f) = cf, \qquad 0 \le m \le M.$$

The phases are defined up to the terms $2\pi k$. We want to find a linear function such that deviation of the initial phases from this linear function is minimal. This leads to the following minimization problem:

$$J(\ell, (k_m)) = \sum_{m=0}^{M} w_m^{\phi} |\phi_m - 2\pi k_m - \ell(mF)|^2 \quad \longrightarrow \quad \min_{\ell(\cdot),(k_m)},$$

where $\ell(f) = kf + b$ is a linear function of the frequency f and the weights $w_m^{\phi} = A_m^2$ are the squared harmonic amplitudes.

The weights $w_m^{\phi} = A_m^2$ determine which phases are more important for interpolation. Numerical minimization of the function J is not easy because it consists of linear quadratic part in c and k and of integer part in $(k_m)_{m=1}^{M}$. A numerical algorithm was implemented and tested.

4   Conclusion

The consonant /z/ has the main energy between 3 kHz and 5 kHz. The spectrum of this signal looks like a noise even on short frames. Nevertheless, It can be successfully described by the harmonic model with a very accurate estimation procedure of amplitudes and frequencies. It was recognised that a rate of the trend of the high frequency harmonics is much faster than that of the low frequency harmonics.

Two new approaches for synthesis of the speech signal after modification of intonation are presented. The first method is based on the nonlinear interpolation between neighbouring complex amplitudes of the source signal spectrum. The second method contains spline interpolation of real amplitudes and a new approach to the linear phase correction. The correction is reduced to the global minimization of the appropriate cost function.

Acknowledgments. The work was supported by Saint Petersburg State University, project 6.37.349.2015.

References

1. Stylianou, Y.: Harmonic plus Noise Models for speech, combined with statistical methods, for speech and speaker modification. Ph.D. Thesis. Ecole Nationale Superieure des Telecommunications. Paris (1996)
2. Degottex, G., Stylianou, Y.: Analysis and synthesis of speech using an adaptive fullband harmonic model. IEEE Trans. Audio Speech Lang. Process. **21**(10), 2085–2095 (2013)
3. Petrovsky, A., Azarov, E., Petrovsky, A.: Hybrid signal decomposition based on instantaneous harmonic parameters and perceptually motivated wavelet packets for scalable audio coding. Signal Process. **91**(6), 1489–1504 (2011)
4. Petrovsky, A., Azarov, E.: Instantaneous harmonic analysis: techniques and applications to speech signal processing. In: Ronzhin, A., Potapova, R., Delic, V. (eds.) SPECOM 2014. LNCS, vol. 8773, pp. 24–33. Springer, Heidelberg (2014)
5. Barabanov, A., Melnikov, A., Magerkin, V., Vikulov, E.: Fast algorithm for precise estimation of fundamental frequency on short time intervals. In: Ronzhin, A., Potapova, R., Fakotakis, N. (eds.) SPECOM 2015. LNCS, vol. 9319, pp. 217–225. Springer, Heidelberg (2015)
6. Shipilo, A., Barabanov, A., Lipkovich, M.: Parametric speech synthesis and user interface for speech modification. In: Železný, M., Habernal, I., Ronzhin, A. (eds.) SPECOM 2013. LNCS, vol. 8113, pp. 249–256. Springer, Heidelberg (2013)

Profiling a Set of Personality Traits of a Text's Author: A Corpus-Based Approach

Tatiana Litvinova[1]([✉]), Olga Zagorovskaya[1], Olga Litvinova[1],
and Pavel Seredin[2]

[1] Voronezh State Pedagogical University, Voronezh, Russia
centr_rus_yaz@mail.ru
[2] Voronezh State University, Voronezh, Russia
paul@phys.vsu.ru

Abstract. Authorship profiling, i.e. revealing information about an unknown author by analyzing their text, is a task of growing importance. Researchers are currently attempting to identify certain psychological characteristics of a text's author (extraversion, openness, etc.). However, it is well-known that a lot of psychological traits mutually correlate making up what is known as a personality psychological profile. The aim of the study is to assess the probability of self-destructive behaviour of an individual as a set of particular traits via formal parameters of their texts. Here we have used corpus *RusPersonality*, which consists of Russian-language texts labeled with information on their authors. A set of correlations between scores on the Freiburg Personality Inventory scales that are known to be indicative of self-destructive behaviour and text variables has been calculated. A mathematical model which predicts the probability of self-destructive behaviour has been obtained.

Keywords: Authorship profiling · Russian language · Corpus linguistics · Predicting personality from text · Regression

1 Introduction

Authorship profiling (also referred to as AP), which is the process of revealing conjectural information about an unknown author (demographics, personality, education, mental health, etc.), just by computer analysis of a given text (on lexical, morphological, syntactical etc. levels), is a task of growing importance – for national security, criminal investigations, and market research. Scientists trying to address this task generally assume, as a given, the sociolinguistic observation that different groups of people speaking or writing in a particular genre and in a particular language use that language differently. To solve authorship profiling problem, text corpora are used for which author details (gender, age, psychological testing results, etc.) are known, and numerical values of particular text parameters (content-based parameters – e.g., proportions of certain vocabulary groups; and style-based parameters – e.g., proportions of prepositions, conjunctions and other function words) are calculated. Correlations between text and personality parameters are identified; based on these, mathematical models are designed by means of mathematical statistical methods (regression methods, computer

© Springer International Publishing Switzerland 2016
A. Ronzhin et al. (Eds.): SPECOM 2016, LNAI 9811, pp. 555–562, 2016.
DOI: 10.1007/978-3-319-43958-7_67

learning methods) with the input data being numerical text parameters and the output data being personality parameters. This is now a common approach. For example, in [2] the researchers show that the right combination of linguistic features and statistical methods enable an automated system to effectively determine the gender, age, native language, and level of neuroticism of an anonymous author.

There has been a growing interest of late in the Author Profiling (AP) task [2, 4, 9, 10]. This is mostly due to a rapid increase in volumes of internet communications, and thus a growing demand for methods which enable the identification of internet communicators. For example, in [2] the authors studied the problem of automatically determining an author's gender by the use of combinations of simple lexical and syntactic features; they achieved an accuracy of about 80 % via this means. Schler et al. [15] studied the effect of age and gender on the writing-style exhibited in blogs; the authors gathered over 71.000 blogs and determined from them a set of relevant stylistic features (e.g. use of non-dictionary words, parts-of-speech, function words and hyper-links), and content features (such as word unigrams with the highest information gain). Analysing the texts using these features, they obtained an accuracy of about 80 % for gender identification and about 75 % for age identification.

There are international competitions which have been instituted in order to reveal the most accurate methods of authorship profiling using numerical parameters of texts [13]. However there remains a great deal which needs to be addressed. One of the major issues facing researchers dealing with text-based personality detection is that of which text parameters are to be analysed. Most studies provide no explanation of the correlations between quantitative text parameters and personality traits; there is thus no theory supporting the choice of any particular parameter (see [9] for review). Furthermore researchers are attempting to identify degrees of certain characteristics (extraversion, friendliness, etc.) based on texts by individuals as a personality's characteristics are known to correlate making up what is known as a personality's psychological profile. For instance, self-destructive behaviour (suicidal behaviour being an extreme form of this) is known to be not just one particular personality trait but a complex personality feature functioning and manifesting itself on different levels. Self-destruction behaviour is associated with spontaneous aggressiveness, high levels of anxiety, and depressiveness [1, 3]. Therefore an important issue is profiling not certain individual characteristics but their combinations. This paper looks at ways of identifying the correlations between the formal parameters of Russian-language texts and personality traits which are determinants of self-destructive behaviour (spontaneous aggressiveness, depressiveness, emotional lability, composedness) and designing a mathematical model which is able to identify proneness to self-destructive behaviour in authors of written texts.

2   Materials and Methods

2.1   Participants

For this study, we used the "Personality Corpus", which consists of Russian-language texts of different genres which are samples of natural written speech (e.g. description of a picture, essays on different topics, etc.) labelled with information on their authors (gender, age, results of psychological tests, and so on) [7, 8].

For the purpose of the current study, each respondent (N = 721, 422 female, mean age 19.8, SD = 3.3, students of Russian universities, all native Russian speakers) was tested using the Freiburg Personality Inventory (FPI) adapted by A.A. Krylov and T.I. Ronginskaya [2]. This questionnaire was chosen as being capable of accurate measurement of determinants of self-destructive behaviour [1]. According to a current view, high scores on "Spontaneous Aggressiveness", "Depressiveness", "Emotional Lability" and low scores on "Composedness" were used as being indicative of self-destructive behaviour [16]. For a further study respondents with severe and low risk of self-destructive behaviour were chosen (Table 1).

Table 1. Characteristics of the respondents

	Respondents with severe risk of self-destructive behaviour	Respondents with low risk of self-destructive behaviour
Testing score	high (7–9) on 3 of 12 scales of FPI: "Spontaneous Aggressiveness", "Depressiveness" (individuals scoring high on psycho pathological depressive syndrome), "Emotional Lability" (high scores are indicative of an unstable emotional condition with affective reactions), and low (1–3) on "Composedness" (low scores are indicative of low stress resistance),	low (1–3) on 3 scales of FPI: "Spontaneous Aggressiveness", "Depressiveness", "Emotional Lability", and high (7–9) on "Composedness",
Demographics	N = 43 (26 females, 17 males, average age is 20, SD = 2.3)	N = 37 (23 females, 14 males, average age is 19.5, SD = 2.2)

2.2   Procedure

Each respondent (N = 80) was asked to produce two texts which were then processed as one text: a letter to a friend about things happening lately, and one to an imaginary employer explaining why they (the respondents) were good for a particular job. Respondents were instructed to write as much as possible: whatever first came into their minds. There was a time limit of 40 min. An average text was 176 words long, SD = 54 words. Texts were divided on experimental set (i.e. used for regression model building) (60 texts) and test set (20 texts). For the analysis, only quantifiable parameters which can be automatically retrieved from texts were selected. The following were on the list:

1. Indices of the readability of the texts:
   1.1. *Flesch readability index.* For the Russian language, this is calculated according to the formula [10]:

$$\text{Flesch index} = 206.835 - 1.3\,\frac{(\text{total of words})}{(\text{total of sentences})}$$
$$- 60.1\,\frac{(\text{total of syllables})}{(\text{total of words})}, \tag{1}$$

the calculation was performed using an online service http://audit.te-st.ru/tests/readability/.

In the texts under consideration this index was in the range from 55 to 88.

1.2. *Hanning Index (or Fog Index).* For the Russian language, this was calculated using the formula [11]:

$$\text{Hanning index} = 0.4 \left[0.78 \left(\frac{(\text{total of words})}{(\text{total of sentences})} \right) \right.$$
$$\left. + 100 \left(\frac{(\text{total of complex words})}{(\text{total of words})} \right) \right], \qquad (2)$$

where the total of complex words is a number of words with more than 4 syllables; 0.78 is a correction coefficient for Russian. The index was automatically calculated using the service http://audit.te-st.ru/tests/readability/ In the texts under consideration the index was in the range from 2 to 7.

1.3. *Average sentence length in words.* This was calculated as the ratio of the total of words to the total of sentences.

2. Index of lexical diversity in the text, i.e. the ratio of the number of different word forms to the total of word forms abstracted to the range 0 to 100. This index was automatically calculated using special software Novel Score (http://sourceforge.net/projects/novelscore/).

3. Frequencies of different parts of speech: *frequencies of function words* (calculated as a ratio of the total of function words to the total number of words in a text Here and further on, the calculation of the frequencies of different parts of speech was made automatic using the designed Python script and morphological analyzer polymorphy2); *frequencies of prepositions; frequencies of conjunctions; frequencies of particles; coefficient of coherence* (calculated using the formula (particles + conjunctions + prepositions)/3 N· sentence [5]); *frequencies of pronouns; frequencies of personal pronouns; pronominalization index* (calculated as a ratio of the total number of pronouns to the total number of nouns); *coefficient indicating the ratio of the total number of verbs and pronouns to the total number of nouns and adjectives* (calculated using the formula (verbs + personal pronouns)/(nouns + adjectives)).

3 Results

The data on numerical values of text parameters and scores on certain scales of FPI was exported into IBM SPSS Statistics 22 [6]and a correlation analysis was performed of numerical values of the selected text parameters and scores of the test scales (for each scale: "Spontaneous Aggressiveness", "Depressiveness", "Emotional Lability", "Composedness"), $p < 0.05$. The correlation analysis revealed that a lot of text variables correlate with several psychological personality traits at a time. Spontaneous aggressiveness correlated with average sentence length ($r = 0.339$, $p = 0.0105$), lexical diversity ($r = -0.503$, $p = 0.000122$), frequencies of prepositions ($r = -0.328$, $p = 0.0137$). Depressiveness correlated with average sentence length ($r = 0.317$, $p = 0.0164$), lexical diversity ($r = -0.493$, $p = 0.000133$), coefficient of coherence ($r = 0.283$, $p = 0.0366$). Composedness correlated with lexical diversity ($r = 0.422$, $p = 0.0164$), frequencies of prepositions ($r = 0.263$, $p = 0.0481$), frequencies of personal pronouns ($r = -0.308$, $p = 0.02$). Emotional lability correlated with average sentence length ($r = 0.307$, $p = 0.0201$), lexical diversity ($r = -0.491$, $p = 0.000164$), frequencies of prepositions and conjunctions ($r = 0.303$, $p = 0.0220$), coefficient of coherence ($r = 0.281$, $p = 0.0376$).

In order to detect self-destructive tendencies (as noted above, a set of personality traits) by means of the obtained correlation coefficients considering multicollinearity, a regression model, which was a system of linear equations (for each personality trait associated with self-destructive behaviour), was designed. Generally the system of linear Eqs. (3) looked like the following:

$$
\begin{aligned}
c_1 &= a_1 b_{11} + a_2 b_{21} + a_3 b_{31} + a_4 b_{41} + a_5 b_{51} \\
c_2 &= a_1 b_{12} + a_2 b_{22} + a_3 b_{32} + a_4 b_{42} + a_5 b_{52} \\
c_3 &= a_1 b_{13} + a_2 b_{23} + a_3 b_{33} + a_4 b_{43} + a_5 b_{53} , \\
c_4 &= a_1 b_{14} + a_2 b_{24} + a_3 b_{34} + a_4 b_{44} + a_5 b_{54}
\end{aligned}
\tag{3}
$$

where a_1 is the average sentence length; a_2 is the index of lexical diversity; a_3 are frequencies of prepositions; a_4 are frequencies of conjunctions; a_5 are frequencies of personal pronouns; c_1 is spontaneous aggressiveness; c_2 is depressiveness; c_3 is composedness; c4 is emotional lability.

The obtained equation system can be handily represented as a matrix (4) with text parameters as the input parameters (row vector A) and personality traits as the output parameters (column vector C), B is a matrix model:

$$
A \times B = C,
$$

$$
(a_1 a_2 a_3 a_4 a_5)
\begin{bmatrix}
b_{11} b_{12} b_{13} b_{14} \\
b_{21} b_{22} b_{23} b_{24} \\
b_{31} b_{32} b_{33} b_{34} \\
b_{41} b_{42} b_{43} b_{44} \\
b_{51} b_{52} b_{53} b_{54}
\end{bmatrix}
=
\begin{pmatrix}
c_1 \\
c_2 \\
c_3 \\
c_4
\end{pmatrix},
\tag{4}
$$

where a_1 is the average sentence length; a_2 is the index of lexical diversity; a_3 are frequencies of prepositions; a_4 are frequencies of conjunctions; a5 are frequencies of personal pronouns; c_1 is spontaneous aggressiveness; c_2 is depressiveness; c_3 is composedness; c_4 is emotional lability.

The solution for these model can be easily found using a Mathematica software by finding a global minimum of the function f(B) = |AB−C|. The matrix elements at which the above system reaches its minimum were identified based on the numerical values of all the text parameters that are included in the study corpus and personality traits of authors. The matrix model (5) identified using minimization for calculating the personality traits based on the selected text parameters is as follows:

$$
B = \begin{bmatrix}
0.501 & 0.475 & 0 & 0.267 \\
1.527 & 0.396 & 7.772 & -1.38 \\
-12.744 & 0 & 9.643 & 0 \\
0 & 0 & 0 & 45.163 \\
0 & 0 & -19.473 & 0
\end{bmatrix}. \tag{5}
$$

The minimization model was proved to be highly efficient. The average deviation from the test results was 2 points (on a 10 scale) for each personality trait (spontaneous aggressiveness; depressiveness; composedness; emotional lability). The accuracy of the model for predicting self-destructive behaviour is about 80 %.

4 Discussion

As correlation-regression analysis show, texts produced by individuals with a greater likelihood of self-destructive behaviour (i.e. those who scored high on spontaneous aggressiveness; depressiveness; emotional lability and low on composedness according to FPI) typically show less lexical diversity, fewer prepositions, more pronouns overall (and particularly personal ones), a higher coefficient of coherence (due to more conjunctions and deictic particles), and a higher average sentence lengths in as compared to texts produced by people with less likelihood of self-destructive behaviour (i.e. those who scored low on spontaneous aggressiveness; depressiveness; emotional lability and high on composedness according to FPI).

Let us try to give a tentative explanation of the established correlations. Using the available data on the neurobiology underlying self-destructive behaviour, we suggested that texts by individuals with high risk of self-destructive behaviour could contain more text elements controlled by the right hemisphere and fewer those for which the left hemisphere is responsible than texts by individuals displaying no such behaviour [14]. Indeed, a lower coefficient of lexical diversity in individuals with a greater likelihood of self-destructive behaviour is consistent with the data indicating less vocabulary in individuals with the activated right hemisphere. A lower percentage of prepositions in the above individuals is accounted for by insufficient activation of the left hemisphere areas known to be responsible for producing more abstract lexical units. A higher pronominalization index, which is characteristics of written speech of people with greater likelihood of self-destructive behaviour, "is commonly observed in weaker paradigmatic language links relying on the cerebellum" [5, p. 82]. It is completely consistent with the neurobiological and neuropsychology data indicating that insufficient activation of the cerebellum is associated with aggressive and suicidal behaviour [14].

We identified correlations between text parameters and personality traits (represented by personality test scores) and designed a mathematical statistical model, which proved to be 80 % accurate. Unlike most studies on AP, this study was concerned with language parameters which were selected on the basis of theoretical findings, i.e. neuroscience data.

5 Conclusions

A worldwide and rapidly developing approach to detecting the personality of authors from their texts, involving the design of predictive models based on the correlations between quantifiable text parameters and individual psychological traits, is not without flaws due to the fact that particular traits are analyzed instead of a set of traits.

We argue that this current research can significantly inform further studies in authorship profiling as: (1) it suggests that it is not a particular personality trait that needs to be analyzed but a whole set of traits, as the neurobiology of personality indicates that self-destructive behaviour is based on a large number of personality traits which share neurobiological foundations and are mutually correlating; (2) a mathematical solution for profiling a set of personality traits using texts is set forth; (3) the problem is addressed using Russian language materials. This has not previously been extensively researched in relation to authorship profiling; (4) a model which predicts the risk of self-destructive behaviour based on formal text parameters is proposed – although we are aware of certain limitations of the study due to the relatively small sample size, as well as the relatively few language parameters which were used for the analysis. Of course, further research is necessary for a more comprehensive assessment of these results. This would involve more respondents and more text parameters. Employing automatic language processing, statistical methods, and neurobiology data in investigating texts produced by individuals who committed suicide [12] is seen as crucial to studying the language correlates of self-destructive behaviour and so designing prognostic models.

Acknowledgments. Funding of the project "Predicting the probability of suicide behavior based on speech analysis" from RF President's grants for young scientists (grant agreement N° MK-4633.2016.6) for T. L. and from the Russian Foundation for Humanities (grant N 15-34-01221 "Lie Detection in a Written Text: A Corpus Study") for O.L. and P.S. is gratefully acknowledged.

References

1. Angst, J., Clayton, P.: Premorbid personality of depressive, bipolar, and schizophrenic patients with special reference to suicidal issues. Compr. Psychiatry 27(6), 511–532 (1986)
2. Argamon, S., Koppel, M., Pennebaker, J., Schler, J.: Automatically profiling the author of an anonymous text. Commun. ACM **52**(2), 119–123 (2009)
3. Batarshev, A.V.: Temperament and Character: Psychological Diagnostics. VLADOS-Press, Moscow (2001). (in Russian)

4. Chung, C.K., Pennebaker, J.W.: The psychological functions of function words. In: Fiedler, K. (ed.) Social Communication, pp. 343–359. Psychology Press, New York (2009)
5. Fotekova, T.A., Akhutina, T.V.: Detecting Speech Impediments in School Children Using Neuropsychological Methods. ARKTI, Moscow (2002). (in Russian)
6. IBM SPSS Statistics 22 Documentation. http://www-01.ibm.com/support/docview.wss?uid= swg27038407#ru
7. Litvinova, T.A., Seredin, P.V., Litvinova, O.A.: Using part-of-speech sequences frequencies in a text to predict author personality: a corpus study. Indian J. Sci. Technol. **8**(9), 93–97 (2015). [S.l.]
8. Litvinova, T.A.: Profiling the author of a written text in Russian. J. Lang. Lit. **5**(4), 210–216 (2014)
9. Nini, A.: Authorship profiling in a forensic context. Ph.D. thesis. Aston University (2014)
10. Noecker Jr., J.W., Ryan, M., Juola, P.: Psychological profiling through textual analysis. Lit Linguist Comput. **28**(3), 382–387 (2013)
11. Oborneva, I.V.: Automatisation of the assessment of perception of a text. Her. J. Mosc. State Pedagogical Univ. **2**(5), 86–92 (2005). (in Russian)
12. Pennebaker, J.W., Stone, L.D.: What was she trying to say? a linguistic analysis of Katie's diaries. In: Lester, D. (ed.) Katie's Diary: Unlocking the Mystery of a Suicide, pp. 55–80. Brunner-Routledge, New York (2004)
13. Rangel, F., Celli, F. Rosso, P.: Overview of the 3rd author profiling task at PAN 2015. In: CEUR Workshop Proceedings (2015). http://www.sensei-conversation.eu/wp-content/uploads/2015/09/15-pan@clef.pdf
14. Rozanov, V.A.: Neurobiuological foundations of suicidal behaviour. Her. J. Biol. Psychiatry **6** (2004) .(in Russian) http://scorcher.ru/neuro/science/data/mem102.php
15. Schler, J., Koppel, M., Argamon, S., Pennebaker, J.: Effects of age and gender on blogging. In: Proceedings of AAAI Spring Symposium on Computational Approaches for Analyzing Weblogs, vol. 6, pp. 199–205 (2006)
16. Yegorov, A.Y.: Coordination of the Activities of the Right Hemisphere of the Human Brain. Abstract of thesis for Ph.D. in Medicine. Saint Petersburg (1999). (in Russian)

Prosody Analysis of Malay Language Storytelling Corpus

Izzad Ramli[1], Noraini Seman[1], Norizah Ardi[2],
and Nursuriati Jamil[1(✉)]

[1] Digital Image, Audio and Speech Technology Research Group,
Faculty of Computer and Mathematical Sciences, Universiti Teknologi MARA,
40450 Shah Alam, Malaysia
zadzed89@gmail.com, norizah@salam.uitm.edu.my,
liza@tmsk.uitm.edu.my
[2] Academy of Language Studies, Universiti Teknologi MARA, 40450 Shah
Alam, Malaysia
aini@tmsk.uitm.edu.my

Abstract. In this paper, the prosody of the storytelling speech corpus is analyzed. The main objective of the analysis is to develop prosody rules to convert
neutral speech to storytelling speech. The speech corpus (neutral and storytelling
speech) contains 464 speech sentences, 4,656 words, and 10,928 syllables. It
was recorded by three female storytellers, one male professional speaker, two
female speakers and two male speakers. The prosodic features considered for
analysis are tempo, pause (sentence and phrase-level), duration, intensity, and
pitch. Further analysis of the word categories exist in storytelling speech such as
verb, adverb, adjective, noun, conjunction and amplifier are also conducted. The
global prosody analysis showed that mean prosodic of storytelling is higher than
neutral speech, especially intensity and pitch. Investigation on the word categories showed that words categorized as adverb, adjective, amplifier and conjunctions have significant number of prominent syllables. Meanwhile, nouns and
verbs do not have significant difference between neutral and storytelling speech.
Positions of the words (i.e. initial, middle, last) in a phrase for different word
categories also proved to have different increasing factor in duration, pitch and
intensity.

Keywords: Neutral speech · Storytelling speech · Prosodic parameters ·
Expressive speech · Prosody rule-set · Text-To-Speech (TTS)

1 Introduction

Speech synthesis is widely used in various applications. However, it produces neutral
speech sound like news reading speech [1]. Therefore, there is a growing need for an
expressive speech synthesis to vary the speaking style speech especially for digital
communication and humanoid robotic [2]. Converting neutral speech to storytelling
speech requires manipulation of speech prosody. The efforts of varying prosody can be
controlled using rule-based methods [3, 4] or data-driven methods [5]. Data-driven
methods are preferred these years. However, it requires a significant amount of training

© Springer International Publishing Switzerland 2016
A. Ronzhin et al. (Eds.): SPECOM 2016, LNAI 9811, pp. 563–570, 2016.
DOI: 10.1007/978-3-319-43958-7_68

data, high cost, and difficulty in recording a large amount of speech with the same quality. The rule-based method, on the other hand, does not require extensive recording data. Therefore, maintaining speech quality is non-existent. Nevertheless, a rule-based method needs a thorough prosody analysis to understand the linguistic nature and describe the prosody characteristics comprehensively by rules [6]. In literature, the development of storytelling speech synthesis was done using the rule-based method with various prosody analysis and rule-set [3, 4, 7].

In general, the prosody analysis in storytelling is based on tempo, pause, duration, intensity and pitch [3]. Theune (2006) in [3] analyzed these prosodic features globally and developed the global rules of storytelling application. The same prosodic features are also analyzed in Hindi storytelling at phrase and sentence level [7]. The prosodic analysis was also done locally at syllable level in adjectives and adverbs [3]. The extra emphasis in adjective and adverb indicates a prominent syllable. This prominent syllable has an extra-long duration, a higher pitch means and rising pitch movement from their local environment [8]. Based on Roekhaut et al. (2010) in [8], the prominent syllable is categorized at initial accents (first syllable of a word or phrase) and final accents (last syllable of a word or phrase). The prominent syllable for final accent is usually detected at noun, adjective, verb or adverbs; and also encountered as initial at several word categories.

Words positioned at initial, middle and final location in a phrase are further analyzed [4]. It is because the storytellers produced a unique intonation at initial, middle and final words of a phrase [4]. As an example, the word at the final phrase has an increased duration compared to a word located at initial and middle of a phrase [4]. These word locations played important roles for manipulating the types of the speaking style [8]. The prosody based on word location (initial, middle, final) are varied by [7] to develop storytelling speech with various emotion.

In this work, we analyzed the prosody of storytelling corpus in the Malay language. The criteria that are considered are tempo, pauses (phrase and sentence level); the last syllable in the adjective, adverb, noun and verb; an initial syllable in potential word categories, and word location (initial, middle, last) in a phrase. Our contribution is the identified modification factors of the prominent syllable in word categories located in different positions in a phrase. This paper is structured as follows. In Sect. 2, the speech corpus is presented. The global prosody analysis of storytelling is elaborated in Sect. 3. Then, local prosody analysis at syllable level is described in Sect. 4. The summary of the results is described in Sect. 5.

2 Storytelling Corpus

In this section, the storytelling corpus used for analysis is discussed. It explains the selection of text corpus, quantitative description of text corpus, storyteller description, the condition of audio recording and audio labeling.

2.1   Text Corpus

The corpus size depends on the language resources and purpose of the collection. Thus, the variations in corpus size existed for different work and languages (i.e. Bengali [4], Hindi [7], Dutch [3], English [2, 9], French [10], Slovak [11] and Spanish [12]) as can be seen in Table 1.

Table 1. Summary of storytelling speech corpus

Authors/Year	Language	Corpus size
Alm&Sproat, 2005	English	2 children stories
Gelin et al., 2010	English	89 short stories
Sarkar et al., 2014	Bengali, Telugu	125 children stories
Theune et al., 2006	Dutch	5 fairy tales
Verma, 2015	Hindi	25 children stories
Přibi&Přibilová, 2008	Slovak	10 children stories
Montano et al., 2013	Spanish	1 story
Doukhan et al., 2011	French	89 children tales

In this research, three narrative children short stories from a classic Malaysia's collections of short stories entitled *'200 kisah teladan haiwan'* (200 animal folklores) [11] are selected for analysis. The number of sentences, words and syllables are depicted in Table 2.

Table 2. Total sentences, words, and syllable in each story

Story	No. of sentences	No. of words	No. of syllables
Si angsa yang berteluremas	12	113	276
Anjing dengan bayang-bayang	9	80	175
Semut dan merpati	8	98	232
Total	**29**	**291**	**683**

The script of three stories made up a total of 29 sentences, 291 words, and 598 syllables. The scripts do not contain any dialogue and description as our scope is the narrative discourse mode. The language used in the stories fulfills the formal Malay language, with simple words easily understood by the children.

2.2   Audio Corpus Recording

The corpus is recorded by three female storytellers, one male professional speaker, two female and two male speakers. The female storytellers are school kindergarten teachers who have the proper training and experience in delivering storytelling. Their ages range from 30 to 45 years old. A 58-year old professional speaker who has more than 30 years delivering lectures and public speeches is also employed as our storyteller. The four speakers are degree college students who are eloquent speakers and have 3 to 5 years experiences giving public speeches. The speech recorded is in two speaking style (neutral and storytelling). The recorded neutral speech is free of all possible stress or emphasis such as news reading. Therefore, the storyteller must maintain their vocal qualities in term of intelligibility, timbre, diction and pronunciation. For storytelling, storyteller needs to narrate the story script with their storytelling style without influence by another storyteller. They can move slightly (e.g., hand movement) to get the mood and inspiration during recorded storytelling speech. Recordings are made in an isolated room in Digital Image, Audio and Speech Technology Group (DIAST) laboratory. The quiet room is equipped with a centralized air conditioner with one door entrance. Background noise of the audio storytelling data was analyzed at 18 dB due to the constant humming of the centralized air-conditioning system. In the end, the speech corpus consists of 48 (8 storyteller × 2 speaking styles × 3 stories) audio. WAV files and down-sampled at 16 kHz with a 16 bits sample size. A total of 464 speech sentences, 4,656 words, and 10,928 syllables are collected from all speakers.

2.3   Corpus Labeling

The corpus was annotated using speech analysis tool known as Praat [13] at the sentence, word, and syllable level producing 48 transcriptions of textgrid files. The speech and non-speech regions are automatically labeled as speech and silence, respectively. The label is used as guidance for manually labeling end point of the sentence-, word-, and syllable-level. The syllables are labeled based on the Malay language syllable structure [1]. The empty labels at word-and syllable- levels are the silence areas which are not annotated and left as blanks.

3   Global Prosody Analysis of Storytelling Speech

For global prosody analysis, 232 neutral sentences and 232 storytelling sentences from eight storytellers are considered. Prosody features such as tempo, pause (phrase and sentence), average syllable duration, average syllable intensity and average syllable pitch are extracted and analyzed as shown in Table 3.

Tempo is also known as the speaking rate of a person and is calculated based on syllable per second (SPS). Previous research showed that the tempo of storytelling is

Table 3. Prosodic comparison between neutral and storytelling speaking style

Prosodic parameter	Neutral	Storytelling
Mean tempo	4.2	4.48
Mean pause (sentence level)	0.81	0.77
Mean pause (phrase level)	0.29	0.37
Mean syllable duration	0.22	0.2
Mean intensity (dB)	66.18	67.89
Mean pitch (Hz)	191.83	210.04

slower than neutral speech [3]. However, our observation showed that storytelling speech tempo is faster than neutral speech. Our speech data showed that six out of eight storytellers have higher tempo than neutral speech. This phenomenon occurs because while recording the neutral speech, the storyteller always puts their attention on each word pronunciations in an utterance which is time-consuming. The similar phenomenon also occurred in [7].

The pause feature is analyzed at phrase and sentence level in second (s). In our work, a phrase is defined as a collection of words and determined by the symbol comma (,) that exists in a sentence. Based on Table 3, the neutral speech has a longer average pause at sentence level compared to storytelling speech. The total average pause at sentence level for neutral speech is longer than storytelling at 0.81 s and 0.77 s, respectively. However, at phrase level, pause for storytelling is longer than neutral speech with the total average of 0.37 s and 0.29 s, respectively. It shows that, at phrase level, storytelling speeches pause longer before continuing to the next phrase.

The syllable's duration determines the tempo of the overall speech. The analysis of the duration is to determine the average syllable's duration for a certain style and storyteller. The average duration for neutral speech is longer than storytelling speech. It is proved by the total average of the syllable's duration of the neutral is 0.22 s, and storytelling speech is 0.20 s. The average of the syllable duration of storytelling is further considered for developing a rule for storytelling speech synthesis.

The intensity of the prosody, calculated in decibels (dB), is a measure of loudness in the utterance [14]. The analysis of the mean intensity of neutral and storytelling speech is 66.18 dB and 67.89 dB. We discover that five storytellers have higher intensity or speech energy compared to neutral speech. It means that a storyteller tends to speak louder when delivering a tale as compared to his/her normal reading style. The analysis based on gender also signifies that male speaks louder than female storyteller for both neutral and storytelling speech.

The analysis of mean pitch between neutral and storytelling speech showed increasing of the pitch from neutral to storytelling from 191.83 Hz to 210.04 Hz. It is because five storytellers have a higher average pitch as compared to their neutral speech. It indicated that storyteller increases their pitch in storytelling speaking style. The analysis on the gender showed that female has a high frequency rather that male storyteller and can manipulate their pitch with ease.

4   Local Prosody Analysis

The literature mentioned that word categories such as noun, verb, adjectives, and adverbs emphasized the last syllable (i.e. final accent) of a particular word during pronunciations. In this research, we also analyzed prominent syllables within conjunction and amplifier (*kata penguat*). Our analysis showed that prominent syllables also existed in both word categories. However, prominent syllable of the amplifier is located at the initial syllable (i.e. initial accent) of a word. The total selected words used in local prosody analysis based on word categories are shown in Fig. 1.

The analysis of each word categories is done by comparing words in neutral speech with the storytelling speech. The prosody parameters compared are duration, intensity

Fig. 1. Number of selected word categories in story for one storyteller

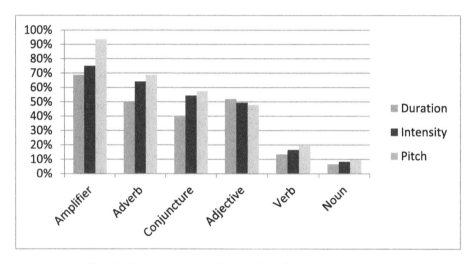

Fig. 2. Percentage of word categories with increased prosody

and pitch. Figure 2 shows the percentage number of words that the storytellers tend to increase their duration, intensity, and pitch.

Figure 2 shows that less than 20 % of verbs and nouns are increased in duration, intensity and pitch at the last syllable from neutral speech to storytelling speaking style. It indicates that only a small percentage of the verb and nouns contain prominent syllables. On the other hand, amplifier words have the highest prominent syllables at more than 65 % compared to other word categories. The overall observation concludes that only certain words in each word category have prominent syllables and these words are used as the basis of the rules.

The words are further examined based on their positions (i.e. initial, middle and last) in a phrase or sentence. Table 4 shows the percentage of increased prosody for prominent syllables in words positioned at the initial, middle or last location in a phrase. The comparison is done between neutral speech and storytelling speech. For an adjective, the prominent syllable at the last word has higher pitch increased that is 40 % as compared to the middle word at 18 %. As an example, the last word *berat* in the sentence *telur itu sangat berat* has a final accent at the last syllable *rat*. The syllable *rat* in storytelling speech has an increased pitch by a factor of 1.4 times from syllable *rat* in

Table 4. Comparison of prominent syllables based on the word position in a phrase

	Adjective			Adverb		
Position	Duration	Intensity	Pitch	Duration	Intensity	Pitch
Initial word	NC	NC	NC	+52 %	+4 %	+21 %
Middle word	+54 %	+6 %	+18 %	+40 %	+6 %	+29 %
Last word	+26 %	+6 %	+40 %	+62 %	+9 %	+24 %
	Amplifier			Conjunction		
Initial word	NC	NC	NC	+49 %	+6 %	+21 %
Middle word	+99 %	+9 %	+31 %	+35 %	+6 %	+20 %
Last word	NC	NC	NC	NC	NC	NC
	Noun			Verb		
Initial word	+36 %	+6 %	+22 %	+103 %	+3 %	+15 %
Middle word	+39 %	+7 %	+26 %	+36 %	+7 %	+28 %
Last word	+45 %	+6 %	+25 %	+31 %	+6 %	+28 %

the neutral speech. However, the duration of the prominent syllable in the middle word is longer than the prominent syllable of the last word.

For adverb word category, there is no significant difference (less than 10 %) of intensity and pitch between initial, middle and last words. However, duration of the prominent syllable in the last word is longer than initial and middle words. As for amplifier word category, there are no changes in duration, intensity and pitch of the initial and last words.

Analysis on the amplifier in the middle position for our speech data is described. It is interesting to note that duration of the amplifier is increased by 99 % for the middle word, which is the highest increment compared to others. A 40 % increase in pitch of the last word and 54 % increase of duration in the middle word of adjectives are observed. No changes (NC) are noted for the initial words. Conjunction words have a slightly higher increase in duration at the initial word compared to middle word. Since there is no occurrence of conjunction at the last word, we described it as no change (NC) for this research.

Even though only 20 % nouns and verbs have prominent syllables, the analysis revealed that noun positioned as the last word showed an increased duration of 45 % that is higher than noun located at the initial and middle word. Intensity and pitch do not show significant difference of less than 5 %. Verbs, however, showed an increase of 103 % duration at the initial word. Nevertheless, it has the lowest intensity increased compared to all the other word categories.

5 Conclusion

In this paper, we have analyzed the prosody of the storytelling as compared to the neutral speech. The corpus has been presented, and the analysis of the corpus has been described. The result discussed the difference in the global prosody of the storytelling and the neutral speech. The analysis in local prosody showed that only certain words in word categories have prominent syllables. The results will be used for modeling rule-based storytelling, which applied the prosodic modification of the neutral Malay TTS to become storytelling TTS. Our future work is to develop the prosody rules of the storytelling based on the data analysis especially on percentage increased of prosody in word categories at different word position which is our contribution in this research.

References

1. Khaw, Y.J., Tan, T., Sciences, C.: Preparation of MaDiTS corpus for Malay dialect translation and speech synthesis system. In: Speech, language and Audio in Multimedia Workshop (SLAM 2014), pp. 53–57 (2014)
2. Gelin, R., D'Alessandro, C., Le, Q.: Towards a storytelling humanoid robot. In: AAAI Fall Symposium Series on Dialog with Robots, pp. 137–138 (2010)
3. Theune, M., Meijs, K., Heylen, D., Ordelman, R.: Generating expressive speech for storytelling applications. IEEE Trans. Audio Speech Lang. Process. **14**, 1099–1108 (2006)
4. Sarkar, P., Haque, A., Dutta, A.K., Gurunath Reddy, M., Harikrishna, D.M., Dhara, P., Verma, R., Narendra, N.P., Sunil Kr., S.B., Yadav, J., Rao, K.S.: Designing Prosody Rule-set for Converting Neutral TTS Speech to storytelling style speech for Indian Languages: Bengali, Hindi and Telugu, p. 4 (2014)
5. Mustafa, M.B., Don, Z.M., Ainon, R.N., Zainuddin, R., Knowles, G.: Developing an HMM-based speech synthesis system for Malay: a comparison of iterative and isolated unit training. IEICE Trans. Inf. Syst. **97**(5), 1273–1282 (2014)
6. Maekawa, K., Koiso, H., Furui, S., Isahara, H.: Spontaneous speech corpus of Japanese. In: Proceedings LREC2000 (Second International Conference on Language Resources and Evaluation), vol. 2, pp. 947–952 , May 2000
7. Verma, R., Sarkar, P., Rao, K. S.: Conversion of neutral speech to storytelling style speech. In: 2015 Eighth International Conference on Advances in Pattern Recognition (ICAPR), pp. 1–6. IEEE, January 2015
8. Roekhaut, S., Goldman, J., Simon, A.C.: A Model for Varying Speaking Style in TTS systems, pp. 4–7 (2010)
9. Sproat, R., Alm, C.O., Sproat, R.: Perceptions of emotions in expressive Perceptions of Emotions in Expressive Storytelling. In: INTERSPEECH, pp. 533–536 (2005)
10. Doukhan, D., Rilliard, A., Rosset, S., Adda-decker, M., Alessandro, C.: Prosodic analysis of a corpus of tales. In: INTERSPEECH, pp. 3129–3132 (2011)
11. Pvribil, J., Pvribilová, A.: Application of expressive speech in TTS system with cepstral description. In: Esposito, A., Bourbakis, N.G., Avouris, N., Hatzilygeroudis, I. (eds.) HH and HM Interaction. LNCS (LNAI), vol. 5042, pp. 200–212. Springer, Heidelberg (2008)
12. Montaño, R., Alías, F., Ferrer, J.: Prosodic analysis of storytelling discourse modes and narrative situations oriented to Text-to-Speech synthesis. In: 8th ISCA Workshop on Speech Synthesis, pp. 171–176 (2013)
13. Boersma, P.: Praat, a system for doing phonetics by computer. Glot int. **5**(9/10), 341–345 (2002)
14. Bulut, M., Narayanan, S.: On the robustness of overall F0- only modifications to the perception of emotions in speech. J. Acoust. Soc. Am. **123**, 4547–4558 (2008)

Quality Assessment of Two Fullband Audio Codecs Supporting Real-Time Communication

M. Maruschke$^{(\boxtimes)}$, O. Jokisch, M. Meszaros, F. Trojahn, and M. Hoffmann

Leipzig University of Telecommunications (HfTL), Leipzig, Germany
{maruschke,jokisch}@hft-leipzig.de
http://www.hft-leipzig.de

Abstract. Recent audio codecs enable high quality signals up to full-band (20 kHz) which is usually associated with the maximal audible bandwidth. Following previous studies on speech coding assessment, we survey in this novel study the music coding ability of two real-time codecs with fullband capability – the IETF standardized Opus codec as well as the 3 GPP specified EVS codec. We tested both codecs with vocal, instrumental and mixed music signals. For evaluation, we predicted human assessments using the instrumental POLQA method which has been primarily designed for speech assessment. Additionally, we performed two listening tests as a reference with a total of 21 young adults. Opus and EVS show a similar music coding performance. The quality assessment mainly depends on the specific music characteristics and on the tested bitrates from 16.4 to 64 kbit/s. The POLQA measure and the listening results are correlating, whereas the absolute ratings of the young listeners achieve much lower MOS values.

Keywords: Opus · EVS · Music coding · POLQA · Listening test

1 Introduction

In the current IP-based real-time communication, two predominant fullband (FB) audio codecs are used – the Internet-driven Opus codec [14] and the telecommunication carrier-patronized codec Enhanced Voice Service (EVS) [1]. In the last years, the widely spread Opus codec has been pre-installed in popular web-browsers such as Google Chrome or Firefox and supports their so called Web-based Real-Time Communication (WebRTC) functionality [5]. Nearly at the same time, the EVS coder standardization was conducted by telecommunication industry – aiming at a flexible and sustainable FB audio codec which is backward compatible to already existing wideband speech codecs in public cellular networks, e.g. Adaptive Multirate-Wideband (AMR-WB). Despite of diverse motivation in the codec developments, both Opus and EVS support several audio bandwidths as shown in Table 1. Both codecs are intended and specified to support different needs – FB audio speech coding as well as high-quality music

© Springer International Publishing Switzerland 2016
A. Ronzhin et al. (Eds.): SPECOM 2016, LNAI 9811, pp. 571–579, 2016.
DOI: 10.1007/978-3-319-43958-7_69

Table 1. Audio bandwidths and corresponding quality expectations.

Acronym	Audio bandwidth	Passband [Hz]	Quality expectation
NB	narrowband	300 ... 3,400	conventional phone voice
WB	wideband	50 ... 7,000	AM radio/ HD voice
SWB	super-wideband	50 ... 14,000	FM radio / full HD voice &music
FB	fullband	20 ... 20,000	CD quality / full HD voice &music

communication applications like live music streaming or web-radio broadcast-ing [1,14]. Therefore, it is reasonable to assess the codec quality of such "all-rounders", most notably for different music characteristics. This contribution focuses on the comparison of the fullband music performance provided by Opus versus EVS and follows our previous reviews on the speech coding performance including some cues on singing voice [10–12].

To create diverging coding challenges, we tested samples in following music categories to detect the audible differences:

- Vocals (a-capella music),
- Musical instruments,
- Mixed music (instrumental and vocal parts).

The test design targeted on bitrate conditions that are adequate for both codecs, Opus and EVS, exclusively in FB mode. We used Perceptual Objec-tive Listening Quality Assessment (POLQA) [8] as an instrumental assessment method, and it should be noted here that the perceptual model of POLQA has not been adapted yet for music assessment which motivated us to test the limits of this method, for the first time. Furthermore, we performed a listening test with human listeners. The widely-used audio quality rating score Mean Opinion Score (MOS) was utilized. Following an overview about previous research related to Opus and EVS in Sect. 2, we introduce the experimental design in Sect. 3. In Sect. 4, we discuss the instrumental and perceptual assessments for Opus and EVS, followed by some conclusions.

Moreover, there are other fullband codecs in the Advanced Audio Coding-Enhanced Low Delay (AAC-ELD) family [4] and also within G.719 [7]. For prac-tical reasons, they are less-spread and missing in the WebRTC environment or public cellular networks.

2   Previous Studies on Opus and EVS

Standardized in RFC 6716 [14] by the Internet Engineering Task Force (IETF), Opus was designed as an all-purpose interactive speech and audio codec. Applica-ble in multiple use cases, Opus is suitable for scenarios like voice over IP, videoconferencing, online-gaming or audio on demand and comprises low bitrate speech coding as well as high quality stereo music coding. To realize both, high quality and dynamic characteristics, Opus combines the linear prediction-based SILK codec and the Modified Discrete Cosine Transform (MDCT)-based Constrained Energy Lapped Transform (CELT) codec. For a flexible use, the Opus codec supports the frequency band types NB, WB, SWB and FB. Consequently, Opus encodes speech and music (alternatively mono or stereo) within a bitrate range from 6 kbit/s to 510 kbit/s with a low delay from 2.5 ms to 60 ms for all relevant sample rates – from 8 kHz up to 48 kHz. Opus supports variable bitrate (VBR as default) and constant bitrate (CBR) modes. After its first appearance in 2011, the Opus codec passed several listening tests – supplemented by comparison to other speech and audio codecs (Speex NB/WB, iLBC, G.722.1/G.722.1C, AMR NB/WB, HE-AAC, Vorbis). The results are summarized in a study of Hoene et al. [6] in which Opus outperformed all codecs – in particular in wider bands if applicable.

EVS was standardized by the 3rd Generation Partnership Project (3 GPP) in 2014 succeeding the AMR-WB codec and designed for packet-switched networks as well as for mobile communication like in Voice over LTE (VoLTE) [1]. It is comparable to Opus as being an all-purpose codec. For achieving high quality and dynamic characteristics, EVS also combines several working modes. It can seamlessly switch between Linear Prediction (LP)-based, frequency domain and inactive signal (Comfort Noise Generation (CNG)) coding. For the applicability in multiple-switched network use cases, EVS provides a higher resilience against packet losses and errors. Furthermore, EVS contains an interactive mode for interoperating with AMR-WB. It supports all frequency band types whereby FB is optional. Similar to Opus, EVS can handle speech and music at a bitrate range from 7.2 kbit/s to 128 kbit/s with low delays from 30.9 ms to 32 ms for all relevant sample rates (8 kHz up to 48 kHz). At the current stage, EVS does not provide stereo music coding.

So far, there are three relevant studies on comparing Opus and EVS under several test conditions. The first contribution by Anssi Rämö et al. (Nokia Networks) [13] focuses on a listening test using a discrete nine-point MOS scale and comparing samples of clean speech and mixed content in a bitrate range from 4.7 kbit/s to 128 kbit/s. The second survey provided by the ITU-T study group 12 includes a P.800 ACR-based listening test to evaluate the prediction performance of the instrumental POLQA assessment method [9] in which the EVS codec has been tested with bitrates from 7.2 kbit/s to 24.4 kbit/s. Based on the MOS values, the prediction performance of POLQA SWB mode has been validated. The third study was provided by 3 GPP itself [2] and consists of an ITU-T P.800 listening test using the five-point MOS scale. These EVS performance experiments were conducted under laboratory conditions including all frequency bands (NB ... FB) with bitrates from 4.7 kbit/s to 24.4 kbit/s.

According to our best knowledge there is no direct comparison between Opus and EVS coded music samples in fullband mode evaluated by listening tests using the five-point MOS scale. A further novelty is our FB assessment by POLQA assistance (whose perceptual model is not including music assessment yet).

3   Test Design and Experiments

3.1   Fullband Testing Concept for Opus and EVS

Both codecs require different minimal bitrates in the FB operating mode –
20 kbit/s (VBR mode of Opus) respectively 16.4 kbit/s (EVS). Additionally, we
tested the codecs with bitrates of 32 kbit/s and 64 kbit/s and provided the original music signals at PCM 16 bit, 48 kHz (768 kbit/s) as reference. We solely
experimented on mono signals because EVS does not support stereo coding yet.
At bitrates higher than 64 kbit/s one can not expect a rising quality since the
codecs reach their saturation curve in mono mode – as demonstrated in [13].

The European Broadcasting Union (EBU) [3] provides their Sound Quality
Assessment Material (SQAM) for listening tests. These EBU SQAM lossless
sound samples are available free of charge for research and development use. To
achieve some balanced variety of music types, we selected six sound examples
from this database (two vocal pieces, two musical instruments and two mixed-
music pieces).

3.2   Evaluation by POLQA Method and Listening Test

The ITU-T recommendation P.863 (POLQA) describes an objective method for
predicting overall listening speech quality from NB up to SWB telecommunication scenarios as perceived by the user in an ITU-T P.800 Absolute Category
Rating (ACR) listening-only test. POLQA supports two operational modes, one
for narrowband and one for super-wideband.

Due to the internal frequency limitation of 14 kHz, the current POLQA version in SWB mode is not able to differentiate between clean, unprocessed audio
14 kHz SWB and 20 kHz FB test signals. Nonetheless, we used the POLQA tool
for our survey to evaluate the general suitability of this method for FB music
testing. In order to validate the POLQA (SWB mode) prediction, we conducted
an ACR listening only test for exactly the same samples.

Figure 1 shows the audio quality measurement in terms of MOS Listening
Quality Objective (LQO) for the POLQA method and MOS ACR for the listening test. For instrumental assessment, we used the software SQuadAnalyzer

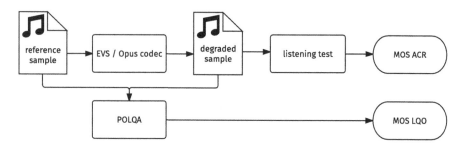

Fig. 1. Experimental setup involving POLQA method and listening assessment.

(version 2.4.0.4) utilizing POLQA in SWB operating mode. The selected stereo sounds from SQAM database were converted into mono *reference samples* and then coded with FB-adequate bitrates, resulting in the *degraded samples.*

3.3 Test Conditions

To evaluate the appropriate listening environment, we conducted two experiments under different acoustic room conditions. The first listening test with eight probands took place in a sound insulating cabinet according to P.800 requirements to minimize background noises. The second experiment – providing the same samples to 13 further probands – was performed in a regular lecture room. Both experimental results differ over all music categories in a range of less than 0.2 on the MOS scale while showing slightly higher values in the lecture room. By summarizing both experiments, following testing conditions were obtained:

- Six different SQAM pieces (violin, glockenspiel, quartet, soprano, two pop music examples incl. vocals vs. w/o vocals),
- Overall 42 audio samples (both codecs Opus/EVS in three different bitrates plus FB reference),
- 21 naive listeners, ICT students in the age range 20 . . . 28,
- Frequent music listeners[1],
- Listening assessment on five point MOS scale,
- Three training samples at the beginning but no further instruction.

According to our test design (group of young probands, frequent music listeners, no training instructions etc.) we intended critical listening decisions to challenge the 'objective' instrumental assessment method and to obtain cues for the further development and optimization of codecs and their assessment.

4 Results and Discussion

4.1 Influence of the Coding Bitrate

The Fig. 2 compares the POLQA and listening test results for both codecs (Opus and EVS) by summarizing the samples of all music categories for the according bitrate. As reference, the average assessments of all 'uncoded' samples at 768 kbit/s (PCM 48 kHz, 16 bit, mono) by POLQA and listeners are shown.

The overall quality degradation between reference and 64 kbit/s samples is obviously low as expected before. The POLQA predictions average out at 4.66 in reference signals versus 4.59 (Opus) or 4.60 (EVS) in 64 kbit/s coding signals. The MOS listening assessment scores to 3.71 (reference) versus 3.72 (Opus) and 3.65 (EVS) at 64 kbit/s. Towards lower bitrates, POLQA and listening test results show a similar tendency for both codecs. The additional degradation at 32 kbit/s amounts to about 0.5 points in the MOS scale but the average assessments

---

[1] Listening to music several hours a day, using different playing techniques – high quality sound system, HD stereo headset etc.

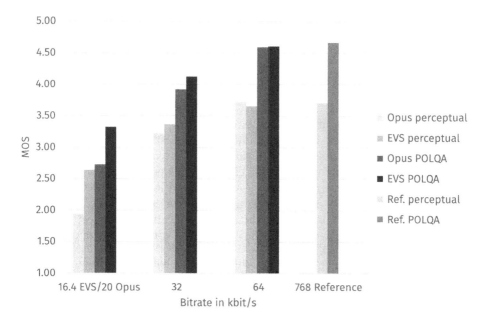

Fig. 2. Overall assessments by POLQA and 21 listeners (in total 42 samples).

stay considerably above 3.00. For the lowest FB bitrate (16.4/20 kbit/s), our assessments suggest an unacceptable audio quality – with the worst MOS = 1.94 (Opus listening test) which is not mirrored by the averaged POLQA predictions of 2.72.

In all tested categories, the absolute POLQA values are significantly too high which probably reflects our challenging listening test – the young target group, unfamiliar mono sounds and no instructions. Age-related assessment differences of about 0.4 in the MOS scale were already observed in our previous studies [10, 11]. The diversified assessments are also manifested in the standard deviations which range from 0.19 for the POLQA measurement of references or Opus/EVS samples at 64 kbit/s to maximal 1.25 for POLQA predictions of Opus samples at 20 kbit/s. The deviations of the listening assessments average out to about 0.7 in all bitrates.

4.2   Effect of the Music Characteristics

To explain the varying coding performance and the assessment deviations in Sect. 4.1, we shortly discuss the music characteristics in the following. Figure 3 illustrates the influence of diverging music pieces if using the Opus codec. Considering the perceptual assessment as a ground truth, we only present the listening results here.

In contrast to the Opus results (Fig. 3), Fig. 4 summarizes the EVS performance on the same music pieces.

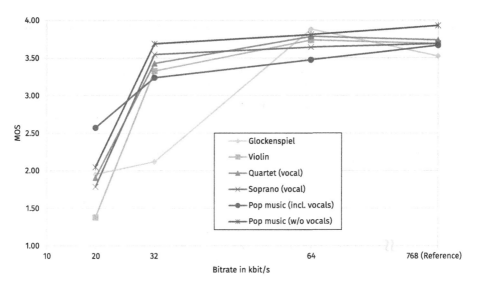

Fig. 3. Music coding by Opus – listening assessments only.

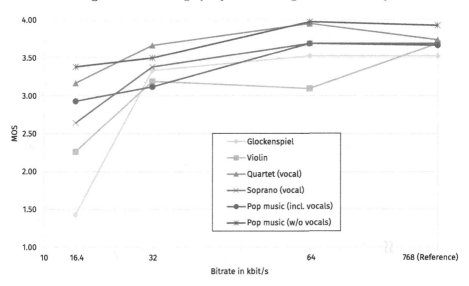

Fig. 4. Music coding by EVS – listening assessments only.

The expected degradation towards lower bitrates can be observed for both codecs and in all music categories. The Opus coding shows more consistent assessments over all music pieces and bitrates than EVS, except for the category "glockenspiel" whose mean assessment is surprisingly improved from original reference to 64 kbit/s and radically reduced at the bitrates of 20 and 32 kbit/s. It can be assumed that the active coding mode in Opus 'harmonizes' some skirl sounds (higher frequency components) of the original glockenspiel signal for listeners at 64 kbit/s but reduces the typical harmonics variety at the lower bitrates of 32 and 20 kbit/s too much.

In general, EVS is performing slightly better, except for the categories "violin" and "glockenspiel" but the scatter band of the assessments is higher than for Opus. For quartet and both categories of pop music, the mean assessment turns out to be higher at 64 kbit/s compared to the original reference. Furthermore, the alternating violin assessments towards lower bitrates are not plausible and require further studies. The explanation may correspond to the hybrid coding characteristics with switching operation modes and potentially different coding principles.

Comparing the performance on mixed characteristics with regard to vocal and music parts, the EVS coding shows a higher assessment tendency towards vocal samples respectively categories including vocals, whereas Opus handles music-only parts slightly better and more consistent to vocal-based assessments. These results are supported by the development history of the Internet-driven Opus derivation versus telecommunication carrier-patronized Enhanced Voice Service, as already illustrated in Sects. 1 and 2.

5   Conclusions and Future Research

We compared the fullband music coding ability of two real-time codecs, Opus and EVS – based on instrumental measures using POLQA and listening assessments as a ground truth. The POLQA predictions are widely plausible and correlating to the listening assessments, although the perceptual model is not adapted for music assessment yet. We will dedicate more experiments into this direction, and we are corresponding with the POLQA developers to support their optimizations for advanced versions. As expected, Opus and EVS showed a similar music coding performance over all bitrates, apparently depending on the music and vocal components in specific music pieces. We need to increase the amount of test data to consolidate the experimental results but we do not expect high improvement potential in the area of "all-rounder" codecs. Another important finding concerns the critical absolute assessments of our probands, in particular the gap to the instrumental assessment. We will run further (e.g. age-related) experiments to survey challenging test cond itions more precisely and to emphasize more research on the interrelations between perceptual and instrumental assessments in the community.

Acknowledgments. We would like to thank SwissQual, a Rhode & Schwarz company in Zuchwil, Switzerland for supplying the POLQA tool SQuadAnalyzer – in particular Jens Berger for the elaborate discussions. Further acknowledgments go to André Schuster for supporting our experiments in the sound insulating cabinet of HfT Leipzig, Germany and to all volunteers in the listening tests.

References

1. 3GPP: EVS Codec General Overview. TS 26.441 v12.1.0, 3rd Generation Partnership Project (3GPP), December 2014. http://www.3gpp.org/DynaReport/26441.htm
2. ETSI: Universal Mobile Telecommunications System (UMTS); LTE; Codec for Enhanced Voice Services (EVS); Performance characterization. TS 126952 v13.0.0, European Telecommunications Standards Institute (ETSI), January 2016. http://www.etsi.org/deliver/etsi_tr/126900_126999/126952/13.00.00_60/tr_126952v130000p.pdf
3. European Broadcasting Union: Sound Quality Assessment Material recordings for subjective tests, October 2008. https://tech.ebu.ch/publications/sqamcd
4. Frauenhofer IIS: The AAC-ELD Family For High Quality Communication Services. Technical paper, Frauenhofer IIS), December 2015
5. Google Inc.: WebRTC, September 2014. http://www.webrtc.org/
6. Hoene, C., Valin, J., Vos, K., Skoglund, J.: Summary of OPUS listening test results draft-ietf-codec-results-03. Internet-Draft, January 2014. http://tools.ietf.org/html/draft-ietf-codeco-results-03
7. ITU-T: Low-complexity, full-band audio coding for high-quality, conversational applications. REC G.719, International Telecommunication Union (Telecommunication Standardization Sector), June 2008. http://www.itu.int/rec/T-REC-G.719-200806-I/en
8. ITU-T: Methods for objective and subjective assessment of speech quality (POLQA): Perceptual Objective Listening Quality Assessment. REC P.863, International Telecommunication Union (Telecommunication Standardization Sector), September 2014. http://www.itu.int/rec/T-REC-P.863-201409-I/en
9. ITU-T: P.Imp863: Implementer's Guide on assessment of EVS coded speech with Recommendation ITU-TP.863, January 2016. http://www.itu.int/rec/T-REC-P.Imp863-201601-I!Oth1/en
10. Jokisch, O., Maruschke, M.: Audio and speech coding/transcoding in web real-time communication. In: Proceedings of International Symposium of Human Life Design, HLD 2016, Kanazawa, Japan, 26–29 March 2016 (2016). http://www.jaist.ac.jp/hld/IntlSymp2016/paper/HLD2016-COM03.pdf
11. Jokisch, O., Maruschke, M., Meszaros, M., Iaroshenko, V.: Audio and speech quality survey of the opus codec in web real-time communication. In: Proceedings of ESSV - 27th Conference of Electronic Signal Processing, ESSV 2016, Leipzig, Germany, 2–4 March 2016, pp. 254–262 (2016). http://www1.hft-leipzig.de/ice/essv2016/files/31%20-%20JokischMaruschke-S.254-262.pdf
12. Maruschke, M., Jokisch, O., Meszaros, M., Iaroshenko, V.: Review of the opus codec in a WebRTC scenario for audio and speech communication. In: Ronzhin, A., Potapova, R., Fakotakis, N. (eds.) SPECOM 2015. LNCS, vol. 9319, pp. 348–355. Springer, Heidelberg (2015)
13. Rämö, A., Toukomaa, H.: Subjective qualitiy evaluation of the 3Gpp EVS codec. In: IEEE International Conference on Acoustics, Speech and Signal Processing, Brisbane, Australia, pp. 5157–5161, April 2015
14. Valin, J., Vos, K., Terriberry, T.: Definition of the Opus Audio Codec. RFC 6716 (Proposed Standard). http://www.ietf.org/rfc/rfc6716.txt

Robust Speech Analysis Based on Source-Filter Model Using Multivariate Empirical Mode Decomposition in Noisy Environments

Surasak Boonkla[1,2](✉), Masashi Unoki[1], and Stanislav S. Makhanov[2]

[1] School of Information Science,
Japan Advanced Institute of Science and Technology, Nomi, Japan
{surasak,unoki}@jaist.ac.jp
[2] Sirindhorn International Institute of Technology,
Thammasat University, Pathum Thani, Thailand
makhanov@siit.tu.ac.th

Abstract. This paper proposes a robust speech analysis method based on source-filter model using multivariate empirical mode decomposition (MEMD) under noisy conditions. The proposed method has two stages. At the first stage, magnitude spectrum of noisy speech signal is decomposed by MEMD into intrinsic mode functions (IMFs), and then IMFs corresponded to noise part are removed from them. At the second stage, log-magnitude spectrum of noise-reduced signals are decomposed into IMFs. Then, these are divided into two groups: the first group characterized by spectral fine structure for fundamental frequency estimation and the second group characterized by frequency response of vocal-tract filter for formant frequencies estimation. As opposed to the conventional linear prediction (LP) and cepstrum methods, the proposed method decomposes noise automatically in magnitude spectral domain and makes noise mixture become sparse in log-magnitude spectral domain. The results show that the proposed method outperforms LP and cepstrum methods under noisy conditions.

Keywords: Multivariate empirical mode decomposition · Speech analysis · Fundamental frequency · Formant frequency · Source-filter model

1 Introduction

Speech analysis is an important core technique normally used in voice activity detection (VAD), automatic speech recognition (ASR), hearing aids, speaker identification, etc. Still, existing speech analysis techniques yield low performance in noisy environments. It is therefore important to improve robustness of speech analysis so that the above applications can work well in noisy conditions.

As a speech signal originates from a glottal-source waveform passing through a vocal-tract filter. The source-filter (SF) model [1] states that the speech signal is resulted from convolution between the glottal-source signal and the impulse

© Springer International Publishing Switzerland 2016
A. Ronzhin et al. (Eds.): SPECOM 2016, LNAI 9811, pp. 580–587, 2016.
DOI: 10.1007/978-3-319-43958-7_70

response of the vocal-tract filter. Most of the speech analysis techniques employ this model. The classical techniques commonly used for speech analysis are the linear prediction (LP) and the cepstrum [1]. LP estimates the vocal-tract filter by assuming that it is an all-pole filter model the coefficients of which are calculated by autocorrelation function (ACF) and covariance methods [1]. Cepstrum is the result of applying the inverse Fourier transform to log-magnitude spectrum of the speech signal. Cepstrum of spectral fine structure corresponding to periodic feature of harmonics (harmonicity) of the glottal-source along frequency axis are peaks in high quefrency range whereas cepstrum of spectral envelope corresponding to the frequency response of vocal-tract filter lies in the low quefrency range [1]. The lifter with proper cut-off quefrency can be applied in order to separate them. The spectral envelope is obtained by keeping the cepstrum of vocal-tract filter and then apply the Fourier transform. Cepstrum has several attractive properties such as robustness in noisy environments. Nowadays, besides LP and cepstrum, several speech analysis methods have been proposed especially STRAIGHT [2] and Praat [3]. STRAIGHT convolves the harmonics of the speech spectrum by the spectral representation of the analysis window and uses that window to interpolate the harmonic peaks of the speech spectrum by means of the summation of the main lobes of the window. Praat is a famous and reliable speech analysis tool which can be used for both glottal-source and vocal-tract filter analysis using analysis techniques proposed within last decade. It was frequently used to define the ground-truth for comparison in several studies.

Most speech analysis methods are required to be able to separately analyze the information of both glottal-source and vocal-tract filter. The majority of the above methods have been used to estimate (i) the fundamental frequency, F_0, of glottal-source and (ii) formants (resonant frequencies) and spectral envelope of the vocal-tract filter. However, the main problem of the above techniques is their robustness in noisy environments because they cannot reduce effects of noise by themselves. Due to this fact, multivariate empirical mode decomposition (MEMD) is thus proposed for speech analysis in noisy conditions based on an idea that MEMD can automatically decompose noise component out from the speech. In previous work [4], MEMD-based method was proposed for clean speech analysis by automatically decomposing glottal-source, and vocal-tract filter. In this paper, we cooperate the previous work with the idea of noise decomposition by MEMD to have a robust speech analysis in noisy conditions.

2   Principles

2.1   Source Filter Model

As stated earlier, speech signal $s(t)$ is resulted from convolution between a glottal-source (excitation) signal $e(t)$ with an impulse response of a vocal-tract filter $v(t)$. In frequency domain, they become multiplication or addition as follows:

$$s(t) = e(t) * v(t), \tag{1}$$

$$S(\omega) = E(\omega)V(\omega) = |E(\omega)|e^{j\angle E(\omega)}|V(\omega)|e^{j\angle V(\omega)}, \tag{2}$$

$$\log S(\omega) = \log|E(\omega)| + \log|V(\omega)| + j(\angle E(\omega) + \angle V(\omega)), \tag{3}$$

where ω is normalized frequency in radians/sample. The Fourier spectra of $s(t)$, $e(t)$, and $v(t)$ are $S(\omega)$, $E(\omega)$, and $V(\omega)$. Log of $S(\omega)$ has real and imaginary parts. The real part has log-magnitude spectrum of glottal-source, $\log|E(\omega)|$, and vocal-tract filter, $\log|V(\omega)|$. The imaginary part is the summation of their phases, $(\angle E(\omega) + \angle V(\omega))$. This research focuses on the log-magnitude spectrum whereas the phase spectrum is untouched.

2.2   Multivariate Empirical Mode Decomposition

MEMD is an adaptive and data-driven signal processing technique for decomposing any non-stationary multivariate signal with n sub-signals, i.e. $\mathbf{x}(t) = \{x_1(t), x_2(t), \ldots, x_n(t)\}$, simultaneously into band-limited oscillating components called intrinsic mode functions (IMFs). So that each sub-signal can be expressed as

$$x_n(t) = \sum_{i=1}^{K} c_i(t) + r(t),\tag{4}$$

where $c_i(t)$ is the i-th IMF, $r(t)$ is the residue or monotonic function, and K is the number of IMFs. An important property of MEMD is that the common mode (frequency components) would align in the same order of IMF [5]. Consider $\mathbf{v}^{\theta_q} = \{v_1^q, v_2^q, \ldots, v_n^q\}$ denoting a set of direction vectors along the directions given by angles $\theta_q = \{\theta_1, \theta_2, \ldots, \theta_Q\}$ on $(n-1)$ sphere where Q is the number of sampling points on the sphere. The following is the algorithm for obtaining the IMFs from $\mathbf{x}(t)$ using MEMD. At the beginning of the algorithm, set $\mathbf{h}(t) = \mathbf{x}(t)$, $\mathbf{r}(t) = \mathbf{x}(t)$, and $i = 1$.

1. Choose a pointset for sampling on an $(n-1)$ sphere.
2. Calculate a projection, denoted by $p^{\theta_q}(t)$ of the input $\mathbf{h}(t)$ along the direction vector $\mathbf{v}^{\theta_q}$ for all q (the whole set of direction vector), giving $p^{\theta_q}(t)\}_{q=1}^{Q}$ as the set of projections.
3. Find the time instants $\{t_i^{\theta_q}\}$ corresponding to the maxima and minima of the set of projected signals $p^{\theta_q}(t)\}_{q=1}^{Q}$.
4. Interpolate $[t_i^{\theta_q}, \mathbf{h}(t_i^{\theta_q})]$ to obtain envelopes $\mathbf{e}_{max}^{\theta_q}(t)\}_{q=1}^{Q}$ and $\mathbf{e}_{min}^{\theta_q}(t)\}_{q=1}^{Q}$.
5. For a set of Q direction vectors, the mean $\mathbf{m}(t)$ of the envelope curves is $\mathbf{m}(t) = \frac{1}{2Q}\sum_{q=1}^{Q} \mathbf{e}_{max}^{\theta_q}(t) + \mathbf{e}_{min}^{\theta_q}(t)$.
6. Extract $\mathbf{d}(t)$ using $\mathbf{d}(t) = \mathbf{h}(t) - \mathbf{m}(t)$. If $\mathbf{d}(t)$ fulfills the properties of IMF or the stopping criterion [5] go to the next step. Otherwise $\mathbf{h}(t) = \mathbf{d}(t)$ and repeat steps 2 to 6.
7. Assign an IMF, $\mathbf{z}_i(t) = \mathbf{d}(t)$, and $i = i+1$. Subtract the IMF from the residual $\mathbf{r}(t) = \mathbf{r}(t) - \mathbf{z}_i(t)$.
8. Stop if $\mathbf{r}(t)$ is monotonic. Otherwise, assign $\mathbf{h}(t) = \mathbf{r}(t)$ and go to step 2 for extracting other IMF.

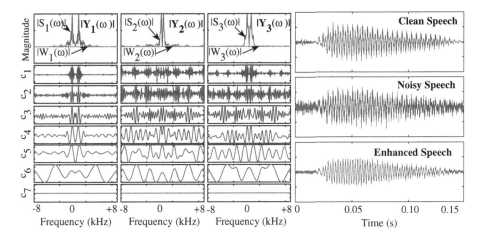

Fig. 1. Decomposition noise speech using MEMD. The flat shape of noise spectrum is separated into the last IMFs, c_7. Removing these IMFs results in speech enhancement.

3   Proposed Method

Generally, a noisy speech signal is described as $y(t) = s(t) + w(t)$, where $w(t)$ is background noise. Its magnitude spectrum can be expressed as

$$|Y(\omega)| = |S(\omega)| + |W(\omega)| = \underbrace{\sum_{k=1}^{N} c_k(\omega)}_{\text{Speech}} + \underbrace{\sum_{k=N+1}^{K} c_k(\omega)}_{\text{Noise}}, \qquad (5)$$

where $|W(\omega)|$ is the magnitude spectrum of $w(t)$, $c_k(\omega)$ is the k-th IMF, N is the number that separate IMFs into two groups which are of speech and noise, and K is the total number of IMFs. The value of N is determined using the characteristic of noise. Theoretically, $|W(\omega)|$ is flat over the entire frequency range when $w(t)$ is white noise. After $|Y(\omega)|$ is decomposed by MEMD into IMFs, the flat shape of $|W(\omega)|$ can be decomposed into the monotonic residue as shown in Fig. 1. This flat shape is identified using the common mode alignment property of MEMD and similarity between IMFs. Let $|S_i(\omega)|$, $|W_i(\omega)|$, and $|Y_i(\omega)|$ are the magnitude spectrum of clean speech, white noise, and noisy speech of the i-th frame. Based on an assumption that white noise is stationary but clean speech is non-stationary. Therefore, $|W_i(\omega)| = |W(\omega)|$ which means that $|W_i(\omega)|$s are mutually dependent but $|S_i(\omega)|$s are mutually independent. This assumption can be met by setting a short analysis window and each frame is far away to each others. Decomposing $|Y_i(\omega)|$ using MEMD results in IMFs as shown in Fig. 1. According to the common mode alignment property of MEMD, the common component would align in the same order of IMF. Since only noise is common to all frames, its flat shape of spectrum aligns in the same order of IMF, say $c_7(\omega)$, in Fig. 1. These flat shape of noise can be detected by similarity measurement such as correlation coefficient across the column. As a result, the value of N of Eq. (5) is 6 in this case.

After removing noise component by omitting the second term of Eq. (5), the enhanced speech is assumed to be equivalent to clean speech. According to Eq. (3), the log-magnitude spectrum of a voiced speech contains two terms. After it is decomposed into IMFs, the IMFs can be divided into two groups corresponding to the glottal-source and vocal-tract filter. That is

$$\log|S(\omega)| = \log|E(\omega)| + \log|V(\omega)| = \underbrace{\sum_{k=1}^{M} c_k(\omega)}_{\text{Source}} + \underbrace{\sum_{k=M+1}^{L} c_k(\omega)}_{\text{Filter}}, \qquad (6)$$

where M is a variable dividing IMFs into two groups and L is the number of IMFs. To determine the value of M, we also use the common mode alignment property of MEMD. The proposed method takes three adjacent frames of speech signal with overlap so that there is a common mode which is harmonicity of glottal-source. Three log-magnitude spectra are decomposed into three sets of IMFs as shown in the first three column of Fig. 2. A the beginning, we roughly divides the IMFs into two groups by autocorrelation function (ACF) of IMF. Let denote the location of the **second peak** of ACF of the **k-th** IMF as Fp_k. If Fp_k is in the normal range of F_0 of human voice (85–400 Hz), the k-th IMF is considered as the first group. Otherwise that IMF is belonged to the second group. The IMFs having common harmonicity are noticeable at c_3 in Fig. 2. These IMFs of common harmonicity would have high correlation coefficient across columns. The value of M is consequently 3 in this case. The result of source-filter separation is shown in the most right column in Fig. 2 where the spectral envelope obtained by the proposed method is shown in blue compared with those obtained by LP (red) and cepstrum (green) based methods.

After source-filter separation, we can estimate important features of glottal-source and vocal-tract from summation of the first and second groups respectively. The peaks of ACF of the summation of the first group is used for F_0 estimation and the peak picking technique is used for formant estimation. The results of F_0, formants estimation, and comparison of spectral envelope before and after noise removal are illustrated in Figs. 3(a)–(c). In the experiment, we will test the robustness of speech analysis before and after noise reduction using MEMD under variation of signal to noise ratios (SNR)s.

4   Experiments and Evaluations

The experiments were carried out before and after noise reduction. The estimation of F_0, formants, and spectral envelope were done because these are important speech features, which most of speech analysis methods can estimate. The F_0 estimation was evaluated using correct rate (CR) which is defined as

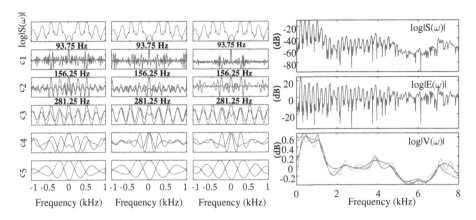

Fig. 2. The result of source-filter separation of a clean speech in log magnitude spectrum domain. IMFs are shown in blue and their ACF are plotted in red. $\log|V(\omega)|$ obtained by the proposed method is shown in blue compared with LP (red) and cepstrum (green) based methods. (Color figure online)

$$\text{CR} = \frac{N_{F_{0,\text{Est}}}(Err)}{N_{F_{0,\text{Ref}}}} \times 100, \qquad (7)$$

where $F_{0,\text{Est}}$ is the estimated F_0, $F_{0,\text{Ref}}$ is referenced value obtained from clean speech using TEMPO [6]. $N_{F_{0,\text{Est}}}$ is the number of correct estimation that satisfies $|F_{0,\text{Ref}} - F_{0,\text{Est}}|/F_{0,\text{Ref}} \le Err(\%)$, $N_{F_{0,\text{Ref}}}$ is the total number of estimations, and Err is an tolerable error margin which is 10 %.

The formants estimation was evaluated by comparison with formants obtained by LP, cepstrum, and Praat (ground-truth). The shape of spectral envelope was evaluated by correlation coefficient and Euclidean spectral distance measurement. The LP-based spectral envelope was obtained from LP with lp-order of 22 (sampling rate in kHz plus few values) and cepstrum-based spectral envelope was calculated using cut-off quefrency lower than the minimum quefrency of the glottal-source corresponding to the maximum F_0 of human voice, 400 Hz. The referenced spectral envelope for comparison was obtained from clean speech. In noise analysis and reduction, the window length was 10 msec with Hanning window, two adjacent frames were 500 msec apart. In speech analysis, the analysis window was 30 msec length, Hanning, and 50 % frame overlap. The number of frequency sampling was 1024 points. The testing data were from vowel /ey/ of words of /CV/ where C is consonant and V is vowel. The testing data were from randomly selected 5 males and 5 females of TIMIT database [7].

5   Results and Discussion

The results of F_0 and formants estimation are shown in Figs. 3(d)–(f). The correct rate of the proposed method before noise removal and formants estimation

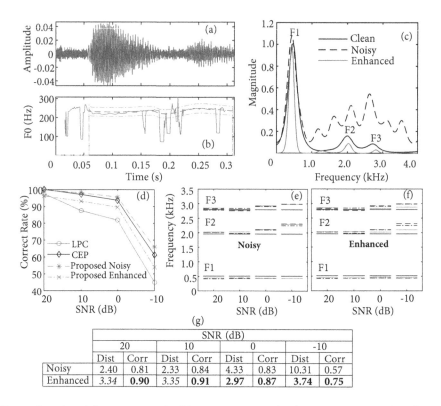

Fig. 3. Results: (a) noisy speech (b) estimated F_0 (red), referenced F_0 (blue), and tolerable error margin (green), (c) magnitude spectrum of vocal-tract filter before and after noise reduction, (d) correct rates using the proposed method before and after noise reduction, (e)–(f) are formant estimation before and after noise reduction, and (g) average spectral distance and correlation coefficient before and after noise reduction. (Color figure online)

after noise removal (SNRs are 0 and −10 dB) outperforms LP and cepstrum based methods. Nevertheless, the correct rate reduces after the noise reduction. The spectral envelope improvement is illustrated in Fig. 3(g) in which average spectral distance and correlation coefficient between spectral envelopes before and after noise removal are summarized. Notice that correlation coefficients are always increased after noise removal but the spectral distance is reduced only when SNRs are 0 and −10 dB.

According to the results, the speech analysis stage is robust against noise for F_0 estimation compared with LP and cepstrum based methods. The robustness come from the fact that decomposition log magnitude spectrum into IMFs makes mixing noise become sparse. The effects from noise are consequently alleviated. The good results obtained after noise removal are more accurate formants estimation and improved shape of spectral envelope. Nevertheless, the correct rate reduces after noise removal and the spectral distance increases when SNRs = 20 and 10 dB. These may be caused by speech distortion after noise reduction.

In sum, the accurate speech features can be obtained by combining these two stages. Therefore, the proposed method is a robust speech analysis in noisy environments.

6   Conclusion

The robust speech analysis method based on source-filter model using MEMD in noisy environments was proposed. The evaluation results showed that it outperforms the linear prediction and cepstrum based methods under noisy conditions. The proposed method could also automatically decomposed noise component which was identified using common mode alignment property of MEMD and mutual dependency of white noise across frames. After noise reduction, the formant estimation and the shape of spectral envelope were improved. In addition, the estimated formants were better than those obtained by LP and cepstrum based method. It was consequently reconfirmed that the proposed method is robust against noisy conditions and can correctly estimate speech features.

Acknowledgments. This work was supported by the Grant-in-Aid for Scientific Research (A) (No. 25240026), and by the Secom Science and Technology Foundation. This was also under a grant in the SIIT-JAIST-NECTEC Dual Doctoral Degree Program.

References

1. Quatieri, T.F.: Discrete-Time Speech Signal Processing: Principles and Practice. Prentice Hall, New Jersey (2001)
2. Kawahara, H., Morise, M., Takahashi, T., Nisimura, R., Irino, T., Banno, H.: Tandem-STRAIGHT: a temporally stable power spectral representation for periodic signals and applications to interference-free spectrum, F0, and aperiodicity estimation. In: IEEE International Conference on Acoustics, Speech, and Signal Processing, Las Vegas, pp. 3933–3936 (2008)
3. Boersma, P., Weenink, D.: Praat: doing Phonetics by computer [Computer Program]. Version 6.0.06 from (2016). http://www.praat.org/
4. Boonkla, S., Unoki, M., Makhanov, S.S., Wutiwiwatchai, C.: Speech analysis method based on source-filter model using multivariate empirical mode decomposition in log-spectrum domain. In: 9th IEEE International Symposium on Chinese Spoken Language Processing, Singapore, pp. 555–559 (2014)
5. Mandic, D.P., Rehman, N.U., Zhaohua, W., Huang, N.E.: Empirical mode decomposition-based time-frequency analysis of multivariate signals: the power of adaptive data analysis. IEEE Sig. Process. Mag. **30**(6), 74–86 (2013)
6. Kawahara, H., Katayose, H., de Cheveigne, A., Patterson, R.D.: Fixed point analysis of frequency to instantaneous frequency mapping for accurate estimation of F0 and periodicity. In: 6th European Conference on Speech Communication and Technology, Hungary, vol. 6, pp. 2781–2784 (1999)
7. Garofolo, J., et al.: TIMIT Acoustic-Phonetic continuous speech corpus. LDC93S1. Web Download. Linguistic Data Consortium, Philadelphia (1993)

Scenarios of Multimodal Information Navigation Services for Users in Cyberphysical Environment

Irina Vatamaniuk, Dmitriy Levonevskiy, Anton Saveliev$^{(\boxtimes)}$, and Alexander Denisov

St. Petersburg Institute for Informatics and Automation of the Russian Academy of Sciences,
39, 14th Line, St. Petersburg 199178, Russian Federation
{vatamaniuk,saveliev}@iias.spb.su, dlewonewski.8781@gmail.com,
sdenisov93@mail.ru

Abstract. Cyberphysical systems (CPS) provide a broad range of possibilities in many fields of human activity such as multimodal human-computer interaction (HCI). The paper discusses the architecture of developing multimodal information navigation system of SPIIRAS, considering an approach of building a corporate information subsystem for tracking events, scheduling and displaying information on a distributed set of stationary monitors. The subsystem architecture was described in detail. The suggested algorithm for generating schedules showed high performance. The subsystem uses standard network technologies, is not tied to any software or hardware platforms, matches extensibility and portability criteria and may be used as a component of the cyberphysical environment in various organizations. Scenarios of user handling depending on user status are presented.

Keywords: Cyberphysical systems · Multimodal interfaces · Information navigation services

1 Introduction

Nowadays cyberphysical systems become widespread due to their possibilities, flexibility and effective interaction with environment [1]. They combine computation, communication and physical dynamics [2]. The CPS is a common expression, which unites developments in many fields such as medicine [3] (health monitoring [4], tele-surgery [5, 6], assistance to elderly and people with disabilities [6]), robotic manufacturing systems [7, 8], robot multi agent control [9], autonomous automotive systems [10, 11], electric power generation and distribution (smart grid) [12, 13], smart spaces [14, 15], Internet of things [16], game and entertainment industry, etc. [2]. A broad overview of the modern CPS is presented in [17].

One of the high demanded fields of CPS application is related to human-computer interaction (HCI) within the smart spaces. The CPS sensors' data fusion allows performing HCI via various modalities (speech, gestures, facial articulation, gaze direction, etc.) The multimodal HCI prevents errors due to redundancy of information and provides the most natural and comfortable way of controlling environment [18, 19]. Smart spaces allow unifying different levels of services, supporting self-organization of services in each level, and providing rules from upper to lower level [20].

© Springer International Publishing Switzerland 2016
A. Ronzhin et al. (Eds.): SPECOM 2016, LNAI 9811, pp. 588–595, 2016.
DOI: 10.1007/978-3-319-43958-7_71

2 Developed Architecture of Multimedia Display Subsystem

The considered approach of distribution of sensory, network, computing and service tasks between components of cyberphysical systems (mobile robots, embedded devices, mobile client devices, stationary equipment, cloud resources) implies that the mobile components perform only those tasks that cannot be solved by stationary devices (for example, guiding a person through the building by a robot) [21–23]. Among the stationary components of the cyberphysical environment there is a corporate information system responsible for tracking events (for example, coming and leaving of employees and guests), visitor registering and recognition, storing their profiles, interacting with them by means of touchscreens, broadcasting information on stationary displays [24–26].

Consider more closely the architecture of the subsystem responsible for tracking events, scheduling and displaying information. Digital signage systems are often used for this purpose. As there are high demands on flexibility, dynamism and extensibility of cyberphysical environment components, the existing open source solutions (Xibo, Concerto v2, Vodigi, etc.) should be carefully examined. It was discovered that those systems have some disadvantages: lack of means of creating templates, i.e. no possibility of automatic building sets of media files from a template using an external data source (for example, employees database); high persistence even correspondingly configured, which is critical if an instant message should be displayed (for example, greeting, alarm, etc.). Client software has implementation issues (for example, Xibo generates high browser load if a large number of objects is present in the schedule), and the ways of defining event activation conditions are not flexible enough. The platform dependency of the software should also be noted.

As a result it was decided to develop a multimedia display subsystem meeting the considered requirements. The implemented subsystem is based on the client-server architecture and consists of the server, monitors and administrator consoles connected via TCP/IP. The central component is the server, its architecture is shown in Fig. 1.

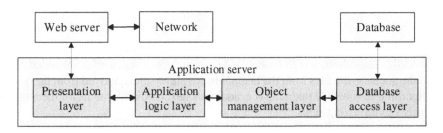

Fig. 1. Server architecture

It stores information about monitors and their groups, users, tracks events, stores media content, forms the media schedule for each monitor, forms and transfers commands, provides the control interface to administrators and operators. Its main components are database server (MySQL) storing data on the subsystem objects, application server (PHP) responsible for the application logic, and web server (Apache) providing access to clients (administrators, operators, monitors).

The algorithms underlying the server functioning are based on the object-oriented data model. On the database layer a single object usually corresponds to a table record. The classes defining objects are arranged into the following structure (Fig. 2). All classes inherit from the base abstract class TGeneric, so it is possible to refer to general properties through a unified interface. The generic operations on objects are: id (getting object identifier, i.e. its unique number); title (getting object name); getAttr, setAttr (getting and setting object properties); create (creating object); delete (removing object); triggerAfterLoad, triggerAfterCreate, etc. (functions invoked on particular operations on object).

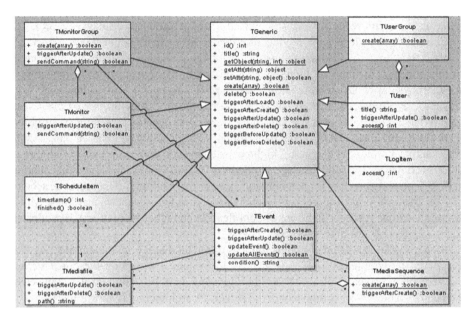

Fig. 2. Class diagram

The principal task of the server is to build and update the media schedule for monitors dynamically. The schedule is an ordered list (a queue). New media files are added to the end of the queue as the files from the beginning are played and removed from the queue. The algorithm of schedule updating (i.e. adding N next media files to it) for the monitor M consists in following steps:

1. Determine the set of active events by testing their activation rules.
2. Determine the set of active events $\{E_M\}$ for the monitor M.
3. Determine the set of active events $\{E_{Gi}\}$ for the monitor groups $G_1, G_2, ..., G_n$, to which the monitor M belongs.
4. Determine the full set of active events related to this monitor:

$$\{E\} = \{E_M\} \cup \{E_{G_1}\} \cup \{E_{G_2}\} \cup ... \cup \{E_{G_n}\}$$

5. Exclude from the schedule all media files that are not associated with events from the set $\{E\}$.
6. Determine the set of media files $\{F\}$ that are associated with $\{E\}$.
7. Sort the set $\{F\}$ by the last activation time (ascending).
8. Add the first N files from $\{F\}$ to the end of the schedule.
9. Update the last activation time for these files.
10. Wait for the next update request.

The algorithm includes carrying out a lot of searching and sorting operations. Such operations are effectively performed by the database server. Transferring the operations with high computational costs to the server allows performing these operations for an acceptable time amount. For instance, steps 1–7 of the algorithm can be fulfilled by a single query. Figure 3 shows the time of executing the query returning 10 media files for a monitor depending on number of files in the database.

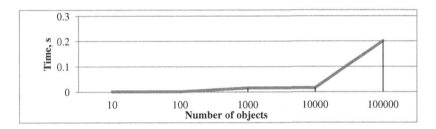

Fig. 3. Query time for different number of media files in the database

Stationary monitors are located in various places of the building. Monitor is a stationary hardware-software complex designed to broadcast media content according to the schedule. It consists of a display and a nettop connected to the server. A web browser with HTML5 support is installed on the nettop to play media files. The web application downloads and displays files from the server. The action sequence diagram describing interaction between server and viewer is shown in Fig. 4.

The design of the monitor web interface is shown in Fig. 5. It consists of viewer and controller. The controller connects to the server, obtains schedule and media and passes it to the viewer. The viewer preloads media, displays them and gives the controller signals about its state. The administrator consoles provide access to manage monitors, events, users and media files via HTTP. Main features of the Web interface include event, file, monitor, group and schedule management, user accounting and viewing log data.

The implemented subsystem is integrated in the corporate cyberphysical environment. It uses standard network technologies, is not tied to any software or hardware platforms and matches extensibility and portability criteria. It may be used as a component of the cyberphysical environment in various organizations.

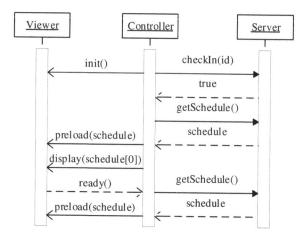

Fig. 4. Diagram of interactions between server and viewer

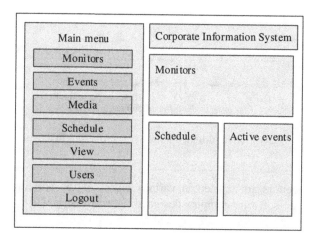

Fig. 5. Web interface of monitor

3   Usage Scenarios of Multimodal Information and Navigation Services

All users of cyberphysical intelligent environment of St. Petersburg Institute for Informatics and Automation of the Russian Academy of Sciences (SPIIRAS) fall into the following categories: employees; students; delegation representatives; single guests; sightseers of museum of K. May school and SPIIRAS museum; other (laborers, couriers, etc.). The main distinction between employees and other categories of users is the fact that they have ID cards and can enter the SPIIRAS at their own discretion. Students have to get on the phone with the professor to enter the SPIIRAS, as well as single guests and laborers. Delegation representatives as well as sightseers are met at the checkpoint by administrative employees by prior arrangement.

The implementation of the cyberphysical intelligent environment allows simplifying this procedure by usage of videoconferencing application at the informational touchscreen at the SPIIRAS checkpoint. The employees pass the turngate after automatic authentication based on face recognition. Other users are suggested to select appropriate menu option in the touchscreen according to the purpose of their visit and follow the further instructions. Scenarios of multimodal informational and navigational services are presented on Fig. 6a, b. The menu proposed to students is shown on Fig. 6c. Delegation representatives, single guests and sightseers are given the menu on Fig. 6d. The system also registers the arrival and leaving time.

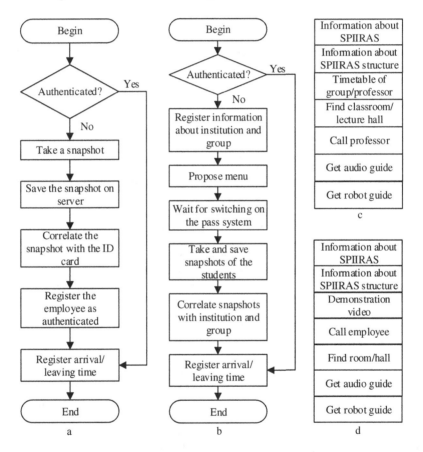

Fig. 6. Scenarios of user registration: a – employees, b – students; visitor menus: c – students, d – other visitors

Other users are suggested to select appropriate menu option in the touchscreen according to the purpose of their visit and follow the further instructions. Scenarios of multimodal informational and navigational services are presented on Fig. 6a, b. The menu proposed to students is shown on Fig. 6c. Delegation representatives, single guests and sightseers are given the menu on Fig. 6d. The system also registers the arrival and leaving time.

4 Conclusion

The informational and navigational services in cyberphysical intelligent environment of SPIIRAS are under implementation. The ensemble of webcams will be involved for processes of registration, authentication and recognition of users. It allows automating work of checkpoint and reception. The developed multimedia display subsystem will help users to get required information quickly and efficiently via monitors and informational touchscreens.

Acknowledgment. The study was performed through the grant of the Russian Science Foundation (project no.16-19-00044).

References

1. Rajeev, A.: Principles of Cyber-Physical Systems. MIT Press, Cambridge (2015)
2. Lee, E.A., Seshia, S.A.: Introduction to Embedded Systems. A Cyber-Physical Systems Approach, 2nd edn. (2015). http://LeeSeshia.org
3. Lee, I., Sokolsky, O.: Medical cyber physical systems. In: Proceedings of the 47th Design Automation Conference, pp. 743–748. ACM, New York (2010)
4. Hackmann, G., Guo, W., Yan, G., Lu, Ch., Dyke, Sh: Cyber-physical codesign of distributed structural health monitoring with wireless sensor networks. IEEE Trans. Parallel Distrib. Syst. **25**(1), 63–72 (2013)
5. Lee, G.S., Thuraisingham, B.: Cyberphysical systems security applied to telesurgical robotics. Comput. Stand. Interfaces **34**(1), 225–229 (2012)
6. Eren, H., Webster, J.G. (eds.): Telemedicine and Electronic Medicine. CRC Press, Boca Raton (2015)
7. Wang, L., Törngren, M., Onori, M.: Current status and advancement of cyber-physical systems in manufacturing. J. Manuf. Syst. **37**(2), 517–527 (2015)
8. Lee, J., Bagheri, B., Kao, H.A.: A cyber-physical systems architecture for industry 4.0-based manufacturing systems. Manuf. Lett. **3**, 18–23 (2015)
9. Fink, J., Ribeiro, A., Kumar, V.: Robust control for mobility and wireless communication in cyber-physical systems with application to robot teams. Proc. IEEE **100**(1), 164–178 (2012)
10. Wan, J., Yan, H., Li, D., Zhou, K., Zeng, L.: Cyber-physical systems for optimal energy management scheme of autonomous electric vehicle. Comput. J. **56**(8), 947–956 (2013)
11. Wan, J., Zhang, D., Zhao, S., Yang, L., Lloret, J.: Context-aware vehicular cyber-physical systems with cloud support: architecture, challenges, and solutions. IEEE Commun. Mag. **52**(8), 106–113 (2014)
12. Bu, S., Yu, F.R.: A game-theoretical scheme in the smart grid with demand-side management: towards a smart cyber-physical power infrastructure. IEEE Trans. Emerg. Top. Comput. **1**(1), 22–32 (2013)

13. Li, H., Lai, L., Poor, H.V.: Multicast routing for decentralized control of cyber physical systems with an application in smart grid. IEEE J. Sel. Areas Commun. **30**(6), 1097–1107 (2012)
14. Zeng, J., Yang, L.T., Ning, H., Ma, J.: A systematic methodology for augmenting quality of experience in smart space design. IEEE Wirel. Commun. **22**(4), 81–87 (2015)
15. Bai, Z.Y., Huang, X.Y.: Design and implementation of a cyber physical system for building smart living spaces. Int. J. Distrib. Sens. Netw. (2012)
16. Kimura, A., Nakae, S., Terano, M., Takenaka, T., Fukuda, K., Yamamoto, Y.: Smart appliance network as cyber physical systems: creating value to meet various consumer lifestyles. In: 2015 IEEE 4th Global Conference on Consumer Electronics (GCCE), pp. 262–264. IEEE (2015)
17. Khaitan, S.K., McCalley, J.D.: Design techniques and applications of cyberphysical systems: a survey. IEEE Syst. J. **9**(2), 350–365 (2015)
18. Sebe, N.: Multimodal interfaces: challenges and perspectives. J. Ambient Intell. Smart Environ. **1**(1), 23–30 (2009)
19. Turk, M.: Multimodal interaction: a review. Pattern Recogn. Lett. **36**, 189–195 (2014)
20. Smirnov, A., Kashevnik, A., Shilov, N.: Cyber-physical-social system self-organization: ontology-based multi-level approach and case study. In: 2015 IEEE 9th International Conference on Self-Adaptive and Self-Organizing Systems (SASO), pp. 168–169. IEEE (2015)
21. Suranova, D.A., Meshcheryakov, R.V.: Personified voice interaction software in billing systems. In: Ronzhin, A., Potapova, R., Delic, V. (eds.) SPECOM 2014. LNCS, vol. 8773, pp. 345–352. Springer, Heidelberg (2014)
22. Motienko, A.I., Makeev, S.M., Basov, O.O.: Analysis and modeling of position choice process for transportation of the sufferer on the basis of Bayesian belief networks. SPIIRAS Proceedings **43**, 135–155 (2015)
23. Karpov, A.A., Ronzhin, A.L.: Information enquiry kiosk with multimodal user interface. Pattern Recogn. Image Anal. **19**(3), 546–558 (2009). MAIK Nauka/Interperiodica, Moscow
24. Yusupov, R.M., Ronzhin, A.L.: From smart devices to smart space. Herald Russ. Acad. Sci. **80**(1), 45–51 (2010). MAIK Nauka
25. Ronzhin, A.L., Budkov, V.Yu.: Multimodal interaction with intelligent meeting room facilities from inside and outside. In: Balandin, S., Moltchanov, D., Koucheryavy, Y. (eds.) ruSMART 2009. LNCS, vol. 5764, pp. 77–88. Springer, Heidelberg (2009)
26. Saveliev, A.I., Vatamaniuk, I.V., Ronzhin, A.L.: Architecture of data exchange with minimal client-server interaction at multipoint video conferencing. In: Balandin, S., Andreev, S., Koucheryavy, Y. (eds.) NEW2AN/ruSMART 2014. LNCS, vol. 8638, pp. 164–174. Springer, Heidelberg (2014)

Scores Calibration in Speaker Recognition Systems

Andrey Shulipa[1(✉)], Sergey Novoselov[1,2], and Yuri Matveev[1,2]

[1] ITMO University, Saint Petersburg, Russia
{shulipa,novoselov}@speechpro.com
[2] Speech Technology Center, Saint Petersburg, Russia
http://en.ifmo.ru/
http://speechpro.com/

Abstract. It is well known that variability of speech signal quality affects the performance of speaker recognition systems. Difference in speech quality between enrollment and test utterances leads to shifting of scores and performance degradation. In order to improve the effectiveness of speaker recognition in these circumstances the scores calibration is required. Speech signal parameters that have a strong impact on speaker recognition performance are total speech duration, signal to noise ratio and reverberation time. Their variability leads to scores shifting and unreliable accept/reject decisions. In this paper we investigate the effects of speech duration variability on the calibration when enroll and test speech utterances originate from the same channel. An effective method of scores stabilization is also presented.

Keywords: Speaker recognition · Calibration scores · Tuning speaker recognition system

1 Introduction

Speaker recognition is an advanced biometric technology that is widely used in different areas, such as government, forensic, and industry [3,10], contact center fraud detection [2], solutions for secure financial transactions [1]. Conventional speaker recognition systems provide the ability to compare voice models of known persons with those of speakers that should be verified or identified. A scalar value, usually called *score*, is used to express speaker similarity and to make decisions based on some threshold value. This score threshold controls the boundary between two types of errors that a speaker recognition system produces [17]. The score calibration procedure is a speaker recognition system tuning technique that allows to choose a threshold value so as to minimize the recognition error and make the scores more reliable [14].

In recent years, the problem of calibration of automatic speaker recognition systems has received more attention, and a number of papers were published that deal with this problem [5,7]. This increased attention is explained by the need to

© Springer International Publishing Switzerland 2016
A. Ronzhin et al. (Eds.): SPECOM 2016, LNAI 9811, pp. 596–603, 2016.
DOI: 10.1007/978-3-319-43958-7_72

get more stable score distributions when the environmental conditions of speech recording are changed. The effect of different factors [5] such as transmission type, vocal effort, noise level, speech duration, etc. is the reason of scores shifting and so it has to be compensated.

The solution to the calibration problem is to determine parameters of score mapping to log likelihood ratios that depend on quality characteristics of speech utterances. The main criteria of the calibration performance of the recognition system is given by the value of the detection cost function at the specified application-independent threshold [4,16,17]. In order to improve calibration performance it is necessary to determine the parameters of the score transformation minimizing the cost function value [9,17]. In [5,13] the investigation of different types of score calibration is presented. Application of generative modeling is proposed in [5] for unsupervised score calibration when supervised data cannot be obtained. A new way of computing scaling parameters for linear calibration by using constrained maximum likelihood Gaussian is reported in [13]. There is an investigation of different calibration approaches in [11].

Other works deal with the scores calibration function where speech duration of enrollment and test speech segments is used as a measure of quality [15,18]. A problem arises if test and enrollment speech segments within the same channel type have high speech duration variability which is larger than variability of other quality measures such as signal to noise ratio, reverberation time and etc.

This paper investigates the effect of speech duration in trial recordings on the scores distribution. The estimation of the distribution parameters with respect to the duration of speech segments is carried out. We propose a method to approximate these parameters, as well as a corresponding approximation function, and compare our results with a similar solution presented in [15]. The state-of-the-art PLDA speaker recognition system was used in our investigations. To train speaker recognition system and to model test conditions we used speech utterances from NIST SRE database recorded only in telephone channel.

2   Speaker Recognition System

In our experiments we used a text independent speaker recognition system that represents speaker voice models as i-vectors in a low dimension space. Modeling of i-vectors distribution was performed by using probabilistic linear discriminant analysis (PLDA). To extract features from speech signal we used 20 ms analysis windows with 10 ms shifting by calculating 13 MFCC parameters. Then we combined the parameters with their first and second derivatives to form a 39-dimensional feature vector.

Voice activity detection is performed by using speech energy based algorithm as described in [12]. Finally, a gender-dependent UBM of 2048 components was applied. The UBM was trained on the NIST SRE-2004, 2005, 2006, Switchboard II and Switchboard Cellular 1, 2 databases. In this paper, we used a gender-dependent 600-dimensional i-vector space which was trained on the same data as the UBM. I-vector length normalization and covariance normalization [8] were applied prior for optimal performance of our system. In PLDA model only the 400 speaker factors were taken into account. Subspace speaker factor matrix in PLDA was trained using the same databases for i-vector space training with speaker labeling.

3   Evaluation Databases

We experimented with speech databases provided by National Institute of Standard and Technology (NIST). All speech data in our experiments were from telephone conversations in English. We used NIST SRE 2008 subset as a development set to train calibration parameters of our system.

Evaluation of calibration performance was carried out on the NIST SRE 2012 (C2 protocol) speech data named as a test set. We applied all possible trials to train calibration parameters by using development speech database. In the telephone speech evaluation protocol we used 2826 target / 161564 imposter trials to evaluate calibration performance. Speech segments from the evaluation set vary in duration from 4 s to 150 s.

4   Calibration

Generally calibration is applied to rescale and shift raw scores minimizing the expectation error at the specified application-independent threshold. After that the calibration scores may be considered as log likelihood ratios and they have a direct probabilistic interpretation.

It can be shown that if the scores are normally distributed with equal variances then calibration mapping is a linear transformation. So calibrated score $\bar{s}$ can be calculated as:

$$\bar{s} = as + b, \tag{1}$$

where s is a raw score. The offset b and scaling a parameters are obtained by solving an optimization problem on a development set.

Accuracy of the speaker recognition system is estimated by the detection cost function that is applied in the NIST speaker recognition evaluations:

$$DCF(\theta) = C_{\mathrm{fr}}P_{\mathrm{fr}}(\theta)\pi + C_{\mathrm{fa}}P_{\mathrm{fa}}(\theta)(1 - \pi), \tag{2}$$

where C_{fr} and C_{fa} are the conditional risk parameters and denote costs of a false-reject and of a false-alarm respectively. Parameter π is a prior probability of target hypothesis. $P_{\mathrm{fr}}(\theta)$ and $P_{\mathrm{fa}}(\theta)$ are false reject and false acceptance errors for the decision threshold θ. In order to evaluate the calibration performance of the speaker recognition system it is necessary to compute the minimal value of the cost function DCF_{min} and the value at the application independent threshold $DCF_{\mathrm{act}} = DCF(\eta)$. If scores are well calibrated then values DCF_{min} and DCF_{act} should be close.

In our research we investigated different ways to take into account the duration of speech segments in the calibration transformation and proposed our decision for the problem. There is a general score transformation for calibration approaches in [15]:

$$\bar{s} = w_0 + w_1 s + Q\left(d_m, d_t, w_2, \dots\right), \tag{3}$$

where calibration parameters are $w_0, w_1, w_2 \dots, Q\left(d_m, d_t, w_2, \dots\right)$ is the quality measure function (QMF) and d_m, d_t are speech durations of model and test segments respectively. We carried out the experiments with Q_{1-3} QMFs proposed in [15]. To train calibration parameters of the QMFs on the development set we used the BOSARIS fusion toolkit [6]. Results of the estimation of the calibration performance are obtained by using Q_{1-3} approaches and are discussed in Sect. 5.

When we were investigating the problem of calibration scores we tried to find an approximation model of statistical parameters of target and imposter score distributions on the speech segment durations. We assumed the distributions to be Gaussian. We also assumed that variances of the distributions are the same and are independent of d_m and d_t so only the expectations have to be approximated. To initialize the common variance we used average value $\sigma = 0.5(\sigma_t + \sigma_i)$, where σ_t and σ_i are variances of target and imposter distributions that are estimated on the development set. So based on the assumptions we can apply the linear form transformation (6) described above for calibration mapping:

$$\bar{s} = y_0 + y_1 s, \tag{4}$$

it is implied that y_0 and y_1 depend on the pair of speech durations d_m, d_t and are defined as:

$$y_0 = -\frac{1}{2\sigma^2}(\mu_{\text{tar}}^2 - \mu_{\text{imp}}^2), \qquad y_1 = \frac{1}{\sigma^2}(\mu_{\text{tar}} - \mu_{\text{imp}}), \tag{5}$$

where σ is the common variance and μ_{tar}, μ_{imp} are expectations of score distributions. In our research we defined approximation models for the expectations that depend on the durations of speech segments. The general form of the most suitable approximation models that we discovered is defined as follows:

$$\mu(d_m, d_t) = C_0 + C_1'(d_m)\sqrt{\log d_t}, \qquad C_1'(d_m) = C_1 + C_2\sqrt{\log d_m}. \tag{6}$$

Finally symmetrizing is needed:

$$\mu(d_m, d_t) = \frac{1}{2}\left[\mu(d_m, d_t) + \mu(d_t, d_m)\right]. \tag{7}$$

To estimate parameters of this approach it is first required to define dependencies of μ expectations on d_t test speech duration at each d_m fixed value of enrollment model speech segments duration from specified set. Then we performed the next approximation step to define function $C_1'(d_m)$. Finally it is required to achieve a symmetrical presentation of $\mu(d_m, d_t)$ relatively to the test and enroll speech segment durations. So the approximation model of the expectations of target and impostor score distributions that we propose is:

$$\mu(d_m, d_t) = C_0 + C_1 \left(\sqrt{\log d_t} + \sqrt{\log d_m} \right) + C_2 \sqrt{\log d_t \log d_m}. \tag{8}$$

It should be noted that this result is obtained in the context of the PLDA approach that allows to assume that the scores are normally distributed. The score representation that we used is explained in [8].

5   Experimental Results

In this section we present the analysis of calibration experiment results. We use a set of trials obtained from the development set to train parameters of the calibration mapping. The trials were performed on all combinations of speech segments durations. Then trial scores were taken into account to define parameters of different QMFs (Table 1) and our approximation model by using the BOSARIS toolkit.

Table 1. Quality measure functions

Name	QMF	Parameters
Q1	$w_1 \lvert \log(\frac{d_m}{d_t}) \rvert$	w_1
Q2	$w_1 \log^2(\frac{d_m}{d_t})$	w_1
Q3	$w_1 \log(\frac{d_m}{d_c}) \log(\frac{d_t}{d_c})$	w_1, d_c

To develop our calibration system we prepared speech segments of different durations by truncating the development utterances to 3, 7, 8, 10, 11 s. These subsets allowed us to generate trials and scores for proposed calibration model training. We estimated the means of the target/imposter score distributions with respect to test and enroll speech segment durations. Then we applied optimization procedure to find approximation parameters by minimizing mean square error (MSE) of the approximation. The results of the parameters approximation of the target/imposter score distributions are demonstrated in Fig. 1. It should be noted that Eqs. eqrefeqn:1 provide an appropriate approximation model that is confirmed by diagrams (Fig. 1).

As mentioned before in our work we used NIST 2012 C2 (only males) evaluation protocol to investigate score stabilization procedures in the speaker recognition systems. We applied different multisession enrollment modes (different session number from 1 to 5) to perform evaluation experiments. In this case the duration of the enrollment model was represented as a sum of speech segments duration of all sessions. In our investigations we focused on several important performance measures which are used in speaker recognition: equal error rate (EER), minimum decision cost function $(minDCF)$ with $C_{miss} = C_{fa} = 1$ and $P_{tar} = 0.01$ and corresponding actual DCF $(actDCF)$ metric.

The main results of the investigation of different score stabilization methods are shown in Table 2. According to those results one can conclude: first, scores

Table 2. Evaluation results

Enroll sessions number	EER [%]	minDCF	actDCF
Non calibrated system			
1	4.58	0.42	0.42
3	3.19	0.31	0.32
5	3.18	0.28	0.28
Q1 function			
1	4.11	0.43	0.43
3	2.90	0.29	0.31
5	2.89	0.25	0.28
Q2 function			
1	4.26	0.41	0.42
3	2.93	0.29	0.30
5	2.91	0.25	0.26
Q3 function			
1	4.59	0.42	0.42
3	3.21	0.31	0.32
5	3.18	0.28	0.29
Proposed calibration			
1	4.13	0.41	0.41
3	2.97	0.29	0.30
5	3.02	0.25	0.26

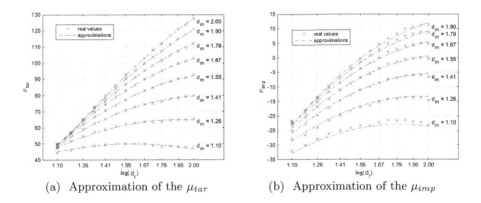

(a) Approximation of the μ_{tar} (b) Approximation of the μ_{imp}

Fig. 1. Approximations of the expectations of score distributions

stabilization procedures help to improve speaker detection system performance; second, Q2-function was found to be the best among all quality measure functions under consideration. The proposed score stabilization method proved to be effective in terms of $actDCF$ for evaluating different types of multisession enroll models. This calibration demonstrates stable leading positions among all QMFs.

6   Conclusion

In this paper we presented the score stabilization method for the state-of-the-art speaker recognition systems. It is based on approximations of the means of target and impostors score distributions that depend on test and enroll speech segment durations. Experiments performed on NIST SRE 2012 C2 evaluation protocol demonstrate the effectiveness of the method in comparison with different heuristic quality measure functions.

Acknowledgments. This work was partially financially supported by the Government of the Russian Federation, Grant 074-U01.

References

1. Sestek, the rise of voice biometrics as a key security solution. Speech Technology Magazine, White paper of SESTEK
2. Averbouch, D., Kahn, J.: Fraud targets the contact center: What now? Speech Technol. Mag. **18**(4), 9 (2013)
3. Batchelor, J., Lee, D., Banks, D., Crosby, D., Moore, K., Kuhn, S., Rodriguez, T., Stephens, A.: Ivestigative report. Florida Department of Law Enforcement (2012)
4. Brümmer, N.: Measuring, refining and calibrating speaker and language information extracted from speech. Ph.D. thesis, Citeseer (2010)
5. Brümmer, N., Garcia-Romero, D.: Generative modelling for unsupervised score calibration. arXiv preprint (2013). arxiv:1311.0707
6. Brümmer, N., de Villiers, E.: The bosaris toolkit: Theory, algorithms and code for surviving the new DCF. arXiv preprint (2013). arxiv:1304.2865
7. Doddington, G.: The role of score calibration in speaker recognition. In: Thirteenth Annual Conference of the International Speech Communication Association (2012)
8. Garcia-Romero, D., Espy-Wilson, C.Y.: Analysis of i-vector length normalization in speaker recognition systems. In: Interspeech, pp. 249–252 (2011)
9. Hautamäki, V., Kinnunen, T., Sedlák, F., Lee, K.A., Ma, B., Li, H.: Sparse classifier fusion for speaker verification. IEEE Trans. Audio Speech Lang. Process. **21**(8), 1622–1631 (2013)
10. Jain, A.K., Ross, A., Prabhakar, S.: An introduction to biometric recognition. IEEE Trans. Circuits Syst. Video Technol. **14**(1), 4–20 (2004)
11. Katz, M., Schafföner, M., Krüger, S.E., Wendemuth, A.: Score calibrating for speaker recognition based on support vector machines and gaussian mixture models. In: SIP. pp. 139–144 (2007)

12. Kozlov, A., Kudashev, O., Matveev, Y., Pekhovsky, T., Simonchik, K., Shulipa, A.: SVID speaker recognition system for NIST SRE 2012. In: Železný, M., Habernal, I., Ronzhin, A. (eds.) SPECOM 2013. LNCS, vol. 8113, pp. 278–285. Springer, Heidelberg (2013)
13. van Leeuwen, D.A., Brümmer, N.: The distribution of calibrated likelihood-ratios in speaker recognition. arXiv preprint (2013). arxiv:1304.1199
14. Mandasari, M.I., Saeidi, R., van Leeuwen, D.A.: Calibration based on duration quality measures function in noise robust speaker recognition for NIST SRE'12. Parameters 1(Q1), w2 (2013)
15. Mandasari, M.I., Saeidi, R., McLaren, M., van Leeuwen, D.A.: Quality measure functions for calibration of speaker recognition systems in various duration conditions. IEEE Trans. Audio Speech Lang. Process. 21(11), 2425–2438 (2013)
16. Martin, A., Doddington, G., Kamm, T., Ordowski, M., Przybocki, M.: The det curve in assessment of detection task performance. Technical report, DTIC Document (1997)
17. van Leeuwen, D.A., Brümmer, N.: An introduction to application-independent evaluation of speaker recognition systems. In: Müller, C. (ed.) Speaker Classification 2007. LNCS (LNAI), vol. 4343, pp. 330–353. Springer, Heidelberg (2007)
18. Villalba, J., Lleida, E., Ortega, A., Miguel, A.: A new bayesian network to assess the reliability of speaker verification decisions (2013)

Selecting Keypoint Detector and Descriptor Combination for Augmented Reality Application

Lukáš Bureš[✉] and Luděk Müller

Faculty of Applied Sciences, New Technologies for the Information Society,
University of West Bohemia, Univerzitní 8, 30614 Pilsen, Czech Republic
{lbures,muller}@ntis.zcu.cz

Abstract. In this paper, we compare the performance of image keypoints detectors and descriptors on well known Oxford dataset. We use evaluation criteria which were presented by Mikolajczyk et al. [12], [13]. We created most of the possible combinations of keypoint detector and descriptor, but in this paper, we present only selected pairs. The best performing detector and descriptor pair are selected for future research, mainly with the focus on augmented reality.

Keywords: Keypoint detector · Keypoint descriptor · Feature extraction · Augmented reality

1 Introduction

Augmented Reality (AR) as a scientific field has been growing dynamically recently. AR has an extraordinary potential which hasn't been still exhausted.

Visualization of 3D human body parts in medical books, badly damaged or ruined historical buildings in cities or addition of an objects in games to the real environment, all of that is just a fragment of using AR.

Extension of real world information is AR and it's realized by feature extraction methods which are able to find and describe visual keypoints. For example, it's important to select the best combination of robust methods and choose the appropriate one for the placing of an virtual object into the augmented space. It is advisable to choose conditions such as real–time capability, stability, etc. which should be fulfilled.

In an application of AR is desirable to choose the best keypoint detector and descriptor combination. Detected keypoints are used for placing augmented objects in the real world. For the best illusion of AR is needed to ensure that objects don't shake on the target position. This depends on stability and robustness of selected keypoints methods.

2 Methods

In this section, we mention detector and descriptor methods. We use these methods for our experiments in Sect. 3.

© Springer International Publishing Switzerland 2016
A. Ronzhin et al. (Eds.): SPECOM 2016, LNAI 9811, pp. 604–612, 2016.
DOI: 10.1007/978-3-319-43958-7_73

2.1 Methods with Detector and Descriptor

Several visual feature extraction algorithms have recently appeared in the literature. Here we mention a group of methods that have feature detector and descriptor.

Scale-invariant feature transform (SIFT) was presented in 2004 by Lowe in paper [10]. Algorithm in the stage of keypoints detecting tries to detect extrema of the result of a difference of Gaussians function applied in scale space to a series of smoothed and resampled images. Then the image of gradient magnitudes and orientations is sampled around keypoint location. Description stage produces descriptor based on orientation and data that was obtained in a small window around the detected keypoint.

Speeded–up robust features (SURF) was proposed by Bay et al. in 2008 [5]. SURF can be considered as a performance extension of SIFT method. SURF uses Haar wavelets and is faster feature detector and descriptor than SIFT.

Another detector and descriptor is oriented FAST and rotated BRIEF (ORB) by Rublee [16] introduced in 2011. It is based on the FAST keypoint detector (see Sect. 2.2) and the visual descriptor BRIEF (see Sect. 2.3). Its aim is to provide a fast and efficient alternative to SIFT.

Binary robust invariant scalable keypoints (BRISK) was proposed by Leutenegger et al. [8]. It provides both scale and rotation invariance. In order to compute the feature locations, it uses the AGAST corner detector [11] which improves FAST by increasing speed while maintaining the same detection performance. For scale invariance, BRISK detects keypoints in a scale–space pyramid, performing non–maximum suppression and interpolation across all scales.

Alcantarilla et al. in 2012 presented KAZE [4] detector and descriptor. This feature extraction method is completely calculated in non–linear scale space. Previously proposed methods like SIFT and SURF find features in the Gaussian scale space, but Gaussian blurring does not respect the natural boundaries of objects. Non–linear scale spaces can be detected and described by non–linear diffusion features keeping important image details and removing noise as long as the image evolves in the scale space. KAZE uses variable conductance diffusion that is one of the simplest non–linear diffusions. The non–linear scale space is built efficiently by means of additive operator splitting.

Accelerated KAZE (AKAZE) was proposed by Alcantarilla et al. in 2013 [3]. AKAZE features use mathematically fast explicit diffusion embedded in a pyramidal framework to speed–up the non–linear scale space computation. It computes a robust modified–local difference binary (M–LDB) descriptor that exploits gradient information from the non–linear scale space. AKAZE is faster than KAZE and the results are comparable.

2.2 Only Detector Methods

We shortly mention a few detector methods which we have tested in our experiments in Sect. 4.

Features from accelerated segment test (FAST) [14,15] are keypoint detector that was originally developed by Rosten and Drummond, and published in 2006. The advantage of FAST keypoint detector is its computational efficiency. FAST is built on machine learning methods and it's fast and indeed, it's faster than many other well–known feature extraction methods, such as difference of Gaussians (DoG) used by SIFT. The FAST detector is very suitable for real–time video processing application because of high–speed performance, that is in any case of augmented reality very critical.

Adaptive and generic accelerated segment test (AGAST) [11] is a highly efficient corner detector based on the same corner test as FAST. It computes a binary decision tree (corner detector) which is generic and does not have to be adapted to new environments. The tree is optimal for a certain probability of similar pixels in the accelerated segment test mask.

Star feature detector is derived from center surrounded extrema (CenSurE) detector [1]. CenSurE uses polygons such as Square, Hexagon, and Octagons as a more computable alternative to circle. Star mimics the circle with two overlapping squares, first one upright and second one 45 degrees rotated. These polygons are bi–level and can be seen as polygons with thick borders. The borders and the enclosed area have weights of opposing signs.

2.3   Only Descriptor Methods

In this last subsection we describe tested descriptor methods very briefly.

Binary Robust Independent Elementary Features (BRIEF) was proposed by Calonder et al. [6]. It uses a sampling pattern consisting of 128, 256, or 512 comparisons (equating to 128, 256, or 512 bits), with sample points selected randomly from an isotropic Gaussian distribution centered at the feature location. Calonder et al. [6] suggests using BRIEF with the efficient CenSurE detector [1].

An efficient dense descriptor applied to wide–baseline stereo (DAISY) was presented by Tola et al. in 2010 [17]. DAISY is a local image descriptor which is robust against many photometric and geometric transformations. It is very efficient to compute densely. DAISY can be used for computing dense depth and occlusion maps from wide–baseline image pairs. This descriptor is inspired from earlier ones such as SIFT but can be computed faster.

Fast Retina Keypoint (FREAK) [2] is a binary descriptor encoding simple image intensity comparisons on a specific pattern at large scale and small scale. This feature descriptor was developed in human–like manner of capturing visual information (coarse in peripheral regions of the retina and fine in the central region). Its main practical interest stems from extremely fast extraction and matching which was long awaited in embedded devices or in large–scale applications.

Locally uniform comparison image descriptor (LUCID) [18] is a simple description method based on linear time permutation distances between the ordering of RGB values of two image patches. It is computable in linear time with respect to the number of pixels and does not require floating point computation.

Learned arrangements of three patch codes (LATCH) [9] is one of current state–of–the–art binary descriptors. It is based on comparing triplets of pixel patches.

3   Experiments

In this section, we describe datasets that we used in our tests and briefly describe them. In Subsect. 3.2 we show criteria that we used for evaluation.

3.1   Datasets

We evaluate the detectors and descriptors on Oxford dataset images which contain different geometric and photometric transformations. This set was originally described in [12,13]. The dataset has since become the standard for evaluating descriptor design capabilities. Example of the dataset[1] is shown in Fig. 1. We evaluate eight different sets which each consist of six images. Each set contains one referential image and five transformed images. The homography matrices of referential to the analyzed image are present, too. In these sets zoom+rotation, viewpoint change, image blur, JPEG compression, light change transformations are present.

Fig. 1. The example of the datasets (from top left): boat: zoom+rotation, bark: zoom+rotation, graffiti: viewpoint change, wall: viewpoint change, bikes: image blur, trees: image blur, ubc: JPEG compression, leuven: light change.

3.2   Evaluation Criterion

A few performance metrics were presented: Mikolajczyk et al. [12,13] proposed to use the metrics of recall, repeatability, and 1–precision. They describe useful characteristics of a feature's performance, which were used as standard measures.

---

[1] The dataset is available at http://www.robots.ox.ac.uk/~vgg/research/affine.

Next metrics was summarized in [7,19]. We selected the following evaluation criteria in our experiments:

The Putative Match Ratio

$$Putative\,Match\,Ratio = \frac{\#Putative\,Matches}{\#Features}, \tag{1}$$

is the selectivity of the descriptor and describes what fraction of the detected features will be initially identified as a match. These matches can be potentially incorrect. The putative match is a single pair of keypoints, where a keypoint cannot be matched to more than one other keypoint. The keypoints that are outside of the bounds of the second image are not counted. This is ensured by transforming keypoint from the first image through ground truth homography matrix to the second image.

The Precision

$$Precision = \frac{\#Correct\,Matches}{\#Putative\,Matches}, \tag{2}$$

quantifies the number of correct matches out of the set of putative matches (the inlier ratio). In Eq. 2, the number of correct matches are those putative matches that are geometrically verified. Verification is based on the known camera positions. Precision is also influenced by many of the same factors like in the case of the putative match ratio, but the consequences are different. For instance, while a less restrictive matching criteria increase the putative match ratio, it will also decrease the precision as a higher number of incorrect matches will be generated.

The Matching Score

$$Matching\,Score = \frac{\#Correct\,Matches}{\#Features}, \tag{3}$$

is the multiplication of the putative match ratio and precision. It describes the number of initial features that will result in correct matches. The matching score describes how well the descriptor is performing and is influenced by the descriptor's robustness to transformations of the data. The matching score can be influenced by indistinct descriptors and the matching criteria.

The Recall

$$Recall = \frac{\#Correct\,Matches}{\#Correspondences}, \tag{4}$$

defines how many of the possible correct matches were actually found. The correspondences are the matches that should have been identified by given the keypoint locations in both images. Recall shares the same influences as the matching score and it is dependent on the detector's ability to generate correspondences. For example, when the matching criterion is too strict, the data is too complex or the descriptors are indistinct that could mean low recall value.

4   Experimental Results

In our experiments, we created the most of the possible combinations of key-point detector and descriptor. In tables below, we show only selected results. All implementation of methods was used from OpenCV 3.1[2]. All detectors and descriptors input parameters were set to default values. For feature matching was used brute–force matcher. Best performing values are shown in bold.

Table 1. Average putative match ratio (from Eq. 1) calculated from full set (consisting of 5 corresponding pairs) of boat, bark, graffiti, wall, bikes, trees, ubc and leuven sets (image dataset order is same as at Fig. 1).

Detector	Descriptor	Average putative match ratio							
sift	sift	0.112	**0.127**	**0.116**	0.204	0.128	0.050	0.262	0.294
surf	surf	0.077	0.050	0.053	0.092	0.197	0.061	0.325	0.262
brisk	brisk	0.036	0.037	0.030	0.035	0.067	0.020	0.193	0.131
kaze	kaze	**0.172**	0.074	0.099	**0.234**	0.364	**0.164**	**0.696**	**0.297**
akaze	akaze	0.060	0.030	0.029	0.083	**0.390**	0.096	0.573	0.281
orb	orb	0.052	0.021	0.022	0.026	0.136	0.040	0.446	0.098
star	surf	0.044	0.039	0.061	0.022	0.116	0.019	0.307	0.130
star	freak	0.019	0.021	0.018	0.017	0.101	0.017	0.340	0.096
agast	latch	0.000	0.000	0.001	0.009	0.044	0.009	0.137	0.153

Table 2. Average precision (from Eq. 2) calculated from full set.

Detector	Descriptor	Average precision							
sift	sift	0.851	**0.940**	0.405	0.737	0.774	0.698	0.942	0.929
surf	surf	0.678	0.879	0.288	0.675	0.798	0.633	0.908	0.874
brisk	brisk	**0.894**	0.931	**0.583**	0.648	0.754	**0.708**	0.955	**0.950**
kaze	kaze	0.858	0.923	0.518	**0.796**	0.838	0.685	0.964	0.905
akaze	akaze	0.503	0.726	0.276	0.514	**0.884**	0.586	0.948	0.910
orb	orb	0.719	0.600	0.329	0.726	0.850	0.660	**0.978**	0.920
star	surf	0.486	0.656	0.226	0.466	0.669	0.433	0.908	0.726
star	freak	0.003	0.683	0.000	0.461	0.009	0.007	0.186	0.021
agast	latch	0.000	0.000	0.000	0.001	0.000	0.000	0.007	0.002

Each table is divided into two sections. In the first section, there are methods which have detector and descriptor. In the second section, there are the mixed detector and descriptor methods.

---

[2] OpenCV is available at http://opencv.org/.

Table 3. Average matching score (from Eq. 3) calculated from full set.

Detector	Descriptor	Average matching score							
sift	sift	0.106	**0.119**	**0.089**	0.194	0.107	0.042	0.255	**0.276**
surf	surf	0.062	0.043	0.031	0.082	0.169	0.047	0.309	0.233
brisk	brisk	0.034	0.034	0.026	0.033	0.056	0.017	0.190	0.126
kaze	kaze	**0.161**	0.066	0.082	**0.218**	0.323	**0.125**	**0.677**	0.272
akaze	akaze	0.041	0.025	0.020	0.068	**0.356**	0.065	0.555	0.261
orb	orb	0.048	0.014	0.018	0.024	0.123	0.033	0.442	0.091
star	surf	0.029	0.027	0.024	0.016	0.087	0.011	0.293	0.101
star	freak	0.000	0.017	0.000	0.014	0.002	0.000	0.084	0.002
agast	latch	0.000	0.000	0.000	0.000	0.000	0.000	0.001	0.000

Table 4. Average recall (from Eq. 4) calculated from full set.

Detector	Descriptor	Average recall							
sift	sift	0.226	**0.358**	**0.189**	0.310	0.580	0.106	0.423	**0.652**
surf	surf	0.142	0.136	0.070	0.148	0.373	0.101	0.436	0.437
brisk	brisk	0.043	0.073	0.038	0.045	0.259	0.029	0.241	0.225
kaze	kaze	**0.237**	0.220	0.133	**0.316**	**0.583**	**0.255**	**0.764**	0.527
akaze	akaze	0.060	0.069	0.027	0.088	0.559	0.125	0.608	0.532
orb	orb	0.062	0.049	0.022	0.040	0.168	0.073	0.482	0.155
star	surf	0.072	0.127	0.055	0.028	0.307	0.031	0.369	0.336
star	freak	0.000	0.075	0.000	0.024	0.004	0.001	0.101	0.007
agast	latch	0.000	0.000	0.000	0.000	0.000	0.000	0.002	0.001

Table 1 shows results of average putative match ratio for each dataset calculated by averaging values from Eq. 1 (Tables 2, 3 and 4).

5   Conclusion

The KAZE detector and descriptor performed the best in our experiments. Our experiments also showed that when detector and descriptor combination is selected badly, the results will be very poor. This is the case of LATCH descriptor.

In future work, we will focus on speed performance experiments for selecting the best detector descriptor and combination for real–time augmented reality application. We will extend our performance experiments, too.

Acknowledgment. This publication was supported by the project LO1506 of the Czech Ministry of Education, Youth and Sports and by grant of the University of West Bohemia, project No. SGS-2016-039.

References

1. Agrawal, M., Konolige, K., Blas, M.R.: CenSurE: center surround extremas for realtime feature detection and matching. In: Forsyth, D., Torr, P., Zisserman, A. (eds.) ECCV 2008, Part IV. LNCS, vol. 5305, pp. 102–115. Springer, Heidelberg (2008)
2. Alahi, A., Ortiz, R., Vandergheynst, P.: Freak: fast retina keypoint. In: 2012 IEEE Conference on Computer Vision and Pattern Recognition (CVPR), pp. 510–517. IEEE (2012)
3. Alcantarilla, P.F., Nuevo, J., Bartoli, A.: Fast explicit diffusion for accelerated features in nonlinear scale spaces. In: British Machine Vision Conference (BMVC) (2013)
4. Alcantarilla, P.F., Bartoli, A., Davison, A.J.: KAZE features. In: Fitzgibbon, A., Lazebnik, S., Perona, P., Sato, Y., Schmid, C. (eds.) ECCV 2012, Part VI. LNCS, vol. 7577, pp. 214–227. Springer, Heidelberg (2012)
5. Bay, H., Ess, A., Tuytelaars, T., Van Gool, L.: Speeded-up robust features (surf). Comput. Vis. Image Underst. **110**(3), 346–359 (2008)
6. Calonder, M., Lepetit, V., Strecha, C., Fua, P.: BRIEF: binary robust independent elementary features. In: Daniilidis, K., Maragos, P., Paragios, N. (eds.) ECCV 2010, Part IV. LNCS, vol. 6314, pp. 778–792. Springer, Heidelberg (2010)
7. Heinly, J., Dunn, E., Frahm, J.-M.: Comparative evaluation of binary features. In: Fitzgibbon, A., Lazebnik, S., Perona, P., Sato, Y., Schmid, C. (eds.) ECCV 2012, Part II. LNCS, vol. 7573, pp. 759–773. Springer, Heidelberg (2012)
8. Leutenegger, S., Chli, M., Siegwart, R.: Brisk: binary robust invariant scalable keypoints. In: Metaxas, D.N., Quan, L., Sanfeliu, A., Gool, L.J.V. (eds.) ICCV, pp. 2548–2555. IEEE Computer Society, Barcelona (2011)
9. Levi, G., Hassner, T.: LATCH: learned arrangements of three patch codes (2015). CoRR abs/1501.03719
10. Lowe, D.G.: Distinctive image features from scale-invariant keypoints. Int. J. Comput. Vis. **60**(2), 91–110 (2004)
11. Mair, E., Hager, G.D., Burschka, D., Suppa, M., Hirzinger, G.: Adaptive and generic corner detection based on the accelerated segment test. In: Daniilidis, K., Maragos, P., Paragios, N. (eds.) ECCV 2010, Part II. LNCS, vol. 6312, pp. 183–196. Springer, Heidelberg (2010)
12. Mikolajczyk, K., Tuytelaars, T., Schmid, C., Zisserman, A., Matas, J., Schaffalitzky, F., Kadir, T., Gool, L.V.: A comparison of affine region detectors. Int. J. Comput. Vision **65**(1–2), 43–72 (2005)
13. Mikolajczyk, K., Schmid, C.: A performance evaluation of local descriptors. IEEE Trans. Pattern Anal. Mach. Intell. **27**(10), 1615–1630 (2005)
14. Rosten, E., Drummond, T.W.: Machine learning for high-speed corner detection. In: Leonardis, A., Bischof, H., Pinz, A. (eds.) ECCV 2006, Part I. LNCS, vol. 3951, pp. 430–443. Springer, Heidelberg (2006)
15. Rosten, E., Porter, R., Drummond, T.: Faster and better: a machine learning approach to corner detection. IEEE Trans. Pattern Anal. Mach. Intell. **32**(1), 105–119 (2010)
16. Rublee, E., Rabaud, V., Konolige, K., Bradski, G.: ORB: an efficient alternative to sift or surf. In: Proceedings of the 2011 International Conference on Computer Vision, pp. 2564–2571. IEEE Computer Society, Washington, DC (2011)

17. Tola, E., Lepetit, V., Fua, P.: DAISY: an efficient dense descriptor applied to wide baseline stereo. IEEE Trans. Pattern Anal. Mach. Intell. **32**(5), 815–830 (2010)
18. Ziegler, A., Christiansen, E., Kriegman, D., Belongie, S.J.: Locally uniform comparison image descriptor. In: Pereira, F., Burges, C.J.C., Bottou, L., Weinberger, K.Q. (eds.) Advances in Neural Information Processing Systems 25, pp. 1–9. Curran Associates, Inc/, Red Hook (2012)
19. Zitnick, C.L., Ramnath, K.: Edge foci interest points. In: Metaxas, D.N., Quan, L., Sanfeliu, A., Gool, L.J.V. (eds.) ICCV, pp. 359–366. IEEE Computer Society (2011)

Semi-automatic Speaker Verification System Based on Analysis of Formant, Durational and Pitch Characteristics

Elena Bulgakova[1,2(✉)] and Aleksey Sholohov[1]

[1] ITMO University, St. Petersburg, Russia
{bulgakova,sholohov}@speechpro.com
[2] Speech Technology Center, St. Petersburg, Russia

Abstract. Modern speaker verification systems take advantage of a number of complementary base classifiers by fusing them to get reliable verification decisions. The paper presents a semi-automatic speaker verification system based on fusion of formant frequencies, phone durations and pitch characteristics. Experimental results demonstrate that combination of these characteristics improves speaker verification performance. For improved and cost-effective performance of the pitch subsystem further we selected the most informative pitch characteristics.

Keywords: Formant frequencies · Phone durations · Pitch characteristics · Speaker verification · Feature selection

1 Introduction

Speech signals carry different information including individual voice characteristics which allows to recognize people by their voice, and therefore to solve a speaker recognition task. This task involves speaker verification in case it is necessary to make a binary (yes or no) decision regarding speaker identity, and speaker identification in case it is necessary to determine which speaker voice is presented on a test recording. In this study we focus on a speaker verification problem. Nowadays human-assisted methods are widely used in forensic speaker recognition [1]. However, the application of these methods is limited by the need of engagement of highly qualified experts. Moreover, human-assisted methods are time consuming that generally complicates their use under time constraints. Furthermore, the final decision is largely subjective since it depends on the personal opinion of the expert [2]. In this paper we continue our research started in [3] and propose a semi-automatic speaker verification system which makes it possible to get over above-mentioned shortcomings. This system includes comparing different voice characteristics: formant frequencies, phone durations and pitch characteristics as well. The final decision concerning identity or difference of speaker voices is made automatically as a result of fusion of the used subsystems. The results of our experiments show that additional use of the pitch

© Springer International Publishing Switzerland 2016
A. Ronzhin et al. (Eds.): SPECOM 2016, LNAI 9811, pp. 613–619, 2016.
DOI: 10.1007/978-3-319-43958-7_74

subsystem proposed in [4] leads to better performance compared with the results of our previous research [3]. For the purpose of increasing verification accuracy and time reduction of comparing speech samples, we found the most distinctive pitch characteristics.

The rest of the paper is organized as follows. Section 2 includes the system description. The experimental results and database descriptions are presented in Sect. 3. Conclusions are considered in Sect. 4.

2   System Description

The proposed speaker verification system consists of three subsystems based on pitch characteristics, formant frequencies and phone durations described in Sects. 2.1, 2.2 and 2.3. Figure 1 shows main modules of the system. The first module in each subsystem extracts speech features from the input speech signal. The second module aggregates these features to represent an entire utterance as a vector of fixed dimension. Given a trial each subsystem outputs a matching score measuring similarity between two utterances. At the fusion stage matching scores are combined into a single score to increase accuracy of the system. The decision module compares the final matched score to a pre-defined threshold. If similarity is above the threshold, the trial is classified as target, otherwise non-target.

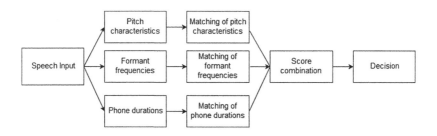

Fig. 1. Block diagram of the speaker verification system

2.1   Pitch Subsystem and Pitch Characteristics

The pitch subsystem compares the characteristics of intonation structures presented in speech samples [4]. The following characteristics were used and described in [4]: initial, final, minimal, maximum and average frequencies of intonation fragments, F0 range, pitch change speed, irregularity coefficient, skewness and kurtosis of distribution of pitch frequencies, duration of intonation fragments, coordinate of minimal, average and maximum frequency values (in percentage of whole duration of chosen fragments). Data analysis includes calculating and correcting pitch curves, segmentation of speech material into comparable intonation structures (fragments) of the utterances (prosodic phrase, head, pre-head, nuclear tone, nucleus + tail) and automatic comparison of pitch characteristics obtained as a result of segmentation. Because of the high labour intensity of this method we conducted segmentation of speech material based on prosodic phrases of 10–15 s duration in an automatic mode without preliminary pitch correction.

2.2   Formant Subsystem and Formant Frequencies

It is well-known that positions of the main spectral peaks in the spectrum of the speech signal depend on the anatomical structure of the vocal tract and the sizes of the resonant cavities. For this reason such spectral characteristics may be applicable to speaker recognition. Since formant frequencies are usually not independent, we use a GMM-UBM framework [5] which is a common tool in speaker verification to approximate complex statistical relationships in multivariate data. It is based on the notion of the universal background model (UBM) which models statistical distribution of features for a large population of speakers [6].

It should be noticed that hand-correcting formant tracks was not carried out. For our experiments we detected the first four formant tracks of six Russian vowels (/i/, /e/, /a/, /u/, /o/, /y/).

2.3   Phone Subsystem and Phone Durations

The phone duration subsystem was presented in [3]. This subsystem includes automatic phonetic segmentation on the basis of recordings and text contents of these files, calculation of average durations for each phone in the phonetic segmentation and calculation of the matching score of speaker voices. Unlike the formant subsystem based on the GMM-UBM framework which enjoys large speech datasets, training the phone subsystem requires transcriptions (typically limited) in addition to speech recordings. Thus smaller amounts of data may lead to over-fitting because of a large number of model parameters. Due to the lack of text contents of speech recordings, we define a simple matching score which has much smaller parameters to tune and hence more robust to over-fitting:

$$s(\boldsymbol{x}_1, \boldsymbol{x}_2) = -\sum_{t=1}^{T} w_i (x_1^t - x_2^t)^2, \tag{1}$$

where $\boldsymbol{x}_1, \boldsymbol{x}_2$ is a pair of feature vectors representing a trial, T is the feature space dimension and w_i are non-negative weights. This formula can be seen as negative Mahalanobis distance. Intuitively greater weights should correspond to more important features (*i.e.* features with higher discriminative ability). We give details how to estimate these weights in the next Section. To the aim of time reduction we did not correct phone boundaries.

3 Experiments

3.1 Experiment – Speaker Verification

Here we describe the experiment on speaker verification. For the experiment presented in this Section we used the database described below. For training we formed the database including Russian quasi-spontaneous speech of 124 male speakers and 70 female speakers recorded over the telephone channel. Each speaker participates in five recording sessions of 3–5 min duration and there is one week gap between sessions. During the recording session every speaker answers questionnaire questions. For training we used the database of 1–3 min natural spontaneous telephone dialogues in Russian. The evaluation set consists of 1037 target and 9397 non-target trials for males and 507 target and 2233 non-target trials for females. To increase reliability of speaker verification the final decision can be made based on decisions of independent subsystems. Such procedure is called a decision fusion at the score-level [7]. For a set of matching scores s_i fusion was done using a convex combination of scores:

$$s = p_1 s_1 + p_2 s_2 + p_3 s_3,$$

where s_i is a matching score of the i-th sub-system, p_i are weight parameters such that $\sum_i p_i = 1$. The values p_i were tuned by hand on a subset of the training set.

The important aspect of fusion is statistical independence of matching scores of combined subsystems. Otherwise the final decision hardly results in a sharp gain in speaker verification performance.

We report speaker verification performance in the form of equal error rate (EER, %) [8]. Table 1 presents the performance evaluation of the considered subsystems.

Table 1. Speaker verification results for two different genders (EER, %)

Subsystem	Male	Female
Pitch characteristics	23.28	27.33
Phone durations	27.57	36.98
Formant frequencies	2.93	4.63
Formant frequencies + Phone durations	2.02	4.49
Formant frequencies + Phone durations + Pitch characteristics	1.41	3.83

As appears from Table 1, the formant subsystem is the most accurate. Pitch characteristics demonstrate the noticeable degradation. Phone durations concede in performance to other characteristics. In our previous research fusion of subsystems based on phone durations and formant frequencies was performed [3]. In this experiment we conducted fusion of all above-described subsystems.

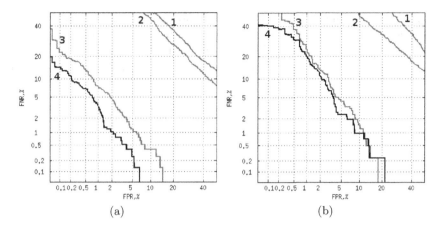

Fig. 2. DET (detection error trade-off)-curves for male (a) and female speakers (b). DET-curve (1) demonstrates the performance of the phone durations subsystem, (2) – pitch subsystem, (3) – formant subsystem, DET-curve (4) shows the whole system performance. FNR (False Negative Rate), FPR (False Positive Rate).

The results presented in Table 1 and Fig. 2 demonstrate that fusion of subsystems based on poorly correlated features (pitch characteristics, formant frequencies and phone durations) leads to a decrease of EER and improves speaker verification performance.

3.2 Experiment – Informative Pitch Characteristics

Feature selection is the crucial step in design semi-automatic speaker recognition systems. It can considerably reduce time of comparing speech samples and even improve speaker verification performance.

We ranked features according to weights calculated as follows:

$$w_i = \frac{\sigma_b^2}{\sigma_w^2}, \qquad (2)$$

where σ_b^2 is between-speaker variance and σ_w^2 is within-speaker variance for the i-th feature. Higher values correspond to features with a higher class separability. To assess selected subsets of features we evaluated speaker verification performance as the function of a number of selected features. We used a dataset consisting of 5102 speech cuts from 195 speakers. Each speaker takes part in 2–5 recording sessions of 3–5 min duration. The database includes male and female spontaneous speech of speakers recorded over a microphone channel in Russian, Tajik, Azerbaijani and Talysh. It should be noticed that prosodic segmentation into intonation fragments was done fully manually. To evaluate verification performance we averaged EERs over 100 random splits of the dataset into equally-sized training and testing parts. First, we estimated system accuracy in terms of EER using subsets of the most informative features. Starting from the top ranked feature we gradually added other features according to the order defined by weights (2). We used the same weights to compute the matching score defined by (1). Then we estimated EERs for each feature separately. Figure 3 demonstrates the results.

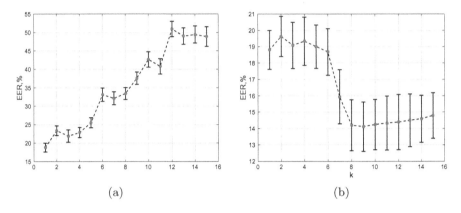

(a)   (b)

Fig. 3. Speaker verification performance (a) with a subset of the top-k most informative pitch characteristics and (b) for each characteristic separately (sorted in the same order).

Figure 3(a) shows individual speaker verification performance for all pitch characteristics ordered according to (2): (1) average, (2) final, (3) minimal, (4) initial, (5) maximum pitch frequencies, (6) F0 range measured in Hertz, (7) irregularity coefficient, (8) pitch change speed, (9) F0 range measured in semitones, (10) kurtosis and (11) skewness of distribution of pitch frequencies, coordinate of (12) minimal, (13) maximum and (14) average frequency values (in percentage of whole duration of chosen fragments), (15) duration of intonation fragments. Thus the first five most informative features are (1–5), while (12–15) are the least distinctive features. However, as can be observed, there is a strong correlation between some features. For this reason the joint use of such characteristics as (1–5) does not improve speaker verification performance that Fig. 3(b) shows. While adding (7) and (8) leads to a noticeable decrease of EER. Interestingly, including the rest of less informative pitch characteristics even slightly decreases accuracy of the pitch subsystem. The results of the additional experiments demonstrate that the joint use of (1), (7) and (8) leads to the best speaker verification performance having the lowest EER of 13 %. Therefore, EER obtained on the reduced feature set is lower than that on the full feature set (14,79 %). It was also experimentally established that the threshold for absolute difference of average pitch frequencies corresponding to equal misses and false alarms equals to 12 Hz. This finding can be useful for rapid comparison of speech samples carried out by experts.

4   Conclusion

In this paper we proposed a semi-automatic speaker verification system based on fusion of formant frequencies, phone durations and pitch characteristics. Experimental results show that including of pitch characteristics improves speaker verification performance compared with an earlier developed system [3]. We found out that use of the reduced set of pitch characteristics (average F0, irregularity coefficient and pitch change speed) leads to increased speaker verification accuracy.

Acknowledgments. This work was financially supported by the Government of the Russian Federation, Grant 074-U01.

References

1. Rose, P.: Forensic Speaker Identification. Taylor and Francis, London (2002)
2. Tanner, D.C., Tanner, M.E.: Forensic Aspects of Speech Patterns: Voice Prints, Speaker Profiling, Lie and Intoxication Detection. Lawyers and Judges Publishing, Tucson (2004)
3. Bulgakova, E., Sholohov, A., Tomashenko, N., Matveev, Y.: Speaker verification using spectral and durational segmental characteristics. In: Ronzhin, A., Potapova, R., Fakotakis, N. (eds.) SPECOM 2015. LNCS, vol. 9319, pp. 397–404. Springer, Heidelberg (2015)
4. Smirnova, N., et al.: Using parameters of identical pitch contour elements for speaker discrimination. In: Proceedings of the 12th International Conference on Speech and Computer, pp. 361–366 (2007)
5. Becker, T., Jessen, M., Grigoras, C.: Forensic speaker verification using formant features and Gaussian mixture models. In: Proceedings of Interspeech, pp. 1505–1508 (2008)
6. Reynolds, D., Quatieri, T., Dunn, R.: Speaker verification using adapted Gaussian mixture models. Digit. Signal Proc. **10**, 19–41 (2000)
7. Jain, A.K., Flynn, P., Ross, A.A. (eds.): Handbook of Biometrics. Springer-Verlag New York, Inc., New York (2008)
8. The NIST year 2010 Speaker Recognition Evaluation plan. http://www.itl.nist.gov/iad/mig/tests/sre/2010/NISTSRE10evalplan.r6.pdf

Speaker-Dependent Bottleneck Features for Egyptian Arabic Speech Recognition

Aleksei Romanenko[1,2(✉)] and Valentin Mendelev[1,2]

[1] ITMO University, Saint-Petersburg, Russia
anromanenko@corp.ifmo.ru, mendelev@speechpro.com
[2] Speech Technology Center Ltd, Saint-Petersburg, Russia

Abstract. In this paper, several ways to improve a speech recognition system for the Egyptian dialect of Arabic language are presented. The research is based on the CALLHOME Egyptian Arabic corpus. We demonstrate the contribution of speaker-dependent bottleneck features trained on other languages and verify the possibility of application of a small Modern Standard Arabic (MSA) corpus to derive phonetic transcriptions. The systems obtained demonstrate good results as compared to those published before.

Keywords: Arabic language · Keyword search · Low resources

1 Introduction

The Arabic language is one of the most widely used in the world [1]. It has multiple variants, including Modern Standard Arabic (MSA) which is predominantly used in written communication, in broadcasting, for religious and official purposes. In everyday life native Arab speakers use various dialects of Arabic language (DA) depending on their origins and place of living.

There are a few studies devoted to automatic speech recognition for dialects. Dealing with natural language processing (NLP) problems for DA is associated with substantial difficulties:

- DA differ significantly from MSA in morphological, phonological, and lexical aspects [2]:
  - High inflectedness of both MSA and DA results in presence of a great amount of words and word forms derived from one root. This greatly increases the out of vocabulary (OOV) rate and makes the estimation of probabilities for language models quite difficult;
  - The numbers of phonemes in MSA and DA often differ. In addition, some phonemes of MSA may be absent in DA or be replaced by other ones. Due to differences in pronunciation of the same words in MSA and DA, it is impossible to specify reliably a pronunciation lexicon;
  - One and the same word in MSA and DA can represent distinct parts of speech [3], which greatly complicates the lexical analysis that would help to find a correct phoneme transcription;

© Springer International Publishing Switzerland 2016
A. Ronzhin et al. (Eds.): SPECOM 2016, LNAI 9811, pp. 620–626, 2016.
DOI: 10.1007/978-3-319-43958-7_75

- Texts in DA often lack diacritics corresponding to short vowels, consonant reduplication, etc. Presence of diacritics would make the process of obtaining the phoneme transcription more easy, but their allocation is a separate complex problem;
- There is a low amount of training data. While the problem of lack of data to construct a language model can be solved with the help of Internet sources [4], the question of obtaining speech corpora for various dialects remains open. The speech recognition for DA is a low resource problem;
- Most of existing tools for analyzing Arabic language are designed specifically for MSA [5], so their application to dialects is very difficult or sometimes impossible.

In recent years, acoustic and language models based on various types of neural networks have demonstrated their efficiency in many fields of NLP.

DNNs with sequence training were used in [6] to build speech recognition systems for various dialects of Arabic language. The reported word error rate (WER) is much lower as compared to HMM-GMM systems. In [7], the combination of an ensemble of DNNs with CNN together with a larger set of training data (about 100 h of speech) and neural network language model (NNLM) shows impressive results in recognition of colloquial Egyptian Arabic. Attempts have also been made to increase the recognition accuracy by taking due account of the above-mentioned peculiarities of DA. In [5], the use of NN morpheme-based feature-rich language model decreases WER by absolute 0.6–0.7 %. The phonemic cross-lingual acoustic modeling [3] is an attempt to obtain correct phonetic transcription for colloquial Egyptian Arabic with the aid of MSA data. This approach yields 41.8 % relative WER reduction.

The automatic continuous speech recognition task is often accompanied by the keyword spotting task. The OpenKWS contest held by National Institute of Standards and Technology (NIST) is focused on rapid development of speech to text (STT) and spoken term detection (STD) systems for new languages under low resource conditions [8].

We present several modifications of a speech recognition system for the Egyptian dialect of Arabic language based on the CALLHOME Egyptian Arabic corpus and demonstrate the contribution of speaker-dependent bottleneck features trained on Russian, English and Levantine Arabic speech corpora. In addition, we try to use a small MSA corpus to derive the phonetic transcriptions.

The remaining part of the paper is organized as follows. In the next section, we describe the datasets. Section 3 describes our automatic speech recognition system. The results of recognition experiments are given in Sect. 4. Conclusion and discussions are presented in Sect. 5.

2   Datasets

In order to train and test the models, we utilize the CALLHOME Arabic dataset (LDC97S45 for the audio and LDC97T19 for the text). This corpus consists of phone conversations between native Egyptian Arabic speakers. There are 120 recordings of up to thirty minutes each. In each recording, a fragment of five or ten minutes length is chosen in an arbitrary way and then transcribed. The whole set is divided into three parts, training, development, and testing. The training set consists of 80 recordings containing 14 h of speech and 130000 words; 20 recordings are used to form the development set of length 3.5 h containing around 32000 words. The remaining 20 recordings constitute the test dataset of roughly 14000 words. In addition, we use LDC2002S37 which contains two hours of audio and LDC2002T38 with almost 16000 words. These data augment the training sets both for the acoustic and language models.

We also make use of the Egyptian Colloquial Arabic Lexicon LDC99L22 as the pronunciation reference. It is worth noticing that the original sets of transcriptions are represented in two versions, namely the romanized transcriptions and Arabic script. The initial lexicon contains almost 52000 romanized word representations and can contain multiple transcriptions. In our study we use the set of 34 phonemes differing from that of the original lexicon. We establish a one-to-one correspondence between the initial phonemes and the phonemes of our set and re-label the lexicon. We thus arrive at a lexicon of roughly 57000 unique entries (romanized representation, Arabic script, phoneme transcription).

To train the bottleneck features extractor, we utilize the Levantine Arabic QT Training Data Set 5 (LDC2006S29 is the audio set, and LDC2006T07 contains the corresponding transcriptions). There are 1660 phone conversations between Levantine Arabic speakers in the corpus (250 h of speech in total). No pronunciation lexicon is provided with this set, so we make use of the G2P model trained on the NEMLAR Speech Synthesis corpus containing about 10 h of speech. The corpus consists of 2032 sentences with roughly 42000 words. Each recording is accompanied with the SAMPA phoneme transcription, so we can compile a training set to train the G2P model. The resulting set contains around 12000 sentences, both with and without diacritics.

3   Experimental Setup

To construct the ASR system we make use of bottleneck features extracted from networks trained on Russian, English (Switchboard-1) and Levantine Arabic (Levantine Arabic QT Training Data Set 5) phone conversations.

As the input features for the extractors we use filter banks with deltas and 50-dimensional i-vectors. The extractor takes as input 11 successive frames (1 central frame and 5 frames from the left and from the right) for each time step. The output features are 80-dimensional bottleneck ones.

To obtain the alignment, we train HMM-GMM models with the use of feature space maximum likelihood linear regression(fMLLR) and speaker adapted training(SAT). The initial acoustic features for the HMM-GMM systems are MFCC with deltas and CMN.

We train a separate DNN for each bottleneck extractor taking features corresponding to 11 successive frames (1 central frame and 5 frames from the left and from the right) as the input, so the input layer size is $80 \times 11 = 880$. Every DNN model has 4 layers, 1536 sigmoidal neurons each. All DNN are trained with the cross-entropy criterion. To obtain the final models, we perform two iterations of sequence training with state-level minimum Bayes risk(sMBR) criterion.

To study the applicability of the pronunciation lexicon obtained with the use of the G2P model trained on MSA dataset, we carry out a complete cycle of training of acoustic models from HMM-GMM to final DNN.

To prepare a 3-gram language model we use the LDC97T19-train and the texts from the supplementary dataset LDC2002T38.

We used Kaldi [9] to perform keyword spotting with the trained models.

4 Results

To carry out the experiment, we make use of two datasets:

- Evaluation set: the length is equal to 1.5 h, the number of words is roughly 15500, 13800 of them belong to the lexicon, and 1700 do not;
- Development set: the length is equal to 3.5 h, the number of words is roughly 33000, 29100 of them belong to the lexicon, and 3900 do not.

The recognition accuracy for some acoustic models is given in Table 1.

Table 1. WER(%) for some acoustic models

Model	Features	Lexicon	WER	
			dev	eval
HMM-GMM fMLLR SAT	39MFCC + deltas + CMN	ECA	59.24	57.64
HMM-GMM fMLLR SAT	39MFCC + deltas + CMN	MSA	63.03	61.83
DNN 4 × 1536	RUS BN	ECA	52.27	52.91
	ENG BN		52.52	52.86
	ARA BN		54.02	54.48
DNN 4 × 1536 sMBR	RUS BN	ECA	49.20	49.84
	ENG BN		51.49	51.33
	ARA BN		51.77	52.26
DNN 4 × 1536	RUS BN	MSA	56.86	56.55
DNN 4 × 1536 sMBR			54.57	54.39

It is obvious that the application of neural network acoustic models significantly increases the recognition accuracy as compared with the classical HMM-GMM. In addition, the sequence-training successively decreases WER. The use of the lexicon constructed by the MSA data lowers the recognition accuracy significantly, but the result remains acceptable.

We perform the keyword search at both the development and evaluation datasets. For each of these sets, we formulate the following search queries:

- 100uni: includes 100 most frequent unigrams in the corpus;
- 50uni35bi15tri: includes 50 most frequent unigrams in the corpus, 35 bigrams, and 15 trigrams.

The results of keyword search are given in Table 2.

Table 2. KWS results

KWS request	Features	Lexicon	dev		eval	
			ATWV	MTWV	ATWV	MTWV
100uni	RUS BN	MSA	0.401	0.6691	0.335	0.3528
		ECA	0.5741	0.8204	0.5413	0.5728
	ENG BN		0.5687	0.8065	0.5211	0.5476
	ARA BN		0.5605	0.7979	0.5177	0.5431
50uni35bi15tri	RUS BN	MSA	0.4424	0.5951	0.4556	0.492
		ECA	0.6558	0.7802	0.5871	0.685
	ENG BN		0.5824	0.7214	0.631	0.7092
	ARA BN		0.6419	0.7634	0.6073	0.6571

The best results obtained with the use of Russian bottleneck features and Egyptian Colloquial Arabic Lexicon are given in Figs. 1 and 2.

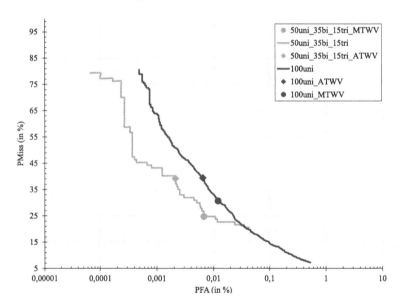

Fig. 1. DET-curve for KWS on evaluation set

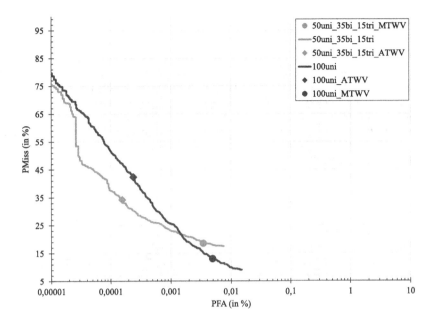

Fig. 2. DET-curve for KWS on development set

5 Conclusions

In this research, we construct an innovative ASR + KWS system for a low-resource language.

The system trained on the Russian bottleneck features shows the best result, which is better than the results of [5] by absolute 6.16 %. It is worth noticing that the Kaldi toolbox includes the callhome egyptian recipe where the final TDNN + iVector system performs worse than the presented system by absolute 2.26 %.

We compare the application of transcriptions of Egyptian Colloquial Arabic Lexicon with those obtained using the grapheme-to-phoneme model trained on the small MSA dataset. The accuracy decrease of 4.5 % is significant but allows us to obviate the need for the Egyptian lexicon and work with the MSA data, which are more readily available.

From our experiments it follows that the Arabic bottleneck features demonstrate the same accuracy as the English bottlenecks, whereas the Russian bottlenecks outperform them by absolute 2 %. We can't yet explain that difference.

The characteristics of keyword search quality given in Table 2 prove that the system built produces meaningful results and can for some cases used in practice.

Acknowledgements. This research was partially financially supported by the Government of the Russian Federation, Grant 074-U01.

References

1. Kirchhoff, K., Bilmes, J., Das, S., Duta, N., Egan, M., Ji, G., He, F., Henderson, J., Liu, D., Noamany, M., Schone, P., Schwartz, R., Vergyri, D.: Novel approaches to Arabic speech recognition: report from the 2002 Johns-Hopkins Summer Workshop. In: Proceeding of the IEEE International Conference on Acoustics, Speech and Signal Processing (ICASSP), vol. 1, pp. 344–347 (2003)
2. Habash, N., Eskander, R., Hawwari, A.: A morphological analyzer for Egyptian Arabic. In: NAACL-HLT 2012 Workshop on Computational Morphology and Phonology (SIGMOR-PHON 2012), pp. 1–9 (2012)
3. Elmahdy, M., Hasegawa-Johnson, M., Mustafawi, E., Duwairi, R., Minker, W.: Challenges and techniques for dialectal Arabic speech recognition and machine translation. In: Proceeding of Qatar Foundation Annual Research Forum, vol. 2011, CSO5, Doha, (2011)
4. Ali, A., Mubarak, H., Vogel, S.: Advances in dialectal Arabic speech recognition: a study using twitter to improve Egyptian ASR. In: Proceeding of International Workshop on Spoken Language Translation (IWSLT 2014), pp. 156–162 (2014)
5. Amr El-Desoky Mousa, Hong-Kwang Jeff Kuo, Mangu, L., Soltau, H.: Morpheme-based feature-rich language models using Deep Neural Networks for LVCSR of Egyptian Arabic. In: Proceeding of 2013 IEEE International Conference on Acoustics Speech and Signal Processing (ICASSP), pp. 8435–8439 (2013)
6. Ali, A., Zhang, Y., Cardinal, P., Dahak, N., Vogel, S., Glass, J.: A complete KALDI recipe for building Arabic speech recognition systems. In: Proceeding of IEEE SLT, pp. 525–529 (2015)
7. Samuel, T., Saon, G., Kuo, Hong-Kwang J., Mangu, L.: The IBM BOLT speech transcription system. In: Proceeding of Sixteenth Annual Conference of the International Speech Communication Association, pp. 3150–3153 (2015)
8. Trmal, J., Chen, G., Povey, D., Khudanpur, S.: A keyword search system using open source software. In: Proceeding of Spoken Language Technology (SLT) Workshop, IEEE (2014)
9. Povey, D., Ghoshal, A., et al.: The Kaldi speech recognition toolkit. In: Proceeding of the IEEE 2011 Workshop on Automatic Speech Recognition and Understanding (ASRU), IEEE Signal Processing Society (2011)

Speech Acts Annotation of Everyday Conversations in the ORD Corpus of Spoken Russian

Tatiana Sherstinova[(✉)]

Saint Petersburg State University, 7/9 Universitetskaya Nab., St. Petersburg 199034, Russia
t.sherstinova@spbu.ru

Abstract. The paper describes annotation principles developed for tagging of speech acts in the "One Day of Speech" (ORD) corpus of Russian everyday speech, with special attention being paid to categories and subcategories of speech acts distinguished in the ORD. Annotation of speech acts is a part of pragmatic annotation of the corpus, which includes as well the tagging of macro- and micro-episodes of verbal communication. Speech acts are annotated on four levels: (1) the orthographic transcript with information on syntagmatic and phrasal boundaries, (2) the speaker's code, (3) the main category of a speech act, and (4) its subcategory. Practical approbation of the proposed annotation scheme has been made on the material of 6 macroepisodes of everyday communication, in which 2250 speech acts have been discerned. Pragmatic annotation of the ORD corpus provides an opportunity to study everyday discourse in terms of speech acts and to study linguistic properties and patterns of speech acts of different types.

Keywords: Corpus linguistics · Speech corpus · Pragmatics · Spoken Russian · Everyday dialogues · Speech acts · Discourse · Annotation

1 Introduction

The ORD corpus is one of the most representative linguistic resources of everyday spoken Russian which contains 1200 h of speech recordings made in real-life settings. The recordings were made by 127 respondents-volunteers (66 men and 61 women) who gave their consent to record their verbal communication during a whole day. The recordings were made at different places – at home, in the office, in educational institutions, in fitness clubs, shops, service centers, restaurants, outdoors, etc. – and refer to various communication situations, both informal and professional [1]. During the day of recording, each respondent had different interlocutors, whose social roles also considerably differed (family members, friends, colleagues, acquaintances, etc.). Such diverse linguistic material provides a wide range of possibilities for linguistic and pragmatic studies of Russian spoken discourse, for "data-driven" research on face-to-face inter-action, spoken communication, conversation analysis, everyday speech variation, etc. Besides, these data may be used for defining and testing statistical models for diverse applied linguistic tasks and speech technologies.

Pragmatic annotation of the corpus data has been introduced in order to facilitate data retrieval from the corpus and its further linguistic, sociolinguistic and pragmatic

© Springer International Publishing Switzerland 2016
A. Ronzhin et al. (Eds.): SPECOM 2016, LNAI 9811, pp. 627–635, 2016.
DOI: 10.1007/978-3-319-43958-7_76

analysis. From the very beginning of the ORD creation, the corpus developers have encountered the necessity to annotate large fragments of respondents' recordings referring to large communication episodes united by setting/scene of communication, social roles of participants and their general activity, which are called *macroepisodes* and may be compared with stages within acts in theatrical plot structure [2].

Each macroepisode gets standardized description in three aspects: (1) *Where does the situation take place?* (2) *What are the participants doing?* and (3) *Who is (are) the main interlocutor(s)?* In the result, annotation of communication situations includes information on scene and type of communication, social roles of participants, and a few other factors [ibid]. Now, more than 2450 macroepisodes have been already annotated. Those episodes, which are to be transcribed are divided into *microepisodes*, united by the topic of communication or its main pragmatic task [3].

The next important step towards pragmatic annotation of the ORD corpus is the development of scheme of speech acts annotation, which is presented in this paper. Taking into consideration communicative diversity of everyday conversations and high dependency of pragmatic issues on the context [4] which is not always evident to researchers, this is a rather challenging task. However, we consider any attempts to speech acts annotating of real-life spontaneous conversations to be extremely important, as they can improve our understanding of the spoken discourse structure and its inner regularities, as well as to reevaluate the existing theoretical conceptions. Moreover, speech act annotation of real-life conversations could be useful for many applications in applied linguistics and speech technologies (e.g., by providing possibility to study linguistic properties and patterns of speech acts of different types, which may be used in elaboration of human-computer spoken dialogue systems, for speech synthesis and recognition systems, etc.) [5].

2   Speech Acts and Approaches to Their Annotation

The idea of "speech acts" was initially suggested by Austin [6], and developed further by Searle [7] and many of their followers. According to the speech act theory, any speech act should have a particular illocutionary force. However, the real data shows that in many cases real-life utterances could not be referred to "speech acts" in traditional terms (cf., for example, one conclusion of the research made on the base of Searle's classification: *"over 70 % of the sentences in our data set have no speech act at all"* [8]).

Having a practical task of pragmatic annotation of everyday discourse, we are more inclined to expect that each utterance should have some pragmatic meaning, and this meaning may be classified. In this perspective, we share the views of Mikhail Bakhtin who wrote that "each rejoinder, regardless of how brief and abrupt, has a specific quality of completion that expresses a particular position of the speaker, to which one may respond or may assume, with respect to it, a responsive position" [9, p. 72]. Because of that, for the ORD annotating, we prefer to understand "speech acts" in a broader meaning, distinct from their traditional interpretation, like many other endeavors in this field.

There are different classifications of speech acts proposed for practical annotation of speech used in corpus linguistics. Thus, Jurafsky considers the interpretation and generation of speech acts to be one of four core inferential problems in pragmatics that have received the most attention in the computational linguistics [10].

The most known approaches towards speech act annotation are the following: (1) Dialogue Act Markup in Several Layers (DAMSL) [11], (2) the tagging scheme in the Speech Act Annotated Corpus (SPAAC) [12, 13], MapTask Coding [14], the International project on Cross-Cultural Study of Speech Act Realization Patterns (CCSARP) [15], the VRM (Verbal Response Modes) system by W. B. Stiles [16].

The empiric work on everyday dialogues which are extremely diverse in terms of topics, intentions, general structure, context and participants, led us to conclusion that the most suitable classification for our task would be a rather detailed classification of utterances proposed by I. N. Borisova [17]. Therefore, it has been used as the basis for the ORD speech act classification. However, this scheme also did not perfectly fit into the real data, so we had to adapt it by introducing several additional categories and uniting subcategories, having much in common.

3   Categories and Subcategories of Speech Acts Distinguished in the ORD Corpus

The main categories of speech acts are determined in the following way. Although the names of some types coincide with that of traditional speech act theory, their meaning in some cases differs from it. Following [17] we distinguish 6 main categories of speech acts: (1) representatives (INF), (2) directives (DIR), (3) commissives (COM), (4) expressives, which include two subcategories — emotives (EMO) and etiquette expressives (ETI), (5) verdictives, containing valuatives (VAL) and suppositives (SUP), and (6) discourse regulatory acts (REG).

Further, the real-life material presented in our data made us to introduce two more auxiliary "categories", which do not allow to determine their pragmatic meaning: (7) an interrupted speech fragment (FRA), which does not have any cues revealing its intended category; and (8) an unintelligible utterance (NER), which could neither be transcribed nor understood by researchers because of some technical gaps in recoding or because of some special circumstances of communication (e.g., when the interlocutor was far from the recorder, or when a high level of ambient noise exists, etc.). Finally, (9) we use the tag (PAR) to label meaningful paralinguistic phenomena (e.g., a sigh or laughter) that may have pragmatic meaning, too.

We are also mindful about such category as "declaration" in terms of Searle classification (e.g., statement declaring war or the utterance like "*I hereby pronounce you man and wife*"), however like some other linguists (cf., [8]) we didn't find such type of speech acts in our everyday speech data until now.

The list of speech acts subcategories, which form the content of main categories has been initially borrowed from [17]. However, it was subject to a certain revision. Thus, the original list of subcategories exceeded 200 items [3], many of which being hardly discernible for expert attribution, so we decided to unite them into larger classes. We have also united the subcategories of speech acts which have much in common but are preferably used in different communication settings, like "command" and "order" (the latter being used primarily in the army or in security forces). In order not to inflate the classification, we omit in its current version those speech act subcategories which seem to us to be extremely rare to occur in everyday dialogues (e.g., "oath" or "confession"). However, in case we discover the necessity for additional labels when annotating the real data, we shall extend the classification scheme.

Below is a list of speech act categories proposed for the ORD annotation with examples of their most frequently used subcategories.

1. Regulative Speech Acts (REG) are used to regulate the process of communication itself. They are peculiar to spoken communication, and it is hardly possible to find them in written language. The following subcategories are the most common here: (1) "backchannel" utterances (RPO), (2) introduction of new topic (INI), (3) hesitation fillers (HES); (4) attracting interlocutor's attention (ATT); (5) capture the communicative initiative (CAP); (6) (self-)motivation, marker of the beginning (TAK), (7) end-marker (END); (8) request for repetition, echo-question (ECH); (9) expressing readiness for communication (RED); (10) repetition (REP), etc.

These tags allow the formal structure of communication to be traced. For example: *"Well?"* (TAK), *"Yeah."* (RPO), *"Let's talk about tomorrow!"* (INI), *"What do you call it..."* (HES).

2. Representative speech acts (INF) are used to perform tasks concerning information exchange. Representatives include the following subcategories: (1) descriptives (describing objects/persons/phenomena) (DES); (2) commentives or comment (commenting/accompanying message) (CMM); (3) constatives, stating existence or presence of some fact/phenomenon (STA); (4) correctives, correcting or improving the previous utterance(s) (COR); (5) announcement (ANN); (6) rogatives: question, request for information, clarifying question (QUE); (7) response to a question (RES); (8) explicatives, including explanation, argumentation, conclusion, illustration, motivation, justification, etc. (EXP); (9) reproductives – retelling, citation, telling an anecdote, etc. (CIT) and some others.

For example: *"How old is your son?"* (QUE), *"They could not afford this house* (STA)*, because it was very expensive* (EXP)."

3. Directive Speech Acts (DIR) "are the attempts <… > by the speaker to get the hearer to do something" [7]. Directives motivate the addressee for action (or try to prevent him from some action) or intend to influence on his worldview, emotions or life patterns. As distinct from Searle's idea, we do not include *questions* in this group, because to our mind they better fit into the second category dealing with information exchange.

Directives include the following subcategories: (1) request, the act of asking for something to be given or done (ASK); (2) imploration (IMP); (3) instruction (INS); (4) command, the act of commanding or ordering, demand (KOM); (5) offer, proposal (OFF); (6) advice (ADV), an opinion or recommendation offered as a guide to action, conduct, etc.; (7) permission to do something (PER); (8) forbiddance, prohibiting the action of a person (PRH); (9) convincing by argument (or evidence) to belief, agreement, consent, or a course of action (CNV); (10) directions (DRC); (11) warning (WAR), etc.

For example: *"Call me tomorrow!"* (ASK), *"Never touch my papers on the desk!"* (PRH), *"You should better forget him!"* (ADV).

4. Commissive Speech Acts (COM) are commitments of a speaker to some future action. It includes a wide range of acts, including the following: (1) promise (PRO), (2) guaranteeing (GAR), (3) "declaration of intent", revealing the speaker's plans (DEC); (4) obligation (OLB), (5) consent to comply with the request (CON), (6) disclaimer (DIS), (7) threat (TRE), etc. The confession of some action in the past also fits in this category (CNF).

For example: *"I promise you that!"* (PRO), *"I guarantee your security."* (GAR), *"It was a joke."* (CNF).

5. Expressive Speech Acts are used to express speaker's attitude or emotions. We distinguish two classes of expressives: emotives and etiquette speech acts.

5.1. Emotive Speech Acts (EMO) convey emotions or feelings of a speaker: (1) positive emotions (EPO), such as joy, pleasure, satisfaction, sympathy, etc.; (2) negative emotions (ENE) – outrage, resentment, anger, disappointment, antipathy, sadness, anxiety, restlessness, etc.; (3) surprise, astonishment (SUR); (4) emotional response to some external source (REA); (5) apathy, indifference (IND), etc.

For example: *"Oh!"*, *"Gosh!"*, *"Oops!"*. Such utterances may refer to different sub-types depending on context. The emotional speech is often accompanied by evaluations of different kind (see below Evaluatives).

5.2. Etiquette Speech Acts (ETI) are used to regulate communication in typical and ritualized situations: (1) greeting (GRE); (2) farewell (BYE); (3) self-representation or introducing other people (ITR); (4) apology (ESC); (5) thanking, gratitude, appreciation (THA); (6) polite addition to requests or commands like *"please"*, *"be so kind"* (PLS); (7) vocative (VOC); (8) congratulation (CGT); (9) wishes (WIS); (10) giving a toast (TOS); (11) expressing sympathy, condolence, affection, etc. (EPR); (12) making a joke (JOK); etc.

6. Verdictive Speech Acts are related with speaker's personal opinion.

6.1. Evaluative Speech Acts (VAL) are used to express the personal opinion of a speaker or his/her value judgments. The most common evaluatives in everyday language seem to be the following subtypes: (1) agreement with interlocutor's opinion or deeds (AGR); (2) objection, disagreement with the interlocutor's opinion, contestation, admonition, denial, disputing (OBJ); (3) appraisal or judgment, estimating or judging the nature or value of something or someone, including reprobation, accusing, exoneration, acquittal, complaint, etc. (JUD); (4) approval, compliment (APP), (5) invective, an insulting or abusive word or expression, a swearing utterance (INV), (6) ironic exaggeration (IRO); (7) mockery of something or someone; causticity; teasing or jeering utterance, etc. (MOC); (8) imitation of other's speech (IMI), etc.

For example: *"This is very bad!"* (JUD), *"No, you are not right!"* (OBJ), *"How nice!"* (IRO).

6.2. Suppositive Speech Acts (SUP) indicate speaker's supposition, consideration of a possibility, suggestion or proposing an idea or plan: (1) supposition (SUP); (2) doubt (DOT); (3) the expressions of speaker's personal opinion, which is not evaluative, such as guess, belief, etc. (OPI).

For example: *"I suppose he is gone"* (SUP); *"I doubt he will come"* (DOT); *"I think it's worth doing!"* (OPI).

4   Speech Acts Annotation

As may be seen from the list of categories listed in previous section, it is not always possible to identify speech acts based on written utterance taken out of context. It is relevant here to cite Martin Weisser asserting that the complexity inherent in pragmatic annotation "is mainly due to the fact that this type of annotation, unlike, for example, POS (part-of-speech) or semantic tagging/annotation, almost always needs to take into account levels above the individual word and may even need to refer to contextual information beyond those textual units that are commonly referred to as a 'sentence' or 'utterance'" [4].

Another, particularly important factor is prosody. Because of that it is extremely important to make annotation manually with a possibility to listen to each utterance and its broader context. Such opportunity is provided by the multimedia annotation tool ELAN [18], in workspace of which the recordings of the ORD corpus are transcribed and annotated [1].

Since each spoken utterance (or a turn, in terms of conversational analysis) consists of one or several speech acts, it should be segmented into correspondent fragments before annotation. Speech acts may be associated (1) with a whole utterance, which may be syntactically and phonetically well-framed, or incomplete, as well as interrupted or unfinished, (2) with a prosodically framed part of an utterance, and (3) with some para-linguistic phenomena. Speech segmentation is made in ELAN.

Speech acts are manually annotated by specially trained linguists on four levels:

1. RAct (speech act): an orthographic transcript with information on syntagmatic and phrasal boundaries. The rules for speech act spelling are the same as for ORD annotation transcripts (see [1] for the details).

2. RActSp (speaker): the unique speaker's code in the corpus.

3. RAGenT (general type): the main speech act category is one of the following (see above): REG, INF, DIR, COM, EMO, ETI, VAL, SUP, FRA, NER, and PAR. When choosing between these categories, the expert should indicate the type which fits the data the most, or is dominating (e.g., making choice between "emotive" and "evaluative" speech act, the decision should be based on what is dominating – emotion or evaluation). When speech acts could not be identified by a single tag, they are marked with two or more labels that are equally appropriate, as all relevant tags should be indicated in annotation.

4. RADetT (detailed type): speech act subcategory. This is also a three-letter code like PRO, INI, HES, CON, etc., the main of which are listed under the corresponding category in the previous section. Double tags are possible here, too.

These "detailed" categories are of special interest because they allow the data between different annotation schemes (as most of them have such tags like "greeting", "question", "answer", etc.) to be compared.

5 Preliminary Results

The pilot speech act annotation has been made on the material of 6 macroepisodes of everyday communication. The manual tagging was made by 6 independent researches (one linguist annotated one macroepisode) and then checked by an expert. In the result, 2250 speech acts have been discerned. 86 % of all speech acts have been unequivocally identified. 4 % of speech acts could not be identified at all being interrupted or unintelligible fragments. Remaining 10 % of speech acts received double tags.

As expected, the most frequent type of speech acts on the given sample turned out to be representative speech acts taking 39.36 % of all data. The discourse regulatory acts numbers 12.37 % and evaluatives – 11.17 %. Directives account for 6.80 %, etiquette speech acts make 4.14 %, and emotives – 3.51 %. Commissive and suppositive speech acts are used less often having 2.89 % and 2.53 % correspondently. Paralinguistic "acts" appeared in 3.55 % of all cases.

As for the subcategories, the most frequent types of speech acts turned out to be the following: (1) questions/"rogatives" speech acts (11.26 %), (2) constatives and statements (8.34 %), and (3) explicative speech acts (7.08 %). All these types are representatives, dealing with information exchange. Among the regulatory speech acts the most frequent are (self-)motivation acts, which usually initiate a conversation (2.45 %) and "backchannel" utterances (1.82 %). The other most "popular" speech acts are the following: agreement with interlocutor's opinion (3.07 %), supposition (2.00 %), and offer (1.78 %).

It is worth noting that practical approbation of the proposed annotation scheme revealed some drawbacks in speech act classification, which became visible in the process of evaluation. Thus, a number of categories are still difficult to distinguish from each other. For example, the agreement speech acts like "*Yes!* (*You are right!*)" in many cases remind "backchannel" speech acts like "*Aha*", however in other contexts they may be quite different. Speech acts introducing new topic are often confused by those marking conversation boundaries. Besides, there were some difficulties in attribution indirect speech acts, and this list may be continued.

Because of that the classification of speech acts presented here could not be considered as an ideal and finite scheme and should be partially reconsidered to become an effective tool for pragmatic annotation of such heterogeneous data as everyday discourse. However, the presented version of the annotation scheme does provide an opportunity to observe and analyze main tendencies in speech act distribution in everyday Russian discourse, as well as to study speaker's preferences in different communication settings.

Acknowledgements. The annotation principles for macro episodes tagging have been developed with support of the Russian Foundation for Humanities (project # 12-04-12017, *"Information System of Communication Scenarios of Russian Spontaneous Speech"*). The presented statistics were obtained within the framework of the project *"Everyday Russian Language in Different Social Groups"* supported by the Russian Science Foundation, project # 14-18-02070.

References

1. Asinovsky, A., Bogdanova, N., Rusakova, M., Ryko, A., Stepanova, S., Sherstinova, T.: The ORD speech corpus of Russian everyday communication "One Speaker's Day": creation principles and annotation. In: Matoušek, V., Mautner, P. (eds.) TSD 2009. LNCS, vol. 5729, pp. 250–257. Springer, Heidelberg (2009)
2. Sherstinova, T.: Macro episodes of Russian everyday oral communication: towards pragmatic annotation of the ORD speech corpus. In: Ronzhin, A., Potapova, R., Fakotakis, N. (eds.) SPECOM 2015. LNCS, vol. 9319, pp. 268–276. Springer, Heidelberg (2015)
3. Sherstinova, T.: Approaches to Pragmatic Annotation in the ORD Corpus: Microepisodes and Speech Acts. In: Proceedings of the International Conference on "Corpus linguistics-2015", pp. 436–446 (2015)
4. Weisser, M.: Speech act annotation. In: Aijmer, K., Rühlemann, C. (eds.) Corpus Pragmatics: a Handbook, pp. 84–111. CUP, Cambridge (2014)
5. Potapova, R.K.: Speech: Communication, Information, Cybernetics. URSS, Moscow (2003) (In Russian)
6. Austin, J.L.: How To Do Things With Words. Oxford University Press, Oxford (1962)
7. Searle, J.R.: A classification of illocutionary acts. Lang. Soc. **5**(1), 1–23 (1976)
8. Qadir, A., Riloff, E.: Classifying sentences as speech acts in message board posts. In: Proceedings of the 2011 Conference on Empirical Methods in Natural Language Processing (EMNLP-2011), pp. 748–758 (2011)
9. Bakhtin, M.M.: Speech Genres and Other Late Essays. University of Texas Press, Austin (1986). Edited by Caryl Emerson and Michael Holquist, Translated by Vern W. McGee
10. Jurafsky, D.: Pragmatics and computational linguistics. In: Horn, L., Ward, G. (eds.) The Handbook of Pragmatics, pp. 578–604. Blackwell, Oxford (2006)
11. Allen, J., Core, M.: Draft of DAMSL: dialog act markup in several layers (1997). https://www.cs.rochester.edu/research/speech/damsl/RevisedManual/
12. Leech, G., Weisser, M.: Generic speech act annotation for task-oriented dialogues. In: Proceedings of the Corpus Linguistics 2003 Conference, vol. 16. UCREL Technical Papers, Lancaster University (2003)
13. Weisser, M.: SPAACy: a semi-automated tool for annotating dialogue acts. Int. J. Corpus Linguist. **8**(1), 63–74 (2003)
14. Carletta, J., Isard, A., Isard, S., Kowtko, J.S., Doherty-Sneddon, G., Anderson, A.H.: The reliability of a dialogue structure coding scheme. Comput. Linguist. **23**, 13–32 (1997)
15. Blum-Kulka, S., Olshtain, E.: Requests and apologies: a cross-cultural study of speech act realization patterns (CCSARP). Appl. Linguist. **5**(3), 196–215 (1984)
16. Stiles, W.: Describing Talk: A Taxonomy of Verbal Response Modes. Sage, Newbury Park (1992)

17. Borisova, I.N.: Russian spoken dialogue. Structure and Dynamics. KomKniga, Moscow (2009) (In Russian)
18. Hellwig, B., Van Uytvanck, D., Hulsbosch, M., et al.: ELAN — Linguistic Annotator. Version 4.9.3 (2014). http://tla.mpi.nl/tools/tla-tools/elan/

Speech Enhancement with Microphone Array Using a Multi Beam Adaptive Noise Suppressor

Mikhail Stolbov[1,2] and Alexander Lavrentyev[1(✉)]

[1] Speech Technology Center, Krasutskogo-4, St. Petersburg 196084, Russia
{stolbov, lavrentyev}@speechpro.com
[2] ITMO University, 49 Kronverkskiy Pr., St. Petersburg 197101, Russia

Abstract. This paper presents a new speech enhancement method with microphone array for the joint suppression of coherent and diffuse noise. The proposed method is based on combined technique: target and noise steering beamforming and adaptive noise suppression. The microphone array forms two beams steered in the directions of target speaker and of noise source. The signal of reference beam is used to suppress the noise in primary channel. The proposed algorithm of Adaptive Noise Suppressor (ANS) is based on the transformation of the signal spectrum of the reference channel into the noise spectrum of the main channel using noise equalizer and algorithm of dual channel spectral subtraction. The effectiveness of the proposed technique is confirmed in varying real life coherent and diffuse noise conditions. The experimental results show that proposed method is an efficient procedure for speech quality improvement in real life noisy and reverberant conditions with SNRs down to −5 dB and reverberation time up to 0.88 s.

Keywords: Speech enhancement · Adaptive interference canceller/suppressor

1 Introduction

Microphone arrays (MA) are widely used technique for speech capturing in noisy environments in all areas of speech processing. In general, the acoustic noise is a combination of diffuse and spatially coherent noise. Coherent direct path noises are produced by point acoustic sources in free space (with unhindered wave propagation). Incoherent diffuse noises are produced by remote or spatially distributed acoustic sources under conditions of reverberation and multipath wave propagation [1, 2].

The basic algorithm of MA is fixed beamforming (FBF). However, this FBF algorithm is not very efficient because part of the environment noise comes to MA output through both main lobe and sidelobes. The problem of speech enhancement is important in a high noise level conditions (sounds of audio devices indoor, art work and traffic sounds outdoor). In these cases, the signal/noise ratio (SNR) of the output signal of MA is low.

A large number of methods for suppression of coherent and diffuse noises are proposed [1–5]. For non-stationary noise environment methods of adaptive noise

A. Ronzhin et al. (Eds.): SPECOM 2016, LNAI 9811, pp. 636–644, 2016.
DOI: 10.1007/978-3-319-43958-7_77

reduction based on extraction of reference noise signal and algorithm of it suppression in noisy target signal are used. Three groups of methods are used for extraction of reference noise signal. (1): null steering beamforming (NSB) in the direction of the noise source [5]. (2): using the reference microphone placed close to the source of interference [6]. (3): forming beams (one or various) in the direction of noise sources [7–9] using the same microphone array or by an auxiliary array [10].

The disadvantage of the first group of methods is the sensitivity to steering errors (misadjustment) of the primary channel and multipath propagation of target signal [1]. The target signal leakage in reference channel results in cancellation of target signal.

A disadvantage of the second group of methods is that the placement of a microphone close to the noise source is not always possible.

The third group of forming beams (one or various) in the direction of noise sources is more robust to steering errors. Our proposed method is based on the formation of beams steered in the directions of target speaker and of noise source.

The second element of the methods of adaptive noise reduction is a signal processing algorithm. The algorithms are divided into two main classes: adaptive noise cancelling (ANC) and adaptive noise suppression (ANS) algorithms.

ANC algorithms better save the target speech signal, but their limitation is that they only suppress the coherent part of the noise. In the case of a diffuse sound field much of noise may be incoherent in main and reference channels, which weakens the effectiveness of noise suppression. ANS algorithms distort the useful signal, but they allow suppress a coherent and diffuse noise.

The main purpose of this research is to improve the microphone array algorithm of both coherent and diffuse noise reduction for speech enhancement.

2 The Proposed Method

The proposed method is based on combined technique: target and noise steering beamforming and adaptive noise suppression. The basis of beamforming is frequency-domain FBF [3]. A general block diagram for an adaptive noise cancellation/suppression (ANC/ANS) system is presented in Fig. 1. The signals of the microphones are segmented into overlapping frames with 50 % overlap. Then Hann window is applied on each segment and a set of Fourier coefficients $X_n(\omega, k)$ using short-time fast Fourier transform (STFT) is generated.

The signals of main and reference beams are calculated as follows:

$$X(\omega, k) = D^T(\theta_M, \omega)X(\omega, k) \qquad R(\omega, k) = D^T(\theta_R, \omega)X(\omega, k), \qquad (1)$$

where ω – is the frequency, k – is the frame time index, θ_M, θ_R – are the angles of the directions to the target speaker and to the noise source respectively, N – is the number of microphones, $D(\theta, \omega) = [d_1(\theta, \omega), d_2(\theta, \omega), \ldots, d_N(\theta, \omega)]^T$ is the steering vector of the microphone array in the direction θ, $X(\omega, k) = [X_1(\omega, k), X_2(\omega, k), \ldots, X_N(\omega, k)]^T$ is the signal vector received by the microphone array.

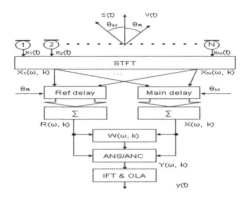

Fig. 1. The structure of the system

Consider the formation of the main signal and reference signal for the case of the target speaker and the noise source. The sound propagation model for each beam can be described as follows:

$$X(\omega, k) = S(\omega, k) + H_v(\omega, k)V(\omega, k) = S(\omega, k) + N_x(\omega, k), \tag{2}$$

$$R(\omega, k) = H_r(\omega, k)V(\omega, k) + H_s(\omega, k)S(\omega, k), \tag{3}$$

where $S(\omega, k)$ – is the signal of the target speaker, $V(\omega, k)$ – is the signal of the noise source arriving to microphone array from the direction θ_v, $H_v(\omega, k)$ – is the transfer function from noise source to main beam of FBF, $H_r(\omega, k)$ - is the transfer function from noise source to reference beam of FBF, $H_s(\omega, k)$ - is the transfer function from target speaker to main beam of FBF.

Adaptive noise suppression algorithm is as follows. ANS algorithm based on an assessment of the amplitude spectrum interference $\widetilde{N_x}(\omega, k)$ in the main channel, which is calculated from the spectrum of the reference channel signal using the noise equalizer:

$$\tilde{N}_x(\omega, k) = W(\omega, k - 1)|R(\omega, k)|, \tag{4}$$

where $W(\omega, k)$ – is the transfer function of equalizer, k – is the time frame index. Estimation of the transfer function is calculated as follows:

$$W(\omega, k) = \begin{cases} (1 + \beta) \times W(\omega, k - 1), |X(\omega, k)| > \tilde{N}_x(\omega, k) \\ (1 - \alpha) \times W(\omega, k - 1), |X(\omega, k)| \le \tilde{N}_x(\omega, k) \end{cases}, \tag{5}$$

where α is the release rate, β is the attack rate.

The algorithm in the absence of a speech signal $|S(\omega, k)| \approx 0$ aligns the noise amplitude spectrum of the reference channel to the noise spectrum in the main channel:

$$|H_v(\omega, k)V(\omega, k)| \approx W(\omega, k)|H_r(\omega, k)V(\omega, k)|. \tag{6}$$

Since the spectrum of noise in the reference channel is usually much greater than the noise spectrum in the main channel: $|H_r(\omega, k)V(\omega, k)| \gg |H_v(\omega, k)V(\omega, k)|$, than $W(\omega, k) \ll 1$. Therefore it is necessary to constrain the maximum values of the transfer function of the equalizer:

$$\tilde{W}(\omega, k) = Min\{W_{max}(\omega), W(\omega, k)\}, \tag{7}$$

where $W_{max}(\omega)$ is the maximum values of the transfer function of the equalizer.

Constraint of the transfer equalizer function prevents unwanted amplification of the target spectral signal components belonging to a reference channel.

The estimation of the noise spectrum of the main channel is used in the algorithm of dual channel spectral subtraction to estimate spectrum of the target signal:

$$|\tilde{S}(\omega, k)| = |X(\omega, k)| - \tilde{N}x(\omega, k) = g(\omega, k) \times |X(\omega, k)|, \tag{8}$$

where $g(\omega, k)$ is the gain function of spectral subtraction:

$$g(\omega, k) = |\tilde{S}(\omega, k)|/|X(\omega, k)| = SNR(\omega, k)/(1 + SNR(\omega, k)), \tag{9}$$

where $SNR(\omega, k) = |\tilde{S}(\omega, k)|/\tilde{N}x(\omega, k)$ are the spectral SNRs. To reduce the residual musical noise we made the following modification of gain function:

$$g(\omega, k) = C \times [SNR(\omega, k)]^2, \tag{10}$$

where $C = 1 \ldots 5$ is the slope of gain function.

In its final form, taking into account constraints of minimum and maximum values the spectral gain is as follows:

$$G(\omega, k) = Min\left\{1, Max\left\{G_0(\omega, k), C \times [SNR(\omega, k)]^2\right\}\right\}, \tag{11}$$

where $G_0(\omega, k)$−suppression spectral floor. Estimation of target signal after noise reduction is as follows:

$$\tilde{S}(\omega, k) = X(\omega, k) \times G(\omega, k). \tag{12}$$

The enhanced signal ŝ(t) is calculated, using Invers Fourier Transform (IFT) and overlap and add (OLA) technique.

3 Simulation Results

The proposed ANS method is compared with the following methods: Fixed Beam-forming (FBF), constrained frequency domain GSC [1], frequency domain Null-Steering Beamformer (NSB) [5] and Adaptive Noise Canceller in time and frequency domain (ANC-T, ANC-F) [11]. The comparison has been done for linear microphone array with 11 microphones with a inter microphone spacing 3.5 cm.

To test the noise reduction performance of these methods, a computer program has been developed. The comparison has done using Noise Reduction (NR) и Speech Distortion (SD) and SNR improvement measure (SNRI).

Noise Reduction. To estimate NR the coherent broadband interference (white Gaussian noise) arriving to the microphone array from the angle $+45°$ was used. It has been set no useful signal $S(\omega, k) = 0$. Main channel beam was steered in the look direction $\theta_M = 0°$, the beam of the reference channel is steered in the direction $\theta_R = +45°$:

$$X(\omega, k) = H_v(\omega, k)V(\omega, k), \qquad R(\omega, k) = H_r(\omega, k)V(\omega, k). \tag{13}$$

The NR was calculated using the residual interference signal power with interference power in a separate microphone:

$$NR\,dB = 10\log[P_{mic}/P_{out}]. \tag{14}$$

In this case, NR_{mic} on a separate microphone is equal to 0 dB [3].

Speech Distortion. To estimate SD the coherent speech signal arriving to the microphone array from the angle $0°$ was used. It has been set no interference signal $V(\omega, k) = 0$. Main channel beam was steered in the look direction $\theta_M = 0°$, the beam from the reference channel is steered in the direction $\theta_R = +45°$:

$$X(\omega, k) = S(\omega, k), \qquad R(\omega, k) = H_s(\omega, k)S(\omega, k). \tag{15}$$

In this case, the output of microphone array FBF is undistorted speech signal:

$$Y_{FBF}(\omega, k) = S(\omega, k). \tag{16}$$

The speech signal is distorted if other methods are used. The ratio of the power of the distorted and undistorted signals y(t) and s(t) is defined as speech distortion:

$$SD\,dB = 10\log[P_S/P_Y] = 10\log[P_{FBF}/P_{out}] \tag{16}$$

SNR Improvement. To estimate SNRI coherent speech signal arriving to the microphone array from the angle of $0°$ and coherent broadband interference (white Gaussian noise) arriving from the angle of $+45°$ were used. Main channel beam was steered in the look direction $\theta_M = 0°$, the beam from the reference channel is steered in the direction $\theta_R = +45°$. The input SNR has been set equal to -5 dB. SNRI evaluation was carried out in accordance with the procedure laid down in [4].

Table 1. NR, SD, SNRI after processing with different methods

Method	NR dB	SD dB	SNRI dB
FBF	10.98	0	5.65
NSB	30.16	7.97	16.86
GSC	14.80	0.11	10.03
ANC-T	45.43	11.78	9.85
ANS	**48.51**	**8.81**	**14.03**

The desired signal s(t) and interference n(t) are superposed with given SNR. The noisy signal x(t) is processed with the noise reduction algorithm. Afterwards the desired and interfering signals are separately processed with the resulting filter coefficients. SNRI was estimated by comparing outputs to inputs of the fixed filters.

The estimations of NR, SD, SNRI with different methods are shown in Table 1.

The proposed ANS method is superior to other methods according to the criterion of NR and close to NSB method for SD, SNRI criteria. Another advantage of the ANS is the ability to suppress diffuse noise. At the same time it is much inferior to GSC method for SD criteria. However, GSC loses its advantage under steering misadjustment, non-ideal microphones and reverberation multipath propagation.

4   Experimental Results in Real Conditions

4.1   Suppression of Partially Ccoherent Noise

We solved the problem of extracting speech speaker on the background of loud music using linear 8-microphone array with inter microphone spacing 5 cm.

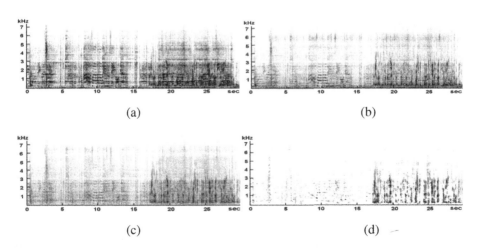

(a)   (b)

(c)   (d)

Fig. 2. Spectrograms for (a) Microphone signal, (b) FBF steered to target speaker, (c) FBF with ANC-T processing, (d) FBF with ANS processing.

Acoustic scenario: Office room size $6 \times 13 \times 3.2$ m, reverberation time $T_{60} \approx 0.66$ s distance to the target speaker 3 m, $\theta_S \approx +10°$, distance to the loudspeaker 4.5 m, $\theta_V \approx -60°$, SNR ≈ -5.3 dB. Background music was a partially coherent, partially diffuse sound field. Background music is present throughout the range the target speaker's speech is present at 17–30 s interval.

The examples of the enhancement of speech with different methods are shown in Fig. 2.

The results of experiment are as follows. ANS gave the highest noise reduction comparing to the others: FBF (8 dB), FBF + ANC-T (11 dB), FBF + ANS (22 … 24 dB). ANS method showed the robustness to errors of microphone array steering on the target speaker and on the source of noise. ANS results reduction of both coherent and diffuse noise components.

4.2   Suppression of Diffuse Speech Interference

We solved the problem of the separation of two remote speakers speech in reverberant room using linear 6×8 microphone array with inter microphone spacing 5 cm. The

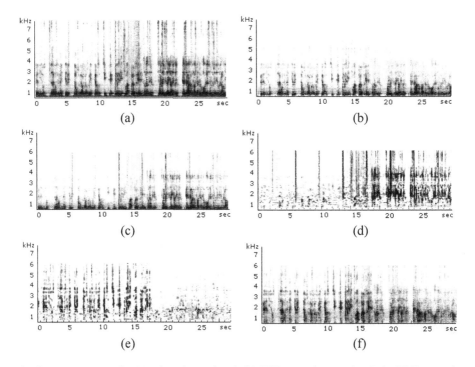

Fig. 3. Spectrograms for (a) microphone signal, (b) FBF steered to speaker 1, (c) FBF steered to speaker 2, (d) FBF with ANS enhancement of speaker 1, (e) FBF with ANS enhancement of speaker 2, (f) FBF with ANC-T enhancement of speaker 1.

low-pass filtering (6 kHz) for elimination of sidelobes was applied when processing signals in the microphone array.

Acoustic scenario: Office room size $6 \times 6.5 \times 3.2$ m, reverberation time $T_{60} \approx$ 0.88 s, distance to the speaker_1 $d1 = 6$ m, $\theta_1 \approx +40°$, distance to the speaker_2 $d2 = 5$ m, $\theta_2 \approx 0°$. The speech was diffuse sound field. The speech of 1-st speaker is present on the time interval 0–15 s, the speech of 2-d speaker is present on the time interval 15–30 s. The examples of the enhancement of speech with different methods are shown in Fig. 3.

The results of experiment are as follows. ANS method allowed separate the remote speakers in reverberant room. Maximum suppression of the target speaker in using ANS is in the frequency range of 0–500 Hz, where the main lobe of array beampattern is broad and leakage of the target signal in the reference channel is the maximum. ANS method suppresses speech of interfering speaker significantly more effectively than the FBF, ANC-T, ANC-F methods.

5 Conclusion

A new speech enhancement method with MA for the joint suppression of coherent and diffuse noise is presented. The method is based on combined target and noise steering beamforming and algorithm of ANS. The ANS is based on the algorithm of dual channel spectral subtraction. The spectral subtraction results in the reduction of coherent and diffuse noise in the target beam signal. The proposed ANS yields better SNR improvement than conventional FBF and GSC algorithms and the best noise reduction comparing FBF, GSC, NSB algorithms and microphone alignment technique [12]. The experimental results show that ANS is an efficient procedure for speech enhancement in real life noisy and reverberant conditions with SNRs down to −5.3 dB and reverberation time up to $T_{60} \approx 0.88$ s. The additional advantages of ANS are its low computational cost that allows real-time speech processing and robustness to errors MA steering on the target speaker and source of noise.

Acknowledgements. This work was partially financially supported by the Government of the Russian Federation, Grant 074-U01.

References

1. Fischer, S., Simmer, K.: An adaptive microphone array for hands–free communication. In: Proceedings of IWAENC-1995, pp. 1–4 (1995)
2. McCowan, I.A.: Robust Speech Recognition using Microphone Arrays. Ph.D. Thesis, Queensland University of Technology, Australia (2001)
3. Brandstein, M., Ward, D. (eds.): Microphone Arrays. Springer, Heidelberg (2001)
4. Benesty, J., Makino, S., Chen, J. (eds.): Speech Enhancement. Springer, Heidelberg (2005)

5. Jonhson, D.H., Dungeon, D.E.: Array Signal Processing: Concepts and Techniques. Prentice-Hall, Upper Saddle River (1993)
6. Spalt, T., Fuller, C., Brooks, T., Humphreys, W.: A Background Noise Reduction Technique using Adaptive Noise Cancellation for Microphone Arrays. American Institute of Aeronautics and Astronautics, pp. 1–16 (2011)
7. Cao, Y., Sridharan, S., Moody, M.P.: Post-microphone-array speech enhancement with adaptive filters for forensic application. In: Proceedings of International Symposium on Speech, Image Processing and Neural Networks, pp.253–255 (1994)
8. Meyer, L., Sydow, C.: Noise cancelling for microphone arrays. In: Proceedings of ICASSP-1997, pp. 211–213 (1997)
9. Jingjing, T. et al.: The algorithm research of adaptive noise cancellation based on dual arrays and particle swarm algorithm. In: Proceedings of International Conference on Environmental Engineering and Technology Advances in Biomedical Engineering, vol. 8, pp. 106–111 (2012)
10. Nathwani, K., Hegde, R.: Joint adaptive beamforming and echo cancellation using a non reference anchor array framework. In: Proceedings of Asilomar 2012, pp.885–889 (2012)
11. Bitzer, J., Brandt, M.: Speech enhancement by adaptive noise cancellation: problems, algorithms, and limits. In: Proceedings of 39-th AES Conference, pp. 109–113 (2010)
12. Stolbov, M., Aleinik, S.: Speech enhancement with microphone array using frequency-domain alignment technique. In: Proceedings of 54-th AES Conference (2014)

Speech Features Evaluation for Small Set Automatic Speaker Verification Using GMM-UBM System

Ivan Rakhmanenko[✉] and Roman Meshcheryakov

Tomsk State University of Control Systems and Radioelectronics, Tomsk, Russia
ria@keva.tusur.ru, mrv@security.tomsk.ru

Abstract. This paper overviews the application sphere of speaker verification systems and illustrates the use of the Gaussian mixture model and the universal background model (GMM-UBM) in an automatic text-independent speaker verification task. The experimental evaluation of the GMM-UBM system using different speech features is conducted on a 50 speaker set and a result is presented. Equal error rate (EER) using 256 component Gaussian mixture model and feature vector containing 14 mel frequency cepstral coefficients (MFCC) and the voicing probability is 0,76 %. Comparing to standard 14 MFCC vector 23,7 % of EER improvement was acquired.

Keywords: Speaker recognition · Speaker verification · Gaussian mixture model · GMM-UBM system · Mel frequency cepstral coefficients · Speech features · Small speaker set · Speech processing

1 Introduction

Automatic speaker recognition task is one of the most challenging problems in speech processing field. Methods that are used in modern speaker recognition systems are not perfect. There are models that work effectively in acoustically clean environment but losing their effectiveness in low signal-noise ratio environment. Requirements for speaker verification systems accuracy are constantly increasing because of the growing spreading of biometric multi-factor authentication systems. These systems include remote voice authentication banking account management systems, access control systems and others. All these systems require high accuracy of speaker recognition in order to satisfy customers' needs.

The application field of currently developed voice authentication systems includes multi-factor (biometric) authentication and access restriction systems, banking account management systems using voice biometrics in order to give speaker access to his banking account, national security and anti-terrorism issues. The use of speaker recognition systems that have even small possibility of mistake in such a sensitive application areas could be very dangerous.

Equal error rate value (EER) is one of the most common speaker verification accuracy measures used nowadays. EER is used both for text-dependent and text-independent automatic voice authentication systems. By now the best speaker recognition systems are characterized by 3–5 % EER values [1]. This accuracy is insufficient for

© Springer International Publishing Switzerland 2016
A. Ronzhin et al. (Eds.): SPECOM 2016, LNAI 9811, pp. 645–650, 2016.
DOI: 10.1007/978-3-319-43958-7_78

modern speaker verification systems because even small probability of false acceptance is critical. If there are many speakers working with such systems, then mistakes will occur definitely, and such mistakes are unacceptable in systems granting access rights to confidential data or banking accounts.

Speaker recognition includes verification and identification. Automatic speaker verification (ASV) is a verification of a person's claimed identity from his voice. In automatic speaker identification (ASI), there is no a priori identity claim, and the system decides who the person is, what group the person is a member of, or (in the open-set case) that the person is unknown [2]. Automatic text-independent speaker verification system that is presented in this paper works with the closed-set verification problem, deciding whether or not claimed speaker was presented on the speech signal. Existence of speakers that are not registered in the system is not taken into consideration.

2 Features Extraction

Mel frequency cepstral coefficients (MFCC), their deltas and double deltas are used very commonly as feature vectors in many scientific works dedicated to speaker recognition. But in case of using ASV system working on a small speaker set this decision should be reconsidered in order to achieve better verification accuracy. Thus, more attention should be devoted to another speech features such as line spectral pair frequencies, perceptual linear predictive cepstral coefficients, short-term energy, formant frequencies, fundamental frequency, voicing probability, zero crossing rate, jitter and shimmer.

Basic feature set used in the presented system is mel frequency cepstral coefficients set. Mel frequency cepstral spectrum transform method was first introduced in [3]. MFCC are used for speaker recognition, speech recognition and other speech related applications. 12 MFCC is most frequently used count of coefficients. In some systems a delta and a double delta features related to the change in cepstral features over time are added. Other features are added to basic mel frequency feature vector.

Feature vectors extraction process is shown in Fig. 1. First step of feature vector extraction is windowing – taking a small part of speech signal instead of the whole signal. Hamming windows were used for MFCC calculation. Window length is 20 ms, window shift is 10 ms. Discrete Fourier Transform (DFT) is performed after windowing.

Next step of feature vector extraction is warping frequencies outputted by DFT to the mel scale defined as:

$$f_{mel} = 1125 \ln (1 + f /700). \tag{1}$$

The mapping between frequency in hertz and the mel scale is linear below 1000 Hz and logarithmic above 1000 Hz [4]. A bank of triangular filters is created for implementing this scaling and the log energy is collected from each of these frequency bands [3]. The final step of MFCC extraction is the inverse Discrete Fourier Transform (IDFT).

Besides MFCC, jitter, shimmer, zero crossing rate (ZCR), perceptual linear predictive cepstral coefficients(PLP CC), short-term energy, voicing probability (V_p), fundamental frequency (F_0), formants, line spectral pair frequencies are added to feature vector (Fig. 1).

Voicing probability is computed as a maximum of the autocorrelation function of the spectrum. Features extraction was done using openSMILE tool [5].

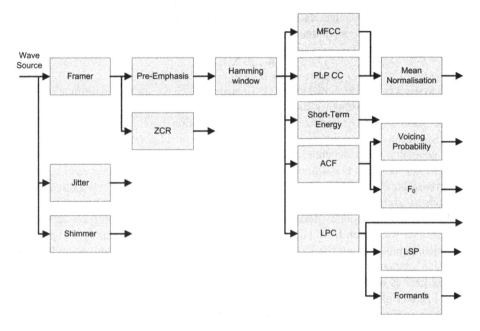

Fig. 1. Features extraction process diagram.

Despite the fact that there are no features in spectrum and cepstrum that could help distinguish speakers, nevertheless it could be effectively used in automatic speaker recognition (ASR) task [6]. This is possible due to the fact that the spectrum reflects the structure of the human vocal tract, which is the main physiological factor that allows us to distinguish voices.

3   GMM-UBM System

The choice of decision rules composition method is very important in ASR task. The most common methods are Gaussian Mixture Model (GMM), Support Vector Machines (SVM), Hidden Markov Models (HMM), neural networks and factor analysis modifications. GMM is used in ASM system presented in this paper.

A Gaussian Mixture Model (GMM) is a parametric probability density function represented as a weighted sum of Gaussian component densities [7]. A GMM with M component Gaussian densities can be presented by the equation

$$p(x|\lambda) = \sum_{i=1}^{M} w_i g(x|\mu_i \Sigma_i), \tag{2}$$

where x is a D-dimensional continuous-valued data vector (i.e. measurement or features), w_i, $i = 1,...,M$, are the mixture weights, and $g(x|\mu_i, \Sigma_i)$, $i = 1,...,M$, are the component Gaussian densities with mean vector μ_i and covariance matrix Σ_i. The complete GMM is parameterized by the mean vectors, covariance matrices and mixture weights from all component densities. It could be represented by the equation:

$$\lambda = \{w_i, \mu_i, \Sigma_i\}. \tag{3}$$

Each speaker is represented by his Gaussian mixture λ for speaker identification task.

There are two reasons for using Gaussian mixture densities as a representation of speaker identity [8]. The first reason is the intuitive notion that the individual component densities of the GMM may model some underlying set of acoustic classes, reflecting some general speaker-dependent vocal tract configurations. The second reason is the empirical observation that a linear combination of Gaussian basis functions is capable of representing a large class of sample distributions. A GMM can form smooth approximations to arbitrarily-shaped densities.

Universal Background Model (UBM) is a GMM trained on large set of speech samples that was taken from big population of speakers expected during recognition. As in [9], parameters for the UBM are trained using the EM algorithm, and a form of Bayesian adaptation is used for training speaker models. Number of mixtures used is 256, as EER is not decreasing for small speaker set when larger mixture numbers are used. Speaker models are derived by MAP adaptation, where only means are adapted with relevance factor $r = 10$. GMM-UBM system described in this section is based on MSR Identity Toolbox [10].

4   Experimental Evaluation

The experiments were conducted using speech database containing collection of speech from 25 male and 25 female speakers. This speech database includes speech samples of sentences from science fiction stories. The total length of speech for each speaker is at least 6 min consisting of 50 speech segments of various lengths. Each speaker was recorded using medium-quality microphone, 8000 Hz sampling rate, 16 Bit sample size.

All 50 speaker set was divided equally for male and female speakers on the UBM training set consisting of 30 speakers and speakers' training set consisting of 20 speakers. For MAP adaptation of speakers' models 40 speech segments was taken. Remaining 10 utterances of each speaker was used for testing verification system. Overall, 4000 tests were done for each feature set, having 10 positive (true speaker) and 190 negative (imposter) tests for each speaker.

After training phase, that consists of UBM training and speakers' models adapting, starts test phase. For each test speech segment verification scores (log-likelihood ratios) are calculated using speaker GMM and UBM models (Eq. 4). Using different decision thresholds hypothesized speaker model was accepted or rejected:

$$\Lambda(X) = \log p(X|\lambda_{hyp}) - \log p(X|\lambda_{ubm}). \tag{4}$$

Two different verification metrics was used for evaluating speaker verification system: EER and minimum detection cost function with SRE 2008 parameters (minDCF). Best results of the experimental evaluation are given in Table 1.

Table 1. Different feature sets verification trials results.

Feature set	%EER	minDCF*100
MFCC + V_p	**0,763**	0,805
MFCC + $_\Delta$+V_p	1,000	**0,699**
MFCC + $_\Delta$ +$_{\Delta\Delta}$ + V_p	1,000	0,803
MFCC	1,000	0,925
MFCC + Shimmer	1,000	1,007
MFCC + $_\Delta$	1,052	0,825
MFCC + JitterDDP	1,131	1,003
MFCC + Zcr	1,131	1,031
MFCC + F_0	1,157	1,161

As the Table 1 shows, best verification results were obtained using feature vector consisting of 14 mel frequency cepstral coefficients and the voicing probability with EER = 0,763 %. Minimum DCF was obtained using 14 mel frequency cepstral

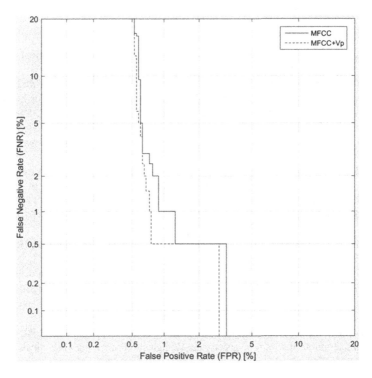

Fig. 2. Detection error trade-off (DET) curve for MFCC and MFCC + voicing probability feature sets

coefficients, their deltas and the voicing probability. Figure 2 shows MFCC and MFCC plus voicing probability feature vectors detection error trade-off (DET) curves. Adding other features to standard MFCC vector had given worse verification results unlike using only MFCC vector. Furthermore, it is noticeable that adding the voicing probability to MFCC vector increases EER or decreasing minDCF. So we could conclude that the voicing probability could increase effectiveness of the GMM-UBM speaker verification system.

5   Conclusion

Speaker verification system based on Gaussian mixture model and universal background model was created. Best verification results were obtained using feature vector consisting of 14 MFCC and the voicing probability giving EER = 0,763 %. Comparing to standard 14 MFCC vector 23,7 % of EER improvement was acquired using this feature vector. It is planned to evaluate presented system on bigger speaker set in order to compare obtained results with small speaker set problem.

This work was supported by the Ministry of Education and Science of the Russian Federation within 1.3 federal program «Research and development in priority areas of scientific-technological complex of Russia for 2014-2020» (grant agreement № 14.577.21.0172 on October 27, 2015; identifier RFMEFI57715X0172).

References

1. Sorokin, V.N., Viugin, V.V., Tananykin, A.A.: Speaker recognition: analytical review. Inf. Processes. **12**, 1–30 (2012)
2. Campbell Jr., J.P.: Speaker recognition: a tutorial. Proc. IEEE **85**(9), 1437–1462 (1997)
3. Davis, S.B., Mermelstein, P.: Comparison of parametric representations for monosyllabic word recognition in continuously spoken sentences. IEEE Trans. Acoust. Speech Signal Process. **28**(4), 357–366 (1980)
4. Jurafsky, D., Martin, J.H.: Speech and Language Processing, 2nd edn. Pearson Education, New Jersey (2009)
5. Eyben, F., Weninger, F., Gross, F., Schuller, B.: Recent developments in opensmile, the munich open-source multimedia feature extractor. In: Proceedings of the 21st ACM International Conference on Multimedia, pp. 835–838. ACM (2013)
6. Atal, B.S.: Automatic recognition of speakers from their voices. Proc. IEEE **64**(4), 460–475 (1976)
7. Reynolds, D.A.: Gaussian mixture models. In: Encyclopedia of Biometric Recognition. Springer, Heidelberg (2008)
8. Reynolds, D.A., Rose, R.C.: Robust text-independent speaker identification using Gaussian mixture speaker models. IEEE Trans. Speech Audio Process. **3**(1), 72–83 (1995)
9. Reynolds, D.A., Quatieri, T.F., Dunn, R.B.: Speaker verification using adapted Gaussian mixture models. Dig. Sig. Proc. **10**(1), 19–41 (2000)
10. Sadjadi, S. O., Slaney, M., Heck, L.: MSR identity toolbox v1. 0: A MATLAB toolbox for speaker-recognition research. Speech and Language Processing Technical Committee Newsletter (2013)

Speech Recognition Combining MFCCs and Image Features

Stamatis Karlos[(✉)], Nikos Fazakis, Katerina Karanikola,
Sotiris Kotsiantis, and Kyriakos Sgarbas

University of Patras, Patras, Greece
{stkarlos,karaink,sgarbas}@upatras.gr,
fazakis@ece.upatras.gr, sotos@math.upatras.gr

Abstract. Automatic speech recognition (ASR) task constitutes a well-known issue among fields like Natural Language Processing (NLP), Digital Signal Processing (DSP) and Machine Learning (ML). In this work, a robust supervised classification model is presented (MFCCs + autocor + SVM) for feature extraction of solo speech signals. Mel Frequency Cepstral Coefficients (MFCCs) are exploited combined with Content Based Image Retrieval (CBIR) features extracted from spectrogram produced by each frame of the speech signal. Improvement of classification accuracy using such extended feature vectors is examined against using only MFCCs with several classifiers for three scenarios of different number of speakers.

Keywords: ASR · MFCCs · Supervised model · Feature extraction · CBIR features

1 Introduction

Recognizing speech signals under either plain or more complicated environments is an important task of Automatic Speech Recognition (ASR) and Automatic Classification field, especially when such tasks are applied on large databases. Albeit speech recognition task is being examined by researchers many decades since now, it still remains an open issue. The main activity of a speech classification system is the procedure of extracting the appropriate features or removing the useless, for reducing both overfitting phenomena and computational resources needed. Besides the simple mathematic attributes that are computed exclusively from one domain, such as auto-correlation or temporal centroid and spectral centroid, skewness or kurtosis from time and frequency domain respectively, several other measures have been proposed for exploiting the enriched content of audio signals. Energy descriptors, harmonic and perceptual features are the most important categories of them [1]. The most well-known groups of attributes used for similar issues are Mel-Frequency Cepstral Coefficients (MFCCs), Linear Predictive Codes (LPCs), Perceptual Linear Prediction (PLP) and PLP-Relative Spectra (PLP-RASTA). MFCCs seem to have met the wider acceptance from researchers, judging by the large amount of works that have been used, either alone or combined with other attributes [2–4]. Theirs high performance is reasonable, since they are

© Springer International Publishing Switzerland 2016
A. Ronzhin et al. (Eds.): SPECOM 2016, LNAI 9811, pp. 651–658, 2016.
DOI: 10.1007/978-3-319-43958-7_79

computed by a well-sophisticated model. Without spending more time on analyzing the mathematical background of this theory, its main ambition is the description of the spectral envelope that is formatted by the phonemes of vocal tract with a few coefficients. All these parameters can also be applied to speech signals. Little modifications are usually needed respecting some generic properties of them. For example, there is necessity for adjusting both the window's length during processing stages and the frequency bands that are examined, since the maximum frequency component of speech signals are usually located below 4 kHz.

However, all these features are collected being mainly focused on the audio nature of signals. Another strategy for exploiting useful information is the mining of images produced by such signals, either examining the full length signal or its frames separately. The most common visualization technique is spectrogram, which represents the intensity of the existing frquencies over time and is computed by rising to the square the magnitude of a windowed Short-Term Fourier Transform (STFT). According to the literature, there are three distinct families of methods in image processing: Content, Feature and Appearance-Based. In this work, extension of feature set by using both MFCCs and image features that are obtained through the Autocorrelogram filter [5] along with large enough window length for recognizing speech signals inside restricted time framework is proposed. A number of comparisons with some specific Content-Based Image Retrieval (CBIR) features, which are described in [6, 7] along with a Java library, are implemented and compared for recognizing speech signals at solo mode that come from 8, 16 and 36 different speakers. Ten different options, together with the proposed, were examined for the CBIR features, which are based on the pixel contents of the tested images. For classification task, three classifiers were used to compare the accuracy of using only MFCCs against *MFCCs + CBIR* scenario. The enhanced behavior achieved by this strategy in the majority of the examined cases proves the need for exploiting different views of the same dataset. The proposed method is the combination of *MFCCs + autocor + SVM* that achieved the best accuracy for all the tested scenarios without lacking in needed training time against the other choices.

2   Related Works

CBIR procedures have been highly exploited for obtaining additional information from sound and/or speech signals, either for composing new recognition techniques or for improving existing methods by extending their feature sets [8, 9]. Extraction of low-level features from whole an image or from its sub-regions are been examined. The basic query is to determine the similarity between two different images by measuring the distance between their feature vectors. The most common kind of data that are used is the color content and the texture information, such as color histogram and directionality of the image pixel, respectively.

Local gradient features [10] on two-dimensional matrices that represent time-frequency attributes of speech signals were compared against MFCC + Delta MFCC, using PCA technique for dimension reduction and HMMs for speech recognition [2]. Ten speakers (5 male/5 female) were used in this work with 25-ms frame length and 10-ms frame sift. The improvement of the proposed technique (HOG + MFCC + Delta MFCC) against MFCC + Delta MFCC and HOG + MFCC as it concerns the word recognition rate (WER) was equal to 0.5 % and 1.5 % for clean speech. Extended experiments have been demonstrated in [11] over a male telephone speaker recognition framework. This dataset consists of 500 speakers. 2D Gabor features were used for this large-scale experiment producing 1357 initial feature dimensions. Reduction procedures are applied so as to reduce the computational time, since Multilayer Perceptron (MLP) classifier was used for training. The results showed that combining MFCC + Gabor features gives an 8 % relative EER improvement over the MFCCs alone. FFNN [12] has been proved as an effective solution when large number of parameters are demanded [13, 14].

Discrimination between music and speech signals is also another familiar task. Wavelet package transform on gray-scale spectrograms and application of Multiple Kernel Learning for subband selection had achieved very good results [15]. Dennis J. has also made in-depth search for sound event recognition in various environments using Spectrogram Image (SI) processing methods [16]. The main process consists of computing higher order central moments from block based partitions applied on SIs. Linear kernel of Support Vector Machine (SVM) classifier performed robust results for the tested mismatched conditions. A method that extracts SI based co-occurrence attributes – using frame width of 256 samples and 50 % overlap factor – along with RANSAC algorithm for discriminating music signal with voice or without voice has also been implemented [17]. Other algorithms for distinguishing music signals or environmental sounds through behaving to SI like texture images have been proposed, either combined with MFCCs [3, 18] or without [9]. The choice of frequency bands also may affect the performance of such algorithms. A work based on speech spectrograms for recognizing stress and emotion using log-Gabor Filter performed better using equivalent rectangular bandwidth (ERB) scale bands against CB and Bark scales [19].

3 Proposed Technique

Integration of attributes from two different views is presented here for increasing classification accuracy rate and the robustness of the final classification model. The first view of the examined speech signals should be the MFCCs, which are being collected according to right chain of Fig. 1. A short-term spectral analysis method is applied on the speech signals, after having been segmented with a large Hamming window – its time duration equals with half a second — and 50 % overlap factor. The highest band edge of Mel filters has been set to 4 kHz. In the sequel, Fast Fourier Transform (FFT) is applied to each segment and its magnitude spectrum is logarithmically scaled in both magnitude and frequency domain. At the end, the appropriate coefficients are obtained by computing the Discrete Cosine Transformation (DCT). In order to integrate information from SIs, we used a WEKA [20, 21] implementation of Lucence Image Retrieval (LIRe), which constitutes an extensible java library for CBIR tasks. The method that seems to fit with the extraction of informative enough features from Sis for classification tasks is the AutoColorCorrelogramFilter (autocor). According to this approach, the spatial correlation of colors from each image is distilled. Since it is not based on purely local properties, it is not too sensitive to big shape changes. It is really effective in recognizing large changes of shape and is really efficient in being computed [5]. Furthermore, this asset to capture the spatial correlation of the tested images outperforms the classical methods that are mainly based on histograms, and this property is harmonized with the manner that SIs are produced.

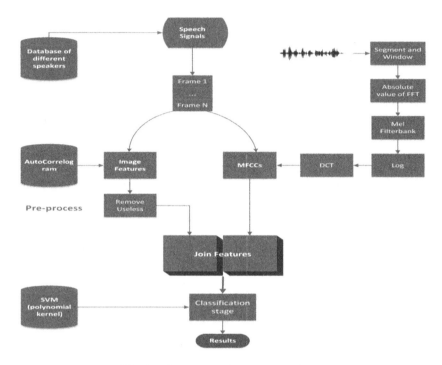

Fig. 1. Flowchart of the proposed scheme

The final stage of this chain contains the right choice of classifier. SVM with polynomial kernel for achieving both accurate and fast enough decisions was chosen, like in other related works [22]. The intermediate stage between extracting CBIR features and joining them with MFCCs is a post-processing procedure for removing useless attributes. The criterion for such a choice is the maximum accepted variance of a feature. Each one that exceeds a predefined threshold is omitted. In our implementation, this threshold value (M) was not differentiated from the default value of WEKA's corresponding filter ($M = 99\%$). The produced features from autocor filter were equal to 1024 but only 57 of them were finally used for describing the SI set. Figure 1 depicts the whole procedure.

4   Experiments

The experiments are based on datasets extracted from the CHAINS Corpus [23]. The selected scenario for our experiments is the 'solo speech', according which the texts are been read at a natural rate. This dataset consists of 36 speakers – 28 of them are from Eastern part of Ireland and the rest 8 are from UK and USA – who read 33 different sentences. All the three different scenarios – 8, 16 and 36 speakers – that have been formatted by the author of this work are examined here. In each task, the number of male and female speakers is equal. The training and the testing subsets consist of 10 and 9 specific wav files, respectively. Since the 10-cross-validation technique has been chosen for performing the experiments, these subsets have been joined to one. The number of the rows of our datasets was reduced to 1298, 2577 and 5818 for the tested cases, because of the selected large window. Having rejected the 0th coefficient, only the next 25 coefficients were used. Consequently, each row consists of 25 MFCCs, the number of features that each filter uses and the class label. Besides the autocor filter, all the rest nine filters that come from LIRe were used and combined with MFCCs for checking their total performance. A short description of them is following: BinaryPatternPyramid (binpyr) [24], ColorLayout (clay) [25], EdgeHistogram (edhist) [7], FCTH (fcth) [26], FuzzyOpponentHistogram (fuzzy) [7], Gabor (gabor) [7], JpegCoef (jpeg) [7], PHOG (phog) [27], SimpleColorHistogram (simlpehist) [7].

Three different classifiers were used in all the cases for evaluating the different approaches. Following the strategies of many similar works [22, 28] SVMs and Neural Networks were used along with LogisticRegression (LogReg), a well-known classifier for a wide variety of tasks. As it concerns SVM classifier, it was used the polynomial kernel with degree equal to 3 via the implementation of LibSVM [29]. The default values of MLP and LogReg were used [20]. Table 1 shows the results of exploiting only MFCCs for fulfilling the identification task compared with the proposed. The required time for building the classification models, measured in seconds, also accompanies the accuracy values. All the experiments were executed on Intel i3 64-bit system with 8 GB ram. Regarding the scenario of combining MFCCs with CBIR features, performance of SVM classifier was increased in all the cases for all the examined scenarios of 8, 16 and 36 speakers. However, the autocor filter managed to boost its accuracy up to 11.5 %, 7.8 % and 9.9 % demanding only half a second, less than a second and about 4 s more than the simplified scenario of using only MFCCs.

Another interesting point is the large deterioration of predictions accuracy that appears in *MFCCs + FCTH* combination for the 16 speakers experiment. Furthermore, the algorithms that mainly depend on local attributes did not manage to score high accuracy improvement against more simplified and less specified approaches, following our tactic to obtain more generalized visualizations of speech signals. The total results could be found in the following link: http://ml.math.upatras.gr/wp-content/uploads/2016/04/results1.xlsx due to lack of space. Moreover, the number of features that were produced for each filter and how many of them were kept after the pre-process stage is referred. For further examining the behavior of all the tested CBIR filters, a statistical comparison was executed [30]. The post-hoc test of Nemenyi was selected for obtaining both a ranking of the methods and the information about which of them are significantly different. These results are shown in Fig. 2 and have been plotted with the help of scmamp library [30]. The length of CD parameter in this figure depicts the minimum distance that must mediate between two participants for being theorized as significantly different. Thus, all the methods that are connected with a horizontal bold line are not obsessed by this property. The combination of *MFCCs + autocor* and *MFCCs + binpyr* achieved the best two performances. Their behaviors were similar enough, but the first one required less computational time than the else in all the tested scenarios.

Table 1. Comparison of MFCCs vs MFCCs + autocor

Classifiers	8 speakers		16 speakers		36 speakers	
	MFCCs	MFCCs + auto cor	MFCCs	MFCCs + auto cor	MFCCs	MFCCs + auto cor
SVM	79.89	87.44	75.90	83.70	66.74	76.64
Time (sec)	0.45	0.88	1.29	2.09	5.93	9.62
MLP	69.49	82.42	69.03	80.36	60.1581	66.33
Time (sec)	10.71	60.80	35.43	121.04	179.89	452.50
LogReg	66.41	76.96	73.38	79.74	60.89	67.13
Time (sec)	0.26	1.08	1.71	4.06	5.46	27.98

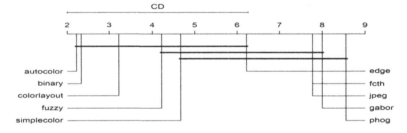

Fig. 2. Critical difference plot of CBIR filters + MFCC against MFCCs

5 Conclusion

A new strategy for increasing speech recognition accuracy based on Mel-frequency cepstral coefficients (MFCCs) exploiting both MFCCs and CBIR features is proposed. The whole procedure is performed by using some well-known algorithms of ML field and the best results – with efficient computation time – were given by SVMs with polynomial kernel and degree equal with three. The results show that by using extended feature sets through image filters over spectrogram visualization can boost the performance up to 10 % for 16 and 36 speakers' task and 11.5 % at most for 8 speakers'. Instead of using small windows for computing the necessary features, long values of windows were used, reducing dramatically the number of frames needed for building the final datasets.

Although this strategy may lack in recording fast transient phenomena though spectrogram representation, rendering the image dataset inefficient to lead to good identification results, their combination with MFCCs enhances the total accuracy rates for speech recognition tasks being recorded on clean conditions. Moreover, the poor accuracy of mining only SI features with large window length for ASR experiments justifies the cardinal role that is possessed by the sound features. This means that more specialized image extraction algorithms could be combined under similar schemes (*MFCCs + SI features*) instead of exploiting just MFCCs, so as to achieve more robust and more accurate behaviors. Parallel implementation of this approach could also accelerate the whole procedure, especially for larger corpus.

The combination of magnitude with phase related features may also increase the accuracy of such algorithms, as in the case of Hartley Phase Spectrum, where enhanced results obtained for specific speech and audio classes [31]. Finally, semi-supervised techniques that respect multi-view theory, such as co-training, could perform well enough in combining sound/speech features along with image attributes on such experiments [32].

References

1. Yu, G.: Audio Classification From Time-Frequency Texture, Massachusetts Institute of Technology. Ecole Polytechnique, Palaiseau Cedex, NSL, Time, pp. 1677–1680 (2009)
2. Muroi, T., Takashima, R., Takiguchi, T., Ariki, Y.: Gradient-based acoustic features for speech recognition. In: International Symposium on Intelligent Signal Processing Communication Systems 2009, ISPACS 2009, pp. 445–448 (2009)
3. Khunarsa, P., Lursinsap, C., Raicharoen, T.: Impulsive environment sound detection by neural classification of spectrogram and mel-frequency coefficient images. In: Zeng, Z., Wang, J. (eds.) Advances in Neural Network Research and Applications. LNEE, vol. 67, pp. 337–346. Springer, Heidelberg (2010)
4. Davis, S.B., Mermelstein, P.: Comparison of parametric representations for monosyllabic word recognition in continuously spoken sentences. Trans. Acoust. Speech Signal Process. **28**(4), 357–366 (1980)
5. Huang, J., Kumar, S.R., Mitra, M., Zhu, W.-J., Zabih, R.: Image indexing using color correlograms. In: Proceedings of IEEE Computer Society Conference on Computer Vision and Pattern Recognition, pp. 762–768 (1997)
6. Lux, M., Chatzichristofis, S.A.: Lire: lucene image retrieval. In: Proceedings of the 16th ACM International Conference on Multimedia - MM 2008, p. 1085 (2008)
7. Lux, M.: Content based image retrieval with LIRe. In: Proceedings of the 19th ACM International Conference on Multimedia, pp. 735–738 (2011)
8. Lux, M., Oge, M.: Visual Information Retrieval using Java and LIRE. Morgan & Claypool, San Rafael (2013)
9. Souli, S., Lachiri, Z.: Environmental sounds spectrogram classification using log-gabor filters and multiclass support vector machines. Int. J. Comput. **9**(4–3), 142–149 (2012)
10. Dalal, N., Triggs, B.: Histograms of oriented gradients for human detection. In: Proceedings of the IEEE Conference on Computer Vision and Pattern Recognition, pp. 720–723 (2007)
11. Lei, H., Meyer, B.T., Mirghafori, N.: Spectro-temporal Gabor features for speaker recognition. In: ICASSP, pp. 4241–4244 (2012)
12. Gramss, T.: Fast algorithms to find invariant features for a word recognizing neural net. Int. J. Speech Technol. **18**(1), 180–184 (2014)
13. Kleinschmidt, M.: Localized spectro-temporal features for automatic speech recognition, pp. 2573–2576 (2003)

14. Kleinschmidt, M.: Methods for capturing spectro-temporal modulations in automatic speech recognition. Acta Acust. - Acust. **88**(3), 416–422 (2002)
15. Nilufar, S., Ray, N., Molla, M.K.I., Hirose, K. Spectrogram based features selection using multiple kernel learning for speech/music discrimination. In: 2012 IEEE International Conference on Acoustics, Speech and Signal Processing (ICASSP), pp. 501–504 (2012)
16. Dennis, J., Tran, H.D., Li, H.: Spectrogram image feature for sound event classification in mismatched conditions. IEEE Signal Process. Lett. **18**(2), 130–133 (2011)
17. Ghosal, A., Chakraborty, R., Dhara, B.C., Saha, S.K.: Song/instrumental classification using spectrogram based contextual features. In: Proceedings of the CUBE International Information Technology Conference - CUBE 2012, p. 21 (2012)
18. Khunarsal, P., Lursinsap, C., Raicharoen, T.: Very short time environmental sound classification based on spectrogram pattern matching. Inf. Sci. (Ny) **243**, 57–74 (2013)
19. He, L., Lech, M., Maddage, N., Allen, N.: Stress and emotion recognition using log-Gabor filter analysis of speech spectrograms. In: Proceedings - 2009 3rd International Conference on Affective Computing and Intelligent Interaction Work. ACII 2009, pp. 1–5 (2009)
20. Hall, M., Frank, E., Holmes, G., Pfahringer, B., Reutemann, P., Witten, I.H.: The WEKA data mining software. In: ACM SIGKDD Explorations Newsletter, vol. 11, no. 1, p. 10 (2009)
21. Mayo, M.: ImageFilter WEKA filter that uses LIRE to extract image features (2015). https://github.com/mmayo888/ImageFilter
22. Georganti, E., May, T., Van De Par, S., Mourjopoulos, J.: Sound source distance estimation in rooms based on statistical properties of binaural signals. IEEE Trans. Audio, Speech Lang. Process. **21**(8), 1727–1741 (2013)
23. Cummins, F., Grimaldi, M., Leonard, T., Simko, J.: The CHAINS speech corpus: CHAracterizing INdividual speakers. In: Proceedings of the SPECOM, pp. 1–6 (2006)
24. Chatzichristofis, S.A., Boutalis, Y.S., Arampatzis, A.: Accelerating image retrieval using Binary Haar Wavelet transform on the color and edge directivity descriptor. In: Proceedings of the 5th International Multi-Conference Computing in the Global Information Technology, ICCGI 2010, vol. 4, no. 1, pp. 41–47 (2010)
25. Jalab, H.: Image retrieval system based on color layout descriptor and Gabor filters. In: IEEE Conference on Open Systems, pp. 32–36 (2011)
26. Chatzichristofis, S.A., Boutalis, Y.S.: FCTH: fuzzy color and texture histogram - a low level feature for accurate image retrieval. In: 2008 Ninth International Workshop on Image Analysis for Multimedia Interactive Services, pp. 191–196 (2008)
27. Bosch, A., Zisserman, A., Munoz, X.: Representing shape with a spatial pyramid kernel. In: CIVR 2007 Proceedings of the 6th ACM International Conference on Image and Video Retrieval, pp. 401–408 (2007)
28. Thiruvengatanadhan, R.: Speech/Music Classification using SVM. Int. J. Comput. Appl. **65**(6), 36–41 (2013)
29. Chang, C., Lin, C.: LIBSVM: a library for support vector machines. ACM Trans. Intell. Syst. Technol. **2**, 1–39 (2011)
30. Demšar, J.: Statistical comparisons of classifiers over multiple data sets. J. Mach. Learn. Res. **7**, 1–30 (2006)
31. Paraskevas, I., Rangoussi, M.: The hartley phase spectrum as an assistive feature for classification. In: Solé-Casals, J., Zaiats, V. (eds.) NOLISP 2009. LNCS, vol. 5933, pp. 51–59. Springer, Heidelberg (2010)
32. Hong, Y., Zhu, W.: Spatial co-training for semi-supervised image classification. Pattern Recognit. Lett. **63**, 59–65 (2015)

Sociolinguistic Extension of the ORD Corpus of Russian Everyday Speech

Natalia Bogdanova-Beglarian, Tatiana Sherstinova$^{(\boxtimes)}$, Olga Blinova, Olga Ermolova, Ekaterina Baeva, Gregory Martynenko, and Anastasia Ryko

Saint Petersburg State University, 7/9 Universitetskaya nab., St. Petersburg 199034, Russia
{n.bogdanova,t.sherstinova,o.blinova,g.martynenko}@spbu.ru,
{o-ermolova,aryko}@mail.ru, ekaterinabaeva@yahoo.com

Abstract. The ORD corpus is one of the largest resources of contemporary spoken Russian. By 2014, its collection numbered about 400 h of recordings made by a group of 40 respondents (20 men and 20 women, of different ages and professions), who volunteered to spend a whole day with a switched-on voice recorder, recording all their verbal communication. The corpus presents the unique linguistic material recorded in natural communicative situations, allowing spoken Russian and the everyday discourse to be studied in many aspects. However, the original sample of respondents was not sufficient enough to study a sociolinguistic variation of speech. Thus, it was decided to launch a large project aiming at the ORD sociolinguistic extension, which was supported by the Russian Science Foundation. The paper describes the general principles for the sociolinguistic extension of the corpus. It defines social groups which should be presented in the corpus in adequate numbers, sets criteria for selecting participants, describes the "recorder's kit" for the respondents and involves the adaptation principles of the ORD annotation and structure. Now, the ORD collection exceeds 1200 h of recordings, presenting speech of 127 respondents and hundreds of their interlocutors. 2450 macro episodes of everyday spoken communication have been already annotated, and the speech transcripts add up to 1 mln words.

Keywords: Speech corpus · Everyday spoken Russian · Oral communication · Sociolinguistics · Social groupings · Sociolects · Speech variation

1 Introduction

In sociolinguistic studies of the last decade one may observe the increasing use of corpora and it is expected that variational linguistics "will increasingly interact with corpus-based approaches to linguistics from other areas" [1]. Some examples of sociolinguistic research performed on the base of linguistic corpora are reviewed in [2, 3]. However, "texts found within most corpora do not contain the kind of material of greatest interest to most sociolinguists, namely, casual everyday speech, often from non-standard language varieties. Large corpora of spontaneously occurring spoken data are still expensive and time-consuming to compile due to problems of transcription and input" [3].

© Springer International Publishing Switzerland 2016
A. Ronzhin et al. (Eds.): SPECOM 2016, LNAI 9811, pp. 659–666, 2016.
DOI: 10.1007/978-3-319-43958-7_80

Current situation with Russian sociolinguistic studies is much alike, as there are not enough linguistic resources of Russian spontaneous speech recordings suitable for research on sociolinguistic variation. For example, the Spoken speech subcorpus in Russian National Corpus does not contain any audio data at all, consisting just of transcripts [4]. The other well-known Night Dream Stories corpus contains both texts and speech recordings which are thoroughly annotated. However, this corpus is rather small (about 2 h of recordings, 14000 words in transcripts) and contains only speech of children and adolescents [5].

The largest resource of contemporary spoken Russian is the ORD corpus [6]. By 2014, its collection numbered about 400 h of recordings made by a group of 40 respondents (20 men and 20 women, of different ages and professions), who volunteered to spend a whole day with a switched-on voice recorder, recording all their oral communication in natural communicative situations [ibid.]. The similar methodology of the long-term recordings had been earlier used for collecting data for the British National Corpus [7] and the JST ESP corpus in Japan [8].

ORD recordings were made at home, in offices, in stores, in bars and restaurants, at the university and in a military college, in parks and outdoors, etc. and contain diverse genres and styles of speech — everyday domestic conversations, professional conversations with colleagues, communications with friends, telephone calls, lectures, workshops, etc. The topics in these conversations have a great range from discussions of teeth problems with a dentist to conversations about family, business, football, politics, religion, etc. [6]. Two professional multimedia annotation tools – ELAN [9] and Praat [10] – are used to annotate the ORD corpus.

The corpus presents the unique linguistic material, allowing spoken Russian and everyday discourse to be studied in many aspects. A number of interdisciplinary studies have been held on its data, among which we can mention several sociolinguistic endeavors (e.g., [11]).

However, the original sample of respondents was not sufficient enough to study sociolinguistic variation of speech. Therefore, it was decided to launch a large project aiming at the ORD sociolinguistic extension, which received the support of the Russian Science Foundation. The paper describes the general principles for the sociolinguistic extension of the corpus. It defines social groups which should be presented in the corpus in adequate numbers, sets criteria for selecting participants, describes the "recorder's kit" for the respondents and involves the adaptation principles of the ORD annotation and structure. It also concerns the preliminary results of the corpus extension and reports its current statistics.

2   Social Groups and Their Categories

First of all, it was essential to define basic social groupings of the contemporary Russian society which the corpus would represent. For this purpose, the sociolinguistic principles that were used in some of the well-known speech corpora such as the British National Corpus, the Australian Database of Spoken Language, the speech subcorpus of the National Corpus of the Russian Language, Perm corpus of spoken Russian in Perm

Region, and the SAT corpus were reviewed [12] and compared to those used by the developers of the ORD corpus.

As a result, a list of social groups to be represented in the corpus was drawn up as follows:

1. **Gender Groups.** We distinguish two gender categories: (1) men, and (2) women.
2. **Age Groups.** The age distributions of the modern society are rapidly changing, thereby altering the ratio between age groups. It was decided to adhere the following distribution of the age groups:
   (1) from 18 to 24 (young adults, junior group): this is a stage of studying and beginning to work, when a person usually leaves home and finds his or her place in social life;
   (2) from 25 to 34 (young adults, senior group): this period of life is frequently characterized by extensive work, career movements, and starting a family;
   (3) from 35 to 44 (mature adults, group I): this is the period of extensive work and — usually — the peak of a person's social maturity;
   (4) from 45 to 59 (mature adults, group II): this period is generally characterized by a high social maturity until retirement;
   (5) 60+ are senior citizens, who generally take less part in social life. One cannot deny that there are people who remain socially and professionally active even after retirement; however, the general activity tends to decrease.
      These groups can be later combined into bigger categories, for instance, in order to compare the speech of "the youth" with that of the "middle-aged and seniors".
3. **Education Level Groups.** Here, we consider it appropriate to differentiate five educational categories: (1) secondary school, (2) secondary professional school, (3) incomplete higher education, (4) higher education, (5) academic degree (PhD).
4. **Professional Groups or Generalized Types of Occupation.** As for the social factor of professional activities, it became obvious that in the framework of an individual research project it is impossible to describe in detail the linguistic diversity of speech of all statistically relevant professional groupings. Moreover, "the number of writers have critiqued the idea that homogenized professional groupings have ever existed. They have argued that the idea of a single professional identity is problematic because people have complex personalities and professional histories" [13]. However, our recent studies have shown that some differences in speech between certain professional groups do exist at least on lexical and syntactic levels [14], and some phonetic distinctions can be traced, too.

   As a compromise, it was decided to analyze speech of several generalized professional groups. For example, the "worker" group would comprise plumbers, builders, mechanics, and other "handyman" professions that demand physical labor, whereas "service sector employee" group would comprise shop assistants, delivery men, waiters, librarians, social services, etc.

   Having reviewed the data of the Federal Statistics Department of St. Petersburg [15], we have chosen ten following generalized professional groups:
   (1) people working in manufacturing and building, doing manual labor (builders, mechanic, plumbers, carpenters, etc.);

(2) service sector employees (shop assistants, cashiers, merchandisers, delivery couriers, waiters, hairdressers, etc.);

(3) people working in education (practicing teachers and lecturers);

(4) people working in military and defense (army officers, police officers, military cadets, security guides);

(5) people of creative professions (photographers, designers, artists, architects, musicians, stage directors, etc.);

(6) office or "white-collar" workers engaged in economy (economists, accountants, logistics managers, finance analysts), advertising business or public relations (market researchers, advertising managers, PR managers, etc.);

(7) IT professionals (IT engineers, programmers);

(8) engineers of different fields;

(9) people engaged in humanities (linguists, archeologists, historians, philosophers, psychologists);

(10) people engaged in natural science (biologists, chemists, astronomers, etc.).

We are aware that the proposed categories may intersect with each other, as one and the same person may be engaged simultaneously in more than one group (e.g., a lecturer in chemistry would be assigned to two professional groups — natural science and education). Thus, it is planned to compare speech features between opposite groups: for instance, "workmen" vs. "scholars", "humanities" vs. "natural sciences", "white-collar workers" vs. "creative professionals", and so on.

5. **Social Status or Job Position Groups.** Here, we distinguish four categories associated with social status and job position: (1) executive managers and employers (directors, deputy directors, heads of departments or private companies, etc.), (2) employees and civil servants, (3) students, including those who combine studies with work, (4) currently unemployed, including those who are retired.

If we compare social groups proposed for this study with the categories by T. Zaslavskaya, which are widely used in Russian sociological research, the proposed sociolinguistic approach is focused in describing everyday Russian language for two major strata of modern Russian society: the "middle layer" and the "base layer" [16].

3   Methodology of Data Collection

3.1   Criteria for Selection of Participants

By the summer of 2014, the ORD corpus consisted of about 400 h of recordings gathered from 40 volunteers, balanced by gender and representing various age groups. The professional categories, however, lacked a proper balance, as those parameters had not been taken into account at the first stage of data collecting. Namely, the corpus lacked speech recordings from workers, creative professionals, IT specialists, and some other professional groups. In the social status category, the data obtained from executive managers, businessmen, and retired persons were insufficient as well.

Taking into consideration that transcribing and processing of speech data is time-consuming, it was decided that the minimum sample size for each professional or status group should be 10 people.

The next task was to determine the list of people for new recordings so that we could close all gaps in the ORD data in terms of particular social groups (see Sect. 2). The list consisting of 60 "vacancies" — which would become representatives of the described above social groups — was compiled. In other words, to make the corpus representative of major socially stratified groupings, its volume of recordings required its extension up to 1000 h.

Additional criteria for selecting participants were defined. The list of compulsory requirements was set as follows: (1) age factor: no people under 18 could become a respondent for ORD recordings, (2) native language factor: in this project, only Russian native speakers could participate, and (3) residence factor: the prospective candidate must be residing in the urban area.

A significant factor in selecting volunteers was their desire and readiness to "live a whole day with a recorder around their neck" and to fill in all the necessary forms and questionnaires.

3.2 Main Principles of Speech Recordings

The methodological background for speech recording remained mostly the same as it was proposed for the first recordings of the ORD which had aim to record everyday Russian speech in natural communicative situations [6]. It was required that nothing should interfere with the usual habits of speakers' communicative behavior when they made recordings. Also, every respondent should speak as he or she normally speaks, e.g. not changing the subjects of topics during the recording [ibid.].

It was settled that the recording would be made by professional voice recorders Roland R09-HR, enhanced with external condenser microphones. In the result of pilot series of long-term recordings, using a variety of recording settings, the optimal recorder settings were proposed which should provide the best possible sound quality in different communicative situations.

3.3 The "Recorder's Kit"

Though participation in ORD recordings is anonymous, all respondents have to fill in several questionnaires, including a sociological one. For this purpose, the "recorder's kit" was compiled, consisting of the following elements:

(1) Sociological questionnaire for the volunteers and their main interlocutors. It was developed based on the data of the Federal Statistics Department of St. Petersburg after having taking into account traditional sociolinguistic issues. This question-naire contains traditional questions about gender, age, place of birth, professions (both past and current), education, the native language and other languages spoken by the informant. In addition, it includes the information about the respondent's parents, their social background, and place of birth. Sociological information

concerning main interlocutors is replenished by indicating their social role in relation to the volunteer respondent.

(2) "A speech diary" is a template where the participant has to note down the details of her/his major communicative speech episodes during the recording day, including the place of communication, main activities, and interlocutors.

(3) "The recorder's guide" was written to provide respondents with principal technical and organizational requirements for the recording. Besides, it contains the legal Agreement to be signed by each respondent for participating in the project.

In addition, every participant is required to take three psychological tests offline (Hans Eysenck test, FPI test and Cattell's test). As it is well-known that there is a correlation between the psychological type of the person and some features of his/her speech, the information obtained from these tests is very important for further speech analysis. Later on, these data may be used for advanced psycholinguistic studies.

4   Adaptation of the ORD Annotation and Structure

The ORD speech corpus consists of three major components: (1) audio files, (2) correspondent annotation files, and (3) information system [17]. Sociolinguistic extension of the corpus implied development and adaptation of all three components, as well as the data processing software.

The major alteration in principles of annotation lies in levels of speech transcripts. It is well-known that natural conversations inevitably have periods when one or more participants talk simultaneously. As usual, the more the number of interlocutors, the greater is the part of overlapping speech. Originally, the ORD annotation was based on linear representation of overlapping fragments, as all speech transcripts had to be written on the single Phrase-tier. This approach for speech transcribing was suitable for earlier ORD tasks.

However, if we have to compare speech between different social groups, it becomes necessary to distinguish more accurately — who is saying what, and when. Here, we need a multilevel transcribing of speech that is similar to that used in conversation analysis. For that purpose, we have elaborated alternative multilevel speech transcription system and developed software tools which should simplify conversion between two types of speech transcribing.

Further, we introduced a number of new annotation symbols referring to paralinguistic phenomena, such as sigh, clattering tongue, yawning, moaning, etc., which is a novelty in the ORD corpus annotation. To perform a multilevel linguistic analysis of speech, particular means of linguistic annotation are developed.

The ORD information system was extended, too. For example, the tables *Informants* (*Participants*) and *Interlocutors* have been expanded by adding extra sociolinguistic fields, including that for normalized codes for each sociolinguistic category (as described above in Sect. 2), and several new tables were introduced: *Microepisodes* (subdivision of macroepisode), *Paralinguistics*, and *Extralinguistics*.

5   Current Statistics of the ORD Corpus

New recordings for ORD started in July, 2014. Since then, we have gathered recordings from 66 new participants (service workers, white-collars, IT-specialists, artists, musicians, businessmen, pensioners, etc.), with the total duration of 842 h. Nowadays, the extended ORD corpus contains more than 1200 h of speech gathered from 127 major participants (66 men and 61 women). The age of participants rangers from 18 to 77 years, with the average value of 39 years. Each professional or social status group introduced in Sect. 2 is presented at least by 10 respondents.

As expected, it turned out to be challenging to find "pure" representatives for individual professional groups. In particular, it may be explained by the fact that in post-perestroika decades many Russian citizens had to change their professional activities or were forced to combine different occupations, frequently from different professional areas. Moreover, representatives from particular professional and status groupings often refused to take part in the recordings. For example, not working pensioners usually argued that they "do not speak much during the day" or that they "are afraid to break a voice recorder".

All recorded data are being segmented into macroepisodes [18], 2450 macroepisodes have been already described, and the speech transcripts add up to 1 mln words. The work on multilevel linguistic annotation of the corpus continues.

Given that the ORD corpus contains everyday private recordings of respondents, an open access to its content is impossible for ethical reasons. However, it is planned to create a website of this resource which should have expanded functions for scientific research for authorized users.

Acknowledgement.   The research is supported by the Russian Science Foundation, project # 14-18-02070 "Everyday Russian Language in Different Social Groups".

References

1. Kendall, T.: Corpora from a sociolinguistic perspective. In: Corpus Studies: Future Directions, Special Iss. of Revista Brasileira de Linguística Aplicada, vol. 11(2), pp. 361–389 (2011)
2. Baker, P.: Sociolinguistics and Corpus Linguistics. Edinburgh University Press, Edinburgh (2010)
3. Romaine, S.: Corpus linguistics and sociolinguistics. In: Lüdeling, A., Kytö, M. (eds.) Corpus Linguistics: An International Handbook, vol. 1, pp. 96–111. Mouton de Gruyter, Berlin-New York (2008)
4. Grishina, E.A.: Spoken speech in the Russian national corpus. In: The Russian National Corpus 2003–2005, pp. 94–110. Indrik Publ., Moscow (2005). (in Russian)
5. Kibrik, A.A., Podlesskaya, V.I. (eds.): Night Dream Stories: a Corpus Study of Spoken Russian Discourse. Languages of Slavic Cultures, Moscow (2009). (in Russian)
6. Asinovsky, A., Bogdanova, N., Rusakova, M., Ryko, A., Stepanova, S., Sherstinova, T.: The ORD speech corpus of Russian everyday communication "One Speaker's Day": creation principles and annotation. In: Matoušek, V., Mautner, P. (eds.) TSD 2009. LNCS, vol. 5729, pp. 250–257. Springer, Heidelberg (2009)

7. Reference Guide for the British National Corpus. http://www.natcorp.ox.ac.uk/docs/URG.xml
8. Campbell, N.: Speech & expression; the value of a longitudinal corpus. In: LREC 2004, pp. 183–186 (2004)
9. Linguistic Annotator ELAN. https://tla.mpi.nl/tools/tla-tools/elan/
10. Praat: doing phonetics by computer. http://www.fon.hum.uva.nl/praat/
11. Bogdanova-Beglarian, N., Martynenko, G., Sherstinova, T.: The "One Day of Speech" corpus: phonetic and syntactic studies of everyday spoken Russian. In: Ronzhin, A., Potapova, R., Fakotakis, N. (eds.) SPECOM 2015. LNCS, vol. 9319, pp. 429–437. Springer, Heidelberg (2015)
12. Baeva, E.M.: On means of sociolingiustic balancing of a spoken corpus (Based on the ORD corpus). Perm Univ. Herald Russ. Foreign Philol. **4**(28), 48–57 (2014). (in Russian)
13. Davis, J.M., Smith, M.: Working in Multi-Professional Contexts: A Practical Guide for Professionals in Children's Services, p. 82. SAGE Publications Ltd., Los Angeles (2012)
14. Bogdanova-Beglarian, N.V. (ed.): Speech Corpus as the Base for Analysis of Russian Speech. Part 2. Theoretical and practical aspects of analysis, 1. Philological Faculty of St. Petersburg State University, St. Petersburg (2014). (in Russian)
15. Social and demographic portrait of Russia: the result of population census of 2010 by Federal Agency of Urban Statistics. Statistics of Russia, Moscow (2012). (in Russian)
16. Zaslavskaya, T.I.: Social structure of modern Russian society. Soc. Sci. Modernity **2**, 5–23 (1997). (in Russian)
17. Sherstinova, T.: The structure of the ORD speech corpus of Russian everyday communication. In: Matoušek, V., Mautner, P. (eds.) TSD 2009. LNCS, vol. 5729, pp. 258–265. Springer, Heidelberg (2009)
18. Sherstinova, T.: Macro episodes of Russian everyday oral communication: towards pragmatic annotation of the ORD speech corpus. In: Ronzhin, A., Potapova, R., Fakotakis, N. (eds.) SPECOM 2015. LNCS (LNAI), vol. 9319, pp. 268–276. Springer, Heidelberg (2015)

Statistical Analysis of Acoustical Parameters in the Voice of Children with Juvenile Dysphonia

Miklós Gábriel Tulics[(✉)], Ferenc Kazinczi, and Klára Vicsi

Laboratory of Speech Acoustics, Department of Telecommunications and Media Informatics, Budapest University of Technology and Economics, Budapest, Hungary
{tulics,kazinczi,vicsi}@tmit.bme.hu

Abstract. The goal of this research is to answer the question: is it necessary to build a completely different system in order to automatically recognize functional dysphonia (FD) in children's cases or is it possible to train the system with healthy and pathological voices of adults? For this reason preliminary statistical analyses were carried out between healthy and functional dysphonia voices of children and healthy children voices with healthy adults'. The statistical analyses draw the conclusion that variations of Jitter and Shimmer values with Harmonics-to-Noise Ratio (HNR) and the first component of the mel-frequency cepstral coefficients (MFCC1) are good indicators to separate Healthy and FD voices in case of children as well. Healthy samples of children and adult voices were compared giving the clear conclusion that differences exist in the examined acoustical parameters even between healthy child and healthy adult groups. It is necessary to carry out the investigations separately on children's voices as well, we cannot use adult voices to make any conclusions to children's voices. Lastly the differences between adult female and male samples were examined. The study results confirmed our assumptions that in order to build an automatic decision making system that recognizes FD it is advisable to build separate systems for adult males, adult females and children.

Keywords: Speech recognition · Voice disorder · Statistical analysis · Acoustic parameters · Juvenile dysphonia

1 Introduction

Articulation disorder can be explained by the neuromuscular dysfunction of the vocal organs. The dysfunction can manifest as either an overdrive in voice performance or its powerlessness. The starting point of the greater part of the functional voice disorder is the repetitive strain of the voice. The unnatural increased activity is asymptomatic for a while, but if the increased activity is maintained the muscle gets tired and operational failure occurs. Voice disorder, present for a long time generated only on a functional basis, causes organic changes such as vocal nodes.

© Springer International Publishing Switzerland 2016
A. Ronzhin et al. (Eds.): SPECOM 2016, LNAI 9811, pp. 667–674, 2016.
DOI: 10.1007/978-3-319-43958-7_81

Dysphonia is the disorder of the articulation as a complex function. It is a patho-logical condition showing varied based symptoms due to several etiologic factors and pathogenesis diversity [1].

The frequency of dysphonia according to Schulze [2] among the 3-10-year-old population can be put between 20–30 %, according to the literature review of Fuchs, 6–25 % appears to be well founded. The data therefore suggest that almost every fourth or fifth child produces a pathological voice. The studies agree that dysphonia is more often found among boys than girls, the ratio being 70–30 %. Symptoms that can cause discomfort associated with dysphonia are: pressure on the neck, forced coughing, shortness of breath. 45–65 % of children suffering from dysphonia have similar complaints [3]. There are several questions regarding whether sustained voice or continuous speech is more effective in distinguishing Healthy from pathological voice [4–9]. Our previous research has confirmed that acoustic parameters like Jitter, Shimmer, HNR (Harmonics-to-Noise Ratio) in the automatic classification of results from the Healthy and pathological voices are improved in a big extent using continuous speech [10].

The differences and the similarities between pathological and healthy speech was also analyzed in adult speech by statistical tests. It was found that in case of the Hungarian vowels marked with SAMPA characters [E] and [o], variations of acoustic parameters like Jitter, Shimmer, HNR show significant differences [15]. In the present study the differences and the similarities between adult and children's voice was analyzed using continuous speech. Different approaches were carried out: acoustic parameters from vowels [E], [o], [O], [A:], [u] were extracted from adult and children's speech samples and compared by statistical analyses. The acoustic parameters were also compared with two sample T-tests in the case of children, between Healthy and pathological group. Furthermore, the differences and similarities of healthy voice samples between the adult and child group was examined. At the beginning of our research male and female samples were treated together, seeing the difference we arrived at the conclusion that it is better to treat them separately.

2   Participants and Methods

2.1   Pathological and Healthy Adults Speech Database

The databases' recordings were made during patient consultations of Dr. Krisztina Mészáros in a consulting room at the Outpatients' Department of the Head and Neck Surgery Department of the National Institute of Oncology. Over the past years several types of diseases occurred. Recordings from healthy people were collected as well. These recordings are used as comparison, and the recordings were collected from people who had attended for unrelated check-ups. Speech samples were recorded by near field microphone (Monacor ECM-100), with Creative Soundblaster Audigy 2 NX: an outer USB sound card with 44,100 Hz sampling rate, at a 16-bit linear coding. The microphone was placed 10 cm from the patient's mouth. The duration of the recordings are about one minute each. Every patient had to read out aloud one of Aesop's Fables, "The North Wind and the Sun". This folktale is frequently used in phoniatrics as an illustration of spoken language. It has been translated into several languages, Hungarian included. A more detailed description of the database is found in [13]. In this work a total of 136 recordings were used from this database: 84 recordings from Healthy people (42 female and 42 male) and 52 recordings from patients suffering from functional dysphonia (FD) (38 female and 14 male).

2.2   Juvenile Dysphonia and Healthy Child Speech Database

For our research it was essential to create a well-structured speech database containing children's speech samples. The database contains samples of children suffering from dysphonia, Healthy and healed children's voices as well. The recordings of children suffering from dysphonia were collected at the Budapest University of Technology Laboratory of Speech Acoustics audiological cab. The audiological cab provides an environment isolated from noise and vibrations by eliminating external sources of interference and suitable to make noise-free recordings. The recordings of Healthy children were made at Albertfalva Don Bosco kindergarten. All the recordings were made in the presence of the children's parents.

During the recordings the children told the poem from Erika Bartos entitled "The Squirrel". The poem was chosen for therapeutic reasons, and because children in the 5–10 year old age group are very fond of the poem and it is easy to learn. All the children from the database are aged 5 to 6.

The recordings were made using a near field microphone (Monacor ECM-100), Creative Soundblaster Audigy 2 NX outer USB sound card, with 44,100 Hz sampling rate and 16-bit linear coding. The duration of the recordings are about 20 s each.

A clinician classified all the recorded speech samples according to the RBH scale, voices where H was given the score 0 were considered Healthy [10]. The database contains 20 Healthy and 12 (1 female and 11 male) recordings from children diagnosed with juvenile dysphonia (furthermore referred as FD children). These records were used in our research.

Note the distribution of the genres of the two databases: where as in the adult database the number of females with functional dysphonia is much higher than the number of males, in the child database the number of males diagnosed with dysphonia is higher. This ratio corresponds to the clinicians' experience.

Both databases were annotated and segmented on phoneme level, using the SAMPA phonetic alphabet [11]. The segmentation was made with the help of an automatic phoneme segmentator, which was developed in our Laboratory, followed by manual corrections.

2.3   Pre-processing Methods

When examining the voice of adults, the middle of vowels were selected, and the typical acoustic parameters were measured there. The vowels were marked with the SAMPA characters during the phoneme levelled segmentation, thus we used this nomination in this article too. Among the 14 Hungarian vowels, [E] and [o] are usually analyzed in case of adults. One of the reasons that justifies this choice is that in the Hungarian language the [E] vowel is the most frequent one and there are approximately 50 [E] vowels in the tale that was read. The [o] vowel is usually used during both sustained and continuous speech based speech therapies by Hungarian professionals. In the case of the children, the vowel [o] is the poem's most frequent one, with 16 pieces, and there are only 9 pieces of the vowel [E]. The statistical analyses were made extracting the vowels [E], [o], [O], [A:], [u] from each database. During the extraction of the vowels, samples shorter than 62 ms were discarded, in order to eliminate sounds containing less than 5 periods. The limit is established based on the sampling frequency 44.1 kHz, and the minimum male fundamental frequency set to 80 Hz. Both in adult and children speech the extracted vowels appeared in different words and contexts.

For the extraction of the acoustic parameters Praat software was used [12]. At the middle of each examined vowel, the following acoustic parameters were measured: Jitter_ddp (the average absolute difference between consecutive differences between consecutive periods, divided by the average period), Shimmer_ddp (the average absolute difference between consecutive differences between the amplitudes of consecutive periods), mean HNR and the first component of the mel-frequency cepstral coefficients (MFCC1). The parameters were selected taking into account the results of our previous research [13].

2.4   Statistical Analyses of Acoustic Parameters

All parameters obtained were disposed by using SPSS20.0 software. Two sample T-tests were used for statistical significance testing for the mean values of the acous-tic parameters between healthy voices and those with functional dysphonia [14]. Where F tests showed significant variances of an acoustic parameter within the groups (with significance level 95 % ($\alpha = 0.05$)), Welch's T-test was used. Welch's T-test is insensitive to equality of the variances regardless of whether the sample sizes are similar. Our assumption is that the distributions are normal, but T tests are relatively robust to moderate violations of the normality assumption.

3   Results

3.1   Comparison of Healthy and FD Children

Acoustic parameters presented in 2.3 were extracted from vowels [E], [o], [O], [A:], [u] from Healthy children and FD children voice samples and were used for statistical analyses. Every sound has been evaluated separately. The results of the two sample T-tests are shown in Table 1. Where the entries are marked with *, the mean difference is significant at the 90 % ($p < 0.1$) level, where entries are marked with **, the mean difference is significant at the 95 % ($p < 0.05$) level, where entries are marked with ***, the mean difference is significant at the 99 % ($p < 0.001$) level, otherwise, there was no significant difference in means ($p > 0.05$) and represents that we accept the null hypothesis, that the means are equal.

Table 1. p – values of T-tests between Healthy and FD children by five vowels, (* p < 0.1; ** p < 0.05; *** p < 0.001)

	Vowels				
	[O]	[A:]	[E]	[o]	[u]
	p - values				
Jitter_ddp	0.000***	0.009**	0.018**	0.000***	0.025**
Shimmer_ddp	0.000***	0.001**	0.000***	0.000***	0.883
mean_HNR	0.000***	0.023**	0.072*	0.003**	0.173
MFCC1	0.000***	0.000***	0.000***	0.000***	0.000***

The vowels [O] and [o] presents the difference the best, possibly because these vowels occurred most often in the poem. The poem contains 15 instances of [O] sounds, 5 instances of [A:] sounds, 9 instances of [E], 16 instances of [o] and 7 in-stances of [u] sounds. When examining vowel [O] tests revealed significant differences in Jitter_ddp (p < 0.001), Shimmer_ddp (p < 0.001), mean_HNR (p < 0.001) and MFCC1 (p < 0.001). When examining vowel [o] the results were only slightly different: Jitter_ddp (p < 0.001), Shimmer_ddp (p < 0.001), mean HNR (p < 0.005), MFCC1 (p < 0.001). This means that all acoustic parameters showed significant differences in means. Table 1 also suggests that choosing another threshold, like $\alpha = 0.01$ (99 % significance level), would give no difference in Jitter_ddp between the groups at vowel [E] and mean_HNR in case of vowel [A:]. Uncertainty in case of different vowels is due to the small amount of data; in addition, the number of occurrences of different vowels is different as well.

Our results show that variations of Jitter and Shimmer values with HNR and MFCC1 are good indicators to separate Healthy and FD voices in case of children as well.

3.2 Comparison of Healthy Adults and Children

We wanted to know if there is a difference in the means of the examined acoustic parameters in the healthy adult and children group, by two of the five vowels. The adult group was divided to healthy females and healthy males. The thought behind this is that our prediction was that female and child samples show more similarity. The reason for this may be that in case of children there is no mutation yet and the child pitch (300–500 Hz) is much closer to the female pitch value (150–300 Hz) as to average male pitch (100–200 Hz). Vowels [o] and [E] were used because vowel [o] has the most number of occurrences in the poem and vowel [E] is the vowel with the most number of occurrences in the tale. Acoustic parameters from the two vowels were extracted from adult and children's speech samples and compared by two2 sample T-tests. Every sound has been evaluated separately. Results of the T-tests revealed significant differences mostly between adult males and children. The null hypothesis is that the means are equal. The detailed results of the statistical analysis between healthy child and healthy adult male groups are given in Table 2.

Table 2. Summary statistics for all measures in between healthy child and healthy male groups by two vowels (* p < 0.1; ** p < 0.05; *** p < 0.001)

	Vowel									
	[o]					[E]				
	Child		Male			Child		Male		
	Mean	Std. Dev.	Mean	Std. Dev.	p-value	Mean	Std. Dev.	Mean	Std. Dev.	p-value
Jitter_ddp	1.095	0.740	1.448	1.533	**0.020****	1.414	1.084	1.986	1.791	**0.000*****
Shimmer_ddp	7.514	3.698	8.654	6.962	0.109	9.669	5.268	12.125	10.070	**0.003****
mean_HNR	17.982	4.232	12.872	4.776	**0.000*****	13.262	3.914	8.337	4.068	**0.000*****
MFCC1	245.977	45.554	265.013	54.779	**0.000*****	175.224	32.372	208.357	51.887	**0.000*****

The detailed results of the statistical analysis between healthy child and healthy adult female groups are given in Table 3.

Table 3. Summary statistics for all measures in between healthy child and healthy female groups by two vowels (* p < 0.1; ** p < 0.05; *** p < 0.001)

	Vowel									
	[o]					[E]				
	Child		Female			Child		Female		
	Mean	Std. Dev.	Mean	Std. Dev.	p-value	Mean	Std. Dev.	Mean	Std. Dev.	p-value
Jitter_ddp	1.095	0.740	0.904	1.026	**0.013****	1.414	1.084	1.173	1.155	**0.011****
Shimmer_ddp	7.514	3.698	5.813	4.653	**0.000*****	9.669	5.268	7.755	5.717	**0.000*****
mean_HNR	17.982	4.232	17.109	5.223	0.370	13.262	3.914	12.764	4.408	0.128
MFCC1	245.977	45.554	249.780	47.506	0.347	175.224	32.372	177.965	43.429	0.320

When examining the differences between health child and healthy male groups at vowel [O], tests revealed significant differences in Jitter_ddp (p < 0.05), mean_HNR (p < 0.001) and MFCC1 (p < 0.001). When the vowel [E] was taken into account significant differences were found at all acoustical parameters. When examining the differences between healthy child and healthy female groups significant differences were only found in Jitter_ddp (p < 0.05) and Shimmer_ddp (p < 0.001). Parameter mean_HNR and MFCC1 showed no significant difference.

From this result it is clear that differences exist in the examined acoustical parameters even between healthy child and healthy adult groups. A decision system that inquiries child's voice trained with adult voice samples would likely detract erroneous conclusions.

3.3   Comparison of Healthy Males and Females

Because the child voice samples showed various differences with adult female and male samples, the differences between adult female and male samples were examined. Results of the T-tests are shown in Table 4.

Table 4. Summary statistics for all measures in between healthy male and healthy female groups by two vowels (* $p < 0.1$; ** $p < 0.05$; *** $p < 0.001$)

	Vowel									
	[o]					[E]				
	Female		Male			Female		Male		
	Mean	Std. Dev.	Mean	Std. Dev.	p-value	Mean	Std. Dev.	Mean	Std. Dev.	p-value
Jitter_ddp	0.904	1.026	1.448	1.533	**0.000*****	1.173	1.155	1.986	1.791	**0.000*****
Shimmer_ddp	5.813	4.653	8.654	6.962	**0.000*****	7.755	5.717	12.125	10.070	**0.000*****
mean_HNR	17.109	5.223	12.872	4.776	**0.000*****	12.764	4.408	8.337	4.068	**0.000*****
MFCC1	249.780	47.506	265.013	54.779	**0.007****	177.965	43.429	208.357	51.887	**0.000*****

All examined acoustic parameters showed differences in means. Because the p-value is very small in each case, it indicates strong evidence against the null hypothesis, so the null hypothesis is rejected, the means are not equal.

It follows that when examining adult voice samples, it is reasonable to separate male and female samples. A separate decision system is needed to be built for adult women, adult men, and children in order to obtain a more precise result.

4   Conclusions

The present study first of all investigated the relationship between healthy and FD voices of children. For this experiment, it was essential to create a well-structured speech database containing children's speech samples, the Juvenile dysphonia and Healthy Child Speech Database was built. The database contains 20 Healthy and 12 child samples with juvenile dysphonia. Acoustic parameters from vowels were extracted from adult and children's speech samples and compared by statistical analyses. The statistical analyses draw the conclusion that variations of Jitter and Shimmer values with HNR and MFCC1 are good indicators to separate Healthy and FD voices in case of children as well. Healthy samples of children and adult voices were compared giving the clear conclusion that differences exist in the examined acoustical parameters even between healthy child and healthy adult groups. It is necessary to carry out the investigations separately on children's voices as well, we cannot use adult voices to make any conclusions to children's voices. Lastly the differences between adult female and male samples were examined. The study results confirmed our assumptions that in order to build an automatic decision making system that recognizes FD it is advisable to build separate systems for adult males, adult females and children. Of course much more data is needed to obtain better results, and further investigations are necessary to decide which acoustical parameters are the best for distinguishing healthy from pathological voice in case of children.

Acknowledgement. We would like to thank Krisztina Mészáros from the Department of Head and Neck Surgery of the National Institute of Oncology for her continued cooperation in helping us collect and evaluate the patient data, which is the basis of our research. We would also like to thank Mária Ágostházy from the Speech Therapy and Vocational Education Service of Újbuda for helping us construct the Juvenile dysphonia and Healthy Child speech database. We hope that our cooperation will last long.

References

1. Hirschberg, J., Hacki, T., és Mészáros, K.: Foniátria és társtudományok: A hangképzés, a beszéd és a nyelv, a hallás és a nyelés élettana, kórtana, diagnosztikája és terápiája (I. kötet). Budapest: Eötvös Kiadó (2013)
2. Schulze, J.: Stimmstörungen im Kindes-und Jugendalter. Schulz-Kirchner, Idstein (2002)
3. Connor, N.P., et al.: Attitudes of children with dysphonia. J. Voice **22**(2), 197–209 (2008)
4. Zhang, Yu., Jiang, J.J.: Acoustic analyses of sustained and running voices from patients with laryngeal pathologies. J. Voice **22**(1), 1–9 (2008)
5. Peng, C., et al.: Pathological voice classification based on a single Vowel's acoustic features. In: 7th IEEE International Conference on Computer and Information Technology. IEEE (2007)
6. Parsa, V., Jamieson, D.G.: Acoustic discrimination of pathological Voice Sustained vowels versus continuous speech. J. Speech, Lang., Hear. Res. **44**(2), 327–339 (2001)
7. Askenfelt, A.G., Hammarberg, B.: Speech waveform perturbation analysis a perceptual-acoustical comparison of seven measures. J. Speech, Lang., Hear. Res. **29**(1), 50–64 (1986)
8. Peng, C., et al.: Pathological voice classification based on a single Vowel's acoustic features. In: 7th IEEE International Conference on Computer and Information Technology. IEEE (2007)
9. Ritchings, R.T., McGillion, M., Moore, C.J.: Pathological voice quality assessment using artificial neural networks. Med. Eng. Phys. **24**(7), 561–564 (2002)
10. Klára, V., Viktor, I., Krisztina, M.: Voice disorder detection on the basis of continuous speech. In: Jobbágy, Á. (ed.) 5th European Conference of the International Federation for Medical and Biological Engineering. IFMBE Proceedings, vol. 37, pp. 86–89. Springer, Heidelberg (2011)
11. Klára, V.: SAMPA computer readable phonetic alphabet, Hungarian (2008)
12. Boersma, P., Weenink, D.: Praat: doing phonetics by computer [Computer program]. Version 6.0.15 (2016). http://www.praat.org/
13. Kazinczi, F., Mészáros, K., Vicsi, K.: Automatic detection of voice disorders. In: Dediu, A.-H., et al. (eds.) SLSP 2015. LNCS, vol. 9449, pp. 143–152. Springer, Heidelberg (2015). doi:10. 1007/978-3-319-25789-1_14
14. Fadem, B.: High-Yield Behavioral Science (High-Yield Series). Lippincott Williams & Wilkins, Hagerstwon (2008)
15. Imre, V.: Acoustical examination of pathological voices, Diploma work. Budapest University of Technology and Economics (2009)

Stress, Arousal, and Stress Detector Trained on Acted Speech Database

Róbert Sabo[1](✉), Milan Rusko[1], Andrej Ridzik[1], and Jakub Rajčáni[2]

[1] Institute of Informatics, Slovak Academy of Sciences, Bratislava, Slovakia
{robert.sabo,milan.rusko,andrej.ridzik}@savba.sk
[2] Department of Psychology, Faculty of Arts, Comenius University, Bratislava, Slovakia
rajcani.jakub@gmail.com

Abstract. This paper reports on initial experiments with the creation of a suitable database for training and testing systems for stress detection in speech and first experimental results. Based on the psychological understanding of the concepts of stress and emotion, we operationalized stress as a level of arousal, which can be detected in speech. We describe here a speech database with three levels of "acted stress" and three levels of soothing. For the very first experiment performed on the database we detect different levels of stress using Gaussian mixture models. The accuracy of detecting three levels of stress was 89 % for speakers included in the training database and 73 % for speakers whose recordings were not used during the adaptation of the GMM models.

Keywords: Stress · Emotions · Stress detection · Tense arousal · Universal background model · Gaussian mixture model

1 Introduction

After the speech processing technologies have achieved good results using linguistic and phonetic features, more and more researchers focus their attention to paralinguistic aspects of speech with the emphasis on the practical application. in automatic speech processing tasks, such as affective speech synthesis, recognition, speaker verification, and others. A number of research works examine the presence of emotions or stress in speech [1–3]. Other studies specify characteristics of speech under stress and emotions [4–6]. In all these papers the choice of research material, methodology, and even the definitions were determined by the intended use of the results and the domain of their future application. In this article we focus on the definition of stress, which is reflected in changes of arousal and therefore also to the measurable speech characteristics.

2 The Concept of Stress in Psychology

Despite an intensive research interest in stress, there is still some inconsistency regarding its definition. For the purpose of this study we will explain some important concepts in the theory of stress and emotions, which affects the procedure used in our research. In general,

© Springer International Publishing Switzerland 2016
A. Ronzhin et al. (Eds.): SPECOM 2016, LNAI 9811, pp. 675–682, 2016.
DOI: 10.1007/978-3-319-43958-7_82

stress can be understood as a real or implied threat to the psychological or physiological integrity of an individual [7]. For understanding the concept, it is important to distinguish the concepts of *stress*, *stressor*, and *adaptive stress response*. *Stress* represents the state of threatened homeostasis, the dynamic internal equilibrium of an organism [8]. *Stressors*, on the other hand, are external or internal adverse forces that serve as threatening stimuli. Stressors vary from physical (e.g. low temperature), chemical, or biological (e.g. infection) to psychological and social stressors (e.g. work demands or problems in relationships). In reaction to a stressor, the individual makes adaptive behavioral and physiological responses, which aim at coping with the threat and preventing bodily or psychological damage. Stress response of an individual is largely determined by the appraisal of the stressful event. Such appraisal, as understood by Lazarus [9], is a universal process evaluating whether the external stimulus is significant to the individual's well-being. The appraisal of threat and safety thus plays an important role in stress response.

Two basic behavioral stress responses recognized by Cannon [10] are: fighting the threat or fleeing from the situation. The "fight or flight" response is associated with emotional and physiological changes. The preparatory activation of stress systems, such as the sympathetic nervous system and the HPA axis [8], help to mobilize resources and prepare an organism for behavioral response. The "Fight or flight" response is also accompanied with a corresponding emotional experience, consisting mainly of emotions such as anger or fear. The terms *stress* and *emotions* are closely related and according to some theorists stress can be included in the concept of emotions [9].

Emotions can be conceptualized by dimensional models based on their position in a two or more dimensional space. Two prevalent dimensions of affect are overall activation or arousal, and valence ranging from pleasurable to non-pleasurable emotions [11]. Emotions associated with the "fight or flight" reaction (e.g. anger or fear) are mostly characterized by high arousal and negative emotional valence. The dimension of arousal also corresponds to the preparatory physiological excitation, which is a part of adaptive stress response [12]. Thayer [13] distinguishes energetic arousal, associated with readiness to vigorous muscular and skeletal activation, and tense arousal or the emergency preparation that is activated by real or imagined danger that prepares the person for "fight or flight."

We presume that the concept of tense arousal in relation to stress and emotions best describes the affective and physiological phenomenon that we want to study in the context of speech. For the purposes of this study we will narrow down the characteristics of stress induced changes in speech to the level of tense arousal. Tense arousal in speech will be addressed as different levels of imperativeness in a crisis related message.

3   Speech Database of "Acted Stress"

The effects of stress on the speech signal have been extensively studied in the last decades. Some of the acoustic characteristics of speech, such as the fundamental frequency, the intensity, the articulation rate, the vocal tract spectral characteristics, and others, are known to be influenced by stress [14]. The notion of stress covers a very wide range of phenomena and their effects on the speech signal are highly non-specific, for example the Lombard speech [15]. In order to be able to observe the specific effect of stress on the speech signal we decided to narrow the definition of stress situations (the choice of stress stimuli) to those that are reflected to the changes of tense arousal in emotional space. Moreover, we needed to be able to control the stress/arousal level in a repeatable way and keep the particular levels consistent in the records of the speech database. As this cannot be achieved in the spontaneous speech under stress, we decided to create an acted database. The different levels of tense arousal were obtained using the same methodology as in [16]. The use of the acted emotional speech is a prevalent research method in the emotional speech research [17].

3.1 Text Resources

All the texts used in this study were in Slovak, recorded by Slovak native speakers. The texts were selected to evoke specific crisis situations in speakers (such as an urgent need to inform people about a threat to human health and life). Crisis situations associated with threats in real life are known to elicit strong stress responses and carry high emotional load.

The texts of 150 warning messages were used for higher tense arousal databases (levels 1, 2, 3) and 150 sentences for lower tense arousal (levels −1, −2, −3) included soothing texts.

3.2 Database Recording

The databases were recorded in an acoustically treated recording studio using a RODE K2 microphone, 48 kHz sampling frequency and 16 bit resolution.

One of the biggest problems with recording acted emotional/stressed speech databases is that the actor is often unable to keep the level of portrayed emotion consistent for a longer time interval. After a while, the expressive load in his/her speech changes. The authors of [16] have designed a three step method of recording an expressive database. In this method the speaker does not try to maintain the same level of expressivity during the entire recording, but s/he rather varies the emotional load in three steps with every sentence. Hence, the speaker produces triplets of lexically identical utterances while trying to keep same steps in tense arousal levels. The authors of [16] think that this leads back to the neutral, natural setting of the speaker's voice functions like a "reset" and gives the speaker a robust reference for further changes in his/her voice in the other two depicted levels of arousal.

The speaker was therefore instructed to utter the message once in a neutral manner (referred to as level 1 of tense arousal), then with higher imperativeness, representing a serious command or a directive (level 2), and finally acting out an extremely urgent command or statement being declared in a situation when human lives are directly in danger (level 3). After recording the message in the third level, the speaker relaxes for several seconds and then s/he starts with a new prompted sentence.

When recording the "lower tense arousal" triplet of databases the speaker was instructed to utter the prompted message once in a natural way, comfortable for him or her. We again assume that this level reflects the neutral state of the speaker at that particular recording session. This first, neutral, reference level of tense arousal is denoted "level −1" to distinguish it from the "level 0" related to the "big" neutral database and "level 1" which is the label of the neutral database from the triplet with increasing arousal. The same sentence is then uttered in the second (decreased) level of expressivity with lower activation (level −2). The speaker is instructed to imagine that s/he has to announce to a group of adult people that the emergency situation has passed, that the alarm was called off and they can calm down and stay at ease.

Finally, the same sentence is uttered with extremely low tense arousal (level −3). The speaker should imagine that s/he is speaking to scared small children, or to a seriously ill or wounded person. His/her speech should not be mimic motherese or whispered speech, but has to be very peaceful. After recording the message in the third level, the speaker relaxes for several seconds and then s/he starts with a new prompted sentence.

At the very beginning of recording, the speaker first tries to act all three levels of arousal. Only when s/he is satisfied with the realization of the sentences s/he starts the recording. This approach helps speakers to set up or "calibrate" the three levels of arousal. The actual recording was realized without the presence of an experimenter so that the less-experienced speaker does not feel ashamed in the presence of another person.

At the moment of writing this article the speech database contains 15 speakers (10 males, 5 females), and the recording of additional speakers continues. Each speaker has recorded approximately 20 min of speech, approx. 7 min of speech in each level (excluding pauses between utterances). Speech samples for each of the six levels of arousal can be found at [18].

To illustrate the differences of the speech signal at different levels of arousal we present in Fig. 1 the long-term average spectrum (LTAS) differences of the speech at all six levels of arousal with respect to neutral speech LTAS (in one speaker (MR)). The areas of biggest differences among the LTAS correspond to the spectral areas that are influenced by the change in the arousal level most significantly.

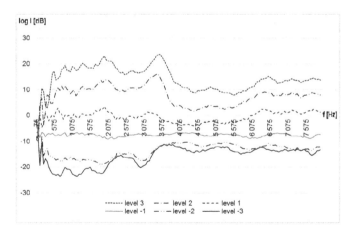

Fig. 1. LTAS differences in the spectra of speech signal stress levels (adopted from [19])

In order to verify the correctness of our methodology, we decided to create a system for speaker independent automatic measurement of stress/arousal level from speech. In the first version, we only consider three levels of arousal - neutral, increased, and high (levels 1, 2, 3).

4 Stress Detection Using Adapted GMM

The method of Gaussian Mixture Model (GMM) adaptation was already widely used in several different fields, such as gender recognition of a speaker [20]. It consists of training a single GMM from a large number of diverse recordings and using it as a Universal Background Model (UBM). The trained UBM is then adapted to only a specific type of recordings t, resulting in a model M_t representing this class. For example, in the case of gender recognition, two separate models M_{male} and M_{female} are created. The process of adaptation may be carried out by applying several iterations of the Expectation–Maximization algorithm, starting from the UBM and using only the data belonging to one class.

During the phase of recognition of an unknown recording x, for each class t the probability $P(x|t)$ is calculated as the probability of the recording being from the class t. The result of the classification can then be made as a maximum a posteriori (MAP) estimate

$$T(x) = \underset{t}{argmax}\, P(x|t). \tag{1}$$

We have decided to employ this approach also to the problem of stress detection using our database of recordings mentioned above, in which each level of stress corresponds to a different class.

5 Experimental Results

In our experiments, we represented the recordings with a set of 19-dimensional features of mel frequency cepstral coefficients (MFCC) with appended delta and delta-delta coefficients. As a background model, we used a gender-independent UBM containing 1024 Gaussians that was trained on the recordings from the LibriSpeech database [21], consisting of recordings of approx. 2500 speakers. This model was then used for the adaptation to three different levels of stress and three GMMs were trained. For each speaker in our database (consisting of 15 speakers), we excluded 30 recordings for each level; and these recordings were not used during the adaptation, but were only used for testing.

In this experiment of classifying a speech utterance as level 1, 2 or 3 we achieved an accuracy of 89.19 %. A more detailed description of the results is shown in Table 1.

Table 1. Test results of identification of three levels of stress on the Crisis acted stress database

	Level 1	Level 2	Level 3
Recall	97.78 %	75.11 %	95.67 %
Precision	86.96 %	91.35 %	89.87 %

As the results show, only 2.22 % of neutral recordings of level 1 were misclassified as containing stress. However, all of these misclassifications were caused by their incorrect classification as level 2. Similarly good performance was also achieved on detecting level 3 recordings, where most of the errors here were also caused by classifying them as level 2. Even though significantly worse results were achieved while detecting recordings of level 2, where almost 25 % of these recordings were incorrectly classified, the classification of level 2 resulted in the best precision. These observations could be the result of a relatively high variance of expressed stress in this level, and thus the adaptation of the corresponding GMM was difficult to achieve.

Based on these observations, we also investigated the ability to differentiate only between neutral speech and speech containing stress. In order to achieve this, we created a new GMM by adapting the UBM to a mixed set of recordings of level 2 and 3. This resulted in a model representing a non-neutral speech, thus speech of any level of stress. In this task of classifying a test speech utterance as being neutral or containing any level of stress, we achieved an overall classification accuracy of 94.74 %.

We have also evaluated the quality of stress detection on speakers whose speech was not used during the process of adaptation. We have tested the system on 553 recordings for each level from 7 new speakers and evaluated the performance. In this scenario we achieved an accuracy of 73.18 %, while more detailed results are shown in Table 2.

Table 2. Test results of identification of three levels of stress on 553 recordings for each level from 7 different speakers

	Level 1	Level 2	Level 3
Recall	92.77 %	51.18 %	75.59 %
Precision	72.97 %	64.46 %	80.85 %

Since the recordings from these speakers were not used during the training process, we see an expected drop in the performance. Additionally, as measured also in the previous experiment, we have detected a significantly lower recall on recordings of level 2, confirming our assumption of higher variance in recordings of this level of stress. As done before, we have also tested the ability to discriminate just between the neutral speech and speech containing stress. This resulted in 85.96 % of accuracy.

6   Conclusions and Future Work

In this paper, we have discussed the possibility of creating a suitable database for training and testing systems for stress detection in speech. Based on the psychological understanding of concepts of stress, emotion and arousal, we decided to operationalize stress induced changes in speech as changes in arousal. To be able to control the stress level (i.e. the level of the tense arousal) we have created a speech database of acted stress. We have recorded 15 speakers (10 male, 5 female) who were instructed to imagine that they were in a crisis situation and they should communicate the warning message to the people being at the risk of life and health. The speaker should read each sentence with three levels of stress/arousal (neutral, raised, high).

In order to verify the correctness of our methodology, we decided to create a system for speaker independent automatic measurement of stress/arousal level from speech. In the first version, we only consider three levels of arousal - neutral, increased, and high (levels 1, 2, 3). The models of speech with different levels of arousal were created by adapting a universal GMM to the specific levels of acted stress. In our first experiment, we tried to detect a specific level of stress in recordings of speakers, whose recordings were also used during the adaptation process. The results have shown that by using this approach, we were able to reliably detect level 1 recordings with recall above 97 % and precision above 86 %, as well as recordings of level 3 with recall above 95 % and precision above 89 %. The accuracy of identifying level 2 recordings was significantly worse (recall of 75 %), which might have been caused by higher variance of expressed stress in this level. The ability to discriminate just between the neutral and any aroused speech was also tested with a resulting accuracy of 94.74 %.

We have also tested the performance on the recordings of 7 other speakers whose data were not used during the adaptation. Similarly to the findings in the previous experiment, this resulted in higher accuracy of recordings of level 1 (recall 93 %, precision 73 %) and level 3 (recall 76 %, precision 81 %), but lower for the problematic level 2 (recall 51 %, precision 64 %). Additionally, we achieved an accuracy of 85.96 %, when differentiating between neutral and aroused speech of speakers whose recordings were not used during the process of adaptation.

As soon as the entire database is finished (at least 20 speakers), we will use the whole database to create a system for stress detection for all six levels with more robust models. The detector will be used and validated in the prototype in the frame of the GAMMA - Global ATM Security Management project.

Acknowledgement. The research leading to the results presented in this paper has received funding from the European Union FP7 under grant agreement no. 312382 (GAMMA - Global ATM Security Management project [22]).

References

1. Macková, L., Čižmár, A., Juhár, J.: A study of acoustic features for emotional speaker recognition in i-vector representation. Acta Electrotechnica et Informatica **15**(2), 15–20 (2015)
2. Vizer, L.M., Zhou, L., Sears, A.: Automated stress detection using keystroke and linguistic features: an exploratory study. Int. J. Hum. Comput. Stud. **67**(10), 870–886 (2009)
3. Kurniawan, H., Maslov, A.V., Pechenizkiy, M.: Stress detection from speech and galvanic skin response signals. In: Computer-Based Medical Systems, pp. 209–214 (2013)
4. Zhang, C., Hansen, J.H.L.: Analysis and classification of speech mode: whispered throughshouted. In: Interspeech 2007, Antwerp, Belgium, pp. 2289–2292 (2007)

5. Ruzanski, E., Hansen, J.H., et al.: Effects of phoneme characteristics on TEO feature-based automatic stress detection in speech. In: ICASSP (1), pp. 357–360 (2005)
6. Womack, B.D., Hansen, J.H.: Classification of speech under stress using target driven features. Speech Commun. **20**(1), 131–150 (1996)
7. McEwen, B.S., Wingfield, J.C.: The concept of allostasis in biology and biomedicine. Horm. Behav. **43**(1), 2–15 (2003)
8. Chrousos, G.P.: Stressors, stress, and neuroendocrine integration of the adaptive response: the 1997 Hans Selye Memorial Lecture. Ann. N. Y. Acad. Sci. **851**(1), 311–335 (1998)
9. Lazarus, R.S.: From psychological stress to the emotions: a history of changing outlooks. Pers. Crit. Concepts Psychol. **4**, 179 (1998)
10. Cannon, W.: The wisdom of the body. Physiol. Rev. **9**, 399–431 (1929)
11. Russell, J.A.: A circumplex model of affect. J. Pers. Soc. Psychol. **39**(6), 1161–1178 (1980)
12. Dougall, A.L., Baum, A.: Stress, coping and immune function. In: Weiner, I.B., et al. (eds.) Handbook of Psychology, vol. 3, pp. 441–456. Wiley, New York (2003, 2009)
13. Thayer, R.E.: The Activation-Deactivation Adjective Check List (AD ACL). APPENDIX I, The Biopsychology of Mood and Arousal. Oxford University Press, New York (1989)
14. Hansen, J.H., Patil, S.: Speech under stress: analysis, modeling and recognition. In: Müller, C. (ed.) Speaker Classification 2007. LNCS (LNAI), vol. 4343, pp. 108–137. Springer, Heidelberg (2007)
15. Šimko, J., Beňuš, Š., Vainio, M.: Hyperarticulation in Lombard speech: global coordination of the jaw, lips and the tongue. J. Acoust. Soc. Am. **139**(1), 151–162 (2016)
16. Rusko, M., Darjaa, S., Trnka, M., Ritomský, M., Sabo, R.: Alert!… Calm Down, There is Nothing to Worry About. Warning and Soothing Speech Synthesis. In: LREC, pp. 1182–1187 (2014)
17. Scherer, K.R.: Vocal communication of emotion: a review of research paradigms. Speech Commun. **40**, 227–256 (2003)
18. http://speech.savba.sk/ArousalDB
19. Rusko, M., Trnka, M., Darjaa, S., Hamar, J.: The dramatic piece reader for the blind and visually impaired. In Proceedings of SLPAT 2013, pp. 83–91 (2013)
20. Gajšek, R., et al.: Gender and affect recognition based on GMM and GMM-UBM modeling with relevance MAP estimation. In: Proceedings of the Interspeech, pp. 2810–2813 (2010)
21. Panayotov, V., Chen, G., Povey, D., Khudanpur, S.: Librispeech: an ASR corpus based on public domain audio books. In: Acoustics, ICASSP 2015, pp. 5206–5210 (2015)
22. http://www.gamma-project.eu

Study on the Improvement of Intelligibility for Elderly Speech Using Formant Frequency Shift Method

Yuto Tanaka$^{(\boxtimes)}$, Mitsunori Mizumachi, and Yoshihisa Nakatoh

Kyushu Institute of Technology, 1-1, Sensui-cho, Tobata-ku, Kitakyushu-shi, Fukuoka, Japan
O595401y@mail.kyutech.jp

Abstract. In general, aging is progressing in developed countries. Elderly people have difficulty controlling their articulation accurately due to aging. We need to improve the quality of elderly speech for smooth communication. In this paper, we analyzed the 1st formant frequency (F1) and 2nd formant frequency (F2) between the more intelligible speech and less intelligible speech of Japanese elderly people. In addition, we improved the intelligibility of less intelligible elderly speech by using the formant frequency shift method. This method is the correcting by shift value of formant frequency based on LPC. The shift value is the magnification such as expanding the F1-F2 size of less intelligible speech.

Keywords: Elderly speech · Intelligibility · Formant frequency shift · Improvement speech quality

1 Introduction

Speech is very important for us to communicate with others in our daily lives. However, because of aging, some people's ways of speaking change. Owing to this, they cannot have conversation smoothly. For an aging society worldwide, this problem is very serious. For smoothing communication, it is necessary to improve the speech of the elderly.

The previous research reported about analyzing Japanese elderly speech, that elderly speech is less intelligible compared with non-elderly speech by listening test [1]. And, there is a correlation between the intelligibility and the difference of transition distance [2].

We study the relationship between intelligibility of auditory impression and acoustic feature, and we study a method of improving speech intelligibility [3].

In this study, we improved the speech of elderly people based on the analysis. As analysis, we investigated the relationship between difference of transition distance and position of articulation in terms of the level of intelligibility. As the method for improving, we used the shift method based on formant frequency. Specifically, the first formant frequency (F1) and the second formant frequency (F2) shift method, which closes intelligible speech to less intelligible speech.

© Springer International Publishing Switzerland 2016
A. Ronzhin et al. (Eds.): SPECOM 2016, LNAI 9811, pp. 683–690, 2016.
DOI: 10.1007/978-3-319-43958-7_83

2   Analysis of Japanese Elderly Speech

This chapter describes the database of elderly speech and the method for selecting subjects.

2.1   Database Elderly Speech

We recorded the speeches of 36 male elderly persons over the age of 60 in order to improve the intelligibility of elderly speech. The recorded words were 543 isolated words which have phoneme balance. The elderly speech was recorded on 16-bit, 24 k sampling. Table 1 shows the recorded number of elderly people by age. For analyzing the influence of aging on intelligibility, we selected the speakers who gave conspicuous impression based on people's feeling impression of subjective characteristics of elderly speech and analyzing the physical features of the speaker's voice.

We conducted a listening test to determine the degree of subjective characteristics of elderly speech that include "rough", "slow speaking", and "less intelligibility" [4]. The subjects were 10 adult males and 10 adult females. The subjects listened to 50 connected words, which were prepared from a phonetically balanced 543-word database, spoken individually by 36 elderly male speakers. Each speaker was labeled by the subjects with the degree of the characteristics based on a five-point scale. Each figure of the degree of characteristics of elderly speech in "less intelligibility" is shown in Fig. 1. The vertical axis expresses the evaluation degree in each impression of characteristics of elderly speech, and the horizontal axis rearranges each evaluation speaker's value according to the degree of an evaluation. In order to analyze elderly speech, we selected six more intelligible speakers and six less intelligible speakers.

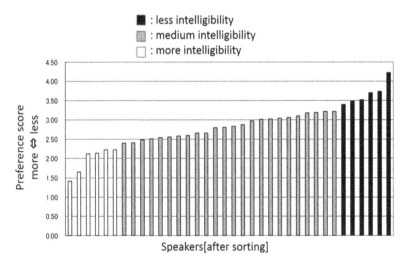

Fig. 1. Preference scores of characteristics of elderly speech on intelligibility. The higher six are the more intelligible group. The lower six are the less intelligible group

2.2   F1-F2 Size of Vowels of Japanese Elderly Speech

We analyzed less intelligible speech by linear predictive coding (LPC) focusing on F1 and F2, and compared more intelligible speech and less intelligible speech. LPC is a tool used mostly in audio signal processing and speech processing to represent the spectral envelope and peak of a digital signal of speech in compressed form.

We calculated mean values of F1 and F2 from the 6 intelligible person's speeches and a less intelligible speech. Figure 2 shows the results of calculating F1 and F2. Figure 2(a) shows the results of initiate phonemes. Figure 2(b) shows the results of medial phonemes. According to Fig. 2, the less intelligible vowels except /u/converge to /u/regardless of the initiate phoneme and medial phoneme. We estimated that due to a decrease in muscle strength with age, the movement of the tongue and mouth become dull, thus the vowels become closer to /u/.

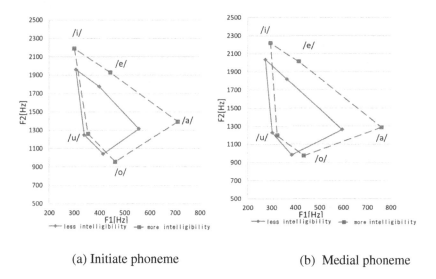

(a) Initiate phoneme   (b) Medial phoneme

Fig. 2. F1 and F2 mean value of more intelligible and less intelligible speech on F1-F2 size. The solid line is the mean value of F1 and F2 of the less intelligible group. The dotted line is the mean value of F1 and F2 of the more intelligible group.

3   Improvement of Speech Intelligibility Based on Formant Frequency Shift

This section describes our proposed method to improve speech intelligibility. To shift F1 and F2, we separated speech in two, vocal cord and vocal tract. We process separated vocal cord to improve speech intelligibility. Finally, we create speech to synthesis vocal cord and processed vocal tract.

3.1 Whole Block Diagram

Figure 3 is the entire process of the shift of F1 and F2. This method of shift F1 and F2 consist of the five key parts:

(1) Time frequency transformation (DCT (Discrete Cosine Transformation)),
(2) Flattening of DCT value by the LPC (Linear Predictive Coding) envelope,
(3) Flattening of DCT value by the spectral of bark scale,
(4) Correcting envelope multiplied by the LPC envelope and DCT envelope transformed bark scale,
(5) Multiplying Flattening DCT value and shifted envelope.

To separate input signal in vocal cord and vocal tract, the input signal x(t) is transformed LPC spectrum envelope F(ω) by LPC block. x(t) is flattered by calculated LPC spectral envelope. However, only LPC envelope cannot be flattered x(t) perfectly. In this paper, we attempt to complete flattering by dividing the flattered signal using the LPC envelope that are converted to the bark scale (G(ω)) on their own.

The shifted envelope is made by shifting the spectral envelope from a value multiplied by the LPC envelope and spectrum converted to bark scale by DCT using shift value. Finally, the shifted signal is made by multiplying the flattened DCT spectrum and the shifted envelope.

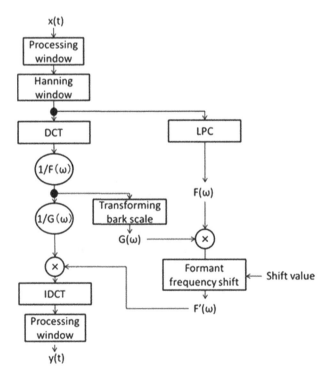

Fig. 3. Whole block diagram

In this paper, we connect vowels to increase the shift value gradually using the 0.03 s before and after in order to smooth the shifted spectral envelope.

3.2 Method of Formant Frequency Shift

Figure 4 shows the process of formant frequency shift block. First, block of peak detection and bottom detection find the peaks and the LPC of the spectral envelope. Up-sampling block up-samples the LPC spectral envelope to expand and contract it. Finally, the shift envelope is made from an up-sampled LPC spectral envelope by the block of data expansion and contraction based on shift value.

The method of expansion and contraction is that the LPC spectral envelope is expanded and contracted as a point of the peak shift while fixing the before and after points of the bottom. Figure 5 is the process image of data expansion and contraction.

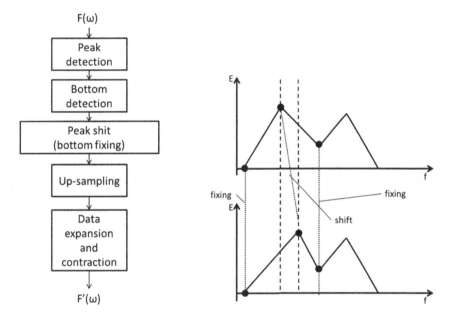

Fig. 4. Block diagram of formant frequency

Fig. 5. Process image of data expansion and contraction

3.3 Decision Shift Value

For improving the intelligibility of less intelligible speech, F1 and F2 must shift close to the F1 and F2 of more intelligible speech. We consider that intelligibility is improved by expanding the size of F1-F2. We improved less intelligible speech by subtracting the mean value of the F1 or F2 of the less intelligible speech from the F1 or F2 of more intelligible speech [5]. In this paper, the shift value is a constant magnification, as F1 and F2 of /u/ is fixed and F1 and F2 of the other vowels move in relation to /u/.

Table 1 is the shift magnification that was used in this study. We defined this magnification from preliminary experiments.

Table 1. Shift magnification as expansion F1-F2 size

	F1	F2
/a/	1.1	1.1
/o/	1.2	0.95
/u/	1.0	1.0
/i/	0.9	1.3
/e/	1.2	1.2

4 Verification of the Effect of Shift Method by Listening Test

In this section, we verify the effect of our proposed method by a listening test using 2 typical elderly speech with less intelligibility.

4.1 Listening Test

In order to verify the effect of improving intelligibility by our shift method, we made an "original speech," "shift speech," and "non-shift speech" for a listening test. The "non-shift speech" is a speech which was synthesized only processing window without shift to the F1 and F2. "Non-shift speech" was prepared as a dummy. We performed a listening test using the three types of speech. The method of comparison is based on the paired comparison called Scheffe (Nakaya's Variation, not considering stimulus order effect). The evaluation words were 4 and contained a few vowels from the database of 543 words. The subjects of corrected by our shift method were two less intelligible speakers. The subjects of listening test are ten male adults.

4.2 Evaluation Method

First, subjects of listening test listened to two speeches at random from "original speech" and "shift speech" and "non-shift speech". Second, the subjects evaluated two speeches at five grades about the degree of intelligibility. The evaluation word was intelligibility without distortion. The number of trials was 5. Figure 6 show example of listening test.

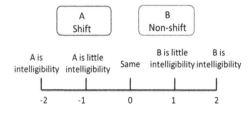

Fig. 6. Example of five grades of evaluation about intelligibility

If the subjects feel "A is intelligibility", speech of A have-2 point. We verify effective of our proposed method to calculate mean value of this preference score.

4.3 Results of Listening Test

We calculated the mean value of preference score and the 95 % confidence interval using the method of paired comparison of Scheffe. Figure 7 shows the result of comparing "original speech" and "shift speech" by listening test in the case of the two subjects. The top side indicates that "shift speech" is good. The bottom side indicates that "original speech" is good. The line is the 95 % confidence interval. The results of the listening test have significance unless the line crosses the zero.

From Fig. 7, in the case of speaker A, the words of /UIUISII/ and /OIOI/ are improved intelligibility by our shift method. However, the words of /AOAO/ and /IMEEJI/ are not improved intelligibility. In the case of speaker B, the all words are improved intelligibility by our shift method. It is assumed that our method is effective in a typical speaker with less intelligibility. In a speech which differ from the trends described in Sect. 2, our method is not effective by processing to expand the area in uniform. From the questionnaire by the subjects of listening test, we found that the distortion due to shift affect the intelligibility because the original speech is not low intelligibility.

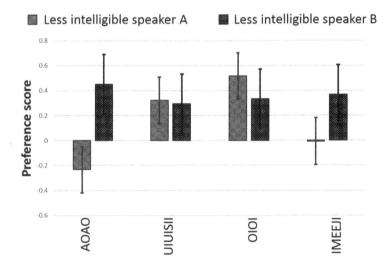

Fig. 7. Preference score of each speeches by the listening test in two less intelligible speakers

5 Conclusion

In this study, we analyzed elderly speeches for intelligibility based on acoustic features. And we improved less intelligible speech by our proposed method. Analysis of the F1 and F2 of more intelligible speech and less intelligible speech showed that the less intelligible vowels except /u/ converge to /u/ when compared to vowels of more intelligible speech. We proposed an envelope shift method to expand the area of the F1-F2 in uniform each vowels. As verification of this shift method, a listening test based on Scheffe's method of paired comparisons was carried out, and the method was effective for less intelligible speech in two elderly speakers with typical less intelligible.

In future works, we will compare to various correction methods, and we will investigate analysis and how to improve of acoustic features of consonants in the elderly speech.

References

1. Miyazaki, T., et al.: Study on auditory impressions of elderly speech. In: Proceeding of ASJ meeting, pp. 427–428 (2008)
2. Yuda, Y., et al.: Investigation on variation of the initial phonemes of Japanese words due to aging. In: ICISIP 2013, pp. 49–52 (2013)
3. Tanaka, Y., et al.: Study of improvement of intelligibility for the elderly speech based on formant frequency shift. Int. J. Comput. Consum. Control 2015 **3**(3), 57–64 (2014)
4. Harada, D., et al.: Analysis of ill-articulated speech by elderly speakers based on temporal transition of amplitude spectrum. In: Proceeding 2010 RISP International Workshop on NCSP, PaperID:40, March 2010
5. Tanaka, Y., et al.: Improvement of speech intelligibility for elderly people based on formant frequency shift. In: Proceeding NCSP 2016, pp. 343–346 (2016)

Text Classification in the Domain of Applied Linguistics as Part of a Pre-editing Module for Machine Translation Systems

Ksenia Oskina[✉]

Institute of Applied and Mathematical Linguistics,
Moscow State Linguistic University, Moscow, Russia
ksenia.oskina@gmail.com

Abstract. This article describes the method of document classification on the basis of a vector space model with regard to the domain of Applied Linguistics for Russian. This method makes it possible to classify input text data in two different categories: applied linguistics texts (AL) and non-applied linguistics texts (nonAL). The proposed method is implemented using the statistical measure of TF-IDF and the evaluation measure of cosine similarity. The study gives promising results and opens up further prospects for the application of this approach to text classification in other languages.

Keywords: Machine translation (MT) · Automatic pre-editing · Domain adaptation · Document classification · TF-IDF term weighting · Vector space model · Cosine similarity

1 Introduction

Present-day machine translation systems are far from being perfect as they provide unsatisfactory results while translating scientific and technical texts. As a rule, the reason for that is the lack of adjustment to a domain (in particular, this article deals with the domain of applied linguistics). It is possible to demonstrate the necessity to improve the semantic component of modern MT systems on the example of translation of a few sentences from the book in applied linguistics [8] performed by the Google translate system [5] (Fig. 1). The highlighted words are the ones which have not been translated by the system correctly, namely (in order of appearance): prosody, prosodeme, prosodics, prosodemics, semiologically, spoken speech, main stress, intonational invariants (II), marked, stressed, post-tonic.

One of the means to acquire the appropriate system settings in a domain and to produce high quality relevant translation is to embed modules of pre- and post-editing and to use a context-based multilingual terminological dictionary [9].

This article presents a domain determination algorithm, as part of the pre-editing module, which reveals whether an input text belongs to the domain of applied linguistics or not (Fig. 2).

© Springer International Publishing Switzerland 2016
A. Ronzhin et al. (Eds.): SPECOM 2016, LNAI 9811, pp. 691–698, 2016.
DOI: 10.1007/978-3-319-43958-7_84

This algorithm was first described in [3] and has already proved its effectiveness, for instance, in [12] where, however, cosine similarity was substituted by the Naïve Bayes classifier. Similar TF-IDF term weighting approaches have been also used in [1,6,13].

Fig. 1. Example of sentences translation in the domain of applied linguistics

The algorithm, which has been implemented for the domain of applied linguistics, can be equally well adapted for any other highly specialized domain either in order to improve machine translation or for the purposes of information retrieval.

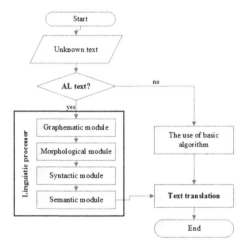

Fig. 2. Pre-editing module for a machine translation system adapted to the domain of applied linguistics

2   Algorithm Implementation

The study has been carried out in 4 steps. The general flowchart is shown in Fig. 3.

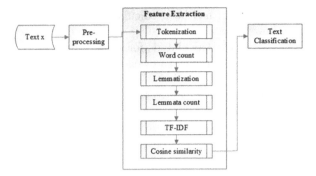

Fig. 3. Unknown text classification flowchart

Step 1. Preparatory Work. At the beginning a list of lemmas and wordforms in the domain of applied linguistics was composed in order to carry out the procedure of lemmatization. This list was formed on the basis of the list of wordforms of the Russian language, taken from [2]. After that by using the script written in Perl [11] a list of terms (which were absent from the list of Russian wordforms) has been retrieved from the book of R.K. Potapova "Speech: communication, information, cybernetics" [8]. These terms have been combined with the above-mentioned list and the resulting list totaled 2,390,327 wordforms. Thus, a list of wordforms from the domain of applied linguistics has been obtained, on the basis of which a list of lemmas and wordforms in the domain of AL has been formed (totaled 1.181 lemmas) and combined with the list of lemmas and wordforms of the Russian language (86.336 lemmas). The overall number of the resulting list made up 87.517 lemmas.

Step 2. The Formation of the Training Sample. On the next step a training sample was formed. It comprised 100 articles, half of which referred to the subject domain of applied linguistics (AL), the other half did not refer to it respectively (nonAL). The articles in the domain of applied linguistics have been taken from journals "Speech technology" [10] and "Computational Linguistics and Intellectual Technologies" [4] of the years 2014–2015. The overall volume of the articles totaled 147.408 tokens (the average volume of an article equaled 2.948 words). Similarly to the AL corpus, the corpus of out-of-domain articles was formed from articles from [7] of the year 2015 and totaled 151.186 tokens (the average volume of an article made up 550 words). The training sample included not only news articles, but also texts on such topics as information technology, economics and a few others in order to create a most representative original sample.

Common stop words, which included prepositions and conjunctions, were removed. After that every article has been processed by the script in Perl: tokenization has been carried out, total amount of terms in every article has been estimated, the procedure of lemmatization has been conducted and the number of uses of every term has been calculated as well. Thus, the obtained data appeared as follows (Fig. 4).

Then TF-IDF has been calculated for every term [3]. TF-IDF is a statistical measure which determines the weight of each element of the formed term-document matrix. A term is selected from every document; its weight is calculated on the basis of the frequency of its occurrence in the document (i.e. its incidence). This statistical measure makes it possible to reduce the weight of terms which occur too often and to increase the weight of less common words.

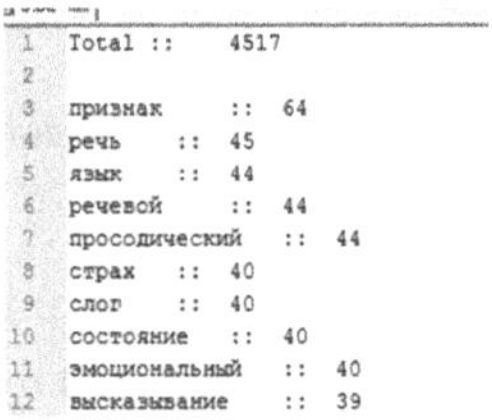

```
1  Total ::     4517
2
3  признак      ::  64
4  речь     ::  45
5  язык     ::  44
6  речевой      ::  44
7  просодический    ::  44
8  страх    ::  40
9  слог     ::  40
10 состояние    ::  40
11 эмоциональный    ::  40
12 высказывание     ::  39
```

Fig. 4. Result of processing an article in applied linguistics

First, TF for each term in every document is calculated separately. TF (term frequency) is the ratio of the number of occurrences of a word to the total number of words in a document. TF is calculated as follows:

$$tf(t, d) = \frac{n_i}{\sum_k n_k}, \tag{1}$$

where t is a term; d is a document; n_i is a number of occurrences of a term in a document; $\sum_k n_k$ is the total number of terms in a document.

TF estimates the importance of the term t_i within a single document. The first ten words for the AL and nonAL corpora are presented in Table 1.

The high TF values for the words "nut" and "fancy" obtained during this study can be preconditioned by the fact that one of the texts in the AL corpus was dedicated to the study of the semantic field of "nut", while another one concerned the concept of "fancy" words. As a result, the program has revealed the high frequency of these terms within a single document and, therefore, it was concluded that these terms belonged to the field of applied linguistics. However, since these words do not reflect the sense of applied linguistics, an expert decided to remove them from the resulting list.

Further on IDF was calculated for every term which made it possible to reduce the number of common words. IDF (inverse document frequency) is the inversion of frequency, with which some word can occur in the document collection. IDF was calculated using the following equation:

$$idf(t, D) = \log \frac{|D|}{|d_i \supset t_i|}, \tag{2}$$

where $|D|$ is the number of documents in the corpus; $|(d_i \supset t_i)|$ is the number of documents where t_i occurs (when $n_i \neq 0$). The selection of the logarithm base in the equation is of no importance, since the change in the base leads to a change in the weight of each word by a constant multiplier that does not affect the balance ratio. Unlike TF, IDF is calculated not for one particular document, but for the corpus in total. The lowest IDF was obtained for words which occurred in every article of the corpus: $be, whole, which, can, he, such, result$ (IDF equalled 0).

Table 1. TF highest value for AL and nonAL corpora

TF (AL)		TF (nonAL)	
verb	0,0692607	he	0,0573770
come	0,0559297	be	0,0402298
sentence	0,0535117	year	0,0370370
nut	0,0467047	vulnerability	0,0355329
word	0,0435075	first	0,0350877
validity	0,0429216	city	0,0344827
fancy	0,0404721	saint	0,0324675
vector	0,0384615	loan	0,0310880

Thus, the measure of TF-IDF is the multiplication of two multipliers:

$$tf{-}idf(t, d, D) = tf(t, d) \times idf(t, D). \tag{3}$$

The largest TF-IDF weight will be obtained by words with high frequency within a particular document and with low frequency of use in other documents. TF-IDF values are deducted for each term in every document separately. Then the obtained values are being normalized (mathematical expectation is counted for the TF-IDF value for every term) for both AL and nonAL validation sets. Table 2 shows 8 most frequently used terms considering TF-IDF weighting.

During the second step two term-document matrices were obtained, in other words two one-dimension arrays, from which two resulting vectors were formed: vector A for the AL corpus (volume = 7561 terms) and vector B for the nonAL corpus (volume = 10488 terms). These values are the reference, on the basis of which the program will make a decision on text classification.

Step 3. The Formation of the Test Sample. In order to form a test sample, a corpus of 200 articles has been collected. 100 articles belonged to the domain of applied linguistics, totaling 388.728 tokens, and the other 100 articles were not on applied linguistics, their total volume made up 128.375 tokens. Articles on applied linguistics have also been collected from "Speech Technology" and "Computational linguistics and intellectual technologies" journals. The nonAL validation set has been collected from [7] as well.

Table 2. 8 most frequently used terms for AL and nonAL corpora

TF-IDF (AL)		TF-IDF (nonAL)	
validity	0,0729226	vulnerability	0,0603694
tongue-twister	0,0548995	saint	0,0551613
invalidity	0,0524531	loan	0,0528177
soundlet (n)	0,0524079	fighter	0,0447097
graph (adj)	0,0512747	flag	0,0447097
recurrent	0,0309804	wolf	0,0434043
introduction	0,0298186	refugee	0,0409390
annotation	0,0294429	hemp	0,0399757

Step 4. Application Development for Test Sample Estimation. During the research an application in Visual Studio 2013 in C++ programming language was developed targeted at unknown text classification. The input to the program is text x. With the help of a Perl script the lemmatization procedure is carried out during which the program determines terms and calculates their number. Then TF-IDF is counted for every term. Upon that the IDF parameter is taken from the classifying samples.

Thus, during the processing of the unknown text two vectors are being obtained: vector C (with the IDF parameter calculated for AL) and vector D (with the IDF parameter calculated for nonAL). After that the cosine similarity between the two resulting vectors and the AL-nonAL vectors is calculated respectively. Cosine similarity is a measure of similarity between two vectors of a pre-Hilbertian space which is used for measuring the cosine of the angle between the two vectors [3]. Actually, cosine similarity reflects the correlation coefficient between the two vectors. If one has two feature vectors (A and B), then cosine similarity $\cos\theta$ can be represented using the scalar product and the norm function:

$$similarity = \cos\theta = \frac{\mathbf{A} \times \mathbf{B}}{||\mathbf{A}||\,||\mathbf{B}||} = \frac{\sum_{i=1}^{n} A_i \times B_i}{\sqrt{\sum_{i=1}^{n}(A_i)^2} \times \sqrt{\sum_{i=1}^{n}(B_i)^2}}. \qquad (4)$$

Next, the obtained vectors C and D are compared to the two reference vectors A and B, which have been pre-determined statistically. Then the cosine similarity between the vectors A and C and B and D is counted. Finally, the decision is taken depending on which vector (A or B) the derived one is closer to. Cosine similarity of two documents varies from 0 to 1 because the frequency of a term (or TF-IDF weight) cannot be negative. Thus, the decision about the classification of the unknown text to this or that category (domain) is made up for the vector, whose cosine similarity turned out to be closer to value 1. An example of AL text classification can be seen in Table 3.

Table 3. Example of text classification in the domain of applied linguistics

	processing	grapho-dynamic	homonymic	semantic	investigation	...	$\cos\theta$
AL	0,001475	0,012818	0,000986	0,000911	0,000153	...	**0.66**
article	0,002927	0,013976	0,000776	0,004433	0,000138	...	

	processing	grapho-dynamic	homonymic	semantic	investigation	...	$\cos\theta$
nonAL	0	0	0	0	0,005661	...	**0.33**
article	0	0	0	0	0,001827	...	

3 Results and Research Perspectives

The percentage of correctly classified texts equals 90 % (it should be noted that the difference between the cosine similarity values is not very large: for one text, for example, the cosine similarity for AL made up 0.62074 and for nonAL 0.606344; for another AL text the cosine similarity equaled 0.625622, for nonAL 0.587069). The cause for the errors in the classification of texts in applied linguistics was an excessive amount of words with negative connotation which related to the semantic fields of war, aggression, and threats, the analysis of which turned out to be the aim of a few articles in the AL validation set. Anyway, the expert opinion corresponds to the results of the program output which indicates the effectiveness of the latter.

Initially the nonAL validation sample was used, the volume of which totaled 16.681 tokens. Further research showed that such a sample was insufficient for obtaining relevant results for the determination of IDF-values. As a consequence, IDF values for such words as, for instance, august, actual, analysis, base, run, input, book, key, kilometer, etc. equaled 1,69897, which led eventually to an error of 24 % in classifying an unknown text. After the validation sample was multiplied by 10 (up to 151 thousand tokens), it enabled one to significantly improve the results (10 % of errors). Moreover, the correlation between the training and the validation sample was marked, that is why, in order for the algorithm to be effective articles with a large number of tokens should be used. The nature of the correlation is planned to be identified in further researches.

This article describes the method of document classification trained on the sample of 100 texts which correctly classifies an input text in the domain of applied linguistics. The method is implemented by Perl and C++ programming languages.

TF-IDF gives good results in terms of weight determination. At the same time it should be borne in mind that texts in applied linguistics may contain different kind of study on semantic fields, whose lexical structure is not typical for the area of applied linguistics in general. Due to the fact that a term may have a high frequency value for one text only, it received an unduly large weight which can skew the results. Therefore, an expert analysis is needed for at least first 20 terms, which have the highest TF values in the training sample.

The above-described approach makes it possible to determine whether a text belongs to the domain of applied linguistics or not. The created application can be integrated as an external module into an MT system and be used as a starting point in determining if a text belongs to some highly specialized domain, which can be further processed by using a list of semantic and grammatical rules typical for any particular domain. These rules can be applied to optimize translation of texts in a given domain.

Acknowledgements. The survey is being carried out with the support of the Russian Foundation for Basic Research in the framework of the project 14-06-00363 at Moscow State Linguistic University (the project is implemented under the supervision of R.K. Potapova).

References

1. Albitar, S., Fournier, S., Espinasse, B.: An effective TF/IDF-based text-to-text semantic similarity measure for text classification. In: Benatallah, B., Bestavros, A., Manolopoulos, Y., Vakali, A., Zhang, Y. (eds.) WISE 2014, Part I. LNCS, vol. 8786, pp. 105–114. Springer, Heidelberg (2014)
2. Arhivy foruma "Govorim po-russki". http://www.speakrus.ru/dict/
3. Manning, C., Raghavan, P., Schtze, H.: An Introduction to Information Retrieval, pp. 109–134. Cambridge University Press, New York (2009)
4. "Computational Linguistics and Intellectual Technologies" journal. http://www.dialog-21.ru/digest/
5. Google Translate. https://translate.google.ru/?hl=ru
6. Kim, H.K., Kim, M.: Model-induced term-weighting schemes for text classification. Appl. Intell. **6**, 1–14 (2016). Springer, New York
7. Lenta.ru. https://lenta.ru/
8. Potapova, R.K.: Rech: kommunikatsiya, informatsiya, kibernetika. Knizhnyiy dom "Librokom", Moskva (2010). (in Russ.)
9. Potapova, R., Oskina, K.: Semantic multilingual differences of terminological definitions regarding the concept "Artificial Intelligence". In: Ronzhin, A., Potapova, R., Fakotakis, N. (eds.) SPECOM 2015. LNCS, vol. 9319, pp. 356–363. Springer, Heidelberg (2015)
10. "Speech Technology" journal. http://speechtechnology.ru/
11. The Perl Programming Language. https://www.perl.org/
12. Yoo, J.Y., Yang, D.: Classification scheme of unstructured text document using TF-IDF and naive bayes classifier. In: COMCOMS 2015. ASTL, vol. 111, pp. 263–266. SERSC, Tasmania (2015)
13. Yun-tao, Z., Ling, G., Yong-cheng, W.: An improved TF-IDF approach for text classification. J. Zhejilang Univ. SCI. **6**(1), 49–55 (2005). Springer, Zhejilang

Tonal Specification of Perceptually Prominent Non-nuclear Pitch Accents in Russian

Nina Volskaya and Tatiana Kachkovskaia[(⊠)]

Saint Petersburg State University, 7/9 Universitetskaya nab.,
St. Petersburg 199034, Russia
{volni,kachkovskaia}@phonetics.pu.ru

Abstract. The paper deals with tonal characteristics of perceptually prominent prosodic words in the pre-nuclear part of the intonational phrase. The research is based on a 20 h part of the annotated Russian speech corpus CORPRES. Non-nuclear prominent words are grouped according to the direction of pitch movement on the stressed syllable. It is shown that the pitch accent shape on these words is highly correlated with the type of pitch movement on the nucleus. Most often, falling pre-nuclear accents occur with the rising nucleus, and rising—with the falling nucleus. Emotional or highly individual speech may contain more complex pitch movements in the pre-nuclear part (e.g. fall-rise), or a sequence of prominent words with the same pattern.

Keywords: Intonation · Russian · Non-nuclear pitch accent · Pitch accent shape · Prominence

1 Introduction

In Russian the accented syllable in a phrase is normally a stressed syllable, but it is not exclusively the nuclear stressed syllable. Pitch accents normally coincide with lexically stressed syllables, and their particular pitch shape depends on the utterance type—declarative or interrogative, and on the degree of its expressivity.

In neutral final declaratives accents form a series of H*L accent shapes superimposed on the declination line. In non-final units (grammatically dependent phrases or clauses) both pitch accents and declination are much less prominent and often absent; in the latter case, which is also observed in interrogatives (yes-no questions), F_0 declination may be absent, which imposes certain limitations on the use of declination reset as a means for gaining prominence, and lexically stressed syllables are made prominent by other prosodic means—intensity and vowel duration, rather than pitch: they are stressed, but unaccented [1].

Nuclear pitch accent is the principal accent of the intonational phrase which performs delimitative, sentence-forming and distinctive function. Other accents do not have such properties: an additional pitch accent on a particular word may convey emphasis or contrast, and it may be present in the intonational phrase along with the nuclear accent [2]. At the same time, in expressive speech every

© Springer International Publishing Switzerland 2016
A. Ronzhin et al. (Eds.): SPECOM 2016, LNAI 9811, pp. 699–705, 2016.
DOI: 10.1007/978-3-319-43958-7_85

word in the intonational phrase may be accented, and this prominence "cannot be described as the contrast between the word carrying the principal (nuclear) pitch accent and the rest, equally accented words" [3].

Since tonal patterns of the accented words vary, they require specification and adequate description, particularly when they add to the expressivity of the utterance and speech in general. Intonation descriptions based on nuclear pitch accents only are not sufficient and adequate.

Thus, in the focus of this study are those prosodic words which are perceptually prominent but do not carry nuclear accent. In order to obtain a tonal specification of such words, we investigate the direction of pitch movement within their stressed syllables.

2   Material

This study is based on the Corpus of Professionally Read Speech (CORPRES) [4] for Russian, containing texts of different speaking styles recorded from 4 male and 4 female speakers. Its total size is 60 h of recorded speech, 50 % of which has been manually segmented into phrases, words and sounds, and fully annotated on the phonetic and prosodic levels. For our analysis we have chosen a 20 h part of this corpus—the recordings from 4 speakers, 2 males (A, M) and 2 females (C, K).

Prosodic information includes pitch movement type in the intonation center, type of pauses, and additional prominence. Each utterance is segmented into intonational phrases (IPs). For each IP, the lexical word carrying a nuclear pitch accent is marked, and the melodic type is assigned based on perceptual and acoustical data, according to the system proposed by Volskaya in [5]. The system is a revision and extension of the well-known Bryzgunova system of intonation constructions (ICs) [6], [7, pp. 90–92].

If the IP contained more than one perceptually prominent word, such additional prominence was marked using the special symbol, [+], before the lexical word. E.g.[1]:

 - у [+]любого из этих [11]людей /p3/ мог быть спасительный [01a]вариант /p5/ ([+]any of these [11]people /pause/ could have a saving [01a]opportunity /pause/)
 - но почему-то [+]моего [11b]мужа /p3/ я люблю [01a]больше /p5/ (but somehow [+]my [11b]husband /pause/ I love [01a]more /pause/)
 - а меня это не [10]волнует /p4/ потому что я живу [+]творческой [01c]жизнью /p5/ (this does not [10]bother me /pause/ since I am living a [+]creative [01c]life /pause/)

During the annotation of the corpus, we used the following criteria in defining a perceptually prominent word in the IP: (1) it should "stand out" from the tonal

---

[1] In these examples, model 11 has a rise-fall nuclear accent used in non-final IPs, 11b—its intensified version; 01a is a low fall used utterance-finally, 10 is a non-low fall used in non-utterance-final IPs, and 01c—a fall from a high to mid or low level often used to establish contact with the listener.

environment; (2) it should be perceived as "prominent" for there must be reasons either subjective (speaker's decision) or objective, semantic (following from the context or situation) with consequences for general communicative meaning of the utterance [8, p. 5].

The corpus also has a pitch tier in two versions: a manually corrected pitch tier with labels on the voiced segments only; a pitch tier with F_0 values on voiceless segments as well, calculated by means of linear approximation, and with microprosody automatically removed.

3 Method

Based on the information about stress on the segmental tier, each utterance was automatically segmented into prosodic words'(PW).[2] Then the boundaries of perceptually prominent pre-nuclear prosodic words and their stressed syllables were retrieved automatically using specially written Python scripts.

For each prominent prosodic word, F_0 values were extracted from the pitch tier within the boundaries of its stressed syllable; the pitch tier used here has labels on both voiced and voiceless segments (see Material). The array of F_0 values was split into rising, falling and level intervals. Within this procedure, the following principles were used: (a) an interval was considered level if the pitch range did not exceed 1 semitone; (b) intervals shorter than 50 ms and smaller than 1 semitone were joined to an adjacent interval; (c) two or more successive intervals with the same direction of pitch movement were joined together.

Thus, for each prosodic word's stressed syllable a stylization of its pitch contour was obtained, e.g. "R" (rising), "RF" (rising-falling), "FRL" (falling-rising-level) etc. For the purposes of this study, level parts were ignored, and the stylization was further simplified, e.g.: "FRL" → "FR".

Prosodic words beginning the intonational phrases were excluded from the analysis due to the phenomenon of initial rise (declination reset) observed frequently in Russian.

Perceptually prominent pre-nuclear prosodic words were grouped according to the melodic type on the *nucleus*: rising vs. falling. The rising nuclei included melodic types which correspond to IC-3, IC-4 and IC-6 in Bryzgunova system [6], and their variants. The falling nuclei included melodic types corresponding to IC-1 and IC-2 in Bryzgunova system, and their variants. (For a detailed description of the prosodic system used in the corpus, see [5].)

4 Results

Tables 1 and 2 show the frequency of falling, rising, falling-rising and rising-falling pitch accent shapes within the stressed syllables of perceptually prominent non-nuclear prosodic words. Table 1 pertains to intonational phrases with

---

[2] We use the term "a prosodic word" in its traditional sense for a content word and its clitics, which include all items that in a particular intonation unit, a phrase or an utterance, lose their lexical stress and thus form one rhythmic unit with a "properly" stressed word.

rising nuclei, Table 2—to intonational phrases with falling nuclei. For simple, unidirectional shapes (rising or falling) mean pitch range of the pitch movement in semitones is provided.

Pitch accent shapes other than those specified in these tables also occurred in the material, but with lower frequencies. They are level tone and falling-rising-falling shape. The presence of level tone on a prominent word implies that tonal changes on the stressed syllable is not the only way of conveying prominence. The cases of falling-rising-falling contours may be further classified according to the prevailing movement, but this requires larger datasets; so far this is still to be investigated.

4.1 Prominence in IPs with Rising vs. Falling Nuclei

Our data reveals the following differences between the pitch contours of prominent prosodic words in IPs with rising and falling nuclei.

For most speakers, a *rise* on the prominent prosodic word occurs mostly in IPs with a *falling* nucleus. A *fall*, on the other hand, is more typical for IPs with a *rising* nucleus. However, the mean intervals (in semitones) of these falls and rises do not differ between the two types of IPs (see Tables 1 and 2).

Rising-falling shapes are observed on prominent prosodic words in IPs with both rising and falling nuclei, being more frequent in the former group. Data on the median difference between the rising and the falling parts of this contour are presented in Table 3. If the value is positive, the rising part prevails, meaning the contour often resembles IC-3 in Bryzgunova notation; a negative value means that the falling part is prevalent, resembling the shape of IC-2 in Bryzgunova notation. As it follows from Table 3, (1) in IPs with a rising nucleus the *falling* part predominates, while (2) in IPs with a falling nucleus the *rising* part outweighs. However, this seems to be speaker-specific—see data for speaker C (Table 3).

Falling-rising shapes occur mostly in IPs with a falling nucleus. In both types of IPs, the rising part is much larger in range (see Table 4), meaning that these shapes resemble IC-4 in Bryzgunova notation—a model which is often associated with negative connotations.

5   Discussion

Speech expressivity adds to the variety of pitch accent shapes. Previous observations over realizations of perceptually prominent syllables in CORPRESS in terms of their deviations from the declination line, revealed several principal tonal patterns for gaining prominence for syllables other than the one carrying the nuclear pitch accent [9]:

1. upstep from the declination line;
2. downstep from the declination line.

Table 1. Frequency of pitch accent shapes on the stressed syllables of perceptually prominent non-nuclear prosodic words in IPs with *rising* nucleus. Mean pitch range is given in semitones, and for simple contours only. For each speaker, sample size is provided.

		Pitch movement			
		Fall	Fall-rise	Rise	Rise-fall
Speaker C, n = 163	Frequency	47%	4%	9%	33%
	Mean pitch range	7.8		5.2	
Speaker K, n = 143	Frequency	46%	2%	17%	28%
	Mean pitch range	7.1		6.5	
Speaker A, n = 230	Frequency	38%	4%	11%	35%
	Mean pitch range	7.0		5.4	
Speaker M, n = 121	Frequency	23%	2%	36%	31%
	Mean pitch range	4.0		4.5	

Table 2. Frequency of pitch accent shapes on the stressed syllables of perceptually prominent non-nuclear prosodic words in IPs with *falling* nucleus. Mean pitch range is given in semitones, and for simple contours only. For each speaker, sample size is provided.

		Pitch movement			
		Fall	Fall-rise	Rise	Rise-fall
Speaker C, n = 163	Frequency	39%	12%	28%	18%
	Mean pitch range	7.9		5.9	
Speaker K, n = 199	Frequency	21%	13%	44%	18%
	Mean pitch range	7.5		7.0	
Speaker A, n = 368	Frequency	27%	11%	27%	24%
	Mean pitch range	6.9		6.4	
Speaker M, n = 268	Frequency	10%	7%	50%	25%
	Mean pitch range	4.3		4.5	

Table 3. Median difference between the rising and falling parts of *rising-falling* pitch accent shapes on perceptually prominent non-nuclear prosodic words (in semitones).

		Speaker C	Speaker K	Speaker A	Speaker M
Type of nucleus in the IP	Rising	−2.48	−0.46	−1.31	0.48
	Falling	−2.8	1.12	0.58	1.78

Table 4. Median difference between the rising and falling parts of *falling-rising* pitch accent shapes on perceptually prominent non-nuclear prosodic words (in semitones).

		Speaker C	Speaker K	Speaker A	Speaker M
Type of nucleus in the IP	Rising	5.09	4.09	3.76	3.22
	Falling	2.69	4.73	3.22	2.76

The results of the present study add more data to the types of pitch shapes of perceptually prominent words. When a word in the pre-nuclear part receives prominence, its tonal pattern can take several forms:

1. falling tone;
2. rising tone;
3. rising-falling tone;
4. falling-rising tone.

All of these kinetic tones are copies of the most frequent nuclear accents: the (high) fall is normally used for logical and emphatic nuclear accent, the rising tone is one of the nuclear tones for non-finality along with most frequent rising-falling tone which is used in general questions as well, the falling-rising tone is observed in non-final intonational phrases and often used to convey negative attitude.

The rising accent type is correlated with the falling nuclear tone, while the second, falling accent regularly appears when the intonational phrase ends in the rising nuclear tone. The rise-fall is observed more often in intonational phrases with the falling nuclear tone.

There are examples of less frequent combination of the pitch accent shapes with the type of the nucleus. Falling-rising shape is used mostly in intonational phrases with the falling nucleus. Level tone, although rather rare, is observed in cases where other parameters must be working to convey prominence.

In general, the localization of these pitch accents is predictable, since a number of words in Russian, like lexical intensifiers for example, are known to attract prominence. In expressive speech the situation changes. At the speaker's will, any word and even all words in the phrase can receive prominence. This is why a detailed specification of pitch accent shapes for perceptually prominent prosodic words is needed for the purposes of both automatic speech recognition and speech synthesis—in order to process and generate speech signal with a high degree of naturalness.

Acknowledgments. The research is supported by Saint Petersburg State University (grant 31.37.353.2015).

References

1. Kocharov, D., Volskaya, N., Skrelin, P.: F0 declination in Russian revisited. In: The Scottish Consortium for ICPhS 2015 (ed.) Proceedings of the 18th International Congress of Phonetic Sciences, pp. 293.1–293.5. The University of Glasgow, Glasgow (2015)
2. Ode, C.: Transcription of Russian intonation, ToRI, an interactive research tool and learning module on the internet. In: Houtzagers, H.P., Kalsbeek, J., Schaeken, J. (eds.) Dutch Contributions to the Fourteenth International Congress of Slavists, Netherlands, pp. 431–450 (2008)
3. Krivnova, O.F.: On the accentual function of melody in Russian [Ob akcentnoj funkcii melodiki (na materiale russkogo jazyka)]. In Intonation [Intonacija], pp. 119–143. Visha Shkola, Kiev (1978)
4. Skrelin, P., Volskaya, N., Kocharov, D., Evgrafova, K., Glotova, O., Evdokimova, V.: CORPRES. In: Sojka, P., Horák, A., Kopeček, I., Pala, K. (eds.) TSD 2010. LNCS, vol. 6231, pp. 392–399. Springer, Heidelberg (2010)
5. Volskaya, N.B., Skrelin, P.A.: Prosodic model for Russian. In: Proceedings of Nordic Prosody X, Helsinki, pp. 249–260 (2009). Frankfurt am Main: Peter Lang
6. Bryzgunova, E.A.: Intonation. In: Shvedova, N. (ed.) Russian Grammar, vol. 2, pp. 96–122. Nauka, Moscow (1980)
7. Cubberley, P.: Russian: A Linguistic Introduction. Cambridge University Press, Cambridge (2002)
8. Nikolaeva, T.M.: Semantics of Accent Allocation [Semantika akcentnogo vydelenija]. Nauka, Moscow (1982)
9. Volskaya, N., Kocharov, D., Skrelin, P., Shumovskaya, E.: Towards automatic detection of various types of prominence in read aloud Russian texts. In: Przepiórkowski, A., Piasecki, M., Jassem, K., Fuglewicz, P. (eds.) Computational Linguistics. SCI, vol. 458, pp. 203–215. Springer, Heidelberg (2013)

Toward Sign Language Motion Capture Dataset Building

Zdeněk Krňoul[1]($\boxtimes$), Pavel Jedlička[2], Jakub Kanis[1], and Miloš Železný[1]

[1] Faculty of Applied Sciences, NTIS - New Technologies for the Information Society,
University of West Bohemia, Univerzitní 8, 306 14 Pilsen, Czech Republic
{zdkrnoul,jkanis,zelezny}@ntis.zcu.cz
[2] Faculty of Applied Sciences, Department of Cybernetics,
University of West Bohemia, Univerzitní 8, 306 14 Pilsen, Czech Republic
jedlicka@kky.zcu.cz

Abstract. The article deals with a recording procedure for motion dataset building mainly for sign language synthesis systems. Data gloves and two types of optical motion capture techniques are considered such as one source of sign language speech data for advanced training of more natural and acceptable body movements of signing avatars. A summary of the state-of-the-art technologies provides an overview of possibilities, and even limiting factors in relation to the sign language recording. The combination of the motion capture technologies overcomes the existing difficulties of such a complex task of recording both manual and non-manual component of the sign language. A result is the recording procedure for simultaneous motion capture of signing subject towards further research yet unexplored phenomenon of sign language production by a human.

Keywords: Corpus building · Sign language · Motion capture

1 Introduction

In these days sign language (SL) translation or TV broadcast is provided by humans. SL synthesis is considered as supplementary communication means of the deaf individuals. One perspective technique is virtual 3D character animation in the form of the signing avatar [5]. However, there is still poor realism of the character animation compared to the standard video of the signing subject causing overall rejection of the signing avatars by the deaf community.

One reason for the rejection is that artificial signing avatars are not able to sign fluently and naturally and, therefore, it is difficult or uncomfortable to understand them. Integration of high-quality motion capture data is essential for any further research and gives certain assumptions to provide accessible SL synthesis [4]. The full body motion capture (mocap) including hand, finger, facial expression, and eye gaze movements may provide spatial-temporally synchronous records of all the channels [2].

© Springer International Publishing Switzerland 2016
A. Ronzhin et al. (Eds.): SPECOM 2016, LNAI 9811, pp. 706–713, 2016.
DOI: 10.1007/978-3-319-43958-7_86

There are different approaches using different technology for body mocap [3]. These approaches are optical, gyroscopic, mechanical, etc. and designed for mocap of different body parts. There are more specialized techniques based on markers fixed on speaker's face or marker-less techniques tracing the face by image processing gray, color and/or depth data[1]. The optical mocap systems are based on special cameras to track active or passive markers in 3D space (e.g. VICON, VICON Cara[2], Qualisys, OptiTrack, Optotrak). Whilst data processing provided by the VICON and VICON Cara systems are very beneficial for SL corpora building, there is a limited functionality of tools for CyberGlove3[3] data glove [6] using for precise finger mocap. The both facial and body capturing by one mocap system may result in noisy positions of the facial markers. Moreover, simultaneous capturing of the body, fingers, and facial data at high-frequency rates cause technical difficulties.

In the paper, we present SL recording procedure allowing the simultaneous body, finger, and facial mocap; flexible setting of the data parameter; spatial-temporally synchronous record; the data glove calibration; and mocap data interpretation by the 3D character model.

2   Combined SL Motion Capturing Method

We consider three mocap systems for the SL data acquisition task: VICON, VICON Cara, and CyberGlove3. The VICON and VICON Cara systems are a marker-based optical system. The optical capture principle was chosen because the signing subject is not wearing any special suit that limits his or her natural movement and the marker-based principle was chosen for its higher precision compared to non-marker approaches. Two CyberGlove3 data gloves provide robust finger mocap using bent sensor principle.

2.1   Body Motion Capturing

In our case, the VICON motion capture system consists of eight T-series cameras measuring a motion of passive spherical retroreflective markers in the infrared spectrum. The T-20 is a high-frequency camera with 2 Mpx resolution and is capable of frame rate 1200 fps (690 fps in full resolution). The system includes also VICON Blade software used for a camera set-up, calibration, and motion capturing itself. There are some limiting factors in consequence of the capturing principles and recording of complex body movement.

The main limiting factor is the tracking of the finger movements. Since the finger markers are close to each other, there is a significant number of overlapping situations (frames with marker swaps), especially the hand contacts have to be resolved during data post-processing. Moreover, such mocap setup requires at least 30 additional finger markers. We observed also negative effects of fixation

---

[1] www.faceshift.com.

[2] https://www.vicon.com/products/camera-systems/cara.

[3] http://www.cyberglovesystems.com/cyberglove-iii/.

Fig. 1. The marker setups for the optical mocap systems. On the left: body mocap consisting of 53 14 mm retroreflective markers for the VICON system, on the right: 54 black passive markers for the VICON Cara system.

of the finger markers when they were not rigid to the particular finger segment during its bending. It causes an inaccuracy in the identification of the skeleton model internally used by the VICON system. On the other hand, there are unwanted losses of the finger markers attached directly to the skin caused by frequent touches of the hands during the signing. We have observed also the higher motion speed of the finger markers mainly for fingertips, which requires higher camera frame rate compared to capturing remaining body parts.

According to our experience, a standard set of 53 passive 14 mm markers fixed on the body of the signing subject is optimal to capture a head, shoulders, arms and wrist including hand/body contacts. The consider marker setup contains 10 markers on each arm and 15 markers on the torso and head providing mocap of any general movement of the whole upper body, see Fig. 1 on the left.

2.2   Hand Motion Capturing

The CyberGlove3 data glove is based on the resistive sensors of finger bending that provide robust measurements of hand shape especially during finger contacts on one or mutually between hands, see Fig. 2. In addition, the data glove measures also palm flex and wrist rotation like pitch and yaw. On the other hand, the reading of one sensor is relative to the preceding finger segment or the wrist and thus does not capture absolute 3D position.

The calibration is needed to found the conversion relationship between the sensor raw data and the actual finger bending. The manual calibration controlled by a protocol is a preferred option for SL mocap corpus building [8]. However, once identified calibration parameters does not provide precise conversion of hand shapes after re-dressing of the gloves by the same subject. This data inconsistency must be taking into account while creating of the SL mocap corpora. The standard CyberGlove3 tool enables the calibration only for common simple hand shapes. The very laborious and time-consuming process is calibration of the thumb touch with the rest of fingers. But the thumb-pinky finger touch was not achieved anyway. There are, moreover, also reported problems of glove sensor cross-coupling [9].

2.3   Facial Motion Capturing

The VICON Cara is a motion capture system considered for the marker-based facial motion capturing. The system consists of a headgear (HeadRig) with four cameras, a processing unit, a storage device, and a battery pack, see Fig. 1 on the right. An integral part is the operating and the post-processing software tool enabling calibration, triggering the Cara device and 3D reconstruction. The HeadRig is equipped with four 720p HD high-speed cameras with the framerate up to 60 fps. It is possible to natively synchronize time-code with the VICON system. Constant light conditions are provided by a custom designed controllable rig of four lights. The cameras have 3 mm F2.0 IR filtered lens. Noise caused by the T-series camera strobes is reduced by the IR filtered lens. The storage device has a recording capacity of 64 GB and two hours battery time.

The markers can be placed on the subject's face in the form of glued circles, drawn by an ink marker, or drawn by a make-up. White or black passive facial markers can be used. The certain positions of the marker are not required and there is also no default SL facial marker set. For example, the MPEG4 standard defines 53 markers as the set of Facial Feature Points, in the SignCom project, there were 41 markers used for mocap of the French SL [1] and the set of 60 markers was used in the Sign3D project [7]. The software tool detects these markers in the record as circular blobs and then finds it's centroids. After that, the 3-D position of each centroid is computed and the set of $(x, y$ and $z)$ positions over time forms the facial mocap data.

2.4   Combining Optical and Data Glove Recording

It is necessary to determine which body parts will be included in the motion capture data. There is a defined connection of the body mocap and the hand mocap and a connection of the body mocap and the facial mocap. The first option for the hand and body mocap connection is to use a mapping of the wrist pitch and jaw sensor to the target model and the VICON system determines only the wrist position and the forearm twist. The preferred option is tracking a full/global wrist rotation by the VICON system and only fingers and palm flex by the data glove. In this case, at least two optical markers on the back of the hand have to be added to the two markers placed on the wrist joint, see Fig. 2. The connection body part of the body mocap and the facial mocap is subjects head. The global position of the head is tracked by the VICON system through the HeadRig of the Cara system and the facial mocap data are relative to the transformation.

2.5   Character Model

The objective of the mocap data for SL synthesis is its proper interpretation by the 3D model. We assume 3D character model created by Autodesk character generator[4], see Fig. 3 on the right. The model overcomes a limitation of the

---

[4] Available at https://charactergenerator.autodesk.com/.

built-in hand model internally used by the CyberGlove3 tool. In addition, the model is appropriate also for the body and the facial mocap data.

The model includes the standard three bones per finger, moreover, index and pinky metacarpal bone, and 21 auxiliary bones of the facial rig. There is a support for the characterization of the body mocap data and it also allows the animation retargeting to the different body proportions (SL speaker/model). The standard skinning method is based on a weighted transformation of each bone and affects vertices of the surface mesh.

The bone-ends of the facial rig are fixed to predefined 3D positions in the model mesh surface. In general, the positions differ from the positions of chosen facial marker set. We consider manual retargeting of the facial mocap data to the character's face. For this purpose *position constraints* were defined by the professional 3D character animation software Autodesk MotionBuilder (MB). One constraint defines the affected bone-end as a constrained object and one or more of the facial markers as source objects. As a result, all the facial markers are transformed by weighting interpolation to the facial rig of the model.

3   SL Recording Procedure

The sign language recording procedure determines suitable steps for feasible and functional simultaneous recording of SL mocap data. The procedure divides the data acquisition to a capturing session and data post-processing.

3.1   Capturing Session

Facial Mocap. First of all, it is necessary to prepare and adjust the VICON Cara system for capturing a particular subject. The position of each camera has to be adjusted and focused on a target part of the subject's face. The next step is a standard calibration of the system. Markers are placed on the subject's face according to the desired model while the HeadRig is removed. After that, the HeadRig is returned on the subject and recording of the range of movement follows.

Hand Mocap. We consider capturing of a raw glove motion data without pre-defined glove calibration. We assume recently developed tools for the control and the communication with the CyberGlove3 gloves [6]. The tools provide an interface for recording with one or two (left and right) gloves at the time and also enables necessary time synchronization between the gloves and the VICON system.

The glove recording session starts by a launching of the above-mentioned tool for the simultaneous recording of both gloves. First, the time-synchronization stamp from the VICON system is set to the gloves. The particular commands for the time set are sent to the gloves at the same time. However, it can be executed by each glove with a slightly different delay depending on the processing unit of each glove. To time-synchronize the data recording we set the same internal time

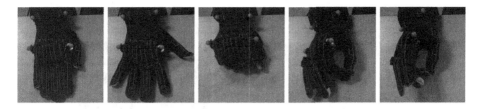

Fig. 2. Calibration take hand shapes.

for both gloves by one command and then start the recording simultaneously with another one command. This procedure allows us to reach the time difference between gloves in a range of a one data frame, i.e. 33.3 ms because there are 30 frames per second. The time difference can be greater and it is recommended to keep the internal time setting until the difference is acceptable. As soon as it is acceptable, we can start the recording.

The first step (and it is beneficial to be the last one too) of the glove recording session is capturing of a calibration take which is essential for the successful glove raw data interpretation. The calibration take consists of five hand shapes: a flat hand, a stretching of all fingers, a fist and two "o" hand shapes, the one with thumb – index touch and the second with thumb – pinky touch respectively, see Fig. 2. The most important feature of the calibration take is to cover the full range of all finger movements. But a researcher can define its own calibration take which better suits his needs. Next, we can launch the standard recording.

Body Mocap. The T-20 cameras are situated and aimed at the captured subject. The camera layout depends on the subject's body proportion and on the complexity (range) of the SL recording material. The next step is the calibration of the system. The markers are placed on the subject according to the body model. Each capturing session starts with the standard recording of the range of movements (ROM).

3.2 Data Post-processing

The data acquired during the session have to be post-processed to get the standard motion capture data. The VICON Cara Post is a software tool used for post-processing data acquired by VICON Cara. The centroids of the markers placed on the subject's face are identified and cleared from an incidental noise. The 3-D reconstruction and the labeling of the final motion capture data are made after that.

The data from T-20 cameras are post-processed in the VICON Blade software tool. The reconstruction of 3-D data is made and necessary manual denoising is needed. The noise can be caused e.g. by body marker occlusions. The labeling of the data and export as the final mocap data follows.

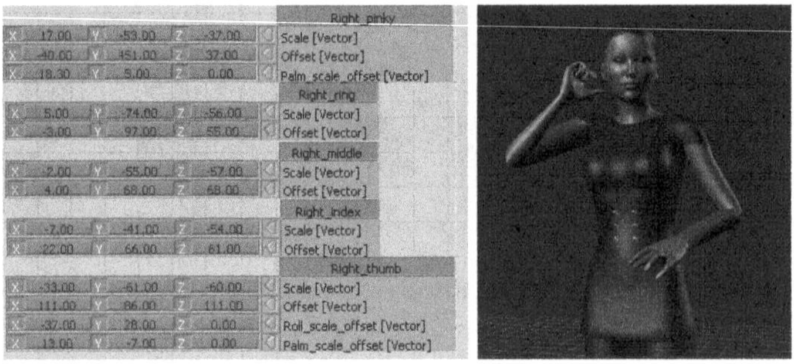

Fig. 3. On the left: right hand manual calibration interface, on the right: the 3D character model.

The glove data post-processing phase allowing interpretation of the raw data and include the glove data calibration. The post-processing starts by the downloading of the recorded data files from the glove internal memory cards (calibration and data takes). The time-corresponding records for the left and right hand are then converted to the XMLTRC format (newly designed XML version of the TRC (Track Row Column[5]) format) and merged to the one corresponding XMLTRC file. An arbitrary XMLTRC file can be anytime later converted to the standard TRC format which is suitable for the processing of the 3D motion data by a standard animation software. The glove data calibration can be done in automatic and/or manual manner. For this purpose, we used the MB with a calibration template integrating the graphical user interface, see Fig. 3. This template allows a manual adjusting of all necessary calibration parameters (all scale and offset linear equation parameters). The TRC file of the merged calibration take is loaded into the MB with the active calibration template. The researcher can then adjust the template parameters until the finger motions of the given 3D model appropriately match the calibration take finger motions. The provided automatic calibration method can be optionally used as a starting point for the manual calibration. To be able to use the automatic calibration tool, the user only needs to identify calibration gesture keyframes in the calibration take by the supplied tool.

4   Conclusion

The recording procedure for motion dataset building is a crucial step to research new methods for the sign language synthesis systems. We combine the data gloves and optical motion capture techniques to collect source data of the sign language. The state-of-the-art technologies VICON, VICON Cara, and Cyber-Glove3 are discussed to summary advantage and also limiting factors in relation to motion capturing of the sign languages. The time-consuming and laborious

---

[5] http://simtk-confluence.stanford.edu:8080/display/OpenSim/ Marker+(.trc)+Files.

calibration of the two gloves is moved from a recording session to the phase of an off-line data post-processing when the presence of the signer is not required. The combination of the motion capture technologies overcomes the existing difficulties of such a complex task. The recording procedure provides instruction for researchers dealing with simultaneous recording both the manual and the non-manual component of the sign language. In this context, further research will be aimed to uncover naturalness of movements provided by the signing human.

Acknowledgments. This work was supported by the project LO1506 of the Czech Ministry of Education, Youth and Sports and by the UWB grant, project No. SGS-2016-039.

References

1. Gibet, S., Courty, N., Duarte, K., Naour, T.L.: The signcom system for data-driven animation of interactive virtual signers: methodology and evaluation. ACM Trans. Interact. Intell. Syst. **1**(1), 6:1–6:23 (2011). http://doi.acm.org/10.1145/2030365.2030371

2. Gibet, S., Lefebvre-Albaret, F., Hamon, L., Brun, R., Turki, A.: Interactive editing in French Sign Language dedicated to virtual signers: requirementsand challenges. Universal Access in the Information Society, September 2015. https://hal.archives-ouvertes.fr/hal-01205742

3. Hasler, N., Rosenhahn, B., Thormahlen, T., Wand, M., Gall, J., Seidel, H.P.: Markerless motion capture with unsynchronized moving cameras. In: Computer Vision and Pattern Recognition, CVPR 2009, pp. 224–231 (2009)

4. Huenerfauth, M., Lu, P., Kacorri, H.: Synthesizing and evaluating animations ofamerican sign language verbs modeled from motion-capture data. In: SLPAT 2015, pp. 22–28. ACL, Dresden (2015). http://www.aclweb.org/anthology/W15-5105

5. Krňoul, Z., Kanis, J., Železný, M., Müller, L.: Czech text-to-sign speech synthesizer. In: Popescu-Belis, A., Renals, S., Bourlard, H. (eds.) MLMI 2007. LNCS, vol. 4892, pp. 180–191. Springer, Heidelberg (2008)

6. Krňoul, Z., Kanis, J., Železný, M., Müller, L.: Semiautomatic data glove calibration for sign language corpora building. In: 7th Workshop on the Representation and Processing of Sign Languages: Corpus Mining, LREC, May 2016, in press

7. Lefebvre-Albaret, F., Gibet, S., Turki, A., Hamon, L., Brun, R.: Overview ofthe Sign3D project high-fidelity 3D recording, indexing and editing of French Sign Language content. In: SLTAT 2013, Chicago, United States (2013). https://hal.archives-ouvertes.fr/hal-00914661

8. Lu, P., Huenerfauth, M.: Accessible motion-capture glove calibration protocolfor recording sign language data from deaf subjects. In: Proceedings of the11th International ACM SIGACCESS Conference on Computers and Accessibility, Assets 2009, pp. 83–90. ACM, New York (2009). http://doi.acm.org/10.1145/1639642.1639658

9. Wang, Y., Neff, M.: Data-driven glove calibration for hand motion capture. In: Proceedings of the 12th ACM SIGGRAPH/Eurographics Symposium on Computer Animation, SCA 2013, pp. 15–24. ACM, New York (2013). http://doi.acm.org/10.1145/2485895.2485901

Trade-Off Between Speed and Accuracy for Noise Variance Minimization (NVM) Pitch Estimation Algorithm

Andrey Barabanov and Aleksandr Melnikov[✉]

Saint Petersburg State University,
Universitetskaya nab., 7/9, Saint Petersburg, Russia
Andrey.Barabanov@gmail.com, melnikov.alex.rus@gmail.com

Abstract. New version of NVM algorithm [3] in case of stationary voice model for precise estimation of the Fundamental frequency on a short time interval is proposed. Its computational complexity is proportional to that of FFT on the same time interval. A precise trade-off between approximation error and numerical speed is established.

Keywords: Frequency estimation · Fast algorithms · Harmonic model

1 Introduction

Precise estimation of the Fundamental frequency is necessary for correct calculation of harmonic amplitudes especially for the high frequency formants. An estimation error causes a multiple error for the high frequency harmonics. Pitch estimation error of 1 sample can completely reject harmonics in the estimated model at the frequency band near 2 kHz.

Such effect can be seen at Fig. 1 that shows a part of spectrum (from 3 to 6.5 kHz) of some voice signal. This signal is first coded and then restored signal is obtained. Here are two cases: the first one corresponds to a precise estimation of Pitch and the second one shows the same computation with 1 Hz error.

The Least Squares approach is successfully implemented for estimation of the complex amplitudes of the harmonic polynomial model of a voiced signal [1,4]. But the Pitch estimation problem remains highly nonlinear with several local minima that can cause a standard multiple frequency error.

A general complexity of the estimation algorithms is proportional to N^2 where N is the window length. Such exhaustive search of admissible Pitch values is too expensive.

The "unbiased criterion" for Pitch estimation was proposed in [2]. Its complexity is proportional to $N \log_2 N$ where N is the frame window length. This criterion is also independent of the additive white noise.

In our previous work [3] the unbiased criterion from [2] for Pitch estimation was generalized to short time intervals. We proposed fast algorithm called Noise Variance Minimization (NVM) for precise estimation of the Fundamental

© Springer International Publishing Switzerland 2016
A. Ronzhin et al. (Eds.): SPECOM 2016, LNAI 9811, pp. 714–721, 2016.
DOI: 10.1007/978-3-319-43958-7_87

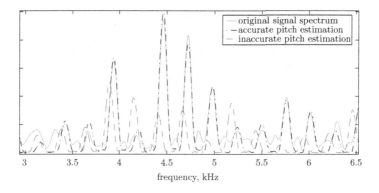

Fig. 1. Effect of pitch determination error

frequency on a short time interval. The new algorithm gives an approximate solution with a complexity of $N \log_2 N$ operations.

In this paper a new generation of the NVM algorithm is proposed. Precise formulation of the trade-off between approximation error and numerical calculation speed is presented.

2   Stationary Model and Cost Function

Let $s = (s_t)_{t=-N/2}^{N/2-1}$ be a voiced signal of the length N. The stationary model of the signal is

$$\widehat{s}_t = \sum_{k=-M}^{M} a_k e^{\frac{2\pi i}{N} F k t} + v_t, \qquad -N/2 \leq t \leq N/2 - 1,$$

where P is the Pitch period of the model, $M = [(P-1)/2]$ is the number of harmonics, a_k are the complex amplitudes and $a_k = \bar{a}_{-k}$ for all k. v_t — white noise with σ^2 variance. The Pitch period P corresponds to the Fundamental frequency $F = N/P$ calculated in periods per frame.

The full set of the model parameter contains the value of P and the vector $A = (a_k)_{k=-M}^{M}$. All these values can be arbitrary. Accuracy of the model can be measured by the squared norm of the windowed estimation error

$$J(A, P) = \frac{1}{N} \sum_{t=-N/2}^{N/2-1} |w_t(s_t - \widehat{s}_t)|^2,$$

where $w_t = [1 + \cos(2\pi t/N)]/2$ is the Hanning window. The estimation problem is then reduced to minimization of the function J by all variables.

It is numerically effective to make a successive minimization:

$$J_{\min}(P) = \min_A J(A, P), \qquad J_{\min}(P) \to \min_P .$$

The first minimization problem is to be solved for all P, and the last minimization in one variable P is made by a constrained search.

As shown in [3] the function $J_{\min}(F)$ can be presented in explicit form (i.e. for the class of stationary models):

$$J_{\min}(F) = \frac{1}{N} \left(\sum_{t=-N/2}^{N/2-1} w_t^2 s_t^2 - \sum_{m=0}^{P-1} \frac{|y_m|^2}{C_m} \right),$$

where

$$y_m(P) = \sum_{n=[\frac{-N/2-m}{P}]_+}^{[\frac{N/2-1-m}{P}]_-} \tilde{s}_{m+nP}, \quad 0 \le m \le P-1,$$

$$C_m(P) = \sum_{n=[\frac{-N/2-m}{P}]_+}^{[\frac{N/2-1-m}{P}]_-} w_{m+nP}^2, \quad 0 \le m \le P-1,$$

$\tilde{s}_t = w_t^2 s_t$, $[\cdot]_+$ means round up and $[\cdot]_-$ — round down.

The minimal admissible value of P in this case corresponds to $F = 1.6$. If the number of signal periods in the frame window is less than 1.6 then a signal cannot be distinguished from the white noise.

The expectation of the minimal cost function is equal to

$$\mathsf{E}J_{\min}(P) = \frac{3}{8}\sigma^2 \left(1 - \frac{h_\infty(F)}{F} \right).$$

On interval $F \in [1.6, 3.0]$ function $h_\infty(F)$ can be approximate by

$$h_\infty^s(F) \approx -1.2635 + 3.0399 \cdot F - 0.9621 \cdot F^2 + 0.1018 \cdot F^3, \qquad 1.6 \le F \le 3.$$

If $F \ge 3$ a good approximation is $h_\infty^s(F) = 1.9444$.

The function $J_{\min}(P)$ cannot be taken for the final decision of the Pitch estimate. The unbiased criterion $\mathcal{E}_{UB}(P)$ derived in [3] corrects the two standard errors: the multiple frequency error and influence of the white noise.

The unbiased criterion in this problem coincides with the Maximum Likelihood criterion: to minimize the unbiased estimate of the noise variance σ^2:

$$\mathcal{E}_{UB}(P) = \frac{J_{\min}(P)}{1 - \frac{h_\infty(F)}{F}}.$$

Next section describes a method of fast computation of cost function.

3 Computation of the Cost Function

Due to high nonlinearity of $\mathcal{E}_{UB}(P)$ with many local minima, it is necessary to perform exhaustive search of global minimum. Search process is divided into two stages. In the first stage, integer pitch candidates are obtained from $\mathcal{E}_{UB}(P)$ for all pitch candidates from desired range. Next, integer pitch candidate is refined over all continuous values.

Thus, at the first stage, it is required to calculate the function (right part for the $J_{\min}(P)$ formulation).

$$\phi(P) = \sum_{m=0}^{P-1} \frac{|y_m(P)|^2}{C_m(P)}$$

for all integer P from the admissible interval $[P_{\min}, P_{\max}]$ where $P_{\min}$ is a fixed small integer and $P_{\max} \approx 5N/8$.

Theorem 1. *Let $F \geq 1.6$. With relative error less than 0.01*

$$\frac{1}{C_m(P)} \approx \frac{8}{3F|K_F|^2} |g_P(z_P^m)|^2, \quad g_P(z) = \sum_{k=0}^{\infty} \alpha_F^k z^k,$$

where

$$K_F = \frac{1}{2}\left(\sqrt{1 + 2\widehat{\eta}_0(F)} + \sqrt{1 - 2\widehat{\eta}_0(F)}\right), \qquad \alpha_F = -\frac{\widehat{\eta}_0(F)}{K_F^2}, \qquad z_P = e^{-\frac{2\pi i}{P}},$$

$$\widehat{\eta}_0(x) = \frac{4\sin(\pi x)}{\pi x(x^2 - 1)(x^2 - 4)}, \quad x \neq 0, \quad x \neq \pm 1, \quad x \neq \pm 2,$$

$$\widehat{\eta}_0(0) = 1, \qquad \widehat{\eta}_0(\pm 1) = \frac{2}{3}, \qquad \widehat{\eta}_0(\pm 2) = \frac{1}{6}.$$

proof is algebraic and omitted here.

According to Theorem 1 it is possible to replace the original function $\phi(P)$ with approximation:

$$\phi(P) \approx \frac{8}{3F|K_F|^2}\phi_0(P), \qquad \phi_0(P) = \sum_{m=0}^{P-1} |g_P(z_P^m)y_m|^2.$$

Now let

$$v_P(t) = s_t w_t^2 g_P(z_P^t), \qquad -\frac{N}{2} \leq t \leq \frac{N}{2} - 1.$$

The following lemma gives the expression of the $\phi_0(P)$ in terms of correlation function of the signal $v_P(t)$:

Lemma 1. *Let P — integer, $1 \leq P < N/2$. Function ϕ_0 may be computed by*

$$\phi_0(P) = r_P(0) + 2 \sum_{k=1}^{[N/P]} r_P(kP),$$

where $r_P(t)$—correlation function of the signal $v_P(t)$, filled with zeros at $|t| \geq N/2$.

proof is omitted here.

4   Complexity vs. Accuracy

According to Theorem 1 and Lemma 1, the problem of computation of $\mathcal{E}_{UB}(P)$ with integer values of P is reduced to the computation of correlation function r_P of the signal $v_P(t)$.

In this section an approximation method for r_P is presented. Let us introduce the following notation for signals

$$\tilde{s}_t = s_t w_t^2, \qquad h_t = \tilde{s}_t |g_P(t)|^2 = s_t w_t^2 |g_P(t)|^2,$$

and for corresponding DFT's

$$\tilde{S}_n = \sum_{t=-N/2}^{N/2-1} \tilde{s}_t e^{-\frac{2\pi i}{2N} tn}, \qquad H_n = \sum_{t=-N/2}^{N/2-1} h_t e^{-\frac{2\pi i}{2N} tn}, \qquad -N \leq n \leq N-1.$$

Introduce two DFT's parametrized by indexes ℓ and j:

$$F_{n,j} = \sum_{t=-N/2}^{N/2-1} \tilde{s}_t \left(\frac{2t}{N}\right)^j e^{-\frac{2\pi i}{2N} tn}, \qquad -N \leq n \leq N-1, \quad j \geq 0,$$

$$\rho_{\ell,j}(\tau) = \frac{1}{2N} \sum_{n=-N}^{N-1} \tilde{S}_n^* F_{n+\ell,j} e^{\frac{2\pi i}{2N} \tau n}, \qquad j \geq 0, \quad \ell \geq 0.$$

Approximation of the correlation function r_P is based on the selection of a set of pairs of non-negative indices $M = \{(\ell, j)\}$ for $\rho_{\ell,j}(\tau)$ calculation:

Theorem 2.

$$\hat{r}_{P,M}(\tau) = \frac{1}{1-\alpha_F^2} \left[\rho_{0,0}(\tau) + 2\Re \sum_{(k,j):(\ell_{2Fk},j)\in M} \alpha_F^k \frac{(-\pi i x_{2Fk}/2)^j}{j!} \rho_{\ell_{2Fk},j}(\tau) \right].$$

where F — frequency with relation to N: $F = N/P$,

$$2Fk = \ell_{2Fk} + x_{2Fk}, \qquad |x_{2Fk}| \leq 1/2.$$

and the total number of Fourier transformations required for computation of the approximation is equal to

$$N_{\text{fft}} = |M| + J_{\max} + 1,$$

proof is omitted.

To improve the quality of approximation, it makes sense to include in the set M all pairs (ℓ, j) with $0 \leq j \leq J(\ell) - 1$ for fixed first component ℓ. We assume that this condition is satisfied.

The initial task of searching pitch period P has been reduced by Lemma 1 to calculation of the $\phi_0(P)$ for correlation function $r_P(\tau)$.

The maximum number of ℓ for which $(\ell, 0) \in M$ is denoted by L. Let P — integer and $F = N/P$. Maximum integer k, for which $2Fk \le L + 0.5$, denoted by $K(P)$. Obviously,

$$K(P) = \left\lfloor \frac{P(2L+1)}{4N} \right\rfloor.$$

the next result gives an estimation of error for approximation from Theorem 2:

Theorem 3. *Approximation accuracy for ϕ_0 is:*

$$|\phi_0(P) - \widehat{\phi}_0(P)| \le \sum_{t=-N/2}^{N/2-1} \gamma_P(t)|\widetilde{s}_t| \left(|\widetilde{s}_t| + 2 \sum_{q=1}^{\lfloor \frac{t}{P} + \frac{F}{2} \rfloor} |\widetilde{s}_{t-qP}| \right),$$

where

$$\gamma_P(t) = \frac{2}{1 - \alpha_F^2} \left[\sum_{k=1}^{K(P)} |\alpha_F|^k \frac{1}{J(\ell_{2Fk})!} \left| \frac{\pi t}{N} x_{2Fk} \right|^{J(\ell_{2Fk})} + |\alpha_F|^{K(P)+1} \frac{1 + |\alpha_F|}{|1 + \alpha_F z_P^t|^2} \right],$$

proof is omitted.

Finally, it is possible to obtain an accuracy estimation depending only on signal energy:

Theorem 4. *For all $P \in [P_{\min}, P_{\max}]$*

$$|\phi_0(P) - \widehat{\phi}_0(P)| \le \lambda \|s_w\|^2,$$

where

$$\lambda = \max_{0 \le k \le P-1} \lambda_k, \quad \lambda_k = \|A\|, \quad a_{i,j} = c_i c_j d_{\max\{i,j\}}, \quad 0 \le i, j \le N_k - 1,$$

$$c_n = w_{t_k^0 + nP}, \quad d_n = \gamma_P(t_k^0 + nP).$$

proof is omitted.

Result from Theorem 4 gives ability for fast computation of error estimation.

5   Pitch Determination Algorithm Description

Results from previous section let us introduce iterative schema for the pitch determination algorithm. One can select initial approximation accuracy and find local minimum and accuracy bounds. If accuracy is not sufficient, the next step of more precise approximation is used.

A rough description of the algorithm scheme is described below:

Data: original signal s

Result: Pitch period P_{pitch}

fix set M, fix search interval $P_{\text{range}} = [P_{\min}; P_{\max}]$;

while *error estimation result do not allow select global minimum* **do**

> calculate $\phi_0(F)$, $J_{\min}(F)$, $\mathcal{E}_{UB}(P)$;
> add local minimums with acceptable accuracy to $P_{\text{candidate}}$;
> reduce search area P_{range} and update set M ;

end

refinement of $P_{\text{candidate}}$ via continuous values and get P_{pitch};

Algorithm 1. Pitch determination

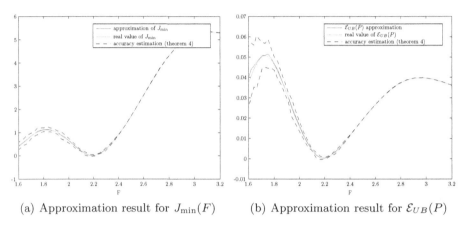

(a) Approximation result for $J_{\min}(F)$ (b) Approximation result for $\mathcal{E}_{UB}(P)$

Fig. 2. Approximation results

The first step of the algorithm calculates an approximation of $\phi_0(F)$. Next, calculation of $J_{\min}(F)$ and $\mathcal{E}_{UB}(P)$ is performed. Figure 2 shows approximation results and errors estimations. It is clear that the approximation is enough to select the global minimum of $\mathcal{E}_{UB}(P)$.

Comparison of NVM algorithm with other pitch determination methods (SWIPE, YIN, RAPT, YAAPT, PEFAC) can be found in our previous work [3].

6   Unbiased Criterion Examples

Unbiased criterion plays a central role in NVM algorithm. In this section several examples of criterion importance are shown. Figure 3 demonstrates cases where the minimum (asterisk mark) of the $J_{\min}(F)$ gives a wrong Pitch candidate, and $\mathcal{E}_{UB}(P)$ corrects this error:

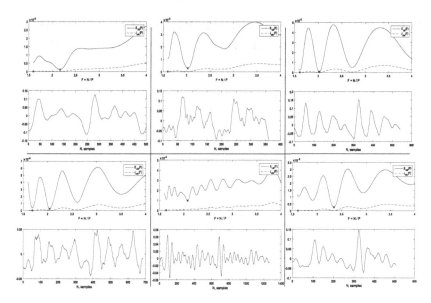

Fig. 3. $J_{\min}(F)$ and $\mathcal{E}_{UB}(P)$ comparison

7   Conclusion

In this paper a new formulation of the NVM algorithm is proposed. Previous work [3] describes a less effective method without accurate error estimation statements. Error estimation by Theorem 4 allows to determine actual global minimum of $\mathcal{E}_{UB}(P)$ only by fast approximation results.

A general complexity of the algorithm is proportional to $N \log_2 N$ where N is the window length.

Acknowledgments. The work was supported by Saint Petersburg State University, project 6.37.349.2015.

References

1. Stylianou, Y.: Harmonic plus Noise Models for speech, combined with statistical methods, for speech and speaker modification. Ph.D. Thesis. Ecole Nationale Superieure des Telecommunications. Paris (1996)
2. Griffin, D.W., Lim, J.S.: Multiband excitation vocoder. IEEE Trans. Acoustic Speech Signal Process. **36**(8), 1223–1235 (1988)
3. Barabanov, A., Melnikov, A., Magerkin, V., Vikulov, E.: Fast algorithm for precise estimation of fundamental frequency on short time intervals. In: Ronzhin, A., Potapova, R., Fakotakis, N. (eds.) SPECOM 2015. LNCS, vol. 9319, pp. 217–225. Springer, Heidelberg (2015)
4. de Cheveigne, A., Kawahara, H.: YIN, a fundamental frequency estimator for speech and music. J. Acoust. Soc. Am. **111**(4), 1917–1930 (2002)

Unsupervised Trained Functional Discourse Parser for e-Learning Materials Scaffolding

Varvara Krayvanova$^{(\boxtimes)}$ and Svetlana Duka

Altai State Technical University, Barnaul, Russia
krayvanova@yandex.ru

Abstract. The article describes the way of automatic segmentation of natural language text into fragments with different functional semantics. The proposed solution is based on the analysis of how the various parts of speech are distributed through the text. The amount and variety of nouns, verbs and adjectives is calculated for a set of sliding windows with the same length. The text is divided into fragments using clustering of windows set. We considered two clustering methods: ISODATA and a method based on the minimum spanning tree. The results of comparison of the methods with each other and with the manually text markup are shown.

Keywords: Automatic text segmentation · Description of the context · Discourse parsing · Clustering methods comparison · Text mining

1 Introduction

Functional discourse parsing is an automatic separation or selection of text fragments which have different functional semantics [11]. The clearest example is the extraction of methods, results, conclusions, etc. from scientific articles. Most of current researchers in this area study this kind of texts. As a rule, special sets of patterns and dictionaries [3,4] and supervised learning are used for this task. Unsupervised techniques apply to short and very formal texts like scientific abstracts [7].

The structure of a long text is heterogeneous and contains large and complex elements of meaning, for which description more and more words should be considered. Supervised training algorithms require annotated samples. Binding to the meanings of certain words increases training samples, which are expensive to develop [5]. In addition to widespread functional elements of a discourse a text can include unique elements, which may be absent in existing corpora, but which should be extracted too. This is especially important if we want to extend the application area of functional discourse parsing algorithms from strictly structured articles of scientific journals to less formal scientific web-articles and blog posts, scientific books and learning materials which use a much wider vocabulary and aless strict structure. Discourse parsing is the traditional task of machine translation [11], but the rapid development of e-learning opens a new challenge

© Springer International Publishing Switzerland 2016
A. Ronzhin et al. (Eds.): SPECOM 2016, LNAI 9811, pp. 722–728, 2016.
DOI: 10.1007/978-3-319-43958-7_88

for the use of these technologies, and in particular, of the functional parsing in the scaffolding of e-learning materials. Let's consider, for example, the task of generating a draft of a presentation. We want to visualize everything that is possible. Figure 1 shows an example of the visualization of individual sentences with the word ДЕЛИТЬСЯ *(TO DIVIDE)*. In case A we see the description of a process, in case B – the description of a certain classification. The semantic nuances of the word "ДЕЛИТЬСЯ" are very important for visualization in this example, and require rather specific knowledge about surrounding nouns. Besides, it is easy to imagine a context in which picture from case A is suitable for sentence from case B.

A "Зигота делится на две клетки"   В "Множество делится на две категории"
(The zygote divides into two cells)   *(The set divides into two categories)*

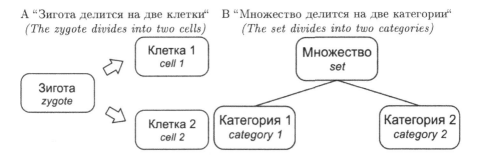

Fig. 1. The meaning nuance of the word "ДЕЛИТЬСЯ"

Thus, it makes sense to look for approaches that, firstly, would allow to produce a functional fragmentation without extensive knowledge of the semantics of some individual words, and secondly, that would not require marked text corpora for training.

It has been shown previously that the problem can be solved using the cluster analysis. However, the suggested method does not provide sufficient accuracy and does not determine the number of clusters automatically [6]. In this paper we compare two methods of clustering for this task, namely ISODATA and Minimum Spanning Tree.

2 Text Model

We assume that the part-of-speech tagging is solved with sufficient quality. Let SP be a set of parts of speech which the parser recognizes. R is a set of syntactic relations, which the parser detects. Text $t = \langle s_i \rangle$ is a sequence of sentences s_i. Each sentence is a pair $s = \langle L_s, R_s \rangle$, where $L_s = \langle w_j \rangle$ is the list of words in order of their appearance in the sentence, $R_s = \{\langle w, u, r \rangle | w, u \in L_s, r \in R\}$ is the list of syntactic relations between the words. The word w is attributed by the part of speech SP_w in the sentence.

Window $W_{i,j} = \langle p_i, ..., p_j \rangle$ is a continuous sequence of sentences in text t, where i – the number of the first sentence, j – the number of the last sentence, $l = j - i + 1$ – the window size.

In the analysis, we use the following six parameters of window $W_{i,j}$.

(1) Total number of nouns P_{Noun}.
(2) Number of different nouns $P_{DiffNoun}$.
(3) Total number of verbs P_{Verb}.
(4) Number of different verbs $P_{DiffVerb}$.
(5) Total number of adjectives P_{Adj}.
(6) Number of different adjectives $P_{DiffAdj}$.

It is known that these parameters are different for various functional styles [1] of texts and allow to define the authorship [9]. If we use this model of text, we can apply methods which are used for image segmentation to the text segmentation task. As it is shown below, the variation of these parameters over the text allows to receive information not only about the text in general, but also about its internal structure.

Sentences in a scientific text consist not only of natural language phrases. The text can contain expressions in formal languages, such as mathematical or chemical formulas. Besides sentences have various length and various purpose in the text. These factors cause great noise in the behaviour of parameters (1)–(6) throughout the text. For most texts the lower bound of value l is between 40 and 60 sentences. With very large values of l clustering loses its sensitivity. The object of analysis is the set of all the windows $\{W_{i,j}\}$ with length l. Let's designate such set as $\{W_i^l\}$, where i is the number of the first sentence in the window. Let $n_t = |t|$ be the amount of sentences in the text. Then $n_w^l = |t| - l + 1$ is the amount of windows with length l.

We considered two methods of clustering: ISODATA [8] and clustering with a minimum spanning tree [2] (we will call this method a tree clustering).

3   Estimation Method

To estimate the resilience and quality of the results of the algorithms we use the following approach.

Let $Cluster(W_i^l)$ be the cluster calculated for window W_i^l. Let $B = \{b_k\} \subset \{W_i^l\}$ be the set of windows, which are the boundaries of clusters, i.e. $b_k = W_i^l$ and $Cluster(W_i^l) \neq Cluster(W_{i+1}^l)$. Let n experiments be made and sets $B_1, \ldots, B_n$ be received. We assume that the boundary is found in the experiment e_1 and in the experiment e_2, if $\exists b_{k_1}, b_{k_2} : |b_{k_1} \in B_{e_1}, b_{k_2} \in B_{e_2}$ and $|b_{k_1} - b_{k_2}| < l/2$, where $|b_{k_1} - b_{k_2}|$ is the number of sentences between the beginning of the windows b_{k_1} and b_{k_2}. We will estimate the detection accuracy of boundary b_k at experiment e_1 and e_2 as $\epsilon = min_{k_2}(|b_{k_1} - b_{k_2}|)/l$.

The experiments were conducted on long scientific and educational texts (more than 20 pages) of natural science and medicine domains from Single Window Access to Educational Resources[1]. To conduct the experiment, we have

---

[1] http://window.edu.ru/.

developed a software system that includes an external parser, an object model of the text, a module for manually labeling of the text and a cluster analysis module.

We use Seman[2] and MyStem[3] for a part-of-speech tagging. Both parsers provide enough quality results for our task and give similar results, but the first one is sensitive to spelling mistakes and syntax errors, and the second one is not open source, so the developed software provides the possibility to replace the parsing module.

We extracted the texts from pdf-files, so they kept extra line breaks, page numbers, as well as fragments of a destructed text: formulas, labels on figures, etc. To prepare the text for parsing, we have created a module which removes fragments that do not contain Russian letters, decodes common abbreviations, restores the sentences integrity and divides the text into sentences.

4   Description of Clustering Methods

ISODATA method is a classical method of a cluster analysis which automatic detects the number of clusters. This method has a list of parameters, and we experimentally choose them as a linear function of standard derivation and variance of distances between windows in space of parameters (1)–(6). The initial positions of cluster centers are chosen randomly from the set of clustered objects. The number of clusters is chosen excessively large in order to ensure coverage of the whole text and to increase the stability of the results. The task structure and method properties assume that the cluster boundaries may vary slightly depending on the initial positions of the centers. The experiments show that the algorithm converges. The accuracy ϵ of determining of fragments boundaries is less than 0.06 of the window size.

Let's consider in more details the tree clustering algorithm applied to our task. The set of windows $\{W_{i,j}\}$ with length l can be represented as a complete graph, where the length of each edge is Euclidean distance in the space of parameters (1)–(6). Let $Tree = \langle W, V, dest \rangle$ be the minimum spanning tree of the windows graph, where $W, V \in \{W_{i,j}\}$, $dest$ – Euclidean distance between W and V in the space of parameters (1)–(6). The tree is constructed using the following algorithm.

1. Choose a tree root from the set of windows $Root_0 \in \{W_{i,j}\}$ randomly.
2. Add the selected window to the tree.
3. From all the windows $W_{i,j} \notin Tree$, which have not been added to the tree yet, look for the nearest one to the tree. The distance to the tree for window $W_{i,j}$ is calculated as the minimum distance for all the windows included into the tree.
4. Add the found window to the tree.
5. Repeat steps 3 and 4 until all the windows are in the tree.

---

[2] http://sourceforge.net/projects/seman/.
[3] https://tech.yandex.ru/mystem/.

Then we calculate the mean M_{dest} and the standard deviation σ_{dest} of the edge length in the tree. Then all the edges which length is less than $M_{dest} + 2\sigma_{dest}$ are removed from the tree. The tree splits into some subtrees which are considered as clusters. If after edges removing the subtrees with only one vertex are formed, these subtrees merge with the nearest subtree.

The results of the tree clustering depend on the window size, but don't depend on the choosing of the root in step 1.

Depending on the text the ISODATA method can select up to 30 % more boundaries than Tree Clustering. There are differences of not more than 7 % of the window size for the boundaries which have been found using the both methods. It confirms the accuracy of the detected boundaries.

5   Results

The applicability of the developed methods for selecting semantically related fragments was verified as follows. We could not find a corpus with functional annotated discourse like BioDRB [10] for the Russian language. Therefore we have created a small corpus in which we manually allocated fragments containing descriptions of specific processes, procedures, and other sequences of actions or events. Let's call such fragments scenarios. Scenarios are located irregularlly in the text, they may be adjacent to each other, and contain a destructed text within themselves (for example, labels on figures). For manually marking, scenario is considered to be a text fragment which satisfies the following conditions.

- Scenario is a fragment of a text containing all the sentences, which describe a certain process.
- Scenario is a continuous fragment, that is, between two sentences of the scenario untagged sentences or sentences from the other scenarios can not exist.
- Scenarios do not overlap, that is, one sentence can not belong to several scenarios.

We apply a conversion formula to translate the sentence number into the window number for comparing the clusters boundaries with the boundaries of scenarios. The numbering of the windows and sentences begins with 0. Let $Window(s_i)$ be the number of the window for sentence s_i:

$$Window(s_i) = \begin{cases} 0, & i < l/2 \\ i - l/2, & l/2 \le i \le n_t - l/2 \\ n_w^l - 1, & i > n_t - l/2 \end{cases} .$$

If the window length l is odd, $l/2$ is rounded down.

Scenarios may contain a destructed text which is usually released into separate fragments during clustering. In addition, a fragment obtained by clustering, can contain several scenarios. The automatic detection of whether a cluster contains a scenario is not a trivial task and requires an additional study that goes beyond the scope of the article. Therefore, we apply the following approach to test the quality of clustering.

Let's divide all the clusters into two groups: clusters which identify the scenario and clusters which identify the absence of a scenario (for example, fragments of other types). We assess the quality of clustering according to the following criteria. Let C be a set of clusters, and $c \in C$ be some cluster. $Scenario(c)$ is a set of sentences which are included both in cluster c and in scenarios; $c \backslash Scenario(c)$ is a set of sentences in cluster c, which are not included in scenarios. If $|Scenario(c)| > |c \backslash Scenario(c)|$, we assume that cluster c identifies a scenario. Otherwise we assume that a cluster identifies the absence of a scenario. Then the number of correct determined sentences for cluster c is calculated by the formula:

$$P_{correct} = \frac{max(|Scenario(c)|, |c \backslash Scenario(c)|)}{|c|}.$$

The number of incorrect determined sentences is calculated by the formula:

$$P_{incorrect} = \frac{min(|Scenario(c)|, |c \backslash Scenario(c)|)}{|c|}.$$

The evaluation results of clustering methods are shown in the Table 1. As we see, clustering allocates the boundaries of fragments of a certain type, such as scenarios, accurately enough. It is necessary to explore further the ratio between the distributions of parameters (1)–(6) for the cluster and for the text to determine the type of fragments allocated to a cluster.

Table 1. Estimation of clustering quality for scenarios detection task

Clustering method	Correct sentences $P_{correct}$	Incorrect sentences $P_{incorrect}$
ISODATA	87 %	13 %
Tree clustering	93 %	7 %

6   Conclusion and Future Work

The experiments show that the suggested methods provide results sufficient for practical application. The dependence between ISODATA algorithm operating time and the amount of windows expressed as $o(In_w^l)$, where I is the number of iterations. The time complexity of the Tree Clustering algorithm is $o((n_w^l)^3)$, that is, much more slowly than ISODATA. However, this is compensated by greater stability and better quality of results.

Low quality of ISODATA results are determined by the fact that the algorithm finds hyperspheres in six-dimensional parameters space, while the clusters observed by visualization using principal component method are significantly elongated in one of the directions. To resolve this contradiction it is necessary to select another measure of distances or to use advanced heuristics. Tree Clustering gives good results.

The suggested algorithms will be used for generating of interactive e-learning materials and illustrations using books from Altai State Technical University e-library. We are going to expand the annotated text corpus and to share it in the Internet. We also develop the algorithm for automatic detection of a fragment type based on the used verbs. We reckon that the verbs is the best way to describe functional semantics.

References

1. Alekseeva, I.: Text and Translation: Theory. Moscow, International relationships (2003)
2. Belim, S., Kutlunin, P.: Boundary extraction in images using a clustering algorithm. Comput. Opt. **39**(1), 119–124 (2015)
3. Bolshakova, E.: Language of lexical and syntactic patterns lspl: using experience and ways of development. In: Software Systems and Tools. Thematic Collection, vol. 15, pp. 15–26. MSU FCMC, Moscow (2014)
4. Guo, Y., Korhonen, A., Liakata, M., Karolinska, I.S., Sun, L., Stenius, U.: Identifying the information structure of scientific abstracts: an investigation of three different schemes. In: Proceedings of the 2010 Workshop on Biomedical Natural Language Processing, BioNLP 2010, pp. 99–107. Association for Computational Linguistics, Stroudsburg, PA, USA (2010). http://dl.acm.org/citation.cfm?id=1869961.1869974
5. Guo, Y., Silins, I., Stenius, U., Korhonen, A.: Active learning-based information structure analysis of full scientific articles and two applications for biomedical literature review. Bioinformatics **29**(11), 1440–1447 (2013)
6. Krayvanova, V., Kryuchkova, E.: Application of automatic fragmentation for the semantic comparison of texts. In: Železný, M., Habernal, I., Ronzhin, A. (eds.) SPECOM 2013. LNCS, vol. 8113, pp. 46–53. Springer, Heidelberg (2013)
7. Lin, J., Karakos, D., Demner-Fushman, D., Khudanpur, S.: Generative content models for structural analysis of medical abstracts. In: Proceedings of the HLT-NAACL BioNLP Workshop on Linking Natural Language and Biology, LNL-BioNLP 2006, Stroudsburg, PA, USA, pp. 65–72. Association for Computational Linguistics (2006). http://dl.acm.org/citation.cfm?id=1654415.1654427
8. Lurie, I., Kosikov, A.: Theory and practice of digital image processing (2003)
9. Lvov, A.: Linguistic analysis of the text and author recognition (2008). http://fantlab.ru/article374
10. Prasad, R., McRoy, S., Frid, N., Joshi, A., YuEmail, H.: The biomedical discourse relation bank. Bioinformatics **12**, 188 (2011)
11. Webber, B., Egg, M., Kordoni, V.: Discourse structure and language technology. J. Nat. Lang. Eng. **01**, 1–40 (2012)

Author Index

Printed in the United States
By Bookmasters